Controlled Substances

Controlled Substances

Crime, Regulation, and Policy

Alex Kreit

ASSOCIATE PROFESSOR OF LAW,
THOMAS JEFFERSON SCHOOL OF LAW

CAROLINA ACADEMIC PRESS
Durham, North Carolina

ISBN: 978-1-59460-871-1
LCCN: 2012950344

Carolina Academic Press
700 Kent Street
Durham, North Carolina 27701
Telephone (919) 489-7486
Fax (919) 493-5668
www.cap-press.com

Printed in the United States of America

In memory of

Lester J. Mazor, Professor Emeritus, Hampshire College
1936 — 2011

The Honorable M. Blane Michael, United States Court of Appeals for the Fourth Circuit
1943 — 2011

"It is not possible to know how far the influence of any amiable honest-hearted duty-doing man flies out into the world; but it is very possible to know how it has touched one's self in going by …"

—Charles Dickens, *Great Expectations*

Contents

Table of Cases

Preface

Forty years ago, President Richard Nixon declared drug abuse "public enemy number one in America"* — "the modern curse of youth, just like the plagues and epidemics of former years."** In the decades since, our drug laws and policies have for the most part closely matched this rhetoric. As a result, the number of Americans incarcerated for drug offenses today is larger than the entire United States prison and jail population was in 1980. Despite the vigorous enforcement of drug prohibition, however, its wisdom and morality continues to be hotly debated. Indeed, a poll by Gallup in late 2011 found that 50% of Americans now favor taxing and regulating marijuana like alcohol.

Yet, while modern drug laws have dramatically changed our criminal justice system, they are strangely absent from the curriculum at most law schools. Every criminal law casebook devotes significant coverage to homicide, property crimes, and rape. But only a handful include a chapter or section on drug offenses. Criminal procedure courses are filled with drug cases. But this is only because so many of the leading Fourth, Fifth, and Sixth Amendment cases happened to involve drug prosecutions. Courses like federal criminal law and international criminal law sometimes include coverage of drug offenses. And there are some schools that offer a seminar or course on drug policy. At most law schools today, however, a student could take every single criminal law-related offering without studying drug law and policy.

It is hard to say why there is such a large gap between the coverage of drug crimes in law schools and the importance of drug crimes to criminal law practice and criminal justice policy. A lack of prepared course materials may be partly to blame. There has not been a casebook dedicated to controlled substances law since the second and final edition of Gerald F. Uelmen and Victor G. Haddox's excellent work *Drug Abuse and the Law: Cases, Text, Materials* in 1983. Another explanation may be that some criminal law teachers mistakenly believe drug offenses are too straightforward to merit much attention. In 2011, for example, prominent criminal law professor Orin Kerr wrote on the *Volokh Conspiracy* blog that because "[t]he elements of drug crimes are trivially simple ... there's no purpose to be served in covering those crimes in a substantive law class." It is not hard to imagine how someone might jump to this conclusion. Drug decriminalization may make for an interesting policy debate, this line of thinking may go, but when a person is found with drugs in their pocket, what legal defense could she possibly have?

Whatever the reason for the inattention to drug laws, teachers and students alike have been the poorer for their absence from law schools. A course on controlled substances provides a uniquely rich mix of complex legal and policy problems. A close look at the law of drug crimes reveals unusually tough challenges in how to define

---

 * Andrew B. Whitford and Jeff Yates, Presidential Rhetoric and the Public Agenda: Constructing the War on Drugs 86 (2009).

 ** Dan Baum, Smoke and Mirrors: The War on Drugs and the Politics of Failure 12 (1997).

them, how to prove them, and how to grade them. Is drug possession meant to punish drug ownership or physical contact with drugs? What sort of evidence is sufficient to ascribe an intent to distribute to someone in possession of drugs? Should we sentence drug offenders based on the type and quantity of drugs involved in their offense or some other metric? The enforcement of drug laws, meanwhile, provides an ideal vehicle for studying a number of important and often overlooked issues like prosecutorial discretion, the use of informants in modern policing, and racial profiling. And, of course, drug prohibition presents one of the most difficult tests for the theories of punishment. Though we may disagree about how much punishment a thief, a killer, or a drunk driver should receive, few question that theft, murder, and driving under the influence should be crimes. Many theorists and policy analysts, however, believe that drug criminalization is unjust or unworkable.

From beginning to end, this course provides an intellectually engaging experience for a wide range of law students. Students who plan on becoming prosecutors or defense attorneys will learn about an area of the law that will inevitably occupy a large percentage of their practice. Others will enjoy debating marijuana legalization or studying the relationship between race and our drug laws.

This book is designed to accommodate a number of different types of courses on drug abuse and the law. I teach the subject as a three-credit lecture course that covers drug policy, drug crimes, and drug regulation, using materials from the first seven chapters of this book. However, this book could also be used in a seminar on drug policy or the "war on drugs," an advanced criminal law course, or a study abroad course on international and comparative drug control. Portions of the book could also be used to supplement a first-year criminal law course. If you are a teacher who is considering this book, please refer to the Teacher's Manual for suggested syllabi or email me if you would like to discuss ideas.

Before I close, a few formatting notes. My chief objective has been to make this book as readable and user-friendly as possible. I have minimized the use of ellipses. Ellipses appear for omitted material within a sentence or paragraph. But I have opted not to use them where whole paragraphs or the beginning or end of a paragraph have been cut. I have deleted most in-text citations and the vast majority of footnotes from the cases and materials. Footnotes that have been retained are marked using the original numbering from the source material. A * indicates a footnote that I have written. Finally, in place of the traditional "notes and questions" sections, I use short narrative essays (usually one or two paragraphs) to link and supplement the materials.

I have found learning about and teaching this subject to be incredibly enjoyable and rewarding. I hope that you will as well.

Alex Kreit
akreit@tjsl.edu
November 2012

Acknowledgments

I am grateful to Kelly Hayes (Thomas Jefferson School of Law, 2013) for her excellent work, including research assistance, suggestions, support in obtaining copyright clearances, and proofreading of the text. I also thank for their valuable contributions, J. Janell Woodbury (Thomas Jefferson School of Law, 2012) for her proofreading of portions of the text; Jenna Hackett (Thomas Jefferson School of Law, 2011) for her research assistance and proofreading of portions of the text; Veronica Inezian (Thomas Jefferson School of Law, 2010) for her research assistance at the beginning of this project, including market research for the book proposal; Catherine Deane (Thomas Jefferson School of Law Library) for all of her help, from tracking difficult-to-find materials to alerting me to many wonderful sources that I had not even thought to look for; Douglas Husak, for providing me with an English-language version of his article *Illicit Drugs: A Test of Joel Feinberg's* The Moral Limits of the Criminal Law; and Anders Kaye, Bridget Kennedy, and Zara Snapp for their thoughtful comments and advice. Thank you to the entire Carolina Academic Press team — I am so fortunate to have such a supportive and dedicated publisher. Finally, I thank all of my students in my 2010, 2011, and 2012 Controlled Substances classes for allowing me to test out and refine these materials with them.

I would also like to thank the following individuals and organizations for their permission to reproduce excerpts from their works in this casebook (listed in order of appearance in this casebook):

FROM CHOCOLATE TO MORPHINE, Copyright © 1983, 1993 by Andrew Weil and Winifred Rosen. Reprinted by permission of Houghton Mifflin Harcourt Publishing Company. All Rights reserved.

SAYING YES: IN DEFENSE OF DRUG USE by Jacob Sullum, copyright © 2003 by Jacob Sullum. Used by permission of Jeremy P. Tarcher, an imprint of Penguin Group (USA) Inc.

Alexander Shulgin and Ann Shulgin (1991), PiHKAL: A Chemical Love Story, Copyright © 1991, 1992, 1995, 1998, 2000, 2003, 2007 by Alexander Shulgin and Ann Shulgin. Reprinted by permission of Transform Press.

Linda C. Fentiman, *Rethinking Addiction: Drugs, Deterrence, and the Neuroscience Revolution*, 14 University of Pennsylvania Journal of Law and Social Change 233 (2011). Reprinted by permission of the author.

Barnard E. Harcourt, *The Collapse of the Harm Principle*, 90 Journal of Criminal Law and Criminology 109 (1999). Reprinted by special permission of Northwestern University School of Law, *The Journal of Criminal Law and Criminology*.

Douglas Husak, *Illicit Drugs: A Test of Joel Feinberg's* The Moral Limits of the Criminal Law, 10 Libertaria (2008). Reprinted by permission of the author.

Steven G. Calabresi, *Render Unto Caesar That Which is Caesar's, and Unto God That Which is God's*, 31 Harvard Journal of Law and Public Policy 495 (2008). Reprinted with permission.

Dan M. Kahan, *The Cognitively Illiberal State*, 60 Stanford Law Review 115 (2007). Reprinted by permission of the journal for a fee via the Copyright Clearance Center.

Jonathan P. Caulkins and Peter Reuter, *Setting Goals for Drug Policy: Harm Reduction or Use Reduction?*, 92 Addiction 1143 (1997). Reprinted by permission of the journal for a fee via the Copyright Clearance Center.

Michael M. O'Hear, *Federalism and Drug Control*, 57 Vanderbilt Law Review 783 (2004). Reprinted by permission of the author.

Ethan A. Nadelmann, *Drug Prohibition in the United States: Costs, Consequences, and Alternatives*, 5 Notre Dame Journal of Law Ethics and Public Policy 783 (1991). Reprinted by permission of the author.

James Q. Wilson, *Against the Legalization of Drugs*, 89 Commentary 21 (1990). Reprinted from COMMENTARY, February 1990, by permission; © 1990 by Commentary, Inc.

Mark A.R. Kleiman & Aaron J. Saiger, *Drug Legalization: The Importance of Asking the Right Question*, 18 Hofstra Law Review 527 (1990). Reprinted with the permission of the *Hofstra Law Review Association*.

Beau Kilmer, Jonathan P. Caulkins, Rosalie Liccardo Pacula, Robert J. MacCoun and Peter H. Reuter, *Altered State: Assessing How Marijuana Legalization in California Could Influence Marijuana Consumption and Public Budgets*, RAND Corporation (2010). Reprinted by permission of the RAND Corporation.

Michael Vitiello, *Legalizing Marijuana: California's Pot of Gold?*, 2009 Wisconsin Law Review 1349. Reprinted by the permission of the Wisconsin Law Review.

David W. Rasmussen and Bruce L. Benson, *Rationalizing Drug Policy Under Federalism*, 50 Florida State University Law Review 679 (2003). Reprinted by permission of the Florida State University Law Review.

Ryan S. King and Marc Mauer, *The War on Marijuana: The Transformation of the War on Drugs in the 1990s*, The Sentencing Project (2005). Reprinted by permission of The Sentencing Project.

Thomas M. Quinn and Gerald T. McLaughlin, *The Evolution of Federal Drug Control Legislation*, 22 Catholic University Law Review 586 (1973). Reprinted by permission of the Catholic University Law Review.

Corey Rayburn Yung, *The Emerging Criminal War on Sex Offenders*, 45 Harvard Civil Rights-Civil Liberties Law Review 435 (2010). Reprinted by permission of the journal for a fee via the Copyright Clearance Center.

Jamie Fellner, *Race, Drugs, and Law Enforcement in the United States*, 20 Stan. L. & Pol'y Rev 257 (2009). Reprinted by permission of the journal for a fee via the Copyright Clearance Center.

William J. Stuntz, *The Pathological Politics of Criminal Law*, 100 MICHIGAN LAW REVIEW 505 (2001).

Michelle Alexander, *The New Jim Crow*, 9 Ohio State Journal of Criminal Law 7 (2011). Reprinted by permission of the author.

Dave Bewley-Taylor, Chris Hallam and Rob Allen, *The Incarceration of Drug Offenders: An Overview*, The Beckley Foundation Drug Policy Programme, Report Sixteen (2009). Reprinted by permission of The Beckley Foundation.

Markus Dirk Dubber, *Policing Possession: The War on Crime and the End of Criminal Law*, 91 Journal of Criminal Law & Criminology 829 (2001). Reprinted by special permission of Northwestern University School of Law, *The Journal of Criminal Law and Criminology*.

Myrna S. Reader, *Single Moms, Battered Women, and Other Sex-Based Anomalies in the Gender-Free World of the Federal Sentencing Guidelines*, 20 Pepperdine Law Review 905 (1993). Reprinted by permission of the author.

David M. Zlotnick, *The Future of Federal Sentencing Policy: Learning Lessons From Republican Judicial Appointees in the Guidelines Era*, 79 U. Colo. L. Rev. 1 (2008). Reprinted with permission of the author and the *University of Colorado Law Review*.

Michael D. Blanchard and Gabriel J. Chin, *Identifying The Enemy in the War on Drugs: A Critique of the Developing Rule Permitting Visual Identification of Indescript White Powder in Narcotics Prosecutions*, 47 AMERICAN UNIVERSITY LAW REVIEW 557 (1998). Reprinted by permission of the authors and the American University Law Review.

L. Buckner Inniss, *A Moving Violation? Hypercriminalized Spaces and Fortuitous Presence in Drug Free School Zones*, 8 Texas Forum on Civil Liberties and Civil Rights 51 (2003). Reprinted by permission of the author.

Tina Wescott Cafaro, *Slipping Through the Cracks: Why Can't We Stop Drugged Driving?*, 32 Western New England Law Review 33 (2010). Reprinted by permission of the author.

Scott Burris, Steffanie A. Strathdee, and Jon S. Vernick, *Lethal Injections: The Law, Science, and Politics of Syringe Access for Injection Drug Users*, 37 University of San Francisco Law Review 813 (2003). Reprinted by permission of the University of San Francisco Law Review.

Lynn M. Paltrow, *Pregnant Drug Users, Fetal Persons, and the Threat to* Roe v. Wade, 62 Albany Law Review 999 (1999). Reprinted by permission of the author and the Albany Law Review.

Douglas A. Berman, *Reconceptualizing Sentencing*, 2005 University of Chicago Legal Forum 1. Originally appearing in the *University of Chicago Legal Forum*, Vol. 2005. Reprinted with permission from the *University of Chicago Legal Forum* and the University of Chicago Law School.

Henry J. Bemporad, An Introduction to Federal Sentencing (12th ed. 2010). Reprinted by permission of the author.

Ian Weinstein, *Fifteen Years After the Federal Sentencing Revolution: How Mandatory Minimums Have Undermined Effective and Just Narcotics Sentencing*, 40 American Criminal Law Review 87 (2003). Reprinted with permission of the publisher, © Georgetown University Law Center.

Paul J. Hofer and Mark H. Allenbaugh, *The Reason Behind the Rules: Finding and Using the Philosophy of the Federal Sentencing Guidelines*, 40 American Criminal Law Review 19 (2003). Reprinted with permission of the publisher, © Georgetown University Law Center.

Kyle O'Dowd, *Weighing the Evidence: Drug Quantity Issues in Mandatory Minimum Cases*, 24 Champion 43 (2000). Reprinted by permission of the National Association of Criminal Defense Lawyers.

Hon. William W. Wilkins, Jr., Phyllis J. Newton and John R. Steer, *Competing Sentencing Policies in a "War on Drugs" Era*, 28 Wake Forest L. Rev. 305 (1993). © *Wake Forest Law Review*, reprinted by permission.

Stephen J. Schulhofer, *Rethinking Mandatory Minimums*, 28 Wake Forest Law Review 199 (1993). © *Wake Forest Law Review*, reprinted by permission.

Sarah French Russell, *Rethinking Recidivist Enhancements: The Role of Prior Drug Convictions in Federal Sentencing*, 43 U.C. Davis Law Review 1134 (2010). Reprinted by permission of the author.

Mark Osler, *Indirect Harms and Proportionality: The Upside-Down World of Federal Sentencing*, 74 Mississippi Law Journal 1 (2004). Reprinted by permission of the Mississippi Law Journal.

Steven D. Clymer, *Unequal Justice: The Federalization of Criminal Law*, 70 Southern California Law Review 643 (1997). Reprinted with the permission of the *Southern California Law Review*.

Eric J. Miller, *Embracing Addiction: Drug Courts and the False Promise of Judicial Intervention*, 65 Ohio State Law Journal 1479 (2004). Reprinted by permission of the author and the Ohio State Law Journal.

Ryan S. King and Jill Pasquarella, *Drug Courts: A Review of the Evidence*, The Sentencing Project (2009). Reprinted by permission of The Sentencing Project.

Josh Bowers, *Contraindicated Drug Courts*, 55 UCLA Law Review 783 (2008). Reprinted by permission of the author.

National Association of Criminal Defense Lawyers (2009), *America's Problem-Solving Courts: The Criminal Costs of Treatment and the Case for Reform*. Reprinted by permission of the National Association of Criminal Defense Lawyers.

Nora V. Demleitner, *"Collateral Damage": No Re-Entry for Drug Offenders*, 47 Villanova Law Review 1027 (2002). Reprinted by permission of the Villanova Law Review.

Radley Balko, *The Forfeiture Racket*, Reason Magazine, February 2010. Reprinted by permission of Reason Magazine.

Eric Blumenson and Eva Nilsen, *Policing for Profit: The Drug War's Hidden Economic Agenda*, 65 University of Chicago Law Review 35 (1998). Reprinted by permission of the journal for a fee via the Copyright Clearance Center.

Elizabeth E. Joh, *Breaking the Law to Enforce It: Undercover Police Participation in Crime*, 62 Stanford Law Review 155 (2009). Reprinted by permission of the journal for a fee via the Copyright Clearance Center.

Randy Barnett, *The Harmful Side Effects of Drug Prohibition*, 2009 Utah Law Review 11. Reprinted by permission of the author.

Alexandra Natapoff, *Deregulating Guilt: The Information Culture of the Criminal System*, 30 Cardozo Law Review 965 (2008). Reprinted by permission of the Cardozo Law Review.

Alexandra Natapoff, *Beyond Unreliable: How Snitches Contribute to Wrongful Convictions*, 37 Golden Gate University Law Review 107 (2006). Reprinted by permission of the Golden Gate University Law Review.

Michael L. Rich, *Coerced Informants and Thirteenth Amendment Limitations on the Police-Informant Relationship*, 50 Santa Clara Law Review 681 (2010). Reprinted by permission of the author.

Lenese C. Herbet, *Can't You See What I'm Saying? Making Expressive Conduct a Crime in High-Crime Areas*, 9 Georgetown Journal of Poverty Law and Policy 135 (2002). Reprinted with permission of the publisher, © Georgetown University Law Center.

Andrew Guthrie Ferguson, *Crime Mapping and the Fourth Amendment: Redrawing "High-Crime Areas"*, 63 Hastings Law Journal 179 (2011). Reprinted by permission of the Hastings Law Journal.

David Rudovsky, *The Impact of the War on Drugs on Procedural Fairness and Racial Equality*, 1994 University of Chicago Legal Forum 237. Originally appearing in the *University of Chicago Legal Forum*, Vol. 1994. Reprinted with permission from the *University of Chicago Legal Forum* and the University of Chicago Law School.

Kevin R. Johnson, *How Racial Profiling in America Became the Law of the Land:* United States v. Brignoni-Ponce *and* Whren v. United States *and the Need for Truly Rebellious Lawyering*, 98 Georgetown Law Journal 1005 (2010). Reprinted by permission of the author.

Jeffrey S. Weiner and Kimberly Homan, *Those Doggone Sniffs Are Often Wrong: The Fourth Amendment Has Gone to the Dogs*, 30 The Champion 12 (2006). Reprinted by permission of the National Association of Criminal Defense Lawyers.

Radley Balko, *Overkill: The Rise of Paramilitary Police Raids in America*, The Cato Institute 2006. Reprinted by permission of the Cato Institute.

Robert J. MacCoun, *Testing Drugs Versus Testing For Drug Use: Private Risk Management in the Shadow of Criminal Law*, 56 DePaul Law Review 507 (2007). Reprinted by permission of the author.

Erik Luna, *Drug Exceptionalism*, 47 Villanova Law Review 753 (2002). Reprinted by permission of the author and the Villanova Law Review.

Paul Finkelman, *The Second Casualty of War: Civil Liberties and the War on Drugs*, 66 Southern California Law Review 1389 (1993). Reprinted with the permission of the *Southern California Law Review*.

Kimani Paul-Emile, *Making Sense of Drug Regulation: A Theory of Law For Drug Control Policy*, 19 Cornell Journal of Law and Public Policy 691 (2010). Reprinted by permission of the Cornell Journal of Law and Public Policy.

Peter J. Cohen, *Medical Marijuana: The Conflict Between Scientific Evidence and Political Ideology*, 2009 Utah Law Review 35. Reprinted by permission of the Cohen family.

Lars Noah, *Challenges in the Federal Regulation of Pain Management Technologies*, 31 Journal of Law, Medicine & Ethics 55 (2003). Reprinted by permission of the American Society of Law, Medicine & Ethics.

Diane E. Hoffmann, *Treating Pain v. Reducing Drug Diversion and Abuse: Recalibrating the Balance in Our Drug Control Laws and Policies*, 18 Saint Louis University Journal of Health Law and Policy 231 (2008). Reprinted with permission of the Saint Louis University Journal of Health Law & Policy © 2008 St. Louis University School of Law, St. Louis, Missouri.

Douglas J. Behr, *Did You Forget to Say You're Sorry? Litigating a Show Cause Hearing for a Physician's DEA Registration*, 9 Quinnipiac Health Law Journal 99 (2005). Reprinted by permission of the author.

Bryan A. Liang and Tim Mackey, *Searching for Safety: Addressing Search Engine, Website, and Provider Accountability for Illicit Online Drug Sales*, 35 American Journal of Law and Medicine 125 (2009). Reprinted by permission of the American Society of Law, Medicine & Ethics.

Richard C. Ausness, *"There's Danger Here, Cherie!": Liability for the Promotion and Marketing of Drugs and Medical Devices for Off-Label Uses*, 73 Brooklyn Law Review 1253. Reprinted by permission of the author.

Ellen M. Weber, *Failure of Physicians to Prescribe Pharmacotherapies for Addiction: Regulatory Restrictions and Physician Resistance*, 13 Journal of Health Care Law and Policy 49 (2010). Reprinted by permission of the author.

Marijuana Policy Project (2011), *State-By-State Medical Marijuana Laws*. Reprinted by permission of the Marijuana Policy Project.

Alex Kreit, *Beyond the Prohibition Debate: Thoughts on Federal Drug Laws in an Age of State Reforms*, 13 Chapman Law Review 555 (2010).

Robert A. Mikos, *A Critical Appraisal of the Department of Justice's New Approach to Medical Marijuana*, 22 Stanford Law and Policy Review 633 (2011). Reprinted by permission of the journal for a fee via the Copyright Clearance Center.

Robert Post, *Federalism, Positive Law, and the Emergence of the American Administrative State: Prohibition in the Taft Court Era*, 48 William and Mary Law Review 1 (2006). Reprinted by permission of the William and Mary Law Review.

Marcia Yablon, *The Prohibition Hangover: Why We Are Still Feeling the Effects of Prohibition*, 13 Virginia Journal of Social Policy and the Law 552 (2006). Reprinted with the Journal's permission.

Micah L. Berman, *Smoking Out the Impact of Tobacco-Related Decisions on Public Health Law*, 75 Brooklyn Law Review 1 (2009). Reprinted by permission of the author.

Karen C. Sokol, *Smoking Abroad and Smokeless at Home: Holding the Tobacco Industry Accountable in a New Era*, 13 New York University Journal of Legislation and Public Policy 81 (2010). Reprinted by permission of the New York University Journal of Legislation and Public Policy.

James G. Hodge, Jr., Megan Scanlon, Alicia Corbett and Andrew Sorensen, *The Consumable Vice: Caffeine, Public Health, and the Law*, 27 Journal of Contemporary Health Law and Policy 76 (2010). Reprinted by permission of the author.

Chantal Thomas, *Disciplining Globalization: International Law, Illegal Trade, and the Case of Narcotics*, 24 Michigan Journal of International Law 549 (2003). Reprinted by permission of the author.

United Nations Office on Drugs and Crime, *World Drug Report, 2011*. Reprinted by permission of the United Nations Office on Drugs and Crime.

Peter H. Reuter, *A Report on Global Illicit Drugs Markets 1998–2007: Assessing the Operation of the Global Drug Market, Report 1*, RAND Corporation, Prepared for the European Commission (2009). A Report on Global Illicit Drugs Markets 1998–2007, © European Communities, 2009. Reprinted by permission of the Publications Office of the European Union.

Seth Harp, Note, *Globalization of the U.S. Black Market: Prohibition, the War on Drugs, and the Case of Mexico*, 85 New York University Law Review 1661 (2010). Reprinted by permission of the New York University Law Review.

Viridiana Ríos and David A. Shirk, *Drug Violence in Mexico: Data and Analysis Through 2010*, University of San Diego Trans-Border Institute. Reprinted by permission of the University of San Diego Trans-Border Institute.

Michael Chertoff, *The Nexus Between Drug Trafficking, Terrorism and Organized Crime*, 13 Chapman Law Review 681 (2010). Reprinted by permission of the author.

Michael Jacobson and Matthew Levitt, *Tracking Narco-Terrorist Networks: The Money Trail*, 34 Fletcher Forum of World Affairs 117 (2010). Reprinted, Courtesy of The Fletcher Forum of World Affairs.

Daniel Heilmann, *The International Control of Illegal Drugs and the U.N. Treaty Regime: Preventing or Causing Human Rights Violations?*, 19 Cardozo Journal of International and Comparative Law 217 (2011). Reprinted by permission of the Cardozo Journal of International and Comparative Law.

Robin Room and Peter Reuter, *How Well Do International Drug Conventions Protect Public Health?*, 379 The Lancet 84 (2012). Reprinted by permission of the journal for a fee via the Copyright Clearance Center.

Yvonne M. Dutton, *Explaining State Commitment to the International Criminal Court: Strong Enforcement Mechanisms as a Credible Threat*, 10 Washington University Global Studies Law Review 477 (2011). Reprinted by permission of the Washington University Global Law Review.

Heather L. Kiefer, *Just Say No: The Case Against Expanding the International Criminal Court's Jurisdiction to Include Drug Trafficking*, 31 Loyola of Los Angeles International and Comparative Law Review 157 (2008). Reprinted by permission of Loyola of Los Angeles International and Comparative Law Review.

Eugene Kontorovich, *Beyond the Article I Horizon: Congress's Enumerated Powers and Universal Jurisdiction Over Drug Crimes*, 93 Minnesota Law Review 1191 (2009). Reprinted by permission of the author and the Minnesota Law Review.

Edward M. Morgan, *Traffic Circles: The Legal Logic of Drug Extraditions*, 31 University of Pennsylvania Journal of International Law 373 (2009). Reprinted by permission of the author.

Kristen McCallion, Comment, *War for Sale! Battlefield Contractors in Latin America & the 'Corporatization' of America's War on Drugs*, 36 University of Miami Inter-American Law Review 317 (2005). Reprinted by permission of the author and the University of Miami Inter-American Law Review.

Joanne Sum-Ping, Note: *A New Approach to Extraterritorial Application of Environmental Statutes?: Uncovering the Effects of Plan Colombia*, 31 Colombia Journal of Environmental Law 139 (2006). Reprinted by permission of the Columbia Journal of Environmental Law.

Raj Bhala, *Fighting Bad Guys with International Trade Law*, 31 University of California Davis Law Review 1 (1997). Reprinted by permission of the author.

Robert J. MacCoun, *What Can We Learn From the Dutch Cannabis Coffeeshop System?*, 106 Addiction 1899 (2011). Reprinted by permission of the journal for a fee via the Copyright Clearance Center.

Alex Kreit, *The Decriminalization Option: Should States Consider Moving From a Criminal to a Civil Drug Court Model?*, 2010 University of Chicago Legal Forum 299. Originally appearing in the *University of Chicago Legal Forum*, Vol. 2010. Reprinted with permission from the *University of Chicago Legal Forum* and the University of Chicago Law School.

James L. Nolan, Jr., *Harm Reduction and the American Difference: Drug Treatment and Problem-Solving Courts in Comparative Perspective*, 13 Journal of Health Care Law and Policy 31 (2010). Reprinted by permission of the author.

Peter Reuter, *Can Heroin Maintenance Help Baltimore?*, The Abell Foundation 2009. Reprinted by permission of the author.

Christopher Hallam, *What Can We Learn From Sweden's Drug Policy Experience?*, The Beckley Foundation Drug Policy Programme, Briefing Paper 20 (2010). Reprinted by permission of the Beckley Foundation.

Part I

It is difficult to think of a development that has had a greater impact on our criminal justice system over the past four decades than the war on drugs. More Americans are arrested for a drug offense each year—approximately 1.5 million in 2011—than for any other category of crime. Drug convictions have helped fuel the explosion in our prison population. The United States has the world's highest incarceration rate, with 750 of every 100,000 Americans in prison or jail as of 2008. Russia is second at 628 per 100,000, while most other countries have far lower rates. England, for example, incarcerates only 148 people per 100,000 and Denmark 67 per 100,000. *See* THE PEW CENTER ON THE STATES, ONE IN 100: BEHIND BARS IN AMERICA 2008, 35. Drug offenders account for almost one quarter of our prison population and the number of Americans incarcerated for drug offenses today is larger than the entire United States prison and jail population was in 1980. Meanwhile, drug investigations have had a dramatic influence on constitutional criminal procedure and policing, leading to (among other things) a rise in the use of informants, pre-textual traffic stops, and no-knock executions of warrants. Some commentators—and even some judges—have gone so far as to argue that courts have developed an implicit "drug exception" to the Constitution.

Although our drug laws are vigorously enforced, the wisdom and morality of drug prohibition remain hotly contested. Some argue that drug use and distribution are consensual, "victimless" activities that should not be criminalized at all. Others view drug prohibition as a moral imperative because of the harms to the community associated with substance abuse. In addition to the debate over whether it is just to criminalize drug transactions, there is widespread disagreement about how to calculate and balance the costs and benefits of prohibition. Does drug prohibition reduce drug use? If so, is the reduction in use substantial enough to be worth the price?

Discussions about the role of race and class in our criminal justice system also tend to focus on drug policy. In her book *The New Jim Crow*, Michelle Alexander argues that "[n]othing has contributed more to the systemic mass incarceration of people of color in the United States than the War on Drugs." MICHELLE ALEXANDER, THE NEW JIM CROW 59 (2010).

In addition to the policy issues raised by modern drug prohibition, drug laws can pose challenging legal problems. Almost every attorney who works in criminal law will encounter drug cases throughout her practice—from handling misdemeanor possession cases as a new attorney to navigating a wiretap drug conspiracy investigation years into practice. As in every area of the law, some drug cases may be straightforward. But even a seemingly run-of-the-mill drug case can be quite complex. Imagine, for example, that the police find drugs in a hotel room with two occupants, neither of whom claims responsibility for the drugs. Are both occupants guilty of drug possession? Neither?

This book provides an overview of the law and policy of controlled substances. Chapter 1 focuses on drugs and drug use by briefly examining the question of what is a drug and offering perspectives on substance use, abuse and addiction. Chapter 2 introduces some of the key policy questions related to drug prohibition in the United States. Chapter 3 moves from policy to legal doctrine with an overview of drug crimes, including: possession, possession with intent to distribute, manufacture, proof of the identity of a substance, and additional offenses like drug paraphernalia laws. Chapter 4 addresses drug sentencing and civil sanctions. Chapter 5 deals with the legal and policy issues raised by drug investigations, from the use of informants to racial profiling. Chapter 6 moves from criminal law to administrative law with an examination of the Controlled Substances Act, the federal law under which drugs of abuse are classified and controlled. Chapter 7 focuses on criminal and regulatory provisions related to the recreational use of medicines. Chapter 8 briefly surveys how the law treats three mind-altering substances that are legal to use recreationally, namely alcohol, tobacco and caffeine. Finally, Chapter 9 concludes with a look at international and comparative drug control law.

Chapter 1

Drugs and Drug Use

A. What Is a Drug?

Politicians and commentators frequently bemoan the problem of "drug" abuse in our society. Indeed, the war on "drugs" is perhaps one of the most recognizable policies in the United States. But what is a drug?

When President Barack Obama says he opposes drug legalization, no one thinks he is advocating a return to alcohol prohibition. Legally, alcohol is not classified as a drug. It is exempted from the Controlled Substances Act of 1970, which was enacted to provide a comprehensive and uniform structure for classifying and regulating drugs of abuse. *See* 21 U.S.C. 802(6) (providing that "[t]he term 'controlled substances'... does not include distilled spirits, wine, malt beverages, or tobacco"). Yet, one recent study that aimed to assess "the harms caused by the misuse of drugs" found that "alcohol was the most harmful drug (overall harm score 72), with heroin (55) and crack cocaine (54) in second and third places." David J. Nutt, Leslie A. King, and Lawrence D. Phillips, *Drug Harms in the UK: A Multicriteria Decision Analysis*, 376 The Lancet 1558 (2010). Is alcohol a "drug"?

How about caffeine? There are few restrictions on the sale and use of caffeine in the United States. Indeed, many public schools sell soft drinks that contain caffeine out of vending machines to children. When one company recently announced plans to sell an inhaler that dispenses breathable caffeine, however, Senator Charles Schumer (D-NY) attacked the product as "nothing more than a club drug designed to give users the ability to drink until they drop" and wrote to the Food and Drug Administration to ask them to review its safety. Anna Edney, *Caffeine Inhaler a Dangerous 'Club Drug,' Says Senator*, USA Today, Dec. 23, 2011. *See also*, Jane E. Brody, *Scientists See Dangers in Energy Drinks*, N.Y. Times, Jan. 31, 2011 (reporting that "a number of scientists are worried about highly caffeinated beverage like Red Bull, Rockstar, Monster and Full Throttle, which are popular among teenagers and young adults").

One recent study in the field of addiction looked at brain activity in response to food. The study asked participants to look at images of either a "luscious chocolate shake" or a "bland no-calorie solution." The researchers found that simply viewing images of the sweets caused participants who had three or more symptoms of food addiction to show increased brain activity in "the amygdala, anterior cingulate cortex and medial orbitofrontal cortex—the same regions that light up in drug addicts who are shown images of drug paraphernalia and drugs." Moreover, "[s]imilar to people suffering from substance abuse, the food-addicted participants also showed reduced activity in brain regions involved with self-control (the lateral orbitofrontal cortex), when they actually ate the ice cream." *See* Maia Szalavitz, *Heroin vs. Häagen-Dazs: What Food Addiction Looks Like in the Brain*, Time, April 4, 2011. Does this study mean that ice cream is a "drug"?

From Chocolate to Morphine:
Everything You Need to Know about Mind-Altering Drugs
Andrew Weil and Winifred Rosen
(1983)

Most people would agree that heroin is a drug. It is a white powder that produces striking changes in the body and mind in tiny doses. But is sugar a drug? Sugar is also a white powder that strongly affects the body, and some experts say it affects mental function and mood as well. Like heroin, it can be addicting. How about chocolate? Most people think of it as a food or flavor, but it contains a chemical related to caffeine, a stimulant, and can also be addicting. Is salt a drug? Many people think they cannot live without it, and it has dramatic effects on the body.

A common definition of the word *drug* is any substance that in small amounts produces significant changes in the body, mind, or both. This definition does not clearly distinguish drugs from some foods. The difference between a drug and a poison is also unclear. All drugs become poisons in high enough doses, and many poisons are useful drugs in low enough doses. Is alcohol a food, a drug, or a poison? The body can burn it as a fuel, just like sugar or starch, but it causes intoxication and can kill in overdose. Many people who drink alcohol crusade against drug abuse, never acknowledging that they themselves are involved with a powerful drug. In the same way, many cigarette addicts have no idea that tobacco is a strong drug, and many people who depend on coffee do not realize that they are addicted to a stimulant.

The decision to call some substances drugs and others not is often arbitrary. In the case of medical drugs — substances such as penicillin, used only to treat physical illness — the distinction may be easier to make. But talking about psychoactive drugs — substances that affect mood, perception, and thought — is tricky.

In the first place, foods, drugs, and poisons are not clear-cut categories. Second, people have strong emotional reactions to them. Food is good. Poison is bad. Drugs may be good or bad, and whether they are seen as good or bad depends on who is looking at them. Many people agree that drugs are good when doctors give them to patients in order to make them better. Some religious groups, such as Christian Scientists, do not share that view, however. They believe that God intends us to deal with illness without drugs.

When people take psychoactive drugs on their own, in order to change their mood or feel pleasure, the question of good or bad gets even thornier. The whole subject of pleasure triggers intense controversy. Should pleasure come as a reward for work or suffering? Should people feel guilty if they experience pleasure without suffering for it in some way? Should work itself be unpleasant? These questions are very important to us, but they do not have easy answers. Different people in different cultures answer them in different ways.

Drug use is universal. Every human culture in every age of history has used one or more psychoactive drugs. (The one exception is the Eskimos, who were unable to grow drug plants and had to wait for white men to bring them alcohol.) In fact, drug-taking is so common that it seems to be a basic human activity. Societies must come to terms with people's fascination with drugs. Usually the use of certain drugs is approved and integrated into the life of a tribe, community, or nation, sometimes in formal rituals and ceremonies. The approval of some drugs for some purposes usually goes hand in hand with the disapproval of other drugs for other purposes. For example, some early Muslim sects encouraged the use of coffee in religious rites, but had strict prohibitions against alcohol. On the other hand, when coffee came to Europe in the seventeenth century, the

Roman Catholic Church opposed it as an evil drug but continued to regard wine as a traditional sacrament.

Everybody is willing to call certain drugs bad, but there is little agreement from one culture to the next as to which these are. In our own society, all nonmedical drugs other than alcohol, tobacco, and caffeine are viewed with suspicion by the majority. There are subgroups within our society, however, that hold very different opinions. Many North American Indians who use peyote and tobacco in religious rituals consider alcohol a curse. The most fervent members of the counterculture that arose in the 1960s regard marijuana and psychedelics as beneficial while rejecting not only alcohol, tobacco, and coffee but most other legal and illegal drugs as well. Classic heroin addicts, or junkies, may reject psychedelics and marijuana as dangerous but think of narcotics as desirable and necessary. Some yogis in India use marijuana ritually, but teach that opiates and alcohol are harmful. Muslims may tolerate the use of opium, marijuana, and qat (a strongly stimulating leaf), but are very strict in their exclusion of alcohol.

Drug Abuse in America: Problem in Perspective, Second Report
National Commission on Marijuana and Drug Abuse
(1973)

The meaning of the word drug often varies with the context in which it is used. From a strictly scientific point of view, a drug is any substance other than food which by its chemical nature affects the structure or function of the living organism. From this perspective, the term includes some agricultural and industrial chemicals. The physician might define drug as any substance used as a medicine in the treatment of physical or mental disease; when treatment of illness is the referent, the lay public may use the word in the same sense. However, when used in the context of drug "abuse" or the drug "problem," the meaning of "drug" becomes social rather than scientific.

In its social sense, drug is not a neutral term. This point is illustrated by the fact that "drug problem" is frequently used not as a descriptive phrase, but a substitute for the word drug. In our visits to communities throughout this country and other nations, we have noted that local leaders often feel compelled to report not simply that drugs are available or that they are used, but that there is a "drug problem."

This value component of the word drug is reflected in the selective application of this term by the general public. Table 1-1, drawn from a Commission-sponsored National Survey illustrates that the public tends uniformly to regard heroin as a drug, as well as other substances associated with the drug problem, such as marijuana, cocaine, the amphetamines and the barbiturates. Some psychoactive substances, such as alcohol and tobacco, are generally not regarded as drugs at all. In neither public law nor public discussion is alcohol regarded as a drug. It may be called a beverage, a food, a social lubricant or a relaxant, but rarely is it called a drug.

The imprecision of the term "drug" has had serious social consequences. Because alcohol is excluded, the public is conditioned to regard a martini as something fundamentally different from a marihuana cigarette, a barbiturate capsule or a bag of heroin. Similarly, because the referents of the word "drug" differ so widely in the therapeutic and social contexts, the public is conditioned to believe that "street" drugs act according to entirely different principles than "medical" drugs. The result is that the risks of the former are exaggerated while the risks of the latter are overlooked.

Table 1-1. Substances Regarded as Drugs

	Adults (N = 2411) (percent)	Youth (N = 880) (percent)
Heroin	95	96
Cocaine	88	86
Barbiturates	83	91
Marihuana	80	80
Amphetamines	79	86
Alcohol	39	34
Tobacco	27	16
No opinion	1	1

This confusion must be dispelled. Alcohol *is* a drug. All drugs act according to the same general principles. Their effects vary with dose. For each drug there is an effective dose (in terms of the desired effect), a toxic dose and a lethal dose. All drugs have multiple effects. The lower the dose, the more important non-drug factors become in determining drug effect. At high dose levels, and for some individuals at much lower dose levels, all drugs may be dangerous. The individual and social consequences of drug use escalate with frequency and duration of use. American drug policy will never be coherent until it is founded on uniform principles such as these, which apply to *all* drugs.

––––––––––

As the material above discusses, the term "drug" is not amenable to a precise definition and may mean different things to different people and in different contexts. This book's title, *Controlled Substances*, signals its focus on drugs that are legally classified as controlled substances. Controlled substances are the drugs that are likely to come to mind when we think of the "war on drugs." The classification of a drug as a controlled substance means that it is a crime to possess, manufacture or distribute the substance for recreational use. Both "street" drugs like marijuana and prescription drugs that have recreational uses are regulated as controlled substances. Strictly medical drugs (like penicillin) or foods that have relatively mild mind-altering effects (like caffeine) are not. Although alcohol and tobacco are drugs used for recreation, both substances are specifically exempted from the federal Controlled Substances Act. 21 U.S.C. § 802(6).

B. Perspectives on Substance Use, Abuse and Addiction

There is an extensive range of artistic and scientific commentary on drug use, abuse and addiction.

Some sources recount positive experiences with mind-altering substances. In his 1954 nonfiction book *The Doors of Perception*, for example, novelist Aldous Huxley describes his use of the hallucinogen mescaline as something of a religious experience: "To be shaken out of the ruts of ordinary perception, to be shown for a few timeless hours the outer and inner world, not as they appear to an animal obsessed with survival or to a human being obsessed with words and notions, but as they are apprehended, directly and un-conditionally, by Mind at Large—this is an experience of inestimable value to everyone and especially to the intellectual." Others, like Irvine Welsh in his 1993 novel about a group of heroin addicts, *Trainspotting*, paint a decidedly grimmer picture. In the film adaptation, the main character describes withdrawal: "Too ill to sleep. Too tired to stay awake, but the sickness is on its way. Sweat, chills, nausea. Pain and craving. A need like nothing else I've ever known will soon take hold of me. It's on its way." There are also less dramatic accounts of drugs and drug use. Take, for example, *Wine Spectator* maga-zine, which features wine ratings and tasting notes. In 2009, *Westword*, a weekly news-paper in Denver, Colorado (where medical marijuana is legal) hired a critic to write similar reviews of marijuana. *See*, Kristen Wyatt, *Marijuana Critic Hired By Colorado Newspaper*, Associated Press, October 20, 2009. Psychologists, neuroscientists and physicians may not capture the popular imagination in the same way as novelists or film directors. But the scientific literature on substance use and abuse is equally diverse. Researchers in these fields work to, among other things, examine the pharmacology of different drugs, assess different drug treatment models, and provide diagnostic tools for identifying substance abuse and addiction.

The following excerpts provide a sampling of different perspectives on substance use, abuse and addiction. For additional readings, see e.g., Mike Jay, Artificial Paradises: A Drugs Reader (2000); Rebecca Shannonhouse and Pete Hamill, Under the In-fluence: The Literature of Addiction (2003). As you read through the material, re-flect on your own views and experiences. How does your perspective on substance use and abuse shape your beliefs about drug policy?

John Barleycorn
Jack London
(1913)

It all came to me one election day. It was on a warm California afternoon, and I had ridden down into the Valley of the Moon from the ranch to the little village to vote Yes and No to a host of proposed amendments to the Constitution of the State of Califor-nia. Because of the warmth of the day I had had several drinks before casting my ballot, and divers drinks after casting it. Then I had ridden up through the vine-clad hills and rolling pastures of the ranch, and arrived at the farm-house in time for another drink and supper.

"How did you vote on the suffrage amendment?" Charmian asked.

"I voted for it."

She uttered an exclamation of surprise. For, be it known, in my younger days, despite my ardent democracy, I had been opposed to woman suffrage. In my later and more tol-erant years I had been unenthusiastic in my acceptance of it as an inevitable social phenomenon.

"Now just why did you vote for it?" Charmian asked.

I answered. I answered at length. I answered indignantly. The more I answered, the more indignant I became. (No; I was not drunk. The horse I had ridden was well named "The Outlaw." I'd like to see any drunken man ride her.)

And yet—how shall I say?—I was lighted up, I was feeling "good," I was pleasantly jingled.

"When the women get the ballot, they will vote for prohibition," I said. "It is the wives, and sisters, and mothers, and they only, who will drive the nails into the coffin of John Barleycorn——"

"But I thought you were a friend to John Barleycorn," Charmian interpolated.

"I am. I was. I am not. I never am. I am never less his friend than when he is with me and when I seem most his friend. He is the king of liars. He is the frankest truthsayer. He is the august companion with whom one walks with the gods. He is also in league with the Noseless One. His way leads to truth naked, and to death. He gives clear vision, and muddy dreams. He is the enemy of life, and the teacher of wisdom beyond life's wisdom. He is a red-handed killer, and he slays youth."

And Charmian looked at me, and I knew she wondered where I had got it.

I continued to talk. As I say, I was lighted up. In my brain every thought was at home. Every thought, in its little cell, crouched ready-dressed at the door, like prisoners at midnight waiting a jail-break. And every thought was a vision, bright-imaged, sharp-cut, unmistakable. My brain was illuminated by the clear, white light of alcohol. John Barleycorn was on a truth-telling rampage, giving away the choicest secrets on himself. And I was his spokesman. There moved the multitudes of memories of my past life, all orderly arranged like soldiers in some vast review. It was mine to pick and choose. I was a lord of thought, the master of my vocabulary and of the totality of my experience, unerringly capable of selecting my data and building my exposition. For so John Barleycorn tricks and lures, setting the maggots of intelligence gnawing, whispering his fatal intuitions of truth, flinging purple passages into the monotony of one's days.

I outlined my life to Charmian, and expounded the make-up of my constitution. I was no hereditary alcoholic. I had been born with no organic, chemical predisposition toward alcohol. In this matter I was normal in my generation. Alcohol was an acquired taste. It had been painfully acquired. Alcohol had been a dreadfully repugnant thing——more nauseous than any physic. Even now I did not like the taste of it. I drank it only for its "kick." And from the age of five to that of twenty-five I had not learned to care for its kick. Twenty years of unwilling apprenticeship had been required to make my system rebelliously tolerant of alcohol, to make me, in the heart and the deeps of me, desirous of alcohol.

I sketched my first contacts with alcohol, told of my first intoxications and revulsions, and pointed out always the one thing that in the end had won me over——namely, the accessibility of alcohol. Not only had it always been accessible, but every interest of my developing life had drawn me to it. A newsboy on the streets, a sailor, a miner, a wanderer in far lands, always where men came together to exchange ideas, to laugh and boast and dare, to relax, to forget the dull toil of tiresome nights and days, always they came together over alcohol. The saloon was the place of congregation. Men gathered to it as primitive men gathered about the fire of the squatting place or the fire at the mouth of the cave.

I reminded Charmian of the canoe houses from which she had been barred in the South Pacific, where the kinky-haired cannibals escaped from their womenkind and feasted and drank by themselves, the sacred precincts taboo to women under pain of death. As a youth, by way of the saloon I had escaped from the narrowness of woman's influence into the wide free world of men. All ways led to the saloon. The thousand roads of romance and adventure drew together in the saloon, and thence led out and on over the world.

"The point is," I concluded my sermon, "that it is the accessibility of alcohol that has given me my taste for alcohol. I did not care for it. I used to laugh at it. Yet here I am, at the last, possessed with the drinker's desire. It took twenty years to implant that desire; and for ten years more that desire has grown. And the effect of satisfying that desire is anything but good. Temperamentally I am wholesome-hearted and merry. Yet when I walk with John Barleycorn I suffer all the damnation of intellectual pessimism."

"But," I hastened to add (I always hasten to add), "John Barleycorn must have his due. He does tell the truth. That is the curse of it. The so-called truths of life are not true. They are the vital lies by which life lives, and John Barleycorn gives them the lie."

"Which does not make toward life," Charmian said.

"Very true," I answered. "And that is the perfectest hell of it. John Barleycorn makes toward death. That is why I voted for the amendment to-day. I read back in my life and saw how the accessibility of alcohol had given me the taste for it. You see, comparatively few alcoholics are born in a generation. And by alcoholic I mean a man whose chemistry craves alcohol and drives him resistlessly to it. The great majority of habitual drinkers are born not only without desire for alcohol, but with actual repugnance toward it. Not the first, nor the twentieth, nor the hundredth drink, succeeded in giving them the liking. But they learned, just as men learn to smoke; though it is far easier to learn to smoke than to learn to drink. They learned because alcohol was so accessible. The women know the game. They pay for it—the wives and sisters and mothers. And when they come to vote, they will vote for prohibition. And the best of it is that there will be no hardship worked on the coming generation. Not having access to alcohol, not being predisposed toward alcohol, it will never miss alcohol. It will mean life more abundant for the manhood of the young boys born and growing up—ay, and life more abundant for the young girls born and growing up to share the lives of the young men."

"Why not write all this up for the sake of the men and women coming?" Charmian asked. "Why not write it so as to help the wives and sisters and mothers to the way they should vote?"

"The 'Memoirs of an Alcoholic,'" I sneered—or, rather, John Barleycorn sneered; for he sat with me there at table in my pleasant, philanthropic jingle, and it is a trick of John Barleycorn to turn the smile to a sneer without an instant's warning.

"No," said Charmian, ignoring John Barleycorn's roughness, as so many women have learned to do. "You have shown yourself no alcoholic, no dipsomaniac, but merely an habitual drinker, one who has made John Barleycorn's acquaintance through long years of rubbing shoulders with him. Write it up and call it 'Alcoholic Memoirs.'"

Confessions of an English Opium Eater
Thomas De Quincey
(1821)

I have often been asked how I first came to be a regular opium-eater, and have suffered, very unjustly, in the opinion of my acquaintance from being reputed to have brought upon myself all the sufferings which I shall have to record, by a long course of indulgence in this practice purely for the sake of creating an artificial state of pleasurable excitement. This, however, is a misrepresentation of my case. True it is that for nearly ten years I did occasionally take opium for the sake of the exquisite pleasure it gave me; but so long as I took it with this view I was effectually protected from all material bad consequences by the necessity of interposing long intervals between the several acts of indulgence, in order to renew the pleasurable sensations. It was not for the purpose of creating pleasure, but of mitigating pain in the severest degree, that I first began to use opium as an article of daily diet. In the twenty-eighth year of my age a most painful affection of the stomach, which I had first experienced about ten years before, attacked me in great strength. This affection had originally been caused by extremities of hunger, suffered in my boyish days. During the season of hope and redundant happiness which succeeded (that is, from eighteen to twenty-four) it had slumbered; for the three following years it had revived at intervals; and now, under unfavourable circumstances, from depression of spirits, it attacked me with a violence that yielded to no remedies but opium.

It is so long since I first took opium that if it had been a trifling incident in my life I might have forgotten its date; but cardinal events are not to be forgotten, and from circumstances connected with it I remember that it must be referred to the autumn of 1804. During that season I was in London, having come thither for the first time since my entrance at college. And my introduction to opium arose in the following way. From an early age I had been accustomed to wash my head in cold water at least once a day: being suddenly seized with toothache, I attributed it to some relaxation caused by an accidental intermission of that practice, jumped out of bed, plunged my head into a basin of cold water, and with hair thus wetted went to sleep. The next morning, as I need hardly say, I awoke with excruciating rheumatic pains of the head and face, from which I had hardly any respite for about twenty days. On the twenty-first day I think it was, and on a Sunday, that I went out into the streets, rather to run away, if possible, from my torments, than with any distinct purpose. By accident I met a college acquaintance, who recommended opium. Opium! dread agent of unimaginable pleasure and pain! I had heard of it as I had of manna or of ambrosia, but no further. How unmeaning a sound was it at that time: what solemn chords does it now strike upon my heart! what heart-quaking vibrations of sad and happy remembrances! Reverting for a moment to these, I feel a mystic importance attached to the minutest circumstances connected with the place and the time and the man (if man he was) that first laid open to me the Paradise of Opium-eaters. It was a Sunday afternoon, wet and cheerless: and a duller spectacle this earth of ours has not to show than a rainy Sunday in London. My road homewards lay through Oxford Street; and near "the *stately* Pantheon" (as Mr. Wordsworth has obligingly called it) I saw a druggist's shop. The druggist — unconscious minister of celestial pleasures! — as if in sympathy with the rainy Sunday, looked dull and stupid, just as any mortal druggist might be expected to look on a Sunday; and when I asked for the tincture of opium, he gave it to me as any other man might do, and furthermore, out of my shilling returned me what seemed to be real copper halfpence, taken out of a real wooden drawer. Nevertheless, in spite of such indications of humanity, he has ever since existed in my mind as the beatific vision of an immortal druggist, sent down to earth on a special mission to myself. And it confirms me in this way of considering him, that when I next came up to London I sought him near the stately Pantheon, and found him not; and thus to me, who knew not his name (if indeed he had one), he seemed rather to have vanished from Oxford Street than to have removed in any bodily fashion. The reader may choose to think of him as possibly no more than a sublunary druggist; it may be so, but my faith is better — I believe him to have evanesced, or evaporated. So unwillingly would I connect any mortal remembrances with that hour, and place, and creature, that first brought me acquainted with the celestial drug.

Arrived at my lodgings, it may be supposed that I lost not a moment in taking the quantity prescribed. I was necessarily ignorant of the whole art and mystery of opium-taking, and what I took I took under every disadvantage. But I took it — and in an hour — oh, heavens! what a revulsion! what an upheaving, from its lowest depths, of inner spirit! what an apocalypse of the world within me! That my pains had vanished was now a trifle in my eyes: this negative effect was swallowed up in the immensity of those positive effects which had opened before me — in the abyss of divine enjoyment thus suddenly revealed. Here was a panacea ... for all human woes; here was the secret of happiness, about which philosophers had disputed for so many ages, at once discovered: happiness might now be bought for a penny, and carried in the waistcoat pocket; portable ecstacies might be had corked up in a pint bottle, and peace of mind could be sent down in gallons by the mail-coach. But if I talk in this way the reader will think I am laughing, and I can assure him that nobody will laugh long who deals much with opium: its pleasures even are of a grave and solemn complexion, and in his happiest state the opium-eater cannot present himself in the character of *l'Allegro* [the cheerful man]: even then he speaks and thinks as becomes *Il Penseroso* [the pensive man]. Nevertheless, I have a very reprehensible way of jesting at times in the midst of my own misery; and unless when I am checked by some more powerful feelings, I am afraid I shall be guilty of this indecent practice even in these annals of suffering or enjoyment. The reader must allow a little to my infirm nature in this respect; and with a few indulgences of that sort I shall endeavour to be as grave, if not drowsy, as fits a theme like opium, so anti-mercurial as it really is, and so drowsy as it is falsely reputed.

Saying Yes: In Defense of Drug Use
Jacob Sullum
(2003)

Peter B. Lewis, who stepped down in 2001 after thirty-six years as CEO of Progressive Insurance, is widely admired as a hard-driving, innovative executive who transformed his company from a tiny player into the nation's fifth-largest auto-insurer — "a prodigiously growing, solidly successful stock market standout," as *Fortune* put it. Originally specializing in coverage for high-risk drivers, an area where it quickly became a leader, Progressive later moved into other types of auto insurance, making a name for itself through direct sales, candid price comparisons, and fast claims service. Between 1990 and 1999, the company had compounded growth of more than 23 percent, compared to an industry average of less than 5 percent. Progressive was the first insurer with a website and the first to sell policies online, pioneering forays that paid off dramatically: Its revenues jumped from $3.4 billion in 1996 to $6.1 billion three years later.

Lewis, the man who accomplished all this, still serves as Progressive's chairman and owns about 13 percent of the company, making him a billionaire. Observers call him a perfectionist, "an extraordinary businessman," and "an absolutist about untiring effort." They also call him a "functioning pothead."

Although he declined to comment on the question while he was CEO, friends said Lewis was a regular marijuana smoker. In 2000 these reports were confirmed in a very public way: Lewis was arrested for marijuana and hashish possession at the Auckland, New Zealand, airport. The authorities released him after he made a donation to the local drug rehabilitation center. The next year, when he was interviewed by the *Wall Street Journal* about his financial support for drug policy reform, he observed, "My personal experience lets me understand and have a view of the relative effects of some of these substances."

With his remarkable record of achievement, Lewis does not quite fit the pothead stereotype promoted in taxpayer-funded public service announcements: the lazy, stupid loser who can't get it together. A knowledge engineer in his early thirties who smoked marijuana about once a week summed up the official message this way: "Pot will destroy your life, and you'll end up sitting in a living room, not caring about anything, watching TV, unemployed, and broke." Most marijuana users do not become billionaires, of course, but neither do most of them lead empty unproductive lives. As misleading as it may be to hold Peter Lewis's career up as an example of what marijuana can do, it is equally misleading to cite users who never amount to anything as evidence of the drug's effects. The typical pot smoker lies somewhere between these two extremes.

Yet the failures spring to mind when people think about marijuana, mainly because they're conspicuous. They call attention to themselves through excessive, ostentatious indulgence that gets them into trouble at school and work. Responsible users, by contrast, have something to lose and therefore tend to be circumspect. If they acknowledge their drug user, they risk being tarred by stereotypes that manifestly do not apply to them. In 2001, Nick Gillespie, editor of *Reason* magazine (where I work), wrote an editorial in which he mentioned his own recreational use of drugs and observed: "Far from our drugs controlling us, by and large we control our drugs, as with alcohol, the primary motivation in taking drugs is to enjoy ourselves, not to destroy ourselves…. There is such a thing as responsible drug use, and it is the rule, not the exception." He and his colleagues were later mocked by editors of the *Wall Street Journal*'s opinion pages, who wrote, "We imagine the editorial meetings at *Reason* consisting of a brunch in earnest, well-scrubbed young wonks in bow ties sitting around a table debating the fine points of Social Security reform amid a haze of marijuana smoke." The humor here (such as it is) hinges on the idea that pot smokers are the sort of people who think nothing of getting stoned at work. If Gillespie had admitted a fondness for single-malt Scotch whiskey, the *Journal*'s editors presumably would not have imagined the *Reason* staff conducting their business in a drunken stupor.

During his 2000 presidential campaign, Steve Forbes neatly summed up this understanding of drugs as forces of evil. "Drugs are wrong," he said, "because they destroy the body, enslave the soul, and take away people's freedom to think and choose for themselves." According to this view, a drug user is not an independent moral agent because his will has been hijacked by a chemical.

If some drugs really do turn people into zombies, it makes no sense to expect self-control. But if voodoo pharmacology is a myth, it's reasonable to talk about illegal drugs the way we talk about alcohol. Anyone who is familiar with alcohol understands that there is nothing inevitable about the damage that drinkers can do to themselves and others. Reactions to alcohol depend upon individual characteristics and social context. Some people find that alcohol stimulates their thinking, while others find that it makes them stupid. There are happy drunks and sad drunks, outgoing drunks and shy drunks, loud drunks and quiet drunks, mean drunks and maudlin drunks, violent drunks and affectionate drunks, amorous drunks and impotent drunks. Not only do reactions vary from one person to another, but the same individual may display dramatically different reactions on different occasions.

In their 1969 book *Drunken Comportment*, MacAndrew and Edgerton pointed out that the behavior of drinkers varies between individuals in the same culture, across situations in the same individual, over time in the same individual, across cultures, across situations in the same culture, and over time in the same society. Their most interesting evidence came from cross-cultural comparisons, including societies in North America, South America, Africa, and Asia. They cited examples of societies where people would get falling-down drunk without any dramatic changes in demeanor and others where people routinely got into bloody fights after drinking. Within the same society, people drinking in a ceremonial context would be peaceful and friendly, while people drinking in a less structured situation would be raucous and violent, even though the amounts consumed were comparable. MacAndrew and Edgerton concluded that "drunken comportment is essentially a *learned* affair…. The way people comport themselves when drunk is determined not by alcohol's toxic assault upon the seat of moral judgment, conscious, or the like, but by what their society makes of and imparts to them concerning their state of drunkenness."

The psychiatrist Norman Zinberg made a similar point when he talked about the three factors that shape a drug's perceived effects. In addition to the drug itself, Zinberg said, the user's experience is influenced by his personality, expectations, and emotional state—the "set"—and by the physical, social, and cultural environment—the "setting." As another keen observer of human behavior once noted, "A drug is neither moral nor immoral—it's a chemical compound. The compound itself is not a menace to society until a human being treats it as if consumption bestowed a temporary license to act like an asshole." In other words, drugs do not cause behavior. How a person acts after taking drugs is determined by a complex interaction of variables, a process in which the user's beliefs and choices play crucial roles.

Scientists who are interested in looking at drug use as something other than a problem are not likely to get funding from the government, which has no interest in raising questions about its war on drugs, or from academic institutions that rely on government money. In a 1999 letter to *Harper's*, a researcher at Northern Illinois University reported that he and a colleague had been unable to obtain funding for a study of why people use drugs. He suggested that "no one in the anti-drug complex wants to learn that the choice to do drugs is for most people a rationale one, that users see themselves, rightly or wrongly, as benefiting from doing so."

As mainstream drug policy experts, such as UCLA's Mark Kleiman, have long concluded, the vast majority of illegal drug users do not become addicts, and the vast majority do not harm themselves or others. There's no denying that drug use carries risks, but those risks do not preclude a discussion of moderate use. To the contrary, they show the need for such a discussion.

PiHKAL: A Chemical Love Story
Alexander Shulgin and Ann Shulgin
(1991)

I am a pharmacologist and a chemist. I have spent most of my adult life investigating the actions of drugs; how they are discovered, what they are, what they do, how they can be helpful—or harmful. But my interests lie somewhat outside the mainstream of pharmacology, in the area I have found most fascinating and rewarding, that of the psychedelic drugs. Psychedelics might best be defined as physically non-addictive compounds which temporarily alter the state of one's consciousness.

The prevailing opinion in this country is that there are drugs that have legal status and are either relatively safe or at least have acceptable risks, and there are other drugs that are illegal and have no legitimate place at all in our society. Although this opinion is widely held and vigorously promoted, I sincerely believe that it is wrong. It is an effort to paint things either black or white, when, in this area, as in most of real life, truth is colored grey.

Let me give the reasons for my belief.

Every drug, legal or illegal, provides some reward. Every drug presents some risk. And every drug can be abused. Ultimately, in my opinion, it is up to each of us to measure the reward against the risk and decide which outweighs the other. The rewards cover a wide spectrum. They include such things as curing of disease, the softening of physical and emotional pain, intoxication, and relaxation. Certain drugs—those known as the psychedelics—allow for increased personal insight and expansion of one's mental and emotional horizons.

The risks are equally varied, ranging from physical damage to psychological disruption, dependency, and a violation of the law. Just as there are different rewards with different people, there are also different risks. An adult must make his own decision as to whether or not he should expose himself to a specific drug, be it available by prescription or proscribed by law, by measuring the potential good and bad with his own personal yardstick. And it is here that being well informed plays an indispensable role. My philosophy can be distilled into four words: be informed, then choose.

I personally have chosen some drugs to be of sufficient value to be worth the risks; others, I deem not to be of sufficient value. For instance, I use a moderate amount of alcohol, generally in the form of wine—and at the present time—my liver function tests are completely normal. I do not smoke tobacco. I used to, quite heavily, then gave it up. It was not the health risk that swayed me, but rather the fact that I had become completely dependent upon it. That was, in my view, a case of the price being unacceptably high.

Each such decision is my own, based on what I know of the drug and what I know about myself.

Among the drugs that are currently illegal, I have chosen not to use marijuana, as I feel the light-headed intoxication and benign alteration of consciousness does not adequately compensate for an uncomfortable feeling that I am wasting time.

I have tried heroin. This drug, of course, is one of the major concerns in our society, at the present time. In me, it produces a dreamy peacefulness, with no rough edges of worry, stress or concern. But there is also a loss of motivation, of alertness, and of the urge to get things done. It is not any fear of addiction that causes me to decide against heroin; it is the fact that, under its influence, nothing seems to be particularly important to me.

I have also tried cocaine. This drug, particularly in its notorious "crack" form, is the cause celebre of today. To me, cocaine is an aggressive pusher, a stimulant which gives me a sense of power and of being completely with it, on top of the world. But there is also the inescapable knowledge, underneath, that it is not true power, that I am not really on top of the world, and that, when the drug's effects have disappeared, I will have gained nothing. There is a strange sense of falseness about the state. There is no insight. There is no learning. In its own distinctive way, I find cocaine to be as much an escape drug as heroin. With either one, you escape from who you are, or—even more to the point—from who you are not. In either case you are relieved for a short time from awareness of your inadequacies. I frankly would rather address mine than escape them; there is, ultimately, far greater satisfaction that way.

With the psychedelic drugs, I believe that, for me, the modest risks (an occasional difficult experience or perhaps some body malaise) are more than balanced by the potential for learning. And that is why I have chosen to explore this particular area of pharmacology.

I am completely convinced that there is a wealth of information built into us, with miles of intuitive knowledge tucked away in the genetic material of every one of our cells. Something akin to a library containing uncountable reference volumes, but without any obvious route of entry. And, without some means of access, there is no way to even begin to guess at the extent and quality of what is there. The psychedelic drugs allow exploration of this interior world, and insights into its nature.

Rethinking Addiction: Drugs, Deterrence, and the Neuroscience Revolution
Linda C. Fentiman
14 University of Pennsylvania Journal of Law and Social Change 233 (2011)

In recent years, neuroscience research has provided astounding insight into the biochemical and physical processes through which people become dependent on addictive drugs. Drugs affect the brain at the most basic levels, causing changes in gene expression, neuronal firing, and brain circuitry, which in turn are linked to subsequent behaviors. All drugs affect neurotransmitters, the chemicals that send messages between individual neurons. Many scientists see dopamine, a particularly important neurotransmitter, as a key to understanding the puzzle of addiction because all drugs, including alcohol and nicotine, affect it. Dopamine plays an essential role in the normal pleasurable sensations humans feel—when eating, falling in love, and having sex—but the quality and quantity of dopamine produced by drug use far surpasses the amounts released in these naturally pleasurable moments. Many researchers posit that this is precisely why drugs are so attractive: they can deliver unique euphoric effects not otherwise achievable.

Scientists are still debating the exact mechanisms by which drugs become addictive. Many researchers have concluded that drug use establishes reward circuits that dopamine and other chemicals mediate, which become hard-wired into the brain. This is an example of the more general phenomenon of "neural plasticity:" the idea that portions of the brain change and grow in response to repeated activity. Environmental stimuli, including stress, also shape brain development, and dopamine and other brain chemicals mediate the impact of stress.

All addictive drugs affect the limbic region of the brain, which is believed to be the physical site where learning and memory, as well as emotional reactions, occur. That drug reward circuits are centered in the limbic area, a more "primitive" portion of the brain, suggests that they may be harder to change than neurological circuits found in parts of the brain devoted to higher order reasoning and speech. Indeed, there is a very high correlation between drugs that humans abuse and drugs that laboratory animals will learn to "self-administer."

Different drugs act through different mechanisms and at multiple brain sites, but generally the brain responds to drug administration by either enhancing or diminishing the production and availability of dopamine. Drugs such as cocaine, amphetamines, methamphetamines, and ecstasy appear to directly increase the concentration of dopamine in the limbic region, while other drugs, including alcohol, nicotine, opiates, and marijuana, appear to act indirectly by inducing the firing of brain neurons and the release of dopamine to specific drug-sensitive neural receptors.

Leading neuroscience researchers George Koob and Michel Le Moal have hypothesized a three stage cycle of addiction: the "preoccupation/anticipation" stage, the "binge/intoxication" stage, and the "withdrawal/negative affect" stage. In their view, addiction involves a progression from an "impulsive" to a "compulsive" disorder. Koob and Le Moal's theory involves a feedback loop of two "opponent processes," in which drug use leads both to a short-lived positive response, the dopamine-infused "high," and a negative response of greater duration, the comedown or "crash" after the high. These much longer-lasting negative feelings predispose a drug user to take more drugs in order to eliminate the feelings.

Other researchers hypothesize that a drug's reinforcing power is not due to direct changes in the amount of dopamine available, but to indirect changes in which drug use and exposure predict future rewards. Under these theories, repeated drug use gives certain previously neutral environmental stimuli "salience," stimulating desire for the drug. For example, regular cocaine users showed increased brain activity in the limbic system and the prefrontal cortex (the site of "executive functioning") when they were exposed to images of drugs and drug paraphernalia, even when the exposure was too short to permit them to identify the image.

Neuroscience research has also illuminated multiple contributors to relapse. "Drug-priming" (e.g., taking one drink) after a long period of abstinence quickly reinstates drug cravings. In addition, drug users frequently relapse not only in an effort to avoid the negative effects of drug withdrawal (e.g., a Bloody Mary in the morning to cure a hangover), but also because they are affected by environmental stimuli, including cues associated with drug use, as noted above. Stress, mediated through brain chemicals, also precipitates relapse, and the limbic system features prominently in this process. Since the amygdala, and the limbic system generally, is the locus of emotional memory and "fear conditioning," researchers have speculated that the limbic system plays a role in the process of relapse.

Even as neuroscience research increases our understanding of the neurophysiology of drug addiction, it does not provide a complete picture. Other researchers, particularly psychologists and other behaviorists, have built on neuroscience to develop a theory with a different emphasis. While acknowledging that repeated drug use is involved in the development of reinforcement pathways in the brain, they suggest that drugs work no differently from other reinforcing stimuli. They assert that drug addiction is merely one kind of learned behavior, which is acquired (and can be extinguished) in the same way as other behaviors. [T]heir work relies on principles of classical conditioning, studies showing that humans as well as animals respond to positive rewards, and empirical data showing that many addicts "age out" of excessive drug-taking.

Individuals' genetic make-up can make them more vulnerable to drug addiction, as chronic drug exposure appears to affect gene expression. While scientists have long recognized that alcoholism and other types of substance abuse seem to run in families, today it is clear that the genetic contribution to addiction is highly complex, affecting both an individual's biology and personality—thus one's genes may increase or decrease the risk that one will try drugs, use them frequently, become tolerant of their effects, seek more of them, and relapse. On the biological side, for example, some genetic risk factors for addiction or substance abuse appear to be physiological. For example, many Chinese people have inherited a gene ... that affects their ability to metabolize alcohol and increases the likelihood that they will become ill even when consuming small amounts of alcohol. There are also genetic variations in the extent to which stopping drug use causes dopamine levels to drop, which may prompt relapse.

Other genetic factors appear to be more psychological or behavioral. Thus, one's genes may increase or decrease the risk that one will try drugs, use them frequently, become tolerant of their effects, seek more of them, and relapse. Some scientists speculate that certain genes predispose people to risk-taking, making them more likely to experiment with drugs and to otherwise live "on the edge." Others hypothesize that having genes that make one less likely to be inhibited or more likely to engage in oppositional behavior can increase vulnerability to drug use and abuse. Researchers have even found a genetic predisposition for "going along with the crowd" when in a group of heavy drinkers. Behaviorists accept these genetic links, but suggest that it is not only addicts' genetic predispositions but also their prior learning histories and greater exposure to drugs that increase the odds that drugs will be particularly reinforcing to them, particularly if competing reinforcers are less powerful.

Environmental factors are also crucial in determining whether people who experiment with alcohol and other drugs will go on to become addicts. A constellation of related factors make drug abuse and addiction more likely. These include neighborhood poverty, physical and sexual abuse, a lack of parental support, lower socioeconomic status, stress, and widespread access to drugs. Studies have shown a strong correlation between childhood stressors, such as sexual and physical abuse, domestic violence, parental alcoholism and mental illness, and the incidence of many adult health problems.

Some researchers question whether a biologically-focused disease model of addiction can completely explain why people do or do not become addicted, and why certain people find it easier to stop using drugs than others. These researchers accept studies showing that continued drug use causes chemical and structural changes in the brain, but ask whether this necessarily means that drug addiction is involuntary. As psychologist Gene Heyman notes in his recent book, *Addiction: A Disorder of Choice*, the majority of substance abuse researchers and clinicians contend that drug abuse is a chronic illness caused by changes in the brain due to drug ingestion, which set up the user to want to use more drugs more frequently. This group further asserts that because addiction has a biological basis it is most appropriately treated like other chronic illnesses, such as diabetes or Alzheimer's disease.

Heyman and others challenge this view, arguing instead that addiction results, at least in part, from differences in individual decision-making styles. Heyman notes that epidemiological data shows that most drug addicts decide, at some point, to reduce or give up their drug use, a phenomenon known as "aging out," because of the adverse consequences threatened by continued use. In his view, this evidence suggests that people are capable of choosing not to use drugs when it becomes apparent that it is in their self-interest. Heyman further asserts that addiction is but one example of a larger pattern of impaired decision-making, which he describes as the problem of "local" versus "global" choice. Local choice is the immediate choice, and most people prefer something that immediately provides a positive reward. Global choice, on the other hand, involves being able to take a longer-term view, which leads to an outcome more favorable in the aggregate and over time, even if some of the near-term consequences are less desirable. Heyman argues that those who succeed in quitting do so because they adopt a global choice perspective. Many make a conscious choice to quit because it is necessary to feed their families, keep their job, or avoid arrest. In contrast, Heyman observes, those people who continue to use drugs frequently suffer from co-existing mental or physical illnesses which make it harder for them to limit their drug use.

One way to encourage addicts to transition from "local" to "global" decision-making is to provide financial incentives for healthy behavior. Incentive-based programs have been quite successful in encouraging and supporting drug addicts to abstain from or reduce their use of drugs. Drawing upon classical learning theory and the principles of operant conditioning, these "contingency management interventions" target specific desired behaviors and offer concrete rewards for engaging in them. Not only have these incentives effectively helped addicts refrain from drug use during the critical period at the beginning of drug treatment, but they also have been shown to have an impact long after the intervention has ended. The most successful incentive programs do not simply reward desired behavior, such as drug-free urine samples or attendance at substance abuse treatment sessions, but do so in a progressive manner, so that each time program participants meet the behavioral goal, the reward for subsequent compliance increases.

Contingency management interventions are an effective supplement to traditional substance abuse treatment because they enable addicts to abstain from drug use in the early stages of recovery while other aspects of treatment, such as medication, counseling, and skills training, make long-term abstinence more likely.

While contingency management programs have not yet been tried extensively with pregnant drug users, preliminary studies have shown that incentives increase women's participation in prenatal care and contribute to better birth outcomes. One promising study examined the effect of contingent vouchers on pregnant smokers who were interested in quitting. The "contingent" group — those who were given vouchers if, and only if, their urinalysis demonstrated they had not smoked recently — had rates of abstinence that were five times greater than the group who received vouchers whenever they had a clinic visit. Other studies that offered incentives to pregnant women to quit smoking also had positive outcomes, which were particularly impressive because they involved low-income women with little education, a group that has long resisted smoking cessation efforts. Contingent incentive programs that rewarded pregnant heroin and cocaine addicts who attended treatment sessions and provided "clean" urine samples were also successful, although this was true only when the incentives increased in response to each successive positive result. While researchers have noted the concern that incentives could be expensive, local merchants and other community groups donated the necessary goods or cash in many studies. In addition, while some might object that it is morally inappropriate to pay people to do what they ought to be doing anyway, the results of contingency management programs — and, indeed, the complicated nature of addiction described herein — suggest that it is prudent to pay for incentives now to prevent future undesired behavior, which will be costly in terms of human suffering and taxpayer dollars.

Indeed, physicians, health insurers, and policymakers, both in the United States and abroad, are finding that incentives are cost-effective in a wide range of scenarios. For example, studies have found that American patients who take blood thinners to avoid strokes increase compliance with their medication regimen when they receive small financial payments. India recently announced the success of a major initiative that improved maternal and infant mortality by paying mothers to deliver their babies in hospitals rather than at home. Some Mexican cities have successfully implemented dietary incentive programs to help police officers lose weight.

In sum, it is critical to understand that biology in general, and neuroscience in particular, provides only a partial explanation of why certain people become, and remain, drug abusers and addicts. Behavioral researchers have offered persuasive evidence that changes in the brain caused by drug exposure need not be permanent, and that incentives and other behavioral interventions may encourage addicts to end their dependence on drugs. However, in order to develop effective strategies to reduce addiction and minimize its harmful consequences, researchers must also consider other factors that affect addiction.

Chapter 2

Perspectives on Prohibition and Its Alternatives

Beliefs about what sort of conduct should be the subject of criminal punishment typically fall into one of two categories: consequentialist and deontological.

Consequentialist arguments are focused on outcomes. Under the chief consequentialist theory of punishment, utilitarianism, punishment is justified if the benefits to society outweigh the costs. This formulation is easy enough to state but exceedingly difficult to apply. This is because there are a wide range of costs and benefits involved in criminal punishment and many of the figures depend on predictions about the future (like how many would-be criminals will be deterred by a given law) or involve considerations that are not easily quantifiable (like the emotional pain experienced by a crime victim or by a child of someone who is incarcerated).

Deontological philosophies, like retribution, are not concerned with results. Retributivists believe that moral blameworthiness justifies punishment, regardless of any costs or benefits to society. As Immanuel Kant famously put it: "Even if a Civil Society resolved to dissolve itself with the consent of all its members ... the last Murderer lying in the prison ought to be executed before the resolution was carried out." IMMANUEL KANT, THE PHILOSOPHY OF LAW 198 (1887).

Though there are some who subscribe only to one theory of punishment, in practice most discussions about when criminal punishment is justified involve a mixture of utilitarian and retributivist arguments.

Whatever moral philosophy one subscribes to, retributivists and utilitarians alike generally agree that the conduct covered by most criminal statutes calls for criminal punishment. To be sure, there is often strong disagreement about *how much* punishment a robber should receive. But, few object to the existence of criminal laws against robbery (or sexual assault or homicide).

The shape of the debate over drug crimes is much different. Though criminal laws against the possession, distribution and manufacture of controlled substances are well established, there is a vigorous and ongoing debate over whether this sort of activity should be criminalized at all. The material below sketches the main arguments in this debate. It is roughly divided into two sections covering deontological (is drug criminalization just?) and consequentialist (does drug criminalization work?) perspectives.

A. Is Drug Criminalization Just?

One of the most prominent objections to criminal drug laws is that they punish "victimless" conduct. Are drug crimes truly "victimless"?

Wisconsin v. Hoseman

Court of Appeals of Wisconsin
2011 WI App 88

Anderson, J.

Seeking to escape responsibility for damages that rendered an 1885 Victorian home uninhabitable, Michael S. Hoseman appeals from a judgment of conviction in which the court included an order that he pay a $25,000 portion of restitution totaling $106,409.63. Hoseman asserts that the manufacture of marijuana is a "victimless" crime; therefore, he reasons the owners of the residence are not "direct victims" of his criminal conduct. We reject Hoseman's argument and affirm that his unauthorized alterations to the residence in order to construct and operate a hydroponic growing operation were at the heart of the extensive damages that made the residence uninhabitable.

Along with four other individuals, Hoseman was charged with a single count of conspiracy to manufacture between 2500 and 10,000 grams of marijuana. The charge arose after law enforcement uncovered a sophisticated marijuana growing operation in Walworth county.

The State and Hoseman reached a plea agreement under which Hoseman pled guilty to a lesser charge of conspiracy to manufacture between 200 and 1000 grams of marijuana. The trial court imposed three years' initial confinement and three years' extended supervision. It also tentatively held Hoseman was jointly and severally liable for restitution of $106,409.63 in property damages.

The underlying facts are not in dispute. The growing operation was set up in an 1885 Victorian home owned by Tom and Lisa Burbey. Initially, the Burbeys had the house on the market for sale but without any potential buyers, they decided to rent out the house. Hoseman, posing as the son of co-conspirator John G. Olson, approached the Burbeys seeking to rent the house as a weekend retreat and represented that the long-range plan was to move to the house and purchase it from the Burbeys. After Tom Burbey finalized the lease, he moved to Las Vegas, Nevada, to join his wife.

Olson provided almost $180,000 in capital for the development of the hydroponic growing operation and Hoseman served as the on-scene architect. Two upstairs bedrooms were converted to grow rooms using nutrients from Canada; hydroponic growing equipment purchased from suppliers in California—including buckets, lights, ballasts, fertilizer and a growing medium. Starting with marijuana seeds from Amsterdam, the original fifty plants were cloned to produce 200 plants with a street value of $300,000 to $500,000. To prepare the two grow rooms, blankets covered all the windows and sheets were stapled to the walls to reflect the grow lights. Hoses and electrical wiring ran up the stairs. Fifty-gallon drums that held the nutrients and residual acids from the operation were drained into toilets and sinks. The exhaust gases from the growing operation were vented directly into the house. For security, closed circuit televisions were mounted in the house to provide coverage of the outside lot.

After not receiving rental payments from Hoseman for several months, Tom Burbey returned to Walworth county to begin an eviction action. Upon arriving at the house, he had to break in because the locks had been changed. After discovering the growing operation, Burbey notified law enforcement.

The Burbeys filed a restitution claim for property damage in the amount of $106,409.63. The damage they documented stated that high humidity from the operation encouraged mold and mildew damage to the walls, fixtures, wood and curtains. The huge barrels of chemicals needed for the operation ruined wood floors, carpeting and an antique rug. There were hundreds of staple holes in the walls as the result of stapling reflective sheets. THC resin saturated many surfaces; there was testimony that the "[s]ticky sappy stuff doesn't wash off that sticks to your hands, it leaves your handprint on it when you touch it and smells like marijuana and stinks like marijuana and never goes away." Draining acidic chemicals into the toilets and sinks created stains; the toilets were also stopped up with plant material. Finally, the furnace was not working, resulting in frozen water pipes. In their claim for restitution, the Burbeys asserted that as a result of the damages, their residence was uninhabitable.

After sentencing, Hoseman and his co-conspirators filed a motion demanding an evidentiary hearing on the Burbeys' claim for restitution. When the hearing began, the co-conspirators objected to the court's authority to hear the claim for restitution, insisting that the Burbeys were not victims of a crime.

> Judge, first of all, in a drug case there — in fact, I had a sentencing before you last week where even the state asserted in a drug case there is no victim. Number one, if this were a burglary matter, sexual assault, homicide, something of that nature, then this person could claim to be a victim. This is a civil matter with civil damages, and they have not asserted in any way.

The Burbeys' attorney responded, the house "was not rented to operate a marijuana greenhouse. It was operated as a residential rental. It was a home. They used my clients' house, water, electricity, heat, all of the equipment, the fixtures, everything in my clients' house for that enterprise. That makes my client[s] [] victim[s]."

The trial court denied the motion, holding that the use of the Burbeys' house was a part of the conspiracy to manufacture marijuana. The court concluded that conducting the criminal enterprise in the Burbeys' house made them victims as defined in Wis. Stat. § 950.02(4)(a)(1), entitling them to restitution under Wis. Stat. § 973.20. The court went on to conduct an evidentiary hearing that lasted over two days. At the conclusion of the hearing, the court determined that restitution damages totaled $106,409.63. It set Hoseman's restitution at $25,000, based on his ability to pay during the six-year term of his sentence. Hoseman appeals.

On appeal, Hoseman continues with his theme that the manufacture of marijuana is a "victimless" crime; specifically, he argues that the Burbeys are not victims under Wis. Stat. § 973.20 and are not allowed to receive restitution. He contends that the term "victim" as defined in the statutes is "a person against whom a crime has been committed" and does not include all of those who suffered pecuniary losses caused by a defendant's crime.

The scope of the trial court's authority to order restitution is a question of statutory interpretation. The interpretation of a statute is a question of law which this court reviews de novo.

Restitution is governed by Wis. Stat. § 973.20. It provides, in relevant part:

> When imposing sentence or ordering probation for any crime ... for which the defendant was convicted, the court ... shall order the defendant to make full or partial restitution under this section to any victim of a crime considered at sen-

tencing ... unless the court finds substantial reason not to do so and states the reason on the record....

Because the restitution statute does not define the term "victim," we turn to Wis. Stat. §950.02(4)(a), which is a related statute. Section 950.02(4)(a)(1) provides that "victim" means "[a] person against whom a crime has been committed."

Case law arising under the restitution statute informs us that there are two components to the question of whether restitution can be ordered. First, the claimant of restitution must be a "direct victim" of the crime. Second, there must be a causal connection between the defendant's conduct and harm suffered by the claimant.

To answer the first component of the analysis, we are required to determine who is "a person against whom a crime has been committed." In *State v. Vanbeek,* 316 Wis. 2d 527, we discussed who is a "direct victim" of a crime. Vanbeek left a bomb scare note in a lunch room threatening to harm school property, forcing the school district to evacuate students and staff to another location. After Vanbeek was found guilty of making a bomb scare, the school district sought restitution, including the salaries and benefits of teachers and staff. We affirmed the circuit court's order for restitution.

In opposing restitution, "Vanbeek argue[d] that the persons occupying the school were the direct victims of his crime, and that the school district was only collaterally impacted." We rejected his attack:

> This argument misses the mark. Vanbeek conveyed a false threat to destroy school district property, which resulted in an evacuation and a direct loss to the school district. There is no doubt that the conduct involved in the crime considered at sentencing—conveying a threat to destroy school district property by means of explosives—was directed at the school district. Vanbeek left the bomb scare note on school district property and the note threatened to destroy school district property.

Hoseman makes an argument similar to Vanbeek's that the Burbeys were not directly impacted by the manufacture of marijuana:

> [T]he defendant was not convicted of any crime related to the damage of property. The offense of manufacturing with intent to deliver THC is not a crime committed against or directed against the homeowners, and thus, under Wisconsin law, the homeowners should not have been awarded restitution under Wis. Stat. §973.20.

Like Vanbeek, Hoseman relies on cases that considered "whether the government (on behalf of law enforcement agencies) or police officers were direct victims, and we determined that the government claimant was not a direct victim entitled to restitution." He argues that *State v. Ortiz,* 247 Wis. 2d 836, "hammers home how stringent Wisconsin courts have delineated between direct victims" and "closely related parties." In *Ortiz* we rejected a city's request for restitution of overtime costs incurred in mobilizing a SWAT team to arrest Ortiz who refused to come out of his house. We held that the police officers were the direct victims of Ortiz's criminal conduct and not the city:

> [T]he fact remains that it was the police, not the city, who were the direct and actual victims of Ortiz's crimes. Ortiz did not threaten to injure the city—he threatened to injure the police officers. Ortiz did not fail to comply with an attempt by the city to take him into custody—he failed to comply with the police effort to take him into custody. Ortiz did not obstruct the city—he obstructed the police. And finally, Ortiz's disorderly conduct was not targeted at the city—it was targeted at the police.

Hoseman also relies on *State v. Lee,* 314 Wis. 2d 764, where we held that a police officer who was injured chasing the defendant from the scene of an armed burglary and armed robbery was not a direct victim because he was not the target of the crime of conviction. He argues that *Lee* supports his thesis that because he was not charged with damaging the Burbeys' property, they are not the direct victims of the crime of conviction.

To further support his argument, Hoseman states that "the record does not indicate that there was any direct victim to the crime sentenced upon, in that there was no evidence presented of any purchasers of the defendant's THC product."

The cases Hoseman relies upon are inapposite under the facts of this case; they stand for the proposition that governmental entities are not entitled to restitution for collateral expenses incurred in the normal course of law enforcement. Hoseman is convicted of conspiracy to manufacture marijuana; in furtherance of that conspiracy, Hoseman rented the Burbeys' residence using a ruse, he converted two upstairs rooms into grow rooms for hydroponic growing equipment, he allowed exhaust gases to vent directly into the residence, he ran hoses and electrical wiring up the stairs, and he drained chemicals into the toilets and sinks of the residence. This is not similar to the situation in *Ortiz* where the city tried to ride on the coattails of the police officers who were the targets of Ortiz's criminal conduct. Likewise, this is not similar to *Lee* where the police officer's injury as collateral damage arising after the crime of conviction was committed. What distinguishes this case from those relied upon by Hoseman is the Burbeys, as owners of the residence, were the direct targets of the conspiracy to manufacture marijuana; it was their residence that was altered and made uninhabitable to further the goal of the conspiracy. If the alterations to the Burbeys' residence had not been made, Hoseman and his co-conspirators could not have manufactured marijuana. The alterations are not collateral to the manufacture of marijuana, they are integral. As the Burbeys' attorney so eloquently argued, the house "was not rented to operate a marijuana greenhouse. It was operated as a residential rental. It was a home. They used my clients' house, water, electricity, heat, all of the equipment, the fixtures, everything in my clients' house for that enterprise. That makes my client[s] [] victim[s]."

The Washington Court of Appeals reached the same result in *State v. Coe,* 939 P.2d 715 (Wash. Ct. App. 1997). Like Hoseman, Coe argued "that growing marijuana is a 'victimless' crime and that the State's failure to charge him with vandalism or some other crime that includes an element of property damage makes restitution inappropriate." The court promptly rejected this argument because there was substantial evidence establishing that Coe made "unauthorized alterations to the house's electrical and ventilation systems to facilitate the manufacture of marijuana." Similar to Coe, Hoseman made unauthorized alterations to the residence in order to construct and operate a hydroponic growing operation.

Having concluded that the Burbeys were direct victims of the conspiracy to manufacture marijuana, we turn to the second component of our analysis—whether there is a causal connection between the defendant's entire course of conduct and harm suffered by the claimant.

We have previously summarized the extensive damage to the Burbeys' residence that made it uninhabitable and Hoseman does not seriously challenge the inescapable conclusion that the actions taken in furtherance of the conspiracy to manufacture marijuana caused the damage to the residence.

Hoseman's unauthorized alterations to the residence and unauthorized operation of a marijuana growing operation were integral to the damages that rendered the residence uninhabitable. And Hoseman's conduct of turning an 1885 Victorian home into a twenty-first century hydroponic marijuana growing operation was the substantial factor in causing the damages incurred by the Burbeys.

By the Court. — Judgment affirmed.

It is clear that Hoseman caused damage to the Burbeys' home. But were the Burbeys victims of Hoseman's cultivation of marijuana in the same sense that someone whose wallet is stolen is a victim of theft? It certainly would have been possible for Hoseman to grow marijuana without damaging the Burbeys' home by, for example, growing a smaller number of plants or designing his operation with greater care. Similarly, Hoseman could have caused just as much damage to the Burbeys' home if he had grown a legal plant in the same fashion as he had the marijuana. What principles should guide the definition of "victim" in the criminal law?

The argument that drug crimes should not be punished because they are victimless is rooted in the harm principle. The harm principle posits that criminal punishment should be reserved for conduct that harms others. John Stuart Mill provided the most well-known and enduring description of the harm principle in his 1859 essay *On Liberty*.

On Liberty
John Stuart Mill
(1859)

The object of this Essay is to assert one very simple principle, as entitled to govern absolutely the dealings of society with the individual in the way of compulsion and control, whether the means used be physical force in the form of legal penalties, or the moral coercion of public opinion. That principle is, that the sole end for which mankind are warranted, individually or collectively in interfering with the liberty of action of any of their number, is self-protection. That the only purpose for which power can be rightfully exercised over any member of a civilized community, against his will, is to prevent harm to others. His own good, either physical or moral, is not a sufficient warrant. He cannot rightfully be compelled to do or forbear because it will be better for him to do so, because it will make him happier, because, in the opinions of others, to do so would be wise, or even right. These are good reasons for remonstrating with him, or reasoning with him, or persuading him, or entreating him, but not for compelling him, or visiting him with any evil, in case he do otherwise. To justify that, the conduct from which it is desired to deter him must be calculated to produce evil to some one else. The only part of the conduct of any one, for which he is amenable to society, is that which concerns others. In the part which merely concerns himself, his independence is, of right, absolute. Over himself, over his own body and mind, the individual is sovereign.

It is proper to state that I forego any advantage which could be derived to my argument from the idea of abstract right as a thing independent of utility. I regard utility as the ultimate appeal on all ethical questions; but it must be utility in the largest sense, grounded on the permanent interests of man as a progressive being. Those interests, I contend, authorize the subjection of individual spontaneity to external control, only in respect to those actions of each, which concern the interest of other people. If any one does an act hurtful to others, there is a prima facie case for punishing him, by law, or, where legal penalties are not safely applicable, by general disapprobation. There are also many positive acts for the benefit of others, which he may rightfully be compelled to perform; such as, to give evidence in a court of justice; to bear his fair share in the common defence, or in any other joint work necessary to the interest of the society of which he enjoys the protection; and to perform certain acts of individual beneficence, such as saving a fellow-creature's life, or interposing to protect the defenceless against ill-usage, things which whenever it is obviously a man's duty to do, he may rightfully be made responsible to society for not doing. A person may cause evil to others not only by his actions but by his inaction, and in neither case he is justly accountable to them for the injury. The latter case, it is true, requires a much more cautious exercise of compulsion than the former. To make any one answerable for doing evil to others, is the rule; to make him answerable for not preventing evil, is, comparatively speaking, the exception. Yet there are many cases clear enough and grave enough to justify that exception. In all things which regard the external relations of the individual, he is de jure amenable to those whose interests are concerned, and if need be, to society as their protector. There are often good reasons for not holding him to the responsibility; but these reasons must arise from the special expediencies of the case: either because it is a kind of case in which he is on the whole likely to act better, when left to his own discretion, than when controlled in any way in which society have it in their power to control him; or because the attempt to exercise control would produce other evils, greater than those which it would prevent. When such reasons as these preclude the enforcement of responsibility, the conscience of the agent himself should step into the vacant judgment-seat, and protect those interests of others which have no external protection; judging himself all the more rigidly, because the case does not admit of his being made accountable to the judgment of his fellow creatures.

But there is a sphere of action in which society, as distinguished from the individual, has, if any, only an indirect interest; comprehending all that portion of a person's life and conduct which affects only himself, or, if it also affects others, only with their free, voluntary, and undeceived consent and participation. When I say only himself, I mean directly, and in the first instance: for whatever affects himself, may affect others through himself; and the objection which may be grounded on this contingency, will receive consideration in the sequel. This, then, is the appropriate region of human liberty. It comprises, first, the inward domain of consciousness; demanding liberty of conscience, in the most comprehensive sense; liberty of thought and feeling; absolute freedom of opinion and sentiment on all subjects, practical or speculative, scientific, moral, or theological.

No society in which these liberties are not, on the whole, respected, is free, whatever may be its form of government; and none is completely free in which they do not exist absolute and unqualified. The only freedom which deserves the name, is that of pursuing our own good in our own way, so long as we do not attempt to deprive others of theirs, or impede their efforts to obtain it. Each is the proper guardian of his own health, whether bodily, or mental or spiritual. Mankind are greater gainers by suffering each other to live as seems good to themselves, than by compelling each to live as seems good to the rest.

Though this doctrine is anything but new, and, to some persons, may have the air of a truism, there is no doctrine which stands more directly opposed to the general tendency of existing opinion and practice. Society has expended fully as much effort in the attempt (according to its lights) to compel people to conform to its notions of personal, as of social excellence. The ancient commonwealths thought themselves entitled to practise, and the ancient philosophers countenanced, the regulation of every part of private conduct by public authority, on the ground that the State had a deep interest in the whole bodily and mental discipline of every one of its citizens, a mode of thinking which may have been admissible in small republics surrounded by powerful enemies, in constant peril of being subverted by foreign attack or internal commotion, and to which even a short interval of relaxed energy and self-command might so easily be fatal, that they could not afford to wait for the salutary permanent effects of freedom. In the modern world, the greater size of political communities, and above all, the separation between the spiritual and temporal authority (which placed the direction of men's consciences in other hands than those which controlled their worldly affairs), prevented so great an interference by law in the details of private life; but the engines of moral repression have been wielded more strenuously against divergence from the reigning opinion in self-regarding, than even in social matters; religion, the most powerful of the elements which have entered into the formation of moral feeling, having almost always been governed either by the ambition of a hierarchy, seeking control over every department of human conduct, or by the spirit of Puritanism.

Under the name of preventing intemperance the people of one English colony, and of nearly half the United States, have been interdicted by law from making any use whatever of fermented drinks, except for medical purposes: for prohibition of their sale is in fact, as it is intended to be, prohibition of their use. And though the impracticability of executing the law has caused its repeal in several of the States which had adopted it, including the one from which it derives its name, an attempt has notwithstanding been commenced, and is prosecuted with considerable zeal by many of the professed philanthropists, to agitate for a similar law in this country. The association, or "Alliance" as it terms itself, which has been formed for this purpose, has acquired some notoriety through the publicity given to a correspondence between its Secretary and one of the very few English public men who hold that a politician's opinions ought to be founded on principles. Lord Stanley's share in this correspondence is calculated to strengthen the hopes already built on him, by those who know how rare such qualities as are manifested in some of his public appearances, unhappily are among those who figure in political life. The organ of the Alliance, who would "deeply deplore the recognition of any principle which could be wrested to justify bigotry and persecution," undertakes to point out the "broad and impassable barrier" which divides such principles from those of the association. "All matters relating to thought, opinion, conscience, appear to me," he says, "to be without the sphere of legislation; all pertaining to social act, habit, relation, subject only to a discretionary power vested in the State itself, and not in the individual, to be within it." No mention is made of a third class, different from either of these, viz., acts and habits which are not social, but individual; although it is to this class, surely, that the act of drinking fermented liquors belongs. Selling fermented liquors, however, is trading, and trading is a social act. But the infringement complained of is not on the liberty of the seller, but on that of the buyer and consumer; since the State might just as well forbid him to drink wine, as purposely make it impossible for him to obtain it. The Secretary, however, says, "I claim, as a citizen, a right to legislate whenever my social rights are invaded by the social act of another." And now for the definition of these "social rights." "If anything invades my social rights, certainly the traffic in strong drink does. It destroys my primary right of security, by constantly creating and stimulating social disorder. It invades my right of equality, by deriving a profit from the creation of a misery, I am taxed to support. It impedes my right to free moral and intellectual development, by surrounding my path with dangers, and by weakening and demoralizing society, from which I have a right to claim mutual aid and intercourse." A theory of "social rights," the like of which probably never before found its way into distinct language — being nothing short of this — that it is the absolute social right of every individual, that every other individual shall act in every respect exactly as he ought; that whosoever fails thereof in the smallest particular, violates my social right, and entitles me to demand from the legislature the removal of the grievance. So monstrous a principle is far more dangerous than any single interference with liberty; there is no violation of liberty which it would not justify; it acknowledges no right to any freedom whatever, except perhaps to that of holding opinions in secret, without ever disclosing them; for the moment an opinion which I consider noxious, passes any one's lips, it invades all the "social rights" attributed to me by the Alliance. The doctrine ascribes to all mankind a vested interest in each other's moral, intellectual, and even physical perfection, to be defined by each claimant according to his own standard.

———————

There are two potential responses to those who believe that the harm principle precludes criminal punishment for drug use, manufacture, and sale. First, proponents of drug prohibition might reject the harm principle outright and argue that it is appropriate to use the criminal law to pursue goals such as the advancement of traditional values. Second, drug prohibitionists might argue that criminal laws against drug activity are perfectly consistent with the harm principle because the sale and use of drugs causes harm.

The Collapse of the Harm Principle
Barnard E. Harcourt
90 Journal of Criminal Law and Criminology 109 (1999)

As we approach the end of the twentieth century, we are witnessing a remarkable development in the debate over the legal enforcement of morality. The harm principle is effectively collapsing under the weight of its own success. Claims of harm have become so pervasive that the harm principle has become meaningless: the harm principle no longer serves the function of a critical principle because non-trivial harm arguments permeate the debate. Today, the issue is no longer whether a moral offense causes harm, but rather what type and what amount of harms the challenged conduct causes, and how the harms compare. On those issues, the harm principle is silent. This is a radical departure from the liberal theoretic, progressive discourse of the 1960s.

[I]n the writings of John Stuart Mill, H.L.A. Hart and Joel Feinberg, the harm principle acted as a necessary but not sufficient condition for legal enforcement. The harm principle was used to exclude certain categories of activities from legal enforcement (necessary condition), but it did not determine what to include (but not sufficient condition), insofar as practical, constitutional or other factors weighed into the ultimate decision whether to regulate a moral offense. Today, although the harm principle formally remains a necessary but not sufficient condition, harm is no longer in fact a necessary condition because non-trivial harm arguments are being made about practically every moral offense. As a result, today, we no longer focus on the existence or non-existence of harm. Instead, we focus on the types of harm, the amounts of harms, and the balance of harms. As to these questions, the harm principle offers no guidance. It does not tell us how to compare harms. It served only as a threshold determination, and that threshold is being satisfied in most categories of moral offense. As a result, the harm principle no longer acts today as a limiting principle with regard to the legal enforcement of morality.

The collapse of the harm principle has significantly altered the map of liberal legal and political theory in the debate over the legal enforcement of morality. To be sure, the liberal criteria themselves have not changed. As in the 1960s, it is still possible today to define "liberalism," in the specific context of the legal enforcement of morality, on the basis of the same three criteria, namely (1) that it is a justifiable reason to limit an individual's freedom of action if their action causes harm to other persons (the harm principle), (2) that it is also a justifiable reason to limit someone's activities in order to prevent serious offense to other persons (the offense principle), and (3) that it is generally not a justifiable reason to limit harmless conduct on the ground that it is immoral. The criteria are the same today.

But the map of liberalism has changed. In the 1960s and '70s, liberalism was predominantly progressive in relation to moral offenses: liberal theory was dominated by progressives, like H.L.A. Hart, Joel Feinberg, and Ronald Dworkin, who were favorably inclined, by and large, toward the relaxation of sexual morality in the area of homosexuality, fornication, and pornography. In the 1960s and '70s, liberalism was opposed, chiefly, by moral conservatives, like Lord Patrick Devlin, who were theoretically illiberal insofar as they espoused legal moralist principles. Today, liberalism is the domain of progressives and conservatives. Conservatives have adopted the harm principle, and increasingly are making harm arguments. As a result, liberal theory itself is no longer formally opposed. Liberal theory has colonized moral conservatism and, it would appear, is being colonized by conservatives in return. The net effect is the emergence of what I will call conservative liberalism.

The harm principle traces back to John Stuart Mill's essay On Liberty. Mill succinctly stated the principle in a now-famous passage in the opening pages of the essay:

> The object of this essay is to assert one very simple principle, as entitled to govern absolutely the dealings of society with the individual in the way of compulsion and control.... That principle is that the sole end for which mankind are warranted, individually or collectively, in interfering with the liberty of action of any of their number is self-protection. That the only purpose for which power can be rightfully exercised over any member of a civilized community, against his will, is to prevent harm to others.

Though simple at first blush, the harm principle actually was far more complicated than it looked, and, over the course of the essay, it took on many nuances. The argument in fact became more complex with each restatement. In Mill's short essay, the harm principle metamorphosed from a simple inquiry into harm, to a more complex analysis of interests (self-regarding and other regarding interests), and eventually to a quasi-legal determination of rights. In his final restatement of the harm principle, Mill ultimately defined the concept of harm on the basis of recognized or legal rights. Mill wrote:

> Though society is not founded on a contract ... the fact of living in society renders it indispensable that each should be bound to observe a certain line of conduct toward the rest. This conduct consists, first, in not injuring the interests of one another, or rather certain interests which, either by express legal provision or by tacit understanding, ought to be considered as rights; and secondly, in each person's bearing his share (to be fixed on some equitable principle) of the labors and sacrifices incurred for defending the society or its members from injury and molestation.

As Mill explained elsewhere, the notion of rights embodied in this final restatement rested on a modified utilitarian calculus grounded on the permanent interests of man as a progressive being.

In Mill's writings, then, the original, simple harm principle evolved into a more cumbersome principle. Mill nevertheless applied the principle and justified, on its basis, a large number of regulations and prohibitions. The harm principle, in Mill's own hands, produced a blueprint for a highly regulated society: a society that regulated the sale of potential instruments of crime, that taxed the sale of alcohol and regulated the public consumption of alcohol, that regulated education and even procreation, and that prohibited public intoxication and indecency.

Beginning at least in the 1950s, liberal theorists, most prominently Professors H.L.A. Hart and Joel Feinberg, returned to Mill's original, simple statement of the harm principle. The context was the debate over the legal enforcement of morality. In England, this debate was reignited by the recommendation of the Committee on Homosexual Offences and Prostitution (the "Wolfenden Report") that private homosexual acts between consenting adults no longer be criminalized. In the United States, the debate was reignited by the Supreme Court's struggle over the definition and treatment of obscenity and the drafting of the Model Penal Code. In both countries, the debate was fueled by the perception among liberal theorists that legal moralist principles were experiencing a rejuvenation and were threatening to encroach on liberalism. More than anyone else, Lord Patrick Devlin catalyzed this perceived threat. In his Maccabaean Lecture, delivered to the British Academy in 1959, Lord Devlin argued that purportedly immoral activities, like homosexuality and prostitution, should remain criminal offenses. Lord Devlin published his lecture and other essays under the title *The Enforcement of Morals*, and Devlin soon became associated with the principle of legal moralism—the principle that moral offenses should be regulated because they are immoral.

The Hart-Devlin exchange structured the debate over the legal enforcement of morality, and thus there emerged, in the 1960s, a pairing of two familiar arguments—the harm principle and legal moralism. All the participants at the time recognized, naturally, that this structure was a recurrence of a very similar pairing of arguments that had set the contours of the debate a hundred years earlier. The Hart-Devlin debate replicated, in many ways, the earlier debate between Mill and another famous British jurist, Lord James Fitzjames Stephen. In 1873, in a book entitled *Liberty, Equality, Fraternity*, Lord Stephen had published a scathing attack on Mill's essay and strenuously advocated legal moralism. Stephen described his argument as "absolutely inconsistent with and contradictory to Mr. Mill's." Stephen's argument, like Mill's, was best captured in a now-famous passage: "[T]here are acts of wickedness so gross and outrageous that, self-protection apart, they must be prevented as far as possible at any cost to the offender, and punished, if they occur, with exemplary severity."

Professor Hart immediately underscored the similar structure of the emerging debate. "Though a century divides these two legal writers," Hart observed, referring to Lords Stephen and Devlin, "the similarity in the general tone and sometimes in the detail of their arguments is very great." In his defense, Devlin responded that at the time he delivered the Maccabaean lecture he "did not then know that the same ground had already been covered by Mr. Justice Stephen...." Nevertheless, Devlin conceded that there was "great similarity between [Lord Stephen's] view and mine on the principles that should affect the use of the criminal law for the enforcement of morals." Devlin also noted the similarity between Hart, Mill, and the Wolfenden Report. Referring to the Wolfenden Report, Devlin observed that "this use of the [harm] principle is, as Professor Hart observed, 'strikingly similar' to Mill's doctrine."

Though the paired structure of arguments was similar, it was not exactly the same. In contrast to Stephen's straightforward legal moralist argument, Lord Devlin's argument in *The Enforcement of Morality* was ambiguous and susceptible to competing interpretations. Devlin's argument played on the ambivalence in the notion of harm—at times courting the idea of social harm, at other times aligning more closely with the legal moralism of his predecessor. As a result, the conservative position began to fragment and there developed at least two interpretations of Devlin's argument: the first relied on public harm, the second on legal moralism.

In large part, the source of the ambiguity stemmed from the fact that Devlin defined public morality in terms of harm to society. In several key passages, Devlin strongly suggested that public morality necessarily encompassed conduct that affected society as a whole. Devlin wrote, for instance, that "[t]here is a case for a collective [moral] judgement ... only if society is affected." "[B]efore a society can put a practice beyond the limits of tolerance," Devlin emphasized, "there must be a deliberate judgement that the practice is injurious to society." In these and numerous other passages, Devlin made clear that public morality would necessarily involve injury to society, and that the injury was precisely "what gives the law its locus standi." This overlap of harm and morality significantly exacerbated the ambiguity in the debate, and the struggle for the meaning of harm.

Under the more extreme reading, Devlin's argument was much closer to the earlier statement of legal moralism in Lord Stephen's book, Liberty, Equality, Fraternity. Certain key passages in Devlin's writings supported this reading, especially the concluding sentence of the Maccabaean lecture:

> So the law must base itself on Christian morals and to the limit of its ability enforce them, not simply because they are the morals of most of us, nor simply because they are the morals which are taught by the established Church—on these points the law recognizes the right to dissent—but for the compelling reason that without the help of Christian teaching the law will fail.

These were ominous and somewhat bewildering words. "Christian morals." "The law will fail." To what extent was this a prediction of actual social harm or a traditional argument about legal moralism? Could they even be distinguished anymore? Was legal moralism, in reality, a harm argument? In which direction was Devlin going? Unsure, Hart and other liberal theorists returned to Mill's essay On Liberty and to the original, simple statement of the harm principle. Ironically, that rhetorical move would further ambiguate the conception of harm. The simplicity of the original harm principle would veil an intense struggle for the meaning of harm.

In *Law, Liberty, and Morality*, a set of lectures delivered at Stanford University in 1962 in response to Lord Devlin, Hart rehearsed Mill's harm principle, but carefully pared the argument down to its original, simple, and succinct statement. Right after posing the central question of his lectures—"Ought immorality as such to be a crime?"—Hart immediately cited Mill in support of his position. "To this question," Hart responded, "John Stuart Mill gave an emphatic negative answer in his essay *On Liberty* one hundred years ago, and the famous sentence in which he frames this answer expresses the central doctrine of his essay." Then Hart repeated the famous sentence: "He said, 'The only purpose for which power can rightfully be exercised over any member of a civilised community against his will is to prevent harm to others.'" Hart endorsed the simple harm argument, and declared that, "on the narrower issue relevant to the enforcement of morality Mill seems to me to be right."

Similarly, in an early essay in 1973 entitled *Moral Enforcement and the Harm Principle*—an essay which would sketch the contours of his later four-volume treatise on *The Moral Limits of the Criminal Law*—Professor Joel Feinberg rehearsed Mill's harm principle and he, too, pared the principle down to its original, simple formulation. Feinberg emphasized the importance of distinguishing between direct and indirect harm, but went no further, at the time, in developing the harm argument. Feinberg endorsed the argument and wrote that the distinction, "as Mill intended it to be understood, does seem at least roughly serviceable, and unlikely to invite massive social interference in private affairs."

Eleven years later, Feinberg published the first volume of *The Moral Limits of the Criminal Law*, entitled *Harm to Others*. Feinberg explored there the contours of the harm principle and developed fifteen supplementary criteria, or what he called "mediating maxims," to assist in the application of the harm principle. Throughout the four-volume treatise, Feinberg maintained that the harm argument, as refined by the mediating maxims, was one of only two considerations (the other being the offense principle) that were always a good reason for prohibiting purportedly immoral activity.

Feinberg's experience with the harm principle mirrored, in significant ways, Mill's own experience. Like Mill, Feinberg's confidence in the robustness of the original harm principle eroded somewhat over the course of his writings. Whereas Feinberg originally defined liberalism, in his own words, "boldly," relying exclusively on the harm principle (supplemented by an offense principle), Feinberg concluded the fourth and last volume of *The Moral Limits of the Criminal Law* by softening his claims about the critical role of the harm principle. But even under the more cautious version proposed by Feinberg at the end of his treatise, the qualified harm principle still played a dominant role. Feinberg concluded his treatise with the following "cautious" definition of liberalism:

> [W]e can define liberalism cautiously as the view that as a class, harm and offense prevention are far and away the best reasons that can be produced in support of criminal prohibitions, and the only ones that frequently outweigh the case for liberty. They are, in short, the only considerations that are always good reasons for criminalization. The other principles [moralist or paternalist] state considerations that are at most sometimes (but rarely) good reasons, depending for example on exactly what the non-grievance evil is whose prevention is supposed to support criminalization.

As this passage makes clear, the original harm principle remained, even by the end of Feinberg's treatise, one of the two main limits on state regulation of moral offenses.

Gradually, over the course of the 1960s, '70s, and '80s, Mill's famous sentence began to dominate the legal philosophic debate over the enforcement of morality. Harm became the critical principle used to police the line between law and morality within Anglo-American philosophy of law. Most prominent theorists who participated in the debate either relied on the harm principle or made favorable reference to the argument.

Over time, the harm principle essentially prevailed in the legal philosophic debate over the legal enforcement of morality. From one end of the spectrum to the other, there arose a consensus that Hart had carried the day. At the liberal end of the spectrum, Professor Ronald Dworkin reported that Devlin's argument "was widely attacked" and that his thesis was, ultimately, "very implausible." On the other end of the spectrum, Professor Robert George would report that "many ... perhaps even most [commentators] think that Hart carried the day...." Professor Jeffrie Murphy—who is today a skeptic of the harm principle—captured well the prevailing consensus. "I believed, along with most of the people with whom I talked about legal philosophy," Murphy wrote, "that legal moralism had been properly killed off, that liberalism had once again been vindicated against the forces of superstition and oppression, and that legal philosophy could now move on to new and more important topics."

This is not to suggest that the controversy simply disappeared from philosophic circles. There were attempts to rehabilitate Devlin's position. There were even attempts to radicalize Devlin's argument. And still today, Devlin has supporters. In fact, just this year, Professor Gerald Dworkin published a provocative essay entitled *Devlin Was Right*. In the essay, Dworkin sides with Devlin "in believing that there is no principled line following the contours of the distinction between immoral and harmful conduct such that only grounds referring to the latter may be invoked to justify criminalization." Dworkin argues that Devlin was right in criticizing the line between immoral and harmful conduct, and offers his own justification for criminalizing immoral conduct—namely, that the term "wrongful" connotes conduct that "ought not to be done" in the very same way that the terms "harmful" or "offensive" do. Nevertheless, even Gerald Dworkin's provocative essay does not significantly alter the equation. To a certain extent, Dworkin's argument in fact reflects the fragmentation on the conservative side of the debate. In several key passages of his essay, Dworkin seems to premise his argument on the assumption that harmless wrongdoing is simply not possible. If that is true, of course, then his argument collapses into the public harm thesis—and legal moralism is indistinguishable from the harm principle. In any event, and more importantly for present purposes, Dworkin is willing to concede in his essay that he is swimming against the liberal tide. He readily acknowledges that he is practically alone today in defending Lord Devlin. The fact is that, over time, a consensus emerged that the liberal harm principle prevailed in the legal philosophic debate over the enforcement of morality.

As the harm principle began to dominate the legal philosophic debate, the principle also began to dominate criminal law scholarship and legal rhetoric. Most of the leading criminal law scholars either adopted the harm principle or incorporated it in their writings. Herbert Packer, in his famous book published in 1968, entitled *The Limits of the Criminal Sanction*, included the harm principle in his list of limiting criteria that justified the criminal sanction. Although Packer did not focus primarily on the harm principle—focusing instead on the effectiveness and social consequences of policing certain activities—he did incorporate it into his work and argued that "[t]he harm to others formula seems to me to have ... uses that justify its inclusion in a list of limiting criteria for invocation of the criminal sanction."

The simple harm principle also permeated the rhetoric of the criminal law itself. This was reflected most clearly in the drafting of the Model Penal Code by the American Law Institute, which was begun in 1952 and completed in 1962. Professor Herbert Wechsler, the chief reporter and intellectual father of the Model Penal Code, strongly endorsed harm as the guiding principle of criminal liability. As early as 1955, Wechsler wrote: "All would agree, I think, that there is no defensible foundation for declaring conduct criminal unless it injures or threatens to injure an important human interest...." In his scholarly writings, Wechsler consistently emphasized the harm principle: conduct "is not deemed to be a proper subject of a penal prohibition" unless it "unjustifiably and inexcusably inflicts or threatens substantial harm...." This was, Wechsler emphasized, "a declaration designed to be given weight in the interpretation of the [Model Penal] Code."

The language of the Model Penal Code reflected this emphasis on the harm principle. In the preliminary article, section 1.02, the drafters addressed the purposes of criminal law and stated, as the very first principle, the objective "to forbid and prevent conduct that unjustifiably and inexcusably inflicts or threatens substantial harm to individual or public interests."

The harm principle was also reflected in the definition of crimes, especially moral offenses and public decency crimes. "The Model Penal Code does not attempt to enforce private morality," the drafters explained. "Thus, none of the provisions contained in Article 251 purports to regulate sexual behavior generally."

With regard to each moral offense, the drafters specifically discussed harm. In the case of prostitution, the drafters retained the criminal sanction specifically because of the potential harm in the spread of syphilis and gonorrhea. "Of special importance to the continuation of penal repression," the drafters emphasized, "was the perceived relationship between prostitution and venereal disease." In the case of consensual homosexual activity, the drafters rejected criminal responsibility on the ground of lack of harm. The drafters canvassed the moral grounds for sanctioning sodomy, but ultimately rejected them because of the "absence of harm to the secular interests of the community occasioned by atypical sexuality between consenting adults." With regard to obscenity, the drafters paid special attention to the relationship between obscene materials and overt misbehavior. The drafters noted that "in another era, spiritual error may have been a sufficient ground for penal repression, but in an age of many faiths and none, society tends to look to more objective criteria to determine what is harmful." Even the proposed definition of public drunkenness incorporated the harm (and offense) principles. In the Model Penal Code, the offense of public intoxication "differs from prior law principally in requiring that the person be under the influence of alcohol or other drug 'to the degree that he may endanger himself or other persons or property, or annoy persons in his vicinity.'"

During the course of the last two decades, the proponents of legal enforcement have increasingly deployed the rhetoric of harm. Armed with social science studies, with empirical data, and with anecdotal evidence, the proponents of regulation and prohibition have shed the 1960s rhetoric of legal moralism and adopted, instead, the harm principle. Whether they have been motivated by moral conviction or by sincere adherence to the harm principle, the result is the same: the harm principle has undergone an ideological shift — or, what Professor Balkin would call "ideological drift" — from its progressive origins.

Today, the harm principle is being used increasingly by conservatives who justify laws against prostitution, pornography, public drinking, drugs, and loitering, as well as regulation of homosexual and heterosexual conduct, on the basis of harm to others. The conservative harm arguments are powerful. By endorsing the harm principle and simultaneously making harm arguments, the proponents of legal enforcement have disarmed the progressive position and the traditional progressive reliance on the harm principle. This has significantly changed the structure of the debate over the legal enforcement of morality.

[For example, t]he structure of the debate over the criminalization of the use of psychoactive drugs has … changed significantly since the 1960s. The early progressive argument that the use of marijuana was a "victimless crime" was countered in the late 1970s and 1980s by a campaign against drug use that emphasized the harms to society, and justified an all-out war on drugs. The proponents of legal enforcement — in this case modeled on military enforcement — forcefully deployed the harm argument. Here, again, the harm principle experienced an ideological shift from its progressive origins: today, the debate over drug use pits conservative harm arguments against new progressive arguments about "harm reduction."

The progressive position in the 1960s and early 1970s was characterized by the argument that marijuana use was essentially a "victimless" crime. In his 1968 book, *The Limits of the Criminal Sanction*, Herbert Packer emphasized the "fact" that "the available scientific evidence strongly suggests that marijuana is less injurious than alcohol and may even be less injurious than ordinary cigarettes." Packer refuted, one-by-one, the various claims of harm — including the claims that marijuana use stimulates aggression, causes anti-social behavior, and leads to the use of stronger narcotics. "[T] here is a total lack of solid evidence connecting its use with the commission of other crimes in a causative way," Packer argued. Professor John Kaplan, in his 1970 book *Marijuana — The New Prohibition*, similarly offered a point-by-point rebuttal of practically every possible harm argument associated with the use of marijuana. My colleague, Ted Schneyer, suggested that

Kaplan's "treatment of these issues is unassailable and, on the basis of existing evidence, Kaplan's conclusion seems warranted—marijuana use can be considered no more harmful to users and other members of society than the use of alcohol." Schneyer remarked that Kaplan's arguments "are applicable ... to policymaking in the general area of 'victimless' crime." Joel Feinberg placed the case of the use of psychoactive drugs under the rubric of "legal paternalism"—the principle that justifies criminal sanctions where an activity causes possible harm to the actor, but no harm to others.

All that has changed today. The conservative harm arguments disarmed the traditional progressive position. Today, the opponents of drug prohibition—a loosely grouped coalition critical of current anti-drug enforcement policies—argue about "harm reduction." The term "harm reduction" was crafted in the early 1990s as an alternative to "legalization." Ethan Nadelmann, the director of the Lindesmith Center (a drug policy reform center established in New York City with funding from George Soros) and a leading spokesperson for the reform coalition, explains the "harm reduction" argument: we must "[a]ccept that drug use is here to stay and that we have no choice but to learn to live with drugs so that they cause the least possible harm." Rather than continue the war on drugs, Nadelmann argues, "[t]he more sensible and realistic approach today would be one based on the principles of 'harm reduction.' It's a policy that seeks to reduce the negative consequences of both drug use and drug prohibition, acknowledging that both are likely to persist for the foreseeable future." Nadelmann explains:

> What does "harm reduction" mean in practice? ... "Harm reduction" means designing policies that are likely to do more good than harm, and trying to anticipate the consequences of new policy initiatives.... "Harm reduction" requires governments to keep public health precepts and objectives front and center in its drug control policies, and to banish the racist and xenophobic impulses that stirred prohibitionist sentiments and laws earlier in this century.... "Harm reduction" means keeping our priorities in order.

In fact, the "harm reduction" movement has cleverly turned the table on the conservative harm arguments, focusing instead on the harms caused by the policies prohibiting drug use. "[M]any, perhaps most, 'drug problems' in the Americas are the results not of drug use per se but of our prohibitionist policies," Nadelmann claims. The greater harms, then, are "the harms that flow from our prohibitionist policies." Nadelmann emphasizes: "[Milton] Friedman, [Thomas] Szasz and I agree on many points, among them that U.S. drug prohibition, like alcohol Prohibition decades ago, generates extraordinary harms."

The concept of "harm reduction" traces its origins to alternative public policies adopted in the late 1970s and early 1980s in the Netherlands and Great Britain. Policies there were designed to render drug use safer and thereby reduce the harms associated with illicit drug use—including the transmission of diseases like AIDS or hepatitis, and the risks of overdose. Policies were also developed to separate out certain drug markets (marijuana and hashish) from others (heroin), and to relax, but still regulate, the possession and sale of small quantities of marijuana. These policies became part of a public health approach to drug use that now includes methadone programs, needle exchange programs, and community outreach programs, in contrast to the more punitive measures associated with the war on drugs. And they are now part of the domestic "harm reduction" agenda.

The counter-argument from proponents of the enforcement of anti-drug laws has been to argue even greater harm. Barry McCaffrey, director of the Office of National Drug Control Policy and better known as the current "Drug Czar," responds to the "harm reduction" argument: "The plain fact is that drug abuse wrecks lives." "[E]ach year drug use contributes to 50,000 deaths and costs our society $110 billion in social costs." McCaffrey also extolls the benefits of prohibition: "In the past 20 years, drug use in the United States decreased by half and casual cocaine use by 70%." McCaffrey's response, in a nut-shell, is that "[a]ddictive drugs were criminalized because they are harmful; they are not harmful because they were criminalized."

In testimony before Congress, McCaffrey has referred to the "harm reduction" movement as "a carefully-camouflaged, well-funded, tightly-knit core of people whose goal is to legalize drug use in the United States. It is critical to understand that whatever they say to gain respectability in social circles, or to gain credibility in the media and academia, their common goal is to legalize drugs." And, in a recent editorial, McCaffrey argues that:

> The so-called harm-reduction approach to drugs confuses people with terminology. All drug policies claim to reduce harm. No reasonable person advocates a position consciously designed to be harmful. The real question is which policies actually decrease harm and increase good. The approach advocated by people who say they favor "harm reduction" would in fact harm Americans.

As a result, today, both conservatives and progressives are making harm arguments. The debate is over which harms are worse. In that debate, the harm principle is silent.

———————

Bernard E. Harcourt argues that "[c]laims of harm have become so pervasive that the harm principle has become meaningless: the harm principle no longer serves the function of a critical principle because non-trivial harm arguments permeate the debate." Can a meaningful distinction be drawn between harms cited in defense of drug prohibition (such as child neglect due to drug use) and harms that everyone agrees satisfy the harm principle (such as the harm an armed robber causes to her victim)?

Illicit Drugs: A Test of Joel Feinberg's The Moral Limits of the Criminal Law
Douglas Husak
10 *Libertaria* (2008)

The test of any theory is its application to practice. A theory is not valuable if it tells us only what we already know. We do not require a theory about the moral limits of the criminal law to tell us that a state may prohibit murder and rape, but may not prohibit political speech or membership in the Catholic Church. A theory is valuable if it provides insights on issues about which we are likely to be confused and undecided.

If so, statutes prohibiting the use of designated drugs provide an ideal test of the liberal theory of law defended by Joel Feinberg's celebrated four-volume treatise on the moral limits of the criminal sanction.

Can prohibitions against drug use for recreational purposes be justified on the ground that drug use causes harm to others? If so, we would have the most secure justification for drug proscriptions that could possibly be provided. But the first and most important point to notice in applying this potential rationale is that the use of a drug *need* not cause harm to anyone, including the user himself. That is, no one need be harmed by my use of a drug—even the most dangerous of the illicit drugs. Therefore, if we are to apply a harm-to-others rationale, statutes proscribing the use of drugs must be conceptualized as examples of *inchoate* offenses. I understand an offense to be *consummate* if it proscribes conduct that is harmful on each and every occasion in which it is performed. More precisely, each act-token of an act-type proscribed by a consummate offense produces a harm or evil. It is not surprising that most of the principles venerated by criminal theorists have been developed with consummate offenses in mind. Core crimes — arson, rape, murder, and the like — are examples of consummate offenses. Each commission of these crimes violates the rights of others and thus causes them harm. Not all offenses, however, are comparable. An offense is inchoate if it proscribes conduct that does *not* cause harm on each and every occasion in which it is performed. More precisely, some act-tokens of the act-type proscribed by an inchoate offense do not produce harm. Even though these statutes are not designed to reduce the occurrence of harm itself, they *are* designed to reduce something that is almost as bad: a *risk* of harm that might materialize. Perhaps illicit drugs should be criminalized because their use increases the probability that a subsequent harm will result.

No state should repeal all inchoate offenses. The crime of attempt, for example, exists and ought to exist in all jurisdictions. Still, several principles are needed to identify the conditions under which the state is justified in prohibiting conduct on the ground that it prevents a risk of harm rather than harm itself. In what follows, I will defend four such principles, and discuss their application to the case of drug prohibitions.

The first two principles are clear and need little elaboration. First, all criminal laws must promote a *substantial* state interest. Since any reasonable person must agree with Feinberg that the prevention of trivial harms cannot justify a penal law, it is apparent that the prevention of trivial risks provides even less of a rationale. I call this constraint the *substantial risk* requirement. Since virtually all behavior involves *some* level of risk, criminal liability to prevent insubstantial risks would threaten to punish all human activity. How should we apply this first principle? In assessing whether the use of any given drug exceeds whatever level of harm is required, we must decide whether the relevant variable is the *aggregate* amount of harm that drug causes, or whether the relevant variable is the amount of harm that drug causes *per incidence of use*. This determination is difficult. On the one hand, it seems strange to conclude that a given drug causes a trivial amount of harm because almost no harm results from particular instances of use. Tobacco causes lots of disease, but only because smokers tend to consume large amounts of tobacco through the course of their lives. On the other hand, it seems equally strange to suppose that a given drug causes massive amounts of harm because people who use it tend to do so frequently. After all, the criminal offense we seek to justify prohibits a single incidence of drug use, even if the offender never elects to use that drug again. I admit, however, that deciding whether to aggregate or to individuate harms for purposes of applying the substantial risk requirement pose one of the many thorny problems that arise in deciding whether proscriptions of illicit drugs may be justified under a harm-to-others rationale.

Second, criminal statutes must directly advance the state's interest. I call this constraint the *empirical* requirement. When applied to inchoate offenses, this requirement entails that the proscription in question must actually decrease the likelihood that a subsequent harm will occur. If enacting the inchoate offense did not make the incidence of the subsequent harm less probable, the state interest in preventing that harm could hardly justify the proscription. In other words, drug proscriptions cannot be justified if they are ineffective or counterproductive.

A third and fourth requirement must be met before an inchoate offense is justified. I call the third condition the *consummate harm* requirement. According to this principle, the state may not proscribe conduct to reduce the risk of a given harm unless the state would be permitted to proscribe conduct that intentionally and directly causes that same harm. In other words, no theory of criminalization should justify an inchoate offense prohibiting an act that creates the risk of some undesirable state of affairs unless a consummate offense prohibiting an act that intentionally and directly causes that very state of affairs would also be justified. The importance of the consummate harm requirement may escape notice because its truth is generally taken for granted. For example, liability for an attempt presupposes that what is attempted is a crime; persons who attempt to perform an act that is not a crime simply have not committed a criminal attempt. If the crime attempted is precluded by a theory of the penal sanction, no one would propose to retain a separate offense of attempting to commit that crime.

The rationale for the consummate harm requirement is straightforward. It cannot be worse to risk bringing about an undesirable state of affairs than to engage in conduct that deliberately and directly brings about that same state of affairs. In any hierarchy of culpable states, recklessness is less culpable than intention (or purpose). If the act of intentionally and directly causing a result should not be criminalized, the state cannot be justified in enacting an inchoate offense to prevent persons from merely creating a risk of that result. For example, since the act of intentionally failing to save money neither is nor ought to be a criminal offense, an inchoate offense designed to prevent persons from engaging in conduct that increases the risk that they will fail to save money would be incompatible with the consummate harm requirement and thus precluded by a theory of criminalization.

Applications of the consummate harm requirement jeopardize the crime of drug use. As I have indicated, when conceptualized under a harm-to-others rationale, these laws are designed to reduce the probability of a subsequent harm. The *nature* of this subsequent harm, however, is not identified by the statute itself. Frankly, the nature of this harm is mysterious. It will prove convenient to give a name to the ultimate harm the offenses of drug possession, use, and distribution are designed to proscribe. To avoid question-begging, I will refer to this elusive harm as *harm X*. No one should be confident about his ability to identify harm X. Many candidates have been proposed. If we hope to specify harm X, we have little alternative but to rely on the opinions of commentators who defend this law. Consider, for example, the opinions of Daniel Lungren, former Attorney General of California. He protests against "legalizing drugs" by predicting that repeal of these proscriptions would increase "homelessness, unemployment, welfare, lost productivity, disability payments, school dropouts, lawsuits, medical care costs, chronic mental illness, accidents, crime, child abuse, and child neglect."

I am skeptical that many of these rationales for drug prohibition would survive a test of criminalization that includes the consummate harm requirement. Let us suppose that Lungren is correct that the failure to punish illicit drug possession would lead to each of the undesirable states of affairs he mentions — even though solid empirical evidence for these claims seldom is provided.[3] Even granting this contested supposition, most of his allegations fail to provide a viable defense of the prohibition. The consummate harm requirement enables us to appreciate what is unpersuasive about many

---

3. Does illicit drug use cause greater amounts of crime, for example? Many criminologists think not. Even James Q. Wilson — a steadfast opponent of drug decriminalization — admits that drug prohibitions probably cause more crime than drug use. He contends: "It is not clear that enforcing the laws against drug use would reduce crime. On the contrary, crime may be caused by such enforcement." See James Q. Wilson: "Drugs and Crime," in Michael Tonry and James Q. Wilson, eds: *Drugs and Crime* (Chicago: University of Chicago Press, 1990), p. 522.

(but not all) of Lungren's allegations. We are not justified in proscribing drug possession because use leads to lost productivity, for example, since conduct that deliberately and directly causes lost productivity neither is nor ought to be criminalized. Since no one proposes to prohibit acts that make workers less productive—such as deliberately quitting one's job and becoming unemployed—it follows that conduct that merely increases the risk of becoming less productive should not be a crime. Proscribing conduct that causes the risk of an undesirable outcome while failing to proscribe conduct that directly and deliberately brings about that very outcome is incompatible with the consummate harm requirement—a requirement that any test of criminalization should include.

But we have not yet completed that part of a theory of criminalization that pertains to inchoate offenses. A fourth principle, which I call the *culpability* constraint, is needed. Criminal laws should not be more extensive than necessary to achieve their objectives. This condition imposes a presumption against overinclusive criminal legislation—a presumption that jeopardizes a great many inchoate offenses. A statute is overinclusive when its justificatory rationale applies to some but not all of the conduct proscribed. Since the purpose of an inchoate offense is to reduce the probability of a subsequent harm, a given offense of risk-imposition is overinclusive when a defendant can breach it *without* increasing the likelihood of that harm. No theory of criminalization should allow such a person to be punished.

Drug proscriptions probably fail the culpability constraint. To support my suspicions, return to Lungren's several attempts to specify what I have called harm X. Recall his allegation that illicit drug use increases child abuse. I admit that this rationale for drug proscriptions satisfies the consummate harm requirement. Still, Lungren's rationale fails to show that existing drug proscriptions are no more extensive than necessary to accomplish their objective. After all, the overwhelming majority of adults can and do use drugs without creating a substantial risk that any children will be abused. Therefore, this statute is overinclusive and presumptively unjustified. A statute punishing all drug users because some drug users increase the risk of child abuse, when the two classes of users are easily distinguished, is more extensive than necessary to accomplish Lungren's objective.

It is apparent that a great deal of guesswork is needed to show that given inchoate offenses—like drug proscriptions—fail any or all of the four principles in our test of criminalization. Still, it is clear that many drug offenses are almost certainly overinclusive, with little need for conjecture. Consider statutes prohibiting drug possession or distribution in proximity to a school zone. Although the proscribed acts may seem especially culpable and important to deter, almost none of the cases in which this charge is brought involve sales of drugs to minors. These statutes have been construed so broadly that virtually all drug offenses in urban areas fall within their parameters. It is nearly impossible to find a place in a municipality that is *not* within 1000 feet of a school zone. In one case, a defendant was convicted of this offense even though she distributed drugs within a prison that happened to be near a school. The risk that schoolchildren will use drugs is not increased in this kind of situation. It is difficult to imagine that schoolchildren would break into prison to procure drugs.

How can problems of overinclusion be remedied? Isn't overinclusion inevitable as long as law consists of rules? Many possible solutions to this problem might be defended. I propose that no one should be criminally liable for engaging in conduct that increases the risk of a subsequent harm X unless he acts with culpability about the occurrence of X. Thus, no one would be liable for using a drug because his drug use would increase the risk of child abuse unless he was reckless (or perhaps negligent) about that risk. No one should complain about the overinclusiveness of an inchoate offense if he is culpable with respect to the very harm this statute seeks to prevent. Requiring that defendants are culpable with respect to the subsequent harm these inchoate offenses are designed to prevent would help to justify such laws within a liberal framework that limits the reach of the criminal sanction.

Feinberg offers his only extended discussion of drug prohibitions in his treatment of paternalism. In rejecting "hard paternalism," Feinberg maintains "the state has the right to prevent self-regarding harmful conduct *when but only when* that conduct is substantially nonvoluntary." Unless the person suffers from some cognitive or volitional deficiency, his choice to use drugs is not subject to paternalistic intervention.

Feinberg illustrates his position by presenting three scenarios in which Mr. Roe discusses with Dr. Doe his decision to use a dangerous recreational drug called *x*. In the first example, Roe mistakenly believes that using x will not cause him harm. Feinberg concludes that Roe's decision to use x is nonvoluntary because he does not intend to ingest a substance that will actually harm him. In the second example, Roe is aware that x is harmful but indicates that he actually intends to harm himself. Feinberg claims that Roe's decision is so odd that it creates a presumption of nonvoluntariness. If further examination does not reveal independent evidence of incapacitation, however, Roe should be allowed to proceed. In the third and final example, Roe understands the risks of x, has no desire to harm himself, and states: "I don't care if it causes me physical harm. I'll get a lot of pleasure first, so much pleasure in fact, that it is well worth the risk.'" Feinberg concludes that this latter case is "easy", and he is correct.

To which of these three scenarios do most instances of drug use in the real world conform? I assume that almost no drug user intends to harm himself. If he did, it is hard to see how threats of punishment could be expected to deter him. But do drug users really understand the risks of illicit drug use? Empirical evidence confirms that the vast majority of persons know that drug use may be harmful. Why else would they think that drugs are illegal? In fact, most drug users tend to *over*estimate rather than *under*estimate the hazards of the substances they consume. And even those few adults who act *in* ignorance seldom act *because* of ignorance. In other words, more accurate information about the hazards of drugs is unlikely to change their behavior. Studies testing the efficacy of educational programs for adolescents support this conclusion. Efforts to present factual information about the risks of specific substances do not reduce the prevalence of drug use and may actually increase it. Drug prohibitionists tend to agree that lack of information by drug users is not at the heart of the problem. As William Bennett, America's first and most famous "drug czar" states: "If ignorance is the problem, knowledge is the cure. I don't believe that for a large number of kids out there who use drugs, that ignorance is the problem." What is true of "kids" is even more likely to be true of adults. If I am correct so far, most illicit drug use by adults conforms to the third scenario—the scenario Feinberg aptly describes as "easy." Like any number of hazardous activities in which persons engage for recreational purposes, drug users typically believe the pleasure is worth the risk. If we reject hard paternalism, drug prohibitions cannot be justified on paternalistic grounds.

Arguably, the most widely accepted rationale for criminalization does not depend on the *effects* or *consequences* of illicit drugs. Instead, punishing drug users might represent a *moral* imperative. William Bennett writes: "I find no merit in the legalizers' case. The simple fact is that drug use is wrong. And the moral argument, in the end, is the most compelling argument." James Q. Wilson expresses this view eloquently. He writes: "Even now, when the dangers of drug use are well-understood, many educated people still discuss the drug problem in almost every way except the right way. They talk about the 'costs' of drug use and the 'socioeconomic factors' that shape that use. They rarely speak plainly—drug use is wrong because it is immoral and it is immoral because it enslaves the mind and destroys the soul." Polls suggest that most people in the United States agree with this moral judgment.

Many legal philosophers would quickly dismiss this rationale out of hand because they do not accept its major premise: *legal moralism.* Feinberg, of course, would join those who reject it. To my mind, however, the ... premise [that recreational drug use is immoral] ... is even less plausible than the first. In other words, I see no reason to believe that the recreational use of illicit drugs is immoral. Of course, I may be mistaken in my belief; debates about morality are notoriously hard to resolve. Because *I* see no reason to believe that the recreational use of illicit drugs is immoral does not show that no such reason exists.

Why should we believe that the recreational use of illicit drugs is immoral? Sometimes, prohibitionists offer historical explanations. They remind Americans of our puritan legacy, of our longstanding suspicion of pleasure and fun, of our alleged "hedonism taboo." But how are these points supposed to advance our inquiry? They cannot be taken seriously as a *justification* for criminalization. Whatever may have been true at an earlier period in our history, no one continues to believe that an activity is immoral simply because it produces pleasure. No one denounces other activities as wrongful—spectator sports and television, for example—on the ground that they are recreational.

How *might* a moral case against recreational drug use be constructed? Someone could believe this activity to be wrongful for either of two kinds of reasons. First, drugs might be thought to be immoral because of the psychological states they cause. In other words, the "high" of drugs might be wrongful for people to experience. This alternative seems improbable. In the first place, it is not altogether clear how a psychological state *could* be immoral to experience. Moreover, the euphoria produced by licit drugs and prescription medications almost never are condemned as wrongful. In addition, psychological states that may be indistinguishable from those caused by drugs—a "runner's high," for example—are not denounced. Therefore, the moral case against drugs is unlikely to be based on the nature of the experiences they cause. A second explanation for the immorality of drug use is more probable. Perhaps the alleged immorality consists in the behavior of persons under the influence of drugs. Specifically, drugs produce risks that users will behave badly. But this case against drugs flounders in light of empirical considerations. Worst-case scenarios aside, few drug users jeopardize the welfare of children, commit crimes, endanger their health to a substantial degree, or otherwise behave in ways that merit blame or condemnation. Since neither of these two explanations of the immorality of drug use seem plausible, it is hard to see how a persuasive case *could* be constructed.

I am not saying that no sensible moral objections have ever been raised against recreational drug use. Instead, I am saying that the *kinds* of moral objections that are plausible provide a poor rationale for criminalization. Let me explain. In my judgment, the most serious moral questions about recreational drug use invoke a conception of human virtue. Philosophers have long disagreed about the details of a theory of human excellence. Greek philosophers and Christian theologians, for example, have offered very different accounts of perfection in human beings. All philosophers, however, agree that the ideal person cultivates his physical and intellectual talents. Drug use, especially when excessive, undermines this aspiration; these users tend to make less of their lives than they might. Heavy drug use might be described as a *handicap.* Those who use drugs excessively for an extended period of time are destined to fall short of an ideal. According to this school of thought, heavy drug use is a moral *vice*—the opposite of a virtue.

Whether *all* recreational drug use is a vice is far more controversial. Philosophers who develop accounts of human excellence disagree about the extent to which the pursuit of pleasure is consistent with the attainment of virtue. Notwithstanding ascetic accounts of virtue—which condemn all pleasurable activities—I see no reason to believe that those who aspire to perfection cannot pursue recreational activities at least occasionally. Perhaps recreational *drug* use, unlike other recreational pursuits, is incompatible with virtue. But this claim needs to be defended rather than assumed.

In any event, the difficulty with this kind of moral position should be evident. No one ... seriously proposes to criminalize all vice. It is one thing to say that we deserve to be punished when we behave immorally, but quite another to say that we deserve to be punished when we handicap ourselves or fall short of an ideal. Sloth and gluttony are at odds with the development of our physical and intellectual talents, but almost all of us would be subject to punishment if these vices were criminalized. A rationale for criminalization must show that drug use is *wrongful*—not that it is contrary to virtue or excellence. The criminal law establishes a floor beneath which we are not permitted to sink, rather than a ceiling to which we are encouraged to aspire.

A few prohibitionists have risen to the challenge and endeavored to explain why they believe that the recreational use of illicit drugs is immoral, whereas the recreational use of licit drugs is not. James Q. Wilson writes:

> "If we believe—as I do—that dependency on certain mind-altering drugs is a moral issue, and that their illegality rests in part on their immorality, then legalizing them undercuts, if it does not eliminate altogether, the moral message. That message is at the root of the distinction we now make between nicotine and cocaine. Both are highly addictive; both have harmful physical effects. But we treat the two drugs differently, not simply because nicotine is so widely used to be beyond the reach of effective prohibition, but because its use does not destroy the user's essential humanity. Tobacco shortens one's life, cocaine debases it. Nicotine alters one's habits, cocaine alters one's soul."

How are we to understand this attempt to differentiate between the morality of licit and illicit drug use? After all, Wilson does not mention the protection of youth, a rise in crime, a decline in health, or a general deterioration in society to support the distinction he draws. Wilson's reference to the "soul" provides the key to an answer. The use of illicit drugs is said to "alter" or "destroy" the soul. On the basis of this allegation, Wilson is prepared to send illicit drug users to prison, while sparing those who use licit drugs like tobacco and alcohol. How might his argument be assessed? Millions of living Americans and Europeans have used cocaine and heroin. If we examine their souls, would we find them to be altered or destroyed? Would we find the souls of users of licit drugs to be preserved and intact?

I cannot really believe that Wilson is intending to make an empirical claim about what doctors and scientists would discover if they examined the souls of illicit drug users. Instead, I believe he is using religious grounds to object to the use of illicit drugs. Contemporary discussions of drug policy rarely mention religion explicitly. I believe this neglect is unfortunate; religion plays an absolutely central role in shaping contemporary drug policy in the United States today. Attitudes about drugs and drug policy correlate with age, race, geographical location, education, political affiliation, and gender. But no demographic variable correlates nearly as strongly with attitudes about illicit drugs in the United States as religion. Lifetime abstainers frequently mention religion when asked to explain how they have managed to resist the lure of illicit drugs. Polls indicate that a majority of respondents who identify themselves as having "no religion" believe that marijuana should be "made legal." Protestants, by contrast, oppose legalization by a 69–26 margin. The United States is probably more religious than any Western industrialized democracy; it is no coincidence that the United States has the most punitive drug policy. We should not be surprised that issues closely linked to religion are impossible to resolve by rational argument. In this respect, attitudes about drugs resemble those about abortion, where religion plays an even more central role. Religious belief, almost by definition, is the product of faith rather than reason. We live in a secular state in which people should not be punished for behaving in ways that are contrary to the teachings of religion. A justification for punishment must not presuppose that we all share the same religious faith.

One of the frustrating aspects of debating an issue that is influenced by religion is that those who take sides are not always candid about why they hold their opinions. Few are willing to say, "I believe that drug users should be punished because of my religious convictions." Instead, they often disguise the reasons for their beliefs by citing some other liberty-limiting principle. Debates will have no impact as long as we focus on issues that do not really explain why parties to the debate feel as they do. Thus I would like to make one more point before we leave this rationale behind. Prohibitionists pretend to occupy the high moral ground in debates about illicit drug use. Unlike their opponents, they profess to stand up against immorality. Those who oppose criminalization are seemingly placed in the uncomfortable and awkward position of condoning behavior that is suspect from a moral point of view. I contend that the moral high ground should *not* be conceded to those who favor prohibition. Disagreement about the immorality of recreational drug use might be reasonable. But there can be no disagreement about the immorality of punishing people without excellent reasons to do so. Punishment is the most powerful weapon in the state arsenal, and we must always be vigilant to ensure that it is not inflicted without adequate justification. The entire thrust of this paper is that this weapon is invoked without good reason against recreational drug users. If I am correct, prohibitionists are more clearly guilty of immorality than their opponents. The wrongfulness of recreational drug use, if it exists at all, pales against the immorality of punishing drug users. How much harm to drug users and to society are prohibitionists willing to tolerate in their efforts to prevent people from using drugs? I conclude that those who punish drug users perpetrate a far greater immorality than those who use drugs.

Render Unto Caesar That Which Is Caesar's, and Unto God That Which Is God's
Steven G. Calabresi
31 Harvard Journal of Law and Public Policy 495 (2008)

At some level government and law ought to promote morality for the laws to be just and to command our support. This is most obviously true of those laws preventing one person from directly harming another person by depriving that person of life, liberty, or property. There is widespread consensus in the West today that laws preventing one person from directly harming another person are desirable ways for government to promote morality.

A harder question over the last 150 years concerns laws seeking to promote morality when an individual has not directly harmed another. This includes government efforts to promote morality by preventing people from harming themselves by, for example, drinking alcohol, smoking cigarettes, cigars, and pipes, using other dangerous drugs like heroin, opium, or cocaine, gambling, engaging in prostitution, committing suicide, consuming obscene pornography, driving cars without seatbelts on, or engaging in consensual dueling, professional boxing, gladiatorial matches to the death, or for that matter playing professional football. Should these "victimless" but dangerous and self-destructive activities be legalized where they are now outlawed, or ought we to decline to criminalize them where they are not currently illegal? Some activities—alcohol and tobacco consumption, professional boxing, and gambling—are mostly legal. Other activities—assisted suicide and dealing in and possessing drugs—are still illegal, although the laws are imperfectly enforced. Is this situation good? Ought government to promote morality by outlawing these supposedly victimless behaviors?

To begin, the behaviors in question are not, in fact, totally victimless. The most common victims of so-called victimless behavior are the children and other family of the perpetrator. When people abuse alcohol, tobacco, or drugs, commit suicide, or behave in other self-destructive ways, they hurt their children, spouse, parents, siblings, and friends. The victimless crime is to some extent a fiction. Self-destructive behavior often harms others.

People who engage in these activities also damage themselves, another moral and religious wrong, albeit not one that ought always to be legally policed. Our religious obligations to love God and to love our neighbors as ourselves require that we not abuse our bodies or our souls. Actively harming oneself is morally problematic, although there are admittedly gray areas where risky behavior may be warranted. That is, after all, why we outlaw dueling but allow professional boxing and football, or why we outlaw obscenity but protect the artistic depiction of nude bodies. Can the law police risky, self-destructive behavior to allow what is valuable and prohibit what is not without bringing on the suffocation of a totalitarian state? The answer is a qualified yes—provided that we recognize several major limitations of the law when it comes to paternalistic regulation.

The first important limitation is that government efforts to out-law so-called victimless crimes may give prosecutors enormous discretion in enforcement—discretion that can and will be abused to the detriment of unpopular individuals and minorities. For example, the problem with a law against buying alcohol is that a lot of people will violate it at some point, but not everyone will be prosecuted and jailed. The people who are prosecuted and jailed may be selected for reasons that turn out to be fairly arbitrary, and when that happens they may deserve to be released.

Second, some paternalistic laws are widely disobeyed, causing many people to hold the legal system in low regard. Widely disobeyed laws foster disrespect for the entire legal system, leading some people at the margins to disobey other laws. It is not costless to put laws on the books that nobody follows. This argues against paternalistic laws as ambitious as was Prohibition.

Third, rare enforcement of laws may not provide the individuals against whom they are enforced with actual notice that what they did was prosecutable. A due process question arises when the government prosecutes people for laws not usually enforced. This suggests that we need a doctrine of desuetude to deal with laws that have become nullities as a result of decades of non-enforcement.

The conclusion usually drawn from the reservations just mentioned is that "victimless" offenses ought to be made legal. Thus, many libertarians argue for legalizing drugs, prostitution, and assisted suicide, just as the repeal of Prohibition legalized the sale of alcohol.

I oppose this solution. Too many people look to the law for guidance regarding what is right and moral for outright, blanket legalization of morals offenses to be desirable.

There was an explosion in gambling when it was legalized in the 1970s. Many people concluded that because gambling was legal, it was also morally unproblematic. Even state governments became confused about the issue. Indeed, many state governments now sponsor gambling in the form of lotteries and encourage their citizens to gamble through lottery advertising. In my humble opinion, the legalization of gambling was a mistake. We should learn from that mistake and not repeat it with other victimless behaviors.

Legalizing drugs, prostitution, and assisted suicide could and probably would produce an explosion of such self-destructive behavior. After legalization, the government could itself encourage immoral behavior: (1) by selling drugs in state-owned, for-profit stores (the way some states continue to sell alcohol), (2) by running state-owned brothels to raise tax revenue, or (3) by encouraging elderly Medicare patients to consider assisted suicide to keep welfare costs down. Like it or not, the law teaches moral lessons, and people, especially in America, are quite prone to believe that what is legal is also moral.

One solution is to keep legal prohibitions on traditionally proscribed self-destructive adult consensual behavior in place but to make the penalties better proportioned to the offenses than we in the United States have done up until now. I agree with that course of action.

Thus, while I oppose legalization of heroin, opium, or cocaine, I also adamantly oppose the draconian sentences that we impose for narcotics offenses. I oppose legalization of prostitution, but I also oppose jail sentences, as opposed to fines, for prostitutes or their customers. There are many ways in which the law can send a moral message without imposing punishments that are disproportionate to the offenses committed.

Ah Lim v. The Territory of Washington

Supreme Court of Washington
1 Wash. 156 (1890)

Dunbar, J.

The defendant was indicted at the August term of the district court for King county, for the crime of smoking opium, as follows, to wit: "The said Ah Lim, on the 27th day of September, A. D. 1889, in the county of King, in the district aforesaid, then and there being, did then and there willfully and unlawfully smoke opium, by then and there burning said opium and inhaling the fumes thereof through an instrument commonly known as an opium pipe, contrary to the form of the statute," etc.

To this indictment the defendant interposed a demurrer specifying several grounds, but the one relied upon by the defendant, and the one to be considered here, is, that the statute upon which the indictment is based is unconstitutional as being in violation of the inalienable right to life, liberty and pursuit of happiness; and that it involves a deprivation of liberty and property, through a limitation upon the means and ways of enjoyment, without due process of law.

[T]he doctrine is well established, that the power of the legislature cannot be restrained by the courts upon considerations of policy or supposed natural equity. Were this power given to the courts, the law, instead of being administered and decided upon uniform principles, would be decided according to the particular bent or inclination of mind of the ruling judge. What would appeal to one judge as natural equity would not be so received by another, and the different views of what constitutes a natural equity would only be equaled in number by the number of judges on the bench, each judge following his own ideas of abstract right, not limited to any well-defined path of investigation, but controlled and impelled only by his personal ideas of what ought or ought not to be allowed in a particular case; pointed in no definite direction, but drifting aimlessly like mariners at sea under a clouded sky with neither compass nor log.

In the case at bar no special constitutional limitation or inhibition is pointed out with which the law in question is in conflict, but it is contended by the defense that the right of liberty and pursuit of happiness is violated by the prohibition of any act which does not involve direct and immediate injury to another.

The state has an undisputed right to, and does provide gymnasium attachments to its schools, and prescribes calisthenic exercises for the muscular development of school children. The object to be obtained is not for the exclusive benefit of the child. The state has an interest in the health of its citizens, and has a right to see to it that its citizens are self-supporting. It is burdened with taxation to build and maintain jails and penitentiaries for the safe keeping of its criminals, and to protect its law-abiding subjects from their ravages. It is taxed to maintain insane asylums for the safe-keeping and care of those who become insane through vicious habits or otherwise. It is compelled to maintain hospitals for its sick, and poorhouses for the indigent and helpless, and surely it ought to have no small interest in, and no small control over, the moral, mental and physical condition of its citizens.

If the state concludes that a given habit is detrimental to either the moral, mental or physical well-being of one of its citizens to such an extent that it is liable to become a burden upon society, it has an undoubted right to restrain the citizen from the commission of that act; and fair and equitable consideration of the rights of other citizens make it not only its right, but its duty, to restrain him. If a man willfully cuts off his hand or maims himself in such a way that he is liable to become a public charge, no one will doubt the right of the state to punish him; and if he smokes opium, thereby destroying his intellect and shattering his nerves, it is difficult to see why a limitation of power should be imposed upon the state in such a case. But it is urged by the defense that a moderate use of opium, or that the moderate use of an opium pipe, is not deleterious, and consequently cannot be prohibited. We answer that this is a question of fact which can only be inquired into by the legislature. Smoking opium is a recognized evil in this country. It is a matter of general information that it is an insidious and dangerous vice, a loathsome, disgusting and degrading habit that is becoming dangerously common with the youth of the country, and that its usual concomitants are imbecility, pauperism and crime. It has been regarded as a proper subject of legislation in every western state, and it is admitted by counsel for the defense in the argument of this case that the statute in relation to the suppression of joints kept for the purpose of smoking opium was constitutional and right.

Granted that this is a proper subject for legislative enactment and control, no limit can be placed on the legislative discretion. It is for the legislature to place on foot the inquiry as to just in what degree the use is injurious; to collate all the information and to make all the needful and necessary calculations. These are questions of fact with which the court cannot deal.

It is common to indulge in a great deal of loose talk about natural rights and liberties, as if these were terms of well-defined and unchangeable meaning. There is no such thing as an absolute or unqualified right or liberty guaranteed to any member of society. Natural rights and liberties of a subject are relative expressions and have relative or changeable meanings. What would be a right of liberty in one state of society would be an undue license in another. The natural rights of the subject or his rightful exercise of liberty in the pursuit of happiness, depends largely upon the amount of protection which he receives from the government. Governments in their earlier existence afforded but little protection to their subjects, consequently the subject had a right to pursue his happiness without much regard to the rights of the government. The reciprocal relations were not large—he yielded up but little and received but little. If he was strong enough to buffet successfully with the world, all well and good; if not, he must live on the charity of individuals or die neglected on the highway. But now all civilized governments make provisions for their unfortunates; and progress in this direction has been wonderful even since noted sages like Blackstone lectured upon the inalienable rights of man. Not only is the protection of individual property becoming more secure, but the vicious are restrained and controlled, and the indigent and unfortunate are maintained at the expense of the government, in comfort and decency, and the natural liberties and rights of the subject must yield up something to each one of these burthens which advancing civilization is imposing upon the state. It is not an encroachment upon the time-honored rights of the individual, but it is simply an adjustment of the relative rights and responsibilities incident to the changing condition of society.

Our conclusion is, that the law in question involves no inalienable right. It may be radical, injudicious and wrong; but, as we have before indicated, these are questions solely for legislative investigation and discretion, and as has been said by Judge Story, "Judges should regard it as their duty to interpret laws and not to wander off into speculations upon their policy."

The judgment of the court below is affirmed.

Scott, J., dissenting.

I cannot agree with the decision rendered in this case. That part of the act upon which the indictment is founded, is, in my opinion, void. It is as follows: "Any person or persons who shall smoke or inhale opium ... shall be deemed guilty of a misdemeanor," etc.

Legislation ... has ordinarily been confined to those cases where the act of the person directly and clearly affected the public in some manner. But here a single inhalation of opium, even by a person in the seclusion of his own house, away from the sight and without the knowledge of any other person, constitutes a criminal offense under this statute. And this regardless of the actual effect of the particular act upon the individual, whether beneficial or injurious.

It is admitted that this law can only be sustained upon some one or more of the following grounds, viz.: That smoking or inhaling opium injures the health of the individual, and in this way weakens the state. That it tends to the increase of pauperism. That it destroys the moral sentiment and leads to the commission of crime. In other words, that it has an injurious effect upon the individual, and, consequently, results indirectly in an injury to the community. And it is claimed that we must presume that the legislature had some one or more of these objects in view in enacting the law, although there is nothing upon the face of the act to indicate the legislative intention. This is going to a very great and dangerous extent to sustain legislation, in this most important branch of our social structure.

[I]f the act in question declared that no man should willfully injure himself by smoking or inhaling opium, thereby limiting its scope to such cases where injury resulted, there would be strong, and I think valid, reasons for sustaining it upon some one or more of the grounds mentioned. Every act of the individual which has a direct tendency to render him unfit to perform the duties he owes to society, is a rightful subject of legislation. The principle is a just and legal one. A man has no right to do that which will render himself an imbecile, or a pauper. Society has an interest in the promotion and preservation of the bodily, mental and moral health of each individual citizen. And laws tending to such results should be upheld in all reasonable ways.

A body politic is a social compact by which the whole people covenants with each citizen, and each citizen with the whole people, that all shall be governed by certain laws for the common good. This does not confer power upon the whole people to control rights which are purely and exclusively private, but it does authorize the establishing of laws requiring each citizen to so conduct himself and so use his own property as not unnecessarily to injure another. This is the very essence of government.

It is contended here that the legislature, being the sole and absolute judge of the effect upon the individual, of the act forbidden, has decided every act of smoking or inhaling opium to be injurious to the person so doing, no matter how long or how short the duration, or how great or how small the quantity, or under what conditions or circumstances the same might have been used, and that there is no right of appeal to the courts in this particular. Such a construction of the law makes the legislature the sole judge of the constitutionality of its own acts of this character.

There must be a right of review or control, to some extent, in the courts. Each citizen is entitled to the protection of all the branches of the government. A declaration by the legislature as to what the law shall be, is not necessarily a conclusion reached by the state. The legislature is not the state, although a very important or essential part of it. The power to protect the rights of the citizen from the wrongful effect of such legislation is peculiarly adapted to, and within the province of, the judicial branch of the government[.]

To declare any private act or omission of the citizen to be a crime, which does not result in any injury to the person and could not possibly affect society ... would be an unwarranted infringement of individual rights, and therefore unconstitutional. Individual desires are too sacred to be ruthlessly violated where only acts are involved which purely appertain to the person, and which do not clearly result in an injury to society, unless, possibly, thus rendered necessary in order to prevent others from like actions which to them are injurious.

A great principle is involved in this character of legislation. Suppose the legislature had forbidden the use of opium in any manner. If the unqualified right to prohibit its use in one way exists, this carries with it the right to prohibit its use entirely. Substitute any other substance, whether commonly used as medicine, food or drink, and still such a statute must be upheld if the courts have no right of review. It is no answer to say that the legislature would do nothing unreasonable. No man knows as to this. The question is, has it the arbitrary power and right?

I make no question but that the habit of smoking opium may be repulsive and degrading. That its effect would be to shatter the nerves and destroy the intellect; and that it may tend to the increase of pauperism and crime. But there is a vast difference between the commission of a single act, and a confirmed habit. There is a distinction to be recognized between the use and abuse of any article or substance.

It is also a well-known fact that opium, in its different forms, is frequently administered as a medicine with beneficial results; and while it may not be customary to administer it by way of inhalation, yet the legislature should not arbitrarily prevent its use in such a manner. If this act must be held valid it is hard to conceive of any legislative action affecting the personal conduct, or privileges of the individual citizen, that must not be upheld. We have been cited to no law, which has been sustained, that goes to the extent that this one does. It has no reference to the manufacture or sale of the substance. It is not based upon any pernicious example that the commission of the act might be to others. The prohibited act cannot affect the public in any way except through the primary personal injury to the individual, if it occasions him any injury. It looks like a new and extreme step under our government in the field of legislation, if it really was passed for any of the purposes upon which that character of legislation can be sustained, if at all.

In former times laws were sometimes passed limiting individual conduct in ways that are now considered ridiculous. Such as regarding the number of courses permissible at dinner. The length of pikes that might be worn on the shoes, etc. But these were founded on the pique or whims of an exacting and tyrannical aristocracy, rather than on reason. Or, as in the case of the Connecticut blue laws, upon views of propriety or religion that do not now obtain with anything like the former degree of strictness.

Judge Cooley, in his admirable work on Constitutional Limitations ... says: "In former times sumptuary laws were sometimes passed, and they were even deemed essential in republics to restrain the luxury so fatal to that species of government. But the ideas which suggested such laws are now exploded utterly, and no one would seriously attempt to justify them in the present age. The right of every man to do what he will with his own, not interfering with the reciprocal right of others, is accepted among the fundamentals of our law. The instances of attempt to interfere with it have not been numerous since the early colonial days."

From the best investigation I have been able to give this subject, I am forced to the conclusion that the judgment of the court below should have been reversed, and the defendant discharged.

The Cognitively Illiberal State
Dan M. Kahan
60 Stanford Law Review 115 (2007)

Cultural cognition refers to a collection of psychological mechanisms that moor our perceptions of societal danger to our cultural values. In appraising societal risks, for example, we rely critically on value-pervaded emotions such as fear and disgust. To minimize dissonance, we more readily notice and recall instances of calamity that appear to be occasioned by behavior we abhor than by behavior we revere. Where members of society disagree about the harmfulness of a particular form of conduct, we instinctively trust those who share our values—and whose judgments are likely to be biased in a particular direction by emotion, dissonance avoidance, and related mechanisms.

These dynamics confront the liberal aspiration with a special dilemma. As a result of cultural cognition, we naturally view behavior that denigrates our moral norms as endangering public health, undermining civil order, and impeding the accumulation of societal wealth. Under these circumstances, the promise not to interfere with the liberty of individuals except to prevent harm to others is likely to be rendered meaningless: whenever individuals deviate from dominant understandings of virtue, they will be perceived as sources of harm. Even lawmakers who honestly focus their attention only on promoting secular goods—ones of value to all citizens, irrespective of their worldviews—will be impelled to create a system of repressive regulation that expresses and reinforces a partisan moral orthodoxy.

This condition of cognitive illiberalism, I'm convinced, is endemic in our law today. Indeed, we can all readily perceive instances of coercive regulation that rest on empirical claims about harm accepted only because they are congenial to the partisan worldviews of those who favor such regulation. The problem is that we have highly polarized understandings of what those regulations are—criminalization of marijuana, the banning of (or refusal to ban) possession of handguns, exclusion of gays from the military, the moratorium on construction of nuclear power plants—precisely because we subscribe to competing cultural worldviews. The selective apprehension of cognitive illiberalism is part and parcel of the phenomenon itself.

The equation of vice with danger is a familiar characteristic of premodern cosmologies. Emperor Justinian banned sodomy in the sixth century to protect his subjects from pestilence, famine, and earthquake. The ancient Jews observed the commandments of Yahweh lest he "strike [them] with consumption, and with fever and with inflammation and with fiery heat and with the sword and with blight and with mildew." The Cheyenne believed the scent of a tribe member who had murdered a fellow tribe member would drive away the buffalo and thus spoil the hunt. In the primitive world, "the laws of nature are dragged in to sanction the moral code: this kind of disease is caused by adultery, that by incest; this meteorological disaster is the effect of political disloyalty, that the effect of impiety." In this way, "the whole universe is harnessed to men's attempts to force one another into good citizenship."

We moderns are no less disposed to believe that moral transgressions threaten societal harm. This perception is not, as is conventionally supposed, a product of superstition or unreasoning faith in authority. Rather it is the predictable consequence of the limited state of any individual's experience with natural and social causation, and the role that cultural commitments inevitably play in helping to compensate for this incompleteness in knowledge. What truly distinguishes ours from the premodern condition in this sense is not the advent of modern science; it is the multiplication of cultural worldviews, competition among which has generated historically unprecedented conflict over how to protect society from harm at the very same time that science has progressively enlarged our understandings of how our world works.

Start with a puzzle: how do ordinary people figure out what sorts of activities are harmful, either for them individually or for their communities collectively? Personal experience—Did I (or my children) contract leukemia from living in the vicinity of a toxic waste dump? Did I get shot by a violent criminal because my state failed to adopt a "right to carry" law? Will my planet suffer catastrophic environmental consequences if global warming isn't reversed in the next decade?—provides necessarily inconclusive (not to mention untimely) guidance. Scientists have amassed a wealth of empirical data on many putative dangers. But very few people have the time or inclination to sort through such studies, or the capacity to understand the technical information they contain and to evaluate their relative quality when they reach conflicting results.

We nevertheless manage to form beliefs about harm—usually supremely confident ones—through heuristics. Some of these belief-formation strategies are relatively straightforward and deliberate: confronted with competing claims about the hazards of a particular technology or medical procedure, or the efficacy of a disputed policy, we sample the views of those whom we have associated with, or defer to the opinions of experts whose judgment we trust. Others are more complex and less observable. We instinctively impute danger, for example, to activities that evoke negative emotions—such as fear, dread, anger, and disgust. We form estimations of the relative magnitude of risks based on how readily we can recall or imagine instances of the harms with which they are associated. While hardly foolproof, such mechanisms allow us to form judgments about hazards that we are unable to investigate in a more systematic and detached fashion.

The theory of cultural cognition posits that the heuristic processing of risk information interacts decisively with individuals' defining group commitments. Whether we regard putatively harmful activities (deviant sexual practices, gun possession, nuclear power) with fear or admiration, with disgust or equanimity, with dread or indifference, expresses the cultural valuations we attach to those activities. Accordingly, to the extent that it is driven by affect, risk perception is necessarily conditioned by culture.

Culture likewise interacts with the contribution that ease of recollection, or "availability," makes to estimations of risk. To avoid cognitive dissonance, we are much more likely to take note of and assign significance to instances of harm associated with behavior we despise than those associated with conduct we revere. We thus end up with culturally skewed inventories of readily recalled and imagined misfortunes, and as a result naturally form culturally biased estimations of the danger of deviant behavior.

Finally, and most importantly, culture interacts with the role that social influence has in formation of perceptions of harm. Individuals generally conform their beliefs to those held by their associates—both because those are the persons from whom they obtain most of their information and because those are the ones whose respect they most desire. The people we are most inclined to associate with are those who share our cultural outlooks. The predictable result is highly uniform views of societal harms among persons of shared cultural persuasions.

Cognitive illiberalism is not invisible to us. But we do perceive it selectively.

Imagine persons forbidden to engage in a species of behavior that is integral to their understanding of the good life but that is widely viewed as morally abhorrent. Such a group is unlikely to be mollified by the explanation that the State enacted the prohibition because a majority of citizens believed the behavior posed grave risks of harm to society. In that case, the dissenting minority will not only perceive a law motivated by fear to be equivalent in its impact to a law motivated by disgust, its members will also suspect that the majority's disgust is what disposed it to be fearful. Social psychologists have documented that persons readily, and correctly, discern that individuals who hold factual beliefs different from their own have formed those views to fit their group commitments.

The complaint that their perception of harm is motivated by animus is unlikely to have much impact on members of the majority, however. The same research that shows that people often discern the effect of group commitments on the factual views of others finds that people usually don't discern the distorting effect of such commitments on their own beliefs. Social psychologists call this dynamic "naive realism."

This experience—of simultaneously perceiving and not perceiving cognitive illiberalism—is a ubiquitous feature of our political experience. Because our society is genuinely pluralistic, nearly every citizen belongs simultaneously to (potentially shifting) majorities and minorities in moral debates. As a result, we can all identify some species of regulation we object to on the ground that its secular rationale is either a pretext for, or a rationalization of, aversion to disfavored values. And by the same token, we all support regulations the secular justifications for which are perceived by others as pretexts or rationalizations.

Disputes over who is being "realistic" and who "naive" about the relationship between cultural commitments and perceptions of harm is another familiar form of illiberal status competition in our society. To illustrate its ubiquity, I will consider how egalitarians and hierarchs, individualists and communitarians, take turns advancing and denying charges of cognitive illiberalism across a diverse set of issues.

Both same-sex intimacy and the use of (certain) recreational drugs are deeply woven into visions of the good life that defy traditional, largely hierarchical norms. For that reason, these forms of behavior provoke revulsion among hierarchically inclined persons.

Egalitarians and individualists, in turn, have invoked liberal values to attack antisodomy and drug laws, depicting them as the equivalent of cultural alien and sedition acts.

It would be a mistake, though, to infer that moral aversion to the values same-sex sodomy and drugs respectively express has ever been offered as the sole basis for prohibiting them. Instead, consistent with the cultural cognition of harm, proponents of regulation have always rested their case on (or at least amply fortified it with) the contribution such laws make to avoiding secular harms. It is said, for example, that drug use generates crime, leads to mental and physical disorders (which nonusers end up paying to treat), detracts from worker productivity (visiting economic losses on society at large), and interferes with responsible parenting. Before being struck down as unconstitutional in *Lawrence v. Texas*, same-sex sodomy laws were defended on the ground that homosexuality spreads disease, conduces to child molestation, and risks social disorder.

Sodomy and drug law opponents have never simply taken these harm rationales at face value. Instead, they have tested them with a series of argumentative techniques aimed at showing that they are either the product of bad faith or delusion.

One of these is akin to an evidentiary burden of proof. "Most philosophers"—or at least most liberal ones—"begin with a 'presumption of freedom,' or liberty, which places the onus of justification on those who would interfere with what a person wants to do." Dire speculations unsupported by empirical evidence—such as Lord Devlin's "social disintegration thesis," or the claim that homosexual sodomy leads to child molestation— are clearly inadequate to discharge this justificatory burden. But so too are harm-prevention rationales supported by reasonably disputed empirical evidence. In the face of reasonable "scientific doubts" about the public health and safety effects of marijuana use and "volumes [of writings] supporting one hypothesis or another" on the effects of drug laws in combating crime, the presumption of liberty should prevail.

Another technique focuses less on the weight of the evidence supporting the secular rationales for regulation than on the plausibility of them as motivations for regulation. Drug use is less dangerous than a host of other activities, from motorcycle riding to mountain climbing to alcohol consumption. If they were truly motivated by the threat that drugs pose to public health, prohibitionists would be just as intent on banning these other activities. Likewise, if the defenders of same-sex sodomy laws had been genuinely concerned to prevent the spread of AIDS, they'd have been just as intent on regulating heterosexual as homosexual sodomy—and would actually have had no interest in regulating lesbian sex. Indeed, they'd actually support homosexual marriage, which conduces to monogamy and hence to the reduction of sexually transmitted diseases.

The selectivity with which they are applied, critics conclude, reveals that the harm-prevention rationales for drug and antisodomy laws are nothing more than "post hoc empirical makeweights for … moralistic and paternalistic arguments." Because they so plainly lack support and cogency, these rationales, even if honestly believed by their deluded sponsors, do nothing, critics maintain, to acquit such laws of the charge that they are the instruments of cultural orthodoxy.

The regulation of smoking also excites charges of cognitive illiberalism. Defenders of hefty sales taxes, public smoking bans, and other restrictions (many arising from settlement of the historic governmental lawsuit against the tobacco industry) invoke secular rationales: reducing the public health costs of treating lung cancer victims, and abating the risk of disease or the simple annoyance associated with ingesting "second-hand smoke." But behind these rationales opponents detect the unmistakable signature of animus toward the cultural values that smoking expresses.

The social meaning of smoking has undergone immense transformation in the last three decades. The broad appeal of smoking for much of the twentieth century was underwritten by a melange of symbolic connotations — "the independent Marlboro Man" and "liberated Virginia Slim," "continental sophistication" and "outright rebelliousness" — that made cigarettes congenial to a diverse array of cultural styles. Today, however, cigarettes bear a more univocal, individualistic connotation. That meaning continues to resonate for a cultural style that prizes the "authenticity of impulse and risk." But for others, the individualistic aura of the cigarette denotes a constellation of negative values, such as weakness, crudeness, and irrationality, along with a culpable heedlessness of social obligation.

In addition, like the secular rationales for regulating drugs, same-sex sodomy, and guns, the rationales for public smoking bans are over-inclusive. There are (of course) scientifically credible grounds for doubting the claims of harm attributed to passive smoke ingestion in enclosed, not to mention open-air, public facilities. But however sound, no study suggests that allowing smoking patrons of a bar to light up creates nearly as much danger for nonsmoking patrons as permitting both to drink at such an establishment does for members of the public, who as a result face an increased risk of being killed by intoxicated drivers. Why so much less solicitude for the latter, who have so much less control over the risk they are being exposed to than do consumers who want to avoid smoky restaurants and bars? If smoking weren't banned at the workplace, employees could still choose not to work at firms that don't have privately enforced bans; why so much more solicitude for these risk-averse individuals than for persons who work in jobs that expose them to obviously greater hazards and whom we expect to protect themselves through market self-help? Why consider banning drivers from smoking but not from listening to music when studies show that the distraction associated with adjusting a radio or CD player results in twelve times as many accidents as lighting up on the road?

For critics of smoking regulation, the answer to these questions is again the unstated, and maybe even unappreciated influence, of regulators' moral aversion to smoking. Antismokers, one such critic writes, bridle at the style of "the entrepreneurial businessman and others … who promote, celebrate, engage in, reward, and profit from daring and passionate risk-courting (or gambling) and bold and creative individualism." They "find the choice to smoke, its array of sensual and social pleasures, and its deliberate courting of death to be perverse, incomprehensible, and alien." "It is one of the peculiarities of paternalism in the modern liberal state that its charges of perversion are described in rationalist, consequentialist terms, with scientific evidence adduced for its conclusions."

Ought, it is said, implies can. Contrary to the central injunction of liberalism, we cannot, as a cognitive matter, justify laws on grounds that are genuinely free of our attachments to competing understandings of the good life. But through a more sophisticated understanding of social psychology, it remains possible to construct a form of political discourse that conveys genuine respect for our cultural diversity.

B. Does Drug Criminalization Work?

Those who object to drug criminalization on moral grounds would presumably oppose even the most successful prohibition policy. For others, their views on prohibition laws may depend on how well they think the laws work. Of course, the answer to this question can also be strongly influenced by moral intuitions. Someone who finds drug use relatively unobjectionable may think that a reduction in drug use rates is worth very little. This person might support a prohibition model only if it dramatically lowered drug use at a minimal cost. On the other side of the spectrum, there are those who believe that preventing drug use is such a strong moral imperative that they would favor spending large amounts of money to vigorously enforce drug criminalization laws even if the effort only resulted in a modest decline in drug use. Similarly, people may disagree about what our objectives should be in setting drug policy. Should drug laws aim to reduce overall use rates for all illegal drugs or to reduce use among certain populations (e.g., young people) or of certain substances? Or, should drug laws focus on reducing the harms associated with drug abuse first (e.g., drug overdoses) as opposed to reducing drug use rates? Should we strive for an idealized goal like a "drug free America"?

The consequentialist discussion of the merits of drug criminalization is inevitably complicated by the wide-range of possible objectives and policy options. Even if it were possible to agree on a common objective for our drug laws, any attempt to measure their effectiveness will need to account for a number of considerations beyond drug use rates or drug-related hospital admissions. What value, if any, should be placed on principles like individual choice or privacy in a cost-benefit analysis? How should the unintended consequences of drug criminalization laws—for example, the violence associated with black markets—be measured and factored into the assessment?

With so much room for disagreement over how to define and measure success in drug policy, it should come as no surprise that two people might look at the same set of data and come to different conclusions about what it means. To one person, a 5 percent reduction in marijuana use and availability at a cost of $1 billion dollars might qualify as a resounding success. Another might consider that same result to be a dismal failure.

Setting Goals for Drug Policy: Harm Reduction or Use Reduction?
Jonathan P. Caulkins and Peter Reuter
92 Addiction 1143 (1997)

Correct, well-defined and generally understood goals can help individuals and organizations perform effectively. In some domains (e.g. prison administration), even if goals are not well articulated, responding to situational imperatives seems to work reasonably well. Such "muddling through" is unlikely to be effective for making policy toward illicit drugs. Drug policy making is fragmented across dozens of federal agencies, hundreds of state offices and thousands, if not tens of thousands, of divisions of local government, community groups, schools and private companies. Without some common vision of purpose, many of these organizations will work ineffectively, if not at cross-purposes.

The US government has developed a set of simple and transparent goals for drug policy. Even though these goals have real policy consequences, there has been little discussion of their merits or how they compare to alternatives. Debate has focused more on policies (e.g. concerning needle exchange or legalization) than on goals, yet goals promote clarity in debate. This paper compares the two most prominent alternatives: use reduction (current US policy) and harm reduction.

A commonly articulated goal has been a "Drug Free America". Few dispute that this would be a desirable end-state. Unfortunately it is no more feasible than a "Crime Free America" or a "Schizophrenia Free America". Use of psychoactive substances by some fraction of the population is nearly universal, spanning centuries and cultures.

Infeasible goals are not uncommon. Environmentalists call for "zero-discharge", consumers' groups for "zero cancer risk", and local activists for absolute guarantees that a new facility will pose no danger. Japanese and American manufacturers may have found the relentless pursuit of zero-defect production to be good business practice, but in government fanatical pursuit of noble causes frequently carries a high opportunity cost. Prison cells emptied to make room for drug offenders could have housed violent felons. Cocaine treatment counselors could have been treating alcoholics, and school-based prevention programs take time away from traditional academic subjects. Unattainable goals also offer little assistance to decision makers. How should one choose from among three competing proposals, none of which has any hope of meeting the goal?

More practical goals are needed. The 1988 Anti-Drug Omnibus Control Act demanded a strategy that included "long range goals for reducing drug abuse in the United States" and "short-term measurable objectives". The first (1989) National Strategy made a clear statement as to goals: "The highest priority of our drug policy must be a stubborn determination to reduce the overall level of drug use nationwide—experimental first use, 'casual' use, regular use and addiction alike". This emphasis on use reduction was reflected in the measurable objectives enunciated in the first Strategy and confirmed by its three successors.

The Clinton Administration's Strategies have reaffirmed that there was "one overarching goal—the reduction of drug use", although they have dropped quantitative measures, so the goals again became rhetorical.

These strategies could have established other goals: minimizing drugs' threat to civil liberties, increasing drug control efforts by a certain amount, or developing and disseminating more accurate information about drugs to allow individuals to make better informed choices. The alternative goal discussed here is to reduce the harm done by the production, distribution and consumption of drugs and by the drug policies and programs themselves. For example, although the British government's first strategy eschews the word "goals", it substitutes a "Statement of Purpose" that articulates three central goals, to: "increase the safety of communities from drug related crime; reduce the acceptability and availability of drugs to young people; and reduce the health risks and other damage related to drug misuse."

A literalist might object that this is not pure harm reduction, but note the lack of emphasis on prevalence of drug use. The first and third goals are clearly specified in terms of harms; the second is more instrumental, aimed at reducing prevalence. The document's specific objectives retain this harm orientation.

Inasmuch as this paper contrasts use reduction (Robert MacCoun's phrase for the current US approach) and harm reduction, it is important to ask whether these goals truly differ. After all, zero use will generate zero harm; perhaps no reduction in harm can be attained without a reduction in use. This turns out not to be the case, however, because not all use is equally harmful.

Consider a pregnant, recovering addict who visits a shooting gallery for the first time since leaving treatment and injects heroin with an HIV-contaminated needle. Contrast that with an employed, emotionally stable adult with no dependents who uses marijuana in the privacy of his or her own home on a Friday night to relax after a week of work. Both individuals used a Schedule I prohibited drug, but by most measures the first use session involves greater harm to the user, friends and family of the user, and the rest of society.

These examples are extreme, but the principle that trends in harm and use can differ is supported by empirical evidence. A classic example is the contrasting trends observed in the National Household Survey on Drug Abuse (NHSDA) and the Drug Abuse Warning Network (DAWN). DAWN emergency room mentions of cocaine increased dramatically even as the NHSDA showed striking declines in the number of people reporting use of cocaine.

Reconciling these trends is straightforward. Seeking emergency medical attention is a rare event, even for cocaine users. In the 1991 NHSDA fewer than 4% of past-year cocaine users reported seeking emergency room help for their drug use in the previous year. The number of people using cocaine in a way that puts them at risk for needing emergency medical attention can increase even as the (much larger) number of less seriously involved cocaine users declines.

What is important, though, is not the explanation but the fact that trends in a measure of cocaine use can differ dramatically from trends in a measure of harm. Reducing use need not imply harm will go down or vice versa.

This reflects the observation that much of what is thought of as the "drug problem" is only indirectly related to use. For example, most market violence and political instability in source countries is not related directly to use; indeed, one can provide sensible scenarios in which interdiction programs which reduce drug use in the United States actually increase, at least in the short term, harms in source countries. Similarly, adverse impacts on quality of life can be as much a function of public sales and public use as they are of use in and of itself.

There are three concepts of use that could be targeted for reduction: (1) prevalence; the number of people who consume a drug within a certain period of time or who define themselves as drug users, (2) quantity; e.g. the weight consumed, number of use sessions or number of hours of intoxication; (3) expenditures; the amount users spend on drugs and, hence, the amount drug sellers receive.

Choice among these three has substantial programmatic consequences. Treating heavy users is a low priority for the prevalence goal since a distressingly small fraction of treated heavy users become abstinent. If all users are considered equal, the incentive is to focus on individuals whose behavior is easiest to change, so-called light or recreational users.

In contrast, since heavy or compulsive users consume so much per capita, the quantity objective makes treating heavy users probably the most cost-effective of all programs. For cocaine, it appears that just the reduction in consumption obtained during treatment of heavy users—even if every user resumes full consumption after leaving treatment—is enough to make treatment more cost-effective than source country control, interdiction or domestic enforcement at reducing consumption.

An expenditure goal provides little incentive for price-raising enforcement programs. Higher prices reduce consumption and prevalence, but the impact on spending is less favorable because spending per unit increases. Indeed, if demand is relatively inelastic, then driving up prices would actually increase, not decrease, total spending. Enforcement programs that raise nonmonetary costs of drug use, e.g. by increasing user search time, are positively regarded in all three regimes.

Similarly, there are several conceptually distinct ways of defining the total harm which is to be reduced. Should the benefits of drug use be included as negative harms? Should harms that adults impose on themselves be included? Some argue the government has neither the responsibility nor the right to protect people from themselves. Others argue that "drug consumers may be less capable than other consumers of protecting their own interests". Similar arguments can be made and different conclusions reached for people presumptively less capable of looking after their own interests, such as adolescents, those with mental health problems and (possibly) people who are already addicted.

Confusion over which harms to count arises in part from uncertainty over who are the legitimate stakeholders. In particular, do criminals have a stake in the making of policies pertaining to the laws they are breaking? On one hand, most drug-law violators are US citizens and, conversely, many citizens have broken some law. On the other hand, once convicted, criminals' rights are greatly curtailed, most notably by denying their freedom and, in some states, by forfeiting their right to vote.

Beliefs about the standing of drug-law offenders help determine which form of harm reduction is most appealing. At one extreme, a strict social utilitarian would count the benefits of drug use as well as the costs. Such a person might consider much casual drug use to be good, not bad, and the tremendous reductions in casual use since 1980 as a failure, not progress.

Most people would exclude the benefits of drug use, but deciding whether to include harms people impose on themselves is also consequential. Enforcement makes users worse off directly by imposing sanctions and indirectly by raising prices, reducing availability and increasing variability in potency. In contrast, treatment programs help users break the cycle of addiction and avoid some of the harshest consequences of use. Hence, one is more likely to favor treatment over enforcement if users are seen as legitimate stakeholders.

The full utility of goals cannot be realized until they are associated with tangible measures, which allow one to assess a situation, monitor progress and evaluate interventions.

Estimating even the most basic measure of use, prevalence, is difficult and expensive. The US spends about $12 million/year surveying the household population and $2 million/year surveying high school seniors to learn about their drug use. These surveys primarily generate national prevalence figures, but for many programmatic purposes city or community level figures are more relevant. Furthermore, the data have significant limitations, most notably that they rely on self-reports of activities which are both widely disapproved of and legally prohibited. Also, only a small fraction of people use illicit drugs, particularly hard drugs, and use is more common among difficult to reach populations such as high school dropouts and the homeless.

There are many other sources of prevalence information. However, even after combining all such information, prevalence estimates are still highly suspect.

Estimates of the quantity consumed can be made from the demand-side or supply-side. Demand-side estimates are based on the same sources as prevalence estimates and, hence, inherit all their limitations and more. For instance, although some surveys ask respondents how much they use, people are rather poor at estimating their own consumption and heterogeneity in consumption makes it hard to determine what level of use is average.

Supply-side estimates subtract the quantity seized from estimates of total production (based, e.g. on acreage under cultivation) and assume the remainder is consumed. This procedure worked reasonably well for US cocaine consumption in the early 1980s when the United States consumed most of the world's cocaine. It works less well for current cocaine consumption and is virtually useless for heroin since US heroin consumption only accounts for about 7% of the world heroin export market.

The basic method for estimating spending on illicit drugs is to multiply estimates of the quantity consumed by price. Hence, spending estimates cannot be any better than estimates of consumption and finding the average price paid is non-trivial. Thus, high quality, transparent, reliable measures are not available for any of the use reduction goals.

Difficult as it is to find suitable measures for use reduction, it is much harder to find measures for harm reduction. Measures of each form of harm are poor. For example,

DAWN is often looked to as a source of information about drug-related morbidity, but it is poorly suited for this task. Only limited data are available on the share of property crime and violence that is "drug-related". The large literature on domestic violence is rather weak quantitatively and methodologically, making estimates of drug-related domestic violence tenuous. It is difficult even to imagine calculating aggressive street enforcement's toll on civil liberties or the social cost flagrant dealing imposes on neighborhoods.

Even if perfect data existed on individual harms, there is no way to aggregate them. With what common unit can one denominate both battered children and burglaries? It is simply not possible to report a scalar, aggregate measure of drug-related harm.

Since use reduction and harm reduction are clearly different goals, it is natural to ask which is better? Keeney advises that goals be selected based on one's ultimate values. Following that argument, harm reduction makes more sense for people who do not care about drug use per se, but care about use because it contributes to health problems, poverty, spread of infectious diseases, property crime, violence, reduced productivity, etc.

Others view drug use itself as "bad". They view as bad even a hypothetical situation in which an adult user could freely choose to use a psychoactive that has absolutely zero risk of damaging self or others, directly or indirectly, in the short- or long-term. For such people, use reduction may be the ultimate goal.

Besides relation to ultimate values, other relevant criteria include the extent to which goals are: (1) objectively defensible, (2) integrative, (3) politically feasible, (4) inspirational and (5) relevant to policy decisions.

Striving to reduce harm is closely related to maximizing societal welfare, which is one responsibility of government, so harm reduction has intrinsic appeal. Use reduction goals are more problematic because it is not clear how to decide which drug's use is inherently wrong and to justify that decision. Alcohol can be just as intoxicating and tobacco just as addictive as some of the currently prohibited drugs but, arguably, we do not make reducing alcohol use a national goal. If alcohol and tobacco should be included as drugs whose use is inherently wrong, should one also include caffeine? Xanthines in chocolate? It is difficult to divine a simple rule for judging which substances are inherently bad that neither condemns benign substances nor condones dangerous ones, and there is ample opportunity for cultural prejudice to color those judgments.

Ideally national goals should unite people in a common struggle. Goals which ally the government with one group against another are rarely productive in the long term, particularly when they divide the populace along racial or religious lines. The Cultural Revolution in China is an extreme example.

Use reduction goals tend to be divisive. They make it easy to think about drug offenders themselves — not their actions — as the problem, perhaps even as the "enemy" in a "War on Drugs". Such labels can exaggerate and solidify the breach between drug offenders and the rest of society. In theory, harm reduction goals are more pragmatic, less judgmental and, hence, more conducive to reintegrating offenders into mainstream society. Pragmatically harm reduction goals would also be divisive, for political reasons.

Goals should be chosen such that the responsible individuals and agencies can affect the extent to which the goals are attained. No one would suggest giving the National Weather Service the goal of increasing the number of sunny days by 20%, yet only slightly more plausible goals are common. Politicians pledge to reduce high school drop out rates, yet in a democratic society, individuals and families make decisions that are largely beyond the control of the government let alone any single official.

Setting drug policy goals is similar to setting educational targets in this sense. It is easy for the government to outlaw consensual crime, but hard to prevent it. Drug use is characterized by long-term cycles of greater and lesser use. Government interventions certainly affect the quality of these cycles (e.g. whether use is severely punished or grudgingly tolerated) and they presumably have some impact on their magnitude and length, but the larger trends are a function of demand. Demand is the summation of the tastes and preferences of hundreds of millions of potential consumers, not a policy variable which the government can easily control.

Both use reduction and harm reduction are inferior to process-orientated goals in this respect. For example, the government could be held accountable for the extent to which it achieved a goal such as providing treatment on demand to all users. This is not an endorsement of process goals which have other, obvious limitations. The comparison illustrates, however, that neither use nor harm reduction goals are particularly good "score cards" with which one can evaluate the government's performance; too many factors outside the government's control also affect use and harm.

Federalism and Drug Control
Michael M. O'Hear
57 Vanderbilt Law Review 783 (2004)

Four competing paradigms of drug control policy have emerged in recent years as especially influential: public-health generalism, legalism, cost-benefit specifism, and rights-based. The public-health approach regards drug abuse as a disease and seeks to reduce the social harms (overdoses, births of addicted babies, and so forth) caused by that disease. Under this paradigm, all abusable substances, whether currently lawful (alcohol, tobacco) or not (cocaine, heroin), should be handled in much the same manner. For those who abuse such substances, the public-health viewpoint emphasizes treatment and eschews moralism. Proponents of this approach do not necessarily reject criminalization as one component of a broader harm-reduction strategy—a strategy that would also include significant public education and treatment components—but, by and large, they tend to be skeptical of the effectiveness of the criminal justice system in reducing the incidence of substance abuse.

The legalist approach, by contrast, has been the dominant paradigm in federal drug policy. This approach focuses on "the threat that illegal drugs represent to the established order and political authority structure. In this view, it is the consumption of the prohibited substance rather than any secondary consequences that might ensue that is the heart of the matter. The taking of drugs prohibited by the government is an act of rebellion, of defiance of lawful authority, that threatens the social fabric."

Thus, for the legalist, the distinction between lawful and unlawful substances carries great weight; people who consume unlawful substances make a morally wrong decision regardless of whether any tangible harm results. The legalist is skeptical of treatment, preferring law enforcement approaches that are intended to reduce supply. For purposes of public education, the message is simple and straightforward: "illegal drugs are a bad thing and ... drug takers are bad people." Decriminalization is unthinkable: "The central inflexibility is that there is no way to change the terms of the criminal law regarding drugs without admitting defeat in the power struggle between good and evil that is the essence of this account of drug use and abuse."

Much like public-health generalism, cost-benefit specifism rejects moral absolutism and questions the established boundaries between licit and illicit substances. Under the cost-benefit paradigm, however, not all abusable substances are created equal. Proponents of this approach "see drug policy as requiring a balance between the costs of abuse and the likelihood of reducing them by means of legal prohibition, and the manifold costs of enforcing those prohibitive laws." This balancing process must be made on a drug-by-drug basis, with careful attention to social context. Thus, while the public-health generalist might regard treatment as the public policy response of first resort with respect to any type of substance abuse problem, the cost-benefit specifist might, for instance, favor tough criminal sanctions for heroin, public education for cocaine, decriminalization for marijuana, and treatment for all juvenile users. The cost-benefit approach has been embodied in state laws and proposed initiatives that would narrowly decriminalize a particular drug or particular uses of a drug, such as the medical marijuana laws.

Finally, the rights-based paradigm is premised on the existence of a moral or legal right to recreational drug use. This fundamental right might be an adjunct of the right to privacy, or based more broadly on each person's right to be treated by the state as a "responsible moral agent." Like the public-health and cost-benefit perspectives, the rights-based perspective calls into question the existing legal framework of drug control at the federal level, but on different grounds. It rejects the purported moral neutrality of the public-health and cost-benefit perspectives, and finds hidden (and perhaps dubious) moral judgments in their counting and weighing of social harms. Proponents tend to favor legalization, but are not necessarily opposed to all drug regulation. After all, in our legal system, we are accustomed to the notion of state infringement on fundamental rights, so long as the infringement is sufficiently limited in scope and justified by a compelling state interest. A broad criminal prohibition on drug use, however, is unlikely to be justifiable from the rights-based point of view.

As should be clear by now, participants in drug policy debates disagree on even the most fundamental premises of the debate. While a legalist, for instance, might assume that the appropriate target of a "drug" policy is limited to illicit substances, a public-health generalist would want to include alcohol and tobacco in the discussion. While a public-health generalist might view addiction as the fundamental harm to be addressed by drug policy, a critic from the legalist or rights-based perspectives might question whether there is even such a phenomenon as "drug addiction," at least insofar as the term connotes a diminished degree of moral responsibility.

Any attempt to answer the question whether drug criminalization works must also take the available alternatives into account. It is possible, for example, for a person to think that drug criminalization produces only modest benefits at a high cost while nevertheless supporting criminalization because she believes the other policy options would be even worse. Legalization and decriminalization are two frequently discussed alternatives to prohibition. But what do those concepts mean? Are they distinct from the idea of harm reduction?

Consider heroin maintenance programs, which have been employed in a handful of locations outside of the United States, including Switzerland and Vancouver, Canada. Under heroin maintenance policies, heroin-dependent people are given medical prescriptions for the drug and allowed to use it in a safe, controlled environment. "The programs, by design, offer a very sterile, indeed clinical, environment. Operators make every effort to reduce the experience to medicine rather than recreation. Patients must turn up on time, take the drug promptly, and leave the premises. There is to be no congregating or socializing. For example, in one facility there are few chairs in the waiting room; the aim is to move patients in and out as soon as they have recovered from their dose." Peter Reuter, *Can Heroin Maintenance Help Baltimore?: What Baltimore Can Learn From the Experiences of Other Countries* (Abell Foundation, 2009). Participants in the programs must use the drug at the maintenance site and it remains illegal for them to possess heroin away from the facility. Only those who are already heroin-dependent are eligible to be admitted into the program.

How should heroin maintenance programs be characterized? In the early 1970s New York City Mayor John Lindsay suggested investigating the implementation of a heroin maintenance program. New York Congressman Charles Rangel attacked Lindsay's proposal as a plan to "legalize heroin." *See* JOSEPH A. CALIFANO, JR., HIGH SOCIETY: HOW SUBSTANCE ABUSE RAVAGES AMERICA AND WHAT TO DO ABOUT IT 130 (2007). Is heroin maintenance a form of heroin "legalization" or a harm reduction measure? Or both? How important do you think the characterization of a program like this as legalization or as something else would be to its political viability?

Just as some drug policy programs are not easily classified, the terms legalization and decriminalization can encompass a range of policy options. As federal Judge Juan R. Torruella has observed, "legalization" and "decriminalization," "although technically distinct, are often used almost interchangeably." Juan R. Torruella, *One Judge's Attempt at a Rational Discussion of the So-Called War on Drugs*, 6 B.U. PUB. INT'L L. J. 1, 12–13 (1996). That said, the line between the two concepts is fairly well delineated at least in theory. Decriminalizing a drug generally means removing criminal penalties for its use and possession in small amounts. Manufacture and sale of the drug remain prohibited under a decriminalization regime and, in some cases, users may still incur civil penalties (such as fines or coerced treatment). Legalization, by contrast, typically refers to a system in which the sale and manufacture of a substance is taxed and regulated. *See, e.g.,* ROBERT J. MACCOUN AND PETER REUTER, DRUG WAR HERESIES: LEARNING FROM OTHER VICES, TIMES, AND PLACES 40 (2001); Eric E. Sterling, *The Sentencing Boomerang: Drug Prohibition, Politics and Reform,* 40 VILLANOVA L. REV. 383 (1995) (discussing the different meanings assigned to terms like legalization and prohibition).

Drug Prohibition in the United States: Costs, Consequences, and Alternatives
Ethan A. Nadelmann
5 Notre Dame Journal of Law Ethics and Public Policy 783 (1991)

There is no one legalization option. At one extreme, some libertarians advocate the removal of all criminal sanctions and taxes on the production and sale of all psychoactive substances—with the possible exception of restrictions on sales to children. The alternative extremes are more varied. Some would limit legalization to one of the safest (relatively speaking) of all illicit substances: marijuana. Others prefer a "medical" oversight model similar to today's methadone maintenance programs. The middle ground combines legal availability of some or all illicit drugs with vigorous efforts to restrict consumption by means other than resort to criminal sanctions. Many supporters of this dual approach simultaneously advocate greater efforts to limit tobacco consumption and the abuse of alcohol as well as a transfer of government resources from anti-drug law enforcement to drug prevention and treatment. Indeed, the best model for this view of drug legalization is precisely the tobacco control model advocated by those who want to do everything possible to discourage tobacco consumption short of criminalizing the production, sale, and use of tobacco.

Clearly, neither drug legalization nor enforcement of anti-drug laws promises to "solve" the drug problem. Nor is there any question that legalization presents certain risks. Legalization would almost certainly increase the availability of drugs, decrease their price, and remove the deterrent power of the criminal sanction—all of which invite increases in drug use and abuse. There are at least three reasons, however, why these risks are worth taking. First, drug control strategies that rely primarily on criminal justice measures are significantly and inherently limited in their capacity to curtail drug abuse. Second, many law enforcement efforts are not only of limited value but also highly costly and counter-productive; indeed, many of the drug-related evils that most people identify as part and parcel of "the drug problem" are in fact the costs of drug prohibition policies. Third, the risks of legalization may well be less than most people assume, particularly if intelligent alternative measures are implemented.

Few law enforcement officials any longer contend that their efforts can do much more than they are already doing to reduce drug abuse in the United States. This is true of international drug enforcement efforts, interdiction, and both high-level and street-level domestic drug enforcement efforts.

The United States seeks to limit the export of illicit drugs to this country by a combination of crop eradication and crop substitution programs, financial inducements to growers to abstain from the illicit business, and punitive measures against producers, traffickers, and others involved in the drug traffic. These efforts have met with scant success in the past and show few indications of succeeding in the future. The obstacles are many: marijuana and opium can be grown in a wide variety of locales and even the coca plant "can be grown in virtually any subtropical region of the world which gets between 40 and 240 inches of rain per year, where it never freezes, and where the land is not so swampy as to be waterlogged. In South America this comes to [approximately] 2,500,000 square miles," of which less than 700 square miles are currently being used to cultivate coca. Producers in many countries have reacted to crop eradication programs by engaging in "guerrilla" farming methods, cultivating their crops in relatively inaccessible hinterlands, and camouflaging them with legitimate crops. Some illicit drug-production regions are controlled not by the central government but by drug trafficking gangs or political insurgents, thereby rendering eradication efforts even more difficult and hazardous.

Even where eradication efforts prove relatively successful in an individual country, other countries will emerge as new producers, as has occurred with both the international marijuana and heroin markets during the past two decades and can be expected to follow from planned coca eradication programs. The foreign export price of illicit drugs is such a tiny fraction of the retail price in the United States [approximately 4% with cocaine, 1% with marijuana, and much less than 1% with heroin] that international drug control efforts are not even successful in raising the cost of illicit drugs to U.S. consumers. U.S. efforts to control drugs overseas also confront substantial, and in some cases well-organized, political opposition in foreign countries. Major drug traffickers retain the power to bribe and intimidate government officials into ignoring or even cooperating with their enterprises. Particularly in many Latin American and Asian countries, the illicit drug traffic is an important source of income and employment, bringing in billions of dollars in hard currency each year and providing liveable wages for many hundreds of thousands. The illicit drug business has been described—not entirely in jest—as the best means ever devised by the United States for exporting the capitalist ethic to potentially revolutionary Third World peasants. By contrast, United States-sponsored eradication efforts risk depriving those same peasants of their livelihoods, thereby stimulating support for communist insurgencies ranging from Peru's Shining Path to the variety of ethnic and communist organizations active in drug-producing countries such as Colombia and Burma. Moreover, many of those involved in producing illicit drugs overseas do not perceive their moral obligation as preventing decadent gringos from consuming cocaine or heroin; rather it is to earn the best living possible for themselves and their families. In the final analysis, there is little the U.S. government can do to change this perception.

Interdiction efforts have shown little success in stemming the flow of cocaine and heroin into the United States. Indeed, during the past decade, the wholesale price of a kilo of cocaine has dropped by 80% even as the retail purity of a gram of cocaine has quintupled from 12 to about 60%; the trend with heroin over the past few years has been similar if less dramatic. Easily transported in a variety of large and small aircraft and sea vessels, carried across the Mexican border by legal and illegal border crossers, hidden in everything from furniture, flowers, and automobiles to private body parts and cadavers, heroin and cocaine shipments are extraordinarily difficult to detect. Despite powerful congressional support for dramatically increasing the role of the military in drug interdiction, military leaders insist that they can do little to make a difference. The Coast Guard and U.S. Customs continue to expand their efforts in this area, but they too concede that they will never seize more than a small percentage of total shipments. Because cocaine and heroin are worth more than their weight in gold, the incentives to transport these drugs to the United States are so great that we can safely assume that there will never be a shortage of those willing to take the risk.

The one success that interdiction efforts can claim concerns marijuana. Because marijuana is far bulkier per dollar of value than either cocaine or heroin, it is harder to conceal and easier to detect. Stepped-up interdiction efforts in recent years appear to have increased its price to the American consumer. The unintended consequences of this success are twofold: the United States has emerged as one of the world's leading producers of marijuana; indeed, U.S. producers are now believed to produce among the finest strains in the world; and many international drug traffickers appear to have redirected their efforts from marijuana to cocaine. The principal consequence of the U.S. drug interdiction effort, many would contend, has been a glut of increasingly potent cocaine and a shortage of comparatively benign marijuana.

Domestic law enforcement efforts have proven increasingly successful in apprehending and imprisoning rapidly growing numbers of illicit drug merchants, ranging from the most sophisticated international traffickers to the most common street-level drug dealers. The principal benefit of law enforcement efforts directed at major drug trafficking organizations is probably the rapidly rising value of drug trafficker assets forfeited to the government. There is, however, little indication that such efforts have any significant impact on the price or availability of illicit drugs. Intensive and highly costly street-level law enforcement efforts such as those mounted by many urban police departments in recent years have resulted in the arrests of thousands of low-level drug dealers and users and helped improve the quality of life in targeted neighborhoods. In most large urban centers, however, these efforts have had little impact on the overall availability of illicit drugs.

The logical conclusion of the foregoing analysis is not that criminal justice efforts to stop drug trafficking do not work at all; rather, it is that even substantial fluctuations in those efforts have little effect on the price, availability, and consumption of illicit drugs. The mere existence of criminal laws combined with minimal levels of enforcement is sufficient to deter many potential users and to reduce the availability and increase the price of drugs. Law enforcement officials acknowledge that they alone cannot solve the drug problem but contend that their role is nonetheless essential to the overall effort to reduce illicit drug use and abuse. What they are less ready to acknowledge, however, is that the very criminalization of the drug market has proven highly costly and counterproductive in much the same way that the national prohibition of alcohol did 60 years ago.

Total government expenditures devoted to enforcement of drug laws amounted to a minimum of $10 billion in 1987. Between 1981 and 1987, federal expenditures on anti-drug law enforcement more than tripled, from less that $1 billion per year to about $3 billion. State and local law enforcement agencies spent an estimated $5 billion, amounting to about one-fifth of their total investigative resources, on drug enforcement activities in 1986. Drug law violators currently account for approximately 10% of the roughly 550,000 inmates in state prisons, more than one-third of the 50,000 federal prison inmates, and a significant (albeit undetermined) proportion of the approximately 300,000 individuals confined in municipal jails. The U.S. Sentencing Commission has predicted that in 15 years the federal prison population will total 100,000 to 150,000 inmates, of whom one-half will be incarcerated for drug law violations. Among the 40,000 inmates in New York State prisons, drug law violations surpassed first-degree robbery in 1987 as the number one cause of incarceration, accounting for 20% of the total prison population. Nationwide, drug trafficking and drug possession offenses accounted for approximately 135,000 (23%) of the 583,000 individuals convicted of felonies in state courts in 1986. State and local governments spent a minimum of $2 billion last year to incarcerate drug offenders. The costs, in terms of alternative social expenditures foregone and other types of criminals not imprisoned, are perhaps even more severe.

Police have made about 750,000 arrests for violations of the drug laws during each of the last few years. Slightly more than three-quarters of these have been not for manufacturing or dealing drugs but solely for possession of an illicit drug, typically marijuana. (Those arrested, it is worth noting, represent less than 2% of the 35 to 40 million Americans estimated to have illegally consumed a drug during each of the past years.) On the one hand, these arrests have clogged many urban criminal justice systems: in New York City, drug law violations in 1987 accounted for more than 40% of all felony indictments, up from 25% in 1985; in Washington D.C., the figure was 52% in 1986, up from 13% in 1981. On the other hand, they have distracted criminal justice officials from concentrating greater resources on violent offenses and property crimes. In many cities, urban law enforcement has become virtually synonymous with drug enforcement.

The greatest beneficiaries of the drug laws are organized and unorganized drug traffickers. The criminalization of the drug market effectively imposes a de facto value-added tax that is enforced and occasionally augmented by the law enforcement establishment and collected by the drug traffickers. More than half of all organized crime revenues are believed to derive from the illicit drug business; estimates of the dollar value range between $10 and $50 billion per year. By contrast, annual revenues from cigarette bootlegging, which persists principally because of differences among states in their cigarette tax rates, are estimated at between $200 million and $400 million. If the marijuana, cocaine, and heroin markets were legal, state and federal governments would collect billions of dollars annually in tax revenues. Instead, they expend billions in what amounts to a subsidy of organized criminals.

The connection between drugs and crime is one that continues to resist coherent analysis both because cause and effect are so difficult to distinguish and because the role of the drug prohibition laws in causing and labeling "drug-related crime" is so often ignored. There are five possible connections between drugs and crime, at least three of which would be much diminished if the drug prohibition laws were repealed. First, the production, sale, purchase, and possession of marijuana, cocaine, heroin, and other strictly controlled and banned substances are crimes in and of themselves, which occur billions of times each year in the United States alone. In the absence of drug prohibition laws, these activities would largely cease to be considered crimes. Selling drugs to children would, of course, continue to be criminalized, and other evasions of government regulation of a legal market would continue to be prosecuted, but by and large the connection between drugs and crime that now accounts for all of the criminal justice costs noted above would be severed.

Second, many illicit drug users commit crimes such as robbery and burglary, as well as other vice crimes such as drug dealing, prostitution, and numbers running, to earn enough money to purchase cocaine, heroin, and other illicit drugs—drugs that cost far more than alcohol and tobacco not because they cost much more to produce but because they are illegal. Because legalization would inevitably lead to a reduction in the cost of the drugs that are now illicit, it would also invite a significant reduction in this drug-crime connection. At the same time, current methadone maintenance programs represent a limited form of drug legalization that attempts to break this connection between drugs and crime by providing an addictive opiate at little or no cost to addicts who might otherwise steal to support their illicit heroin habits.

The third connection between drugs and crime is more coincidental than causal in nature. Although most illicit drug users do not engage in crime aside from their drug use, and although many criminals do not use or abuse illicit drugs or alcohol, substance abuse clearly is much higher among criminals than among noncriminals. A 1986 survey of state prison inmates found that 43% were using illegal drugs on a daily or near daily basis in the month before they committed the crime for which they were incarcerated; it also found that roughly one-half of the inmates who had used an illicit drug did not do so until after their first arrest. Perhaps many of the same factors that lead individuals into lives of crime also push them in the direction of substance abuse. It is possible that legalization would diminish this connection by removing from the criminal subculture the lucrative opportunities that now derive from the illegality of the drug market. But it is also safe to assume that the criminal milieu will continue to claim a disproportionately large share of drug abusers regardless of whether or not drugs are legalized.

The fourth link between drugs and crime is the commission of violent and other crimes by people under the influence of illicit drugs. It is this connection that seems to most infect the popular imagination. Clearly, some drugs do "cause" some people to commit crimes by reducing normal inhibitions, unleashing aggressive and other asocial tendencies, and lessening senses of responsibility. Cocaine, particularly in the form of "crack," has gained such a reputation in recent years, just as heroin did in the 1960s and 1970s and marijuana did in the years before that. Crack cocaine's reputation for inspiring violent behavior may well be more deserved than were those of marijuana and heroin, although the evidence has yet to substantiate media depictions. No illicit drug, however, is as strongly associated with violent behavior as is alcohol. According to Justice Department statistics, 54% of all jail inmates convicted of violent crimes in 1983 reported having used alcohol just prior to committing their offense." The impact of drug legalization on this aspect of the drug-crime connection is the most difficult to assess, largely because changes in the overall level and nature of drug consumption are so difficult to predict.

The fifth connection is the violent, intimidating, and corrupting behavior of the drug traffickers. In many Latin American countries, most notably Colombia, this connection virtually defines the "drug problem." But even within the United States, drug trafficker violence is rapidly becoming a major concern of criminal justice officials and the public at large. The connection is not difficult to explain. Illegal markets tend to breed violence, both because they attract criminally minded and violent individuals and because participants in the market have no resort to legal institutions to resolve their disputes. During Prohibition, violent struggles: between bootlegging gangs and hijackings of booze-laden trucks and sea vessels were frequent and notorious occurrences. Today's equivalents are the booby traps that surround some marijuana fields, the pirates of the Caribbean looking to rob drug-laden vessels en route to the shores of the United States, the machine gun battles and executions of the more sordid drug gangs, and the generally high levels of violence that attend many illicit drug relationships; the victims include not just drug dealers but witnesses, bystanders, and law enforcement officials. Most law enforcement authorities agree that the dramatic increases in urban murder rates during the past few years can be explained almost entirely by the rise in drug dealer killings, mostly of one another. At the same time, the powerful allure of illicit drug dollars is responsible for rising levels of corruption not just in Latin America and the Caribbean but also in federal, state and local criminal justice systems throughout the United States. A drug legalization strategy would certainly deal a severe blow to this link between drugs and crime.

Perhaps the most unfortunate victims of the drug prohibition policies have been the poor and law-abiding residents of urban ghettos. Those policies have proven largely futile in deterring large numbers of ghetto dwellers from becoming drug abusers but they do account for much of what ghetto residents identify as the drug problem. In many neighborhoods, it often seems to be the aggressive gun-toting drug dealers who upset law-abiding residents far more than the addicts nodding out in doorways. At the same time, the increasingly harsh criminal penalties imposed on adult drug dealers have led to the widespread recruiting of juveniles by drug traffickers. Where once children started dealing drugs only after they had been using them for a few years, today the sequence is often reversed. Many children start to use illegal drugs now only after they have worked for older drug dealers for a while.

Perhaps the most difficult costs to evaluate are those that relate to the widespread defiance of the drug prohibition laws: the effects of labeling as criminals the tens of millions of people who use drugs illicitly, subjecting them to the risks of criminal sanction, and obliging many of those same people to enter into relationships with drug dealers (who may be criminals in many more senses of the word) in order to purchase their drugs; the cynicism that such laws generate toward other laws and the law in general; and the sense of hostility and suspicion that many otherwise law-abiding individuals feel toward law enforcement officials. It was costs such as these that strongly influenced many of Prohibition's more conservative opponents.

Among the most dangerous consequences of the drug laws are the harms that stem from the unregulated nature of illicit drug production and sale. Many marijuana smokers are worse off for having smoked cannabis that was grown with dangerous fertilizers, sprayed with the herbicide paraquat, or mixed with more dangerous substances. Consumers of heroin and the various synthetic substances sold on the street face even more severe consequences, including fatal overdoses and poisonings from unexpectedly potent or impure drug supplies. In short, nothing resembling an underground Food and Drug Administration has arisen to impose quality control on the illegal drug market and provide users with accurate information on the drugs they consume. More often than not, the quality of a drug addict's life depends greatly on his or her access to reliable supplies. Drug enforcement operations that succeed in temporarily disrupting supply networks are thus a double-edged sword: they encourage some addicts to seek admission into drug treatment programs, but they oblige others to seek out new and hence less reliable suppliers, with the result that more, not fewer, drug-related emergencies and deaths occur.

Among the strongest arguments in favor of legalization are the moral ones. On the one hand, the standard refrain regarding the immorality of drug use crumbles in the face of most Americans' tolerance for alcohol and tobacco use. Only the Mormons and a few other like-minded sects, who regard as immoral any intake of substances to alter one's state of consciousness or otherwise cause pleasure, are consistent in this respect; they eschew not just the illicit drugs but also alcohol, tobacco, caffeinated coffee and tea, and even chocolate. "Moral" condemnation by the majority of Americans of some substances and not others is little more than a transient prejudice in favor of some drugs and against others.

On the other hand, drug enforcement involves its own immoralities.

Indeed, enforcement of drug laws makes a mockery of an essential principle of a free society, that those who do no harm to others should not be harmed by others, and particularly not by the state. Most of the nearly 40 million Americans who illegally consume drugs each year do no direct harm to anyone else; indeed, most do relatively little harm even to themselves. Directing criminal and other sanctions at them, and rationalizing the justice of such sanctions, may well represent the greatest societal cost of our current drug prohibition system.

Repealing the drug prohibition laws clearly promises tremendous advantages. Between reduced government expenditures on enforcing drug laws and new tax revenue from legal drug production and sales, public treasuries would enjoy a net benefit of at least $10 billion per year and possibly much more; thus billions in new revenues would be available, and ideally targeted, for funding much-needed drug treatment programs as well as the types of social and educational programs that often prove most effective in creating incentives for children not to abuse drugs. The quality of urban life would rise significantly. Homicide rates would decline. So would robbery and burglary rates. Organized criminal groups, particularly the up-and-coming ones that have yet to diversify into nondrug areas, would be dealt a devastating setback. The police, prosecutors, and courts would focus their resources on combating the types of crimes that people cannot walk away from. More ghetto residents would turn their backs on criminal careers and seek out legitimate opportunities instead. And the health and quality of life of many drug users and even drug abusers would improve significantly. Internationally, U.S. foreign policymakers would get on with more important and realistic objectives, and foreign governments would reclaim the authority that they have lost to the drug traffickers.

All the benefits of legalization would be for naught, however, if millions more people were to become drug abusers.

Our experience with alcohol and tobacco provides ample warnings. Today, alcohol is consumed by 140 million Americans and tobacco by 50 million. All of the health costs associated with abuse of the illicit drugs pale in comparison with those resulting from tobacco and alcohol abuse.

The impact of legalization on the nature and level of consumption of those drugs that are currently illegal is impossible to predict with any accuracy. On the one hand, legalization implies greater availability, lower prices, and the elimination (particularly for adults) of the deterrent power of the criminal sanction—all of which would suggest higher levels of use. Indeed, some fear that the extent of drug abuse and its attendant costs would rise to those currently associated with alcohol and tobacco. On the other hand, there are many reasons to doubt that a well-designed and implemented policy of controlled drug legalization would yield such costly consequences.

The logic of legalization depends in part upon two assumptions: that most illegal drugs are not as dangerous as is commonly believed; and that those types of drugs and methods of consumption that are most risky are unlikely to prove appealing to many people precisely because they are so obviously dangerous. Consider marijuana. Among the roughly 60 million Americans who have smoked marijuana, not one has died from a marijuana overdose, a striking contrast with alcohol, which is involved in approximately 10,000 overdose deaths annually, half in combination with other drugs. Although there are good health reasons for people not to smoke marijuana daily, and for children, pregnant women, and some others not to smoke at all, there still appears to be little evidence that occasional marijuana consumption does much harm at all. Certainly, it is not healthy to inhale marijuana smoke into one's lungs; indeed, the National Institute on Drug Abuse (NIDA) has declared that "marijuana smoke contains more cancer-causing agents than is found in tobacco smoke." On the other hand, the number of "joints" smoked by all but a very small percentage of marijuana smokers is a tiny fraction of the 20 cigarettes a day smoked by the average cigarette smoker; indeed, the average may be closer to one or two joints per week than one or two per day. Note that the NIDA defines "heavy" marijuana smoker as one who consumes at least two joints "daily." A heavy tobacco smoker, by contrast, smokes about 40 cigarettes per day.

The dangers associated with cocaine, heroin, the hallucinogens, and other illicit substances are greater than those posed by marijuana but not nearly so great as many people seem to think. Consider the case of cocaine. In 1986, NIDA reported that over 20 million Americans had tried cocaine, that 12.2 million had consumed it at least once during 1985, and that nearly 5.8 million had used it within the past month. Among 18- to 25-year-olds, 8.2 million had tried cocaine; 5.3 million had used it within the past year; 2.5 million had used it within the past month; and 250,000 had used it on the average weekly. One could extrapolate from these figures that a quarter of a million young Americans are potential problem users. But one could also conclude that only 3% of those 18- to 25-year-olds who had ever tried the drug fell into that category, and that only 10% of those who had used cocaine monthly were at risk.

All of this is not to say that cocaine is not a potentially dangerous drug, especially when it is injected, smoked in the form of "crack," or consumed in tandem with other powerful substances. Clearly, many tens of thousands of Americans have suffered severely from their abuse of cocaine and a tiny fraction have died. But there is also overwhelming evidence that most users of cocaine do not get into trouble with the drug. So much of the media attention has focused on the relatively small percentage of cocaine users who become addicted that the popular perception of how most people use cocaine has become badly distorted.

With respect to the hallucinogens such as LSD and psilocybic mushrooms, their potential for addiction is virtually nil. The dangers arise primarily from using them irresponsibly on individual occasions. Although many of those who have used hallucinogens have experienced "bad trips," far more have reported positive experiences and very few have suffered any long-term harm. As for the great assortment of stimulants, depressants, and tranquilizers produced illegally or diverted from licit channels, each evidences varying capacities to create addiction, harm the user, or be used safely.

Until recently, no drugs were regarded with as much horror as the opiates, and in particular heroin. As with most drugs, it can be eaten, snorted, smoked, or injected. The custom among most Americans, unfortunately, is the last of these options[.] There is no question that heroin is potentially highly addictive, perhaps as addictive as nicotine. But despite the popular association of heroin use with the most down-and-out inhabitants of urban ghettos, heroin causes relatively little physical harm to the human body. Consumed on an occasional or regular basis under sanitary conditions, its worst side effect, apart from the fact of being addicted, is constipation. That is one reason why many doctors in early 20th-century America saw opiate addiction as preferable to alcoholism and prescribed the former as treatment for the latter where abstinence did not seem a realistic option. It is both insightful and important to think about the illicit drugs as we do about alcohol and tobacco. Like tobacco, some illicit substances are highly addictive but can be consumed on a regular basis for decades without any demonstrable harm. Like alcohol, many of the substances can be, and are, used by most consumers in moderation, with little in the way of harmful effects; but like alcohol they also lend themselves to abuse by a minority of users who become addicted or otherwise harm themselves or others as a consequence. And like both the legal substances, the psychoactive effects of each of the illegal drugs vary greatly from one person to another. To be sure, the pharmacology of the substance is important, as is its purity and the manner in which it is consumed. But much also depends upon not just the physiology and psychology of the consumer but his expectations regarding the drug, his social milieu, and the broader cultural environment, what Harvard University psychiatrist Norman Zinberg called the "set and setting" of the drug. It is factors such as these that might change dramatically, albeit in indeterminate ways, were the illicit drugs made legally available.

It is thus impossible to predict whether or not legalization would lead to much greater levels of drug abuse. The lessons that can be drawn from other societies are mixed. China's experience with the British opium pushers of the 19th century, when millions reportedly became addicted to the drug, offers one worst-case scenario. The devastation of many native American tribes by alcohol presents another. On the other hand, the decriminalization of marijuana by 11 states in the United States during the mid-1970s does not appear to have led to increases in marijuana consumption. In the Netherlands, which went even further in decriminalizing cannabis during the 1970s, consumption has actually declined significantly; in 1976, 3% of 15- and 16-year-olds and 10% of 17- and 18-year-olds used cannabis occasionally; by 1985, the percentages had declined to 2 and 6%, respectively. The policy has succeeded, as the government intended, "in making drug use boring." Finally, late 19-century America is an example of a society in which there were almost no drug laws or even drug regulations but levels of drug use were about what they are today. Drug abuse was regarded as a relatively serious problem, but the criminal justice system was not regarded as part of the solution.

There are, however, strong reasons to believe that none of the currently illicit substances would become as popular as alcohol or tobacco even if they were legalized. Alcohol has long been the principal intoxicant in most societies, including many in which other substances have been legally available. Presumably, its diverse properties account for its popularity: it quenches thirst, goes well with food, often pleases the palate, promotes appetite as well as sociability, and so on. The widespread use of tobacco probably stems not just from its powerful addictive qualities but from the fact that its psychoactive effects are sufficiently subtle that cigarettes can be integrated with most other human activities. None of the illicit substances now popular in the United States share either of these qualities to the same extent, nor is it likely that they would acquire them if they were legalized. Moreover, none of the illicit substances can compete with alcohol's special place in American culture and history, one that it retained even during Prohibition.

Much of the damage caused by illegal drugs today stems from their consumption in particularly potent and dangerous ways. There is good reason to doubt that many Americans would inject cocaine or heroin into their veins even if given the chance to do so legally.

Perhaps the most reassuring reason for believing that repeal of the drug prohibition laws will not lead to tremendous increases in drug abuse levels is the fact that we have learned something from our past experiences with alcohol and tobacco abuse. We now know, for instance, that consumption taxes are an effective method for limiting consumption rates and related costs, especially among young people. Substantial evidence also suggests that restrictions and bans on advertising, as well as promotion of negative advertising, can make a difference. The same seems to be true of other government measures, including restrictions on time and place of sale, bans on vending machines, prohibitions of consumption in public places, packaging requirements, mandated adjustments in insurance policies, crackdowns on driving while under the influence, and laws holding bartenders and hosts responsible for the drinking of customers and guests. There is even some evidence that some education programs about the dangers of cigarette smoking have deterred many children from beginning to smoke. At the same time, we also have come to recognize the great harms that can result when drug control policies are undermined by powerful lobbies such as those that now block efforts to lessen the harms caused by abuse of alcohol and tobacco.

Legalization thus affords far greater opportunities to control drug use and abuse than do current criminalization policies. The current strategy is one in which the type, price, purity, and potency of illicit drugs, as well as the participants in the business, are largely determined by drug dealers, the peculiar competitive dynamics of an illicit market, and the perverse interplay of drug enforcement strategies and drug trafficking tactics.

A drug control policy based predominantly on approaches other than criminal justice thus offers a number of significant advantages over the current criminal justice focus in controlling drug use and abuse. It shifts control of production, distribution, and, to a lesser extent, consumption out of the hands of criminals and into the hands of government and government licenses. It affords consumers the opportunity to make far more informed decisions about the drugs they buy than is currently the case. It dramatically lessens the likelihood that drug consumers will be harmed by impure, unexpectedly potent, or misidentified drugs. It corrects the hypocritical and dangerous message that alcohol and tobacco are somehow safer than many illicit drugs. It reduces by billions of dollars annually government expenditures on drug enforcement and simultaneously raises additional billions in tax revenues. And it allows government the opportunity to shape consumption patterns toward relatively safer psychoactive substances and modes of consumption.

Toward the end of the 1920s, when the debate over repealing Prohibition rapidly gained momentum, numerous scholars, journalists, and private and government commissions undertook thorough evaluations of Prohibition and the potential alternatives. Prominent among these were the Wickersham Commission appointed by President Herbert Hoover and the study of alcohol regulation abroad directed by the leading police scholar in the United States, Raymond Fosdick, and commissioned by John D. Rockefeller. These efforts examined the successes and failings of Prohibition in the United States and evaluated the wide array of alternative regimes for controlling the distribution and use of beer, wine, and liquor. They played a major role in stimulating the public reevaluation of Prohibition and in envisioning alternatives. Precisely the same sorts of efforts are required today.

The controlled drug legalization option is not an all-or-nothing alternative to current policies. Indeed, political realities ensure that any shift toward legalization will evolve gradually, with ample opportunity to halt, reevaluate, and redirect drug policies that begin to prove too costly or counterproductive. The federal government need not play the leading role in devising alternatives; it need only clear the way to allow state and local governments the legal power to implement their own drug legalization policies. The first steps are relatively risk-free: legalization of marijuana, easier availability of illegal and strictly controlled drugs for treatment of pain and other medical purposes, tougher tobacco and alcohol control policies, and a broader and more available array of drug treatment programs.

There is no question that legalization is a risky policy, one that may indeed lead to an increase in the number of people who abuse drugs. But that risk is by no means a certainty. At the same time, current drug control policies are showing little progress and new proposals promise only to be more costly and more repressive. We know that repealing the drug prohibition laws would eliminate or greatly reduce many of the ills that people commonly identify as part and parcel of the "drug problem." Yet that option is repeatedly and vociferously dismissed without any attempt to evaluate it openly and objectively. The past 20 years have demonstrated that a drug policy shaped by rhetoric and fear-mongering can only lead to our current disaster. Unless we are willing to honestly evaluate all our options, including various legalization strategies, there is a good chance that we will never identify the best solutions for our drug problems.

Against the Legalization of Drugs
James Q. Wilson
89 Commentary 21 (1990)

In 1972, the president appointed me chairman of the National Advisory Council for Drug Abuse Prevention. Created by Congress, the Council was charged with providing guidance on how best to coordinate the national war on drugs. (Yes, we called it a war then, too.) In those days, the drug we were chiefly concerned with was heroin. When I took office, heroin use had been increasing dramatically. Everybody was worried that this increase would continue. Such phrases as "heroin epidemic" were commonplace.

That same year, the eminent economist Milton Friedman published an essay in *Newsweek* in which he called for legalizing heroin. His argument was on two grounds: As a matter of ethics, the government has no right to tell people not to use heroin (or to drink or to commit suicide); as a matter of economics, the prohibition of drug use imposes costs on society that far exceed the benefits. Others, such as the psychoanalyst Thomas Szasz, made the same argument.

We did not take Friedman's advice. (Government commissions rarely do.) I do not recall that we even discussed legalizing heroin, though we did discuss (but did not take action on) legalizing a drug, cocaine, that many people then argued was benign. Our marching orders were to figure out how to win the war on heroin, not to run up the white flag of surrender.

That was 1972. Today, we have the same number of heroin addicts that we had then—half a million, give or take a few thousand. Having that many heroin addicts is no trivial matter; these people deserve our attention. But not having had an increase in that number for over fifteen years is also something that deserves our attention. What happened to the "heroin epidemic" that many people once thought would overwhelm us?

The facts are clear: A more or less stable pool of heroin addicts has been getting older, with relatively few new recruits. In 1976 the average age of heroin users who appeared in hospital emergency rooms was about twenty-seven; ten years later it was thirty-two. More than two-thirds of all heroin users appearing in emergency rooms are now over the age of thirty. Back in the early 1970s, when heroin got onto the national political agenda, the typical heroin addict was much younger, often a teenager. Household surveys show the same thing—the rate of opiate use (which includes heroin) has been flat for the better part of two decades. More fine-grained studies of inner-city neighborhoods confirm this. John Boyle and Ann Brunswick found that the percentage of young blacks in Harlem who use heroin fell from 8 percent in 1970–71 to about 3 percent in 1975–76.

Why did heroin lose its appeal for young people? When the young blacks in Harlem were asked why they stopped, more than half mentioned "trouble with the law" or "high cost" (and high cost is, of course, directly the result of law enforcement). Two-thirds said that heroin hurt their health; nearly all said they had had a bad experience with it. We need not rely, however, simply on what they said. In New York City in 1973–75, the street price of heroin rose dramatically and its purity sharply declined, probably as a result of the heroin shortage caused by the success of the Turkish government in reducing the supply of opium base and of the French government in closing down heroin-processing laboratories located in and around Marseilles. These were short-lived gains for, just as Friedman predicted, alternative sources of supply—mostly in Mexico—quickly emerged. But the three-year heroin shortage interrupted the easy recruitment of new users.

Health and related problems were no doubt part of the reason for the reduced flow of recruits. Over the preceding years, Harlem youth had watched as more and more heroin users died of overdoses, were poisoned by adulterated doses, or acquired hepatitis from dirty needles. The word got around: Heroin can kill you. By 1974 new hepatitis cases and drug-overdose deaths had dropped to a fraction of what they had been in 1970.

Alas, treatment did not seem to explain much of the cessation in drug use. Treatment programs can and do help heroin addicts, but treatment did not explain the drop in the number of new users (who by definition had never been in treatment) nor even much of the reduction in the number of experienced users.

No one knows how much of the decline to attribute to personal observation as opposed to high prices or reduced supply. But other evidence suggests strongly that price and supply played a large role. In 1972 the National Advisory Council was especially worried by the prospect that U.S. servicemen returning to this country from Vietnam would bring their heroin habits with them. Fortunately, a brilliant study by Lee Robins of Washington University in St. Louis put that fear to rest. She measured drug use of Vietnam veterans shortly after they had returned home. Though many had used heroin regularly while in Southeast Asia, most gave up the habit when back in the United States. The reason: Here, heroin was less available and sanctions on its use were more pronounced. Of course, if a veteran had been willing to pay enough—which might have meant traveling to another city and would certainly have meant making an illegal contact with a disreputable dealer in a threatening neighborhood in order to acquire a (possibly) dangerous dose—he could have sustained his drug habit. Most veterans were unwilling to pay this price, and so their drug use declined or disappeared.

Suppose we had taken Friedman's advice in 1972. What would have happened? We cannot be entirely certain, but at a minimum we would have placed the young heroin addicts (and, above all, the prospective addicts) in a very different position from the one in which they actually found themselves. Heroin would have been legal. Its price would have been reduced by 95 percent (minus whatever we chose to recover in taxes). Now that it could be sold by the same people who make aspirin, its quality would have been assured—no poisons, no adulterants. Sterile hypodermic needles would have been readily available at the neighborhood drugstore, probably at the same counter where the heroin was sold. No need to travel to big cities or unfamiliar neighborhoods—heroin could have been purchased anywhere, perhaps by mail order.

There would no longer have been any financial or medical reason to avoid heroin use. Anybody could have afforded it. We might have tried to prevent children from buying it, but as we have learned from our efforts to prevent minors from buying alcohol and tobacco, young people have a way of penetrating markets theoretically reserved for adults. Returning Vietnam veterans would have discovered that Omaha and Raleigh had been converted into the pharmaceutical equivalent of Saigon.

Under these circumstances, can we doubt for a moment that heroin use would have grown exponentially? Or that a vastly larger supply of new users would have been recruited? Professor Friedman is a Nobel Prize-winning economist whose understanding of market forces is profound. What did he think would happen to consumption under his legalized regime? Here are his words: "Legalizing drugs might increase the number of addicts, but it is not clear that it would. Forbidden fruit is attractive, particularly to the young."

Really? I suppose that we should expect no increase in Porsche sales if we cut the price by 95 percent, no increase in whiskey sales if we cut the price by a comparable amount—because young people only want fast cars and strong liquor when they are "forbidden." Perhaps Friedman's uncharacteristic lapse from the obvious implications of price theory can be explained by a misunderstanding of how drug users are recruited. In his 1972 essay he said that "drug addicts are deliberately made by pushers, who give likely prospects their first few doses free." If drugs were legal it would not pay anybody to produce addicts, because everybody would buy from the cheapest source. But as every drug expert knows, pushers do not produce addicts. Friends or acquaintances do. In fact, pushers are usually reluctant to deal with nonusers because a nonuser could be an undercover cop. Drug use spreads in the same way any fad or fashion spreads: Somebody who is already a user urges his friends to try, or simply shows already-eager friends how to do it.

But we need not rely on speculation, however plausible, that lowered prices and more abundant supplies would have increased heroin usage. Great Britain once followed such a policy and with almost exactly those results. Until the mid-1960s, British physicians were allowed to prescribe heroin to certain classes of addicts. (Possessing these drugs without a doctor's prescription remained a criminal offense.) For many years this policy worked well enough because the addict patients were typically middle-class people who had become dependent on opiate painkillers while undergoing hospital treatment. There was no drug culture. The British system worked for many years, not because it prevented drug abuse but because there was no problem of drug abuse that would test the system.

All that changed in the 1960s. A few unscrupulous doctors began passing out heroin in wholesale amounts. One doctor prescribed almost six hundred thousand heroin tablets—that is, over thirteen pounds—in just one year. A youthful drug culture emerged with a demand for drugs far different from that of the older addicts. As a result, the British government required doctors to refer users to government-run clinics to receive their heroin.

But the shift to clinics did not curtail the growth in heroin use. Throughout the 1960s the number of addicts increased—the late John Kaplan of Stanford estimated by fivefold—in part as a result of the diversion of heroin from clinic patients to new users on the streets. An addict would bargain with the clinic doctor over how big a dose he would receive. The patient wanted as much as he could get, the doctor wanted to give as little as was needed. The patient had an advantage in this conflict because the doctor could not be certain how much was really needed. Many patients would use some of their "maintenance" dose and sell the remaining part to friends, thereby recruiting new addicts. As the clinics learned of this, they began to shift their treatment away from heroin and toward methadone, an addictive drug that, when taken orally, does not produce a "high" but will block the withdrawal pains associated with heroin abstinence.

Whether what happened in England in the 1960s was a miniepidemic or an epidemic depends on whether one looks at numbers or at rates of change. Compared to the United States, the numbers were small. In 1960 there were sixty-eight heroin addicts known to the British government; by 1968 there were two thousand in treatment and many more who refused treatment. (They would refuse in part because they did not want to get methadone at a clinic if they could get heroin on the street.) Richard Hartnoll estimates that the actual number of addicts in England is five times the number officially registered. At a minimum, the number of British addicts increased by thirtyfold in ten years; the actual increase may have been much larger.

In the early 1980s the numbers began to rise again, and this time nobody doubted that a real epidemic was at hand. The increase was estimated to be 40 percent a year. By 1982 there were thought to be twenty thousand heroin users in London alone. Geoffrey Pearson reports that many cities—Glasgow, Liverpool, Manchester, and Sheffield among them—were now experiencing a drug problem that once had been largely confined to London. The problem, again, was supply. The country was being flooded with cheap, high-quality heroin, first from Iran and then from Southeast Asia.

The United States began the 1960s with a much larger number of heroin addicts and probably a bigger at-risk population than was the case in Great Britain. Even though it would be foolhardy to suppose that the British system, if installed here, would have worked the same way or with the same results, it would be equally foolhardy to suppose that a combination of heroin available from leaky clinics and from street dealers who faced only minimal law-enforcement risks would not have produced a much greater increase in heroin use than we actually experienced. My guess is that if we had allowed either doctors or clinics to prescribe heroin, we would have had far worse results than were produced in Britain, if for no other reason than the vastly larger number of addicts with which we began. We would have had to find some way to police thousands (not scores) of physicians and hundreds (not dozens) of clinics. If the British civil service found it difficult to keep heroin in the hands of addicts and out of the hands of recruits when it was dealing with a few hundred people, how well would the American civil service have accomplished the same tasks when dealing with tens of thousands of people?

Now cocaine, especially in its potent form, crack, is the focus of attention. Now as in 1972 the government is trying to reduce its use. Now as then some people are advocating legalization. Is there any more reason to yield to those arguments today than there was almost two decades ago?

I think not. If we had yielded in 1972 we almost certainly would have had today a permanent population of several million, not several hundred thousand, heroin addicts. If we yield now we will have a far more serious problem with cocaine.

Crack is worse than heroin by almost any measure. Heroin produces a pleasant drowsiness and, if hygienically administered, has only the physical side effects of constipation and sexual impotence. Regular heroin use incapacitates many users, especially poor ones, for any productive work or social responsibility. They will sit nodding on a street corner, helpless but at least harmless. By contrast, regular cocaine use leaves the user neither helpless nor harmless. When smoked (as with crack) or injected, cocaine produces instant, intense, and short-lived euphoria. The experience generates a powerful desire to repeat it. If the drug is readily available, repeat use will occur.

The notion that abusing drugs such as cocaine is a "victimless crime" is not only absurd but dangerous. Even ignoring the fetal drug syndrome, crack-dependent people are, like heroin addicts, individuals who regularly victimize their children by neglect, their spouses by improvidence, their employers by lethargy, and their co-workers by carelessness. Society is not and could never be a collection of autonomous individuals.

We all have a stake in ensuring that each of us displays a minimal level of dignity, responsibility, and empathy. We cannot, of course, coerce people into goodness, but we can and should insist that some standards must be met if society itself—on which the very existence of the human personality depends—is to persist. Drawing the line that defines those standards is difficult and contentious, but if crack and heroin use do not fall below it, what does?

The advocates of legalization will respond by suggesting that my picture is overdrawn. Ethan Nadelmann of Princeton argues that the risk of legalization is less than most people suppose. Over twenty million Americans between the ages of eighteen and twenty-five have tried cocaine (according to a government survey), but only a quarter million use it daily. From this Nadelmann concludes that at most 3 percent of all young people who try cocaine develop a problem with it. The implication is clear: Make the drug legal and we only have to worry about 3 percent of our youth.

The implication rests on a logical fallacy[.] The fallacy is this: The percentage of occasional cocaine users who become binge users when the drug is illegal (and thus expensive and hard to find) tells us nothing about the percentage who will become dependent when the drug is legal (and thus cheap and abundant). Drs. Gawin and Ellinwood report, in common with several other researchers, that controlled or occasional use of cocaine changes to compulsive and frequent use "when access to the drug increases" or when the user switches from snorting to smoking. More cocaine more potently administered alters, perhaps sharply, the proportion of "controlled" users who become heavy users.

It is possible that some people will not become heavy users even when the drug is readily available in its most potent form. So far there are no scientific grounds for predicting who will and who will not become dependent. Neither socioeconomic background nor personality traits differentiate between casual and intensive users. Thus, the only way to settle the question of who is correct about the effect of easy availability on drug use, Nadelmann or Gawin and Ellinwood, is to try it and see. But the social experiment is so risky as to be no experiment at all, for if cocaine is legalized and if the rate of its abusive use increases dramatically, there is no way to put the genie back in the bottle, and it is not a kindly genie.

Many people who agree that there are risks in legalizing cocaine or heroin still favor it because, they think, we have lost the war on drugs. "Nothing we have done has worked" and the current federal policy is just "more of the same." Whatever the costs of greater drug use, surely they would be less than the costs of our present, failed efforts.

That is exactly what I was told in 1972—and heroin is not quite as bad a drug as cocaine. We did not surrender and we did not lose. We did not win, either. What the nation accomplished then was what most efforts to save people from themselves accomplish: The problem was contained and the number of victims minimized, all at a considerable cost in law enforcement and increased crime. Was the cost worth it? I think so, but others may disagree. What are the lives of would-be addicts worth? I recall some people saying to me then, "Let them kill themselves." I was appalled. Happily, such views did not prevail.

Have we lost today? Not at all. High-rate cocaine use is not commonplace. The National Institute of Drug Abuse (NIDA) reports that less than 5 percent of high-school seniors used cocaine within the last thirty days. Of course this survey misses young people who have dropped out of school and miscounts those who lie on the questionnaire, but even if we inflate the NIDA estimate by some plausible percentage, it is still not much above 5 percent. Medical examiners reported in 1987 that about 1,500 died from cocaine use; hospital emergency rooms reported about 30,000 admissions related to cocaine abuse.

These are not small numbers, but neither are they evidence of a nationwide plague that threatens to engulf us all.

It took about ten years to contain heroin. We have had experience with crack for only about three or four years. Each year we spend perhaps $11 billion on law enforcement (and some of that goes to deal with marijuana) and perhaps $2 billion on treatment. Large sums, but not sums that should lead anyone to say, "We just can't afford this any more."

The illegality of drugs increases crime, partly because some users turn to crime to pay for their habits, partly because some users are stimulated by certain drugs (such as crack or PCP) to act more violently or ruthlessly than they otherwise would, and partly because criminal organizations seeking to control drug supplies use force to manage their markets. These also are serious costs, but no one knows how much they would be reduced if drugs were legalized. Addicts would no longer steal to pay black-market prices for drugs, a real gain. But some, perhaps a great deal, of that gain would be offset by the great increase in the number of addicts. These people, nodding on heroin or living in the delusion-ridden high of cocaine, would hardly be ideal employees. Many would steal simply to support themselves, since snatch-and-grab, opportunistic crime can be managed even by people unable to hold a regular job or plan an elaborate crime.

Proponents of legalization claim that the costs of having more addicts around would be largely if not entirely offset by having more money available with which to treat and care for them. The money would come from taxes levied on the sale of heroin and cocaine.

To obtain this fiscal dividend, however, legalization's supporters must first solve an economic dilemma. If they want to raise a lot of money to pay for welfare and treatment, the tax rate on the drugs will have to be quite high. Even if they themselves do not want a high rate, the politicians' love of "sin taxes" would probably guarantee that it would be high anyway. But the higher the tax, the higher the price of the drug, and the higher the price the greater the likelihood that addicts will turn to crime to find the money for it and that criminal organizations will be formed to sell tax-free drugs at below-market rates. If we managed to keep taxes (and thus prices) low, we would get that much less money to pay for welfare and treatment and more people could afford to become addicts. There may be an optimal tax rate for drugs that maximizes revenue while minimizing crime, bootlegging, and the recruitment of new addicts, but our experience with alcohol does not suggest that we know how to find it.

The advocates of legalization find nothing to be said in favor of the current system except, possibly, that it keeps the number of addicts smaller than it would otherwise be. In fact, the benefits are more substantial than that.

We are now investing substantially in drug-education programs in the schools. Though we do not yet know for certain what will work, there are some promising leads. But I wonder how credible such programs would be if they were aimed at dissuading children from doing something perfectly legal. We could, of course, treat drug education like smoking education: Inhaling crack and inhaling tobacco are both legal, but you should not do it because it is bad for you. That tobacco is bad for you is easily shown; the Surgeon General has seen to that. But what do we say about crack? It is pleasurable, but devoting yourself to so much pleasure is not a good idea (though perfectly legal)? Unlike tobacco, cocaine will not give you cancer or emphysema, but it will lead you to neglect your duties to family, job, and neighborhood? Everybody is doing cocaine, but you should not?

Again, it might be possible under a legalized regime to have effective drug-prevention programs, but their effectiveness would depend heavily, I think, on first having decided that cocaine use, like tobacco use, is purely a matter of practical consequences; no fundamental moral significance attaches to either. But if we believe—as I do—that dependency on certain mind-altering drugs is a moral issue and that their illegality rests in part on their immorality, then legalizing them undercuts, if it does not eliminate altogether, the moral message.

That message is at the root of the distinction we now make between nicotine and cocaine. Both are highly addictive; both have harmful physical effects. But we treat the two drugs differently, not simply because nicotine is so widely used as to be beyond the reach of effective prohibition, but because its use does not destroy the user's essential humanity. Tobacco shortens one's life, cocaine debases it. Nicotine alters one's habits, cocaine alters one's soul. The heavy use of crack, unlike the heavy use of tobacco, corrodes those natural sentiments of sympathy and duty that constitute our human nature and make possible our social life. To say, as does Nadelmann, that distinguishing morally between tobacco and cocaine is "little more than a transient prejudice" is close to saying that morality itself is but a prejudice.

Now we have arrived where many arguments about legalizing drugs begin: Is there any reason to treat heroin and cocaine differently from the way we treat alcohol?

There is no easy answer to that question because, as with so many human problems, one cannot decide simply on the basis either of moral principles or of individual consequences; one has to temper any policy by a commonsense judgment of what is possible. Alcohol, like heroin, cocaine, PCP, and marijuana, is a drug—that is, a mood-altering substance—and consumed to excess it certainly has harmful consequences: auto accidents, barroom fights, bedroom shootings. It is also, for some people, addictive. We cannot confidently compare the addictive powers of these drugs, but the best evidence suggests that crack and heroin are much more addictive than alcohol.

Many people, Nadelmann included, argue that since the health and financial costs of alcohol abuse are so much higher than those of cocaine or heroin abuse, it is hypocritical folly to devote our efforts to preventing cocaine or drug use. But as Mark Kleiman of Harvard has pointed out, this comparison is quite misleading. What Nadelmann is doing is showing that a *legalized* drug (alcohol) produces greater social harm than *illegal* ones (cocaine and heroin). But of course. Suppose that in the 1920s we had made heroin and cocaine legal and alcohol illegal. Can anyone doubt that Nadelmann would now be writing that it is folly to continue our ban on alcohol because cocaine and heroin are so much more harmful?

Perform the following mental experiment: Suppose we legalized heroin and cocaine in this country. In what proportion of auto fatalities would the state police report that the driver was nodding off on heroin or recklessly driving on a coke high? In what proportion of spouse-assault and child-abuse cases would the local police report that crack was involved? In what proportion of industrial accidents would safety investigators report that the forklift or drill-press operator was in a drug-induced stupor or frenzy? We do not know exactly what the proportion would be, but anyone who asserts that it would not be much higher than it is now would have to believe that these drugs have little appeal except when they are illegal. And that is nonsense.

Suppose that today we had, not fifteen million alcohol abusers, but half a million. Suppose that we already knew what we have learned from our long experience with the widespread use of alcohol. Would we make whiskey legal? I do not know, but I suspect there would be a lively debate. The Surgeon General would remind us of the risks alcohol poses to pregnant women. The National Highway Traffic Safety Administration would point to the likelihood of more highway fatalities caused by drunk drivers. The Food and Drug Administration might find that there is a nontrivial increase in cancer associated with alcohol consumption. At the same time the police would report great difficulty in keeping illegal whiskey out of our cities, officers being corrupted by bootleggers, and alcohol addicts often resorting to crime to feed their habit. Libertarians, for their part, would argue that every citizen has a right to drink anything he wishes and that drinking is, in any event, a "victimless crime."

However the debate might turn out, the central fact would be that the problem was still, at that point, a small one. The government cannot legislate away the addictive tendencies in all of us, nor can it remove completely even the most dangerous addictive substances. But it can cope with harms when the harms are still manageable.

No one can know what our society would be like if we changed the law to make access to cocaine, heroin, and PCP easier. I believe, for reasons given, that the result would be a sharp increase in use, a more widespread degradation of the human personality, and a greater rate of accidents and violence.

I may be wrong. If I am, then we will needlessly have incurred heavy costs in law enforcement and some forms of criminality. But if I am right, and the legalizers prevail anyway, then we will have consigned millions of people, hundreds of thousands of infants, and hundreds of neighborhoods to a life of oblivion and disease. To the lives and families destroyed by alcohol we will have added countless more destroyed by cocaine, heroin, PCP, and whatever else a basement scientist can invent.

Human character is formed by society; indeed, human character is inconceivable without society, and good character is less likely in a bad society. Will we, in the name of an abstract doctrine of radical individualism, and with the false comfort of suspect predictions, decide to take the chance that somehow individual decency can survive amid a more general level of degradation?

I think not. The American people are too wise for that, whatever the academic essayists and cocktail-party pundits may say. But if Americans today are less wise than I suppose, then Americans at some future time will look back on us now and wonder, what kind of people were they that they could have done such a thing?

Drug Legalization: The Importance of Asking the Right Question
Mark A.R. Kleiman and Aaron J. Saiger
18 Hofstra Law Review 527 (1990)

Ethan Nadelmann, a prominent advocate of legalization, asks his readers to compare today's commerce in licit tobacco to the state of the world if the production, sale and possession of tobacco were made illegal. As millions of newly criminal nicotine addicts searched for ways to feed their addiction, black-market dealers would take over. Revenue which now flows to the states as cigarette excise taxes would, instead, feed the coffers of criminal organizations. A large, expensive and corruptible "Tobacco Enforcement Administration" would need to be created. Courts would be clogged with users caught with tobacco, and with dealers caught selling it to them. The nation would suddenly confront a daunting, dangerous, and expensive "tobacco problem."

Nadelmann, and other proponents of drug legalization, contend that this allegory of illicit tobacco closely resembles the reality of illicit drugs. Their argument rests on the proposition that the social costs of prohibiting some drugs, and enforcing that prohibition, exceeds the value of the goals which that prohibition achieves (i.e., the social cost it avoids). Such arguments maintain that making psychoactive drugs illegal simply creates a dangerous and menacing black market without significantly diminishing the quantity consumed. On this view, legalization would make the streets safer, put the black-market dealers out of business, and focus attention on the medical problem of addiction rather than the legal problem of drug dealing.

In reply, supporters of existing prohibitions contend that the benefits of prohibition justify its costs. Some of these supporters claim that safer neighborhoods and lower law enforcement budgets would not balance the damage to the public health and well-being that increased consumption of legal drugs would create. Others hold that the damage done by prohibition is not as significant as legalization advocates assert.

On this level, the argument between advocates and opponents of legalization involves different predictions about the results of alternative policies and different value weightings of those results. For example, legalizers are likely to stress crime reduction, whereas prohibitionists would emphasize the protection of users' health. But both sides can agree that policies are to be judged by their predictable consequences, and that the balance of advantage ought to determine the choice. Drugs ought to be prohibited if, and to the extent that, the benefits of prohibition outweigh its costs.

This sort of argument requires both analysis and evaluation. It must both identify the probable consequences of a range of possible policies, and suggest which bundles are "better" and which are "worse."

Neither the analysis nor the evaluation is straightforward. Like other major social problems, the drug problem has costs that resist quantification and even description. Costs range from the obvious and the assignable—lung cancer deaths, dealer violence—to problems to which drugs may or may not contribute, such as the weakening of the traditional family structure or the undermining of the work ethic. Comparing these costs is even more difficult. How much liberty is worth sacrificing to prevent how many drug-related deaths? How much drug intoxication would be accepted to empty ten percent of the prison cells?

This Article's critique of legalization proposals downplays the problem of what weights to assign different kinds of harm. Instead, it emphasizes the analytic side of the problem, identifying the probable consequences of various policies. Thus the close evaluative questions, with important values on both sides, are left unanswered.

A central accomplishment of the consequentialist proponents of legalization has been to stress the vital distinction between the costs of drug abuse and the costs of drug control. Drug use is one problem. It makes some users sicker, poorer, more dangerous, and less responsible. On the other hand, state control of drug use creates different problems: crowded prisons, unsafe neighborhoods, wealthy criminal consortia, corrupt officials. These problems should not be confused; prison overcrowding should not be treated as if it were a pharmacological result of cocaine use.

Equally important, legalization advocates have refused to treat currently legal drugs as conceptually distinct from currently illegal ones. Alcohol and tobacco, like marijuana and heroin, are drugs with significant costs of abuse and costs of control. Tobacco is an important special case: addictive and health damaging. But the rhetoric of the "war on drugs" attempts to obscure this fact, as if there were chemical categories of "legal" and "illegal" drugs. Reminding us to treat alcohol and tobacco as drugs, in both explanatory and comparative contexts, is therefore an important service.

Current consequentialist arguments for legalization, however, suffer from grave weaknesses.

Legalization advocates have pointed out that some costs that appear to be the costs of drug abuse are in fact costs of its control. However, the discovery that prohibition has significant costs appears to have obscured, for these advocates, its possible benefits. Some advocates of legalization simply argue that prohibition has no effect on consumption, and, thus, that legalization can shrink the drug problem at a stroke by legislating away a whole category of costs. In short, while illegal drugs have costs of abuse and costs of control, legal ones would have only costs of abuse. Other, more sophisticated accounts simply minimize prohibition's effects.

The problem legalization advocates face in accounting for the effects of prohibition is illustrated by their treatment of alcohol and tobacco. Correctly, they use the heavy load of damage associated with the currently licit drugs to point up the arbitrariness, perhaps irrationality, of the current categorization of drugs into forbidden and permitted. But unless one thinks that drug policies are made under Murphy's Law, the fact that the licit substances cause more health damage than the currently forbidden ones suggests that prohibition tends, on balance, to protect health. From a public health standpoint, creating a cocaine problem the size of the current alcohol problem or the current tobacco problem would be a major disaster. Yet it is far from clear that legal cocaine would be less attractive, or do less damage to users' health, than alcohol or tobacco. Alcohol and tobacco are indeed instructive, but they make a point quite opposite to the one legalization's advocates intend: they demonstrate that legal availability can carry costs at least as significant as those of prohibition.

Drugs that are currently legal provide a convenient set of models for the legalization debate. Examining licit drug control allows us to consider real-life, working, regulatory regimes, rather than the artists' sketches now passing as legalization proposals. Alcohol provides a superb example of legalization gone awry. Regulations governing alcohol, the nation's premier recreational psychoactive, are fantastically permissive, measured against either the rules for other drugs or benefit-cost criteria.

Alcohol is a very dangerous drug. Had Congress failed to specifically exempt it from the provisions of the Controlled Substances Act, it could be placed along with marijuana and heroin in Schedule I, as a psychoactive drug with no accepted medical use and great potential for harm. Indeed, as a product unsafe in its intended use, it could perhaps be vulnerable to challenge under the Consumer Product Safety Act.

When compared with other drugs, casual or experimental alcohol users are at significant risk of progressing to heavy, chronic use or to alcoholic bingeing. An estimated eighteen million Americans, out of 140 million total current drinkers, have significant drinking problems. Many of these "problem" drinkers find that their alcohol use is no longer fully under their deliberate control, and some of them are the victims of a physical dependency that makes them actively ill if they do not get a daily ration of their drug—they are alcohol addicts, alcoholics. Heavy chronic alcohol use is associated with a wide variety of diseases, and alcohol has been estimated to cause approximately twenty thousand excess disease deaths per year. More than one-third of all crime leading to state prison sentences is committed under the influence of alcohol, as is an even greater proportion of domestic assault, sexual assault, and the physical and sexual abuse of children, all of which are under-reported and under-punished. Tens of thousands die annually and many more are maimed in alcohol-related traffic accidents, drownings, and fires, including thousands of people who were not drinking themselves. Alcohol's contribution to industrial accidents and decreased economic productivity is unknown.

One possible conclusion to be drawn from this catalogue of catastrophes would be that alcohol should be assigned its rightful place in Schedule I of the Controlled Substances Act. This is a conclusion with some appeal. But just as the costs of controlling illicit drugs do not of themselves justify legalization, the extensive damage caused by alcohol abuse is not, in and of itself, sufficient to justify re-Prohibition. The costs of criminalizing alcohol would be high; there are other means of reducing alcohol-related damage; and not all alcohol users incur, or cause, harm related to their drug use. Many users testify that they derive pleasure and relaxation from drinking, that it contributes to sociability, and that they drink responsibly and behave responsibly while drinking, doing no harm to others and suffering nothing worse than an occasional hangover.

This testimony need not be taken at face value. Drug users can and do deceive themselves about the damage they incur and the damage they do to others. However, neither should such testimony be ignored. Benefits are an essential part of a cost-benefit calculation, and consumers—even drug consumers—have information about benefits. However, an explanation and analysis of the purported benefits of drug use is notably absent from the debate over legalization.

Even if it turned out that the total benefits of alcohol availability—the sum of consumers' and producers' surpluses from its use and sale—were exceeded by its total costs, that alone would not establish the case for its re-prohibition. It would still have to be shown that the excess of costs (including black market and enforcement costs) over benefits would be less under some practicable form of prohibition than it is now. The larger the existing market, the higher those added costs of implementing prohibition are likely to be. One can regret Repeal without wishing to reverse it.

But consider those "other means" of reducing the costs alcohol imposes on drinkers and others. What are they? To what extent can they reduce costs while preserving benefits?

The only regulatory institution now in force which has significant potential as a mechanism for controlling alcohol abuse is alcohol taxation. Such taxation discourages consumption by making the drug more expensive, but American alcohol taxes have been declining in real terms since the Korean War. Even if the social costs of crime and costs to the drinkers are excluded, alcohol taxes fall markedly short of the costs to society of alcohol consumption. It has been estimated by one study that there is an external social cost, excluding tax, of forty-eight cents per ounce of alcohol, while the average sale and excise taxes (federal and state) add up to only twenty-three cents per ounce. Beer, the alcohol product most widely used by adolescents, is particularly undertaxed, with the result that cheap beer is less expensive at the retail level than many name-brand soft drinks.

Alcohol taxes ought to be significantly higher and alcohol in beer should be taxed as heavily as alcohol in liquor. Fixing the magnitude of an increase, however, is complex. The costs of raising taxes include lost consumers' surplus, some redistribution of the total tax burden toward the poor, and further impoverishment of those who cannot or do not quit heavy drinking. A very steep tax increase might also lead to the development of a black market in untaxed alcohol with attendant costs of enforcement and likely injury caused by adulterated products.

The central problem with taxation is that it is by nature nondiscriminating. In theory, every drink should be taxed according to its own social costs. Some drinks do no harm, and therefore ought not be taxed; other drinks impose extraordinary costs, and thus should be taxed heavily. However, the practical barriers to multiple levels of taxation are all but insurmountable. Taxation set to cover average social cost is sure to put too high a price on most use and not enough on some. Another mechanism is therefore required.

The obvious solution is to prohibit drinking entirely by persons whose drinking carries social costs above the level set by taxation. Youthful drinking is not the only type of drinking which causes disproportionate harm. Heavy drinking by anyone, drinking by "compulsive" users (i.e., those whose drinking is no longer under their deliberate self-control) and drinking by those who commit crimes or act recklessly while intoxicated all fall into this category.

All of these types of use could be prohibited. Children and those whose use has led to crime or recklessness could be forbidden from purchasing alcohol entirely, and there could be an absolute limit as to the maximum quantity of alcohol anyone could purchase in a given period. A central database of ineligible purchasers could be maintained, or, if that proved costly or infeasible, all persons could be licensed to purchase alcohol as they are to drive, with licenses revocable for alcohol-related offenses, including resale to unlicensed individuals.

Such "positive" licensure is an attractive strategy. It could be conditioned on passing a written test on drinking safety, as is now done for driving. The drinkers' licenses might be issued in conjunction with drivers' licenses, and might in fact be the same documents with different colors. Licensure could allow relatively easy enforcement of personal quantity limits by a system similar to the system used to keep credit card holders within their credit limits. It could allow "teetotalers" to identify themselves—and thus, perhaps, to make themselves eligible for lower auto, life and health insurance premiums—and it could allow those who wish to become teetotalers the crutch of tearing up their drinkers' licenses.

But licensure would have its costs as well. A number of practical problems, some more difficult than others, suggest themselves immediately. State licensing would interfere with interstate travel and, therefore, a national system might be required. The administration of quantity restrictions would require a central computer, and appropriate safeguards would need to be instituted to protect confidentiality. Everyone, not just young adults, would need to be "carded" in bars, in liquor stores, and at social functions where alcohol was distributed without charge.

Finally, licensure would involve significant enforcement costs, especially because access to alcohol is made, in some cases, inversely proportional to the motivation for obtaining it. Leakage is sure to be significant, though its specific features depend on regulatory details. For example, if personal alcohol limits were high, light drinkers would have a strong incentive to sell their excess to others at a profit; if the limits were low, much harmless drinking would be curtailed, and a black market encouraged.

Despite these problems, a regime consisting of taxation and licensure has strong potential to control the costs of alcohol use, including the costs of its own enforcement, while maintaining most of the benefits of legal availability.

This regime departs from the dichotomy which currently governs American drug control: prohibition or free commerce. It concedes that the social costs of a flat ban are too great to justify prohibition, but does not replace it with free drug commerce and offers a middle way, one that might be called "grudging toleration," with strict controls to decrease consumption and minimize harms.

If the category of "grudgingly tolerated vice" could be successfully institutionalized, over time it might provide a framework for the control of some other licit and illicit drugs. With a working alcohol control regime in place, the alcohol problem would be considerably smaller, at which time a proposal to make our marijuana problem more like our alcohol problem might sound attractive, or at least more attractive than it does now.

But at the moment, there is no socially recognized category of "grudgingly tolerated vice," nor are there working models. In the absence of such models, new legalization regimes are likely to tend towards the relatively unrestricted availability which characterizes alcohol. The costs of such availability suggest that those who advocate the legalization of now-illicit drugs might best begin the process of drug control reform by proposing and testing reforms of current alcohol policy.

If one of the currently illicit drugs had to be chosen for legalization, marijuana would be the most obvious candidate. Indeed, those who argue in favor of legalizing "drugs" often argue as if marijuana is the typical case, while opponents of legalization concentrate their fire on heroin and cocaine. Several facts combine to make marijuana prohibition look like a questionable bargain:

• Marijuana is the most widely used of the illicit drugs.

• Despite its prohibited status, marijuana is very easy to obtain. Thus, a substantial fraction of those who would use marijuana if it were legal are probably using it currently.

• Government expenditures on marijuana enforcement are quite high. It is estimated that the Federal Government alone has spent $636 million on marijuana enforcement in 1986. Similar calculations suggest that expenditures in 1988 were $968 million. Thus, prohibition is expensive.

• Marijuana has by far the lowest ratio of measured harm to total use of all the illicit drugs. A substantial fraction of all regular marijuana users become at least daily users for some period of time, but this becomes a chronic condition for relatively few. The most frightening fact about marijuana is that the number of heavy daily users, people who spend most of their waking hours under the influence, is quite large: a few million Americans at any given time. But even the existence of this rather obvious "problem" population must be inferred from data about the drug market rather than being directly observed in the form of deaths, injuries, crimes or skid-row personal collapse. Thus, even if prohibition and enforcement were very successful in reducing marijuana consumption, questions could still be raised about the benefits of that reduction.

Marijuana prohibition, then, seems like an expensive, largely ineffective effort to control a relatively modest problem. It is no wonder that legalization of marijuana is offered as an obvious and relatively risk-free "first step" in the deployment of legalization. Nevertheless our experience with alcohol should make us skeptical of claims that any drug legalization is "risk-free." Even the best control regimes have significant costs, and the control regime that actually emerges from a legalization process might not be the best one.

Such a regime could tax marijuana, license users, limit quantity and potency and so on. It is plausible that such a regime, constructed on the model of grudging toleration, would have the effect of vastly reducing the enforcement problem, even though this potential benefit is reduced by the fact that marijuana use is so great among age groups for whom it would presumably remain illegal under a regulatory regime. Several billion dollars in annual revenue would become available to various levels of government, most of it transferred from the revenues of illicit businesses.

However, legalization could, at the same time, lead to dramatic increases in consumption. Under prohibition, marijuana is available to a determined buyer but still far less easy to find and of a less consistent quality than most legal commodities. Under a regulatory regime, it would become vastly more available. Buying marijuana would be as quick and easy as buying a chocolate bar.

Some proponents are likely to reply that any resulting consumption increase would be of little significance. Like occasional and moderate drinking, occasional and moderate marijuana use is without evident harm. However, there are two sorts of use which have significant social costs: use by children and very heavy use. Preventing growth of either of these user populations must be a design criterion for any legalization strategy.

Effective prevention of such growth would require taxation, licensing, and quantity restrictions similar to those described for alcohol, with all their associated problems. In particular, there would be laws proscribing sale to minors, who now make up a large minority of marijuana users. If enforcement of this law were lax, consumption would grow; if it were severe, enforcement levels might not decrease much from the current regime. Some of the details might differ: because marijuana is so much more compact than alcohol, marijuana leakage from adults to children and other ineligible users could more easily take on the characteristics of illicit enterprise than does the leakage of alcohol. Because marijuana legalization involves a change in legal status, it would also have important social effects, including the effects of use by role models. It may be that such acceptability would make marijuana use no worse a problem than cigarette smoking; but making the marijuana problem more like the cigarette problem is not a desideratum.

Marijuana varies widely in its potency. The concentrations of tetrahydrocannabinol (THC), marijuana's main active principle, vary from less than three percent to more than ten percent. There is reason to think that the more potent product poses greater risks of overintoxication, though less potent marijuana exposes its users to more lung damage for the same drug experience. Marijuana users believe the subjective effects of high potency "connoisseur" grade to be qualitatively different from the commercial product. This raises another policy design problem. Should there be limits, beyond labelling requirements, on marijuana potency? If so, a black market might develop in illegal high-potency marijuana; if not, the newly legal marijuana industry might compete to provide more potent (and therefore possibly more psychologically dangerous) forms of the drug. Perhaps tax rates could be adjusted to discourage very-high-potency marijuana without flatly forbidding it.

Setting tax rates itself poses a difficult problem. Untaxed or lightly taxed marijuana would be significantly cheaper than it is on the current black market; a pre-rolled "joint" might cost a few cents, like a tobacco cigarette or a tea bag. Significant increases in consumption could be expected to result from such a sharp decline in price.

Heavy taxation, however, risks the possibility that the black market would continue to profit from selling untaxed marijuana. Some heavy users who now pay for their marijuana from their earnings as marijuana dealers might turn to property crime instead. At best, heavy taxation would require serious enforcement efforts.

Marijuana legalization, then, has the potential to make some things better and others worse. The magnitude of these changes under any specific regulatory regime is a matter for further conjecture and analysis; whether they add up to a good or bad trade depends on what is likely to happen and on what weights are assigned to different aspects of the problem. But the spectrum of the possible results of marijuana legalization is much broader than some of its proponents seem to believe. Low-tax, high-potency legal marijuana could lead to severe social costs within user populations of the greatest concern; high-tax, low-potency marijuana could sustain black markets and their associated costs while increasing consumption more modestly.

If legalizing marijuana were to lead to modest increases in heavy drug use and drug use by minors (say ten percent), it could reasonably be counted a success. If, instead, those levels were to triple, and marijuana potency were to rise, it would have to be counted as an expensive and difficult-to-reverse failure. In the absence of any quantitative estimate of the probabilities of these two outcomes, legalizing marijuana has to be rated as a gamble, and a high-stakes gamble at that.

The pragmatic question about drug control policy is how to manage the availability of a wide range of existing and potential psychoactives to get the best mix of cost and benefits. Changing drugs' legal status is only one of many possible interventions which can effect that mix. Less dramatic proposals, which offer the potential of real progress with minimal risks, deserve at least equal attention.

Without changing the legal status of alcohol, we could create a new regulatory regime to make it less widely abused and responsible for less crime. Without changing the legal status of marijuana, we could reduce enforcement costs greatly with little or no increase in abuse.

The challenge of drug policy is to find least-cost solutions to the problems created by the age-old fact that some human beings take more of various mind-altering substances than is good for them or their neighbors, and by the modern fact that the variety of available psychoactives is rapidly increasing. To concentrate on changing labels from "legal" to "illegal" is to miss all of the hard work and most of the social importance that accompanies that challenge.

C. The Marijuana Legalization Debate

Though there has been a robust debate among scholars and policy analysts about the merits of drug prohibition, it has taken place mostly outside of the political spotlight. The war on drugs became immensely popular with voters during the 1980s and 1990s and has been enthusiastically supported by most politicians regardless of political party. Public support for the drug war has declined in recent years. A 2008 Zogby poll, for example, found that three quarters of Americans believe the drug war is failing. Still, the perception that supporting changes to current drug laws is politically risky persists today. As United States Senator Jim Webb (D-VA), who has called for a national commission to re-assess criminal justice policy, put it, "few candidates or elected officials these days even dare to mention the mind-boggling inconsistencies and the long-term problems that are inherent in [our criminal justice system]" because they believe that "to be viewed as 'soft on crime' is one of the surest career-killers in American politics." JIM WEBB, A TIME TO FIGHT 216 (2008).

Recently, however, the prohibition debate has moved into the political arena with respect to one controlled substance: marijuana. In 2010, California nearly became the first state to legalize marijuana since its prohibition with 46.5% of voters casting their ballot in favor of Proposition 19, an initiative that would have made adult possession of one ounce of the substance legal statewide and permitted localities to tax and regulate its commercial manufacture and sale. In the aftermath of the loss, the ballot measure's proponents argued it would not be long before they would be able to achieve majority support for their position. *See,* Jesse McKinley, *Backers of Legal Marijuana Find Silver Lining in Defeat of California Measure*, N.Y. TIMES, Nov. 14, 2010, at A24 ("We're going to win," said Aaron Houston, the executive director of Students for Sensible Drug Policy, a nonprofit group in Washington. "And we're going to win a whole lot sooner than anybody thinks."). Just as this book was going to press, voters in Colorado and Washington approved marijuana legalization ballot initiatives in the November 2012 election. Because of the timing of the referenda, it was not possible to incorporate them into the main text, however a short addendum—including the text of Colorado's Amendment 64 and Washington's Initiative 502—is included after Chapter 9, on page 957.

While the ultimate fate of efforts to tax and control marijuana like alcohol remains unknown, marijuana policy is poised to become an increasingly politically salient issue in the coming years. The materials that follow provide an overview of the current debate surrounding marijuana legalization and the enforcement of marijuana prohibition laws. Proposals to legalize marijuana at the state level also raise challenging legal and policy problems in relation to federal marijuana prohibition laws. The interplay between federal and state drug laws is considered in more detail in Chapter 7 in the context of state medical marijuana laws.

Altered State: Assessing How Marijuana Legalization in California Could Influence Marijuana Consumption and Public Budgets
Beau Kilmer, Jonathan P. Caulkins, Rosalie Liccardo Pacula, Robert J. MacCoun and Peter H. Reuter
RAND Corporation (2010)

California has always been on the cutting edge of marijuana policy reform. It was one of the first states to prohibit marijuana in 1913, predating the federal Marihuana Tax Act of 1937 by nearly 25 years. In 1975, California was one of the first states to reduce the maximum sentence for possessing less than an ounce from incarceration to a small fine ($100). In 1996, California was the first state to allow marijuana to be grown and consumed for medicinal purposes. And, in November 2010, California will become the third state to vote on whether marijuana should be legalized and taxed—and potentially the first to pass such legislation.[2]

While Californians have discussed legalization for decades, the idea is now being taken more seriously by policymakers, pundits, and the population at large. It was noteworthy when Republican Governor Arnold Schwarzenegger suggested that "it was time for a debate" about marijuana legalization as a way of increasing state revenues. There has been a flurry of activity in Sacramento, including an October 2009 hearing of the California Assembly Committee on Public Safety and the introduction of two marijuana reform bills in 2010. The debate has gained considerable attention because of the recession and California's budget crisis, and it has been fueled by a report from the California State Board of Equalization (BOE) estimating that legalizing marijuana and taxing it at $50 per ounce would generate $1.4 billion for the state each year.

Within this context, this RAND occasional paper is intended to inform the debate about marijuana legalization in California. Although marijuana legalization could have

---

2. Nevada voters rejected a related proposition in 2006, and Alaska voters rejected two ballot propositions (2000, 2004) that would have allowed the state to regulate marijuana sales.

many consequences, this paper focuses largely on two outcomes that are central to the debate in California: the effect on consumption and public budgets.

Our analysis reveals that projections about the impact of legalizing marijuana in California on consumption and public budgets are subject to considerable uncertainty. Although the state could see large increases in consumption and substantial positive budget effects, it could also see increases in consumption and low revenues due to tax evasion or a "race to the bottom" in terms of local tax rates.

Decisionmakers should view skeptically any projections that claim either precision or accuracy. In particular, we highlight two distinct drivers of uncertainty that surround these estimates of consumption and tax revenues: uncertainty about parameters (such as how legalization will affect production costs and price) and uncertainty about structural assumptions (such as the federal response to a state that allows production and distribution of a substance that would still be illegal under federal law). Such uncertainties are so large that altering just a few key assumptions or parameter values can dramatically change the results.

Marijuana offenses account for most of the drug arrests in the United States, and the number has risen sharply in the past 20 years. More than 80 percent of marijuana arrests are now for simple possession. The rate of possession arrests per capita rose sharply in the United States in the 1990s, from about 89 per 100,000 population in 1991 to 223 in 1997. Since then, the number has risen more slowly, approaching 250 per 100,000 in 2008 (about 750,000 arrests in total). Sales arrests rose much more slowly from 1990 to 2008; instead of the nearly 200-percent increase for possession, sales arrests nationally rose only about 40 percent between 1990 and 2008.

While per capita marijuana arrests were similar for the United States and California in the early 1990s, the subsequent increase was more pronounced outside of California. Still, the arrest data for California also show a dramatic increase from 1990 to 1996. Per capita marijuana arrests in California remained stable between 1996 and 2005 (around 175 per 100,000) and then jumped more than 25 percent between 2005 and 2008.

To provide a sense of the intensity of enforcement, we calculated the risk a marijuana user faces of being arrested for possession. If calculated per joint consumed, the figure nationally is trivial—perhaps one arrest for every 11,000–12,000 joints. However, the relevant risk may be the probability of being arrested during a year of normal consumption. Since marijuana is mostly consumed by individuals who use it at least once a month, we estimated the risk that such individuals face. We know from prior studies that these risks are higher for youth. We observe that the annual risk of misdemeanor arrest for those 12–17 (6.6 percent) is more than twice the rate for the full population (3.0 percent).

Arrest is only the first step in the criminal-justice process. To assess the personal consequences of an arrest and estimate the current costs of marijuana enforcement, it is important to have data on the disposition of these arrests. Unfortunately, we are not aware of data on the number of individuals entering probation or local jails as a consequence of arrest for marijuana possession in California. Since state law indicates that those possessing less than 1 ounce are generally supposed to be cited without booking, we can safely infer that most of those arrested for simple possession are not incarcerated at all. For decades now, California law has specified a fine as the maximum penalty.

There are approximately 1,500 marijuana prisoners in California, but most felony marijuana offenders in California state courts sentenced to incarceration go to jail, not prison. It is important to note, however, that these felony data do not give a precise picture of the flow of marijuana offenders to jail. They exclude those who are sentenced to jail after a misdemeanor conviction, which might be the result of a plea agreement. They also do not include those who spend time in jail before they are sentenced, which may be a more significant omission.

As of July 2010, there are two marijuana-related bills before the California legislature (Senate Bill [SB] 1449 and Assembly Bill [AB] 2254); in addition, in November 2010, Californians will vote on the proposition known as the Regulate, Control, and Tax Cannabis Act of 2010 (the RCTC proposition).

SB 1449 would not legalize marijuana. Rather, it would reduce the penalty for possessing less than 1 ounce to an infraction—the equivalent of a parking violation—instead of a misdemeanor offense. (To distinguish this from legalization, this is sometimes called depenalization.) In addition to making possession merely an infraction, SB 1449 would eliminate the possibility of booking or court-ordered diversion. The bill passed the Senate on June 3, 2010, and it was voted out of the Assembly's Committee on Public Safety on June 22, 2010. It is now being considered by the full Assembly.*

In contrast to SB 1449, AB 2254 and the RCTC proposition would truly legalize marijuana with respect to California, albeit not federal, law, including production and wholesale distribution.

AB 2254, introduced by Assembly member Tom Ammiano and often referred to as the Ammiano bill, would legalize marijuana for those aged 21 and older and task the Department of Alcoholic Beverage Control (ABC) with regulating its possession, sale, and cultivation. Similar to laws governing alcohol, the bill would require ABC to impose a licensing fee on cultivators and wholesalers that will reasonably cover the costs of assuring compliance with the regulations to be issued, but may not exceed five thousand dollars ($5,000) for an initial application, or two thousand five hundred dollars ($2,500) per year for each annual renewal.

The bill would also impose a $50-per-ounce excise tax to be paid at the point of retail (in addition to a sales tax), and it would require that these funds "be expended exclusively for drug education, awareness, and rehabilitation programs under the jurisdiction of the State Department of Alcohol and Drug Programs [ADP]."

The RCTC proposition of 2010 is a voter proposition that will be on the November 2010 ballot. It would change state law and make it legal for those aged 21 and older to possess, process, share, or transport up to 1 ounce of marijuana and to cultivate plants for personal use in an area that does not exceed a 5-foot-by-5-foot plot, subject to certain limitations, such as not using marijuana on school grounds, while operating a vehicle, or when minors are present. A separate and distinct part of the proposition would allow a city or county to permit, license, and regulate the commercial cultivation, processing, distribution, and sales of marijuana. These latter activities would remain illegal in localities that do not opt in. Hence, personal production, possession, sharing, and use would immediately become legal under state law everywhere in California, but larger-scale production and sale would be legal only in jurisdictions that took additional, local action.

Unlike the Ammiano bill, the RCTC proposition does not specify any tax on marijuana, although it would allow *local* governments to establish taxes and fees. It is not clear

---

* SB 1449 was passed by the legislature after publication of the RAND report and was signed into law by Governor Arnold Schwarzenegger on September 30, 2010. [*Footnote by casebook author.*]

whether state taxes would be allowed. The California Legislative Analyst's Office (LAO) notes that there is "significant uncertainty" about revenues and expenditures from the RCTC proposition. A large amount of the uncertainty comes from the fact that marijuana will still be illegal under federal law. As for major fiscal effects, the LAO reports that there will be "[s]avings of up to several tens of millions of dollars annually to state and local governments on the costs of incarcerating and supervising certain marijuana offenders; and unknown but potentially major tax, fee, and benefit assessment revenues to state and local government related to the production and sale of marijuana products."

[P]rojecting the effects of legalizing marijuana on use and on tax revenues hinges on estimates of current consumption, current and future prices, how responsive use is to price changes (its "elasticity"), taxes levied and possibly evaded, and the aggregation of many nonprice effects (such as the elimination of any lawbreaking in consuming marijuana). Each of these components, or parameters, of the model is interesting in its own right[.] Building such a logic model is critical not only in building the production model but also in ensuring that we have systematically examined all the potential factors that may affect outcomes. The exercise itself often identifies connections that are not intuitively obvious but turn out to be very important.

Figure 3.1
How Marijuana Legalization Could Influence Consumption and State and Local Budgets

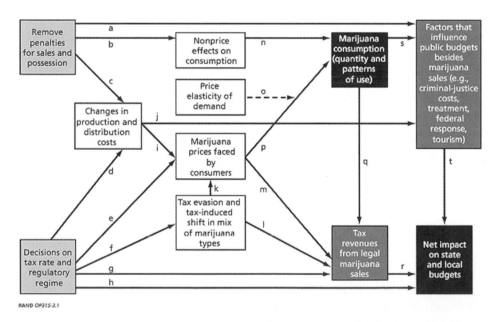

RAND OP315-3.1

Figure 3.1 presents a diagram — what is known as a *logic model* — showing how marijuana legalization could influence marijuana consumption and public budgets in California. The boxes in the far left corners represent the government's decision to legalize, tax, and regulate marijuana, and the black boxes capture our main outcomes of interest in this study: consumption and the net effect on state and local budgets. The other boxes and arrows (labeled with letters) demonstrate the various ways legalization can influence these outcomes. Boxes for tax revenues from legal sales and other factors that influence the budgets (besides legal marijuana sales) are gray to highlight that they are important intermediate outcomes to the final budget figures.

Starting at the top left of the figure, legalization will remove the penalties for selling and possessing marijuana. Doing so will immediately lower production and distribution costs (indicated by arrow c); indeed, an important share of the price currently paid for marijuana comes from having to compensate suppliers for participating in a black market and for the inefficiencies created by having to operate covertly. Post-legalization, users will no longer face this enforcement "tax." Additionally, prices may fall because of shifts in production techniques (e.g., larger and more-efficient plots) and advances in production and processing technologies. There are many ways that legalization could influence consumption besides through its effect on price. The reductions in legal penalties are obvious, but there are other mechanisms, including advertising, a change in social norms, availability, and perceived harmfulness; these are represented by arrow b in the figure.

At the bottom left of the figure, we show that legalizing marijuana will require decisions about the regulatory regime and the tax rate, if any, and these decisions may vary considerably by jurisdiction, since the RCTC proposition gives discretion to the county and municipal governments. There are five arrows coming from the box in the bottom left, and we discuss them in a counterclockwise manner. Since it costs money to regulate and collect taxes, there is a direct link between the light-gray box and black budget box (h). Setting the tax rate also obviously influences tax revenues directly (g), but taxes can also elicit a behavioral response (f), including both tax evasion (purchasing untaxed marijuana from the "gray" market) and a shift in the mix of types of marijuana consumed; a fixed excise tax per ounce may give users an incentive to shift to smaller quantities of higher-potency forms of marijuana. For marijuana purchased in the legal market, tax rates also directly influence the prices faced by consumers (e). The regulation of the industry will also influence the production and distribution costs (d).

The arrows pointing to the marijuana-consumption box come from these nonprice effects (n) and from price (p). The impact of price on consumption (p) will depend not only on how much legalization influences price (e, i, k) but also on how sensitive users and potential users are to price (o; represented by the arrow coming from the price-elasticity-of-demand box).

The story gets even more complex when thinking about tax revenues from marijuana sales. Revenues will obviously be influenced by the tax rate (g), consumption (q), and price (through the sales tax) (m), but we must also consider the role of tax evasion (l). Tax evasion influences both tax revenues and the average price paid by consumers (k). If the gray-market price (the price for untaxed marijuana) is substantially different from the prices charged in the legal market, this evasion-induced price decrease could lead to a further increase in consumption.

The gray box at the top right corner represents the factors that could influence state and local budgets besides tax revenue from legal sales. These would include changes in government expenditures on law enforcement (a), changes in government expenditures on drug treatment, or tax revenues from other goods that are purchased (or not purchased) because of a change in marijuana consumption and production (j, s; e.g., bongs, fertilizer, alcohol). This box would include the impacts of tourism, and it also captures the possibility of a federal intervention (e.g., making federal highway funds contingent on states not legalizing marijuana—similar to what was done to make sure all states imposed a legal drinking age of 21 years). It is this box (t) in combination with tax revenues (r) and the regulation costs (h) that generate the net impact on state and local budgets.

Legalizing Marijuana: California's Pot of Gold?
Michael Vitiello

2009 Wisconsin Law Review 1349

In early 2009, California Assembly member Tom Ammiano authored A.B. 390, which proposes legalizing marijuana production and taxing its sales.

Not surprisingly, Ammiano's bill has produced a heated debate. Supporters of legalizing marijuana marshal powerful arguments for its legalization, including projected revenues of over a billion dollars, with savings of another billion dollars in reduced prison costs. Opponents predict widespread marijuana use, including a dramatic increase in use by California's youth, with no significant reduction in prison costs or significant increases in revenue. As is typical of debates about important policy questions today, the debate surrounding A.B. 390 has generated much heat and little light.

Support for legalizing marijuana is not new. But demographic changes may favor reforming marijuana laws. With its widespread use among college students beginning in the 1960s, marijuana is no longer a drug associated with fringes of society. Today, the National Organization for the Reform of Marijuana Laws (NORML), the most visible organization lobbying for its legalization, claims that nearly 100 million Americans have used marijuana. A World Health Organization study reports that over 40 percent of Americans have tried it. Proponents of legalizing marijuana can point to the current hypocrisy among politicians: possibly three Presidents, a Supreme Court Justice, California's Governor, and numerous prominent—and often conservative—members of Congress have admitted using marijuana. Despite that, few are willing to advocate for its legalization.

Proponents of legalizing marijuana can also point to the selective enforcement of drug laws. Despite survey data suggesting that the same proportion of whites, Hispanics, and African Americans use illegal drugs, enforcement falls far more heavily on minority communities. Saddled with criminal records, young minority adults bear yet another disability when they attempt to enter the mainstream of American society.

Further, proponents have long argued that, unlike alcohol, marijuana use is not associated with violent crime. And while smoking marijuana involves similar risks to those involved in the use of tobacco, marijuana users are not likely to smoke as much as cigarette users. And while both tobacco and alcohol are listed among the ten most dangerous substances, marijuana does not make that list. As a result, marijuana seems to cause less harm than do two legal substances widely used in America.

These arguments have been around for some time. Apart from occasional efforts to legalize marijuana, most proponents have concentrated efforts on legalizing marijuana for medical use. To date, fourteen states have adopted compassionate-use statutes, allowing seriously ill individuals to use marijuana. No doubt, many advocates of medical marijuana see it as a stepping stone towards the legalization of marijuana. But until Ammiano's bill, the legalization movement in California had been relatively quiet.

My fear is that the debate will be dominated by the passionate advocates for prohibition or legalization. Legalizing marijuana does create risks. But many of those risks, like widespread use by teenagers, already exist. And thoughtful legislation can reduce many of those risks. But creating thoughtful legislation is hard work—the product of genuine debate among policy experts, not just vested interests. Further, legalizing marijuana does generate some benefits, including increased revenue. Whether the benefits outweigh the risks—the question that we ought to be asking—is dependent on careful scrutiny of the risks and benefits. This [paper] does not answer all of the questions that it poses. But it does suggest some of the hard issues that California faces in trying to decide whether to legalize marijuana.

The debate about marijuana has become interesting because of the current economic crisis. Californians face a crushing deficit, which forces unpleasant choices. The requirement of a balanced budget in bad economic times certainly contradicts Keynesian theory, but for many states, balanced budgets are a reality. Cutting education and other social services at a time of need seems especially shortsighted and, in some instances, cruel. In that context, [marijuana legalization] may look like a silver bullet.

A Board of Equalization (BOE) spokesperson has estimated the value of California's marijuana crop at $4 billion. Ammiano's bill got a boost from BOE Chairwoman Betty Yee, when she publicly supported A.B. 390. She estimated that the bill would raise about $1.3 billion per year ($990 million from a licensing fee and $349 million in sales tax). In addition to income from taxes, proponents contend that the state would receive significant savings in reduced prison costs.

Unlike previous attempts to legalize or de-criminalize marijuana, Ammiano has captured media interest. Ammiano's backers include several people already critical of the war on drugs. For example, former Orange County Superior Court Judge James P. Gray, a long-time opponent of the war on drugs, has appeared on radio talk shows debating against A.B. 390's opponents. In addition to listing his various books, Gray's Web site includes endorsements of his book on the failed war on drugs from several prominent public figures. The list includes the late Milton Friedman, George Schultz, Adrianna Huffington, and Walter Cronkite. Mainstream publications like *The Economist* have editorialized in favor of ending the failed war on drugs. Some TV pundits, including Glenn Beck (Fox) and Jack Cafferty (CNN) have questioned the wisdom of the war on drugs. Many proponents advance the financial wisdom of legalization, not just personal-choice arguments.

Proponents also focus on prison savings and better allocation of law-enforcement resources. Proponents project a savings of about a billion dollars based on estimates of the number of offenders in California's prisons for marijuana offenses. While proponents and opponents clash on whether any offenders are currently in California's prisons for possession of marijuana, no one denies that, statewide, law-enforcement officials arrest and prosecute many offenders for marijuana offenses, with many of them ending up in county jails. Estimates vary on the amount of those savings. Further, proponents argue that even if few, if any, offenders are in prison merely on possession of marijuana charges, many end up back in prison for parole violations based on failed urine tests that show marijuana usage. They also contend that A.B. 390 would allow reallocation of law-enforcement resources away from fighting marijuana towards fighting more serious criminal conduct.

Beyond these significant savings, proponents contend that legalizing marijuana would "declaw powerful and violent Mexican drug cartels." As argued in *The Economist*, "far from reducing crime, prohibition has fostered gangsterism on a scale that the world has never seen before. According to the U.N.'s perhaps inflated estimate, the illegal drug industry is worth some $320 billion a year." Some proponents analogize to the post-Prohibition era, when legalizing alcohol weakened the power of mobsters around the country. In addition to undercutting the drug cartels, legalizing marijuana may reduce corruption among law-enforcement officials in the United States as well.

Finally, the medical marijuana experiment seems to have worked. That is, many Americans—and especially Californians—have seen that marijuana can be made available, regulated, and used responsibly. That fact, in combination with the economic arguments and the demographic changes, helps to explain why increasing numbers of Americans and 54 percent of Californians favor legalizing marijuana.

[T]he proponent literature includes an even rosier picture of the post-legalized world. For example, NORML, the best known and probably oldest organization advocating legalization, makes some sweeping claims about the benefits flowing from legalization. A brief summary follows.

Beyond the tax revenue, California NORML sees additional benefits. It argues that beyond retail sales of marijuana, the total economic impact should include "spinoff industries such as coffeehouses, paraphernalia, and industrial hemp." Analogizing to the wine industry, that organization argues that legalized marijuana could generate four times as much economic activity as its retail sales. "If the marijuana industry were just one-third the size of the wine industry, it would generate 50,000 jobs and $1.4 billion in wages, along with additional income and business tax revenues for the state." It estimates that industrial hemp could become a business comparable to the $3.4-billion cotton industry in California. Meanwhile, hemp is better for the environment than cotton. Growers need fewer pesticides for hemp than for cotton and the fields are virtually weed-free after harvest.

California NORML recognizes that legalizing marijuana will drive down the price, but the decrease would be offset by increased consumption. NORML also argues that marijuana is far less destructive than alcohol and tobacco. As a result, one might expect lower human and health-care costs associated with marijuana use than with alcohol and tobacco use.

Further, although not highlighted by proponents of A.B. 390, some commentators argue that tax revenue will increase from a second source. Employees of illegal drug dealers do not report income and, as a result, do not pay taxes on that income. Legalizing marijuana production and sales would add revenue from legal workers through their state and federal taxes.

Many critics of A.B. 390 rehash traditional arguments against legalizing marijuana. But to be effective in the current debate surrounding A.B. 390, they must start by directly rebutting the claims that legalization of marijuana will increase revenue and reduce violent gang activity. Those are the kinds of issues that have increased public support for legalization. For example, in a debate that may presage future heated discussions about A.B. 390, John Lovell, a lobbyist for the California Police Officers' Association, has argued that the estimates of revenue—and prison and law enforcement savings—are illusory.

On the question of revenue, Lovell contends that the street price for illegal marijuana will always be less than the price for legally purchased marijuana. His contention is based on the fact that [under A.B. 390's tax structure] legal marijuana will always carry a $50 surcharge, making it more expensive than the street variety. Further, he contends that legal producers will have to comply with various state regulations, like California Occupational Safety and Health Administration (OSHA) and minimum wage laws, driving up their costs.

Lovell, like the Office of National Drug Control Policy, rebuts claims that our prisons house thousands of felons convicted of possession of marijuana. He insists that no one is in prison for smoking marijuana. While he cannot contend that marijuana offenders do not end up in jail, he argues that the only marijuana offenders in prison are those involved in drug trafficking. Further, according to Lovell, parole officers do not "roll over" parolees merely for urine tests indicating marijuana use.

Opponents see no savings in law-enforcement efforts or in a reduction of violence among drug cartels. Lovell argues, for example, that police are not targeting small users of marijuana but instead more serious criminal actors. Offenders may be charged with marijuana offenses when the police arrest them for other more serious charges. Because a prosecutor may end up offering a plea agreement for a possession offense, rather than a more serious drug-related offense or other criminal offense, some offenders who appear in the statistics as marijuana offenders are in fact more serious criminals.

Drug cartels will continue to present a problem even if California legalizes marijuana. That is so because they are involved in the drug trade generally, not just in the marijuana trade. Thus, even if they no longer dominate the marijuana trade (something that some, like Lovell, contest), they will continue to engage in violence as they fight over territory in which to distribute other illegal drugs.

Opponents to legalizing marijuana also question whether society ought to legalize another mind-altering drug. Some of the debate is philosophical: for example, Lovell criticizes libertarians as narcissistic, unwilling to accept their social responsibilities to one's neighbors. He is critical of alcohol use as well (one of the other mind-alerting drugs he targets as a social evil). While that kind of neo-prohibitionist philosophy is not likely to gain traction with many Americans as they consume high quality wine, critics point out that problem drinking is already a significant national problem, leading to more than 100,000 deaths a year and costing an estimated $184.6 billion a year. Alcohol costs businesses hundreds of billions in lost productivity, premature death, and crime. Further, a report by the National Center on Addiction and Substance Abuse at Columbia University focused on the billions of dollars that states spend on coping with the fallout of drug and alcohol abuse: for example, the report estimated that states spend 96 cents of each dollar the federal government spent on substance abuse and addiction went to "shoveling up" the wreckage caused by substance abuse and addiction, including the abuse visited on children of abusing parents. Legalizing marijuana, and thereby presumably increasing its use, can only exacerbate these problems.

Lovell argues that A.B. 390 will increase marijuana use exponentially. He relies on a study from the Midwest, indicating that when legislation allowed wine to be sold in grocery stories (making it more readily available to consumers), wine consumption went up 700 percent in the first year, and 300 percent over time. Not only will use go up among adults, but because A.B. 390 reduces penalties for selling drugs to teenagers, their use will also increase.

Thus, according to critics, legalizing marijuana will lead to increased hardship and damage. Because legal marijuana will be more expensive than the illegal product, A.B. 390 will not provide revenue and will not address prison overcrowding. Instead, the bill is a drug dealers' bill of rights.

Sorting through charges and countercharges presents a daunting task for a number of reasons. Good data are hard to find, making an honest assessment of costs and benefits difficult. Further, proponents and opponents seldom engage directly on the same point. Like the cliched ships passing in the night, the two sides of the debate often fall back on familiar themes that are not fully responsive to each others' main concerns. At a minimum, a healthy dose of skepticism may bring clarity to the debate.

The debate surrounding A.B. 390 does not prove that civil discourse has gone downhill in recent years. But as someone who was undecided on the question of legalization when I began focusing on the question, I have found the debate unhelpful. Almost all of the discussion about legalization is passionate advocacy, not reasoned debate. Even after considering the questionable assumptions about savings in prison costs or the supposed dramatic increase in use of marijuana, I am a tepid supporter of legalization.

Legalizing marijuana would bring the law in line with the behavior of millions of Americans. For most of them, it has produced little harm. American law favors freedom of choice, absent compelling arguments to the contrary. I must tolerate a great deal of behavior that I do not believe in for myself, but have little say in those matters. That is a cost of freedom.

In deciding whether to make some conduct unlawful, legislatures often do a cost-benefit analysis of the legislation. A cost-benefit analysis seems to support legalizing marijuana.

Part of the problem with the current debate is that opponents of marijuana focus on the total cost to society associated with marijuana use. That is the wrong place to start. Years of an expensive war on drugs has not and cannot eradicate marijuana use. In California, as long as marijuana is available for medical use, eradicating marijuana use is simply not going to happen. As a result, the right cost figure in the legalization debate is the marginal rate of increased use, with marginal increased health costs. Thus, the cost is considerably less than opponents contend.

But what about the benefit side of the equation? To state the obvious, California is in bad financial shape. Indeed, anyone who witnessed the spectacle of the legislature's budget morass during the past year might hope for a quick fix, marijuana or stronger! I cannot fault the proponents of A.B. 390 for trying to find free money to help the state resolve its financial woes. But A.B. 390 would probably not generate as much money as its proponents contend, if only because it would not produce the reduced prisons costs, and without continued law-enforcement efforts against illegal sellers of marijuana, tax revenue would be far lower than projected.

Nonetheless, properly done, legalizing marijuana might generate some revenue and depending on how the law was structured, policy-makers could reduce some of the risks created by legalizing marijuana. The best outcome of all might be the generation of substance abuse funds. Even if more Californians use marijuana after its legalization, a very small number would become chronic users. The best outcome for all Californians would be if legalization generated enough money to put in place real drug-treatment programs for substance abusers. That kind of legislation would be worth backing with enthusiasm.

As the material above indicates, the number of variables involved makes it impossible to estimate with any precision how marijuana legalization might impact consumption and state budgets, not to mention other considerations like the extent to which legalization might reduce black market violence or how shifting law enforcement resources away from marijuana arrests might impact the overall crime rate. In the RAND Corporation study excerpted above, for example, the authors concluded that marijuana "[c]onsumption will increase [under legalization], but it is unclear how much because we know neither the shape of the demand curve nor the level of tax evasion (which reduces revenues and the prices that consumers face)." Beau Kilmer, et al., *Altered State: Assessing How Marijuana Legalization in California Could Influence Marijuana Consumption and Public Budgets*, RAND Corporation 53 (2010).

Assuming that marijuana consumption did rise substantially under legalization, it is also unclear whether this would increase the overall rate of substance use or whether the increase in marijuana use would come as the result of users substituting marijuana for other substances they currently use (such as alcohol). Indeed, some proponents of marijuana legalization argue that if increased marijuana use led to a corresponding reduction in alcohol consumption this could be viewed as a positive outcome. For example, in the book *Marijuana is Safer, So Why Are We Driving People to Drink?* (2009), Steve Fox, Paul Armentano and Mason Tvert argue in favor of marijuana legalization because it would "provid[e] adults with a safer and less harmful recreational alternative to alcohol."

Rationalizing Drug Policy Under Federalism
David W. Rasmussen and Bruce L. Benson
50 Florida State University Law Review 679 (2003)

[E]nforcement might reduce the quantity of illicit drugs demanded, but this potential benefit is much more elusive than our analysis of the direct impact of raising price (and even full price) suggests. Economic theory is based on the proposition that individuals respond to incentives and that, on the margin, prices play an important role in guiding individual choice. Advocates of the drug war often seem to believe that drug users will only respond to the rising price by reducing or stopping use, but ... there is no reliable evidence that this earnest hope is warranted.

The demand for mind-altering substances seems to be persistent; in fact, it is alleged to be common among many species. If individuals consume drugs to achieve an altered mental state then anything that raises the full price of the drug of choice will give consumers an incentive to seek alternative, relatively low-priced drugs that provide a similar effect. This tendency can also explain the life cycle of individual drugs. New drugs are often attractive to users because their intoxication effects are immediately apparent while the consequences of using them are not. As experience of adverse consequences accumulates, the full price of use becomes more apparent and the drug loses popularity. Similarly, if enforcement increases the price of an illicit drug, consumers often can shift to alternative illegal substances or to new products that have not yet been declared illegal.

Persistence of demand for mind-altering substances can be responsible for substantial unintended consequences of enforcement that undermine efforts to reduce the harms of drug use. When a specific drug is viewed as a particular problem, a policy of increased enforcement to combat its use may appear attractive because the resulting higher price will curtail its use. However, users of this drug are likely to adjust their consumption patterns by looking for alternative psychoactive substances, and there can be no presumption that the alternative is less harmful than the substance being targeted for increased enforcement.

Critical to understanding the impact of enforcement on drug use is determining the extent to which various drugs are substitutes for one another. Unfortunately, the literature on this point is not definitive due to data limitations and the fact that these relationships almost surely vary by type of drug and characteristics of users. Given that the absolute value of the price elasticity of demand is inversely related to the percent of income spent on a good, we would expect heavy drug users who spend most of their income on drugs to be very sensitive to changes in relative drug prices while young, infrequent experimenters' drug of choice may not be very sensitive to such changes. For most youth, the relevant choice among drugs is between alcohol, marijuana, and hashish. Recognizing that it is not realistic to expect social policy to ever get youth to "just say no" to all mind-altering substances, it follows that a crucial dimension of this policy debate rests in how we assess the relative costs of using and abusing alcohol and cannabis. Current policy obviously favors the former over the latter, but it is not clear that an objective evaluation would support policies that increase the full price of cannabis relative to alcohol.

According to a leading think-tank on substance abuse, "research has not established a direct causal relationship between substance abuse and ... social problems" related to criminal justice, social service expenditures, and business. An estimate of the economic costs of alcohol in terms of direct healthcare costs and the indirect burden of productivity losses shows that in Canada they are about six times greater than the corresponding costs of illicit drugs. The same study estimates that almost 98% of direct costs due to traffic accidents arising from substance abuse are associated with alcohol with the remainder attributed to illicit drugs. Since alcohol tends to impair drivers more than marijuana, the most frequently used illicit drug, this result is not surprising. Adding to this evidence is the fact that there are no recorded overdose deaths associated with marijuana, while acute alcohol poisoning is a relatively common occurrence. Thus substantial evidence suggests that using enforcement to raise the full price of marijuana, relative to alcohol, may enhance the harms of substance abuse.

Drug suppliers can also shift to the production and distribution of other drugs when faced with effective enforcement, a response called "output substitution." Such changes in output can increase the harms associated with drug use rather than reduce them. Efforts to intercept drugs in the Miami area in 1984 were highly successful against the importation of marijuana, no doubt because this product is bulky and relatively difficult to conceal. Smugglers did not change their occupation. Instead they simply changed the product being smuggled, shifting to a lower risk commodity, cocaine. Successful interdiction of marijuana thus increased the supply of cocaine, and youth correspondingly reported that this drug was more readily available.

Increasing enforcement against the illicit drug industry also has a tendency to increase the potency of mind-altering substances. This first became apparent during America's alcohol prohibition experiment. During Prohibition, consumption of high-alcohol content spirits rose sharply relative to beer because spirits were relatively easy to conceal and transport, thereby making them more attractive to consumers and producers alike. Prior to Prohibition (from 1911 to 1916), the ratio of expenditures on spirits to expenditures on beer was fairly stable, ranging from 0.70 to 0.78, but there was a dramatic shift in these spending patterns with Prohibition. It is estimated that by 1925 consumers spent about seven times as much on spirits as they did on beer. Furthermore, some of the bootleg whiskey contained as much as twice the alcohol found in commercial brands.

The incentives to produce and consume more powerful alcohol during Prohibition are also inherent in our current drug laws. Low dosage drugs such as marijuana are bulkier and more easily detected than harder drugs, providing the incentives already noted to increase the supply of more potent drugs. Furthermore, because the penalties for possessing and selling drugs are related to weight rather than strength, the legal system provides a strong incentive to avoid handling low-dose products that have been cut. But beyond this, drug entrepreneurs can produce stronger drugs just as more potent alcohol emerged during Prohibition.

Trends in the potency of marijuana are consistent with the proposition that greater enforcement efforts lead to increased potency. Thornton reports that the average potency of marijuana increased by a factor of eight between 1974 and 1984, and he provides evidence suggesting that marijuana potency is positively correlated with law enforcement expenditures.

Clearly, unintended negative consequences of drug enforcement are common as both drug users and suppliers respond to relative prices in hopes of limiting its impact on their activities. Furthermore, the magnitude of the alleged harms of some drug use is probably substantially less than is popularly perceived, while the hidden costs of criminal justice drug control efforts are substantially greater than a simple summation of the budgetary outlays for drug enforcement suggests.

Though it is difficult to estimate how marijuana legalization might affect use rates and state budgets, statistical information on the enforcement of current marijuana laws is much less speculative. Marijuana arrests and prosecutions have risen substantially since the early 1980s.

The War on Marijuana:
The Transformation of the War on Drugs in the 1990s
Ryan S. King and Marc Mauer
The Sentencing Project (2005)

Despite decades of discussion and intense media coverage, there remains considerable confusion regarding how the criminal justice system treats marijuana offenders. This misunderstanding has catalyzed a contentious debate that has been characterized by disagreements about the appropriate legal status of marijuana, the suitable level of punishment, and the most effective distribution of institutional resources to address marijuana use. This has been coupled with a fundamental difference of opinion about the true dangers that marijuana use poses to American society. In light of international developments in which a number of countries have reduced punishment for marijuana use, as well as the growth in the domestic decriminalization movement culminating in local ballot initiatives and proposals to amend state law, the struggle over the appropriate criminal justice response to marijuana has become a key policy concern.

Drug war advocates such as John Walters and former Attorney General John Ashcroft have frequently remarked that the current criminal justice approach to drug abuse represents an efficient use of resources. Walters, the head of the Office of National Drug Control Policy, has lamented that persons who claim that prisons are full of low-level drug offenders are incorrect and have misinformed the debate on drug policy.

In order to provide a framework for assessing the role of marijuana enforcement in the criminal justice system, we have conducted a national analysis of marijuana offenders for the period of 1990 to 2002. This includes an assessment of trends in arrest, sentencing, and incarceration, along with an evaluation of the impact of these developments on marijuana price and availability, and the use of crime control resources. Our analysis indicates that the "war on drugs" in the 1990s was, essentially, a "war on marijuana."

The findings in this report call for a national discussion regarding the zealous prosecution of marijuana use and its consequences for allocation of criminal justice resources and public safety. Law enforcement has focused disproportionately on low-level possession charges as a result of the nation's lack of a thoughtful strategy about how best to address the consequences of marijuana use. Consequently, police spend a significant amount of time arresting marijuana users, many of whom do not merit being charged in court. This diverts efforts away from more significant criminal activity while having no appreciable impact on marijuana cost, availability, or use. As state and federal resources become more limited, a rational consideration of the most efficient way to address marijuana use is critical; this discussion should take place outside the realm of political rhetoric. The findings in this study can inform that conversation with sound, empirical analysis of more than a decade's worth of data on the criminal justice system's treatment of marijuana offenders.

[F]rom 1990 to 2002, drug arrests nationally increased by 41%, from 1,089,500 to 1,538,800. During this time, the total number of marijuana arrests more than doubled from 327,000 to 697,000, an increase of 113%. All non-marijuana drug arrests increased by only 10%. The percentage of arrests for all offenses comprised of marijuana more than doubled from 2.3% in 1990 to 5.1% in 2002.

This significant expansion of the drug war was fueled almost entirely by a focus on marijuana. Of the 450,000 increase in arrests for drugs, 82.4% was solely from marijuana arrests, and 78.7% from marijuana possession arrests.

Since 1990, there have been 6.2 million arrests for marijuana possession and an additional 1 million for marijuana trafficking. As of 2002, marijuana arrests comprised 45% of all drug arrests, and of these, possession arrests constituted 88% of all marijuana arrests. While marijuana trafficking arrests declined as a proportion of all drug arrests during this period (from 6.1% in 1990 to 5.4% in 2002), the proportion for marijuana possession increased by two-thirds (24% in 1990 to 40% in 2002).

[O]verall arrests declined by 3% from 1990 to 2002, while marijuana arrests rose by 113%. The incongruent arrest patterns between marijuana and other criminal offenses require further analysis to understand the trends at work. Overall Index I crimes, defined as the most serious and costly to society, dropped by 24% during this period, a time when the United States was experiencing the lowest crime rates since the 1970s.

From a policy perspective, for this growth to be tenable, one must assume that marijuana use and marijuana market trends ran counter to all national crime trends, including patterns in overall drug arrests. As this is rather unlikely, this growth is probably better understood as the result of selective enforcement decisions. There is no indication from national drug survey data that a dramatic decrease in the use of other drugs led to law enforcement agencies shifting resources to marijuana. Indeed, there was a slight increase in the use of all illicit drugs by adult users between 1992 and 2001 (5.9% to 6.6%). Over that same period, emergency room admissions for heroin continued to increase. Thus, there are no explicit indications of dramatic shifts in drug use that might explain the law enforcement trend toward marijuana enforcement in the 1990s.

An examination of historical drug arrest patterns illustrates the role of policy decisions in shaping the trends of the 1990s. [I]n 1982, marijuana comprised 72% of all drug arrests. At that point, the "war on drugs" began in earnest and there was a shift in the distribution of arrests for drug abuse violations. By 1992, marijuana arrests made up only 28% of all drug arrests. During that same period, the proportion of cocaine and heroin arrests increased from 13% to 55%.

However, over the course of the 1990s a tangible shift toward arrest patterns of the early 1980s began to reemerge. Law enforcement agencies arrested fewer people for cocaine and heroin offenses and began to arrest more people for marijuana possession and sale. By 1996, marijuana had once again surpassed heroin and cocaine as the primary drug of arrest, a gap which has widened since then. Early pursuit of the "war on drugs" targeted heroin and cocaine (drugs deemed to be hard, costly, or dangerous), but the current manifestation of the drug war, from the law enforcement perspective, is targeted disproportionately at marijuana use.

Despite a 113% increase in marijuana arrests, almost exclusively for possession, marijuana costs have decreased, and purity increased as have use and perceived availability. If increased law enforcement and an expanded use of arrests were successful in restricting the supply of marijuana, then an increase in its price would be expected. Instead, marijuana prices fell continuously during the 1990s even as marijuana arrests reached unprecedented levels. This trend suggests that the growth in marijuana arrests in the 1990s has had no measurable impact on price, access, or availability.

The drug war has been predicated on arresting high-ranking narco-traffickers. However, the data indicate that this has not been the practice. During the 1990s the focus of law enforcement has been on low-level marijuana offenders. In fact, some law enforcement officials acknowledge that they target low-level offenders as part of a larger strategy known as "quality of life," or order maintenance, policing. This approach emphasizes the use of police officers to stop and frisk pedestrians under the assumption that such encounters will deter people from carrying contraband. In practice, this approach often targets low-level offenses as a means of identifying more substantial criminal behavior. Former New York City Police Commissioner Howard Safir remarked, in defense of this strategy, "[o]ur plan is to attack it on all levels. We're not just going after the major traffickers; we're gonna harass the little guys on a daily basis."

The growth of marijuana arrests results in substantial costs for law enforcement. Since 1991, the domestic law enforcement component of the federal drug control budget has increased from $4.6 billion (or 42% of the federal drug control budget) to $9.5 billion (or 51% of the federal drug control budget) in 2002. This increase of $4.9 billion (107%) has occurred during a period when most of the growth in drug arrests has been for marijuana.

Of the total law enforcement budget for 2001 of $72.4 billion, we estimate that $2.1 billion, or 2.9% of the entire law enforcement budget nationally, is spent on marijuana arrests. Of this, approximately $430 million is spent on marijuana trafficking and $1.7 billion on marijuana possession arrests.

In addition to cost, a significant consequence of these tactics includes reduced law enforcement attention to other criminal behavior. Law enforcement resources come from a finite pool of funding in the general revenue fund. It is the responsibility of the legislature to determine how these resources will be allocated (law enforcement, corrections, education, roads, etc.). If the role of law enforcement is to be expanded, there are three options available to accomplish this: 1) increase the size of the common pool (raise taxes); 2) alter the distribution within the common pool (draw monies away from a different program and direct additional funding towards law enforcement); or 3) alter the approach of law enforcement patterns (practice selective enforcement of offenses).

Economists Rasmussen and Benson believe that the latter is the most likely solution. "[I]ndividual police officers and police departments as a whole must decide which laws to attempt to enforce and how rigorously." Increased resources directed towards a specific type of offense, such as drugs, lead inevitably to a decrease in resources dedicated to another offense. Law enforcement resource allocation is a zero-sum game, and any difference in appropriation is likely to manifest itself in delayed response times. "As drug crimes receive more attention from police ... the queues for other offenses must move slower as fewer resources are allocated to them." This is of particular concern in light of recent developments which indicate that many cities and municipalities are losing police officers in response to budgetary constraints.

The shift in the 1990s towards more aggressive policing of marijuana may have siphoned law enforcement resources away from certain Index crimes. Rasmussen and Benson suggest that not only is this a possible scenario, but that there are institutional incentives in place that encourage the pursuit of drug crimes. Civil asset forfeiture, which permits law enforcement agencies to seize all or a portion of property obtained during a drug investigation, creates an incentive for administrators to dedicate more resources to drug enforcement. "[L]aw enforcement agencies focus resources on enforcement of drug laws because of the financial gains for the agencies arising from forfeitures." Indeed, a recent analysis of arrest patterns in police departments that are permitted to retain a portion of seized assets discovered that this policy resulted in an increase of drug arrests by 18%, and drug arrests as a portion of all arrests by 20%.

The geographical variation in marijuana arrest patterns at the local level illustrates the critical role of discretion in defining a law enforcement agency's policy. [Between 1990 and 2002, e]very major county except for Fairfax, Virginia experienced an increase in marijuana arrests[.] In nearly every county in the sample, the growth rate for possession arrests far exceeded that for sales or manufacturing. Despite the similarities, there are variations in the degree of growth, and there are also a number of counties that experienced a decline in some types of marijuana arrests. In the ten most populous counties, the growth in arrests ranged from 20% (San Diego) to 418% (King, WA). This variation was affected by the size of the county and the degree to which each had been pursuing marijuana violations in 1990 versus 2002. It also underscores the importance of individual policymakers and practitioners making decisions that shift the emphasis in enforcement policy. Short of a localized, rapid increase in marijuana sales and use, for a county to experience the size of growth witnessed in Clark (Nevada), Shelby (Tennessee), or most of the counties in this sample, a tangible modification of marijuana arrest policies is the most likely cause.

Given the dramatic growth in marijuana arrests, it is instructive to examine how these cases have been handled by the court system. The primary source for national level sentencing data is the National Judicial Reporting Program, which issues a biennial survey of felony sentences in state courts. We collected NJRP data from 1990 and 2000, analyzing the processing of marijuana offenders in the state court system. Perhaps surprisingly considering the growth in the arrest rate, state court systems did not experience any rapid increase in marijuana offenders being sentenced for a felony offense. The proportion of all persons sentenced for a marijuana felony in state courts in 2000 was 3.6%, which is 39% higher than the proportion in 1990 (2.6%), but far below the 113% growth in arrests during this period.

The state sentencing figures in 2000 indicate a similar pattern as in 1990, suggesting that pre-trial dismissals and the fact that most arrests were for low-level misdemeanors dramatically mediated the shift in law enforcement treatment of marijuana over the decade. For example, in 2000 there were 734,000 marijuana arrests and approximately 41,000 felony convictions in state and federal courts. Thus, only 1 of every 18 arrests results in some type of felony sentence.

Considering the significant growth in arrests during this period and the relative stasis in felony sentences for marijuana in the state court system, it is apparent that the vast majority of the more than 700,000 arrests for marijuana in 2000 are for misdemeanors, or are dismissed for one or more of a variety of reasons.

In 2000, persons convicted of felony marijuana offenses were likely to be incarcerated. Half (51%) of the convictions for possession led to a prison or jail term, as did two-thirds (63%) of the trafficking convictions. Overall, one-third of all felony marijuana convictions resulted in a prison term of at least one year. This rate was the same for both marijuana trafficking and possession, raising questions regarding the charging phase of the proceedings.

Conventional wisdom suggests that individuals sentenced to prison for possession are repeat offenders with significant criminal histories. Although this may be true of many sentences, some states mandate incarceration even for some types of first-time marijuana possession. In Alabama, a 2004 report by the state's sentencing commission found that 328 people were sentenced to prison for marijuana possession, and only one-third were repeat offenders.

D. The "War on Drugs"

The United States has pursued a particularly forceful brand of drug prohibition. There is some disagreement about when the "war on drugs" began. Although President Richard Nixon first used the phrase in 1971, many of the policies most closely associated with the drug war strategy were put in place under President Ronald Reagan. As a result, while most sources point to 1971 as the start date for the war on drugs, the early 1980s is also occasionally cited.

Whatever its start date, the war on drugs is at once one of the most recognizable social policies of the last fifty years and one of the most difficult to define with precision. After all, federal and state drug prohibition laws pre-date the drug war by many decades. What, if anything, distinguishes the drug war from drug prohibition?

Arguably, the guiding tenets of the "war on drugs" strategy have been the vision of a "drug free" society and the belief that vigorous enforcement of uncompromising criminal justice measures is the most effective method for achieving it. This philosophy has manifested itself in an unrelenting focus on supply-side initiatives, including the incarceration of drug offenders at all levels of offense severity in an effort to deter domestic drug manufacture and distribution, combined with a militaristic approach to eradicating drug production abroad. The theory is that these policies will help to "keep drugs off our streets," and thereby lead to a reduction in drug use and drug-related crime. Efforts aimed directly at demand reduction have largely followed the same philosophy by increasing the number of arrests for drug possession and addressing drug use and addiction problems primarily within the criminal justice system.

This description of the drug war philosophy still does not tell us much about the drug war from a legal or policy perspective, however. Is the drug war a coherent set of laws and policies that is substantially different from standard drug prohibition? Or, is the drug war primarily a rhetorical device that describes a general outlook on how drug prohibition laws should be enforced?

In his first interview after being confirmed as the Director of the Office of National Drug Control Policy in 2009, Gil Kerlikowske said he thought it was time to retire the "drug war" concept in favor of a "public health approach" to drug policy. Two years later, Kerlikowske described his outlook in even bolder terms, telling a Seattle reporter "we certainly ended the drug war almost two years ago." *See* Jacob Sullum, *End 'War on Drugs' by Legalizing Drugs*, CHICAGO SUN-TIMES, June 14, 2011. Thus far, no significant changes in law or policy have accompanied Kerlikowske's comments and President Barack Obama's annual drug strategies have largely mirrored those of his predecessors. Nevertheless, the possibility that the drug war may be coming to an end makes the task of identifying the defining characteristics of the war on drugs all the more important.

1. Drug Prohibition and the Drug War

The Evolution of Federal Drug Control Legislation
Thomas M. Quinn and Gerald T. McLaughlin
22 Catholic University Law Review 586 (1973)

The earliest mention of opium (or for that matter, any narcotic drug) in Federal legislation appears in the Tariff Act of 1832. The Act-exempting opium from all import duties-attempted neither to interdict the flow of drugs nor produce substantial revenue. Ten years later in 1842, however, the narcotic was placed on the tariff lists for the first time and a duty of seventy-five cents per pound was levied on all imported opium. In 1862, morphine was added to the tariff list and taxed at the rate of two dollars per pound. The tariff rates on medicinal or raw opium and morphine fluctuated throughout the nineteenth century. Raw opium even reappeared on the duty free list in 1890. This use of imported opium as a source of governmental revenue was consistent with the flourishing international opium traffic of the nineteenth century. British traffic in opium had led to the Opium Wars with China and generated a series of diplomatic concessions extorted from the Chinese, concessions which assured continuance of the lucrative opium trade. For example, in an 1858 treaty between China and the United States, China agreed to remove opium from its list of contraband items, permitting American merchants to sell the drug at various Chinese ports. With opium traffic so open and obvious, it was not surprising that the Unite States government should view opium as nothing more than another imported item to be taxed.

Smoking opium, however, was singled out for special treatment during this earliest period of federal concern. [S]moking opium was first associated with the Chinese immigrant but gradually, as the practice spread, it became a national concern. The response was an eighty per cent ad valorem tax on all imported smoking opium. In succeeding years, it continued to be taxed at ever increasing rates, reflecting the growing fear with which the practice was regarded.

A second and quite different theme in federal narcotic drug control appeared on the scene in 1906. It came in response to a growing national concern with the use of patent medicines. These commodities—heavily laced with opium, morphine and cocaine—were widely sold throughout the country and served as familiar preparations for such ailments as headaches, menstrual pains, cold symptoms, alcoholism, and general fatigue. What resulted from the heavy dependence on such patented medicines was a widespread pattern of national addiction. The federal response conceived of the patent medicine problem as one of consumer deception. Thus, to control the trade in these medicines, Congress enacted labeling regulations in 1906, the idea being that an informed consumer could protect himself if he chose to do so.

The Pure Food and Drug Act of 1906 prohibited the interstate shipment of misbranded or adulterated food and drugs. An article of food or drugs was considered to be misbranded if it contained any alcohol, morphine, cocaine, heroin, or any derivatives or preparations of these substances where such ingredients were not clearly marked on the label. Similarly, confectionaries were considered to be adulterated if they contained any narcotic drug as an ingredient. The Act also provided that food would be considered adulterated if it contained any added poisonous or deleterious ingredients which might be injurious to health. By requiring labeling of medicines which contained opium and cocaine, and by prohibiting outright the interstate shipment of food containing deleterious substances, the Act exposed to public view the dangerous and addictive capacities of non-prescription medicines and sodas being marketed in the country. It should be noted, however, that this legislation was entirely consistent with a legitimate domestic traffic in opium, morphine, heroin, and cocaine. Indeed, heroin was sold by one pharmaceutical company under the heroin trade name and widely touted; morphine could be purchased over the counter along with opium or cocaine. While the Pure Food and Drug Act alerted consumers to the presence of narcotic drugs in various products, the sales of these drugs continued to flourish. For example, a 1910 pharmaceutical journal reported that one drug store earned a profit of $60 a day from sales of cocaine alone.

In 1909 the federal government shifted from its earlier pattern of taxing opium to outright suppression of the traffic in the drug. In response to the Shanghai Opium Conference in 1909, the United States banned the importation of all smoking opium and restricted the importation of all other opium except for limited amounts authorized by the Secretary of the Treasury for medical purposes. This had the effect of closing the United States ports of entry to the legal flow of opium except in controlled quantities for regulated purposes. Since the Act also forbade any person from receiving or selling illegally imported opium knowing it to be illegally imported, the Act represented the first serious federal attempt to use the criminal law to curtail domestic trafficking in opium.

Five years later, the United States took a second major step in the border control of opium traffic when it set controls on the export of opium. With these controls, Congress effectively took the United States out of the international drug traffic by prohibiting the use of its ports for either the import or export of opium and other harmful drugs. Controls on export, like the earlier controls on import, came in response to international pressures. At the Hague International Opium Conference in 1912, the signatory powers, including the United States, had agreed to place various restrictions on prepared opium, cocaine, and morphine—one of these restrictions was to align export controls with the import controls of other nations. Consequently, Congress enacted the Narcotic Drug Export Act, absolutely prohibiting any smoking opium from being admitted into the United States for transshipment to another country and, more importantly, banning the export of cocaine and opium—other than smoking opium, the export of which was absolutely forbidden—to any country which did not regulate the importation of these drugs. On the very same day that it passed the Narcotic Drug Export Act, Congress also adopted a statute which levied a prohibitive tax of $300 per pound on all opium manufactured in the United States for smoking purposes. Thus, Congress had now forbidden the import or export of smoking opium, heavily taxed its domestic manufacture, and severely restricted the import of other forms of opium.

With the Harrison Act the federal government interjected itself decisively into the domestic traffic in narcotic drugs. This statute was by far the most significant of all the early federal drug control laws, setting the main lines for domestic narcotic control and regulation which persisted until 1970. The thrust of the Harrison Act was twofold. First the Act sought to expose to federal surveillance the legal traffic in narcotics from its point of entry or manufacture to its point of consumption. Second, the Act provided criminal penalties for any trafficking in narcotics outside the legally established patterns. The stage was thus set for the regulation of the legal narcotic flow and the suppression of the illegal flow.

To achieve such broad purposes, the actual legislative scheme of the Harrison Act might be considered cumbersome to say the least. Congress chose to assert jurisdiction through its revenue powers rather than through its power to regulate interstate commerce. This rather curious approach was justified, however, since in 1914 the interstate commerce clause was still read rather restrictively by the courts. In all probability, that clause would not have supported any congressional controls over local drug manufacturers or distributors. Of course, Congress' decision to use its revenue powers placed the domestic control of narcotics in the hands of the Internal Revenue Service, then deeply involved in the enforcement of the newly created federal income tax, and later the Prohibition laws. Contrary to certain state patterns of narcotic control, this placed enforcement of the Harrison Act in the hands of a special enforcement unit rather than in the hands of general law enforcement officers.

By its terms, the Harrison Act required registration with the local Internal Revenue Collector and payment of a special occupational tax by every person, with certain exceptions, who produced, imported, manufactured, compounded, dealt in, dispensed, sold, distributed, or gave away opium or coca leaves or any compound or preparation of these drugs. The Act also stipulated that any sale, exchange, or transfer of these drugs must be pursuant to the written order of the person to whom the drugs were to be transferred. Written orders could only be executed on forms specially provided by the Commissioner of Internal Revenue and the forms themselves could only be purchased by a registered person. Everyone in the drug distribution system was subject to stringent record-keeping. Finally, it was unlawful for any unregistered or unpaid person to possess or control any restricted drug; such possession or control was presumptive evidence of failure to register and pay the occupational tax.

The Harrison Act was amended in 1919[.] The 1919 amendments made it unlawful for any person to purchase, sell, dispense or distribute any of the aforementioned drugs or their compounds except in the original stamped packages or from the original stamped packages. The absence of appropriate tax-paid stamps became prima facie evidence of a violation of the Harrison Act.

From the viewpoint of federal law enforcement officer, there was one glaring gap in the coverage of the Harrison Act—the medical profession. Section 2 of the Act specifically exempted from its coverage the dispensing or distribution of drugs "to a patient by a physician ... in the course of his professional practice only." With narcotics tightly regulated, the physician represented the sole legitimate source of supply open to the addict. For the unscrupulous doctor, this presented a lucrative opportunity to push drugs legitimately under the guise of practicing medicine.

Huge profits could be made. The "script doctor," as he came to be called, became a prime concern of the early Internal Revenue Service personnel charged with enforcement of the Harrison Act. For the responsible physician, the Harrison exemption was not a source of new income; if anything, it was a source of unexpected problems. As long as an addict was not confined to a hospital for treatment, a doctor could minister to him in one of two ways—either by personally administering the drug to the addict in his office or by prescribing the drug for the addict to administer to himself at home. If he treated the addict in his office, the physician could minimize possible drug diversion into the illicit market but at the expense of turning his office into a drug clinic with long lines of addicts awaiting treatment. If he prescribed drugs for self administration, the doctor created serious problems of illegal diversion. The dilemma was real and with no apparent solution. Because of the possibility of diversion, law enforcement officials soon began to move to curtail the medical profession's freedom to prescribe narcotics in the treatment of addicts. The unfortunate consequence of this policy was to drive from the field of drug treatment not only the unethical "script doctor" but the legitimate doctor as well.

At the outset, the Harrison Act was not interpreted as interfering with the physician's medical treatment of the addict, whether by prescription or otherwise. Thus, for example, providing an addict with morphine in the treatment of his addiction was considered valid medical treatment to the extent that it suppressed and alleviated withdrawal symptoms. In 1919, however, with the Supreme Court's decision in *Webb v. United States*, a series of cases maintained otherwise. Although Webb was a "script doctor," the Court was asked to decide whether a practicing physician's order for morphine was exempt as a physician's prescription within the meaning of section 2 where the order was not in the course of professional treatment in an attempt to cure the addict but solely to keep the addict comfortable by maintaining his customary use? The Court said no: "[T]o call such an order for the use of morphine a physician's prescription would be so plain a perversion of meaning that no discussion of the subject is required."

One year later, in *Jin Fuey Moy v. United States*, the Supreme Court was faced with another case involving a "script doctor." In elaborating on its holding in *Webb*, the Court stated that the Harrison Act's immunity for physicians dispensing or distributing drugs in the course of their professional practice did not "include a sale to a dealer or a distribution intended to cater to the appetite or satisfy the craving of one addicted to the use of the drug. A "prescription" issued for either of the latter purposes protects neither the physician who issues it, nor the dealer who knowingly accepts and fills it."

The most controversial decision in this area, however, was neither *Webb* nor *Jin Fuey Moy*, but *United States v. Behrman*, decided in 1922. Behrman, a physician like Webb and Jin Fuey Moy, dispensed drugs indiscriminately. At one time, for instance, he had given an addict prescriptions for 150 grains of heroin, 360 grains of morphine and 210 grains of cocaine. The Government, however, grounded its indictment on a holding that "prescribing drugs for an addict was a crime regardless of the physician's intent in the matter." Although the Supreme Court stressed the large amount of the drugs dispensed by Behrman, the decision could be read by nervous physicians as prohibiting all doctors from prescribing, in good faith, even small quantities of narcotics for self-administration in an attempt to treat an addict. After *Behrman*, it seemed that a physician could only prescribe narcotics for conditions such as ulcers or cancer, but not for relief of addiction itself.

The *Behrman* holding was soon tested in *Linder v. United States*. Dr. Linder had personally dispensed to one of his patients one tablet of morphine and three tablets of cocaine. Limiting the *Behrman* rationale, the Court stated: "[The Harrison Act] says nothing of 'addicts' and does not undertake to prescribe methods for their medical treatment. They are diseased and proper subjects for such treatment, and we cannot possibly conclude that a physician acted improperly or unwisely or for other than medical purposes solely because he has dispensed to one of them, in the ordinary course and in good faith, four small tablets of morphine or cocaine for relief of conditions incident to addiction."

The Court further asserted that *Behrman* could not be interpreted as precluding a physician, acting in good faith and according to fair medical standards, from ever giving an addict moderate amounts of drugs for self-administration in order to relieve the conditions incident to addiction.

Although the language in *Linder* could be read to repudiate *Behrman*, doctors were genuinely afraid to treat addicts. This fear increased as lower federal courts seemingly disregarded the clear intent of the *Linder* rationale. Now the addict could no longer turn to the medical profession for help: he was forced to turn to a new source of supply—the growing illicit drug market. As Rufus King remarks: "The addict-patient vanished; the addict-criminal emerged in his place."

In 1922, Congress passed the Narcotic Drug Import and Export Act which continued the existing ban on opium importation while adding cocaine to the list of drugs which were forbidden entry into the country. Limited amounts of crude opium and coca leaves, however, were permitted to be imported for medical and other legitimate needs. It is interesting to note that, for the first time, all restricted drugs were classified under the generic category of "narcotic drugs." A Federal Narcotics Control Board (composed of three Cabinet members) was created to administer various provisions of the Act. For instance, the Board was empowered to determine exactly what amounts of crude opium and coca leaves were needed to be imported for legitimate and medical purposes.

By the late twenties, the federal government was faced with a new problem—large numbers of addicts in its prison system. As the patterns of addiction grew and became associated with domestic crime, it was perhaps inevitable that the addict population in prisons would increase. Congress responded to the problem by enacting the Porter Act in 1929. The Act established two United States Narcotic Farms designed to provide care and treatment of convicted addicts. The first was opened in Lexington, Kentucky in 1935; the second at Fort Worth, Texas in 1938.

The growing narcotic problem also led to the emergence of a new federal agency within the Treasury Department. Enforcement of the Harrison Act of 1914 was entrusted to the narcotics division of the prohibition unit of the Internal Revenue Service. In 1927 this division was incorporated into the newly created Prohibition Bureau of the Treasury Department. In 1930 law enforcement in the federal narcotics field was further developed and consolidated into its own separate agency, the Federal Bureau of Narcotics. Of equal importance with the establishment of the agency was the appointment of Harry J. Anslinger as the new agency's first commissioner. Anslinger had risen through the diplomatic service and established himself later at the Department of the Treasury as Assistant Commissioner of Prohibition. With the establishment of the Bureau of Narcotics, Anslinger shifted his main concern from prohibition to narcotic law enforcement. Under his vigorous leadership the Bureau of Narcotics was shaped and developed into a powerful law enforcement agency.

While the Harrison Act was cast in terms of a regulatory statute designed to publicly expose the legitimate narcotic drug flow on the domestic scene, its collateral and less obvious goal was to interdict the domestic flow of illegal narcotics. This latter purpose obviously led to heavy criminal law enforcement work. To facilitate this effort the Commissioner of Narcotics was empowered by Congress in 1930 to pay informers for information concerning violations of the drug laws.

Although early federal legislation was mainly concerned with controlling opium and cocaine, a new "drug menace" had appeared by the 1930s—that "menace" was marihuana. In 1937, under the prodding of the newly created Federal Bureau of Narcotics, Congress passed the Marihuana Tax Act—which was similar, in many respects, to the Harrison Act. The Marihuana Tax Act required those in the chain of marihuana distribution to register and pay an occupational tax. A commodity tax of $1.00 per ounce was levied on transfers of marihuana to persons registered under the Act. Unlike the Harrison Act where transfers could only be made to registered persons, the Marihuana Tax Act allowed transfers to non-registered persons but provided ample deterrents to such transfers by a prohibitive tax of $100 an ounce. To effect a legal transfer both registered and non-registered persons were required to file special order forms. Increasing federal control over marihuana distribution even further, various reports and record-keeping requirements were mandated. In short, Congress placed virtually identical controls over marihuana as over the narcotic drugs.

Like the Informers Act of 1930, the Vehicle Seizure Act of 1939 attested to the continuing efforts of the Bureau of Narcotics to extend its control over the growing black market in illegal drugs. By its terms, the Act made it unlawful to transport, carry, or convey any contraband article in, upon, or by means of any vessel, vehicle, or aircraft. A contraband article was defined as any narcotic drug which has been or is possessed with intent to sell or offer for sale in violation of the law, or which is sold in violation of the law, or which does not bear appropriate tax paid Internal Revenue Stamps. Any vessel, vehicle, or aircraft (with certain exceptions) which has been or is being used in violation of the Act was subject to seizure and forfeiture.

The unintended effect of the Harrison Act and its subsequent enforcement was the closing of legitimate sources of supply to the addict, resulting in the rise to a flourishing black market in illegal drugs. With the repeal of Prohibition, organized crime in turn became more involved with the illegal distribution of drugs. The inevitable result was an expanding drug problem. The years between 1946 and 1960 were times of a rising drug trade in the United States and, equally important, times of growing fears regarding the drug problem.

Not the least of these fears was that drug use was reaching epidemic proportions among minors. In 1951, for example, a Special Senate Committee on Organized Crime became concerned with the increasing number of drug addicts among young people. The Committee found that, in 1946, only three percent of the patient-addicts at the United States Public Health Service Hospital at Lexington, Kentucky, were below the age of 21, while just five years later the percentage had increased to eighteen percent. Congress responded with the escalation of penalties for narcotic violations, first in 1951 under the vigorous leadership of Congressman Hale Boggs, and again in 1956.

The Harrison Act and subsequent statutes established the basic approach to drug control by the federal government. The legislation of the 1950s did not alter that approach. What prompted this legislation was the belief that tougher penalties would deter involvement in the traffic by severely punishing those who did not heed the warning. To this end, penalties were sharply increased. Mandatory minimum sentences were instituted to prevent "soft" judges from ameliorating the harshness of these strictures. In addition, a drug offender's right to a suspended sentence or probation was curtailed.

In 1960 the federal government once again broke new ground in the field of narcotics control. For approximately forty years, the United States had closed its ports of entry to the import and export of narcotic drugs and then regulated and controlled the internal distribution processes with the Harrison Act. However, the Act exercised no direct control over the quantities of narcotic drugs legally manufactured within the country itself. The Narcotic Manufacturing Act of 1960 sought to remedy this. Under this Act the Secretary of the Treasury was empowered to license manufacturers of narcotic drugs and to set an individual quota for each drug classification. The Government could not be assured that only those quantities of narcotic drugs actually required for legitimate needs would be domestically manufactured.

This Act was significant in another respect. Before 1960, licensing was always viewed as a peculiarly local concern left to the several states. Now Congress asserted jurisdiction over licensing and, interestingly enough, based its power—at least in part—on the interstate commerce clause, an approach which had been rejected in 1914 when the Harrison Act was enacted. The cumbersome fiction of a tax statute to justify local control over drug distribution was no longer needed.

Still more new ground was broken with the Narcotic Addict Rehabilitation Act of 1966. This Act, patterned on state legislation found in California and New York, was based on two existing approaches to drug rehabilitative treatment. The first, embodied in the Porter Act of 1929, had led to the creation of federal hospitals at Lexington and Fort Worth as places for confinement and treatment of the addict-criminal. The second was the longstanding concept that the mentally ill, the alcoholic, and the addict could be legally confined and treated even in the absence of overt criminal behavior. NARA was designed to funnel accused and convicted criminals out of the court and prison systems and into re-habilitative confinement. Even where no overt criminal conduct was involved, the Act provided rehabilitative confinement for addicts who voluntarily committed themselves or who were involuntarily committed by relatives.

Dangerous drugs are not to be confused with narcotic drugs which have been previously discussed[.] Dangerous drugs include basically three categories of drug—depressants [including barbituates and tranquillizers], stimulants, and hallucinogens.

When compared to narcotics, dangerous drugs became subject to federal regulation rather late in time. It was not until 1965—with the amendments to the Federal Food, Drug and Cosmetic Act—that Congress imposed controls on the distribution of these drugs comparable to those in the Harrison Act. Before this time, individuals who unlawfully dispensed dangerous drugs could only be prosecuted through certain misbranding provisions of the Food, Drug and Cosmetic Act.

The 1965 amendments cover all dangerous drugs—whether in interstate or intrastate commerce. Unlike the Harrison Act which was based on federal taxing powers, Congress justified intrastate regulation of dangerous drugs on interstate commerce theories.

The amendments categorize[d] dangerous drugs as either depressants or stimulants. Depressant drugs include all drugs containing "any quantity of barbituric acid or any of the salts of barbituric acid" (a definition which does not encompass many common tranquilizers); stimulant drugs are those containing "any quantity of amphetamine, any of its optical isomers, or any salt of amphetamine." The definition of a depressant or stimulant drug, however, includes the following significant language: "any drug which contains any quantity which the Secretary, after investigation, has found to have, and by regulation designates as having, a potential for abuse because of its depressant or stimulant effect on the central nervous system or its hallucinogenic effect[.]"

This language [provided] the authority for controlling hallucinogens and nonbarbituric tranquilizers under the amendments.

With certain exceptions the 1965 amendments forbade the manufacture of depressant or stimulant drugs. Permitted to manufacture, however, were manufacturers who were properly registered and who produced drugs for use in research, teaching, medicine or for chemical analysis. Sales were prohibited except by those legitimately in the chain of distribution and only in the ordinary and authorized course of their business. Finally, possession (a) other than for personal use of the possessor or a member of his household or (b) for administration to an animal owned by him or by a member of his household, was forbidden.

It is interesting that enforcement of the dangerous drug laws was first placed in the hands of the Food and Drug Administration in the Department of Health, Education, and Welfare—an agency responsible for the general health and not particularly involved with law enforcement. In 1968, however, jurisdiction over dangerous drugs was transferred from the FDA to the Justice Department.

These amendments were the final piece of legislation which preceded the Comprehensive Drug Abuse Prevention and Control Act of 1970, with Title II of that Act otherwise known as the Controlled Substances Act.

The Comprehensive Drug Abuse Prevention and Control Act of 1970 repealed almost all prior federal drug legislation and created a new and comprehensive scheme for federal drug control. For the first time, one statute governed both narcotics and dangerous drugs. Enforcement of all drug laws was placed in the hands of the Bureau of Narcotics and Dangerous Drugs (BNDD)—an agency created in the Justice Department in 1968 to combine the enforcement powers of the Bureau of Narcotics in the Department of Treasury and the Drug Abuse Control Bureau of the FDA in the Department of Health, Education, and Welfare. Although the 1970 Act totally revamped the existing pattern of drug control, a great deal was borrowed from prior legislation[.]

The regulatory component of the 1970 Controlled Substances Act, which continues to serve as the foundation for federal drug laws today, is covered in detail in Chapter 6.

The Emerging Criminal War on Sex Offenders
Corey Rayburn Yung
45 Harvard Civil Rights-Civil Liberties Law Review 435 (2010)

In 1971, Richard Nixon officially declared the War on Drugs in America. However, laws enabling that criminal war were enacted years before Nixon's speech formally initiated the new conflict. In 1968, Lyndon Johnson established the Bureau of Narcotics and Dangerous Drugs, which came to be known as the Drug Enforcement Agency ("DEA"), to lead the charge against domestic drug use and distribution. The next year, efforts to limit drug smuggling from Mexico culminated in Operation Intercept, which nearly led to a complete closing of the southern border of the United States. When Nixon took over the Presidency, he signed into law the Comprehensive Drug Abuse Prevention and Control Act, which established the categorization system for regulating drugs. At the same time, the National Organization for the Reform of Marijuana Laws ("NORML"), was founded to counter the shifting policy priorities of the criminal justice system. By the time of Nixon's official declaration, the War on Drugs was substantially underway.

There is almost no theoretical work concerning when ordinary law enforcement escalates into a criminal war. While many scholars have written about the War on Drugs, a general war on crime, or other specific criminal wars, the definition of a "criminal war" has largely been taken for granted. This has likely led to some overuse of the phrase since "criminal wars" have been relative rarities in the United States. It might even be contended that the difference between a "criminal war" and general law enforcement is based only upon form, not substance. However, the American experience with the War on Drugs illustrates how a criminal war should be distinguished from even the most heightened levels of ordinary law enforcement.

While there have been other crime-fighting efforts called "wars," the War on Drugs stands out as the quintessential example of a war on crime in the United States. As news of heavy drug use among American soldiers in Vietnam reached the United States, so began the War on Drugs. Like the War on Poverty and other domestic wars, the War on Drugs had no specific enemy—it targeted a "noun." As the War unfolded, the emphasis on treatment for drug users disappeared, replaced with increased criminal penalties. As time passed, the War on Drugs became much bigger than its relatively modest beginnings.

Even in hindsight, it is still difficult to see how America reached the present point in the drug war. In all, $2.5 trillion government dollars have been spent[.] With recent drug violence in Mexico reaching American borders, the United States seems to be in a worse position than when it launched Operation Intercept in 1969 to stanch the flow of drugs across the border. Drug violence in Mexico is so prevalent that the Mexican authorities had to declare that the nation was not a "failed state," perhaps the surest sign that country may well be.

To understand how America arrived at this moment in the War on Drugs, it is helpful to review a few key historical points in the conflict. While the official start date of the War on Drugs was Nixon's declaration in 1971, the war became an "all-out" conflict in 1973 when the DEA was formed out of the Bureau of Narcotics and Dangerous Drugs. The DEA became the primary vehicle for investigating and controlling the domestic drug trade. Under President Reagan, the drug war reached new heights. As the war expanded, the costs in personnel, money, and other resources became a substantial burden on the United States government. To maintain public support for the effort, the government inflamed the public fears of drug use by tapping already existing myths. In 1986, the Anti-Drug Abuse Act allocated $1.7 billion for the conflict while establishing the system of mandatory minimum penalties for drug crimes.

The Reagan administration also started an anti-drug propaganda campaign largely popularized by First Lady Nancy Reagan. In particular, Mrs. Reagan's "Just Say No" slogan had societal resonance and became a rallying call for supporters of the War on Drugs. Other private and public entities joined the Reagan propaganda campaign. The Drug Abuse Resistance Education ("D.A.R.E.") program, which started in Los Angeles, grew into a national organization. Perhaps the most famous message disseminated during the era appeared in a commercial by the Partnership for a Drug-Free America that showed a frying egg and told viewers that the image depicted "your brain on drugs." Despite mounting evidence that the propaganda and drug-education programs did little or nothing to abate drug use, the efforts were deemed successful because they increased public support for the War on Drugs.

The first Bush presidency continued Reagan-era policies. With the end of the Cold War, the War on Drugs provided an alternative focus for some of the resources that had previously targeted the Soviet Union. President Bush also established the Office of National Drug Control Policy and appointed as its head William Bennett, America's first "drug czar."

The Clinton years kept the drug war on track as some of the harshest punishments for drug offenders, including use of the death penalty in non-homicide cases, were signed into law. In 1995, the United States Sentencing Commission recommended that mandatory minimums be adjusted to diminish or eliminate what was known as the crack/cocaine disparity. However, because of the fervor still surrounding the War on Drugs, Congress, for the first time, rejected the Commission's recommendation. The Clinton administration claimed many successes in the War on Drugs, but statistical evidence did not support those conclusions. Nonetheless, federal efforts in support of the criminal war were expanded based upon those supposed victories.

While the War on Terror became the highest priority for the second Bush presidency, investment in the failing drug war continued. President Bush pledged to decrease drug use among Americans by 25%. While marijuana use declined by 6%, use of the other major drugs increased during the same period. National drug policy forged ahead, despite the lack of data available to evaluate its effectiveness. As with many other reports before, the government did not alter its course.

The War on Drugs presents nearly forty years of policy, public reaction, and law to examine. From the drug war experience, three essential elements of a criminal war emerge: marshalling of resources, myth creation, and exception making. The first two are prerequisites for the war to begin, and the third is an inevitable result. They are each discussed below in turn.

One of the clearest signs that a war has truly begun is that the government provides a substantial budget, seeks to employ persons to fight, and attempts to find political support for the use of these resources. This is as true in fighting an international war as it is in fighting a criminal war. The direct cost of the War on Drugs, estimated at $2.5 trillion, paints only part of the picture. One record places the cost of the War on Drugs at $600 per second in 2003. America's prisons are filled with persons captured as part of the war. Indeed, without the drug war, America would not have the ignominious label of being the country with the most persons incarcerated per capita. Someone in the United States is arrested for a drug crime every twenty seconds. Nearly two million people are arrested for non-violent drug crimes every year.

The drug war largely began when the Nixon Administration decided to make it a high priority item through the allocation of government resources. The Reagan administration escalated the conflict again through the allocation of more resources to the effort. Without this intentional diversion of resources, no criminal war can occur. The money and other capital provide the means for turning law enforcement into a war-fighting effort.

The marshalling of resources is also found in the way the legal regime surrounding the criminal war is constructed. In the War on Drugs, the establishment of an agency, the Bureau of Narcotics and Dangerous Drugs, was significant because the agency hired a substantial number of law enforcement agents to focus solely on drug investigations and arrests. The federalization of drug laws with the passage of the Comprehensive Drug Abuse Prevention and Control Act replaced the disorganized, piecemeal approaches that made a criminal war unsustainable. Although there have been amendments and supplements to the main War on Drugs statutes, the basic legal architecture for the conflict was in place even before the formal declaration of war.

The drug war has featured the creation of substantial myths about the danger of procuring and using various illegal drugs. The myths have been supported by rhetoric that in turn has constructed both the contours and details of a criminal war. They were disseminated through a variety of media and created an environment that fueled continued support for the allocation of substantial government resources to the War on Drugs. Whether this propaganda effort was warranted is beside the point—the key issue is that government went above and beyond traditional crime-fighting techniques when it utilized propaganda as part of law enforcement.

A variety of advertising campaigns created a series of myths about drugs, including a recent campaign which stated that purchasers of marijuana were facilitating terrorism around the world. This connection is tenuous at best. Further, a powerful argument by legalization advocates has been that the War on Drugs creates drug-sponsored terrorism, which would not exist absent the aggressive U.S. campaign against illegal drugs.

These government facilitated myths, encouraged the demonization of drug suppliers and, in many cases, users. This propaganda bears some similarities to efforts by the government in international military conflicts. In those cases, demonization of the enemy, exaggeration of harms, and misstatements about the state of the world are common. The same characteristics can be identified in criminal wars.

For example, after President Nixon made his initial declaration of war, he stated that drugs were "public enemy [number] 1." The entire campaign of the War on Drugs was filled with language more commonly found during armed conflicts. This language has repeatedly served to reinforce the assumptions of the war in the public's mind while creating the reality of the criminal war itself. William Elwood explained that: "One rhetorical idea that applies to ... the War on Drugs is condensation symbols: names, words, phrases, or maxims that evoke discrete, vivid impressions in each listener's mind and also involve the listener's most basic values.... War is a potent condensation symbol that connotes heroes and enemies, battles and battlefields, and war-sized allocation of resources to guarantee ultimate victory over the enemy."

Politicians and the media have not been the only sources for drug war myths and rhetoric. Notably, the Supreme Court has adopted the idea that the War on Drugs creates special circumstances which warrant different rules. The majority opinion in *Board of Education v. Earls*, held that drug testing of students participating in extracurricular activities was constitutional because the "drug epidemic makes the war against drugs a pressing concern in every school." In *Morse v. Frederick*, the Court held that there was no infringement of a student's right to free speech based upon his suspension for displaying a banner reading "BONG HiTS 4 JESUS" due to Congress' decision to give unique status to the war on drugs. Similar reasoning led Justice John Paul Stevens to write, "no impartial observer could criticize this Court for hindering the progress of the war on drugs. On the contrary ... this Court has become a loyal foot soldier in the Executive's fight against crime."

The tone, messages, and effects of war rhetoric differ from that used in ordinary law enforcement which is not explained to the public in the same manner. The purpose of these rhetorical techniques in the drug war context is to maintain public consent, if not active support, for the conflict. As one commentator recently noted, the policy effects of drug war rhetoric have been substantial: "War implies a threat so existential, so dire to our way of life, that we citizens should be ready to sign over some of our basic rights, be expected to make significant sacrifices, and endure collateral damage in order to defeat it."

An empirical study showed that Presidential rhetoric in particular had "real and substantial" effects on the priorities of law enforcement and directly resulted in more drug arrests. Further, the government continued to claim victories in the ongoing conflict by distorting and misrepresenting evidence. The media often served to reinforce the messages of the government, enabling the criminal war to grow.

Notably, the new "drug czar" in the Obama administration has rejected the use of "war" rhetoric, and many have seen this as a sign that the conflict is finally deescalating. Without the underlying rhetoric and myths being propagated, the attempts to diminish drug use in the United States can return to the domain of ordinary law enforcement.

As in international wars, criminal wars are marked by deviations from normal codes of conduct. With the recent international War on Terror, there have been debates about the permissibility of torture, inapplicability of the Geneva Conventions, application of the Foreign Intelligence Surveillance Act, and the utilization of private corporations in acquiring personal information of citizens. The mentality of exception making in the War on Terror culminated in the oft-stated belief that "the Constitution is not a suicide pact." Thus, constitutional guarantees of liberty were to be sacrificed when policymakers perceived a threat to national security.

Similarly, in criminal wars, exceptions are crafted into normal law enforcement rules. In the constitutional context, it has been argued extensively that the War on Drugs has created a substantial set of exceptions to the Fourth, Fifth, Sixth, Eighth, and Fourteenth Amendments. However, the First Amendment's protections for speech and free exercise of religion have also been subject to unusual exceptions due to the drug war. Even the right to bear arms under the Second Amendment has not been unscathed by the War on Drugs. The drug war also expanded to federal criminal jurisdiction in ways that required another exception to federalism doctrines. Outside of the constitutional context, law enforcement was given a variety of weapons unique to the drug war context. The emergence of heavily armed SWAT teams, inter-departmental and inter-governmental coordination, aerial surveillance, and extensive sting operations are the result of the War on Drugs. Further, the growth of federal criminal law can largely be attributed to the desire to stamp out drug distribution and use in the United States.

This exception-making attribute of criminal wars has long-term effects beyond the immediate scenarios which were used to justify the exceptions. Once the government gained the exceptional tools used in the drug war, it was able to use those tools in other contexts as well. The constitutional and non-constitutional exceptions eventually became rules. Now, SWAT teams are utilized in a variety of situations, the Fourth Amendment has lost its force in many cases, the federal government is free to pass criminal laws with little concern about overreaching under the Commerce Clause, and undercover operations are used for any high-priority law enforcement project. What started as exceptions supported by "unique" circumstances have become tools available outside of the drug war context. With signs that the War on Drugs might be abating, some are already wondering who or what the next war will target.

2. Race, Class and the Drug War

In *From Chocolate to Morphine*, Andrew Weil and Winifred Rosen observe that "[e]verybody is willing to call certain drugs bad, but there is little agreement from one culture to the next as to which these are." If opinions about drugs are largely cultural, do cultural considerations also influence drug laws?

There is a good deal of evidence that many early U.S. drug laws were enacted, at least in part, because of racial and cultural animus. In *Ex parte Yung Jon*, 28 F. 308 (D. Ore. 1886), for example, the court considered the constitutionality of a law outlawing "opium dens." In upholding the law, Judge Deady explained: "Smoking opium is not our vice, and therefore it may be that this legislation proceeds more from a desire to vex and annoy the 'Heathen Chinee' in this respect, than to protect the people from the evil habit. But the motives of legislators cannot be the subject of judicial investigation for the purposes of affecting the validity of their acts." *Id.* at 312.

Similarly, in *The Forbidden Fruit and the Tree of Knowledge: An Inquiry into the Legal History of American Marijuana Prohibition*, 56 Va. L. Rev. 971 (1970), Richard J. Bonnie and Charles H. Whitebread conclude that "racial prejudice" was the "most prominent" factor in the passage of the first marijuana prohibition laws. As they explain it, at the time these early marijuana prohibition laws were passed, "not only did few middle-class Americans know about marijuana and its use, but what little 'information' was available provided an automatic association of the drug with Mexican immigration, crime and the deviant life style in the Black ghettos. Naturally, the impending drug legislation ... became entangled with society's views of these minority groups." Among the examples cited by Bonnie and Whitebread is a *Montana Standard* newspaper article about a 1929 marijuana prohibition bill, which reported: "There was fun in the House Committee during the week when the Marihuana bill came up for consideration. Marihuana is Mexican opium, a plant used by Mexicans and cultivated for sale by Indians. 'When some beet field peon takes a few rares of this stuff,' explained Dr. Fred Fulsher of Mineral County, 'He thinks he has just been elected president of Mexico so he starts out to execute all his political enemies. I understand that over in Butte where the Mexicans often go for the winter they stage imaginary bullfights in the 'Bower of Roses' or put on tournaments for the favor of

'Spanish Rose' after a couple of whiffs of Marijuana. The Silver Bow and Yellowstone delegations both deplore these international complications.' Everybody laughed and the bill was recommended for passage."

It is rare to see this sort of conscious and overt racism regarding drug laws today. Nevertheless, drug law enforcement continues to have a disproportionate impact on people of color.

Race, Drugs, and Law Enforcement in the United States
Jamie Fellner
20 Stan. L. & Pol'y Rev 257 (2009)

Race has been and remains inextricably involved in drug law enforcement, shaping the public perception of and response to the drug problem. A recent study in Seattle is illustrative. Although the majority of those who shared, sold, or transferred serious drugs in Seattle are white (indeed seventy percent of the general Seattle population is white), almost two-thirds (64.2%) of drug arrestees are black. The racially disproportionate drug arrests result from the police department's emphasis on the outdoor drug market in the racially diverse downtown area of the city, its lack of attention to other outdoor markets that are predominantly white, and its emphasis on crack. Three-quarters of the drug arrests were crack-related even though only an estimated one-third of the city's drug transactions involved crack. Whites constitute the majority of those who deliver methamphetamine, ecstasy, powder cocaine, and heroin in Seattle; blacks are the majority of those who deliver crack. Not surprisingly then, seventy-nine percent of those arrested on crack charges were black. The researchers could not find a "racially neutral" explanation for the police prioritization of the downtown drug markets and crack. The focus on crack offenders, for example, did not appear to be a function of the frequency of crack transactions compared to other drugs, public safety or public health concerns, crime rates, or citizen complaints. The researchers ultimately concluded that the Seattle Police Department's drug law enforcement efforts "reflect implicit racial bias: the unconscious impact of race on official perceptions of who and what constitutes Seattle's drug problem.... Indeed, the widespread racial typification of drug offenders as racialized "others" has deep historical roots and was intensified by the diffusion of potent cultural images of dangerous black crack offenders. These images appear to have had a powerful impact on popular perceptions of potential drug offenders, and, as a result, law enforcement practices in Seattle."

The racial dynamics reflected in Seattle's current drug law enforcement priorities are long-standing and can be found across the country. Indeed, they provided the impetus for the "war on drugs" that began in the mid-1980s. Spearheaded by federal drug policy initiatives that significantly increased federal penalties for drug offenses and markedly increased federal funds for state anti-drug efforts, the drug war reflected the popularity of "tough on crime" policies emphasizing harsh punishments as the key to curbing drugs and restoring law and order in America. The drug of principal concern was crack cocaine, erroneously believed to be a drug used primarily by black Americans. The use of cocaine, primarily powder cocaine, had increased in the late 1970s and early 1980s, particularly among whites, but powder cocaine use did not provoke the "orgy of media and political attention" that occurred in the mid-1980s when a cheaper, smokable cocaine in the form of crack appeared.

Crack was the latest in a series of drugs that since the late nineteenth century have preoccupied policy makers in the United States. In each case, "the drug of primary concern was strongly associated in the white public mind with a particular racial minority." Race was the lens through which drug problems in the United States were viewed, coloring both the definition of the problem and the proposed solutions. As the case of Seattle exemplifies, race continues today to influence the perceptions of the danger posed by those who use and sell illicit drugs, the choice of drugs that warrant the most public attention, and the choice of communities in which to concentrate drug law enforcement resources.

Although the use of crack was by no means limited to low-income, urban, minority neighborhoods, it was those neighborhoods which more visibly suffered from crack addiction, and the nuisance and violence that accompanied the struggle of different drug-dealing groups to establish control over its distribution in the 1980s and 1990s. The dismay of local residents, however, was exceeded by the censure and outrage from outsiders fanned by sensationalist media stories and by politicians eager to seek electoral advantage. With politicians and the media focused on the putative effects of crack in inner-city neighborhoods—although many of those effects were subsequently proven to have been greatly exaggerated or just plain wrong—those neighborhoods became and remain the principal "fronts" in the war on drugs.

Crack in black neighborhoods was a lightning rod for a complicated and deep-rooted set of racial, class, political, social, and moral dynamics. Politicians were able to woo a white electorate anxious about its declining status through the race-coded language of "drugs" and "crime." "Public discourse focused on addiction and violence but the subtext was understood as that of race. Crack cocaine was perceived as a drug of the Black inner-city urban poor, while powder cocaine, with its higher costs, was a drug of wealthy whites.... This framing of the drug in class and race-based terms provides important context when evaluating the legislative response." That response, most notoriously, included the federal Anti-Drug Abuse Act of 1986 and the Anti-Drug Abuse Act of 1988, which imposed far higher penalties for possession or sale of crack cocaine than powder cocaine, as well as state laws that required prison sentences even for low level drug offenses.

The legislative and law enforcement responses to crack "cannot be attributed solely to objective levels of criminal danger, but [also reflect] the way in which minority behaviors are symbolically constructed and subjected to official social control." Law enforcement efforts against crack in poor minority neighborhoods reinforced control of the urban "underclass," a group deemed by the political and white majority to be particularly "dangerous, offensive and undesirable." The conflation of the underclass with crack offenders meant the perceived dangerousness of one increased the perceived threat of the other. Urban blacks, the population most burdened by concentrated socio-economic disadvantage, became the population at which the war on drugs was targeted.

When asked to close their eyes and envision a drug offender, Americans did not picture a white middle class man snorting powder cocaine or college students smoking marijuana. They pictured unkempt African-American men and women slouched in alleyways or young blacks hanging around urban street corners. At least for the last twenty years, however, whites have engaged in drug offenses at rates higher than blacks.

According to the 2006 surveys conducted by the federal Substance Abuse and Mental Health Services Administration (SAMHSA), an estimated 49% of whites and 42.9% of blacks age twelve or older have used illicit drugs in their lifetimes; 14.5% of whites and 16% of blacks have used them in the past year; and 8.5% of whites and 9.8% of blacks have used them in the past month. Because the white population is more than six times greater than the black population, the absolute number of white drug offenders is far greater than that of black drug offenders. SAMHSA estimates that 111,774,000 people in the United States age twelve or older have used illicit drugs during their lifetime, of whom 82,587,000 are white and 12,477,000 are black. Even among powder and crack cocaine users—which remain a principal focus of law enforcement—there are more whites than blacks. According to SAMHSA's calculations, there are 27,083,000 whites who have used cocaine during their lifetime, compared to 2,618,000 blacks and, indeed, 5,553,000 whites who have used crack cocaine, compared to 1,537,000 blacks.

According to the most recent SAMHSA survey, if black and white drug users are combined, blacks account for 13% of the total who have ever used an illicit drug, 8% of those who have ever used cocaine, and 21% of those who have ever used crack cocaine.

By definition, drug users violate laws against drug possession. They also frequently engage in illegal drug distribution activities—e.g., selling drugs for cash or providing them to friends. If blacks constitute a relatively small proportion of those who use drugs (between 13% and 20% depending on the drug), they likely constitute a comparable proportion of those who engage in other illegal drug-related activities. Although there is little direct research on the race of drug sellers, for example, that which exists suggests a racial breakdown among sellers similar to that among users. National surveys of drug abuse conducted by the federal Substance Abuse and Mental Health Services Administration have sometimes included questions on drug selling. In 1991, 0.7% of adult whites and 1.4% of adult blacks reported selling drugs in the past twelve months. Although the proportion of sellers was twice that among blacks than among whites, in absolute numbers far more whites (939,345) reported drug selling than blacks (268,170). Black sellers constituted 12% of the combined number of self-reported black and white sellers. Fifteen years later, 1.6% of whites and 2.8% of blacks surveyed in 2006 reported they had sold drugs in the past twelve months, or an estimated 2,461,797 whites, and 712,044 blacks. Blacks thus represented 14% of the combined black and white sellers.

Evidence regarding the race of drug sellers also emerges from research in specific urban drug markets. For example, the study of Seattle's drug market, discussed above, indicates that the majority of the drug sellers are white (as are a majority of the users). In fact, research suggests that drug users tend to obtain their drugs from people of the same race as themselves. As one researcher addressing racial congruity in drug activities concluded, "Dealers with direct contact with their customers … are likely to look like the customers …"

Some might question whether blacks constitute a higher percentage than whites of persons occupying higher ranks in the drug business, e.g. major traffickers. Empirical research addressing this question is not available, but experts suggest that higher positions in the drug trade are not likely to be held by black individuals. The race of persons in the upper echelons of the drug trade is also not particularly relevant, because the overwhelming preponderance of drug offenders entering the criminal justice system are low-level non-violent offenders. For example, between 1980 and the present, arrests for drug sales, possession with intent to sell, manufacturing, transportation, or importing have never constituted more than 36% of all drug arrests. Drug offenders who are incarcerated are mostly street-level dealers, couriers, and other bit players in the drug trade.

All other things being equal, if blacks constitute an estimated 13% to 20% of the total of black and white drug offenders, they, should constitute a roughly similar proportion of the total number of blacks and whites who are arrested, convicted, and sent to prison for drug law violations. But all other things are not equal. The data demonstrate clearly and consistently that blacks have been and remain more likely to be arrested for drug offending behavior relative to their percentage among drug offenders than whites who engage in the same behavior. There are many reasons for the racial disparities in drug arrests, including demographics, the extent of community complaints, police allocation of resources, racial profiling, and the relative ease of making drug arrests in minority urban areas compared to white areas. One analyst has observed that in the war on drugs: "Racial profiling is almost inevitable. Race becomes one of the readily observable visual clues to help identify drug suspects, along with age, gender and location. There is a certain rationality to this—if you are in poor black neighborhoods, drug dealers are more likely to be black. Local distribution networks are often monoracial; downscale markets are often neighborhood-based; and downscale urban neighborhoods are often segregated.... The law and practice of drug enforcement is market-specific, and the markets are divided by race and class."

Former New York Police Commissioner Lee Brown explained the police concentration in certain neighborhoods and the consequent racial impact as follows: "In most large cities, the police focus their attention on where they see conspicuous drug use—street-corner drug sales—and where they get the most complaints. Conspicuous drug use is generally in your low-income neighborhoods that generally turn out to be your minority neighborhoods.... It's easier for police to make an arrest when you have people selling drugs on the street corner than those who are [selling or buying drugs] in the suburbs or in office buildings. The end result is that more blacks are arrested than whites because of the relative ease in making those arrests."

Between 1980 and 2007, there were more than twenty-five million adult drug arrests in the United States. The percentage of arrests that involved black men and women increased from 27% in 1980 to a high ranging from 40% to 42% between 1989 and 1993, and then declined more or less steadily to the current percentage of 35%. Relative to population, blacks have been arrested on drug charges at consistently higher rates than whites. In 1980 blacks were arrested at rates almost three (2.9) times the rate of whites. In the years with the worst disparities, between 1988 and 1993, blacks were arrested at rates more than five times the rate of whites. In the last six years, the ratio of black to white drug arrest rates has ranged between 3.5 and 3.9.

Although the ratio of black to white arrests has decreased somewhat since the mid 1990s when it was at its highest, racial disparity in drug arrests has continued despite changes in drug use and law enforcement priorities. As the crack cocaine market began to constrict in urban areas and the use of cocaine stabilized, "Law enforcement shifted its emphasis toward marijuana." Methamphetamine manufacture and use emerged as law enforcement concerns in the late 1990s. Yet although marijuana use is prevalent across races, and methamphetamine is used primarily by whites, blacks continue to be disproportionately arrested.

The difference between the black proportion of drug offenders and the black proportion of drug arrests reflects the ongoing salience of urban drug law enforcement, or, more specifically, drug law enforcement in black urban neighborhoods. In 2007, for example, 77% of drug arrests occurred in cities. Although urban blacks account for approximately 6% of the national population, they constituted 29.8% of all drug arrests in 2007. A longitudinal analysis of urban drug arrests by race shows that in the largest American cities, drug arrests for African Americans rose at three times the rate for whites between 1980 and 2003, 225% compared to 70%. In eleven cities, black drug arrests rose by more than 500%. In the seventy-five largest counties in the United States, blacks in 2002 accounted for 46% of drug offense arrests, even though they represented only 15.6% of the population. New York State provides a particularly striking example: blacks in New York City represent 10.7% of the state population, yet accounted for 42.1% of drug arrests statewide.

The racial disparities evident in drug arrests grow larger as cases wind their way through the criminal justice system. Blacks constitute 43% and whites 55% of persons convicted of drug felonies in state courts, and blacks account for 53.5% and whites for 33.3% of persons admitted to state prison with new convictions for drug offenses. In 2007, blacks accounted for 33.2% of people entering federal prison for drug offenses.

A comparison of the rates, relative to population, at which blacks and whites are sent to state prison for drug offenses offers what may be the most compelling evidence of the diste racial impact of drug control policies: the black rate (256.2 per 100,000 black adults) is ten times greater than the white rate (25.3 per 100,000 white adults). Disaggregating these rates by gender reveals that black men were sent to prison on drug charges at 11.8 times the rate of white men and black women are sent to prison on drug charges at 4.8 times the rate of white women.

Just as conscious and unconscious racial notions helped define the drug problem, they have also helped shape political and policy responses to that problem. The legislative history of federal crack sentencing laws, for example, provides reason "to suspect that regardless of the objectives Congress was pursuing, it would have shown more restraint in fashioning the crack penalties or more interest in amending them in ensuing years, if the penalties did not apply almost exclusively to blacks." To the extent that the white majority in the United States identified both crime and drugs with racialized "others," it has no doubt been easier to endorse or at least acquiesce to punitive penal policies that might have been rejected if applied at equivalent rates to members of their own families and communities. Politicians have been able to reap the electoral rewards of endorsing harsh drug policies because the group that suffered most from those policies — black Americans — lacked the numbers to use the political process to secure a different strategy.

Throughout the modern war on drugs, measures to battle the use and sale of drugs have emphasized arrest and incarceration rather than prevention and treatment. The emphasis on harsh penal sanctions cannot be divorced from the widespread and deeply rooted public association of racial minorities with crime and drugs, just as the choice of crack as an ongoing priority for law enforcement cannot be divorced from public association of crack with blacks.

Faced with concerns about crack, the United States could have emphasized a public health and harm reduction approach prioritizing drug education, substance abuse treatment, and increased access to medical assistance. It could have sought to stem the spread of drug use and the temptations of the drug trade in deteriorating inner cities by making investments to reduce poverty, build social infrastructure, improve education, increase medical and mental health treatment, combat homelessness, increase employment, and provide more support to vulnerable families. It could have restricted prison to only the most serious drug offenders (e.g., major traffickers).

Instead, federal and state governments embraced harsh penal sanctions to battle the use of drugs and their sale to consumers. They adopted policies that increased the arrest rates of low-level drug offenders, the likelihood of a prison sentence upon conviction of a drug offense, and the length of such prison sentences.

Defenders of anti-drug efforts claim they want to protect poor minority neighborhoods from addiction and violence. But the choice of arrest and imprisonment as the primary anti-drug strategy evokes the infamous phrase from the Vietnam War: "It became necessary to destroy the town in order to save it." Noted criminologist Michael Tonry has pointed out that unless and until drug control policies are less destructive, the life prospects for many disadvantaged blacks and their communities will remain bleak.

In a fair, equitable, and non-discriminatory criminal justice system, sanctions should be imposed equally on offending populations. Yet the racial patterns of persons arrested and incarcerated on drug charges are distantly related, at best, to racial patterns of drug offending.

The Pathological Politics of Criminal Law
William J. Stuntz
100 MICHIGAN LAW REVIEW 505 (2001)

Relative to other Western legal systems, America's criminal justice system has long had a strong focus on vice—prostitution and gambling a century ago, alcohol in the 1920s, and drugs more recently. That focus is usually attributed to America's moralism. It is also a consequence of the interacting incentives of law enforcers and legislators.

Most criminal litigation deals with crimes that nearly all non-offenders believe should be crimes. Prosecutors may make sorting errors in burglary cases, and criminalizing the possession of burglars' tools may make those sorting errors more likely. But there will be no dispute about whether burglars should be punished. The huge majority of the population thinks the relevant behavior wrong and, importantly, the huge majority of the population has no desire to engage in the relevant behavior themselves. For crimes like these, the lawmaking dynamic yields broader liability rules but does not change the nature of the behavior the system is seeking to punish.

With vice, the story is different. Gambling, sex for hire, and intoxicants are all things that a large portion of the public wants, and these goods and services are sufficiently cheap, at least in some forms, that people of all social classes can afford them. At the same time, these things generate both intense disapproval among another large slice of the population, and substantial social costs that tend to concentrate in poor communities. The result is complicated: anti-vice crusades tend to have strong public support, but only so long as the crusades are targeted at a fairly small subset of the population. Our tradition of giving police and prosecutors basically unregulated enforcement discretion makes that targeting easy. Which in turn permits legislatures to define criminal liability in ways that might otherwise be politically impossible.

One sees hints of this dynamic with each of the major vice crimes that have occupied the criminal justice system over the past century. Begin with prostitution. Before the late nineteenth century, most jurisdictions had no prostitution statutes; the relevant crime was running a "disorderly house," a more circumscribed offense. The period after about 1880 saw the growth of a powerful urban reform movement that led first to prostitution statutes, and then to broader solicitation and procurement statutes. But when some urban police forces tried to enforce those laws generally—when they actually tried to shut down prostitution, across neighborhoods and classes—they generated a significant backlash, in Lawrence Friedman's words, from the "silent army" of middle-class customers who frequented the more upscale houses. There were two typical results: non-enforcement coupled with graft, with the police using the prostitution laws as devices for extracting payoffs, or enforcement targeted mostly at poor immigrant neighborhoods.

The story with respect to gambling is similar. For a long time the market for illegal games tended to segment by class, with numbers businesses dominating the downscale market, and bookmaking and illegal casinos playing the same role in the upscale market. Throughout this time, in most jurisdictions the criminal law of gambling was all-encompassing. Enforcement was not. In those times and places when police and prosecutors took gambling seriously, they almost always targeted numbers operations, which were in turn concentrated in poor urban neighborhoods.

Prohibition was likewise legally all-encompassing, banning manufacture and sale of beer and wine as well as hard liquors. There, too, the illegal market tended to segment by class (there is some evidence that Prohibition made beer the working-class drink of choice, as liquor was priced out of reach for urban factory workers). And there, too, enforcement was largely class-based: contemporaneous accounts report that blacks were the prime focus of alcohol enforcement and prosecution in the South; in Northern cities, it was working-class white ethnics.

Notice the pattern. For each of these three classic vice crimes, a majority of the population seems to have supported the ban, but a sizeable minority, cutting across classes and ethnic groups, wished to participate in the illegal market. Given the size of that minority—and, consequently, the sheer number of illegal transactions—across-the-board enforcement of the ban was unsustainable. The solution was enforcement aimed primarily at lower-class markets: street prostitutes, numbers operations, and working-class beer distribution networks. That tended to be a relatively popular solution, at least for a time, for two reasons. First, the social harms associated with these transactions—violence, impoverishment, disease—tended to correlate not only with the illegal transactions but with class as well. Second, lower-class neighborhoods were often politically convenient targets. Hostility to blacks in the South and to working-class immigrants in Northern cities were strong themes of turn-of-the-century American politics.

Notice, too, how hard that solution would be to define legislatively. Had legislatures sought to capture the difference between downscale and upscale gambling, they probably would have banned some kinds of games but not others. But that strategy would have had limited effect, for the downscale market could simply have shifted from illegal games to legal ones. Had street solicitation but not prostitution been criminalized, prostitutes in poor neighborhoods could have retreated to fixed houses—as they did in most American cities through much of the nineteenth century. Had beer but not liquor been banned, working-class consumption would have moved, perversely, toward products with a higher alcohol content. That kind of flexibility is probably in the nature of markets for pleasurable-but-sometimes-harmful goods and services. As a consequence, serious criminal enforcement of vice may depend on broad criminalization, coupled with equally broad law enforcement power to target particular neighborhoods and, inevitably, particular racial or ethnic groups. Without enforcement discretion, criminalization might be impossible.

Contemporary drug law and drug enforcement paint a complex picture, but one sees elements of the same pattern there as well. Not only are classically "hard" drugs like cocaine and heroin banned, but so are a wide variety of "softer" drugs like marijuana. Enforcement tends to be more aggressive than with past anti-vice crusades. Drug sentences are more severe than were sentences for gambling or illegal alcohol earlier this century, and the policing of upscale drug markets appears to be more persistent than policing of other upscale illegal markets over the course of the past hundred years. To that extent, the pattern breaks down; support for drug criminalization is probably both broader and deeper than support for earlier crusades against prostitutes, gamblers, or saloonkeepers. Yet class-based, and hence to some degree race-based, enforcement remains common. Thus, crack markets in urban black neighborhoods are targeted, while more upscale, and whiter, drug markets receive less law enforcement attention.

Once again, that type of enforcement strategy, and that type of criminal law, would be much harder in a regime with limited police and prosecutorial discretion. Perhaps one reason support for drug criminalization remains so high—and surely one reason why the scope of drug criminalization remains so broad—lies in legislatures' ability to prohibit without fear that the prohibition will be applied equally everywhere.

The New Jim Crow
Michelle Alexander
9 Ohio State Journal of Criminal Law 7 (2011)

I find that when I tell people that mass incarceration amounts to a New Jim Crow, I am frequently met with shocked disbelief. The standard reply is: "How can you say that a racial caste system exists? Just look at Barack Obama! Just look at Oprah Winfrey! Just look at the black middle class!"

The reaction is understandable. But we ought to question our emotional reflexes. The mere fact that some African Americans have experienced great success in recent years does not mean that something akin to a caste system no longer exists. No caste system in the United States has ever governed all black people. There have always been "free blacks" and black success stories, even during slavery and Jim Crow. During slavery, there were some black slave owners—not many, but some. And during Jim Crow, there were some black lawyers and doctors—not many, but some. The unprecedented nature of black achievement in formerly white domains today certainly suggests that the old Jim Crow is dead, but it does not necessarily mean the end of racial caste. If history is any guide, it may have simply taken a different form.

Any honest observer of American racial history must acknowledge that racism is highly adaptable. The rules and reasons the legal system employs to enforce status relations of any kind evolve and change as they are challenged. Since our nation's founding, African Americans have been repeatedly controlled through institutions, such as slavery and Jim Crow, which appear to die, but then are reborn in new form-tailored to the needs and constraints of the time.

For example, following the collapse of slavery, the system of convict leasing was instituted—a system many historians believe was worse than slavery. After the Civil War, black men were arrested by the thousands for minor crimes, such as loitering and vagrancy, and sent to prison. They were then leased to plantations. It was our nation's first prison boom. The idea was that prisoners leased to plantations were supposed to earn their freedom. But the catch was they could never earn enough to pay back the plantation owner the cost of their food, clothing and shelter to the owner's satisfaction, and thus they were effectively re-enslaved, sometimes for the rest of their lives. It was a system more brutal in many respects than slavery, because plantation owners had no economic incentive to keep convicts healthy or even alive. They could always get another one.

Today, I believe the criminal justice system has been used once again in a manner that effectively re-creates caste in America. Our criminal justice system functions more like a caste system than a system of crime control.

For those who find that claim difficult to swallow, consider the facts. Our prison system has quintupled for reasons that have stunningly little to do with crime. In less than 30 years, the U.S. penal population exploded from around 300,000 to more than 2 million. The United States now has the highest rate of incarceration in the world, dwarfing the rates of nearly every developed country, including highly repressive regimes like China and Iran.

In fact, if our nation were to return to the incarceration rates of the 1970s—a time, by the way, when civil rights activists thought that imprisonment rates were egregiously high—we would have to release four out of five people who are in prison today. More than a million people employed by the criminal justice system could lose their jobs. That is how enormous and deeply entrenched the new system has become in a very short period of time.

As staggering as those figures are, they actually obscure the severity of the crisis in poor communities of color. Professor Loïc Wacquant has argued that the term "mass incarceration" itself is a misnomer, since it implies that nearly everyone has been subject to the new system of control. But, of course that is not the case. The overwhelming majority of the increase in imprisonment has been poor people of color, with the most astonishing rates of incarceration found among black men. It was estimated several years ago that, in Washington, D.C.—our nation's capital-three out of four young black men (and nearly all those in the poorest neighborhoods) could expect to serve time in prison. Rates of incarceration nearly as shocking can be found in other communities of color across America.

So what accounts for this vast new system of control? Crime rates? That is the common answer. But no, crime rates have remarkably little to do with skyrocketing incarceration rates. Crime rates have fluctuated over the past thirty years, and are currently at historical lows, but incarceration rates have consistently soared. Most criminologists and sociologists today acknowledge that crime rates and incarceration rates have, for the most part, moved independently of one another. Rates of imprisonment—especially black imprisonment—have soared regardless of whether crime has been rising or falling in any given community or the nation as a whole.

So what does explain this vast new system of control, if not crime rates? The War on Drugs. The War on Drugs and the "get tough" movement explain the explosion in incarceration in the United States and the emergence of a vast, new racial undercaste. In fact, drug convictions alone accounted for about two-thirds of the increase in the federal system, and more than half of the increase in the state prison population between 1985 and 2000. Drug convictions have increased more than 1000% since the drug war began, an increase that bears no relationship to patterns of drug use or sales.

People of all races use and sell drugs at remarkably similar rates, but the enemy in this war has been racially defined. The drug war has been waged almost exclusively in poor communities of color, despite the fact that studies consistently indicate that people of all races use and sell drugs at remarkably similar rates. This evidence defies our basic stereotype of a drug dealer, as a black kid standing on a street corner, with his pants hanging down. Drug dealing happens in the ghetto, to be sure, but it happens everywhere else in America as well. Illegal drug markets, it turns out—like American society generally—are relatively segregated by race. Blacks tend to sell to blacks, whites to whites, Latinos sell to each other. University students sell to each other. People of all races use and sell drugs. A kid in rural Kansas does not drive to the 'hood to get his pot, or meth, or cocaine, he buys it from somebody down the road. In fact, the research suggests that where significant differences by race can be found, white youth are more likely to commit drug crimes than youth of color.

But that is not what you would guess when entering our nation's prisons and jails, overflowing as they are with black and brown drug offenders. In the United States, those who do time for drug crime are overwhelmingly black and brown. In some states, African Americans constitute 80 to 90% of all drug offenders sent to prison.

I find that many people are willing to concede these racial disparities once they see the data. Even so, they tend to insist that the drug war is motivated by concern over violent crime. They say: just look at our prisons. Nearly half of the people behind bars are violent offenders. Typically this is where the discussion ends.

The problem with this abbreviated analysis is that violent crime is not responsible for the prison boom. Violent offenders tend to get longer sentences than nonviolent offenders, which is why they comprise such a large share of the prison population. One study suggests that the entire increase in imprisonment can be explained by sentence length, not increases in crime. To get a sense of how large a contribution the drug war has made to mass incarceration, consider this: there are more people in prison today just for drug offenses than were incarcerated in 1980 for all reasons. The reality is that the overwhelming majority of people who are swept into this system are non-violent offenders.

In this regard, it is important to keep in mind that most people who are under correctional control are not in prison or jail. As of 2008, there were approximately 2.3 million people in prisons and jails, and a staggering 5.1 million people under "community correctional supervision"—i.e., on probation or parole. Millions more have felony records and spend their lives cycling in and out of prison, unable to find work or shelter, unable to vote or to serve on juries. This system depends on the prison label, not prison time. It does not matter whether you have actually spent time in prison; your second-class citizenship begins the moment you are branded a felon. It is this badge of inferiority—the criminal record—that ushers you into a parallel social universe in which discrimination is, once again, perfectly legal.

How did this extraordinary system of control, unprecedented in world history, come to pass? Most people insist upon a benign motive. They seem to believe that the War on Drugs was launched in response to rising drug crime and the emergence of crack cocaine in inner city communities. For a long time, I believed that too. But that is not the case. Drug crime was actually declining, not rising, when President Ronald Reagan officially declared the drug war in 1982. President Richard Nixon was the first to coin the term a "war on drugs," but President Reagan turned the rhetorical war into a literal one. From the outset, the war had little to do with drug crime and much to do with racial politics.

The drug war was part of a grand and highly successful Republican Party strategy—often known as the Southern Strategy—of using racially coded political appeals on issues of crime and welfare to attract poor and working class white voters who were resentful of, and threatened by, desegregation, busing, and affirmative action. Poor and working class whites had their world rocked by the Civil Rights Movement. White elites could send their kids to private schools and give them all of the advantages wealth has to offer. But poor and working class whites were faced with a social demotion. It was their kids who might be bused across town, and forced to compete for the first time with a new group of people they had long believed to be inferior for decent jobs and educational opportunities. Affirmative action, busing, and desegregation created an understandable feeling of vulnerability, fear, and anxiety among a group already struggling for survival.

Republican party strategists found that thinly veiled promises to "get tough" on "them"—the racially defined others—could be highly successful in persuading poor and working class whites to defect from the Democratic New Deal Coalition and join the Republican Party. H.R. Haldeman, President Richard Nixon's former Chief of Staff, reportedly summed up the strategy: "[T]he whole problem is really the blacks. The key is to devise a system that recognizes this while not appearing to."

A couple years after the drug war was announced, crack cocaine hit the streets of inner-city communities. The Reagan administration seized on this development with glee, hiring staff who were responsible for publicizing inner-city crack babies, crack mothers, the so-called "crack whores," and drug-related violence. The goal was to make inner-city crack abuse and violence a media sensation that, it was hoped, would bolster public support for the drug war and would lead Congress to devote millions of dollars in additional funding to it.

The plan worked like a charm. For more than a decade, black drug dealers and users became regulars in newspaper stories and saturated the evening TV news-forever changing our conception of who the drug users and dealers are. Once the enemy in the war was racially defined, a wave of punitiveness took over. Congress and state legislatures nationwide devoted billions of dollars to the drug war and passed harsh mandatory minimum sentences for drug crimes-sentences longer than murderers receive in many countries. Many black politicians joined the "get tough" bandwagon, apparently oblivious to their complicity with the emergence of a system of social control that would, in less than two decades, become unprecedented in world history.

Almost immediately, Democrats began competing with Republicans to prove that they could be even tougher on "them." In President Bill Clinton's boastful words, "I can be nicked on a lot, but no one can say I'm soft on crime." The facts bear him out. Clinton's "'tough on crime' policies resulted in the largest increases in federal and state prison inmates of any president in American history." But Clinton was not satisfied with exploding prison populations. In an effort to appeal to the "white swing voters," he and the so-called "new Democrats" championed legislation banning drug felons from public housing (no matter how minor the offense) and denying them basic public benefits, including food stamps, for life. Discrimination in virtually every aspect of political, economic, and social life is now perfectly legal, once you're labeled a felon.

All of this has been justified on the grounds that getting brutally tough on "them" is the only way to root out violent offenders or drug kingpins. The media images of violence in ghetto communities—particularly when crack first hit the street—led many to believe that the drug war was focused on the most serious offenders. Yet nothing could be further from the truth. Federal funding has flowed to those state and local law enforcement agencies that increase dramatically the volume of drug arrests, not the agencies most successful in bringing down the bosses. What has been rewarded in this war is sheer numbers—the sheer volume of drug arrests.

The results are predictable. People of color have been rounded up en masse for relatively minor, non-violent drug offenses. In 2005, for example, four out of five drug arrests were for possession, only one out of five for sales. Most people in state prison for drug offenses have no history of violence or even of significant selling activity. In fact, during the 1990s—the period of the most dramatic expansion of the drug war—nearly 80% of the increase in drug arrests was for marijuana possession, a drug generally considered less harmful than alcohol or tobacco and at least as prevalent in middle-class white communities as in the inner city.

In this way, a new racial undercaste has been created in an astonishingly short period of time. Millions of people of color are now saddled with criminal records and legally denied the very rights that were supposedly won in the Civil Rights Movement.

None of this is to say, of course, that mass incarceration and Jim Crow are the "same." There are significant differences between mass incarceration and earlier forms of racial control, to be sure. Just as there were vast differences between slavery and Jim Crow, there are important differences between Jim Crow and mass incarceration. Yet all three (slavery, Jim Crow, and mass incarceration) have operated as tightly networked systems of laws, policies, customs, and institutions that operate collectively to ensure the subordinate status of a group defined largely by race. When we step back and view the system of mass incarceration as a whole, there is a profound sense of deja vu. There is a familiar stigma and shame. There is an elaborate system of control, complete with political disenfranchisement and legalized discrimination in every major realm of economic and social life. And there is the production of racial meaning and racial boundaries.

If someone were to visit the United States from another country (or another planet) and ask: "Is the U.S. criminal justice system some kind of tool of racial control?", most Americans would swiftly deny it. Numerous reasons would leap to mind why that could not possibly be the case. The visitor would be told that crime rates, black culture, or bad schools were to blame. "The system is not run by a bunch of racists," the apologist would explain. They would say, "It is run by people who are trying to fight crime." Because mass incarceration is officially colorblind, and because most people today do not think of themselves as racist, it seems inconceivable that the system could function much like a racial caste system.

But more than forty-five years ago, Martin Luther King Jr. warned of the danger of precisely this kind of thinking. He insisted that blindness and indifference to racial groups is actually more important than racial hostility to the creation and maintenance of systems of racial control. Those who supported slavery and Jim Crow, he argued, typically were not bad or evil people; they were just blind. Many segregationists were kind to their black shoe shiners and maids and genuinely wished them well. Even the Justices who decided the infamous Dred Scott case, which ruled "that the Negro had no rights which the white man was bound to respect," were not wicked men, he said. On the whole, they were decent and dedicated men. But, he hastened to add, "They were victims of spiritual and intellectual blindness. They knew not what they did. The whole system of slavery was largely perpetuated by sincere though spiritually ignorant persons."

The same is true today. People of good will—and bad—have been unwilling to see black and brown men, in their humanness, as entitled to the same care, compassion, and concern that would be extended to one's friends, neighbors, or loved ones.

After all, who among us would want a loved one struggling with drug abuse to be put in a cage, labeled a felon, and then subjected to a lifetime of discrimination, scorn and social exclusion? Most Americans would not wish that fate on anyone they cared about. But whom do we care about? In America, the answer to that question is still linked to race. Dr. King recognized that it was this indifference to the plight of African Americans that supported the institutions of slavery and Jim Crow. And this callous racial indifference supports mass incarceration today.

3. Incarceration and the Drug War

The Incarceration of Drug Offenders: An Overview
Dave Bewley-Taylor, Chris Hallam and Rob Allen
The Beckley Foundation Drug Policy Programme, Report Sixteen (2009)

Imprisonment continues to play an important part in the crime policy of every country, but its use varies between different regions and between countries within regions. As Stern noted at the end of the last century, some nations use it lavishly while others use it with considerable parsimony. Today over 10 million people are held in penal institutions throughout the world. [E]vidence shows that recent years have seen increasing numbers of people arrested for drug related offences being sent to prison. The steepest rise has been in the US, where the increased use of imprisonment as a policy option in general has led one author to give it the title "The Great Incarcerator". Today over half of Federal inmates in the United States are in prison due to a drug charge. Less spectacular rises have also taken place in other nations including many in Europe, Asia, Africa, Oceania and the Americas. It has been noted that law enforcement oriented approaches in most of Western Europe have caused persons sentenced for drug law offences to make up an increasing percentage of prison populations.

As one of those nations most explicitly using incarceration as a drug policy tool, data and research from the United States provides many useful insights into the use of the policy option to reduce levels of illicit drug use. In an attempt to reduce drug use and dealing, US administrations have for many years pursued punitive drug control policies; often collectively labelled the "war on drugs." As we note in The Beckley Foundation Drug Policy Programme Report Three, *Law Enforcement and Supply Reduction,* a central objective of contemporary US drug policy is to reduce the scope and scale of drug markets via supply-side initiatives, particularly tough and uncompromising law enforcement. The difficulties in achieving sustained and widespread success in the reduction of both foreign production and the flow of illicit drugs into the country have meant that US policymakers augment the supply-side policies overseas with punitive measures at home.

A key component of this approach has involved the threat of arrest and incarceration. Over the first 70 years of the twentieth century the US incarceration rate was characterized by a relative stability, with approximately 100 per 100,000 citizens suffering imprisonment at a given moment. The following 35 year period has seen a steep rise in this rate, with the figure reaching 491 per 100,000 in 2005. More recent data suggests that this has risen still further since then. This rise has been largely fuelled by policies associated with the "war on drugs", and has been particularly acute since the early 1980s, when concern about cocaine became prominent. Figures show that drug arrests have more than tripled in the last 25 years, reaching a record of some 1.8 million in 2005; in 1980 there were 581,000 drug law arrests, climbing to a total of 1,846,351 in 2005. 81.7% of these arrests were for possession offences, and 42.6% of arrests were for marijuana offences. Of the 450,000 increase in drug arrests during the period 1990–2002, 82% of the growth was for marijuana, with 79% for marijuana possession alone. These figures reflect the shifting law enforcement emphasis towards the drug since the early 1990s. The upward trend in arrest rates has been accompanied by a greater increase in the number of drug offence related commitments to state and federal prison. These rose approximately ten-fold between 1980 and 2000. This upward trend can be explained in large part by mandatory sentencing statutes. These were the product of a stepping up of the "war on drugs" during the Reagan presidency. Mandatory minimums at both the state and federal levels lead to people serving a prison sentence after being convicted of possession of relatively small amounts of illegal substances.

It is important to note that arrest and punishment is not the only aspect of US drug policy—drug treatment and drug prevention strategies do have their place within US domestic policies. Indeed, the US Government spends more on drug prevention and treatment than any other country. Furthermore, recent years have seen an expansion of the drug court movement in which judges oversee the treatment of drug dependent offenders in community based or residential settings as an alternative to short periods of imprisonment. Nonetheless, it is the vigorous pursuit of law enforcement and criminal justice measures that remain dominant.

At both the federal and state levels the US domestic "war on drugs" has increasingly relied upon incarceration as a deterrent. Indeed, in 2000 a Human Rights Watch report concluded that drug control policies bore "primary responsibility for the quadrupling of the [US] national prison population since 1980 and a soaring incarceration rate, the highest among western democracies ...". In that same year, nearly one in four persons imprisoned in the US was imprisoned for a drug offence, with a significant proportion of these individuals being non-violent offenders. In 2000, the number of persons behind bars for drug offences was roughly the same as the entire US prison and jail population only twenty years earlier. For comparative purposes, it is noteworthy that at the beginning of the Twenty-First century, there were 100,000 more persons imprisoned in the US for drug offences than the total number of prisoners in the EU, even though the EU had 100 million more citizens than the US. Today, almost half a million dealers and users are under incarceration in the US.

There is an extensive body of evidence to show that the costs of such drug laws do not fall equally across all segments of US society. Between 1985 and 1995, for instance, there was an increase of 200 percent in the number of females incarcerated in state and federal institutions, most for non-violent offences. Many commentators agree that much of this was the result of stricter enforcement, increased penalties and mandatory prison sentences for drug offenders. Additionally, while punitive US drug policies can be seen to have significantly affected the imprisonment of women in general, the greatest increase in the percentage of inmates incarcerated for drug offences is seen in African American women.

Figures concerning African-American women reflect the more general finding that it is predominantly minorities arrested for drug selling. By way of example, the year-end figures for 2005 demonstrate that of the 253,300 state prisoners serving sentences for drug offences, 113,500 were black, 51,100 were Hispanic and 72,300 were white. In percentage terms, the figures are, respectively, 44.8%, 20.2% and 28.5%. These may be contrasted with the ethnic make-up of the US population in general, which, according to the CIA World Fact Book, is, by percentage: black 12.85%, Hispanic approximately 15.1% and white 79.96%. According to US government statistics in 1990, African-Americans constituted only 15–20% of the nation's drug users, but in most urban areas constituted half to two-thirds of those arrested for drug offences. This relationship is also reflected with reference to marijuana in particular. African-Americans represent 14% of marijuana users in the general population, but 30% of arrests. A similar disproportion can also be seen in the composition of prison sentence statistics. In certain specific American states, the disparities can be much greater. New Jersey leads the US in terms of its record of imprisoning non-violent drug offenders. Nearly half of those entering the system in 2003 (the last year for which detailed data exist) were drug law violators, whereas the national average is 31%. Some 62% of incoming prisoners in New Jersey are African American, while for drug law offenders the figure is almost three-quarters (70%). To put these figures into context, African Americans make up about 13% of New Jersey's population. A similar pattern is repeated in New York City. The trend toward a law enforcement focus on cannabis is striking, with 353,000 people arrested for possession of small amounts of the drug between 1997 and 2006. Of these arrests, 52% were black, who make up about 26% of the city's population; 31% were Hispanic (from 27% of the population) and 15% were white (35% of the population).

While the US is one of the main exponents of incarceration as a policy tool both in terms of rhetoric and application, many other governments echo US-style rhetoric and logic without actually implementing heavy sanctions in the vast majority of cases. In the UK, for instance, under the 1971 Misuse of Drugs Act (MDA) potential custodial sentences for the possession and supply of illegal drugs range from two years to life. However, of the 104,400 people who committed drug offences under the MDA in the year 2000 only nine percent were imprisoned, and the vast majority of these received sentences of less than one year.

Although the drug war has resulted in an exponential increase in the number of drug offenders in prison, it is important to keep the impact of drug enforcement on the overall U.S. incarceration rate in perspective. As John F. Pfaff has observed, the "increase in drug incarcerations explain only a fraction of prison growth, so any reduction in drug commitments will have only a moderate effect on prison population size." John F. Pfaff, *The Micro and Macro Causes of Prison Growth*, 28 Ga. St. U. L. Rev. 1239, 1272 (2012). To be sure, drug offenders account for approximately 20% of our prison population. But, "[e]ven if we released every offender currently serving time for a drug conviction, the US prison population would remain above 1 million[.]" *Id.* at 1270.

Part II

Chapter 3

Drug Crimes

A. Drug Possession

The United States addresses drug use and abuse primarily through laws against simple drug possession. In 2011, there were just over 1.25 million arrests for drug possession offenses in the United States, more than for any other single crime except larceny (1.26 million). Indeed, arrests for simple drug possession made up 10% of *all* arrests nationwide in 2011. These figures tell us drug possession as measured by its impact on the criminal justice system is undeniably one of the most important crimes in the United States today. But what legal issues arise in the context of drug possession offenses?

On the surface, drug possession might seem to be a fairly straightforward crime that is unlikely to raise interesting or difficult questions of law. After all, someone who is found with drugs on their person or in their car or home would seem to present a classic "open and shut" case. To be sure, if the police discovered the drugs as the result of an illegal search or seizure, the defendant could seek to exclude them from evidence. But, in the absence of a Fourth Amendment claim, what defense could a drug possession defendant possibly have?

While it is true that some drug possession cases are clear-cut, others can present surprisingly complicated and fascinating problems. Consider, for example, the following scenarios:

Problem 1

Dave, a youth soccer coach, arrives at Bushrod Park early to get everything set up for his team's weekly practice. As Dave is putting down some cones for a drill, he notices a little baggie lying on the ground. He picks it up and sees that the small bag contains marijuana. Dave walks over to a garbage can across the field to throw it away. Just as Dave is about to reach the garbage can, however, Officer Walters approaches him. Walters notices the baggie in Dave's hand and arrests him for possession of marijuana.

Problem 2

Pam and Paul are a couple in their mid-40s raising three children. Tammy, their oldest, just turned 16 and has begun experimenting with drugs and alcohol. Pam and Paul have done everything they can to convince Tammy to stop her substance use but to no avail. One night, Tammy tells her parents that she is going out to see a movie but does not return and, in response to text messages from Paul and Pam, tells them: "Stop treating me like a baby. I'm having fun and will come home tomorrow morning." Frustrated, Pam and Paul decide to search through Tammy's room. Inside one of the dresser drawers, they discover what appears to be a bag of 20 "ecstasy" (MDMA) pills. Paul puts the pills in his pocket so that he and Pam can confront Tammy with them when she comes home. An hour later, Paul experiences chest pains and calls 911. When the medical crew responds, they discover the ecstasy pills in Paul's pocket and notify the police who arrest Paul for possession of ecstasy.

Problem 3

Southgate is in charge of a small cocaine operation in Indianapolis, Indiana. Southgate has set up a somewhat sophisticated procedure in order to try and avoid arrest and prosecution. Instead of selling the cocaine himself, Southgate employs two lieutenants: Victor, who collects money from the customers and Beatrice, who gives the customers their cocaine. Victor, Beatrice and Southgate operate on a corner in front of an abandoned building. After Victor takes a customer's money, he sends the customer to Beatrice and flashes her a hand signal to let her know how much cocaine the customer has purchased. Beatrice usually carries no more than enough cocaine on her person to supply five customers. The group keeps the rest of the product in a little spot underneath the steps of the abandoned building. Southgate sits on the stoop to guard the cocaine and watch over Victor and Beatrice. Southgate is careful never to touch the cocaine or the money in public and only collects his share of the money from Victor at the end of each day. After receiving complaints from neighbors, the police go to observe Southgate's operations from within an unmarked vehicle. The police quickly identify the activity as a drug operation and they would like to arrest Southgate for possession of cocaine. But, after three hours of observation, they have not seen Southgate so much as lay a finger on the cocaine.

Based on your intuitions, which (if any) of the individuals in these problems do you think has committed a drug possession crime? On the one hand, Southgate seems to be more culpable either than Paul or Dave. On the other hand, Paul and Dave were both found with illegal drugs on their person and Southgate was not. Keep these Problems in mind as you read through the cases in this section and think about how the criminal law should define "possession."

1. An Introduction to Drug Possession

Policing Possession:
The War on Crime and the End of Criminal Law
Markus Dirk Dubber
91 Journal of Criminal Law & Criminology 829 (2001)

Possession offenses have not attracted much attention. Yet they are everywhere in modern American criminal law, on the books and in action. They fill our statute books, our arrest statistics, and, eventually, our prisons. By last count, New York law recognized no fewer than 153 possession offenses; one in every five prison or jail sentences handed out by New York courts in 1998 was imposed for a possession offense. That same year, possession offenses accounted for over 100,000 arrests in New York State, while drug possession offenses alone resulted in over 1.2 million arrests nationwide.

The dominant role of possession offenses in the war on crime is also reflected in the criminal jurisprudence of the U.S. Supreme Court. They are the common thread that connects the Court's sprawling and discombobulated criminal procedure jurisprudence of the past thirty years. [V]irtually every major search and seizure case before the Court, from 1968's *Terry v. Ohio* (which relaxed Fourth Amendment requirements for so-called Terry stops and frisks) to last term's *Illinois v. Wardlow* (which relaxed Terry's relaxed requirements in "high crime areas"), involved a possession offense of one kind or another, in one way or another.

So broad is the reach of possession offenses, and so easy are they to detect and then to prove, that possession has replaced vagrancy as the sweep offense of choice. Unlike vagrancy, however, possession offenses promise more than a slap on the wrist. Backed by a wide range of penalties, they can remove undesirables for extended periods of time, even for life. Also unlike vagrancy, possession offenses so far have been insulated against constitutional attack, even though they too break virtually every law in the book of cherished criminal law principles.

While drug possession is a popular and extremely powerful policing tool, other possession offenses also make significant contributions to the crime war effort.

Millions of people commit one of its variants every day, from possessing firearms and all sorts of other weapons, dangerous weapons, instruments, appliances, or substances, including toy guns, air pistols and rifles, tear gas, ammunition, body vests, and anti-security items, to burglary tools or stolen property, and of course drugs, and everything associated with them, including drug paraphernalia, drug precursors, not to mention instruments of crime, graffiti instruments, computer related material, counterfeit trademarks, unauthorized recordings of a performance, public benefit cards, forged instruments, forgery devices, embossing machines (to forge credit cards), slugs, vehicle identification numbers, vehicle titles without complete assignment, gambling devices, gambling records, usurious loan records, prison contraband, obscene material, obscene sexual performances by a child, "premises which [one] knows are being used for prostitution purposes," eavesdropping devices, fireworks, noxious materials, and taximeter accelerating devices (in New York), spearfishing equipment (in Florida), or undersized catfish (in Louisiana), and the list could go on and on.

[P]ossession is, on the face of it, neither a status offense nor a conduct offense. It is the phantom offense of modern American criminal law, everywhere yet nowhere, an offense so flexible that it no longer is an offense, but a scheme, a means of surreptitiously expanding the reach of existing criminal prohibitions, of transforming them into instruments of incapacitation. Neither fish nor foul, possession is sui generis, the general part of criminal law as police control of undesirables, the paradigmatic modern police offense.

To appreciate its function, and the complexity of its operation, one must scratch the surface of this apparently bland, yet ubiquitous and potent offense. Normally, the offense goes about its work unnoticed as it disappears in its myriad particular manifestations. So, discussions of the "legalization" of drugs as a rule ignore the technique by which drugs are "criminalized." But the criminalization of drugs means the criminalization of their possession. Similarly, any debate about gun "control" always also is a debate about possession offenses.

———————

Conceptually, possession cases usually fall into one of two categories: "actual" possession or "constructive" possession. These categories do not represent separate offenses. Rather, they denote two different scenarios in which a person may be shown to have committed the crime of possession. Actual possession refers to situations in which an individual has drugs on their person. Constructive possession, by contrast, involves circumstances where illegal drugs are found *near* a person—such as in a person's car or home.

Although possession is an age-old concept in property law, courts first began to seriously grapple with the idea of possession in the criminal context during alcohol prohibition. These prohibition era possession cases employed a somewhat narrow definition of the term in which possession was almost synonymous with ownership. Courts consistently found, for example, that holding a bottle of liquor in one's hand to take a drink from it did not constitute "possession" of the liquor, at least where the person taking the drink did not own the liquor. As Judge Samford of the Alabama Court of Appeals put it: "Possession of whisky within the meaning of the prohibition law contemplates a control over the whisky, whereas when the whisky is in the man the whisky controls the man." *Evans v. State*, 24 Ala. App. 196, 197 (1931).

The prohibition era understanding of possession was abandoned, however, during the 1960s and 1970s as courts began to redefine the term in the context of drug laws. The following case provides an example of the contrasting views.

Hawaii v. Hogue
Supreme Court of Hawaii
52 Haw. 660 (1971)

Marumoto, J.

Defendant was convicted after a jury trial in the circuit court of knowingly possessing marihuana in violation of H[awaii] R[evised] S[tatute] § 329-5. The portion of the statute relevant to this case reads as follows:

> "No person shall knowingly plant, cultivate, produce, manufacture, possess, have under his control, prescribe, administer, or compound any narcotic drug as defined by section 329-1 except as provided in this chapter."

The case was submitted to the jury upon the following stipulation of facts:

> "That the State is able to prove by the testimony of the three arresting officers, upon the trial of Gregory Dale Hogue, that the defendant Gregory Dale Hogue on or about the 5th day of March, 1970, in the County of Kauai, State of Hawaii, did then and there at the invitation of a friend, one Charles Glagolich, who was the owner of a pipe containing marihuana in hashish form while sitted at a picnic table at Lydgate Park with Mr. Glagolich and three other friends, Stephanie Kay Stearns, Johnny Ray Griffith and Georgia Marie Shannon, did knowingly take two puffs from a pipe containing marihuana in hashish form.

> "That the three officers will testify that, prior to the arrest, they observed Charles Glagolich turn over a pipe containing marihuana in hashish form to one Stephanie Kay Stearns, who after a couple of puffs turned it over to one Johnny Ray Griffith, who after a couple of puffs turned it over to defendant Gregory Dale Hogue. That defendant Gregory Dale Hogue was observed by the three arresting officers with a hashish pipe in his hands, no one else was holding it, and did take two puffs from said pipe knowing it to contain marihuana in hashish form. That after the pipe had been passed and the actions were observed by the three arresting officers, defendant together with his friends were placed under arrest for unlawful possession or control of marihuana. Defendants were properly advised of their constitutional rights.

> "That the State's contention is that the offense committed by defendant Gregory Dale Hogue is the knowingly taking of two puffs from a pipe containing

marihuana in hashish form owned by one Charles Glagolich. Defendant, if called, will testify that he took only one puff from said pipe.

"That the residue within the pipe was analyzed by Dr. Quentin Belles. Said analysis revealed an oily residue which a chemical test showed was charred marihuana."

Among the instructions given by the circuit court to the jury were the following:

"Hawaii statutes do not state that smoking marihuana, per se, is legal or illegal. It does state that possession or control of marihuana, in its various forms, is illegal.

"Considering the totality of the circumstances, a person may smoke marihuana *without* 'possessing' or 'controlling' it, or he may smoke marihuana in such a way that he *does* have possession or control over it.

"To 'possess' means to have the actual control, care and management of the marihuana (hashish), and not a passing control fleeting and shadowy in its nature."

[This] appeal is based on the denial by the circuit court of [a] motion to dismiss made before the trial.

The motion for dismissal was made on the ground that the mere passing and puffing from a marihuana pipe owned and supplied by another was insufficient as a matter of law to constitute a possession of marihuana proscribed in HRS §329-5. The stipulation quoted above provided the factual basis for the motion.

The stipulation stated that the defendant was observed by three police officers "with a hashish pipe in his hands, no one else was holding it, and did take two puffs from said pipe knowing it to contain marihuana in hashish form", after two other persons sitting at the same table took two puffs each from the same pipe. The facts stipulated, as having been observed by the officers, show conscious and substantial possession, not a mere involuntary or superficial possession, and much more than a passing control, fleeting and shadowy in nature.

Thus, the circuit court did not err in denying the motion to dismiss.

The defense argues that the legislature has not expressly outlawed the smoking of marihuana, that its silence in this regard suggests that it was more concerned with curbing the dealer and supplier than with the user at the end of the supply chain, and that in an area where the legislature has remained silent it appears to be a proper judicial function "to dilute the number of marihuana defendants down to only the owner-user while freeing the non-owner user."

The answer to the argument is that the question before us is in an area where the legislature has spoken, not where it has remained silent. In an area where the legislature has spoken, our function is to give effect to the legislative will.

The acts proscribed in HRS §329-5 are basically those which are prohibited in §2 of the Uniform Narcotic Drug Act. Contention has frequently been advanced that the word "possess," as used in §2 of the uniform act, does not refer to possession of a narcotic drug for the personal use of the possessor. Courts have rejected such contention. It is stated in *State* v. *Reed* as follows, as one of the reasons for rejection:

"[S]ection 4 of the Drug Act provides that 'it shall be unlawful for any person to possess any narcotic drug, *except as authorized by this chapter.*' There follows a number of sections which permit possession under certain conditions by physicians, pharmacists, and others who must handle narcotics in the regular course of business. Section 36 expressly permits possession for the possessor's personal consumption or use if he has obtained the drug from an authorized dispenser for medical treatment and if he keeps the unused drug in the container in which he received it. This exception shows that the Legislature considered the problem of possession by a user." [34 N.J. 554 (1961).]

Furthermore, the concern of the legislature with dealers and suppliers of narcotic drugs is shown specifically in its enactment of HRS § 329-3, which reads: "It shall be unlawful for any person to possess *with the intent to sell or to sell or dispense* any narcotic drug, except as provided in this chapter." (Emphasis supplied) The legislature would have had no reason to enact [HRS § 329-3] if [HRS § 329-5] were directed solely against dealers and suppliers.

Affirmed.

Levinson, J., dissenting.

I would reverse the appellant's conviction on the ground that a person who receives from another a pipe containing marihuana for the sole purpose of inhaling therefrom and subsequently returning it does not, as a matter of law, unlawfully "possess" or "have under his control" a narcotic drug, within the meaning of HRS § 329-5. That statute provides in relevant part:

> No person shall knowingly plant, cultivate, produce, manufacture, possess, have under his control, prescribe, administer, or compound any narcotic drug as defined by section 329-1 except as provided in this chapter.

The Narcotics Act, of which the above provision is a part, does not define the words "possess" or "control." It falls upon this court, therefore, to give these words a sensible and reasonable meaning within the context of the Act. To do so it is first necessary, I believe, to determine the regulatory purposes of the Narcotics Act. Specifically, does the Act disclose any discernible pattern of legislative concern which would throw light on whether the appellant's brief dominion over the pipe containing marihuana amounted to possession or control as proscribed by HRS § 329-5? My analysis of the Narcotics Act and the case law relevant to illegal possession leads me to conclude that the possession and control contemplated by the legislature is of a more substantial character than the momentary possession necessary to take one or two puffs.

I do not believe that the possession or control contemplated by the legislature was meant to encompass the mere taking in hand of a pipe or cigarette for the immediate purpose of smoking marihuana. Instead I think that the possession and control prohibited by the statute is the *power to distribute* the drugs as the possessor sees fit. In the instant case this status belonged to the owner of the marihuana who offered it to the appellant for the latter's immediate consumption. At all times control over distribution remained in the offeror. He is the one, not the mere user, who falls within the prohibition of the Act.

The majority does not agree with this analysis. It does concede, however, that mere "superficial possession" and "passing control" are exempt from the operation of the statute. Nevertheless it holds that the present conduct is not "superficial" or "passing." I am at a loss to conceive what these phrases import if they do not describe the appellant's acts in the present case. What possession could be more superficial, or what control more passing, than the fleeting act of holding and puffing on a marihuana pipe and "passing" it to another? A sensible construction of HRS § 329-5, consistent with the statutory scheme of regulating the marketing and distribution of narcotic drugs, requires that possession be equated with ownership, and control be defined as such management or dominion over the prohibited substance as gives to the controller the power to dispose of it to others. Such an interpretation sweeps broad enough to encompass those in a position to dispense the prohibited drugs, while passing over persons whose only contact is immediate consumption. In addition, this construction of the Narcotics Act is supported by the case law dealing with fact situations closely analogous to the instant case.

During the "Great Experiment" of the Prohibition era numerous cases arose where a group of persons would be arrested for passing and drinking from a bottle of illegal liquor owned and distributed by one member of the group. The defendants in such cases were charged with unlawful possession of liquor, under statutes worded similarly to our own. The courts were called upon to construe the meaning of possession within the context of a statute aimed at controlling the traffic in intoxicating liquor. Adopting a statutory analysis which parallels the one asserted above, these courts concluded that possession did not include the mere taking in hand for drinking purposes. What was prohibited was ownership or control of such a degree as to give the controller the power of distribution to others.

[In] *State v. Jones*, 114 Wash. 144, 148 (1921), the Washington Supreme Court held that:

> [P]ossession, as the word is used in the statute, means something more than the mere taking in the hand for the purpose of immediately drinking the thing thus possessed upon the express invitation of the owner so to do ... the court should at least have defined possession as including control of the thing possessed with the right to dispose of it in any manner the possessor saw fit. As we understand the laws of hospitality, when one is offered a glass of liquor, he has a right to accept and drink it, or refuse it, and his possession, if he accepts it, is not broader than the invitation upon which he acts.

Similarly, one who is offered a pipe of marihuana for immediate consumption obtains only the dominion necessary for that act. Actual possession and control lies at all times in the offeror. It is he, as the distributor of the prohibited substance, who falls within the regulatory purposes of the Act.

In effect, the majority opinion's definition of possession extends the coverage of the Narcotics Act to penalize the smoking or use of marihuana. This result is, I believe, clearly beyond that contemplated by the legislature. This belief is supported by the Narcotics Act itself because the provisions of the Act indicate that at the time the legislature acted it was familiar with the specific limiting language necessary to deal with the consumption of marihuana. Yet it chose not to employ this language to prohibit the use of narcotic drugs.

HRS § 329-4 of the Narcotics Act prohibits the sale of narcotic drugs to minors. This provision also makes it a crime to induce "any person under the age of twenty years to buy, traffic in, receive, *take, inject, inhale, or smoke* any narcotic drug...." (emphasis added). This is the language the legislature would have used had it desired to prohibit the acts of the appellant. The legislature chose, however, not to proscribe the "taking," "inhaling," "injecting," or "smoking" of marihuana because it was not concerned with penalizing the user of drugs. Therefore, if the legislature did not intend to prohibit the use of marihuana directly, this court should not indirectly do so by broadly defining possession so as to include the superficial custody required for the immediate inhalation of marihuana.

In deciding this case it is important to recognize what is not in issue. The appellant does not contend that possession as used in HRS § 329-5 is limited only to dealers and suppliers of narcotic drugs. Nor is it argued that a person falls outside the statute if he possesses narcotic drugs for his personal consumption. The motive for possession as the word is used in this section is irrelevant. What is important is the power to dispense narcotic drugs to others. This is what is meant by unlawful possession. Thus one who buys a single marihuana cigarette, even for his own immediate consumption, violates the statute because he has acquired the power to dispense, not necessarily by sale, to others. Similarly one who lacks this power does not have unlawful possession, even though he takes a puff on a marihuana pipe. What this case puts in issue is not whether possession for personal use violates the statute but whether personal use without possession has been made a crime.

The majority opinion attempts to answer this question by arguing that all contact with marihuana is prohibited unless specifically authorized by HRS ch. 329. The cases cited in support of this position are based upon different factual situations since they deal only with the question whether ownership for personal use constitutes unlawful possession. Nevertheless, the decision in *State v. Reed*, one of the cases cited by my Brother Marumoto, is enlightening for its analysis of the reasons behind defining unlawful possession so as to include possession for personal use.

> [T]he inclusion of unauthorized possession for personal consumption within the proscriptions of the Drug Act seems necessary to fulfill the legislative goal of suppressing illegal narcotics traffic. Every possessor of narcotics has the power to dispense them to another. That power in the hands of any person is a potential source of illegal traffic.

As we have seen, by holding in his hand and puffing on the marihuana pipe in the presence, at the invitation, and under the control of the owner, the appellant did not acquire this statutorily proscribed power to dispense to another. Therefore, as the New Jersey Supreme Court points out, he does not fall within the class of persons whom the legislature desired to penalize for unlawful possession.

Currently the wisdom of dealing with the problem of marihuana use through the criminal process is being assiduously questioned. There may even exist a serious question as to the constitutionality of marihuana laws.[11] At the very least, scholars who have studied the problem raise grave doubts as to the social utility of criminalizing marihuana use. As Professor John Kaplan of the Stanford University Law School concludes, in his excellent book, *Marijuana: The New Prohibition* (1970), "the social and financial costs directly and indirectly attributable to the criminalization of marijuana far outweigh the benefits of this policy." In addition, Professor Kaplan warns in his book, "[t]he most serious cost of the criminalization of marijuana is probably that it make felons of a large portion of our population, especially our youth."[14]

This court need not be blind to the practical consequences of its interpretations of law. As the above analysis indicates the purposes of the Narcotics Act will not be undermined if the temptation is resisted to extend the coverage of the Act so as to penalize persons who, perhaps through social pressures, accept an invitation to puff on a marihuana pipe or cigarette. I see little social value in the majority opinion's rigid interpretation of existing drug laws. As Professor Michael P. Rosenthal cogently noted, *A Plea for Amelioration of the Marihuana Laws*, 47 Tex. L. Rev. 1359, 1372 (1969):

---

11. M. Town, "*Privacy and the Marijuana Laws*," reprinted in The New Social Drug (1970); Wallenstein, *Marijuana Possession as an Aspect of the Right to Privacy*, 5 Crim. L. Bull. 59 (1969), Note *Marijuana and the Law: The Constitutional Challenge to Marijuana Laws in Light of the Social Aspects of Marijuana Use*, 13 Vill. L. Rev. 851 (1968).

14. Professor Kaplan reports that recent studies indicate that approximately thirty percent of California's high school students and sixty-nine percent of the students at Stanford University have used marihuana at least once. J. Kaplan, *supra* note 10, at 23. Studies have not yet been conducted in Hawaii. Nevertheless, extrapolating from the available information, I do not believe that in enacting HRS ch. 329 the legislature contemplated that it would be used to label as criminals one-third of today's high school students and two-thirds of today's college students.

Certainly, the consequences of criminalization would seem to be least warranted in the case of the experimenter. A small transgression or even a small number of transgressions, especially—but not exclusively—when committed by the young and developing, should not be the basis for permanently scarring a person's life. This is part of the rehabilitative ideal. While that ideal is usually spoken of in connection with sentencing after conviction of a crime, it should be given weight in formulating definitions of criminality also.

Based on the above statutory analysis, case law and policy considerations, I would reverse the appellant's conviction.

2. Possession for Disposal

Under *Hogue*'s interpretation of possession, a person need not own or have lasting authority over an item to possess it. It is enough that she holds the object in her hand, even if only for an instant. The dissent in *Hogue* argues that this definition of possession is flawed because it criminalizes casual drug users who do not exert any lasting control over the drugs that they use.

Problems 1 and 2 from the beginning of this section indicate that this view of possession has the potential to sweep even further than the *Hogue* dissent envisions, however, by making criminals out of people like our hypothetical good Samaritan soccer coach or concerned parents. After all, if knowingly holding drugs in one's hand is all that is required to commit the crime of drug possession, then the person who takes a bag of marijuana from the ground in order to throw it in the trash would seem to be just as guilty as the person who takes a marijuana cigarette from their friend in order to smoke it.

To address this problem, courts have developed the "possession for disposal" doctrine (also sometimes referred to as the "fleeting" or "temporary" possession doctrine). This doctrine provides a defense to individuals who possess a controlled substance for the sole purpose of disposing of it, at least in some circumstances.

a. The Basic Rule

Stanton v. Florida provides an introduction to the "possession for disposal" rule. In reading *Stanton*, it is useful to consider what distinguishes Stanton's case from Hogue's. If the answer is that Stanton possessed drugs for an admirable purpose, does that mean the definition of possession turns entirely on the defendant's motive? If so, what is the basis for incorporating motive into the definition of criminal possession?

Stanton v. Florida

Court of Appeal of Florida, Third District
746 So. 2d 1229 (1999)

Cope, J.

David Stanton appeals his conviction for possession of cocaine. We conclude that the evidence was legally insufficient to support the conviction, and reverse it.

The very unusual facts of the case are that defendant Stanton was in an area of Key West during the Goombay Festival. He encountered a drug dealer who asked what defendant was looking for, meaning what drugs the defendant was looking for. After repeatedly saying that he was not looking for any drugs, the drug dealer handed defendant a rock of crack cocaine, saying that it was "on the house," and if defendant wanted more, he should come back.

Defendant, who testified that he had a long-standing cocaine problem but had managed to stay clear of cocaine for some time, decided to turn the drug dealer in. He accepted the cocaine rock and walked to the first police officer he could find. He put the cocaine rock down on a barricade by which the police officer was standing. There is some disagreement about the details of the conversation, but the defendant indicated that he wanted to assist the police in apprehending the drug dealer, such as by acting as an undercover buyer.

The police arrested the defendant for possession of cocaine and did not take up the offer of assistance in arresting the drug dealer. The State took the position at trial that since the defendant was in physical possession of a cocaine rock, it followed that he had committed the crime of possession of cocaine, regardless of the circumstances.

We do not think that a person who takes temporary possession of contraband for the sole purpose of turning it into the authorities, and promptly does so, is guilty of a crime. If a person finds contraband washed up on the beach, or floating in the sea, and takes the contraband forthwith to the authorities, we do not think that the law does, or is intended to, criminalize temporary possession for that purpose. Likewise if a parent discovers contraband in possession of his or her child, and disposes of it, we do not think the law criminalizes the parent's temporary possession.

In the trial court, the State's position was that if defendant had physical possession of the contraband, he was guilty; that the circumstances did not matter; and that his motive for turning the cocaine over to the police were not relevant and could not be considered by the jury.

On this appeal, the State concedes, correctly, that it is not a crime for a citizen to take temporary possession of contraband in order to turn it over to the police. The State argues, however, that there are some factual differences in the testimony of the arresting officer and the defendant, which created issues for consideration by the jury. We find that argument unpersuasive.

The undisputed fact is that the defendant voluntarily approached a uniformed police officer and turned over a cocaine rock. We are unable to see any plausible explanation for this act, other than, as defendant said, to turn it over to proper authorities and offer to assist in the apprehension of the drug dealer.

We conclude that the evidence is legally insufficient to support the conviction.

Reversed.

––––––––––

Many readers will find themselves agreeing with the result in *Stanton*. But does the possession for disposal concept have any basis in law or is it something judges invented from thin air in order to avoid reaching results they would personally consider to be unjust? Whatever the answer, nearly every court that has considered the possession for disposal rule has decided to adopt it. *But see, Kansas v. Calvert*, 27 Kan. App. 2d 390, 392 (Kan. Ct. App. 2000) (declining to adopt "the so-called innocent possession defense" but stating "[o]ur ruling does not prevent a defendant from presenting a common-sense defense to a charge of a possessory crime").

While *Stanton* presents a straightforward example of the possession for disposal rule, cases in which a defendant seeks to raise the defense can often pose difficult line-drawing problems for courts. These problems are arguably exacerbated by the fact that the possession for disposal rule is judge-made and so there is no statutory definition of the concept that might help to provide answers.

b. Length of Possession

Perhaps the most common problem that courts wrestle with in possession for disposal cases concerns the length of time that one may possess an item and still benefit from the defense. Thinking back to Problems 1 and 2 above, for example, the defendants in both situations possessed drugs in order to dispose of them. In Problem 2, however, the defendant possessed drugs for a much longer time. Rather than immediately throwing the drugs away or turning them over to the authorities, the parents in that hypothetical example decided to keep them temporarily so that they could confront their daughter. Should this distinction matter? On the one hand, the defendants in both Problems would appear to stand on equal footing in terms of their blameworthiness. On the other hand, is there a danger that the absence of a time-limitation could open the door for every drug possession defendant to simply make up a possession for disposal defense?

Courts that recognize the possession for disposal defense have answered the length of possession problem in different ways.

In *People v. Cole*, the police found a bag containing .651 grams of cocaine in a safe in defendant Richard Andrew Cole's home along with a small amount of cocaine in the purse of Cole's 18-year-old daughter Jennifer. At trial, Jennifer testified that the cocaine in the safe was also hers. "She said that her father confiscated it the day before the search when he caught her using it in the bathroom. According to Jennifer, appellant took the cocaine, stormed out of the bathroom, and threatened to call the police. She was already on juvenile court probation for drug use." Andrew Cole testified that "[h]e told his wife, when he seized the baggies from Jennifer, that he was going to call the police, but his wife urged him not to do so. She wanted to dispose of the drugs immediately but later agreed to discuss the matter with him over the weekend and then to decide whether to discard the cocaine or turn it over to the police." Cole's wife also corroborated this version of events and testified "she had asked appellant not to call the police because she feared Jennifer would be removed from their home since she was already on probation." The police found the cocaine in the safe the day after Andrew's confrontation with Jennifer. The trial court instructed the jury that the possession for disposal theory required acquittal if Cole "handl[ed] the controlled substance for only brief moments for the purpose of disposal[.]" The appellate court reversed, finding that the defense "is not limited to possession for 'brief moments' only," but encompasses any "possession of illegal drugs *solely for the purpose of disposal*[.]" 202 Cal. App. 3d (1988) (emphasis in original). According to *Cole*, the length of time the defendant had the drugs should be, at most, one factor for the jury to consider in assessing the credibility of the defendant's claimed purpose.

Thirteen years later, in *People v. Martin*, the California Supreme Court overruled *Cole* and adopted a length-based limitation on the possession for disposal rule.

California v. Martin

Supreme Court of California
25 Cal. 4th 1180 (2001)

Baxter, J.

In *People v. Mijares* (1971), this court held that, under limited circumstances, momentary or transitory possession of an unlawful narcotic for the sole purpose of disposing of it can constitute a defense to a charge of criminal possession of the controlled substance. Nearly two decades later, [a lower California appellate] court in *People v. Cole* (1988) read our decision in *Mijares* as holding that "possession of illegal drugs *solely for the purpose of disposal* does not constitute unlawful possession," and further concluded the defense "is not limited to possession for 'brief moments' only."

To date, with the exception of one published decision that, in dicta, seemingly accepted the rationale and holding of *Cole*, every court that has considered the issue has rejected *Cole*'s expansive reading of *Mijares*'s transitory possession defense. We granted review to clarify the nature and scope of the affirmative defense of transitory possession for disposal first announced in *Mijares*. We conclude the rationale and holding of *Cole* misconstrues the defense as devised in *Mijares*, and that *Cole* should therefore be disapproved. Accordingly, the judgment of the Court of Appeal will be affirmed.

On June 3, 1997, defendant Robert Louis Martin was living with his girlfriend, Janelle Davis, and her 19-year-old son, Guy Davis, in Hemet, California. Sometime in the late afternoon a family altercation commenced at the home during a visit by Janelle's nephew, Charles Trip, and his wife, Nicole Trip. Defendant returned home with his three young children shortly after Charles and Nicole arrived. According to Janelle, who testified for the defense, when defendant entered the house she called him into the kitchen, handed him a small packet of white powder she had just discovered in Guy's room, which she suspected to be drugs, and asked defendant to "[g]et rid of it." The two then returned to the living room and began arguing with the visitors.

The melee escalated. Guy Davis entered the argument and, according to his mother's testimony, hit defendant with a pipe, accidentally hitting her as well. Nicole Trip testified Guy was wielding a small "bat" and defendant had picked up a chair and was holding it over his head in a threatening manner. As the visitors and a neighbor, Kenneth Biggs, became involved in the fracas, defendant yelled for everyone to get out of the house. Defendant's children ran from the house, and most of the adults also exited, including defendant. Ultimately, defendant wound up outside in the alley behind the house, facing a group of adults comprised of family members and neighbors as he screamed and swung a metal pipe around himself in an arc, as one would swing a baseball bat. Defendant also picked up and threw rocks at the group, hitting a neighbor, Naomi Biggs, in the leg. Nicole Trip testified that as she tried to go past defendant to enter the house to call police,[2] defendant stepped in her direction and took a "full swing" at her with the pipe. She "jump[ed] back" and the pipe missed her by three or four feet. Defendant did not actually hit anyone with the pipe during the episode.

Police officers Randy Jahn and Scott Jernagan arrived on the scene at 7:00 p.m. They found defendant and a neighbor, Kenneth Biggs, in a fighting stance with others standing around. A three-foot length of pipe was recovered from the ground six inches from where defendant was standing. After questioning defendant and the others at the scene for approximately 30 minutes, Officer Jahn handcuffed defendant and took him into custody, and Officer Jernagan transported him to the Hemet police station. At the station Officer Jernagan searched defendant's pants pockets and discovered a "bindle" containing .12 grams of methamphetamine. When Officer Jahn questioned defendant about the methamphetamine, he responded, "I don't know how I got it, and it's not mine. I don't know how it got there."

Defendant was charged with two felonies and two misdemeanors: assault with a deadly weapon (swinging the pipe at victim Nicole Trip); possession of methamphetamine; mis-

---

2. There was also evidence that defendant himself, at Janelle's request, had called the police when the argument first erupted.

demeanor battery (hitting Naomi Biggs with rocks); and misdemeanor fighting in public. The misdemeanor charge of fighting in public was dismissed pursuant to section 1385 prior to the start of trial. Defendant was found guilty by a jury of the three remaining charges.

The Court of Appeal ... rejected defendant's claim that the trial court erred in refusing to give a defense-requested [jury instruction] pertaining to the possession of methamphetamine charge (the standard version was given) and affirmed the judgment and sentence in all other respects.

The essential elements of unlawful possession of a controlled substance are "dominion and control of the substance in a quantity usable for consumption or sale, with knowledge of its presence and of its restricted dangerous drug character. Each of these elements may be established circumstantially." It has been observed that the statute proscribing the unlawful possession of controlled substances "makes possession illegal without regard to the specific intent in possessing the substance." *People v. Sullivan* 215 Cal. App. 3d 1446, 1452 (1989). Although the possessor's knowledge of the presence of the controlled substance and its nature as a restricted dangerous drug must be shown, no further showing of a subjective mental state is required.

Intent to possess the controlled substance for a minimally prescribed period of time has never been an element of the statutes criminalizing simple possession. Nonetheless, in *Mijares*, we held that, under limited circumstances, facts showing only a "brief," "transitory" or "momentary" possession could constitute a complete defense to the crime.[5]

In *Mijares* the principal question presented was whether the act of momentarily handling a narcotic for the sole purpose of disposal constituted unlawful "possession" within the meaning of Health and Safety Code former section 11500. Defendant Mijares was observed by a woman bystander as he leaned inside a parked car and slapped the passenger (his friend) across the face. Moments later he was seen removing an object from the passenger compartment of the car, which he threw into a nearby field. He then drove his friend, who was suffering from a heroin overdose, to a fire station. The friend, who was not breathing, was revived and taken away by ambulance while Mijares waited at the station for the police. The authorities recovered the object tossed into the field and determined it contained heroin and related paraphernalia, whereupon Mijares was arrested for possession of narcotics. At trial Mijares claimed he believed his friend was overdosing and needed medical help. Suspecting the friend might still have narcotics on his person if he had recently taken drugs, Mijares looked inside the friend's pockets, found the narcotics outfit, and threw it out of the car before driving to the fire station for help.

We explained in *Mijares* that "in throwing the heroin out of the car, defendant Mijares maintained momentary possession for the sole purpose of putting an end to the unlawful possession of [his friend]." We concluded that the physical control inherent "during the brief moment involved in abandoning the narcotic" was not possession for purposes of the statute. We reasoned that if such transitory control were to constitute possession, "manifest injustice to admittedly innocent individuals" could result. As an example, we referred to the witness who saw the defendant throw the object. Had she "briefly picked up the package and identified the substance as heroin and then placed the outfit back on the ground, during the time after which she had realized its narcotic character she, too, would have been guilty of possession under an unduly strict reading of [the statute], notwithstanding the fact that her transitory handling of the contraband might have been

---

5. The *Mijares* theory has been alternately described as the "temporary possession defense," the "momentary possession defense," the "transitory possession defense," and the "disposal defense."

motivated solely by curiosity." We refused to "read the possession statutes to authorize convictions under such guileless circumstances." We further relied on certain federal court decisions that had rejected the notion that criminal possession under federal statutes includes such transitory activity as the momentary handling of drugs. We noted that the Seventh Circuit Court of Appeals had reversed a federal narcotics conviction, declaring, "To 'possess' means to have actual control, care and management of, and not a passing control, fleeting and shadowy in its nature."[6]

Our decision in *Mijares* gave rise to the initial version of [California Jury Instruction No. 12.06], entitled Momentary Possession as Not Unlawful.[7] Nearly two decades later, the court in *Cole* concluded the core holding of our decision in *Mijares* was that "possession of illegal drugs *solely for the purpose of disposal* does not constitute unlawful possession," and that the defense recognized in *Mijares* "is not limited to possession for 'brief moments' only." Defendant Cole claimed he had seized cocaine from his teenage daughter and placed it in his safe while he and his wife decided how to dispose of it. The cocaine was found in the safe by police the following day during a search pursuant to a warrant. The *Cole* court concluded the trial court had erred in defining constructive possession for the jury followed by an instruction based on *Mijares* because the jury might have accepted Cole's claim—that he had only "momentarily handled the cocaine for purposes of disposal or abandonment"—but nevertheless felt it had to convict him because the drugs remained "in his constructive possession in the safe for more than 'brief moments.' ..."

The court held: "For guidance on retrial, we suggest the instruction could be tailored as follows: If the defendant physically controlled the substance solely for the purpose of its disposal, such possession would not be unlawful even though he knew its nature as a controlled substance. Length of time of possession is one of the factors which may be considered when deciding whether the defendant physically handled the substance solely for disposal."

Accordingly, [California Jury Instruction No. 12.06] was revised in the wake of *Cole*. The instruction was renamed Possession—Not Unlawful, reference to "momentary possession" was deleted, and a paragraph was added pursuant to the suggested language in *Cole* stating that, "Length of time of possession is one of the factors that may be considered in deciding whether the defendant physically handled the substance solely for abandonment, disposal, or destruction."

[W]ithin one year after *Cole* was decided a different [California] appellate court disagreed with *Cole*'s expansive reading of the *Mijares* defense [in *People v. Sullivan*]. The defendant in *Sullivan* was stopped for Vehicle Code violations, whereupon it was quickly

---

6. We also found support for defendant Mijares's position in a Prohibition era case, *Garland v. State* (1933) 165 Miss. 136, in which the Mississippi Supreme Court declared that a wife who had been arrested for throwing out a jug of illegal alcohol had possessed it for the sole purpose of putting an end to the unlawful possession of the liquor by her husband. Paraphrasing *Garland*, we observed that "in throwing the heroin out of the car, defendant Mijares maintained momentary possession for the sole purpose of putting an end to the unlawful possession of [his passenger]", and that Mijares's jury therefore should have been instructed that the possession prohibited by Health and Safety Code former section 11500 "does not include mere[] handling for only brief moments prior to abandoning the narcotic."

7. The instruction provided that possession of an item is not unlawful where (1) possession is "momentary" and "based on neither ownership nor the right to exercise control over" the item; (2) the item is "possessed in furtherance of its abandonment or destruction"; (3) the item is possessed "for the purpose of terminating the unlawful possession of it by another person or preventing another person from acquiring possession of it"; and (4) "control is not exercised over the [item] for the purpose of preventing its imminent seizure by law enforcement."

discovered that his Land Cruiser contained chemicals, a gram scale, plastic baggies and other items commonly associated with the manufacture of methamphetamine. He was searched and found in possession of a quantity of methamphetamine. The police proceeded to Sullivan's house and searched a locked shed in which they found more chemicals and paraphernalia associated with methamphetamine labs. Sullivan's defense was that all the chemicals, paraphernalia and quantities of methamphetamine belonged to a person who rented the shed behind his house. Since he (Sullivan) was on probation for a drug offense, he was afraid to call the police. Knowing the methamphetamine materials were dangerous, and fearful for his children, Sullivan loaded them into his Land Cruiser and was heading to an industrial park to dispose of them in a dumpster when he was stopped by police a quarter-mile from his house.

Sullivan contended on appeal that the trial court had erred in refusing his requested instruction, purportedly derived from the holding of *Mijares*, that "'Limited handling of contraband, such as for the purpose of abandonment, will not support a conviction for possession.'" The trial court had rejected the requested instruction because the facts did not indicate a "fleeting possession" such as occurred in *Mijares*. Sullivan therefore sought to invoke the holding of *Cole* which, he urged, held that "fleeting possession" was not a necessary prerequisite for the *Mijares* instruction.

The *Sullivan* court disagreed, reasoning as follows: "We think the *Cole* court, by abandoning the requirement the possession be 'fleeting,' has unreasonably expanded the *Mijares* rule. *Mijares*'s rule arose from a situation involving a fleeting, de minimis possession and a reflexive act of abandonment. The Supreme Court's holding was that this de minimis possession and reflexive response was not a criminal possession[.] [T]his rule is one which is an understandable and simple rule. *Cole* complicates the rule by bringing in inquiries into the defendant's subjective intent in possessing the contraband. These inquiries are not suggested by *Mijares* or supported by the language of the statute. *Mijares*'s focus was on the fleeting nature of the possession (during the instant of abandonment), not on the subjective mental state of the defendant. The statute makes possession illegal without regard to the specific intent in possessing the substance. We conclude the *Cole* court misinterpreted the *Mijares* decision and erred in deleting the 'momentary' possession requirement. We therefore decline to follow *Cole*, preferring instead to apply pure *Mijares*."

We agree with the decision[] in *Sullivan* that reject[ed] *Cole*'s expansive reading of our opinion in *Mijares*. As noted, the statutes (past and present) at issue in the cases we have reviewed all make unlawful the possession of enumerated controlled substances "without regard to the [possessor's] specific intent in possessing the substance." As aptly explained in *People v. Spry*[:] "When a defendant relies on the *Mijares* defense, he or she essentially admits the commission of the offense of simple possession of narcotics: The defendant exercised control over the narcotics, he or she knew of its nature and presence, and possessed a usable amount. However, the defendant additionally asserts that he or she possessed the narcotics for the limited purpose of disposal, abandonment, or destruction. *Mijares* does not serve to negate an element of the offense of possession of narcotics. Instead, it offers a judicially created exception of lawful possession under certain specific circumstances as a matter of public policy, similar to the defenses of entrapment and necessity."

We agree that recognition of a "momentary possession" defense serves the salutary purpose and sound public policy of encouraging disposal and discouraging retention of dangerous items such as controlled substances and firearms. The theory of defense to unlawful possession of narcotics announced in *Mijares* "arose from a situation involving a fleeting, de minimis possession and a reflexive act of abandonment. [Our] holding was that this de minimis possession and reflexive response was not a criminal possession."

Throughout our opinion we repeatedly focused on the fleeting and transitory nature of Mijares's possession of his passenger's "narcotics outfit" during the instant he removed it from the latter's person and threw it into the nearby field. We concluded in *Mijares* that such momentary or transitory handling or possession, coupled with intent to dispose, could establish a defense to the crime of unlawful possession of narcotics. *Cole*'s expansion of the momentary possession defense to lengthier possession incidental to the defendant's intent to dispose of controlled substances effectively rewrites the statutory requirements of unlawful possession by introducing a new element of "specific intent to retain."[9]

We conclude that the defense of transitory possession devised in *Mijares* applies only to momentary or transitory possession of contraband for the purpose of disposal, and that the trial court did not err in refusing defendant's requested instruction based on the holding in *Cole*. To the extent *People v. Cole* [is] inconsistent with the views expressed herein, [it is] disapproved.

Returning to the facts of this case, even assuming arguendo the jury fully credited Janelle Davis's testimony that she found the methamphetamine bindle in her son Guy's room and handed it over to defendant with a request that he dispose of it, defendant was still not entitled to even the pre-*Cole* version of the *Mijares* transitory possession instruction that he received. The Court of Appeal concluded as much as four hours had elapsed between the time Davis first gave the narcotics to defendant (when he first returned to the home at approximately 3:00 p.m., 20 minutes after the Tripps had arrived) and the time of the arrival of the officers on the scene of the altercation at 7:00 p.m. Defendant vigorously contested the Court of Appeal's conclusion that the time of possession was as long as four hours. We agree that the testimony in the record upon which that conclusion was based is equivocal. We note, however, that at the instruction-settling conference, defense counsel conceded the relevant time of possession was "not a fleeting instantaneous possession, such as in *Sullivan*."[11] In any event, according to the officers' testimony, an additional 30 minutes elapsed between the time they arrived and questioned defendant and others, and the time defendant was placed under arrest. At least another 10 minutes elapsed from the time defendant was arrested and transported to the police station until the point he was searched, leading to discovery of the narcotics in his pants pocket. There is no indication in the record that during these periods defendant made any attempt, or took any physical action, to dispose of the methamphetamine bindle, much less enlist the assistance of the officers in doing so. Indeed, there is nothing in the record from which to infer that defendant would have voluntarily relinquished possession of the drugs were it not for the search conducted incident to his arrest and booking that led to recovery of the methamphetamine bindle. On these facts, defendant was not entitled to a *Mijares* instruction on transitory possession for the purpose of disposal.

The judgment of the Court of Appeal is affirmed.

Kennard, J., concurring.

I concur in the result.

In *People v. Mijares* this court held that momentary handling of a controlled substance for the sole purpose of disposal is not possession. Although the majority repeatedly states

---

9. We reiterate: although there is no such specific intent element in the crime of simple possession of controlled substances, brief or transitory possession of narcotics *with the intent to dispose of the contraband* can establish the *Mijares* defense of transitory possession.

11. In oral argument before this court, appellate counsel likewise acknowledged that as far as *Mijares*'s brief or momentary time requirement, the facts of this case do not meet the *Mijares* test. Appellate counsel urged that we instead follow *Cole* and conclude "it all boils down to an issue of intent."

that in *Mijares* this court held that momentary handling of a controlled substance is a "defense" to a charge of possessing that substance, this court did not there create or recognize any affirmative defense to such a charge. Rather, this court in *Mijares* simply noted that the issue of momentary handling "goes to the very essence of the offense." Thus, unlike the majority, I would reaffirm *Mijares* without modification.

––––––––––

The *Martin* court argued that "*Cole*'s expansion of the momentary possession defense to lengthier possession incidental to the defendant's intent to dispose of controlled substances effectively rewrites the statutory requirements of unlawful possession by introducing a new element of 'specific intent to retain.'" In footnote 9, however, *Martin* emphasizes that "although there is no such specific intent element in the crime of simple possession of controlled substances, brief or transitory possession of narcotics *with the intent to dispose of the contraband* can establish the *Mijares* defense of transitory possession." Do you agree that there is a principled distinction between the use of intent in *Martin*'s test and *Cole*'s? Or do both tests interject a defendant's "specific intent" into the crime of possession?

While the *Martin* court clearly disapproves of the rule adopted in *Cole*, does the decision articulate a clear standard to govern future cases? The court holds that the possession for disposal defense "applies only to momentary or transitory possession of contraband." But what constitutes "momentary or transitory" possession? The court does not provide a direct answer, though its analysis indicates that possession for just a few hours may be too long as a matter of law.

Utah v. Miller presents another take on the possession for disposal rule.

Utah v. Miller

Supreme Court of Utah
2008 UT 61

Durrant, J.

Following a jury trial, Curtis Miller ("Miller") was convicted of two counts of felony possession of a controlled substance in violation of Utah Code section 58-37-8(2)(a)(I) (the "possession statute"). Miller seeks to have his conviction reversed and his case remanded for a new trial. He claims that the trial court erred in failing to instruct the jury on his proposed defense of innocent possession. For the reasons detailed below, we remand for a new trial in which Miller will be entitled to an instruction on the defense of innocent possession.

The material facts are not in dispute. Miller works as a general contractor, and in April 2004, he had a crew of about ten men working for him on a basement remodel project. Among the crew were Jason Lemon and Vincent Henderson. On April 10, the crew finished the project and had a party at Miller's house to celebrate. About twenty people, including Lemon and Henderson, came to Miller's home that night.

According to Miller, by 2:00 a.m., only one of Miller's friends, who was asleep on Miller's sofa, remained at his home. Then, at 2:30 a.m., a woman arrived at Miller's door asking if he had called an escort.[1] Miller said, "no," but the woman demanded that he pay her $85.00 for "showing up." Miller refused.

––––––––––

1. Jason Lemon testified that while at the party, Vincent Henderson was "really wasted ... [and] excited that he had called this escort service." He also testified that Henderson "announced it to everybody," but left the party before anyone from the escort service arrived.

After the woman left, Miller started cleaning up his apartment in preparation for a visit from his grandchildren the next day. Fifteen minutes later, the same woman returned with "two other guys," who were yelling and "kicking the door." After Miller opened the door and told the group he was calling 911, they left. Miller did not call 911 at that time. The men returned shortly thereafter and "were even louder[,].... [were] kicking [Miller's] door[,]" and "were very threatening, saying that they were going to beat [him] and make [him] pay." In response to this, Miller called 911 for the first of four times that night.

Sergeant John Beener responded to Miller's first call, checked around the home's exterior, but found no one. Sergeant Beener then entered Miller's home and talked with Miller, who appeared to be "extremely intoxicated, [with] bloodshot, watery eyes, slurred[,] interrupted speech, a lack of comprehension, [and] a loss of balance." Miller told Sergeant Beener about the threats he had received from the escort service. When Sergeant Beener attempted to get more information from Miller, Miller accused Sergeant Beener of being "on the take" from the escort service. Sergeant Beener left Miller's home because he did not consider the issue to be a police matter. He got into his police car and pulled into a parking lot across the street from Miller's home to complete paperwork.

After Sergeant Beener left, Miller began cleaning up again and found a glass pipe and a pill bottle on his coffee table. He recognized the pill bottle as one containing a prescription medication, so he put it in his pants pocket with the intention of later putting it in his medicine cabinet—out of the reach of his grandchildren—and then returning it to its owner. Although Miller did not look at the name on the bottle before placing it in his pocket, he learned after his arrest that it belonged to Henderson. Miller also put the glass pipe in his pants pocket. As Miller was cleaning, the escort service called Miller's home one or two times to demand payment. In response, Miller called 911 the second and third times. Sergeant Beener did not respond to Miller's second and third calls because he "was sitting there staring at the residence" and could see that no one was at Miller's home. When Miller called the fourth time, Sergeant Beener returned to Miller's home and arrested him for abuse of the 911 system and for intoxication.

In a search incident to Miller's arrest, Sergeant Beener found the glass pipe and the prescription bottle with Vincent Henderson's name on it in Miller's pants pocket. The bottle contained four pills of oxycodone, four pills of hydrocodone, and one pill for gastro-intestinal problems.

Sergeant Beener prepared to take Miller to jail and, at Miller's request, went to Miller's bedroom to get Miller's shoes and keys. While Sergeant Beener was in the bedroom, he found "a mirror and a pipe laying out."

Miller was charged with two counts of possession of a controlled substance, both third degree felonies; one count of possession of drug paraphernalia, a class B misdemeanor; emergency reporting abuse, a class B misdemeanor; and intoxication, a class C misdemeanor. In November 2004, Miller was bound over on all charges and was tried to a jury in June 2006.

At the close of Miller's jury trial, the trial court excused the jury, and Miller's counsel proposed that the court give the jury an instruction on the defense of innocent possession. The proposed instruction, which was based on a weapons charge defense, provided that possession was innocent if "(1) the firearm was attained innocently and held with no illicit or illegal purpose, and (2) ... the possession of the firearm was transitory; that is that the defendant took adequate measures to rid himself of possession of the firearm as promptly as reasonably possible."

The trial court rejected the proposed instruction. The jury found Miller guilty of two counts of possession of a controlled substance and possession of drug paraphernalia but acquitted him of abusing the reporting system and intoxication. The court sentenced Miller to two terms of zero to five years, suspended the terms, and ordered Miller to report to jail to serve 365 days followed by thirty-six months probation.

Miller timely appealed, claiming that the court erred in refusing to instruct the jury on his proposed defense of innocent possession of the controlled substances.[2] Miller claims that he was entitled to an instruction on this defense because the evidence supported his claim that "his possession of the drugs was innocent, where he did not take control of the drugs for any illegal purpose; rather, he took possession of the bottle in order to return it to its lawful owner."

"Whether a jury instruction correctly states the law presents a question of law which we review for correctness."

Our analysis focuses on Utah Code section 58-37-8(2)(a)(I), the possession statute under which Miller was charged.

Miller was charged under a statute that prohibits possession of certain controlled substances, including oxycodone and hydrocodone. Utah Code section 58-37-8(2)(a)(I) provides that a defendant is guilty of the crime of possession if he (1) knowingly and intentionally, (2) possesses, (3) a controlled substance.

Utah's criminal law is statutory. Thus, all criminal defenses "must be grounded in the specific code sections" under which the defendant is charged. The possession statute under which Miller was charged provides an affirmative defense to the crime of possession in only one instance—if the controlled substance "was obtained under a valid prescription or order, directly from a practitioner." Because this possession statute does not provide an explicit affirmative defense of innocent possession, the defense exists only if the statute implicitly includes it. And the State concedes that—at least in some measure—the statute does.

During oral argument, the State was asked how Miller, or any homeowner, could avoid criminal liability if a house guest inadvertently leaves a bottle of controlled substance prescription pills in the homeowner's home. The State responded that a homeowner would not violate the possession statute if he or she immediately called the police or the owner of the medication. But during either call, the homeowner would clearly "possess" the medication.[9] By admitting that certain types of possession do not violate the statute, the State conceded that some form of innocent possession defense exists. We agree.

The plain language of the possession statute provides that a defendant is guilty of the crime of possession if he (1) knowingly and intentionally, (2) possesses, (3) a controlled substance. The Controlled Substance Act defines "possession" using terms such as "retaining" and "maintaining," and it provides that possession may be inferred if the person charged has "the ability and the intent to exercise dominion and control over" the item. This definition does not, however, clarify whether the term "possess," as it is used in the possession statute, includes the type of innocent possession at issue here—temporary

---

2. Miller has not appealed his conviction for possession of drug paraphernalia; therefore, we limit our discussion and application of the innocent possession defense to Miller's possession of the controlled substances.

9. Under the theory of constructive possession, a person may be found guilty of possession where drugs or contraband are in the person's home even if not on his or her person. *See e.g.,* State v. Layman, 1999 UT 79 (2000), 985 P.2d 911.

possession for the purpose of returning a controlled substance to its lawful owner. And when we "find a provision that causes doubt or uncertainty in its application, we must analyze the act in its entirety and harmonize its provisions in accordance with the legislative intent and purpose."

In this case, the legislature has clearly evinced its intent regarding how courts are to interpret the penal code. Most important is the legislature's directive that the penal code shall not "be strictly construed." Rather, courts are to construe the code's provisions "according to the fair import of their terms *to promote justice* and to effect the objects of the law and the general purposes of Section 76-1-104." Section 76-1-104 further advises courts to construe the code to "[d]efine adequately the conduct and mental state which constitute each offense and *safeguard conduct that is without fault from condemnation.*"

Strictly construing the term "possess" to include every type of possession, whether culpable or innocent, contradicts the legislature's directive to avoid strictly construing the code, and it is contrary to the policy goals of safeguarding faultless conduct and promoting justice. This is most apparent in the many examples of injustices that may result from strictly construing the term "possess." A daughter who no longer lives at home but who picks up her sick mother's prescription medication and drives it to her mother's home, for example, could be guilty of felony possession under a strict construction of the term "possess."[19] And, as this case demonstrates, a house guest who inadvertently leaves a prescription bottle of pills at a homeowner's home creates an impossible situation for the homeowner wherein she could do nothing short of immediately fleeing her home to avoid "possessing" the pills. Because construing the term "possess" to include brief, innocent possession contradicts the legislature's interpretative guidelines and creates a myriad of absurd prosecutorial possibilities, we hold that the term "possess," as it is used in section 58-37-8(2)(a)(I), excludes transitory possession of a controlled substance for the purpose of returning it to its lawful owner. That is, we hold that the possession statute implicitly includes the defense of innocent possession.[20] We next address the parameters of that defense.

Miller proposed an instruction for the innocent possession of drugs based on an instruction that the Court of Appeals for the District of Columbia recognizes for the innocent possession of firearms. Tailoring the innocent possession of firearms defense to a controlled substance possession charge, the defense applies if (1) the controlled substance was attained innocently and held with no illicit or illegal purpose, and (2) the possession of the controlled substance was transitory; that is, that the defendant took adequate measures to rid himself of possession of the controlled substance as promptly as reasonably possible.

This is an appropriate instruction. It requires that a standard of reasonableness be applied to the innocent possession of a controlled substance, and in so doing, does not im-

---

19. Universally, courts that recognize an innocent possession defense cite public policy reasons for doing so, chiefly to "prevent a conviction for an innocent act." *People v. E.C.,* 761 N.Y.S.2d 443, 445 (Sup. Ct. 2003). In *People v. E.C.,* the New York appellate court recognized an innocent possession defense and hypothesized that a juror who handles illegal drugs as part of a review of the evidence would be guilty of possession under a strict interpretation of the possession statute. *Id.* California also recognizes the innocent possession defense and applies it to "fleeting and transitory" possession of illegal drugs "for the purpose of disposal." *People v. Martin,* 25 P.3d 1081, 1088–89, n.9 (Cal. 2001).

20. We also note that the legislature has provided the statutory defense of justification. The justification defense protects from prosecution conduct that is "justified for *any ... reason* under the laws of this state." Utah Code Ann. §76-2-401(1)(e). This is a broad catchall provision that allows courts to ensure that justice is done. In this case, we believe that justice requires interpreting the possession statute to include the defense of innocent possession.

pose an obligation on individuals to focus their efforts exclusively on returning a controlled substance to its lawful owner once it comes into their possession. Nor does this instruction impose an arbitrary time limit for return of a controlled substance or require only fleeting or momentary possession that may not be practical given the circumstance. If a possessor of a controlled substance takes reasonable action to return that substance to its lawful owner, possession may be longer than momentary, yet the possessor would still be entitled to an instruction on the defense of innocent possession. The instruction leaves to the jury the question of whether a defendant took adequate measures to rid himself of a controlled substance as promptly as reasonably possible.

Because the trial court refused Miller's proposed instruction, we remand for a new trial at which Miller is entitled to the following innocent possession defense instruction: the defendant's possession of the controlled substances found in his pocket did not violate Utah Code subsection 58-37-8(2)(a)(i) if (1) the controlled substance was obtained innocently and held with no illicit or illegal purpose, and (2) the possession of the controlled substance was transitory; that is, the defendant took adequate measures to rid himself of possession of the controlled substance as promptly as reasonably possible. It will be for the jury to decide whether, given this instruction along with the facts Miller presents, his possession was innocent.

c. What Qualifies as Disposal?

In *Miller*, the Utah Supreme Court applied the possession for disposal defense where the defendant sought to return a lawfully prescribed controlled substance to its owner. Should the defense apply to transitory possession of an illegal drug like marijuana for purposes of returning it to its "owner"? Or should the defense be limited to cases where an individual plans to throw the substance away or turn it over to the police? In the next case, *Adams v. Alaska*, the Court of Appeals of Alaska adopts an unusually forgiving interpretation of what counts as "disposal." Though other jurisdictions have not followed the *Adams* court's approach, the case is useful for thinking about what sort of purpose a defendant ought to have in order to qualify for the innocent possession defense.

Adams v. Alaska
Court of Appeals of Alaska
706 P.2d 1183 (1985)

Coats, J.

Daniel Adams was convicted, following a jury trial, of one count of misconduct involving a controlled substance in the third degree, and two counts of misconduct involving a controlled substance in the fourth degree. The misconduct involving a controlled substance in the third degree count consisted of a charge that on August 3, 1983 Adams possessed approximately three and one-half ounces of cocaine with the intent to deliver that substance. The two counts of misconduct involving a controlled substance in the fourth degree involved charges that Adams possessed approximately one-fourth of an ounce of cocaine on August 23, 1983, and that Adams possessed approximately one-eighth of an ounce of cocaine on August 25, 1983. Judge Victor Carlson imposed a sentence of seven years with three years suspended on the possession with intent to deliver count, and sentences of three years with one year suspended on the possession of cocaine counts. The sentences were all concurrent. Adams appeals his convictions and sentences. We reverse Adams' conviction for possession of cocaine with intent to deliver but affirm his convictions and sentences for possession of cocaine.

The trial in this case focused mainly on the charge that, on August 3, 1983, Adams possessed approximately three and one-half ounces of cocaine with the intent to deliver that substance. Adams testified that he was a user of cocaine, and admitted possessing cocaine on August 25, 1983. Adams additionally indicated that he could have had the one-quarter ounce of cocaine on August 23, 1983. However, Adams testified that his possession of the three and one-half ounces of cocaine on August 3, 1983 was involuntary.

In support of his contention that he involuntarily possessed the cocaine Adams testified that Alex Resek was a cocaine dealer and that he got his cocaine from Resek. On August 3, 1983 both Alex Resek and his family and Adams and his family were in Campbell Creek Park. Daniel Adams' car, a Corvette, was parked in the lot; the top was down and the windows were open. According to Adams, Alex Resek borrowed his keys so he could listen to the radio in the Corvette. After going to the car, Resek came back to Adams and told Adams to watch the car because there was something in it. Adams testified that he concluded that Resek had left cocaine in the car, and that he told Resek to get it out. Resek refused and said he would be back. Alex Resek then left the park and did not return. Adams discovered that Resek had left a brown bag in Adams' car. Adams testified that he did not look inside the bag.

Approximately forty-five minutes after Alex Resek placed the bag in the car Mark Flechsing arrived. Flechsing was one of Alex Resek's closest collaborators in the cocaine selling operation and, unknown to Adams or Resek, was also operating as a police informant. Flechsing testified that when he arrived at the park, Alex Resek was gone. Adams gave Flechsing the brown paper bag from the car and told him to get the package out of there. Additionally, Adams instructed Flechsing to meet him at the Hall Closet, a business that Adams owned which sold drug paraphernalia. Flechsing drove off and secretly met with a police officer who took a sample of the contents of the brown package. The sample was tested. It was cocaine. Flechsing then drove to meet Adams. After Flechsing reached the Hall Closet, Alex Resek arrived and had Flechsing place the brown package in his car. The package was not taken into the Hall Closet.

Adams' defense at trial was that he had never voluntarily possessed the cocaine found in his car. He contended that Resek placed the cocaine in his car without his permission, and that when he found out it was in his car he attempted to have Resek take the cocaine out of the car. When that failed he gave the cocaine to Flechsing to return to Resek. On the other hand, the state argued that Adams was deeply involved in Resek's cocaine selling business and that Adams' possession of the cocaine had been entirely voluntary. The state presented evidence that during the time the cocaine was in Adams' car an off-duty police officer coincidently happened to come into the park and talk to another police officer in a marked police car. The state argued that Adams had panicked and had the cocaine removed from his car because of the presence of the police, not because he involuntarily possessed the cocaine.

Judge Carlson instructed the jury on what constituted possession: "'possess' means having physical possession or the exercise of dominion or control over property. A passing control, fleeting and shadowy in nature does not constitute possession." After some deliberation the jury asked for an explanation of "passing control." The court gave the following supplemental instruction, which defense counsel objected to:

SUPPLEMENTAL INSTRUCTION NO. 1

"Passing control" of a controlled substance is control for only such a period of time as is reasonably necessary for the possessor to learn of the nature of the substance and to make a *legal disposition of it by throwing it away, destroying it, or by giving it to police.*

If you find that the defendant had control of a controlled substance only for the purpose of putting to an end another's illegal possession, you may not find him guilty of a crime. For example, if a person finds a heroin addict unconscious on the street, empties the addict's pockets of heroin and throws the heroin away before taking the heroin addict to the hospital, that person may not be convicted for that brief control of the heroin. Similarly, if a person finds a package on the street, opens it, finds cocaine and then puts the package back down and walks away, that person may not be convicted for that brief control of the cocaine.

If you find that the defendant had control of a controlled substance only because another forced it upon him, *you may find the defendant guilty only if you find he did not act reasonably in disposing of it.*

"Passing control" is not a defense for the person who, having possession of a substance he knows is a controlled substance and fearing that he is about to be apprehended by police, removes the controlled substance from his immediate possession.

If you find beyond a reasonable doubt that the defendant possessed a controlled substance long enough after knowing it was a controlled substance to have had a reasonable opportunity to dispose of it through legal channels (be throwing it away or giving it to police, for example), then you may find the defendant guilty; if this has not been proved beyond a reasonable doubt, you must find the defendant not guilty.

Adams argued at trial, and now argues on appeal, that the supplemental instruction was erroneous because it unduly restricted ways in which a person could have "passing control." Adams argues that if the jury believed him that Resek forced the cocaine on him by placing it in his car, the jury could have read the supplemental instruction as requiring him to get rid of the cocaine by "throwing it away, destroying it, or by giving it to the police." He argues that the jury therefore could have believed him that he got rid of the cocaine by returning it to Resek through Flechsing, and yet have convicted him under the supplemental instruction because he did not dispose of the cocaine as the instruction required.

We agree with Adams that it is a reasonable interpretation of the jury instruction that a person who has cocaine forced upon him must throw it away, destroy it, or give it to the police. Therefore, we agree that under the given jury instruction the jury could have believed Adams' version that he came into possession of the cocaine involuntarily and that he got rid of it as soon as possible by giving it to Flechsing to return to Resek, and still have convicted him under the supplemental instruction. The next question is whether Adams' version of events, if believed, constitutes possession of cocaine with intent to distribute. Alaska case authority on this issue appears to be sparse. In *Moreau v. State*, 588 P.2d 275 (Alaska 1978), the supreme court dealt with a case where the defendant momentarily possessed a napkin which contained heroin residue. Moreau was staying in a house which the police entered under a search warrant. When her co-defendant, Stone, spit out the napkin, Moreau picked the napkin up and may have attempted to move towards the bathroom. The police grabbed her and took the napkin. The supreme court held that there was insufficient evidence to convict Moreau of possession of heroin. The court held that momentary possession for purposes of disposing of a controlled substance did not constitute possession. In its holding, the court approved of the definition of possession in *United States v. Landry*, 257 F.2d 425, 431 (7th Cir. 1958):

To "possess" means to have actual control, care and management of, and not a passing control, fleeting and shadowy in nature. (Citation omitted.)

The *Moreau* court also relied on *People v. Mijares*, 6 Cal. 3d 415 (1971). In that case the defendant testified that in attempting to help a friend who had overdosed on drugs, he discovered a handkerchief which contained heroin. He threw the heroin out of the window of a car. The *Mijares* court held that the defendant's version, if believed, was not possession of heroin in violation of the statute.

In addition to the authority that the defendant cites, we have also considered the Model Penal Code. Section 201(4) of the Model Penal Code states, "possession is an act, within the meaning of this section, if the possessor knowingly procured or received the thing possessed or was aware of his control thereof for a sufficient period to have been able to terminate his possession."

The authorities to which the parties have cited us and our own research have not clearly resolved the problem. However, it is clear that more is required than momentary or fleeting possession of a controlled substance; some sort of dominion or control of the substance is required. We note that the state has not cited any cases standing for the proposition that a person who has drugs forced upon him is required to dispose of the drugs by throwing them away or giving them to the police.

It appears to us that if the jury believed Adams' version of the events, Adams was not in possession of cocaine because he was not aware of his control of the cocaine "for a sufficient period to have been able to terminate his possession[.]" Under Adams' version the cocaine belonged to Alex Resek. Adams came into possession involuntarily and terminated his possession as soon as reasonably possible by returning it to Alex Resek through Flechsing. This appears to us to be the sort of fleeting possession which the cases allow. We do not believe that he was required to turn the cocaine over to the police or destroy it in order to not be in possession. His returning it promptly to Resek through Flechsing would be sufficient to terminate his possession.

Since the jury could have understood the trial court's instructions to require Adams to terminate his possession of the cocaine by "throwing it away, destroying it, or by giving it to the police," we reverse Adams' conviction for possession of cocaine with intent to distribute. However, we affirm Adams' two convictions for possession of cocaine since he essentially admitted the incidents on which those convictions were based. Those convictions could not have been affected by the supplemental instruction.

The conviction for misconduct involving a controlled substance in the third degree is REVERSED. The convictions and sentences for misconduct involving a controlled substance in the fourth degree are AFFIRMED.

The possession for disposal doctrine can sometimes work its way into a criminal defense attorney's practice in unexpected ways. How should a criminal defense attorney respond to a client who asks him to take possession of contraband? A recent case from Connecticut presented this problem in the context of possession of child pornography. A church found pornographic pictures of children on its choirmaster's laptop. The church took the laptop to its attorney, Phillip Russell, and told him that it did not want to report the crime. "So Russell chose what he likely saw as the only remaining option to protect the church from illegal possession of the images—he destroyed the hard drive. Federal prosecutors indicted Russell on two counts of obstruction of justice, each carrying a twenty-year prison term." Stephen Gillers, *Guns, Fruits, Drugs, and Documents: A Criminal Defense Lawyer's Responsibility for Real Evidence*, 63 STAN. L. REV. 813 (2011) (discussing the legal and ethical problems that criminal attorneys face when asked by a client to take possession of contraband, stolen property, or evidence of a crime).

3. Actual Possession

Most sufficiency of the evidence problems in possession cases arise in the context of constructive possession (discussed below). This is because the great majority of actual possession cases involve instances where the defendant has been found by the police with drugs on his or her person. Nevertheless, questions of proof can arise in actual possession cases as well. What happens, for example, if an individual confesses to the police that she is a drug user and has been in possession of illegal drugs every day for the past year, but at the time of the confession, she doesn't have any drugs on her? In *Adams*, the court affirmed two possession convictions on just this sort of evidence, reasoning Adams had "essentially admitted the incidents on which those convictions were based." In *United States v. Baggett*, the United States Court of Appeals for the Tenth Circuit determined that a defendant's confession to possessing a controlled substance was *not* enough to sustain her conviction.

United States v. Baggett
United States Court of Appeals for the Tenth Circuit
890 F.2d 1095 (1989)

Seymour, J.

After a jury trial, defendant Barbara Lynn Baggett was found guilty of simple possession of heroin under 21 U.S.C. § 844(a). Defendant argues that there is insufficient evidence to support the jury's verdict on the possession count. We agree and we therefore reverse the conviction.

On November 23, 1987, Barbara Baggett made the first of a number of phone calls to Steve Daniels, a suspected drug dealer. On November 29, she made three more calls to Daniels, all recorded by the police, in which she arranged to purchase some cocaine and heroin, and to meet Daniels at a specified time and place. At the prescribed location, an Oklahoma City police officer and an agent with the Oklahoma Bureau of Narcotics and Dangerous Drugs twice observed Steve Daniels meeting with a "white female" driving a car registered to Barbara Baggett. It is during these two meetings that the exchange of heroin allegedly occurred, and it is on this day, November 29, that Baggett is charged with the possession of heroin and with making three telephone calls to facilitate the distribution of the drug.

In assessing the sufficiency of the evidence for a criminal conviction, we must view all the evidence, both direct and circumstantial, in the light most favorable to the Government. Taken together with all reasonable inferences to be drawn from such evidence, we must determine whether the evidence is sufficient to establish guilt beyond a reasonable doubt. In addition, "our review here does not include assessing the credibility of witnesses; that task is reserved for the jury."

It is not necessary that the Government have direct evidence to support a conviction for possession. But where, as in this case, the Government fails to seize and analyze the chemical composition of the alleged narcotic substance, there must be enough circumstantial evidence to support an inference that the defendant actually did possess the drugs in question. *See, e.g., United States v. Hill*, 589 F.2d 1344, 1348–50 (8th Cir. 1979); *United States v. Iacopelli*, 483 F.2d 159, 161 (2d Cir. 1973).

The circumstantial evidence that Baggett actually possessed the drugs in question is not strong. The three telephone calls of November 29 do make clear that she arranged for a purchase of a controlled substance on that day. Additionally, some four months later, on

March 31, 1988, Baggett confessed to two police officers that during November of 1987 she had used "about a half a pill or balloon of heroin a day and that towards the end of the month she was up to using a whole pill or balloon of heroin per day." However, the Government must put forth some evidence to show that Baggett actually possessed heroin on the day in question. Such evidence may include:

> "evidence of the physical appearance of the substance involved in the transaction, evidence that the substance produced the expected effects when sampled by someone familiar with the illicit drug, evidence that the substance was used in the same manner as the illicit drug, testimony that a high price was paid in cash for the substance, evidence that transactions involving the substance were carried on with secrecy or deviousness, and evidence that the substance was called by the name of the illegal narcotic by the defendant or others in [her] presence...."

United States v. Dolan, 544 F.2d 1219, 1221 (4th Cir. 1976). *See also United States v. Scott,* 725 F.2d 43, 44–46 (4th Cir. 1984).

Little of the relevant information listed in *Dolan* has been presented as evidence here. Both Detective Janice Stupka and Agent Lonnie Wright observed a meeting between Steve Daniels and a "white female." The first meeting took place inside Daniels' car and lasted for about three minutes; the second occurred outside the vehicles, and consisted of only "a brief contact with each other." Neither Wright nor Stupka saw any money or narcotics exchanged at either of the two meetings. No witness for the Government testified to seeing a drug exchange between Daniels and Baggett, or to seeing Baggett with heroin at any time on November 29. The Government put forward no evidence other than Stupka and Wright's testimony to show that a transaction actually took place.

If the prosecution is not going to present direct evidence of drug possession, its circumstantial evidence must include some testimony linking defendant to an observed substance that a jury can infer to be a narcotic. The Government here has presented us with no case in which a conviction was upheld without evidence that the defendant possessed a substance and that the substance was a narcotic. Courts typically require much stronger evidence before holding it sufficient to meet the Government's burden of proof. *See, e.g., Scott,* 725 F.2d at 46 (finding that "every fact listed in *Dolan* for establishing circumstantially the illegal character of the [substance] possessed by the defendant was present").

In *Iacopelli*, a conviction was affirmed although no substance was actually observed at the time the defendant allegedly obtained possession of a controlled substance by misrepresentation or deception. 483 F.2d at 161. But in that case, records showed that the defendant, a pharmacist, had ordered a box of a controlled substance, sodium secobarbital; a company "traffic manager" had observed the delivery of a box with outside descriptions consistent with the order; records reflected that sodium secobarbital had, in fact, been delivered; and records revealed that the defendant had been the one to pick up the box. The defendant also later gave a witness a capsule-filled bottle with a "label denoting the contents as sodium secobarbital and bearing the same control number as the control number on the sealed box." Such strong circumstantial evidence is not present in this case.

In sum, we conclude that the Government's evidence is insufficient to sustain the possession conviction.[2]

---

2. The Government's case has several other weaknesses. Agent Wright was over a block away from the place of Daniels' and Baggett's alleged transaction, and he could not describe the "white female" with any detail. Officer Stupka was closer to the two people and she could identify Daniels, but she was unable to identify the observed white female as Barbara Baggett. Additionally, both Stupka and Wright incorrectly described the color of the car later identified as Baggett's.

Why wasn't Baggett's admission that she was using "about a half a pill or balloon of heroin a day and that towards the end of the month she was up to using a whole pill or balloon of heroin per day" sufficient evidence to convict her? If the answer is Baggett did not confess to possessing heroin on the particular day in question, why should that fact be controlling?

Another question that has arisen with some regularity in this area is whether a positive drug test is sufficient evidence upon which to base a conviction for possession. Most courts have held it is not. *See, e.g., North Carolina v. Harris*, 178 N.C. App. 723, 725–26 (2006) (collecting cases). As the Kansas Supreme Court explained in *Kansas v. Flinchpaugh*, 232 Kan. 831 (1983):

> Once a controlled substance is within a person's system, the power of the person to control, possess, use, dispose of, or cause harm is at an end. The drug is assimilated by the body. The ability to control the drug is beyond human capabilities. The essential element of control is absent.

> Discovery of a drug in a person's blood is circumstantial evidence tending to prove prior possession of the drug, but it is not sufficient evidence to establish guilt beyond a reasonable doubt. The absence of proof to evince knowledgeable possession is the key. The drug might have been injected involuntarily, or introduced by artifice, into the defendant's system. In the narrow holding of this case, we find that evidence of a controlled substance assimilated in one's blood does not establish possession of that substance, nor is it adequate circumstantial evidence to show prior possession by that person.

Though *Flinchpaugh* represents the majority interpretation, a few states have adopted laws that directly criminalize internal possession of a controlled substance. South Dakota, for example, amended its drug laws in 2001 to provide that "the term [controlled substances] includes an altered state of a drug or substance … absorbed into the human body." *See South Dakota v. Schroeder*, 2004 S.D. 21 (holding that the 2001 amendment "permits a defendant to be convicted of 'unauthorized possession' of a controlled drug or substance when the only evidence is from the ingested or absorbed unauthorized substance in the defendant's body"). Utah makes it a crime for a person to "knowingly and intentionally" have "any measurable amount of a controlled substance in [his or her] body." *See Utah v. Robinson*, 2011 UT 30 (rejecting a constitutional challenge to the "measurable quantity" law).

Courts are more closely split on the questions of if and when a person found with less than a "usable quantity" of a drug—for example, a small amount of drug residue—may be convicted of drug possession. In most jurisdictions, possession of any amount is sufficient to support a conviction for possession. Others, however, provide that a usable amount is required, at least in some circumstances. *Compare, e.g., Richardson v. Colorado*, 25 P.3d 54, 58 (Colo. 2001) ("[W]e reject the defendant's argument that evidence of less than a usable amount creates an inference against knowing possession by the defendant.") *with Harbison v. Arkansas*, 302 Ark. 315, 322 (1990) ("The intent of the legislation prohibiting possession of a controlled substance is to prevent use of and trafficking in those substances. Possession of a trace amount or residue which cannot be used and which the accused may not even know is on his person or within his control contributes to neither evil.") *and Arizona v. Cheramie*, 218 Ariz. 447, 451 (2008) ("A 'usable quantity' is neither an element of the possession offense nor necessary to sustain a conviction for it. Rather, it is simply evidence from which a factfinder may infer intent.").

4. Constructive Possession

a. Introduction to Constructive Possession

Constructive possession cases can present particularly vexing problems for courts and juries. In a typical constructive possession case, authorities find a controlled substance in an area that more than one person has access to, such as a shared home or a car. Imagine, for example, that the police pull over a vehicle for a traffic violation and see marijuana in plain view sitting on the console between the passenger and the driver. There is little doubt that the marijuana belongs to either the driver or the passenger (or both). But is this evidence standing alone sufficient to prove *beyond a reasonable doubt* that both of them possessed the marijuana?

Courts have struggled to create a doctrine that neatly distinguishes between individuals found near drugs who are simply in the wrong place at the wrong time from those who exercise dominion and control over them. *See, e.g.,* Charles H. Whitebread and Ronald Stevens, *Constructive Possession in Narcotics Cases: To Have and Have Not*, 58 VA. L. REV. 751 (1972) (arguing that constructive possession cases "have engendered such conceptual confusion and given rise to so many conflicting rulings 'that for the practitioner the problems are difficult to understand and apparently for the courts impossible to master.'") In 1971, Judge Edward Tamm of the U.S. Court of Appeals for the District of Columbia Circuit questioned whether courts are guided by a coherent set of principles in constructive possession cases: "The rhetorical legerdemain compounded in this area of the law invokes abstractions which appear more designed to achieve a particular result in an individual case than to stabilize and formalize a workable index of objective standards. The more cases one reads on constructive possession the deeper is he plunged into a thicket of subjectivity. Successive cases enumerate a continuing re-interpretation which can only be described as judicial whimsy.... Both prosecutor and defendant's attorney present their cases with the unfortunate knowledge that the law of constructive possession is what we will say it is in our next opinion." *United States v. Holland*, 445 F.2d 701, 703–04 (D.C. Cir. 1971) (Tamm, J., concurring).

Though constructive possession cases remain filled with conflicts, most jurisdictions today have coalesced around at least one basic principle: proximity to contraband, by itself, is insufficient to prove possession. Not all courts agree with even this basic premise, however. In *People v. Valot*, presented below, the Court of Appeals of Michigan adopted a less stringent standard. Though the *Valot* court's approach represents the exception rather than the rule, it remains helpful for thinking about the consequences that a low evidentiary standard for constructive possession cases might have.

Michigan v. Valot
Court of Appeals of Michigan
33 Mich. App. 49 (1971)

Churchill, J.

Defendant, Harold Valot, was charged with having had possession and control of marijuana contrary to the provisions of MCLA § 335.153. He was convicted by nonjury trial.

Defendant asserts on appeal that there was no evidence of his possession or control of the drug to support the conviction.

Three Redford Township policemen went to a motel in their township in response to a call from a motel employee. Upon answering they learned from the motel manager that he was concerned about the continued use of one of the motel rooms by a number of "hippie-type people". The room had been rented about three days before. The rent was paid until noon of that day. The police were called and arrived in the early afternoon. The officers examined the registration card and learned that the motel room was registered in the name of Harold Valot. One officer recognized the name as the name of an escapee from the Detroit House of Correction. They learned that an auto, identified on the registration card, was parked in the motel parking lot. They learned that a man answering Valot's description had been seen entering the room. They were unable to learn if he had left the room. The police were informed that efforts to contact the room by motel employees by telephone were unsuccessful.

The policemen went to the room with the motel manager. The manager knocked on the door. There was no response. The manager opened the door with a key. The manager and the policemen walked in and observed five persons in the room, all apparently asleep on or in beds. One of the officers recognized the defendant by description and the officers observed marijuana about the room. Defendant was arrested. The marijuana was seized.

Defendant personally registered for the room on September 27, 1968, three days before the arrest, and paid one day's room rent. A girl paid rent on the day before the arrest. Defendant testified that he rented the room for two other persons, and that he had been sleeping there since about 7 a.m. or 8 a.m. on the day of the arrest. He said that he knew that Paul Silver carried and used marijuana and that he, Valot, previously chased Silver out, but that Silver was there when he was aroused by the police. He said that he was unaware of the presence of marijuana in the room until that time.

The room, upon police entry, was in complete disarray. There was a strong odor of marijuana in the room. There were four hand rolled marijuana cigarettes and a brass water pipe of a type used for smoking marijuana on tables, including one on a table next to the bed occupied by defendant and another. Later examination disclosed traces of marijuana on the pipe. Two marijuana cigarette butts were in the room, one of them being on the floor beside defendant's bed. Defendant's record player was in the room.

The legislature used the words "possession" and "control" in the narcotics statute in their commonly understood sense, and not in a restricted, technical sense. The trial judge conceded the possibility that someone, unbeknownst to defendant, brought the marijuana into the room, but nevertheless did not have a reasonable or fair doubt as to defendant's control thereof. It was a fact question. There was strong circumstantial evidence to support the court's findings. Defendant's control of the marijuana in the room was a fact reasonably inferred from the evidence.

His conviction is affirmed.

Levin, J., dissenting.

I dissent because it is not a crime to be in control of a room where marijuana is found and because the people failed to prove that the defendant, Harold Eugene Valot, Jr., was in possession or control of marijuana.

Time and again the courts of this and other states have ruled that where the people's case is based on circumstantial evidence the prosecution has the burden of proving "that there is no innocent theory possible which will, without violation of reason, accord with the facts". In this case the people failed to negate every reasonable theory consistent with Valot's innocence of the crime charged.

When the police entered the motel room they observed five persons all apparently asleep. There were four marijuana cigarettes on a desk. There was also a water pipe, with marijuana residue in the pipe near where Valot and his girlfriend were sleeping. Next to the water pipe was a marijuana cigarette butt. On another bed a man was sleeping and near him on the floor was another marijuana cigarette butt. Sprawled on the floor somewhere was another man and another woman. Valot had paid the rent for the room for one day. His girlfriend paid the rent for the second day; he offered to reimburse her but she refused. The rent for the third day had not been paid.

The trial judge found that Valot was in control of the room and was aware at least of the fact that others in the room had marijuana. Those inferences and findings are reasonably supported by the evidence. From the fact that Valot had paid the rent for the first day, had offered to pay for the second day and, by his own testimony, had kicked someone out of the room, it is reasonable to conclude that he was in control of the room. In the light of the manager's testimony that shortly before his arrest Valot was awake,[3] it is reasonable to conclude that he was aware that marijuana was being used or, at least, that it had been used in the room.

One or more of the persons in the room possessed or controlled the marijuana that was in it. There was, however, no evidence as to who brought the marijuana into the room or who used it. The people did not prove by direct or circumstantial evidence that Valot, rather than another person or persons in the room, was himself in actual possession of the marijuana found in the room. There was no evidence, direct or circumstantial, that Valot ever used marijuana or did so on this occasion. The trier of fact's disbelief of Valot's testimony does not support a conclusion that the opposite of his testimony is true in the absence of independent evidence affirmatively supporting that conclusion.

If Valot did not bring the marijuana into the room or smoke it—and, again, there was no evidence that he had—then someone else did. It is not reasonable to infer from Valot's *control of the room* and his knowledge that others in the room possessed or were using marijuana, and I quote from the majority opinion, that Valot, rather than one or another of the other persons in the room, was in "control of the marijuana in the room".

In *Delgado v. United States* (CA 9, 1964), 327 F2d 641, 642, the defendants were living together as husband (Rodriguez) and wife (Delgado) with their two children. Seven marijuana cigarettes and loose marijuana were found in a drawer of the nightstand in their bedroom. In reversing their convictions of receiving and concealing marijuana, the United States Court of Appeals for the Ninth Circuit declared:

> "It is fundamental to our system of criminal law that guilt is individual. Here, that means that there must be sufficient evidence to support a finding, as to each defendant, that he or she had possession of the marijuana. Possession can be joint as well as several, 'constructive' as well as 'actual'. It must also be knowing. But here it is pure speculation as to whether Rodriguez alone, or Delgado alone, or both of them, had possession. No doubt one of them did; perhaps both did. But proof that does not give a rational basis for resolving the doubts necessarily present in the situation pictured to the jury in this case is not sufficient."

Of course, it is entirely true that the marijuana could have been in the joint possession or joint control of all those who were in the motel room. But, unless the trier of fact has the discretion to convict any one who was in the room essentially of the crime of being in a room where marijuana is in use, knowing that it is in use, then there must be some

---

3. The manager of the motel testified that Valot went out on the balcony sometime between 12 noon and 3 p.m. The arrest was made at 4 p.m.

independent evidence of the joint enterprise—evidence in addition to the evidence that the persons charged were all present in the room when the marijuana was used.[8]

The rented motel room bore the earmarks of a crash pad. The ebb and flow of humanity in and out of the room indicates a somewhat unconventional living style. Conventional notions as to control and possession are simply inapplicable to crash-pad communal life. I think we should know a great deal more about such societal patterns than we do before we declare our satisfaction that it is reasonable to infer that whoever happens to have paid the rent for a motel room occupied by a number of persons is in control or possession of marijuana or other property belonging to the persons moving in and out of the room.

But, even if we apply conventional notions of control and possession, Valot's conviction should not be affirmed.

The trial judge inferred that Valot was in control of marijuana possessed by other persons in the room from the facts that Valot was in control of the room and he knew that they were using marijuana. The issue which separates my colleagues and me, reduced to its essence, is whether that is a reasonable inference. It has been said that in a criminal case "not only must each of the facts from which the inference is drawn be proved beyond a reasonable doubt, but the inference itself must be such as admits of no other rational conclusion".

Allowing a trier of fact to draw an inference in a criminal case only if the inference follows with "impelling certainty" enforces the requirement, alluded to at the outset of this opinion, that, where the people's case is based on circumstantial evidence, the prosecution must negate every reasonable theory (*i.e.*, every reasonable inference) consistent with the defendant's innocence of the crime charged.

Plainly, the prosecution failed in this case to negate the reasonable inference that persons in the room other than Valot were in control of the marijuana in the room. Plainly, to infer from the fact that a person is in control of a room that he is in control of marijuana in the possession of other persons in the room is not a reasonable inference. It is not a reasonable inference beyond a reasonable doubt. It is not even more probable than not (the probable-cause standard) that Valot was in control of marijuana possessed by others in the room.

I recognize that leaving the matter at large so that prosecutors can charge whomever they wish and judges and juries can convict those who seem culpable without differentiable proof facilitates law enforcement.

The legislature may, if it wishes, amend the statute to make presence in a room where marijuana is in use a crime.[9] In the meantime, enforcement of the law prohibiting pos-

---

8. Parenthetically, there was no evidence that Valot was present when the marijuana was used. While there is evidence placing him in the room a few hours before his arrest at 4 o'clock p.m. (see fn 3), there was no evidence of how long he had been in the room or when the marijuana was smoked.

9. The Massachusetts legislature has so enacted. See 3A Annotated Laws of Massachusetts, 1970 Cum Supp, C 94, § 213A, which provides:

"Whoever is present at a place where he knows a narcotic drug is illegally kept or deposited, or whoever is in the company of a person, knowing that said person is illegally in possession of a narcotic drug, or whoever conspires with another person to violate the narcotic drugs law, may be arrested without a warrant by an officer or inspector whose duty it is to enforce the narcotic drugs law, and may be punished by imprisonment in the state prison for not more than five years, or by imprisonment in a jail or house of correction for not more than two years or by a fine of not less than five hundred dollars nor more than five thousand dollars."

session and control of marijuana is not, in my opinion, of sufficient overriding public importance to justify departure from fundamental principles long established.

The legislature made possession and control of marijuana a crime. It is not a crime for one in possession or control of a motel room to invite or allow hippy types in the room or to fail to evict guests smoking marijuana. The legislature has not yet made a citizen responsible for the indulgence of others in his presence.

In *Valot*, the dissent argues that the legislature could "amend the statute to make presence in a room where marijuana is in use a crime," citing to a Massachusetts statute that did just that for support. Massachusetts is not alone in having attempted to make it a crime to be in the presence of drugs. A California statute, for example, provides that "[i]t is unlawful to visit or to be in any room or place where any controlled substances ... are being unlawfully smoked or used with knowledge that such activity is occurring." Cal. Health & Saf. Code § 11365 (2012). Constitutional concerns about these laws have led courts either to construe them very narrowly or to strike them down entirely. As the California Supreme Court explained: "We recognize that a literal reading of [the law] could proscribe some kinds of conduct which cannot constitutionally be considered criminal.... An individual might find himself in situations such as at a party, theater, or dance hall, or in a hotel lobby, bus, apartment, or taxi, or even in a private automobile, where he had no relation to the acts of others who might be disposed to use marijuana. As this court has held: If the defendant did not aid, assist, or abet, the perpetration of the crime, he is guilty of no violation of law from the mere fact that he was present and knew of its commission." *California v. Cressey*, 2 Cal. 3d 836 (1970) (citations omitted). *See also, e.g., Nebraska v. Adkins*, 196 Neb. 76 (1976) (collecting cases and finding unconstitutional a statute that made it a crime "for any person ... [t]o visit or be in any room, dwelling house, vehicle, or place where any controlled substance is used"); Lawrence C. Wright, Note, *No Place for "Being in a Place": The Vanishing of Health and Safety Code 11,556*, 23 STAN. L. REV. 1009 (1971) (providing a history of California's law).

With respect to drug possession, most jurisdictions require more to sustain a conviction than did the court in *Valot*. In *Taylor v. Maryland*, for example, a Maryland appellate court reversed a conviction under circumstances that were remarkably similar to those in *Valot*. Richard Jamison Taylor had been convicted of marijuana possession after he and four friends were found inside a hotel room with marijuana. The court reversed Taylor's conviction, finding that the evidence was sufficient to prove only that "Taylor was present in a room where marijuana had been smoked recently, that he was aware that it had been smoked, and that Taylor was in proximity to the contraband that was concealed in a container belonging to another." The court explained that "[p]ossession requires more than being in the presence of other persons having possession; it requires the exercise of dominion or control over the thing possessed." 346 Md. 452 (1997).

The basic concept articulated in *Taylor* is straightforward: if a defendant is found in a location (such as a car, a home, or a street corner) with contraband and others have access to that location as well, the defendant's proximity to the contraband or his control over the location are not sufficient to prove he was in possession of the contraband. This principle makes a great deal of sense. If the rule were otherwise, a defendant could be convicted of possession simply because she was at a party where others were using illegal drugs in her presence or because she was in a car with another passenger who had placed drugs on the vehicle's floor.

But, if proximity to a controlled substance along with knowledge of its presence is insufficient to sustain a conviction for possession, what more is needed? On this issue, courts have continued to have difficulty settling on a consistent set of rules or principles. The materials that follow consider constructive possession cases in three distinct areas: vehicles, open-air drug markets, and go-betweens. As you read each case, consider whether you believe courts have been able to create an objective set of standards to govern constructive possession cases or whether you agree with Judge Tamm's view that "[t]he more cases one reads on constructive possession the deeper [he or she] is plunged into a thicket of subjectivity."

b. Constructive Possession in Vehicles

Turner v. Georgia

Court of Appeals of Georgia
276 Ga. App. 381 (2005)

Blackburn, J.

Following a bench trial, Gregory Turner appeals his conviction of possession of cocaine, challenging the sufficiency of the evidence. Because the sole evidence of possession was Turner's ownership and driving of the vehicle in which the cocaine was found under the passenger seat, and because the passenger in Turner's car had equal access to that cocaine, we reverse.

"On appeal from a criminal conviction, the evidence must be construed in a light most favorable to the verdict, and [Turner] no longer enjoys a presumption of innocence." So viewed, the record shows that officers on routine patrol spotted Turner's car entering the parking lot of a hotel at approximately 3:00 a.m. in a high drug trafficking area. They ran his tag, which came back registered to a different car. The officers pulled Turner over and asked him to explain the tag discrepancy. Turner responded that he had "owned the car for a while" and produced a five-month-old bill of sale. While talking to Turner, the officers noticed an open container of an alcoholic beverage in the car. They asked Turner and his passenger to step out of the vehicle and obtained permission from Turner to search the car. The search uncovered a bag of cocaine weighing less than one ounce hidden under the passenger's seat.

Turner, but not his passenger, was arrested and charged with possession of cocaine. He was convicted following a bench trial in which the sole evidence that he possessed the cocaine was his ownership and driving of the vehicle. His only enumeration on appeal is that evidence of equal access prevents a finding of constructive possession of the cocaine beyond a reasonable doubt.

The State relied solely on the rebuttable presumption that the driver and owner of an automobile has possession and control of contraband found in the automobile. "However, as to automobiles, the rule does not apply where there is evidence in the case that others have had access to it."

Howren v. State recently summarized this principle: "The equal access rule *entitles a defendant to acquittal* when (1) the sole evidence of his possession of contraband is his possession of a vehicle in which contraband is found; and (2) others have equal access to the area where the contraband is found or the vehicle has recently been in the possession of others." (Emphasis supplied.) Because these two criteria apply in the present case, we must reverse. *Howren v. State,* 271 Ga. App. 55, 58 (2004).

The State counters that other evidence showed that Turner was in possession of the cocaine. Specifically, the State claims that "the evidence also shows that the cocaine was easily within Turner's reach; Turner was driving with an unidentified woman in an area known for prostitution and illegal drug activity; Turner was driving with a stolen tag on his car; and Turner was driving with an open beer in the console of his car." But the only item in this list that in any way connects Turner to the possession of the cocaine found in the vehicle was that, though hidden under the passenger seat, the cocaine was within Turner's reach. As [we have] stated in [a previous case], "[a] finding of constructive possession must be based upon some connection between the defendant and the contraband *other than spatial proximity.*"

Though not argued by the State, we recognize that the equal access rule does not apply to eliminate the presumption of possession where "all persons allegedly having equal access to the contraband are alleged to have been in joint constructive possession of that contraband." Here the State attempted to rely upon its jury argument of joint possession to eliminate the application of the equal access rule. However the police released the passenger and did not identify her or charge her with joint possession of the cocaine. Where the State does not charge the other occupant of the vehicle who is contended to be in joint possession, the State bears the burden of showing that the defendant "was in *sole* constructive possession of the drugs." The State's passing reference in its closing argument that Turner may have been in joint constructive possession of the cocaine is insufficient; formal charges against the other occupant are required.

Accordingly, the evidence did not sustain the conviction. We must reverse.

Rivas v. United States

District of Columbia Court of Appeals
783 A.2d 125 (2001)

Glickman, J.

Applying principles of constructive possession, a jury convicted appellant Baltazar Rivas and his codefendant Jose Melgar of possessing, with intent to distribute, cocaine found in plastic bags that lay between them in the console of a car in which Melgar was the driver and Rivas the front seat passenger. A division of this court affirmed both convictions in *Rivas v. United States,* 734 A.2d 655 (D.C. 1999) *(Rivas I).* We granted Rivas's petition for rehearing en banc in order to reconsider a rule followed in *Rivas I* and other recent cases that appears to ease the government's burden of proving constructive possession when drugs are found in the "close confines" of an automobile, as distinct from, say, a dwelling. The division relied upon this special "automobile" rule in rejecting Rivas's challenge to the sufficiency of the evidence that he intended to exercise dominion or control over the cocaine in Melgar's car, stating that "our decisions leave no doubt that the requisite intent may be inferred from the presence of contraband in an automobile, in plain view, conveniently accessible to the defendant."

We agree with Rivas that no categorical distinction based on where drugs are found—and certainly no lessening of the government's burden of proving constructive possession on that basis—is justified. A defendant's close proximity to drugs in plain view is certainly probative in determining not only whether he knew of the drugs and had the ability to exert control over them, but also whether he had the necessary intent to control (individually or with others) their use or destiny. Nevertheless, we make clear today that there is no "automobile" exception to the settled general rule that knowledge and proximity alone are insufficient to prove constructive possession of drugs beyond a reasonable doubt. A passenger in someone else's car, who is not the driver and who does not have exclusive control over the vehicle or its contents, may not be convicted *solely* on the basis that drugs were in plain view and conveniently accessible in the passenger compartment. As in all other constructive possession cases, there must be something more in the totality of the circumstances—a word or deed, a relationship or other probative factor—that, considered in conjunction with the evidence of proximity and knowledge, proves beyond a reasonable doubt that the passenger *intended* to exercise dominion or control over the drugs, and was not a mere bystander.

Viewed in the light most favorable to the government, the evidence showed that two police officers in uniform, in a marked police cruiser, were patrolling on Hyatt Place, N.W., at around 1:00 a.m. when they saw an automobile stopped in the middle of the street. The officers pulled up behind the car, a two-door Honda occupied by the driver (Melgar, who was also the registered owner of the vehicle), a front seat passenger (Rivas), and two rear seat passengers. Seconds later the passenger-side door opened and Rivas stepped out; leaving the door open, he walked to the sidewalk where he engaged another man in conversation. Soon afterwards the Honda pulled over to the curb. The police officers activated their overhead emergency lights and moved in behind the parked car. As they did so, Rivas, who evidently saw the officers approach, left the man he was speaking with and walked a short distance around the corner onto Park Road. There he remained to talk with someone else, out of sight of the police until he was apprehended a few minutes later.

In the meantime, as the officers approached the car on foot, Officer Mitchell looked in on the passenger side and saw an open container of alcohol on the rear floorboard. The occupants were ordered out of the car, and as Mitchell reached in to retrieve the container, he saw two plastic bags containing a visible white rock substance in the console between the two front seats. Mitchell, who could see the bags because a streetlight illuminated the interior of the car, told his partner to secure the other occupants while he went looking for Rivas. He found him in the midst of conversation some twenty to thirty feet from the corner of Hyatt Place and Park Road.

The plastic bags taken from the console of the car were later determined to contain twelve and six rocks of crack cocaine, respectively, weighing in the aggregate 1,951 milligrams. This was enough, according to a police expert, to furnish 195 separate "hits" or uses of the cocaine. The expert opined, hypothetically, that if the eighteen rocks weighed the same they would sell individually for about twenty dollars on the street; in other words, that the cocaine had a total street value of a few hundred dollars. In the expert's opinion, the amount and configuration of the drugs (in small rocks) were inconsistent with possession for personal consumption.

There was no evidence to show how long Rivas had been in Melgar's car when the police arrived on the scene, or what he or anyone else in the car had been doing. No evidence was presented that Rivas's fingerprints were found on the bags of cocaine seized from the car, or that Rivas had ever handled the bags or engaged in a drug transaction. No incriminating evidence was taken from Rivas's person,[2] and he said nothing to inculpate himself.

To prove constructive possession, the prosecution was required to show that Rivas knew that the cocaine was present in the car and that he had both the ability and the intent to exercise dominion or control over it. Constructive possession may be sole or joint and may be proven by direct or circumstantial evidence.

---

2. Melgar had $236 in small denominations of bills on his person.

No one disputes that the jury permissibly could find that Rivas *knew* the cocaine was in the console (given that it was in plain view), and that he had the *ability* to exercise dominion and control over it (given his proximity to it).[4] The question before us is whether the jury rationally could find beyond a reasonable doubt that Rivas *intended* to exercise that power, in other words that he in fact "had a substantial voice vis-a-vis the drug[s]." In general, the settled rule in constructive possession cases is that "mere presence of the accused on the premises, or simply his proximity to the drug, does not itself enable ... a deduction" beyond a reasonable doubt that he had the requisite intent. "Nor is mere association with another, standing alone, enough even when the other is known to possess the drug." Rather, there must be something more in the totality of the circumstances that—together with proximity and knowledge—establishes that the accused meant to exercise dominion or control over the narcotics:

> There must be some action, some word, or some conduct that links the individual to the narcotics and indicates that he had some stake in them, some power over them. There must be something to prove that the individual was not merely an incidental bystander. It may be foolish to stand by when others are acting illegally, or to associate with those who have committed a crime. Such conduct or association, however, *without more,* does not establish the offenses here charged. *United States v. Pardo,* 636 F.2d 535, 549 (1980) (emphasis in the original).

In recent years, decisions of this court have attempted to distill at least one principle from constructive possession cases, which, when compared to one another, can sometimes seem "a thicket of subjectivity." *United States v. Holland,* 445 F.2d 701, 703 (1971) (Tamm, J., concurring). Recognizing the normal difference in size between a room in a house or other building and the interior of an automobile, our decisions have stated that "the requisite inferences [of dominion or control] may be drawn from the location of weapons [or other contraband] in plain view and substantially within a defendant's reach in the closer confines of an automobile." In *In re F.T J.,* 578 A.2d 1161, 1163 (D.C. 1990), we declared that "our decisions ... leave no doubt that the requisite intent may be inferred from the presence of contraband in an automobile, in plain view, conveniently accessible to the defendant"—a declaration that the division echoed in *Rivas I,* as mentioned earlier. We have suggested that "it is reasonable to expect the law to require a somewhat higher degree of proof [of intent] where an apartment visitor is alleged to have possessed contraband located somewhere within the large space of an apartment, as opposed to that required for an automobile occupant who knows a pistol [or other contraband] is within easy reach under or behind the seat."

Rivas criticizes these statements, contending that they amount to an unjustified relaxation of the proof requirements when persons are found near drugs in automobiles. Rivas observes that there is nothing "about the nature of a car, except its limited size, that would necessitate a different standard [of proof] in constructive possession cases." Limited size, however, is of questionable significance in this context. Rivas persuasively argues that physical proximity to drugs in the "close confines" of a car, at least one occupied jointly with other persons, may be *less* probative of possession than proximity in some larger enclosure because a passenger "is greatly restricted in her ability to distance herself from contraband in plain view. There is simply nowhere to go," especially when the car is in mo-

---

4. Nor is it disputed that, if Rivas constructively possessed the cocaine, he did so with the intent to distribute it. *See, e.g., Earle v. United States*, 612 A.2d 1258, 1270 (D.C. 1992) (packaging of drugs "in ziplock bags, in amounts regularly sold and purchased on the street," sufficient to establish intent to distribute).

tion. Moreover, Rivas points out, "the relationship of a 'visitor' in a car may be far more attenuated than a visitor to a house or apartment":

> People offer or accept rides from colleagues or acquaintances solely because they are travelling to a common destination. We might pick someone up in bad weather, merely recognizing them as a neighbor. We arrange car pools, and drive people home from parties knowing only that we have friends in common. In all these circumstances, we find ourselves in cars with people whom we might never have occasion to invite into the privacy of our own homes. There is no reason to conclude that a "visitor" in a car, as a general rule, has any greater relationship to its contents than a visitor to a home.

We agree with these reasons why any categorical distinction between cars and other enclosed places in deciding issues of constructive possession is untenable. Whether constructive possession has been proven beyond a reasonable doubt in any given case depends, as the parties before us agree, on a fact-specific inquiry into all of the circumstances. A special exception for automobiles does not stand up to scrutiny. Thus, to the extent that language in our decisions may have implied from the normal size of a passenger compartment that proximity to exposed drugs in a car, without more, is sufficient to prove (beyond a reasonable doubt) the requisite intention to exercise dominion or control, we disavow that language.

Lest our holding be misconstrued, we do not mean to suggest that close proximity to exposed contraband—whether in a car or in a room—has no bearing on the issue of control. It plainly does. Nor do we mean to say that inferences of possession may not be drawn more readily from a person's presence in a car with contraband in plain sight, particularly if that presence is more than momentary, than in other circumstances. To acknowledge no such distinction between a car and other surroundings would ignore the judgment and common experience[.]

Acknowledging, then, the relevance of the evidence that Rivas was seen in close proximity to exposed drugs in the confined space of an automobile, we turn to the remaining issue. Was the evidence adduced in this case sufficient to prove possession by Rivas beyond a reasonable doubt? We hold that it was not.

Before discussing the sufficiency of that evidence, we think it useful to review the principles that must guide our evaluation; for this truly is a case that turns not on the absence of proof, but on the difference between the reasonable doubt standard and less stringent standards of proof.

The reasonable doubt standard of proof requires the factfinder "to reach a subjective state of near certitude of the guilt of the accused." *Jackson v. Virginia,* 443 U.S. 307, 315 (1979). Proof of a fact beyond a reasonable doubt is thus "more powerful" than proof that the fact is "more likely true than not;" more powerful, even, than proof "that its truth is highly probable." This requirement, a component of due process, "'plays a vital role in the American scheme of criminal procedure,' because it operates to give 'concrete substance' to the presumption of innocence, to ensure against unjust convictions, and to reduce the risk of factual error in a criminal proceeding." *Jackson,* 443 U.S. at 315 (quoting *In re Winship,* 397 U.S. 358, 363 (1970)).

Proof beyond a reasonable doubt is not merely a guideline for the trier of fact; it also furnishes a standard for judicial review of the sufficiency of the evidence. We have an obligation to take seriously the requirement that the evidence in a criminal prosecution must be strong enough that a jury behaving rationally really could find it persuasive beyond a reasonable doubt.

Turning now to the evidence in this case, it has the quality of a snapshot—a frozen instant in time and space, crystallized but devoid of explanatory context. The police discovered two bags of cocaine, worth a few hundred dollars on the street, lying exposed to view in the front console of Melgar's vehicle. Rivas had just been seen sitting for a few moments in the front passenger seat, in the company of Melgar himself and two other passengers. But there was no evidence as to how long Rivas had been in the car, how he had come to be there, or what he had been doing. There was no evidence that the occupants of the car were actively engaged in distributing drugs or preparing them for distribution when Rivas was present. When the police arrived, Rivas made no gestures toward the drugs and did not signal in any other way an intent to hide or dispose of them. No other evidence was presented that linked Rivas to the cocaine.

There is no serious doubt that at least one of the car's occupants was in possession of the drugs, and the jury could reasonably infer that Melgar, who was the owner and driver of the automobile and who was found with $236 in cash on his person, had control over its contents. But that does not mean that any of the other occupants shared possession of the cocaine with Melgar (indeed, the government did not charge the two rear seat passengers with possession), nor that Rivas in particular had a stake in it.

The government argues that the jury could find that Rivas jointly possessed the cocaine with Melgar in light of three factors. First and foremost, the government points to Rivas's proximity to drugs lying unconcealed next to him as one factor the jury could rely on to conclude, that he possessed them. Second, the government argues that the jury could infer that Rivas was Melgar's ally in distributing drugs from his car from the fact that Melgar apparently entrusted Rivas with immediate access to the drugs. And third, the government argues that Rivas's actions after the police arrived suggested a person distancing himself from drugs in his possession; for having left the car door open, Rivas evidently intended to return to the car, but he changed his mind and took evasive action when the police signaled their intent to investigate.

Could a reasonable jury find that these factors add up to proof beyond a reasonable doubt that Rivas knowingly had the ability and the intention to exercise control over the cocaine? Knowledge of the cocaine, yes; ability, yes; but intention to exercise control over the cocaine, no—not beyond a reasonable doubt. A reasonable jury perhaps could find it *more likely than not* that Rivas jointly possessed the cocaine with Melgar. But that is where we think any reasonable jury would have to draw the line. In the record before us there is no *substantial* evidence of "some action, some word, or some conduct that links [Rivas] to the narcotics and indicates that he had some stake in them, some power over them." If the standard of proof beyond a reasonable doubt means anything, the factors on which the government relies are not compelling enough to permit a reasonable jury to find Rivas guilty.

The first factor, Rivas's immediate proximity to unconcealed drugs in an automobile, certainly does make it more probable that he possessed the drugs. If the standard of proof were less rigorous, this evidence alone might have been enough to support Rivas's conviction. But the evidence that Rivas knowingly sat next to the cocaine in Jose Melgar's car did not by itself prove beyond a reasonable doubt that he "was not merely an incidental bystander." Perhaps, for example, Rivas accepted a ride with Melgar not knowing there were drugs present until some time after he got in the car. Or Rivas may have been aware that Melgar had cocaine in his vehicle, but rode in the car anyway, intending to do nothing more than (foolishly) ride around with a friend who was also a drug dealer.[10] The

---

10. As Judge Farrell ruefully observed in his concurrence in *Rivas I,* "perhaps, especially in today's culture, the fact that a passenger has taken no steps to distance himself from drugs visibly meant for

3 · DRUG CRIMES

critical question is whether the other factors cited by the government add anything substantial to the mix, i.e., whether they reasonably combine with knowing presence to permit an inference of joint possession *beyond a reasonable doubt.*

The second factor on which the government relies is not about Rivas's state of mind; it is about Melgar's. The argument is that Melgar would not have been likely to let Rivas sit in the car next to the cocaine unless Rivas was part of his criminal operations. But whatever assumptions a jury might reasonably make about the usual operating procedures of drug dealers in general, and particularly those displaying large quantities of drugs, it is pure speculation that in this particular case Melgar—about whom we know nothing—was cautious rather than careless. Indeed, even if Melgar was cautious, he could have had many reasons to trust Rivas without Rivas having been part of his drug trafficking operation or having joint possession of his drugs. If knowing proximity to drugs is insufficient to prove guilt, being permitted to be in proximity adds virtually nothing unless the evidence also divulges *why* permission was granted. Melgar's unexplained willingness to let Rivas near his drugs in the circumstances of this case does not illuminate the intent of Rivas.

The government's third factor is Rivas's conduct after the police arrived: exiting the car when he (presumably) saw them drive up, leaving the door open behind him, and walking around the corner and out of sight when the officers approached the car on foot. We find these facts to be too equivocal to be informative on the central question of Rivas's intentions vis-a-vis the drugs. Rivas's behavior may have been evasive (though hardly stealthy or precipitous), but "in our cases, we have looked for more than 'walking away' to find manifestation of a consciousness of guilt." We have appreciated that even "leaving a scene hastily may be inspired by innocent fear, or by a legitimate desire to avoid contact with the police." "Headlong flight" may be "the consummate act of evasion: ... not necessarily indicative of wrongdoing, but ... certainly suggestive of such." *Illinois v. Wardlow,* 528 U.S. 119, 124 (2000). But Rivas did not engage in headlong flight or anything close. Assuming that the jury could conclude that Rivas did mean to distance himself while the police were around, that might reinforce the implication that he knew there was cocaine in the car and did not want to be connected with it,[11] but it does not show also that he "had some stake in" the drugs himself. The additional fact that Rivas left the car door open, while perhaps suggesting that he planned to re-enter the car and hence that he may have been more than a momentary or casual occupant, is marginally significant

---

sale lying inches from him in a car driven by a friend says nothing, or too little, about whether he personally has 'some stake in [the drugs], some power over them.'" 734 A.2d at 659 (citation omitted). In this vein, Rivas complains that the government's position improperly "imposes on innocent citizens an affirmative obligation to distance themselves from contraband" that they are aware is at hand. The government counters that a jury *should* be able to draw guilty inferences from a person's failure to utilize readily available means of separating himself from marketable drugs, and that our cases have recognized as much. *See Brown,* 546 A.2d at 397 ("in full knowledge that [his codefendant] was carrying the pistol, appellant knowingly and voluntarily continued his association with him"); *Parker,* 601 A.2d at 52 ("each [defendant] had control of whether to be present with the other at all"). We need not enter this debate in this case. Assuming that a passenger might remain in a vehicle containing contraband for so long a time and in such distinctive circumstances that his constructive possession of the contraband could be inferred, no such inference can be drawn in this case, given the total absence of evidence as to how long Rivas had been in Melgar's car and as to what he and the car had been doing before the police arrived.

11. Although we indulge this interpretation of Rivas's behavior under our deferential standard of review, an alternative interpretation, also reasonable but favorable to Rivas rather than to the government, is that he left the car door open (knowingly exposing its interior to police inspection) and did not run away when he had the chance because he had no idea there were drugs in the vehicle.

at best. If Rivas's guilt cannot be inferred from the fact that he was in Melgar's car for an unknown length of time, it cannot be inferred from the fact that he expected to continue to be in Melgar's car.

In short, an innocent person in Rivas's shoes might have acted exactly as he did when the police arrived. On the issue of whether he exercised control over the cocaine, Rivas's actions were insolubly ambiguous. *Cf. Speight v. United States,* 599 A.2d 794, 798 (D.C. 1991).[12]

When the government proves the presence of contraband in an automobile, in plain view, conveniently accessible to a passenger defendant, the additional evidence necessary to prove constructive possession is comparatively minimal. As Rivas acknowledges in his brief,

> it could be a furtive gesture indicating an attempt to access, hide or dispose of the object, flight or other evidence of consciousness of guilt, evidence of participation in an ongoing criminal venture involving the contraband, an inculpatory statement, evidence of prior possession of the item, actual possession of paraphernalia relating to the use or sale of the contraband, control of the area or container in which the contraband is found, or the like.[13]

In this case, however, such additional probative evidence was lacking. The jury could only speculate about whether Rivas possessed the critical intent to exercise dominion or control over the cocaine in Melgar's car, or just happened to be present in the wrong place at the wrong time. The circumstances were suspicious, and perhaps Rivas is *probably* guilty; but on the thin record of this case, a reasonable doubt about his guilt ineluctably remains. The risk that an innocent man was convicted is therefore unacceptably large under our system of justice. Fidelity to the requirement of proof beyond a reasonable doubt in criminal cases requires that we reverse Rivas's conviction for insufficiency of the evidence.

So ordered.

Ruiz, J., concurring.

The doctrine of constructive possession is a judicially developed theory of liability designed to be a "proxy" for actual possession. *Burnette v. United States,* 600 A.2d 1082,

---

12. In *Speight,* this court deemed the evidence of constructive possession insufficient even though the appellant, who was found with others in a private apartment standing a few feet away from drugs and drug paraphernalia in plain view, gave a false name in order to conceal his identity at the time of his arrest. While we fully appreciated that engaging in elusive behavior to avoid detection can "indicate" consciousness of guilt, we held that appellant's use of an alias, combined with his proximity to drugs in plain view, "falls short ... in establishing that appellant intended to exercise any dominion and control over the contraband in question or to guide its destiny." 599 A.2d at 796, 798. In words that might be applied almost verbatim to the present case, this court concluded:

Based on what the government has presented, there are at least three plausible explanations for appellant's presence: (1) he was innocently visiting a neighbor who happened to be engaged in illegal drug trafficking; (2) he was present in order to purchase drugs; or, (3) he was actively involved in the drug trafficking. The jury could only speculate as to appellant's actual role. We conclude that no reasonable juror could find that appellant's role was as a participant in drug trafficking in light of other plausible reasons for his presence. *Id.* at 798.

13. Needless to say, Rivas's listing of additional evidence that would, together with proximity to contraband in plain view, support a conviction for constructive possession is not exhaustive. We think it appropriate to add, as has already been intimated, that a claim of innocent presence becomes decidedly less plausible in an environment (vehicular or otherwise) that is rife with evidence of ongoing drug production or distribution, such as a manufacturing or cutting facility, a warehouse, or a staging or preparation area where a large quantity of drugs or drug paraphernalia is exposed to view.

1084 (D.C. 1991). As early as fifteen years ago we noted that our case law on "the question of who may be held responsible when the police find an illegal item in a location together with more than one individual demonstrates some inconsistency." Cases decided since then have likewise failed to craft a coherent methodology in approaching this question. This case presents a good opportunity to review and clarify our constructive possession jurisprudence.

I write separately to explain how the decision we reach today fits in our jurisprudence on constructive possession, and why I think it correctly confines us to our judicial role, and away from policy-making in an area properly left to the legislature.

This court has had numerous opportunities to consider what evidence is necessary to sustain a conviction under a constructive possession theory. For example, recognizing that innocent presence or even guilty knowledge are insufficient to sustain a conviction for constructive possession, we regularly have stated that "mere presence at the scene, association with one in possession, or proximity to the drugs do not in themselves substantiate a finding of constructive possession." We have noted the particular ambiguity of situations where more than one person is in the presence, but not in actual possession, of drugs, and that "any legitimate inference which can be drawn from such presence, proximity, or association is considerably weakened where the accused is one of several people gathered in the place where the contraband is found." We have also demonstrated an unwillingness to impute possession of an illegal item to a visitor or even to "a resident of premises to which others have access ... without proof that the accused is actually involved in some criminal enterprise of which the contraband is a part."

Even though we continuously stressed that proximity to contraband in plain view in an apartment or house fails to support an inference of intent, our case law developed, without much explanation, to allow proximity to contraband in plain view to support an inference of intent when the contraband was "substantially within, a defendant's reach in the closer confines of an automobile." In *In re F.T.J.*, the court explicitly recognized that "our decisions ... leave no doubt that the requisite intent may be inferred from the presence of contraband in an automobile, in plain view, conveniently accessible to the defendant."

Having reconsidered the issue, we now abandon the standard announced in *In re F.T.J.* and hold today that there is no special rule for automobiles that allows a sufficient inference of intent to control or exercise dominion over contraband to be derived merely from the fact of presence and proximity to that contraband in plain view. We are right to do so.

Although proximity to drugs can be probative of intent to control the drugs, proximity is a relative concept that must be evaluated in the context of the totality of the circumstances in a particular case. As the majority notes, a categorical distinction between knowing proximity to drugs in a car, as opposed to a house or apartment, does not withstand scrutiny. The closer proximity to drugs (or any item) in an automobile, where a passenger's ability to remove him or herself from the presence of contraband is limited by the car's close space and mobility, may be less probative of intent than proximity in a house or an apartment, where an individual has greater freedom of movement and may therefore choose where to be in relation to the item in question. Therefore, just as caution is in order before possession of an illegal item is imputed to a visitor in a house or apartment without some further proof, at least a like caution should operate before imputing possession to one of several passengers in an automobile. Absent additional evidence that proximity is probative of intent in the totality of the circumstances of a defendant's situation, in the ambiguous situation involving more than one person with access to contraband, physical proximity alone is insufficient to establish the intent element of constructive possession beyond a reasonable doubt.[22] There is no distinction in the quantum of proof required to prove the element of intent under a theory of constructive possession whether the contraband be found in a house, apartment or automobile.

Finally, an important consideration for me is that a less demanding standard has too great a potential to impose criminal liability on a person who simply fails to disassociate from, or has mere knowledge of, the presence of contraband. This would ignore the reality that there is a broad range of what may be considered tolerable exposure to criminal activity. *See Rivas,* 734 A.2d at 659 (Farrell, J., concurring) ("Perhaps, especially in today's culture, the fact that a passenger has taken no steps to distance himself from drugs visibly meant for sale lying inches from him in a car driven by a friend says nothing, or too little, about whether he personally has some stake in the drugs."). Moreover, a person's living conditions, relatives and friends may not permit the luxury of safe distance from criminal behavior in a crowded, harsh and sometimes inescapable urban environment. If we permit too low an evidentiary threshold for constructive possession, we would in essence be setting a heightened standard of behavior, on pain of criminal sanction, for individuals faced with close proximity to contraband in plain view. If knowing proximity to contraband is to be a crime, it is for the legislature to declare it. What we must do is ensure that in setting the evidentiary minimum to establish the judge-made elements of constructive possession as a proxy for actual possession, the jury does not stray from the offense of drug *possession* that the legislature has criminalized, as possession is normally understood.[24]

I agree with the majority's analysis that the evidence in this case is insufficient to meet the demanding standard of guilt beyond a reasonable doubt because the jurors must have had a reasonable doubt about Rivas' guilt. I add some comments about evidence and arguments not discussed by the majority, and to respond to the dissent.

The dissent argues that the manner in which Rivas distanced himself from the car shows a guilty conscience, particularly because Rivas exited the car right after the police pulled up behind, while the car was still in the middle of the street. The evidence taken as a whole significantly weakens the inference the dissent would permit the jury to draw, that Rivas left the car because he was aware of the police presence. Co-defendant Melgar testified that he was out driving that night with three friends when his car "died out" in the middle of the street. After attending to the carburetor for one minute, Melgar was able to restart the car. With the car running again, Melgar was just about to drive on to Park Road when he noticed the police cruiser behind him with its emergency lights on. Upon seeing the police, he pulled his car over to the curb. The evidence was therefore undisputed from Officer Mitchell's and Melgar's testimony that the police did not turn on their lights and make their presence known until *after* Rivas had exited the car where it was stopped in the middle of the road. Although the jury could discount Melgar's tes-

---

22. In situations where there is only one person in possible constructive possession, the ambiguity is lessened, although not necessarily eliminated. It then also becomes relevant to know the period of time during which the person has been in "exclusive" proximity, and evidence that others may have been responsible for the contraband's presence may render the situation just as ambiguous as when more than one person is present.

24. The majority states it does not need to "enter the debate in this case" about whether criminal intent may be inferred from failure to separate from contraband. My position is that it is not for the court—in this case or in any other—to decide whether a person's failure to distance himself or herself from contraband constitutes a criminal act. As the statute is currently worded in terms of "possession," it will not allow such an attenuated proof.

timony that the car had stalled and not draw the inference that the car's stalling prompted Rivas to exit the car where he did, there was scant evidence from which the jury could infer that Rivas left the car in the middle of the road in order to distance himself from the drugs once the presence of the police became known. To infer that Rivas exhibited a guilty conscience because he left the vehicle within a "couple of seconds" of the unannounced arrival of a police cruiser behind the car in which he was a passenger is too slim a reed to support an inference of intent beyond a reasonable doubt.

In this case, the reason for Rivas' action of leaving the passenger door open when he exited the car is particularly opaque. Although the government argues that it evidences Rivas' intent to return, not only to the car, but to the drugs, it is equally possible that, although Rivas might well have intended to return to the car, he left momentarily not to avoid trouble with the police, but to seek help moving the car, which had stalled in the middle of the road. Further, to the extent that the government's argument is premised on the assumption that Rivas acted once he was aware of the police's presence, it would be anomalous for a person who knows he has drugs in the car to leave the door open, making it easier for police to spot the contraband, as happened here, where Officer Mitchell testified that he was able to see the drugs because of the light from street lamps, no doubt aided by the car's open door. An inference that Rivas intended to maintain dominion and control over the drugs from the fact that he left the passenger door open also requires speculation because it assumes a fact as to which there was no direct evidence, that the drugs were on the console before Rivas left the vehicle a full five minutes prior to their discovery — time during which any of the three other passengers in the car who by then had a better basis than Rivas to be aware of the police's presence might have tried to dispossess themselves of the drugs.

The government's expert testified that drug dealers "sometimes" work together with other people; that they do not always personally carry the drugs they intend to sell or the money they make from distribution, but instead use a "stash or hiding place"; and that drug dealers working together "sometimes" have different responsibilities, "somebody might hold the narcotics, somebody might hold the money." The generalized expert testimony presented in this case can meet only part of the government's burden to prove intent to possess beyond a reasonable doubt; the government must prove also that Rivas was acting pursuant to such shared division of labor with Melgar.

Our prior cases have recognized, and we reaffirm today, that "presence, proximity or association may establish a prima facie case of ... possession when colored by evidence linking the accused to an ongoing criminal operation of which that possession is a part." "The proof of such an ongoing criminal operation need not be explicit or strong," but there must be evidence "linking the accused to [the] ongoing criminal operation." We have cautioned, however, of the risk "that the patina of expert testimony will endow purely innocent activity with criminal attributes merely because that activity is 'consistent' with actions of criminals"

The evidence presented in this case is readily distinguishable from that presented in *Carpenter v. United States,* 475 A.2d 369 (D.C. 1984), in which an expert on drug transactions testified that "a common arrangement in drug transactions is for one man ..., to have control of the drugs, and for another man ... to have control of the money, while one or more additional persons ("runners") act as go-betweens...." In addition to the expert testimony, evidence was presented that the appellant's movements "were fully consistent with the role of 'runner.'" The appellant was observed approaching vehicles, receiving money, going to another party making "hand-to-hand contact," then to another from which he received "a small white object" that he in turn gave to the driver of the vehicle.

Likewise, in *Bullock v. United States,* 709 A.2d 87, 90 (D.C. 1998), expert testimony that "explained how open-air drug enterprises tend to operate," was related to the case at hand by eyewitness testimony that the appellant "physically gave a bundle of cellophane packets" later found to contain heroin and "periodically emerged from [an] alley to check" on the distribution. In each of these cases, the expert testimony described the appellant's affirmative actions as part of an overall ongoing criminal enterprise consistent with expert testimony.

Apart from Rivas' presence in the car, there is no evidence in this case that links Rivas to an ongoing criminal operation of which possession of the rock cocaine is a part. Notably, in this case there was no evidence presented of the relationship between Rivas and the driver of the vehicle; nor was there evidence that the car was stopped in an area known for drug trafficking, that the car in which Rivas was a passenger had any of the characteristics of those driven by drug dealers as the expert testified in *Parker,* or that Rivas' movements were consistent with the roles described by the government expert, that "somebody might hold the narcotics, somebody might hold the money." Although Melgar was found with $236 on his person, suggesting that he could be the "money" man, the facts do not indicate that Rivas was "holding" the drugs; the drugs were neither in a "stash or hiding place" nor in Rivas' personal possession. Indeed, the facts are at least equally consistent, if not more consistent, with the possibility that Melgar, in whose car the drugs were found in a location under his control as driver, was in charge of both the money and the drugs.

In sum, the factors relied upon by the government, neither singly or in combination, permitted the jury reasonably to infer beyond a reasonable doubt that Rivas intended to possess the drugs found some five minutes after he exited the car where he had been a passenger. Although the jury is allowed leeway to weigh the evidence and make inferences, to be beyond a reasonable doubt, its findings must be based on the evidence or lack of evidence. In this case, the jury did not have sufficient evidence from which it could, without engaging in impermissible speculation, dispel a reasonable doubt that Rivas may have been an innocent bystander to the drugs found on the brake console.

Steadman, J., with whom Wagner, CJ. and Terry, J. join, concurring in part and dissenting in part.

I concur in [the legal principles set forth in the majority opinion.] My disagreement is with the application of those principles to the specific facts of this case in order to determine the sufficiency issue.[1]

The task of ruling on constitutional sufficiency "does not require a court to ask itself whether *it* believes that the evidence at trial established guilt beyond a reasonable doubt. Instead, the relevant question is whether, after viewing the evidence in the light most favorable to the prosecution, *any* rational trier of fact could have found the essential elements of the crime beyond a reasonable doubt." *Jackson v. Virginia,* 443 U.S. 307, 318–19 (1979).

Applying that test, I am unable to conclude on the record here that *no* rational trier of fact could have found appellant guilty under the requisite standard. The majority opin-

---

1. This issue standing alone would hardly justify review by the en banc court. See D.C. App. R. 40(e) (rehearing en banc will not ordinarily be ordered except where necessary to maintain uniformity of decisions or where proceeding involves a question of exceptional importance). The en banc opinion having resolved the possible conflict in our prior decisions, I would have been quite willing to remand the case to the panel for application of the relevant principles to this specific case. However, since the en banc court has determined to deal with the appeal as a whole, I will do likewise.

ion lays out the factual elements, and I note most particularly the actions of appellant in exiting the automobile and departing the scene in the presence of police. This behavior, in the context of the entire circumstances, admitted of a reasonable conclusion and inference that the actions were those of a person increasingly disassociating himself from drugs in his possession with the growing involvement of the police; that is, an initial act of distancing himself—but not too far—from the car followed by his abrupt departure from sight when he saw that the police were serious about investigating. Furthermore, the nature of the exit itself from the car bears note: the Honda was stopped in the middle of the street late at night, the police car pulled up behind it, and at that point, presumably having observed the police car, the appellant left the car still parked in the middle of the street, leaving the door open in a manner suggesting an intention to return and maintain ready access to the inside of that vehicle where the drugs were in plain view next to where he had been sitting,

As the Supreme Court reasserted in the above-cited case, in which it ultimately concluded that the evidence was constitutionally sufficient, the prosecutor is not under an affirmative duty to rule out every hypothesis except that of guilt.

No claim is made that the jury here was not fully and correctly instructed on the meaning of the concept of "proof beyond a reasonable doubt." While I do not doubt the duty of this court to strike down convictions that fail to meet the constitutional standard of proof, I cannot say that the twelve members of the jury who heard all the evidence first-hand acted irrationally in finding the appellant guilty beyond a reasonable doubt or that the trial court twice erred in coming to a like conclusion in denying the repeated motions for a judgment of acquittal.

Rivas demonstrates the difficulty of crafting a consistent and principled set of factors for analyzing constructive possession cases. The majority, concurrence and dissent all agree on the basic premise that proximity and knowledge alone are not sufficient to sustain a conviction for drug possession. Likewise, all of the judges in *Rivas* appear to agree that in *some* instances proximity and knowledge combined with evasive action may be enough evidence to prove drug possession. It is at this point, however, that the judges part ways.

The majority and concurrence find the fact that Rivas left the car when the police approached it to be insufficient to sustain his conviction. Would the result have been different if Rivas had engaged in "headlong flight" from the vehicle? The majority opinion implies that it would. But, the majority also explains, even "[a]ssuming that the jury could conclude that Rivas did mean to distance himself while the police were around, that might reinforce the implication that he knew there was cocaine in the car and did not want to be connected with it." Couldn't the same be said of headlong flight?

Though the sufficiency of the evidence for the driver, Jose Melgar, was not at issue in this appeal, the court distinguishes Melgar's situation from Rivas's by explaining that "the jury could reasonably infer that Melgar, who was the owner and driver of the automobile and who was found with $236 in cash on his person, had control over its contents." What evidence was there, however, to indicate that the drugs belonged to Melgar and not Rivas (or, for that matter, one of the passengers in the back seat)? If the presence of money on Melgar's person is what differentiates his case from Rivas's, why is Melgar's $236 in cash any more inculpatory than Rivas's open-door exit from the vehicle? If the distinction is that Melgar was the driver and owner of the vehicle, does that put the *Rivas* court's decision at odds with *Turner* (above)?

c. Constructive Possession in Open-Air Drug Markets

Bullock v. United States

District of Columbia Court of Appeals

709 A.2d 87 (1998)

Steadman, J.

Appellant Jay Bullock was convicted by a jury of one count of unlawful distribution of a controlled substance and one count of unlawful possession with intent to distribute a controlled substance ("PWID"). At the same trial, appellant Kenneth V. Rawlinson was convicted of one count of PWID. All charges relate to a quantity of heroin that was stashed beside a tree near the corner of Georgia Avenue and Otis Place, N.W.

On the morning of March 12, 1994, Officer Richard Fitzgerald of the Metropolitan Police Department manned an observation post near the "high drug area" of Georgia Avenue and Otis Place, N.W. From approximately 10:20 a.m. until 11:10 a.m., Fitzgerald observed the two appellants and a third person, Cynthia Davis,[2] through binoculars.

At around 10:20 a.m., appellant Bullock emerged from an alley known for drug trafficking, engaged Davis in conversation, and gave her a bundle of objects wrapped in a plastic band. Fitzgerald believed the objects were cellophane ziplock bags. Through his binoculars, Fitzgerald watched Davis count out ten objects by "flipping through" the bundle. Davis stashed the bundle at the base of a nearby tree. Davis remained near the tree while Bullock wandered up and down the street, often looking back toward the tree.

Shortly after Bullock gave the bundle to Davis, appellant Rawlinson entered the scene. Rawlinson approached Davis and struck up a conversation. Fitzgerald could not hear what was said, but he observed Davis gesture toward the base of the tree with her head. Rawlinson nodded in response to this gesture, and he and Davis walked a short distance together. Rawlinson continued to associate with Davis throughout the surveillance period. Fitzgerald testified that Rawlinson once "motioned and directed" a passerby to Davis, who then appeared to sell drugs from the stash to the passerby.

During the fifty minutes of Fitzgerald's surveillance, a total of five or six pedestrians appeared to buy drugs from Davis. After every one or two sales, Davis would approach Bullock, appear to give him money, and then return to the tree while Bullock disappeared into the alley. Fitzgerald testified that Bullock appeared to be "more or less overlooking what [was] going on, supervising his troops." Fitzgerald also saw Rawlinson appear to make two or three drug sales to different passersby, although his testimony was unclear as to whether these sales were linked to the stash by the tree or to a different source. At one point during the observation, all three suspects conferred in a group.

At 11:10 a.m., two arrest teams moved into the area and apprehended Bullock, Rawlinson, and Davis. After Bullock's arrest, police found $115 in one of his pockets. Police found no drugs on Bullock's person, and they did not find drugs or money in the alley. Police recovered neither drugs nor money from Rawlinson after his arrest. A police officer searched the base of the tree and found two small cellophane ziplock bags hidden inside a bottle-cap. There were no other items of significance beneath the tree. The contents of the ziplock bags were identified as heroin in a field test.

---

2. Davis was indicted with Bullock and Rawlinson for PWID, but she pled guilty before trial.

At trial, an expert explained how open-air drug enterprises tend to operate. The expert identified a common pattern in which one individual, designated a "runner," would solicit potential customers and direct them to the "holder," who supervised the supply of drugs. A holder in an enterprise rarely keeps the drugs on his or her person for fear of being caught with incriminating evidence. Instead, the holder might stash the drugs in a vehicle, near a tree, or in a bag amongst litter. For the same reason, the participants in an open-air drug enterprise might arrange to have incoming cash stashed separately. Finally, the expert identified "an executive lieutenant or captain who will pass [the drugs] out to the street lieutenants for selling on the street."

Neither defendant presented any evidence.

Bullock claims the evidence was insufficient to convict him of distribution and PWID, and, for that reason, contends that the trial court erred in denying his motion for judgment of acquittal ("MJOA"). In reviewing the denial of an MJOA, we view the evidence "in the light most favorable to the government, with due regard for the jury's right to weigh the evidence and assess credibility."

As for the distribution, the government presented eyewitness testimony that Bullock physically gave Davis a bundle of cellophane packets, which she deposited by the tree. Davis exchanged some of these packets with various passersby over the course of fifty minutes, but two packets remained when the police moved in. The contents of these two packets field-tested positive for heroin. The delivery of a controlled substance between two participants in a drug enterprise, whether or not an agency relationship exists, is a distribution. The identification testimony of even a single eyewitness is sufficient to sustain a conviction for distribution, "coupled, of course, with other evidence identifying the substance itself." A reasonable factfinder could conclude that Bullock distributed heroin to Davis.

Bullock's PWID conviction was based on a theory of constructive possession of the stash after it was distributed to Davis. "To establish constructive possession, the government must prove that the accused (1) knew the location of the drugs, (2) had the ability to exercise dominion and control over them, and (3) intended to exercise such dominion and control." "Constructive possession may be established by circumstantial as well as direct evidence, and may be sole or joint possession."

There was eyewitness testimony from which a jury could infer all three elements of constructive possession. Bullock appeared to know the location of the drugs because he saw Davis place them by the tree and he periodically emerged from the alley to check on Davis and Rawlinson. There was expert testimony that a drug enterprise often includes an "executive lieutenant or captain" who keeps an eye on the runner and holder. Moreover, the packaging of the drugs, the operation of the enterprise, and the fact that he periodically accepted incoming cash from Davis would allow the inference that Bullock intended to distribute the remainder of the stash. From the government's evidence, a reasonable factfinder could conclude that Bullock continued to have both the ability and the intent to exercise dominion and control over the stash.

Having established that the evidence was sufficient as to each offense, we now address Bullock's more novel contention that he cannot remain convicted of both. Bullock argues that logically he cannot continue to possess the same heroin he already distributed to Davis; alternatively, he cannot be said to have distributed the heroin to Davis if, as the government alleged, he retained dominion and control over the stash during the fifty minutes of surveillance. To remain convicted of both distribution and PWID with respect to the same drugs, he claims, is a "legal impossibility."

We rejected a similar claim in *Allen v. United States,* 580 A.2d 653 (D.C. 1990), where we affirmed convictions for both PWID and distribution even when they concerned the same contraband. The appellant in *Allen* had offered a tinfoil packet of cocaine to a passerby, but changed his mind and withdrew the packet when he saw a police car approach. He tried to resume, but did not complete, the transaction after he thought the police car had passed. The police had not left but remained and caught him with a total of three tinfoil packets of cocaine. He was convicted of distribution as to the first incident[4] and PWID as to the second.

Not unlike Bullock, the appellant in *Allen* contended that he could not remain convicted of PWID and distribution of "the same drugs in the same place to the same person at approximately the same time." We disagreed and held that the offenses arose from separate acts. The key factor in *Allen* was the passage of time between the first incident and the second, which were interrupted by the passing of a police car.

> Sometime during that interval, appellant reached the "fork in the road".... After the [police] car disappeared around the corner, appellant could have chosen to put his drugs away and go home. Instead, however, he decided to try again to distribute his drugs to a prospective customer. This decision, made after the first attempt was completed, was the product of a new criminal impulse and thus was punishable separately from the earlier act....

We find the *Allen* analysis appropriate to Bullock's case. Bullock gave a bundle of heroin packets to Davis, thus completing the distribution offense. At that point, Bullock reached the "fork in the road." He could have ended his participation in the enterprise and gone home, but instead, for over fifty minutes, he continued to supervise the others and periodically receive money from Davis. These acts reflected a renewed criminal impulse with respect to the heroin stash and are thus punishable separately from the earlier offense.

There is nothing "legally impossible" about holding an individual responsible for both distribution and PWID of the same drugs on these facts.[5] Distribution is a physical act. Possession with intent to distribute, particularly under a theory of constructive possession, is a conceptual act. An individual commits the offense of distribution upon transferring physical control of the drugs. But he or she may continue to "possess" the drugs because constructive possession may encompass joint possession. Thus in certain circumstances our law would permit convictions of both offenses, even with respect to the same quantity of drugs.[6]

We repeat our admonition in *Allen* that "we would not look kindly upon a prosecution that attempted to subdivide [a single transaction] into two parts, focusing first on the period before the sale (and charging PWID) and then on the sale itself (and charging distribution)." However, given the particular circumstances here, we conclude that the passage of time between Bullock's distribution of the heroin to Davis and his continuing exercise of dominion and control over the stash was enough to render the PWID a separate offense.

---

4. The statutory definition of distribution includes attempted distribution.

5. We note in passing that Bullock's sentences for the two offenses are concurrent, not consecutive.

6. No claim has been made in this case that at the time Bullock physically handed the drugs to Davis, she was already in joint constructive possession of them. We express no view as to whether the transfer of contraband into the physical possession of a party can constitute distribution if, prior to the transfer, the recipient possessed the contraband constructively.

Finally, we address appellant Rawlinson's single contention that the trial court should have granted his MJOA because the evidence was insufficient to convict him of PWID.

Rawlinson's case was submitted to the jury under two alternative theories, as a principal and as an aider and abettor. We conclude that the evidence was sufficient to support a conviction under either theory.

First, a reasonable jury could find Rawlinson guilty as a principal offender under a theory of constructive possession. The eyewitness testimony showed that Rawlinson (1) approached Davis soon after she stashed the heroin by the tree, (2) engaged her in conversation and nodded in response to her gesture to the stash, (3) associated with Davis throughout the fifty-minute surveillance, (4) conferred with both Davis and Bullock, and (5) "motioned and directed" a pedestrian to Davis, who then appeared to sell drugs to the pedestrian from the stash. The government's expert explained the role of a runner, who refers potential customers to the holder in an open-air drug enterprise.

From this evidence, the jury could infer that Rawlinson knew the location of the stash and that he shared both the ability and the intent to exercise dominion and control over the stash by the tree. Rawlinson's referral of a customer to Davis is further proof of his intent to distribute the remaining heroin. In short, Rawlinson's activities fit the expert's description of a runner. "The failure of police to find any money or drugs on [appellant] at the time of his arrest in no way detracts from the strength of that evidence," particularly where there was expert testimony as to the reluctance of open-air drug dealers to keep their product and its proceeds on their person.

Second, the same evidence also would have been sufficient to support Rawlinson's PWID conviction as an aider and abettor. To establish that Rawlinson aided and abetted possession with intent to distribute heroin, the government must prove that (1) someone committed the PWID offense as a principal and (2) appellant knowingly assisted or participated in the principal's offense.

The government's evidence was sufficient to permit a reasonable juror to find both prongs of aiding and abetting PWID. First, there was evidence that *someone* possessed the stash by the tree with the intent to distribute it, whether that someone was Davis, whose participation in the enterprise was known to the jury, or Bullock, whom the jury had convicted of PWID before it reached a decision as to Rawlinson. The trial court instructed the jurors that if they considered the aiding and abetting theory, they must agree on the identity of the principal that Rawlinson aided and abetted, whether Davis or Bullock. Second, the jury could infer from the government's evidence that Rawlinson knowingly assisted or participated in the PWID offense by acting as a runner. Davis showed Rawlinson the stash, Rawlinson nodded, and Rawlinson referred at least one buyer to Davis during the surveillance.

In *Lowman v. United States*, 632 A.2d 88, 90–92 (D.C. 1993), we held that a runner aids and abets the offense of distribution when she directs a potential buyer to the holder.[9] Rawlinson's case is somewhat different because his PWID conviction is based on the quantity of heroin that remained in the stash *after* his participation in that particular sale.

---

9. The concerns expressed by the dissenting judge in *Lowman* are absent from Rawlinson's case. The dissent was concerned that the runner in that case was acting more as an agent of the buyer than as an agent of the seller. Here, however, the evidence collected during the fifty minutes of surveillance more clearly established links between the runner and the others in the enterprise than the evidence in *Lowman*.

Nevertheless, in light of both the eyewitness and expert testimony, a reasonable juror could infer that Rawlinson intended to assist in further sales of heroin from the stash.

For the foregoing reasons, the convictions of both appellants are

Affirmed.

d. Constructive Possession by Go-Betweens

United States v. Manzella

United States Court of Appeals for the Seventh Circuit
791 F.2d 1263 (1986)

Posner, J.

A jury convicted Louis Manzella of one count of possession of cocaine with intent to distribute it, in violation of 21 U.S.C. §841(a)(1), and one count of conspiracy to distribute cocaine and to possess it with intent to distribute it, in violation of 21 U.S.C. §846. Manzella appeals, arguing that there was insufficient evidence to convict him on either count.

Lopez, an undercover agent of the Drug Enforcement Administration, began negotiating with Ernest Rizzo to buy a kilogram of cocaine. At a meeting with Tom Apuzzo, Manzella told Apuzzo that Rizzo would need a new source for the cocaine that he wanted to sell to Lopez. Later the same day, Rizzo told Lopez on the phone that Manzella "has to bring the guy [with the cocaine] to me." Lopez and Rizzo agreed to meet the next day at a restaurant to complete the sale. When Lopez arrived at the appointed time, Manzella was there with Rizzo. Manzella told Lopez that he would make a phone call and the cocaine would arrive in 15 minutes. Manzella went to make the call and came back and said the cocaine was en route. When it did not arrive Manzella became angry. Eventually he received a phone call at the restaurant and was overheard saying, "The package won't be ready?" Manzella then told Lopez that the people who had the cocaine couldn't do the deal. Another meeting was set up—this time in a conversation between Lopez and Manzella—but was later postponed because Manzella was unable to procure the cocaine. During this period Manzella was negotiating with Apuzzo, who had found a possible source for the cocaine, Richard Weiss. Eventually Manzella told Lopez that the deal was set for the next day and that he should call Rizzo. Rizzo and Lopez then arranged another restaurant meeting. At the meeting Apuzzo showed up at last with cocaine that Weiss had supplied him, and Apuzzo and Rizzo were then arrested. At trial Manzella testified that he had sought a source for the cocaine out of friendship for Rizzo, and not for money.

The evidence was ample to show that Manzella conspired with Rizzo and Apuzzo to sell cocaine to Lopez. Manzella's role as broker probably was essential and certainly was helpful to the consummation of the transaction. He was as much a part of the conspiracy as a real estate broker is a part of the deal to sell a house. It makes no difference that Manzella was not present at the sale; he had played a significant role, through his negotiations with Apuzzo, in bringing about Weiss's sale to Lopez.

But in the analogy to the real estate broker we encounter the greatest weakness in the government's case—the lack of evidence that Manzella possessed cocaine; for remember that he was convicted for possession as well as conspiracy. A real estate broker does not possess the house he is trying to sell, or a loan broker the money of the bank whose funds he is trying to get for his customer; and while a stock broker often will have custody of his customer's stocks, rarely will he possess the stocks before buying them for the customer. Manzella knew where the cocaine was. He arranged (at first unsuccessfully) for it to be transported to the place of sale. But he never had control over it.

There is, it is true, a doctrine of constructive possession, under which a person can be convicted for possessing cocaine though he does not possess it in a literal sense. The doctrine creates a legal fiction to take care of such cases as that of a drug dealer who operates through hirelings who have physical possession of the drugs. It would be odd if a dealer could not be guilty of possession, merely because he had the resources to hire a flunky to have custody of the drugs. Of course he might be guilty of many other things, not only conspiracy but also violation of the drug "kingpin" statute, 21 U.S.C. §848, which carries the heaviest noncapital penalties in the federal criminal code; but he would also be guilty of possession with intent to distribute. See, e.g., *United States v. Caspers,* 736 F.2d 1246, 1249 (8th Cir. 1984); *United States v. Caballero,* 712 F.2d 126, 130–31 (5th Cir. 1983).

But as this example suggests, the essential point is that the defendant have the ultimate control over the drugs. He need not have them literally in his hands or on premises that he occupies but he must have the right (not the legal right, but the recognized authority in his criminal milieu) to possess them, as the owner of a safe deposit box has legal possession of the contents even though the bank has actual custody. Mere association with those who possess the drugs is not good enough. There is no evidence that Manzella had possession in this sense. His was the role of a finder, a broker, a bringer together of seller and buyer. Manzella was furious when his principals in the first transaction pooped out but there is no suggestion that he thought that by failing to show up with the drugs as arranged the people who had the drugs had stolen them from him, as would have been the case if he had been the possessor and they the custodians. He had no right to control Weiss's cocaine. Weiss, and later Apuzzo, had the possessory interest in that cocaine. Manzella was again just a broker, a finder working for Rizzo.

The line between broker and seller in the murky depths of the underworld is of course a fine one, and many cases have upheld convictions of middlemen for possession in circumstances superficially like those in the present case. But we can find no case in which the evidence was so weak. In *United States v. Esdaille,* 769 F.2d 104 (2d Cir. 1985), the defendant was identified to the buyer of the cocaine as a supplier, led the buyer to an apartment, and emerged a short time later with the cocaine; this was held to be enough evidence that he constructively possessed the cocaine in the apartment. *United States v. Davis,* 679 F.2d 845 (11th Cir. 1982), is similar; the evidence supported an inference that the defendant was part of a group of conspirators who jointly controlled the cocaine. There is no indication that Manzella had any control, individually or jointly, over the cocaine that he tried to obtain for Rizzo. In *United States v. White,* 660 F.2d 1178 (7th Cir. 1981), where we acknowledged that the evidence of defendant Rogers' constructive possession was much weaker than that relating to his codefendant White, Rogers was present in White's apartment when the sale of heroin was made and accompanied the buyer to her car to get the money for it, so again the evidence pointed to a conspiracy in which the coconspirators jointly controlled the drugs. In *United States v. Virciglio,* 441 F.2d 1295 (5th Cir. 1971), the defendant collected, and retained half of, the purchase price of the machine gun that he was accused of constructively possessing. He had actual possession of many other illegal guns. The court said that, jointly with others, he had "the intention and the power to exercise dominion and control over the machine gun." The same cannot be said about Manzella in regard to Weiss's cocaine.

Admittedly there is language in some cases which if taken literally would allow Manzella to be convicted of constructive possession; for he "instigated the sale, negotiated the price, and caused the drug to be produced for the customer," *United States v. Felts,* 497 F.2d 80,

82 (5th Cir. 1974), and he "likely had some appreciable ability to guide the destiny of the drug," *United States v. Staten,* 581 F.2d 878, 883 (D.C. Cir. 1978). But in each of these cases the evidence of constructive possession was stronger than in this case. If the quoted language were taken literally, every broker would be guilty of constructive possession, a result inconsistent with the fundamental proposition that constructive possession requires the right or power to control. Some cases hold that ability to assure delivery is enough, in combination with association with the actual possessors, to convict of constructive possession. See, e.g., *United States v. Weisser,* 737 F.2d 729, 732 (8th Cir. 1984). We have no quarrel with this formulation; he who can *assure* the delivery of a good controls it. But given the difficulties Manzella had in arranging delivery, it can hardly be inferred that he could assure delivery at the time and place of his choosing; the extent of his association with the actual possessors was also more limited (so far as the record shows) than in the cases we have cited.

[W]e affirm Manzella's conviction for conspiracy but reverse his conviction for possession.

5. When Does a Drug Buyer Acquire Possession?

One particularly vexing possession problem is how to determine when a buyer has acquired possession from a seller. This scenario relates to both "actual" and "constructive" possession and is especially useful for considering the difference between the two theories of possession. It also adds a new twist to the constructive possession inquiry. The disputed issue in most of the constructive possession cases above was the defendant's intent to exercise control over the contraband. In *Epps v. Georgia,* by contrast, there is no question the defendants eventually intended to exercise control over the cocaine but it is not clear whether they had the *power* to do so.

Epps v. Georgia
Court of Appeals of Georgia
251 Ga. App. 645 (2001)

Phipps, J.

William Epps, Rogelio Angulo, Dwayne Brayboy, and Fondel Barr were arrested by a drug task force conducting a reverse sting (wherein undercover police officers pose as drug dealers, sell drugs to purchasers, and then arrest the purchasers for possession of the drugs). The arrestees were charged with trafficking in cocaine and other offenses. Epps, Angulo, and Brayboy appeal their convictions of trafficking in cocaine. Because possession of cocaine is an essential element of trafficking in cocaine, and because law enforcement authorities arrested appellants before they acquired possession of the cocaine, we must reverse their convictions based on an insufficiency of supporting evidence.

Construed in a light most favorable to support the verdict, the evidence showed that a City of Doraville police sergeant was told by a confidential informant that a man later identified as Angulo wanted to purchase a kilogram of cocaine. The sergeant decided to conduct a reverse sting with the assistance of a DeKalb County drug task force. The sting was conducted at an apartment complex in Doraville where Brayboy resided. The informant met Angulo at the apartment complex entrance. They were driving their respective cars. The informant was in possession of a block of cocaine weighing almost 998 grams.

Epps and Barr later arrived in Epps's truck with the purchase money. After going to Brayboy's apartment, Epps and Angulo returned with Brayboy to the informant's car. Epps and Angulo went to the rear of the vehicle and asked to see the cocaine. The informant had put the cocaine on the backseat of his car, and he took it out and showed it to Epps and Angulo. At Epps's request, the informant unsealed the cocaine. The informant also cut a piece out of it. Epps then bent down, smelled the cocaine, and took a piece of it to test at Brayboy's apartment.

After Epps, Angulo, and Brayboy went back to Brayboy's apartment and tested the cocaine, they returned to the area of the informant's car to make the purchase. Epps and Angulo approached the car while Brayboy remained in the background. Angulo placed the money in the backseat of the car. The informant, however, had put the cocaine in the trunk of his car at the direction of the police sergeant who wanted to hide the cocaine from the appellants because he was concerned they might try to steal it. Observing that the cocaine had been moved from its prior location, Angulo asked where it was. The informant asked where the money was. When Angulo told the informant the whereabouts of the money, the informant alerted task force officers by prearranged signal that the buy had been completed. The informant continued giving the signal while telling the appellants that the cocaine was in his trunk. When the informant opened the trunk, the officers converged on the scene and arrested Epps, Angulo, and Brayboy. As the trunk was opened, Epps and Angulo stood approximately three feet from the informant's car.

The relevant element of trafficking in cocaine is knowing possession of 28 grams or more of cocaine. Possession may be joint or exclusive and actual or constructive. A person who knowingly has direct physical control over a thing at a given time is in actual possession of it. A person who, though not in actual possession, knowingly has both the power and the intention at a given time to exercise dominion or control over a thing is then in constructive possession of it. If one person alone has actual or constructive possession of a thing, possession is sole. If two or more persons share actual or constructive possession of a thing, possession is joint. Spatial proximity alone is insufficient to prove joint constructive possession of contraband.

The State argues that the evidence in this case supports a finding that when Epps inspected the cocaine and acquired actual possession of a piece of it, he and the other appellants, along with the informant, were in joint constructive possession of the entire block of cocaine. Alternatively, the State argues that once the appellants paid the purchase price for the cocaine, they obtained constructive possession of it as a result of their apparent ability to overpower the informant and take the cocaine from him.

We cannot agree with either of these arguments. The appellants could not have been in constructive possession of the entire kilogram of cocaine when Epps conducted his inspection, because they indisputably lacked the intention to exercise dominion or control over it until they had tested the sample. Upon tendering the purchase price to the informant, the appellants clearly possessed the intent to exercise control over all of the cocaine, but the evidence is insufficient to show that they ever acquired the power of control so as to give them constructive possession, as the informant hid the cocaine from them by placing it in his closed trunk until the police arrived to make the arrests. This is simply a case in which authorities conducting a sting arrested the subjects before they acquired possession of the drug and then obtained convictions against them for an offense which has possession of the drug as an element. Applying the law to the facts as established by the evidence, we must reverse the convictions for trafficking in cocaine.

Judgments reversed.

Smith, J., dissenting.

I respectfully dissent. Whether sufficient evidence was presented from which the jury could have convicted the defendants of the crime charged is a close question. But given the circumstances of this case, I believe the issue of whether the defendants had the ability to exercise control over the contraband, even though it was in the trunk of the informant's vehicle, was properly submitted to the jury and that evidence existed from which a rational trier of fact could have concluded that the defendants were in constructive possession of the cocaine.

United States v. Kitchen

United States Court of Appeals for the Seventh Circuit
57 F.3d 516 (1995)

Cudahy, J.

Isiah Kitchen was associated with the El Rukn street gang. For activities arising out of that association, a grand jury charged Kitchen with the possession of cocaine with intent to distribute and with the possession of firearms by a felon. A jury convicted Kitchen of both offenses. Kitchen appeals, suggesting that the evidence is insufficient to support either conviction. We accept the jury verdict as to the conviction for the possession of the firearm. We believe, however, that the evidence was insufficient to support the conviction for the possession of cocaine. We therefore affirm in part and reverse in part.

The police arrested Isiah Kitchen as part of an undercover narcotics operation. In March, 1989, undercover agents posing as drug dealers apprehended him during the course of a sale—also termed a "reverse buy"—of cocaine. Later that day, federal agents recovered two firearms from the house that Kitchen shared with his girlfriend. These events form the basis for Kitchen's convictions.

The specifics of the reverse buy are largely undisputed. The government engineered the setup by contacting Lawrence Griffin, a long-time acquaintance of Kitchen and an associate of the El Rukn street gang. Griffin was, at that time, incarcerated at the Cook County Jail. Griffin and Kitchen had several discussions over a three-month period. A number of these discussions proved to be fruitless, ultimately failing to result in a scheduled transaction. Griffin and Kitchen stayed in touch, however, with Kitchen able to page Griffin (actually federal agents) at a number Griffin had provided. Finally, Griffin and Kitchen agreed to a sale. Griffin told Kitchen that he would be released from prison soon, and that at that time, he would be able to deal narcotics. After further negotiations, Kitchen agreed to purchase two kilograms of cocaine from Griffin. The parties decided to transact the deal the next day for a total price of $28,000. Kitchen was to bring $14,000 to the deal, with Griffin "fronting" him the remainder of the cocaine for payment at a later date.

The next day, authorities removed Griffin from prison for the purpose of conducting the transaction. Griffin telephoned Kitchen. The two men agreed to meet at Montrose Harbor at 3:00 p.m. that afternoon. At the scheduled time, Griffin traveled to the Harbor with Special Agent Michael Casali, who was posing as a drug trafficker. Griffin and Casali waited for Kitchen to arrive. Kitchen arrived with an individual named Kenneth Dowdell and parked his car behind the undercover vehicle. Griffin and Casali entered Kitchen's vehicle. At that point, Kitchen and Dowdell produced $14,000 in cash in a series of envelopes. Kitchen left the cash with Dowdell and accompanied Casali to the location of the cocaine in order to "check the merchandise." Griffin and Dowdell stayed with the cash in Kitchen's vehicle. Another special agent, Eduardo Fernandez (Fernandez), was waiting at a different location with two kilograms of cocaine in the trunk of his car.

Casali and Kitchen pulled up to the right of Fernandez's car. The three men then met at the rear of that car, where Fernandez had popped the hatchback. A white garbage bag containing two kilograms of cocaine sat in the trunk. One of the agents opened the bag to reveal two packages of cocaine. The parties dispute exactly what happened next. Kitchen contends that he never touched the cocaine. The government suggests that Kitchen picked up one of the kilograms of cocaine for "two or three seconds." All agree that Kitchen made a comment expressing concern about the drug's purity—that he was worried about "slabs" (apparently one of the most desirable forms of cocaine). At that point, Casali and Fernandez placed Kitchen under arrest.

Following the arrest, agents served a search warrant on Mary Williams's residence in Chicago. The search uncovered a fully loaded .357 magnum revolver and a .9 millimeter semiautomatic handgun. Both weapons were found in a bedroom on the first floor of the residence. The .357 magnum was discovered in the bed area, leaning up against the back of the headboard. The .9 millimeter was recovered from a dresser drawer along with an additional magazine of ammunition.

In the same bedroom, agents found both men's and women's clothing, shoes and toiletries. They also found miscellaneous papers and invoices bearing the name "Ike Kitchen." Among these papers were some containing handwritten numerical figures like those on papers seized from Dowdell at the scene of the arrest. In addition, agents located a gold bracelet with Kitchen's El Rukn nickname lying on the dresser.

Whether Kitchen actually lived with Williams is the subject of some dispute. Kitchen claims to have been residing with his mother in Robbins, Illinois. He denies living with Williams and suggests that he only stayed overnight with her occasionally. The government points to evidence of Kitchen's presence at Williams's house. Kitchen apparently gave Williams's telephone number to Griffin, and was observed at Williams's address on a number of occasions. In addition, the government suggests that Kitchen was responsible for $10,000 worth of repairs on Williams's basement.

The jury ultimately found the government's version of events credible. They found Kitchen guilty of possession of cocaine with intent to distribute in violation of 21 U.S.C. §841(a)(1), and of possession of a firearm by a felon in violation of 18 U.S.C. §922(g)(1). Kitchen appeals, suggesting that the evidence was insufficient to support both determinations.

A defendant challenging the sufficiency of the evidence supporting a jury's verdict bears a "heavy burden." Both the evidence and all of the reasonable inferences that can be drawn from the evidence are viewed in the light most favorable to the government. After applying this standard, we must uphold the verdict if a rational trier of fact could have found the existence of each element of the crime beyond a reasonable doubt. Here, Kitchen mounts challenges to both counts of his conviction—that for possession of cocaine and that for possession of a firearm. He suggests, particularly, that the element of possession was not established in either case.

To convict Kitchen of the unlawful possession of a firearm by a felon, the government had the burden of proving: (1) that he had a previous felony conviction, (2) that he possessed a firearm and (3) that the firearm had traveled in or affected interstate commerce. Kitchen does not contest the first and third elements of his conviction, but he does contend that evidence supporting the second element is lacking.

Under the doctrine of constructive possession, the jury could have determined that Kitchen possessed the weapons. The evidence adduced at trial suggested that Kitchen was something more than a casual visitor at Williams's home. In many of the recorded drug conversations with Kitchen, agents had reached him by calling the telephone number at that address. According to the government, Kitchen had stated that he lived at that address. Agents in fact saw Kitchen at that address on numerous occasions. The search revealed, in addition to the firearms, a number of Kitchen's possessions — his El Rukn bracelet, bills and papers bearing his name and various articles of men's clothing. Finally, the government also came forward with evidence suggesting that Kitchen had spent about $10,000 on repairs to Williams's basement. Kitchen argues that he in fact lived with his mother in Robbins, Illinois, and only visited Williams occasionally. But the jury was under no obligation to accept his testimony on this point. It could have instead concluded that Kitchen shared the residence with Williams.

Such a conclusion supports the determination that Kitchen constructively possessed the handguns found at the residence. "Constructive possession can be established by a showing that the firearm was seized at the defendant's residence." It is not material, contrary to Kitchen's assertions, that he was incarcerated at the time the agents actually seized the guns. The jury might nevertheless have determined that he constructively possessed the guns before he was incarcerated, despite the fact that the guns were seized later. If he in fact resided at Williams's home, then he had the power to exercise control over the two firearms.

Neither is it material that other adults had access to the residence and may have had the same power to exercise control over the firearms that Kitchen had. Constructive possession may be either sole or joint. The fact that Williams, too, had access to the firearms fails to negate the inference that Kitchen did as well. The law recognizes the possibility of joint possession.

The evidence is therefore sufficient to support Kitchen's conviction for a felon's possession of a firearm under Section 922(g)(1). The jury might have determined that he lived at the residence and occupied the bedroom where the guns were located. Under these circumstances, we believe that Kitchen constructively possessed the guns in question.

The sufficiency of the evidence supporting Kitchen's conviction for the possession of cocaine under 21 U.S.C. § 841(a)(1) gives us more pause, however. In order to sustain a conviction under 21 U.S.C. § 841(a)(1), the government must show that: (1) the defendant knowingly or intentionally possessed cocaine, (2) he possessed cocaine with the intent to distribute it and (3) he knew that the material was a controlled substance. Here, again, the only element that Kitchen contests is possession, and the issue is a close one.

As the foregoing discussion demonstrates, the doctrine of "possession" contains concepts that can become almost metaphysical. Few would suggest that "possession" of an object should be confined to instances of physical holding. The second part of this case raises the opposite, yet related, question: is any physical holding — no matter the circumstances — sufficient to establish possession? It is the government's position that Kitchen actually possessed the cocaine because he picked up one of the kilograms for 2 or 3 seconds.[1]

Possession, again, may be either "actual" or "constructive." It is the government's position that actual possession is established if a defendant picks a controlled substance up

---

1. Kitchen contends that he never actually touched the cocaine and points to an expert's inability to locate his fingerprints on the bags containing the substance. Given the standard for our review of a jury's verdict, we are constrained to accept the government's version of events on this point. Assuming Kitchen did pick up the cocaine for two or three seconds, therefore, we will examine whether the requirements of possession have been satisfied.

for "one fleeting moment"—or 2 or 3 seconds, as seems to have occurred here. This position, the government asserts, is supported by cases such as *United States v. Toro,* 840 F.2d 1221 (5th Cir. 1988), *United States v. Jones,* 676 F.2d 327 (8th Cir.) and *United States v. Posner,* 868 F.2d 720 (5th Cir. 1989).

These cases do discuss actual possession, each ultimately suggesting that the government need not risk a defendant's escape in order to produce evidence for a later charge of possession. The common theme in each case is the court's refusal to define possession in "a manner that affords [a defendant] an opportunity to escape with the contraband." And in each case, the court rejects the argument that a defendant cannot have possessed the controlled substance in light of the presence of federal agents. But these cases hardly establish that Kitchen's "fleeting moment" of contact with the narcotics demonstrates actual possession. The record here in no way suggests that Kitchen was preparing to leave with the drugs. And Kitchen does not argue that the presence and authority of federal agents alone should stand in the way of a possession conviction.

Toro and *Jones* and *Posner* do not otherwise support the government's position, which we understand to be some extraordinarily literal application of the definition of "possession." The government suggests that any time a defendant has an object in his hands, the law should recognize his "possession" of it. Yet none of the cases upon which the government relies embraces such an application of the doctrine. Instead, in each, the defendant engaged in some act that was clearly consistent with transporting the narcotics away from the scene of the transaction. In *Toro,* the defendant took the cocaine from the government agent and put it in a briefcase which he then locked. In *Jones,* the defendant loaded bales of marijuana into his van. And in *Posner,* the defendant's coconspirator accepted keys to a van containing marijuana, got into the van and attempted to start it. These cases all involve conduct over and above a defendant's momentary handling of a controlled substance.

This conduct—all acts indicating that transportation of narcotics is imminent—is important precisely because it is unequivocal. By taking delivery of the drug and loading it into a briefcase or a van, a defendant clearly demonstrates his assent to the drug transaction. Here, however, we have no indication of assent. The record is devoid of evidence that Kitchen intended to walk away with the narcotics or otherwise transport them. This factual distinction might not be dispositive if the record revealed *any* evidence that Kitchen had completed the sale or indicated some sort of unequivocal agreement to complete the drug transaction. Given that sort of clear evidence, perhaps a momentary holding, without more, would be sufficient to demonstrate actual possession. But that is not the case before us now.

The undisputed evidence in Kitchen's case tells a strikingly different story—different, ultimately, because here, the sale of the drugs remained incomplete at the time of arrest, and the record reveals no other indication that Kitchen would have proceeded with the drug sale. On the day of the proposed transaction, Kitchen and his coconspirator Dowdell met the government informant Griffin and the undercover agent Casali at a predetermined location. There, the four men got into Kitchen's car. The stated plan was for Kitchen to pay for one kilogram of cocaine and have the remaining kilogram "fronted" to him for payment at a later date. Kitchen showed Casali the money and then handed it to his coconspirator, Dowdell. Casali admitted that at no point did either Kitchen or Dowdell offer Griffin or him the money or attempt to hand the money over. Instead, Kitchen left the money with Dowdell and proceeded to another location with Casali to examine the drugs.

Both at the initial meeting and en route to the second location, Casali repeatedly urged Kitchen to "check out the merchandise" or otherwise inspect the narcotics. Griffin, too, suggested that Kitchen should satisfy himself by inspecting the drugs. It is clear that Kitchen proceeded to the second location with Casali to do just this.

It is also clear, however, that at the second location, no transaction occurred. Casali admitted that Kitchen never stated that he would complete the transaction or made a similar affirmative comment to that effect. Instead, Kitchen made a statement expressing doubt about the quality of the cocaine. These factors indicate that the transaction simply had not been completed at the time of Kitchen's arrest. Absent evidence suggesting that the transaction was in any sense final or certain, we are quite uncomfortable with the notion that momentary contact with narcotics establishes actual possession.

Our discomfort stems from a number of sources. First, the cases upholding convictions for possession do so only in the context of some sort of unequivocal conduct on the part of the defendants. Often, as in *Toro, Jones* and *Posner,* that conduct will consist of actions consistent with transporting the drug away from the site of the deal. In other circumstances, however, the conduct may be more idiosyncratic. In *United States v. Santiago,* 889 F.2d 371 (1st Cir. 1989), for instance, the court fastened upon the fact that one of the defendants was leaving to purchase a pair of shoes to replace the government informant's shoes, which secreted illegal drugs. "The informant had unequivocally given up his shoes, and petitioner was about to go buy him new shoes. Delivery was complete." *See also O'Connor,* 737 F.2d at 818 (performance of tests on each of thirty one-kilo bags of cocaine over a two-hour period established possession).

We do not attempt to use the present case to formulate a rule workable for all circumstances. Nor, by focusing on the incomplete nature of the narcotics deal here, do we wish to suggest that all drug transactions must be "complete" in order to later establish possession at trial. Of necessity, the particulars of a given drug transaction will drive the determination that a certain aspect of the defendant's conduct is unequivocal enough to establish possession. But here, nothing in the record convinces us that Kitchen's momentary holding constitutes possession of the drugs. Money had not yet changed hands, and Kitchen had not otherwise assented to the deal. Instead, Kitchen's momentary holding was in the context of inspection, not delivery.

[H]ere, the essential proof of possession that we require is *some factor* indicating that Kitchen had the authority or the ability to exercise control over the contraband. This demand is hardly foreign to the doctrine of possession. Constructive possession, as developed in this circuit, expressly demands this sort of showing. The government suggests that this factor is not relevant in light of Kitchen's momentary holding of the narcotics. Yet the cases discussing actual possession do not support this argument; in each, as demonstrated, some sort of unequivocal conduct indicating acceptance of the drug or assent to the transaction was present. We suspect, in any event, that the notion of control is not absent from the concept of actual possession.[2] In most cases of actual possession, because the defendant physically holds or carries the narcotics, his control over them is presumed. But to state that control is presumed is not to suggest that actual possession can be established when it is completely absent.

The facts suggest that it was absent in this case. The constructive possession cases teach that a defendant must have ultimate control over the drugs. This requirement translates into the right, or the recognized authority within the "criminal milieu," to possess the

---

2. Implicit in a common-sense understanding of possession—both actual and constructive—is the notion that a defendant has some right or ability to control the disposition of an object. An approved jury instruction on actual possession, for instance, states that a "person who knowingly has direct physical control over a thing, at a given time, is then in actual possession of it."

drugs in question. *Manzella,* 791 F.2d at 1266. This authority is not necessarily established when a defendant acts as a broker in a drug transaction. As we noted in *Manzella,* "a stock broker often will have custody of his customer's stocks, [but] rarely will he possess the stocks before buying them for the customer." Neither is this authority established merely because a defendant has the power or the opportunity to make off with another's property, because "the power to make off with someone else's property is not equivalent to a right to the property." *United States v. Ortega,* 44 F.3d 505 (7th Cir. 1995).

The government does, however, point to evidence of Kitchen's *intent* to transact a drug deal. And it suggests that the jury concluded that Kitchen *intended* to purchase the cocaine. It further suggests that various indicia of Kitchen's intent should be sufficient to establish possession of the narcotics. In support of this conclusion, the government highlights the repeated phone conversations between Kitchen and Griffin discussing potential transactions; Kitchen's various admissions about unrelated drug dealings; and Kitchen's arrival at the scene with the required cash in hand. Yet these factors establish only that Kitchen intended to purchase cocaine, and Kitchen's intent to purchase, without more, is insufficient to establish possession because it overlooks the required element of dominion or control.

By reading the element of control out of the equation, we risk confusing possession with attempted possession. It is well-established that intent is a key element of the doctrine of attempted possession. *United States v. Weaver,* 8 F.3d 1240 (7th Cir. 1993) ("Because attempt to possess a controlled substance is an inchoate crime, it does not require completion of the act of possession.").

The intent to engage in a drug transaction, without more, cannot support a conviction for possession. The missing link in this case is the ability to control the contraband. Had the evidence indicated some sort of unequivocal assent to the transaction, then a momentary holding might have been sufficient to establish the required element of control. But the momentary holding upon which the government relies here simply is not adequate to overcome our concerns. There simply is no evidence—such as payment of the purchase price or verbal agreement—that the drug transaction was in any sense certain or complete. We believe that although Kitchen held the drugs for a moment, he neither controlled them nor had recognized authority over them. His conduct was consistent with inspection—but nothing more. Lack of control is dispositive under both the doctrines of actual and constructive possession. We therefore find the evidence insufficient to support Kitchen's conviction for possession of cocaine.

Because the evidence established that Kitchen resided in the home in which the police located the firearms, it was sufficient to support Kitchen's conviction for the possession of a firearm. We therefore AFFIRM in part. We are not, however, persuaded that the momentary holding that occurred here established Kitchen's possession—either actual or constructive—of the cocaine. Kitchen's conviction for possession of cocaine is therefore REVERSED.

B. Trafficking Offenses

1. Distinguishing between Users and Sellers

Federal and state drug laws both purport to draw a sharp distinction between users and sellers. The Supreme Court recently had the opportunity to revisit and apply this principle in the context of a law that criminalizes the use of a communication facility in facilitating certain drug offenses.

Abuelhawa v. United States

Supreme Court of the United States
129 S. Ct. 2101 (2009)

Souter, J., delivered the opinion for a unanimous Court.

The Controlled Substances Act (CSA) makes it a felony "to use any communication facility in committing or in causing or facilitating" certain felonies prohibited by the statute. 21 U.S.C. § 843(b). The question here is whether someone violates § 843(b) in making a misdemeanor drug purchase because his phone call to the dealer can be said to facilitate the felony of drug distribution. The answer is no.

FBI agents believed Mohammed Said was selling cocaine and got a warrant to tap his cell phone. In the course of listening in, they recorded six calls between Said and petitioner Salman Khade Abuelhawa, during which Abuelhawa arranged to buy cocaine from Said in two separate transactions, each time a single gram. Abuelhawa's two purchases were misdemeanors while Said's two sales were felonies. The Government nonetheless charged Abuelhawa with six felonies on the theory that each of the phone calls, whether placed by Abuelhawa or by Said, had been made "in causing or facilitating" Said's felonies, in violation of § 843(b).[1] Abuelhawa moved for acquittal as a matter of law, arguing that his efforts to commit the misdemeanors of buying cocaine could not be treated as causing or facilitating Said's felonies, but the District Court denied his motion and the jury convicted him on all six felony counts.

Abuelhawa argued the same point to the Court of Appeals for the Fourth Circuit, with as much success. The Circuit reasoned that "for purposes of § 843(b), 'facilitate' should be given its 'common meaning — to make easier or less difficult, or to assist or aid.'" The court said Abuelhawa's use of a phone to buy cocaine counted as ordinary facilitation because it "undoubtedly made Said's cocaine distribution easier; in fact, 'it made the sale possible.'" We granted certiorari, to resolve a split among the Courts of Appeals on the scope of § 843(b), and we now reverse.

The Government's argument is a reprise of the Fourth Circuit's opinion, that Abuelhawa's use of his cell phone satisfies the plain meaning of "facilitate" because it "allow[ed] the transaction to take place more efficiently, and with less risk of detection, than if the purchaser and seller had to meet in person." And of course on the literal plane, the phone calls could be described as "facilitating" drug distribution; they "undoubtedly made … distribution easier." But stopping there would ignore the rule that, because statutes are not read as a collection of isolated phrases, "[a] word in a statute may or may not extend to the outer limits of its definitional possibilities." We think the word here does not.

---

1. In full, § 843(b) provides: "It shall be unlawful for any person knowingly or intentionally to use any communication facility in committing or in causing or facilitating the commission of any act or acts constituting a felony under any provision of this subchapter or subchapter II of this chapter. Each separate use of a communication facility shall be a separate offense under this subsection. For purposes of this subsection, the term 'communication facility' means any and all public and private instrumentalities used or useful in the transmission of writing, signs, signals, pictures, or sounds of all kinds and includes mail, telephone, wire, radio, and all other means of communication." Section 843(d) provides, subject to exceptions not at issue here, that "any person who violates this section shall be sentenced to a term of imprisonment of not more than 4 years, a fine…, or both."

To begin with, the Government's literal sweep of "facilitate" sits uncomfortably with common usage. Where a transaction like a sale necessarily presupposes two parties with specific roles, it would be odd to speak of one party as facilitating the conduct of the other. A buyer does not just make a sale easier; he makes the sale possible. No buyer, no sale; the buyer's part is already implied by the term "sale," and the word "facilitate" adds nothing. We would not say that the borrower facilitates the bank loan.

The Government, however, replies that using the instrument of communication under § 843(b) is different from borrowing the money or merely handing over the sale price for cocaine. Drugs can be sold without anyone's mailing a letter or using a cell phone. Because cell phones, say, really do make it easier for dealers to break the law, Congress probably meant to ratchet up the culpability of the buyer who calls ahead. But we think that argument comes up short against several more reasons that count against the Government's position.

The common usage that limits "facilitate" to the efforts of someone other than a primary or necessary actor in the commission of a substantive crime has its parallel in the decided cases. The traditional law is that where a statute treats one side of a bilateral transaction more leniently, adding to the penalty of the party on that side for facilitating the action by the other would upend the calibration of punishment set by the legislature, a line of reasoning exemplified in the courts' consistent refusal to treat noncriminal liquor purchases as falling under the prohibition against aiding or abetting the illegal sale of alcohol. See *Lott v. United States*, 205 F. 28, 29–31 (9th Cir. 1913) (collecting cases). And this Court followed the same course in rejecting the broadest possible reading of a similar provision in *Gebardi v. United States*, 287 U.S. 112 (1932). The question there was whether a woman who voluntarily crossed a state line with a man to engage in "illicit sexual relations" could be tagged with "aid[ing] or assist[ing] in ... transporting, in interstate or foreign commerce ... any woman or girl for the purpose of prostitution or of debauchery, or for any other immoral purpose" in violation of the Mann Act. Since the statutory penalties were "clearly directed against the acts of the transporter as distinguished from the consent of the subject of the transportation," we refused to "infer that the mere acquiescence of the woman transported was intended to be condemned by the general language punishing those who aid and assist the transporter, any more than it has been inferred that the purchaser of liquor was to be regarded as an abettor of the illegal sale."

These cases do not strictly control the outcome of this one, but we think they have a bearing here, in two ways. As we have said many times, we presume legislatures act with case law in mind, and we presume here that when Congress enacted § 843(b), it was familiar with the traditional judicial limitation on applying terms like "aid," "abet," and "assist." We thus think it likely that Congress had comparable scope in mind when it used the term "facilitate," a word with equivalent meaning, compare Black's Law Dictionary 76 (8th ed. 2004) (defining "aid and abet" as to "facilitate the commission of a crime") with *id.*, at 627 (defining "facilitation" as "[t]he act or an instance of aiding or helping; ... the act of making it easier for another person to commit a crime").

And applying the presumption is supported significantly by the fact that here, as in the earlier cases, any broader reading of "facilitate" would for practical purposes skew the congressional calibration of respective buyer-seller penalties. When the statute was enacted, the use of land lines in drug transactions was common, and in these days when everyone over the age of three seems to carry a cell phone, the Government's interpretation would skew the calibration of penalties very substantially. The respect owed to that penalty calibration cannot be minimized. Prior to 1970, Congress punished the receipt, concealment, purchase, or sale of any narcotic drug as a felony, see 21 U.S.C. § 174 (1964 ed.)

(repealed), and on top of that added a minimum of two years, and up to five, for using a communication facility in committing, causing, or facilitating, any drug "offense," 18 U.S.C. § 1403 (1964 ed.). In 1970, however, the CSA downgraded simple possession of a controlled substance to a misdemeanor and simultaneously limited the communications provision to prohibiting only the facilitation of a drug "felony." This history drives home what is already clear in the current statutory text: Congress meant to treat purchasing drugs for personal use more leniently than the felony of distributing drugs, and to narrow the scope of the communications provision to cover only those who facilitate a drug felony. Yet, under the Government's reading of § 843(b), in a substantial number of cases Congress would for all practical purposes simultaneously have graded back up to felony status with the left hand the same offense it had dropped to a misdemeanor with the right. As the Government sees it, Abuelhawa's use of a phone in making two small drug purchases would subject him, in fact, to six felony counts and a potential sentence of 24 years in prison, even though buying the same drugs minus the phone would have supported only two misdemeanor counts and two years of prison. Given the CSA's distinction between simple possession and distribution, and the background history of these offenses, it is impossible to believe that Congress intended "facilitating" to cause that twelve-fold quantum leap in punishment for simple drug possessors.[3]

The Government suggests that this background usage and the 1970 choice to reduce culpability for possession is beside the point because Congress sometimes incorporates aggravating factors into the Criminal Code, and the phone use here is just one of them; the Government mentions possession by a prior drug offender, a felony punishable by up to two years' imprisonment. And, for perspective, the Government points to unauthorized possession of flunitrazepim, a drug used to incapacitate rape victims, which is punishable by imprisonment up to three years. It would not be strange, the Government says, for Congress to "decid[e] to treat the use of a communication facility in a drug transaction as a significant act warranting additional punishment" because "[t]oday's communication facilities ... make illicit drug transactions easier and more efficient.... [and] greatly reduce the risk that the participants will be detected while negotiating a transaction."

We are skeptical. There is no question that Congress intended § 843(b) to impede illicit drug transactions by penalizing the use of communication devices in coordinating illegal drug operations, and no doubt that its purpose will be served regardless of the outcome in this case. But it does not follow that Congress also meant a first-time buyer's phone calls to get two small quantities of drugs for personal use to expose him to punishment 12 times more severe than a purchase by a recidivist offender and 8 times more severe than the unauthorized possession of a drug used by rapists. To the contrary, Congress used no language spelling out a purpose so improbable, but legislated against a background usage of terms such as "aid," "abet," and "assist" that points in the opposite direction and accords with the CSA's choice to classify small purchases as misdemeanors. The Government's position is just too unlikely.

---

3. The Government's suggestion that a result like this is not anomalous because a prosecutor could exercise his discretion to seek a lower sentence, see Tr. of Oral Arg. 41, simply begs the question. Of course, Congress legislates against a background assumption of prosecutorial discretion, but this tells us nothing about the boundaries of punishment within which Congress intended the discretion to be exercised; prosecutorial discretion is not a reason for courts to give improbable breadth to criminal statutes. And it ill behooves the Government to invoke discretionary power in this case, with the prosecutor seeking a sentencing potential of 24 years when the primary offense is the purchase of two ounces of cocaine. For that matter, see *id.*, at 41–43 (concession by Government that current Department of Justice guidelines require individual prosecutors who bring charges to charge the maximum crime supported by the facts in a case).

The judgment of the Court of Appeals for the Fourth Circuit is reversed, and the case is remanded for further proceedings consistent with this opinion.

2. Distribution and Possession with the Intent to Distribute

a. Proving an Intent to Distribute

One of the most frequently prosecuted trafficking offenses is possession with the intent to distribute.* As an initial matter, it is worth asking why the law divides "possession with the intent to distribute" and "possession" into separate offenses in the first place. Why isn't the crime of distribution (or sale) a sufficient mechanism for distinguishing between users and sellers? What does the offense of "possession with the intent to distribute" add that "distribution" does not? Perhaps the most obvious answer is that criminalizing possession with the intent to distribute allows the government to reach would-be sellers before a sale has occurred (though, wouldn't "attempted distribution" also meet this goal?). Another important advantage that possession with the intent to distribute has— at least from the government's perspective—is that it is typically much easier to prove than distribution or attempted distribution. The government does not need to show that the defendant sold drugs or took a substantial step toward selling drugs; a mere intent to distribute the drugs possessed is enough.

But, if a defendant hasn't distributed or attempted to distribute drugs, how can we be sure what her intention is in possessing them? Consider the following scenario: The police execute a search warrant on Denise's home and uncover a large quantity of an intoxicating substance—enough for one year of daily use by an addict, according to the government's expert. In addition, the police find $500 in small bills and a passport belonging to Denise in a safe. In the garage, they discover a gun registered to Denise and bags that are commonly used to package the substance. Is this evidence sufficient to prove that Denise intended to distribute the substance? If you believe that it is, what fact(s) are determinative for you? Would the quantity of the substance alone be sufficient to prove her intent to distribute?

Would your answer to the hypothetical above change if you learned that the intoxicating substance the police found at Denise's home was alcohol? (Of course, it is perfectly legal to possess alcohol today. Our concern for purposes of this thought exercise is not the substance's legal status but what the circumstances surrounding Denise's possession might tell us about her *intent* in possessing the substance.) Isn't it as likely Denise is an alcoholic, or a wine collector, or preparing to throw a big party—though, as we'll soon see, serving a controlled substance to social guests constitutes distribution under today's drug laws—as it is that she is planning to sell the alcohol?

As the example above indicates, trying to determine what a person intends to do with an item in her possession can sometimes be a difficult and uncertain endeavor. Of course, in other cases intent may be much clearer.

---

* Though federal law and most states use the term "distribution" in their statutes, some states criminalize "sale" rather than "distribution." This distinction can carry important legal consequences in some factual settings. In most cases, however, the terms are essentially interchangeable. For the sake of simplicity, this section uses the term "distribution" to refer to both "sale" and "distribution" statutes unless otherwise noted.

California v. Peck

Court of Appeal of California
52 Cal. App. 4th 351 (1996)

Richli, J.

Defendant is a member of a church which uses marijuana as a sacrament. He was convicted of transportation of more than 28.5 grams of marijuana in violation of Health and Safety Code section 11360, subdivision (a), and of possession of marijuana for sale in violation of section 11359 of that code.

Defendant was apprehended at the border patrol checkpoint in Temecula driving a car with 40 pounds of marijuana in the trunk. The marijuana was divided into bags of about one pound each. Cash in the amount of $2,350 was found under the dash cover. The wholesale value of the marijuana was about $40,000.

Defendant is president and a priest of the Israel Zion Coptic Church (IZCC). The IZCC has about 200 or 250 members. The IZCC is an offshoot of the Ethiopian Zion Coptic Church, commonly known as the Rastafarians.

The IZCC uses marijuana as a sacrament. The purpose of using the marijuana is to make the users aware of their sins. Typically, marijuana would be used approximately three times a day.

Defendant had grown marijuana for use in the IZCC, but had been criminally prosecuted and convicted for it. (See *State v. Peck* (1988) 143 Wis.2d 624.) Defendant and the other members of the IZCC then began buying small amounts of marijuana in Wisconsin for church use, but considered it too expensive. Therefore, defendant and two other members contributed a total of about $30,000, so that defendant could buy a large quantity of marijuana in San Diego, where defendant had grown up. Defendant was returning to Wisconsin when he was stopped.

The court, sitting without a jury, found defendant guilty of transportation of and possession for sale of marijuana.

Possession of illegal drugs for sale requires that the defendant have the intent to sell the drugs. During grand jury proceedings, which the parties stipulated the court could consider at trial, a sheriff's investigator gave the opinion that defendant possessed the marijuana for sale, based on the quantity. Such an opinion is sufficient to support a conviction of possession for sale.

Defendant argues the evidence of intent to sell was insufficient, despite the officer's opinion, because defendant testified without contradiction he intended only to give the marijuana away, not to sell it. We find the evidence sufficient, for at least two reasons. First, defendant testified that when he provided marijuana for use in the church, members were "free and welcomed to put some money in" towards the cost of the marijuana, and that they did so from time to time. A sale of an illegal drug is "a transfer of possession of such a drug to another for cash." At least with respect to the members who contributed money, defendant made such a transfer. The court reasonably could infer defendant intended to follow the same practice with respect to the marijuana he bought in California.

Second, a "sale" of drugs "includes transfers other than for money." The record shows defendant received a quantity of marijuana himself, over and above the amount he paid for with his own money, in return for providing it to the other members. Defendant testified that if he had not been apprehended, he would have received more than one-quarter of the marijuana, despite the fact he paid less than one-quarter of the total price, for getting the marijuana. Receiving a valuable commodity—here, the additional marijuana beyond the amount defendant paid for—in return for providing the commodity to another qualifies as a sale.

The judgment is affirmed.

———————

Peck introduces two important principles in this area of the law. First, most courts have held that a law enforcement officer's opinion that the quantity of drugs possessed is consistent with an intent to distribute can be sufficient to support a conviction, at least in some circumstances. Second, *Peck* indicates the terms "sale" and "distribution" can encompass a broader range of activity than the exchange of drugs for money.

Beyond these basic principles, however, things can become more difficult. The next case, *Hunt*, raises the problem of drug quantity and expert testimony in a much more nuanced setting. *Hunt* also highlights some additional factors that courts have held may be relevant for proving an intent to distribute.

United States v. Hunt
United States Court of Appeals for the Fifth Circuit
129 F.3d 739 (1997)

Garza, J.

Latarsha Hunt appeals her conviction for possession of cocaine base with intent to distribute in violation of 21 U.S.C. §841(a)(1). Finding insufficient evidence to support the verdict, we reverse, vacate the sentence, and remand for sentencing on the lesser included offense of simple possession.

A confidential informant told police that marijuana was being sold out of 832 Arthur Walk, which police identified as property leased to Hunt. Executing a search warrant on those premises, police officers discovered a brown paper bag containing marijuana on a coffee table in the living room along with loose tobacco and cigar labels on the floor. In addition, they found a loaded handgun under the couch. In Hunt's bedroom, they discovered 7.998 grams of cocaine base (or "crack") and a razor blade on a plate on the top of a dresser. The cocaine was broken into one large rock and several smaller pieces. Hunt, Dashanta Burton, who is a friend of Hunt's, and an unidentified male juvenile were present when the police entered the house. Hunt was standing near the front door when police entered, and, according to the testimony of the officers, did not appear to be expecting the police.

Detective Ruben Rodriguez testified that the cocaine was worth about $200, an amount that could be doubled depending on how it was cut, and that it was a distributable amount. Furthermore, he stated that each of the smaller rocks would be "a lot of crack for a crack head" and that the rocks are available in sizes smaller than that size. Brian Cho, a forensic drug analyst, stated that the amount of cocaine base he usually receives for testing is around 100 to 200 mg per submission, usually in the form of one small rock.

Detective Rodriguez also stated, however, that a cocaine base addict may smoke close to $500 worth in one day. He explained that although a junkie who had a rock as big as the largest one "would be in heaven," it would produce only a three-second high. When questioned about the razor blade that was found with the cocaine, he testified that a razor blade is necessary to cut the cocaine base, either for distribution or, as he conceded on cross-examination, for personal use (i.e., to fit in a smoking device).

When questioned about drug paraphernalia, Detective Rodriguez testified that crack users will smoke from homemade crack pipes, which can be made from objects such as broken car antennas, aluminum cans, and aluminum foil. The officers did not find any smoking devices, such as a smoke pipe, and, according to Detective Rodriguez, this indicated that no crack cocaine smokers were present. Furthermore, in his opinion, the tobacco and cigar wrappings they found were evidence of "blunts" being sold out of Hunt's house. He explained that blunts are made by taking the tobacco out of cigars and replacing it with marijuana and that "primos" are made by adding crack cocaine to the marijuana. He stated that in the area of town where Hunt's house was located, marijuana and crack are usually sold hand in hand, "like a little drug store." On recross, however, he stated that "primos" are one way that cocaine users smoke cocaine.

Hunt testified that she arrived at home just before the police officers and that she had not yet entered her bedroom, where the police officers found the cocaine. She admitted that she used marijuana, but claimed she did not "indulge" in crack cocaine. She said she knew the marijuana was in the house, but denied knowledge of the cocaine being there. She also denied allegations that she had ever sold drugs. She said she had given a key to the house to Burton, who was also living in the house, and that Burton had obtained the marijuana for a "get-together" they were going to have with a few friends that night. She also admitted she owned the gun, but denied owning the tobacco. Wendy Wilson, Hunt's neighbor and friend, testified that she had never seen Hunt use or deal crack cocaine.

Hunt was indicted under § 841(a)(1) for possession of cocaine base with intent to distribute. The first trial resulted in a hung jury. During the first and second trials, neither the government nor the defendant requested that the lesser included offense of possession be submitted to the jury. Moreover, neither the government nor Hunt challenged the instructions at trial or on appeal. In the second trial, the jury returned a verdict of guilty.

On appeal, Hunt contends that the evidence is insufficient to support the jury's verdict regarding the element of intent to distribute. She does not contend that the evidence was insufficient to support possession. In reviewing a challenge to the sufficiency of the evidence in a criminal case, we will affirm a conviction if a rational trier of fact could have found that the evidence established the essential elements of the offense beyond a reasonable doubt.

To establish a violation of 21 U.S.C. § 841(a)(1), the government must prove the knowing possession of a controlled substance with the intent to distribute. The elements of the offense may be proved either by direct or circumstantial evidence.

Intent to distribute may be inferred solely from the possession of an amount of controlled substance too large to be used by the possessor alone. On the other hand, a quantity that is consistent with personal use does not raise such an inference in the absence of other evidence. *See Skipper,* 74 F.3d at 611 (holding as a matter of law that 2.89 grams of crack cocaine alone was insufficient to prove intent, despite testimony indicating that amount could suggest drug dealing, because it was "not clearly inconsistent with personal use"); *see also Turner v. United States,* 396 U.S. 398, 423 (1970) (holding that a small quantity of cocaine, which could be for the defendant's personal use as well as for sale, does not support an inference of distribution).

Hunt contends that the 7.998 grams of crack cocaine that the police discovered in her house is insufficient as a matter of law to infer intent, and we agree. Although the government introduced testimony that this amount is a distributable amount and that the individual rocks may be larger than those that Detective Rodriguez believes are usually smoked or that Cho, the forensic analyst, usually tests, the testimony also indicated, as in *Skipper*, that this amount was also consistent with personal use. In particular, Detective Rodriguez testified that a crack cocaine user may smoke, in one day alone, close to $500 worth, an amount that exceeds even the highest value he assigned to the cocaine found in Hunt's house. Furthermore, at oral argument, the government conceded that "the amount alone, by itself, is not sufficient" to support an inference of intent to distribute.[1]

We must therefore examine the other evidence to determine whether it, in conjunction with the quantity of cocaine found, suffices to establish the requisite intent to distribute. *See United States v. Munoz,* 957 F.2d 171, 174 (5th Cir. 1992) (noting that even a small quantity of cocaine is sufficient to infer intent when augmented by the presence of evidence such as distribution paraphernalia or large quantities of cash). As with the quantity of drugs, however, "paraphernalia that could be consistent with personal use does not provide a sound basis for inferring intent to distribute." As evidence of intent to distribute, the government points to the razor blade, the absence of smoking pipes or other such instruments, the evidence of blunts, the gun, and Hunt's testimony. In *Skipper*, the government similarly argued that a straight-edged razor and the absence of smoking paraphernalia suggested the intent to distribute. We held that, even viewed in the light most favorable to the government, the evidence was insufficient to prove intent beyond a reasonable doubt. The same conclusion is warranted here. Detective Rodriguez testified that although a razor blade is needed to cut crack cocaine for distribution, it is also needed to cut the cocaine for personal use. Furthermore, even though Rodriguez testified that the evidence of blunts indicated drug sales, he also said that the evidence indicated use, namely, the smoking of cocaine in the form of primos. Because this evidence is also consistent with personal use, we do not believe it provides a sound basis for inferring that Hunt intended to distribute the cocaine.

The government also points to the gun found under her couch as evidence of Hunt's intent to distribute. We have often recognized that guns are tools of the trade in the drug business. In *United States v. Lucien,* 61 F.3d 366, 375 (5th Cir. 1995), the government argued that three guns that were found in the defendant's apartment were evidence that he was distributing cocaine base. In response, we noted that "although we do not discount

---

1. In considering the quantity of crack cocaine found in Hunt's house, we note that, in a few cases, other circuit courts rested their decisions that the evidence was sufficient to support an inference of intent in large part on quantities comparable to this amount. In *United States v. Lamarr,* 75 F.3d 964, 973 (4th Cir. 1996), the court quoted a letter to the editor of the Washington Post (regarding sentencing), which stated that "'five grams of crack cocaine is the equivalent of 50 street doses'" and that "'anybody holding that much crack is dealing.'" The court concluded that the 5.72 grams the defendant possessed was roughly the amount a strong user would use in two months and held that, combined with testimony that the defendant was dealing, the evidence was sufficient to infer intent. *See also United States v. Haney,* 23 F.3d 1413 (8th Cir. 1994) (emphasizing the testimony of a criminologist that if an addict ingested 6.57 grams of crack in one or two days he would probably die; but also relying on confidential informant's information that defendant would be selling crack in exchange for food stamps, the $371 cash and $97 in food stamps found on defendant, and the fact that cocaine was cut into $20 pieces). Here, however, the only testimony the jury heard regarding the quantity of drugs was that a crack cocaine user can consume in one day, a value of crack greater than that found in Hunt's house and that the size of the individual rocks may be larger than those usually smoked by crack users or those tested by Brian Cho. Furthermore, we note again the government's concession at oral argument that this amount, by itself, is not sufficient to support an inference of intent. Therefore, although we recognize the import of the quantity in determining the intent to distribute controlled substances, we conclude that the quantity of cocaine base at issue here, as evaluated by the testimony presented, does not support an inference of intent to distribute.

the prevalence of guns in drug trafficking, we do not place undue weight on the presence of the guns in this case because [the defendants] could have untold reasons, nefarious and otherwise, for keeping guns in the apartment." The reasoning in *Lucien* applies with equal force to this case. Hunt's gun was found in her residence, under a couch, and not with the cocaine. Furthermore, Hunt made no move toward the gun when the police entered, and she admitted when asked that she did have a gun in the house. This evidence can be contrasted with cases in which a weapon was found in a more incriminating context. *See, e.g., United States v. Harrison,* 55 F.3d 163, 165 (5th Cir.) (noting that loaded .22 caliber pistol and ammunition were found next to 49.32 grams of cocaine base in dresser drawer); *United States v. Perez,* 648 F.2d 219, 220–21 (5th Cir. Unit B June 1981) (noting that when defendant noticed police observing him feeding bales of marijuana on conveyor belt to boat, he ran into house and was apprehended as he reached toward a shelf on which there were two loaded weapons). Unconnected with any such circumstances, however, the gun is no more probative of distribution of drugs than of other, non-nefarious purposes for which one may keep a gun. We therefore cannot affirm Hunt's conviction based on the presence of the gun.

The government also argues that the jury could have rejected Hunt's testimony that she had no knowledge of the cocaine and that Hunt's denial of use of cocaine necessitates a conclusion that the cocaine was kept on the premises for distribution. On appeal, however, Hunt does not challenge the jury's finding that she possessed the cocaine. Furthermore, although denial of personal consumption may be a factor in inferring intent to distribute in certain circumstances, we have stated that a defendant's "denial of guilt itself should not be permitted to become evidence of guilt." *United States v. Sutherland,* 428 F.2d 1152, 1157 (5th Cir. 1970). Accordingly, we reject the government's argument that Hunt's denial of use leads to the inference that she intended to distribute the crack.

When we have concluded that the evidence presented at trial was sufficient to support an inference of intent to distribute, we have pointed to evidence that is not as equally probative of possession as of distribution. *See, e.g., Lucien,* 61 F.3d at 376 (over $1200 cash, three weapons, and a plastic bag with several aluminum foil packets); *United States v. Pigrum,* 922 F.2d 249, 251 (5th Cir. 1991) (two sets of scales, coffee cup containing a test tube, cutting agent); *United States v. Onick,* 889 F.2d 1425, 1430–31 (5th 1989) (drug paraphernalia, particularly 4,063 empty gelcaps, and testimony that dealers package drugs in these gelcaps for street distribution); *United States v. Prieto-Tejas,* 779 F.2d 1098, 1101 (5th Cir. 1986) (value of cocaine between $2,200 and $9,000). We do not, however, see any evidence in this case, viewed individually or collectively, that is more probative of distribution than of possession. We therefore hold that a reasonable jury could not conclude beyond a reasonable doubt that Hunt intended to distribute the cocaine. We accordingly reverse Hunt's conviction for possession with intent to distribute.

The government asked us to remand for entry of judgment and for sentencing on the lesser included offense of simple possession if we found the evidence insufficient to support the element of intent to distribute.

In certain limited circumstances, we may exercise our power under 28 U.S.C. § 2106 and reduce a conviction to a lesser included offense.

Hunt has conceded the element of possession on appeal, challenging only the element of intent. We therefore find that reducing Hunt's conviction to possession will occasion her no undue prejudice.

For the foregoing reasons, Hunt's conviction is REVERSED, the sentence is VACATED, and the cause is REMANDED with instructions.

The *Hunt* court concluded that 7.998 grams of cocaine base was insufficient to demonstrate an intent to distribute. But in *United States v. Lamarr* (cited by *Hunt* in footnote 1), the Fourth Circuit found sufficient evidence to prove an intent to distribute where the defendant was found with 5.72 grams of crack. In *Lamarr*, the court concluded that 5.72 grams was enough to last a "strong user" two months. In *Hunt*, however, the officer testified that a crack user might smoke more than 7.998 grams "in one day alone."

The contrast between *Lamarr* and *Hunt* highlights two important and interrelated issues in this area. The first is the frequency with which law enforcement officers provide expert testimony in intent to distribute cases. Critics argue that members of law enforcement are likely to be biased against defendants and that this bias might color their testimony. In a similar vein, juries may be too quick to defer to an officer's testimony that a given drug quantity or a certain piece of evidence is indicia of an intent to sell. Finally, while police officers may be likely to have expert knowledge about some aspects of the drug trade, their familiarity with issues like the amount of drugs an average user consumes is arguably more tenuous. Perhaps as a result of these issues, it is not uncommon to see the same drug quantity described as a two month supply in one case and a one day supply in another, as in *Lamarr* and *Hunt*. Despite these concerns, the use of police officers as experts in "intent to distribute" cases remains widespread. While evidentiary rules place limits on the scope of police officer testimony in these cases, most courts have rejected arguments that officers should not be allowed to give their opinion about whether circumstances are consistent with an intent to distribute drugs. *See, e.g.,* Dana R. Hassin, *How Much is Too Much? Rule 704(b) Opinions on Personal Use vs. Intent to Distribute*, 55 U. Miami L. Rev. 667 (2001) (discussing the federal evidentiary rule against "ultimate issue" testimony and its impact on police officer testimony in drug cases). For a forceful argument that courts have been too lenient in permitting police officers to testify as experts in drug cases, see Brian R. Gallini, *To Serve and Protect? Officers As Expert Witnesses in Federal Drug Prosecutions*, 19 Geo. Mason L. Rev. 363 (2012) (arguing that "courts should limit officers' expert testimony in federal drug prosecutions to law enforcement members who did not also participate in the underlying criminal investigation").

The second issue highlighted by *Lamarr* and *Hunt* is the extent to which judgments about a defendant's intent to distribute should be based on the quantity of drugs involved. The inconsistencies that can arise from a case-by-case approach to the relationship between drug quantity and intent to distribute might suggest that legislatures should adopt numerical limits to govern intent to distribute cases. Some legislatures have done just that. But statutorily enshrined drug quantity presumptions raise their own set of problems. If an individual is found with enough drugs for a six-month supply, can we be sure she is engaged in distribution? Arguably, it is not uncommon for individuals to have an equivalent amount of alcohol for their own use. A wine connoisseur might have a cellar full of bottles. Someone who enjoys making a variety of different cocktails might keep enough hard liquor in their home bar to last for months. A number of defendants have brought constitutional challenges to intent-to-distribute-presumption laws. These challenges have generally been unsuccessful, however. *See, e.g., Stone v. Arkansas*, 254 Ark. 1011 (1973) (upholding a state law that created a rebuttable presumption of an intent to deliver for anyone found with a quantity of heroin in excess of 100 milligrams).

At least one state responded to difficulties posed by the crime of possession with the intent to distribute by abandoning it in favor of an alternative approach. In 1989, Minnesota adopted a scheme in which "[t]he crime of possession with intent to sell … vanished, except in cases where small amounts of drugs are involved." Philip Leavenworth, Note, *Illegal Drugs, New Laws, and Justice: An Examination of Five Recently Enacted Minnesota Statutes,* 16 WM. MITCHELL L. REV. 523, 521 (1990). In its place, the new law separated the offense of drug possession into five degrees based on the amount and type of drug possessed. *Id.* at 523 (noting that the law was developed because "police and prosecutors were frustrated with the burden of proving the intent element of the crime of possession with intent to sell").

b. Is Sharing between Users Distribution?

Hunt addresses the question of how to determine whether a person found in possession of drugs intended to distribute them. But what actions qualify as "distribution"? Clearly, the exchange of drugs for money amounts to distribution. But does passing a marijuana cigarette to a friend at a party constitute distribution of the cigarette? In *New Jersey v. Morrison* the Supreme Court of New Jersey considered the meaning of the term distribute in a tragic factual setting.

New Jersey v. Morrison

Supreme Court of New Jersey

902 A.2d 860 (2006)

Albin, J.

In the early morning hours of September 27, 2002, Daniel Shore and his friend defendant Lewis B. Morrison trolled the streets of Plainfield for drugs. When they found a dealer, defendant took their pooled money and bought four decks of heroin — little glassine packets containing the powdery substance. Afterwards, defendant gave two of the decks to Shore. Later that day, Shore died of a heroin overdose.

A grand jury returned an indictment charging defendant with distributing the heroin to Shore and, as such, with causing Shore's drug-induced death. Based on the grand jury record, the trial court concluded that the evidence could not support a finding that defendant distributed the heroin to Shore, but only that defendant and Shore jointly purchased and possessed the drugs for their personal use. For that reason, the court dismissed the distribution and drug-induced death charges. The Appellate Division overruled the trial court, finding that the evidence raised a jury issue, and reinstated the charges. We now reverse. We agree with the trial court that the evidence revealed only that defendant and Shore were joint purchasers and possessors of the heroin and therefore no act of distribution occurred between the two. Accordingly, we hold that the trial court did not abuse its discretion in dismissing the distribution and strict liability for drug-induced death charges.

On the evening of September 26, 2002, Shore and defendant Morrison, both twenty-four years old, were playing in a band together. After band practice, which ended between 1:00 and 2:00 a.m., they went to defendant's home in Raritan Township. Defendant lived there with his parents, who apparently were not home at the time. At approximately 3:00 a.m., with defendant behind the wheel, defendant and Shore drove to Plainfield to buy heroin. Defendant was a heroin addict, and Shore had experimented with the drug on an infrequent basis. To make the purchase, they pooled their money, Shore contributing thirty dollars and defendant ten dollars. Seemingly familiar with the area, defendant drove around Plainfield until an unknown man appeared on a bicycle. They honked the horn and, in return, the man whistled. In exchange for forty dollars, the man gave defendant four decks of heroin. Defendant placed the decks in his pocket and, after driving out of the city, gave one to Shore. While still in the car, Shore snorted half of the deck. When they returned to defendant's home, defendant handed Shore a second deck of heroin. Shore entered a downstairs bathroom and shut the door, where he presumably ingested the remainder of the heroin. At the same time, defendant walked upstairs where he injected his two bags of heroin. When defendant returned downstairs, he and Shore "talked about how messed up they both were." The two young men then went to sleep. Sometime that afternoon, defendant injected another dose of heroin from the remnants of two bags he had purchased earlier and fell back asleep.

At about 6:00 p.m., defendant went outside to feed his horses. On his return, he found Shore lying on the couch, blue and not breathing. [D]efendant dialed 911, and shortly afterwards, Raritan Township Police Department officers and paramedics responded to the scene. When Patrolmen David Carson and Gary Brewer arrived, they observed defendant attempting to perform CPR on Shore, who was lying face up in the driveway. Patrolmen Carson and Brewer, both trained Emergency Medical Technicians, took over the CPR efforts. In response to questioning from Patrolman Carson, defendant repeatedly denied that Shore had taken an "illegal drug," mentioning only that Shore was on some prescription medications. Significantly, an off-duty paramedic on the scene had with him a drug called Narcan, which is administered to counter the effects of a heroin overdose. Because of defendant's deceptive responses, the Narcan was not immediately given to Shore.

Upon his arrival, Raritan Township Police Detective Benedict Donaruma, Jr., also questioned defendant, who again "denied any knowledge of any type of illegal narcotics." Based on defendant's constricted pupils and slow speech, it was obvious to Detective Donaruma that defendant was on drugs and not being truthful. Despite defendant's misleading responses, paramedics by that time had administered the Narcan.

Police officers next took defendant to headquarters, where he was advised of his *Miranda* rights. After a brief line of questioning by Detective Donaruma, defendant broke down crying. Defendant explained that he had a heroin addiction, had been dishonest in his earlier answers, and wanted to tell the truth. Defendant next provided a narrative of the trip that he and Shore took to Plainfield and the events that unfolded.

In the meantime, Shore had been transported to a hospital, where he was pronounced dead. Dr. Daksha Shah of the Hunterdon County Medical Examiner's Office conducted an autopsy and determined that Shore had died of a heroin overdose.

Defendant was charged with both distribution of a controlled dangerous substance (heroin) to Shore, in violation of N.J.S.A. 2C:35-5(a)(1) and N.J.S.A. 2C:35-5(b)(3), and strict liability for Shore's drug-induced death on the basis of the alleged heroin distribution, in violation of N.J.S.A. 2C:35-9. Both crimes require proof of an act of drug distribution. The distribution statute provides that "it shall be unlawful for any person knowingly or purposely ... [to] distribute or dispense ... a controlled dangerous substance." The drug-induced death statute provides that "[a]ny person who ... distributes or dispenses [heroin or other classified controlled dangerous substances], in violation of [the distribution statute], is strictly liable for a death which results from the injection, inhalation or ingestion of that substance."

The key issue here is whether defendant distributed the heroin to Shore or whether both jointly possessed the heroin at the time defendant purchased the drug from the street dealer. To address that issue, we must understand the meaning of the concepts of distribution, possession, and joint possession of a controlled dangerous substance under the

Comprehensive Drug Reform Act. Under the Act, distribution is defined as "the actual, constructive, or attempted transfer from one person to another of a controlled dangerous substance" for other than lawful medical or research purposes. It hardly requires stating that the "transfer" of a controlled dangerous substance cannot occur under N.J.S.A. 2C:35-2 if the intended recipient already possesses that substance.

The law recognizes three distinct forms of possession, actual, constructive, and joint. A person has actual possession of "an object when he has physical or manual control of it." Alternatively, a person has constructive possession of "an object when, although he lacks 'physical or manual control,' the circumstances permit a reasonable inference that he has knowledge of its presence, and intends and has the capacity to exercise physical control or dominion over it during a span of time." Two persons have joint possession of an object when they "share actual or constructive knowing possession of" that object.

Relying on those basic concepts, a number of jurisdictions have concluded that when "two individuals simultaneously and jointly acquire possession of a drug for their own use, intending only to share it together, their only crime is personal drug abuse—simple joint possession, without any intent to distribute the drug further." *United States v. Swiderski,* 548 F.2d 445, 450 (2d Cir. 1977); *accord Commonwealth v. Johnson,* 413 Mass. 598, 602, 602 (Mass. 1992); *People v. Schultz,* 246 Mich. App. 695 (Mich. Ct. App. 2001).

In the seminal case of *United States v. Swiderski,* the defendant and his codefendant fiancee, accompanied by a government informant, went to a studio apartment in New York City to purchase cocaine. There, a drug supplier gave the defendant a package containing cocaine, which both he and his fiancee sampled. The defendant purchased the package for $1,250, put it in his pocket, and left with his fiancee and the informant. Shortly afterwards, government agents stopped the van in which they were traveling and arrested them. The codefendant fiancee had the cocaine in her purse along with a substantial amount of cash. The defendant had in his possession only $529. Both were charged with possession with intent to distribute cocaine in violation of 21 U.S.C.A. § 841(a). At trial, the government and the defendants disputed whether the defendants intended to sell the cocaine to third parties.

In summation, the Assistant United States Attorney argued that "even if the defendants bought the cocaine with a view to sharing it between themselves as users, ... this proof would be sufficient to establish possession 'with intent to distribute.'" In instructing the jury, the court "made it clear over defense objections that distribution could be satisfied solely by a transfer between [the defendant] and [his fiancee]." Both defendants were found guilty by the jury of possession with intent to distribute. The Second Circuit Court of Appeals reversed the convictions, concluding that, in enacting the Comprehensive Drug Abuse Prevention and Control Act, Congress did not intend to make "the exchange of physical possession between two persons who jointly acquired and hold the drug for their own use" an act of distribution under 21 U.S.C.A. § 841(a).

The Second Circuit limited its holding to "the passing of a drug between joint possessors who simultaneously acquired possession at the outset for their own use."[4] The Second

---

4. A number of jurisdictions have limited *Swiderski* to its precise holding. *See, e.g., United States v. Speer,* 30 F.3d 605, 609 (5th Cir. 1994) (stating that court "need not pass on the validity of the *Swiderski* doctrine" because it was "undisputed that at least some of the cocaine was intended ... to be subsequently distributed to [a person] who was not at or near the scene of the transaction"); *Long v. United States,* 623 A.2d 1144, 1150–51 (D.C. 1993) (declining government's "invitation to reject *Swiderski* as incorrectly decided" but agreeing with government that *Swiderski* did not apply because defendant brought drugs home to his friends and thus served "'as a link in the chain of distribution'"

Circuit distinguished its decision from *United States v. Branch,* 483 F.2d 955 (9th Cir. 1973), in which the Ninth Circuit Court of Appeals held that an act of distribution under 21 U.S.C.A. §841(a) occurred when "the defendant had handed over a small amount of marijuana to an informer for smoking purposes." The Second Circuit did not "quarrel" with the result in *Branch* because in that case "there was no evidence that the informer-friend had jointly and simultaneously acquired possession of the drug at the outset." Unlike in *Swiderski,* "sole possession in *Branch* rested with the defendant" and therefore the transfer of the drug to the informer, whether a "friend or not," constituted an act of distribution.

Our Appellate Division applied "the *Swiderski* principle" in *State v. Lopez* and held that "the sharing of drugs by individuals in joint possession ... does not constitute 'intent to distribute' within the meaning of N.J.S.A. 2C:35-5 and N.J.S.A. 2C:35-7." In that case, in executing a warrant to search an apartment shared by Lopez and Garcia, the police discovered, in all, 7.37 grams of marijuana, 0.41 grams of cocaine, and drug paraphernalia. In particular, the police found remnants of three hand-rolled marijuana cigarettes in the living room, a few grams of loose marijuana and a marijuana cigarette in Lopez's bedroom, and the cocaine in the kitchen. Lopez and Garcia were charged with and convicted of a number of crimes, including possession and possession with intent to distribute cocaine and marijuana.

The appellate panel noted that "[t]he prosecution's theory of culpability as to the element of 'possession' was based on joint possession by both defendants of the marijuana and the cocaine." Nevertheless, the prosecutor argued in summation that "'the sharing of this marijuana by the two of them is possession with the intent to distribute.'" The panel found the prosecutor's remarks, suggesting that distribution occurs when two persons in joint possession of drugs share those same drugs with each other, to be a misstatement of law. The panel explained:

> The legal concept of "joint possession" is premised upon a metaphysical event in which two or more persons simultaneously possess an entire object, without leaving any piece of it outside the joint possessors' control. A corollary of this proposition is that one cannot acquire something one already possesses. Having an object with the intent to distribute presumes that the intended recipient does not have possession of it. Therefore, as a matter of law, two or more defendants cannot intend to distribute to each other drugs they jointly possess. Stated differently, the element of "intent to distribute" under either N.J.S.A. 2C:35-5 or N.J.S.A. 2C:35-7 cannot be established on the basis of the sharing of drugs between or among joint possessors.

Because the prosecutor's statement conflicted with those principles of law and was clearly capable of producing an unjust result, the Appellate Division reversed the possession with intent to distribute convictions.

We accept the self-evident precept in *Lopez* that "one cannot acquire something one already possesses" and thus two or more persons cannot "distribute to each other drugs they jointly possess." We also accept the limited *Swiderski* principle that when "two individuals simultaneously and jointly acquire possession of a drug for their own use, intending only to share it together," they have not committed the crime of distribution, in violation of N.J.S.A. 2C:35-5. We note that the appellate panel in this case, although sus-

---

(quoting *Swiderski, supra, 548 F.2d at 450*)); *State v. Moore,* 529 N.W.2d 264, 266–67 (Iowa 1995) (declining to apply *Swiderski* where both participants did not "actively participate[] in the drug purchase" but rather one "purchase[d] drugs and later share[d] them with others," noting that in those circumstances delivery has occurred "even if joint funds have been used to finance the purchase").

taining the indictment, accepted the basic principles enunciated in *Swiderski* and *Lopez* as discussed above.

We also note that in enacting New Jersey's Comprehensive Drug Reform Act, the Legislature made findings and declarations that shed some light on how distinctions should be made concerning culpability. The Legislature stated that "it is the policy of this State to distinguish between drug offenders based on the seriousness of the offense, considering principally the nature, quantity and purity of the controlled substance involved, and the role of the actor in the overall drug distribution network." In passing the Act, the Legislature deemed the sentencing guidelines under the old drug laws inadequate in "identify[ing] the most serious offenders and offenses and [in] guard[ing] against sentencing disparity." The consequences of a finding of distribution are significantly greater than that of possession. Whereas the maximum term of imprisonment for distributing heroin that causes a person's drug-induced death is twenty years, the maximum term for possession of heroin is only five years. The Legislature expected the criminal culpability of parties to bear some proportion to their conduct. We are mindful, as well, that criminal statutes are to be strictly construed.

We now apply the concepts and principles discussed to the facts of this case. In determining whether there are any facts to support the indictment charging defendant with distributing two decks of heroin to Shore, we must engage in a fact-sensitive analysis based on the totality of the circumstances. Among the factors to be considered are whether the relationship of the parties is commercial or personal, the statements and conduct of the parties, the degree of control exercised by one over the other, whether the parties traveled and purchased the drugs together, the quantity of the drugs involved, and whether one party had sole possession of the controlled dangerous substance for any significant length of time. *Cf. Swiderski*, 548 F.2d at 450 (discussing factors to consider in determining whether fair inference can be drawn that party possessed drugs with intent to distribute).

The grand jury testimony revealed that defendant and Shore played in a band together and enjoyed a friendly relationship. After band practice, in the early morning hours of September 27, 2002, they traveled to defendant's home and from there to Plainfield in search of heroin. Defendant had a heroin addiction, and Shore had dabbled with the drug in the past. They drove together and pooled their money, Shore contributing thirty dollars and defendant ten dollars. Despite the Appellate Division's speculation that the division of proceeds "could be interpreted as compensation for defendant finding the drug seller and making the purchase," nothing in the grand jury record even remotely suggests that defendant and Shore's relationship was commercial in nature. Considering that defendant provided the transportation and the place for the evening, the difference in their monetary contributions is not an overriding factor, transforming a case of simple joint possession into distribution. Here were two friends on a misguided and ill-fated venture. They found the street dealer together, but as a practical matter only one could actually conduct the purchase for the two of them.

In reality, defendant was nothing more than Shore's designee, making the buy for both. Typically, when two persons jointly purchase drugs, the one who gives the money for the drugs will necessarily have the drugs in his possession before he hands a portion over to his companion. To accept the State's strained view would lead to the absurd result that an act of distribution between defendant and Shore depended solely on the fortuity of who first took in hand the drugs from the dealer. Both defendant and Shore acted for a common purpose, and both were simultaneously present at the time of the drug purchase. Shore had the intent and capacity to take control of his share of the heroin. The evidence clearly implies that when defendant bought the four decks both were in joint possession of the drugs—that is, defendant had actual possession and Shore constructive possession of the heroin. Viewing the evidence in the light most favorable to the State, we agree with the trial court that because defendant and Shore simultaneously and jointly acquired possession of the drugs for their own use, intending only to share it together, defendant cannot be charged with the crime of distribution.

To summarize, we agree with the trial court that there is insufficient evidence in the grand jury record to support count one charging defendant with strict liability for Shore's drug-induced death and count three charging distribution of a controlled dangerous substance. We therefore find that the trial court did not abuse its discretion in dismissing those counts of the indictment. We reverse the judgment of the Appellate Division and remand to the trial court for entry of an order consistent with this opinion.

Justice RIVERA-SOTO, dissenting.

I am entirely in accord with *Swiderski's, Lopez's,* the majority's and the panel's legal reasoning that the joint possession of controlled substances is inconsistent with the intent to distribute statutorily required for the crimes for which defendant stands charged. However, I part company with the majority's conclusion because, as the Appellate Division correctly acknowledged, great deference is due to our constitutionally mandated grand jury process. Unless the basic protective guidelines applied to that process are violated, and there is no intimation here that they were violated in any way, the adversary process started by an indictment must be allowed to proceed. Viewed differently, the issue of whether defendant's and his victim's possession of the heroin that claimed that victim's life was joint is a matter of defense at trial, and was not an element of the charges returned against defendant. Therefore, the resolution of this issue should not be addressed prematurely via a motion to dismiss the indictment, but at the ripe time for the determination of defenses: at trial.

I respectfully dissent.

New Jersey's strict liability drug-induced death statute, and the prosecutor's decision to charge Morrison under it, represents one possible legal response to heroin overdoses. At the other end of the spectrum, some states and a number of colleges and universities have recently adopted "good Samaritan" (or "medical amnesty") policies. These policies provide protection from prosecution for some drug offenses to anyone who calls 911 during an overdose emergency. *See, e.g.,* Deborah K. Lewis & Timothy C. Marchell, *Safety First: A Medical Amnesty Approach to Alcohol Poisoning at a U.S. University*, 17 INT. J. OF DRUG POL'Y 329 (2006) (examining Cornell University's medical amnesty policy in the context of alcohol overdoses and abuse).

Which approach do you think is the better one? Should the state provide immunity for people like Morrison in order to encourage them to call for help and honestly answer paramedics' questions? Or, should the state prosecute people in Morrison's position as vigorously as possible in an effort to try and deter heroin abuse (and, consequently, overdoses)?

United States v. Wallace

U.S. Court of Appeals for the Second Circuit
532 F.3d 126 (2008)

Jacobs, J.

In May, 2003, a confidential informant made two controlled purchases of cocaine base at an apartment in Rochester, New York. Each time, the seller took the cash, went into a bedroom, and came back with one or two small ziplock bags containing cocaine base. A week later, Rochester police executed a search warrant at the apartment, in which Wallace lived with his father. During the search, Wallace advised the officers that he lived in the apartment, that he was unemployed, and that he had a shotgun in his bedroom. From his bedroom, the police recovered ziplock bags containing a total of 1.5 grams of cocaine base, a quantity of new unused ziplock bags, 91.22 grams of marijuana, an AK-47 semi-automatic assault weapon and ammunition compatible with it, and $460 in cash.

After his arrest, Wallace waived his *Miranda* rights and made several statements to the police: that he had cocaine base and marijuana to use and share with his friends, but was not a drug dealer; that he used the ziplock bags to store the drugs for his own use; that he kept the AK-47 to protect himself and his bed-ridden father; and that he knew the weapon was illegal, but made sure to keep it unloaded. These statements were admitted at trial.[1]

Wallace testified to the following at trial. He was unemployed; however, his father received disability and Social Security checks, which Wallace (who had power of attorney) would cash to pay the monthly $400 rent and utilities for the apartment. The narcotics and ziplock bags belonged to him, while the gun belonged to his father. He purchased $50 worth of cocaine base every month or so. He had purchased about $600 worth of marijuana two or three years earlier, the remains of which were seized by the police. He had the drugs for his personal use and, on occasion, to share with friends. He purchased ziplock bags in bulk. It was his practice to break the cocaine base into smaller pieces and place them in the ziplock bags so that his visitors would not know how much he had and try to "use it all up." Wallace's girlfriend and his father got the AK-47 from "a boss" and brought it to the apartment. To prevent it from hurting anyone, he "put it up for safety," keeping it under his mattress and putting the ammunition in an empty baby wipes container.

On April 9, 2004, the jury convicted Wallace of possession of cocaine base with intent to distribute, possession of a firearm as a convicted felon and possession of marijuana.

Wallace argues that the evidence was insufficient to support his conviction for possession with the intent to distribute cocaine because the government failed to prove that he held (or shared) drugs with a commercial purpose.

On the same legal theory, Wallace challenges the district court's supplemental jury instruction that "[s]haring drugs with another constitutes distribution."

This Circuit has not yet decided whether the social sharing of a small quantity of drugs, without consideration, constitutes the distribution of drugs within the meaning of 21 U.S.C. § 841(a). *See United States v. Williams*, 247 F.3d 353, 358 n.6 (2d Cir. 2001) ("Drugs intended for personal use are not for distribution. It may be, however, that drugs held to be shared gratis with family and friends, though not for personal use, are also not for 'distribution,' pursuant to 21 U.S.C. § 841. On this point, we take no position whatsoever.").

Several of our sister circuits, however, have concluded that distribution within the meaning of 21 U.S.C. § 841(a) can take place without a sale. *See, e.g., United States v. Cormier*, 468 F.3d 63, 70 n.3 (1st Cir. 2006) ("It is well accepted that drugs may be distributed by giving them away for free; 21 U.S.C. § 841(a)(1) imposes no requirement that a sale take place."); *United States v. Fregoso*, 60 F.3d 1314, 1325 (8th Cir. 1995) ("No 'sale' is required to violate the statute."); *United States v. Vincent*, 20 F.3d 229, 233 (6th Cir. 1994) ("In order to establish the knowing or intentional distribution of a controlled substance, the government needed only to show that defendant knowingly or intentionally

---

1. No evidence of the confidential informant's controlled purchases was admitted at trial.

delivered a controlled substance. It was irrelevant for the government to also show that defendant was paid for the delivery."); *United States v. Washington,* 41 F.3d 917, 919 (4th Cir. 1994) (holding that the defendant's "intent to share the cocaine with others is sufficient for a court to find that he possessed drugs with intent to distribute"); *United States Ramirez,* 608 F.2d 1261, 1264 (9th Cir. 1979) ("[T]here is direct evidence that appellant engaged in the 'distribution' of cocaine; although apparently no commercial scheme is involved, his sharing the cocaine ... constitutes 'distribution' for purposes of 21 U.S.C. § 841(a)(1).").

We now join this sound majority and hold that the sharing of drugs, without a sale, constitutes distribution for purposes of 21 U.S.C. § 841(a), which makes it illegal to "possess with intent to manufacture, distribute, or dispense, a controlled substance." The word "distribute" means "to deliver," and "deliver" means "the actual, constructive, or attempted transfer of a controlled substance[.]" These definitions, which take no account of consideration, bespeak a congressional intent "to proscribe a range of conduct broader than the mere sale of narcotics."

This reading respects the line between "possession" and "distribution." Simple possession, in violation of 21 U.S.C. § 844, refers to "possession for one's own use," *United States v. Dovalina,* 525 F.2d 952, 958 (5th Cir. 1976), whereas distribution, in violation of 21 U.S.C. § 841(a), "can only be ultimately accomplished by 'delivery' to a distributee," *United States v. Binkley,* 903 F.2d 1130, 1138 (7th Cir. 1990). Thus a defendant who holds narcotics solely for personal use is in possession; one who delivers or transfers narcotics to another — for consideration or gratis — is distributing.

Wallace testified that he purchased cocaine base and marijuana for his own personal use, and also shared the drugs with friends[:] "Most of the time I used it by myself ... but if a lady friend come by we use it together, you know, have some and relax...." This testimony is direct evidence that Wallace engaged in the distribution of cocaine base.

Accordingly, we reject Wallace's sufficiency challenge. We likewise reject his challenge to the supplemental jury charge that "[s]haring drugs with another constitutes distribution" — the charge is sound.

Wallace contends that *United States v. Swiderski,* 548 F.2d 445 (2d Cir. 1977), indicates that a felony drug offense must be commercial in nature. *Swiderski* held that "where two individuals simultaneously and jointly acquire possession of a drug for their own use, intending only to share it together, their only crime is personal drug abuse — simple joint possession, without any intent to distribute the drug further." Since neither one of the joint possessors "serves as a link in the chain of distribution," we concluded that "simple joint possession does not pose any of the evils which Congress sought to deter and punish through the more severe penalties provided for those engaged in a 'continuing criminal enterprise' or in drug distribution."

Wallace never testified that he shared his drugs with anyone as "joint possessors" within the meaning of *Swiderski.* The rule announced in *Swiderski* is expressly limited "to the passing of a drug between joint possessors who simultaneously acquired possession at the outset for their own use." We advised that the rule would not apply where the evidence showed that the defendant "handed over a small amount of marijuana ... for smoking purposes" to another individual without proof that the other individual "had jointly and simultaneously acquired possession of the drug at the outset." Rather, since "sole possession" in such a case would rest with the defendant, "his transfer of the drug to a third person, friend or not," would violate the prohibition on drug distribution. Wallace had "sole possession" of the drugs, even if he "handed over a small amount" to his occasional visitor.

Nor can Wallace find refuge in cases in which convictions under 21 U.S.C. §841(a) were reversed for want of evidence that the possession of narcotics was with the intent to distribute. In *United States v. Boissoneault,* 926 F.2d 230 (2d Cir. 1991), we reversed a conviction on sufficiency grounds where "the quantity of cocaine at issue, 5.31 grams (.19 oz.), was not inconsistent with personal use." But in that case, and other similar cases, it mattered that defendant had none of the tools of the trade. Thus there was no proof that Boissoneault had "scales, beepers, and other devices," or the "materials needed to process cocaine or to package it in druggist folds," or "a gun or other weapon, which would have helped sustain an inference that he was engaged in the dangerous business of drug trafficking."

This is not the *Boissoneault* case. When the Rochester police searched Wallace's bedroom, they found (among other things) 1.5 grams of cocaine base parceled out in more than a dozen small ziplock bags; a dinner plate holding numerous new and unused small ziplock bags; a ziplock bag containing numerous new and unused small ziplock bags bearing green dollar signs; a dresser drawer full of empty and unused glassine ziplock bags; and a semi-automatic assault weapon and ammunition for it. Viewed in the light most favorable to the government, this evidence supports the inference that Wallace had the intent to distribute narcotics. *See United States v. Gamble,* 388 F.3d 74, 77 (2d Cir. 2004) (affirming finding of intent to distribute where "[l]aw enforcement officers found 1.7 grams of cocaine base (with a purity of 79 percent), packaged in twenty-six zip-lock bags, ... along with hundreds of empty zip-lock bags," and evidence showed "an unusually high volume of pedestrian traffic at [the defendant's] apartment in the weeks preceding the search"); *United States v. Garrett,* 903 F.2d 1105, 1113 (7th Cir. 1990) ("Intent to distribute has been inferred in cases where small amounts of drugs have been packaged in a manner consistent with distribution or have been possessed in conjunction with other indicia of drug distribution, such as a weapon." (footnote omitted)).

Also seized was $460 in cash. Wallace testified that he was unemployed, and that he relied on his father's disability checks to pay the $400 monthly rent, the utility bills and medical expenses. These facts made it permissible to infer that Wallace lacked any legitimate income to purchase the cocaine base for his personal use and for sharing with friends.

For the reasons stated in this opinion, the judgment is AFFIRMED.

———————

If two or more people acquire drugs together then they are considered to be "joint users" and sharing between them does not constitute distribution. *Wallace,* however, demonstrates the narrow construction many courts have given to the "joint user" doctrine. Most federal courts have held that if one friend shares a controlled substance socially with another, it constitutes "distribution" unless the users acquired the drugs together at the same time. In *United States v. Wright,* for example, the Ninth Circuit held the defendant was not entitled to the "joint user" defense to possession with intent to distribute where a friend "asked him to procure heroin so that they might use it together; she gave him $20 with which to buy the heroin but did not tell him where to buy it; he left her dwelling and procured the heroin; then he brought the heroin back and they 'snorted' it together." 593 F.2d 105, 108 (1979). Because Wright and his friend had not acquired the heroin "simultaneously," the court found Wright's conduct constituted "distribution." The *Wallace* court reasoned that this interpretation of the term distribution "respects the line between 'possession' and 'distribution'" because "a defendant who holds narcotics solely for personal use is in possession; one who delivers or transfers narcotics to another—for consideration or gratis—is distributing."

In light of the fact that many drug users (including users of alcohol) share the substance with friends, however, doesn't *Wallace*'s approach to distribution have the potential to turn most users into distributors in the eyes of the law? If so, is such a result consistent with the policy objectives underlying the distinction between users and distributors discussed by the Supreme Court in *Abuelhawa*?

Some states take a more forgiving approach than federal courts to the joint user defense. *See, e.g., Minnesota v. Carithers*, 490 N.W.2d 620 (1992) ("That the absent spouse did not exercise physical control over the substance at the moment of acquisition is an irrelevancy when there is no question that the absent spouse was *entitled* to exercise joint physical possession.").

Another common scenario that arises in the context of distribution offenses is that of the so-called "purchasing agent." A purchasing agent is an individual who helps a buyer secure drugs, literally acting as an agent for the purchaser. Prior to passage of the Controlled Substances Act in 1970, a substantial number—perhaps a majority—of jurisdictions recognized a "purchasing agent" defense, which provided that someone who acts as a buyer's agent has not committed a distribution offense. Under this doctrine, a purchasing agent is considered to be an accomplice of the buyer (in other words, an accomplice to the crime of possession) rather than an accomplice of the seller. Today, only a handful of courts continue to recognize the defense. *See*, Scott W. Parker, Note: *An Argument for Preserving the Agency Defense As Applied to Prosecutions for Unlawful Sale, Delivery, and Possession of Drugs*, 66 Fordham L. Rev. 2649 (1998) (detailing the history of the defense and its demise); New York v. Roche, 45 N.Y.2d 78 (1978) (providing a detailed exploration of the defense); Yuval Simchi-Levi, *The Agency Defense: Can the Legislature Help?*, 59 Buffalo L. Rev. 1109 (2011) (arguing that "[c]ourts in New York are struggling to consistently apply the agency defense").

Elaine M. Chiu has argued that the agency defense raises intriguing questions about the role of motive in the criminal law because "its litmus test is expressed directly in terms of a defendant's motive." As Chiu describes the defense, "[i]n order to be treated as an agent, a jury must conclude that the defendant is motivated" by a desire to help the purchaser, rather than a desire to help the seller. *See* Elaine M. Chiu, *The Challenge of Motive in the Criminal Law*, 8 Buff. Crim. L. Rev. 653 (2005). Is the agency defense's reliance on motive unusual in the criminal law? If so, does that help to explain why most jurisdictions no longer recognize the defense?

3. Manufacture

Our examination of drug trafficking offenses began with the crime of possession with intent to distribute both because of its prevalence and the many difficult legal problems that it raises. But, of course, before a controlled substance can be distributed it must first be manufactured. The following cases provide an overview of the legal requirements and issues that arise in the crime of manufacture.

a. Manufacture of Naturally Occurring Substances

North Carolina v. Childers

Court of Appeals of North Carolina
41 N.C. App. 729 (1979)

Martin, J.

Defendant first assigns as error the failure of the trial court to instruct the jury that defendant could not be found guilty of manufacturing marijuana if it were found that she was growing the plants for her personal use. She contends that in order for her to be found guilty of the offense of manufacturing marijuana, it must be proved beyond a reasonable doubt by the State that she was manufacturing it with intent to distribute.

N.C. Gen. Stats. § 90-95(a) provides that "it is unlawful for any person: (1) To manufacture ... a controlled substance." Marijuana is a controlled substance under Schedule VI of the North Carolina Controlled Substances Act, pursuant to the provisions of N.C. Gen. Stats. § 90-94. N.C. Gen. Stats. § 90-87(15) defines "manufacture" as:

> ... the production, preparation, propagation, compounding, conversion or processing of a controlled substance by any means, whether directly or indirectly, artificially or naturally, or by extraction from substances of a natural origin, or independently by means of chemical synthesis, or by a combination of extraction and chemical synthesis; and "manufacture" further includes any packaging or repackaging of the substance or labeling or relabeling of its container except that this term does not include the preparation or compounding of a controlled substance by an individual for his own use ...

N.C. Gen. Stats. § 90-87(24) defines "production" as including "the manufacture, planting, cultivation, growing, or harvesting of a controlled substance." "Preparation" is defined by *Webster's Third New International Dictionary* as being "the action or process of making something ready for use or service." The same source provides, in addition, definitions as stated for the following terms: (1) propagation: causing to continue or increase by natural reproduction; (2) compounding: the putting together of elements, ingredients or parts to form a whole; (3) conversion: changing [of a substance] from one form, state or character into another; (4) processing: to subject [something] to a particular method, system or technique of preparation, handling or other treatment designed to effect a particular result.

N.C. Gen. Stats. § 90-87(15), in defining the term "manufacture" used six specific terms to illustrate what activity was being proscribed. It excepts "preparation or compounding of a controlled substance by an individual for his own use." Defendant argues that, because these two activities are excepted, any manufacture of a controlled substance for personal use would not be "manufacturing" within the contemplation of the statute. With this contention we cannot agree. The plain meaning of the exception is to avoid making an individual liable for the felony of manufacturing controlled substance in the situation where, being already in possession of a controlled substance, he makes it ready for use (*i.e.*, rolling marijuana into cigarettes for smoking) or combines it with other ingredients for use (*i.e.*, making the so-called "Alice B. Toklas" brownies containing marijuana). The four activities not excepted by this proviso contemplate a significantly higher degree of activity involving the controlled substance (*i.e.*, planting, growing, cultivating or harvesting a controlled substance or creating it by any synthetic process or mixture of processes, or taking a controlled substance and, by any process or conversion, changing the form of the controlled substance or concentrating it) and thus are more appropriately made felonies without regard to the intent of the person charged with the offense as to whether the controlled substance so "manufactured" was for personal use or for distribution.

We are aware that our interpretation of the statute may lead to some apparently anomalous results, where a person cultivating one marijuana plant weighing less than one ounce would be subject to conviction for a felony, while possessing less than one ounce of the final product of the plant would constitute only a misdemeanor. However, the Legislature has chosen, in its wisdom, to impose a higher penalty for manufacturing even small quantities of controlled substances than for merely possessing them. We may not presume to contravene that legislative intent. Should a revision of the present manufacturing statute be deemed advisable such an action must be done by the Legislature itself.

Like North Carolina, federal law and the law in nearly every state includes the production of naturally occurring substances like marijuana under the crime of "manufacture." In New Mexico, however, the legislature appears to have consciously decided to exclude the production of naturally occurring substances from its manufacture statute. Can you think of reasons why the New Mexico legislature would have made this choice?

New Mexico v. Pratt
Court of Appeals of New Mexico
138 N.M. 161 (2005)

Wechsler, J.

Defendant appeals his conviction of trafficking psilocybin mushrooms by manufacture contrary to NMSA 1978, § 30-31-20(A)(1) (1990) of the Controlled Substances Act (CSA). He argues that his conviction should be reversed because the legislature did not intend to punish the act of growing mushrooms as "manufacturing" when it enacted Section 30-31-20(A)(1). We agree and reverse Defendant's conviction.

The facts are not in dispute. On June 6, 2002, police, on information obtained from a confidential informant, obtained and executed a search warrant on Defendant's home. Throughout the house, they found glass mason jars containing psilocybin mushrooms at varying stages of maturity. Some of the jars had psilocybin spores growing on top of a rice cake mixture. The officers also found syringes filled with spores, which were allegedly used to inoculate the rice cake mixture. In the kitchen, the officers found a white styrofoam cooler containing a "bubbling apparatus," which was apparently used by Defendant as a humidifier for growing the psilocybin mushrooms. The machine was "turned on and pumping" when the officers found it. The officers also found "recipes" with instructions on growing psilocybin mushrooms. A message was written on the cooler stating "Remember to be patient!!!! Pinning might take a few weeks."

After a jury trial, Defendant was convicted of trafficking psilocybin mushrooms by manufacture and possession of drug paraphernalia. Defendant does not appeal the possession conviction. We will address the remaining facts as they pertain to the issue on appeal.

The State argues that Defendant "manufactured" psilocybin mushrooms by growing them artificially using special equipment. Defendant, relying primarily on our holding in *State v. Shaulis-Powell*, 127 N.M. 667 argues that the mushrooms "were in a natural state of mushroomness" when they were seized by police and that "assisting a growing plant or a fungus by providing [a] growing medium and water" is not "manufacture" as proscribed by Section 30-31-20(A)(1).

The question of whether Defendant's conduct of artificially growing psilocybin mushrooms falls within the ambit of Section 30-31-20(A)(1) is a legal question subject to de novo review. When we interpret a statute, our goal is to give effect to the intent of the legislature. "We do this by giving effect to the plain meaning of the words of [the] statute, unless this leads to an absurd or unreasonable result."

The CSA prohibits, as intentional trafficking, the "manufacture of any controlled substance enumerated in Schedules I through V or any controlled substance analog as defined in Subsection W of Section 30-31-2." Section 30-31-20(A)(1). "Manufacture" is defined in Section 30-31-2(M) in relevant part as:

> the production, preparation, compounding, conversion or processing of a controlled substance or controlled substance analog by extraction from substances of natural origin or independently by means of chemical synthesis or by a combination of extraction and chemical synthesis and includes any packaging or repackaging of the substance or labeling or relabeling of its container.

Section 30-31-20(A)(1) is silent as to its applicability to the act of artificially growing psilocybin mushrooms. However, *Shaulis-Powell* is instructive in deciding this issue. In Shaulis-Powell, one defendant was convicted of violating Section 30-31-20(A)(1) by growing eight marijuana plants in his yard. In reversing that defendant's conviction for trafficking by manufacture, we stated that "the plain meaning of 'manufacture' does not include simply growing marijuana. Without more, growing marijuana does not constitute manufacture."

The State seeks to distinguish Shaulis-Powell on its facts by arguing that: (1) mushrooms are different from marijuana plants, which were at issue in Shaulis-Powell, and (2) the mushrooms found in Defendant's possession were not in their natural state. In making these arguments, the State relies primarily on the testimony at trial of its expert witness.

The witness, a forensic scientist with the Minnesota Bureau of Criminal Apprehension Forensic Science Laboratory, testified that "Mushrooms are fungi, and so they are different from plants [in] that they don't have seeds; they have spores that they start out with.... Spores are ... the seeds of the mushroom; they're the reproductive cells." The witness also stated that the four stages that make up the life cycle of the mushroom are the spores, the mycelium, the primordia, and the mature fruit. The witness detailed an experiment she conducted in an attempt to duplicate the process Defendant used to grow psilocybin mushrooms. She prepared a substrate using distilled water, brown rice powder, and vermiculite. She placed this mixture into glass jars and inoculated the substrate with psilocybin mushroom spores she purchased legally from an advertisement in High Times Magazine. The witness stated that the mushroom spores were legal because they did not contain psilocybin. However, she detected psilocybin at the "mycelium knot" stage of mushroom development during her experiment. The witness also stated that the process is labor intensive, and, if not followed carefully, the mushrooms will not grow. Based on this evidence, the State argues that Defendant "manufactured" mushrooms as defined by Section 30-31-20(A)(1) and Section 30-31-2(M).

Although Shaulis-Powell noted that the marijuana plants at issue "were growing in their natural state when the officers seized them," we based our holding in the case on the statutory definition of "manufacture." We stated that "even if growing marijuana could be considered 'production' under the statute, 'production' is modified by the phrase 'by extraction from substances of natural origin or independently by means of chemical synthesis.'" The same statutory analysis applies in this case. We do not agree with the State that Defendant's actions met the chemical synthesis requirement of "manufacture" by "using a specialized process [thereby manufacturing] illegal ... mushrooms from the legal spores ... received in the mail." This argument is controverted by the State's own expert witness who testified that "spores are ... the seeds of the mushroom" and that the drug was produced naturally in the mushrooms at the mycelium knot stage. Because there is no evidence that Defendant engaged in "extraction from substances of natural origin or ... chemical synthesis" as defined by Section 30-31-2(M), his acts of cultivating or growing mushrooms, even if by artificial means, are not prohibited by Section 30-31-

20(A)(1). To interpret Section 30-31-20(A)(1) otherwise, as the State suggests, would require us to read language into the statute that is not there. See *Marshall,* 2004 NMCA 104, PP 10, 13 (refusing to read a personal use exception into the CSA, reasoning that to do so "would impermissibly read language into a statute that makes sense as written").

Our holding is also supported by an analysis of the federal counterpart to Section 30-31-20(A)(1), 21 U.S.C. § 841(a)(1) of the Federal Drug Abuse Prevention and Control Act (federal act). See *State v. Carr,* 95 N.M. 755, 760 (Ct. App. 1981) (recognizing that the [New Mexico] CSA is patterned after the federal act and relying on federal interpretation to the extent that the statutes are similar). The federal act, in pertinent part, proscribes any person from knowingly or intentionally manufacturing, distributing, dispensing, or possessing "with intent to manufacture, distribute, or dispense, a controlled substance." Its definitional section, which is virtually identical to Section 30-31-2(M), defines "manufacture" in pertinent part as:

> the production, preparation, propagation, compounding, or processing of a drug or other substance, either directly or indirectly or by extraction from substances of natural origin, or independently by means of chemical synthesis or by a combination of extraction and chemical synthesis, and includes any packaging or repackaging of such substance or labeling or relabeling of its container. 21 U.S.C. § 802(15).

However, the federal act specifically includes a separate definition of "production" as the "planting, cultivation, growing, or harvesting of a controlled substance." 21 U.S.C. § 802(22); see also *United States v. Klein,* 850 F.2d 404, 405 (8th Cir. 1988) (affirming the defendant's conviction of the "manufacture" of marijuana when the defendant grew ninety-four marijuana plants in the basement of his home using fluorescent lights, light fixtures, a heater, planting pots, and soil testing equipment). Because the CSA is patterned after the federal act, we believe the legislature acted intentionally when it omitted a similar definition of "production," criminalizing as manufacture the "planting, cultivation, growing, or harvesting of a controlled substance," from the CSA. [S]ee also *State v. Bennett,* 134 N.M. 705 ("We presume that the legislature knows the law when enacting a statute.").

Because Defendant's conduct did not fall within the ambit of Section 30-31-20(A)(1), we reverse his conviction. We remand for proceedings consistent with this opinion.

b. Proof of Manufacture

Saul v. Arkansas

Supreme Court of Arkansas

365 Ark. 77 (2006)

Brown, J.

On February 13, 2002, Officer Andy Lee of the Bentonville Police Department stopped Saul for speeding in a white van in Bentonville. After running a warrants check on Saul, he discovered that Saul had an outstanding misdemeanor warrant for forging checks. Officer Lee arrested Saul based on the warrant, searched the van, and found a blue plastic container in the rear of the vehicle. He opened the container and found items and substances he associated with a methamphetamine lab. After that discovery, Officer Lee backed away from the van and secured the scene. He also called in another investigator to assist him with the processing of the found items. Evidence was collected, following which some of the items from the blue container were sent to the crime lab and other items were sent to an environmental agency for disposal. When Officer Lee later questioned

Saul at the jail about the blue container, Saul denied ever having seen it before. Officer Lee described Saul's denial in his affidavit of probable cause dated February 20, 2002. Saul was charged with manufacturing methamphetamine, based on the contents of the blue container, and also as a habitual offender with two prior convictions for possession of drug paraphernalia.

On November 3, 2003, Saul was tried before a jury on the charge of manufacturing methamphetamine which derived from the February 13, 2002 traffic stop. The State introduced, as part of its case-in-chief, the testimony of Officer Lee, Detective Woodruff, and Officer Allen, as well as testimony from a representative of the Arkansas State Crime Lab, Matthew Sarver. Saul testified in his defense that he had been at work all day on February 13, 2002, and that he was on his way to have dinner with his ex-wife and children at the time he was stopped by Officer Lee. Saul denied any ownership or knowledge of the blue container that was found in his vehicle. The jury found Saul guilty of manufacturing methamphetamine and sentenced him to thirty years.

Saul appealed his judgment of conviction to the court of appeals, and that court reversed based. We subsequently granted review.

Saul first claims that his motion for a directed verdict should have been granted because the evidence at trial was insufficient to prove that he had actually engaged in the manufacture of methamphetamine. Saul cites this court to *Chapman v. State*, 343 Ark. 643 (2001), where he claims that this court held the evidence sufficient to prove manufacture of methamphetamine after the state had presented evidence that all of the ingredients, solvents, chemicals, and hardware necessary to manufacture methamphetamine had been found, together with the additional factor of the defendant's attempted flight from the scene. Saul also relies on *Ford v. State*, 75 Ark. App. 126 (2001), where the court of appeals found the evidence insufficient that the defendant was an accomplice to manufacturing methamphetamine, when the State was unable to prove that the process had actually taken place.

Saul also argues that there was no direct evidence that he actually had manufactured methamphetamine. In this regard, he explains that there was no heat source found among the items in the blue container and that Officer Lee testified that a heat source was necessary for the type of manufacturing process that was alleged in this case (the red phosphorus method). Additionally, Saul notes that there were other items necessary for the manufacturing process that were not found in the blue container, including no empty or used bottles of hydrogen peroxide; no used striker plates; no baggies for packaging the unfinished product; no clean coffee filters to filter the unfinished product; and no powder methamphetamine (the finished product). He further emphasizes that no objects were sent to the crime lab for fingerprinting. As a final point, he contends that the blue container did not belong to him. In sum, Saul claims that the circumstantial evidence presented at trial clearly allows for other reasonable explanations consistent with innocence, and that the jury had to resort to surmise and conjecture to find him guilty of manufacturing methamphetamine.

Saul was convicted of manufacturing methamphetamine, in violation of Ark. Code Ann. 5-64-401(a). Section 5-64-101(m) of the Arkansas Code Annotated defines "manufacture":

> "Manufacture" means the production, preparation, propagation, compounding, conversion, or processing of a controlled substance, either directly or indirectly by extraction from substances of natural origin, or independently by means of chemical synthesis, or by a combination of extraction and chemical synthesis, and includes any packaging or repackaging of the substance or labeling or relabeling of its container[.]

We agree with the State that the evidence supporting Saul's conviction is more than sufficient. The arresting officer, Officer Lee, was extensively trained, certified, and experienced in the identification of methamphetamine labs and the production of methamphetamine. Officer Lee testified that he smelled a strong chemical odor coming from Saul's van after he stopped Saul. Inside the van, Officer Lee found a blue plastic container that contained what he recognized as a methamphetamine lab. The State lists dozens of items found in the blue plastic container which are associated with producing methamphetamine by the red phosphorus method, including jars, tubing, funnels, lye, filters stained with red sludge, filters containing iodine crystals, hydrogen peroxide, camping fuel, acetone, hand scales, materials used as a hydrogen chloride gas generator, and items for cutting such as scissors, knives, and razor blades.

In addition, Matthew Sarver, a chemist for the crime lab who was trained and certified in the testing of methamphetamine labs, testified that the evidence in this case indicated that the lab discovered by Officer Lee was used for the red phosphorous method of producing methamphetamine. Mr. Sarver testified that the results of his tests showed iodine and phosphorous on the coffee filters, and he explained that the sludge left on the filters was what is left after methamphetamine has been "cooked." He also stated that tests of the samples taken from the liquid in a plastic bottle showed pseudoephedrine and methanol, and that the liquid appeared to be a "pill soak," which is used in the first stage of manufacturing methamphetamine by combining pills with alcohol. Sarver went on to describe the liquid found in other plastic bottles as organic solvent and acid, both of which are used throughout the process of manufacturing methamphetamine. According to Sarver, tests of samples taken from still another jar showed methamphetamine with an organic solvent. He pointed out that the liquid contained in this jar was actually methamphetamine and that the substance found in the jar is the result of one of the final stages of the manufacturing process.

We do not view the fact that Saul was not apprehended in the process of "cooking meth" as being determinative. In *Stone v. State*, 348 Ark. 661 (2002), police officers found ingredients for making methamphetamine as well as containers the officers suspected to be involved in the manufacture of methamphetamine at the defendant's home. The defendant was later convicted of manufacturing methamphetamine. He appealed and in a challenge to the sufficiency of the evidence, this court found that the State had "produced sufficient evidence that Stone was indeed manufacturing methamphetamine by means of the necessary ingredients and required apparatus." We held that this was so even though the defendant was not caught in the actual act of manufacturing methamphetamine.

We further note that the case of *Chapman v. State* is not helpful to Saul. In that case, this court found the evidence to be sufficient to support the defendant's conviction for manufacturing methamphetamine where the state had presented evidence that all of the ingredients, solvents, chemicals, and hardware necessary to manufacture methamphetamine were found on defendant's property, and where the defendant's attempted flight at the scene of the search provided additional evidence of guilt. Saul now contends that the proof introduced in *Chapman* is the standard against which the proof in the instant case must be weighed. We disagree. As already stated, the multiple ingredients and devices used in methamphetamine production which were found together with the by-products of such production and the actual methamphetamine discovered as well as the testimony of the police officers more than suffices as substantial evidence.

Although Saul concludes that the fact no heat source was found in the blue container is significant, the items found in Saul's van could well have been used with a heat source at a different location to produce the methamphetamine. Simply because a heat source was not present in Saul's van does not lead ineluctably to the conclusion that no heat source had been previously used to manufacture methamphetamine.

Affirmed. Court of appeals reversed.

————————

The items in Saul's possession were certainly suspicious, but did they really prove that Saul had already manufactured methamphetamine or only that Saul *planned* to manufacture methamphetamine? Wouldn't the evidence in this case be more consistent with proof of an attempt to manufacture methamphetamine rather than manufacture?

C. Precursor Chemicals

In addition to criminalizing the manufacture of controlled substances, federal and state laws also regulate and criminalize some of the chemicals that are used in the production of controlled substances. In recent years, lawmakers and drug enforcement agencies have particularly focused on precursor chemicals used to manufacture methamphetamine. *See, e.g.,* Note: *Cooking Up Solutions to a Cooked Up Menace: Responses to Methamphetamine in a Federal System*, 119 HARV. L. REV. 2508 (2006); John A. Gilbert, Jr., *DEA Regulation of Controlled Substances and Listed Chemicals*, 65 FOOD & DRUG L. J. 623, 628–29 (2010) (discussing the federal regulation of "listed chemicals" which are "chemicals that can be either directly used to illicitly manufacture controlled substances ... or chemicals that are important to the manufacture of controlled substances").

United States v. Kim
United States Court of Appeals for the Ninth Circuit
449 F.3d 933 (2006)

Berzon, J.

Pseudoephedrine, a "listed chemical" under a federal drug statute, 21 U.S.C. § 802(33) & (34)(K), is an ingredient in many over-the-counter cold medications. It can also be used to manufacture methamphetamine, a controlled substance under 21 U.S.C. § 812. Both the United States and California have statutes prohibiting over-the-counter sales of drugs containing pseudoephedrine in certain instances.

This case concerns the conviction of the proprietor of a small pharmacy for selling cold remedies containing pseudoephedrine. Jae Gab Kim was convicted of violating 21 U.S.C. § 841(c)(2), which prohibits the distribution of listed chemicals, including pseudoephedrine, "knowing, or having reasonable cause to believe, that [the pseudoephedrine] will be used to manufacture a controlled substance." He argues that, because drugs containing pseudoephedrine can be legally sold over the counter and there is no bright line in the law demarcating a legal sale from an illegal sale, the law allowing conviction upon "reasonable cause to believe" is unconstitutionally vague. We have previously held that § 841(c)(2) contains a mens rea requirement. With that mens rea standard, the statute is not unconstitutionally vague. We therefore affirm Kim's conviction.

Kim owned and operated the San Jacinto Pharmacy. After receiving information about the law regarding the sale of pseudoephedrine from an industry newsletter, Kim instructed his clerk, Virginia García, not to sell more than 150 sixty-milligram pills per person, per day. Kim believed that sales under this quantity were legal.

Kim purchased drugs containing pseudoephedrine from Bergen Brunswig. In May 2000, the Drug Enforcement Administration (DEA) received a report from Bergen Brunswig that Kim's purchases of drugs containing pseudoephedrine had sharply increased.[1]

The DEA began an investigation of Kim, sending undercover agents to purchase cold remedies containing pseudoephedrine from his pharmacy. Two transactions are relevant to this appeal:[2] On January 4, 2001, three undercover agents entered Kim's pharmacy. Kim was standing in an elevated section at the rear of the pharmacy, filling prescriptions. Kim nodded and smiled at the three agents. The agents attempted to purchase all the packages of cold medication on display. After Garcia started to tell the agents that one person could not buy all the medication, Kim interjected to ask what was going on and who was buying what. Kim instructed them to return some of the medication so that his stock would not be depleted. The three agents returned some of the boxes and divided the remainder for purchase. Ultimately, the agents were each allowed to purchase two boxes of 96-count thirty-milligram tablets and one box of 24-count thirty-milligram tablets, for a total of around 6 grams of pseudoephedrine. Additionally, in Kim's presence and conspicuously, the men inquired about and purchased hydrogen peroxide, iodine, and rubbing alcohol, all of which are used to manufacture methamphetamine. One of the men mumbled, in connection with the purchase of alcohol, that he needed alcohol to "break it down." One of the agents provided all the money for the purchases, although the purchases were rung up separately. There were confusing statements as to whether the person who supplied the money was holding the others' money for them or, instead, paying for all the purchases himself.

As Garcia was completing the transaction, one of the agents asked, "Can we get some more of this tomorrow?" Garcia answered, "Well hopefully." Kim, however, answered, "We're not selling every day." He added that the purchase "lasts for you, normally."

The next day, January 5, 2001, the same three undercover officers returned to the pharmacy. Kim again nodded to them as they entered. Although the officers assumed that he recognized them, there is no direct evidence that he did. One officer attempted to purchase multiple bottles of pseudoephedrine. Again, Garcia would not allow this sale to proceed. She did, however, allow each man to purchase one 100-count sixty-milligram bottle. As on the previous day, one officer held all the money initially and handed it to the other two so they could pay for their pseudoephedrine. Afterwards, the officers also each purchased two 24-count boxes of thirty-milligram pseudoephedrine, for a total of about 7.5 grams each. Kim was not involved in this transaction, but he was in the store at the time.

Kim was indicted for violating 21 U.S.C. §841(c)(2), for distributing a listed chemical when the merchant "knows or has reasonable cause to believe" that the chemical will be used to manufacture illicit drugs. At trial, at the close of the government's case-in-chief, the district court granted Kim's motion for judgment of acquittal on three counts.

---

1. Evidence at trial showed that Kim's purchases increased from a total of 347.28 grams in December 1999 to 1712.16 grams in April 2000. The quantity continued to increase, reaching a high of 4396.32 grams in July 2000. Kim's purchases of the larger-count bottles (stock bottles) also increased drastically over the same time period.

2. There were seven total purchases by undercover agents, each one eventually resulting in a count in Kim's indictment. As noted below, Kim was ultimately convicted of only two counts in the indictment.

The jury found Kim not guilty of another count. The district court later granted a post-verdict judgment of acquittal as to yet another count. In the end, Kim was convicted only on counts six and seven, covering the incidents described above.

Both after the government's case-in-chief and after the jury returned its verdict, Kim challenged the vagueness of the statute under which he was indicted. The district court denied both motions. Kim was sentenced to five months incarceration, three years supervised release — during which he was to spend five months in home detention — and a $15,000 fine. We were informed at oral argument that he lost his pharmacist's license as a result of the convictions.

The federal statute under which Kim was convicted provides that "[a]ny person who knowingly or intentionally ... possesses or distributes a listed chemical knowing, or having reasonable cause to believe, that the listed chemical will be used to manufacture a controlled substance except as authorized by this subchapter" shall be fined or imprisoned, or both. 21 U.S.C. § 841(c)(2). The federal law also contains a requirement that sales of certain packages of pseudoephedrine be recorded.[5] The recording statute contains a confusing maze of rules, exceptions to the rules, and exceptions to the exceptions. First, "[e]ach regulated person who engages in a regulated transaction involving a listed chemical ... shall keep a record of the transaction for two years after the date of the transaction." 21 U.S.C. § 830(a)(1). Not all sales of listed chemicals, however, are considered "regulated transactions." "[A]ny sale of ordinary over-the-counter pseudoephedrine ... by retail distributors shall not be a regulated transaction." § 802(39)(A)(iv)(I)(aa). Over-the-counter sales of pseudoephedrine that are not "ordinary," however, may be regulated transactions, because they are not necessarily included in the exemption from regulated transactions.[6] With respect to pseudoephedrine in particular, "The term 'ordinary over-the-counter pseudoephedrine ... product' means any product containing pseudoephedrine ... sold in package sizes of not more than 3.0 grams of pseudoephedrine base ... that is packaged in blister packs, each blister containing not more than two dosage units, or where the use of blister packs is technically infeasible, that is packaged in unit dose packets or pouches." § 802(45)(B)(i).[7] Additionally, sales of twenty-four grams or more of pseudoephedrine were automatically subject to the recording requirements of § 830. § 802(39)(A)(iv)(II). The upshot is that over-the-counter sales of pseudoephedrine

---

5. Certain of those sales that must be recorded must also be *reported* to the government. "Each regulated person shall report to the Attorney General ... any regulated transaction involving an extraordinary quantity of a listed chemical, an uncommon method of payment or delivery, or any other circumstance that the regulated person believes may indicate that the listed chemical will be used in violation of this subchapter." 21 U.S.C. § 830(b)(1)(A). The statute contains no definition of "extraordinary quantity."

6. The definition of "regulated transaction" generally allows the "Attorney General [to] establish[ ] a threshold amount for a specific listed chemical." § 802(39)(A). Section 802(39)(A)(iv)(II) provided at the time of Kim's offense "the threshold for any sale of products containing pseudoephedrine ... products by retail distributors or by distributors required to submit reports by section 830(b)(3) of this title shall be 24 grams of pseudoephedrine ... in a single transaction."

At the time of the relevant transactions in this case, the Attorney General had not established single transaction thresholds for retail sales of pseudoephedrine, but he has done so since then. *Compare* 21 C.F.R. 1310.04(f) (2000) with 21 C.F.R. 1310.04(f) (2006). The details of the quantity or quality of pseudoephedrine that must be recorded and reported are not dispositive in this case and the statute has been amended recently, *see* infra note 8, so we do not address the recording and reporting requirements further.

7. In the case of liquids, however, if they are "sold in package sizes of not more than 3.0 grams of pseudoephedrine base," they qualify as "ordinary over-the-counter" sales. § 802(45)(B)(ii).

had to be recorded if the items purchased totaled twenty-four grams or more and (1) were not in blister packs or (2) were in packages of more than three grams per package.[8]

California makes it a felony for people to sell certain substances "with knowledge or the intent that the recipient will use the substance to unlawfully manufacture a controlled substance." Cal. Health & Safety Code § 11104(a). The prohibited substances, which include pseudoephedrine, are listed in California Health and Safety Code section 11100(a), which also requires merchants to report sales of regulated substances. The California reporting statute, section 11100, incorporates federal law by exempting from its reporting requirements those transactions involving chemicals "lawfully sold, transferred, or furnished over the counter without a prescription pursuant to the federal Food, Drug, and Cosmetic Act (21 U.S.C. Sec. 301 et seq.) or regulations adopted thereunder." The California statute, however, specifically *does not exempt* from its reporting requirement sales "where the individual transaction involves more than three packages or nine grams of" pseudoephedrine. Thus, a pharmacist who sells more than nine grams of pseudoephedrine must report the sale to the California government, whereas a pharmacist who sells less must only report the sale to California if the drugs were sold in violation of the federal law—a category which would include, as we have noted, sales made "knowing or having reasonable cause to believe" that the purchase of drugs would be used to manufacture methamphetamine.

The upshot is that neither state nor federal law specifies any "safe harbor" amount of pseudoephedrine that may be sold over the counter. Instead, the seller's actual or imputed knowledge that the chemical will be used to manufacture methamphetamine is determinative of criminal liability, regardless of the amount sold.

Kim sold quantities below the per se reporting limits of the California statute, never selling to the undercover DEA agents more than three packages or nine grams of pseudoephedrine during a single transaction. Kim argues that because the California provision makes a sale of nine grams "otherwise authorized," he did not have adequate notice that a sale of less than nine grams could subject him to federal prosecution.[10] We reject Kim's claim.

First, Kim points to no support for his assumption that the federal statute exempts from criminal liability transactions permitted under state law. There is no provision in the federal law providing a safe harbor for transactions "otherwise authorized"; the term is entirely of Kim's own construction. Furthermore, unless a federal law states otherwise, state law cannot empower a citizen to act contrary to a federal prohibition.

Second, Kim appears to have confused the reporting requirements under California law with the criminal liability standards. The California provision does not "authorize[ ]" single transactions of less than nine grams. As noted above, the California law requires merchants to report to the California Department of Justice transactions involving sales

---

8. The federal law has very recently been amended. On March 9, 2006, President Bush signed into law an amendment to the USA PATRIOT Improvement and Reauthorization Act of 2005, which contained a section entitled the Combat Methamphetamine Epidemic Act of 2005. The Combat Methamphetamine Epidemic Act strengthened the recording requirements of the federal statute and further restricted sales of pseudoephedrine. It contains no amendment, however, to § 841(c)(2), the criminal liability section.

10. Kim does not challenge the sufficiency of the evidence on his conviction. In particular, he does not argue that because he did not directly participate in the January 5 transaction, he could not be guilty of distributing pseudoephedrine with any knowledge or reasonable cause to believe that this particular sale would result in the production of methamphetamine. We therefore do not decide whether a supervising pharmacist or proprietor who does not participate directly in a specific transaction can be criminally liable under § 841(c)(2).

of certain chemicals. A merchant need not report a *lawful* (under federal law) sale of less than nine grams; he or she *must* report a sale of more than nine grams, whether or not lawful under federal law. The more-than-nine-grams standard is thus significant for the purposes of California law only because it delineates those sales that must automatically be reported from those that *may* not need to be reported.

The California *felony* provision covering sales of pseudoephedrine, in contrast, contains *no* dosage safe harbor. Section 11104(a), the criminal liability provision, makes it a felony conviction to sell certain chemicals "with knowledge or the intent" that those chemicals will be used to manufacture illicit drugs. A sale of *any* quantity can violate California law if it is entered into with the requisite mental state; the quantity is irrelevant except as circumstantial evidence of intent. Although Kim allowed the undercover agents to purchase only quantities of pseudoephedrine below the per se *reporting* requirement of the California statute, he was not necessarily acting within the bounds of state law by consummating the sale for those quantities.

Kim argues that there is inadequate notice "of where (and how) the line is drawn to indicate when an [over-the-counter] sale that is otherwise authorized becomes one that is unlawful." As noted above, however, Kim's sales were *not* authorized by the California statute, although they were not explicitly prohibited either; the mens rea requirement was determinative.

Third, Kim's arguments based solely on federal law fare no better. He contends that because pseudoephedrine is legally sold over-the-counter for personal use, he must have protection against criminal liability under federal law for those personal use sales that are below the level at which they must be recorded. Pointing to provisions of federal law that mention "legitimate medical use" and "personal use," § 802(46)(A) & (B), Kim contends that "other than limiting the dosage level, there is nothing in the law to provide a retail distributor with assurance or guidance as to what is required for his over-the-counter sales to be deemed sales for legitimate medical use."

Kim is correct that, under federal law, a retail distributor is one who engages in sales for personal use, which are "below-threshold" sales for legitimate medical purposes. 21 U.S.C. § 802(46). He forgets, however, that retail distributors are *only* exempted from the definition of "regulated transaction" (which triggers the *recording* requirements of § 830) when they sell "not more than 3.0 grams of pseudoephedrine base ... that is packaged in blister packs, each blister containing not more than two dosage units, or where the use of blister packs is technically infeasible, that is packaged in unit dose packets or pouches." § 802(45)(B)(i).

Kim is therefore correct that a bright-line rule exists establishing a threshold for sales of pseudoephedrine. This bright-line rule, however, applies only to the recording requirements and *not* to the criminal liability provision. The criminal liability provision contains no cross-reference to the recording requirements, nor does it include the terms "legitimate medical use" or "personal use." Whether the over-the-counter sale was for a legitimate medical purpose within the meaning of the recording requirement is therefore technically irrelevant to the criminal liability provision at issue here. In practical terms, however, when a pharmacist knows or has reasonable cause to believe that a below-threshold quantity of pseudoephedrine will be used for the production of methamphetamine, that is not a legitimate medical use.

In any event, whether or not Kim had to report the sales he entered into with the undercover DEA agents to the U.S. Attorney General, he could still be subject to criminal prosecution if those sales violated § 841(c)(2). Kim's criminal liability instead turns on whether he "kn[e]w or ha[d] reasonable cause to believe" that his conduct would lead to manufacture of illicit drugs. §841(c)(2). As is true with other criminal statutes, conduct is prohibited not solely because of its objective contours, but because of the defendant's state of mind regarding such an effect. There is no quantity threshold exempting a merchant from criminal liability under §841(c)(2).

Kim argues that, construed as containing no quantity threshold, the statute is unconstitutionally vague because it does not provide a reasonably intelligent person with sufficient notice concerning whether he is violating it. Essentially, he argues that absent designation of a "safe harbor" amount that he may sell to each individual each day, he cannot be expected to conform his behavior to legal requirements and thus avoid criminal liability. There is, however, no constitutional principle—and Kim points to none—requiring the federal government to spell out a specific amount of pseudoephedrine that pharmacists may sell in each transaction without incurring criminal liability. Nor do more general vagueness principles support his contention.

Vague laws that do not infringe upon First Amendment rights have two principle evils: (1) they do not give a "person of ordinary intelligence a reasonable opportunity to know what is prohibited, so that he may act accordingly"; and (2) they encourage arbitrary and discriminatory enforcement by not providing explicit standards for policemen, judges, and juries. Thus, if a statute is not sufficiently clear to provide guidance to citizens concerning how they can avoid violating it and to provide authorities with principles governing enforcement, a defendant cannot be punished for violating that statute.[16]

We have previously held that §841(c)(2) contains a mens rea requirement. *United States v. Johal*, 428 F.3d 823, 827 (9th Cir. 2005). The statute "requires that a defendant subjectively know facts that either cause him or would cause a reasonable person to believe that the ingredients are being used to produce illegal drugs." Whether a defendant is guilty of having "reasonable cause to believe" that the pseudoephedrine will be used to produce illicit drugs "turns on *the facts actually known by the defendant* in a particular case." Also, the requirement includes the specification that the defendant had reasonable cause to believe that the chemical he sold "*will be used* to manufacture a controlled substance," §841(c)(2) (emphasis added); mere probability of use is insufficient.[17] For all these reasons, the statutory "reasonable cause to believe" mens rea standard "limits the likelihood that a defendant will be prosecuted for mere inadvertent conduct and is consistent with the longstanding principle presuming a mens rea requirement for criminal activity." *Johal*, 428 F.3d at 827.

The holding in *Johal* forecasts our decision here, because "a scienter requirement may mitigate a law's vagueness, especially with respect to the adequacy of notice to the complainant that his conduct is proscribed." Significantly, here, a person of ordinary intelligence can base his behavior on his factual knowledge of the situation at hand and thereby avoid violating the law.

Kim argues that larger chain stores escape liability because of their larger size and mechanized checkouts, demonstrating that the statute is subject to arbitrary enforcement

---

16. As we noted earlier, we are assuming sufficient evidence because sufficiency was not challenged.

17. *Johal* rejected the defendant's contention that the "statute requires the actual production of methamphetamine." *Johal*, 428 F.3d at 828. It is therefore of no consequence that Kim sold the pseudoephedrine to undercover federal agents who presumably did not actually manufacture illicit drugs with their purchases. The key question is whether *Kim* had "reasonable cause to believe the chemical will be used to make drugs." The inquiry therefore centers on defendant's understanding, or imputed understanding, of the situation at the time of the sale.

and therefore vague. We do not have any evidence on the record supporting Kim's differential enforcement accusation. Even assuming that it is accurate, however, lack of prosecution of some cases that could be covered by a statute "is not sufficient reason to hold the language too ambiguous to define a criminal offense." *United States v. Petrillo,* 332 U.S. 1, 7 (1947).

Furthermore, any discrepancy in enforcement could well be the result of a structural difference between the chain stores and small pharmacies, rather than of arbitrary enforcement. It is not that the statute has no guidelines, such that the authorities can arbitrarily prosecute one class of merchants instead of another, but rather that the statute allows for a situation in which a store's structure can, intentionally or not, cause its employees and managers to avoid criminal liability. The disincentive to prosecute may be a matter of proof — that it is difficult for the government to prove the existence of an actor in the chain stores who knows or has reasonable cause to believe that a sale of pseudoephedrine will lead to the manufacture of methamphetamine, because checkout stands are covered by many different people at different times or not covered at all. Alternatively, the reason for any discrepancy in prosecution may be a matter of there not *being* an actor in the store who has such mens rea, because the larger stores have ways of monitoring their sales to assure that suspicious sales do not occur. Or it may be that the smaller, nonchain stores are targeted by the methamphetamine manufacturers themselves and so are more likely to come on the DEA's radar screen through pseudoephedrine manufacturers' reports or personal observation. As these examples show, given the reach of prosecutorial discretion, there are many explanations for differential prosecution — not all of them indicative of the most efficient policy — other than the vagueness of the statute involved.

Kim has misinterpreted, whether deliberately or not, his obligations under the federal and state laws restricting the sale of pseudoephedrine. We clarify here that the recording and reporting statutes establish no safe harbor from prosecution under §841(c)(2). Instead, retailers must refrain from selling *any* amount of pseudoephedrine knowing or having reasonable cause to believe that the buyer intends to use the chemical to manufacture methamphetamine. Here, the jury determined that Kim knew or had reasonable cause to believe that the sales to the undercover DEA agents would lead to the manufacture of methamphetamine. Kim apparently thought he could rely on some magic formula, rather than his own informed observation of his customers, to decide which sales were legal and which were not. Congress has chosen not to provide such a formula. Balancing its desire to continue to allow sales of cold medicines without a prescription against the apparent propensity of methamphetamine manufacturers to accumulate chemicals for their manufacturing processes through purchases from ordinary retail stores, Congress has placed responsibility to monitor pseudoephedrine sales on those who are profiting from them.

There may be circumstances more marginal than this one in which that approach could yield an unfair result. Careful attention to the sufficiency of the evidence in cases under §841(c)(2) is therefore of critical importance, so as not to dissuade legitimate retailers from selling these useful home remedies at all, for fear of prosecution.[18] That Kim was acquit-

---

18. Although he did not raise a sufficiency argument, Kim's case is somewhat close compared to others that have been reported. There was, however sufficient evidence supporting the jury's conclusion, at least to the January 4 offense: Before the sting operation, Kim was warned by investigators from the California Pharmacy Board about the dangers of pseudoephedrine and his potential liability. There was a large spike in his sales, especially of the larger stock bottles. On January 4, Kim directly encountered three men who were acting suspiciously while purchasing substantial quantities of pseudoephedrine — specifically, stating a desire to "break it down"; purchasing alcohol, hydrogen peroxide, *and* iodine; attempting to purchase the entire supply of pseudoephedrine packages; and paying through

ted by the judge and the jury on most of the counts against him indicates that such care was taken in this case.

In sum, we conclude that because it has a sufficiently clear mens rea provision, §841(c)(2) is not unconstitutionally vague. Kim's conviction was therefore valid.

AFFIRMED.

4. Conspiracy and Continuing Criminal Enterprise

The crime of conspiracy is by no means unique to drug offenses and receives significant consideration in many criminal law courses. Nevertheless, drug conspiracy prosecutions deserve individual attention both because of the important role they play in drug enforcement and because they can raise unique problems. Because drug crimes occur within a marketplace, drug conspiracies are often much more sprawling than a conspiracy to rob a bank. This fact, in combination with the practice of sentencing offenders based primarily on drug type and quantity (discussed in Chapter 4), can sometimes result in lengthy sentences for peripheral participants in drug conspiracies. It can also make it difficult to decide what conspiratorial group a particular defendant belongs to. For example, is the mid-level drug dealer a co-conspirator of the drug wholesaler or is he a co-conspirator of the street level dealer?

a. Drug Conspiracies and Minimally Involved Participants

United States v. Brigham

United States Court of Appeals for the Seventh Circuit
977 F.2d 317 (1992)

Easterbrook, J.

Steep penalties await those who deal in drugs. Buying or selling 10 kilograms of cocaine—even agreeing to do so, without carrying through—means a minimum penalty of 10 years' imprisonment, without possibility of parole.

The "mandatory" minimum is mandatory only from the perspective of judges. To the parties, the sentence is negotiable. Did a marginal participant in a conspiracy really understand that a 10-kilo deal lay in store? A prosecutor may charge a lesser crime, if he offers something in return. Let's make a deal. Does the participant have valuable information; can he offer other assistance? Congress authorized prosecutors to pay for aid with sentences below the "floor." Let's make a deal.

Bold dealers may turn on their former comrades, setting up phony sales and testifying at the ensuing trials. Timorous dealers may provide information about their sources and customers. Drones of the organization—the runners, mules, drivers, and lookouts—have nothing comparable to offer. They lack the contacts and trust necessary to set up big deals, and they know little information of value. Whatever tales they have to tell, their bosses will have related. Defendants unlucky enough to be innocent have no information at all and are more likely to want vindication at trial, losing not only the opportunity to make a deal but also the 2-level reduction the sentencing guidelines provide for accepting responsibility.

---

a single person, suggesting one transaction rather than three—and yet he allowed the sale to proceed.

Mandatory minimum penalties, combined with a power to grant exceptions, create a prospect of inverted sentencing. The more serious the defendant's crimes, the lower the sentence—because the greater his wrongs, the more information and assistance he has to offer to a prosecutor. Discounts for the top dogs have the virtue of necessity, because rewards for assistance are essential to the business of detecting and punishing crime. But what makes the post-discount sentencing structure topsy-turvy is the mandatory minimum, binding only for the hangers on. What is to be said for such terms, which can visit draconian penalties on the small fry without increasing prosecutors' ability to wring information from their bosses?

Our case illustrates a sentencing inversion. Such an outcome is neither illegal nor unconstitutional, because offenders have no right to be sentenced in proportion to their wrongs. Still, meting out the harshest penalties to those least culpable is troubling, because it accords with no one's theory of appropriate punishments.

Agents of the Drug Enforcement Agency learned from an informant that Craig Thompson was in the market to buy 10 kilograms of cocaine. The DEA's undercover agents feigned willingness to supply him. During negotiations, Thompson said that he had just sold 17 kilograms and needed 10 more that very day to tide his organization over until the arrival of a shipment that he was expecting. Thompson and the agents did not trust one another. Jeffrey Carter, one of Thompson's goons, searched an agent; the agent's gun, normal in the business, did not trouble Carter, but a transmitter or recorder would mean big trouble. Carter was not very good at his job; he didn't find the concealed recorder. Thompson ultimately agreed to pay $30,000 per kilogram, a premium price for quick service. After the agents let on that they didn't trust Thompson any more than Thompson trusted them, Thompson agreed to let the agents hold his Rolls Royce as collateral until payment. In the agents' presence, Thompson called Tyrone Amos and told him to pick up "ten of those things today" at a suburban motel. Thompson and Carter would hand over the Rolls in a different suburb.

At the appointed time, less than five hours after the agents first met Thompson, one team descended on a restaurant to receive the Rolls Royce and another decamped to the motel to "deliver" the cocaine. Amos arrived at the motel in a car driven by Anthony Brigham. Amos and the agents at the motel had a conversation; Brigham stayed in the car. Carter had not appeared at the restaurant with the Rolls Royce, so everyone settled down to wait. Brigham looked around the parking lot but scrunched down in his seat when the agents' Corvette drove slowly by. At the restaurant Thompson and the agents discussed future deals of 50–100 kilograms per month. At the motel Brigham paced nervously in the lobby. After touring the parking lot again, lingering over the Corvette, Brigham joined Amos at a nearby gas station, where Amos placed a phone call. The two had a conversation and returned to the motel, where Amos told the agents that Carter and the Rolls were still missing. While Amos and one agent were dining together some distance from the motel, Thompson paged Amos with news that the Rolls had arrived.

Back at the motel, the agents went through the motions of delivering cocaine. As Amos headed for the agents' car to retrieve the drug from the trunk, Brigham moved his car to a location from which he could keep the delivery in sight. But there was no cocaine. Before Amos could open the trunk other agents moved in, arresting Amos and Brigham, just as they pinched Thompson and Carter at the restaurant.

All but Brigham pleaded guilty and provided valuable assistance to prosecutors. All but Brigham were sentenced to less than the "mandatory" minimum. Thompson received 84 months' imprisonment and Amos 75 months', after the prosecutor made motions

under §3553(e). Carter, who was allowed to plead to a charge that did not carry a minimum term, received 4 years' probation, 4 months of which were to be in a work-release
program run by the Salvation Army. That left Brigham, who went to trial, was convicted,
and received the "mandatory" term of 120 months' imprisonment.

Was the evidence sufficient? Appellate judges do not serve as additional jurors. After
a jury convicts, the question becomes whether any sensible person could find, beyond a
reasonable doubt, that the defendant committed the crime.

Brigham emphasizes that "mere" presence at the scene of a crime does not implicate
the bystander in that offense. Conspiracy is agreement and what proof of agreement did
the prosecutor present? Brigham arrived with Amos, conferred with Amos, and was in position to watch an exchange occur. No one testified that Brigham had any role in the exchange or Thompson's organization. Although the prosecutor portrayed Brigham as a
lookout, he asks: What kind of lookout would be unarmed, without radio, pager, cellu-
lar phone, or any other way to give or receive alerts? What countersurveillance operative
would hunker down in the car rather than keep a hawk-eyed watch? Thompson, Carter,
and Amos, who reaped rewards for their assistance, were conspicuously absent at Brigham's
trial. Had they no evidence to offer against him?

No one questions the rule that "mere presence" at the scene of a crime does not prove
conspiracy. "Mere" presence differs from, say, "revealing" presence. Like many a weasel
word, "mere" summarizes a conclusion rather than assisting in analysis. When the evidence
does not permit an inference that the defendant was part of the criminal organization, the
court applies the label "mere presence." So we must examine the evidence, taking inferences
in the light most favorable to the jury's verdict, rather than resting content with slogans.

Brigham shows up on short notice with Amos, who the jury could conclude was there
to receive 10 kilograms of cocaine from strangers whom Thompson and Amos do not trust.
Is Amos likely to come alone? Is a companion apt to be ignorant of the nature and risks of
the transaction? For almost three hours Brigham remains at the motel, generally obser-
vant and generally nervous; he follows Amos to a pay phone where a telephone call and conversation ensue. Amos reveals the contents of this conversation to the agents; the jury could
conclude that he revealed it to Brigham too. While Amos and an agent go to dinner, Brigham
keeps watch. After Amos returns, eye contact and a nod from Amos lead Brigham to take
up position where he can watch the trunk of the agents' car. Just what *was* Brigham doing
for three hours in the lobby and parking lot of the motel, if not assisting Amos? He was not
exactly passing through while a drug deal went down around him. Brigham did not testify,
and his lawyer offered no hypothesis at trial. At oral argument of this appeal the best his
counsel could do was to suggest that Brigham might have believed that Amos was picking
up counterfeit money rather than drugs. Tell us another! The jury was entitled to conclude
that Brigham knew about, and joined, a conspiracy to distribute cocaine.

Thin the evidence was, but it was also sufficient.

Wise exercise of prosecutorial discretion can prevent egregious sentencing inversions.
How that discretion is to be exercised is a subject for the political branches. Brigham
joined the conspiracy and received a sentence authorized by Congress. His judicial remedies are at a close.

AFFIRMED.

Bauer, J., dissenting.

I respectfully dissent. Taking all the evidence as described in the majority opinion as
absolutely true, and viewing it in the light most favorable to the government, I still do not

find that any sensible juror could find Brigham guilty of the crime of conspiracy beyond a reasonable doubt. At oral argument, counsel for Brigham could only suggest, in answer to a question from the bench as to what explanation he could give for Brigham's actions on the day in question, "that Brigham might have believed that Amos was picking up counterfeit money rather than drugs." An unbelievable scenario. The fact is, no one testified as to what exactly Brigham was doing or why he was doing it; no one, in spite of the marvelous totally cooperating witnesses who, if the government's theory is correct, could have nailed Brigham's hide to the jailhouse wall. But they didn't. And it is not Brigham's missing explanation that is fatal; it is the government's inability to explain that creates the problem.

Tell us another, indeed, but only if it is the government tale; the accused has absolutely no burden to explain anything. The government accuses, the defendant says "prove it," and the government says the suspicious activity is enough to convince and convict.

And so it proved.

I would have directed a verdict of "not guilty" had I been the trial judge and I construe my role in review to be the same. I do not believe the evidence sufficient to convince a sensible juror of proof beyond a reasonable doubt. The existence of cooperating witnesses who knew all and told nothing virtually implies the missing witness analysis: you had the control, you didn't produce, I infer the testimony would have been adverse to you.

I would reverse.

United States v. Burgos

United States Court of Appeals for the Fourth Circuit
94 F.3d 849 (1996)

Williams, J.

Frank Burgos appeal[s] [his] conviction[] for conspiracy to possess with intent to distribute cocaine base, in violation of 21 U.S.C.A. §§ 841(a)(1) and 846, contending that the evidence was insufficient to sustain [his] conviction.

Taken in the light most favorable to the Government, the evidence adduced at Burgos's trial established the following facts. On January 25, 1993, law enforcement officers Berkley Blanks and Daniel Kaplan were performing narcotics interdiction at the train station in Greensboro, North Carolina, focusing on a train arriving from New York, New York, a known source city for contraband narcotics. Officers Blanks and Kaplan observed Burgos, [Alexio] Gobern, and Anthony Gonzales disembark together from the train, but walk separately into the terminal. Officer Blanks testified that he initiated a conversation with Gonzales, who informed Officer Blanks he was traveling alone from New York, denied familiarity with Gobern, and presented a train ticket bearing the name "Anthony Flores." Officer Kaplan testified that he spoke with Burgos, who produced a train ticket bearing his own name. According to Officer Blanks, Gobern carried a knapsack and a package wrapped in Christmas paper but which bore no ribbon, bow, or card; also, Gobern carefully observed Officer Blanks's conversation with Gonzales.

As Officer Blanks and Gonzales walked to the front of the terminal, Gobern followed them, continued to observe them, halted when Officer Blanks and Gonzales halted, and with the Christmas package and knapsack, proceeded into the terminal lavatory, where he remained one to two minutes; this lavatory was small, measuring 9.5 feet square. Gobern then exited the lavatory without the Christmas package, but still carrying the knapsack. Officers Blanks and Kaplan testified unequivocally that no one else entered, occupied, or exited the lavatory while Gobern occupied it. On exiting the lavatory, Gobern, at Officer Kaplan's request, produced his train ticket, which, like Gonzales's ticket, bore the name "Anthony Flores," stated that he was traveling alone from New York, and denied that he and Gonzales knew each other. Interestingly, Gonzales's and Gobern's train tickets bore consecutive numbers, were purchased simultaneously at the same locale, and were both round-trip tickets from New York, New York, to Greensboro, North Carolina, issued on January 25, 1993, with a return date of January 27, 1993.

After concluding their conversation with Gobern, Officers Blanks and Kaplan proceeded immediately to the lavatory just exited by Gobern while Officer Cameron Piner, who had recently arrived at the train terminal, watched Burgos, Gobern, and Gonzales. On the sink, Officers Blanks and Kaplan found the Christmas package and a cereal box, both of which were ripped open, and crumpled newsprint dated January 9, 1993 from *The Daily News*, a New York newspaper. Pages from the same edition of *The Daily News* were found on the floor and in the wastebasket of the lavatory. Also in the wastebasket were pieces of the Christmas paper in which the Christmas package had been wrapped, as well as remnants of the package itself. Secreted behind the commode was a mass of wadded newsprint, which concealed aluminum foil, which, in turn, concealed a plastic bag containing 78.5 grams of cocaine base, an amount which Officers Blanks and Kaplan testified was a distribution quantity. Significantly, the newspaper concealing the foil and plastic bag was from the same edition of *The Daily News* that was on the sink, scattered around the floor, and in the wastebasket. Not only was this wadded mass of newsprint from *The Daily News*, but it complemented and completed perfectly the newspaper edition found near the sink. Officers Blanks and Kaplan exited the lavatory, and Officer Blanks observed Burgos, Gobern, and Gonzales attempt to board the same taxicab. Before they could depart, Gobern was arrested, and Burgos and Gonzales agreed to accompany Officers Blanks and Kaplan for questioning. Burgos was then questioned by Special Agent Wayne Kowalski of the Drug Enforcement Agency.

At Burgos's trial, Special Agent Kowalski testified that Burgos stated: (1) he knew Gonzales, but not Gobern; (2) he conversed with Gonzales and Gobern on the train; (3) he knew that cocaine base was in the Christmas package, which Gobern possessed since leaving New York; and (4) he knew that the cocaine base was to be distributed at a college in Greensboro, North Carolina. Specifically, Special Agent Kowalski avowed that Burgos admitted that "Gobern ... carried the package *wrapped* as a Christmas package ... *throughout the trip down*." Moreover, "Burgos ... knew that they had dope.... It was his understanding they were going to sell the dope at the A&T University." Dispelling any doubt that Burgos knew that the plastic bag containing the cocaine base was in the Christmas package since the trio left New York, Special Agent Kowalski testified that he asked Burgos "whether he knew that there was crack cocaine in the package" and Burgos "said that he knew they had it, but he didn't see it." Additionally, Special Agent Kowalski testified that Burgos stated that he was in Greensboro visiting a friend, but did not mention traveling to Laurinburg, North Carolina, to play basketball with his former schoolmates, as Burgos testified at trial; indeed, the train on which the men traveled did not stop at Laurinburg. Also introduced at Burgos's trial was forensic evidence revealing that Gobern's fingerprints were on the Christmas wrapping paper, and that Burgos's fingerprint was impressed on the sealing mechanism at the top of the plastic bag which contained the cocaine base, although forensic analysis did not establish when Burgos's fingerprint was impressed on the plastic bag.

Burgos's testimony differed dramatically from Special Agent Kowalski's. Burgos testified that while purchasing his train ticket, Gonzales, whom Burgos knew only by the alias

"Tone," requested that Burgos purchase two train tickets for him and gave Burgos a piece of paper with a reservation number and the name "Flores" written on it. Burgos and Gonzales also exchanged telephone numbers. Burgos purchased three round-trip train tickets: One for himself in his own name and the other two for Gonzales in the name of "Anthony Flores," the two for Gonzales each having a two-day stay in Greensboro and returning to New York City on January 27, 1993. Burgos testified further that Gonzales was alone when he solicited Burgos to purchase his train tickets. According to Burgos, he then boarded the train by himself. While on board, he was approached by Gonzales, Gobern, whom Burgos denied knowing, and two women, who have remained nameless and faceless, all of whom sat behind Burgos. Testifying further, Burgos stated that he carried with him on the train sandwiches, cookies, and potato chips, all of which were wrapped in plastic bags similar to the plastic bag bearing his fingerprint in which the cocaine base was found. Burgos, however, did not consume all of the food he brought, but rather shared it with Gonzales, Gobern, and the women. Specifically, he gave sandwiches, still encased in the plastic bags, to Gonzales and Gobern and gave the cookies to the women.

Moreover, Burgos avowed that he had no discussions with Gonzales and Gobern concerning narcotics while on the train. Regarding his intentions in North Carolina, Burgos testified that after visiting friends for one day in Greensboro, he intended to play basketball with former schoolmates in Laurinburg. With respect to the Christmas package, Burgos testified that Gobern carried no such Christmas package, yet on cross-examination he testified that Gobern wrapped no packages on the train nor did Gobern possess any implements used to wrap packages, such as paper, tape, or scissors. Likewise, on cross-examination, Burgos could offer no explanation for his fingerprint on the plastic bag containing the cocaine base, nor could Burgos explain the glaring, direct contradictions between his testimony and that of Special Agent Kowalski.

Burgos was convicted of conspiracy to possess with intent to distribute cocaine base, in violation of 21 U.S.C.A. §§ 841(a)(1), 846, possession with intent to distribute cocaine base, in violation of 18 U.S.C.A. § 2 and 21 U.S.C.A. § 841(a)(1), and aiding and abetting, and sentenced to 131 months imprisonment. Burgos appeals his convictions, challenging the sufficiency of the evidence, but he does not appeal his sentence.

To prove conspiracy to possess cocaine base with intent to distribute, the Government must establish that: (1) an agreement to possess cocaine with intent to distribute existed between two or more persons; (2) the defendant knew of the conspiracy; and (3) the defendant knowingly and voluntarily became a part of this conspiracy. In *United States v. Laughman,* 618 F.2d 1067, 1074 (4th Cir. 1980) we explained that the "gravamen of the crime of conspiracy is an *agreement* to effectuate a criminal act." By its very nature, a conspiracy is clandestine and covert, thereby frequently resulting in little direct evidence of such an agreement. Hence, a conspiracy generally is proved by circumstantial evidence and the context in which the circumstantial evidence is adduced.

The preceding precepts demonstrate that a conspiracy can have an elusive quality and that a defendant may be convicted of conspiracy with little or no knowledge of the entire breadth of the criminal enterprise:

> It is of course elementary that one may be a member of a conspiracy without knowing its full scope, or all its members, and without taking part in the full range of its activities or over the whole period of its existence. Critically, it is not necessary to proof of a conspiracy that it have a discrete, identifiable organizational structure; the requisite agreement to act in concert need not result in any such formal structure[.] Indeed[,] … contemporary drug conspiracies [can] con-

template[] ... only a loosely-knit association of members linked only by their mutual interest in sustaining the overall enterprise of catering to the ultimate demands of a particular drug consumption market.... *United States v. Banks,* 10 F.3d 1044, 1054 (4th Cir. 1993).

Of course, in addition to proving the existence of a conspiracy beyond a reasonable doubt, the Government must also prove a defendant's connection to the conspiracy beyond a reasonable doubt. To satisfy that burden, the Government need not prove that the defendant knew the particulars of the conspiracy or all of his coconspirators.

In addition to selling narcotics, that participation may assume a myriad of other forms, such as supplying firearms or purchasing money orders for coconspirators or permitting them to store narcotics and other contraband in one's home, or purchasing plane tickets for coconspirators. Thus, a variety of conduct, apart from selling narcotics, can constitute participation in a conspiracy sufficient to sustain a conviction.

Moreover, our precedents have mandated that "once it has been shown that a conspiracy exists, the evidence need only establish a slight connection between the defendant and the conspiracy to support conviction." We have adhered repeatedly to this principle, explaining that while the existence of the conspiracy and the defendant's connection to it must be proved beyond a reasonable doubt, the defendant's connection to the conspiracy need only be "slight." Requiring that the defendant's connection to the conspiracy be "slight" in no way alleviates the Government's burden of proving the existence of the conspiracy and the defendant's connection to it beyond a reasonable doubt. The term "slight" does not describe the *quantum* of evidence that the Government must elicit in order to establish the conspiracy, but rather the *connection* that the defendant maintains with the conspiracy. Requiring a "slight connection" between the defendant and the established conspiracy complements the canons of conspiracy law that a defendant need not know all of his coconspirators, comprehend the reach of the conspiracy, participate in all the enterprises of the conspiracy, or have joined the conspiracy from its inception.

Guided by the preceding principles, we address Burgos's challenges to the sufficiency of the evidence to sustain his conspiracy conviction. Burgos asserts that his conviction must be reversed because the Government failed to prove that he participated in any conspiracy. We disagree. Viewing all of the evidence and the inferences to be drawn therefrom that were adduced at Burgos's trial in the light most favorable to the Government, we conclude that the evidence against Burgos is sufficient for a jury to find beyond a reasonable doubt that he participated in a conspiracy with Gobern and Gonzales to distribute cocaine base at North Carolina A&T University. Indeed, the dissent does not disagree that a conspiracy existed between Gobern and Gonzales, but merely takes issue with the sufficiency of the evidence regarding Burgos's participation in this conspiracy.

The most damning physical evidence establishing Burgos's participation in the conspiracy is that his left index fingerprint was impressed on the sealing mechanism at the top of the ziplock plastic bag in which the cocaine base was located. This plastic bag was wrapped in foil, which, in turn, was wrapped in newspaper, which was packaged in a box, which was wrapped in Christmas paper; in short, the cocaine base was intentionally and thoroughly concealed. Burgos devotes much energy to denigrating the fingerprint evidence, particularly because, he posits, this evidence is the sole evidence linking him to the conspiracy, a position that we find frivolous, considering all of the evidence before the jury.

Federal appellate courts consistently have concluded that fingerprints constitute material, cogent proof in sustaining conspiracy convictions for contraband narcotics, particularly when viewed in the context of other circumstantial evidence. Burgos's finger-print impressed on the sealing mechanism of the plastic bag containing cocaine base, which was concealed inside a wrapped package, is a significant piece of evidence establishing his knowing and willful participation in the conspiracy.

The factual circumstances adduced from the testimony likewise give rise to the reasonable inference that Burgos knowingly and voluntarily participated in the conspiracy. Special Agent Kowalski testified that Burgos told him that Gobern possessed the wrapped Christmas package from the inception of the journey in New York:

> Q: Did [Burgos] say whether he talked to Gonzales and Gobern while they were on the train?

> A: Yes, [Burgos] did. He rode with them. He told me that Mr. Gobern was the one who carried the *package wrapped as a Christmas package.*

> Q: All right. Did he make any statements as to how long Mr. Gobern had this package?

> A: He said Mr. Gobern *had the package throughout the trip down.*

> Q: All right. And did he tell you anything about what Mr. Burgos or Mr Gonzales — what Mr. Gonzales or Mr. Gobern told him about what was in the package during the train trip?

> A: *What Mr. Burgos told me was that he knew that they had dope, although he didn't see it. And it was his understanding — this is what he told me — it was his understanding they were going to sell the dope at the A&T University.*

In addition, Special Agent Kowalski testified that he fingerprinted Burgos and one of Burgos's fingerprints was on the plastic bag. Moreover, Burgos himself testified that Gobern, Gonzales, and the women sat behind him for the entire trip, he did not see anyone transfer material into a plastic bag, wrap or rewrap the package, nor did he leave his seat except for the occasional visit to the train lavatory. Thus, not only was there *positive* testimony of Burgos's knowing and willful participation in the conspiracy, but the testimony contradicted Burgos's trial testimony, permitting the jury to infer that he had perjured himself.

The dissent erroneously posits that there is no evidence establishing that Burgos assisted in packaging the cocaine base prior to boarding the train in New York. [A] reasonable jury could infer from the facts that Burgos did assist in packaging the cocaine base before boarding the train in New York. How else could Burgos's fingerprint be found on an item *inside a wrapped package* that was wrapped since the inception of the trip from New York? Regardless, the jury was free to draw either conclusion, and substantial evidence supports the conclusion of guilt.

Despite the evidence and inferences establishing Burgos's knowing and willful participation in the conspiracy, our dissenting colleagues assert that we have excised from conspiracy jurisprudence the requirement that substantial evidence support the jury's finding that a defendant knowingly and willfully participated in a conspiracy. To the contrary, we specifically recognize this requirement of the offense, and explain that the Government must prove it beyond a reasonable doubt. While reciting the fundamental tenets of conspiracy law, the dissent fails to apply the principles that a defendant may be a member of a conspiracy without knowledge of or participation in its full scope and that a conspiracy need not be a tightly-knit organization run with precision. Only by viewing Special Agent Kowalski's testimony and all the evidence adduced at trial in a light most favorable to Burgos and by faulting the Government for not disproving Burgos's contradictory and vague explanations for the fingerprint evidence can the dissent conclude as a matter of law that no rational jury could draw the foregoing inferences. Viewed in a light most favorable to the Government, the evidence established that Burgos was not a mere traveling companion, but a knowing, willful participant in this narcotics distribution conspiracy.

To reiterate, Burgos's fingerprint was impressed on the sealing mechanism of a plastic bag wrapped in aluminum foil, packed in newspaper, and encased in a wrapped package. At trial, Burgos explained the presence of his fingerprint on the sealing mechanism of the plastic bag by testifying that Gobern apparently consumed a sandwich Burgos prepared, and, unbeknownst to Burgos, placed the cocaine base in the plastic bag without leaving any of his own fingerprints on it. Burgos testified further that although he sat in front of Gobern during the trip from New York, he never saw the Christmas package prior to disembarking from the train. To accept Burgos's rendition of the testimony, the jury would have had to find that Gobern saved the plastic bag, entered the lavatory, tore open the Christmas package and the cereal box, unwrapped the newspaper and aluminum foil from the cocaine base, placed the cocaine base in the plastic bag without leaving his fingerprint, wrapped the plastic bag in aluminum foil, swaddled the aluminum foil in the newspaper, and secreted the cocaine base behind the commode. The implausibility of this transpiring within two minutes runs deep, as the dissent concedes. Regardless, while this account of events strikes us as highly implausible, material for our purposes is the fact that the jury disbelieved this version of the events, and its disbelief was rational, particularly given the context and content of the testimony of Officers Blanks and Kaplan and Special Agent Kowalski.

Yet another circumstance supporting a guilty verdict is the fact that Burgos, Gobern, and Gonzales boarded a train from New York City. We have steadfastly acknowledged that New York City is a known source city for contraband drugs.[7] Additionally, all three men traveled together on the train, Gobern and Gonzales scheduled the same return trip, and Burgos's travel plans enabled him to accompany them, which is circumstantial evidence bolstering an inference of guilt in a drug distribution conspiracy. This circumstantial evidence assumes greater import here because Burgos's testimony that the men traveled separately was contradicted by Special Agent Kowalski, tending to illustrate further Burgos's guilt.

Not only did Burgos, Gobern, and Gonzales travel together from a source city, but it was Burgos who purchased Gobern's and Gonzales's tickets so that the three men could travel aboard the same train, adding more circumstantial evidence tending to prove Burgos's participation in the conspiracy. *See, e.g., James,* 40 F.3d at 873 (observing that purchasing airline tickets for conspirators is cogent circumstantial evidence tending to establish a conspiracy and illustrating that not every participant in a drug trafficking conspiracy actually sells drugs, but many participants furnish goods or services for the conspiracy, such as providing money-orders, firearms, or shelter). Furthermore, according to his own testimony, Burgos was acquainted with Gonzales, all three men apparently were from the same neighborhood in New York, and Burgos and Gonzales exchanged telephone numbers. This type of familiarity constitutes further circumstantial evidence that Burgos participated in the conspiracy. *See James,* 40 F.3d at 873 (recognizing that acquaintance and ability to contact others associated with the conspiracy permits a jury to conclude that a defendant participated in the conspiracy).

---

7. Contrary to the dissent's mischaracterization, we do not hold that traveling from a source city automatically renders one a narcotics conspirator. Rather, we simply note that traveling from a source city is a valid consideration that enters the calculus of guilt.

While some of this evidence, if viewed in isolation, could appear innocuous, "such [an] argument misses the mark; our inquiry is whether *any* reasonable jury could find the elements of the crime, on these facts, beyond a reasonable doubt, not whether Burgos is plausibly not guilty." Construing all of this evidence and its reasonable inferences in favor of the Government leads inexorably to the conclusion that substantial evidence supports Burgos's conspiracy conviction. Based on the plethora of evidence, we conclude that a rational jury could find beyond a reasonable doubt that Burgos participated in the conspiracy; indeed, we would be hard-pressed to accept that a jury could conclude otherwise. In this respect, the dissent disregards yet another precept of conspiracy jurisprudence: We do not analyze evidence in a piecemeal manner, but must consider its cumulative effect, which is precisely what we have accomplished. Conversely, the dissent dissects the direct and circumstantial evidence by separately dismissing selective pieces, not by analyzing all of the evidence in context. We, therefore, affirm Burgos's conviction for conspiracy to possess with intent to distribute cocaine base.

Michael, J., dissenting.

Nearly a half century ago, Justice Jackson expressed concern that the history of the law of conspiracy "exemplifies the 'tendency of a principle to expand itself to the limit of its logic.'" *Krulewitch v. United States*, 336 U.S. 440, 445 (1949) (Jackson, J., concurring) (quoting B. Cardozo, *The Nature of the Judicial Process* 51). Justice Jackson further warned that:

> The unavailing protest of courts against the growing habit to indict for conspiracy in lieu of prosecuting for the substantive offense itself, or in addition thereto, suggests that loose practice as to this offense constitutes a threat to fairness in our administration of justice.

Unfortunately, I believe that today's majority opinion confirms the fears expressed by Justice Jackson. The majority has turned the law of conspiracy—at least in the context of alleged drug conspiracies—into the law of "mere association." Burgos's conviction stands simply because he hung around with the wrong people on a long train ride. Indeed, as of today there seems to be little that does not allow inference of conspiracy. I, therefore, respectfully dissent insofar as the majority opinion affirms Burgos's conviction.

At Burgos's trial the following facts were presented to the jury. On January 25, 1993, three men, Alexio B. Gobern, Anthony Gonzales, and Frank K. Burgos, traveled on the same train from New York City to Greensboro, North Carolina. Gobern, Gonzales, and Burgos got off the train at the AmTrak station in Greensboro. Burgos was first off, followed by Gonzales and then Gobern. They did not walk together on the platform. Gobern carried a Christmas-wrapped package and a blue knapsack. Although the package was not elaborately wrapped, it had no loose ends.

As part of routine drug interdiction work, Police Officer Daniel Kaplan stopped and questioned Burgos before he reached the terminal building. Burgos produced his train ticket, which was in his name. Police Officer Berkley Blanks stopped and questioned Gonzales, and Gobern paused to watch the questioning of Gonzales. Officer Blanks and Gonzales then walked to the front of the terminal building, and Gobern followed and watched. At Officer Blanks' request, Gonzales produced his train ticket, which was in the name of "Anthony Flores." By this time, Officer Kaplan had finished questioning Burgos and had joined Officer Blanks and Gonzales in front of the terminal building.

Gobern then entered the terminal building and walked to the men's restroom with the wrapped package and the knapsack. Approximately one to two minutes later, Gobern came out of the restroom with the knapsack but without the wrapped package. No one else entered or exited the restroom during this time. After Gobern exited the restroom, Officer Kaplan stopped and questioned him. Officer Kaplan asked for Gobern's train ticket, which was also in the name of "Anthony Flores." Both Gobern and Gonzales denied that they knew each other or that they were traveling together. However, both Gobern's and Gonzales's tickets were in sequential order, bore the same name, were issued on January 25, and had identical return dates of January 27.

Officers Kaplan and Blanks then searched the restroom after telling Officer Cameron Piner to watch Gobern, Gonzales, and Burgos. Inside the restroom the officers saw the Christmas package and a cereal box torn open on the sink, and they found a balled-up New York City newspaper, *The Daily News*, behind the commode. Inside the newspaper, the officers found aluminum foil; inside the aluminum foil was a ziploc plastic bag containing "crack" cocaine. After finding the cocaine, Officers Kaplan and Blanks went outside and saw Gobern, Burgos, and Gonzales standing near a pay phone. There was a cab with an open door, and it appeared that Gobern, Burgos, and Gonzales were preparing to leave. Gobern was arrested, and Burgos and Gonzales were asked to go to the police station. At the police station all three men were questioned and fingerprinted. Special Agent Wayne Kowalski of the DEA conducted the questioning and fingerprinting. At the end of the evening Gobern was detained, and Burgos and Gonzales were released.

The Greensboro Police sent the wrapping paper, cereal box, newspaper, and aluminum foil to a North Carolina lab for fingerprint analysis. Agent Kowalski sent the cocaine and plastic bag to a DEA lab in Miami for analysis. Three of Gobern's prints were found on the wrapping paper, and one of Burgos's prints was found on the plastic bag. It could not be determined when the cocaine was placed in the bag or when Burgos touched the bag. The aluminum foil was not tested for cocaine residue.

At Burgos's trial Agent Kowalski testified that when he questioned Burgos on January 25, Burgos said (1) that he (Burgos) knew Gonzales but did not know Gobern, (2) that Burgos "drove down on the train with Gonzales and Gobern from New York," (3) that "Gobern had the package throughout the trip down," (4) that Gobern and Gonzales "had dope although Burgos did not see it," and (5) that Gobern and Gonzales "were going to sell the dope at the A&T University."

In his defense Burgos testified that he was currently attending college in New York City and that he was traveling to North Carolina to visit friends. He planned to spend a day in Greensboro, but his ultimate destination was Laurinburg Institute, a prep school he had attended.

Burgos boarded the train in New York City. While near the front of the ticket line at Penn Station, he was approached by Anthony Gonzales. Burgos knew Gonzales from his neighborhood as "Tone," though he did not know Gonzales's last name. Because he was running late, Gonzales asked Burgos to get his (Gonzales's) tickets, and he gave Burgos the ticket money and a piece of paper with the reservation numbers. The tickets were in the name of "Anthony Flores," and not knowing Gonzales's last name, Burgos thought nothing of it. He gave Gonzales the tickets, boarded the train, and sat down by himself. After he was seated, Gonzales, Gobern, and two young women came by. Gonzales introduced Burgos to Gobern. Gonzales, Gobern, and the two women sat behind Burgos on the train.

The trip from New York to Greensboro lasted approximately twelve hours, and Burgos had brought sandwiches and snacks to eat. He had packed the food in ziploc bags. He offered some of his food to Gonzales, Gobern, and the women. Eventually, Gonzales and Gobern ate some of the sandwiches. Burgos did not see what they did with the ziploc bags after they ate the food. According to Burgos, the ziploc bags were of the same type as the one found containing the cocaine.

In contrast to the testimony provided by Agent Kowalski, Burgos testified that there was no conversation about drugs on the train and that he did not see the wrapped package until Gonzales and Gobern were being questioned by the police at the train station. Burgos explained that he called a cab after Officer Blanks told him in a hostile manner to leave the train station. He called the cab for himself, not for Gobern and Gonzales. When the cab arrived, Burgos moved to open the door, but Officer Piner stopped him and told him not to leave. After Burgos stepped back to the platform, Officers Kaplan and Blanks came out of the train station and arrested Gobern.

Robert Lewis, a friend of Burgos's and a student at North Carolina A&T University, testified that Burgos called him a few days before the train trip. Burgos told Lewis that although he was coming down to visit him in Greensboro, his main purpose was to visit Laurinburg Institute. In addition, Vernon Johnson, a dormitory director at Laurinburg Institute testified that Burgos called him in January 1993 and said that he (Burgos) was coming down to Laurinburg Institute to play basketball, which he had done in the past. Burgos's final witness was a character witness, Frank McDuffy, the headmaster of Laurinburg Institute. McDuffy testified that he and Burgos had developed a relationship like that between father and son, that Burgos was in his opinion truthful, and that Burgos would visit Laurinburg when he was in North Carolina.

Based on this evidence, the jury convicted Burgos of conspiracy to possess cocaine base with intent to distribute. The jury also convicted Burgos of possession of cocaine base with intent to distribute. He was sentenced to 131 months imprisonment.

At the outset, I emphasize that I agree with the majority's conclusion that once a conspiracy has been established, the Government need only show a "slight connection" between the defendant and the established conspiracy. In addition, while the majority does not expressly state what it believes to constitute a "slight connection," I assume the majority agrees that to establish a "slight connection" the Government must present substantial evidence showing that the defendant knowingly and willfully participated in the conspiracy.

With that said, however, I believe that the majority has confused the concept of what elements make a conspiracy with the principles by which we determine whether sufficient evidence has been presented to establish those elements.

To hold, as the majority does, that "elastic, ad hoc principles" govern the application of the law of conspiracy to the facts of a case is to condone decisionmaking without clear principles—decisionmaking that is particularly ill-suited for determining whether any crime has been committed. Indeed, one need look no further than the cases presented here to be certain that under the majority's approach *any* fact that shows that individuals associated together (or were simply acquainted) may be turned into evidence showing the existence of a conspiracy and a defendant's participation therein. I will mention just a few examples at this point (the rest are discussed in detail *infra*): as the majority sees it, (1) that Burgos was acquainted with Gonzales, (2) that Burgos, Gonzales, and Gobern were from the same neighborhood, and (3) that Burgos and Gonzales exchanged phone numbers are all facts showing that Burgos participated in a conspiracy. While I believe one would be hard-pressed to say that these facts show anything more than mere association, and a very weak association at that, under the majority's "elastic, ad hoc principles," these are all facts that establish Burgos's guilt.

Needless to say, analysis such as that represents the kind of "loose practice" that Justice Jackson specifically warned against in *Krulewitch*, a practice that "constitutes a threat to fairness in our administration of justice." 336 U.S. at 446 (Jackson, J., concurring). *See also United States v. Falcone,* 109 F.2d 579, 581 (2d Cir.) (Hand, J.) ("so many prosecutors seek to sweep within the drag-net of conspiracy all those who have been associated in any degree whatever with the main offenders. That there are opportunities of great oppression in such a doctrine is very plain, and it is only by circumscribing the scope of such all comprehensive indictments that they can be avoided."). In short, reliance on "elastic, ad hoc principles" allows for conspiracy convictions to be based on no more than a defendant's "mere association" with alleged co-conspirators, rather than substantial evidence establishing the existence of a conspiracy and a defendant's knowing and willful participation therein.

At Burgos's trial the Government presented substantial evidence to the jury showing that Burgos *associated* with Gobern and Gonzales. I think it clear, however, that the Government failed to present substantial evidence that Burgos knowingly and willfully participated in a Gobern/Gonzales drug conspiracy to possess crack cocaine with intent to distribute.

Viewed in the light most favorable to the Government, the evidence at Burgos's trial established the existence of a conspiracy between Gobern and Gonzales. Most importantly, Agent Kowalski's testimony about Burgos's alleged admissions shows that Gobern and Gonzales traveled together from New York City with the intent to distribute crack cocaine in Greensboro, North Carolina.[6]

Agent Kowalski's testimony further shows (as does Burgos's) that Burgos associated with Gobern and Gonzales during the trip from New York City. Indeed, Burgos does not deny that he bought two train tickets on Gonzales' behalf, that he sat near Gobern and Gonzales throughout the trip, or that he talked with Gobern and Gonzales during the trip. What, of course, Burgos does deny is that he participated in a Gobern/Gonzales conspiracy, and Burgos has denied any such participation from the moment he was questioned by Agent Kowalski. Thus, the Government had to prove beyond a reasonable doubt that Burgos willfully joined and participated in the Gobern/Gonzales conspiracy with the intent to further, promote, and accomplish its criminal purpose.

At trial, however, the Government offered no testimony, admission, or co-conspirator declaration showing that Burgos willfully joined and participated in the Gobern/Gonzales conspiracy. The Government offered no evidence that Burgos possessed tools of the drug trade (*e.g.,* firearms or unexplained cash). The Government offered no evidence that drugs were found in Burgos's possession. The Government offered no evidence that Burgos used an alias. The Government offered no evidence that Burgos was scheduled to travel back to New York on the same train as Gobern and Gonzales. The Government offered no evidence that Burgos made reservations to travel with Gobern and Gonzales.

---

6. Agent Kowalski's testimony on this point does, however, raise a question that was not explored at Burgos's trial. If, when questioned by Agent Kowalski on the night of Gobern's arrest, Burgos did in fact implicate Gobern and Gonzales in a conspiracy to possess and distribute crack cocaine, why then was *Gonzales* released by the police? Indeed, to this day Gonzales has never been indicted on the crimes for which Burgos and Gobern were charged. I want to make clear that my central question here is not, as the majority believes, why Gonzales was never prosecuted, but rather it is why Gonzales was released by the police right after Burgos made his alleged admissions. Also, I raise this point not to suggest that the police handled these cases improperly in any way, but merely to suggest that Agent Kowalski's testimony at Burgos's trial does raise some inconsistencies which have never been explained.

And the Government offered no evidence that Burgos knew Gobern prior to the time of the train trip.

There are thus only two facts offered by the Government to show that Burgos participated in a Gobern/Gonzales conspiracy. First, Burgos's fingerprint was discovered on the plastic bag that contained the crack cocaine, and second, Burgos, Gobern, and Gonzales were traveling "together" on January 25, 1993. Despite the majority's attempt to weave these two fibers into a cloak of guilt, these facts (separately or together) do not provide substantial evidence that Burgos knowingly and wilfully participated in a Gobern/Gonzales conspiracy.

The Government says the fingerprint is probative evidence that Burgos participated in the conspiracy because the jury could rationally infer that the fingerprint was impressed on the baggie when it contained crack cocaine. Although the Government's fingerprint expert acknowledged he did not know whether Burgos touched the bag when it contained crack, the Government argues that the inference nevertheless can be drawn.

The majority agrees with the Government and points out that Gobern did not have sufficient time to transfer the crack cocaine to the plastic bag during his one or two minutes in the train station restroom. The majority also points to the testimony of Agent Kowalski and contends that "a reasonable jury could infer from the facts that Burgos did assist in packaging the cocaine base before boarding the train in New York." And, in particular, the majority believes that because Agent Kowalski testified that Burgos had knowledge of the conspiracy and did not see wrapping materials on board the train, a rational juror could infer that Burgos touched the plastic bag while it contained crack and that he assisted in the packaging before the men boarded the train in New York. The majority then rhetorically asks, "How else could Burgos's fingerprint be found on an item *inside a wrapped package* that was wrapped since the inception of the trip from New York?"

Obviously, I agree with the majority to the extent that it is implausible to think that Gobern put the cocaine base in the plastic bag during the one or two minutes he spent in the restroom. Where, however, I do disagree with the majority is on its contention that the evidence and reasonable inferences show that Burgos must have assisted in the packaging of the crack cocaine *prior* to boarding the train in New York. A rational juror would disagree on this too.

I do not dispute that the jury could infer that Burgos touched the bag when it contained cocaine *if* there was evidence that the cocaine was in the wrapped package throughout the entire trip from New York. There is, however, no such evidence. While Agent Kowalski testified that Burgos said that Gobern possessed the package throughout the trip down from New York, Agent Kowalski *never* testified that Burgos said that the plastic bag containing the cocaine was inside the wrapped package throughout the entire trip. Gobern may have carried a wrapped package all the way from New York. He may also have carried the crack all the way from New York. Still there is no evidence that Gobern carried the plastic bag inside the wrapped package "since the inception of the trip from New York[.]" Accordingly, there is no evidence to support the majority's assertion that Burgos assisted in the packaging of the cocaine. Gobern was on the train for twelve hours, so he did not have just one or two minutes to put the cocaine in the plastic bag, he had half a day.

Indeed, the fact that Burgos testified that he did not see any materials with which Gobern could wrap or rewrap the package aboard the train does not mean that Gobern did not wrap or open and close the package during the half day he spent on the train. Any child that has ever looked at presents under a Christmas tree before Christmas morning knows that packages can be opened and closed without the aid of scissors, wrapping paper, or tape. Here, there are several different reasons why Gobern may have handled and packaged or repackaged the crack cocaine during the train trip from New York.

Nonetheless, could a reasonable juror still infer (and believe it true beyond a reasonable doubt) that Burgos must have assisted in the packaging of the cocaine prior to boarding the train in New York? I think not. Because there was no testimony from Agent Kowalski (or anyone else) that the cocaine was in the wrapped package throughout the entire trip from New York, there is no evidence that Gobern did not put the cocaine into an empty plastic bag bearing Burgos's fingerprint during the twelve hour train ride from New York. Indeed, all a rational juror could know and infer based on the evidence presented here is that the plastic baggie was placed inside the wrapped package at some unknown time before Gobern got off the train.

Furthermore, suppose that I am wrong and that a rational juror could reasonably infer that Burgos did in fact touch or hold Gobern's crack-filled bag at some point before the men boarded the train (or during the train trip itself).[8] How does a juror jump from the fingerprint to a conclusion that Burgos willfully joined and participated in the Gobern/Gonzales conspiracy with the intent to further and accomplish its criminal purpose? Although a juror could speculate that one who simply touched another's container of drugs had the intent to join in and associate himself with an endeavor to possess and ultimately distribute those drugs, I do not think this would qualify as a rational inference. I therefore think it clear that Burgos's conviction cannot be sustained based on the fingerprint evidence.

The question, of course, remains whether the Government's other evidence somehow bridges the gap between the fingerprint and Burgos's alleged intent to participate in the Gobern/Gonzales conspiracy. Viewed in the light most favorable to the Government, the other evidence showed the following: Burgos, Gonzales, and Gobern were all from New York; Burgos was acquainted with Gonzales in New York prior to the train ride; Burgos sat near Gobern and Gonzales on the train ride; Burgos and Gonzales exchanged telephone numbers; Burgos was told they had drugs; the three men got off the train one after the other; and the three men were seen getting into a cab together when the police arrested Gobern.

That being said, not a single witness testified that Burgos had ever met Gobern before the train ride. Also, while Burgos said he was acquainted with Gonzales in New York, no evidence was presented on the scope of their relationship, save for the fact that Burgos and Gonzales exchanged telephone numbers while on the train—a fact that shows that Burgos had hardly any relationship with Gonzales, much less a conspiratorial one.

Likewise, the Government presented no witnesses from New York or the train ride. The Government presented no evidence to show that Burgos had planned to travel to Greensboro with Gobern and Gonzales. There was no evidence that Burgos had previously engaged in any drug activity with Gobern and Gonzales or anyone else. And, as stated above, Burgos was not found to be in possession of any drugs, any weapon, any large amount of cash, or any other items that might indicate an involvement with drugs or the other two men.

---

8. Again, the Government's fingerprint expert testified he had no idea how long Burgos's fingerprint was on the bag. *See United States v. Townley*, 942 F.2d 1324, 1326 (8th Cir. 1991) ("There is no evidence when or where the fingerprints [on tape wrapping a bar of cocaine] were made. The police fingerprint expert testified that fingerprints 'can last for a long time'; 'it's possible' 'even as long as a year.'").

Indeed, evidence that Burgos traveled on the same train with Gobern and Gonzales, while going far to show that Burgos associated with Gobern and Gonzales, does little to show that Burgos knowingly and willfully participated in a Gobern/Gonzales drug conspiracy.

Nevertheless, to buttress its conclusion that Burgos participated in a Gobern/Gonzales conspiracy, the majority attempts to distill a number of discrete facts and inferences from the single fact that Burgos, Gobern, and Gonzales traveled on the same train. For example, the majority evidently believes that persons traveling from "source cities," such as New York City, are more likely to be drug conspirators; and, according to the majority, traveling from such a city is affirmative evidence of guilt. While I might agree that traveling from a "source city" is a fact that has bearing on whether law enforcement officials have a "reasonable suspicion" that drugs are being smuggled, I fail to see how our Fourth Amendment jurisprudence bears on the question of whether sufficient evidence was presented showing that Burgos (or anyone else traveling from New York City) knowingly and willfully participated in a drug conspiracy.

Similarly, that Burgos picked up Gobern's and Gonzales's train tickets, that Burgos knew Gonzales, that Burgos, Gonzales, and Gobern were from the same neighborhood in New York, that Burgos and Gobern exchanged telephone numbers, and that the three appeared to be leaving the train station in a cab together are all "facts" that the majority believes help prove Burgos's guilt. Yet, these are facts that when taken together (or separately) are innocent on their face. They provide little, if any, evidence that Burgos participated in a drug conspiracy.

In addition, while Burgos, Gobern, and Gonzales were on the same train from New York City, there is no evidence showing that Burgos scheduled the same return trip with Gobern and Gonzales, that Burgos lied to Agent Kowalski when he said he was not traveling with Gobern and Gonzales, or that Burgos remained seated near Gobern and Gonzales because they were his co-conspirators. Also, while Gobern and Gonzales possessed sequentially numbered train tickets, both in the name of "Anthony Flores," Burgos's ticket was in his own name and evidently not in sequential order with the tickets of Gobern and Gonzales. Indeed, even when taken in the light most favorable to the Government, these facts undercut, rather than support, the majority's conclusion that Burgos participated in a drug conspiracy.

Could then the association evidence and the fingerprint evidence, taken together, lead a juror rationally to conclude beyond a reasonable doubt that Burgos willfully participated in, and intended to further and accomplish the purpose of, the Gobern/Gonzales conspiracy? Again, I think not. If the fact that a defendant merely associates with a drug dealer is insufficient to prove a conspiracy, I doubt the evidence would suddenly be propelled into the realm of sufficiency by the additional fact that the defendant at one time touched the container that stored the dealer's drugs (especially when the Government has not shown that the defendant touched the container while it contained the drugs).

The Ninth Circuit's decision in *United States v. Vasquez-Chan*, 978 F.2d 546 (9th Cir. 1992), is on point. In that case, DEA Agents infiltrated a drug ring and identified several persons who were suspected of participating in drug trafficking. Eventually, the DEA seized over six hundred kilograms of cocaine found in a house in which the defendants were temporarily residing. One defendant, Vasquez, was the housekeeper, and the other defendant, Gaxiola, was a houseguest. Neither defendant had been mentioned by the co-conspirators as having participated in the drug ring. However, when the DEA agents arrived at the house both defendants were present.

Both Vasquez and Gaxiola, like Burgos, agreed to speak with the law enforcement officials. Vasquez admitted that she had resided in the house for three months. She said that she worked as a caretaker for a man named Peralta and was paid between $300 and $800 every fifteen days; the money arrived by messenger. According to Vasquez, she did not lease or rent the residence, although agents found a utility bill in her name and the name of Peralta. Vasquez also told the officers that the cocaine had been delivered by messengers about three days earlier, although she could not describe them to the police. In addition, Vasquez possessed a false passport.

As for Gaxiola, she told the agents that she had been Vasquez's roommate in Mexico and that she and her infant child had been visiting Vasquez and staying at the house for a few weeks. The vast majority of the cocaine was found in the bedroom where Gaxiola and her child slept. Twelve of Gaxiola's fingerprints were found on the containers in which the cocaine was stored. While no fingerprints were found on the plastic bags inside of the containers, one of Gaxiola's fingerprints was found on the inside surface of the cover for a container housing the cocaine.

Both Vasquez and Gaxiola were indicted and convicted by a jury of conspiracy to possess cocaine with intent to distribute, possession, and aiding and abetting. On appeal they claimed that the evidence was insufficient on all counts. The Ninth Circuit reversed the convictions. On the conspiracy charge, the court held:

> While the government submitted more than enough evidence that a narcotics conspiracy existed among several defendants other that Gaxiola and Vasquez, the evidence does not establish that the defendants here agreed to or knowingly assisted that conspiracy. Gaxiola's and Vasquez's actions are consistent with those of an innocent housekeeper and houseguest who have no involvement in the ongoing narcotics transaction....

As for the fingerprint evidence against Gaxiola, the court said:

> The canisters—some opened, some closed, some empty, some filled with cocaine—were located in her bedroom; it is reasonable to assume that she touched them at some time, including on one occasion the inside lid of a canister, as she passed in and out of the room or made space in the small bedroom so that she and her infant child could have a comfortable place to sleep. The evidence presented at Gaxiola's trial did not establish any reason to believe that an innocent explanation of that evidence was any less likely than the incriminating explanation advanced by the government.... Even when the fingerprint evidence is combined with the other evidence against Gaxiola, it is legally insufficient to establish in the mind of a reasonable juror, *beyond a reasonable doubt*, that she possessed the cocaine located in the house in which she was staying.

Needless to say, the evidence presented against Burgos is no more damning (and actually far less so) than the evidence presented against Vasquez and Gaxiola.

Finally, in making the sufficiency determination, I have not given any credit to Burgos's innocent explanations. Nor have I required the Government to disprove all innocent hypotheses. The law is clear that the Government need not exclude every reasonable hypothesis consistent with innocence.

What we have here is a case where the Government urges inference upon inference, not all of which are rational or supported by the record. The Supreme Court advised long ago that "charges of conspiracy are not to be made out by piling inference upon inference," *Direct Sales Co. v. United States*, 319 U.S. 703, 711 (1943). Viewed in the light most favorable to the Government, the evidence here was insufficient for a rational juror to conclude to a "near certitude," that Burgos willfully participated in the Gobern/Gonzales conspiracy. Consequently, the evidence was insufficient as a matter of law to sustain Burgos's conspiracy conviction.

I respectfully dissent from the majority's affirmance of Burgos's conviction.

Despite their differences with respect to the sufficiency of the evidence, both the *Burgos* dissent and majority agree "the Government need only show a 'slight connection' between the defendant and the established conspiracy." Indeed, the "slight connection" concept is a relatively well-settled principle in the law of conspiracy. In the context of ongoing market-based criminal enterprises like drug operations, however, this principle can lead to an especially broad application of the crime of conspiracy. One of the most striking examples of this has been the so-called "girlfriend" drug conspiracy cases. In these cases, significant others of drug dealers (often wives or girlfriends) have been convicted of conspiracy and received lengthy prison sentences for arguably minor involvement in the drug operations of their boyfriends or husbands.

Single Moms, Battered Women, and Other Sex-Based Anomalies in the Gender-Free World of the Federal Sentencing Guidelines
Myrna S. Reader
20 Pepperdine Law Review 905 (1993)

The most troubling gender questions concerning female offenders are raised by simply reading the published facts of many drug cases, which identify women by their relationships with men. Such females are typically married to, living with, or intimately involved with males who are described as being central to the conspiracies in question. In contrast, the women often have relatively minor roles in the conspiracies: facilitating drug deals by answering the telephone, opening the door, or acting as couriers for their male intimates. While the mate of a white-collar criminal may be shielded from his crime in the suites, the live-in companion of a drug dealer who sells his wares on the streets or at home is not equally sheltered. Mere presence is easily converted to membership in a conspiracy by the number of ways in which women have been socialized to further their relationships with men. Thus, indigent women can become active participants in crime by permitting drugs in the home, answering the door or the telephone, and by giving or bringing contraband to buyers.

Given the nature of such women's relationships, unless a female leaves her mate who is dealing drugs, it may be difficult for her to totally disassociate herself from the conspiracy. In other words, she is likely to be aware of his criminal endeavors and familial actions on her part often promote his criminal activities. Undoubtedly, such females do receive the benefit of drug money, and have enough involvement with illicit activity to be charged and convicted of crime. However, while the mates of drug dealers and mates of men accused of white-collar crime equally receive the benefits of tainted money, mates of drug dealers usually live at the scene of criminal activity. Therefore, some women who are poor may be sucked into crime, whereas richer women who associate with white-collar felons do not face sacrificing their relationships in order to remain crime-free.

The interrelationship of gender to crime and sentencing is fairly complex in such situations and raises a number of policy questions. When charging conspiracies, how do prosecutors determine which women to arrest? Are some women really arrested to provide leverage for plea bargaining with the more culpable male, either to provide information and testimony in exchange for immunity, or to be dismissed in exchange for the male's plea? Since decisions concerning the nature of the charge and plea bargaining rest with the prosecutor, gender questions concerning a woman's culpability are often not raised at the appellate level because evidence supporting the verdict will always exist. For example, one female defendant who moved to Minneapolis to marry her male codefendant claimed she had no criminal intent to join the conspiracy, but found herself counting money and writing messages for him. Large quantities of drugs and money were found in their residence and she admitted to maintaining ledgers. Needless to say, the jury convicted her. Similarly, another women who pleaded guilty to a drug conspiracy agreed to accompany her boyfriend of five years on a drug buy and carry the purchase money. While she claimed it was the first time she had actively participated in his drug dealing, she admitted that for two years she suspected his illegal earnings were drug-related.

It is obvious that such women are not really innocent. However, unless the prosecutor permits them to plead to lesser offenses, they become subject to long mandatory minimums which are disproportionate to their culpability as a member of the conspiracy. Men can similarly show circumstances in which they are given sentences that have no relationship to their activities in a conspiracy, but such arguments will depend on the facts in a given case rather than on gender-based role patterns.

The Future of Federal Sentencing Policy: Learning Lessons from Republican Judicial Appointees in the Guidelines Era
David M. Zlotnick
79 University of Colorado Law Review 1 (2008)

Of all the low-level offender cases, the so-called "girlfriend" cases seemed to bother Republican [federal judicial] appointees the most. Generally, these female defendants had a minor role in the offense. They may have taken messages, stored drugs, assisted in transport, or sometimes engaged in small quantity sales activity. However, they rarely made a substantial profit and their primary motivation for criminal conduct was their relationship with a man who was a drug dealer. Moreover, even if the quantity of drugs in the conspiracy was reasonably foreseeable to them, they rarely had any influence over the scope of the operation.

A poignant illustration of a ... "girlfriend" case comes from a 2002 case before Reagan appointee Judge James D. Todd (W.D. Tenn.). The defendant, Lakisha Murphy, had been with her boyfriend, Cedric Robertson, since she was fifteen. Cedric was a member of the "Crips" and a drug dealer. He was also a paraplegic and Lakisha was his primary caretaker, who fed and bathed him. Because Lakisha spent most of her time caring for Cedric at his house, she clearly was aware of Cedric's illegal activities, as he was still a principal of the group despite his disability. In the course of the investigation, Lakisha admitted she occasionally helped Cedric with his drug business and even made a few retail sales when none of Cedric's gang mates were around; however, when she was not helping Cedric with his health needs, she usually had a job as a cashier to support herself and was not considered to be a full-time employee of the conspiracy by the government.

Because more than fifty grams of crack was involved in the offense, Lakisha faced a ten-year mandatory minimum sentence. Perhaps on principle, or out of love or fear, Lakisha refused to cooperate with the police. Thus, although Cedric received a longer sentence than her, four of her male co-defendants, who were far more culpable, received less time than Lakisha because they received substantial assistance motions from the government. Judge Todd noted this disparity, stating "it seems unfortunate in this case that you're doing more time than some of these guys did ... and there's nothing I can do about it." Judge Todd also spoke directly to Lakisha at the sentencing hearing before he imposed the ten-year sentence, saying:

> The tragedy of this [case], Ms. Murphy, is that you made a very poor choice of boyfriends ...
>
> I have no doubt that this was Cedric Robertson's drug operation.... [But] a woman can stand by her man without becoming a criminal herself.... But you had the misfortune in this case of having a boyfriend who couldn't use his arms and his legs and couldn't care for himself, so you became his arms and his legs. And in doing so, you did, in fact, become a criminal[.]

b. Recommending a Source from Which to Buy Drugs

United States v. Tyler

United States Court of Appeals for the Second Circuit
758 F.2d 66 (1985)

Meskill, J.

Warren Tyler appeals from a judgment of conviction entered in the United States District Court for the Southern District of New York on a jury verdict. Following a two day trial, the jury found Tyler guilty of conspiracy to distribute heroin in violation of 21 U.S.C. §846 and of aiding and abetting the distribution of heroin in violation of 18 U.S.C. §2 and 21 U.S.C. §841. Tyler was sentenced to concurrent terms of two years imprisonment on each of the two counts, to be followed by a five year special parole term on the aiding and abetting count. He is currently serving his sentence.

Tyler's arrest, indictment and conviction stemmed from a purchase of heroin by New York City Police Detective Cleveland Baxter. Baxter made the actual purchase of heroin from James Bennett. Tyler was arrested because Baxter identified Tyler as the man who had introduced him to Bennett. Tyler was charged in two counts of a four count indictment. Count one charged conspiracy to distribute heroin and count two charged aiding and abetting the distribution of heroin.

At trial, Baxter was the government's main witness. He testified that on May 10, 1984, he went over to Harlem as part of an undercover narcotics operation. His goal was to make at least two purchases of drugs. As he was walking along the street he encountered Tyler. After an exchange of greetings, Tyler asked Baxter "if everything was all right." Baxter told Tyler that he "was looking for some good dope." (Dope is the street name for heroin.) Tyler told Baxter that "he would take care of [him]."

The two began to walk down the street. They stopped and Tyler went off to the side and spoke briefly to an unidentified individual. Tyler returned to Baxter and told him that "he was trying to get [him] something that was good, because there was a lot of dope on the street that was not good." The two then continued to walk down the street.

They next encountered Bennett. Tyler and Bennett stepped off to the side and had a brief conversation, after which Bennett walked over to Baxter and asked "how many did [he] want." Baxter told him three. Baxter and Bennett then began to walk down the street. As they were walking, they exchanged three glassine envelopes containing heroin for thirty dollars.

After completing the transaction with Bennett, Baxter turned around and walked back up the street. As he was walking away, Tyler approached him and asked him for some change. Baxter told him that he was low on cash and "that maybe he could check with [Bennett] and [Bennett would] take care of him." Baxter testified that Tyler replied "yes, but he just wanted to have more change, he was trying to get something." Baxter gave Tyler seventy-five cents and the two parted company. Baxter reported the buy to his back-up team and they arrested Tyler approximately twenty minutes later. At the time of his arrest, Tyler was carrying two dollars and seventy-five cents.

Tyler was the only witness called by the defense. He testified that although Baxter asked him about drugs, he did not take Baxter to Bennett nor did he have any role in the sale. He did testify, however, that he saw the sale take place and that after it was completed he approached Baxter to ask him for some money.

After two days of deliberations the jury found Tyler guilty on both the conspiracy count and the aiding and abetting count. Tyler's motion for entry of judgment of acquittal notwithstanding the verdict or for a new trial was denied. The appeal before us ensued.

Tyler's first argument is that there was insufficient evidence of an agreement between himself and Baxter to establish the existence of a conspiracy to distribute heroin.

[W]e have recognized that "'[a] conspiracy by its very nature is a secretive operation.'" Thus, we have held that the existence of "a conspiracy ... may be established ... through circumstantial evidence." Moreover, to be sufficient "the evidence need not have excluded every possible hypothesis of innocence."

Our narrow standard of review, however, does not require us to affirm all conspiracy convictions. On the contrary, we have found the evidence insufficient to sustain a conspiracy conviction in a number of cases. Likewise, we find the evidence in the instant case insufficient to sustain Tyler's conspiracy conviction.

The government's evidence against Tyler consisted mainly of Baxter's testimony. According to Baxter's version of the transaction, Tyler told Baxter that he would get him some good dope. After making some type of inquiry of an unidentified individual, Tyler encountered Bennett. Tyler had a brief side conversation with Bennett and Bennett then approached Baxter. Bennett and Baxter walked away from Tyler and consummated their deal. The two then separated and Tyler walked up to Baxter and asked him for some change. Conspicuously absent from this scenario is any evidence that Tyler asked Baxter how much heroin he sought to purchase, that Tyler indicated that he had a specific source of heroin in mind for Baxter, that Tyler knew where to find Bennett or expected him to be in the area, or that Tyler had made any previous deals with Bennett.[1]

The evidence adduced by the government merely shows that Tyler helped a willing buyer locate a willing seller. As we have stated in the past, such evidence, standing alone, is insufficient to establish the existence of an agreement between the facilitator and the seller. *United States v. Hysohion*, 448 F.2d 343, 347 (2d Cir. 1971) ("The fact that Rimbaud told Everett, a willing buyer, how to make contact with a willing seller does not necessarily imply that there was an agreement between that seller ... and Rimbaud."); *United States v. Torres*, 519 F.2d 723, 726 (2d Cir.) ("membership in a conspiracy is not established ... by the fact that a defendant told a willing buyer how to make contact with a willing seller").

---

1. The government argues that the jury could have concluded that two dollars of the two dollars and seventy-five cents Tyler was carrying at the time of his arrest came from Bennett. From this, the government claims that the jury could have inferred that Tyler had a stake in the outcome of Bennett's sale. The evidentiary support for these inferences along with the other evidence in this case is simply not substantial enough to establish a conspiracy between Tyler and Bennett.

In an attempt to fill in the holes in its case, the government relies on the jury's obvious disbelief of Tyler's testimony to support the conspiracy conviction. We also agree that the jury has a right to consider the defendant's lack of credibility in reaching its verdict.

Th[is] proposition[], however, [is] not helpful to the government's case here. In each of the cases in which the jury's disbelief was relied on as a factor supporting affirmance, the evidence apart from the incredibility of the defendant's testimony was sufficient or very close to sufficient. We merely added that the defendant's incredible story was another circumstance that the jury was entitled to consider. Here, on the other hand, the evidence of an agreement between Tyler and Bennett was nonexistent. Thus, although the jury's disbelief of a defendant's testimony may supplement already existing evidence and help make the evidence in a borderline case sufficient, in the instant case there was simply no existing evidence to supplement.

In sum, even viewing the evidence in the light most favorable to the government, the evidence shows no more than that Tyler helped a willing buyer find a willing seller. Under the law of this Circuit, such evidence is insufficient to prove the existence of a conspiratorial agreement between Tyler and the seller. Thus, Tyler's conspiracy conviction must be reversed.

Tyler also urges us to reverse his aiding and abetting conviction. He argues that because the government failed to prove that he had a stake in the outcome of Bennett's sale the evidence was insufficient to establish aiding and abetting. We do not find this argument compelling.

[T]he requirements for the offense of aiding and abetting are "'that [a defendant] in some sort associate himself with the venture, that he participate in it as in something that he wishes to bring about, [and] that he seek by his action to make it succeed.'"

Looking at the evidence in the light most favorable to the government, we concluded that these requirements have been satisfied. Tyler told Baxter that he would find him some good dope; he approached the unidentified individual, apparently in an effort to locate drugs; he continued to assist Baxter until they encountered Bennett; he apparently told Bennett what Baxter was seeking; and after Baxter and Bennett made their deal he asked Baxter for some change, apparently seeking a reward for his making good on his claim that he would find Baxter some good dope. From this evidence the jury was entitled to conclude that Tyler associated himself with the criminal venture, participated in it as something he wished to bring about and sought by his actions to make it succeed. Therefore, "there was enough evidence here to support the conclusion that [Tyler] was an aider and abettor. He had sufficient ability, influence and control here to bring about a sale that, without his participation, would not have been made."

Finally, we note that there is nothing inconsistent in our determination that the evidence was insufficient with respect to the conspiracy count but sufficient with respect to the aiding and abetting count. The two offenses are separate and distinct.

The essence of conspiracy is proof of a conspiratorial agreement while aiding and abetting requires there be a "community of unlawful intent" between the aider and abettor and the principal. While a community of unlawful intent is similar to an agreement, it is not the same. Thus, a defendant may wittingly aid a criminal act and be liable as an aider and abettor ... but not be liable for conspiracy, which requires knowledge of and voluntary participation in an agreement to do an illegal act.

For the foregoing reasons, Tyler's conviction on the conspiracy count is reversed and his conviction on the aiding and abetting count is affirmed.

c. When Do Purchasers Become Co-Conspirators with Sellers?

United States v. Colon

United States Court of Appeals for the Seventh Circuit
549 F.3d 565 (2008)

Posner, J.

The defendant was convicted by a jury of possessing cocaine with intent to sell it, conspiring to possess cocaine with intent to sell it, and aiding and abetting the conspiracy, and he was sentenced to 135 months in prison. The principal ground of his appeal is that he was not a conspirator or an aider and abettor of a conspiracy, but was merely a purchaser from a conspirator, and that the jury's contrary finding lacked sufficient basis in the evidence to stand.

The evidence of his guilt of these offenses, as summarized in the government's brief, is that the "defendant regularly obtained distribution quantities of cocaine from Saucedo and Rodriguez.... The dealings between ... [the defendant and Saucedo, with whom alone the defendant dealt] were standardized and exhibited mutual trust. Saucedo and Rodriguez had a stake in defendant's distribution activities as well as their ongoing arrangement, given that their profits depended on the success of defendant's distribution efforts.... [The defendant and Saucedo] conducted regular, standardized transactions through which defendant obtained cocaine in quantities of either 4.5 or 9 ounces at consistent prices, and distributed it to customers. Defendant and Saucedo regularly arranged deliveries by telephone," with defendant being the caller, using Saucedo's cellphone number.

The government's summary describes a routine buyer/seller relationship, as in *United States v. Mercer,* 165 F.3d 1331, 1336 (11th Cir. 1999), where the court remarked that "the evidence shows simply that his co-defendant Miller knew that Mercer sold drugs and that he had sources from which he could get drugs, that Mercer had a source for drugs and if that source failed he would 'go somewhere else,' that he bought quantities of cocaine from some unknown source and sold it to police agents presumably at a profit." The relationship in the present case was "standardized" only in the sense that because seller and buyer dealt regularly with each other, the sales formed a regular pattern, as one would expect in any repeat purchase, legal or illegal. The length of the sales relationship is unclear; it may have been as long as six weeks, but the total number of sales was no more than six or seven, involving a total of 30 to 35 ounces of cocaine.

In any event, how "regular" purchases on "standard" terms can transform a customer into a co-conspirator mystifies us. "[A]greement—the crime of conspiracy—cannot be equated with repeated transactions." *United States v. Thomas,* 150 F.3d 743, 745 (7th Cir. 1998). The government either is confusing buying with conspiring or believes that a seller and buyer who fail to wrangle over each sale aren't dealing at arms' length and therefore lack mutual trust. But "mutual trust" is already a factor in the conventional analysis of conspiracy; an act that is merely evidence of mutual trust cannot be a separate factor. And anyway repeat transactions need not imply greater mutual trust than is required in any buyer-seller relationship. If you buy from Wal-Mart your transactions will be highly regular and utterly standardized, but there will be no mutual trust suggestive of a relationship other than that of buyer and seller.

It is different if, as in *United States. v. Sax*, 39 F.3d 1380, 1385–86 (7th Cir. 1994), a seller assists his customers in establishing the methods by which they will take delivery from him, for then he is more than just a seller; he is helping to create a distribution system for his illegal product. But the defendant in our case (a buyer, not a seller) did nothing to help Saucedo and Rodriguez establish a delivery system that would enable them to serve him, or serve him better.

The fact that in his conversations with Rodriguez, Saucedo referred to Colon as "Dude" or "Old Boy," rather than calling him by his name, is not, as the government believes, indicative of intimacy or a pre-existing relationship; it is for obvious reasons a convention in the drug trade not to refer to a customer by his real name. There were no sales on credit to the defendant, or other evidence of mutual trust or dependence, and he had no dealings with — indeed, he never met or spoke to — Rodriguez, Saucedo's unquestioned co-conspirator, although the defendant knew that they worked together. There is no suggestion that the defendant could expect to receive any part of the income that Saucedo obtained from selling cocaine to other customers. There was no "stimulation, instigation," or "encouragement" by the defendant of Saucedo and Rodriguez's business, no "informed and interested cooperation" between that business and the defendant's retail drug business. In his conversations with Rodriguez, Saucedo referred to the defendant only as a "customer," not as an associate, colleague, pal, or "one of us." The prosecutor in closing argument described the defendant as the conspirators' customer, and its own witnesses denied that Saucedo had ever asked the defendant to sell cocaine for him or Rodriguez.

Of course Saucedo and Rodriguez had, as the government says, "a stake in defendant's distribution activities." Every seller to a distributor has a stake in the distributor's activities; a person who buys for resale will not enrich his seller if his resale business dries up. Saucedo and Rodriguez had other customers; we do not know how many, or what the defendant's volume of purchases was relative to that of other customers.

Cases in this and other circuits list factors such as we have discussed, along with others, as indicative of participation in a conspiracy. But in every case such factors have to be placed in context before an inference of participation in a conspiracy can be drawn. In *United States v. Hicks,* 368 F.3d 801, 805 (7th Cir. 2004), for example, we listed a number of these factors but added "prolonged cooperation" between the parties (a quotation from *Direct Sales Co. v. United States,* 319 U.S. at 713, the Supreme Court's leading case on the difference between a conspiracy and a mere buyer-seller relationship) and "sales on credit," factors that strengthen an inference of participation drawn from observing circumstances also found in a routine buyer-seller relationship.

So the government's theory of conspiracy, when stripped of its redundancies and irrelevancies, reduces to an assertion that a wholesale customer of a conspiracy is a coconspirator per se. The implication is that during Prohibition a speakeasy was a co-conspirator of the smuggler who provided it with its supply of booze. And the logic of the government's position does not stop with the customer who is a wholesale purchaser rather than a retail one. Had the defendant been purchasing for his personal consumption, he would still have had "regular, standardized" transactions with Saucedo, as in our Wal-Mart example, and Saucedo would have had a stake in whatever activity the defendant engaged in to obtain the money to buy cocaine. There would have been the same level of "mutual trust" as required in any illegal sale because either buyer or seller might be a government informant or turn violent. The mutual trust in this case was less than it would have been had Saucedo "fronted" cocaine to the defendant (a factor mentioned in almost all the cases) rather than being paid in cash at the time of sale. With fronting, the seller becomes the buyer's creditor, adding a dimension to the relationship that goes beyond a spot sale for cash.

There are practical reasons for not conflating sale with conspiracy. "A sale, by definition, requires two parties; their combination for that limited purpose does not increase the likelihood that the sale will take place, so conspiracy liability would be inappropriate." *United States v. Townsend,* 924 F.2d 1385, 1394 (7th Cir. 1991). As we put it in *United States v. Manzella,* 791 F.2d 1263, 1265 (7th Cir. 1986), "A conspiracy involves more people and can therefore commit more crimes; and it can do so more efficiently, by exploiting the division of labor and by arranging concealment more effectively—sometimes through suborning law enforcers." There is nothing like that here, so far as the defendant's involvement was concerned. And the situation is not altered just because he was a buyer for resale rather than for his personal consumption. As the plurality opinion in *United States v. Lechuga,* 994 F.2d 346 (7th Cir. 1993) (en banc), explains, "before today, it was widely assumed that a conviction for participation in a drug conspiracy could be affirmed with no more evidence than that the defendant had sold in a quantity too large to be intended for his buyer's personal consumption, though some of our cases ... tugged the other way. Today we resolve the conflict in our cases by holding that 'large quantities of controlled substances, without more, cannot sustain a conspiracy conviction.' What is necessary and sufficient is proof of an agreement to commit a crime other than the crime that consists of the sale itself."

The Eleventh Circuit pointed out in *United States v. Dekle* that "what distinguishes a conspiracy from its substantive predicate offense is not just the presence of any agreement, but an agreement with the same joint criminal objective—here the joint objective of distributing drugs. This joint objective is missing where the conspiracy is based simply on an agreement between a buyer and a seller for the sale of drugs. Although the parties to the sales agreement may both agree to commit a crime, they do not have the joint criminal objective of distributing drugs." This would be a different case, therefore, had the defendant agreed to look for other customers for Saucedo and Rodriguez, had received a commission on sales to those customers, had advised Saucedo and Rodriguez on the conduct of their business, or had agreed to warn them of threats to their business from competing dealers or from law-enforcement authorities. It would be a different case if "Lechuga [the seller] had told Pinto [the buyer] that he needed a good distributor on the south side of Chicago and wanted to enter into a long-term relationship with Pinto to that end. Then it would be as if Lechuga had hired Pinto to assist him in reaching his market." *United States v. Lechuga,* 994 F.2d at 349.

All these would be settings in which, in the Eleventh Circuit's terminology, Saucedo, Rodriguez, and the defendant would have had "the same joint criminal objective ... of distributing drugs." But in our case there is no evidence of a relationship other than a conventional sales relationship between the defendant and the conspiracy from which he bought drugs. It is true that after discarding, in his flight from the police, the cocaine he had just bought from Saucedo, the defendant called Saucedo and told him what had happened. But there is no suggestion that he was warning Saucedo, in order to help the latter evade capture, rather than merely reporting an incident that might affect the defendant's future purchases. A drug runner employed by Saucedo phoned the defendant and told him he'd been stopped by the police after delivering cocaine to him, but that is not evidence of the defendant's participation in a conspiracy either.

The muddle that was the government's theory of the case was mirrored in the jury instructions, which after correctly noting that the defendant's purchase of drugs from another person for resale was insufficient evidence that the defendant had conspired with that person, told the jury to consider whether "the parties had an understanding that the cocaine would be sold" and whether "the transaction involved large quantities of cocaine."

If the defendant was a middleman, as he was, the parties would understand that he would be reselling the cocaine; and as a middleman he would be likely to buy in quantities greater than one would buy for one's personal consumption, and therefore "large." The jury was also asked to consider whether the parties had "a standardized way of doing business over time," whether they had "a continuing relationship," "whether the sales were on credit or on consignment," and whether the seller had a "financial steak [*sic*] in a resale by the buyer." Only the question about credit or consignment was germane, for reasons that we've indicated, and that question could only have confused the jury, since all the transactions with the defendant were cash transactions. And the judge made no effort to relate the factors that she told the jury to consider to the difference between a customer and a conspirator. It is no surprise that the jury convicted; given the warped instructions, the conviction does nothing to advance the government's argument that the evidence of conspiracy was sufficient for a reasonable jury to convict.

Nor was the defendant proved to be an aider or abettor of the Saucedo-Rodriguez conspiracy. An aider and abettor is conventionally defined as one who knowingly assists an illegal activity, wanting it to succeed. This is a general definition, however, and like most legal generalizations requires qualification in particular cases. Suppose you own and operate a store that sells women's clothing. Every month the same young woman buys a red dress from your store. You happen to know that she's a prostitute and wears the dress to signal her occupation to prospective customers. By selling her the dress at your normal price you assist her illegal activity, and probably you want the activity to succeed since if it fails she'll stop buying the dress and your income will be less. But you are not an aider and abettor of prostitution because if you refused to sell to her she would buy her red dress from another clothing store, one whose proprietor and staff didn't know her profession. So you're not *really* helping her or promoting prostitution, as you would be if you recommended customers to her in exchange for a commission.

It is the same here, so far as the record reveals. By buying from Saucedo, the defendant was assisting an illegal activity, which he doubtless wanted to be successful as otherwise he would have to find another seller. If that is enough to establish aiding and abetting, every buyer from a drug conspiracy is an aider and abettor of a conspiracy and is therefore to be treated by the law exactly as a member of the conspiracy would be treated. Yet as with the sale of the red dress, there is no basis for thinking that the defendant really helped Saucedo and Rodriguez's drug conspiracy—that he made a difference—because so far as appears they could have found another customer for the modest amount of cocaine that they sold to him.

The government relies on *United States v. Kasvin,* 757 F.2d 887 (7th Cir. 1985), but omits mention of the part of the opinion that shows how different that case is from this one. Kasvin, the buyer defendant, "for several years ... had visited the headquarters of the conspiracy several times weekly, had been assigned a number just as some of the admitted members of the conspiracy had been assigned, his telephone number had been encoded, on occasion he provided the organization with marijuana for use in its business, his transactions with the conspiracy ran into hundreds of thousands of dollars annually but unlike an ordinary customer of a business, he simply picked up quantities of marijuana from headquarters, presumably disposed of it through a distribution network, and brought the money back from time to time in amounts which, so far as the records show, bore no definite relationship to the amounts of marijuana carried away at any particular time." There is nothing like that here.

Even the government has its doubts whether the defendant was a member or an aider and abettor of the Saucedo-Rodriguez conspiracy. A conspirator is liable for the foreseeable crimes that his co-conspirators commit in furtherance of the conspiracy, *Pinkerton v. United States,* 328 U.S. 640, 646–47 (1946), yet the only drug quantity on which the government sought to base the defendant's sentence was the quantity that Saucedo sold him, though he knew that Saucedo and Rodriguez were selling cocaine to others as well as to him. One is led to wonder why the government added charges of conspiracy and of aiding and abetting to the charge of possession with intent to distribute. The guideline ranges were the same and the additional charges were likely to confuse the jury by making the defendant's conduct seem more ominous than it was.

So probably the additional charges added nothing to the charge of possession with intent to distribute. But maybe the government was concerned that in the (unlikely) event that the evidence obtained when the defendant was caught at Saucedo's house was suppressed, the jury might acquit the defendant of possession or the sentence for possession might be based on a smaller quantity of cocaine and therefore be shorter.

Since the defendant was given concurrent sentences on the two counts, it may seem that reversing the conspiracy and aiding and abetting count could not alter his sentence. But the district judge sentenced him very near the top of the applicable guideline range, and in doing so may have been influenced by the fact that the jury had found the defendant guilty of conspiracy and aiding and abetting as well as of possession. So while the defendant's conviction of possession stands, he is entitled to be acquitted on the other count and he must therefore be resentenced.

United States v. Caldwell

United States Court of Appeals for the Tenth Circuit
589 F.3d 1323 (2009)

Lucero, J.

This case is before us on direct appeal of a criminal conviction and sentence. Among other dispositions,[1] Michael Caldwell was convicted by a jury of participating in a three-party conspiracy to distribute marijuana. The government alleged the conspiracy consisted of Caldwell, the defendant; David Anderson, a street dealer of marijuana; and Samuel Herrera, the drug supplier for both Anderson and Caldwell. In its verdict, the jury concluded the three men entered into a single conspiracy — a tripartite conspiracy — to distribute at least 100 kilograms of marijuana over a two-year period. Although Caldwell admits that he conspired with Herrera, he argues that insufficient evidence supports the theory of a tripartite conspiracy. Caldwell maintains that both the jury and the sentencing judge attributed an improper quantity of marijuana to him.

On our review of the record on appeal, we conclude that the evidence presented at Caldwell's trial was indeed sufficient to establish conspiracies between Caldwell and Herrera and between Caldwell and Anderson, but that it was insufficient to establish a tripartite conspiracy among all three. Both the jury and the sentencing court erroneously attributed quantities of marijuana to Caldwell based on the existence of a tripartite conspiracy. Exercising jurisdiction under 28 U.S.C. §1291 and 18 U.S.C. §3742(a)(1), we affirm Caldwell's conviction, but vacate his sentence and remand the case to the district court for resentencing.

Beginning in 1995, the United States Drug Enforcement Administration ("DEA") began investigating a drug ring headed by the Rosales family of El Paso, Texas. The family's

---

1. Caldwell was also convicted of two counts of using a telephone in furtherance of a drug trafficking crime. Caldwell does not appeal those convictions or sentences.

main contact in Oklahoma was Robert Williams, who distributed marijuana to a number of intermediary suppliers in the state. These suppliers distributed the marijuana, mostly on consignment, to street-level dealers.

Herrera was one such intermediary supplier. He sold marijuana to a number of street-level dealers in Oklahoma City, including Caldwell. The first transaction between Herrera and Caldwell took place in 2004. During that transaction, Caldwell received between two to four kilograms of marijuana on consignment. For approximately two years thereafter, Herrera distributed two to seven kilograms of marijuana once every several weeks to Caldwell. Caldwell then resold the marijuana to users.

Anderson, a friend of Caldwell's since early 2005, eventually became another one of Herrera's main customers. Early in their friendship, Anderson dealt drugs to Caldwell: On two or three occasions shortly after they met, Anderson sold Caldwell approximately one kilogram of marijuana on consignment. For roughly one year after these sales occurred, Anderson and Caldwell had no drug-related interaction. Then in early 2006, Anderson's regular supplier was "running short" on marijuana, and Anderson asked Caldwell if he knew of a reliable drug supplier. Caldwell arranged a meeting between Anderson and Herrera. Even though Caldwell was present at the initial meeting, during which Herrera sold approximately 4.5 kilograms of marijuana to Anderson on consignment, Caldwell received no economic benefit from the introduction. From that point on, Anderson and Herrera dealt with one another "one-on-one"—that is, no subsequent drug transactions between Anderson and Herrera involved Caldwell. Anderson received monthly supplies of approximately four to nine kilograms of marijuana from Herrera, generally on consignment.

During the course of its investigation, the DEA intercepted several incriminating calls regarding the distribution of marijuana between Herrera and Caldwell, and a number of similar calls between Herrera and Anderson. It did not intercept any drug-related telephone conversations between Caldwell and Anderson.

In October 2007, a grand jury indicted Caldwell for conspiracy to distribute 100 kilograms or more of marijuana in violation of 21 U.S.C. § 841(a)(1). The indictment listed Caldwell, Herrera, and Anderson as members of the same conspiracy. In exchange for reduced sentences, both Herrera and Anderson testified at trial. A DEA agent also testified that, during the course of the conspiracy, Herrera sold 54 to 163 kilograms of marijuana to Caldwell and 163 to 327 kilograms of marijuana to Anderson.

Caldwell was convicted of conspiracy to distribute marijuana, and the jury returned a special verdict finding that the conspiracy involved 100 kilograms or more of marijuana. During sentencing, the court relied on the special verdict and a presentence investigation report ("PSR"). The PSR attributed 188 kilograms of marijuana to Caldwell. Caldwell objected to the drug quantity determinations of the jury and the PSR, but the court overruled Caldwell's objection. Based on its finding that over 100 kilograms of marijuana was attributable to Caldwell, the court sentenced Caldwell to 130 months' imprisonment.

We must first consider whether the government produced sufficient evidence for a reasonable jury to conclude that Herrera, Caldwell, and Anderson were engaged in a tripartite conspiracy to distribute marijuana. Where "an indictment charges a single conspiracy, but the evidence presented at trial proves only the existence of multiple conspiracies," a variance occurs. In considering a claimed variance, "we view the evidence and draw all reasonable inferences therefrom in the light most favorable to the government, asking whether a reasonable jury could have found [the defendant] guilty of the charged conspirac[y] beyond a reasonable doubt." The existence of a variance that would support acquittal is a matter of law that we review de novo.

As noted, we conclude that Herrera's role as a common supplier, Caldwell's earlier purchase of marijuana from Anderson, and Caldwell's introduction of Anderson to Herrera do not constitute sufficient evidence of a single conspiracy among the three drug dealers. Instead, the evidence presented at trial demonstrates the existence of separate conspiracies between Caldwell and Anderson, and between Caldwell and Herrera. Assuredly, each of the three conspired to distribute marijuana, but a conspiracy did not exist among Herrera, Caldwell, and Anderson as a group.

Distinguishing between a single, large conspiracy and several smaller conspiracies is often difficult; we will generally defer to the jury's determination of the matter. Nonetheless, "we may not uphold a conviction obtained by piling inference upon inference.... The evidence supporting the conviction must be substantial and do more than raise a suspicion of guilt."

To prove a conspiracy, the government must demonstrate: "(1) that two or more persons agreed to violate the law, (2) that the defendant knew at least the essential objectives of the conspiracy, (3) that the defendant knowingly and voluntarily became a part of it, and (4) that the alleged coconspirators were interdependent." In reviewing a jury's determination that a single conspiracy existed, "a focal point of the analysis is whether the alleged coconspirators' conduct exhibited interdependence." Interdependence exists where coconspirators "inten[d] to act together for their shared mutual benefit within the scope of the conspiracy charged." Circumstantial evidence alone is often sufficient to demonstrate interdependence; indeed, it is often the only evidence available to the government. Further, a single act can be sufficient to demonstrate interdependence. *See, e.g., United States v. Hamilton*, 587 F.3d 1199 (10th Cir. 2009) (determining that a single instance of traveling to collect another drug dealer's debts was sufficient to show defendant became a part of a large and wide-reaching conspiracy).

We are told by the government that the relationship between Caldwell, Anderson, and Herrera was a "vertical conspiracy." A vertical conspiracy, or "chain-and-link" conspiracy, involves a series of consecutive buyer-seller relationships. The classic vertical conspiracy involves Supplier A selling contraband to Supplier B, who then sells the contraband to Supplier C. But drug distribution organizations often do not fit neatly into the concept of vertical conspiracy.

In the present case, Caldwell and Anderson were equal-level purchasers rather than links in a vertical chain. After Herrera became their joint supplier, neither Caldwell nor Anderson bought or sold marijuana to the other. Instead, each independently sold marijuana to third parties. Thus, their relationship does not evince the characteristics of a vertical conspiracy. Were we to categorize this alleged conspiracy, it would fit more neatly into the concept of a "hub-and-spoke" conspiracy, in which several separate players all interact with a common central actor, here Herrera. However, because *any* conspiracy requires a showing of interdependence, we prefer to eschew rigid labels and instead engage in the general, yet fact-specific, inquiry of whether there is evidence of interdependence among all alleged coconspirators.

When multiple individuals are involved in the sale of illegal drugs, they are engaged in an inherently illicit enterprise. Consequently, the degree of specificity with which the government must prove interdependence among them may be lower in the drug context than in the context of other types of conspiracies. But even in the drug context, we must "scrupulously safeguard each defendant individually, as far as possible, from loss of identity in the mass."

It is essential that the evidence demonstrate a mutual benefit before we proceed to determine that several drug dealers who interact with one another are involved in a single conspiracy:

It is not enough that a group of people separately intend to distribute drugs in a single area, nor even that their activities occasionally or sporadically place them in contact with each other. People in the same industry in the same locale (even competitors) can occasionally be expected to interact with each other without thereby becoming coconspirators. What is needed is proof that they intended to act *together* for their *shared mutual benefit* within the scope of the conspiracy charged.

For example, we determined in *Powell* that several drug dealers who shared a common supplier and sold to the same customers and wholesalers in a cooperative matter could be found to have engaged in a single conspiracy. However, sharing a common supplier, without more, does not demonstrate that two drug dealers are acting together for their shared mutual benefit. Accordingly, in the case at bar, the fact that Caldwell and Anderson both bought from Herrera is insufficient to establish interdependence among the three.

The government argues that Anderson's sale of a relatively small amount of marijuana to Caldwell, approximately one year before Anderson met Herrera, supports the jury's finding of a tripartite conspiracy. Undoubtedly, the government presented sufficient evidence for a jury to conclude that Caldwell and Anderson were involved in a conspiracy to distribute marijuana in early 2005: Anderson provided Caldwell with two or three kilograms of marijuana on consignment in early 2005. Our court has previously held that providing drugs on credit can be sufficient to demonstrate a conspiracy to distribute drugs. But the question is whether Caldwell's introduction of Anderson to Herrera constituted a continuation of the earlier Caldwell-Anderson conspiracy. If Caldwell and Anderson were still involved in a conspiracy to distribute marijuana when the introduction occurred, that conspiracy (and thus Caldwell as a member) would have benefitted from Anderson being introduced to Herrera.

"[A] conspiracy, once instituted, continues to exist until it is abandoned, succeeds, or is otherwise terminated by some affirmative act, such as withdrawal by the defendant." Although a lapse in time does not necessarily convert a single conspiracy into multiple conspiracies, time in combination with other factors can "sever the single continuous conspiracy alleged in the indictment into two separate conspiracies."

Under the totality of the circumstances present here, a reasonable jury could not have concluded that the introduction of Anderson to Herrera constituted a continuation of the earlier Caldwell-Anderson conspiracy. Approximately one year passed between Anderson's last sale of drugs to Caldwell and the introduction. A relatively small quantity of drugs passed between Anderson and Caldwell, indicating the objectives of their conspiracy were achieved through a discrete sale of marijuana. Unlike the coconspirators in *Williamson*, Anderson and Caldwell did not spend their year apart merely "enjoying the fruits of their proceeds," and Anderson did not stop selling drugs to Caldwell in order to cover up their crimes. To the contrary, Anderson and Caldwell used the year to build separate illicit businesses, wherein each obtained marijuana and sold it to customers. Because this arrangement demonstrates that the two were competing rather than cooperating, the government failed to meet its burden of proving that the earlier Caldwell-Anderson conspiracy "still functioned as a single ongoing entity" when Caldwell introduced Anderson to Herrera.

We now address a question of first impression for the Tenth Circuit: Is the mere introduction of a common supplier, made by one drug dealer to another, sufficient to create a single conspiracy among all the dealers? We conclude that it is not.

The government attempts to equate this case with *United States v. Ivy*, 83 F.3d 1266 (10th Cir. 1996), in which we held that a single conspiracy existed among three drug dealers. There, a jury convicted Kenny Taylor, a street-level drug dealer, of conspiring with

Samuel Norwood and Raymond Hickman to distribute crack cocaine. Norwood sold crack cocaine to Hickman, who in turn sold it to Taylor. We upheld the jury's finding of a single conspiracy in part because Taylor referred a customer to Hickman. In that situation, however, the government used the introduction to demonstrate that Taylor, Norwood, and Hickman were interdependent, not that Taylor and the man he introduced to Hickman were interdependent.[3] By contrast, the government is attempting to use an introduction to show that Caldwell was interdependent with Anderson, the man Caldwell introduced to his supplier.

Having established that *Ivy* does not govern this case, we look to the type of evidence required to uphold a conspiracy conviction. Under our case law, "mere presence is not sufficient in and of itself [to establish a conspiracy], nor is it sufficient for the government to show only mere association with conspirators known to be involved in crime." Likewise, "the government must do more than show there were casual transactions between the defendant and the conspirators." To distinguish a "casual transaction" from an act demonstrating interdependence, we consider the circumstances surrounding the transaction.

Evidence showing that an alleged coconspirator has an economic stake in the outcome of a drug transaction can demonstrate that a transaction is not merely casual. Of course, direct economic benefit for all individuals involved is not necessarily a prerequisite for a jury to find a single conspiracy. But in the profit-driven world of illicit drugs, the fact that several individuals are in an economically symbiotic relationship may demonstrate that transactions among them are in pursuit of mutual benefit. For example, in *Edwards*, we determined that a reasonable jury could have found a single conspiracy existed when multiple defendants pooled their money to negotiate a lower drug price from a supplier.

On the other hand, an act that merely facilitates the distribution of drugs may be insufficient to show that two individuals intend to act together for their mutual benefit. For example, loaning scales to a drug dealer knowing he would use them to weigh crack cocaine is, in isolation, insufficient to establish a conspiracy between the person who loans the scales and the person who uses them. Without more, loaning of scales "could have been merely a gratuitous favor or isolated act among friends."

United States v. Pressler, 256 F.3d 144 (3d Cir. 2001), is instructive in determining whether Caldwell's introduction of Anderson to Herrera was merely a casual favor among friends, or evidence of interdependence among coconspirators. In that case, a jury convicted Scott Shreffler of conspiracy to distribute heroin. Shreffler introduced two other drug dealers, Anthony and Aaron Forshey, to his heroin supplier, Pete Caban. As in the present case, Shreffler did not receive a discount on his own drug purchases or any other economic benefit from Caban or the Forsheys as a result of this introduction. The Third Circuit held that evidence showing "Shreffler introduced the Forsheys to another, superior source of supply from which Shreffler himself had purchased a large amount of heroin" was insufficient to establish that Shreffler had entered into any sort of agreement to distribute heroin to the Forsheys. In a somewhat insouciant comparison, the court stated:

> It is common for people to tell their friends about a good store or restaurant. Though the Government proved that Shreffler was a very good customer to Caban, that he had recommended Caban to others, and that Caban benefitted from Shreffler's patronage, *it did not show that Shreffler and Caban ever agreed to work together on anything.*

---

3. The government also presented more evidence than just the introduction: It demonstrated that Hickman sold Taylor large quantities of crack cocaine, the vast majority of which Hickman had obtained from Norwood.

Similarly, Caldwell's introduction of Anderson to Herrera undoubtedly broadened Herrera's customer base. But the facts surrounding the introduction demonstrate that it was friendly rather than conspiratorial. As in *Pressler*, the government offered no evidence that Caldwell received any economic benefit from the introduction, and Anderson testified that Caldwell received no such benefit. After the introduction, Caldwell was not involved with any drug transaction between Herrera and Anderson. On the facts of this case, Caldwell's introduction alone cannot demonstrate beyond a reasonable doubt that a single conspiracy existed among Caldwell, Anderson, and Herrera. Although the government established that Caldwell was involved in two separate conspiracies, it failed to prove the tripartite conspiracy alleged in the indictment. As a result, a variance occurred.

Not every variance, however, requires reversal. A variance becomes fatal, and thus reversible error, "only if it affects the substantial rights of the accused." We review de novo the question of whether a particular variance constitutes reversible error.

A variance is not fatal "merely because the defendant is convicted upon evidence which tends to show a narrower scheme than that contained in the indictment, provided that the narrower scheme is fully included within the indictment." The primary purpose of the prohibition against variances is "to insure notice of the charges." When an indictment charges a conspiracy among multiple individuals, it generally provides sufficient notice to a defendant that she must defend against the smaller conspiracies. By comparison, a variance may be substantially prejudicial "if the evidence adduced against co-conspirators involved in separate conspiracies was more likely than not imputed to the defendant by the jury in its determination of the defendant's guilt."

Caldwell contends he was substantially prejudiced because the jury must have relied on the amount of marijuana Herrera sold to Anderson in assessing drug quantity. Caldwell's argument fails, however, because "when asking what facts the jury had to find in order to convict, we look to the elements of the crime as defined by law." Moreover, Caldwell admits that the government presented sufficient evidence to prove Caldwell was involved in two separate drug conspiracies. As a result [h]is conviction stands.

Even though Caldwell's conviction is valid, his sentence is not.

In the present case, the jury's determination of drug quantity was clearly erroneous because it was based on an unsupported tripartite conspiracy. The government proved at trial that Herrera sold Caldwell between 54 and 163 kilograms of marijuana, and that Anderson sold Caldwell between 2 and 4 kilograms of marijuana. While these ranges demonstrate that Caldwell could have been responsible for over 100 kilograms of marijuana, they do not demonstrate beyond a reasonable doubt that Caldwell was responsible for that quantity.

Moreover, the PSR attributed approximately 188 kilograms to Caldwell, a quantity that could not have been reached without taking into account the marijuana Herrera sold to Anderson. The sentencing court relied both on this amount and the jury's special verdict in calculating Caldwell's sentence. Consequently, the factual basis for Caldwell's sentence was clearly erroneous, and we remand the matter to the district court for resentencing. In doing so, the district court should not consider the amount of marijuana Herrera sold to Anderson.

d. Continuing Criminal Enterprise and "Drug Kingpin" Laws

In 1970, Congress created a new crime targeted at managers of drug conspiracies, the "continuing criminal enterprise" (or "CCE") offense. 21 U.S.C. § 848. The CCE law requires proof that the defendant engaged in a "continuing series" of federal drug crimes "which are undertaken by such person in concert with five or more other persons with respect to whom such person occupies a position of organizer, a supervisory position, or any other position of management and from which such person obtains substantial income or resources." Though the CCE crime is occasionally referred to as a federal "drug kingpin" law, courts have held that "[a] defendant need not be the dominant organizer or manager of a criminal enterprise; the statute requires only that he occupy some managerial position." *United States v. Becton*, 751 F.2d 250, 255 (8th Cir. 1984).

CCE is rarely prosecuted today. Of the 22,911 defendants sentenced for drug offenses under the federal sentencing guidelines in 2009, a mere 22 had been convicted of CCE. Sourcebook of Criminal Justice Statistics Online, Drug Offenders Sentenced in U.S. District Courts Under the U.S. Sentencing Commission Guidelines, Table 5.39.2009 (2009). Nevertheless, the offense raises interesting questions about vicarious and group criminality. Moreover, the fact that the offense has fallen into disuse may itself be a sign of just how much federal drug enforcement has changed since 1970. When Congress enacted CCE, it provided for much longer terms of imprisonment than were typically available for other federal drug offenses. As discussed in Chapter 4, however, sentences for federal drug offenses like conspiracy and possession with intent to distribute are much longer today than they were in 1970.

United States v. Witek

United States Court of Appeals for the Eleventh Circuit
61 F.3d 819 (1995)

Black, J.

Appellant Ralston Wright was convicted of engaging in a continuing criminal enterprise (CCE) under 21 U.S.C.A. § 848. We must decide whether the Government presented sufficient evidence to prove Wright's guilt beyond a reasonable doubt. We conclude that it did not, and vacate Wright's CCE conviction.

In late 1991 and early 1992, Ralston Wright and his girlfriend, Appellant Claudette Hubbard, sold narcotics from their residence in Cocoa, Florida. Wright and Hubbard would obtain powdered cocaine and marijuana in Dallas, Texas, process most of the cocaine into cocaine base (crack), and then sell the drugs to customers in and around the Cocoa area. Wright and Hubbard's initial supplier was Thomas Semple, but they switched their source to Paul Ohaegbu in March 1992. Ohaegbu entered into a plea agreement with the Government and testified against Wright and Hubbard.

Wright and Hubbard's primary customers were street dealers who operated in and around Cocoa. They included Appellants Alfred Bain, George Calhoun, John Dixon, Tommie Dixon, Earl Green, Reginal Hardy, and Edward Witek; and cooperating witnesses Barbara Chelewski, Siricia Mitchell, and Charles Williams. Generally, sales were negotiated over the phone using code words common to the drug trade. Wright or Hubbard usually delivered the drugs to their buyers at the customer's residence or at some mutually arranged location. Sales were at the going market price and often involved "fronting"— allowing the customer to pay for the drugs after delivery.

In 1992, Wright was arrested and charged with: (1) conspiracy to possess with intent to distribute five kilograms or more of cocaine base in violation of 21 U.S.C. § 846; (2) engaging in a continuing criminal enterprise in violation of 21 U.S.C. § 848; (3) possession with intent to distribute cocaine hydrochloride in violation of 18 U.S.C. § 2 and 21

U.S.C. § 841(a)(1), (b)(1)(C); (4) unlawful use of a communication facility in the commission of a felony in violation of 21 U.S.C. § 843(b); and (5) use of firearms during and in relation to drug trafficking crimes in violation of 18 U.S.C. §§ 2 and 924(c). At trial, Wright's motion for judgment of acquittal was denied and the jury found him guilty on all counts. The district court sentenced Wright to life for the conspiracy and CCE convictions, concurrent twenty and four-year terms for possession and unlawful use of a communication facility, and consecutive five-year enhancements for use of a firearm. This appeal follows.

In order to convict a defendant for engaging in a continuing criminal enterprise, the government must show:

   (1) a felony violation of the federal narcotics laws

   (2) as part of a continuing series of violations

   (3) in concert with five or more persons

   (4) for whom the defendant is an organizer or supervisor

   (5) from which he derives substantial income or resources.

Wright argues that the Government did not adequately demonstrate that he organized or supervised five or more persons as required by the statute. The Government responds that Wright organized or supervised (1) Hubbard, (2) Ohaegbu, and (3) his street-dealing customers, most notably Bain, John Dixon, Tommie Dixon, and Witek.

Section 848(c), which defines a continuing criminal enterprise, requires the government to demonstrate that the defendant "occupies a position of organizer, a supervisory position, or any other position of management" with respect to five other persons engaged in the illegal drug trade. 21 U.S.C.A. § 848(c)(2)(A). This management requirement is disjunctive, allowing the government to meet its burden by showing the defendant functioned "as an organizer *or* a supervisor *or* any other type of manager." Three broad considerations influence our interpretation of the management requirement. First, we must give § 848 a "common-sense reading." Second, we must recall that the statute "is designed to reach the "top brass" in the drug rings, not the lieutenants and foot soldiers." Third, where it is unclear whether particular conduct is prohibited by ambiguous terms in a criminal statute, the rule of lenity requires us to construe that statute narrowly.

It is unnecessary to restate every rule this Court applies when examining § 848's management requirement. At the outset, however, we must make clear what should be obvious from the statute's text: A mere buyer-seller relationship does not satisfy § 848's management requirement. We thereby join with every circuit to consider the issue. A contrary interpretation would do violence to the common-sense meaning of the words "organizer" and "supervisor" and extend § 848's reach beyond the scope Congress intended. Congress knew how to proscribe the mere selling of narcotics when they adopted § 848, *see* 21 U.S.C.A. § 841(a) ("it shall be unlawful ... to ... *distribute, or dispense*"), but did not do so in § 848.[3] We must assume that the use of different language in § 848 was the result of a deliberate choice by Congress.

With these principles in mind, we examine the record to determine whether Wright served as an organizer or supervisor of five or more persons connected to the drug conspiracy in this case.

---

3. Sections 841 and 848 were both enacted as part of Controlled Substances Act of 1970.

1. Hubbard.

Wright insists that Hubbard was at least his equal, and therefore could not be managed or supervised within the meaning of § 848. Although much of the evidence suggests an equal partnership between Wright and Hubbard, that would not prevent the jury from inferring that, at least on some occasions, Wright organized or supervised Hubbard. Section 848 does not require the Government to prove that Wright was the only, or even the dominant, organizer of the Wright-Hubbard operation. Nor does it require the Government to prove that Wright *controlled* Hubbard, because an organizer does not necessarily control those people he organizes, but simply arranges their activities into an orderly operation.

The Government presented enough evidence for the jury to conclude that Wright organized Hubbard's activities within the meaning of § 848. While on a drug-buying trip to Dallas, Wright called Hubbard with instructions to collect money from Tommie Dixon. Hubbard agreed and placed two calls to Dixon asking for payment. Hubbard made other calls for Wright to tell Ohaegbu when to expect Wright in Dallas. Finally, when Charles Williams could not find Wright at an agreed meeting place, Hubbard assisted Wright by directing Williams to the correct location. The evidence is not overwhelming, and could support a conclusion that Wright and Hubbard were equal partners. Nevertheless, viewing the evidence in the light most favorable to the Government, the jury could have believed that this evidence demonstrated that Wright sometimes organized Hubbard's illegal activities.

2. Ohaegbu.

Wright contends that Ohaegbu's role as a narcotics broker does not support a finding that Wright organized or supervised him in any way. We agree. Although there may be cases where a narcotics buyer organizes or supervises his supplier within the meaning of § 848, this is not such a case.

> Every legitimate retail store makes arrangements with its regular suppliers. In one sense it may be said to organize its supply, but does it organize its suppliers? Surely not in the sense of being a manager of its suppliers. To be an organizer within the sense of the statute more is required than simply being a steady customer. *United States v. Jerome,* 942 F.2d 1328, 1331 (9th Cir.1991).

Wright's steady purchases of Ohaegbu's drugs, standing alone, does not satisfy the management requirement of § 848.

A review of the record uncovers no additional evidence from which to infer that Wright organized Ohaegbu's activities. Although Ohaegbu picked up and dropped off Hubbard at the airport on her request,[4] a reasonable factfinder could not interpret this act as evidence of organization or supervision. Buyers and sellers often need to accommodate one another when meeting and arranging for delivery. Such conduct is simply incidental to the buyer-seller relationship. In sum, a reasonable jury could not conclude that Wright, alone or acting through Hubbard, organized or supervised the activities of Ohaegbu.

3. The Street Dealers.

Wright argues that the Government cannot rely on his relationship with customers to sustain the CCE conviction. The Government replies that evidence of Wright and Hubbard's fronting drugs to the street dealers satisfies the management requirement of § 848

---

4. Our conclusion that Wright organized Hubbard's activities allows us to treat her actions on behalf of the Wright-Hubbard enterprise as attributable to Wright for § 848 purposes.

and brings the number of persons organized above the five required by the statute.[5] Although evidence of fronting is certainly relevant to the question of organization or supervision under § 848, this Court has never sustained a CCE conviction based solely on fronting. We now join the circuits which have held that evidence of fronting, *without more,* is insufficient to satisfy the management requirement of § 848.

The Government's reliance on *United States v. Aguilar,* 843 F.2d 155 (3rd Cir.), *United States v. Cruz,* 785 F.2d 399 (2nd Cir.1986), and *United States v. Adamo,* 742 F.2d 927 (6th Cir.1984), is misplaced. In these cases, the defendants' arrangement with their dealers went beyond simple fronting and constituted a consignment or franchise type of operation, with the defendants retaining ultimate control and authority over the drugs. In *Aguilar,* for example, the evidence showed that when a dealer was unable to repay on time, the defendant would reclaim the drugs. Wright and Hubbard never operated at such a level of sophistication.

Just as importantly, in *Aguilar, Cruz,* and *Adamo,* other substantial evidence helped satisfy § 848's management requirement. As the Sixth Circuit noted in distinguishing *Adamo* from a case where fronting was the sole evidence, "the government proved many other facts about the organization's activities in *Adamo.*" Finally, to the extent that these cases can be interpreted to sustain a conviction based on fronting alone, we must disagree. Such an expansive reading of § 848 does not comport with the plain meaning of the terms "organize" or "supervise," goes beyond the scope intended by Congress, and violates the rule of lenity. Thus, the evidence of fronting relied on by the Government does not satisfy § 848's management requirement.

In sum, the Government did not produce enough evidence for a reasonable jury to conclude that Wright organized or supervised the street dealers. The record, viewed in the light most favorable to the Government, only supports a conclusion that Wright organized or supervised Hubbard, four short of the minimum number required by § 848.

We hold that the record does not contain sufficient evidence for a reasonable jury to conclude, beyond a reasonable doubt, that Wright was guilty of engaging in a continuing criminal enterprise. Consequently, we vacate Wright's CCE conviction.[8] We affirm the other convictions and sentences involved in this appeal.

New Jersey v. Alexander

Supreme Court of New Jersey
136 N.J. 563 (1994)

Handler, J.

A jury convicted defendant of several drug-related offenses, including a charge of violating N.J.S.A. 2C:35-3, commonly known as the "drug kingpin" statute. The Appellate Division reversed the "drug kingpin" conviction because it found error in the trial court's instructions to the jury. Specifically, the court below held that in a prosecution for violation of N.J.S.A. 2C:35-3, the trial court must instruct the jury that the State bears the burden of proving that "the defendant functioned as an 'upper echelon member' of an or-

---

5. Viewed in a light most favorable to the Government, Wright and Hubbard fronted cocaine to Bain, Chelewski, John Dixon, Tommie Dixon, and Witek.

8. As we affirm Wright's other convictions, the only collateral consequence of vacating his CCE conviction is eliminating the $250 special assessment imposed for that count. Nevertheless, the presence of a special assessment required us to review Wright's CCE conviction.

ganized 'drug trafficking network' ..." and must define for the jury certain other terms contained in the statute. We granted the State's petition for certification to review that determination.

Defendant, Ryan Lee Alexander, hired Anthony Harewood to sell crack cocaine in Hackensack, introduced Harewood to his customers, and supplied Harewood daily with thirty to seventy baggies of crack. Harewood sold the baggies at $10 each and gave seventy percent of his gross receipts to defendant or to Chris Kittrell, defendant's cousin and an unindicted coconspirator. Harewood's paramour, Sandra Palmer, assisted him by carrying the crack and by delivering the drugs to buyers after they had paid Harewood. Making between $300 and $1,500 per day, Harewood gave up to $5,000 per week to Alexander, and kept up to $2,000.

A confidential informant identified Harewood to an undercover narcotics officer as a drug seller. The officer gave $100 to Harewood, who directed him to Palmer for completion of the drug transaction. Palmer gave the officer nine baggies containing what was later identified as crack cocaine. When Harewood and Palmer were arrested, they had 7.34 grams of cocaine contained in nine $100 baggies and $341.02 in cash. They identified defendant as their supplier, described the commission arrangement, and said that they had sold crack five to six days per week. A search of defendant's apartment yielded 11.08 grams of cocaine contained in forty-two baggies that matched those sold by Harewood and Palmer. The State charged Alexander with possession of cocaine; with possession of cocaine with intent to distribute; and with being a leader of a drug-trafficking network in violation of N.J.S.A. 2C:35-3. The State also charged Harewood and Palmer with various counts of possession of cocaine and of possession of cocaine with intent to distribute.

At trial, Harewood and Palmer testified against defendant, and the jury convicted him on all counts. The trial court sentenced defendant to the mandatory term of life imprisonment with a twenty-five-year parole disqualifier on his conviction for being a leader of a narcotics-trafficking network, and to two five-year sentences on the charges of possession of cocaine and possession of cocaine with intent to distribute, to run concurrently with the life sentence.

The Appellate Division affirmed in part and reversed and remanded in part. Other than merging defendant's conviction for possession of cocaine into his conviction for possession of cocaine with intent to distribute, the court below rejected all defendant's arguments except those directed at the N.J.S.A. 2C:35-3 charge. That statute provides in pertinent part as follows:

> A person is a leader of a narcotics trafficking network if he conspires with others as an organizer, supervisor, financier or manager, to engage for profit in a scheme or course of conduct to unlawfully manufacture, distribute, dispense, bring into or transport in this State methamphetamine, lysergic acid diethylamide, phencyclidine or any controlled dangerous substance classified in Schedule I or II, or any controlled substance analog thereof. Leader of narcotics trafficking network is a crime of the first degree and upon conviction thereof * * * a person shall be sentenced to an ordinary term of life imprisonment during which the person must serve 25 years before being eligible for parole. * * *

> Notwithstanding the provisions of N.J.S.A. 2C:1-8, a conviction of leader of a narcotics trafficking network shall not merge with the conviction for any offense [that] is the object of the conspiracy. * * *

It shall not be necessary in any prosecution under this section for the State to prove that any intended profit was actually realized. The trier of fact may infer that a particular scheme or course of conduct was undertaken for profit from all of the attendant circumstances, including but not limited to the number of persons involved in the scheme or course of conduct, the actor's net worth and his expenditures in relation to his legitimate sources of income, the amount or purity of the specified controlled dangerous substance or controlled dangerous substance analog involved, or the amount of cash or currency involved.

According to the Appellate Division, a correct jury instruction should define "'[o]rganized "drug trafficking net-work"' ... as a group of individuals who, by reason of their number and interrelationships, constitute a structured organization or system engaged in the manufacture or distribution of illegal drugs," and should define "'[u]pper echelon member'... as someone who stands on an upper level of the chain of command of a drug trafficking network, exercising command authority over members of that organization whose status is subordinate to his." Finally, the Appellate Division held that the jury charge should define an "upper" level as "a level [that] is superior to street-level distributors and to their immediate supervisors or suppliers."

On its appeal to this Court from the Appellate Division's reversal of the N.J.S.A. 2C:35-3 conviction, the State argues that the court below erred by "engraft[ing] a declaration of legislative policy onto the drug kingpin statute so as to redefine the elements of the offense," and by requiring that the jury find beyond a reasonable doubt that the State had established each of those newly-defined elements.

N.J.S.A. 2C:35-3 is an unusually-constructed criminal statute. It describes the offense by giving a label to the offender: leader of a narcotics-trafficking network. It then lists the activities that will result in one being branded with that label, namely, (1) that the defendant conspired with at least two others; (2) that the defendant was an organizer, supervisor, financier, or manager; (3) that the defendant engaged in the conspiracy for profit; and (4) that the conspiracy included a scheme or course of conduct unlawfully to manufacture, distribute, dispense, or transport a controlled dangerous substance or analog. Those enumerated activities constitute the material elements of the crime.

When the Legislature enacted the "Comprehensive Drug Reform Act of 1986," it included a statement of policy that is set forth at N.J.S.A. 2C:35-1.1. That statement declares in part that

> to be effective, the battle against drug abuse and drug-related crime must be waged aggressively at every level along the drug distribution chain, but in particular, our criminal laws must target for expedited prosecution and enhanced punishment those repeat drug offenders and upper echelon members of organized narcotics trafficking networks who pose the greatest danger to society.... [T]o ensure the most efficient and effective dedication of limited investigative, prosecutorial, judicial and correctional resources, it is the policy of this State to distinguish between drug offenders based on the seriousness of the offense, considering principally the nature, quantum and purity of the controlled substance involved and the role of the actor in the overall drug distribution network. It is the intention of the Legislature to provide for the strict punishment, deterrence and incapacitation of the most culpable and dangerous drug offenders.

The State argues that in a prosecution for violating N.J.S.A. 2C:35-3, to include as part of the basic definition and as a specific element of the crime in the jury instructions any reference to the role of the defendant as an "upper echelon member" in the overall drug-distribution network improperly redefines the statutory crime. It reasons that the inclusion of that element is at odds with the elements of the offense that are set forth in N.J.S.A. 2C:35-3. Thus, the State contends that the Appellate Division's proposed instruction rewrites the drug-kingpin statute by requiring the State to prove beyond a reasonable doubt a material element that the Legislature did not include in its definition of the offense.

N.J.S.A. 2C:35-3 does not include some of the important factors used in the statutory statement of purpose to describe the drug-kingpin crime, and, to that extent, does not completely convey the full legislative understanding in creating this crime. The statement of purpose expressly makes the defendant's "upper-level" role in a drug network central to the activity criminalized by the Legislature. The prominence of the upper-level status of the defendant in the description and explanation of the purpose of the crime clearly evidences the Legislature's intent that the status or the position of the defendant in the drug trafficking network is a substantive part of the crime. Consistent with that intent, the status or position of the defendant should be considered a material element of the crime. Accordingly, we conclude that a trial court, in a prosecution pursuant to N.J.S.A. 2C:35-3, should instruct the jury that it must find that the defendant occupies a high-level position, that is, a position of superior authority or control over other persons, in a scheme or organization of drug distribution (or manufacture or dispensing or transporting), and that in that position the defendant exercised supervisory power or control over others engaged in an organized drug-trafficking network.

That conclusion is based largely on the fact that the words of the statute alone under N.J.S.A. 2C:35-3, whether their meaning is "plain" or "clear" for constitutional purposes, without any further explanation would not fully convey to the jury the nature of the actual elements of the conduct that the Legislature intended to criminalize. Those elements, in addition to the activities enumerated in N.J.S.A. 2C:35-3, such as supervision, management, financing, and the like, include the role of the defendant as an "upper-level member" of a drug operation.

The recognition of the upper-level position of the defendant as an essential element of the crime under the drug-kingpin statute does not, as the State believes, entail a rewriting of the statute.

This Court has made abundantly clear that correct jury instructions are at the heart of the proper execution of the jury function in a criminal trial: "'[a]ppropriate and proper charges to a jury are essential for a fair trial.'" A court's obligation properly to instruct and to guide a jury includes the duty to clarify statutory language that prescribes the elements of a crime when clarification is essential to ensure that the jury will fully understand and actually find those elements in determining the defendant's guilt.

For the purpose of instructing and guiding juries, courts regularly explain and define statutory language consistent with legislative intent. Courts commonly clarify statutory language to give more precise meaning to statutory terms to effect the legislative intent and to make sure that juries carry out that intent in determining criminal culpability.

Courts follow that approach even when statutory terms have common or well-understood meanings based on ordinary experience. In a prosecution under N.J.S.A. 2C:35-5 for possession of a controlled dangerous substance (C.D.S.) with the intent to distribute, for example, the model jury instruction includes a long definition of a relatively common term—"possession." That definition of possession does not appear anywhere in N.J.S.A. 2C:35-5. Rather, the definition reflects this Court's numerous expositions of the meaning of "possession." The model jury instruction's definition of "possession" includes the situation in which a person "is aware of the presence of the [C.D.S.] and is able to exercise intentional control or dominion over it." The language of "intentional control or dominion" comes not from the literal language of N.J.S.A. 2C:35-5 but from this Court's interpretation of that statute.

Further, statutes containing words whose meanings are ordinary and understandable often require a judicial determination with respect to their intended scope of application. *State v. Thomas,* 132 N.J. 247, 254 (1993) (defining use of school property for school purposes as "essential element" of school-zone drug offense); *State v. Ivory,* 124 N.J. 582, 587–92, 592 A.2d 205 (1991) (defining property that constitutes "school property used for school purposes" for purposes of school-zone drug offense); *see also State ex rel. M.T.S.,* 129 N.J. 422, 609 A.2d 1266 (1992) (finding that legislative history was relevant to under-standing of legislative intent that principles of criminal assault were relevant in defining element of force and role of consent for crime of second-degree sexual assault).

An instruction that makes explicit the implicit elements of the crime does not involve rewriting the statute or redefining, modifying, amending, or adding to the substantive elements prescribed by the statute because that instructional definition conforms to the legislative intent and carries out that intent. Thus, a proper instruction should, in addition to reciting the statutory language of N.J.S.A. 2C:35-3, at least inform the jury that it must find that the defendant occupies a high-level position of authority in the scheme of distribution (or manufacture or dispensing or transporting, as the evidence may permit). A court should instruct the jury that a defendant's position and status must be at a superior or high level in relation to other persons in the drug trafficking network and that the defendant's role must be that of a "leader" in the drug organization or system and, in that capacity, the defendant exercised supervisory power or control over others engaged in the organized drug-trafficking network.

Under the statute a drug-trafficking network need not have any specific configuration or chain of command. Such a network is not to be understood primarily or exclusively as a vertical, in contrast to a horizontal, organization. Rather, it is to be considered as an organization of persons who are collectively engaged in drug activities. A "high-level" or "upper-echelon" "leader" of such an organization is one who occupies a significant or important position in the organization and exercises substantial authority and control over its operations. Neither the specific elements enumerated in the provisions of N.J.S.A. 2C:35-3 nor the additional requirements extrapolated from the statute's statement of purpose indicate that a drug operator exercising authority and controlling other people in an organization or network, even at the street level, could not be a "leader" or "drug kingpin" within the contemplation of the Legislature. Rather, the role of a defendant as a leader or drug kingpin turns more on the nature of that person's authority, the magnitude or extent of control, and the number of persons over whom that power is exercised.

An appropriate instruction should also amplify the other statutory terms that are expressed as material elements of the crime under N.J.S.A. 2C:35-3. Thus, the statutory terms "organizer, supervisor, financier or manager" should be explained so that the meaning of those terms is more fully understood by the jury. For example, the court might define an "organizer" as a person who arranges, devises, or plans a drug-trafficking network; a "supervisor" as one who oversees the operation of a drug-trafficking network; a "financier" as one who is responsible for providing the funds or resources necessary to operate a drug-trafficking network; and a "manager" as one who directs the operations of a drug-trafficking network.

We affirm so much of the judgment of the Appellate Division as reverses defendant's conviction and remands for a new trial. We modify the terms of the remand with respect to the proper jury charge.

Clifford, J., dissenting.

This Court does not have to love a statute, but we do have to apply it unless it is invalid. I fear that the majority's hostility to the enactment that the Legislature has given us has caused the Court to rewrite the "drug kingpin" statute — an illicit exercise bad enough in itself, made worse by the Court's botching of a job for which it is demonstrably ill-suited.

I would apply the statute as written and would reinstate the conviction of this $1500-to-$9000-per-week drug entrepreneur as a "leader of a drug trafficking network."

We are told that "without any further explanation" the words of section 35-3 alone "would not fully convey to the jury the nature of the actual elements of the conduct that the Legislature intended to criminalize." And so, relying on a separate statutory section, N.J.S.A. 2C:35-1.1 (section 35-1.1), the court has added to section 35-3's list of criminal elements yet another "essential element of the crime under the drug-kingpin statute," characterized variously as a defendant's "high-level position" in the nefarious scheme, or a defendant's "role * * * as an 'upper-level member' of a drug operation."

Reliance on section 35-1.1 as justification for the court's stunning addition of a defendant's "upper-level position" as "an *essential element* of the crime under the drug-kingpin statute," is badly misplaced. Section 35-1.1c, quoted in essential part in the majority opinion does nothing more than set forth the Legislature's findings and its declaration of public policy. Section 35-1.1c does not criminalize any conduct, define any elements of any offense, provide for any penalties, or otherwise display any of the identifying features of a criminal statute. Those functions are left to N.J.S.A. 2C:35-2 to -16, in which the Legislature got down to the business of defining and grading the related criminal offenses. Section 35-1, which precedes those sections, is only what it purports to be, nothing more: a statement, an announcement of the Legislature's intent in creating certain crimes and prescribing the penalties therefor, an identification of the targets at which the Comprehensive Drug Reform Act of 1986 is aimed.

Facing the dilemma created when the Legislature writes a statute whose operative provisions are crystal clear but whose operative provisions may not conform with the Legislature's explicit statement of legislative purpose, the Court attempts to remedy the situation by rewriting the operative provisions. We will never know why the Legislature, having so clearly indicated its intention that the statute should apply only to high-level drug dealers, went on to define the crime in a way that would permit conviction of drug dealers at a lower level. What we do know, however, is that one part of the statute is a declaration of legislative intent and purpose, not a definition of a crime, and that another section of the statute is unmistakably the definition of the crime. The crime defined is "leader of narcotics trafficking network." The Legislature says so: "leader of narcotics trafficking network is a crime of the first degree and upon conviction thereof * * * a person shall be sentenced to an ordinary term of life imprisonment during which the person must serve 25 years before being eligible for parole." That is the crime. The Legislature also left no doubt about the elements of that crime:

> A person is a leader of a narcotics trafficking network if he conspires with others as an organizer, supervisor, financier or manager, to engage for profit in a scheme or course of conduct to unlawfully manufacture, distribute, dispense, bring into or transport in this State methamphetamine, lysergic acid diethy-

lamide, phencyclidine or any controlled dangerous substance classified in Schedule I or II, or any controlled substance analog thereof.

One need not twist and turn to figure out what the Legislature meant by "leader of a narcotics trafficking network." It is there in black and white. The crime is named by the Legislature "leader of a narcotics trafficking network," and the crime is defined by the Legislature. As much as section 35-3 may not conform to section 35-1.1c's statement of legislative purpose and intent, that circumstance is for the Legislature, not for this Court, to remedy; for when this Court attempts to remedy it, as no case better shows than this, the Court drafts a new statute. Whether that new statute comes closer to the legislative intent or wanders farther from it is immaterial. The important point is that the Court's gratuitous and painfully inept amendment now becomes the law — not of the people of New Jersey, not of the Legislature, but of this Court.

But, says the Court, a jury is left in the dark by a charge that simply instructs in the language of the criminal statute as dutifully delivered by the trial court in this case. And so, to pierce the newly-developed fog of language, the Court declares that in addition to reciting the statutory language of section 35-3, the trial court must "at least inform the jury that it must find that the defendant occupies a high-level position of authority in the scheme of distribution * * *." Presumably as a definition of what it means by "a high-level position of authority," the Court, in the very next sentence, rules that a trial court should instruct the jury that a "defendant's role must be that of a 'leader' in the drug organization or system and, in that capacity, the defendant exercised supervisory power or control over others engaged in the organized drug-trafficking network," an almost verbatim repetition of the definition provided earlier, in the Court's explanation of why a defendant's "upper-level" role in a drug network is "a substantive part of the crime."

Stop right there. Either the court has added a new element — high-level position of authority — to the criminal offense, or it has introduced a requirement for a "clarifying" jury instruction whose most conspicuous attribute is a limitless potential for jury confusion and for production of inconsistent verdicts on similar facts. Either result is assiduously to be avoided.

I tend to think that the majority rewrites the statute and redefines the elements of the offense by engrafting a declaration of legislative policy onto the operative or criminalizing section. Most of the discussion thus far seeks to support that conclusion. But assuming that the Court's endeavor is only to give more complete definition to the Legislature's terms, without adding any essential elements to the offense itself, that effort has, I suggest, produced more chaos than clarification. The majority unearths no novel concept, clarifies nothing, illuminates no shadowy corners of the "drug-kingpin" statute by declaring that in a prosecution under that statute the State must demonstrate that the defendant occupies "a position of superior authority or control over other persons * * * and that in that position the defendant exercised supervisory power or control over others engaged in an organized drug-trafficking network."

What, then, are we to make of the Court's holding that the trial court here committed plain error in failing to instruct the jury that defendant occupied a "high-level" or "upper-echelon" position? Furnishing no definition of those terms, the Court leaves jurors at sea, with no judicial guidance on how they should determine whether the defendants in the cases before them are "high-level" or "upper-echelon" players in the drug-trafficking scheme. Those terms, unlike the language of section 35-3, are not terms of the street, not in common usage. Including them as elements of a criminal statute in which they nowhere appear represents judicial mucking about in an area in which we have neither authority nor competence.

I would reverse and remand to the Law Division for reinstatement of defendant's conviction for violation of the "drug kingpin" statute.

C. *Mens Rea*: Knowledge in Drug Offenses

If a defendant is found with a three-year supply of heroin in his car, the quantity alone may be sufficient to show an intent to distribute. To obtain a conviction, however, the government will also need to prove that the defendant knew the contraband was there.

To get a sense of the problems that can arise in this area, consider the case of Lisette Lee, a 28-year-old California woman, who was arrested at an airport in Ohio with 506 pounds of marijuana. Lee was traveling on a chartered private plane with a bodyguard and two personal assistants. The marijuana was contained in 13 suitcases. Lee told Drug Enforcement Administration agents that a friend had paid her $60,000 to transport the suitcases from Los Angeles and leave them in a hotel room in Columbus. Lee said she had been told the suitcases contained equipment for a horse farm but that she knew that story was false. Instead, she suspected the people paying her were involved with "weapons and money laundering or something." *See,* Jeannie Nuss, *Lissette Lee Arrested for 506 Pounds of Pot on Private Jet*, Associated Press, June 16, 2010.

Assuming that a jury believed Lee's story, should she still be held criminally liable? If so, what crime should she be convicted of? Even if one were to conclude that Lee "knew" she was transporting contraband of some kind, it seems clear that she did not know *what* or exactly *how much* contraband was in her possession.

1. Willful Blindness

United States v. Heredia
United States Court of Appeals for the Ninth Circuit
483 F.3d 913 (2007)

Kozinski, J.

We revisit *United States v. Jewell,* 532 F.2d 697 (9th Cir. 1976) [in which the Ninth Circuit adopted the willful blindness doctrine], and the body of caselaw applying it.

Defendant Carmen Heredia was stopped at an inland Border Patrol checkpoint while driving from Nogales to Tucson, Arizona. Heredia was at the wheel and her two children, mother and one of her aunts were passengers. The border agent at the scene noticed what he described as a "very strong perfume odor" emanating from the car. A second agent searched the trunk and found 349.2 pounds of marijuana surrounded by dryer sheets, apparently used to mask the odor. Heredia was arrested and charged with possessing a controlled substance with intent to distribute under 21 U.S.C. §841(a)(1).

At trial, Heredia testified that on the day of her arrest she had accompanied her mother on a bus trip from Tucson to Nogales, where her mother had a dentist's appointment. After the appointment, she borrowed her Aunt Belia's car to transport her mother back to Tucson.[1] Heredia told DEA Agent Travis Birney at the time of her arrest that, while still in Nogales, she had noticed a "detergent" smell in the car as she prepared for the trip and asked Belia to explain. Belia told her that she had spilled Downey fabric softener in the car a few days earlier, but Heredia found this explanation incredible.

Heredia admitted on the stand that she suspected there might be drugs in the car, based on the fact that her mother was visibly nervous during the trip and carried a large amount of cash, even though she wasn't working at the time. However, Heredia claimed that her suspicions were not aroused until she had passed the last freeway exit before the checkpoint, by which time it was too dangerous to pull over and investigate.

The government requested a deliberate ignorance instruction, and the judge obliged, overruling Heredia's objection. The instruction read as follows:

> You may find that the defendant acted knowingly if you find beyond a reasonable doubt that the defendant was aware of a high probability that drugs were in the vehicle driven by the defendant and deliberately avoided learning the truth. You may not find such knowledge, however, if you find that the defendant actually believed that no drugs were in the vehicle driven by the defendant, or if you find that the defendant was simply careless.

On appeal, defendant asks us to overrule *Jewell* and hold that section 841(a)(1) extends liability only to individuals who act with actual knowledge. Should *Jewell* remain good law, she asks us to reverse her conviction because the instruction given to the jury was defective and because there was an insufficient factual basis for issuing the instruction in the first place.

While *Jewell* has spawned a great deal of commentary and a somewhat perplexing body of caselaw, its core holding was a rather straightforward matter of statutory interpretation: "'[K]nowingly' in criminal statutes is not limited to positive knowledge, but includes the state of mind of one who does not possess positive knowledge only because he consciously avoided it." In other words, when Congress made it a crime to "knowingly ... possess with intent to manufacture, distribute, or dispense, a controlled substance," it meant to punish not only those who know they possess a controlled substance, but also those who don't know because they don't want to know.[4]

Overturning a long-standing precedent is never to be done lightly, and particularly not "in the area of statutory construction, where Congress is free to change [an] interpretation of its legislation." Even in the criminal context, where private reliance interests are less compelling, stare decisis concerns still carry great weight, particularly when a precedent is as deeply entrenched as *Jewell*. Since *Jewell* was decided in 1976, every regional circuit—with the exception of the D.C. Circuit—has adopted its central holding. Indeed, many colloquially refer to the deliberate ignorance instruction as the "*Jewell* instruction." Congress has amended section 841 many times since *Jewell* was handed down, but not in a way that would cast doubt on our ruling. Given the widespread acceptance of *Jewell*

---

1. Belia was not the aunt in the car with Heredia at the time she was stopped at the checkpoint. Belia was traveling on the same interstate at about the same time, but in a separate car.

4. As our cases have recognized, deliberate ignorance, otherwise known as willful blindness, is categorically different from negligence or recklessness. A willfully blind defendant is one who took *deliberate* actions to avoid confirming suspicions of criminality. A reckless defendant is one who merely knew of a substantial and unjustifiable risk that his conduct was criminal; a negligent defendant is one who should have had similar suspicions but, in fact, did not.

across the federal judiciary, of which Congress must surely have been aware, we construe Congress's inaction as acquiescence.[6]

That said, there are circumstances when a precedent becomes so unworkable that keeping it on the books actually undermines the values of evenhandedness and predictability that the doctrine of stare decisis aims to advance. Here, we recognize that many of our post-*Jewell* cases have created a vexing thicket of precedent that has been difficult for litigants to follow and for district courts—and ourselves—to apply with consistency. But, rather than overturn *Jewell*, we conclude that the better course is to clear away the underbrush that surrounds it.

The parties have pointed out one area where our cases have not been consistent: Whether the jury must be instructed that defendant's motive in deliberately failing to learn the truth was to give himself a defense in case he should be charged with the crime.[8] *Jewell* itself speculated that defendant's motive for failing to learn the truth in that case was to "avoid responsibility in the event of discovery." Yet the opinion did not define motive as a separate prong of the deliberate ignorance instruction. And we affirmed, even though the instruction given at Jewell's trial made no mention of motive. Since then, we've upheld two-pronged instructions, similar to the one given here, in at least four other published opinions.

The first mention of the motive prong came in a dissent by then-Judge [and current Supreme Court Justice] Kennedy, who also authored the dissent in *Jewell*. *See United States v. Murrieta-Bejarano*, 552 F.2d 1323, 1326 (9th Cir. 1977) (Kennedy, J., dissenting). Judge Kennedy's chief concern was with what he viewed as the absence of *deliberate* avoidance on the part of the defendant in that case. At any rate, he was not writing for the court. Yet some of our opinions seem to have adopted the motive prong, providing little justification for doing so other than citation to Judge Kennedy's dissent. Three other federal circuits have followed suit. *See United States v. Puche*, 350 F.3d 1137, 1149 (11th Cir. 2003); *United States v. Willis*, 277 F.3d 1026, 1032 (8th Cir. 2002); *United States v. Delreal-Ordones*, 213 F.3d 1263, 1268–69 (10th Cir. 2000).

Heredia argues that the motive prong is necessary to avoid punishing individuals who fail to investigate because circumstances render it unsafe or impractical to do so. She claims that she is within this group, because her suspicions did not arise until she was driving on an open highway where it would have been too dangerous to pull over. She thus claims that she had a motive *other* than avoiding criminal culpability for failing to discover the contraband concealed in the trunk.

---

6. Our dissenting colleague seeks support for her position from the fact that Congress has, on occasion, defined the scienter requirement in some criminal statutes as "knows, or has reasonable grounds to believe." But "has reasonable grounds to believe" defines a mental state that is less than actual knowledge. By contrast, *Jewell* defines willful blindness as knowledge—and sets a much higher standard for satisfying it. Thus, under *Jewell*, the prosecution must prove that defendant was aware of a "high probability" that he is in the possession of contraband, and that he "deliberately avoided learning the truth." This standard focuses on defendant's actual beliefs and actions, whereas "has reasonable grounds to believe" is an objective standard that could be satisfied by showing what a reasonable person would believe, regardless of defendant's actual beliefs. That Congress chose to set a lower scienter requirement in some criminal statutes tells us nothing about our interpretation of "knowledge" in *Jewell*. It certainly provides an insufficient basis for rejecting an interpretation that Congress has left undisturbed for three decades and that has since been adopted by ten of our sister circuits.

8. The motive prong usually requires the jury to find that defendant was deliberately ignorant "in order to provide himself with a defense in the event of prosecution."

We believe, however, that the second prong of the instruction, the requirement that defendant have *deliberately* avoided learning the truth, provides sufficient protections for defendants in these situations. A deliberate action is one that is "[i]ntentional; premeditated; fully considered." *Black's Law Dictionary* 459 (8th ed. 2004). A decision influenced by coercion, exigent circumstances or lack of meaningful choice is, perforce, not deliberate. A defendant who fails to investigate for these reasons has not deliberately chosen to avoid learning the truth.[10]

We conclude, therefore, that the two-pronged instruction given at defendant's trial met the requirements of *Jewell* and, to the extent some of our cases have suggested more is required they are overruled. A district judge, in the exercise of his discretion, may say more to tailor the instruction to the particular facts of the case. Here, for example, the judge might have instructed the jury that it could find Heredia did not act deliberately if it believed that her failure to investigate was motivated by safety concerns. Heredia did not ask for such an instruction and the district judge had no obligation to give it sua sponte. Even when defendant asks for such a supplemental instruction, it is within the district court's broad discretion whether to comply.

Defendant also claims there was insufficient foundation to give the *Jewell* instruction.

In deciding whether to give a particular instruction, the district court must view the evidence in the light most favorable to the party requesting it. When knowledge is at issue in a criminal case, the court must first determine whether the evidence of defendant's mental state, if viewed in the light most favorable to the government, will support a finding of actual knowledge.[13] If so, the court must instruct the jury on this theory. Actual knowledge, of course, is inconsistent with willful blindness. The deliberate ignorance instruction only comes into play, therefore, if the jury rejects the government's case as to actual knowledge. In deciding whether to give a willful blindness instruction, in addition to an actual knowledge instruction, the district court must determine whether the jury could rationally find willful blindness even though it has rejected the government's evidence of actual knowledge. If so, the court may also give a *Jewell* instruction.

This case well illustrates the point. Taking the evidence in the light most favorable to the government, a reasonable jury could certainly have found that Heredia actually knew about the drugs. Not only was she driving a car with several hundred pounds of marijuana in the trunk, but everyone else who might have put the drugs there—her mother, her aunt, her husband—had a close personal relationship with Heredia. Moreover, there was ev-

---

10. The concurrence would add the third prong to the *Jewell* instruction in order to protect defendants who have "innocent" motives for deliberately avoiding the truth. But the deliberate ignorance instruction defines when an individual has sufficient information so that he can be deemed to "know" something, even though he does not take the final step to confirm that knowledge. The *reason* the individual fails to take that final step has no bearing on whether he has sufficient information so he can properly be deemed to "know" the fact. An innocent motive for being deliberately ignorant no more vitiates the knowledge element of a crime than does an innocent motive vitiate any other element.

Equally misplaced is the concurrence's concern about FedEx and similar package carriers. The fact that a tiny percentage of the tens of thousands of packages FedEx transports every day may contain contraband hardly establishes a high probability that any particular package contains contraband. Of course, if a particular package leaks a white powder or gives any other particularized and unmistakable indication that it contains contraband, and the carrier fails to investigate, it may be held liable— and properly so.

13. As previously noted, willful blindness is tantamount to knowledge. We use the phrase "actual knowledge" to describe the state of mind when defendant, in fact, knows of the existence of the contraband rather than being willfully blind to its existence.

idence that Heredia and her husband had sole possession of the car for about an hour prior to setting out on the trip to Tucson. Based on this evidence, a jury could easily have inferred that Heredia actually knew about the drugs in the car because she was involved in putting them there.

The analysis in the foregoing paragraph presupposes that the jury believed the government's case in its entirety, and disbelieved all of Heredia's exculpatory statements. While this would have been *a* rational course for the jury to take, it was not the only one. For example, a rational jury might have bought Heredia's basic claim that she didn't know about the drugs in the trunk, yet disbelieved other aspects of her story. The jury could, for example, have disbelieved Heredia's story about *when* she first began to suspect she was transporting drugs. The jury could have found that her suspicions were aroused when Belia gave her the unsatisfactory explanation for the "detergent" scent,[15] or while she drove to Tucson but before the last exit preceding the checkpoint. Or, the jury might have believed Heredia that she became suspicious only after she had passed the last exit before the checkpoint but disbelieved that concerns about safety motivated her failure to stop.

All of these are scenarios the jury could rationally have drawn from the evidence presented, depending on how credible they deemed Heredia's testimony in relation to the other evidence presented. The government has no way of knowing which version of the facts the jury will believe, and it is entitled (like any other litigant) to have the jury instructed in conformity with each of these rational possibilities. That these possibilities are mutually exclusive is of no consequence. A party may present alternative factual theories, and is entitled to instructions supporting all rational inferences the jury might draw from the evidence.

We do not share the worry that giving both an actual knowledge and a deliberate ignorance instruction is likely to confuse the jury. A jury is presumed to follow the instructions given to it and we see no reason to fear that juries will be less able to do so when trying to sort out a criminal defendant's state of mind than any other issue. Nor do we agree that the *Jewell* instruction risks lessening the state of mind that a jury must find to something akin to recklessness or negligence. The instruction requires the jury to find beyond a reasonable doubt that defendant "was aware of a high probability" of criminality and "deliberately avoided learning the truth." Indeed, the instruction actually given in this case told the jurors to acquit if they believed defendant was "simply careless." Recklessness or negligence never comes into play, and there is little reason to suspect that juries will import these concepts, as to which they are not instructed, into their deliberations.

Even if the factual predicates of the instruction are present, the district judge has discretion to refuse it. In cases where the government does not present a deliberate ignorance theory, the judge might conclude that the instruction will confuse the jury. Concerns of this nature are best dealt with by the district judge, whose familiarity with the evidence and the events at trial is necessarily superior to our own. We will second guess his decision only in those rare cases where we find an abuse of discretion. For the reasons explained, the district court did not abuse its discretion by giving the *Jewell* instruction here.

We decline the invitation to overrule *Jewell*, and further hold that district judges are owed the usual degree of deference in deciding when a deliberate ignorance instruction

---

15. Some of our cases have suggested that irregular or strong scents are not enough to support the inference that defendant suspected he might be transporting drugs. This rule is a byproduct of the hands-on approach to reviewing *Jewell* cases we eschew today and does not survive our opinion. Whether an irregular scent provides a sufficient foundation for the first prong of the *Jewell* instruction depends on the evidence in each case. It is a matter committed to the sound discretion of the district court. Contrary statements in our opinions are disapproved.

is warranted. While the particular form of the instruction can vary, it must, at a minimum, contain the two prongs of suspicion and deliberate avoidance. The district judge may say more, if he deems it advisable to do so, or deny the instruction altogether. We review such decisions for abuse of discretion. The instruction given at defendant's trial met these requirements, and the district judge did not abuse his discretion in issuing it.

Kleinfeld, J., concurring in the result.

Suppose Heredia were a witness rather than defendant, perhaps because the government had charged her aunt who owned the car instead of her. If Heredia were asked "was there marijuana in the car," counsel would have objected for lack of foundation, and the objection would have been sustained.[1] Heredia's suspicion would not be enough to let her testify to knowledge. Yet she can be convicted under a statute that requires her to have knowledge. This is not impossible, but it is a troubling paradox for criminal knowledge to require *less* than evidentiary knowledge. To avoid injustice, the jury needs to be instructed that they must find a motivation to avoid criminal responsibility to be the reason for lack of knowledge.

In our en banc decision in *United States v. Jewell*, a man offered to sell marijuana to the defendant and his friend in a Tijuana bar, and then to pay defendant $100 to drive a car across the border. The friend refused, saying that "it didn't sound right," and he "wanted no part of driving the vehicle." But the defendant accepted the offer, even though he "thought there was probably something illegal in the vehicle." The defendant determined that there was no contraband in the glove compartment, under the front seat, or in the trunk, so he concluded that "the people at the border wouldn't find anything either." He admitted to seeing a secret compartment in the trunk (where 110 pounds of marijuana was later found), but did not attempt to open it.

We held that, in these circumstances, the knowledge element in the applicable drug statutes could be satisfied without positive, confirmed personal knowledge that the marijuana was in the trunk. We took particular note of the motive in such deliberate avoidance of knowledge cases "to avoid responsibility in the event of discovery":

> [T]he jury could conclude that ... although appellant knew of the presence of the secret compartment and had knowledge of facts indicating that it contained marijuana, he deliberately avoided positive knowledge of the presence of the contraband *to avoid responsibility in the event of discovery*. If ... positive knowledge is required to convict, the jury would have no choice consistent with its oath but to find appellant not guilty even though he deliberately contrived his lack of positive knowledge.

We described such blindness as "wilful" and not merely negligence, foolishness or recklessness, differing from positive knowledge "only so far as necessary to encompass a calculated effort to avoid the sanctions of the statute while violating its substance."

> A court can properly find wilful blindness only where it can almost be said that the defendant actually knew. He suspected the fact; he realised its probability; but he refrained from obtaining the final confirmation because he wanted in the event to be able to deny knowledge. This, and this alone, is wilful blindness. It requires in effect a finding that the defendant intended to cheat the administration of justice. Any wider definition would make the doctrine of wilful blindness indistinguishable from the civil doctrine of negligence in not obtaining knowledge.

---

1. *See* F.R.E. 602 ("A witness may not testify to a matter unless evidence is introduced sufficient to support a finding that the witness has personal knowledge of the matter.").

Then-judge Kennedy, joined by Judges Ely, Hufstedler and Wallace, vigorously dissented. They presciently warned that the majority opened the door too wide to suspicion as a substitute for scienter.

"Wilfulness" requires a "purpose of violating a known legal duty," or, at the very least, "a bad purpose." That is why wilful blindness is "equally culpable" to, and may be substituted for, positive knowledge. But to allow conviction without positive knowledge or wilful avoidance of such knowledge is to erase the scienter requirement from the statute. And we do not have the authority to do this: "The definition of the elements of a criminal offense is entrusted to the legislature, particularly in the case of federal crimes, which are solely creatures of statute." The statute made it a crime for Heredia to "knowingly or intentionally" possess the marijuana in the trunk of her aunt's car with an intent to distribute it (that is, give the car back to her aunt or to someone else). If she did not act "knowingly or intentionally," then she did not commit the crime.

The majority converts the statutory element that the possession be "knowing" into something much less—a requirement that the defendant be suspicious and deliberately avoid investigating. The imposition on people who intend no crime of a duty to investigate has no statutory basis. The majority says that its requirement is enough to protect defendants who cannot investigate because of "coercion, exigent circumstances or lack of meaningful choice." I am not sure what the latter two novelties mean (especially the term "meaningful" choice) or how a jury would be instructed to give them concrete meaning. The majority's statement that "[a]n innocent motive for being deliberately ignorant" does not bar conviction under its rule seems to contradict its proposition that coercion or exigent circumstances excuse failure to investigate. The majority seems to mean that if someone can investigate, they must. A criminal duty to investigate the wrongdoing of others to avoid wrongdoing of one's own is a novelty in the criminal law.

The majority's "coercion, exigent circumstances or lack of meaningful choice" justifications for failure to investigate are too few. The government has not conscripted the citizenry as investigators, and the statute does not impose that unpleasant and sometimes risky obligation on people. Shall someone who thinks his mother is carrying a stash of marijuana in her suitcase be obligated, when he helps her with it, to rummage through her things? Should Heredia have carried tools with her, so that (if her story was true) she could open the trunk for which she had no key? Shall all of us who give a ride to child's friend search her purse or his backpack?

No "coercion, exigent circumstances, or lack of meaningful choice" prevents FedEx from opening packages before accepting them, or prevents bus companies from going through the luggage of suspicious looking passengers. But these businesses are not "knowingly" transporting drugs in any particular package, even though they know that in a volume business in all likelihood they sometimes must be. They forego inspection to save time, or money, or offense to customers, not to avoid criminal responsibility. But these reasons for not inspecting are not the ones acceptable to the majority ("coercion, exigent circumstances, or lack of meaningful choice"). The majority opinion apparently makes these businesses felons despite the fact that Congress did not. For that matter, someone driving his mother, a child of the sixties, to Thanksgiving weekend, and putting her suitcase in the trunk, should not have to open it and go through her clothes.

A *Jewell* instruction ought to incorporate what our case law has developed, that the wilful blindness doctrine is meant to punish a defendant who "all but knew" the truth—a defendant who "suspects a fact, realizes its [high] probability, but refrains from obtaining final confirmation in order to be able to deny knowledge if apprehended." "This, and this alone, is wilful blindness." The jury instruction in this case told the jury that Heredia had "knowing" possession of the marijuana in the trunk if she "was aware of a high probability" that drugs were in the car and "deliberately avoided learning the truth." That mental state would fit FedEx and the child of an aging hippy, as well as a drug mule. A *Jewell* instruction ought to require (1) a belief that drugs are present, (2) avoidance of confirmation of the belief, and (3) wilfulness in that avoidance — that is, choosing not to confirm the belief in order to "be able to deny knowledge if apprehended." The instruction should expressly exclude recklessness, negligence and mistake (the one given only excluded "simpl[e] careless[ness]" and an "actual[] belie[f] that no drugs were in the vehicle"). Anything less supports convictions of persons whom Congress excluded from statutory coverage with the word "knowingly." People who possess drugs, but do not do so "knowingly," are what we traditionally refer to as "innocent."

The reason that I concur instead of dissenting is that defendant did not object to these deficiencies in the instruction, and the deficiencies were not "plain." To constitute plain error, "[a]n error ... must be ... obvious or readily apparent."

Our previous cases did not make clear that the instruction had to say these things (they only made clear that the judge must decide there was some evidence of wilfulness before giving the instruction). For that reason, it is not surprising that the instruction given tracked the language of our own form. Defendant's objection was to giving a *Jewell* instruction at all, rather than to the language in the *Jewell* instruction. She argued that "the instruction is not appropriate in this particular case" because "there is no evidence that she did anything ... to deliberately avoid [learning the truth]...." She did not argue in the district court, as she now does on appeal, that the wilful blindness instruction, if given, should include a requirement that a defendant's wilful blindness be motivated by a desire to avoid criminal responsibility.

Graber, J., dissenting.

Assuming the *Jewell* instruction to be proper, I agree with the majority that the standard by which to review a district court's decision to give one is "abuse of discretion" in the light of the evidence presented at trial. But as a matter of statutory construction, I believe that the *Jewell* instruction is not proper because it misconstrues, and misleads the jury about, the mens rea required by 21 U.S.C. § 841(a)(1). Because the legal error of giving a *Jewell* instruction in this case was not harmless beyond a reasonable doubt, I respectfully dissent.

Under 21 U.S.C. § 841(a)(1), it is a crime to "*knowingly or intentionally* ... manufacture, distribute, or dispense, or possess with intent to manufacture, distribute, or dispense, a controlled substance." (Emphasis added.) The plain text of the statute does not make it a crime to have a high probability of awareness of possession — knowledge or intention is required.

The majority recognizes that willful blindness is a mens rea separate and distinct from knowledge. *See* Majority op. ("Actual knowledge, of course, is inconsistent with willful blindness."); *see also United States v. Jewell*, 532 F.2d 697, 705–06 (9th Cir. 1976) (en banc) (Kennedy, J., dissenting) ("The majority opinion justifies the conscious purpose jury instruction as an application of the wilful blindness doctrine recognized primarily by English authorities.... [T]he English authorities seem to consider wilful blindness a state of mind *distinct from, but equally culpable as,* 'actual' knowledge."). Similarly, if not even more obviously, willful blindness is at least one step removed from intention.

Instead of justifying its sleight-of-hand directly, the majority points to the fact that *Jewell* has been on the books for 30 years and that Congress has not amended the statute in a way that repudiates *Jewell* expressly. I find this reasoning unpersuasive. "[C]ongressional inaction lacks persuasive significance because several equally tenable inferences may be drawn from such inaction...."

Whatever relevance congressional *inaction* holds in this case is outweighed by actual congressional *action*. Under 21 U.S.C. § 841(a)(1), a person is guilty of a crime only if the requisite act is performed "knowingly or intentionally." By contrast, both before and after *Jewell*, Congress has defined several other crimes in which the mens rea involves a high probability of awareness—but it has done so in phrases dramatically different than the one here, which lists only knowledge and intent. *See, e.g.*, 18 U.S.C. §§ 175b(b)(1) ("knows or has reasonable cause to believe"), 792 ("knows, or has reasonable grounds to believe or suspect"), 842(h) ("knowing or having reasonable cause to believe"), 2332d(a) ("knowing or having reasonable cause to know"), 2339(a) ("knows, or has reasonable grounds to believe"), 2424(a) ("knowing or in reckless disregard of the fact"). Most importantly, Congress has done so in adjacent sections of the same statute, the Controlled Substances Act, 21 U.S.C. §§ 801–971, and even within the same section of the same statute. *See* 21 U.S.C. §§ 841(c)(2) ("knowing, or having reasonable cause to believe"), 843(a)(6) ("knowing, intending, or having reasonable cause to believe"), 843(a)(7) (same). "It is axiomatic that when Congress uses different text in 'adjacent' statutes it intends that the different terms carry a different meaning." Thus, "[i]f we do our job of reading the statute whole, we have to give effect to [its] plain command, even if doing that will reverse the longstanding practice under the statute and the rule."

The majority recognizes that the *Jewell* instruction embodies a substantive decision that those who possess a controlled substance and "don't know because they don't want to know" are just as culpable as those who knowingly or intentionally possess a controlled substance. But Congress never made this substantive decision about levels of culpability—the *Jewell* court did. By "clear[ing] away the underbrush that surrounds" the instruction, the majority chooses to reaffirm this judge-made substantive decision. In so doing, the majority directly contravenes the principle that "[i]t is the legislature, not the Court, which is to define a crime, and ordain its punishment." *United States v. Wiltberger,* 18 U.S. (5 Wheat.) 76, 95 (1820). "'The spirit of the doctrine which denies to the federal judiciary power to create crimes forthrightly admonishes that we should not enlarge the reach of enacted crimes by constituting them from anything less than the incriminating components contemplated by the words used in the statute.'" *Jewell,* 532 F.2d at 706 n.7 (Kennedy, J., dissenting). The majority creates a duty to investigate for drugs that appears nowhere in the text of the statute, transforming knowledge into a mens rea more closely akin to negligence or recklessness.

I agree with the *Jewell* court that "one 'knows' facts of which he is less than absolutely certain." That being so, the mens rea-reducing *Jewell* instruction not only is wrong, it also is unnecessary in the face of the kind of proof that a prosecutor is likely to produce. For example, if your husband comes home at 1:00 a.m. every Friday (after having left work at 5:00 p.m. the day before as usual), never reveals where he has been, won't look you in the eye on Fridays, and puts Thursday's shirts in the hamper bearing lipstick stains, your friends will agree that you "know" he is having an affair even if you refuse to seek confirmation. The role of a jury is to apply common sense to the facts of a given case. A sensible jury will be persuaded that a drug mule "knows" what she is carrying when confronted with evidence of how mules typically operate and how this mule acted—all without reference to a *Jewell* instruction.

Thus, I would overrule *Jewell* and interpret 21 U.S.C. § 841(a) to require exactly what its text requires—a knowing or intentional mens rea. If Congress wants to criminalize willful ignorance, it is free to amend the statute to say so and, in view of the several examples quoted above, it clearly knows how.

_____

As the *Heredia* court explains, in a willful blindness case the courier is suspicious that there are drugs in the car but "refrain[s] from obtaining the final confirmation" in order "to be able to deny knowledge." In other drug courier cases—so-called "blind mule" cases—the defendant may deny knowledge or suspicion of the contraband entirely. In cases where the defendant advances a blind mule argument, prosecutors have often sought to introduce "expert" testimony by drug agents, who claim that "a blind mule is a 'mythical character.'" *California v. Covarrubias,* 202 Cal. App. 4th 1 (2012). In one recent blind mule case, for example, Immigration Customs Enforcement Special Agent Andrew Flood testified "he had never been involved with, nor heard of, a case involving a blind mule." Agent Flood explained: "You have to look at it not as 193 pounds of marijuana in the car, but say, ... $185,000 of cash in the car. It's a business. You don't—the idea of putting drugs ... on someone and hope to retrieve it somewhere north of the border is—it's guesswork." *Id.* In spring 2012, however, the federal government revealed that the use of blind mules near the San Diego border had in fact become somewhat widespread. According to a news report of the U.S. Immigrations and Customs Enforcement announcement, "[s]mugglers have long advertised work as security guards, housecleaners and cashiers, telling applicants they must drive company cars to the United States. They aren't told the cars are loaded with drugs." Elliot Spagat, *Drug Smugglers Placing Job Ads In Mexican Newspapers*, Associated Press, April 11, 2012. "For drug traffickers, the tactic lowers expenses and, they hope, makes drivers appear less nervous when questioned by border inspectors, said Millie Jones, an assistant special agent in charge of investigations for ICE in San Diego." *Id.* With respect to expenses, the cost-savings appears to be substantial. According to the report, "blind mules" are paid $50 to $200 per-trip compared to $1,500 to $5,000 for a courier who knows she is carrying contraband.

In addition to addressing the willful blindness doctrine, *Heredia* involved a question about the relationship in time between knowledge and possession. The defendant argued that she only became suspicious there might be drugs in the car after she "had passed the last freeway exit before the [border] checkpoint, by which time it was too dangerous to pull over and investigate." Is it possible to reconcile the outcome in *Heredia* with the constructive possession cases that require proof to an intent to exercise dominion and control over the substance in addition to knowledge of its existence?

In a recent San Francisco case, a man charged with drug possession raised a time-based *mens rea* defense of a much different nature. Eric Meoli was acquitted of possessing magic mushrooms "after his lawyer argued that he forgot they were in his backpack, so he could not have knowingly possessed them." Margaret Baum, *San Francisco Jury Acquits Man who Forgot Mushrooms Were in his Backpack*, S.F. Examiner, July 15, 2011. Meoli, an employee at a medical marijuana dispensary, claimed that he "had given $10 of legally-obtained medical marijuana to 'a hippy in Golden Gate Park' suffering from insomnia" and the hippy gave Meoli the mushrooms in return. Meoli then put the mushrooms in a backpack and "forgot all about them" until he was stopped by the police six months later for riding his bicycle on the platform of a subway station and consented to a search of his backpack. Meoli's lawyer, public defender Kimberly Lutes-Koths told the *Examiner*: "One of the elements of the law requires that the defendant know of the presence of the substance. Some people think my argument was unique, but it just seemed logical to me."

2. Knowledge of Drug Type and Quantity

The willful blindness doctrine addresses instances where a defendant is suspicious that he possesses contraband but lacks positive knowledge. What happens in a case where a defendant knows he possesses contraband but is mistaken about the drug type or quantity?

United States v. Gomez

United States Court of Appeals for the Eleventh Circuit
905 F.2d 1513 (1990)

Roney, J.

A defendant can be convicted of a controlled substance offense without proof that he knew the exact drug that was involved. This sentencing case raises the question of whether a mandatory minimum sentence for cocaine can be imposed without proof that the defendant knew the drug involved was cocaine. We hold that it can, and affirm the district court's imposition of a mandatory minimum sentence for cocaine possession in a case where there was no finding that the defendant knew he possessed cocaine.

In exchange for $5,000 in cash offered by two men he had met in a Miami, Florida bar, defendant Alberto Gomez agreed to drive a car from Miami to a hotel parking lot in Detroit, Michigan, and leave the car there for several hours before driving it back to Miami. According to his statement to police, Gomez knew that some kind of drug was hidden in the car, but believed the drug to be marijuana, in a small quantity, because of what the two men had told him. He did acknowledge, however, that the men had supplied him with a packet of cocaine for the purpose of helping him "stay awake" during the drive.

While Gomez was driving to Detroit, a Georgia State Trooper stopped him for speeding on Interstate 75 in northern Georgia's Gordon County. Gomez consented to the Trooper's search of his vehicle, which uncovered the cocaine packet, as well as ten bundles concealed in the vehicle's rear quarter panels, containing more than ten kilograms of cocaine.

Gomez was subsequently charged in a three-count indictment with conspiracy to possess with intent to distribute cocaine, possession with intent to distribute more than five kilograms of cocaine, and possession of cocaine.

During its deliberations following the trial, the jury sent the district judge a note asking whether the defendant had to know that the concealed drug he transported was cocaine in order to be found guilty on the first two counts. The court correctly instructed the jury that defendant's knowledge that he was carrying *some* controlled substance would be sufficient, without his knowing exactly what drug he had. The jury's guilty verdicts on all counts reflected no determination on its part as to whether the defendant knew he was carrying cocaine.

At sentencing, the district court treated counts one and two as falling within 21 U.S.C.A. § 841(b)(1)(A)'s ten-year mandatory minimum sentence provision for offenses involving the distribution of more than 5 kilograms of cocaine, and imposed concurrent ten-year prison terms on each count. Gomez challenged his sentence on the ground that because his theory of defense had been that he believed the drug to be *marijuana*, and since the jury had not found that he knew otherwise, § 841(b)(1)(A)'s mandatory minimum penalty for *cocaine* offenses could not be invoked against him.

As to the conviction itself and the district court's instruction, it is well-settled that to sustain a conviction for possession with intent to distribute a controlled substance, it need not be proved that the defendant had knowledge of the particular drug involved, as long as he knew he was dealing with a controlled substance.

As to sentencing, it is now equally well-settled that a defendant need not know the *quantity* of drug involved in the offense in order to be subject to a mandatory minimum sentence based on quantity under § 841(b)(1).

This is the first time we have held that a defendant need not be found to know the particular drug involved in order to receive a mandatory sentence based on the kind of drug under § 841(b)(1).

The rationale for this decision is essentially the same as that articulated in the cases cited above: those who, acting with a deliberate anti-social purpose in mind, become involved in illegal drug transactions, assume the risk that their actions will subject them to enhanced criminal liability.

The imposition of greater penalties for certain classes of offenses is routinely grounded in a legislative judgment that those who commit such offenses pose an enhanced threat to society at large. In this case, it is undisputed that Gomez knew he was engaging in conduct designed to introduce *some* illegal substance into the stream of commerce. He was doing this at the behest of two individuals whom, he claimed, he hardly knew. Yet he lacked even the minimal consideration for the public welfare that would have caused him to determine the substance's true identity before agreeing to transport it. One who demonstrates a lack of even this minimal societal consciousness shows himself to pose an alarming menace to the public safety, because he readily allows himself to become the instrument for others' criminal designs "so long as the price is right." Accordingly, where the facts concerning the type and quantity of drug involved in such a one's conduct ultimately prove to fit within § 841(b)(1), that defendant is properly given the enhanced sentence prescribed by that statute.

As in *Gomez*, the overwhelming majority of courts have held that a defendant may be convicted and sentenced based upon the quantity and type of controlled substance he actually possessed, even if he believed he possessed a much smaller amount of a different substance. In one notable exception, New York's highest court reached the opposite conclusion in *New York v. Ryan*, 82 N.Y. 2d 497 (1993). The *Ryan* Court explained that "[t]o ascribe to the Legislature an intent to mete out drastic differences in punishment without a basis in culpability would be inconsistent with notions of individual responsibility and proportionality prevailing in the Penal Law." Less than 18 months after *Ryan*, however, New York lawmakers passed legislation that effectively overruled the decision. *See*, Alum Griffiths, Comment, People v. Ryan: *A Trap For The Unwary*, 61 BROOK. L. REV. 1101 (1995). *See also*, United States v. Cordoba-Hincapie, 825 F. Supp. 485 (E.D.N.Y. 1993) (making a detailed argument that drug defendants should not be held strictly liable for drug type and quantity).

A fascinating knowledge problem has arisen in the context of khat, an East African plant than contains the mild stimulant alkaloid cathinone. Although cathinone is a controlled substance under federal law, the khat plant itself is *not* listed as a controlled substance. As a result of this odd state of affairs, courts have been left to decide whether a defendant can be convicted of a controlled substances offense based upon proof that he knew he was in possession of khat or whether the government must also prove the defendant knew that khat contains the controlled substance cathinone. The khat cases raise perplexing due process, knowledge, and mistake of law questions and courts have yet to reach consensus on how to answer them. *United States v. Caseer* provides one of the more detailed discussions of the khat issue.

United States v. Caseer

United States Court of Appeals for the Sixth Circuit
399 F. 3d 828 (2005)

Moore, J.

For centuries, persons in East African and Arabian Peninsular countries such as Somalia, Kenya, and Yemen have chewed or made tea from the stems of the native khat shrub (*Catha edulis*), which is known to have stimulant properties. Khat is often consumed in social settings, and many men in the East African/Arabian Peninsular region use khat. Khat is legal in many parts of East Africa, the Middle East, and Europe; however, khat is illegal in the United States because it contains cathinone, a Schedule I controlled substance, and cathine, a Schedule IV controlled substance. *See* 21 C.F.R. § 1308.11(f) (listing cathinone as a Schedule I stimulant); 21 C.F.R. § 1308.14(e) (listing cathine as a Schedule IV stimulant). State and federal prosecutions relating to khat seem to be a recent phenomenon, with the first reported cases appearing in the mid-1990s.

At the time of his trial in 2001, Daahir Caseer had lived in the United States for approximately three years, having spent the first sixteen years of his life in Somalia and seven years in Kenya. The events in question began in the spring of 2000, when Caseer approached John Eldridge, a bookkeeper at the Nashville, Tennessee taxicab company where Caseer worked, about the possibility of Eldridge traveling to Amsterdam, the Netherlands, to transport about fifty pieces of khat to the United States. Caseer explained to Eldridge that he could not make the trip himself because of visa issues. Caseer assured Eldridge that khat was an agricultural product and, at worst, customs might confiscate the khat and assess a fine.[2] At trial, Eldridge testified that taxicab drivers in Nashville (80% to 90% of whom he believed to be of Somali or East African descent) frequently chewed khat and that, from his observations, khat was no stronger than caffeine.

Eldridge agreed to go to Amsterdam along with his girlfriend, Shannon Adams. Eldridge would receive $200.00 to compensate him for a day of missed work, and Eldridge and Adams's travel expenses would be covered by Caseer and several other taxicab drivers who would be dividing the khat. Caseer also admitted during trial that three weeks before Eldridge's trip, $1,500.00 had been sent to Amsterdam via Western Union. However, Caseer explained that the money wired to Amsterdam was unrelated to the khat and was bound for Somalia and that the khat was a gift from a Mr. Awale and three or four other people.

After arriving in Amsterdam on June 3, 2000, Eldridge and Adams met with Awale, who removed the contents of their luggage and left with the empty bags. The morning that Eldridge and Adams were to fly back to the United States, Awale returned with the three bags, now containing approximately 285 bundles of khat, or roughly 14,250 stems.

Eldridge and Adams returned to the United States on June 5, 2000, landing at the airport in Detroit, Michigan. A drug-detection dog at the Detroit airport alerted on one of the bags filled with khat, and a Drug Enforcement Agency ("DEA") agent approached Eldridge and Adams. The pair agreed to cooperate with the investigation, and Eldridge placed a recorded telephone call to Caseer informing him that he had arrived and had cleared customs. At trial, Eldridge testified that during the telephone call, he complained about the

---

2. Douglas Panning, an agent with the United States Customs Service, testified that the U.S. Customs Service's practice at that time was to levy $500.00 fines for small amounts of khat intended for personal use if federal or local authorities decided not to prosecute.

amount of khat being greater than Caseer had indicated and reiterated his understanding that Caseer would pay his travel and related expenses. Caseer told Eldridge to trust him and that Eldridge did not need to discuss the matter with anyone else. Eldridge also testified that he met with Caseer after returning to Nashville and that Caseer told him they had not done anything illegal and would not be prosecuted, that he would take care of it, and that Eldridge should just stay quiet and not say anything about Caseer's involvement.

Agent Panning then traveled to Nashville and arrested Caseer. During questioning, Caseer admitted knowing Eldridge, Adams, and Awale. Caseer initially stated that Eldridge had purchased the airplane tickets; however, Caseer later said that a Hussein Abugar had made the purchase. At trial, Caseer stated that he may have lied to Agent Panning, but that he only did so because he was shaky and scared.

A sample of the khat seized by the DEA was sent to the Michigan State Police for analysis. Jurgen Switalski, a chemist employed by the Michigan State Police, tested the khat and concluded that it contained cathinone and cathine, but did not determine in what amounts. Switalski testified that, once khat has been harvested, the cathinone begins to dissipate and the cathine level rises; however, Switalski stated that he did not know how long it would take for the cathinone to degrade.

Eldridge, Adams, and Caseer were indicted on two counts: (1) conspiracy to import cathinone; and (2) importation of cathinone, and aiding and abetting the importation of cathinone. Eldridge agreed to testify against Caseer and pleaded guilty to misdemeanor possession of cathinone pursuant to a plea agreement recommending six months' probation. Caseer waived his right to trial by jury and was tried before a district judge for the Eastern District of Michigan.

At the conclusion of the prosecution's case-in-chief, Caseer filed a motion for judgment of acquittal pursuant to Federal Rule of Criminal Procedure 29, claiming: (1) that his constitutional right to due process had been violated because he had not been fairly warned of the criminality of his actions; (2) that khat qualified as a food item not subject to regulation by the Controlled Substances Act; and (3) that the evidence presented at trial was insufficient to prove beyond a reasonable doubt that Caseer intended to import cathinone. The district court took Caseer's motion under advisement, later denying the motion and finding Caseer guilty on both counts. The district court sentenced Caseer to two years' probation. Caseer now appeals his conviction, asserting the fair warning and insufficiency-of-the-evidence claims first raised in his motion for judgment of acquittal.

A. Fair Warning

Caseer first appeals his conviction on the basis that, because the schedule of controlled substances in 21 C.F.R. § 1308.11(f) lists cathinone as a controlled substance without making explicit reference to "khat," he was not fairly warned that importing khat into the United States was illegal and thus his conviction violates due process. Whether a criminal statute is unconstitutionally vague is a legal question which we review de novo.

1. Establishment of Cathinone as a Controlled Substance

Section 812 of the Controlled Substances Act, 21 U.S.C. § 812, sets forth five schedules of controlled substances which are revised annually by rules promulgated by the Administrator of the DEA and published in 21 C.F.R. § 1308.01 et seq. Cathinone was not listed in the original Controlled Substances Act schedules but was added by agency rule as a Schedule I controlled substance in 1993:

> (f) *Stimulants.* Unless specifically excepted or unless listed in another schedule,
> any material, compound, mixture, or preparation which contains any quantity

of the following substances having a stimulant effect on the central nervous system, including its salts, isomers, and salts of isomers:

* * *

(3) Cathinone ... 1235 Some trade or other names: 2-amino-1-phenyl-1-propanone, alphaaminopropiophenone, 2-aminopropiophenone, and norephedrone

Although 21 C.F.R. § 1308.11(f) makes clear that cathinone is a controlled substance, neither the U.S. Code nor the Code of Federal Regulations controlled substances schedules refers to the plant from which cathinone is derived, *Catha edulis,* commonly known as "khat." In contrast, several other chemicals classified as controlled substances are listed in the schedules along with their botanical sources. *See, e.g.,* 21 C.F.R. § 1308.11(d)(23) (listing "peyote" as a controlled hallucinogenic substance and explaining that this listing refers to "all parts of the plant presently classified botanically as *Lophophora williamsii Lemaire,* whether growing or not, the seeds thereof, any extract from any part of such plant, and every compound, manufacture, salts, derivative, mixture, or preparation of such plant, its seeds or extracts"); 21 C.F.R. § 1308.11(d)(28) (stating that the term "tetrahydrocannabinols" means "tetrahydrocannabinols naturally contained in a plant of the genus Cannabis (cannabis plant), as well as synthetic equivalents of the substances contained in the cannabis plant or in the resinous extractives of such plant, and/or synthetic substances, derivatives, and their isomers with similar chemical structure and pharmacological activity to those substances contained in the plant"); 21 C.F.R. § 1308.12(b)(4) (listing in Schedule II "coca leaves (9040) and any salt, compound, derivative or preparation of coca leaves (including cocaine (9041) and ecgonine (9180) and their salts, isomers, derivatives and salts of isomers and derivatives), and any salt, compound, derivative, or preparation thereof which is chemically equivalent or identical with any of these substances, except that the substances shall not include decocainized coca leaves or extraction of coca leaves, which extractions do not contain cocaine or ecgonine.").

However, the Supplementary Information published in the Federal Register along with the text of the rule adding cathinone as a Schedule I substance does explain the connection between khat and cathinone. 58 Fed. Reg. at 4,317 ("Cathinone is the major psychoactive component of the plant Catha edulis (khat). The young leaves of khat are chewed for a stimulant effect. Enactment of this rule results in the placement of any material which contains cathinone into Schedule I. When khat contains cathinone, khat is a Schedule I substance. During either the maturation or the decomposition of the plant material, cathinone is converted to cathine, a Schedule IV substance. In a previously published final rule, the Administrator stated that khat will be subject to the same Schedule IV controls as cathine. When khat does not contain cathinone, but does contain cathine, khat is a Schedule IV substance."). The U.S. Sentencing Guidelines also provide for marijuana equivalency with respect to khat-related offenses, but do not reference the chemical "cathinone." United States Sentencing Guidelines Manual § 2D1.1 (Commentary) (2003) (listing one gram of khat as equivalent to 0.01 grams of marijuana).

2. Application of Fair-Warning Doctrine to Khat-Related Offenses

At the heart of the fair-warning doctrine is one of the central tenets of American legal jurisprudence, that "living under a rule of law entails various suppositions, one of which is that '(all persons) are entitled to be informed as to what the State commands or forbids.'" *Papachristou v. City of Jacksonville,* 405 U.S. 156, 162 (1972).

Although the doctrine of fair warning emphasizes the importance of citizens under-standing what conduct is and is not prohibited, courts also frequently invoke the maxim that ignorance of the law is no defense. *See Lambert v. California,* 355 U.S. 225, 228 (1957) (noting that the "the rule that 'ignorance of the law will not excuse' is deep in our law....").

The case at bar differs from most fair-warning cases in that the criminal provision at issue here is not ambiguous in the traditional sense. Neither party has challenged the fact that 21 C.F.R. § 1308.11(f)(3) on its face explicitly establishes cathinone as a Schedule I controlled substance. Rather, the asserted constitutional defect of this provision is that through the definition of prohibited conduct by the use of an obscure scientific term, i.e., "cathi-none," persons of ordinary intelligence, even after reading the statutory text, would be unaware that khat is a controlled substance. In other words, the controlled substances schedule's vagueness derives not from the language's imprecision but rather from the schedule essentially being written in a language foreign to persons of ordinary intelli-gence. When a statute is precise on its face yet latently vague, the danger of persons being caught unaware of the criminality of their conduct is high. *Cf. Bouie v. City of Columbia,* 378 U.S. 347, 352 (1964) ("When a statute on its face is vague or overbroad, it at least gives a potential defendant some notice, by virtue of this very characteristic, that a question may arise as to its coverage, and that it may be held to cover his contemplated conduct. When a statute on its face is narrow and precise, however, it lulls the potential defendant into a false sense of security, giving him no reason even to suspect that conduct clearly out-side the scope of the statute as written will be retroactively brought within it by an act of judicial construction.").

We have previously noted that the "general rule that citizens are presumed to know the requirements of the law ... is not absolute, and may be abrogated when a law is 'so technical or obscure that it threatens to ensnare individuals engaged in apparently inno-cent conduct,' because to presume knowledge of such a law would violate a core due process principle, namely that citizens are entitled to fair warning that their conduct may be criminal."

The use of scientific or technical terminology or terms of art common in a regulated field does not automatically render a statute unconstitutionally vague. However, when we evaluate a provision, like the one at issue here, that regulates the conduct of the pub-lic at large and not a particular industry or subgroup, we do not impute specialized knowl-edge to the "person of ordinary intelligence" by whom we judge the statute's vagueness. As the Supreme Court explained in *Connally*:

> The precise point of differentiation in some instances is not easy of statement; but ... generally ... the decisions of the court, upholding statutes as sufficiently certain, rested upon the conclusion that they employed words or phrases having a technical or other special meaning, well enough known to enable those within their reach to correctly apply them, or a well-settled common law meaning, notwithstanding an element of degree in the definition as to which estimates might differ, or ... that, for reasons found to result either from the text of the statutes involved or the subjects with which they dealt, a standard of some sort was afforded.

Here, the term "cathinone" is sufficiently obscure that persons of ordinary intelligence reading the controlled substances schedules probably would not discern that possession of khat containing cathinone and/or cathine constitutes possession of a controlled sub-stance. Persons seeking clarification of 21 C.F.R. § 1308.11(f) would be unaided by many mainstream dictionaries, as they contain no definitions for "cathinone" and make no reference to the chemical in their definitions of "khat." *See* American Heritage Dictionary of the English Language 294, 961 (4th ed. 2000) (including no definition for "cathinone" and defining "khat" as "1. An evergreen shrub (*Catha edulis*) native to tropical East Africa, having dark green opposite leaves that are chewed fresh for their stimulating effects. 2. A tea like beverage prepared from the leaves of this plant.").[5]

Despite these concerns, we are mindful of the fact that "the classification of a federal statute as void for vagueness is a significant matter. The Supreme Court has held that every reasonable construction must be resorted to, in order to save a statute from unconstitutionality." Crimes arising out of the importation of controlled substances require proof that the defendant "knowingly or intentionally imported ... a controlled substance...." 21 U.S.C. §960(a)(1). Thus, the concern that a person of ordinary intelligence could unwittingly expose himself or herself to criminal penalties due to the vagueness of the controlled substances schedules with respect to khat is overcome here because, as discussed below, conviction requires a showing of actual knowledge that khat contains a controlled substance. Although the requirement of specific intent in this case mitigates any constitutional infirmity resulting from the vagueness of the controlled substances schedules, we caution against the drafting of criminal statutes, targeted at the general populace, that rely on obscure technical or scientific terms foreign to ordinary persons, lest we "sanction[] the practice of Caligula who 'published the law, but it was written in a very small hand, and posted up in a corner, so that no one could make a copy of it.'" *Screws*, 325 U.S. at 96.

B. Sufficiency of the Evidence

Caseer also asserts that his conviction cannot stand because the district court erred in denying his motion for judgment of acquittal and convicting him on the basis that he had sufficient notice and knowledge to satisfy the scienter requirement. Where, as here, the district court has conducted a bench trial, this court reviews the district court's findings of fact for clear error and its conclusions of law de novo.

As we concluded above in our analysis of Caseer's fair-warning claim, the criminal provisions at issue here are saved from potential unconstitutionality because 21 U.S.C. §960 establishes as an element of the offenses that the accused knowingly or intentionally imported a controlled substance. Thus, to convict Caseer properly of the charged offenses, the district court would need to have found beyond a reasonable doubt that Caseer actually knew that khat contained a controlled substance.[8] *See United States v. Restrepo-Granda*, 575 F.2d 524, 527 (5th Cir.) ("Although knowledge that the substance imported

---

5. We also note that the failure to include a reference to the khat shrub in the controlled substances schedule is not, as the government contends, akin to omitting street names or slang terms. In *United States v. Levy*, we rejected a challenge to the use of the term "cocaine base" in lieu of "crack cocaine," stating that, "The fact that a type of contraband may have various nicknames on the street does not render a statute punishing possession of that contraband invalid simply because it fails to list all of the then-current nicknames." 904 F.2d 1026, 1033 n.1 (6th Cir. 1990). Here, in contrast, referring to the botanical source of cathinone as "khat" is not a passing fad that would require repeated amendment of the controlled substances schedules, but rather is the commonly accepted method of referencing the plant *Catha edulis*.

8. This is not to suggest that in all Controlled Substances Act prosecutions the government must prove beyond a reasonable doubt that the defendant had actual knowledge that the substance at issue is controlled. For substances such as cocaine that are controlled per se under the controlled substances schedules and for which there are no due process fair-warning concerns, constructive knowledge inferred from the listing of the substance in the controlled substances schedules may suffice. However, when a targeted item, such as khat, is not itself listed in the controlled substances schedules, due process requires that the government prove beyond a reasonable doubt that the defendant had actual

is a particular narcotic need not be proven, 21 U.S.C. 952(a) is a 'specific intent' statute and requires knowledge that such substance is a controlled substance."). Keeping in mind that the government must prove beyond a reasonable doubt that Caseer knew khat contained a controlled substance, we now turn to the facts identified by the district court as supporting its finding of scienter, considering whether the district court clearly erred in making any individual fact findings and whether the evidence taken as a whole is sufficient that a reasonable trial judge could conclude beyond a reasonable doubt that Caseer had the requisite intent for conviction.

First, the district court points to the 1971 United Nations Convention on Psychotropic Substances and several Federal Register publications that explain that khat contains cathine and cathinone, that establish marijuana equivalency for sentencing of khat-related crimes, and that indicate that khat may be subject to FDA regulation. Although Caseer might be charged with constructive knowledge of the contents of these documents, the mere existence of these documents does not speak to whether Caseer had actual knowledge of their contents. The district court made no finding, and the record furnishes no evidence, that Caseer read or was otherwise familiar with any of these publications. Thus, the existence of the United Nations and Federal Register publications provides no support for a finding of scienter in this case.

Second, the district court cites this court's decision in *Hofstatter* and several state prosecutions for khat-related offenses as evidence that Caseer knew khat was a controlled substance. In *Hofstatter*, we affirmed the convictions of two defendants charged with possessing and conspiring to possess listed precursor chemicals with the intent to manufacture controlled substance analogues. We noted in passing that during a search of one of the defendants' automobiles, DEA agents:

> found two bags containing personal papers, notebooks, and envelopes in the name of [the codefendant]. The documents described "khat" (an East African plant containing cathinone) and methylaminorex.... Formulae for the manufacture of methylcathinone were found in the car, as was a Federal Register notice indicating that methylaminorex was to be scheduled as a controlled substance by the DEA.

In the absence of proof that Caseer read or was otherwise aware of our decision in *Hofstatter*, concluding that this single reference in *Hofstatter* to khat furnished the actual notice to Caseer required for conviction in the present case would be clear error. Moreover, the state cases referenced by the district court, all pertain to state, not federal, controlled substances statutes, and there is no evidence to suggest that Caseer had ever been subject to the laws of these three states. Hence, it cannot be inferred from the existence of these four cases that Caseer knew that khat contains controlled substances regulated by the federal government.

Third, the district court found that Caseer was "aware of the stimulant effect of khat" based on Caseer's trial testimony that "khat is a stimulant and gives energy like tea or coffee." Although actual knowledge that a substance is controlled might in some cases be inferred from the physical effects caused by the substance, in this case the stimulant effect of khat is too mild to permit a reasonable inference that Caseer knew that khat contained a controlled substance. The district court's opinion indicates that Caseer knew only that khat had a mild stimulant effect and indeed seems to suggest that

---

knowledge that the targeted item contained a controlled substance regulated under federal drug abuse laws. *See United States v. Hussein,* 351 F.3d 9, 17–19 (1st Cir. 2003).

chewing khat is the Somali equivalent of drinking coffee or tea in the United States. The seeming ubiquity of coffee houses in the United States attests to the fact that consuming products with stimulating effects is common custom in the United States, and the average American coffee drinker most likely does not pause to consider while drinking his or her morning "cup of Joe" whether he or she may be subject to criminal sanction for possession of a controlled substance. *See Lambert v. California,* 355 U.S. 225, 229–30 (1957) (reversing conviction for failure to comply with felon-registration ordinance, explaining that, "As Holmes wrote in The Common Law, 'A law which punished conduct which would not be blameworthy in the average member of the community would be too severe for that community to bear.' Its severity lies in the absence of an opportunity either to avoid the consequences of the law or to defend any prosecution brought under it. Where a person did not know of the duty to register and where there was no proof of the probability of such knowledge, he may not be convicted consistently with due process. Were it otherwise, the evil would be as great as it is when the law is written in print too fine to read or in a language foreign to the community."). Thus, Caseer's awareness of the mild stimulant effect of khat provides little support for the conclusion that Caseer actually knew that the khat he was importing was a controlled substance.

Finally, the district court found that, although Caseer "testified that he did not know that khat or cathinone was illegal, he was aware that khat could be seized or confiscated at Customs." Not all items that may be seized by the U.S. Customs Service, however, are classified as controlled substances pursuant to 21 U.S.C. § 812 and 21 C.F.R. § 1308.11. Thus, while the district court could reasonably infer from Caseer's testimony that Caseer knew importation of khat violated U.S. customs laws, it is less reasonable to infer that Caseer knew he would be violating U.S. drug laws by importing a controlled substance.[10]

In sum, the evidence cited by the district court in its determination of whether Caseer had the requisite scienter for conviction lends, at best, only tenuous support for the conclusion that Caseer knew that he was participating in the importation of a controlled substance. Even drawing all inferences in the light most favorable to the government, a rational trier of fact would have reasonable doubt that Caseer knew that khat was a controlled substance. Thus, Caseer's conviction cannot stand.

For the reasons set forth above, we conclude that, although the criminal provisions at issue are not unconstitutional for failure to furnish fair warning, we must REVERSE the judgment of conviction because of the insufficiency of the evidence and REMAND the case to the district court for further proceedings consistent with this decision.

---

10. The government also contends that it is reasonable to infer from Caseer's behavior in arranging for the importation of khat and his subsequent conduct during the government's investigation that Caseer knew khat was a controlled substance. The district court did not make any findings regarding Caseer's state of mind based on such behavior, and arguably such conduct is consistent with that of a recent immigrant concerned with violating U.S. customs laws. Any inference from this evidence that Caseer knew he would be importing a controlled substance, and not simply an agricultural product regulated by customs laws, would be weak at best and insufficient to permit a rational trier of fact to conclude beyond a reasonable doubt that Caseer had actual knowledge that the khat he imported was a controlled substance. *See Hussein,* 351 F.3d at 20–21 (finding "very close" the question of whether sufficient evidence of scienter had been presented to sustain conviction, notwithstanding that the defendant: (1) "was a knowledgeable individual; he was not a recent immigrant, but a successful businessman who had been in the United States for a number of years;" (2) knew that khat was a stimulant; (3) had made prior trips to pick up khat for a local distributor; and (4) knew that the methods for sending and receiving packages, including mislabeling, use of fake addresses, and recruitment of multiple couriers, were "elaborately contrived to avoid detection").

Boggs, J., concurring in part and dissenting in part.

I concur in Judge Moore's well-reasoned opinion with respect to the interpretation and constitutionality of the language of the federal drug laws, as they apply to the substance khat. Since the application of the drug laws to Mr. Caseer is constitutional so long as the statutory requirement of *scienter* is met, the question of *scienter* is crucial. I dissent, however, from the court's conclusion that there was insufficient evidence of *scienter*.

In this case the government had presented evidence that:

1. Caseer had been in this country for three years, and had been immersed in an employment and ethnic culture in which consumption of khat was widespread.

2. Even though Caseer himself had recently gone to Europe, he recruited and paid apparently unwitting persons to go to Europe and courier a large quantity of khat back to him.

3. Immediately before the trip, he had wired $1,500 to an acquaintance in Amsterdam, who was the person who supplied the khat to the couriers. Although Caseer later provided an explanation for the sending of this money, that explanation was uncorroborated and the court was under no obligation to accept it.

4. Caseer coached the couriers in silence with respect to law enforcement officers, and took steps to prevent his name from being connected with the khat, both before and after the couriers were apprehended. Even when Caseer thought the couriers had successfully cleared customs and delivered the khat, he continued to counsel them to silence.

As seen in a variety of other cases, evidence of evasion and consciousness of guilt can support a finding of *scienter*. In this case, such evidence is present in abundance. Caseer's best argument to the contrary is that his questionable actions were all because he feared simple confiscation of his cargo under the agricultural laws, not because he had any idea that he was trafficking in controlled substances, of whatever variety. Indeed, his brief argues that "many things people bring in from other countries, such as apples or bottles of liquor, can be confiscated at customs without being controlled substances."

However, his attempts at insulating himself from connection with the khat went far beyond what would be consistent with bringing in illicit apples, or at least the district judge, as finder of fact, was entitled to make such a judgment. And in denying the Rule 29 motion, the judge, as determiner of law, was entitled, contrary to this panel, to determine that she was rational in so doing.

While Caseer's explanation is ingenious, the judge was not obliged to believe it, any more than the judge in *Barnes* was required to believe that the person who arranged for a "swallower" to import a substance in ingested condoms actually thought he was dealing in gold rather than in heroin.

In addition, at the time of the Rule 29 motion, there was evidence that the "street value" of the khat imported was upward of $100,000. This would be strong additional support for the *scienter* that there was something considerably more sinister involved than illegal fruit importation. The judge could take that testimony at face value at the time of the initial submission of the Rule 29 motion.

The value figure was contradicted, though not demolished, in Caseer's own testimony, but when judging the final verdict of guilt we may, as did the district judge, take into account Caseer's own testimony, and the unbelievability of some parts of it, such as his explanations of why he recently went to Germany, but just didn't have time to pick up khat, and couldn't go to Amsterdam himself, but had to use a courier, as well as his explanation that the money wired to the khat supplier, just before the importation, had nothing to do with the almost contemporaneous supplying of the khat.

Under these circumstances *some* rational finder of fact could determine that Caseer's clandestine efforts to avoid detection and thwart law enforcement, coupled with his knowledge of the khat culture, constitutes adequate circumstantial evidence that he knew that he was importing a controlled substance. I do not believe Judge Hood erred in being such a rational fact finder.

In a relatively comparable case, albeit involving a person who was only a courier, the First Circuit found, in *Hussein*, that the finder of fact could find sufficient evidence of *scienter* based on

> four key facts. First, the appellant was a knowledgeable individual; he was not a recent immigrant, but a successful businessman who had been in the United States for a number of years. Second, he knew that what he possessed was khat and that khat was used as a stimulant. Third, this was not his first trip for Mohamed. Last—but far from least—he knew that the arrangements for shipping and retrieving the packages were elaborately contrived to avoid detection.

Hussein, 351 F.3d at 20. Although the First Circuit found the case to be a close one, as I find this case, I would come to the same conclusion. In our case, there are several factors that are even stronger than in *Hussein*, primarily that Caseer was not a mere courier, but was the organizer, recipient, and paymaster for the operation and that Caseer here testified, permitting the finder of fact to assess the credibility of his explanations. Although in the *Hussein* case the court also noted the repeat nature of Hussein's involvement, that factor, when weighed against the other similarities (including knowledge of the nature of khat as a stimulant and elaborate measures to evade detection) lead me to the same conclusion.

On balance, the case against Caseer is at least as strong, and the *Hussein* case would therefore counsel toward an affirmance of the district court judgment. I would so hold, and I therefore respectfully dissent.

Holschuh, J., concurring in part and dissenting in part.

Judge Moore's opinion is not only a thorough and well-written recitation of the facts and a careful analysis of the law, it also is very balanced in its consideration of the two major issues in this appeal, the constitutionality of the regulations that make the possession of cathinone and cathine criminal offenses and the sufficiency of the evidence in this case to support appellant's conviction for the importation of cathinone. I totally agree with Judge Moore that there was insufficient evidence to show that the appellant knew that the khat plant contained a controlled substance. My dissent is based on my firm belief that the due process requirement of fair warning has not been met, and that this constitutional failure is not overcome by the fact that conviction of a defendant violating the regulation at issue requires a showing of actual knowledge that the khat plant contains a controlled substance.

Whether a law does or does not give fair warning to a person of ordinary intelligence requires, in my opinion, a consideration of not just the text of the law, but also the nature of the subject of the law and the persons who are subjected to it.

Cathinone is a psychoactive substance that is produced naturally in the khat plant. The khat plant is unique in that it produces naturally two different chemical components relevant to this case. When it is cut, the khat plant contains a substance identified as cathinone, which begins to degrade after the plant is cut. What remains in the plant is a substance identified as cathine, which has a lesser stimulant effect than cathinone. The Controlled Substances Act ("CSA") does not list cathinone or cathine as a controlled substance, but subsequent regulations place these two substances, emanating from the same plant, in different controlled substances schedules.

The regulations that place cathinone and cathine in different schedules do not mention the khat plant and do not give growers or users of the khat plant even a hint that the khat plant contains *any* controlled substance, much less two different types of controlled substances. Anyone looking at the regulations, however, would readily see that *some plants* that contain controlled substances *are themselves* listed in the schedules by their commonly known names.

Marihuana,[5] the common name for a plant of the genus Cannabis, is specifically listed in the statute as a Schedule I controlled substance. In addition to listing the plant itself, both the statute and the regulations specifically list Tetrahydrocannabinols ("THC"), which is the main psychoactive substance produced naturally by the marihuana plant.

Peyote, a small spineless cactus, is specifically listed in the statute. In addition to listing the plant itself, the regulations specifically list mescaline, the main psychoactive substance produced naturally by the peyote cactus plant, as a controlled substance.

The poppy plant is specifically listed in the statute as a Schedule II controlled substance. In addition to listing the plant itself, the regulations list specific psychoactive substances produced naturally by the opium poppy plant, *e.g.*, morphine, and codeine, as well as opium derivatives, *e.g.*, heroin, and opiates.

The leaves of the coca plant are specifically listed in the statute. In addition to listing the leaves of the coca plant themselves, both the statute and the regulations specifically list cocaine and ecgonine (products of the cocaine alkaloid, a psychoactive substance produced naturally by the coca plant) as controlled substances.

The regulations, therefore, list a number of specific plants as being themselves controlled substances, giving clear warning that possession of these plants is illegal, regardless of whether the person is aware that the plant contains a particular chemical substance that has a psychoactive effect. Remarkably—and in my opinion, fatally—absent from the regulations is the khat plant. Any person who wants to know whether it is illegal to make a cup of tea from the khat plant would find that, in contrast to other plants such as the marihuana plant, the peyote cactus plant, the poppy plant, and the coca plant, there is no reference of any kind to the khat plant any place in the law of the United States, *i.e.*, either in statutes or in regulations. I totally agree with the majority's statement that "the term 'cathinone' is sufficiently obscure that persons of ordinary intelligence reading the controlled substances schedules probably would not discern that possession of khat constitutes possession of a controlled substance."[9] I would go further, however, because it is my opinion that persons of ordinary intelligence reading the controlled substances schedules could reasonably conclude that possession of the khat plant is clearly *not illegal* because, unlike other plants containing naturally-produced psychoactive substances, the khat plant is not listed.

---

5. Although the more common spelling is "marijuana," the spelling found in the CSA and the regulations is used in this opinion.

9. The Government's expert witness, a forensic chemist with a PhD in chemistry, had been employed by the Michigan State Police scientific laboratory for 22 years. He had never heard the word "cathinone" until five years before his testimony in May, 2001. Other than forensic chemists, he knew of no one outside his area of expertise who "would have the faintest idea what cathinone would be."

The failure to include in the regulations the khat plant as a controlled substance itself (a seemingly logical inclusion) may stem from the fact that the Convention on Psychotropic Substances listed only cathinone and cathine as controlled substances. But whatever the reason for the omission, the result is a failure to give fair warning to a person of ordinary intelligence that possession of the khat plant is unlawful, and hence a denial of the due process guaranteed by the Constitution.

There is absolutely no evidence that the khat plant with its cathinone and cathine ingredients presented a significant problem to the population of the United States when the regulations in question were promulgated by the Drug Enforcement Administration ("DEA") of the Department of Justice. In 1986, the United Nations Commission on Narcotic Drugs included cathinone and cathine in the schedules of the Convention on Psychotropic Substances ("Convention"), to which the United States is a signatory. In 1987, the DEA Administrator found that cathinone and cathine "must be controlled under the CSA in order to meet the requirements imposed by the Convention on Psychotropic Substances."

According to the DEA, khat has been used since antiquity as a recreational and religious drug by natives of Eastern Africa, the Arabian Peninsula, and the Middle East. Khat is legal in many countries, and has long been an acceptable substitute for alcohol among Muslims. During the period of Ramadan, the use of khat is popular to alleviate fatigue and reduce hunger. Although khat can be abused, it is often used in a social context similar to the manner in which coffee is consumed in other parts of the world. While the amount of khat seized in the United States has been steadily increasing, the increase appears to be related to the increasing number of immigrants from Somalia, Ethiopia, Yemen, Eritrea, and other countries where khat use is common. It does not seem likely that khat use will expand beyond the ethnic Somalian, Ethiopian, Yemeni, and Eritrea communities. According to the DEA, there is no indication that khat is marketed outside these ethnic communities, although it appears to be readily available.

While every person, regardless of nationality and ethnic background, is obviously subject to the controlled substances regulations, I believe it is nevertheless a relevant factor, when considering the due process requirement of fair notice, that the khat plant has had widespread acceptance as a recreational and religious drug by millions of people in a number of nations, primarily in Africa, the Arabian Peninsula and the Middle East, where its use has been an important part of the cultures of those areas for centuries. Immigrants understandably bring that culture with them when they enter the United States. While the regulations at issue present the same fair warning problem for everyone, they unquestionably severely impact those ethnic groups who traditionally use khat in the same manner as others in the United States use legal stimulants such as coffee and tobacco. The regulations, however, do not mention khat or serve in the slightest way to warn anyone that it is illegal to chew khat, make tea from khat, or possess khat for any purpose whatsoever, including recreational and religious purposes. They truly, in my opinion, constitute a trap for the innocent.

I respectfully disagree with the majority's conclusion that the lack of fair warning is overcome by the requirement to prove scienter, *i.e.*, in this case, that the defendant knew that the khat plant contained a controlled substance.

It is, of course, true that certain statutes have been saved from a finding of unconstitutionality, due to a failure to give fair warning, by the fact that the statute in question required a specific intent to do the prohibited act.

The present case, however, does not fall in the group of cases in which the statute or regulation is subject to a void-for-vagueness attack. There is nothing vague in the listing of cathinone as a controlled substance. The due process problem with this regulation is not a vagueness problem, but the *manner* in which the DEA has chosen to list controlled substances in the schedules. While it has chosen to list some specific plants by their commonly known names as well as their psychoactive substances, it has chosen to list only the psychoactive substances found in the khat plant—substances that are not found in any mainstream dictionaries—and failed to include or mention in any way the khat plant. A person of ordinary intelligence desiring to know whether it is illegal to chew khat during Ramadan or to join friends for a cup of khat tea would not find khat mentioned any place in the laws of the United States. Worse yet, that person, examining the DEA's regulations could reasonably conclude that possession of khat—by reason of its omission from schedules that contain other plants—is *not* a crime.

In my view, it is not enough to excuse this omission by the familiar recitation that while the drafters might have chosen clearer and more precise language, this does not mean that the poorly drafted regulation is unconstitutionally vague. The regulation in the present case is aimed at groups of immigrants from Somalia, Ethiopia, Yemen, Eritrea and other countries where use of the khat plant is an accepted and important part of the lifestyles of the people in those regions. This regulation is not just poorly drafted. It is placed in the context of regulations that would make persons of ordinary intelligence reasonably believe that they can lawfully possess the khat plant.

[I]n the present case, because the regulation on its face is narrow and precise, it lulls a potential defendant into a false sense of security. The fact that the khat plant contains listed illegal psychoactive substances is not revealed to a person of ordinary intelligence until that person is arrested, indicted and endures a criminal prosecution based on the expert testimony of a DEA chemist.

While I appreciate the fact that "a scienter requirement may *mitigate* a law's *vagueness,* especially with respect to the adequacy of notice to the complainant that his conduct is proscribed," I don't believe that a scienter requirement serves to save any and all criminal statutes and regulations from being in violation of the Due Process Clause of the Fifth and Fourteenth Amendments. Otherwise, the "constitutional vice" referred to in *Screws,* "the essential injustice to the accused of placing him on trial for an offense, the nature of which the statute does not define and hence of which it gives him no warning," 325 U.S. at 101, becomes virtually non-existent. I believe that due process issues require that each case be considered on its own unique facts, including not just the text of a regulation, but also the subject matter of that regulation and the persons who are targeted by its enactment. In this case, I seriously doubt that Mr. Caseer, who was indicted and burdened with the cost, both emotionally and financially, of a criminal trial and the fear of possibly being imprisoned, would appreciate the argument that his due process rights under the Constitution of the United States can be satisfied by requiring the government to prove at trial that he knew that the khat plant contained a controlled substance.

For the reasons stated, I believe that 21 C.F.R. § 1308.11(f)(3), listing cathinone as a Schedule I stimulant, and 21 C.F.R. § 1308.14(e)(1) listing cathine as a Schedule IV stimulant, do not provide fair notice to persons of ordinary intelligence that possession of the khat plant is a criminal offense. In my opinion, these regulations do not meet the due process requirements of the Fifth and Fourteenth Amendments, and I therefore respectfully dissent from the majority's conclusion to the contrary. I join Judge Moore, however, in finding that there was insufficient evidence to show that the defendant knew that the khat plant contained a controlled substance, and that the judgment of conviction consequently must be vacated.

3. Is Knowledge Constitutionally Required?

As *United States v. Gomez* demonstrates, a defendant may be convicted and sentenced based upon the quantity and type of controlled substance he actually possessed, even if he believed he possessed a much smaller amount of a substance that would carry a lower penalty. But can the government do away with the knowledge element for a drug possession or distribution offense entirely? A federal district court recently addressed this question in *Shelton v. Dept. of Corrections*. At the time this book was going to press, the decision in *Shelton* was on appeal before the U.S. Court of Appeals for the Eleventh Circuit.

Shelton v. Department of Corrections
United States District Court for the Middle District of Florida
802 F. Supp. 2d 1289 (2011)

Scriven, J.

"Actus non facit reum nisi mens sit rea"—except in Florida.[2]

Prior to May 2002, Florida law provided, *inter alia*:

(1)(a) Except as authorized by this chapter and chapter 499, it is unlawful for any person to sell, manufacture, or deliver, or possess with intent to sell, manufacture, or deliver, a controlled substance.

(6)(a) It is unlawful for any person to be in actual or constructive possession of a controlled substance unless such controlled substance was lawfully obtained from a practitioner or pursuant to a valid prescription or order of a practitioner while acting in the course of his professional practice or to be in actual or constructive possession of a controlled substance except as otherwise authorized by this chapter. Any person who violates this provision commits a felony of the third degree[.] Fla. Stat. § 893.13(1)(a),(6)(a) (2000).

Addressing whether § 893.13 included guilty knowledge as an element of the offense, the Florida Supreme Court opined: "We believe it was the intent of the legislature to prohibit the knowing possession of illicit items and to prevent persons from doing so by attaching a substantial criminal penalty to such conduct." *Chicone v. State*, 684 So. 2d 736, 744 (Fla. 1996). Subsequently, in *Scott v. State*, 808 So. 2d 166, 170–72 (Fla. 2002), the Florida Supreme Court made clear that "knowledge is an element of the crime of possession of a controlled substance, a defendant is entitled to an instruction on that element, and ... [i]t is error to fail to give an instruction even if the defendant did not explicitly say he did not have knowledge of the illicit nature of the substance."

In direct and express response to the Court's holdings in *Chicone* and *Scott*, in May 2002, the Florida legislature enacted amendments to Florida's Drug Abuse Prevention and Control law:

(1) The Legislature finds that the cases of *Scott v. State*, 808 So. 2d 166 (Fla. 2002) and *Chicone v. State*, 684 So. 2d 736 (Fla. 1996), holding that the state must prove that the defendant knew of the illicit nature of a controlled substance found in his or her actual or constructive possession, were contrary to legislative intent.

---

2. Florida exempts itself from the age-old axiom: "The act does not make a person guilty unless the mind be also guilty."

(2) The Legislature finds that knowledge of the illicit nature of a controlled substance is not an element of any offense under this chapter. Lack of knowledge of the illicit nature of a controlled substance is an affirmative defense to the offenses of this chapter.

(3) In those instances in which a defendant asserts the affirmative defense described in this section, the possession of a controlled substance, whether actual or constructive, shall give rise to a permissive presumption that the possessor knew of the illicit nature of the substance. It is the intent of the Legislature that, in those cases where such an affirmative defense is raised, the jury shall be instructed on the permissive presumption provided in this subsection. FLA. STAT. § 893.101.

As explained by one Florida court: "The statute does two things: it makes possession of a controlled substance a general intent crime, no longer requiring the state to prove that a violator be aware that the contraband is illegal, and, second, it allows a defendant to assert lack of knowledge as an affirmative defense. There is a caveat that, once this door is opened, either actual or constructive possession of the controlled substance will give rise to a permissive presumption that the possessor knew of the substance's illicit nature, and the jury instructions will include this presumption. The knowledge element does not need to be proven, but if the defendant puts it at issue, then the jury is going to hear about it, and the defendant must work to rebut the presumption." *Wright v. State*, 920 So. 2d 21, 24 (Fla. 4th DCA 2005).

Not surprisingly, Florida stands alone in its express elimination of *mens rea* as an element of a drug offense.[4] Other states have rejected such a draconian and unreasonable construction of the law that would criminalize the "unknowing" possession of a controlled substance. See, e.g., *State v. Brown*, 389 So. 2d 48, 51 (La. 1980) (concluding drug possession cannot be a strict liability crime because it would impermissibly criminalize unknowing possession of a controlled substance and permit a person to be convicted "without ever being aware of the nature of the substance he was given."). In stark contrast, under Florida's statute, a person is guilty of a drug offense if he delivers a controlled substance without regard to whether he does so purposefully, knowingly, recklessly, or negligently. Thus, in the absence of a *mens rea* requirement, delivery of cocaine it is a strict liability crime under Florida law.

Petitioner was arrested on October 5, 2004, and charged with eight counts ... [including] delivery of cocaine. Because Petitioner was convicted of Count IV — delivery of cocaine — after the May 2002 changes to Florida's Drug Abuse Prevention and Control law, the jury was not instructed as to knowledge as an element of that offense.

Petitioner appealed his sentence and conviction and Florida's Fifth District Court of Appeal affirmed *per curiam*. On August 22, 2006, Petitioner filed a Motion for Post-Conviction Relief. The trial court denied Petitioner's Motion for Post-Conviction Relief, and Florida's Fifth District Court of Appeal affirmed on March 6, 2007. Notably, neither of the appellate decisions analyzed or discussed the federal constitutional issue raised by

---

4. The State of Washington adopted the Uniform Controlled Substances Act, but its legislature has deleted the "knowingly and intentionally" language from the model act's mere possession statute. Thus, *mens rea* was eliminated as an element of the offense of possession of a controlled substance under Washington law by implication not express intent of the legislature. See *State v. Bradshaw*, 98 P.3d 1190, 1194–95 (Wash. 2004). North Dakota had done so but retreated from this unwise course in 1989 by abandoning a strict liability regime and amending its drug laws to include the culpability requirement of "willfully" as an element of the offense. *State v. Bell*, 649 N.W. 2d 243, 252 (2002).

Petitioner—each court simply affirmed the decisions below. On May 18, 2007, Plaintiff filed the instant petition for federal habeas corpus relief.

Petitioner[] claim[s] that FLA. STAT. § 893.13 is facially unconstitutional because it entirely eliminates *mens rea* as an element of a drug offense and creates a strict liability offense under which Petitioner was sentenced to eighteen years in prison.

"The writ of habeas corpus stands as a safeguard against imprisonment of those held in violation of the law." *Harrington v. Richter,* 131 S. Ct. 770, 780 (2011). Pursuant to 28 U.S.C. § 2254(a), a district court may grant an application for writ of habeas corpus if the petitioner "is in custody in violation of the Constitution or laws or treaties of the United States." Under certain circumstances, a district court must grant deference to the state court's decision[.]

As noted in the procedural history . . . , Florida's Fifth District Court of Appeal issued decisions affirming the rulings of the trial court without opinion and without a merits-based analysis of the federal constitutional claims, and thus its *per curiam* affirmances do not constitute an adjudication of Petitioner's facial challenge to the constitutionality of FLA. STAT. § 893.13 on the merits. Therefore, no deference is due to the state court's decision.

As such, this Court reviews *de novo* Plaintiff's constitutional challenge . . . and finds the statute to be facially unconstitutional, as it is violative of the Constitution's due process clause.[6]

The requirement to prove some *mens rea* to establish guilt for conduct that is criminalized is firmly rooted in Supreme Court jurisprudence and, as reflected in the ineffectual response by the State to this petition, cannot be gainsaid here. Well established principles of American criminal law provide: "The contention that an injury can amount to a crime only when inflicted by intention is no provincial or transient notion. It is as universal and persistent in mature systems of law as belief in freedom of the human will and a consequent ability and duty of the normal individual to choose between good and evil." *Morissette v. United States,* 342 U.S. 246, 250 (1952).

To be sure, the law recognizes the authority of government to fashion laws that punish without proof of intent, but not without severe constraints and constitutional safeguards.

Thus, while the State is correct that the legislature has the authority to declare the elements of an offense, it "must act within any applicable constitutional constraints in defining criminal offenses." As discussed further, *infra*, a strict liability offense has only been held constitutional if: (1) the penalty imposed is slight; (2) a conviction does not result in substantial stigma; and (3) the statute regulates inherently dangerous or deleterious conduct. See *Staples v. United States,* 511 U.S. 600, 619–20 (1994).

Because it is rare that a legislative body would deign to expunge knowledge or intent from a felony statute expressly, as the Florida legislature has done here, the issue typically arises where a statute is silent as to knowledge and the courts are called upon to determine whether knowledge is a prerequisite to the constitutional enforcement of the challenged statute. In such cases, courts engraft a knowledge requirement to cure

---

6. The same result would obtain under a deferential standard as the legal authority relied upon herein has long established that some level of culpable *scienter* is an essential element of any felony offense that punishes otherwise innocuous conduct, carries substantial penalties and imposes grievous stigma. In the absence of an articulated basis to ignore these settled principles and precedents, the state decision cannot stand.

the statute's infirmity and follow the common-law presumption against penalizing defendants who have "knowledge only of traditionally lawful conduct." *Staples,* 511 U.S. at 618.

In the seminal case on this issue, *Staples,* the United States Supreme Court held that under the National Firearms Act, which establishes a ten-year maximum sentence for a person who possesses a machine gun that is not properly registered, the government must prove that the defendant knew that the gun was a machine gun. The Supreme Court explained that when a statute is silent as to the mental state required for a violation, the existence of a *mens rea* requirement is the rule rather than the exception. It also explained that without such a requirement in § 5861(d), the statute potentially would impose criminal sanctions on innocent persons. Further, the Supreme Court emphasized that the potentially harsh penalty attached to a statutory violation supported a *mens rea* requirement.

Subsequently, in *United States v. X-Citement Video, Inc.,* 513 U.S. 64, 68 (1994), the Supreme Court considered whether knowledge should be an element of an offense under 18 U.S.C. § 2252, which prohibits the transportation, shipping, reception, or distribution of pornography produced using underage individuals. Although the statute contained the word "knowingly," the Ninth Circuit reasoned that the placement of the word was such that it modified transportation, distribution and receipt, but it did require knowledge by the defendant that the visual depictions involved minors. The Ninth Circuit, finding that there was no *scienter* requirement as to the age of the performers in the videos, struck down the statute as a violation of the First Amendment.

Applying its analysis in Staples, the Supreme Court examined the presumption that "some form of *scienter* is to be implied in a criminal statute even if not expressed" and, because of the added constitutional dimension "a statute is to be construed where fairly possible so as to avoid substantial constitutional questions." *X-Citement Video,* 513 U.S. at 69. Thus, the Supreme Court read *Staples* and its antecedents as "instruct[ing] that the presumption in favor of a *scienter* requirement should apply to each of the statutory elements that criminalize otherwise innocent conduct." Because "the age of the performers is the crucial element separating legal innocence from wrongful conduct," the Supreme Court found a strong presumption in favor of a *scienter* requirement as to that element. The Court reasoned that this presumption was further necessitated because "a statute completely bereft of a *scienter* requirement as to the age of the performers would raise serious constitutional doubts." Thus, the Court found it "incumbent upon [itself] to read the statute to eliminate those doubts so long as such a reading is not plainly contrary to the intent of Congress."[8]

From this body of law it is clear that while "strict liability offenses are not unknown to the criminal law and do not invariably offend constitutional requirements," their use is very limited and they are accorded a "generally disfavored status." *United States v. U.S. Gypsum Co.,* 438 U.S. 422, 437–38 (1978). The Supreme Court has upheld strict liability offenses in "public welfare" cases which involve statutes that regulate inherently dangerous items/conduct and which provide for only slight penalties, such as fines or short jail sentences. In such cases, there is no due process violation because "the accused, if he does not will the violation, usually is in a position to prevent it

---

8. Of course, where, as here, the legislative intent clearly eliminates the *mens rea* requirement, the Court is powerless to cure the statute by engrafting a knowledge requirement that is squarely contrary to that intent. It is precisely that act of engrafting that prompted the legislature to amend the statute. Thus, the Court must consider the statute's constitutionality bereft of *mens rea.*

with no more care than society might reasonably expect and no more exertion than it might reasonably exact from one who assumed his responsibilities." Thus, under *Staples* and its progeny, the tripartite analysis for evaluating a strict liability offense under the strictures of the Constitution involves consideration of: (1) the penalty imposed; (2) the stigma associated with conviction; and (3) the type of conduct purportedly regulated.

Evaluated under this framework, the Florida drug statute fails completely.

It cannot reasonably be asserted that the penalty for violating Florida's drug statute is "relatively small." A violation of § 893.13(1)(a)(1), for delivery of a controlled substance as defined in Schedule I is a second degree felony, ordinarily punishable by imprisonment for up to fifteen years. For habitual violent felony offenders, such as Petitioner, a violation of § 893.13(1)(a)(1) is punishable by imprisonment for up to thirty years and includes a ten-year mandatory minimum sentence. Other provisions of Florida's drug statute subject offenders to even harsher penalties, including ordinary imprisonment for thirty years for first time offenders and life imprisonment for recidivists.

No strict liability statute carrying penalties of the magnitude of FLA. STAT. § 893.13 has ever been upheld under federal law. In fact, the Supreme Court has considered a penalty of up to three years' imprisonment or a fine not exceeding $100,000.00 too harsh to impose on a strict liability offense. In *Gypsum*, the Supreme Court considered the penalties for an individual violation of the Sherman Antitrust Act and opined, "[t]he severity of these sanctions provides further support for our conclusion that the [Act] should not be construed as creating strict-liability crimes." Similarly, in *Staples*, the Supreme Court declined to construe the National Firearms Act as a strict liability statute given its "harsh" penalty of up to ten years' imprisonment. Other federal courts have reached similar conclusions regarding even lighter penalties. For example, in *United States v. Wulff*, 758 F.2d 1121 (6th Cir. 1985), the Sixth Circuit concluded the felony provision of the Migratory Bird Treaty Act ("MBTA") was unconstitutional where the maximum penalty was two years' imprisonment. Specifically, the Sixth Circuit recognized that a two-year sentence was not "relatively small" and that a felony conviction "irreparably damages one's reputation."

[In a different case,] the Third Circuit opted to permit a penalty of two years' imprisonment for strict liability offenses that are part of "a regulatory measure in the interest of public safety, which may well be premised on the theory that one would hardly be surprised to learn that [the prohibited conduct] is not an innocent act." Because the "capture and sale of species protected by the MBTA is not 'conduct that is wholly passive,' but more closely resembles conduct 'that one would hardly be surprised to learn ... is not innocent,'" the Third Circuit upheld the constitutionality of the MTBA's two-year penalty.

Thus, while the Third and Sixth Circuits disagree over whether the outer bounds of due process lie at a one or two-year strict liability sentence, the State does not cite, and the Court has not located, any precedent applying federal law to sustain a penalty of fifteen years, thirty years, and/or life imprisonment for a strict liability offense.

[T]he State suggests that the statute is not unconstitutional as applied because Petitioner's "sentence is not the direct result of or reasonably related to the alleged infirmity in chapter 893." Rather, the State contends Petitioner's "sentence was the result of the habitual violent offender statute." This argument is flawed in three respects. First, Petitioner asserts a facial challenge to Florida's drug statute, not an as-applied challenge as the State implies. Second, Petitioner's "enhanceable" status was triggered by his conviction under § 893.13, a facially unconstitutional statute. Thirdly, the fifteen-year maximum sentence that the statute imposes is not "relatively small" even when considered without regard to the enhancement Petitioner faced, and it cannot reasonably be contended otherwise.

As Petitioner so aptly explained, "a ruling upholding penalties on the order permitted by the statute would leave literally nowhere else to go to draw a meaningful Constitutional line. Even if there is uncertainty about precisely where this line is drawn, that hardly matters here because by any measure sentences of fifteen years to life are on the wrong side of it." The Court agrees. Sentences of fifteen years, thirty years, and life imprisonment are not by any measure "relatively small." Accordingly, the Court concludes that the penalties imposed by Florida's strict liability drug statute are too severe to pass constitutional muster, and doubly so when considered in conjunction with the other two factors in the tripartite analysis.

[T]here can be little question that a conviction for a second degree felony coupled with a sentence of fifteen to thirty years tends to "gravely besmirch" a person's reputation. As the Supreme Court noted, a felony is "as bad a word as you can give to a man or thing." *Morissette,* 342 U.S. at 260. Convicted felons cannot vote, sit on a jury, serve in public office, possess a firearm, obtain certain professional licenses, or obtain federal student loan assistance. The label of "convicted felon" combined with a proclamation that the defendant is so vile that he must be separated from society for fifteen to thirty years, creates irreparable damage to the defendant's reputation and standing in the community. This social stigma precludes, for example, the ability of a convicted felon to reside in any neighborhood of his choosing or to obtain certain employment.

Finally, Florida's strict liability drug statute also runs afoul of due process limits when viewed from the perspective of the nature of the activity regulated. Where laws proscribe conduct that is neither inherently dangerous nor likely to be regulated, the Supreme Court has consistently either invalidated them or construed them to require proof of *mens rea* in order to avoid criminalizing "a broad range of apparently innocent conduct." *Liparota v. United States,* 471 U.S. 419, 426 (1985). Under this reasoning, not even a small criminal penalty may constitutionally be imposed without proof of guilty knowledge where the conduct at issue includes a wide array of innocuous behavior or behavior not inherently likely to be regulated.

In *Lambert,* the Supreme Court held that a strict liability felon registration ordinance, punishable by six months' imprisonment, violated due process. The felon registration ordinance required a convicted felon to register with law enforcement within five days of entering Los Angeles, but it did not require proof that the defendant knew of the registration requirement. The Supreme Court reversed the defendant's conviction because being in Los Angeles is not inherently unlawful, and thus the defendant had no reason to believe that her conduct might be proscribed.

While the Supreme Court has upheld statutes regulating inherently dangerous conduct without requiring *mens rea* as to every element, such instances, unlike the present one, did not involve pure strict liability offenses; rather, they involved statutes that included at least some *mens rea* requirement. For example, in *Balint,* the Supreme Court addressed the requisite *mens rea* for a violation of the Narcotic Act of 1914. The statute at issue in *Balint* was not a true strict liability statute because it required proof that the defendant knew that he was selling "dangerous narcotics." The Supreme Court held that due process was satisfied without proof of the additional fact that the defendant knew that the specific narcotics he was selling were within the ambit of the statute because "where one deals with others and his mere negligence may be dangerous to them, as in selling diseased food or poison, the policy of the law may, in order to stimulate proper care, require the punishment of the negligent person though he be ignorant of the noxious character of what he sells." By contrast, Florida's statute does not require even the minimal showing that the Defendant knew he was delivering any illicit substance as an element of the offense charged.[10]

Knowledge of the hazardous character of substances has also been sufficient to sustain liability in the shipping context. In this context, because "dangerous or deleterious devices or products or obnoxious waste materials are involved, probability of regulation is so great that anyone who is aware that he is in possession of them or dealing with them has to be presumed to be aware of the regulation" requiring classification of property on shipping papers.

Under this analytical framework, FLA. STAT. § 893.13 cannot survive constitutional scrutiny when considered in relation to the conduct it regulates—the delivery of any substance. To state the obvious, there is a long tradition throughout human existence of lawful delivery and transfer of containers that might contain substances under innumerable facts and circumstances: carrying luggage on and off of public transportation; carrying bags in and out of stores and buildings; carrying book bags and purses in schools and places of business and work; transporting boxes via commercial transportation—the list extends *ad infinitum*. Under Florida's statute, that conduct is rendered immediately criminal if it turns out that the substance is a controlled substance, without regard to the deliverer's knowledge or intent.

The State's only rebuttal to this point is a citation to a footnote in *Staples*: "Of course, if Congress thinks it necessary to reduce the Government's burden at trial to ensure proper enforcement of the Act, it remains free to amend § 5861 (d) by explicitly eliminating a *mens rea* requirement." This, the State suggests, is an express pronouncement that "the legislature's abolition of a *mens rea* requirement does not render [FLA. STAT. § 893.13] ... unconstitutional" because it is within the legislature's power to "do away with a *mens rea* requirement." [T]he Supreme Court's dicta in *Staples* that a legislature is free to eliminate *mens rea* in defining the elements of an offense does not dispense with its prior holdings requiring constitutional scrutiny of any such promulgation. As the Court explained in *Patterson*, 432 U.S. at 210, even if the legislative bodies choose to eliminate elements from criminal offenses "*there are obviously constitutional limits beyond which the States may not go in this regard.*" (emphasis added). The State of Florida exceeded those bounds in this instance.

In a final effort to salvage § 893.13, Respondents suggest any constitutional infirmity should be overlooked because: (1) the defendant may raise lack of knowledge as an affirmative defense, [rendering] the statute something other than a strict liability offense; or, alternatively, (2) "it is difficult to conceive of large numbers of people 'innocently' selling or purchasing flour and sugar in plastic baggies for cash on a streetcorner." Each of these arguments is discussed in turn.

In a vacillating and legally unsupported argument, the State contends that the question of whether the statute results in a strict liability offense cannot be answered in "a simple 'yes' or 'no.'" However, the Florida Legislature's removal of a *mens rea* requirement from drug offenses could not be more clear. The statute explicitly provides "knowledge of the illicit nature of a controlled substance is not an element of any offense under this chapter." On its face the statute punishes actual, constructive, and/or attempted delivery without any proof of knowledge—not only of the illicit nature of the substance but, apparently, even of its delivery in fact.

---

10. Curiously, according to Florida's Standard Criminal Jury Instructions, if charged with the crime of possession, the State would at least have to prove that the Defendant had knowledge of the presence of the substance, but again, not that it was an illicit substance.

Despite the clear language of the statute and the unequivocal impetus for its promulgation, the State seems to contend that the offense is not a strict liability crime because the defendant may raise lack of knowledge as an affirmative defense. This contention fails for two reasons. First, even if knowledge could be properly relegated to an affirmative defense for such an onerous felony as drug distribution, it does not change the character of the statute from a strict liability statute. Whether a statute is viewed as one of strict liability is determined by reference to its elements not available affirmative defenses.

Second, if this averment is offered to suggest that knowledge becomes an element of the offense if raised by the Defendant as an affirmative defense, the State is hoisted on its own petard. By the plain import of the statute, the Defendant bears the burden of raising and proving the affirmative defense of knowledge, and the State enjoys a presumption against the proof that a Defendant might proffer. But, as the State well knows, it cannot shift the burden of proof to a Defendant on an essential element of an offense. *Patterson,* 432 U.S. at 215 (recognizing that "a State must prove every ingredient of an offense beyond a reasonable doubt ... it may not shift the burden of proof to the defendant by presuming that ingredient upon proof of the other elements of the offense.... Such shifting of the burden of persuasion with respect to a fact which the State deems so important that it must be either proved or presumed is impermissible under the Due Process Clause.").

What is more, if this affirmative defense is somehow transformed into an element of the offense, it would fail constitutional review for the additional reason that it purports to dispense with the fundamental precept underlying the American system of justice — the "presumption of innocence." By its terms, the statute permits the jury to presume the presence of knowledge and forces the Defendant to overcome the presumption. Thus, either the statute does not require *mens rea*, rendering it a strict liability offense, or it does require proof of *mens rea*, in which case the proof of that element could not constitutionally be shifted to the Defendant under the guise of an affirmative defense.

Additionally, the State argues that FLA. STAT. §893.13 does not regulate innocuous conduct since "the possession of cocaine is never legal," and the imposition of harsh penalties without proof of *mens rea* is simply a risk drug dealers undertake for selling or delivering cocaine. By this assertion, the State confirms Professor Sanford H. Kadish's hypothesis that the basis for strict liability crimes is often simply a backhanded retort — "tough luck" to those who engage in criminal activity. Sanford H. Kadish, *Excusing Crime,* 75 Cal. L. Rev. 257, 267–68 (1987).

But, in this suggestion, the State ignores that Florida's statute is not a "drug dealer beware" statute but a "citizen beware statute." Consider the student in whose book bag a classmate hastily stashes his drugs to avoid imminent detection. The bag is then given to another for safekeeping. Caught in the act, the hapless victim is guilty based upon the only two elements of the statute: delivery (actual, constructive, or attempted) and the illicit nature of the substance. The victim would be faced with the Hobson's choice of pleading guilty or going to trial where he is presumed guilty because he is in fact guilty of the two elements. He must then prove his innocence for lack of knowledge against the permissive presumption the statute imposes that he does in fact have guilty knowledge. Such an outcome is not countenanced under applicable constitutional proscriptions.[12]

---

12. The Court notes with some consternation that if the Florida legislature can by edict and without constitutional restriction eliminate the element of *mens rea* from a drug statute with penalties of this magnitude, it is hard to imagine what other statutes it could not similarly affect. Could the state prove felony theft by proving that a Defendant was in possession of an item that belonged to another, leaving the Defendant to prove he did not take it, overcoming a permissive presumption that he did?

The Court declines to grant the State broad, sweeping authority to impose such an outcome in direct contravention of well-established principles of American criminal jurisprudence—that no individual should be subjected to condemnation and prolonged deprivation of liberty unless he acts with criminal intent—and binding Supreme Court precedent governing the constitutional analysis of strict liability offenses. Because FLA. STAT. § 893.13 imposes harsh penalties, gravely besmirches an individual's reputation, and regulates and punishes otherwise innocuous conduct without proof of knowledge or other criminal intent, the Court finds it violates the due process clause and that the statute is unconstitutional on its face. Accordingly, Petitioner's request for habeas relief on claim one is GRANTED.

D. Proof of the Identity of a Substance

In most cases, the government can conduct a chemical analysis to prove the identity of a controlled substance. What happens, however, if the government does not have physical possession of the drug? Should courts accept a police officer's visual identification of a substance as proof that it is a controlled substance?

Surely, one might think, a police officer can tell the difference between an illegal drug and an innocuous look-a-like substance. But just how reliable is an officer's on-the-scene assessment of a suspected controlled substance? Consider two recent cases.

In New York, the police mistakenly arrested two men for possession of crack cocaine. The pair sat in jail for nearly a week before the Bronx District Attorney's office dropped the charges after tests revealed that what the arresting officers had believed to be crack was, in fact, coconut candy. At the time of the arrest, one of the men asked the officers to "test" or "taste" the item, telling them "It's only candy!" but the officers refused. *See* Erin Calabrese and Murray Weiss, *Two Bronx Men Free After 'Drugs' Turn Out to Be Candy*, NEW YORK POST, Jan. 22, 2010.

In Corpus Christie, Texas, what authorities "initially thought to be one of the largest marijuana plant seizures in the police department's history turned into what amounted to a city park cleanup" after tests revealed that the plants were not marijuana. Law enforcement was alerted to the suspected marijuana by a teen who noticed the plants while riding his bike through a park. Police officers then spent "more than an hour removing and tagging" 300–400 plants. They stopped their search after nightfall with plans to return the next morning "to look around for more." Before the officers could resume their efforts, however, "testing revealed that none of it was marijuana at all." *See* Bart Bedsole, *Marijuana Seizure Turns Into Yardwork*, KRISTV.COM, May 20, 2010, *available at* http://www.kristv.com/news/marijuana-seizure-turns-into-yardwork/.

Identifying the Enemy in the War on Drugs:
A Critique of the Developing Rule Permitting Visual Identification
of Indescript White Powder in Narcotics Prosecutions
Michael D. Blanchard and Gabriel J. Chin
47 AMERICAN UNIVERSITY LAW REVIEW 557 (1998)

Imagine the following scenario: The arresting officer in a prosecution for sale of a controlled substance testifies that he observed the defendant behaving in a manner consistent with narco-trafficking. The officer is qualified to render such an observation as an expert based on his training and years of experience investigating narcotics crimes. The only element of the crime not yet established is that the white powder seized from the defendant was in fact a controlled substance regulated by law. When the prosecutor asks the officer: "In your opinion, what is that white powder?," the defense objects: "Your honor, not even a trained chemist can identify the chemical composition of a white power simply by looking at it." According to a recent line of appellate cases from around the country, the objection will be overruled. The officer will be qualified by the court as an expert in visually identifying white powdered narcotic substances because he had testified to participating in hundreds of arrests and because of his ability to "pick out cocaine from a line-up of various powdery substances." The officer's opinion may be admitted as the only evidence that the substance is indeed a controlled substance, and on that basis the defendant can be convicted.

Until recently, most courts agreed that proof of the identity of a suspected controlled substance could not rest on an opinion based solely on visual inspection. Courts reasoned that it was impossible to ascertain the chemical composition of a substance just by looking at it. In the past decade or so, however, a growing number of appellate courts have held or suggested that an opinion based on visual inspection is admissible and sufficient to prove the identity of the substance.

The general prohibition on visual identification of controlled substances began to disintegrate during the late 1980s, at the height of the drug war. One leading case is *Commonwealth v. Dawson*, where the Supreme Judicial Court of Massachusetts considered whether a substance can be identified as a controlled drug "through the testimony of experienced police officers or the users of the drug rather than through laboratory analysis or testimony by a qualified chemist." The court concluded that a chemical test was not absolutely necessary for most courts hold that circumstantial evidence can, in some cases, be enough. However, the court went on to state that "we suspect it would be a rare case in which a witness's statement that a particular substance looked like a controlled substance would alone be sufficient to support a conviction." The court's opinion therefore suggested that testimony that a substance appeared to be a controlled substance is admissible, and could even be sufficient to prove the identity of the substance beyond a reasonable doubt if a court finds that the witness is qualified.

During the 1990s, these once-isolated cases have become much more common.

The growing tolerance for admitting opinion testimony based solely on visual inspection is troubling, initially, because it simply cannot be done; no one can reliably identify an unknown substance simply by looking at it. The trend is also problematic because of the increasing problem of imitation drugs, which are designed to appear to be controlled substances but are actually fraudulent substitutes. Given these circumstances, visual opinion testimony is likely to be highly unreliable.

There are literally millions of chemical substances that can be made into a white powder; only a comparative handful of these are controlled substances. Perhaps Superman with his x-ray vision could tell them apart, but there seems to be a scientific consensus that narcotics do not display external physical characteristics discernible to mere mortals that can be reliably used to distinguish them.

Dr. James Tong, a Professor and Director of the Forensic Chemistry Program at Ohio State University who earned his Ph.D. from the University of California at Berkeley, has worked for both the prosecution and defense in various criminal cases. As he explains:

there are countless white powders. Even under microscopic examination, you can't tell which is which. Why do we buy instruments that may cost hundreds of thousands of dollars (such as a GCMS, a gas chromatograph mass spectrometer) to identify substances, if we can tell what they are just by looking at them? Why have analytical chemistry at all if we can tell what something is based on appearance?

The rise of criminal prohibitions on sale of imitation narcotics is also evidence of the tremendous practical problem that would arise from wider adoption of the visual identification rule. Trafficking in "look-alike" imitation controlled substances is so pervasive that legislatures have enacted criminal statutes proscribing their sale. By 1991, all but two states had adopted provisions addressing "imitation controlled substances."

These statutes and cases make two things very clear. First, there will be cases in which substances appear to be heroin, cocaine, methamphetamine or other controlled substances, but are not. Second, the fact that there is a market for imitation drugs suggests that simple observation is not an effective way to identify powders, even by people with strong incentives to guess correctly. Drug buyers are likely to know what drugs look like; indeed, user testimony about the effects of narcotic substances are one of the most common methods of expert identification. If addicts can be fooled, anyone can be fooled.

The disturbing trend in narcotics cases, identified here as the visual identification rule, begs explanation. Why would prosecutors introduce baseless police testimony to prove an element of a crime in their case in chief? Why have trial courts permitted irrational and unreliable testimony by police officers to establish the identity of controlled substances? Why have appellate courts nodded in approval of such practices? The answer to these questions may lie in the substance of the offenses in question—i.e., these cases are sui generis because they involve drugs.

United States policy toward illicit substances in the twentieth century has been formulated under the perception that the "drug problem" constitutes a societal crisis warranting emergency measures in response. During the 1980s, the nation's anti-drug efforts reached a fever pitch in the "War on Drugs." The drastic intensification of drug enforcement yielded increases in arrests and incarcerations for drug offenses, but not without significant costs. The "emergency" of the drug war served as justification for the rollback of constitutional protections. Further, increased volume in criminal drug arrests and prosecutions, unaccompanied by proportionate increases in law enforcement and judicial resources, strained the criminal justice system's capacity to process their caseloads. Given these circumstances, the criminal justice system has been forced to improve efficiency in drug prosecutions, possibly at the expense of the quality of justice for drug offense defendants.

Ohio v. McKee

Supreme Court of Ohio
91 Ohio St. 3d 292 (2001)

Sweeney, J.

Defendant-appellee, Cassandra N. McKee, was indicted on two counts of corrupting another with drugs, in violation of R.C. 2925.02. At her trial, two girls, Tiffany Friar and Melissa Austin, ages thirteen and fourteen at the time of the alleged crime, testified that appellee, the girlfriend of Tiffany's father, shared a marijuana joint with them while they were traveling in appellee's car.

The incident was discovered when Tiffany wrote a note to another friend, Stacy Cole, and mentioned that she might obtain marijuana from appellee. Stacy's mother found this note in Stacy's bookbag and gave it to Tiffany's mother. Tiffany's mother contacted the sheriff's department. An investigation ensued, and these charges were brought against appellee. Based upon this evidence, the jury convicted appellee as charged.

Upon appeal, the court of appeals reversed appellee's convictions, finding no evidence that the substance involved was marijuana after excluding the girls' testimony identifying it. However, finding its judgment in conflict with that of the Fifth District Court of Appeals in *State v. Coffey,* 1995 Ohio App. LEXIS 5908 (Oct. 16, 1995), (where the court upheld the use of lay testimony to prove that a substance furnished to minors was marijuana), the appellate court entered an order certifying a conflict. The cause is now before this court upon our determination that a conflict exists and pursuant to the allowance of a discretionary appeal.

The appellate court certified the following issue for our review and resolution: "Is there insufficient evidence as a matter of law to convict a defendant for corrupting another with drugs in violation of R.C. 2925.02, when the alleged drug in question is marihuana, and at trial there is no expert witness or laboratory analysis presented to identify the substance alleged to be marihuana, and the only identification of the substance is the testimony of the juveniles who allegedly smoked the substance?" While we affirm the court of appeals' decision reversing appellee's convictions, we do not believe the issue as framed is dispositive of the case. Because we believe that lay opinion testimony, if properly qualified, may be sufficient to sustain a conviction, we necessarily answer the certified question in the negative.

Appellee was convicted of two counts of corrupting another with drugs in violation of R.C. 2925.02(A)(4)(a), which provides, "No person shall knowingly * * * furnish or administer a controlled substance to a juvenile who is at least two years the offender's junior, when the offender knows the age of the juvenile or is reckless in that regard." Of these elements, the only one in dispute is that the substance in issue was marijuana, a controlled substance according to R.C. 3719.41 Schedule I, (C)(17). The state offered the testimony of the girls to prove this element of the offense.

[W]e must decide whether a person can be convicted for corrupting another with drugs based on identification of the controlled substance solely by the person to whom the substance was given.

The state argues that under either Evid.R. 701 or Evid.R. 702, the girls' testimony was properly admitted. Appellee, however, maintains that according to *State v. Maupin* (1975), 42 Ohio St. 2d 473, 71, Ohio law requires either laboratory analysis or other expert testimony to prove the identity of the drug. Since the record does not establish that the girls were more than novice users, they could not be considered experts. Thus, in the absence of laboratory testing or expert testimony, appellee argues, the state failed to prove its case.

Maupin does not fully answer the issue here. In *Maupin,* the court was asked to decide whether scientific analysis is required for the identification of the substance. In concluding that it is not, the court first determined that a drug may be identified by circumstantial evidence. Yet the court recognized that the identity of a controlled substance is beyond the common experience and knowledge of juries. At the time *Maupin* was decided, the Rules of Evidence, which govern lay and expert testimony, had yet to be adopted. Therefore, the court followed the established common law and held that expert testimony in some form is required. In this regard, the court considered cases where experienced police officers or drug addicts had been found to be experts and cases where casual drug use was found insufficient for qualification. Based upon these cases, the court concluded that the police officer's testimony in question was properly admitted as expert testimony.

However, since the adoption of the Rules of Evidence, both on the state and federal levels, many courts have used an Evid.R. 701 analysis and have allowed lay witnesses to testify about the identity of a drug. For example, in *United States v. Westbrook* (C.A.8, 1990), 896 F.2d 330, the court permitted lay testimony from two witnesses who used the substance at issue and had extensive experience with that type of drug. Courts have considered familiarity with effects of a drug coupled with similar effects from the substance at issue. All these cases, however, recognize the importance of a foundation of sufficient familiarity with the substance to support the opinion. To understand why a foundation is necessary before this testimony is admitted, it is important to consider the language of Evid.R. 701 and its jurisprudence.

Evid.R. 701 provides:

"If the witness is not testifying as an expert, his testimony in the form of opinions or inferences is limited to those opinions or inferences which are (1) rationally based on the perception of the witness and (2) helpful to a clear understanding of his testimony or the determination of a fact in issue."

At common law, lay witnesses were required to testify to facts rather than opinions. However, the practical possibility of distinguishing between fact and opinion proved to be elusive, if not impossible to draw, and led to extensive litigation and pervasive criticism by commentators. Consequently, former Fed.Evid.R. 701, upon which Ohio Evid.R. 701 is based, was adopted, and it "obviated the common law requirement for rigid compartmentalization of lay witness testimony into fact or opinion." Although at first Evid.R. 701 contemplated testimony about such ordinary things as the color, speed, type of vehicle, identity of a person, a person's health, age, or appearance, or even testimony regarding a person's sanity or intoxication under controlled situations, as case law developed, the rule was interpreted to allow for "' "shorthand renditions" of a total situation, or [for] statements of collective facts.'" Although the line between fact and opinion began to blur, all these situations met the core requirements—that the opinion is rationally based upon personal knowledge and is helpful to the trier of fact. Moving further from this core of "shorthand statements," courts began to permit witnesses with firsthand knowledge to offer lay opinion testimony "where they have a reasonable basis—grounded either in experience or specialized knowledge—for arriving at the opinion expressed." Before this type of opinion testimony has been allowed, however, the trial court has made an initial determination that the witness possessed sufficient experience or specialized knowledge, thus satisfying the rule's requirements that the opinion be both "helpful to a clear understanding * * * of a fact in issue" and "rationally based" upon the witness's perception.

It is consistent with this emerging view of Evid.R. 701 that courts have permitted lay witnesses to express their opinions in areas in which it would ordinarily be expected that an expert must be qualified under Evid.R. 702. The situation presented in this case fits into this classification. Although these cases are of a technical nature in that they allow lay opinion testimony on a subject outside the realm of common knowledge, they still fall within the ambit of the rule's requirement that a lay witness's opinion be rationally based on firsthand observations and helpful in determining a fact in issue. These cases are not based on specialized knowledge within the scope of Evid.R. 702,[2] but rather are based upon a layperson's personal knowledge and experience.

---

2. In contrast to Evid.R. 701, Evid.R. 702 authorizes expert testimony. The distinction between lay and expert witness opinion testimony is that lay testimony "results from a process of reasoning familiar in everyday life," while expert testimony "results from a process of reasoning which can be mastered only by specialists in the field."

We follow this line of cases and hold that the experience and knowledge of a drug user lay witness can establish his or her competence to express an opinion on the identity of a controlled substance if a foundation for this testimony is first established. This meets the requirements of Evid.R. 701. It is testimony rationally based on a person's perceptions and helpful to a clear understanding of a fact in issue.

Applying our holding to the facts of this case, we find that the evidence was insufficient to show that the girls were qualified to testify as lay witnesses. Their testimony was sketchy and conclusory. Melissa testified that she "assumed it was" marijuana without explaining in detail how she arrived at this conclusion. There was no evidence as to how many prior experiences the girls had had with the drug. While the girls testified that the marijuana was in a "joint" form, neither girl testified as to the actual appearance of the drug itself. Moreover, while Melissa testified in general terms as to the effects of marijuana, she did not explicitly say whether she experienced those effects this time. We conclude that there was an insufficient foundation of experience or knowledge to support their opinions. Without a proper foundation, this evidence should have been excluded. The trial court abused its discretion in permitting this lay opinion testimony. Once the evidence is excluded, there is no remaining evidence of this element of the crime. When evidence of an element of the crime is deemed insufficient on appeal, the conviction must be reversed.

––––––––––––

Even where the government has subjected a substance to chemical analysis, this does not necessarily end the matter. The testing method itself may be flawed. Or the government agent administering it may improperly conduct the test or even intentionally falsify evidence.

One study on false positives in drug identification, for example, recounts the story of Don Bolles, drummer for the punk band, *The Germs.* In the spring of 2007, Bolles "was arrested and jailed for three and a half days because the bottle of Dr. Bronner's Magic Soap found in his possession tested positive for the drug GHB. Police tested the soap at the scene using the NarcoPouch 928 field drug kit. Subsequent testing found that a wide variety of natural soaps as well as soy milk tested positive for GBH [using the kit.]" John Kelly, FALSE POSITIVES EQUAL FALSE JUSTICE at 3 (2008). *See also*, Alan Harris, Comment: *A Test of a Different Color: The Limited Value of Presumptive Field Drug Tests and Why That Value Demands Their Exclusion from Trial,* 40 Sw. L. REV. 531 (2011) (discussing field drug tests and arguing that "courts should exclude the results of such tests for the purpose of establishing positive identification and further exclude such results altogether because of the risk of undue prejudice to criminal defendants"); Tim Evans, *Indiana Lacks Answers on Toxicology Lab Tests Used in Criminal Cases,* INDIANAPOLIS STAR, March 30, 2012 (reporting that an independent check of blood tests in Indiana found no trace of drugs in 30% of the samples that had been "reported to prosecutors as positive for marijuana or cocaine").

In *State v. Roche,* the Washington Court of Appeals reversed a methamphetamine conviction after it was discovered that the state chemist who testified at Roche's trial had routinely tampered with evidence in order to hide his own heroin addiction. 114 Wn. App. 424 (2002). The chemist had been "self-medicating with heroin sent to the crime lab for testing purposes" and had "reduc[ed] his workload by testing a single purified sample and applying the results across a number of cases, a practice known as 'dry labbing.'" 114 Wn. App. 424 (2002). In a similar story, prosecutors in San Francisco had to "drop hundreds of narcotics cases" after it was discovered that a police drug analyst had been skimming cocaine and possibly other drugs for her own use from the crime lab. *See* Jason Van Derbeken, *Drug Lab Scandal Could Undermine Murder Case,* S.F. CHRON., April 6, 2010.

In the 2009, the United States Supreme Court held defendants have a constitutional right to confront the government agents who conduct chemical analysis at trial. *See* Melendez-Diaz v. Massachusetts, 129 S. Ct. 2527 (2009).

E. Additional Controlled Substances Offenses

Fueled in part by the war on drugs, legislatures have created a range of additional drug crimes to supplement the more traditional and frequently prosecuted offenses. The number and variety of additional offenses is too large to permit a survey of them all in this book. They range from "controlled substances murder" statutes (such as the law discussed above in *New Jersey v. Morrison*) to drug paraphernalia laws. Other laws, such as money laundering, are often used to target drug offenders, though they apply in other contexts as well. This section introduces a sampling of these additional offenses. When reading the material, consider what (if anything) each offense adds to the foundational drug offenses, like possession for sale and manufacture, addressed above.

1. Maintaining a Drug-Involved Premises

21 U.S.C. § 856

Maintaining drug-involved premises

(a) Except as authorized by this title, it shall be unlawful to—

(1) knowingly open, lease, rent, use, or maintain any place, whether permanently or temporarily, for the purpose of manufacturing, distributing, or using any controlled substance;

(2) manage or control any place, whether permanently or temporarily, either as an owner, lessee, agent, employee, occupant, or mortgagee, and knowingly and intentionally rent, lease, profit from, or make available for use, with or without compensation, the place for the purpose of unlawfully manufacturing, storing, distributing, or using a controlled substance.

United States v. Wilson

United States Court of Appeals for the Second Circuit
503 F.3d 195 (2007)

Per Curiam:

Defendant-Appellant Maletha Wilson appeals from a judgment of conviction entered in the United States District Court for the Western District of New York, convicting her after a jury trial of two counts of knowingly and intentionally making her residence available for use for the purpose of unlawfully manufacturing, storing, distributing, or using a controlled substance, in violation of 21 U.S.C. § 856(a)(2). She shared two apartments with a drug dealer, and acknowledges that there were drugs, along with drug-related paraphernalia, at both premises; but she argues that the evidence was insufficient chiefly on the ground that the government failed to prove that she herself intended that the premises would be used for the unlawful purpose.

On October 3, 2002, Rochester police officers arrested one Yusef Blocker outside 323 Arnett Boulevard, where he was living with Wilson. Wilson allowed the police to enter her apartment, told them that she wanted to check on her baby in a back bedroom, and was followed there by the police. There, they saw—in plain view—two plastic bags containing a white rock substance. At trial, Wilson stipulated that the substance was 12.836 grams of cocaine base. Also in the bedroom were unused Ziploc bags and a razor blade in the baby's coat, as well as a second razor blade and a plate inside the top drawer of a dresser.

On May 7, 2004, Rochester police officers executed a search warrant at 35 Jackson Street, where Wilson was then living. No one was present when the officers entered and found a digital scale and unused Ziploc bags in the master bedroom closet. In another bedroom, the officers found a cigar box containing a substance which they suspected was cocaine. At trial, Wilson stipulated that the substance consisted of 61.690 grams of powder cocaine and 31.648 grams of cocaine base.

On February 23, 2005, Wilson was interviewed by a special agent of the Bureau of Alcohol, Tobacco and Firearms. She said that she was living with Yusef Blocker in the apartment on Arnett Boulevard when it was searched in October 2002, and that she was living with Blocker at 35 Jackson Street when it was searched in May 2004. Evidence at trial also indicated that her name was on both leases. The Department of Social Services paid half the rent (and her mother the other half) at each location.

Wilson argues that the evidence against her was insufficient to support her conviction.

In the main, Wilson contends that under 21 U.S.C. §856(a)(2), the government had to prove that, in making her home available to others, it was Wilson's own purpose to allow them to engage in narcotics trafficking there. This is a fundamental misreading of subsection (a)(2).

Section 856(a)(2) makes it unlawful for a person to:

> manage or control any place, whether permanently or temporarily, either as an owner, lessee, agent, employee, occupant, or mortgagee, and knowingly and intentionally rent, lease, profit from, or make available for use, with or without compensation, the place for the purpose of unlawfully manufacturing, storing, distributing, or using a controlled substance.

The law thus prohibits a person with a premises from knowingly and intentionally allowing its use for the purpose of manufacturing, storing or distributing drugs. The intent of the prohibition is "to prohibit an owner from providing a place for illegal conduct, and yet to escape liability on the basis either of lack of illegal purpose, or of deliberate ignorance". *United States v. Tamez*, 941 F.2d 770, 774 (9th Cir. 1991). Accordingly, "under §856(a)(2), the person who manages or controls the building and then rents to others, need not have the express purpose in doing so that drug related activity take place; rather such activity is engaged in by others (*i.e.*, others have the purpose)." *United States v. Chen*, 913 F.2d 183, 190 (5th Cir. 1990). The phrase "for the purpose," as used in this provision, references the purpose and design *not* of the person with the premises, but rather of those who are permitted to engage in drug-related activities there.

This interpretation is compelled by the preceding subsection, 856(a)(1), in which the phrase "for the purpose" applies to the intent of the person with an interest in the premises. That is, subsection 856(a)(1) makes it illegal to:

> knowingly open, lease, rent, use, or maintain any place, whether permanently or temporarily, for the purpose of manufacturing, distributing, or using any controlled substance.

Under Wilson's reading, both *subsections*—(a)(1) and (a)(2)—would proscribe the same conduct. But it would be impermissible to conflate these two subsections, rendering one superfluous. *See Williams v. Taylor,* 529 U.S. 362, 404, (2000) ("It is … a cardinal principle of statutory construction that we must give effect, if possible, to every clause and word of a statute.").

Wilson also challenges the sufficiency of the evidence to prove that she knew her residence was being used for drug trafficking. Our review of the trial record discloses sufficient evidence to support Wilson's conviction. A cooperating witness testified that on numerous occasions, he and Blocker engaged in drug manufacturing activities at both of Wilson's residences, and that he overheard Blocker ask Wilson for Ziploc bags and a Pyrex dish, two items used for those activities. Wilson admitted to the police that she knew Blocker sold drugs. And crack cocaine, cocaine powder and drug paraphernalia were found in her residences, including a razor and Ziploc bags in baby clothes in her bedroom. Given this evidence, a reasonable jury could—and did—conclude that Wilson knowingly allowed others to use those residences for the manufacture, storage and distribution of narcotics.

For the foregoing reasons, the judgment of the district court is affirmed.

2. Firearms and Controlled Substances

United States v. Doody

600 F.3d 752 (2010)
United States Court of Appeals for the Seventh Circuit

Flaum, J.

The defendant, Alduff Doody, was charged with possessing a firearm in furtherance of a drug trafficking crime, in violation of 18 U.S.C. §924(c). Unlike the defendants most commonly charged under §924(c), Doody did not possess the firearm for protection. Instead, he accepted the gun as collateral to secure a drug debt. Thus, he argues, his conduct did not violate §924(c). Because Doody took possession of a firearm in manner that facilitated a drug transaction, we affirm.

On March 11, 2009, Doody was indicted by a grand jury on one count of possessing a firearm in furtherance of a drug trafficking crime in violation of 18 U.S.C. §924(c) and one count of distributing cocaine in violation of 21 U.S.C. §841(a)(1). Although he originally pleaded not guilty to both counts, on May 20, 2009, Doody agreed to plead guilty to Count 2 of the indictment, distributing a controlled substance. The parties also agreed that Count 1 would be submitted to the district court in a bench trial on stipulated facts. Doody waived his right to appeal, except for the right to appeal an adverse decision as to guilt or innocence as a result of the bench trial on Count 1. On May 27, 2009, the district court approved the plea agreement.

According to the stipulated facts, Doody distributed powder cocaine from about April 2008 through February 2009 in Marshall County, Indiana. He distributed a little over a kilogram of powder cocaine during that ten-month period. On August 5, 2008 and February 24, 2009, Doody distributed cocaine to two confidential informants working with the Bureau of Alcohol, Tobacco, and Firearms. In a separate transaction in the fall of 2008, Doody distributed one-sixteenth of an ounce of cocaine to Gil Rodriguez, who did not at that time have the money to pay for it. Rodriguez instead offered his nine-millimeter pistol as collateral to secure the drug debt. Doody took possession of the firearm and held it for four or five days until Rodriguez paid him $60 for the cocaine. Doody then returned the firearm to Rodriguez. When agents searched Doody's residence on February 24, 2009, they found nine-millimeter ammunition and a nine-millimeter magazine.

The district court conducted the bench trial on June 8, 2009. Based exclusively on the stipulated facts, the district court denied Doody's motion for an acquittal and found Doody guilty of Count 1 of the indictment. On August 20, 2009, the district court sentenced Doody to 60 months of imprisonment on Count 1 of the indictment and 51 months of imprisonment on Count 2 of the indictment, with the terms to run consecutively. Doody appeals his conviction on Count 1.

Here, because the facts were stipulated before trial, [this case] turn[s] on the legal question of whether a defendant who accepts a firearm as collateral to secure a drug debt can be said to possess that firearm "in furtherance" of a drug trafficking crime and thus be convicted under 18 U.S.C. § 924(c).

Section 924(c) provides for a mandatory minimum sentence of five years for any person "who, during and in relation to any ... drug trafficking crime ... uses or carries a firearm, or who in furtherance of any such crime, possesses a firearm...." 18 U.S.C. § 924(c)(1)(A). The "uses" prong of § 924(c) has been the subject of a line of Supreme Court cases, culminating in a case addressing the receipt of a firearm in exchange for drugs. First, in *Smith v. United States*, 508 U.S. 223 (1993), the Supreme Court held that a person who trades his firearm for drugs "uses" the firearm "during and in relation to ... [a] drug trafficking crime." Two years later, in *Bailey v. United States*, 516 U.S. 137 (1995), the Court suggested it would follow a more restrictive interpretation of "use," holding that a defendant who had a loaded firearm locked in a bag in the trunk of his car and a defendant who had an unloaded pistol locked in a trunk in her bedroom closet did not "use" the firearms during and in relation to their drug-dealing activities because they did not "actively employ" them. Finally, in *Watson v. United States*, 552 U.S. 74 (2004), a unanimous Court held that a defendant who receives a gun as payment for drugs does not "use" a gun for the purposes of § 924(c). By the time the Court decided *Watson*, Congress had responded to *Bailey* by amending § 924(c) to its present form, adding the prohibition on possessing a firearm in furtherance of a drug trafficking crime. Because the defendant in *Watson* was charged under only the "use" prong of § 924(c), the Court reserved the question of whether he could have been found guilty of possessing a gun "in furtherance of" his drug trafficking.

Since *Watson*, six courts of appeals have considered whether a defendant who receives a firearm in exchange for drugs possesses that firearm in furtherance of a drug trafficking crime, and all six have decided or assumed without deciding that such a defendant does violate § 924(c).

We have not previously addressed this question, but we have considered the "in furtherance of" prong of § 924(c) in other situations. In *United States v. Castillo*, 406 F.3d 806 (7th Cir. 2005), we considered what might be the archetypical possession of a gun in furtherance of drug trafficking: possessing a gun to protect the drugs and the dealer and to serve as a warning to those who might attempt to steal the drugs. We interpreted the phrase "in furtherance of" to mean "furthering, advancing, or helping forward." *Castillo* places the burden on the government to "present a viable theory as to how the gun furthered the [drug distribution] ... and it must present specific, non-theoretical evidence to tie that gun and the drug crime together under that theory." Applying this standard, we concluded that the government had established that the defendant had possessed a gun for protection during a drug offense and thus violated § 924(c).

In *United States v. Vaughn,* 585 F.3d 1024 (7th Cir. 2009), we applied the standard articulated in *Castillo* to a more unusual scenario. In *Vaughn,* the defendant had previously acquired a rifle from a man named Gee, who often bought drugs from him. Gee later became a confidential informant and asked if he could buy back the rifle. Vaughn declined to sell him the rifle, but said he would give the rifle back to Gee if Gee sold six pounds of marijuana for him. Gee agreed, and Vaughn gave him the rifle after Gee paid him for the marijuana. We held that by offering the rifle as an incentive for selling marijuana, Vaughn possessed it in furtherance of a drug trafficking crime. We acknowledged that this was a "novel" use of §924(c) but held that Vaughn's possession of the rifle "helped forward" the sale of six pounds of marijuana by acting as an incentive to sell the marijuana, speeding payment for the marijuana, and assuring the full payment of the marijuana's purchase price.

Castillo and *Vaughn* lead us to the same interpretation of §924(c) as our sister circuits: when a defendant receives a gun for drugs, he takes possession of the firearm in a way that "further[s], advance[s], or help[s] forward" the distribution of drugs. As the Sixth Circuit observed, "If the defendant did not accept possession of the gun, and instead insisted on being paid fully in cash for his drugs, some drug sales—and therefore some drug trafficking crimes—would not take place." The same is true when the defendant holds the gun only as collateral, rather than taking permanent ownership of it. Without the gun serving as security for the drug debt, some drug dealers would refuse to extend credit to their customers, and some drug transactions would not take place. Receiving a gun in exchange for drugs—whether as payment or collateral—facilitates the drug transaction.

Doody makes two closely related arguments against this interpretation of §924(c). First, he relies on the holding in *Watson* that mere "receipt" is not "use" and on 18 U.S.C. §§922(g) & (h), both of which make it a crime to "receive" a firearm or ammunition under certain circumstances. This, Doody suggests, means that Congress must use the word "receipt," not "possession," to criminalize accepting a gun for drugs. Second, he argues that he did not possess the pistol "during and in relation to" the drug trafficking crime, because he did not possess the gun during the drug distribution or possessed it only momentarily (the record is silent on whether the gun or the contraband was handed over first), after which he possessed the gun only "'in furtherance of' a secured debt."

Doody's reliance on *Watson* is misplaced. *Watson* rested on the plain meaning of the word "use"—one who receives something in a bartering transaction is not ordinarily said to use the object he received in relation to trade. Here, Doody "possessed" the pistol in the ordinary meaning of the word: he held it and controlled it. Whatever the merits in another context of Doody's argument that Congress intended to distinguish "possession" from "receipt," the distinction makes no difference here. After receiving the gun, Doody possessed it. And unless Doody had been willing to take possession of the gun in exchange for drugs, the transaction could not have taken place. Thus, Doody's eventual possession furthered his drug trafficking crime.

Finally, we must address Doody's argument that he did not violate §924(c) because he did not take possession of the gun until after he distributed the drugs. This argument rests on a misreading of the text of §924(c). The mandatory minimum applies to a defendant "*who,* during and in relation to any ... drug trafficking crime..., uses or carries a firearm, *or who,* in furtherance of any such crime, possesses a firearm...." 18 U.S.C. §924(c)(1)(A) (emphasis added). The repetition of the subject "who" in this parallel construction makes clear that "during and in relation to" applies only to those defendants accused of using or carrying a firearm. For those who are charged with possessing a firearm, the only limit is that the possession be "in furtherance of" the drug trafficking crime. Thus, Doody cannot rely on the fact that his possession of the firearm may not have come until after the drugs were distributed. Even if it did not come until after the drugs were distributed, Doody's possession of the pistol made the drug transaction possible, and thus furthered it, and § 924(c) requires no more.

The district court's judgment of conviction is AFFIRMED.

Section 924(c) targets people who use or carry a firearm "in furtherance" of a drug trafficking crime. There are a number of other criminal statutes and doctrines that link guns to drugs. For example, 18 U.S.C. § 922(g)(3) focuses on drug users, making it a crime for anyone "who is an unlawful user of or addicted to any controlled substance ... to possess in or affecting commerce, any firearm or ammunition." In the wake of the Supreme Court's decision in *District of Columbia v. Heller,* 554 U.S. 570 (2008), a number of defendants have challenged the constitutionality of the "unlawful user" gun law on Second Amendment grounds. Thus far, courts have been quick to reject these challenges, relying on the Court's statement in *Heller* that its opinion did not "cast doubt on long-standing prohibitions on the possession of firearms by convicted felons and the mentally ill[.]" *Id.* at 626–27. As the Ninth Circuit recently held, "we see the same amount of danger in allowing habitual drug users to traffic in firearms as we see in allowing felons and mentally ill people to do so." *United States v. Dugan,* 657 F.3d 998, 999 (9th Cir. 2011).

3. Drug Free School Zones

A Moving Violation? Hypercriminalized Spaces and Fortuitous Presence in Drug Free School Zones
L. Buckner Inniss
8 Texas Forum on Civil Liberties and Civil Rights 51 (2003)

Over the last thirty years, both the federal government and a majority of states have enacted statutes that prohibit certain types of conduct involving illicit drugs in or near schools, school buses, or other youth or family-related facilities and locales. These statutes vary from jurisdiction to jurisdiction in terms of whether they stand alone as separate offenses or serve as a sentencing enhancement and in terms of the defenses available. The net effect of such statutes in either case is to "hypercriminalize" certain areas or spaces where drug activity takes place by increasing the length of incarceration after conviction. Such statutes have been subject to a number of challenges over the years. Chief among them are constitutional claims that such statutes are an invalid exercise of legislative or police power, violate due process and equal protection guarantees, violate the Eighth Amendment's prohibition on punishment that is grossly disproportionate to the crime, violate double jeopardy provisions, or are overbroad. A number of other claims have been based upon the allegedly vague and arbitrary nature of statutes that punish persons who were found with drugs in their vehicles while passing through school zones. A third set of claims point to the lack of a requirement that the offender intended to be present in the drug-prohibited zone. To date, virtually none of these challenges have succeeded, and both federal and state schoolyard statutes are widely hailed as major weaponry in the war against drugs.

Both federal and state [drug] schoolyard statutes take to high art form the notion of criminalizing spaces. Indeed, the ambit of federal and state schoolyard statutes usually includes both public and private spaces, as the creation of perimeters around schools or other facilities does not make allowances for activities which occur in private homes and some provisions criminalize certain drug activities around publicly funded housing projects.

The federal schoolyard statute was enacted its original form in 1984. It provided for an enhanced penalty for the distribution of drugs within 1,000 feet of a school. The 1984 statute, introduced by Senator Paula Hawkins of Florida, was intended to reduce the presence of drugs in the schools by threatening those who distributed drugs near schools with heavy penalties. In 1986, the statute was amended to prohibit both manufacturing and distributing within 1,000 feet of a school. The 1986 amendment also broadened the scope of educational institutions where such penalties applied. A particular concern of the drafters of the 1986 amendments was the threat of crack cocaine near schools. In 1988, the statute again underwent changes, this time to prohibit possession with intent to distribute within 1,000 feet of a school. The impetus of Congress seems to have again been the fear of having large quantities of drugs near schools.

Several cases at both the federal and state level, which raise equal protection or substantive due process claims, involve defendants who argue that their living conditions are such that they cannot reasonably live outside of a drug prohibited zone. Their presence is, to a great degree, merely happenstance. Thus, they argue, they are treated differently than persons who are able to live elsewhere. For example, in *United States v. White*, the defendant raised substantive due process and equal protection claims based upon a portion of an indictment charging him with violation of 21 U.S.C. Section 845a. This statute provides for sentence enhancement for a conviction of narcotics distribution within 1,000 feet of a school. The alleged narcotics distribution took place in the city of New Haven, Connecticut, where almost all the city falls within the protected 1,000 foot school zone. The defendant argued that the existence of such widespread prohibited zones failed to comport with the intent of the legislation, which was to create drug free zones around schools in particular. The court disagreed with the defendant, finding that application of the statute met with legislative intent, and that there was no reason to "carve out an exception" for New Haven even given its numerous schools throughout the city.

A similar happenstance or fortuitous presence claim was raised in *United States v. Nieves*. There, a defendant argued that the schoolyard statute denied him equal protection of the laws because the statute's enhanced penalties had a greater impact upon racial minorities who, he argued, were more likely to live in high density inner city areas where there are likely to be more schools than in other places. The court, however, rejected this argument, finding that even assuming there to be some statistical validity to defendant's claim, this disparate impact alone would not be the basis of an equal protection claim.

United States v. Agilar

United States Court of Appeals for the Second Circuit
779 F.2d 123 (1985)

Newman, J.

Anthony Agilar appeals from a judgment of the District Court for the Southern District of New York convicting him, after a bench trial, of distributing heroin within 1,000 feet of a public elementary school in violation of 21 U.S.C. §§ 812, 841(a)(1), and 841(b)(1)(B) (1982) and 21 U.S.C. § 845a. Appellant primarily challenges the constitutionality of section 845a, the so-called "schoolyard" provision, which increases penalties for distribution of narcotics within 1,000 feet of a public or private elementary or secondary school. We affirm.

The evidence disclosed that Agilar sold three glassine envelopes containing heroin for $30 to Maritza Ortiz, an undercover New York City police officer. Ortiz had first approached Agilar's co-defendant, Edwin Jimenez, at the corner of Second Avenue and 118th Street in Manhattan and asked for heroin, specifically requesting the brand name "Checkmate," which is sold at that location. Jimenez said, "I will take you to the man." He led Ortiz only 25 feet along 118th Street to a location where Agilar was selling heroin to customers waiting in line. Agilar told Jimenez that Ortiz would have to wait her turn at the end of the line. While she was waiting, Agilar asked her how many glassine envelopes she wanted. She said she wanted three, and he replied, "I am going to take care of you." When Ortiz reached the head of the line, she purchased three envelopes for $30, using money that had been photocopied to record the serial numbers.

Promptly after the sale, Ortiz radioed a backup police officer and gave a description of the seller. The officer arrived on the scene a minute later, arrested Jiminez, and stopped three men, including Agilar, who met the description given by Ortiz. When the three were brought to the undercover officer's presence, she immediately identified Agilar as the seller. Agilar was arrested and searched; he had $140 in cash, but none of the bills that Ortiz had used in the heroin purchase. The evidence also revealed that Agilar, while waiting outside the office of a United States Magistrate the following day, was overheard admonishing Jimenez for bringing an "undercover" to him.

Though the case was developed by New York City police officers, concerns readily visible criminal conduct requiring no special investigatory resources or equipment, and involves a $30 transaction, the matter became the subject of a federal criminal prosecution because it occurred on "federal day," the day of the week when federal law enforcement authorities have decided to convert garden-variety state law drug offenses into federal offenses. Though we are urged in other contexts to tolerate missed deadlines because of the enormous burdens placed upon limited numbers of federal law enforcement personnel, on "federal day" there are apparently enough federal prosecutors available with sufficient time to devote to $30 drug cases that have been developed solely by state law enforcement officers. Be that as it may, the case is lawfully within the jurisdiction of the federal courts and must be decided. It poses issues concerning the constitutionality of the federal "schoolyard" statute because Agilar had the double misfortune to sell to a customer who happened to be an undercover police officer and to make the sale at a location that happened to be within 1,000 feet of a public elementary school.

We have thus far encountered the schoolyard statute on two occasions, ruling in *United States v. Falu,* 776 F.2d 46 (2d Cir. 1985), that the statute does not require knowledge of the proximity of a school and in *United States v. Jones,* 779 F.2d 121 (2d Cir. 1985), that the statute does not require evidence that the specific location of the sale, within the 1,000-foot zone, is one where school children are present or likely to congregate. Agilar's constitutional challenge is no more substantial than the statutory arguments rejected in *Falu* and *Jones.*

Agilar contends that the statute offends the Due Process Clause by creating an unwarranted irrebuttable presumption that every sale of narcotics within 1,000 feet of a school has the detrimental effects upon school children that Congress sought to avoid by enacting section 845a. The cases condemning irrebuttable presumptions that lack rationality do not require that the means chosen by Congress to deal with a problem score a notable success in every application of the statute. Congress wanted to lessen the risk that drugs would be readily available to school children. It is surely rational to achieve that goal by increasing penalties for those who sell drugs near schools. Whether or not each sale within the 1,000-foot zone, if not deterred, would have led to acquisition of drugs by school children, the proscription of sales within the environs of schools is a rational means of reducing the risk of easy availability that can lead to such acquisition.

Nor is the statute constitutionally vulnerable because of appellant's doubt that the increased penalties will in practice add any incremental deterrence to that arising from the already substantial penalties Congress has provided for selling narcotics. Congress is entitled to add higher penalties in the hope of providing further deterrence, whether or not much success is thereby achieved. Appellant's final due process challenge alleges that the 1,000-foot demarcation line is not sufficiently ascertainable by the average person. Since the statute is violated whether or not the seller knows he is within the prohibited zone, this argument has no force. And since there is no protected right to sell narcotics anywhere, there need be no concern for the person who removes his selling activity a considerable distance from a school in order to avoid the risk of being within the 1,000-foot zone.

Agilar also challenges section 845a on equal protection grounds on the strained theory that the statute has a disproportionate impact on members of racial minorities, more of whom live, it is asserted, within 1,000 feet of schools than do non-minority residents, a smaller proportion of whom live in densely populated urban areas. The argument fails, among other reasons, for lack of any claim, much less showing, of a discriminatory purpose.

The judgment of the District Court is affirmed.

4. Driving Under the Influence

Driving under the influence (also known in some states as driving while intoxicated) presents a variety of legal issues. Many private criminal defense attorneys specialize in handling DUI cases, with some devoting their entire practice to it. Though a detailed look at DUI law is beyond the scope of this book, the California Supreme Court case *Burg v. Municipal Court* provides a useful history of drunk driving statutes as well as a glimpse at the blood-alcohol-content-based approach employed in modern DUI laws.

Burg v. Municipal Court
Supreme Court of California
35 Cal. 3d 257 (1983)

Mosk, J.

Richard Joseph Burg, hereafter defendant, appeals from a judgment denying his petition for a writ of prohibition. He contends that Vehicle Code section 23152, subdivision (b),[1] fails to give constitutionally adequate notice of the conduct it prohibits, and that the municipal court erred in overruling his demurrer to that effect. We conclude that section 23152, subdivision (b), is constitutional, and therefore affirm the judgment.

---

1. All statutory references are to the Vehicle Code unless otherwise indicated.

Defendant was arrested at 2:25 in the morning of March 27, 1982, for violation of section 23152, subdivision (a) (driving while under the influence of alcohol). A chemical test administered 50 minutes later revealed a blood-alcohol content of 0.23 percent. He was charged with violating section 23152, subdivision (b), i.e., driving a vehicle while having 0.10 percent or more, by weight, of alcohol in one's body. The complaint also alleged a prior conviction of former section 23102, subdivision (a) (driving while under the influence of alcohol).

Defendant demurred on the ground that section 23152, subdivision (b), gives constitutionally inadequate notice of the conduct proscribed. The municipal court overruled his demurrer, and defendant sought a writ of prohibition in the superior court. The petition was denied on the merits, and this appeal followed.

Eighty years ago an editorialist complained, "Inebriates and moderate drinkers are the most incapable of all persons to drive motor wagons. The general palsy and diminished power of control of both the reason and the senses are certain to invite disaster in every attempt to guide such wagons." In the ensuing decades motor vehicles have become faster, heavier, and ubiquitous, with proportionately tragic consequences to the victims of drinking drivers. Nearly half of the traffic deaths in California between 1976–1980 involved drinking drivers. Nearly one-quarter of all traffic accidents resulting in injury involved the use of alcohol. Traffic deaths in the United States exceed 50,000 annually, and approximately one-half of those fatalities are alcohol-related.

The drunk driver cuts a wide swath of death, pain, grief, and untold physical and emotional injury across the roads of California and the nation. The monstrous proportions of the problem have often been lamented in graphic terms by this court and the United States Supreme Court. As observed in *Breithaupt v. Abram* (1957) 352 U.S. 432, "[the] increasing slaughter on our highways, most of which should be avoidable, now reaches the astounding figures only heard of on the battlefield." Indeed, in the years 1976 to 1980 there were many more injuries to California residents in alcohol-related traffic accidents than were suffered by the entire Union Army during the Civil War, and more were killed than in the bloodiest year of the Vietnam War. Given this setting, our observation that "[drunken] drivers are extremely dangerous people" seems almost to understate the horrific risk posed by those who drink and drive.

Recognizing the effect of alcohol on drivers, state legislatures early in the century attempted to regulate such conduct. Because "both popular and legal views of the problem centered on the grossly intoxicated driver", the laws also reflected that conception. Thus, California's first statute on the topic read simply, "No *intoxicated* person shall operate or drive a motor vehicle or other vehicle upon any public highway within this state." (Italics added.)

A more satisfactory means of defining the problem of drinking and driving emerged in the middle decades of this century, with the development of scientific measurement of blood-alcohol levels. Research on alcohol's effect on both motor skills and judgment revealed that impairment occurred at alcohol concentrations as low as 0.05 percent, considerably below the point at which typical clinical symptoms of intoxication appear in most persons. Thus, in 1969, after a number of intervening amendments that attempted to refine definitions and specified penalties, California's "driving under the influence" statute was fortified by the addition of former section 23126, which created a presumption of being under the influence if a driver had 0.10 percent or more by weight of alcohol in his blood. By 1972, 47 states had similar statutes. (Murray & Aitken, *The Constitutionality of California's Under-the-Influence-of-Alcohol Presumption* (1972) 45 So. Cal. L. Rev. 955, 958, fn. 8.)

Even these laws, which considerably assisted the prosecution of "driving under the influence" cases, proved inadequate in many respects. Under them, the ultimate question was defined in terms of the defendant's subjective behavior and condition: "Was the defendant under the influence at the time he drove?" Celerity and certainty of punishment were frustrated by the ambiguity of the legal criteria; no matter what his blood-alcohol level, a defendant could escape conviction merely by raising a doubt as to his intoxication.

In response to this continuing problem, in the past decade most states enacted additional legislation supplementing existing "driving under the influence" statutes and fashioned after what has been termed the "Scandinavian model." These statutes — which are most frequently subdivisions of a general "driving and alcohol" statute — define the substantive offense not by the subjective term "driving under the influence," but instead as the act of driving with a specified blood-alcohol level. Under these laws, proof of being "under the influence" is unnecessary. The statutes represent a legislative determination that public safety is endangered when a person drives a motor vehicle while having a specified percentage (typically 0.10) or more by weight of alcohol in his blood.

As noted, former section 23102 made it illegal to drive while under the influence of alcohol. Conviction required a showing that alcohol had "so far affected the nervous system, the brain, or muscles as to impair to an appreciable degree the ability to operate a vehicle in a manner like that of an ordinarily prudent and cautious person in full possession of his faculties." As explained above, prosecution under this section was facilitated by former section 23126, which established a presumption that a person with a blood alcohol level of 0.10 or more was under the influence of alcohol.

In an attempt to address the continuing threat to public safety posed by drinking drivers, in 1981 the Legislature retained the "driving under the influence" statute, renumbered it section 23152, subdivision (a), and added the statute at issue here, section 23152, subdivision (b), which provides: "It is unlawful for any person who has 0.10 percent or more, by weight, of alcohol in his or her blood to drive a vehicle. For purposes of this subdivision, percent, by weight, of alcohol shall be based upon grams of alcohol per 100 milliliters of blood."

At the urging of Congress,[3] statutes of this kind have recently been enacted in 28 states and the District of Columbia. Depending on the statutory scheme, these enactments create either a new offense, or an alternative definition of "driving under the influence," or a lesser included offense within driving under the influence. Our statute establishes a new and separate offense.

Contrary to assertions by amici curiae, some commentators, and one court, section 23152, subdivision (b), does not create a conclusive presumption of intoxication, nor does it "eliminate[] the prosecutor's burden of proof when the accused is found to have [0.10] percent, by weight, of alcohol in [his] blood." Instead, the statute defines, in precise terms, the conduct proscribed. In other states that have enacted a statute similar to section 23152, subdivision (b), the courts have drawn the same conclusion, notably the Washington Supreme Court which declared, "The statute does not presume, it defines."

---

3. 23 United States Code Annotated, section 408(e)(1)(C) (making enactment of a 0.10 percent blood-alcohol law mandatory for any state wishing to receive federal highway funds to support alcohol traffic safety programs).

Although under section 23152, subdivision (b), it is no longer necessary to prove that the defendant was in fact under the influence, the People still must prove beyond a reasonable doubt that at the time he was driving his blood alcohol exceeded 0.10 percent.[10]

Scientific evidence and sad experience demonstrate that any driver with 0.10 percent blood alcohol is a threat to the safety of the public and to himself. At least two states and several foreign countries have established standards between 0.05 percent and 0.08 percent. We have no difficulty concluding that the 0.10 percent figure fixed by section 23152, subdivision (b), is rationally related to exercise of the state's legitimate police power.

Five of our sister states have addressed claims of unconstitutional indefiniteness with respect to analogous 0.10 percent statutes, and all have found the contentions meritless. Defendant asserts, however, that we should not be persuaded by these decisions, because they fail to sufficiently analyze the issues and justify the results. We proceed to review defendant's claim that section 23152, subdivision (b), is void for vagueness.

Both article I, section 7, of the California Constitution and the Fourteenth Amendment to the United States Constitution declare that no person shall be deprived of life, liberty or property without due process of law. It has been recognized for over 80 years that due process requires inter alia some level of definiteness in criminal statutes. (Note, *Due Process Requirements of Definiteness in Statutes* (1948) 62 Harv. L. Rev. 77, 77, fn. 2.) Today it is established that due process requires a statute to be definite enough to provide (1) a standard of conduct for those whose activities are proscribed and (2) a standard for police enforcement and for ascertainment of guilt. *Connally v. General Const. Co.* (1926) 269 U.S. 385, 391.[15]

To begin with the second component, the statute could not be more precise as a standard for law enforcement. (Freund, *The Use of Indefinite Terms in Statutes* (1921) 30 Yale L.J. 437, 437.) It gives no discretion whatever to the police, and thus is not susceptible of arbitrary enforcement. Indeed, the very precision of the standard assures the statute's validity in this respect.

Turning now to the "fair notice" component of the void-for-vagueness doctrine, we observe that the real thrust of defendant's argument is that the statute is in effect "void for preciseness." His complaint is not that the language of the statute is vague or ambiguous, but that it is too exact. His novel theory is that the statute fails to notify potential violators of the condition it proscribes, because it is impossible for a person to determine by means of his senses whether his blood-alcohol level is a "legal" 0.09 percent or an "illegal" 0.10 percent. The latter observation is probably true as a matter of fact, but it does not affect the constitutionality of the statute.

---

10. Section 23152, subdivision (b), prohibits driving a vehicle with a blood-alcohol level of 0.10 percent or higher; it does not prohibit driving a vehicle when a subsequent test shows a level of 0.10 percent or more. Circumstantial evidence will generally be necessary to establish the requisite blood-alcohol level called for by the statute. A test for the proportion of alcohol in the blood will, obviously, be the usual type of circumstantial evidence, but of course the test is not conclusive: the defendant remains free to challenge the accuracy of the test result, the manner in which it was administered, and by whom. Of course, both parties may also adduce other circumstantial evidence tending to establish that the defendant did or did not have a 0.10 percent blood-alcohol level while driving.

15. The United States Supreme Court recently observed that "[although] the [void-for-vagueness] doctrine focuses both on actual notice to citizens and arbitrary enforcement, we have recognized recently that the more important aspect of vagueness doctrine 'is not actual notice, but the other principal element of the doctrine—the requirement that a legislature establish minimal guidelines to govern law enforcement.'" *Kolender v. Lawson* (1983) 461 U.S. 352.

Defendant's theory would render the void-for-vagueness doctrine internally inconsistent: the notice requirement would compete with the need to provide precise standards for law enforcement. When, as in the present case, a statutory standard requires scientific measurement, the very factor that assures due process under the "standards" component would violate due process under the "notice" component.

It is apparently defendant's contention that due process requires notice that is subjectively verifiable, according to the terms of the statute, at the instant before the alleged violation. He claims the statute is invalid because it is impossible for ordinary persons actually to know when their blood alcohol reaches the proscribed point. No court, however, has interpreted the notice requirement so strictly; indeed, such a view would invalidate many other criminal laws, violations of which depend on an after-the-fact determination by a judge or jury as to the defendant's state of mind or the reasonableness of his behavior.

"Fair notice" requires only that a violation be described with a "'reasonable degree of certainty'" so that "ordinary people can understand what conduct is prohibited." The notice provided must be such that prosecution does not "trap the innocent" without "fair warning."

One who drives a vehicle after having ingested sufficient alcohol to approach or exceed the level proscribed is neither "innocent" within the meaning of *Grayned*, nor is he without "fair warning." His behavior is not "innocent" because one who drives with a blood-alcohol content above 0.05 percent is in jeopardy of violating section 23152, subdivision (a), i.e., driving while under the influence. Indeed, in a number of states such a driver would be prima facie impaired well before he reached 0.10 percent. It is difficult to sympathize with an "unsuspecting" defendant who did not know if he could take a last sip without crossing the line, but who decided to do so anyway.

The very fact that he has consumed a quantity of alcohol should notify a person of ordinary intelligence that he is in jeopardy of violating the statute. Those who drink a substantial amount of alcohol within a relatively short period of time are given clear warning that to avoid possible criminal behavior they must refrain from driving. Although this factor alone sustains our determination that the statute provides adequate warning to potential violators, we find some further support in this regard from the existence for over 15 years of an analogous "0.10 percent" rebuttable presumption of being under the influence of alcohol pursuant to section 23155 and its predecessor, section 23126. Considering also today's heightened level of public awareness regarding the problem, we cannot believe that any person who drives after drinking would be unaware of the possibility that his blood-alcohol level might equal or exceed the statutory standard.

We decline to frustrate the Legislature's clear and legitimate purpose in enacting the statute involved here. We conclude that under both the federal and state Constitutions, section 23152, subdivision (b), provides adequate notice of the conduct proscribed, and is not void for vagueness.[21]

The judgment is affirmed.

---

21. We also reject the contentions of amici curiae that section 23152, subdivision (b), constitutes an impermissible discrimination against "those adult drivers who consume alcohol," or that it has an impermissible "chilling effect" on the right to travel. Equally untenable are assertions that the statute "invests the police with unlimited discretion to randomly stop and detain drivers," or that it somehow denies equal protection of the laws, or that it is invalid because mixed drinks from different bartenders may contain different amounts of alcohol.

Slipping Through the Cracks: Why Can't We Stop Drugged Driving?
Tina Wescott Cafaro

32 Western New England Law Review 33 (2010)

If you think about the dangerous people you share the roadways with when you get behind the wheel of your car and drive, you will likely consider the inattentive driver, the unskilled driver, the reckless driver, the cell-phone-talking-and-texting driver, and the drunk driver. But, how often do you contemplate a scenario where the driver of the vehicle next to you is under the influence of drugs? Many would argue not often enough. Little is heard of the dangerous crime of operating a motor vehicle while under the influence of drugs (OUI drugs), also called drugged driving.

Efforts to stop alcohol-impaired driving include numerous public-awareness campaigns, the expenditure of millions of dollars by both the government and private organizations, the demand for strict new legislation, and nation-wide implementation of uniform laws. While this has by no means eradicated the crime of alcohol-impaired driving, it has reduced the number of deaths on the highways. Unfortunately, the same focus has not been placed on stopping individuals from using drugs and driving a car. Typically, drugs are used for medicinal purposes, but some are also used for recreational purposes, mostly because of their psychoactive properties. Whether used for medicinal or recreational purposes, many drugs can impair a person's ability to drive. Millions of people in the United States and worldwide continue to take drugs, both licit and illicit, before driving a car.

Unfortunately, the fight against drugged driving must overcome many obstacles. One of the biggest problems is the lack of uniformity regarding what exactly constitutes the crime of drugged driving.

Nationwide, three different standards have been drafted in legislation defining what constitutes OUI drugs: two "effect-based" laws and one "per se" law. The first effect-based law requires that an OUI drug motorist be rendered incapable of driving due to drug use. The second effect-based law requires a demonstration that an OUI drug motorist's ability to operate a motor vehicle is impaired or that the motorist is under the influence or affected by an intoxicating drug while driving. Some per se laws set a limit on the amount of drug or drug metabolite in the driver's system at the time of the arrest. However, there was a lack of consensus as to the particular levels. As a result, states with per se laws now employ a "zero tolerance" per se law. This zero tolerance per se law prohibits motorists from operating a motor vehicle if there is any detectable level of illicit drug or drug metabolite in their body, regardless of whether the motorist operated the motor vehicle in an impaired manner.

While all fifty states have laws that include sanctions for OUI drugs, these laws differ dramatically both in substance and application. The majority of states have effect-based or "under the influence" statutes.

Proving impairment or incapacity in OUI drug cases is often very challenging because it is difficult to establish "a nexus between the observed impairment and a drug as required by most state statutes." Effect-based laws require law enforcement officers to employ a "driving under the influence of alcohol" approach, where officers evaluate a motorist suspected of driving under the influence of a drug in the same manner as they do an OUI alcohol suspect. This includes making observations of the motorist's driving, appearance, behavior, and coordination, and typically involves evidence regarding the defendant's performance on standardized field sobriety tests. The officer will then be asked to give an opinion as to the motorist's state of sobriety. Under these statutes, the prosecution must typically produce evidence that identifies the specific drug used by the suspect. With this comes a plethora of issues regarding opinion, expert, and scientific testimony.

A per se law that sets specific limits of concentrations of drugs that are permissible in a person's system, similar to the .08% blood alcohol content (BAC) limit in OUI alcohol cases, is easier to establish than an effect-based standard. [But], several factors make setting per se levels difficult: the sheer number of different drugs that need to be tested to determine specific concentration limits; the science behind the correlation between the effects of drugs and blood plasma levels; individual sensitivities and tolerance levels; individual differences in absorption, distribution, and metabolism; acute versus chronic administration of the drugs; the effect of accumulation; and the effect of combining drugs, both illicit and licit.

A zero tolerance law is the easiest standard to prove, as this law makes it a criminal act to operate a motor vehicle while any proscribed substance is in one's blood or system, regardless of the impact the drug has on one's ability to drive. Under zero tolerance laws, motorists only need to have a detectable amount of drug in their system to be guilty of OUI drugs. Opponents of the zero tolerance law argue that the law is unjust because an individual would be guilty of OUI drugs if they have even a miniscule amount of drugs in their system regardless of the issue of impairment. The example most often used is marijuana. Marijuana's primary active chemical is THC (delta-9-tetrahydrocannabinol), which is found in all forms of marijuana that are psychoactive. Because THC is absorbed and stored in fatty body tissue, including the brain, and due to the varying concentrations of THC, it is difficult to know the exact length of time traces are detectable in the body. However, full elimination of THC from the body can take several weeks while the peak effects of the drug appear after thirty to sixty minutes and typically last for two to four hours. For that reason, a motorist tested one week after using marijuana may still test positive although the effects have long worn off.

Given the magnitude of the number of combinations of different types of drugs and alcohol, it is easy to see why it is complicated to make a determination that an individual is under the influence of drugs. Even absent polysubstance use, it is difficult for a law enforcement officer to make a determination that a motorist is under the influence of drugs. Often times, the officer at first believes a motorist is under the influence of alcohol. It is not until the motorist takes a breathalyzer test resulting in a BAC indicating the absence of alcohol or a small amount of alcohol that the officer realizes that another substance may be in play. It is at this point in the investigation that a roadside device to test for the presence of drugs would be useful.

Unfortunately, a traditional breathalyzer test will not establish that one is under the influence of drugs. In order to establish that drugs are present in one's system, other tests such as blood, saliva, urine, sweat, and hair must be used. Theoretically, a law enforcement officer at the roadside can ask for any one of these samples of a suspected OUI drug motorist. Realistically, the easiest samples to collect and test are sweat, saliva, and, if proper facilities are available, urine. Developing devices, called roadside testing devices or point-of-contact-testing devices, that screen suspects for drug use and immediately provide drug test results has long been touted as one of the most important advances necessary to combat OUI drugs. Such testing devices do exist, and researchers continue to develop saliva and urine tests that will facilitate roadside testing for drugs. However, the question remains as to exactly what type of drugs these tests should screen for. Presently, most devices only screen for illicit narcotics, but many prescription and some over-the-counter drugs can also impair an individual's ability to operate a motor vehicle.

The European Union, with cooperation from four individual states of the United States, conducted a study from 2003 until 2005 to evaluate the usability and analytical reliability of roadside saliva drug-testing devices. The study evaluated nine different brands of devices administered to 2,046 subjects. Throughout the course of the study, 2,605 device evaluations were performed. All of the devices tested for the presence of the following illicit drugs: amphetamines, methamphetamine, marijuana, cocaine, and opiates, while three devices also had a test for prescription benzodiazepines. The study found that saliva was a good screening fluid for the presence or absence of amphetamines, marijuana, cocaine, and opiates in the body. However, the study exposed a number of impediments to the use of the devices: the failure rate of the devices, the sometimes too lengthy and complicated testing procedures, and the problems associated with the use of these devices during cold and rainy weather. "At the [conclusion] of the study, no device was considered to be reliable enough in order to be recommended for roadside screening of [motorists]." While research appears promising that saliva and other bodily fluid roadside testing can be accurate and indicative of drug use, further technological development and validation is needed before this testing will be generally accepted.

5. Drug Paraphernalia

South Dakota v. Holway

Supreme Court of South Dakota
644 N.W. 2d 624 (2002)

Gilbertson, CJ.

Thomas Holway is a co-owner of Video Blue, an adult bookstore in Rapid City, South Dakota. Ellie Holway is an employee at Video Blue. The Holways attended a trade show in Las Vegas and determined that it would be "very lucrative" to carry certain smoking devices for sale in the store. Thomas Holway contacted the Pennington County State's Attorney, Glenn Brenner (Brenner), to determine if selling the devices would be legal. Brenner read the statute to him and informed him that if it could be proven that the devices could be used for smoking marijuana, law enforcement would be involved.

When Thomas contacted Brenner a second time and showed him a "sample" pipe, Brenner referred him to Todd Love, the drug prosecutor for the Attorney General's Office. One of the Holways did contact Love with the same questions presented to Brenner. Love informed the Video Blue representative that it is illegal to deliver, or to possess with the intent to deliver, any drug paraphernalia. He also informed him that he would not be able to claim immunity based upon anything Brenner had said to them. Love explained that the State Attorney General's Office could prosecute Video Blue's owners and employees for drug violations even if the Pennington County State's Attorney did not.

In April 2000, the devices were put out for sale in two display cases at Video Blue. The display cases contained various items used for smoking including: pipes, water pipes, bongs, wood dugouts, and carburetors. They also contained roach clips and pipes disguised to look like cigarette lighters, lipstick containers, and hi-liter felt tip markers. Each display case had a sign stating "All paraphernalia sales are only sold with the understanding that the purchaser has only legal intent for its use." Yet, no cigarette or pipe tobacco was sold in the store.

On April 14, 2000, the South Dakota Division of Criminal Investigation (DCI) began investigating Video Blue based on allegations that drug paraphernalia was being sold there. Four officers were involved in the investigation: Deputy Sheriff Jeff Whittle (Whittle), Deputy Sheriff Martin Graves (Graves), Detective Dale McCabe (McCabe), and DCI Supervising Agent Robert Overturf (Overturf).

Whittle entered the store on April 14, 2000, and purchased a "one-hitter," a small water pipe, and a wood "dug-out" pipe from Ellie. Ellie gave him a free package of screens, which are commonly used to prevent a marijuana smoker from inhaling the seeds and stems. When Whittle made a comment about how a friend of his got caught selling items like these, Ellie pointed to the sign. Whittle mockingly replied that he, of course, had only legal intent. Ellie raised her hands and said, "Well, I don't want to know about it." She also acknowledged Whittle's comment about a wood dug-out being an "old standard."

Graves entered the store on April 18, 2000, and purchased a red bong and a metal pipe from Ellie. McCabe also entered the store on April 18. He purchased a school bus pipe and a blue hi-liter pipe from Ellie. McCabe asked Ellie if they made a pipe that looked like a police car. She replied "They would probably frown upon that." McCabe also inquired whether he could get a discount. Ellie spoke with Thomas, who agreed to the discount. She also gave McCabe a free package of screens.

Thomas and Ellie were each charged with seven counts of delivery of drug paraphernalia in violation of SDCL 22-42A-4 and SDCL 22-3-3. The two were tried together before a jury on June 5–6, 2001. Thomas and Ellie were each convicted on three of the seven counts and sentenced to 90 days in jail on count I, and two years in prison on counts III and VII. The terms were to run consecutively, with execution of the prison sentences suspended.

SDCL 22-42A-4 sets forth the elements for the crime of delivering drug paraphernalia:

> No person, knowing the drug[-]related nature of the object, may deliver, possess with intent to deliver, or manufacture with intent to deliver, drug paraphernalia, knowing, or under circumstances where one reasonably should know, that it will be used to ... contain, conceal, inject, ingest, inhale, or otherwise introduce into the human body a controlled substance or marijuana in violation of this chapter. Any person who violates any provision of this section is guilty of a Class 6 felony.

The term "drug paraphernalia" means any equipment, products and materials of any kind which are primarily used, intended for use or designed for use by the person in possession of them, ... containing, concealing, injecting, ingesting, inhaling or otherwise introducing into the human body any controlled substance or marijuana in violation of the provisions of this chapter. It includes, but is not limited to:

* * *

(10) Objects used, intended for use or designed for use in ingesting, inhaling or otherwise introducing marijuana, cocaine, hashish or hashish oil into the human body, such as:

(a) Metal, wooden, acrylic, glass, stone, plastic or ceramic pipes with or without screens, permanent screens, hashish heads or punctured metal bowls;

(b) Water pipes;

(c) Carburetion tubes and devices;

(d) Smoking and carburetion masks;

(e) Roach clips: meaning objects used to hold burning material, such as a marijuana cigarette, that has become too small or too short to be held in the hand;

(f) Miniature cocaine spoons and cocaine vials;

(g) Chamber pipes;

(h) Carburetor pipes;

(i) Electric pipes;

(j) Air-driven pipes;

(k) Chillums;

(l) Bongs; and

(m) Ice pipes or chillers.

Therefore, to sustain a conviction, the State is required to prove that: (1) the defendant delivered or possessed with the intent to deliver an object; (2) that object is drug paraphernalia; (3) the defendant knew of the drug-related nature of the object; and (4) the defendant knew or reasonably should have known that the object would be used to introduce illegal drugs into the human body.

The Holways claim that they cannot be guilty because SDCL 22-42A-1 requires those in possession to intend the objects for drug use. They claim that because they did not intend the items for drug use and the undercover officers to whom they sold the objects did not intend or actually use them for drugs, the conviction cannot be sustained. We disagree. The statute identifies drug paraphernalia in the disjunctive. It includes objects "primarily used" for drug use, objects intended for drug use by the person in possession of them, or objects designed for drug use by the person in possession of them. The Holways cannot escape liability by pretending to ignore the most common use of such objects.

While the Holways claim that the objects could have been used to smoke tobacco, we agree with the trial court's characterization of the items herein as being "primarily used" to introduce illegal drugs into the human body. The Holways also assert that they did not know of the objects' drug-related nature. But the jury was justifiably incredulous. It is difficult to believe that those who chose to sell such items because they would be "very lucrative," but who first made inquiries to the State's Attorney and the Attorney General to determine how they could escape liability, did not have a clue as to the drug-related and *illegal* nature of such items.

Ellie actually sold the items at issue. She gave both Whittle and McCabe the free packages of screens, which are commonly used for smoking marijuana, when they purchased the pipes. She indicated that she recognized a wood dug-out as being an "old standard." Yet, an expert witness testified that it certainly is not an "old standard" for smoking tobacco. When Whittle commented on the possible illegality of selling the items, she pointed to the sign and informed him that she did not want to know about his supposedly "legal intent." Her reply to McCabe's question of whether she had any pipes shaped like police cars indicates that she knew law enforcement would "frown upon" having a pipe, used for smoking marijuana, designed in such a shape.

Thomas not only owned the store that the items were sold in, but he was also intricately involved in stocking the items for sale. His statements to Brenner are indicative of his knowledge that the items he wished to sell were legally questionable, at best. The fact that he approved the discount to McCabe indicates he supervised the sales of the items. There was evidence that he displayed the items at issue with many others specifically enumerated within SDCL 22-42A-1(10) as constituting drug paraphernalia. Copies of *Cannabis*

Culture and *High Times*, magazines advocating drug use, show photographs advertising the very same objects.

The facts laid out above give sufficient reason for a jury to believe, beyond a reasonable doubt, that not only were the objects drug paraphernalia, but that Thomas and Ellie knew or reasonably should have known of the objects' drug-related nature. Accepting, as we must, the evidence and the most favorable inferences to be drawn therefrom in favor of the verdict, we do not see that the judgment was in error. Therefore, we affirm the decision of the trial court.

Village of Hoffman Estates v. The Flipside

Supreme Court of the United States
455 U.S. 489 (1982)

Justice Marshall delivered the opinion of the Court.

For more than three years prior to May 1, 1978, appellee The Flipside sold a variety of merchandise, including phonographic records, smoking accessories, novelty devices, and jewelry, in its store located in the village of Hoffman Estates, Ill. On February 20, 1978, the village enacted an ordinance regulating drug paraphernalia, to be effective May 1, 1978. The ordinance makes it unlawful for any person "to sell any items, effect, paraphernalia, accessory or thing which is designed or marketed for use with illegal cannabis or drugs, as defined by Illinois Revised Statutes, without obtaining a license therefor." The license fee is $150. A business must also file affidavits that the licensee and its employees have not been convicted of a drug-related offense. Moreover, the business must keep a record of each sale of a regulated item, including the name and address of the purchaser, to be open to police inspection. No regulated item may be sold to a minor. A violation is subject to a fine of not less than $10 and not more than $500, and each day that a violation continues gives rise to a separate offense. A series of licensing guidelines prepared by the Village Attorney define "Paper," "Roach Clips," "Pipes," and "Paraphernalia," the sale of which is required to be licensed.

After an administrative inquiry, the village determined that Flipside and one other store appeared to be in violation of the ordinance. The Village Attorney notified Flipside of the existence of the ordinance, and made a copy of the ordinance and guidelines available to Flipside. Flipside's owner asked for guidance concerning which items were covered by the ordinance; the Village Attorney advised him to remove items in a certain section of the store "for his protection," and he did so. The items included, according to Flipside's description, a clamp, chain ornaments, an "alligator" clip, key chains, necklaces, earrings, cigarette holders, glove stretchers, scales, strainers, a pulverizer, squeeze bottles, pipes, water pipes, pins, an herb sifter, mirrors, vials, cigarette rolling papers, and tobacco snuff. On May 30, 1978, instead of applying for a license or seeking clarification via the administrative procedures that the village had established for its licensing ordinances, Flipside filed this lawsuit in the United States District Court for the Northern District of Illinois.

The complaint alleged, *inter alia*, that the ordinance is unconstitutionally vague and overbroad, and requested injunctive and declaratory relief and damages. The District Court ... issued an opinion upholding the constitutionality of the ordinance, and awarded judgment to the village defendants.

The Court of Appeals reversed on the ground that the ordinance is unconstitutionally vague on its face. The court reviewed the language of the ordinance and guidelines and found it vague with respect to certain conceivable applications, such as ordinary pipes or "paper clips sold next to *Rolling Stone* magazine." It also suggested that the "subjective" nature of the "marketing" test creates a danger of arbitrary and discriminatory enforcement against those with alternative lifestyles. Finally, the court determined that the availability of administrative review or guidelines cannot cure the defect. Thus, it concluded that the ordinance is impermissibly vague on its face.

In a facial challenge to the overbreadth and vagueness of a law,[5] a court's first task is to determine whether the enactment reaches a substantial amount of constitutionally protected conduct. If it does not, then the overbreadth challenge must fail. A plaintiff who engages in some conduct that is clearly proscribed cannot complain of the vagueness of the law as applied to the conduct of others. A court should therefore examine the complainant's conduct before analyzing other hypothetical applications of the law.

We first examine whether the ordinance infringes Flipside's First Amendment rights or is overbroad because it inhibits the First Amendment rights of other parties. Flipside makes the exorbitant claim that the village has imposed a "prior restraint" on speech because the guidelines treat the proximity of drug-related literature as an indicium that paraphernalia are "marketed for use with illegal cannabis or drugs." Flipside also argues that because the presence of drug-related designs, logos, or slogans on paraphernalia may trigger enforcement, the ordinance infringes "protected symbolic speech."

These arguments do not long detain us. First, the village has not directly infringed the noncommercial speech of Flipside or other parties. The ordinance licenses and regulates the sale of items displayed "with" or "within proximity of" "literature encouraging illegal use of cannabis or illegal drugs," but does not prohibit or otherwise regulate the sale of literature itself. Although drug-related designs or names on cigarette papers may subject those items to regulation, the village does not restrict speech as such, but simply regulates the commercial marketing of items that the labels reveal may be used for an illicit purpose. The scope of the ordinance therefore does not embrace noncommercial speech.

Second, insofar as any *commercial* speech interest is implicated here, it is only the attenuated interest in displaying and marketing merchandise in the manner that the retailer desires. We doubt that the village's restriction on the manner of marketing appreciably limits Flipside's communication of information—with one obvious and telling exception. The ordinance is expressly directed at commercial activity promoting or encouraging illegal drug use. If that activity is deemed "speech," then it is speech proposing an illegal transaction, which a government may regulate or ban entirely.

A law that does not reach constitutionally protected conduct and therefore satisfies the overbreadth test may nevertheless be challenged on its face as unduly vague, in violation of due process. To succeed, however, the complainant must demonstrate that the law is impermissibly vague in all of its applications. Flipside makes no such showing.

Flipside's facial challenge fails because, under the test appropriate to either a quasi-criminal or a criminal law, the ordinance is sufficiently clear as applied to Flipside.

---

5. A "facial" challenge, in this context, means a claim that the law is "invalid *in toto*—and therefore incapable of any valid application." *Steffel v. Thompson,* 415 U.S. 452, 474 (1974).

The ordinance requires Flipside to obtain a license if it sells "any items, effect, paraphernalia, accessory or thing which is designed or marketed for use with illegal cannabis or drugs, as defined by the Illinois Revised Statutes." Flipside expresses no uncertainty about which drugs this description encompasses; as the District Court noted, Illinois law clearly defines cannabis and numerous other controlled drugs, including cocaine. On the other hand, the words "items, effect, paraphernalia, accessory or thing" do not identify the type of merchandise that the village desires to regulate. Flipside's challenge thus appropriately focuses on the language "designed or marketed for use." Under either the "designed for use" or "marketed for use" standard, we conclude that at least some of the items sold by Flipside are covered. Thus, Flipside's facial challenge is unavailing.

The Court of Appeals objected that "designed ... for use" is ambiguous with respect to whether items must be inherently suited only for drug use; whether the retailer's intent or manner of display is relevant; and whether the intent of a third party, the manufacturer, is critical, since the manufacturer is the "designer." For the reasons that follow, we conclude that this language is not unconstitutionally vague on its face.

The Court of Appeals' speculation about the meaning of "design" is largely unfounded. The guidelines refer to "paper of colorful design" and to other specific items as conclusively "designed" or not "designed" for illegal use. A principal meaning of "design" is "[to] fashion according to a plan." It is therefore plain that the standard encompasses at least an item that is principally used with illegal drugs by virtue of its objective features, *i.e.*, features designed by the manufacturer. A business person of ordinary intelligence would understand that this term refers to the design of the manufacturer, not the intent of the retailer or customer. It is also sufficiently clear that items which are principally used for nondrug purposes, such as ordinary pipes, are not "designed for use" with illegal drugs. Moreover, no issue of fair warning is present in this case, since Flipside concedes that the phrase refers to structural characteristics of an item.

The ordinance and guidelines do contain ambiguities. Nevertheless, the "designed for use" standard is sufficiently clear to cover at least some of the items that Flipside sold. The ordinance, through the guidelines, explicitly regulates "roach clips." Flipside's co-operator admitted that the store sold such items and the village Chief of Police testified that he had never seen a "roach clip" used for any purpose other than to smoke cannabis. The Chief also testified that a specially designed pipe that Flipside marketed is typically used to smoke marihuana. Whether further guidelines, administrative rules, or enforcement policy will clarify the more ambiguous scope of the standard in other respects is of no concern in this facial challenge.

Whatever ambiguities the "designed ... for use" standard may engender, the alternative "marketed for use" standard is transparently clear: it describes a retailer's intentional display and marketing of merchandise. The guidelines refer to the display of paraphernalia, and to the proximity of covered items to otherwise uncovered items. A retail store therefore must obtain a license if it deliberately displays its wares in a manner that appeals to or encourages illegal drug use. The standard requires scienter, since a retailer could scarcely "market" items "for" a particular use without intending that use.

Under this test, Flipside had ample warning that its marketing activities required a license. Flipside displayed the magazine *High Times* and books entitled *Marijuana Grower's Guide, Children's Garden of Grass*, and *The Pleasures of Cocaine*, physically close to pipes and colored rolling papers, in clear violation of the guidelines. As noted above, Flipside's co-operator admitted that his store sold "roach clips," which are principally used for illegal purposes. Finally, in the same section of the store, Flipside had posted the sign, "You must be 18 or older to purchase any head supplies."[20]

The Court of Appeals also held that the ordinance provides insufficient standards for enforcement. Specifically, the court feared that the ordinance might be used to harass individuals with alternative lifestyles and views. In reviewing a business regulation for facial vagueness, however, the principal inquiry is whether the law affords fair warning of what is proscribed. Moreover, this emphasis is almost inescapable in reviewing a pre-enforcement challenge to a law. Here, no evidence has been, or could be, introduced to indicate whether the ordinance has been enforced in a discriminatory manner or with the aim of inhibiting unpopular speech. The language of the ordinance is sufficiently clear that the speculative danger of arbitrary enforcement does not render the ordinance void for vagueness.

We do not suggest that the risk of discriminatory enforcement is insignificant here. Testimony of the Village Attorney who drafted the ordinance, the village President, and the Police Chief revealed confusion over whether the ordinance applies to certain items, as well as extensive reliance on the "judgment" of police officers to give meaning to the ordinance and to enforce it fairly. At this stage, however, we are not prepared to hold that this risk jeopardizes the entire ordinance.[21]

"Although it is possible that specific future applications ... may engender concrete problems of constitutional dimension, it will be time enough to consider any such problems when they arise." *Joseph E. Seagram & Sons, Inc.* v. *Hostetter*, 384 U.S. 35, 52 (1966).[22]

Many American communities have recently enacted laws regulating or prohibiting the sale of drug paraphernalia. To determine whether these laws are wise or effective is not, of course, the province of this Court. We hold only that such legislation is not facially overbroad or vague if it does not reach constitutionally protected conduct and is reasonably clear in its application to the complainant.

The application of drug paraphernalia laws to syringes has been particularly controversial. While syringes, when used to inject illegal drugs, would easily meet the definition of many drug paraphernalia statutes, there is a great deal of evidence that suggests giving injection drug users access to clean syringes helps reduce the spread of blood borne infections such as HIV. The following excerpt provides an overview of some of the legal and policy issues related to the distribution of syringes to injection drug users.

---

20. The American Heritage Dictionary of the English Language 606 (1980) gives the following alternative definition of "head": "Slang. One who is a frequent user of drugs."

21. The theoretical possibility that the village will enforce its ordinance against a paper clip placed next to *Rolling Stone* magazine is of no due process significance unless the possibility ripens into a prosecution.

22. The Court of Appeals also referred to potential Fourth Amendment problems resulting from the recordkeeping requirement, which "implies that a customer who purchases an item 'designed or marketed for use with illegal cannabis or drugs' intends to *use* the item with illegal cannabis or drugs. A further implication could be that a customer is subject to police scrutiny or even to a search warrant on the basis of the purchase of a legal item." We will not address these Fourth Amendment issues here. In a pre-enforcement challenge it is difficult to determine whether Fourth Amendment rights are seriously threatened. Flipside offered no evidence of a concrete threat below. In a postenforcement proceeding Flipside may attempt to demonstrate that the ordinance is being employed in such an unconstitutional manner, and that it has standing to raise the objection. It is appropriate to defer resolution of these problems until such a showing is made.

Lethal Injections: The Law, Science, and Politics of Syringe Access for Injection Drug Users
Scott Burris, Steffanie A. Strathdee, and Jon S. Vernick
37 University of San Francisco Law Review 813 (2003)

Access to sterile syringes through syringe exchange programs (SEPs) has been associated with decreased rates of needle sharing, decreased prevalence and incidence of blood borne infections such as HIV and hepatitis B and C, and increased rates of entry into drug treatment among injection drug users (IDUs). There is no evidence that such programs increase crime, drug use or the number of discarded needles on the street. Pharmacies, syringe vending machines, and deregulating syringe access can further expand sterile syringe coverage to IDUs, thereby increasing the potential to achieve these positive public health outcomes.

Despite its public health value, however, syringe access has been politically controversial in the United States. In our political culture, driven by symbols and perceptions, improved syringe access has been painted as "soft on drugs," a retreat from zero tolerance that will be seen as an endorsement of drug use. Polls continue to show that only a little more than half of respondents support enhanced syringe access—a majority, but evidently one that is too narrow or uncommitted to counterbalance the intense symbolic force of the syringe access issue in policy-making. Syringe access, then, is quite a familiar public health policy dilemma: science and professional judgment point to an intervention that is unsettling, if not absolutely unacceptable, to a significant part of the United States public and its political leaders.

Syringe access is regulated by state law. The legal regulation of syringe access varies from state to state but takes one or more of three forms: syringe prescription laws and regulations; other pharmacy regulations or miscellaneous statutes imposing a variety of restrictions on the sale of syringes by pharmacists or others; and drug paraphernalia laws prohibiting the sale or possession of items intended to be used to consume illegal drugs. Laws on drug possession also may be applied in a manner that in practical terms regulate the possession of syringes and so must also be considered for their possible effects on syringe access.

Access to injection equipment has been regulated at the state level for many years. The hypodermic syringe came into common usage in the latter half of the nineteenth century, often as a means for injecting opiates such as morphine and heroin. As rates of opiate addiction began to increase, states responded with legislation making it more difficult for drug users to obtain syringes. New York State enacted the first such law in 1911. Among other provisions, New York's law required a written order from a physician before a syringe could be obtained. Beginning in 1915, several other states, mostly in the east, followed New York's lead and enacted their own laws limiting the availability of syringes.

Legislative efforts to restrict access to injection equipment were not limited to the early part of the past century, however. Another important flurry of activity occurred in the 1970s with the rapid adoption of state laws criminalizing the possession of certain devices, including syringes, used to inject illegal drugs. These so-called "drug paraphernalia" laws were often patterned after a Model Drug Paraphernalia Act (MDPA) written by the Drug Enforcement Agency in 1979 at the request of President Carter. They were originally intended to provide a means of prosecuting operators of "head shops"—stores specializing in equipment for drug users. By 1976, it was estimated that between fifteen and thirty thousand of these stores were doing an annual three billion dollar business in such items as cigarette rolling papers, bongs, and freebasing kits. Syringes were not generally mentioned in the legislative debates or court challenges to these laws, nor is it even clear that syringes were being sold in head shops. Debate about the laws usually focused on their breadth and the danger that innocent sellers of items with both legal and illegal uses (such as rolling papers or scales) might be prosecuted. In a few states, the model law was amended to explicitly exclude pharmacists, but in most states the possibility that pharmacists would be covered through the laws' reference to needles was apparently not considered. Until the emergence of HIV, these laws were seen exclusively in the context of the control of drug abuse.

HIV changed that as transmission through drug injection was recognized as a serious threat to public health. The first syringe exchange program (SEP) was introduced in Amsterdam, the Netherlands, in 1984. The program, initiated by a drug user organization whose name may loosely be translated as the Junkies' Union, was soon adopted by the Municipal Health Department of Amsterdam, where it became a fundamental component of HIV prevention activities among IDUs. In the late 1980s, SEPs were introduced in the United Kingdom, Australia, Canada, and several other European countries. Global expansion of SEPs has occurred in both developed and developing countries, including China, Russia, the Ukraine, Kyrgyzstan, Nepal, Bangladesh, India, Pakistan, and Colombia. "As of December 2000, there were at least 46 regions, countries and territories that reported having at least one SEP."

In the United States, the first SEP was introduced in 1988, in Tacoma, Washington, and spread with the help of non-governmental organizations such as the National AIDS Brigade, the North American Syringe Exchange Network, and Act-Up. Expert reviews of the science supported syringe exchange, but early commentators generally assumed that syringe exchange was illegal in the United States unless explicitly authorized by state law. By 1995, there were at least 60 SEPs operating in 46 cities in 21 states. A review of the legal strategies used to implement these SEPs found that 27 programs in ten jurisdictions had been authorized by law or court decision, or were in a state without a syringe-related law. Thirteen programs were operating without any change in law, backed by local governments exercising their legal authority to protect public health. At least nine SEPs were operating without any claim to legal authorization.

Since the beginning of the HIV epidemic, twelve states (Connecticut, Hawaii, Illinois, Maine, Minnesota, New Hampshire, New Mexico, New York, Oregon, Rhode Island, Washington, and Wisconsin) have deregulated the sale or possession of at least some number of syringes. In others, notably California, efforts at deregulation have been unsuccessful. To date, no state that has liberalized syringe access in response to HIV has rescinded the change, but change continues to be a controversial matter in states that maintain restrictive access policies.

Public health authorities recommend that injection drug users use a new, sterile syringe for every injection. Despite the continued growth of syringe exchange, and the deregulation of syringes in one-fifth of the states, the United States has consistently fallen far short of this public health goal. In the third decade of its HIV epidemic, the United States continues to debate whether and how to make syringes available to injection drug users.

Thirteen states and the Virgin Islands impose some form of syringe prescription requirement by statute. Pennsylvania requires a prescription by pharmacy board regulation, not by statute. The prescription requirement stands as a substantial barrier to syringe access in only six of these jurisdictions: California, Delaware, Massachusetts, New Jersey, Pennsylvania, and the Virgin Islands. In Florida and Virginia, a prescription is required only for minors. In Nevada, a prescription is not required for syringes to be used for asthma, diabetes, or other medical conditions; these exceptions, in combination with a favorable view of syringe sales from the pharmacy board, have reportedly led to reasonably liberal syringe access in the state. The remaining five prescription-law states — Connecticut, Illinois, New Hampshire, New York, and Maine — have partially deregulated syringes and now allow non-prescription sale and possession of syringes in limited numbers. Illinois, like Florida and Virginia, does not permit non-prescription sale to minors.

Four other types of restriction on the sale of syringes appear in state law, usually but not always within the Pharmacy Code. Twenty-two states allow only pharmacies to sell syringes. Nine require the seller to determine, or the buyer to produce information about, how the syringe will be used. Fourteen require records of some type to be kept. Eleven require the buyer to show identification. Finally, twelve states specify limits on the display of syringes in retail establishments, normally requiring that they be kept behind the counter.

The District of Columbia and every jurisdiction studied except Alaska and Puerto Rico have drug paraphernalia laws. Most of these laws were passed in the 1970s and 1980s to regulate an increasing retail trade in drug-use equipment, and closely followed a model paraphernalia law drafted by the United States Department of Justice. The typical statute defines drug paraphernalia to include all equipment, products, and materials of any kind which are used, intended for use, or designed for use to "manufacture, inject, ingest, inhale, or otherwise introduce into the human body a controlled substance" in violation of law. It then provides an exemplary list of items that could be considered drug paraphernalia in some intended uses. In the majority of states, this list includes "hypodermic syringes, needles, and other objects used, intended for use, and designed for use in parenterally injecting controlled substances into the human body." Under this definition, the status of any item as paraphernalia depends not just on the characteristics of the item itself but also on the intention or acts of the defendant. To commit a crime, the seller must not only transfer possession of the syringe, but must do so knowing of the intended drug-related use. Paraphernalia laws usually create two basic offenses: manufacturing or distributing and possessing paraphernalia. Not every state has created both offenses. The crime is typically a misdemeanor.

Nearly all state paraphernalia laws follow the same pattern, though there are small but important differences in many states that influence the applicability of paraphernalia laws to syringes. In addition to the states ... that have fully or partially deregulated syringes as a public health measure, a significant minority of states have provisions that, at least on paper, make it legal under some circumstances for a seller knowingly to dispense a syringe to an IDU. These exemptions ... take several forms. Ten state paraphernalia laws explicitly or implicitly exempt the possession of syringes in at least some quantity. Indiana's statute, for example, exempts items "historically and customarily used in connection with the ... injecting ... of ... lawful substances," thus, at least in theory, legalizing over-the-counter pharmacy sales of syringes. In nine states, pharmacists and in some instances other health care providers are exempt from the law. In four states with laws based on the Justice Department's model act, the drafters of the paraphernalia law chose to depart from the model and did not refer to injection or syringes in the text of the law. Although the broad definition of paraphernalia reasonably could be deemed to include syringes even without explicit reference, the decision to omit the references while otherwise adopting the Justice Department model could be read by a judge as evidence of a legislative decision not to prohibit syringe sale and possession. In a fifth state, South Carolina, the statute was not based on the model act: it does not allude to injection or syringes, and more importantly does not apply to items to be used in the consumption of heroin. In states that have both paraphernalia and prescription laws, the interaction of the two must be assessed individually.

Paraphernalia laws were broadly written to criminalize sale or possession of any item intended to be used to facilitate illegal drug use. In theory, items that are used in drug injection — like cotton and small vessels used to dissolve drugs ("cookers") and even bleach kits — are legally indistinguishable from syringes. Because items used in drug preparation have also been implicated in the spread of blood borne diseases, especially hepatitis C virus, public health agencies and syringe exchange programs have routinely distributed them along with syringes. In areas where syringe exchange has not been authorized, some agencies distribute bleach kits as an alternative harm reduction measure. With the political focus on syringe access, the potential legal ambiguity of these other activities was largely ignored. In recent years, however, there have been anecdotal reports of SEPs being deterred from offering, and IDUs being arrested for possessing, sterile cookers and cotton. Efforts to import specially designed sterile cookers that have been used in other countries' public health efforts have been affected by concern about the potential application of paraphernalia laws. The problem does not appear to be widespread, but does illustrate the potential scope of drug paraphernalia laws.

6. Pregnancy and Substance Use

Pregnant Drug Users, Fetal Persons, and the Threat to Roe v. Wade
Lynn M. Paltrow
62 Albany Law Review 999 (1999)

Since the late 1980s, legislatures have considered numerous bills concerning pregnant women who use drugs or alcohol. Legislative proposals ranged from bills that would increase services and treatment to pregnant women and their children, to ones that would make it a crime for a pregnant woman with a substance abuse problem to give birth. For most of the late 1980s and 1990s, legislatures rejected the most punitive approaches. For example, in 1990, thirty-four states debated bills relating to prenatal exposure to drugs. Fourteen states passed bills designed to help pregnant women through prevention and education. Six states established studies to determine the extent of the problem. Eight states considered, but failed to pass, legislation that would make it a crime to be addicted and to give birth.

Many states, however, began to amend their civil child abuse laws to mandate reporting of pregnant women or newborns who tested positive for drugs. The result put women into the civil child welfare system as suspected child abusers, often resulting in temporary or permanent loss of custody based on nothing more than a single positive drug test. Today, twelve states require that evidence of a woman's drug use during pregnancy be reported to child welfare agencies, and these, along with three other states, now require drug testing of newborns or pregnant women. In some other states women are reported as a matter of policy. In addition, some states, even without legislation, have attempted to expand the scope of their civil child abuse laws to include a woman's conduct during pregnancy.

Despite the fact that no state passed a law criminalizing pregnancy and drug addiction, an estimated 200 women have been prosecuted around the country on theories of fetal abuse. Police and prosecutors attempted to expand the reach of existing criminal laws to punish pregnant women, relying on child abuse, drug delivery, manslaughter, homicide and assault-with-a-deadly-weapon statutes.

During the late 1980s, the public was saturated with media reports about crack cocaine. Unsupported and highly misleading stories, specifically on the effects of prenatal exposure to cocaine, also received widespread coverage. These stories often reported preliminary research studies suggesting potential harm to developing fetuses as conclusive findings of permanent and severe damage to every child exposed prenatally. These studies, typical of an emerging area of medical research, were not rigorous, and given their preliminary nature, raised as many questions as they answered. Unfortunately, in the media frenzy around "crack" this research was reported widely to the public without relaying any caution about the limitations and preliminary nature of the research.

More rigorous research, however, disproved much of the early work, but was not widely reported. As research physicians in the field have observed: "Children exposed to cocaine prenatally ... have been portrayed in the popular media as inevitably and permanently damaged ... The public outcry for the punishment of substance-using mothers and the disenfranchisement of their children as unsalvageable almost demonic "biologic underclass" rests not on scientific findings but upon media hysteria fueled by selected anecdotes."

Kentucky v. Welch

Supreme Court of Kentucky
864 S.W. 2d 280 (1993)

Leibson, J.

Connie Welch was arrested on November 7, 1989, when police, while executing a warrant at the home of a suspected drug dealer, found Welch in possession of oxycodone, a Schedule II narcotic, and syringes. Welch was under the influence of the oxycodone, having just injected some into her jugular vein. Because she was eight months pregnant when arrested, she was not taken into custody but simply given a date to appear in court.

On December 1, 1989, Welch gave birth to a son. Because Welch informed the attending physician of her continued drug dependency, even after arrest, he admitted the baby to the neonatal intensive care unit to be observed for neonatal abstinence syndrome. The toxicology report was negative for oxycodone, but positive for nicotine and caffeine.

The baby was born full term, without birth defects, and his size and weight were appropriate for his gestational age. Further, there was no evidence the baby was going to have a long-term disability, but the baby suffered from symptoms diagnosed as neonatal abstinence syndrome attributed to the baby having become passively addicted to drugs by being exposed through the mother's drug abuse during pregnancy. When the baby was delivered the drug supply was cut off by the act of severing the umbilical cord. The symptoms were: mild temperature, irritable, tremulous and jittery, cried a lot, and some mottling of the skin. Neonatal abstinence syndrome carries with it the possibility of much more serious complications which did not occur, including convulsions and seizures which could cause the cessation of breathing and result in permanent brain damage or death. The baby was released to its mother on December 11, 1989, in good health.

On January 11, 1990, the Boyd County Grand Jury returned an indictment charging Welch with criminal abuse in the second degree, possession of a Schedule II narcotic, and possession of drug paraphernalia. The criminal abuse count, as amended, alleged the baby had suffered neonatal abstinence syndrome and the "abuse" continued up through and including December 11, 1989, when Welch and the baby were released from the hospital.

On May 23, 1990, Welch was found guilty of all charges.

The Court of Appeals affirmed her convictions for possession of a controlled substance and of drug paraphernalia, and vacated her conviction on the criminal abuse charge. We granted the Commonwealth's petition for review of that portion of the opinion reversing the criminal abuse charge. For reasons to be stated, we affirm the decision of the Court of Appeals.

Welch's counsel presents various arguments as to why the criminal abuse statute does not apply to the present fact situation: (1) under the authority of *Hollis v. Commonwealth*, 652 S.W.2d 61 (1983) and *Jones v. Commonwealth*, 830 S.W.2d 877 (1992), a fetus is not a "person" as that word is used in KRS 508.110, the criminal abuse statute used to prosecute Welch; (2) construing KRS 508.110 to cover the present fact situation violates the statute's intent; (3) the statute so construed violates the due process guarantee of fair notice, i.e., it would be unconstitutionally vague; (4) the statute so construed operates as a constitutionally impermissible *ex post facto* law; and (5) the prosecutor's application of the statutes leads to results that are irrational and counterproductive of legislative intent as expressed through H.B. 192, Ch. 442, 1992 Acts, the Maternal Health Act.

The Court of Appeals limited its opinion to the first of these arguments, finding that our decision in the *Hollis* case was controlling and excluded abuse of a fetus from the purview of the criminal abuse statute, albeit the fetus was later born alive and suffered from symptoms causally related to the mother's previous drug abuse.

Applying *Hollis* to the present case, the Court of Appeals reasoned that criminal abuse of a fetus, like murder of the fetus, is not punishable as a discrete criminal offense separate from the crime committed against the mother, however morally reprehensible it may be.

The Commonwealth attacks this conclusion because in this instance the baby was born alive and the effects of past criminal activity caused the baby to suffer postpartum from neonatal abstinence syndrome.

When we look for valid reasons upon which to decide this case, we find two separate problems raised by the facts.

The first problem is: did the General Assembly intend to include within the scope of the criminal abuse statutes prenatal abuse causing injury which carries over the postpartum state? To further complicate this first issue, here the particular mode of abuse, the mother's use of drugs, was *not* a direct cause of postpartum injury but an indirect cause: it was the *withdrawal* of drugs to which the baby had become passively addicted, rather than the *absorption* of these drugs, which was the immediate cause of the baby's neonatal abstinence syndrome.

We will not undertake to engage the complexities of this first problem because the second problem is dispositive of the case. The second problem is: did the General Assembly intend to include prenatal injury from a pregnant woman's self-abuse as well as injury inflicted by a third person? In *Hollis* the neonatal injury was caused by a blow administered by an outsider; the issue here is the mother's self-abuse, which also had the effect of transmitting drugs to the baby through the umbilical cord.

The mother was a drug addict. But, for that matter, she could have been a pregnant alcoholic, causing fetal alcohol syndrome; or she could have been addicted to self abuse by smoking, or by abusing prescription painkillers, or over-the-counter medicine; or for that matter she could have been addicted to downhill skiing or some other sport creating serious risk of prenatal injury, risk which the mother wantonly disregarded as a matter of self-indulgence. What if a pregnant woman drives over the speed limit, or as a matter of vanity doesn't wear the prescription lenses she knows she needs to see the dangers of the road? The defense asks where do we draw the line on self-abuse by a pregnant woman that wantonly exposes to risk her unborn baby? The Commonwealth replies that the General Assembly probably intended to draw the line at conduct that qualifies as criminal, and then leave it to the prosecutor to decide when such conduct should be prosecuted as child abuse in addition to the crime actually committed.

However, it is inflicting intentional or wanton injury upon the child that makes the conduct criminal under the child abuse statutes, not the criminality of the conduct *per se*. The Commonwealth's approach would exclude alcohol abuse, however devastating to the baby in the womb, unless the Commonwealth could prove an act of drunk driving; but it is the mother's alcoholism, not the act of driving that causes the fetal alcohol syndrome. The "case-by-case" approach suggested by the Commonwealth is so arbitrary that, if the criminal child abuse statutes are construed to support it, the statutes transgress reasonably identifiable limits; they lack fair notice and violate constitutional due process limits against statutory vagueness. As stated recently and persuasively by a Pennsylvania trial court in a case factually similar to this one:

> "If the statutes at issue are applied to women's conduct during pregnancy, they could have an unlimited scope and create an indefinite number of new 'crimes.'... In short, the District Attorney's interpretation of the statutes, if validated, might lead to a 'slippery slope' whereby the law could be construed as covering the full range of a pregnant woman's behavior—a plainly unconstitutional result that would, among other things, render the statutes void for vagueness."

For the foregoing reasons, the decision of the Court of Appeals is affirmed.

F. Constitutional Limitations on the Criminalization of Drug Use and Addiction

From the Fourth Amendment to the free exercise of religion under the First Amendment to the scope of Congress' Commerce power, drug laws and their enforcement have impacted a range of constitutional provisions. Constitutional cases involving drug laws appear throughout this book. This section focuses on the constitutional boundaries of the criminalization of drug use and addiction. With nearly one and a half million drug possession arrests every year, the constitutionality of making drug possession a crime seems self-evident. But in the 1968 case *Powell v. Texas*, four members of the United States Supreme Court argued in dissent that punishing an addict for conduct which is "part of the pattern of his disease" is inconsistent with the Eighth Amendment. If just one more Justice had adopted the dissent's view in *Powell*, the constitutionality of prosecuting drug addicts for possessing their substance of addiction would have been in serious question. Six years before *Powell*, in *Robinson v. California*, a majority of the Court struck down a law that made it a crime to "be addicted to the use of narcotics."

1. The Prohibition Against "Status" Crimes

Robinson v. California
United State Supreme Court
370 U.S. 660 (1962)

Mr. Justice Stewart delivered the opinion of the Court.

A California statute makes it a criminal offense for a person to "be addicted to the use of narcotics." This appeal draws into question the constitutionality of that provision of the state law, as construed by the California courts in the present case.

The appellant was convicted after a jury trial in the Municipal Court of Los Angeles. The evidence against him was given by two Los Angeles police officers. Officer Brown testified that he had had occasion to examine the appellant's arms one evening on a street in Los Angeles some four months before the trial. The officer testified that at that time he had observed "scar tissue and discoloration on the inside" of the appellant's right arm, and "what appeared to be numerous needle marks and a scab which was approximately three inches below the crook of the elbow" on the appellant's left arm. The officer also testified that the appellant under questioning had admitted to the occasional use of narcotics.

Officer Lindquist testified that he had examined the appellant the following morning in the Central Jail in Los Angeles. The officer stated that at that time he had observed discolorations and scabs on the appellant's arms, and he identified photographs which had been taken of the appellant's arms shortly after his arrest the night before. Based upon more than ten years of experience as a member of the Narcotic Division of the Los Angeles Police Department, the witness gave his opinion that "these marks and the discoloration were the result of the injection of hypodermic needles into the tissue into the vein that was not sterile." He stated that the scabs were several days old at the time of his examination, and that the appellant was neither under the influence of narcotics nor suffering withdrawal symptoms at the time he saw him. This witness also testified that the appellant had admitted using narcotics in the past.

The appellant testified in his own behalf, denying the alleged conversations with the police officers and denying that he had ever used narcotics or been addicted to their use. He explained the marks on his arms as resulting from an allergic condition contracted during his military service. His testimony was corroborated by two witnesses.

The jury returned a verdict finding the appellant "guilty of the offense charged." An appeal was taken to the Appellate Department of the Los Angeles County Superior Court, "the highest court of a State in which a decision could be had" in this case. Although expressing some doubt as to the constitutionality of "the crime of being a narcotic addict," the reviewing court in an unreported opinion affirmed the judgment of conviction, citing two of its own previous unreported decisions which had upheld the constitutionality of the statute. We noted probable jurisdiction of this appeal because it squarely presents the issue whether the statute as construed by the California courts in this case is repugnant to the Fourteenth Amendment of the Constitution.

The broad power of a State to regulate the narcotic drugs traffic within its borders is not here in issue. More than forty years ago, in *Whipple v. Martinson,* 256 U.S. 41, this Court explicitly recognized the validity of that power: "There can be no question of the authority of the State in the exercise of its police power to regulate the administration, sale, prescription and use of dangerous and habit-forming drugs.... The right to exercise this power is so manifest in the interest of the public health and welfare, that it is unnecessary to enter upon a discussion of it beyond saying that it is too firmly established to be successfully called in question."

Such regulation, it can be assumed, could take a variety of valid forms. A State might impose criminal sanctions, for example, against the unauthorized manufacture, prescription, sale, purchase, or possession of narcotics within its borders. In the interest of discouraging the violation of such laws, or in the interest of the general health or welfare of its inhabitants, a State might establish a program of compulsory treatment for those addicted to narcotics.[7] Such a program of treatment might require periods of involuntary confinement. And penal sanctions might be imposed for failure to comply with established compulsory treatment procedures. Cf. *Jacobson v. Massachusetts,* 197 U.S. 11. Or a State might choose to attack the evils of narcotics traffic on broader fronts also — through public health education, for example, or by efforts to ameliorate the economic and social conditions under which those evils might be thought to flourish. In short, the range of valid choice which a State might make in this area is undoubtedly a wide one, and the wisdom of any particular choice within the allowable spectrum is not for us to decide. Upon that premise we turn to the California law in issue here.

It would be possible to construe the statute under which the appellant was convicted as one which is operative only upon proof of the actual use of narcotics within the State's jurisdiction. But the California courts have not so construed this law. Although there was evidence in the present case that the appellant had used narcotics in Los Angeles, the jury were instructed that they could convict him even if they disbelieved that evidence. The appellant could be convicted, they were told, if they found simply that the appellant's "status" or "chronic condition" was that of being "addicted to the use of narcotics." And it is impossible to know from the jury's verdict that the defendant was not convicted upon precisely such a finding.

This statute, therefore, is not one which punishes a person for the use of narcotics, for their purchase, sale or possession, or for antisocial or disorderly behavior resulting from their administration. It is not a law which even purports to provide or require medical treatment. Rather, we deal with a statute which makes the "status" of narcotic addiction a criminal offense, for which the offender may be prosecuted "at any time before he reforms." California has said that a person can be continuously guilty of this offense, whether or not he has ever used or possessed any narcotics within the State, and whether or not he has been guilty of any antisocial behavior there.

It is unlikely that any State at this moment in history would attempt to make it a criminal offense for a person to be mentally ill, or a leper, or to be afflicted with a venereal disease. A State might determine that the general health and welfare require that the victims of these and other human afflictions be dealt with by compulsory treatment, involving quarantine, confinement, or sequestration. But, in the light of contemporary human knowledge, a law which made a criminal offense of such a disease would doubtless be universally thought to be an infliction of cruel and unusual punishment in violation of the Eighth and Fourteenth Amendments.

---

7. California appears to have established just such a program in §§ 5350–5361 of its Welfare and Institutions Code. The record contains no explanation of why the civil procedures authorized by this legislation were not utilized in the present case.

We cannot but consider the statute before us as of the same category. In this Court counsel for the State recognized that narcotic addiction is an illness.[8] Indeed, it is apparently an illness which may be contracted innocently or involuntarily.[9] We hold that a state law which imprisons a person thus afflicted as a criminal, even though he has never touched any narcotic drug within the State or been guilty of any irregular behavior there, inflicts a cruel and unusual punishment in violation of the Fourteenth Amendment. To be sure, imprisonment for ninety days is not, in the abstract, a punishment which is either cruel or unusual. But the question cannot be considered in the abstract. Even one day in prison would be a cruel and unusual punishment for the "crime" of having a common cold.

We are not unmindful that the vicious evils of the narcotics traffic have occasioned the grave concern of government. There are, as we have said, countless fronts on which those evils may be legitimately attacked. We deal in this case only with an individual provision of a particularized local law as it has so far been interpreted by the California courts.

Reversed.

Mr. Justice Harlan, concurring.

I am not prepared to hold that on the present state of medical knowledge it is completely irrational and hence unconstitutional for a State to conclude that narcotics addiction is something other than an illness nor that it amounts to cruel and unusual punishment for the State to subject narcotics addicts to its criminal law. Insofar as addiction may be identified with the use or possession of narcotics within the State (or, I would suppose, without the State), in violation of local statutes prohibiting such acts, it may surely be reached by the State's criminal law. But in this case the trial court's instructions permitted the jury to find the appellant guilty on no more proof than that he was present in California while he was addicted to narcotics. Since addiction alone cannot reasonably be thought to amount to more than a compelling propensity to use narcotics, the effect of this instruction was to authorize criminal punishment for a bare desire to commit a criminal act.

If the California statute reaches this type of conduct, and for present purposes we must accept the trial court's construction as binding, it is an arbitrary imposition which exceeds the power that a State may exercise in enacting its criminal law. Accordingly, I agree that the application of the California statute was unconstitutional in this case and join the judgment of reversal.

Mr. Justice Clark, dissenting.

The Court finds § 11721 of California's Health and Safety Code, making it an offense to "be addicted to the use of narcotics," violative of due process as "a cruel and unusual punishment." I cannot agree.

The statute must first be placed in perspective. California has a comprehensive and enlightened program for the control of narcotism based on the overriding policy of prevention and cure. It is the product of an extensive investigation made in the mid-Fifties

---

8. In its brief the appellee stated: "Of course it is generally conceded that a narcotic addict, particularly one addicted to the use of heroin, is in a state of mental and physical illness. So is an alcoholic." Thirty-seven years ago this Court recognized that persons addicted to narcotics "are diseased and proper subjects for [medical] treatment." *Linder v. United States,* 268 U.S. 5, 18.

9. Not only may addiction innocently result from the use of medically prescribed narcotics, but a person may even be a narcotics addict from the moment of his birth. See Schneck, Narcotic Withdrawal Symptoms in the Newborn Infant Resulting from Maternal Addiction, 52 Journal of Pediatrics 584 (1958).

by a committee of distinguished scientists, doctors, law enforcement officers and laymen appointed by the then Attorney General, now Governor, of California. The committee filed a detailed study entitled "Report on Narcotic Addiction" which was given considerable attention. No recommendation was made therein for the repeal of § 11721, and the State Legislature in its discretion continued the policy of that section.

Apart from prohibiting specific acts such as the purchase, possession and sale of narcotics, California has taken certain legislative steps in regard to the status of being a narcotic addict—a condition commonly recognized as a threat to the State and to the individual. The Code deals with this problem in realistic stages. At its incipiency narcotic addiction is handled under § 11721 of the Health and Safety Code which is at issue here. It provides that a person found to be addicted to the use of narcotics shall serve a term in the county jail of not less than 90 days nor more than one year, with the minimum 90-day confinement applying in all cases without exception. Provision is made for parole with periodic tests to detect readdiction.

Where narcotic addiction has progressed beyond the incipient, volitional stage, California provides for commitment of three months to two years in a state hospital. For the purposes of this provision, a narcotic addict is defined as "any person who habitually takes or otherwise uses *to the extent of having lost the power of self-control* any opium, morphine, cocaine, or other narcotic drug as defined in Article 1 of Chapter 1 of Division 10 of the Health and Safety Code."

This proceeding is clearly civil in nature with a purpose of rehabilitation and cure. Significantly, if it is found that a person committed under § 5355 will not receive substantial benefit from further hospital treatment and is not dangerous to society, he may be discharged—but only after a minimum confinement of three months.

The majority strikes down the conviction primarily on the grounds that petitioner was denied due process by the imposition of criminal penalties for nothing more than being in a status. This viewpoint is premised upon the theme that § 11721 is a "criminal" provision authorizing a punishment, for the majority admits that "a State might establish a program of compulsory treatment for those addicted to narcotics" which "might require periods of involuntary confinement." I submit that California has done exactly that. The majority's error is in instructing the California Legislature that hospitalization is the *only treatment* for narcotics addiction—that anything less is a punishment denying due process. California has found otherwise after a study which I suggest was more extensive than that conducted by the Court. Even in California's program for hospital commitment of non-volitional narcotic addicts—which the majority approves—it is recognized that some addicts will not respond to or do not need hospital treatment. As to these persons its provisions are identical to those of § 11721—confinement for a period of not less than 90 days. Section 11721 provides this confinement as treatment for the volitional addicts to whom its provisions apply, in addition to parole with frequent tests to detect and prevent further use of drugs. The fact that § 11721 might be labeled "criminal" seems irrelevant,[1] not only to the majority's own "treatment" test but to the "concept of ordered liberty" to which the States must attain under the Fourteenth Amendment. The test is the overall purpose and effect of a State's act, and I submit that California's program relative to narcotic addicts—including both the "criminal" and "civil" provisions—is inherently one of treatment and lies well within the power of a State.

---

1. Any reliance upon the "stigma" of a misdemeanor conviction in this context is misplaced, as it would hardly be different from the stigma of a civil commitment for narcotics addiction.

However, the case in support of the judgment below need not rest solely on this reading of California law. For even if the overall statutory scheme is ignored and a purpose and effect of punishment is attached to § 11721, that provision still does not violate the Fourteenth Amendment. The majority acknowledges, as it must, that a State can punish persons who purchase, possess or use narcotics. Although none of these acts are harmful to society *in themselves*, the State constitutionally may attempt to deter and prevent them through punishment because of the grave threat of future harmful conduct which they pose. Narcotics addiction—including the incipient, volitional addiction to which this provision speaks—is no different. California courts have taken judicial notice that "the inordinate use of a narcotic drug tends to create an irresistible craving and forms a habit for its continued use until one becomes an addict, and he respects no convention or obligation and will lie, steal, or use any other base means to gratify his passion for the drug, being lost to all considerations of duty or social position." Can this Court deny the legislative and judicial judgment of California that incipient, volitional narcotic addiction poses a threat of serious crime similar to the threat inherent in the purchase or possession of narcotics? And if such a threat is inherent in addiction, can this Court say that California is powerless to deter it by punishment?

The argument that the statute constitutes a cruel and unusual punishment is governed by the discussion above. Properly construed, the statute provides a treatment rather than a punishment. But even if interpreted as penal, the sanction of incarceration for 3 to 12 months is not unreasonable when applied to a person who has voluntarily placed himself in a condition posing a serious threat to the State. Under either theory, its provisions for 3 to 12 months' confinement can hardly be deemed unreasonable when compared to the provisions for 3 to 24 months' confinement under § 5355 which the majority approves.

I would affirm the judgment.

Mr. Justice White, dissenting.

If appellant's conviction rested upon sheer status, condition or illness or if he was convicted for being an addict who had lost his power of self-control, I would have other thoughts about this case. But this record presents neither situation. And I believe the Court has departed from its wise rule of not deciding constitutional questions except where necessary and from its equally sound practice of construing state statutes, where possible, in a manner saving their constitutionality.

I am not at all ready to place the use of narcotics beyond the reach of the States' criminal laws. I do not consider appellant's conviction to be a punishment for having an illness or for simply being in some status or condition, but rather a conviction for the regular, repeated or habitual use of narcotics immediately prior to his arrest and in violation of the California law. As defined by the trial court,[2] addiction *is* the regular use of narcotics and can be proved only by evidence of such use. To find addiction in this case the jury had to believe that appellant had frequently used narcotics in the recent past.[3]

---

2. The court instructed the jury that, "The word 'addicted' means, strongly disposed to some taste or practice or habituated, especially to drugs. In order to inquire as to whether a person is addicted to the use of narcotics is in effect an inquiry as to his habit in that regard.... To use them often or daily is, according to the ordinary acceptance of those words, to use them habitually."

3. This is not a case where a defendant is convicted "even though he has never touched any narcotic drug within the State or been guilty of any irregular behavior there." The evidence was that appellant lived and worked in Los Angeles. He admitted before trial that he had used narcotics for three or four months, three or four times a week, usually at his place with his friends. He stated to the police that he had last used narcotics at 54th and Central in the City of Los Angeles on January 27, 8 days before his arrest. According to the State's expert, no needle mark or scab found on appellant's arms was newer than 3 days old and the most recent mark might have been as old as 10 days, which was

The Court has not merely tidied up California's law by removing some irritating vestige of an outmoded approach to the control of narcotics. At the very least, it has effectively removed California's power to deal effectively with the recurring case under the statute where there is ample evidence of use but no evidence of the precise location of use. Beyond this it has cast serious doubt upon the power of any State to forbid the use of narcotics under threat of criminal punishment. I cannot believe that the Court would forbid the application of the criminal laws to the use of narcotics under any circumstances. But the States, as well as the Federal Government, are now on notice. They will have to await a final answer in another case.

I respectfully dissent.

Powell v. Texas

Supreme Court of the United States
392 U.S. 514 (1968)

Mr. Justice Marshall announced the judgment of the Court and delivered an opinion in which The Chief Justice, Mr. Justice Black, and Mr. Justice Harlan join.

In late December 1966, appellant was arrested and charged with being found in a state of intoxication in a public place, in violation of Texas Penal Code, Art. 477, which reads as follows:

"Whoever shall get drunk or be found in a state of intoxication in any public place, or at any private house except his own, shall be fined not exceeding one hundred dollars."

Appellant was tried in the Corporation Court of Austin, Texas, found guilty, and fined $20. He appealed to the County Court at Law No. 1 of Travis County, Texas, where a trial *de novo* was held. His counsel urged that appellant was "afflicted with the disease of chronic alcoholism," that "his appearance in public [while drunk was] ... not of his own volition," and therefore that to punish him criminally for that conduct would be cruel and unusual, in violation of the Eighth and Fourteenth Amendments to the United States Constitution.

The trial judge in the county court, sitting without a jury ruled as a matter of law that chronic alcoholism was not a defense to the charge. He found appellant guilty, and fined him $50. There being no further right to appeal within the Texas judicial system, appellant appealed to this Court.

Despite the comparatively primitive state of our knowledge on the subject, it cannot be denied that the destructive use of alcoholic beverages is one of our principal social and public health problems. The lowest current informed estimate places the number of "alcoholics" in America (definitional problems aside) at 4,000,000, and most authorities are inclined to put the figure considerably higher. The problem is compounded by the fact that a very large percentage of the alcoholics in this country are "invisible" — they possess the means to keep their drinking problems secret, and the traditionally uncharitable attitude of our society toward alcoholics causes many of them to refrain from seeking treatment from any source. Nor can it be gainsaid that the legislative response to this enormous problem has in general been inadequate.

There is as yet no known generally effective method for treating the vast number of alcoholics in our society. Some individual alcoholics have responded to particular forms of

---

consistent with appellant's own pretrial admissions. The State's evidence was that appellant had used narcotics at least 7 times in the 15 days immediately preceding his arrest.

therapy with remissions of their symptomatic dependence upon the drug. But just as there is no agreement among doctors and social workers with respect to the causes of alcoholism, there is no consensus as to why particular treatments have been effective in particular cases and there is no generally agreed-upon approach to the problem of treatment on a large scale. Most psychiatrists are apparently of the opinion that alcoholism is far more difficult to treat than other forms of behavioral disorders, and some believe it is impossible to cure by means of psychotherapy; indeed, the medical profession as a whole, and psychiatrists in particular, have been severely criticized for the prevailing reluctance to undertake the treatment of drinking problems. Thus it is entirely possible that, even were the manpower and facilities available for a full-scale attack upon chronic alcoholism, we would find ourselves unable to help the vast bulk of our "visible"—let alone our "invisible"—alcoholic population.

However, facilities for the attempted treatment of indigent alcoholics are woefully lacking throughout the country. It would be tragic to return large numbers of helpless, sometimes dangerous and frequently unsanitary inebriates to the streets of our cities without even the opportunity to sober up adequately which a brief jail term provides. Presumably no State or city will tolerate such a state of affairs. Yet the medical profession cannot, and does not, tell us with any assurance that, even if the buildings, equipment and trained personnel were made available, it could provide anything more than slightly higher-class jails for our indigent habitual inebriates. Thus we run the grave risk that nothing will be accomplished beyond the hanging of a new sign—reading "hospital"—over one wing of the jailhouse.

One virtue of the criminal process is, at least, that the duration of penal incarceration typically has some outside statutory limit; this is universally true in the case of petty offenses, such as public drunkenness, where jail terms are quite short on the whole. "Therapeutic civil commitment" lacks this feature; one is typically committed until one is "cured." Thus, to do otherwise than affirm might subject indigent alcoholics to the risk that they may be locked up for an indefinite period of time under the same conditions as before, with no more hope than before of receiving effective treatment and no prospect of periodic "freedom."[24]

Faced with this unpleasant reality, we are unable to assert that the use of the criminal process as a means of dealing with the public aspects of problem drinking can never be defended as rational. The picture of the penniless drunk propelled aimlessly and endlessly through the law's "revolving door" of arrest, incarceration, release and re-arrest is not a pretty one. But before we condemn the present practice across-the-board, perhaps we ought to be able to point to some clear promise of a better world for these unfortunate people. Unfortunately, no such promise has yet been forthcoming. If, in addition to the absence of a coherent approach to the problem of treatment, we consider the almost complete absence of facilities and manpower for the implementation of a rehabilitation program, it is difficult to say in the present context that the criminal process is utterly

---

24. Counsel for *amici curiae* ACLU et al., who has been extremely active in the recent spate of litigation dealing with public intoxication statutes and the chronic inebriate, recently told an annual meeting of the National Council on Alcoholism:

"We have not fought for two years to extract DeWitt Easter, Joe Driver, and their colleagues from jail, only to have them involuntarily committed for an even longer period of time, with no assurance of appropriate rehabilitative help and treatment.... The euphemistic name 'civil commitment' can easily hide nothing more than permanent incarceration.... I would caution those who might rush headlong to adopt civil commitment procedures and remind them that just as difficult legal problems exist there as with the ordinary jail sentence."

lacking in social value. This Court has never held that anything in the Constitution requires that penal sanctions be designed solely to achieve therapeutic or rehabilitative effects, and it can hardly be said with assurance that incarceration serves such purposes any better for the general run of criminals than it does for public drunks.

Appellant claims that his conviction on the facts of this case would violate the Cruel and Unusual Punishment Clause of the Eighth Amendment as applied to the States through the Fourteenth Amendment. The primary purpose of that clause has always been considered, and properly so, to be directed at the method or kind of punishment imposed for the violation of criminal statutes; the nature of the conduct made criminal is ordinarily relevant only to the fitness of the punishment imposed.

Appellant, however, seeks to come within the application of the Cruel and Unusual Punishment Clause announced in *Robinson v. California,* 370 U.S. 660 (1962), which involved a state statute making it a crime to "be addicted to the use of narcotics." This Court held there that "a state law which imprisons a person thus afflicted [with narcotic addiction] as a criminal, even though he has never touched any narcotic drug within the State or been guilty of any irregular behavior there, inflicts a cruel and unusual punishment...."

On its face the present case does not fall within that holding, since appellant was convicted, not for being a chronic alcoholic, but for being in public while drunk on a particular occasion. The State of Texas thus has not sought to punish a mere status, as California did in *Robinson;* nor has it attempted to regulate appellant's behavior in the privacy of his own home. Rather, it has imposed upon appellant a criminal sanction for public behavior which may create substantial health and safety hazards, both for appellant and for members of the general public, and which offends the moral and esthetic sensibilities of a large segment of the community. This seems a far cry from convicting one for being an addict, being a chronic alcoholic, being "mentally ill, or a leper...."

Robinson so viewed brings this Court but a very small way into the substantive criminal law. And unless *Robinson* is so viewed it is difficult to see any limiting principle that would serve to prevent this Court from becoming, under the aegis of the Cruel and Unusual Punishment Clause, the ultimate arbiter of the standards of criminal responsibility, in diverse areas of the criminal law, throughout the country.

It is suggested in dissent that *Robinson* stands for the "simple" but "subtle" principle that "[criminal] penalties may not be inflicted upon a person for being in a condition he is powerless to change." In that view, appellant's "condition" of public intoxication was "occasioned by a compulsion symptomatic of the disease" of chronic alcoholism, and thus, apparently, his behavior lacked the critical element of *mens rea.* Whatever may be the merits of such a doctrine of criminal responsibility, it surely cannot be said to follow from *Robinson.* The entire thrust of *Robinson's* interpretation of the Cruel and Unusual Punishment Clause is that criminal penalties may be inflicted only if the accused has committed some act, has engaged in some behavior, which society has an interest in preventing, or perhaps in historical common law terms, has committed some *actus reus.* It thus does not deal with the question of whether certain conduct cannot constitutionally be punished because it is, in some sense, "involuntary" or "occasioned by a compulsion."

Likewise, as the dissent acknowledges, there is a substantial definitional distinction between a "status," as in *Robinson,* and a "condition," which is said to be involved in this case. Whatever may be the merits of an attempt to distinguish between behavior and a condition, it is perfectly clear that the crucial element in this case, so far as the dissent is concerned, is whether or not appellant can legally be held responsible for his appearance in public in a state of intoxication. The only relevance of *Robinson* to this issue is that because the Court interpreted the statute there involved as making a "status" criminal, it was able to suggest that the statute would cover even a situation in which addiction had been acquired involuntarily. That this factor was not determinative in the case is shown by the fact that there was no indication of how Robinson himself had become an addict.

Ultimately, then, the most troubling aspects of this case, were *Robinson* to be extended to meet it, would be the scope and content of what could only be a constitutional doctrine of criminal responsibility. In dissent it is urged that the decision could be limited to conduct which is "a characteristic and involuntary part of the pattern of the disease as it afflicts" the particular individual, and that "[it] is not foreseeable" that it would be applied "in the case of offenses such as driving a car while intoxicated, assault, theft, or robbery." That is limitation by fiat. In the first place, nothing in the logic of the dissent would limit its application to chronic alcoholics. If Leroy Powell cannot be convicted of public intoxication, it is difficult to see how a State can convict an individual for murder, if that individual, while exhibiting normal behavior in all other respects, suffers from a "compulsion" to kill, which is an "exceedingly strong influence," but "not completely overpowering." Even if we limit our consideration to chronic alcoholics, it would seem impossible to confine the principle within the arbitrary bounds which the dissent seems to envision.

Affirmed.

Mr. Justice Black, whom Mr. Justice Harlan joins, concurring.

While I agree that the grounds set forth in Mr. Justice Marshall's opinion are sufficient to require affirmance of the judgment here, I wish to amplify my reasons for concurring.

The rule of constitutional law urged by appellant is not required by *Robinson v. California*, 370 U.S. 660 (1962). In that case we held that a person could not be punished for the mere status of being a narcotics addict. We explicitly limited our holding to the situation where no conduct of any kind is involved, stating:

"We hold that a state law which imprisons a person thus afflicted as a criminal, *even though he has never touched any narcotic drug within the State or been guilty of any irregular behavior there,* inflicts a cruel and unusual punishment in violation of the Fourteenth Amendment." (Emphasis added.)

The argument is made that appellant comes within the terms of our holding in *Robinson* because being drunk in public is a mere status or "condition." Despite this many-faceted use of the concept of "condition," this argument would require converting *Robinson* into a case protecting actual behavior, a step we explicitly refused to take in that decision.

A different question, I admit, is whether our attempt in *Robinson* to limit our holding to pure status crimes, involving no conduct whatever, was a sound one. I believe it was. Although some of our objections to the statute in *Robinson* are equally applicable to statutes that punish conduct "symptomatic" of a disease, any attempt to explain *Robinson* as based solely on the lack of voluntariness encounters a number of logical difficulties.[3] Other problems raised by status crimes are in no way involved when the State attempts to punish for conduct, and these other problems were, in my view, the controlling aspects of our decision.

---

3. Although we noted in *Robinson* that narcotics addiction apparently is an illness that can be contracted innocently or involuntarily, we barred punishment for addiction even when it could be proved that the defendant had voluntarily become addicted. And we compared addiction to the status of having a common cold, a condition that most people can either avoid or quickly cure when it is important enough for them to do so.

Punishment for a status is particularly obnoxious, and in many instances can reasonably be called cruel and unusual, because it involves punishment for a mere propensity, a desire to commit an offense; the mental element is not simply one part of the crime but may constitute all of it. This is a situation universally sought to be avoided in our criminal law; the fundamental requirement that some action be proved is solidly established even for offenses most heavily based on propensity, such as attempt, conspiracy, and recidivist crimes. In fact, one eminent authority has found only one isolated instance, in all of Anglo-American jurisprudence, in which criminal responsibility was imposed in the absence of any act at all.

The reasons for this refusal to permit conviction without proof of an act are difficult to spell out, but they are nonetheless perceived and universally expressed in our criminal law. Evidence of propensity can be considered relatively unreliable and more difficult for a defendant to rebut; the requirement of a specific act thus provides some protection against false charges. See 4 Blackstone, Commentaries 21. Perhaps more fundamental is the difficulty of distinguishing, in the absence of any conduct, between desires of the day-dream variety and fixed intentions that may pose a real threat to society; extending the criminal law to cover both types of desire would be unthinkable, since "[there] can hardly be anyone who has never thought evil. When a desire is inhibited it may find expression in fantasy; but it would be absurd to condemn this natural psychological mechanism as illegal."

In contrast, crimes that require the State to prove that the defendant actually committed some proscribed act involve none of these special problems. In addition, the question whether an act is "involuntary" is, as I have already indicated, an inherently elusive question, and one which the State may, for good reasons, wish to regard as irrelevant. In light of all these considerations, our limitation of our *Robinson* holding to pure status crimes seems to me entirely proper.

The rule of constitutional law urged upon us by appellant would have a revolutionary impact on the criminal law, and any possible limits proposed for the rule would be wholly illusory. If the original boundaries of *Robinson* are to be discarded, any new limits too would soon fall by the wayside and the Court would be forced to hold the States powerless to punish any conduct that could be shown to result from a "compulsion," in the complex, psychological meaning of that term.

[E]ven if we were to limit any holding in this field to "compulsions" that are "symptomatic" of a "disease," in the words of the findings of the trial court, the sweep of that holding would still be startling. Such a ruling would make it clear beyond any doubt that a narcotics addict could not be punished for "being" in possession of drugs or, for that matter, for "being" guilty of using them.

I would confess the limits of my own ability to answer the age-old questions of the criminal law's ethical foundations and practical effectiveness. I would hold that *Robinson* v. *California* establishes a firm and impenetrable barrier to the punishment of persons who, whatever their bare desires and propensities, have committed no proscribed wrongful act. But I would refuse to plunge from the concrete and almost universally recognized premises of *Robinson* into the murky problems raised by the insistence that chronic alcoholics cannot be punished for public drunkenness, problems that no person, whether layman or expert, can claim to understand, and with consequences that no one can safely predict. I join in affirmance of this conviction.

Mr. Justice White, concurring in the result.

If it cannot be a crime to have an irresistible compulsion to use narcotics, *Robinson v. California,* 370 U.S. 660, I do not see how it can constitutionally be a crime to yield to such a compulsion. Punishing an addict for using drugs convicts for addiction under a different name. Distinguishing between the two crimes is like forbidding criminal conviction for being sick with flu or epilepsy but permitting punishment for running a fever or having a convulsion. Unless *Robinson* is to be abandoned, the use of narcotics by an addict must be beyond the reach of the criminal law. Similarly, the chronic alcoholic with an irresistible urge to consume alcohol should not be punishable for drinking or for being drunk.

Powell's conviction was for the different crime of being drunk in a public place. Thus even if Powell was compelled to drink, and so could not constitutionally be convicted for drinking, his conviction in this case can be invalidated only if there is a constitutional basis for saying that he may not be punished for being in public while drunk. The statute involved here, which aims at keeping drunks off the street for their own welfare and that of others, is not challenged on the ground that it interferes unconstitutionally with the right to frequent public places. No question is raised about applying this statute to the nonchronic drunk, who has no compulsion to drink, who need not drink to excess, and who could have arranged to do his drinking in private or, if he began drinking in public, could have removed himself at an appropriate point on the path toward complete inebriation.

Whether or not Powell established that he could not have resisted becoming drunk on December 19, 1966, nothing in the record indicates that he could not have done his drinking in private or that he was so inebriated at the time that he had lost control of his movements and wandered into the public street. Indeed, the evidence in the record strongly suggests that Powell could have drunk at home and made plans while sober to prevent ending up in a public place. Powell had a home and wife, and if there were reasons why he had to drink in public or be drunk there, they do not appear in the record.

It is unnecessary to pursue at this point the further definition of the circumstances or the state of intoxication which might bar conviction of a chronic alcoholic for being drunk in a public place. For the purposes of this case, it is necessary to say only that Powell showed nothing more than that he was to some degree compelled to drink and that he was drunk at the time of his arrest. He made no showing that he was unable to stay off the streets on the night in question.[5]

Because Powell did not show that his conviction offended the Constitution, I concur in the judgment affirming the Travis County court.

Mr. Justice Fortas, with whom Mr. Justice Douglas, Mr. Justice Brennan, and Mr. Justice Stewart join, dissenting.

The issue posed in this case is a narrow one. There is no challenge here to the validity of public intoxication statutes in general or to the Texas public intoxication statute in particular. This case does not concern the infliction of punishment upon the "social" drinker—or upon anyone other than a "chronic alcoholic" who, as the trier of fact here found, cannot "resist the constant, excessive consumption of alcohol." Nor does it relate to any offense other than the crime of public intoxication.

---

5. I do not question the power of the State to remove a helplessly intoxicated person from a public street, although against his will, and to hold him until he has regained his powers. The person's own safety and the public interest require this much. A statute such as the one challenged in this case is constitutional insofar as it authorizes a police officer to arrest any seriously intoxicated person when he is encountered in a public place. Whether such a person may be charged and convicted for violating the statute will depend upon whether he is entitled to the protection of the Eighth Amendment.

The sole question presented is whether a criminal penalty may be imposed upon a person suffering the disease of "chronic alcoholism" for a condition—being "in a state of intoxication" in public—which is a characteristic part of the pattern of his disease and which, the trial court found, was not the consequence of appellant's volition but of "a compulsion symptomatic of the disease of chronic alcoholism." We must consider whether the Eighth Amendment, made applicable to the States through the Fourteenth Amendment, prohibits the imposition of this penalty in these rather special circumstances as "cruel and unusual punishment." This case does not raise any question as to the right of the police to stop and detain those who are intoxicated in public, whether as a result of the disease or otherwise; or as to the State's power to commit chronic alcoholics for treatment. Nor does it concern the responsibility of an alcoholic for criminal *acts*. We deal here with the mere *condition* of being intoxicated in public.[2]

It is true, of course, that there is a great deal that remains to be discovered about chronic alcoholism. Although many aspects of the disease remain obscure, there are some hard facts—medical and, especially, legal facts—that are accessible to us and that provide a context in which the instant case may be analyzed. We are similarly woefully deficient in our medical, diagnostic, and therapeutic knowledge of mental disease and the problem of insanity; but few would urge that, because of this, we should totally reject the legal significance of what we do know about these phenomena.

The manifestations of alcoholism are reasonably well identified. It is well established that alcohol may be habituative and "can be physically addicting." It has been said that "the main point for the nonprofessional is that alcoholism is not within the control of the person involved. He is not willfully drinking."

It is entirely clear that the jailing of chronic alcoholics is punishment. It is not defended as therapeutic, nor is there any basis for claiming that it is therapeutic (or indeed a deterrent). The alcoholic offender is caught in a "revolving door"—leading from arrest on the street through a brief, unprofitable sojourn in jail, back to the street and, eventually, another arrest. The jails, overcrowded and put to a use for which they are not suitable, have a destructive effect upon alcoholic inmates.

It bears emphasis that these data provide only a context for consideration of the instant case. They should not dictate our conclusion. The questions for this Court are not settled by reference to medicine or penology. Our task is to determine whether the principles embodied in the Constitution of the United States place any limitations upon the circumstances under which punishment may be inflicted, and, if so, whether, in the case now before us, those principles preclude the imposition of such punishment.

It is settled that the Federal Constitution places some substantive limitation upon the power of state legislatures to define crimes for which the imposition of punishment is ordered. In *Robinson v. California,* 370 U.S. 660 (1962), the Court considered a conviction under a California statute making it a criminal offense for a person to "be addicted to the use of narcotics." At Robinson's trial, it was developed that the defendant had been a user of narcotics. The trial court instructed the jury that "[to] be addicted to the use of narcotics

---

2. It is not foreseeable that findings such as those which are decisive here—namely that the appellant's being intoxicated in public was a part of the pattern of his disease and due to a compulsion symptomatic of that disease—could or would be made in the case of offenses such as driving a car while intoxicated, assault, theft, or robbery. Such offenses require independent acts or conduct and do not typically flow from and are not part of the syndrome of the disease of chronic alcoholism. If an alcoholic should be convicted for criminal conduct which is not a characteristic and involuntary part of the pattern of the disease as it afflicts him, nothing herein would prevent his punishment.

is said to be a status or condition and not an act. It is a continuing offense and differs from most other offenses in the fact that [it] is chronic rather than acute; that it continues after it is complete and subjects the offender to arrest at any time before he reforms."

This Court reversed Robinson's conviction on the ground that punishment under the law in question was cruel and unusual, in violation of the Eighth Amendment of the Constitution as applied to the States through the Fourteenth Amendment. The Court noted that narcotic addiction is considered to be an illness and that California had recognized it as such. It held that the State could not make it a crime for a person to be ill. Although Robinson had been sentenced to only 90 days in prison for his offense, it was beyond the power of the State to prescribe such punishment. As Mr. Justice Stewart, speaking for the Court, said: "[even] one day in prison would be a cruel and unusual punishment for the 'crime' of having a common cold."

Robinson stands upon a principle which, despite its subtlety, must be simply stated and respectfully applied because it is the foundation of individual liberty and the cornerstone of the relations between a civilized state and its citizens: Criminal penalties may not be inflicted upon a person for being in a condition he is powerless to change. In all probability, Robinson at some time before his conviction elected to take narcotics. But the crime as defined did not punish this conduct.[29] The statute imposed a penalty for the offense of "addiction"—a condition which Robinson could not control. Once Robinson had become an addict, he was utterly powerless to avoid criminal guilt. He was powerless to choose not to violate the law.

In the present case, appellant is charged with a crime composed of two elements—being intoxicated and being found in a public place while in that condition. The crime, so defined, differs from that in *Robinson.* The statute covers more than a mere status. But the essential constitutional defect here is the same as in *Robinson,* for in both cases the particular defendant was accused of being in a condition which he had no capacity to change or avoid. The trial judge sitting as trier of fact found, upon the medical and other relevant testimony, that Powell is a "chronic alcoholic." He defined appellant's "chronic alcoholism" as "a disease which destroys the afflicted person's will power to resist the constant, excessive consumption of alcohol." He also found that "a chronic alcoholic does not appear in public by his own volition but under a compulsion symptomatic of the disease of chronic alcoholism." I read these findings to mean that appellant was powerless to avoid drinking; that having taken his first drink, he had "an uncontrollable compulsion to drink" to the point of intoxication; and that, once intoxicated, he could not prevent himself from appearing in public places.

Article 477 of the Texas Penal Code is specifically directed to the accused's presence while in a state of intoxication, "in any public place, or at any private house except his own." This is the essence of the crime. Ordinarily when the State proves such presence in a state of intoxication, this will be sufficient for conviction, and the punishment prescribed by the State may, of course, be validly imposed. But here the findings of the trial judge call into play the principle that a person may not be punished if the condition essential to constitute the defined crime is part of the pattern of his disease and is occasioned by a com-

---

29. The Court noted in *Robinson* that narcotic addiction "is apparently an illness which may be contracted innocently or involuntarily." In the case of alcoholism it is even more likely that the disease may be innocently contracted, since the drinking of alcoholic beverages is a common activity, generally accepted in our society, while the purchasing and taking of drugs are crimes. As in *Robinson,* the State has not argued here that Powell's conviction may be supported by his "voluntary" action in becoming afflicted.

pulsion symptomatic of the disease. This principle, narrow in scope and applicability, is implemented by the Eighth Amendment's prohibition of "cruel and unusual punishment," as we construed that command in *Robinson*.

The findings in this case, read against the background of the medical and sociological data to which I have referred, compel the conclusion that the infliction upon appellant of a criminal penalty for being intoxicated in a public place would be "cruel and inhuman punishment" within the prohibition of the Eighth Amendment. This conclusion follows because appellant is a "chronic alcoholic" who, according to the trier of fact, cannot resist the "constant excessive consumption of alcohol" and does not appear in public by his own volition but under a "compulsion" which is part of his condition.

I would reverse the judgment below.

———————

Although *Robinson* provides that the State may not make addiction itself a crime, civil commitment based on addiction alone is permissible. Most states have civil commitment statutes for addicts but they are rarely used today. *See, e.g.,* M. Susan Ridgely & Martin Y. Iguchi, *Coercive Use of Vaccines Against Drug Addiction: Is It Permissible and Is It Good Public Policy?*, 12 VA. J. SOC. POL'Y & L. 260 (2004) (describing the history of laws permitting the civil commitment of alcohol and drug abusers in the United States); John C. Kramer, *The State Versus The Addict: Uncivil Commitment*, 50 B.U. L. REV. 1 (1970) (arguing that California's post-*Robinson* civil commitment scheme "entirely resembles prison programs and has almost no elements which resemble hospital programs").

2. The Right to Privacy

Throughout the years, laws criminalizing drug possession—particularly in the home—have faced a number of challenges based on a substantive due process "right to privacy" theory. In the United States, courts have nearly universally rejected these challenges. *See* Eric Blumenson and Eva Nilsen, *Liberty Lost: The Moral Case for Marijuana Law Reform*, 85 IND. L.J. 279, 282 at n. 8 (2010) (describing courts' rejection of constitutional challenges to marijuana laws). In Alaska, however, the State Supreme Court held in 1970 that the right to privacy contained in Alaska's Constitution protects marijuana possession in the home.

Ravin v. Alaska
Supreme Court of Alaska
537 P.2d 494 (1975)

Rabinowitz, J.

The constitutionality of Alaska's statute prohibiting possession of marijuana is put in issue in this case. Petitioner Ravin was arrested in 1972 and charged with violating AS 17.12.010. Before trial Ravin attacked the constitutionality of AS 17.12.010 by a motion to dismiss in which he asserted that the State had violated his right of privacy under both the federal and Alaska constitutions.

Ravin's basic thesis is that there exists under the federal and Alaska constitutions a fundamental right to privacy, the scope of which is sufficiently broad to encompass and protect the possession of marijuana for personal use. Given this fundamental constitutional right, the State would then have the burden of demonstrating a compelling state interest in prohibiting possession of marijuana. In light of these controlling principles, petitioner argues that the evidence submitted below by both sides demonstrates that marijuana is a relatively innocuous substance, at least as compared with other less-restricted substances, and that nothing even approaching a compelling state interest was proven by the State.

Ravin's arguments necessitate a close examination of the contours of the asserted right to privacy and the scope of this court's review of the legislature's determination to criminalize possession of marijuana.

We have previously stated the tests to be applied when a claim is made that state action encroaches upon an individual's constitutional rights. In *Breese v. Smith,* 501 P.2d 159 (Alaska 1972), we had before us a school hair length regulation which encroached on what we determined to be the individual's fundamental right to determine his own personal appearance. There we stated:

> Once a fundamental right under the constitution of Alaska has been shown to be involved and it has been further shown that this constitutionally protected right has been impaired by governmental action, then the government must come forward and meet its substantial burden of establishing that the abridgement in question was justified by a compelling governmental interest.

When, on the other hand, governmental action interferes with an individual's freedom in an area which is not characterized as fundamental, a less stringent test is ordinarily applied. In such cases our task is to determine whether the legislative enactment has a reasonable relationship to a legitimate governmental purpose. Under this latter test, which is sometimes referred to as the "rational basis" test, the State need only demonstrate the existence of facts which can serve as a rational basis for belief that the measure would properly serve the public interest.

Thus, our undertaking is two-fold: we must first determine the nature of Ravin's rights, if any, abridged by AS 17.12.010, and, if any rights have been infringed upon, then resolve the further question as to whether the statutory impingement is justified.

As we have mentioned, Ravin's argument that he has a fundamental right to possess marijuana for personal use rests on both federal and state law, and centers on what may broadly be called the right to privacy. This "right" is increasingly the subject of litigation and commentary and is still a developing legal concept.

In Ravin's view, the right to privacy involved here is an autonomous right which gains special significance when its situs is found in a specially protected area, such as the home. Ravin begins his privacy argument by citation of and reliance upon *Griswold v. Connecticut,* in which the Supreme Court of the United States struck down as unconstitutional a state statute effectively barring the dispensation of birth control information to married persons. Writing for five members of the Court, Mr. Justice Douglas noted that rights protected by the Constitution are not limited to those specifically enumerated in the Constitution. In order to secure the enumerated rights, certain peripheral rights must be recognized. In other words, the "specific guarantees in the Bill of Rights have penumbras, formed by emanations from those guarantees that help give them life and substance." Certain of these penumbral rights create "zones of privacy", for example, First Amendment rights of association, Third and Fourth Amendment rights pertaining to the security of the home, and the Fifth Amendment right against self-incrimination. The Supreme Court of the United States then proceeded to find a right to privacy in marriage which antedates the Bill of Rights and yet lies within the zone of privacy created by several fundamental constitutional guarantees. It was left unclear whether this particular right to privacy exists independently, or comes into being only because of its connection with fundamental enumerated rights.

The next important Supreme Court opinion regarding privacy is *Stanley v. Georgia,* in which a state conviction for possession of obscene matter was overturned as violative of the First and Fourteenth Amendments. The Supreme Court had previously held that obscenity is not protected by the First Amendment. But in *Stanley* the Count made a distinction between commercial distribution of obscene matter and the private enjoyment of it at home. The Constitution, it said, protects the fundamental right to receive information and ideas, regardless of their worth. Moreover, the Supreme Court said,

> .... in the context of this case — a prosecution for mere possession of printed or filmed matter in the privacy of a person's own home — that right takes on an added dimension. For also fundamental is the right to be free, except in very limited circumstances, from unwanted governmental intrusions into one's privacy.

The Supreme Court concluded that the First Amendment means a state has no business telling a man, sitting alone in his own home, what books he may read or what films he may watch. The Court took care to limit its holding to mere possession of obscene materials by the individual in his own home. It noted that it did not intend to restrict the power of the state or federal government to make illegal the possession of items such as narcotics, firearms, or stolen goods.

In Alaska this court has dealt with the concept of privacy on only a few occasions. One of the most significant decisions in this area is *Breese v. Smith,* where we considered the applicability of the guarantee of "life, liberty, the pursuit of happiness" found in the Alaska Constitution, to a school hair length regulation. Noting that hairstyles are a highly personal matter in which the individual is traditionally autonomous, we concluded that governmental control of personal appearance would be antithetical to the concept of personal liberty under Alaska's constitution. Since the student would be forced to choose between controlling his own personal appearance and asserting his right to an education if the regulations were upheld, we concluded that the constitutional language quoted above embodied an affirmative grant of liberty to public school students to choose their own hairstyles, for "at the core of [the concept of liberty] is the notion of total personal immunity from government control: the right 'to be let alone.'" That right is not absolute, however; we also noted that this "liberty" must yield where it "intrude[s] upon the freedom of others."

Subsequent to our decision in *Breese,* a right to privacy amendment was added to the Alaska Constitution. Article I, section · 22 reads:

> The right of the people to privacy is recognized and shall not be infringed. The legislature shall implement this section.

The effect of this amendment is to place privacy among the specifically enumerated rights in Alaska's constitution. But this fact alone does not, in and of itself, yield answers concerning what scope should be accorded to this right of privacy. We have suggested that the right to privacy may afford less than absolute protection to "the ingestion of food, beverages or other substances." For any such protection must be limited by the legitimate needs of the State to protect the health and welfare of its citizens.[25]

Although a number of other jurisdictions have considered the privacy issue as it applies to marijuana prosecutions, they provide little help in defining the scope of article I,

---

25. If the State were required, for instance, to carry the extremely heavy burden of showing a compelling state interest before it could regulate the purity of foodstuffs and medicines, the result would be a practical inability to protect the public from health threats which consumers could neither know about nor protect themselves against.

section 22 of Alaska's constitution. In Hawaii, whose constitution also contains an express guarantee of the right to privacy, the supreme court has faced a similar issue. In *State v. Kantner,* the Supreme Court of Hawaii upheld a conviction for possession of marijuana by a 3–2 vote, with one member of the majority concurring only because he thought the constitutional issue had not been properly raised. A majority rejected the claim that application of the statute violated guarantees of equal protection and due process, and two members of the court rejected the claim of violation of "fundamental liberty" based on *Griswold.* In dissent, Justice Levinson emphasized the guarantees of privacy and personal autonomy which he found in both the Hawaii Constitution and the due process clause of the Fourteenth Amendment to the United States Constitution. He found that the right to privacy "guarantees to the individual the full measure of control over his own personality consistent with the security of himself and others." The experiences generated by use of marijuana are mental in nature, he wrote, and thus among the most personal and private experiences possible. So long as conduct does not produce detrimental results, the right of privacy protects the individual's conduct designed to affect these inner areas of the personality. The state failed to show, he found, any harm to the user or others from the private, personal use of marijuana, and so the statute infringed on the right to personal autonomy.

In a Michigan case the same year, a conviction for possession of marijuana was overturned by a unanimous court, though for a variety of reasons. One of the justices in *People v. Sinclair,* Justice T. G. Kavanagh, rested his opinion squarely on the basic right of the individual to be free from government intrusions. He found the marijuana possession statute to be "an impermissible intrusion on the fundamental rights to liberty and the pursuit of happiness, and is an unwarranted interference with the right to possess and use private property." He noted the basic freedom of the individual to be free to do as he pleases so long as his actions do not interfere with the rights of his neighbor or of society. ".... 'Big Brother' cannot, in the name of *Public* health, dictate to anyone what he can eat or drink or smoke in the *privacy* of his own home."

Generally, however, privacy as a constitutional defense in marijuana cases has not met with much favor. It was rejected, for instance, by the Massachusetts Supreme Judicial Court in *Commonwealth v. Leis,* where the court held that there was no constitutional right to smoke marijuana, that smoking marijuana was not fundamental to the American scheme of justice or necessary to a regime of ordered liberty, and that smoking marijuana was not locatable in any "zone of privacy." Furthermore, the court said, there is no constitutional right to become intoxicated.

Assuming this court were to continue to utilize the fundamental right-compelling state interest test in resolving privacy issues under article I, section 22 of Alaska's constitution, we would conclude that there is not a fundamental constitutional right to possess or ingest marijuana in Alaska. For in our view, the right to privacy amendment to the Alaska Constitution cannot be read so as to make the possession or ingestion of marijuana itself a fundamental right. Nor can we conclude that such a fundamental right is shown by virtue of the analysis we employed in *Breese.* In that case, the student's traditional liberty pertaining to autonomy in personal appearance was threatened in such a way that his constitutionally guaranteed right to an education was jeopardized. Hairstyle, as emphasized in *Breese,* is a highly personal matter involving the individual and his body. In this sense this aspect of liberty-privacy is akin to the significantly personal areas at stake in *Griswold* and *Eisenstadt v. Baird.* Few would believe they have been deprived of something of critical importance if deprived of marijuana, though they would if stripped of control over their personal appearance. And, as mentioned previously, a discrete federal right of privacy separate from the penumbras of specifically enumerated constitutional rights has not as yet been articulated by the Supreme Court of the United States. Therefore, if we were employing our former test, we would hold that there is no fundamental right, either under the Alaska or federal constitutions, either to possess or ingest marijuana.

The foregoing does not complete our analysis of the right to privacy issues. For in *Gray* we stated that the right of privacy amendment of the Alaska Constitution "clearly it shields the ingestion of food, beverages or other substances," but that this right may be held to be subordinate to public health and welfare measures. Thus, Ravin's right to privacy contentions are not susceptible to disposition solely in terms of answering the question whether there is a general fundamental constitutional right to possess or smoke marijuana. This leads us to a more detailed examination of the right to privacy and the relevancy of where the right is exercised.

At one end of the scale of the scope of the right to privacy is possession or ingestion in the individual's home. If there is any area of human activity to which a right to privacy pertains more than any other, it is the home. The importance of the home has been amply demonstrated in constitutional law. Among the enumerated rights in the federal Bill of Rights are the guarantee against quartering of troops in a private house in peacetime (Third Amendment) and the right to be "secure in their.... houses.... against unreasonable searches and seizures...." (Fourth Amendment). The First Amendment has been held to protect the right to "privacy and freedom of association in the home." The Fifth Amendment has been described as providing protection against all governmental invasions "of the sanctity of a man's home and the privacies of life." The protection of the right to receive birth control information in *Griswold* was predicated on the sanctity of the marriage relationship and the harm to this fundamental area of privacy if police were allowed to "search the sacred precincts of marital bedrooms." And in *Stanley v. Georgia,* the Court emphasized the home as the situs of protected "private activities." The right to receive information and ideas was found in *Stanley* to take on an added dimension precisely because it was a prosecution for possession in the home: "For also fundamental is the right to be free, except in very limited circumstances, from unwanted governmental intrusions into one's privacy." In a later case, the Supreme Court noted that *Stanley* was not based on the notion that the obscene matter was itself protected by a constitutional penumbra of privacy, but rather was a "reaffirmation that 'a man's home is his castle.'"

In Alaska we have also recognized the distinctive nature of the home as a place where the individual's privacy receives special protection. This court has consistently recognized that the home is constitutionally protected from unreasonable searches and seizures, reasoning that the home itself retains a protected status under the Fourth Amendment and Alaska's constitution distinct from that of the occupant's person. The privacy amendment to the Alaska Constitution was intended to give recognition and protection to the home. Such a reading is consonant with the character of life in Alaska. Our territory and now state has traditionally been the home of people who prize their individuality and who have chosen to settle or to continue living here in order to achieve a measure of control over their own lifestyles which is now virtually unattainable in many of our sister states.

The home, then, carries with it associations and meanings which make it particularly important as the situs of privacy. Privacy in the home is a fundamental right, under both the federal and Alaska constitutions. We do not mean by this that a person may do anything at anytime as long as the activity takes place within a person's home. There are two important limitations on this facet of the right to privacy. First, we agree with the Supreme Court of the United States, which has strictly limited the *Stanley* guarantee to possession for purely private, noncommercial use in the home. And secondly, we think this right must yield when it interferes in a serious manner with the health, safety, rights and privileges of others or with the public welfare. No one has an absolute right to do things in the privacy of his own home which will affect himself or others adversely. Indeed, one aspect of a private matter is that it *is* private, that is, that it does not adversely affect persons beyond the actor, and hence is none of their business. When a matter does affect the public, directly or indirectly, it loses its wholly private character, and can be made to yield when an appropriate public need is demonstrated.

Thus, we conclude that citizens of the State of Alaska have a basic right to privacy in their homes under Alaska's constitution. This right to privacy would encompass the possession and ingestion of substances such as marijuana in a purely personal, non-commercial context in the home unless the state can meet its substantial burden and show that proscription of possession of marijuana in the home is supportable by achievement of a legitimate state interest.

This leads us to the second facet of our inquiry, namely, whether the State has demonstrated sufficient justification for the prohibition of possession of marijuana in general in the interest of public welfare; and further, whether the State has met the greater burden of showing a close and substantial relationship between the public welfare and control of ingestion or possession of marijuana in the home for personal use.

The evidence which was presented at the hearing before the district court consisted primarily of several expert witnesses familiar with various medical and social aspects of marijuana use. Numerous written reports and books were also introduced into evidence.

According to figures published by the National Commission on Marihuana and Drug Abuse in 1973, an estimated 26 million Americans have used marijuana at least once. The incidence generally cuts across social and economic classes, though use is greatest among young persons (55% of 18–21 year-olds have used it). Only about 2% of the adults who have used it were classified by the National Commission as "heavy users" (more than once daily). The experience in Alaska seems to be similar. A report published in the Journal of the American Medical Association in 1971 indicated that 24% of Anchorage school children in grades six through twelve had used marijuana, as had 46% in grades eleven and twelve.

Scientific testimony on the physiological and psychological effects of marijuana on humans generally stresses the variability of effects upon different individuals and on any one individual at different times. The setting and psychological state of the user can affect his responses. Responses also vary with the amount of marijuana one has used in the past. A new user, for instance, often feels no effects at all.

The short-term physiological effects are relatively undisputed. An immediate slight increase in the pulse, decrease in salivation, and a slight reddening of the eyes are usually noted. There is also impairment of psychomotor control. These effects generally end within two to three hours of the end of smoking.

Long-term physiological effects raise more controversy among the experts. The National Commission on Marihuana and Drug Abuse reported that among users "no significant physical, biochemical, or mental abnormalities could be attributed solely to their marijuana smoking." Certain researchers have pointed to possible deleterious effects on the body's immune defenses, on the chromosomal structures of users, and on testosterone levels in the body. The methodology of certain of these studies has been extensively criticized by other qualified medical scientists, however. It should be noted that most of the damage suggested by these studies comes in the context of intensive use of concentrated forms of THC. It appears that the use of marijuana, as it is presently used in the United States today, does not constitute a public health problem of any significant dimensions. It is, for instance, far more innocuous in terms of physiological and social damage than alcohol or tobacco. But the studies suggesting dangers in intensive cannabis use do raise valid doubts which cannot be dismissed or discounted.

The experts generally agree that the early widely-held belief that marijuana use directly causes criminal behavior, and particularly violent, aggressive behavior, has no validity. On the contrary, the National Commission found indications that marijuana inhibits "the expression of aggressive impulses by pacifying the user, interfering with muscle coordination, reducing psychomotor activities and generally producing states of drowsiness, lethargy, timidity and passivity." Moreover, the Commission and most other authorities agree that there is little validity to the theory that marijuana use leads to use of more potent and dangerous drugs. Although it has been stated that the more heavily a user smokes marijuana, the greater the probability that he has used or will use other drugs, "it has been suggested that such use is related to 'drug use proneness' and involvement in drug subcultures rather than to the characteristics of cannabis, *per se.*"

While there is no confirmed report of a human ever having died from an overdose of cannabis, the toxic levels of THC have been determined from tests on animals. The lethal dose for marijuana is approximately 40,000 times the dose needed to achieve intoxication. The equivalent ratio of intoxicating to lethal doses for alcohol is 4/10 and for barbiturates is 3/50.

The number of persons arrested for marijuana possession has climbed steeply in recent years. In 1973, over 400,000 marijuana arrests occurred, a 43% rise over the previous year. It should also be noted that 81% of persons arrested for marijuana-related crimes have never been convicted of any crime in the past, and 91% have never been convicted of a drug-related crime.

The justifications offered by the State to uphold AS 17.12.010 are generally that marijuana is a psychoactive drug; that it is not a harmless substance; that heavy use has concomitant risk; that it is capable of precipitating a psychotic reaction in at least individuals who are predisposed towards such reaction; and that its use adversely affects the user's ability to operate an automobile. The State relies upon a number of medical researchers who have raised questions as to the substance's effect on the body's immune system, on chromosomal structure, and on the functioning of the brain. On the other hand, in almost every instance of reports of potential danger arising from marijuana use, reports can be found reaching contradictory results. It appears that there is no firm evidence that marijuana, as presently used in this country, is generally a danger to the user or to others. But neither is there conclusive evidence to the effect that it is harmless. The one significant risk in use of marijuana which we do find established to a reasonable degree of certainty is the effect of marijuana intoxication on driving.

Possibly implicit in the State's catalogue of possible dangers of marijuana use is the assumption that the State has the authority to protect the individual from his own folly, that is, that the State can control activities which present no harm to anyone except those enjoying them. Although some courts have found the "public interest" to be broad enough to justify protecting the individual against himself, most have found inherent limitations on the police power of the state. An apposite example is the litigation regarding the constitutionality of laws requiring motorcyclists to wear helmets. Most of the courts addressing the issue, including this one, have resolved it by finding a connection between the helmet requirement and the safety of other motorists, but a significant number of courts have explicitly rejected such restrictive measures as beyond the police power of the state because they do not benefit the public.

We glean from these cases the general proposition that the authority of the state to exert control over the individual extends only to activities of the individual which affect others or the public at large as it relates to matters of public health or safety, or to provide for the general welfare. We believe this tenet to be basic to a free society. The state cannot impose its own notions of morality, propriety, or fashion on individuals when the public has no legitimate interest in the affairs of those individuals. The right of the individual to do as he pleases is not absolute, of course: it can be made to yield when it begins to infringe on the rights and welfare of others.

Further, the authority of the state to control the activities of its citizens is not limited to activities which have a present and immediate impact on the public health or welfare. It is conceivable, for example, that a drug could so seriously develop in its user a withdrawal or amotivational syndrome, that widespread use of the drug could significantly debilitate the fabric of our society. Faced with a substantial possibility of such a result, the state could take measures to combat the possibility. The state is under no obligation to allow otherwise "private" activity which will result in numbers of people becoming public charges or otherwise burdening the public welfare. But we do not find that such a situation exists today regarding marijuana. It appears that effects of marijuana on the individual are not serious enough to justify widespread concern, at least as compared with the far more dangerous effects of alcohol, barbiturates and amphetamines. Moreover, the current patterns of use in the United States are not such as would warrant concern that in the future consumption patterns are likely to change.

But one way in which use of marijuana most clearly does affect the general public is in regard to its effect on driving. All of which brings us to the opposite (from the home) end of the scale of the right to privacy in the context of ingestion or possession of marijuana, namely, when the individual is operating a motor vehicle. Recent research has produced increasing evidence of significant impairment of the driving ability of persons under the influence of cannabis. Distortion of time perception, impairment of psychomotor function, and increased selectivity in attentiveness to surroundings apparently can combine to lower driver ability. In this regard, Ravin points out that marijuana usually produces passivity and inactivity, in contrast to alcohol, which increases aggressiveness and is likely to result in overconfidence in one's driving ability. Although a person under the influence of marijuana may be less likely to attempt to drive than a person under the influence of alcohol, there exists the potential for serious harm to the health and safety of the general public.

In view of the foregoing, we believe that at present, the need for control of drivers under the influence of marijuana and the existing doubts as to the safety of marijuana, demonstrate a sufficient justification for the prohibition found in AS 17.12.010 as an exercise of the state's police power for the public welfare. Given the evidence of the effect of marijuana on driving an individual's right to possess or ingest marijuana while driving would be subject to the prohibition provided for in AS 17.12.010. However, given the relative insignificance of marijuana consumption as a health problem in our society at present, we do not believe that the potential harm generated by drivers under the influence of marijuana, standing alone, creates a close and substantial relationship between the public welfare and control of ingestion of marijuana or possession of it in the home for personal use. Thus we conclude that no adequate justification for the state's intrusion into the citizen's right to privacy by its prohibition of possession of marijuana by an adult for personal consumption in the home has been shown. The privacy of the individual's home cannot be breached absent a persuasive showing of a close and substantial relationship of the intrusion to a legitimate governmental interest. Here, mere scientific doubts will not suffice. The state must demonstrate a need based on proof that the public health or welfare will in fact suffer if the controls are not applied.

The state has a legitimate concern with avoiding the spread of marijuana use to adolescents who may not be equipped with the maturity to handle the experience prudently, as well as a legitimate concern with the problem of driving under the influence of marijuana. Yet these interests are insufficient to justify intrusions into the rights of adults in the privacy of their own homes. Further, neither the federal or Alaska constitution affords protection for the buying or selling of marijuana, nor absolute protection for its use or possession in public. Possession at home of amounts of marijuana indicative of intent to sell rather than possession for personal use is likewise unprotected.

In view of our holding that possession of marijuana by adults at home for personal use is constitutionally protected, we wish to make clear that we do not mean to condone the use of marijuana. The experts who testified below, including petitioner's witnesses, were unanimously opposed to the use of any psychoactive drugs. We agree completely. It is the responsibility of every individual to consider carefully the ramifications for himself and for those around him of using such substances. With the freedom which our society offers to each of us to order our lives as we see fit goes the duty to live responsibly, for our own sakes and for society's. This result can best be achieved, we believe, without the use of psychoactive substances.

Chapter 4

Sentencing and Civil Sanctions

A. An Introduction to Sentencing

An examination of the sentencing of drug offenders is necessarily complicated by the diverse approaches to sentencing in the United States today. Each state has its own sentencing system, as does the federal government, and these schemes can differ in significant ways. Indeed, many law schools offer a course devoted specifically to sentencing law and policy. *See, e.g.,* Douglas A. Berman, Nora Demleitner, Marc Miller and Ronald Wright, Sentencing Law and Policy: Cases, Statutes and Guidelines (3rd ed. forthcoming 2013).

Though the statutory schemes in which drug sentencing issues arise can vary, jurisdictions across the country wrestle with many of the same issues when sentencing drug offenders. Sentencing problems common to drug cases are the focus of this Chapter. Nevertheless, an appreciation of the basic principles of sentencing law in the United States today, with a particular focus on the federal sentencing system, is essential to contextualizing and understanding drug sentencing problems.

Speech at the American Bar Association Annual Meeting
An Address by Anthony M. Kennedy,
Associate Justice, Supreme Court of the United States
August 9, 2003

Were we to enter the hidden world of punishment, we should be startled by what we see. Consider its remarkable scale. The nationwide inmate population today is about 2.1 million people. In California, even as we meet, this State alone keeps over 160,000 persons behind bars. In countries such as England, Italy, France and Germany, the incarceration rate is about 1 in 1,000 persons. In the United States it is about 1 in 143.

We must confront another reality. Nationwide, more than 40% of the prison population consists of African-American inmates. About 10% of African-American men in their mid-to-late 20s are behind bars. In some cities more than 50% of young African-American men are under the supervision of the criminal justice system.

While economic costs, defined in simple dollar terms, are secondary to human costs, they do illustrate the scale of the criminal justice system. The cost of housing, feeding and caring for the inmate population in the United States is over 40 billion dollars per year. In the State of California alone, the cost of maintaining each inmate in the correctional system is about $26,000 per year. And despite the high expenditures in prison, there remain urgent, unmet needs in the prison system.

To compare prison costs with the cost of educating school children is, to some extent, to compare apples with oranges, because the State must assume the full burden of housing, subsistence, and medical care for prisoners, yet the statistics are troubling. When it costs so much more to incarcerate a prisoner than to educate a child, we should take special care to ensure that we are not incarcerating too many persons for too long.

It requires one with more expertise in the area than I possess to offer a complete analysis, but it does seem justified to say this: Our resources are misspent, our punishments too severe, our sentences too long.

In the federal system the sentencing guidelines are responsible in part for the increase in prison terms. In my view the guidelines were, and are, necessary. Before they were in place, a wide disparity existed among the sentences given by different judges, and even among sentences given by a single judge. As my colleague Justice Breyer has pointed out, however, the compromise that led to the guidelines led also to an increase in the length of prison terms. We should revisit this compromise. The Federal Sentencing Guidelines should be revised downward.

By contrast to the guidelines, I can accept neither the necessity nor the wisdom of federal mandatory minimum sentences. In too many cases, mandatory minimum sentences are unwise and unjust.

Consider this case: A young man with no previous serious offense is stopped on the George Washington Memorial Parkway near Washington D.C. by United States Park Police. He is stopped for not wearing a seatbelt. A search of the car follows and leads to the discovery of just over 5 grams of crack cocaine in the trunk. The young man is indicted in federal court. He faces a mandatory minimum sentence of five years. If he had taken an exit and left the federal road, his sentence likely would have been measured in terms of months, not years.

United States Marshals can recount the experience of leading a young man away from his family to begin serving his term. His mother says, "How long will my boy be gone?" They say "Ten years" or "15 years." Ladies and gentlemen, I submit to you that a 20-year-old does not know how long ten or fifteen years is. One day in prison is longer than almost any day you and I have had to endure.

Reconceptualizing Sentencing
Douglas A. Berman
2005 University of Chicago Legal Forum 1

The transformation of the sentencing enterprise throughout the United States over the past three decades has been remarkable. The field of sentencing, once rightly accused of being "lawless," is now replete with law. Legislatures and sentencing commissions have replaced the discretionary indeterminate sentencing systems that had been dominant for nearly a century with an array of structured or guideline systems to govern sentencing decisionmaking. These modern sentencing developments constitute one of the most dynamic and important law reform stories in recent American legal history—a veritable sentencing revolution.

Beginning in the late nineteenth century and throughout the first three-quarters of the twentieth century, a highly discretionary system was the dominant approach to sentencing. Trial judges in both federal and state systems had nearly unfettered discretion to impose upon defendants any sentence from within the broad statutory ranges provided for criminal offenses; parole officials likewise possessed unfettered discretion to decide precisely when offenders were to be allowed to leave prison.

Though lacking a fundamental legal structure, this model of sentencing was formally and fully conceptualized around the "rehabilitative ideal." Trial judges were afforded broad discretion in the imposition of sentencing terms, and parole officials exercised similar discretion concerning prison release dates, for a clear and defined purpose: to allow sentences to be tailored to the rehabilitation prospects and progress of each individual offender. The rehabilitative ideal often was conceived and discussed in medical terms, with offenders described as "sick" and punishments aspiring to "cure the patient." Sentencing judges and parole officials were thought to have unique insights and expertise in deciding what sorts and lengths of punishments were necessary to best serve each criminal offender's rehabilitation potential. Sentencing was conceived procedurally as a form of administrative decisionmaking in which sentencing experts, aided by complete information about offenders, and possessing unfettered discretion, were expected to craft individualized sentences "almost like a doctor or social worker exercising clinical judgment."

In 1949, the United States Supreme Court constitutionally approved this philosophical and procedural approach to sentencing in *Williams v. New York*. The trial judge in *Williams* sentenced to death a defendant convicted of first-degree murder, despite a jury recommendation of life imprisonment. The trial court relied upon information about the defendant's illegal and unsavory activities that was not presented at trial, but rather appeared in a pre-sentence report. Rejecting a claim that Williams had a right to confront and cross-examine the witnesses against him, the Supreme Court emphasized that "reformation and rehabilitation of offenders have become important goals of criminal jurisprudence." The Court spoke approvingly of judges and parole boards exercising broad discretion in order to further the "prevalent modern philosophy of penology that the punishment should fit the offender and not merely the crime."

While the theory and procedures of the rehabilitative model of sentencing were being sanctioned in the United States Supreme Court, in other quarters they were being questioned. Through the 1960s and 1970s, criminal justice scholars grew concerned about the unpredictable and disparate sentences that highly discretionary sentencing systems could produce. Evidence suggested that broad judicial sentencing discretion resulted in substantial and undue differences in the lengths and types of sentences meted out to similar defendants. Some studies found that personal factors, such as an offender's race, gender, and socioeconomic status, impacted sentencing outcomes and accounted for certain disparities.

Driven by concerns about the disparities resulting from highly discretionary sentencing practices—which dovetailed with concerns about increasing crime rates and broad criticisms of the entire rehabilitative model of punishment and corrections—criminal justice experts and scholars proposed reforms to bring greater consistency and certainty to the sentencing enterprise. Led by the groundbreaking and highly influential work of Judge Marvin Frankel, many reformers came to propose or endorse some form of sentencing guidelines to govern sentence determinations. Reformers also suggested creating specialized commissions to develop these guidelines.

The calls for reform were soon heeded. Through the late 1970s and early 1980s, a few states adopted a form of sentencing guidelines when legislatures passed determinate sentencing statutes that abolished parole and created presumptive sentencing ranges for various classes of offenses. Minnesota became the first state to adopt comprehensively the guidelines reform model in 1978, when the Minnesota legislature established the Minnesota Sentencing Guidelines Commission to develop sentencing guidelines. Pennsylvania and Washington followed suit by creating their own distinctive forms of sentencing commissions and guidelines in 1982 and 1983 respectively. The federal government soon thereafter joined this sentencing reform movement through the passage of the Sentencing Reform Act of 1984 ("SRA"), which created the United States Sentencing Commission to develop guidelines for federal sentencing. Throughout the next two decades, many more states adopted some form of structured sentencing. Though some states did so only through a few mandatory sentencing statutes, many states created sentencing commissions to develop comprehensive guidelines schemes.

Though there is considerable variation in the form and impact of structured sentencing reforms, these developments can be viewed as a "sentencing revolution" that has altered criminal justice practices and outcomes as much as, if not more than, the "criminal procedure revolution" that the United States Supreme Court engineered in the 1960s and 1970s.

An Introduction to Federal Sentencing
Henry J. Bemporad
(12th ed. 2010)

The [federal] Sentencing Reform Act created determinate sentences: by eliminating parole and greatly restricting good time credit, it ensured that defendants would serve nearly all of the sentence that the court imposed. The responsibility for shaping these determinate sentences was delegated to the United States Sentencing Commission, an independent expert body located in the judicial branch. This delegation of authority to the Commission did not, however, end congressional or judicial involvement. Over the years, Congress has mandated particular punishment for certain offenses, specifically directed the Commission to promulgate or amend particular guidelines, and even drafted guidelines itself. Meanwhile, the courts have repeatedly reviewed and interpreted the Act, culminating in the judicial excisions of [the 2005 United States Supreme Court case *United States v.*] *Booker* [543 U.S. 220 (2005)].

As originally written, the Sentencing Reform Act directed the sentencing court to consider a broad variety of purposes and factors, including "guidelines" and "policy statements" promulgated by the Commission. But while it provided for a broad range of sentencing considerations, the Act did not allow an equally broad range of sentencing discretion. Instead, the Act cabined the court's discretion within a grid of sentencing ranges specified by the guidelines, ranges that were mandatory absent a valid ground for departure. A departure from the applicable range was authorized only when the court found "an aggravating or mitigating circumstance of a kind, or to a degree, not adequately taken into consideration by the Sentencing Commission in formulating the guidelines that should result in a sentence different from that described." In determining whether a circumstance was adequately considered, the court's review was restricted to the Commission's guidelines, policy statements, and official commentary.

The Supreme Court's decision in *Booker* fundamentally changed [the federal sentencing guidelines]. Applying a line of recent constitutional decisions, *Booker* held that the mandatory guidelines system triggered the Sixth Amendment right to jury trial with respect to sentencing determinations. Rather than require jury findings, however, the Court excised § 3553(b)(1). The result was a truly advisory guidelines system.

After Booker, the sentencing court must consider the Commission's guidelines and policy statements, but it need not follow them. They are just one of the many sentencing factors to be considered under § 3553(a), along with the nature and circumstances of the offense, the history and characteristics of the defendant, the kinds of sentences available, the need to avoid unwarranted sentencing disparities and provide restitution, and others. The only restriction § 3553(a) places on the sentencing court is the "parsimony" provision, which requires the court to "impose a sentence sufficient, but not greater than necessary," to achieve a specific set of sentencing purposes[.] Beyond this requirement, and the procedural requirement that the court give reasons for the sentence it selects, § 3553(c), the Sentencing Reform Act as modified by Booker places no restriction on the sentence the court may impose within the limits of the statute of conviction. And the sentence the court chooses is subject to appellate review only for "unreasonableness."

While Booker increased the courts' discretion to sentence outside the guidelines, it did not supersede the statutory sentencing limits for the offense of conviction. Even if the guidelines or other § 3553(a) factors appear to warrant a sentence below the statutory minimum, or above the statutory maximum, the statutory limit controls. *Cf.* United States Sentencing Guideline (USSG) § 5G1.1 (explaining interaction between guideline and statutory limits).

Numerous federal statutes include minimum prison sentences; some, like the federal "three strikes" law, 18 U.S.C. § 3559(c), mandate life imprisonment. Defendants often face statutory minimum sentences in three types of federal prosecutions: drugs, firearms, and child-sex offenses.

The federal drug statutes include two types of commonly applied mandatory minimum sentences: drug-amount-based minimums, and recidivism-based minimums. For certain drugs in certain quantities, 21 U.S.C. §§ 841(b) and 960(b) provide minimum sentences of 5 or 10 years' imprisonment. The circuits are divided over whether drug amount must be alleged in the indictment and proved to the jury to trigger these mandatory minimum sentences.

For a defendant who has previously been convicted of one or more drug offenses, the statutes set out a series of minimum sentences up to life imprisonment.

The Guidelines Manual ... contains the Sentencing Commission guidelines, policy statements, and commentary that the court must consider when it imposes sentence in a federal case. The Manual establishes two numerical values for each guidelines case: an offense level and a criminal history category. The two values correspond to the axes of a grid, called the sentencing table; together, they specify a sentencing range for each case. The Manual provides rules for sentencing within the range, and for departures outside of it.

While *Booker* returned a large measure of sentencing discretion to the court, it did not diminish the importance of understanding the guidelines' application in a particular case. This is not just because the guidelines remain the "starting point and the initial benchmark" for the sentencing decision. Statistics show that, while the percentage of guideline sentences has decreased since Booker, courts still follow the guidelines' recommendation more often than not.

The guideline section applicable to a particular case is usually determined by the conduct "charged in the count of the indictment or information of which the defendant was convicted."

Although the initial choice of guideline section is tied to the offense of conviction, critical guideline determinations are frequently made according to the much broader concept of relevant conduct. The Commission developed this concept as part of its effort to create a modified "real offense" sentencing system—a system under which the court punishes the defendant based on its determination of the "real" conduct, not the more limited conduct of which the defendant may have been charged or convicted.

The relevant-conduct guideline requires sentencing based on "all acts and omissions committed, aided, abetted, counseled, commanded, induced, procured, or willfully caused

SENTENCING TABLE
(in months of imprisonment)

Zone	Offense Level	Criminal History Category (Criminal History Points)					
		I (0 or 1)	II (2 or 3)	III (4, 5, 6)	IV (7, 8, 9)	V (10, 11, 12)	VI (13 or more)
	1	0-6	0-6	0-6	0-6	0-6	0-6
	2	0-6	0-6	0-6	0-6	0-6	1-7
	3	0-6	0-6	0-6	0-6	2-8	3-9
Zone A	4	0-6	0-6	0-6	2-8	4-10	6-12
	5	0-6	0-6	1-7	4-10	6-12	9-15
	6	0-6	1-7	2-8	6-12	9-15	12-18
	7	0-6	2-8	4-10	8-14	12-18	15-21
	8	0-6	4-10	6-12	10-16	15-21	18-24
Zone B	9	4-10	6-12	8-14	12-18	18-24	21-27
	10	6-12	8-14	10-16	15-21	21-27	24-30
Zone C	11	8-14	10-16	12-18	18-24	24-30	27-33
	12	10-16	12-18	15-21	21-27	27-33	30-37
	13	12-18	15-21	18-24	24-30	30-37	33-41
	14	15-21	18-24	21-27	27-33	33-41	37-46
	15	18-24	21-27	24-30	30-37	37-46	41-51
	16	21-27	24-30	27-33	33-41	41-51	46-57
	17	24-30	27-33	30-37	37-46	46-57	51-63
	18	27-33	30-37	33-41	41-51	51-63	57-71
	19	30-37	33-41	37-46	46-57	57-71	63-78
	20	33-41	37-46	41-51	51-63	63-78	70-87
	21	37-46	41-51	46-57	57-71	70-87	77-96
	22	41-51	46-57	51-63	63-78	77-96	84-105
	23	46-57	51-63	57-71	70-87	84-105	92-115
	24	51-63	57-71	63-78	77-96	92-115	100-125
	25	57-71	63-78	70-87	84-105	100-125	110-137
	26	63-78	70-87	78-97	92-115	110-137	120-150
	27	70-87	78-97	87-108	100-125	120-150	130-162
Zone D	28	78-97	87-108	97-121	110-137	130-162	140-175
	29	87-108	97-121	108-135	121-151	140-175	151-188
	30	97-121	108-135	121-151	135-168	151-188	168-210
	31	108-135	121-151	135-168	151-188	168-210	188-235
	32	121-151	135-168	151-188	168-210	188-235	210-262
	33	135-168	151-188	168-210	188-235	210-262	235-293
	34	151-188	168-210	188-235	210-262	235-293	262-327
	35	168-210	188-235	210-262	235-293	262-327	292-365
	36	188-235	210-262	235-293	262-327	292-365	324-405
	37	210-262	235-293	262-327	292-365	324-405	360-life
	38	235-293	262-327	292-365	324-405	360-life	360-life
	39	262-327	292-365	324-405	360-life	360-life	360-life
	40	292-365	324-405	360-life	360-life	360-life	360-life
	41	324-405	360-life	360-life	360-life	360-life	360-life
	42	360-life	360-life	360-life	360-life	360-life	360-life
	43	life	life	life	life	life	life

by the defendant ... that occurred during the commission of the offense of conviction, in preparation for that offense, or in the course of attempting to avoid detection or responsibility for that offense." For many offenses, such as drug crimes, relevant conduct extends further, to "acts and omissions" that were not part of the offense of conviction but "were part of the same course of conduct or common scheme or plan as the offense of conviction."

When others were involved in the offense, § 1B1.3 includes their conduct—whether or not a conspiracy is charged—so long as the conduct was (1) reasonably foreseeable and (2) in furtherance of the jointly undertaken criminal activity. The scope of the jointly undertaken criminal activity is not necessarily the same as the scope of the entire conspiracy, and it may not be the same for each defendant. Relevant conduct does not include the conduct of other conspiracy members before the defendant joined, even if the defendant knew of that conduct.

In drug and drug-conspiracy cases, the offense level is generally determined by drug type and quantity, as set out in the drug quantity table in guideline § 2D1.1(c). The table includes a very wide range of offense levels, from a low of 6 to a high of 38; for defendants who played a mitigating role in the offense, the top four offense levels are reduced by 2 to 4 levels.

Unless otherwise specified, drug quantity is determined from "the entire weight of any mixture or substance containing a detectable amount of the controlled substance." "Mixture or substance" does not include "materials that must be separated from the controlled substance" before it can be used. When no drugs are seized or "the amount seized does not reflect the scale of the offense," the court must "approximate the quantity." In conspiracy cases, and other cases involving agreements to sell controlled substances, the agreed-upon quantity is used to determine the offense level, unless the completed transaction establishes a different quantity, or the defendant demonstrates that he did not intend to provide or purchase the negotiated amount or was not reasonably capable of doing so. Drug purity is not a factor in determining the offense level, with four exceptions: methamphetamine, amphetamine, pcp, and oxycodone. For other drugs "unusually high purity may warrant an upward departure" from the guideline range.

The drug guidelines include provisions that raise the offense level for specific aggravating factors, such as death, serious bodily injury, or possession of a firearm. Guideline § 2D1.1(b)(11) provides a 2-level reduction if the defendant meets the criteria of the safety-valve guideline, § 5C1.2.

Criminal history forms the horizontal axis of the sentencing table. The table divides criminal history into six categories, from I (the lowest) to VI (the highest). The guidelines in Chapter Four, Part A, translate the defendant's prior record into one of these categories by assigning points for prior sentences and juvenile adjudications. The number of points scored for a prior sentence is based primarily on the sentence's length. Points are added for committing the instant offense while under any form of criminal justice sentence.

B. Drug Quantity

Formulating a method for sentencing drug offenders is complicated by the ambiguous nature of many drug offenses. For crimes like murder, burglary or rape, the essence of what makes the offense wrongful is easy to grasp. As a result, though there is surely disagreement about how to differentiate more serious from less serious offenses in these areas, the contours of the debate tend to present themselves naturally. Take homicide offenses as an example. Few would disagree that a person who kills "recklessly" should generally receive a lower sentence than a person who kills "intentionally" because the reckless killer is typically less culpable and dangerous than the intentional killer. We may debate how much more severely intentional killings should be punished, or whether certain types of intentional killings such as those that are "willful, deliberate, and premeditated" should be considered more culpable than other types of intentional killings. But there is broad consensus that a primary factor in determining a homicide offender's blameworthiness (and hence her sentence) is her mental state.

By contrast, because drug offenses lack a direct victim and often involve conduct that is more extensive than a discrete act like a homicide or a burglary, there is greater room for disagreement about what makes them fundamentally wrongful. Consider the following scenario: Kingpin is a marijuana distributor in San Diego. He purchases 39 kilos of marijuana from Mexico and pays Addict $1,000 to drive the marijuana across the border in a hidden compartment in Addict's car. Addict makes it across the border successfully and arrives at Kingpin's warehouse. At the warehouse, Addict pays Day Laborer $100 to help her unload the marijuana. Acting on a tip, the police go to the warehouse while Addict and Day Laborer are unloading the marijuana and arrest them both. Kingpin, Addict, and Day Laborer have all committed the crimes of conspiracy and possession with intent to distribute. Should each of them receive the same sentence for their crimes? If not, why not? What objective factors could we use to distinguish each offender's sentence?

As discussed in the Bemporad excerpt above, the sentencing range for a drug offense under the Federal Sentencing Guidelines is determined by the drug type and drug quantity involved. The same is true in most states. Drug sentencing schemes often take other factors into account, of course, but drug type and quantity provide the starting point for determining an offender's sentence in the vast majority of jurisdictions. This section considers the role of drug type and quantity in sentencing.

1. The Importance of Drug Type and Quantity in Sentencing

Fifteen Years after the Federal Sentencing Revolution: How Mandatory Minimums Have Undermined Effective and Just Narcotics Sentencing
Ian Weinstein
40 American Criminal Law Review 87 (2003)

One explicit goal of the sentencing reforms of the 1980s was to increase the severity of federal sentences, particularly for narcotics offenses. This goal has been achieved. Between 1980 and 1995, the average narcotics sentence imposed by federal judges almost doubled, from about forty months to eighty months, despite the abolition of parole. As defendants were typically paroled after serving about forty per cent of the sentences imposed under the old law, the time defendants actually served more than tripled between 1980 and 1995. Although incomplete data prevents comparison of actual sentences served going back to 1980, actual time in prison for narcotics offenses tripled from twenty-seven months in 1984 to seventy-nine months in 1993. Sentences for violent crimes doubled in that period and sentences for firearms offenses nearly tripled.

Another goal of sentencing reform was to decrease unwarranted disparity among sentenced defendants. Of course, there remains very significant debate about the difference between warranted and unwarranted disparity. In practice, however, sentence length is somewhat more predictable today. Differences in sentence length from defendant to defendant turn less on relative culpability and more on the scope of the overall offense in which the defendant was involved. As part of the Guidelines' quest for sentencing factors easily reduced to quantifiable and therefore readily compared scales, the central determinant of sentence length in drug cases is the weight of the narcotics reasonably foreseeable to the defendant who participates in a deal or conspiracy. Thus, a defendant who does no more than help to unload a truck with a ton of cocaine starts at the same sentence level as those who arranged the shipment or who negotiated the sale or purchase of the drugs. Although the Guidelines permit some differentiation among participants, a first-time offender paid one hundred dollars to unload those boxes can face a ten-year mandatory minimum and a guideline sentence of 151 to 188 months following trial. Proof that the defendant who unloaded the boxes also drove another participant to a meeting and made a supportive comment could increase the range to 235 to 293 months. A defendant with a significant criminal history who is the central figure in a plan to sell one kilogram of cocaine could face a sentencing range of seventy-eight to ninety-seven months after trial. Justice is not served by relying on the quantity of drugs as the central element in allocating punishment.

Federal narcotics sentencing is now characterized by harsh and often inequitable sentences. Discussion of the relative increase over the past fifteen years obscures the real impact of the changes. The average time actually served by federal narcotics defendants increased by a factor of three from 1984 to 1992, but defendants' life spans did not change. Their families do not age any more slowly. Thus, the real-life impact for those who face these sentences and their families must be considered and cannot be overstated.

The Reason Behind the Rules: Finding and Using the Philosophy of the Federal Sentencing Guidelines
Paul J. Hofer and Mark H. Allenbaugh
40 American Criminal Law Review 19 (2003)

A case can be made that the [Federal Sentencing] Guidelines underappreciate the importance of culpability as a mitigating factor.

Such a case was made by Judge Jack Weinstein and Fred Bernstein in a policy critique of the Guidelines' approach to *mens rea* in drug sentencing. They noted that *knowledge* that one is engaging in a criminal act is a prerequisite for criminal liability in most circumstances; for example, one can be convicted of possession of a machine gun only if one knows that the gun can be fired automatically. But under the Guidelines, sentences can be increased regardless of whether the offender had knowledge that an aggravating factor was present. A drug defendant can be sentenced for the full amount of drugs she actually carried into the country, even if some of the drugs had been hidden in her luggage without her knowledge. The defendant's state of mind regarding the aggravating circumstance is irrelevant.

Other critics have complained that the Guidelines ignore important aspects of offenders' culpability. Minor members of a large-scale conspiracy can be held accountable for substantial amounts of drugs that they neither owned nor profited from. Economic hardship, drug addiction, a history of physical or sexual abuse, or a lack of guidance as a youth—for many, highly relevant to assessing an offender's culpability—are ignored by the Guidelines and even actively discouraged as grounds for departure.

In their concern to design a workable system and to minimize disparity, the original Commission clearly preferred objective factors, such as drug weight or dollar amount, to subjective ones, such as the offender's role or state of mind, which might be applied inconsistently. The result, however, is that important moral questions of culpability are relatively neglected, while more easily quantifiable issues of harm are elevated to a significance and exactitude beyond their worth. Even former Commissioners have noted that requiring judges to determine the exact amount of drugs or monetary loss involved in an offense gives the Guidelines a false precision.

A great deal of the dissatisfaction with the Guideline system can be traced to one particular guideline: section 2D1.1 concerning drug trafficking. Commentators have argued that this guideline's purpose is unclear, and that it frequently results in lengthy and disproportionate prison terms, particularly for low-level, non-violent drug offenders. Considerable criticism is leveled at the guideline's emphasis on drug quantity, which along with drug type is the primary determinant of sentences under the guideline. We agree that the role of quantity is problematic, but not because the purpose of the drug trafficking guideline is unclear. The purpose of this guideline is the same as other Chapter Two guidelines: proportionate punishment based on the harm of the offense and the culpability of the offender. The confusion arises because both Congress and the Commission have said contradictory things about how drug quantity is related to harm and culpability.

Quantity can be a measure of a drug trafficking crime's *harm*, just as the amount of toxic substance released into a river can be a measure of an environmental crime's harm. The seriousness of different drug crimes then depends on the harmfulness of the drugs that were distributed and the amount for which each offender was responsible. This interpretation is the only way to make sense of the Drug Quantity Table's seventeen different quantity levels and incremental punishment increases. But quantity can also be a rough measure of an offender's *culpability* to the extent it reflects the offender's position within the drug distribution network. In theory, leaders of drug distribution operations will be linked to large amounts, while underlings will be linked only to smaller amounts reflecting their position as wholesale distributer, street-level retail dealer, etc. Congress appears to have understood the relation between quantity and offense seriousness in this way. The legislative history surrounding the Anti-Drug Abuse Act of 1986 describes the quantities tied to ten-year mandatory minimum penalties as typical of "kingpins," "masterminds," those "who are responsible for creating and delivering very large quantities." The quantities tied to five-year minimum penalties were thought to be typical of "managers of the retail traffic," "the person who is filling the bags of heroin, packaging crack cocaine into vials ... and doing so in substantial street quantities."

Having two different ways that quantity might measure a drug crime's seriousness is not better than having one. With no consistent understanding of the reasoning behind the rule, judges are left just to weigh the drugs and mechanically compute the offense level. There is no way to evaluate the guideline or to recognize when it fails to produce the desired result.

———

The use of drug type and quantity in sentencing is especially controversial in drug courier cases because couriers often possess significant quantities of drugs even though they are on the periphery of the drug trade. Critics argue that this can result in punishments that are only minimally related to the defendant's culpability. Imagine, for example, two drug couriers who are each paid $1,500 to drive vehicles across the border. Neither courier is told the drug type or quantity in his vehicle. They are both caught at the border and arrested. Courier A's car turns out to have a moderate amount of marijuana inside of it. In Courier B's car, the agents find a large amount of methamphetamine. In this hypothetical, Courier B is likely to receive a significantly longer sentence than Courier A, even though their cases are arguably indistinguishable from the perspective of moral blameworthiness.

Supporters of the current system typically point to utilitarian considerations. They argue that calibrating drug courier sentences to the drug type and quantity involved in the offense is necessary to sufficiently deter drug importation. If couriers were to receive the same or very similar sentences regardless of what they were carrying, the argument goes, drug cartels would have a strong incentive to give couriers as large a quantity of drugs as logistically possible.

For those who object to current drug courier sentencing practices on retributivist grounds, utilitarian justifications are unlikely to be persuasive. Putting retributivist objections to one side, however, the effectiveness of the current system is also debatable. A recent study by Caleb Mason and David Bjerk shines some light on this issue by analyzing data from probable cause statements for every federal drug smuggling case along the Southwest border of the United States between 2006 and 2010. The authors will be examining the data in a series of forthcoming articles. Their preliminary conclusion, however, is that "the data shows the cartels do compensate [couriers] for differential sentencing risk [based on drug type and quantity], but that doing so is actually quite cheap. As a fraction of the cargo value, it is a drop in the bucket." Caleb Mason, *International Cooperation, Drug Mule Sentences, and Deterrence: Preliminary Thoughts From the Cross-Border Drug Mule Survey*, 18 Sw. J. Int'l L 189 (2011). *See also, e.g.,* Jonathan P. Caulkins, C. Peter Rydell, William L. Schwabe, and James Chiesa, *Mandatory Minimum Drug Sentences: Throwing Away the Key or the Taxpayers' Money?*, RAND (1997) (estimating that arresting, prosecuting, and sentencing more dealers to standard prison terms would be more cost effective than sentencing fewer dealers to longer, mandatory terms).

Though drug sentences are largely driven by drug type and quantity, most sentencing schemes allow for additional factors to influence the final sentence. The federal sentencing guidelines, for example, take offender characteristics like role in the offense or acceptance of responsibility into account for sentencing. In federal drug courier cases, a frequently litigated issue is the extent to which a courier may receive a sentencing reduction under the Guidelines for having played a "minimal" or "minor" role in the offense. *See,* U.S.S.G. § 3B1.2. Under the Guidelines, minimal participants may receive a "four-level" reduction while minor participation yields a "two-level" reduction. Drug couriers who hope to receive these reductions can face an uphill battle in many jurisdictions.

United States v. De Varon
United States Court of Appeals for the Eleventh Circuit
175 F.3d 930 (1999)

Marcus, J.

The central issue presented in this appeal is whether the district court clearly erred in denying a drug courier who imported 512.4 grams of 85 percent pure heroin from Colombia into the United States a two-point downward adjustment for her minor role in the offense under § 3B1.2 of the United States Sentencing Guidelines. U.S. Sentencing Guidelines Manual § 3B1.2 (1996) [hereinafter U.S.S.G.]. We hold that the district court did not commit clear error, that there was in fact ample evidence in the record to support its determination that the defendant did not play a minor role in the offense. Accordingly, we affirm the judgment of the district court.

On June 12, 1996, Isabelle Rodriguez De Varon ("De Varon") smuggled 70 heroin-filled pellets into the United States. She had ingested the pellets and smuggled them from Colombia into the United States inside her body. Upon arrival, De Varon reported to United States Customs. Suspecting that she was an internal carrier of narcotics, the customs officials confronted De Varon and she confessed. The government then accompanied De Varon to a hospital and ultimately recovered 512.4 grams of 85 percent pure heroin. At the time of her arrest, De Varon was carrying $2,350. De Varon admitted that a woman identified only as "Nancy" provided her with $1,350 of travel advance money and instructed her to bring an additional $1,000 of her own money to cover her expenses. De Varon said that upon delivery of the drugs in Miami she had expected to receive $6,000.

A federal grand jury returned a two-count indictment against De Varon, charging her with importing heroin into the United States and with possessing heroin with the intent to distribute it. Pursuant to a plea agreement with the government, De Varon pled guilty to the allegations in Count I and agreed to forfeit the $2,350 she was carrying at the time of her arrest in return for the government agreeing to dismiss Count II. The government also agreed that it would not oppose De Varon's request for a three-level sentence reduction for timely acceptance of responsibility, *see* U.S.S.G. § 3E1.1, or her application for the "safety valve" protection provided in the Guidelines if she met all of the requirements.

The district court accepted the plea and ordered a probation officer to prepare a Presentence Investigation Report ("PSI"). The PSI set De Varon's base offense level under the Guidelines at 28. The officer then deducted two levels because De Varon qualified for the "safety valve" provision and three more levels for De Varon's timely acceptance of responsibility for her conduct. After these adjustments, De Varon's resulting offense level was 23. The probation officer then assigned De Varon a criminal history category of I because she had no prior criminal convictions. The sentencing guideline range for an offense level of 23 with a criminal history of I is 46 to 57 months.

De Varon objected to the PSI's assessment and claimed, *inter alia,* that she should be granted a downward adjustment for her minor role in the offense under U.S.S.G. § 3B1.2. In support of her claim, De Varon argued that she was an internal carrier of narcotics and that she was recruited by another, more culpable participant. Specifically, De Varon relied on the oral statement that she had given to the probation officer who prepared her PSI. That statement is recounted in De Varon's PSI as follows:

> [De Varon] reports that she met a lady by the name of Nancy at the office where she works in Colombia. Nancy inquired about moving some items with the trucking company [that employed De Varon]. After several visits to the company, Nancy asked [De Varon] if she possessed a visa. [De Varon] reports that Nancy knew that [De Varon] was having financial problems. [De Varon] reports that her son is mentally retarded and requires medical attention. Nancy asked [De Varon] if she would bring drugs to the United States. [De Varon] was told that she would have to swallow some pills and that [she] would be paid $6,000. [De Varon] relates that she agreed to swallow the drugs because she needed the money for her ill child. [De Varon] states that she knew what she did was wrong and regrets her actions.

At sentencing, De Varon's counsel further said that De Varon was "prepared to testify to that statement before the Court today, if the Court so chooses." De Varon did not present any other information or evidence in support of her claim.

The district court then denied De Varon's request for a minor role reduction[.]

The district court subsequently sentenced De Varon to 46 months of imprisonment, three years of supervised release, and a $100 assessment. The district court also ordered that De Varon be deported as a condition of her supervised release. De Varon appealed her sentence on the ground that the district court erred in failing to reduce her sentence based on her minor role as a heroin courier.

On appeal, a panel of this Court vacated De Varon's sentence and remanded the case to the district court for resentencing. Following the issuance of the panel's opinion, the government filed a suggestion of rehearing *en banc* with this Court. On May 29, 1998, this Court granted the government's petition, entered an order vacating the panel's decision, and set the case for *en banc* rehearing.

This Court has long and repeatedly held that a district court's determination of a defendant's role in the offense is a finding of fact to be reviewed only for clear error.

The sentence imposed for a particular offense is based upon the applicable sentencing offense levels set forth in Chapter Two (Offense Conduct) of the Sentencing Guidelines. A sentence adjustment for "the role the defendant played in committing the offense" (either mitigating or aggravating) may also be available. Specifically, a defendant may receive a two to four level reduction in her base offense level where her role in the offense can be described as minimal, minor, or somewhere in between. *See* U.S.S.G. § 3B1.2. Minimal participants may receive a four-level reduction, minor participants may receive a two-level reduction, and those whose participation falls in between may receive a three-level reduction. The commentary to the Guidelines instructs that a four-level reduction "is intended to cover defendants who are plainly among the least culpable of those involved in the conduct of a group.... [and their] lack of knowledge or understanding of the scope and structure of the enterprise and of the activities of others is indicative of a role as minimal participant." The application note provides, for example, that a four-level reduction would be appropriate "for someone who played no other role in a very large drug smuggling operation than to off-load part of a single marihuana shipment, or in a case where an individual was recruited as a courier for a single smuggling transaction involving a small amount of drugs." In contrast, a minor role in the offense "means any participant who is less culpable than most other participants, but whose role could not be described as minimal." U.S.S.G. § 3B1.2, comment. (n.3).

The proponent of the downward adjustment—here the defendant—always bears the burden of proving a mitigating role in the offense by a preponderance of the evidence.

Notwithstanding our deference to the district court's discretion in this uniquely fact-intensive inquiry, the district court's ultimate determination of the defendant's role in the offense should be informed by two principles discerned from the Guidelines: first, the defendant's role in the relevant conduct for which she has been held accountable at sentencing, and, second, her role as compared to that of other participants in her relevant conduct. We address each of these principles in turn.

First and foremost, the district court must measure the defendant's role against the relevant conduct for which she has been held accountable. This measurement is compelled by both the Guidelines and our case precedent. The Guidelines provide that the district court should evaluate the defendant's role in the offense "on the basis of all conduct within the scope of § 1B1.3 (Relevant Conduct), *i.e.,* all conduct included under § 1B1.3(a)(1)–(4), and not solely on the basis of elements and acts cited in the count of conviction." In other words, the district court must assess whether the defendant is a minor or minimal participant in relation to the relevant conduct attributed to the defendant in calculating her base offense level.

We believe that this principle of symmetry of relevant conduct is analytically sound. One main purpose of the Guidelines is to punish similarly situated defendants in a like-minded way. However, given the relatively broad definition of relevant conduct under § 1B1.3, some defendants may be held accountable for conduct that is much broader than their specific acts. A conspiracy conviction is the classic example of this phenomenon. In such cases, a defendant's relevant conduct may be coextensive with the entire conspiracy even though her role in that conspiracy was relatively minor. Under these circumstances, a district court may adjust the defendant's sentence for her mitigating role in this broad criminal conspiracy. This adjustment allows a district court to impose a sentence that more closely mirrors the defendant's actual conduct, furthering the Guidelines' goal of imposing comparable sentences for similar acts. However, such an adjustment only makes sense analytically if the defendant can establish that her role was minor as compared to the relevant conduct *attributed to her*. Otherwise, a defendant could argue that her relevant conduct was narrow for the purpose of calculating base offense level, but was broad for determining her role in the offense. A defendant cannot have it both ways. Application note four illustrates this principle by analogy: "If a defendant has received a lower offense level by virtue of being convicted of an offense significantly less serious than warranted by his actual criminal conduct, a reduction for a mitigating role under this section ordinarily is not warranted because such defendant is not substantially less culpable than a defendant whose only conduct involved the less serious offense." According to this example, a defendant must prove that she played a minor role in the relevant conduct attributed to her. Where her actual conduct is more serious than her base offense level suggests, a defendant will not be able to meet this burden. Similarly, where the relevant conduct attributed to a defendant is identical to her actual conduct, she cannot prove that she is entitled to a minor role adjustment simply by pointing to some broader criminal scheme in which she was a minor participant but for which she was not held accountable.

Moreover, a defendant's status as a drug courier does not alter the principle that the district court must assess the defendant's role in light of the relevant conduct attributed to her. In [a prior case], we recognized that courier status in and of itself is not dispositive of whether a defendant is entitled to or precluded from receiving a downward adjustment for role in the offense. Simply put, the drug courier may or may not qualify for a minor role reduction. Having posited this unremarkable proposition, however, it is perfectly legitimate for a district court to consider *any* fact related to a defendant's conduct as a courier in an importation scheme, including her status and assigned tasks in that scheme. Indeed, in many drug courier cases these are the *only* discernable facts. Therefore, when a drug courier's relevant conduct is limited to her own act of importation, a district court may legitimately conclude that the courier played an important or essential role in the importation of those drugs. This is permissible even though facts related to the defendant's status as a drug courier form the basis for this determination. We do not create a presumption that drug couriers are never minor or minimal participants, any more than that they are always minor or minimal. Rather, we hold only that the district court must assess all of the facts probative of the defendant's role in her relevant conduct in evaluating the defendant's role in the offense.

We further note, in the drug courier context, that the amount of drugs imported is a material consideration in assessing a defendant's role in her relevant conduct. Indeed, because the amount of drugs in a courier's possession—whether very large or very small— may be the best indication of the magnitude of the courier's participation in the criminal enterprise, we do not foreclose the possibility that amount of drugs may be dispositive—in and of itself—in the extreme case.

Indeed, the Guidelines explicitly recognize that amount of drugs may be determinative in the context of minimal participants. Application note two states that an adjustment for minimal participation "would be appropriate, for example, for someone who played no other role in a very large drug smuggling operation than to off-load part of a single marihuana shipment, or in a case where an individual was recruited as a courier for a single smuggling transaction involving a small amount of drugs." U.S.S.G. § 3B1.2, comment. (n.2). We do not believe that the Guidelines intended to preclude a district court from considering the amount of drugs as a factor in the context of minor participants.

To reiterate, in determining a defendant's role in the offense, a district court must measure the defendant's role against the relevant conduct attributed to her in calculating her base offense level. This methodology is essential to any evaluation of mitigating role. Only if the defendant can establish that she played a relatively minor role in the conduct for which she has already been held accountable — not a minor role in any larger criminal conspiracy — should the district court grant a downward adjustment for minor role in the offense.

The second principle we derive from the text of the Guidelines is that the district court may also measure the defendant's culpability in comparison to that of other participants in the relevant conduct. We draw this principle from two application notes. Application note one states that minimal participants are those "who are plainly among the least culpable of those involved in the conduct of a group." U.S.S.G. § 3B1.2, comment. (n.1). Application note three says that "a minor participant means any participant who is less culpable than most other participants, but whose role could not be described as minimal." U.S.S.G. § 3B1.2, comment. (n.3). These definitions clearly contemplate some assessment of relative culpability. However, not all participants may be relevant to this inquiry. First, the district court should look to other participants only to the extent that they are identifiable or discernable from the evidence. This is a fact-intensive inquiry. Second, the district court may consider only those participants who were involved in the relevant conduct attributed to the defendant. The conduct of participants in any larger criminal conspiracy is irrelevant.

Relative culpability does not end the inquiry, however. The fact that a defendant's role may be less than that of other participants engaged in the relevant conduct may not be dispositive of role in the offense, since it is possible that none are minor or minimal participants.

In sum, we believe that a district court's determination of a defendant's mitigating role in the offense should be informed by two modes of analysis: First, and most importantly, the district court must measure the defendant's role against the relevant conduct for which she was held accountable at sentencing; we recognize that in many cases this method of analysis will be dispositive. Second, the district court may also measure the defendant's role against the other participants, to the extent that they are discernable, in that relevant conduct.

In making the ultimate finding as to role in the offense, the district court should look to each of these principles and measure the discernable facts against them. In the drug courier context, examples of some relevant factual considerations include: amount of drugs, fair market value of drugs, amount of money to be paid to the courier, equity interest in the drugs, role in planning the criminal scheme, and role in the distribution. This is not an exhaustive list, nor does it suggest that any one factor is more important than another. In the final analysis, this decision falls within the sound discretion of the trial court. Indeed, we acknowledge that a similar fact pattern may on occasion give rise to two reasonable and different constructions. This is inherent in the fact-intensive inquiry specifically contemplated by the Guidelines. As the Supreme Court has recognized, a trial court's choice between "two permissible views of the evidence" is the very essence of the clear error standard of review. So long as the basis of the trial court's decision is supported by the record *and* does not involve a misapplication of a rule of law, we believe that it will be rare for an appellate court to conclude that the sentencing court's determination is clearly erroneous.

Applying the aforementioned analysis to the instant case, the district court's determination that De Varon did not play a minor role in the relevant conduct of heroin importation was not clearly erroneous.

The record amply supports the district court's finding that De Varon did not play a minor role in her offense of heroin importation. First, De Varon played an important or essential role in her relevant conduct of importing 512.4 grams of 85 percent pure heroin from Colombia into the United States. De Varon knowingly and intentionally entered the United States with the entire amount of drugs in her possession. Although De Varon claims that she did not supply the heroin, we believe that it was within the trial court's discretion to conclude that her participation was central to the importation scheme. Second, De Varon's relevant conduct involved carrying a substantial amount of heroin of high purity. Third, although De Varon was, by one construction of the evidence, arguably less culpable than the only other known participant, Nancy, it is altogether possible on this abbreviated record for the trial court to have concluded that Nancy was no more than a messenger and of relatively equal culpability to De Varon. The facts, as recounted by De Varon, even if fully credited by the trial court, establish no more than that she was hired by someone (Nancy) to smuggle one-half kilogram of heroin into the United States, and to deliver the drugs to someone else—albeit unidentified—in Miami. This bare record does not compel the conclusion that Nancy was sufficiently more culpable than De Varon. At all events, these choices fell within the district court's discretion under U.S.S.G. § 3B1.2. Fourth, De Varon's admission that she furnished $1000 of her own money to finance the smuggling enterprise may likewise be taken as support for the district court's conclusion, notwithstanding De Varon's claim that she became involved in the enterprise because of financial problems.

We reiterate that the burden of establishing a minor role in the offense rests with the proponent. De Varon was free to put on evidence in support of her position, and the district court was free to find, as it plainly did, that De Varon failed to meet this burden.

Moreover, the defendant's alternate suggestion that the district court was obligated to investigate and make detailed findings concerning the relative roles of all who may participate in a far-flung narcotics enterprise—that may stretch from the grower, to the manufacturer in a foreign land, through the distribution mechanism, to the final street-level distributor in the United States—is similarly without merit.

On the basis of this record and consonant with this Circuit's longstanding view affording substantial deference to the district court, we conclude that the district court's determination that De Varon was not entitled to a downward adjustment for her minor role in the offense was not clearly erroneous. Accordingly, De Varon's sentence must be, and is, AFFIRMED.

Barkett, J., dissenting.

In applying the law to the facts to determine whether a § 3B1.2 minor role reduction is warranted, a district court should be guided by the spirit and the letter of the Sentencing Guidelines. The "guidance" offered by the majority in this regard is not supported by either, and in fact, conflicts with both.

The majority offers two "principles" which should guide the inquiry: "first, the defendant's role in the relevant conduct for which she has been held accountable at sentencing, and second, her role as compared to that of other participants in her relevant conduct." As the Guidelines make clear, a defendant's "relevant conduct" for purposes of § 3B1.2 includes not just the defendant's *own* acts but also, in the case of jointly undertaken criminal activity, the acts of any other participants in the offense of conviction taken "during the commission of the offense of conviction, [or] in preparation for that offense," whether or not the case is charged as a conspiracy.

This broad understanding of a defendant's "relevant conduct" as expressed in the Guidelines reflects an awareness of two factors of significance here: (1) many criminal endeavors, even those not charged as conspiracies, are joint undertakings involving several participants; and (2) different levels of culpability may be appropriately ascribed to participants in a joint criminal enterprise when those participants perform different tasks in furtherance of the crime charged.

Perhaps no crime illustrates these considerations as effectively as that of importing narcotics through the use of swallowers like De Varon. It is of course true that the completion of this crime requires the participation of a courier, but the actions of a courier are hardly the only components of the crime. Rather, several other significant tasks must be undertaken to complete even the simple crime of importation. Someone must, for example, formulate the plan, recruit the participants, coordinate their actions, locate suppliers, procure the drugs, purchase the tickets, arrange for a drop-off on the other side, and finance the whole venture. All of these activities, which may or may not involve only one person, constitute "relevant conduct" with respect to the crime of importation, "whether or not charged as a conspiracy." U.S.S.G. § 1B1.3 comment. (n.2).

The task of district courts in cases like De Varon's is therefore to determine the relative culpability of the courier as compared to those other participants, if any, who performed the additional tasks necessary to the importation scheme. In a given case, the same person may be found to have performed all the many tasks necessary to complete the crime of drug importation—the masterminding, financing, recruiting, coordinating, procuring, etc. In such a case, that person would plainly not be entitled to a § 3B1.2 role reduction as a minor participant. In other cases, however, the tasks necessary to carry out the crime of importing narcotics will be undertaken by several different participants. Here, if the court finds the defendant "less culpable than most other participants" although her "role could not be described as minimal," it must likewise conclude that a § 3B1.2 minor role reduction is appropriate. Indeed, it is precisely for such cases that § 3B1.2 was intended.

In this case, the district court reasoned that but for the acts of couriers like De Varon there would be no crime of importation, thus essentially rejecting the suggestion that a courier could ever be a minor participant in this crime. Yet this "but for" analysis could be applied to most criminal acts prosecuted, treating all those defendants performing acts necessary to accomplish the crime as equally culpable. The Guidelines, however, reject this categorical approach and instead support the principle of relative culpability by enhancing the punishment for those with greater responsibility in the criminal enterprise and reducing the punishment for those less culpable. Specifically, the commentary to § 3B1.1 identifies characteristics which would make a participant "integral and essential" to the enterprise and therefore more culpable, including the exercise of decision making authority, the nature of participation in the commission of the offense, the recruitment of accomplices, the claimed right to a larger share of the fruits of the crime, the degree of participation in planning or organizing the offense, the nature and scope of the illegal activity, and the degree of control and authority exercised over others.

These same factors also help distinguish those individuals who play only a minor role in the criminal activity from the leaders and other mid-level criminal actors, clearly indicating the Sentencing Commission's view that foot soldiers who actually carry out the crime are less culpable than the "organizers, leaders, managers or supervisors." Under the facts of a given case, a foot soldier may well not receive a § 3B1.2 reduction, but it is wrong to assume that by virtue of his or her participation he or she is automatically to be considered "integral or essential" to the crime.

It is important to recognize what this Guidelines scheme does *not* entail. The majority fears that a defendant could "argue that her relevant conduct was narrow for the purpose of calculating base offense level, but was broad for determining her role in the offense." I agree with the majority that our opinion in *United States v. Fernandez*, 92 F.3d 1121 (11th Cir.1996), in which we reject the defendant's suggestion that his role in the offense could be determined on the basis of an *uncharged conspiracy,* forecloses such an argument. However, under the definition of "relevant conduct" established in the Guidelines, a defendant whose *charged crime* required the performance of several different tasks and whose own actions toward the common goal were minor in relation to the other participants could well be found to be *a minor participant in the conduct on which her base offense level was calculated.* This is directly acknowledged in the Guidelines, which broadly defines an individual defendant's "relevant conduct" for purposes of establishing the base offense level to include "all reasonably foreseeable acts and omissions of others in furtherance of the jointly undertaken criminal activity." U.S.S.G. § 1B1.3(a)(1)(B). *See also* U.S.S.G. § 1B1.3 comment. (n.2) (defining a "jointly undertaken criminal activity" as a criminal plan "undertaken by the defendant in concert with others, whether or not charged as a conspiracy").

Therefore, it seems clear that, under the Guidelines, if a drug courier is found to have acted in concert with others, his or her acts in furtherance of the charged conduct are to be measured against the acts of those others, regardless of whether the offense was charged as a conspiracy or a simple count of importation.

I am also troubled by the suggestion that *in and of itself* the amount of drugs attributed to a defendant has any bearing on whether that defendant is entitled to a minor role reduction. The amount involved may be taken into account, but always as part of the inquiry into relative culpability. The majority asserts that "the amount of drugs in a courier's possession ... may be the best indication of the magnitude of the courier's participation in the criminal enterprise." This may or may not be the case, however, depending on how the amount informs the evidence, viewed in light of § 3B1.2's emphasis on the relative culpability of the defendant to be sentenced. The majority does not explain how it is that the culpability of a drug courier *as compared with* "*most other participants*" in the offense, U.S.S.G. § 3B1.2 comment. (n.3) (emphasis added), would be affected by the amount of drugs with which she was caught. Whatever amount the courier sought to smuggle will be the same amount that defines the offense, and the same amount that must therefore be attributed to the other participants in the scheme. De Varon, for example, was convicted of importing 512.4 grams of 85 percent pure heroin. This is the same amount given to her by "Nancy" and organized by Nancy or others for her to carry. The amount, in other words, remains constant throughout the court's assessment of De Varon's role in the relevant conduct relative to the other participants in the offense. For this reason, when assessing the relative culpability of the participants—the guiding consideration for courts considering requests for minor role reductions—the amount of drugs may well be beside the point.

Finally, I must also dissent from the reasoning used by the majority to uphold the district court's conclusion that De Varon was not entitled to a minor role reduction. First, the district court made no credibility determination regarding De Varon's testimony, and we are in no position to do so here. The most generous interpretation of the district court's ruling on this record is that it provided no indication as to the court's view of the defendant's credibility.

Moreover, assuming that there was such a "finding," which I believe the record refutes, I cannot agree with the majority's analysis concluding that the record in this case "amply supports the district court's finding that De Varon did not play a minor role in her offense of heroin importation." The majority explains that "[t]he facts, as recounted by De Varon, even if fully credited by the trial court, establish no more than that she was hired by someone (Nancy) to smuggle one-half kilogram of heroin into the United States, and to deliver the drugs to someone else — albeit unidentified — in Miami. This bare record does not compel the conclusion that Nancy was sufficiently more culpable than De Varon.

I find this logic flawed. According to De Varon's testimony, if De Varon were to be believed, we know that someone else — maybe Nancy,[6] maybe one or more other participants — masterminded and financed the operation, called the shots, recruited and coordinated the several players, procured the drugs, bought the tickets, and arranged for a drop-off in Miami. In light of this knowledge, De Varon's inability to provide the names of the other participants should not be allowed to render her ineligible for a minor role reduction. Yet rather than assessing De Varon's role in the offense in light of all the relevant conduct suggested by both the law and common sense, the majority implicitly crafts a rule to the effect that, for purposes of § 3B1.2, an unnamed participant to the crime is no participant at all.

The majority's implicit requirement that a defendant must provide the names of all the participants to the crime has the paradoxical and troubling effect of rendering defendants with little inside knowledge or understanding of the larger scheme less likely to receive a minor participant reduction, while allowing those defendants with sufficient knowledge to name all the players and the tasks performed by each to widen the range of participants against whose actions theirs will be judged, thus making them more likely to receive the reduction. Yet as the Guidelines explicitly recognize, a "defendant's lack of knowledge or understanding of the scope and structure of the enterprise and of the activities of others is indicative of a role as minimal participant." U.S.S.G. § 3B1.2 comment. (n.1). This is not to say that where the concerted criminal act involves a single leader and many actors with small roles, the minor players would necessarily be entitled to reductions as "less culpable than most other participants." At the same time, however, minimal knowledge of the larger scheme should not automatically defeat the very defendants who might be most entitled to a § 3B1.2 reduction.

Either a witness who professes to possess limited information about the larger scheme is telling the truth, or she is not. If the judge finds it to be the latter, the judge is free to deny the reduction. But if the judge finds the witness credible and the testimony consistent, the judge may on the basis of the testimony alone determine that the defendant is entitled to a reduction. The judge would, in that instance, consider all of those factors which we know to impact upon the concept of relative culpability, including the defendant's level of education and sophistication, prior involvement in criminal activity, and manner of involvement in the concerted criminal activity relative to other participants.

---

6. If "Nancy was no more than a messenger and of relatively equal culpability as De Varon," this may only go to show merely that both Nancy *and* De Varon were minor participants in the relevant conduct.

With regard to the manner in which De Varon participated in the crime at issue, I am troubled by the complete exclusion from the majority's discussion of any consideration of what, exactly, De Varon *did,* and what is done by an unfortunately high number of the men and women apprehended as drug smugglers at our nation's borders. She swallowed and carried in her intestinal tract 512.4 grams of 85 percent pure heroin, risking not just an extended stay in an American prison, but her very life.[9] This is not a reason that De Varon should not be held responsible for the act she undertook. But the Guidelines direct courts to determine a defendant's relative culpability, and no one can debate the position of a courier like De Varon in the hierarchy of the criminal enterprise. If De Varon was part of a larger enterprise, it is clear that, as a swallower, she was considered by definition as expendable to that organization, for no organization, illicit or otherwise, would risk the lives of its central or valuable members in this way. The fact that De Varon filled the role of swallower in the importation scheme cannot be totally ignored in considering whether she was a minor player.

For all the foregoing reasons, I would reverse the district court's denial of De Varon's request for a § 3B1.2 minor participant reduction, and remand for the court to consider whether De Varon met her burden of demonstrating that she was less culpable than most other participants in the offense.

————————

The mitigating role provision of the federal sentencing guidelines at issue in *De Varon* is just one of many factors that may be taken into account when sentencing drug offenders under the Guidelines. *See,* William J. Wilkins, Jr., Phyllis J. Newton and John R. Steer, *Competing Sentencing Policies in a "War on Drugs" Era,* 28 WAKE FOREST L. REV. 305 (1993) (describing how the federal sentencing guidelines apply in drug cases). The U.S. Court of Appeals for the Ninth Circuit, for example, permits district courts to consider a downward departure under the Guidelines if the defendant "had no control over, or knowledge of, the purity of the [drugs] that he delivered." *United States v. Mendoza,* 121 F.3d 510 (9th Cir. 1997). Other circuits have rejected this approach, however. *See, e.g., United States v. Beltran,* 122 F.3d 1156 (8th Cir. 1997) (holding that the sentencing court could not depart downward based on drug purity).

Because sentencing schemes vary from state to state, the extent to which factors other than drug type and quantity are considered at sentencing is different in every state. In general, however, the type and quantity of drugs involved in the offense plays a central role in state drug sentencing laws.

The United States is not alone in emphasizing drug type and quantity in sentencing. In the United Kingdom, for example, "the weight and class of drug captured [also] largely determine the sentence." Jennifer Fleetwood, *Five Kilos,* 51 BRIT. J. CRIMINOLOGY 375 (2011). Although drug type and quantity may play a similar role for sentencing in other countries, the United States often imposes longer sentences than other countries for comparable drug amounts. *See, e.g.,* MaryBeth Lipp, *A New Perspective on the "War on Drugs": Comparing the Consequences of Sentencing Policies in the United States and England,* 37

————————

9. *See United States v. Purchess,* 107 F.3d 1261, 1263–64, 1270–71 (7th Cir.1997) (affirming a § 5K2.1 upward departure for conduct resulting in death, where the defendant was convicted of organizing the importation of drugs through the use of swallowers and one of his couriers died en route of "body packer syndrome" after a "deadly amount of cocaine [] leaked from the [ingested drug-filled] pellets"); *Huguez v. United States,* 406 F.2d 366, 391 (9th Cir.1968) (explaining that "the acidic nature of the gastric juices in the [stomach] makes the swallowing of almost any flexible container of narcotics quite dangerous").

Loy. L.A. L. Rev. 979 (2004) ("In Britain, an offender possessing five grams of crack could serve from zero to six months' incarceration, while in the United States, the same first-time offender must serve five years' incarceration.").

2. Measuring Drug Quantity

a. Carrier Mediums and Cutting Agents

Chapman v. United States

Supreme Court of the United States
500 U.S. 453 (1991)

Chief Justice Rehnquist delivered the opinion of the Court.

Section 841(b)(1)(B)(v) of Title 21 of the United States Code calls for a mandatory minimum sentence of five years for the offense of distributing more than one gram of a "mixture or substance containing a detectable amount of lysergic acid diethylamide (LSD)." We hold that it is the weight of the blotter paper containing LSD, and not the weight of the pure LSD, which determines eligibility for the minimum sentence.

Petitioners Richard L. Chapman, John M. Schoenecker, and Patrick Brumm were convicted of selling 10 sheets (1,000 doses) of blotter paper containing LSD, in violation of §841(a). The District Court included the total weight of the paper and LSD in determining the weight of the drug to be used in calculating petitioners' sentences. Accordingly, although the weight of the LSD alone was approximately 50 milligrams, the 5.7 grams combined weight of LSD and blotter paper resulted in the imposition of the mandatory minimum sentence of five years required by §841(b)(1)(B)(v) for distributing more than 1 gram of a mixture or substance containing a detectable amount of LSD. The entire 5.7 grams was also used to determine the base offense level under the United States Sentencing Commission, Guidelines Manual (1990) (Sentencing Guidelines). Petitioners appealed, claiming that the blotter paper is only a carrier medium, and that its weight should not be included in the weight of the drug for sentencing purposes. Alternatively, they argued that if the statute and Sentencing Guidelines were construed so as to require inclusion of the blotter paper or other carrier medium when calculating the weight of the drug, this would violate the right to equal protection incorporated in the Due Process Clause of the Fifth Amendment.

Title 21 U. S. C. §841(b)(1)(B) provides that

> "any person who violates subsection (a) of this section [making it unlawful to knowingly or intentionally manufacture, distribute, dispense, or possess with intent to manufacture, distribute, or dispense, a controlled substance] shall be sentenced as follows:
>
> ....
>
> "(1)(B) In the case of a violation of subsection (a) of this section involving—
>
> ....
>
> "(v) 1 gram or more of a mixture or substance containing a detectable amount of lysergic acid diethylamide (LSD);
>
> ....
>
> "such person shall be sentenced to a term of imprisonment which may not be less than 5 years...."

Section 841(b)(1)(A)(v) provides for a mandatory minimum of 10 years' imprisonment for a violation of subsection (a) involving "10 grams or more of a mixture or substance containing a detectable amount of [LSD]." Section 2D1.1(c) of the United States Sentencing Commission, Guidelines Manual parallels the statutory language and requires the base offense level to be determined based upon the weight of a "mixture or substance containing a detectable amount of" LSD.

According to the Sentencing Commission, the LSD in an average dose weighs 0.05 milligrams; there are therefore 20,000 pure doses in a gram. The pure dose is such an infinitesimal amount that it must be sold to retail customers in a "carrier." Pure LSD is dissolved in a solvent such as alcohol, and either the solution is sprayed on paper or gelatin, or paper is dipped in the solution. The solvent evaporates, leaving minute amounts of LSD trapped in the paper or gel. Then the paper or gel is cut into "one-dose" squares and sold by the dose. Users either swallow the squares, lick them until the drug is released, or drop them into a beverage, thereby releasing the drug. Although gelatin and paper are light, they weigh much more than the LSD. The ten sheets of blotter paper carrying the 1,000 doses sold by petitioners weighed 5.7 grams; the LSD by itself weighed only about 50 milligrams, not even close to the one gram necessary to trigger the 5-year mandatory minimum of § 841(b)(1)(B)(v).

Petitioners argue that § 841(b) should not require that the weight of the carrier be included when computing the appropriate sentence for LSD distribution, for the words "mixture or substance" are ambiguous and should not be construed to reach an illogical result. Because LSD is sold by dose, rather than by weight, the weight of the LSD carrier should not be included when determining a defendant's sentence because it is irrelevant to culpability. They argue that including the weight of the carrier leads to anomalous results, viz: a major wholesaler caught with 19,999 doses of pure LSD would not be subject to the 5-year mandatory minimum sentence, while a minor pusher with 200 doses on blotter paper, or even one dose on a sugar cube, would be subject to the mandatory minimum sentence.[2] Thus, they contend, the weight of the carrier should be excluded, the weight of the pure LSD should be determined, and that weight should be used to set the appropriate sentence.

We think that petitioners' reading of the statute—a reading that makes the penalty turn on the net weight of the drug rather than the gross weight of the carrier and drug together—is not a plausible one. The statute refers to a "mixture or substance containing a detectable amount." So long as it contains a detectable amount, the entire mixture or substance is to be weighed when calculating the sentence.

This reading is confirmed by the structure of the statute. With respect to various drugs, including heroin, cocaine, and LSD, it provides for mandatory minimum sentences for crimes involving certain weights of a "mixture or substance containing a detectable amount" of the drugs. With respect to other drugs, however, namely phencyclidine (PCP) or methamphetamine, it provides for a mandatory minimum sentence based *either* on

---

2. Likewise, under the Sentencing Guidelines, those selling the same number of doses would be subject to widely varying sentences depending upon which carrier medium was used. For example, those selling 100 doses would receive the following disparate sentences:

Carrier	Weight of 100 doses	Base offense level	Guidelines range (months)
Sugar cube	227 gr.	36	188–235
Blotter paper	1.4 gr.	26	63–78
Gelatin capsule	225 mg.	18	27–33
[Pure LSD]	5 mg.	12	10–16

the weight of a *mixture or substance* containing a detectable amount of the drug, *or* on lower weights of *pure* PCP or methamphetamine. For example, § 841(b)(1)(A)(iv) provides for a mandatory 10-year minimum sentence for any person who distributes "100 grams or more of ... PCP ... or 1 kilogram or more of a mixture or substance containing a detectable amount of ... PCP...." Thus, with respect to these two drugs, Congress clearly distinguished between the pure drug and a "mixture or substance containing a detectable amount of" the pure drug. But with respect to drugs such as LSD, which petitioners distributed, Congress declared that sentences should be based exclusively on the weight of the "mixture or substance." Congress knew how to indicate that the weight of the pure drug was to be used to determine the sentence, and did not make that distinction with respect to LSD.

Petitioners maintain that Congress could not have intended to include the weight of an LSD carrier for sentencing purposes because the carrier will constitute nearly all of the weight of the entire unit, and the sentence will, therefore, be based on the weight of the carrier, rather than the drug. The same point can be made about drugs like heroin and cocaine, however, and Congress clearly intended the dilutent, cutting agent, or carrier medium to be included in the weight of those drugs for sentencing purposes. Inactive ingredients are combined with pure heroin or cocaine, and the mixture is then sold to consumers as a heavily diluted form of the drug. In some cases, the concentration of the drug in the mixture is very low. *E.g., United States v. Buggs,* 904 F.2d 1070 (CA7 1990) (1.2% heroin); *United States v. Dorsey,* 192 U.S. App. D.C. 313, 591 F.2d 922 (1978) (2% heroin); *United States v. Smith,* 601 F.2d 972 (CA8) (2.7% and 8.5% heroin) (1979). But, if the carrier is a "mixture or substance containing a detectable amount of the drug," then under the language of the statute the weight of the mixture or substance, and not the weight of the pure drug, is controlling.

The history of Congress' attempts to control illegal drug distribution shows why Congress chose the course that it did with respect to sentencing. The Comprehensive Drug Abuse Prevention and Control Act of 1970 divided drugs by schedules according to potential for abuse. LSD was listed in schedule I(c), which listed "any material, compound, mixture, or preparation, which contains any quantity of the following hallucinogenic substances," including LSD. That law did not link penalties to the quantity of the drug possessed; penalties instead depended upon whether the drug was classified as a narcotic or not.

The Controlled Substances Penalties Amendments Act of 1984, which was a chapter of the Comprehensive Crime Control Act of 1984, first made punishment dependent upon the quantity of the controlled substance involved. The maximum sentence for distribution of five grams or more of LSD was set at 20 years. The 1984 amendments were intended "to provide a more rational penalty structure for the major drug trafficking offenses" by eliminating sentencing disparities caused by classifying drugs as narcotic and nonnarcotic. Penalties were based instead upon the weight of the pure drug involved.

The current penalties for LSD distribution originated in the Anti-Drug Abuse Act of 1986, Congress adopted a "market-oriented" approach to punishing drug trafficking, under which the total quantity of what is distributed, rather than the amount of pure drug involved, is used to determine the length of the sentence. To implement that principle, Congress set mandatory minimum sentences corresponding to the weight of a "mixture or substance containing a detectable amount of" the various controlled substances, including LSD. It intended the penalties for drug trafficking to be graduated according to the weight of the drugs in whatever form they were found—cut or uncut, pure or impure, ready for wholesale or ready for distribution at the retail level. Congress did not want to punish retail traffickers less severely, even though they deal in smaller quantities of the pure drug, because such traffickers keep the street markets going.

We think that the blotter paper used in this case, and blotter paper customarily used to distribute LSD, is a "mixture or substance containing a detectable amount" of LSD. Neither the statute nor the Sentencing Guidelines define the terms "mixture" and "substance," nor do they have any established common law meaning. Those terms, therefore, must be given their ordinary meaning. A "mixture" is defined to include "a portion of matter consisting of two or more components that do not bear a fixed proportion to one another and that however thoroughly commingled are regarded as retaining a separate existence." Webster's Third New International Dictionary 1449 (1986). A "mixture" may also consist of two substances blended together so that the particles of one are diffused among the particles of the other. 9 Oxford English Dictionary 921 (2d ed. 1989). LSD is applied to blotter paper in a solvent, which is absorbed into the paper and ultimately evaporates. After the solvent evaporates, the LSD is left behind in a form that can be said to "mix" with the paper. The LSD crystals are inside of the paper, so that they are commingled with it, but the LSD does not chemically combine with the paper. Thus, it retains a separate existence and can be released by dropping the paper into a liquid or by swallowing the paper itself. The LSD is diffused among the fibers of the paper. Like heroin or cocaine mixed with cutting agents, the LSD cannot be distinguished from the blotter paper, nor easily separated from it. Like cutting agents used with other drugs that are ingested, the blotter paper, gel, or sugar cube carrying LSD can be and often is ingested with the drug.

Petitioners argue that the terms "mixture" or "substance" cannot be given their dictionary meaning because then the clause could be interpreted to include carriers like a glass vial or an automobile in which the drugs are being transported, thus making the phrase nonsensical. But such nonsense is not the necessary result of giving the term "mixture" its dictionary meaning. The term does not include LSD in a bottle, or LSD in a car, because the drug is easily distinguished from, and separated from, such a "container." The drug is clearly not mixed with a glass vial or automobile; nor has the drug chemically bonded with the vial or car. It may be true that the weights of containers and packaging materials generally are not included in determining a sentence for drug distribution, but that is because those items are also clearly not mixed or otherwise combined with the drug.

Petitioners argue that the due process of law guaranteed them by the Fifth Amendment is violated by determining the lengths of their sentences in accordance with the weight of the LSD "carrier," a factor which they insist is arbitrary. They argue preliminarily that the right to be free from deprivations of liberty as a result of arbitrary sentences is fundamental, and therefore the statutory provision at issue may be upheld only if the Government has a compelling interest in the classification in question. But we have never subjected the criminal process to this sort of truncated analysis, and we decline to do so now. Every person has a fundamental right to liberty in the sense that the Government may not punish him unless and until it proves his guilt beyond a reasonable doubt at a criminal trial conducted in accordance with the relevant constitutional guarantees. But a person who *has* been so convicted is eligible for, and the court may impose, whatever punishment is authorized by statute for his offense, so long as that penalty is not cruel and unusual and so long as the penalty is not based on an arbitrary distinction that would violate the Due Process Clause of the Fifth Amendment.

We find that Congress had a rational basis for its choice of penalties for LSD distribution. The penalty scheme set out in the Anti-Drug Abuse Act of 1986 is intended to punish severely large-volume drug traffickers at any level. It assigns more severe penalties to the distribution of larger quantities of drugs. By measuring the quantity of the drugs according to the "street weight" of the drugs in the diluted form in which they are sold, rather than according to the net weight of the active component, the statute and the Sentencing Guidelines increase the penalty for persons who possess large quantities of drugs, regardless of their purity. That is a rational sentencing scheme.

This is as true with respect to LSD as it is with respect to other drugs. Although LSD is not sold by weight, but by dose, and a carrier medium is not, strictly speaking, used to "dilute" the drug, that medium is used to facilitate the distribution of the drug. Blotter paper makes LSD easier to transport, store, conceal, and sell. It is a tool of the trade for those who traffic in the drug, and therefore it was rational for Congress to set penalties based on this chosen tool. Congress was also justified in seeking to avoid arguments about the accurate weight of pure drugs which might have been extracted from blotter paper had it chosen to calibrate sentences according to that weight.

Petitioners do not claim that the sentencing scheme at issue here has actually produced an arbitrary array of sentences, nor did their motions in District Court contain any proof of actual disparities in sentencing. Rather, they challenge the Act on its face on the ground that it will inevitably lead to arbitrary punishments. While hypothetical cases can be imagined involving very heavy carriers and very little LSD, those cases are of no import in considering a claim by persons such as petitioners, who used a standard LSD carrier. Blotter paper seems to be the carrier of choice, and the vast majority of cases will therefore do exactly what the sentencing scheme was designed to do—punish more heavily those who deal in larger amounts of drugs.

Petitioners argue that those selling different numbers of doses, and, therefore, with different degrees of culpability, will be subject to the same minimum sentence because of choosing different carriers.[6] The same objection could be made to a statute that imposed a fixed sentence for distributing any quantity of LSD, in any form, with any carrier. Such a sentencing scheme—not considering individual degrees of culpability—would clearly be constitutional. Congress has the power to define criminal punishments without giving the courts any sentencing discretion. Determinate sentences were found in this country's penal codes from its inception and some have remained until the present. A sentencing scheme providing for "individualized sentences rests not on constitutional commands, but on public policy enacted into statutes." That distributors of varying degrees of culpability might be subject to the same sentence does not mean that the penalty system for LSD distribution is unconstitutional.

We hold that the statute requires the weight of the carrier medium to be included when determining the appropriate sentence for trafficking in LSD. Accordingly, the judgment of the Court of Appeals is

Affirmed.

Justice Stevens, with whom Justice Marshall joins, dissenting.

The consequences of the majority's construction of 21 U. S. C. § 841 are so bizarre that I cannot believe they were intended by Congress. Neither the ambiguous language of the statute nor its sparse legislative history supports the interpretation reached by the majority today. Indeed, the majority's construction of the statute will necessarily produce sentences that are so anomalous that they will undermine the very uniformity that Congress sought to achieve when it authorized the Sentencing Guidelines.

---

6. We note that distributors of LSD make their own choice of carrier and could act to minimize their potential sentences. As it is, almost all distributors choose blotter paper, rather than the heavier and bulkier sugar cubes.

This was the conclusion reached by five Circuit Judges in their two opinions dissenting from the holding of the majority of the Court of Appeals for the Seventh Circuit sitting en banc in this case. In one of the dissenting opinions, Judge Cummings pointed out that there is no evidence that Congress intended the weight of the carrier to be considered in the sentence determination in LSD cases, and that there is good reason to believe Congress was unaware of the inequitable consequences of the Court's interpretation of the statute. *United States v. Marshall*, 908 F.2d 1312, 1327–1328 (CA7 1990). As Judge Posner noted in the other dissenting opinion, the severity of the sentences in LSD cases would be comparable to those in other drug cases only if the weight of the LSD carrier were disregarded.

If we begin with the language of the statute, as did those judges who dissented from the Seventh Circuit's en banc decision, it becomes immediately apparent that the phrase "mixture or substance" is far from clear. As the majority notes, neither the statute nor the Sentencing Guidelines define the terms "mixture" or "substance." The majority initially resists identifying the LSD and carrier as either a mixture or a substance; instead, it simply refers to the combination, using the language of the statute, as a "mixture or substance containing a detectable amount" of the drug. Eventually, however, the majority does identify the combination as a mixture: "After the solvent evaporates, the LSD is left behind in a form that can be said to 'mix' with the paper. The LSD crystals are inside of the paper, so that they are commingled with it, but the LSD does not chemically combine with the paper." Although it is true that ink which is absorbed by a blotter "can be said to 'mix' with the paper," I would not describe a used blotter as a "mixture" of ink and paper. So here, I do not believe the word "mixture" comfortably describes the relatively large blotter which carries the grains of LSD that adhere to its surface.

Because I do not believe that the term "mixture" encompasses the LSD and carrier at issue here, and because I, like the majority, do not think that the term "substance" describes the combination any more accurately, I turn to the legislative history to see if it provides any guidance as to congressional intent or purpose. As the Seventh Circuit observed, the legislative history is sparse, and the only reference to LSD in the debates preceding the passage of the 1986 amendments to § 841 was a reference that addresses neither quantities nor weights of drugs.

Perhaps more telling in this case is the subsequent legislative history. In a letter to Senator Joseph R. Biden, Jr., dated April 26, 1989, the Chairman of the Sentencing Commission, William W. Wilkens, Jr., commented on the ambiguity of the statute:

> "'With respect to LSD, it is unclear whether Congress intended the carrier to be considered as a packaging material, or, since it is commonly consumed along with the illicit drug, as a dilutant ingredient in the drug mixture.... The Commission suggests that Congress may wish to further consider the LSD carrier issue in order to clarify legislative intent as to whether the weight of the carrier should or should not be considered in determining the quantity of LSD mixture for punishment purposes.'"

Presumably in response, Senator Biden offered a technical amendment, the purpose of which was to correct an inequity that had become apparent from several recent court decisions. According to Senator Biden: "The amendment remedies this inequity by removing the weight of the carrier from the calculation of the weight of the mixture or substance." Although Senator Biden's amendment was adopted as part of Amendment No. 976 to S. 1711, the bill never passed the House of Representatives. Senator Kennedy also tried to clarify the language of 21 U. S. C. § 841. He proposed the following amendment:

"CLARIFICATION OF 'MIXTURE OR SUBSTANCE.'

"Section 841(b)(1) of title 21, United States Code, is amended by inserting the following new subsection at the end thereof:

"'(E) In determining the weight of a "mixture or substance" under this section, the court shall not include the weight of the carrier upon which the controlled substance is placed, or by which it is transported.'" 136 Cong. Rec. 12454 (1990).

Although such subsequent legislation must be approached with circumspection because it can neither clarify what the enacting Congress had contemplated nor speak to whether the clarifications will ever be passed, the amendments, at the very least, indicate that the language of the statute is far from clear or plain.

In light of the ambiguity of the phrase "mixture or substance" and the lack of legislative history to guide us, it is necessary to examine the congressional purpose behind the statute and to determine whether the majority's reading of the statute leads to results that Congress clearly could not have intended. The figures [contained] in [the table in footnote 2] of the Court's opinion are sufficient to show that the majority's construction will lead to anomalous sentences that are contrary to one of the central purposes of the Sentencing Guidelines, which was to eliminate disparity in sentencing. As the majority's chart makes clear, widely divergent sentences may be imposed for the sale of identical amounts of a controlled substance simply because of the nature of the carrier. If 100 doses of LSD were sold on sugar cubes, the sentence would range from 188–235 months, whereas if the same dosage were sold in its pure liquid form, the sentence would range only from 10–16 months. The absurdity and inequity of this result is emphasized in Judge Posner's dissent:

"A person who sells LSD on blotter paper is not a worse criminal than one who sells the same number of doses on gelatin cubes, but he is subject to a heavier punishment. A person who sells five doses of LSD on sugar cubes is not a worse person than a manufacturer of LSD who is caught with 19,999 doses in pure form, but the former is subject to a ten-year mandatory minimum noparole sentence while the latter is not even subject to the five-year minimum. If defendant Chapman, who received five years for selling a thousand doses of LSD on blotter paper, had sold the same number of doses in pure form, his Guidelines sentence would have been fourteen months. And defendant Marshall's sentence for selling almost 12,000 doses would have been four years rather than twenty. The defendant in *United States v. Rose,* 881 F.2d 386, 387 (7th Cir. 1989), must have bought an unusually heavy blotter paper, for he sold only 472 doses, yet his blotter paper weighed 7.3 grams—more than Chapman's, although Chapman sold more than twice as many doses. Depending on the weight of the carrier medium (zero when the stuff is sold in pure form), and excluding the orange juice case, the Guidelines range for selling 198 doses (the amount in *Dean*) or 472 doses (the amount in *Rose*) stretches from ten months to 365 months; for selling a thousand doses (*Chapman*), from fifteen to 365 months; and for selling 11,751 doses (*Marshall*), from 33 months to life. In none of these computations, by the way, does the weight of the LSD itself make a difference—so slight is its weight relative to that of the carrier—except of course when it is sold in pure form. Congress might as well have said: if there is a carrier, weigh the carrier and forget the LSD.

"This is a quilt the pattern whereof no one has been able to discern. The legislative history is silent, and since even the Justice Department cannot explain the why of the punishment scheme that it is defending, the most plausible inference is that Congress simply did not realize how LSD is sold."

Sentencing disparities that have been described as "crazy," and "loony" could well be avoided if the majority did not insist upon stretching the definition of "mixture" to include the carrier along with the LSD. It does not make sense to include a carrier in calculating the weight of the LSD because LSD, unlike drugs such as cocaine or marijuana, is sold by dosage rather than by weight. Thus, whether one dose of LSD is added to a glass of orange juice or to a pitcher of orange juice, it is still only one dose that has been added. But if the weight of the orange juice is to be added to the calculation, then the person who sells the single dose of LSD in a pitcher rather than in a glass will receive a substantially higher sentence. If the weight of the carrier is included in the calculation not only does it lead to huge disparities in sentences among LSD offenders, but also it leads to disparities when LSD sentences are compared to sentences for other drugs.

There is nothing in our jurisprudence that compels us to interpret an ambiguous statute to reach such an absurd result. In construing a statute, Learned Hand wisely counseled us to look first to the words of the statute, but "not to make a fortress out of the dictionary; but to remember that statutes always have some purpose or object to accomplish, whose sympathetic and imaginative discovery is the surest guide to their meaning." In the past, we have recognized that "frequently words of general meaning are used in a statute, words broad enough to include an act in question, and yet a consideration of ... the absurd results which follow from giving such broad meaning to the words, makes it unreasonable to believe that the legislator intended to include the particular act."

Undoubtedly, Congress intended to punish drug traffickers severely, and in particular, Congress intended to punish those who sell large quantities of drugs more severely than those who sell small quantities. But it did not express any intention to treat those who sell LSD differently from those who sell other dangerous drugs. The majority's construction of the statute fails to embody these legitimate goals of Congress. Instead of punishing more severely those who sell large quantities of LSD, the Court would punish more severely those who sell small quantities of LSD in weighty carriers, and instead of sentencing in comparable ways those who sell different types of drugs, the Court would sentence those who sell LSD to longer terms than those who sell proportionately equivalent quantities of other equally dangerous drugs. The Court today shows little respect for Congress' handiwork when it construes a statute to undermine the very goals that Congress sought to achieve.

I respectfully dissent.

––––––––––

Most states follow the federal law's approach and measure quantity based on the weight of the total "mixture or substance" rather than the pure controlled substance alone. *Chapman* presents a hard question about how far to extend this principle. But where "cutting agents" are used (such as in the sale of heroin or cocaine), application of the rule is straightforward and relatively uncontroversial. In dissent, Justice Stevens argues that "[t]he consequences of the majority's construction of 21 U. S. C. § 841 are so bizarre that I cannot believe they were intended by Congress." But if cutting agents are included in the measurement of heroin or cocaine, what makes including the weight of the carrier paper (or sugar cube) when weighing LSD bizarre? If the weight of the carrier relative to the weight of the LSD is the answer, what is the response to the case referenced by Justice Rehnquist where the amount of heroin in the overall mixture was only 1.2%? Is the difference between carrier paper and cutting agents simply one of degree?

Not all are in agreement with *Chapman*'s application of "mixture or substance" in the context of carrier mediums. The federal Sentencing Commission, for example, disavowed the approach, instructing: "[i]n the case of LSD on a carrier medium (e.g., a sheet of blotter paper), do not use the weight of the LSD/carrier medium. Instead, treat each dose of LSD on the carrier medium as equal to 0.4 mg of LSD for the purposes of the [Guidelines'] Drug Quantity Table." U.S.S.G. § 2D1.1(c) note g. *Chapman* remains good law, however, for purposes of mandatory minimum sentencing. The result is somewhat peculiar and cumbersome: the weight of an LSD carrier medium is included when applying federal mandatory minimum sentencing provisions but not when applying the federal Sentencing Guidelines. *See* United States v. Morgan, 292 F.3d 460, 465 (5th Cir. 2002) (explaining that the "[a]mendments to the Guidelines to not override *Chapman* for the purpose of statutory mandatory minimums").

Minnesota v. Peck

Supreme Court of Minnesota
773 N.W. 2d 768 (2009)

Anderson, G. Barry, Justice.

A person commits a first-degree controlled-substance crime if that person possesses one or more "mixtures" that contain a controlled substance and that weigh 25 grams or more. Minn. Stat. § 152.021, subd. 2(1) (2008). In this appeal we consider whether the term "mixture" applies to bong water that tests positive for the presence of a controlled substance. Appellant State of Minnesota charged respondent Sara Ruth Peck with several drug-related offenses, including first-degree possession of a controlled substance. The first-degree possession charge alleged that Peck possessed 37.17 grams of bong water that tested positive for the presence of methamphetamine. Peck moved to dismiss the first-degree controlled-substance charge for lack of probable cause, arguing that as a matter of law the 37.17 grams of bong water did not constitute a "mixture" under Minn. Stat. § 152.01, subd. 9a (2008). The district court granted Peck's motion. The State filed a pretrial appeal. The court of appeals affirmed. We granted the State's petition for further review.

On August 30, 2007, the Rice County Sheriff's Department executed a search warrant for Peck's residence located in Rice County, Minnesota. Peck and her two minor children were home at the time of the search. During the search, police seized several items, including a small plastic bag found in Peck's purse containing a substance that tested positive for methamphetamine, another plastic bag containing "crystalline residue," a digital scale, a spoon with residue, a glass pipe with apparent methamphetamine residue, and a glass water bong with liquid in it.

Photographs taken of the glass water bong indicate that the police found it with a small button placed over the opening. The police transferred the bong water to a glass jar and submitted the water to the St. Paul Police Department Crime Laboratory for testing. On September 4, 2007, the crime lab issued a report indicating that the jar contained a "pink liquid exhibiting a fruity odor," and that the liquid weighed 37.17 grams and tested positive for the presence of methamphetamine.

On September 5, 2007, the Rice County Attorney filed a complaint against Peck charging her with first-degree possession of a controlled substance under Minn. Stat. § 152.021, subd. 2(1), fifth-degree possession of a controlled substance under Minn. Stat. § 152.025, subd. 2(1), and child endangerment under Minn. Stat. § 609.378, subd. 1(b)(2). On January 24, 2008, Peck filed a motion challenging the State's probable cause on the first-degree controlled-substance charge. Peck argued that as a matter of law the 37.17 grams of bong water did not constitute a "mixture" under Minn. Stat. § 152.01, subd. 9a (defining "mixture" as "a preparation, compound, mixture, or substance containing a controlled substance, regardless of purity").

An omnibus hearing was held on February 29, 2008, and the State presented its evidence through the testimony of Minnesota State Patrol Trooper Douglas Rauenhorst. Rauenhorst was not involved in the search and seizure in Peck's case, but testified based on his experience and training as a certified narcotics K-9 handler. Rauenhorst explained that he and his K-9 partner had responded to more than 1,000 narcotic-related incidents. Rauenhorst testified that he reviewed the information, reports, and photographs pertaining to the case. Through Rauenhorst, the State introduced the report of the St. Paul Police Department Crime Laboratory.

Rauenhorst also testified about the common usage of a bong. He explained that a bong is often used to smoke controlled substances. Rauenhorst testified that while a person can use a bong without water, it is normally used with water. Rauenhorst explained that the water "is used in sucking the smoke from the end of the ball of the [bong] through the water up to the consumer." Rauenhorst agreed that "[w]hen a person is smoking with a bong pipe, they don't ordinarily inhale the water ... [o]r ingest the water."

Rauenhorst further testified that the pink coloring and fruity odor of the liquid discovered in Peck's bong was significant. He explained that bong water is not normally colored or scented. When asked why a narcotics user would keep bong water, Rauenhorst replied, "for future use ... either drinking it or shooting it in the veins." Rauenhorst further testified that he had actual knowledge of narcotics users consuming water with methamphetamine. On cross-examination, Rauenhorst was unsure whether bong users might flavor the water in order to flavor the smoke.

On March 27, 2008, the district court issued its order granting Peck's motion to dismiss the first-degree controlled-substance charge for lack of probable cause. The State filed a pretrial appeal to the Minnesota Court of Appeals, which affirmed the district court decision. The State filed a petition for review, which we granted.

The issue is whether the water containing methamphetamine stored in Peck's bong falls within the definition of "mixture" set forth in Minn. Stat. § 152.01, subd. 9a.[3] The de novo standard controls our review of statutory interpretation issues. When interpreting a statute we must give the statute's words and phrases their plain and ordinary meaning. When analyzing the plain and ordinary meaning of words or phrases, we have considered dictionary definitions.

The threshold issue in any statutory interpretation analysis is whether the statute's language is ambiguous. If the "words of a law in their application to an existing situation are clear and free from all ambiguity, the letter of the law shall not be disregarded under

---

3. The issue in this case is one of statutory interpretation, not whether we approve of the prosecutor's charging decision. The dissent clearly disagrees with the prosecutor's decision, and there is certainly room to debate the wisdom of that decision. But we may intrude onto the executive branch charging function only in very limited circumstances. *State v. Krotzer,* 548 N.W.2d 252, 254 (Minn. 1996) ("Under established separation of powers rules, absent evidence of selective or discriminatory prosecutorial intent, or an abuse of prosecutorial discretion, the judiciary is powerless to interfere with the prosecutor's charging authority."). While the dissent protests, based on commentary from a United States Senator from the Commonwealth of Virginia, that the State's charging decision here "is counterproductive to the purposes of our criminal justice system," the dissent makes no effort to show that the decision here satisfies the standard we articulated in *Krotzer.*

the pretext of pursuing the spirit." A statute is ambiguous if its language is subject to more than one reasonable interpretation. The State argues that the statutory definition of "mixture" is unambiguous. We agree.

Minnesota Statutes § 152.01, subdivision 9a, defines "mixture" as "a preparation, compound, mixture, or substance containing a controlled substance, regardless of purity." A "preparation" is a "substance, such as a medicine, prepared for a particular purpose." The American Heritage Dictionary 1386 (4th ed. 2000). A "compound" is a "combination of two or more elements or parts." *Id.* at 379. A "mixture" is "[s]omething produced by mixing." *Id.* at 1128. A "substance" is "[t]hat which has mass and occupies space; matter. A material of a particular kind or constitution." *Id.* at 1726.

We conclude that when applied to the water containing methamphetamine stored in the bong, the phrase "preparation, compound, mixture, or substance" is clear and free from all ambiguity. Bong water is plainly a "substance" because it is material of a particular kind or constitution. The bong water is a "mixture" because it is a "substance containing a controlled substance"—methamphetamine.

The court of appeals reached the opposite conclusion because it determined that the phrase "preparation, compound, mixture, or substance" excludes a water-based combination such as bong water. But this construction reads out the phrase "regardless of purity" from the definition of "mixture." We have no opportunity to ignore part of the legislature's definition.

Unlike the dissent, we conclude that the water containing methamphetamine stored in the bong does not reasonably fit the definition of drug paraphernalia, which includes any material intentionally or knowingly used to inject, ingest, or inhale a controlled substance. Although a person may add "water" to a bong to facilitate the ingestion or inhalation of methamphetamine, a person does not add "water containing methamphetamine" to a bong to facilitate the ingestion or inhalation of methamphetamine. Unconsumed residual controlled substances are not materials used to inject, ingest, or inhale a controlled substance. In addition, holding that "water containing methamphetamine found in a bong" is part of the bong because "water" is added to the bong to facilitate ingestion or inhalation would lead to absurd results—a mixture of water and heroin found in a syringe would become a part of the syringe because a person must add water, or some comparable liquid, to a syringe to facilitate the injection of the heroin.

We conclude that the definition of "mixture" in Minn. Stat. § 152.01, subd. 9a, as applied to bong water that tests positive for the presence of a controlled substance, is clear and free from all ambiguity. Because the water containing methamphetamine stored in Peck's bong falls within the statutory definition of "mixture," we reverse the lower court decisions and remand for further proceedings consistent with this opinion.

Reversed and remanded.

Anderson, Paul H., Justice (dissenting).

I respectfully dissent from the majority's decision for two reasons. First, I conclude the law does not support the result reached by the majority. The majority's decision to permit bong water to be used to support a first-degree felony controlled-substance charge runs counter to the legislative structure of our drug laws, does not make common sense, and borders on the absurd. The majority reaches its conclusion because it misapplies the plain-meaning rule and fails to consider the statutory language in its application to the facts at hand and in the context of the statute as a whole. The result is a decision that has the potential to undermine public confidence in our criminal justice system.

Second, I dissent because the decision of Rice County to charge Sara Ruth Peck with a first-degree felony offense—an offense that has a presumptive sentence of 86 months in prison—for possession of two and one-half tablespoons of bong water is not only contrary to the law, it is counterproductive to the purposes of our criminal justice system. In a recent article addressing problems with our nation's criminal justice system, Senator Jim Webb (D. Va.) said:

> The United States has by far the world's highest incarceration rate. With 5% of the world's population, our country now houses nearly 25% of the world's reported prisoners. We currently incarcerate 756 inmates per 100,000 residents, a rate nearly five times the average worldwide of 158 for every 100,000....
>
> ....
>
> With so many of our citizens in prison compared with the rest of the world, there are only two possibilities: Either we are home to the most evil people on earth or we are doing something different—and vastly counterproductive. Obviously, the answer is the latter.

Senator Jim Webb, *Why We Must Fix Our Prisons,* Parade, Mar. 29, 2009, at 4. I agree with Senator Webb—Americans are not the most evil people on earth. Rather, we must be doing something "vastly counterproductive." Rice County's decision to charge Peck in a manner far more serious than what was intended by the legislature represents the kind of counterproductive activity that leads unnecessarily to increasing incarceration rates and wasted taxpayer money. I conclude that Rice County's actions are not permitted by law, were not intended by the legislature, and do not benefit the citizens of the State of Minnesota.

As is common throughout the country, Minnesota drug offenses are charged based on weight. Methamphetamine dosages for users range from 100 to 1,000 milligrams a day, depending on the user's tolerance level. Based on such usage levels, a person found in possession of 25 grams or more of methamphetamine is guilty of the most serious drug offense under Minnesota law—a first-degree controlled-substance crime. Based on the weight of the bong water it seized, Rice County charged Peck with a first-degree controlled-substance crime, which is a felony charge carrying a presumptive sentence of 86 months. Peck made a probable cause challenge, arguing that the bong water could not be used to sustain a first-degree controlled-substance charge.

At the probable cause hearing only one witness testified, a witness for the State—Minnesota State Trooper Douglas Rauenhorst. Rauenhorst did not participate in the execution of the search warrant at Peck's residence or have personal knowledge of Peck's case. Rather, Rauenhorst testified based on his general experience, information, and knowledge as a law enforcement officer and the reports provided to him by Rice County.

Rauenhorst testified that users do not ordinarily inhale or ingest bong water when smoking a bong pipe. Rauenhorst explained that "most of the time [the bong water] is not in the bong anymore when they get done smoking and the water is gone," presumably meaning that users typically discard the bong water. When asked why a user would keep bong water, Rauenhorst replied the user would be "[k]eeping the liquid containing methamphetamine for future use."[2] The Rice County prosecutor then asked, "what are *some* of those uses based on your training and experience?" Rauenhorst responded, "either

---

2. It appears that Rauenhorst did not consider the possibility that some drug users are not tidy housekeepers and might not immediately discard their bong water, nor did defense counsel pursue such a line of questioning.

drinking it or shooting it in the veins." Rauenhorst later added that users may consume urine as well.

The Rice County prosecutor also asked Rauenhorst about the pink color and fruity odor of the bong water. Rauenhorst testified that based on his training and expertise, bong water is not normally pink and fruity, and that sugar does not alter the high felt by a user. When defense counsel inquired into whether bong water was ever altered so as to flavor the smoke, Rauenhorst responded, "I'm not sure. I haven't—I don't have prior experience in smoking methamphetamine so I don't know."[3]

There is limited evidence in the record as to how a bong operates, but information on the use of a bong is helpful in understanding the essence of this case. A bong is essentially a water pipe that can be used to inhale various substances, including tobacco, marijuana, and methamphetamine. The standard bong is a tube or cylinder, where one end of the cylinder is sealed shut. The bong cylinder is partially filled with water. The substance to be smoked is packed into a separate bowl with a stem. The stem of the bowl is inserted in the side of the bong cylinder such that the base of the stem rests in the water inside the bong.

The substance packed in the bowl piece is then ignited by the smoker. The smoker then places his or her mouth over the open end of the tube, creates a seal, and then inhales. As the smoker inhales, smoke from the burning substance is pulled through the water in the cylinder. As the smoke passes through the water, the water filters the smoke and cools it. Once the cylinder is filled with smoke, the smoker releases the seal, usually by pulling the bowl and its stem out of the cylinder. The smoker can then inhale the smoke trapped in the cylinder. This process is repeated until the substance in the bowl is entirely smoked. After a smoker is done, both the remaining ashes of the burned substance and the bong water are typically discarded.

Rice County argues that it is within its discretion to charge Peck with a first-degree possession charge because the bong water used to sustain the first-degree charge is a "mixture[] of a total weight of 25 grams or more containing ... methamphetamine." A mixture is defined by statute as "a preparation, compound, mixture, or substance containing a controlled substance, regardless of purity." Rice County argues that the bong water in this case—a liquid which tested positive for the presence of methamphetamine—fits within the plain meaning of the definition of mixture. After making reference to *The American Heritage Dictionary*, the majority agrees with Rice County that bong water is unambiguously a mixture containing methamphetamine.

I disagree, and find ambiguity in applying Minn. Stat. § 152.021, subd. 2(1), to the bong water seized from Peck's residence. The majority employs a very narrow statutory interpretation standard—looking up the word or words in question in the dictionary and determining whether the dictionary definition applies. But Minn. Stat. § 645.16 requires courts to look beyond dictionaries. More specifically, the majority ignores the parameters for statutory construction set out by the legislature and deviates from the manner by which we have historically performed statutory construction.

Focusing on the "language, on its face" permits the majority to declare the statutory language at issue in this case is unambiguous based on a dictionary definition. Of course, every word used in a Minnesota law has a dictionary meaning, so if the majority's plain-meaning approach is taken to its logical conclusion, no word is ambiguous. But the ma-

---

3. A quick and rudimentary Internet search suggests that bong water is commonly altered using fruity flavors in an effort to mask the chemical flavor common to methamphetamine.

jority's formalistic version of the plain-meaning rule is not the standard the legislature has instructed courts to apply when interpreting statutory language. [Minnesota's statutory interpretation provision] does not instruct us to only look at the language; rather, it instructs us to look at "the words of a law *in their application* to an existing situation." As a result, it is not enough to simply look up a definition in the nearest dictionary; rather, we must consider whether the words used in the statute are ambiguous as applied to the facts of the case at hand.

More importantly, the majority does not consider whether the statute's relation to and interaction with other provisions in the statutory scheme create ambiguity. It has long been recognized that "[w]e are to read and construe a statute as a whole and must interpret each section in light of the surrounding sections to avoid conflicting interpretations." We must, therefore, look beyond an isolated word or term and view the statute as a whole in order to determine whether the law at issue is ambiguous as applied.

Taking into account the full standard for statutory interpretation and the facts of this case, ambiguity does arise. Here the police seized a bong and the liquid in it. While the seized liquid can fit the definition of a mixture—"a preparation, compound, mixture, or substance containing a controlled substance"—it also can fit the definition of drug paraphernalia—a material "knowingly or intentionally used" to ingest or inhale a controlled substance.[5] While the bong water fits either definition, the consequences of the various interpretations are dramatically different.

If we treat bong water as a mixture, the weight of which raises the crime to a first-degree felony controlled-substance crime, the presumed sentence for a first-time offender would be 86 months—just over 7 years—and the offender would have a felony drug offense on his or her record. But if we treat the bong water as paraphernalia, the same defendant would receive a fine of no more than $300 dollars and a petty misdemeanor conviction that would not go on his or her criminal record. The disparity in the severity of the sentence between these two possible charges is enormous. This enormous disparity in sentencing severity creates ambiguity as to how the legislature intended the drug statutes to apply to the facts of this case.

Minnesota's current controlled-substance statutory framework was enacted in 1989 and established five tiers of weight-based offenses. One of the sponsors of the 1989 Act explained that the Act was "aimed at fighting a war on drugs in Minnesota, to preserve the safety and stability of our society." The sponsor further explained that the Act was designed so that "[t]he more crack or cocaine that an individual possess or sells, the stiffer the penalties under the provisions of this bill."

One of the commentators at the hearings on the bill was James Kamin, Assistant Hennepin County Attorney, who explained the purpose behind the weight-based system. Kamin said that the Act "makes the penalties commensurate with the crime. That is,

---

5. The majority asserts that while "water" in a bong may fit the definition of paraphernalia, "water containing methamphetamine" could not be paraphernalia because "a person does not add 'water containing methamphetamine' to a bong to facilitate the ingestion or inhalation of methamphetamine." The majority's assertion presents a distinction without a difference. When "water" is added to a bong and used to facilitate the inhalation of methamphetamine, the smoke from burning the methamphetamine passes through the water, turning the water into "water containing methamphetamine." This raises the question of whether the water ceases to be paraphernalia precisely because it was used as paraphernalia. The majority argues, illogically, that it does.

someone who is possessing 25 grams of crack ought to face a significantly stiffer penalty than someone possessing three or four or five grams of crack."

Kamin also explained that possession was punished along with distribution offenses because "it relieves a burden on law enforcement and prosecutors of showing that possession was with the intent to sell" and because "three grams of crack is an awful lot of havoc sitting there in someone's pocket under any circumstances, and ought to be punished appropriately." The weight classes that were established by the act were intended to correspond to the amounts dealers would possess. For example, a third-degree crime was equivalent to the weight amounts possessed by street dealers, a second-degree crime was correlated to retail dealers, and a first-degree crime was intended to apply to wholesale dealers.

As it relates here, it appears the legislature intended to resolve several problems when it enacted the 1989 Act. First, it appears the legislature wanted to impose more significant penalties on serious drug offenders without also imposing those same penalties on minor offenders. Second, it appears the legislature intended to relieve the State of the burden of having to prove subjective intent and of having to undergo significant scientific testing before being in a position to prosecute serious offenders. The legislature relieved the State of significant scientific testing by defining a mixture as a substance containing a controlled substance, "regardless of purity."

Treating bong water as a mixture capable of sustaining a first-degree felony controlled-substance charge does not meet the purposes, aims, or objectives of the legislature when it established the weight-based system. Bong water is not marketed or sold by dealers, large or small, nor is it purchased by consumers. It is not even ordinarily consumed. Bong water is usually discarded when the smoker is finished with consumption of the smoke filtered through the bong water. A person is not more dangerous, or likely to wreak more havoc, based on the amount of bong water that person possesses. The bong water is no more dangerous than the bong itself, because both are used to facilitate consumption without being consumed. Thus, there is no reason to believe the legislature intended to treat the bong water differently from the bong, and there is even less reason to believe that the legislature intended to treat bong water so seriously as to presumptively mandate a more than 7-year prison sentence for possessing two and one-half tablespoons of bong water. As stated earlier, I believe this result to be absurd and a threat to public confidence in our criminal justice system.

The majority's interpretation results in an unreasonable, and possibly unconstitutional, statutory scheme. It is unreasonable that the same conduct should be subject to such disparate treatment based on the discretion of the county attorney. For example, if a student at a university or college in Hennepin or Ramsey County is caught with a marijuana bong in a moment of youthful indiscretion, the prosecutor in these counties may choose to treat the bong and its water as paraphernalia. That student would be charged with a petty misdemeanor, pay a small fine, and have no criminal record. If another student chose to engage in a similar moment of indiscretion at St. Olaf College or Carlton College, both in Rice County, the result is a felony drug conviction, a presumptive sentence of more than 7 years in prison, and a serious criminal record.

I conclude that it is also unreasonable to interpret our legislature's laws as punishing Peck's possession of two and one-half tablespoons of bong water as a more serious crime than the possession of 24 grams of cocaine, heroin, or methamphetamine. Bong water is normally not consumed, and Peck would likely have disposed of it had the police not seized it. Alternatively, 24 grams of heroin is equal to approximately 60 individual doses, 24 grams of cocaine is equal to approximately 200 to over 2000 doses, and 24 grams of methamphetamine is equal to approximately 24 to 240 doses. Yet a defendant caught with 24 grams of cocaine, heroin, or methamphetamine would face only a second-degree charge, less than the first-degree felony charge Peck is facing here. It is both unreasonable and absurd that Peck would face more significant penalties for possession of bong water.

Finally, Rice County's decision to charge Peck with a first-degree crime, and the majority's decision to uphold that decision, serves neither the law nor the interests of the citizens of Minnesota. Peck's actions in this case do not rise to the level of culpability the legislature intended a first-degree controlled-substance crime to carry. Even though Peck possessed only about two and one-half tablespoons of bong water, Rice County is investing the increased resources required to prosecute Peck for a felony-level crime, not to mention the resources that would be required to incarcerate Peck for approximately 7 years.

In his article in *Parade* magazine, Senator Webb pointed out that "we are locking up too many people who do not belong in jail" while at the same time "not protecting our citizens from the increasing danger of criminals who perpetrate violence and intimidation as a way life." Senator Jim Webb, *Why We Must Fix Our Prisons,* Parade, Mar. 29, 2009, at 5. All societies include people who commit evil and violent acts and are truly dangerous, and these kinds of people need to be segregated from society. Even for less violent offenders, punishment as a consequence of misconduct is necessary for a civil society to maintain the rule of law and sustain its moral equilibrium.

But, we as a society and those of us in the criminal justice system need to do a better job of assessing risk when determining how to charge an alleged wrongdoer and what punishment to impose on a wrongdoer who is found guilty. This need for proper risk assessment is particularly critical when it comes to punishing non-violent drug offenders who are presently swelling our prison populations beyond capacity. I believe that the Minnesota Legislature attempted to make such a risk assessment when it enacted chapter 152, which uses weight to distinguish between less serious and more serious offenders. I also believe the District Court Judge, Thomas Neville, and the Minnesota Court of Appeals properly attempted to apply this law based on its intent and plain common sense. On the other hand, Rice County is taking this law in what I believe to be an improper and counterproductive direction that perpetuates the incarceration crisis that Senator Webb has described. Unfortunately, today's decision by the majority affirms Rice County's error and takes us in the wrong direction under the law and under good public policy. Therefore, I express my strong dissent to the decision of the majority.

Oregon v. Slovik
Court of Appeals of Oregon
71 P.3d 159 (2003)

Kistler, J.

Defendant appeals from a judgment of conviction for manufacturing, delivering, and possessing methamphetamine. He argues, among other things, that the trial court erred in imposing enhanced sentences on those offenses because each offense involved 10 grams or more of "a mixture or substance containing a detectable amount of methamphetamine." We reverse and remand for resentencing.

While performing a valid search on June 30, 1999, police officers found items associated with manufacturing methamphetamine. Among other things, they found a gallon jar with liquid in it, two plastic soda pop bottles with residue, a large brown jar, and numerous pseudoephedrine bottles.[2] One of the jars contained a two-layer liquid, the top layer of which was toluene—a solvent that is evaporated in the methamphetamine manufacturing process. Although laboratory tests revealed that the toluene contained methamphetamine, the tests did not determine the weight of the pure methamphetamine contained in the solvent. Rather, they determined that the solvent and methamphetamine together weighed 7.75 grams.

A second jar contained a three-layer liquid. One layer contained chemicals that had been extracted out of the solvent, tested positive for methamphetamine, and weighed 5.8 grams. The second layer, a solution of oil, water, and a brown substance, also tested positive for methamphetamine and weighed 37.4 grams. The third layer, a crystalline substance, contained no trace of any controlled substance. The liquids that tested positive for methamphetamine were in the manufacturing process; that is, the liquids required additional processing to create usable methamphetamine. Until that occurred, the liquids were poisonous to ingest.

The state charged defendant with, among other things, manufacturing, delivering, and possessing methamphetamine. The indictment alleged that each of those three charges—manufacture, delivery, and possession—involved 10 or more grams of "a mixture or substance containing a detectable amount of methamphetamine"—an allegation that made defendant eligible for an enhanced sentence under ORS 475.996(1)(a)(C) and ORS 475.996(2)(b)(C). At the close of the state's case, defendant moved for a judgment of acquittal because the state failed to prove that the liquid containing methamphetamine was in a usable or saleable form. He reasoned that, when the legislature provided for enhanced sentences for drug crimes involving 10 or more grams of a "mixture or substance containing a detectable amount of methamphetamine," it did so only for those mixtures or substances that were ready for sale and use. It did not intend, defendant asserts, to enhance a person's sentence for possessing 10 or more grams of a mixture or substance that was not in marketable form. The trial court denied defendant's motion, and he was convicted of manufacturing, delivering, and possessing methamphetamine. The court imposed an enhanced sentence on each of those convictions.

The issue that defendant raises on appeal is narrow. Defendant does not dispute that a reasonable juror could find that the liquid the officers discovered in the two jars weighed more than 10 grams and contained an unquantified amount of methamphetamine. Conversely, the state does not argue that the methamphetamine that the officers found was in a usable or saleable form; that is, the state does not dispute that the manufacturing process was still ongoing when the officers found the liquid containing the methamphetamine. The question accordingly reduces to a legal issue: Did the legislature intend to enhance a defendant's sentence for manufacturing, delivering, or possessing "a mixture or substance containing a detectable amount of methamphetamine" when the methamphetamine is not in marketable form?

Defendant contends that the statutory phrase "a mixture or substance" is limited to mixtures or substances that are market ready and in a useable form. He bases his argument in large part on *Chapman v. United States,* 500 U.S. 453, 460 (1991), a case interpreting the federal sentencing guidelines on which Oregon's statute was modeled. Noting that the *Chapman* Court explained that the federal government had "adopted a 'market-oriented' approach to punishing drug trafficking, under which the total quantity of what is distributed * * * is used to determine the length of the sentence," defendant reasons

---

2. Pseudoephedrine is extracted from pseudoephedrine tablets and used to manufacture methamphetamine.

that, when the Oregon legislature enacted ORS 475.996, it understood that the phrase "a mixture or substance" referred only to marketable mixtures or substances — typically mixtures or substances that result from diluting a pure drug with a cutting agent before offering it for sale. The state responds that the text of the statute refers broadly to mixtures or substances containing a detectable amount of methamphetamine; nothing in the text of the statute limits its reach to those mixtures or substances that are marketable.

The parties' dispute turns on an issue of statutory interpretation, and we begin with the text and context of the relevant statutes. ORS 475.996(1)(a) provides for an enhanced sentence if a conviction for manufacturing or delivery involves a specific amount of "a mixture or substance containing a detectable amount of" one of eight controlled substances. When defendant committed his crime, the relevant subparagraph provided for an enhanced sentence for a manufacturing or delivery offense that involved "ten grams or more of a mixture or substance containing a detectable amount of methamphetamine." ORS 475.996(1)(a)(C). ORS 475.996(2)(b)(C) similarly enhances a defendant's sentence for possessing "ten grams or more of a mixture or substance containing a detectable amount of methamphetamine."

The texts of those subparagraphs do not expressly limit the type of mixture or substance that will warrant an enhanced sentence; that is, they do not specifically limit the phrase "a mixture or substance" to marketable mixtures or substances. Although the text, viewed in isolation, supports the state's position, the court has explained that a statute's context may reveal a different focus from its text, and we turn to that inquiry.

Under ORS 475.996, "a mixture or substance" is something that a person either delivers, manufactures, or possesses. Those verbs shed light on the meaning of what is effectively their direct object, and we examine each verb separately. "Deliver" means "the actual, constructive or attempted transfer * * * from one person to another of a controlled substance." Delivery connotes the transfer of "a mixture or substance" that is ready for distribution or sale. Typically, a person does not deliver controlled substances until the manufacturing process has been completed and the completed product is capable of being ingested. Put another way, the legislature's use of the verb "deliver" implicitly qualifies the type of mixture or substance to which the statute refers — those mixtures or substances that are marketable. The same is true for possession. Typically, a person possesses controlled substances that are ready for use; that is, the crime of possession ordinarily refers to the possession of a completed product that is capable of ingestion. In the same way that the verb "deliver" implicitly qualifies the phrase "mixture or substance," so does the verb "possess."

The third verb "manufacture" points in a different direction. Manufacture means "the production, preparation, propagation, compounding, conversion or processing of a controlled substance * * * by means of chemical synthesis, or by a combination of extraction and chemical synthesis[.]" ORS 475.005(14). As we explained in *State v. Brown*, 109 Ore. App. 636, 645 (1991), the prohibition against manufacturing controlled substances "prohibits not simply possession of the controlled substance created by the prohibited means, but [also] those acts that ultimately will result in the creation of a controlled substance." Used with that verb, the phrase "mixture or substance" would appear to refer not only to those mixtures or substances that are ready for distribution and use but also to those mixtures or substances that are still in the midst of the manufacturing process.

Defendant also relies on the Court's opinion in *Chapman* as context. As defendant notes, ORS 475.996 was modeled on the federal sentencing statute, which the Court interpreted in *Chapman*. As defendant also notes, the Court explained in *Chapman* that, in enacting the federal sentencing guidelines, Congress "adopted a 'market-oriented' approach" in which the length of a person's sentence is based on the "total quantity of what is distributed." Similarly, when addressing the defendant's due process challenge, the Court stated that the federal statute "measures the quantity of the drugs according to the 'street weight' of the drugs in the diluted form in which they are sold[.]" Defendant reasons that the discussion of the federal statute in *Chapman* reveals that only marketable mixtures or substances—those mixtures that are in a form ready to be sold—would be used to determine whether a defendant's sentence should be enhanced and that the Oregon legislature is presumed to have adopted that understanding when it modeled our statute on the federal law.

We agree with defendant that the Court's discussion of the federal statute in *Chapman* supports his position. We also note that a majority of the federal courts have read *Chapman* to mean that the phrase "a mixture or substance" is limited to marketable mixtures or substances.[10] Despite that understanding of *Chapman*, we are hesitant to give *Chapman's* statements dispositive weight because the question presented in *Chapman* differs from the question presented here.

The question in *Chapman* was whether the blotter paper on which LSD was distributed was a "mixture or substance," the weight of which should be included in determining whether the defendant possessed a substantial quantity of that drug. There was no dispute in *Chapman* that, if the blotter paper were a mixture or substance, it was marketable. By contrast, in this case, there is no dispute that a reasonable juror could find that the liquid in the two jars was "a mixture or substance." Rather, the question here is whether the legislature intended that the phrase "mixture or substance" would refer to any mixture or substance or only those mixtures or substances that are marketable. Because that question was not squarely at issue in *Chapman*, we hesitate to say, in reliance on *Chapman* alone, that Oregon intended to limit the phrase "mixture or substance" to marketable mixtures or substances. We agree, however, with defendant that the text, considered in context, is ambiguous and turn to the legislative history.

ORS 475.996 was a "legislative fix" for a problem that we recognized in *State v. Moeller*, 105 Ore. App. 434 (1991). The defendant in *Moeller* had challenged a sentencing guidelines rule that provided for enhanced sentences for drug offenses that "'occurred as part of a drug cultivation, manufacture or delivery scheme or network.'" We held that the phrase "scheme or network" violated Article I, sections 20 and 21, of the Oregon Constitution because it gave judges and juries unbridled discretion to determine the sort of conduct that would warrant a higher sentence.

Following *Moeller*, Representative Tom Mason introduced a bill to replace the "scheme or network" rule with a more specific test. As initially proposed, the bill provided for a

---

10. *See United States v. Palacios-Molina*, 7 F.3d 49, 54 (5th Cir 1993) (holding that the weight of cocaine mixed with sangria should not be used for sentencing because the cocaine was not part of a "marketable mixture"; only after the liquid was distilled out would the cocaine be ready for either the wholesale or retail market); *United States v. Jennings*, 945 F.2d 129 (6th Cir 1991) (declining to use weight of mixture containing a small amount of methamphetamine and poisonous by-products because the mixture was not marketable); *United States v. Rolande-Gabriel*, 938 F.2d 1231, 1237 (11th Cir 1991) (concluding that weight of liquor in which cocaine was distilled should not be used in weight calculation); *but see United States v. Walker*, 960 F.2d 409, 412–13 (5th Cir) (1992) (holding, in reliance on pre-*Chapman* precedents, that the total weight of waste water containing cocaine should be used to enhance a defendant's sentence); *United States v. Mahecha-Onofre*, 936 F.2d 623 (1st Cir) (1991) (holding that the weight of a suitcase made from a cocaine-acrylic mixture should be used to determine the defendant's sentence).

presumptive prison sentence if a person either delivered certain controlled substances for consideration or if the state proved specific factors, such as the presence of stolen property, a substantial amount of cash, or a substantial amount of controlled substances. There was some concern that the specific factors were themselves vague, and Judge Harl Haas mentioned that the committee might want to look at the federal sentencing guidelines as a way of defining which drug crimes should be subject to an enhanced sentence.

On February 20, 1991, the Oregon District Attorneys Association (ODAA) pursued the approach that Judge Haas had mentioned. It proposed amending HB 2390 to correspond with the federal sentencing guidelines, and the ODAA's proposed amendment became, with some changes, what is now ORS 475.996(1). The ODAA's amendment provided, as ORS 475.996(1) now provides, for enhanced sentences for delivering or manufacturing specified amounts of mixtures or substances containing detectable amounts of certain controlled substances.

Norm Frink, a representative for the ODAA, told the subcommittee why the district attorneys association had proposed the amendment:

> "First, instead of speaking solely in terms of a quantity of a drug, we spoke in terms of a mixture or compound with detectable amounts of the drug. Now, this change is I think a very significant change in terms of actual operation of law. It is based on the federal experience that it has been almost impossible to litigate quantities and that type of thing. It is also based on my brief discussions with the crime lab where they estimate that if we went to a system where the crime labs around the state had to determine the quantity — in other words, you had to show that there was exactly five grams of actual heroin, as opposed to five grams of heroin and 10 percent of cut, or something like that — they estimate that the budgetary expenses necessary to prepare lab reports in that fashion might be in excess of $500,000.
>
> "So, both the experience in federal court and the projections that I received from the crime lab argued for that change, and that was the reason for that change.
>
> "The second change was going to the specific amounts laid out in subsection 1, which made certain deliveries or manufactures presumptively prison based simply on the quantity of the substance involved. And what we tried to do was to make the quantities in reasonable relation to each other based on street value. We took the first quantity that the committee had laid out — 5 grams of heroin — and we attempted to lay out quantities of these other substances that were more or less appropriate to that in terms of street value and magnitude of operation so that there would be a consistency between the various drugs. We also, as the committee would note, added several drugs that we felt in high quantities were deserving of presumptive prison treatment."

As Frink noted, the amendment (and the bill that was later enacted) provides, for example, for a presumptive prison sentence if a manufacturing or delivery offense involves: (1) five grams or more of a mixture or substance containing heroin; (2) 10 grams or more of a mixture or substance containing cocaine; (3) 10 grams or more of a mixture or substance containing methamphetamine; (4) 150 grams or more of a mixture or substance containing marijuana; or (5) 200 user units or more of LSD. Frink also explained how the association arrived at the amount of each mixture or substance that will result in an enhanced sentence. It used the street value of each mixture or substance to determine the amount that would be equivalent to the street value of a mixture or substance containing five grams of heroin; that is, the calculation that resulted in the amount of each mixture or substance set out in the text of the bill is based on the understanding that each mixture or substance is in a form ready to be sold on the street.

The state argues that we should give Frink's comments regarding "street value" little weight because they "were related to the relative threshold quantities proposed for each drug; they did not relate to the purpose of the 'mixture or substance' language or to the general purposes of the substantial-quantities factor." Additionally, the state contends that his remarks should be discounted because they were merely the comments "of a single witness in a single hearing." On the first point, we note that the amount of each mixture or substance that will warrant an enhanced sentence was based on an understanding about the nature of the mixture or substance that was to be measured. That understanding informs our analysis of the sort of mixture or substance that the legislature had in mind when it enacted House Bill 2390. On the second point, an examination of the remainder of the legislative history demonstrates that Frink's comments were not isolated remarks. Rather, the understanding that informs his testimony recurs throughout the remainder of the hearings.

In the Senate, much of the discussion focused on the amount of a controlled substance that would warrant an enhanced sentence; the committee members wanted to distinguish an amount that was consistent with personal use from an amount that was consistent with selling controlled substances. For example, Senator Hamby wanted to know whether "ten grams is less than a week's supply of meth." When the representative from the Oregon Criminal Defense Lawyers Association explained that it would be a week's supply "for someone who's doing a lot of meth," Senator Hamby asked what a normal dose would be.

Similarly, when one of the senators asked how long five grams of uncut heroin would last, the witness explained that the amounts of drugs in the bill that would enhance a person's sentence were based on the "street level variety" of those drugs. The senator responded, "So we drive policy by identifying street level drugs." When questioned on this point, John Bradley, a deputy district attorney from Multnomah County, explained that the sentencing statutes for most other states and the federal government were based on "the weights of what is sold and possessed." Bradley explained that the federal approach had proved successful and the committee ultimately agreed with him.

Throughout the legislative history, the legislators acted on the understanding that the "mixtures or substances" that would be measured to determine a person's sentence were marketable mixtures or substances. Not only did the ODAA representative explain to the House subcommittee that the specific amounts of each mixture or substance set out in the amendment had been determined using their "street values," but the legislators in the Senate sought to determine the amount of drugs that would distinguish trafficking from personal use. That is, the legislators looked to the marketable form of mixtures or substances containing controlled substances in determining the amount of each mixture or substance that would warrant a presumptive prison sentence. Reading the text, context, and legislative history together, we conclude that, when the Oregon legislature modeled ORS 475.996 on the federal statute, it intended to enhance a defendant's sentence only for marketable mixtures or substances—a holding that is consistent with the discussion of the federal sentencing laws in *Chapman* and the majority of the federal courts that have specifically considered the issue. We accordingly vacate defendant's sentences on counts 1, 3, and 5 and remand for resentencing. We also remand the remainder of defendant's convictions for resentencing.

b. Calculating Drug Quantity in Conspiracy Cases

As discussed in Chapter 3, federal drug conspiracy convictions can sometimes result in lengthy sentences for peripheral participants in drug operations (such as in the so-called "girlfriend cases"). Part of the reason for this is the method for determining drug quantity in a conspiracy, under which a drug conspirator is sentenced based on the drug quantity that was reasonably foreseeable and in furtherance of the conspiracy rather than the amount of drugs with which she was directly involved.

Weighing the Evidence: Drug Quantity Issues in Mandatory Minimum Cases
Kyle O'Dowd
24 Champion 43 (2000)

Federal drug offenders sentenced in 1998 will spend almost three times as much time in prison as did offenders in 1984. There are three conspicuous causes for this threefold increase in sentence severity: (1) the Anti-Drug Abuse Act of 1986, which established most of the mandatory minimum penalties for drug trafficking; (2) the Omnibus Anti-Drug Abuse Act of 1988, which extended the mandatory minimums to conspiracy cases; and (3) the U.S. Sentencing Guidelines, which incorporate the mandatory minimums for drug offenses. Because the federal sentencing guideline for drug trafficking is invariably applied in roughly 40 percent of all cases the last 15 years have witnessed a sea change in the composition of the federal prison population. In 1984, drug law violators constituted 30 percent of the federal prisoner population—a figure which swelled to 60 percent by the end of 1998. This translates to approximately 60,000 federal prisoners who are confined for drug law violations—many of whom are low-level, first-time offenders.

For all their structural and functional differences, federal mandatory minimums and the Sentencing Guidelines have one thing in common: under both schemes, drug quantity is the most significant determinant of sentences for drug trafficking.

The Omnibus Anti-Drug Abuse Act of 1988 amended 21 U.S.C. § 846 to provide that "any person who attempts or conspires to commit any offense defined in this subchapter shall be subject to the same penalties as those" set forth for the object offenses.[28] Prescribing mandatory minimums for drug offenses charged as conspiracies—"that elastic, sprawling and pervasive offense"—greatly increased the risk of low-level defendants receiving the same sentences as defendants with greater roles.

Exacerbating this risk and carrying the new language to its untenable extreme, prosecutors argued that all the defendants in a drug conspiracy should be held accountable for the entire weight distributed by the conspiracy as a whole. According to this interpretation, which no circuit abided, a defendant who helps a large-volume dealer in completing a single, small sale of drugs is liable for the dealer's prior and subsequent activities. The first published decision on point was *Jones v. United States*, in which the Eighth Circuit held that, with respect to a conviction for conspiracy, a mandatory minimum is triggered by the amount of drugs that was reasonably foreseeable to the defendant and within the scope of the defendant's agreement with the other conspirators.

---

28. Prior to this change, § 846 provided that the sentence "may not exceed the maximum punishment prescribed for the ... object of the attempt or conspiracy." 21 U.S.C.A. § 846 (West 1981).

This two-pronged analysis is also employed by the Sentencing Guidelines, a fact which some courts of appeals have claimed is the basis for adopting the approach. A better rationale—one that does not overstate the influence of the guidelines on interpretation of the mandatory minimum statutes—is that "there is nothing to indicate that Congress intended to abandon the theory of conspiratorial liability that has descended from *Pinkerton*." Regardless of which source the decisions identify, all the circuits to have decided the issue require an assessment of each defendant's level of responsibility.

Drug quantity calculations for defendants who are convicted of conspiracy charges often present particularly difficult challenges for courts. In cases where the conspiracy was still in the planning stages at the time of arrest, the amount of drugs that were actually involved may be zero. At the opposite end of the spectrum, a large-scale ongoing drug operation may involve significant quantities of drugs but it is likely that most members of the group are personally involved with only a small portion of the total amount. How should drug quantity be calculated in these circumstances? Courts are split in addressing this problem. *See, e.g.,* Alex Kreit, *Vicarious Criminal Liability and the Constitutional Dimensions of* Pinkerton, 57 Am. U. L. Rev. 585, 624–27 (2008) (discussing a disagreement among federal circuit courts over how to calculate the quantity of drugs attributable to drug conspiracy defendants for sentencing purposes). The following case provides one example of how courts calculate drug quantity in the context of the crime of conspiracy.

United States v. Hickman

United States Court of Appeals for the Fourth Circuit
626 F.3d 756 (2010)

Davis, J.

The evidence offered by the Government in this prosecution resulted from the confluence of two distinct investigations by federal and local law enforcement agencies into heroin distribution activities in Baltimore. In the course of the federal component of the investigation, agents of the Drug Enforcement Administration obtained wiretaps on the phones of Hickman's co-defendants James Jones (also known as "Fat Cat") and James Henderson, among others, and instituted surveillance of an inner-city store known as Fat Cat's Variety Store, run by Jones.

The wiretaps intercepted calls between Tony Caldwell (who was also a co-defendant) and Jones on April 24, 2007, in which Caldwell informed Jones he had found a buyer for him, whom he called "Hookie" (Hickman). Agents then set up surveillance at Fat Cat's Variety Store. Special Agent Bennet Strickland observed Hickman's car arrive at Fat Cat's Variety Store, and the wiretap confirmed that Hickman and Henderson spoke by phone only minutes before.

A few minutes after Hickman's arrival, Jones called Caldwell to ask if the person named "Kevin" at his store was, in fact, "Hookie," and was told that he was. Jones also told Caldwell that he had five more grams of heroin than Hickman could pay for, and asked whether he should give Hickman the extra five; Caldwell instructed him to deliver only "what he [was] supposed to get". Shortly afterward, Caldwell asked Jones, "You all know each other?" and Jones confirmed, "Yeah, yeah, yeah, I know him, I know him. Definitely yeah." Caldwell then told Jones that Hickman was "my co-defendant," (apparently alluding to an earlier drug prosecution in state court). Just after leaving the store, Hickman spoke with Henderson by phone; Henderson asked if he "ever ma[d]e it to the store" and Hickman confirmed that he had.

The investigators directed city police to stop Hickman, and after allowing Hickman to drive a few blocks away from the store so as not to raise suspicion, Baltimore Police Officer Keith Sokolowski stopped Hickman's vehicle for a traffic violation. Hickman was driving and his girlfriend, Claudia Lake, was in the front passenger seat. Officer Sokolowski testified that he discovered and seized 32.14 grams of heroin in the passenger area of the car, which Lake had tried to hide. Subsequent analysis revealed that the heroin was 38% pure. Sokolowski also found 17 gold-topped vials of heroin hidden under the gas cap of the vehicle, though the heroin in the vials was never weighed.

Hickman was arrested and then released on bail. The day of his release, he called Henderson about arranging an additional purchase from Jones. Over the next few days, the two spoke several times about it; though Hickman told Henderson that he had spoken with Jones and was simply waiting on him, the Government produced no evidence that this plan was ever consummated.

Meanwhile, in a search of Caldwell's house on May 8, 2007 arising from a separate investigation, local law enforcement officers seized 139 grams of heroin, later found to be 29% pure. In a subsequent search of Fat Cat's Variety Store on June 7, 2007, federal agents seized more than 25,000 vials and a variety of colored tops, packaged by the hundred. The evidence showed that the vials were of the sort customarily employed to package street-level quantities of heroin (one-tenth of a gram).

Hickman was charged with seven others in an 11-count superseding indictment. He was named in two counts; count one alleged a "conspir[acy] ... to distribute, and possess with intent to distribute, one kilogram or more of ... heroin," and count six alleged "possess[ion] with the intent to distribute a quantity ... of heroin." Although all of Hickman's co-defendants pled guilty, none of them testified at trial, nor did the Government call as a witness any other participant in the overall conspiracy. Rather, the Government adduced the testimony of the following witnesses: Special Agent Strickland, who was conducting surveillance outside of Fat Cat's Variety Store at the time of Hickman's purchase; Officers Sokolowski and Michael Woodlon, who took part in the traffic stop of Hickman; Detective Constantine Passamichalis, who assisted in the raid on Caldwell's residence; and criminologists Anthony Rumber and Theodis Warnick, Jr., who tested the narcotics seized from Hickman and Caldwell.

Perhaps most significant for purposes of this appeal was extensive testimony from Special Agent Brendan O'Meara, who monitored the Jones wiretap and who was accepted by the court as an expert in narcotics investigations. The Government relied heavily on the content of the wiretap recordings, and it was Agent O'Meara who interpreted them for the jury, explaining the vague and coded terminology used by drug dealers. In its effort to prove that the conspiracy (which the indictment alleged subsisted for only four months, from February 2007 through May 2007) involved more than one kilogram of heroin, the Government asked Agent O'Meara to explain how heroin is typically cut down from its raw, high-purity state to user-strength level of approximately 8% via mixture with mannite and quinine. Critical to the Government's theory of the case was O'Meara's opinion that the 25,000 vials seized from Fat Cat's Variety Store would be enough to hold one kilogram of user-strength heroin.

After the Government rested, the defense moved for a judgment of acquittal, which the district court denied. The defense at no time specifically argued that the Government's proof established only a conspiracy involving a lesser amount than one kilogram, and the defense never requested a lesser included offense instruction. Nor did the defense call any witnesses.

The jury found Hickman guilty on both the conspiracy and possession with intent to distribute counts. The jury was asked on the verdict form to determine whether the amount of heroin involved in the conspiracy and reasonably foreseeable to Hickman was (1) one kilogram or more, (2) less than one kilogram but greater than or equal to one hundred grams, or (3) less than one hundred grams. It found the conspiracy involved one kilogram or more and that such amount was foreseeable to Hickman. Because Hickman had two predicate felony drug convictions which the Government had noticed pursuant to 21 U.S.C. § 851, he was sentenced to life imprisonment on the conspiracy count and to a concurrent sentence of 360 months for possession with intent to distribute.

Overwhelming evidence supports the jury's finding that Hickman was a knowing member of the basic conspiracy alleged in Count I of the superseding indictment.

Conviction for conspiracy to distribute narcotics under 21 U.S.C. § 846 requires proof beyond a reasonable doubt of three elements: (1) "an agreement between two or more persons to engage in conduct that violates a federal drug law" — here, to distribute or possess narcotics with intent to distribute; "(2) the defendant's knowledge of the conspiracy; and (3) the defendant's knowing and voluntary participation in the conspiracy." Proof of a conspiratorial agreement need not be by direct evidence, and rather may "be proven inferentially and by circumstantial evidence."

Given the plethora of direct evidence, including but not limited to the content of the telephone communications and the circumstances surrounding the traffic stop of Hickman, only very modest inferences, if any, were required here to show the existence of a conspiratorial agreement and Hickman's knowing membership in a heroin conspiracy. The damning wiretap recordings reveal Hickman and Henderson's coordination before and after Hickman purchased 32 grams of heroin from Jones; Henderson discussing his stake in the transaction;[3] and later exchanges between Hickman and Henderson concerning the possibility of a subsequent transaction after the police seized the heroin initially purchased. Moreover, agents observed Hickman entering and exiting Jones's store; in the interim, wiretaps record Jones discussing the Hickman sale with Caldwell; and a police stop some minutes later found Hickman in possession of those 32 grams. In the face of this mountain of evidence of Hickman's knowing participation in a heroin distribution conspiracy, Hickman's broader challenge to the sufficiency of the evidence is plainly unavailing.[8]

Although there is overwhelming evidence of Hickman's knowing membership in a heroin distribution conspiracy, his challenge to the jury's finding that the conspiracy of which he became a member involved at least one kilogram of heroin has merit. Sufficient evidence supported a finding that Hickman knowingly became a member of a large-scale

---

3. *See* J.A. 426–27 (an hour after the buy, having just learned of Hickman's arrest, Henderson telling an unidentified man that Hickman "had my fucking bread yo" and complains "I ain't even get to get that [i.e., retrieve the narcotics] from him yo").

8. We pause to acknowledge the practical conundrum faced by counsel for Hickman. Rare is the lawyer who wants to make an argument to a jury that, "My client was not involved in a conspiracy, but if you disagree, it was at most a conspiracy involving less than one kilogram of heroin." Thus, in his arguments on the motion for judgment of acquittal, in his request for jury instructions, and in his closing argument to the jury, counsel largely sought to cast Hickman as involved merely in one or more buy-sell transactions rather than in a conspiracy, and that argument is pressed on us in this appeal. Nonetheless, we have no doubt that Hickman's argument on the motion for judgment of acquittal was adequate to alert the district court to the deficiency in the Government's proof of *drug quantity* and to preserve the sufficiency of evidence issue for purposes of this appeal.

heroin distribution conspiracy which involved, at the least Jones, Henderson, and Cald-well, and that many of the acts of the co-conspirators were reasonably foreseeable to Hick-man. Yet, no matter how generously we indulge the available *reasonable* inferences in favor of the Government, adding the post-dilution weight of heroin from all known and reasonably inferable transactions — whether completed, attempted, or merely agreed upon by any of Hickman's co-conspirators — to reach a sum of one kilogram, if not a mathematical impossibility, would require reasoning so attenuated as to provide insuffi-cient support for the jury's verdict on the one-kilogram verdict.

The jury heard evidence of the amounts and purity of heroin seized during the traf-fic stop of Hickman and the raid on Caldwell's home; evidence of discussion between Hickman and Henderson of an attempt in the days after Hickman's initial arrest to "do the same thing [transaction] again," presumably with Jones; and a vague statement the de-fense itself elicited on recross-examination of a Government witness concerning the "re-cover[y] [of] heroin ... the week prior" from someone exiting Jones's store.

The indictment alleged a four-month conspiracy. The only definite amounts of heroin established by the Government were the 32.14 grams of 38% pure heroin recovered dur-ing the stop of Hickman's vehicle; 17 gold-topped vials also recovered during the traffic stop, the contents of which were never weighed; the 5 grams of heroin Jones kept from Hick-man; and 139 grams of 29% pure heroin seized from the raid on Caldwell's apartment. Ex-pert testimony from Agent O'Meara provided a basis for inferring that the coconspirators intended that the heroin be substantially diluted before reaching end-users. To "step on" or "cut down" the heroin, a dealer would mix one part raw heroin with one, two, or three parts of "cut" — the solvent used to dilute the heroin, often mannite or quinine — to reach a concentration fit for most users, which Agent O'Meara estimated to be 8%.

Agent O'Meara's discussion of the dilution process was the jury's only basis for inflat-ing the weight of the recovered heroin, and as such the method of dilution he described must constrain the trier of fact's reasonable inferences. As Agent O'Meara described, raw heroin is said, in the "slang vernacular," to "take[ ] a one, two, or a three" depending on how many parts of solvent are mixed with each part of heroin; because "the drug dealers on the street don't have a laboratory" they are limited to this simple mixing process. Agent O'Meara's lengthy discussion, and the vernacular terms he cites, indicate that this mix-ing of heroin with "cut" is always in the ratio of 1:n, where n is a natural number. This, of course, would bound the maximum dilution of heroin of a given purity: without "a laboratory" capable of more precise measurements and mixtures, dilution to precisely 8% will ordinarily be impossible. Thus the 38% pure heroin recovered from Hickman would only "take a four" — be mixed 1:4 with solvent — since a 1:5 mixture would de-crease the purity below 8%; similarly, the heroin seized from Caldwell, 29% pure, would "take a three."[9] These dilutions would result in 128.56 grams of 9.5% purity and 417

9. We note that 8%, though Agent O'Meara gave it as a "rough" estimate of the "average" for low-est-purity "scramble" heroin in Baltimore City, was the lowest purity discussed at trial. The Govern-ment's criminologist, who had worked for the Baltimore City Police Department for eleven years and tested "thousands" of samples for the presence of controlled dangerous substances put the weakest heroin submitted to the crime lab for testing at "around 9 to about 11" percent. (In fact, Government counsel pegged "[w]hat's on the street" at "10%" during a colloquy with the district judge and de-fense counsel, in which he went on to explain to the judge that the Government's theory was that the seized heroin would have been "cut down further ... [d]own to 10%.") As we view the facts in the light most favorable to the Government, we assume 8% purity was the conspiracy's intended target. But finding, beyond a reasonable doubt, even higher weights via speculation as to a lower purity tar-get would be wholly unreasonable on this record.

grams of 9 2/3% purity—together, approximately 546 grams of heroin. But we will assume, *arguendo*, that the Hickman conspiracy would have diluted this heroin precisely to 8% purity, generating 153 grams and 504 grams for Hickman and Caldwell, respectively. Together with the 5 grams Jones kept from Hickman—which, assuming it was of the same purity as the 32 grams Jones sold him, would add another 23.75 grams—the Government would have established a total of 681 grams.

As for the 17 gold-top vials recovered during the traffic stop of Hickman, their contents were never weighed. Rumber, one of the Government's two criminologists at trial, testified that the gross weight of the vials was 24.30 grams, and confirmed that the net weight—the weight of the heroin itself—was never measured. The only testimony on point is from Agent O'Meara, who explained that a vial of heroin typically contains 0.1 grams. Thus the 17 vials support an additional 1.7 grams of heroin. Added to the 681 grams assumed above, this would support a finding of no more than 683 grams.

Evidence concerning the remaining two potential transactions is scant, to say the least. During the week after Hickman's initial arrest and release, he and Henderson spoke about attempting to "do the *same thing again*" and Hickman claimed he had made several telephone calls to a potential narcotics supplier, apparently Jones. Though Hickman remained free until his arrest in August 2007, no evidence of this transaction was offered. Aside from Henderson's reference to "do[ing] the *same thing again*," there is no evidence concerning the amount of heroin Hickman and Henderson sought. Attributing any more than another 32.14 grams to this potential transaction—like the earlier purchase from Jones—would be purely speculative; thus, at a maximum, the jury could find that the conspiracy involved another 153 grams of "cut" heroin, giving them a hypothetical sum of 836 grams.

Evidence of the final alleged transaction—a brief statement on recross-examination by Agent O'Meara about the seizure of some amount of heroin from some individual exiting Jones's store a week before Hickman's purchase—is extremely vague:

> Q. How many people did you stop coming out of Fat Cat's and recover heroin from?
>
> A. We recovered heroin out of—the week prior. I think it was April 17th.
>
> Q. And you recovered it in terms of the stop of Hickman; is that right?
>
> A. Yes, sir.

There is no evidence that this seizure had anything to do with Hickman, Henderson, or Caldwell. Moreover, given that Jones was in the business of selling drug paraphernalia and so would likely be visited by those who had recently bought (or intended to buy) narcotics elsewhere, there is little reason to believe that the seized heroin had just been sold through Jones's store. That the month-long surveillance of Jones's store bore no more fruit than this single drug seizure further undermines the circumstantial evidence of drug quantity implicating Jones. Even if, squinting our eyes, it were to appear nonspeculative to attach an amount to this earlier seizure and link it to the Count I conspiracy, the evidence could by no means bear any more than the "stepped on" amount of Hickman's purchase from Jones, 153 grams. And even with this final amount, the sum would fall short of one kilogram.

To reach its finding that the Count I conspiracy involved at least one kilogram, the jury would have had to rely on either or both of two grounds: (1) that Hickman was criminally liable for the distribution of heroin by buyers of paraphernalia from Jones—a theory that fails as a matter of law; or that, (2) on account of the conspirators' apparent familiarity with the drug trade, they must have undertaken to distribute some amount beyond the amounts involved in the evidenced transactions. Neither theory can sustain Hickman's conviction on the one-kilogram conspiracy.

The Government told jurors during closing argument that Jones "basically runs a one-stop shop[ ] for heroin," with "thousands and thousands of vials that heroin goes in." Indeed, the evidence well supports the inference that Jones was in the business of selling drug paraphernalia. As Agent O'Meara testified, a raid on Jones's store produced bins containing more than 25,000 glass vials of the sort used to distribute heroin, packaged in groups of one hundred, in various sizes and with variously colored tops, also packaged in groups of one hundred; customers were apprised of the merchandise by a three-ring binder on the counter.

Yet there is absolutely no evidence to support a finding that Hickman is liable for heroin distributions by those who had purchased empty vials from Jones. Indeed, it strains credulity even to think that, on the evidence in the record, Jones himself could be convicted of a widespread conspiracy to distribute heroin on the mere fact that he sells drug paraphernalia and had such packaged merchandise at his store. Finding such conspiracy liability for Jones would have required the trier of fact to find beyond a reasonable doubt that Jones's purchase of paraphernalia for resale evidenced a conspiracy to conspire with future paraphernalia buyers concerning subsequent distribution. While paraphernalia vendors can certainly become parties to the distribution conspiracies of their buyers, such cases present substantial evidence of the vendor's involvement in and/or knowing facilitation of, a distributor's operations.

Tellingly, Agent O'Meara testified that law enforcement "did not stop a lot of people coming out of [Jones's store]" because they knew that Jones was "also selling paraphernalia, like vials, and ... we're not going to go out and arrest a particular person just for having the actual vials ... empty vials." "Unless there is a specific reason, [and] we know that a drug deal is taking place," he testified, "we're not just stopping everybody that's coming out of there and ... trying to pull a bunch of empty vials off the street." In fact, the jury was told that in more than a month of surveillance of Jones's store, only a single patron other than Hickman was found with narcotics on his person. Where the Government failed to present evidence about even a single buyer of the paraphernalia or any plans on the part of Jones to involve himself in the distribution activities of his paraphernalia customers, it would be mere speculation to find that Jones's own distribution activities were coextensive with his paraphernalia business.[11] On this paltry evidence, no reasonable inference as to the scope of Jones's conspiracy to distribute narcotics could be drawn from the amount of paraphernalia merchandise he hoped to sell.

Furthermore, even if the evidence had supported widespread conspiracy liability for Jones on the basis of his trafficking in drug paraphernalia, this liability could not be transferred to Hickman on this record. As an initial matter, while we have assumed that Hickman and Jones conspired together with respect to the distribution chain that included Henderson and Caldwell, no evidence was presented to suggest that the selling of paraphernalia entered into this agreement. Moreover, as there was no evidence that Hickman

---

11. Even where co-conspirators have had no connection to paraphernalia sales, and thus any packaging materials would presumably be used for their own distribution, some circuit courts have been skeptical of relying on unused drug packaging materials to increase drug amounts charged to a conspiracy. *See United States v. Henderson*, 58 F.3d 1145 (7th Cir. 1995) (explaining that the court "question[ed] whether multiple boxes of unused baggies present the same degree of reliability [as the used baggies relied on in an earlier case]" and declining to rely upon them to support lower court's finding as to amount of narcotics within the scope of the conspiracy, where lower court's methodology appeared to lack sufficient indicia of reliability).

had or planned to have any involvement with (or even any knowledge of) Jones's paraphernalia buyers, such a conspiracy (having Jones at the center) would have been a classic "rimless," "hub-and-spokes" conspiracy, which has long been held to make out multiple, distinct conspiracies and not a single, large one. Thus evidence of the number of packaged, empty vials in Jones's store is not a sufficient basis for further inflating the amount of heroin ascribable to the Count I conspiracy.

Nor could the jury properly convict Hickman of the one-kilogram conspiracy in reliance on the Government's repeated assertions during closing argument that the four-month Count I conspiracy encompassed far more drug distribution activity (and that Hickman could reasonably foresee such quantity) than that of which the Government could produce competent evidence. The Government strenuously urged jurors to draw such an inference, claiming that the evidence presented was only "a window into the conspiracy," merely "part of something larger"; that the evidenced transactions were simply "two brief episodes ... in the life of this conspiracy" or "a few days in the life of a heroin conspiracy"; that "this [was] an ongoing course of business," an "ongoing thing." "[I]t's clear," said the prosecutor, "that this is a regular course of business for these gentlemen. It's clear that this isn't the first time they've done this before [sic]. It's clear that this wasn't going to be the last time.... [Hickman] would have continued to [seek out drug transactions]."

This line of argument is troubling, not just because it seems to urge jurors to convict the defendant for what he "would have continued to do" which, to the extent these hypothesized future bad acts were not captured by an agreement within the charged period, is clearly improper, but also because it invites the jury to speculate as to the amount of heroin involved in the conspiracy.

Where no evidence exists to guide the trier of fact in determining the outer scope of a conspiracy, the trier may not simply guess at the magnitude or frequency of unknown criminal activity. Unbridled speculation is an impermissible basis for conviction beyond a reasonable doubt.

Under more than two decades of federal law, it is impermissible to enhance drug amounts without particularized evidence of narcotics transactions. Federal district courts have long struggled with extrapolating drug amounts under the U.S. Sentencing Guidelines, which instruct that, "[w]here ... the amount [of narcotics] seized does not reflect the scale of the offense, the court shall approximate the quantity of the controlled substance." U.S.S.G. § 2D1.1 n.12. In reviewing district courts' findings, the courts of appeals have developed a sizable body of case law narrowing the range of permissible inferences. Its teachings are instructive here.

As the First Circuit has explained, "[w]here drug-quantity extrapolations have been upheld, the Government managed to demonstrate an adequate basis in fact and that the drug quantities were determined in a manner consistent with the accepted standards of reasonable reliability." Concerned about the methodologies district courts employ to calculate their extrapolations, courts have cautioned against using small sample sizes.

To be sure, where courts have evidence of a number of transactions, they have been permitted to multiply that number by an average weight-per-transaction to reach an estimate, *see, e.g., United States v. Correa-Alicea*, 585 F.3d 484 (1st Cir. 2009) (upholding such a calculation using "highly conservative" estimates), though the circuit courts have urged district courts to "make conservative approximations," *United States v. Sklar*, 920 F.2d 107 (1st Cir. 1990) ("[W]hen choosing between a number of plausible estimates of drug quantity ... a court must err on the side of caution.").

Such conservative extrapolation as to the amount sold in *evidenced* transactions is perfectly proper; but the courts of appeals have refused to allow a trier of fact to extend this extrapolation so far as to fabricate transactions of which there is no evidence. Thus the First Circuit has held that evidence that a drug conspiracy "did a substantial amount of narcotics business" was insufficient, "[i]n the absence of *particularized findings*," to support a determination by a preponderance of the evidence of an amount of narcotics that "seem[ed] attainable given the appellant's role in the conspiracy," explaining that a court "cannot uphold a drug quantity calculation on the basis of hunch or intuition."

Here the Government contends, unpersuasively, that Hickman's use of "vague and coded language" establishes "familiar[ity] with drug trafficking" and that "only someone heavily involved in repeated drug trafficking would be so brazen and unrepentant to return almost immediately to trying to find more heroin to sell." In a case like Hickman's, where a lack of evidence would make particularized findings impossible, courts would have reversed a sentencing court's finding—made by a mere preponderance of the evidence—that Hickman's conspiracy involved one kilogram or more of heroin. And if such an inference would have been too speculative to satisfy the Sentencing Guidelines, which merely require an "approximat[ion]," U.S.S.G. §2D1.1 n.12, based on evidence with "sufficient indicia of reliability to support a conclusion that they are probably accurate," U.S.S.G. §6A1.3, then a *fortiori* it would fail to satisfy a rational trier of fact tasked with making findings beyond a reasonable doubt.

In this case, where evidence of unknown transactions was meager and offered virtually no guide as to the amounts that may have been involved, we hold that the jury verdict finding the heroin conspiracy involved one kilogram or more was not supported by sufficient evidence.

Yet it is within our power to direct entry of judgment on a lesser included offense when vacating a greater offense for insufficient evidence.

Because we conclude that the record contains sufficient evidence to persuade a rational fact finder beyond a reasonable doubt of Hickman's guilt on the lesser included offense of conspiracy to distribute one hundred grams or more of heroin, we direct entry of judgment against Hickman under Count I of the indictment for conspiracy to distribute and to possess with intent to distribute heroin in the amount of one hundred grams or more.[12]

Hickman's second contention, that the trial judge erred in rejecting his proposed instructions regarding the amount of heroin attributable to him, is without merit.

At trial, defense counsel requested that the judge instruct the jury that Hickman could only be held responsible for the "amount of drugs that were foreseeable to the Defendant and within the scope of his agreement."

The trial court repeatedly instructed the jury that coconspirators' actual or intended distribution of narcotics could only be charged to Hickman "so long as it was reasonably foreseeable to [him] that such a type and quantity of drugs would be involved in the conspiracy which he joined."

These instructions accord with the principles of *Pinkerton v. United States,* 328 U.S. 640, 66 S. Ct. 1180, 90 L. Ed. 1489 (1946).

---

12. Because Hickman had been convicted of two prior felony drug offenses, the Government filed a notice of enhanced punishment mandating a minimum mandatory sentence for the one-kilogram conspiracy of life imprisonment. We of course express no view as to what might be an appropriate sentence after further proceedings.

To the extent that defendant's proposed instruction differs from the instructions given, it misstates the law. It is true that Hickman is responsible only for the amount of drugs "within the scope of his agreement," if this "scope" is properly understood as encompassing any co-conspirators' conduct in furtherance of the conspiracy and reasonably foreseeable to him; but the trial court instructions adequately covered this. If the requested instruction is taken to mean that Hickman is responsible only for an amount of drugs he personally knew of and explicitly agreed to distribute or have distributed, then it mistakes a basic tenant of our conspiracy law, *see Pinkerton,* 328 U.S. at 647. There was no abuse of discretion in the district court's rejection of Hickman's proposed instruction.

For the reasons explained, we conclude that the evidence was insufficient to establish beyond a reasonable doubt that Hickman knowingly became a member of a conspiracy to distribute or to possess with the intent to distribute more than one kilogram of heroin. On the other hand, there is overwhelming evidence in the record to show, beyond a reasonable doubt, that Hickman knowingly became a member of a lesser included conspiracy involving 100 grams or more of heroin, and that such amount was reasonably foreseeable to Hickman. Accordingly, we vacate the conviction for conspiracy to distribute heroin in the amount of one kilogram or more and the life sentence imposed thereon, and we remand the case to the district court with directions to enter a judgment of sentence as to the lesser offense and to resentence accordingly. In all other respects, the judgment is affirmed.

AFFIRMED IN PART, VACATED IN PART, AND REMANDED WITH INSTRUCTIONS

c. Counting Marijuana Plants

Some drug sentencing provisions measure quantity by the number of doses or plants. This can sometimes raise surprisingly difficult counting problems, particularly in marijuana cases.

Pennsylvania v. Allen

Supreme Court of Pennsylvania

669 A.2d 883 (1995)

Montemuro, J.

Appellant, the Commonwealth of Pennsylvania, appeals from a judgment of sentence entered by the Erie County Court of Common Pleas in which the common pleas court sentenced Appellee, Mark Allen Burnsworth, to six to twelve months imprisonment, followed by forty-eight months of probation. In fashioning such a sentence, the common pleas court refused to impose a minimum mandatory sentence as required by our legislature. Instead, the sentencing court declared that the mandatory sentencing provisions of 18 Pa.C.S. §7508(a)(1)(i), (ii), and (iii), relating to "live plants," were unconstitutional.

Burnsworth was charged with two counts of unlawful manufacturing of marijuana and two counts of possession with intent to deliver marijuana plants. On May 11, 1994, Burnsworth appeared for trial. Nevertheless, after consultation with his attorney, and after being notified that the Commonwealth would be seeking the application of the mandatory sentencing provisions, Burnsworth pled guilty to the offenses. As a specific condition of his plea agreement, Burnsworth retained the right to contest the application of the mandatory sentence provisions, specifically with respect to the number of marijuana plants confiscated.

During the July 8, 1994 sentencing hearing, the Commonwealth presented the testimony of Officer Edward Podpora of the Girard Police Department. Officer Podpora, present when the marijuana plants were confiscated, testified that with respect to Count 2738, sixteen "live" marijuana plants were found at Burnsworth's residence. He stated that the plants were four to five feet high, and that "a majority of them were planted in five gallon pails ... [and that t]here were also a few planted into the ground at the residence." Officer Podpora also testified that in regard to Count 2739, he was again present when sixty-one marijuana plants were confiscated from a nearby fenced-in area.

At the conclusion of Officer Podpora's testimony, Burnsworth introduced the testimony of Dr. Larry Gauriloff, an assistant professor of biology at Mercyhurst College. Dr. Gauriloff testified that in addition to propagation by seed, marijuana will often germinate by a lateral root system, meaning that lateral shoots come up from the roots. The following testimony ensued between defense counsel and Dr. Gauriloff:

> Q: Would the collectivity of these lateral roots and stems shooting up from the roots, is that defined as one plant or multiple plants?
>
> A: That would define as a plant arising from a single seed, so you would consider it one plant. Many people counting them, certainly if they were pulled out of the ground, would count them as individual plants.
>
> Q: Is there anything in the literature, in your expertise — would you view this as a plant, a tap system with multiple stems, would you view it as one plant or multiple plants?
>
> A: From a research point of view as a single plant.

Dr. Gauriloff also offered testimony in regard to the weight of the plants at issue in this case:

> Q: Can you form an opinion based on the collectivity of 61 plants with the description that Officer Podpora gave as to how much wet weight there would be?
>
> A: Total?
>
> Q: Yes.
>
> A: Wet weight on 61 plants, like I said, probably 18 inches tall, the whole plant?
>
> Q: Yes.
>
> A: Figure about 4 grams per plant, you're looking at 240 grams roughly, divided by 28 in terms of ounces.
>
> Q: So could you extrapolate that into pounds?
>
> A: Pounds, you're looking at what, maybe 7, 8 ounces; half a pound.

The court further inquired whether Dr. Gauriloff had an opinion on the weight of the sixteen plants. Dr. Gauriloff responded: "Probably in terms of total weight I would say— I'll give them six, probably seven grams. Yeah, they are real sparse looking. But probably about six, seven grams of wet weight" which would correspond to about "four ounces, three ounces, three, three and a half."

Based upon the evidence presented, the sentencing court declared that the mandatory sentencing provisions of 18 Pa.C.S. §7508(a)(1) were unconstitutional as

> vague and overbroad and fail[] to take into account, among other things, the difference in size, maturity and intoxicating productivity of the plants, fail[] to define what constitutes a plant in terms of height, sex, percent of intoxicating cannibis, or root system and that there is a great disparity which has been pointed out in court by Dr. Gauriloff in the mandatory sentencing statute in the com-

parison between the amount of marijuana in pounds and the weight of marijuana in plant form. And this Court finds that such appears to be totally discretionary with no logical reasonable, or scientific basis for comparison. Therefore, the plant portion of the mandatory sentencing is fundamentally unfair, particularly in comparison with the mandatory sentencing by weight.

Moreover, the sentencing court determined that no rational basis existed for the disparity between the statute's weight and "live" plant provisions. The Commonwealth appealed.

It is well settled that when the language of a statute is clear and unambiguous, the statute must be interpreted in accordance with its plain and common usage.

Herein, the legislature adopted the following sentencing requirements:

§ 7508. Drug trafficking sentencing and penalties

(a) General rule. — Notwithstanding any other provisions of this or any other act to the contrary, the following provisions shall apply:

(1) A person who is convicted of violating section 13(a)(14), (30) or (37) of The Controlled Substance, Drug, Device and Cosmetic Act, where the controlled substance is marijuana shall, upon conviction, be sentenced to a mandatory minimum term of imprisonment and a fine as set forth in this subsection:

(i) when the amount of marijuana involved is a least two pounds, but less than ten pounds, or at least ten live plants but less than 21 live plants; one year in prison and a fine of $5,000 ...;

(ii) when the amount of marijuana involved is at least ten pounds, but less than 50 pounds, or at least 21 live plants but less than 51 live plants; three years in prison and a fine of $15,000 ... ;

(iii) when the amount of marijuana involved is at least 50 pounds, or at least 51 live plants; five years in prison and a fine of $50,000....

(emphasis supplied).

We believe that this language is clear and unambiguous, and as such, that we should construe the term "plant" according to its common usage. Even Dr. Gauriloff testified that while, from a biological and research point of view, lateral roots and stems could be considered as a single plant, "many people counting them, certainly if they were pulled out of the ground, would count them as individual plants." Dr. Gauriloff also stated:

The lateral roots are quite fragile, the main body of the root being underneath each new shoot. As long as they were attached by a lateral root, they would be considered a single plant, but when torn from the ground, the lateral root would break.

In fact, he opined that once the "plant" is torn from the earth, the identity of whether it was a single plant or a shoot from one plant's lateral root structure essentially would be indeterminable.

While not controlling, we find the opinion of the United States Court of Appeals for the Tenth Circuit in *United States v. Eves*, 932 F.2d 856 (10th Cir. 1991), to be instructive. In that case, a very similar argument to the one raised in this case was lodged against a similar federal sentencing statute. From eight parent plants, the defendant grew over 1000 cuttings. The defendant argued that in order to determine if a "plant" was actually a plant, it was necessary to engage in a viability analysis. The Tenth Circuit Court of Appeals disagreed. Instead, the court opined that Congress intended the term "marijuana plant" to

include[] those cuttings accompanied by root balls. Whether the plant could survive on its own would not be an issue; if it looks like a "plant" — that is, if it has a reasonable root system—it will be considered a "plant." No expert need testify, no experiment with instrumentation to monitor whether gaseous exchange is occurring need be conducted, no elaborate trimester or viability system need be established. If a cutting has a root ball attached, it will be considered a plant.

Accordingly, the federal appeals court determined that as a matter of statutory interpretation, the word "plant" should be interpreted consistent with its commonplace meaning,[6] and in so ruling, specifically rejected defendant's argument that a more scientific definition should be applied. Furthermore, in *United States v. Robinson,* 35 F.3d 442 (9th Cir. 1994) the United States Court of Appeals for the Ninth Circuit recognized that an organism should have three readily apparent characteristics in order to be classified as a "plant" pursuant to the ordinary meaning of that word—roots, stems and leaves. As we have already indicated, we agree that such a commonsensical definition of the term "plant" should be applied in this instance.

Another precept of statutory construction is that the legislature cannot be presumed to intend a result that is absurd, impossible of execution or unreasonable. The legislature originally enacted this particular section in an attempt to curb drug trafficking. By adding language to trigger the terms of the mandatory sentence when the marijuana involved is a specified number of plants, it is clear that the legislature intended to deter the growing of marijuana. To conclude, as Burnsworth would have us do, that one "plant" could produce an indefinite number of shoots thereby providing a large quantity of marijuana for harvest, but yet be considered only one plant so as to evade the reach of the statute, would be directly contrary to the obvious intent of the legislature. Accordingly, we do not agree with the Erie County Court of Common Pleas that 18 Pa.C.S. § 7508(a)(1)(i), (ii) and (iii) are unconstitutionally vague.

[T]he opinion of the Erie County Court of Common Pleas is reversed and the case is remanded for sentencing consistent with this opinion.

C. Issues in Federal Drug Sentencing

1. The Federal Mandatory Minimum Provisions

Mandatory minimum drug sentencing laws have been among the most controversial aspects of U.S. drug policy. Mandatory minimum drug sentencing dates back to the 1950s when Congress passed the Boggs Act, which provided for mandatory minimum punishments of 2 years for a first offense under the Narcotic Drugs Import and Export Act or the Marihuana Tax Act, 5 years for a second offense, and 10 years for subsequent offenses. *See,* Richard J. Bonnie and Charles H. Whitebread II, The Marihuana Conviction: A History of Marihuana Prohibition in the United States 206–12 (1974) (describing the passage of federal mandatory minimum drug sentencing provisions in the 1950s); Thomas M. Quinn and Gerald T. McLaughlin, *The Evolution of Federal Drug Control Legislation,* 22 Cath. U. L. Rev. 586, 625 (1973) (noting that the Controlled Substances Act of 1970 repealed the 1950s mandatory minimum sentencing provisions). The

---

6. Judge Aldisert noted the ordinary meaning of the term plant as follows:
   The common everyday meaning of "plant" is a living organism which belongs to the vegetable kingdom in the broad sense. cf. [sic] Websters New International Dictionary, 1881, def. n.3 (2d ed. unabridged 1961).

Boggs Act's federal mandatory minimum drug sentencing provisions were repealed in 1970 with the passage of the Controlled Substances Act. Interestingly, one of the legislators who spoke in favor of eliminating mandatory minimum drug sentences was future-President and then-Congressman George H.W. Bush, who argued that the change would "result in better justice and more appropriate sentences." *Footnote in History: The 1970 Views of Congressman George Bush on the Wisdom of Mandatory Minimum Sentences*, 3 FED. SENTENCING REPORTER 108 (1990) (republishing Bush's statement on the House floor in full).

The shift in federal drug sentencing was short lived, however. Federal mandatory minimum drug laws returned in the 1980s, with most providing for even longer minimum sentences than the Boggs Act. Many states also have mandatory minimum drug sentencing laws. State mandatory minimum provisions are often (though not always) less severe than the federal penalties, however, and some have been repealed or modified in recent years. *See, e.g.,* Nora V. Demleitner, *Smart Public Policy: Replacing Imprisonment with Targeted Nonprison Sentences and Collateral Sanctions*, 58 Stan. L. Rev. 339, 350–51 (2005) ("In recent years a number of states have reduced or even abolished mandatory drug sentences, as such sentences had proven too expensive because they led to the incarceration of low-risk offenders."); Robert Weisberg, *How Sentencing Commissions Turned Out To Be a Good Idea*, 12 BERKELEY J. CRIM. L. 179, 201–05 (2007) (providing an overview of some state mandatory minimum drug laws and relevant reforms).

Competing Sentencing Policies in a "War on Drugs" Era
Hon. William W. Wilkins, Jr.,
Phyllis J. Newton and John R. Steer
28 Wake Forest Law Review 305 (1993)

In the 1970s, members of the public and Congress denounced the ineffectiveness of the "revolving-door" criminal justice system. Offenders often were incarcerated, deemed rehabilitated, and released only to start the cycle anew. At the same time, the combination of unwarranted disparity in the sentencing of similarly situated offenders and deficiencies in the parole process caused many to question the system's certainty and fairness. Still other critics argued that the disparity problem had an even uglier side, with some defendants being treated by the criminal justice system in a discriminatory manner for reasons unrelated to their offense or offender characteristics properly bearing upon punishment.

In response to these concerns and after more than a decade of study and debate, a bipartisan Congress enacted the most far-reaching reform of federal sentencing in this country's history—the Sentencing Reform Act of 1984 (SRA). This legislation directed the creation of a permanent, bipartisan commission to develop and, over time, refine sentencing guidelines to further the basic purposes of criminal sentencing. In response to concerns that similar defendants convicted of similar offenses were being sentenced dissimilarly, the sentencing guidelines were to provide certainty and fairness at sentencing and reduce the unwarranted disparity in sentencing that Congress found "shameful." Within specific criteria established by the sentencing guidelines, similarly situated federal defendants convicted of similar offenses were to be sentenced within the same, relatively narrow sentencing range which, in the case of imprisonment, could not exceed the greater of twenty-five percent or six months.

As Congress put its finishing touches on the sentencing reform package that abolished parole and mandated sentencing guidelines, problems associated with drug abuse took on increasing national prominence. Opinion polls showed that drug abuse far surpassed economic problems as the number one public concern. Glaring headlines, dramatic footage on nightly news programs, and regular reports in all forms of mass media chronicled various battles in the war on drugs.

Heightened public concern raised congressional awareness of the devastating effects of illicit drugs. Frustrated by the alarming, apparently increasing, flow of drugs into the country, Congress sought a broad solution that involved curbing both the supply and demand for drugs. Moreover, because Congress believed that too often major drug traffickers were arrested, prosecuted, and convicted only to reappear quickly on the streets as a result of unduly lenient sentencing practices by the judiciary, Congress turned to statutorily mandated sentencing provisions for drug offenses in an effort to stop this "revolving door process" in the federal criminal justice system. More than simply a message to the federal judiciary, these swift and certain mandatory provisions were viewed as a statement that society would no longer tolerate the illegal drug epidemic. By enacting mandatory penalty provisions, Congress believed serious drug offenders would have no escape from lengthy terms of imprisonment.

As part of this strategy, Congress passed the Anti-Drug Abuse Act of 1986, which contained a number of mandatory minimum statutory provisions for drug-related offenses. These new mandatory provisions were tied to the quantity of drugs involved in the offense. For example, trafficking in one kilogram or more of a mixture or substance containing a detectable amount of heroin triggers a mandatory minimum sentence of ten years' imprisonment without parole, as does five kilograms or more of a mixture or substance containing a detectable amount of cocaine. For those involved in trafficking somewhat smaller quantities, Congress provided five-year mandatory minimum penalties. For example, the five-year mandatory minimums were triggered by trafficking in 100 grams or more of a mixture or substance containing a detectable amount of heroin, or 500 grams or more of a mixture or substance containing a detectable amount of cocaine.

For defendants with a prior conviction for a felony drug offense, the applicable mandatory minimum sentence was set at twice that otherwise applicable. Also, a mandatory minimum sentence of twenty years would apply if death or serious bodily injury resulted from use of the controlled substance. In addition, the 1986 Act provided an increased mandatory minimum penalty if the drug distribution was to a person under age twenty-one or to a pregnant female, occurred near a school or college, or involved a person under age eighteen in the distribution process.

By 1988, drug-related violence was still on the rise, and many major urban areas experienced record increases in homicide rates and gang violence, often prompted by drug trafficking. Looking to areas not specifically highlighted by the Anti-Drug Abuse Act of 1986, Congress focused on the increased violence associated with the drug trade and the growing involvement of youth. Out of concern for public safety, Congress again considered enacting a number of new mandatory penalties and strengthening some that were already in place.

By the time congressional debate began on the 1988 Anti-Drug Abuse Act, however, a number of congressional members had begun to question the wisdom of the mandatory minimum penalty structures, especially in light of the Sentencing Reform Act of 1984. The record of Senate debate regarding the omnibus drug bill reflects the following statement of Senator Kennedy, pointing to the apparent inconsistencies between mandatory minimum penalties and the SRA:

> As the principal author of the Sentencing Reform Act of 1984, ... I am concerned about the effect these mandatory sentencing provisions and others in ex-

isting law will have on the Sentencing Commission concept and its central role in formulating the details of sentencing policy.

. . . .

For example, mandatory minimum penalty statutes appear to be inconsistent with the guidelines system. Such statutes mandate sentences without regard for either the particular circumstances of the offense or important offender characteristics. As a result, similarly situated defendants may receive different sentences and dissimilarly situated defendants may receive the same sentence. This is precisely the injustice we sought to eliminate in 1984.

Nevertheless, Congress ultimately did include several mandatory minimum provisions in the Anti-Drug Abuse Act of 1988. Perhaps the most far-reaching was a provision making the mandatory minimum sentences for drug distribution and importation/exportation offenses also applicable to convictions for attempts and conspiracies to commit those offenses.

Rethinking Mandatory Minimums
Stephen J. Schulhofer
28 Wake Forest Law Review 199 (1993)

Mandatory minimum penalties have been a feature of federal criminal law since 1790. The first Congress mandated capital punishment for a number of offenses, and statutes mandating prison terms for various offenses were enacted from time to time during the nineteenth century. Mandatories remained rare in the federal system, however, until the passage of the Narcotic Control Act of 1956, which imposed stiff mandatory minimum sentences for drug importation and distribution in an effort to more effectively deter those offenses. In 1970, Congress concluded that its effort to deter through mandatory minimum sentences had been a failure, and it repealed virtually all of the drug mandatories. Congress found that these mandatories actually tended to reduce deterrence because in many instances prosecutors viewed them as too severe and accordingly declined to prosecute violators. Among those who supported the 1970 repeal of drug mandatories was Congressman George Bush, who urged that mandatories were ineffective and unjust.

Fourteen years later the pendulum swung again. In 1984, Congress enacted mandatory penalties for a number of drug offenses and directed that any offender who used or carried a gun during a crime of violence serve a mandatory five-year term, consecutive to the sentence on the underlying offense. Every two years thereafter, from 1986 through 1990, Congress enacted additional mandatories and stiffened some of those already on the books.

As a result, the federal code now contains more than 100 separate mandatory minimum sentence provisions, located in sixty different statutes. The great majority of these mandatories are seldom or never used. A comprehensive Sentencing Commission Report on the mandatories established that from 1984 through 1990, almost 60,000 cases were sentenced under mandatory minimum provisions. However, just four of these statutes (covering possession, manufacture, importation and distribution of controlled substances, as well as the enhancement for carrying a gun during another offense) accounted for ninety-four percent of those cases. The fifty-six remaining statutes accounted for only six percent of the cases, and more than half the statutes were never used at all.

The Sentencing Commission Report identified six objectives of mandatory minimum sentences: assuring "just" (i.e., appropriately severe) punishment, more effective deterrence, more effective incapacitation of the serious offender, elimination of sentence disparities, stronger inducements for knowledgeable offenders to cooperate in the investigation of others, and judicial economies resulting from increased pressure on defendants to plead guilty. Of these objectives, just punishment, effective deterrence and disparity reduction have probably been the goals most prominently and openly cited by legislators. Prosecutors who support mandatories tend to share these goals but often also stress the value of mandatories as a tool for inducing cooperation. The goal of facilitating guilty pleas is less often cited, at least overtly, and recent Justice Department policy has sought to discourage the tactic of bargaining away mandatories to induce a plea. Nonetheless, this last goal remains prominently in the background, an objective that may be primary for prosecutors charged with the day-to-day implementation of mandatories, but which stands in tension with the ostensibly dominant objectives of just punishment, effective deterrence and disparity reduction.

Mandatories require the judge to impose a given minimum sentence upon conviction under a specified charge, but they do not necessarily obligate prosecutors to bring such a charge just because the facts support it. Therefore, the most important question in any mandatory minimum statute concerns the prosecutor's role: Does the statute entail a *mandate to prosecute* or merely an *option to bargain*? Legislatures rarely address this crucial threshold issue explicitly. Rather, they in effect delegate to prosecutors the power to decide whether the statute is really a mandate to impose a minimum sentence or instead is only a source of discretion. Prosecutors, in turn, often assume that the statute imposes no mandate *on them*. Mandatories then become little more than a bargaining chip, a "hammer" which the prosecutor can invoke at her option, to obtain more guilty pleas under more favorable terms. Bargaining-chip mandatories help avoid the high process costs of the additional trials that real mandatories can generate, and they may even *reduce* process costs because potentially severe penalties can induce pleas that would not otherwise be forthcoming. Bargaining-chip mandatories also have two important crime-control benefits. Though they do not constrain prosecutors, they do constrain judges, who are sometimes perceived as more likely than prosecutors to be "soft" on crime. Even when bargained away, the mandatories have crime-control value because they tend to increase the severity of sentences that guilty plea defendants will accept. Yet, the deterrence value of both severity effects is undercut by the uncertainty that mandatories will be applied and by the perception among offenders that the mandatory can be manipulated. Moreover, bargaining-chip mandatories tend to increase rather than reduce disparity because their application depends so much on low-visibility prosecutorial choices and because their most severe effects fall not on flagrantly guilty repeat offenders (who avoid the mandatory by their guilty pleas), but rather on first offenders in borderline situations (who may have plausible defenses and are more likely to insist upon trial).

These potential effects of the bargaining-chip approach are dramatically illustrated by recent experience in the Arizona state courts. Prosecutors there have treated mandatories primarily as a bargaining tool and have made clear their willingness, in return for a guilty plea, to drop counts carrying stiff minimum penalties. As a result, the trial rate in Arizona has fallen dramatically, from ten percent in the period just before introduction of mandatories to only four percent currently. Average sentences, prison populations, and, of course, the correctional budget have all risen substantially, but the deterrence pay-off from these effects remains speculative because of the perception that anyone willing to "cop a plea" can avoid the mandatory sentence. At the same time, mandatories have produced severe punishments for offenders of marginal culpability who showed the poor judgment to insist on trial.

When mandatories are actually applied to all fact situations falling within their scope, predictable and severe sentences are achieved. The results are longer prison terms, increased correctional costs, and enhanced deterrence.

The consequences of inflexibility are difficult to categorize because they are inherently unpatterned and unpredictable. But there are four common effects of inattention to context: cliffs, mistakes, misplaced equality, and the cooperation paradox.

Cliffs result when an offender's conduct just barely brings him within the terms of a mandatory minimum. For example, a first offender who helps sell 495 grams of cocaine might be thought to deserve anywhere from two to four years of imprisonment. Under the sentencing guidelines, his presumptive sentence (after allowance for his acceptance of responsibility and minimal role in the offense) would fall in the range of twenty-seven to thirty-three months, or about two and one-half years. For an identical offender who sold just five grams more, the sentence would double, because the five-year mandatory minimum applicable to sales of 500 grams would kick in. Conversely, an offender facing the five-year minimum can obtain a dramatic decrease in his sentence if he can establish a very small reduction in the quantity for which he is held responsible. The cliff effect means that small drug quantities have enormous importance, while all other factors bearing on culpability and dangerousness have no importance at all.

Mistakes occur when mandatory provisions are badly drafted or poorly coordinated with other statutes. Current federal mandatories contain several outright mistakes. For example, under 21 U.S.C. § 844, a defendant convicted of first offense, simple possession of over five grams of crack is subject to a *minimum* sentence of five years imprisonment. The same statute provides that for simple possession of five grams or less, the *maximum* sentence is one year's imprisonment.

Misplaced equality occurs even if all outright mistakes can be eliminated. Ensuring equal treatment of like offenders prevents one form of disparity, but the resulting equal treatment of *unlike* offenders creates another serious problem — *excessive uniformity*. Excessive uniformity is inevitable under mandatories because the statutes necessarily single out just one or a very small number of factors to determine the minimum sentence. Offenders who differ in a host of crucial respects receive inappropriately equal treatment.

For example, a common problem associated with mandatories is the equal treatment of offenders who played sharply different roles in the offense. The ringleader faces the same sentence as a moderately important underling, who in turn gets the same sentence as a young messenger or secretary who had little responsibility or control over the events. Parties who were pressured to provide minor assistance face the same sentence as the most violent and abusive leaders. Since mandatories are usually stated as minimums, they could, in theory, incorporate such factors by permitting an offender's role in the offense to aggravate the applicable sentence. However, this approach would require setting the mandatory penalty at the level appropriate for the least culpable offender, and such a statute would hardly "send a message" in the way that legislators intend. Instead, mandatories are invariably pegged at a level that the legislature considers appropriate for a highly culpable participant. In fact, in some of the federal mandatories, the "minimum" sentence is life imprisonment without parole. Just punishment for lesser roles is inevitably precluded.

The cooperation paradox provides a final example of the serious distortions that result from inattention to context. One universally recognized exception to a mandatory minimum requirement is the situation in which a defendant offers to testify against confederates or to provide leads in other investigations. Informal mechanisms for avoiding mandatories, in federal courts and elsewhere, insure that sentence concessions will be available to those defendants who provide the most information at the earliest possible point in an investigation, thus guaranteeing that mandatories will not choke the flow of cooperation. Indeed, mandatories coupled with an exception for cooperation provide powerful inducements for assistance that might not otherwise be forthcoming. This practice is formalized in 18 U.S.C. § 3553(e), which renders all federal mandatories inoperable and authorizes the judge to impose a sentence below the mandatory minimum, if the government makes a motion for a lower sentence on the basis of a defendant's substantial assistance in the investigation or prosecution of others.

Yet, the escape hatch for cooperation creates a paradox. Defendants who are most in the know, and thus have the most "substantial assistance" to offer, are often those who are most centrally involved in conspiratorial crimes. The highly culpable offender may be the best placed to negotiate a big sentencing break. Minor players, peripherally involved and with little knowledge or responsibility, have little to offer and thus can wind up with far more severe sentences than the boss.

Of course, sentence concessions for helping the government have always been part of American sentencing systems and always will be. The vice of an escape hatch for "substantial assistance" stems from its interaction with the unqualified rigidity that mandatories otherwise impose. The quantity-driven drug mandatories pose this problem in its most acute form. Normal principles holding defendants accountable for the acts of their co-conspirators, even if carefully applied, can leave low-level dealers, middlemen and more important distributors responsible for the same quantity of drugs flowing through the conspiratorial network. On a theory of aiding and abetting liability, the "go-fer" who occasionally helps a drug enterprise may be subject to the same penalty as the kingpin, and in some of these cases, the "minimum" can be life imprisonment. Thus, the inflexibility of mandatories means that all participants tend to face the same high sentence, regardless of their limited role in the offense or any mitigating personal circumstances. The "big fish" and the "minnows" wind up in the same sentencing boat. Enter the statutory escape hatch, with sentence concessions that tend to increase with the knowledge and responsibility of the offender. The big fish get the big breaks, while the minnows are left to face severe and sometimes draconian penalties.

This result makes nonsense of the intuitively plausible scale of punishments that Congress and the ordinary person envisage when they think of sentences linked to drug quantity or other hallmarks of the most serious criminal responsibility. Instead of a pyramid of liability with long sentences for leaders at the top of the organizational ladder, the mandatory system can become an inverted pyramid with stiff sentences for minor players and modest punishments for knowledgeable insiders who can cut favorable deals.

2. The "Safety Valve"

Largely in response to the "cooperation paradox" phenomenon discussed above, in 1994 Congress enacted the "safety valve" law, which established an exception from mandatory minimum sentences for certain federal drug offenders who meet five statutory requirements. Approximately one quarter of federal drug offenders receive relief from mandatory minimum sentences under the safety valve each year today. Some argue, however, that the law still leaves many minimally involved defendants to face unjust mandatory minimum sentences. *See, e.g.,* Molly M. Gill, *Correcting Course: Lessons From the 1970 Repeal of Mandatory Minimums*, 21 Fed. Sent. R. 55 (2008) ("For example, having even one too many prior offenses on one's record—even if the offense is nonviolent or occurred when the person was a juvenile—can be enough to fall outside the scope of the safety valve's protection.").

To be eligible for the safety valve, a defendant must meet the following requirements: (1) have no more than one criminal history point as determined under the sentencing guidelines; (2) not have used violence or possessed a dangerous weapon in connection with the offense; (3) the offense cannot have resulted in death or serious bodily injury to any person; (4) not have played a managerial or supervisory role, as determined by the sentencing guidelines; (5) truthfully provide the government with all information and evidence concerning the offense. 18 U.S.C. §355(f)(1)–(5).

Of these conditions, the requirement to truthfully provide information to the government is "overwhelmingly [the] most frequent area of dispute." George H. Newman, *Fighting for the Safety Valve Reduction (Without Cooperation)*, 33 CHAMPION 24 (2009).

a. *The Requirement to Truthfully Provide Information*
United States v. Reynoso
United States Court of Appeals for the Second Circuit
239 F.3d 143 (2000)

Jose A. Cabranes, J.

The facts relevant to this appeal are essentially undisputed. On July 8, 1998, officers and agents of the High Intensity Drug Task Force, a joint task force of the New York City Police Department ("NYPD") and the United States Drug Enforcement Administration, were conducting an investigation in the area of Broadway and 151st Street in Manhattan. As part of that investigation, a confidential informant ("CI") approached an unidentified male and arranged for Ricky Nesmith, an undercover NYPD detective, to purchase 62 grams of crack cocaine. The CI and Detective Nesmith then took a livery taxi to 605 West 151st Street, where the unidentified male had indicated to the CI that the crack cocaine would be delivered.

Soon after the CI and Detective Nesmith arrived at 605 West 151st Street, Reynoso approached the car. Following a conversation with the CI, Reynoso then left. A short time later, however, she returned carrying a brown bag, and handed the bag, which turned out to contain approximately 44 grams of crack cocaine, to the CI. Reynoso told the CI that there were only 45 grams of crack cocaine in the bag, and instructed the CI and Detective Nesmith that because of police activity in the area they should return later for the remaining 17 grams. Reynoso was arrested almost five months later, on December 7, 1998, and charged in a two-count indictment with conspiracy to distribute and possess with intent to distribute more than fifty grams of crack cocaine, in violation of 21 U.S.C. §846; and distribution and possession with intent to distribute more than five grams of crack cocaine, in violation of 21 U.S.C. §812, 841(a)(1), and 841(b)(1)(B).

On August 13, 1999, Reynoso met with prosecutors for a so-called "safety valve proffer." At the meeting, Reynoso informed the Government that she had been addicted to drugs at the time she distributed the crack cocaine to Detective Nesmith. Although she acknowledged distributing the crack cocaine, Reynoso nevertheless denied having served—on July 8, 1998 or on any other date—as a courier or deliverer of drugs for a Washington Heights drug dealer. Instead, Reynoso steadfastly maintained that she had stolen the crack cocaine at issue from a nearby billiards parlor and that she then had approached the first car she saw to sell the drugs. As Reynoso's counsel concedes, "The objective facts known to the parties did not support Ms. Reynoso's story.... The only logical inference [from the known facts] is that Ms. Reynoso was working for a drug dealer as a courier, not that she had stolen the crack and sold it herself."

Because Reynoso continued to deny having served as a courier or distributor, despite the known facts to the contrary, defense counsel retained Dr. Mark Mills, a forensic psychiatrist, to examine Reynoso. After Dr. Mills briefly examined Reynoso in jail and reviewed the case materials, he reported his findings to defense counsel in September 1999. Dr. Mills concluded that Reynoso had no "psychiatric illness," nor any "major psychiatric issues." Nevertheless, after reviewing Reynoso's accounts of neglect and drug use during her childhood and adolescence, Dr. Mills opined:

> [Reynoso's] history of intoxication, impaired memory and neglect accounts for her behavior at her proffer session. While she was ready to accept responsibility for her criminal behavior, she unconsciously elaborated, the technical term is "confabulated[,]" a story that would account for her behavior given the highly incomplete recollection that she had. Expressed differently, Ms. Reynoso told something that was untrue, *but did not appreciate that it was untrue* because of her organic memory impairment, secondary to cocaine intoxication. Such a pattern of confabulation is common in those with significant organic memory impairment.

On October 6, 1999, Reynoso pleaded guilty to Count Two of the indictment—for distribution and possession with intent to distribute more than five grams of crack cocaine. Thereafter, armed with Dr. Mills's report, Reynoso's counsel made a motion pursuant to the safety valve provision of § 3553(f) for relief from the mandatory minimum sentence of 60 months' imprisonment. Defense counsel conceded that Reynoso had not been "objectively" truthful at her safety valve proffer, but argued that she nevertheless satisfied § 3553(f)(5) — which, as noted, requires that "the defendant has truthfully provided to the Government all information and evidence the defendant has concerning the offense"—because "she did not appreciate the fact that her information was untrue [as a result] 'of organic memory impairment, secondary to cocaine intoxication.'" In opposing the motion, the Government did not contest that Reynoso satisfied the other four requirements for relief under the safety valve provision[1] or challenge the findings of Dr. Mills. Instead, the Government argued that Dr. Mills's findings were irrelevant as a matter of law and that Reynoso could not satisfy § 3553(f)(5) because the information she had provided was "objectively untruthful."

Following oral argument, the District Court denied Reynoso's motion for relief from the mandatory minimum sentence in a ruling from the bench. The District Court agreed to assume *arguendo* that Dr. Mills's findings were valid and that Reynoso "genuinely believes that she was telling the truth." Nevertheless, the District Court concluded, primarily as a matter of plain language and of "policy," that Reynoso did not satisfy the requirement of § 3553(f)(5) because she had provided objectively false information to the Government. Accordingly, the District Court sentenced Reynoso to the statutory minimum of 60 months' imprisonment, followed by four years' supervised release, and imposed a mandatory special assessment of $100. This appeal followed.

The sole question on this appeal is whether Reynoso qualifies for relief under the safety valve statute. The parties agree that this question turns on whether Reynoso satisfies the fifth requirement of the statute, which provides that

---

1. The other four requirements for relief under the safety valve provision are as follows: (1) the defendant does not have more than 1 criminal history point, as determined under the sentencing guidelines; (2) the defendant did not use violence or credible threats of violence or possess a firearm or other dangerous weapon (or induce another participant to do so) in connection with the offense; (3) the offense did not result in death or serious bodily injury to any person; (4) the defendant was not an organizer, leader, manager, or supervisor of others in the offense, as determined under the sentencing guidelines and was not engaged in a continuing criminal enterprise ...

not later than the time of the sentencing hearing, the defendant has truthfully provided to the Government all information and evidence the defendant has concerning the offense or offenses that were part of the same course of conduct or of a common scheme or plan, but the fact that the defendant has no relevant or useful other information to provide or that the Government is already aware of the information shall not preclude a determination by the court that the defendant has complied with this requirement.

Reynoso, who bears the burden of proving that she qualifies for safety valve relief, argues that § 3553(f)(5) requires only that a defendant "subjectively believe[]" information provided to the Government is true. In response, the Government contends that the provision requires a defendant to show that the information he or she provided was objectively true. The proper construction of the statute is a question of law, subject to *de novo* review.

We conclude that Reynoso and the Government are both partially correct — that is, that a defendant seeking to qualify for relief under the safety valve provision must prove *both* that the information he or she provided to the Government was objectively true *and* that he or she subjectively believed that such information was true. This conclusion is supported, first and foremost, by the plain language of § 3553(f)(5). As noted, § 3553(f)(5) states that a defendant qualifies for relief only by "*truthfully* providing to the Government all information and evidence [he or she] has concerning the offense." One authority defines "truthful" as both "telling or disposed to tell the truth" and "accurate and sincere in describing reality." Other dictionaries similarly define the word to encompass both a subjective belief in the truth of information conveyed *and* the conveyance of true information. We see no reason to believe that Congress did not intend for the word "truthfully" in § 3553(f)(5) to encompass both these meanings. Accordingly, we hold that in order to qualify for safety valve relief, a defendant must prove both that the information he or she provided to the Government was objectively true and that he or she subjectively believed that such information was true.

Reynoso and our dissenting colleague emphasize that the statutory language is "truthfully provided" rather than "truthful information," and would have us infer from Congress's use of an adverb that "the emphasis in the statute is on the defendant's state of mind," but we are unpersuaded. In previous cases concerning § 3553(f)(5), we have, except when quoting the statute itself, almost without fail used the adjective "truthful" when articulating the standard to be applied. *See United States v. Schreiber,* 191 F.3d 103, 106 (2d Cir. 1999) (holding that § 3553(f)(5) requires that a defendant provide "to the government complete and truthful information no later than the time of sentencing"). This consistent usage, considered in conjunction with both the dictionary definitions of the term "truthful" quoted above and the ordinary, common-sense meaning of the word, leads ineluctably to the conclusion that Congress intended no legal significance to attach to its use of the words "truthfully provided" rather than "truthful information."

Our conclusion, that § 3553(f)(5) requires both that information provided to the Government be objectively truthful and that a defendant subjectively believe that such information is truthful, is further supported by the legislative history and purposes of the safety valve provision. The legislative history of the Mandatory Minimum Sentencing Reform Act of 1994 ("MMSRA"), which contained the safety valve provision, indicates that one of the principal purposes of the statute was to reform the then "current operation of mandatory minimums [under which] mitigating factors that are recognized in the [sentencing] guidelines and generally are considered in drug cases do not apply to the least culpable offenders except in rare instances." As we have explained, Congress intended "to remedy an inequity in the old system, which allowed relief from statutory minimum sentences" to those defendants who rendered "substantial assistance" to the Government—usually higher-level offenders, "whose greater involvement in criminal activity resulted in their having more information"—but effectively denied such relief to the least culpable offenders, who often "had no new or useful information to trade."

The critical point to draw from this legislative history is that Congress, in enacting the MMSRA, was concerned about the low-level figure in a drug conspiracy who sought to provide the Government with substantial assistance but, by virtue of his or her minor involvement in the criminal activity, "had no new or useful information to trade." Thus, Congress intended to provide relief from statutory minimum sentences to those defendants who, *but for their minor roles in criminal activity*, could (and would) have provided the Government with substantial assistance. To be sure, because a defendant may get safety valve relief even when the information provided is neither "new" nor "useful," the Government cannot legitimately claim an entitlement under § 3553(f)(5) to information of value. However, aided by the legislative history, we read the statute to mean that the Government is entitled under § 3553(f)(5) *not* to be provided with objectively false information, which may well be harmful to the Government. Indeed, we are confident that, in enacting the MMSRA, Congress did not intend to reward the defendant who, for whatever reason, tries "to trade" on objectively false information. Similarly, because Congress was concerned primarily with "the least culpable offenders," we conclude that a defendant must subjectively believe he or she is providing truthful information in order to qualify for safety valve relief.

In sum, we hold that a defendant may not qualify for safety valve relief under 18 U.S.C. § 3553(f) without proving both that information he or she provided to the Government was objectively true and that he or she subjectively believed that such information was true. Because Reynoso concedes that the information she provided to the Government was objectively false, she is not entitled to relief under the safety valve provision. Accordingly, the judgment of the District Court is affirmed.

Calabresi, J, dissenting.

This case presents the question of whether 18 U.S.C. § 3553(f)(5)—which requires a defendant to prove that she has "truthfully provided to the Government all information and evidence [she] has" in order to obtain "safety valve" relief from a statutory minimum sentence—employs an objective or a subjective standard of truthfulness. Put otherwise, we are called upon to determine whether a defendant who provides information that she believes to be true has met the requirements of § 3553(f)(5) and is eligible for safety valve relief, even though the data she gives is objectively false. The majority has determined that she is not. Because I believe that the majority's reading of the safety valve provision finds no support (a) in its language when read according to the most elementary rules of grammar, (b) in prior cases interpreting that language, or (c) in the provision's legislative history, I respectfully dissent.

As with all matters of statutory interpretation, we begin with the language of the statute. Although the majority claims to have analyzed what § 3553(f)(5) says, it does not actually respect the provision's plain language. Section 3553(f)(5) requires that a defendant who has otherwise met the "safety valve" criteria "truthfully provide[] to the Government all the information and evidence the defendant has." The majority interprets this sentence to mean that a defendant must prove *both* "that the information he or she provided to the Government was objectively true and that he or she subjectively believed that such information was true." But § 3553(f)(5) in fact says nothing about the veracity of the information a defendant gives; it requires only that the defendant provide information that she believes to be true.

The majority's interpretation treats the provision as if it stated that the defendant must "truthfully provide[] to the Government all the *truthful information* ... the defendant has." The majority attempts to avoid the problem that the statutory language creates for its interpretation by treating the word "truthfully" both as an *adverb* modifying the verb "provide[]" (which it is) and as an *adjective* modifying the noun "information" (which it is not and grammatically cannot be).

It is, in other words, obvious that the provision as it is written (not as the majority might wish it to be) contains no requirement that the information provided comport with the facts of the case as the court finds them to be. Rather, the provision requires that the defendant "truthfully provide[] all the information ... [she] has." She must, that is, make "*a good faith attempt* to cooperate with the authorities." And the placement and form of the word "truthfully" unmistakably indicates that it is the defendant's state of mind rather than the quality of the information that is at issue.

Further evidence that this is the proper reading of the statute can be found in the remainder of the provision: A defendant must truthfully provide "all the information *the defendant has.*" 18 U.S.C. § 3553(f)(5) (emphasis added). I cannot see how someone *has* information that she does not know about. As a result, when the government, remarkably, conceded that Reynoso genuinely believed what she said, it also necessarily conceded that she had *truthfully provided the evidence she had.* And this remains so even though the evidence she gave is not true.

The majority's opinion is thus doubly wrong linguistically: Not only does the grammatical structure of the statute make it clear that the relevant issue is the defendant's state of mind, but so too does the language requiring her to provide all the information she has. One need not be a philologist to conclude that a person *has* no information that for whatever reason, mental or otherwise, she is *conceded not to have.*

Moreover, neither the majority's lengthy citation of cases that have mentioned "truthful information," nor its reliance on the provision's legislative history, support—and certainly do not justify—its misreading of the plain language of the statute.

In none of the cases the majority cites was the courts' rewriting of the sentence in any way relevant, let alone necessary, to their results, and so such judicial rewriting is of no significance. There is, in fact, not a shred of evidence that the question now before us was even subconsciously in the minds of the courts deciding the cases cited above. It follows that their modifications of the statutory language have no bearing on our decision here.

More important, the only appellate cases that have directly focused on the issue before us have rejected the majority's position. *See United States v. Thompson,* 76 F.3d 166 (7th Cir. 1996) and *United States v. Sherpa,* 110 F.3d 656 (9th Cir. 1997). Of the two cases, *Thompson* is more directly germane. In both *Thompson,* and the instant case, the question is the same: What information did the defendant actually have, given the "limitations on [her] perceptual and analytical abilities." Thompson received safety valve relief when she provided objectively false information that the court found she subjectively believed. As in the case before us, a psychologist evaluated the defendant. The expert found "a diminished capacity to understand complex situations." The court stated that Thompson "gave the government information as she knew it and as she understood it." The Seventh Circuit accepted the district court's reliance "on expert testimony presented at the sentencing hearing concerning limitations on Thompson's perceptual and analytical abilities and conclusion that Thompson was forthright within the range of her ability."

The same is true of this case. Reynoso was convicted of distributing and possessing with intent to distribute crack cocaine to an undercover police detective. Throughout her safety valve proffer, she consistently maintained that she believed she had stolen the drugs that she gave to the undercover detective. Dr. Mark Mills, a forensic psychiatrist retained by Reynoso's counsel, testified that Reynoso's

> history of intoxication, impaired memory and neglect accounts for her behavior at her proffer session. While she was ready to accept responsibility for her criminal behavior, she unconsciously elaborated, the technical term is "confabulated" a story that would account for her behavior given the highly incomplete recollection that she had. Expressed differently, Ms. Reynoso told something that was untrue, but *did not appreciate that it was untrue* because of her organic memory impairment, secondary to cocaine intoxication. Such a pattern of confabulation is common in those with significant memory impairment.

Like Thompson, then, Reynoso "was forthright within the range of her ability." As a result, she provided the government all of the information she possessed. (Indeed, the government has *conceded* as much.) That is all the plain language of § 3553(f)(5) requires.

The majority attempts to justify its deviation from the plain meaning of the statute by reference to the legislative history of § 3553(f). It argues that that history provides only one legitimate justification for a defendant's failure to have (and hence to be able to give) information about the offense: the defendant's limited role. The majority also reads into the legislative history a government entitlement "*not* to be provided with objectively false information."

In fact, the legislative history indicates neither such entitlement, nor any other support for the majority's interpretation. Rather, that history, as is often the case, is inconclusive. Most likely, all it shows is that Congress did not really think about the issue. But, if anything, it cuts against the majority view.

The principal goal behind the safety valve provision was undoubtedly to remedy the irony that "for the very offenders who most warrant proportionally lower sentences—offenders that by guideline definitions are the least culpable—mandatory minimums generally operate to block the sentence from reflecting mitigating factors." H.R. Rep. No. 103-460, at 3 (1994). Ordinarily, downward departures that are grounded in cooperation with the police, because they are based on *substantial* assistance being given to the Government, require that the defendant provide useful information that the Government does not already possess, 18 U.S.C. § 3553(e), U.S.S.G. § 5K1.1. The safety valve provision was enacted to benefit defendants even if they "had no new or useful information to trade." It would seem to follow that defendants may be eligible for safety valve relief regardless of whether they have useful knowledge, useless knowledge, wrong knowledge, or no knowledge at all.

This object of the provision—to ensure proportionality in sentencing for "the least culpable offenders" and provide incentives for them to tell all they know—does not militate in favor of any particular interpretation of the language at issue in the instant case. On the one hand, it is not out of the question that the Government might also hope to gain useful information as a result of safety valve proffers by minor participants. To that extent, the provision of true information might be desirable. On the other hand, the obtaining of information, and hence its quality—whether it is true or false, helpful to future prosecutions or not—is beside the point of the statute.

Underlying the majority's refusal to read § 3553(f)(5) as it is written is a prediction that, under a subjective interpretation, defendants will be "rewarded" for "'trading on' objectively false information". This reflects a fear that allowing those like Reynoso, who profess to believe false information, to benefit from safety valve relief will lead to a mare's nest. As the Government states in its brief: "Permitting such a class of persons to receive the safety valve's benefit could mire district courts in a search for the intent behind a defendant's proffer of information when such information is not in fact truthful but the defendant contends his or her perception is sincerely held." Thus far, the Government continues, courts "'have found it fairly easy to cull serious efforts at full disclosure from mere pretense.'" "Permitting the result advocated by Reynoso would drastically change the courts' abilities in this regard, inviting frequent battles between experts, and rendering a court's fact finding mission exponentially more difficult." The majority, like the Government, is understandably worried about defendants who might take advantage of a reversal in this case to gain safety valve relief without providing truthful information. Lying, the majority warns, "may well be harmful to the Government."

[T]hese fears are misguided. [T]he district courts are already involved in determinations of the credibility of defendants' proffers. *See Gambino, 106 F.3d at 1111* (describing how the district court based its denial of the safety valve motion on "the detailed representations in the government's letter, which the court credited over [defendant's] implausible arguments in rebuttal"). As a result, allowing defendants who provide subjectively believed but objectively false information to receive safety valve relief does not suddenly inject credibility determinations where they have never been required in the past. The fact is, moreover, that defendants willing to lie can, under the majority's own holding, readily take advantage of the safety valve by credibly denying that they have any knowledge at all. This is so since, as all seem to concede, under the safety valve (a) a defendant can say that she thought that she had gotten the drugs in a particular way but frankly couldn't remember, and (b) her lack of memory, if truthfully held, would be a defense. Hence, rather than avoiding credibility fights, all the majority does is to create a perverse incentive to deny knowledge of uncomfortable facts.

Nor are the credibility determinations that must be made in such cases any easier than those to be made in the case before us. To the contrary, they present much the same problems as those the majority fears. As a result, the principle effect of the majority's interpretation is to create the need for Ptolemaic cycles and epicycles to enable courts to distinguish cases of lack of information due specifically to the minor role played by the defendant in the offense, from those due to lack of memory of the offense, and finally from those that, as in the instant case, are due to self-deluding false information.

What makes this case odd, and so raises the problem, is the absurdity of the government's concession, which both the district court and the majority of this panel accept *arguendo*. Let me be absolutely clear. My position in no way suggests that the evidence Reynoso proffered was sufficient to carry her burden of proof. Because, however, the government *conceded* that Reynoso believed she was telling the truth, I have no choice but respectfully to dissent.

United States v. Brownlee

United States Court of Appeals for the Eleventh Circuit
204 F.3d 1302 (2000)

Strom, J.

Appellant, Elliott Brownlee, entered a plea of guilty on August 14, 1997, to six counts involving conspiracy to possess with intent to distribute cocaine base and cocaine under

21 U.S.C. § 846, possession of those substances with intent to distribute under 21 U.S.C. § 841(a)(1), and distribution of those substances under 21 U.S.C. § 841(a)(1). Upon his arrest in January 1997, Brownlee gave a proffer regarding his drug activity to a Drug Enforcement Administration task force agent. In this proffer, Brownlee admitted to his involvement in the sale of cocaine, but he did not truthfully disclose the source of the cocaine at this time, nor on later occasions.

On January 8, 1998, the day before Brownlee's sentencing hearing, Brownlee's trial counsel contacted the prosecutor, telling him that Brownlee would meet with him before the sentencing hearing to disclose information. On the morning of Brownlee's sentencing hearing, Brownlee met with the prosecutor and case agent and disclosed that co-defendant Alfred Wright, Jr. was the source of the cocaine. The district court then conducted the sentencing hearing for co-defendant Alfred Wright, Jr., at which the government called Brownlee as a witness. On the witness stand, Brownlee testified that Alfred Wright was the source of the cocaine. After the district court sentenced Wright, it conducted Brownlee's sentencing hearing. Finding that Brownlee's base offense level was 32, the district court added a two-level enhancement pursuant to U.S.S.G. § 3C1.1 for obstruction of justice, and reduced that level by three offense levels for acceptance of responsibility pursuant to U.S.S.G. § 3E1.1, resulting in a total offense level of 31. The district court sentenced Brownlee to 120 months imprisonment, the mandatory minimum for his offenses. Had the district court applied safety-valve relief for Brownlee, he would have been entitled to a two-level reduction pursuant to U.S.S.G. § 2D1.1(b)(6), resulting in an offense level of 29 and a sentencing range of 87–108 months.

In 1994 Congress enacted a provision allowing district courts to sentence less-culpable defendants without regard to the mandatory minimum sentences in certain cases. This Guideline has been nicknamed the "safety-valve" provision. The safety valve provision requires a district court to sentence a defendant in certain drug-possession cases "without regard to any statutory minimum sentence" if the defendant meets five criteria. If the Court determines that all five criteria are met, "'the court shall impose a sentence pursuant to [the Guidelines] without regard to any statutory minimum sentence.'" There is no dispute in this case that the first four criteria of § 5C1.2 are satisfied. The sole issue on appeal is whether Brownlee satisfied U.S.S.G. § 5C1.2(5), which provides:

> Not later than the time of the sentencing hearing, the defendant has truthfully provided to the Government all information and evidence the defendant had concerning the offense or offenses that were part of the same course of conduct or of a common scheme or plan, but the fact that the defendant has no relevant or useful other information to provide or that the Government is already aware of the information shall not preclude a determination by the court that the defendant has complied with this requirement.

The government argues that the Court should read § 5C1.2(5) as requiring a defendant to disclose all information in good faith. The government further contends that defendant's previous lies about his knowledge do not constitute disclosing information in good faith. *See United States v. Ramunno,* 133 F.3d 476 (7th Cir.1998) (stating that § 5C1.2 benefits only those defendants who have made a good faith attempt to cooperate with the authorities) (citations omitted). We decline to adopt the government's view.

The plain language of 18 U.S.C. § 3553(f) and U.S.S.G. § 5C1.2 provides only one deadline for compliance, "not later than the time of the sentencing hearing." It is undisputed that Brownlee met this deadline. Nothing in the statute suggests that a defendant who previously lied or withheld information from the government is automatically disqualified from safety-valve relief. A similar situation to Brownlee's occurred in *United States v. Tournier,* 171 F.3d 645 (8th Cir.1999). In *Tournier,* the defendant gave three interviews prior to sentencing, each time disclosing information that was untruthful. The defendant later gave a fourth interview prior to sentencing, where she completely and truthfully disclosed the relevant information. Upon such disclosure, the district court granted the defendant safety-valve relief. In affirming that decision, the Eighth Circuit declined to adopt the government's view that safety-valve relief should not apply to defendants who wait until the last minute to fully cooperate. The court held that since the defendant had finally provided truthful and complete information before the sentencing hearing, although the court admitted that obtaining truthful information from that defendant had been "grudging and fitful," like "pulling teeth," she was entitled to safety-valve relief. *See also United States v. Gama-Bastidas,* 142 F.3d 1233 (10th Cir.1998) (holding that defendant's attempt to furnish information to the court and the government in the Judge's chambers prior to the sentencing hearing was not "too late" to be entitled to safety-valve relief). "Moreover, to the extent that the government's interest in disclosure could justify penalizing defendants who lie or withhold information during proffer sessions, a similar scheme already exists independent of the safety valve." *See Schreiber,* 191 F.3d at 108 (citing U.S.S.G. § 3C1.1 (obstruction of justice)). We follow those circuits who have held that lies and omissions do not, as a matter of law, disqualify a defendant from safety-valve relief so long as the defendant makes a complete and truthful proffer not later than the commencement of the sentencing hearing.

This does not mean that the defendant's prior lies are completely irrelevant. In making this determination, the evidence of his lies becomes "part of the total mix of evidence for the district court to consider in evaluating the completeness and truthfulness of the defendant's proffer."

The question of whether the information Brownlee supplied to the government the morning of his sentencing was truthful and complete, however, is a factual finding for the district court. Because the district court disqualified Brownlee from safety-valve relief at the threshold, the district court never considered the factual question of whether his final proffer was complete and truthful.

We therefore VACATE Brownlee's sentence and REMAND with instructions that the district court resentence Brownlee in accordance with this opinion.

b. The Criminal History Provision

Though not as frequently a subject of dispute because its application is often clear-cut, the safety valve's criminal history restriction is an important one and prevents a large number of offenders from taking advantage of the provision. The following case illustrates the mechanistic nature of the safety valve's criminal history cut-off.

United States v. Boddie
United States Court of Appeals for the Third Circuit
318 F.3d 491 (2003)

Sloviter, J.

The issue presented in this case is whether a district court has the authority under the Sentencing Guidelines to apply the safety valve to a defendant whose criminal history category of II overstated the seriousness of the defendant's prior record. This court has not previously spoken to this issue. Seven other courts of appeals have considered the issue, and each has held that the statutory language limiting the availability of the safety valve to defendants with one criminal history point must govern. We turn to the facts of this case before considering the legal issue.

From the late summer of 1999 until March of 2001, Appellant Jermaine Boddie and Saunders Mabrey supplied cocaine to Gregory Armstrong, who distributed about 15 kilograms of the drug in the Western District of Pennsylvania. Boddie and Mabrey, who were located in San Francisco, initially met with Armstrong in California, and later shipped cocaine to him in food cans sent to a store in McKeesport, Pennsylvania. Armstrong repackaged and distributed the cocaine. He paid Boddie and Mabrey approximately $17,000 per kilogram of cocaine.

Armstrong was arrested in March 2001. He told authorities that he was still in touch with his suppliers and that he owed them about $75,000 for the last shipment of cocaine. In August 2001, the Drug Enforcement Administration ("DEA") recorded telephone conversations between Armstrong and Mabrey about their cocaine dealings and the debt that Armstrong owed. On October 3, 2001, one of Armstrong's associates who was working as a confidential informant with the DEA had a recorded conversation with Mabrey, in which the confidential informant told Mabrey that the money to repay the debt had been gathered. On October 4, 2001, DEA agents arrested Boddie and Mabrey, who had arrived in Pittsburgh, Pennsylvania, to collect the $75,000.

On October 31, 2001, a grand jury indicted Boddie and Mabrey, charging them with conspiracy to distribute and possess with intent to distribute in excess of five kilograms of cocaine, in violation of 21 U.S.C. § 846. On February 8, 2002, Boddie and Mabrey pled guilty to the charge pursuant to a plea agreement in which it was agreed, among other things, that the quantity of cocaine attributable to each of them was at least five but less than 15 kilograms. The Government agreed that if Boddie and Mabrey satisfied statutory requirements, it would recommend at sentencing that the District Court apply the safety valve provision and sentence them without regard to the statutory mandatory minimum penalty.

In Boddie's Presentence Investigation Report ("PSR"), the United States Probation Office determined that Boddie has a criminal history category of II based upon three criminal history points, including one point for a 1999 conviction for driving with a suspended license and two points because the present offense occurred during the period of probation imposed for the driving violation. The Probation Office also stated that it appeared that Boddie did not qualify for the safety valve provision and that he was subject to the statutory mandatory minimum sentence of 120 months.

Boddie objected to the PSR, claiming that his criminal history category was overstated based upon the absence of any involvement with the criminal justice system other than driving violations, and that he qualifies for the application of the safety valve provision. The District Court agreed with Boddie that his criminal history category overstates the seriousness of his past criminal conduct and that a criminal history category of I applies. It ruled, however, that Boddie does not qualify for the safety valve provision because he has more than one criminal history point. The District Court sentenced Boddie to the statutory mandatory minimum of 120 months imprisonment and 60 months supervised release, and ordered him to pay a $100.00 special assessment. This appeal followed.[1]

Boddie argues that the Sentencing Guidelines do not prohibit the application of the safety valve provision of U.S.S.G. § 5C1.2 to an individual whose criminal history is found to be

---

1. The District Court sentenced Mabrey to 70 months imprisonment and 60 months supervised release, and ordered him to pay a $100.00 special assessment. Mabrey did not appeal his sentence.

overstated pursuant to § 4A1.3. He contends that the determination of whether a defendant has more than one criminal history point should be made after a downward departure has been applied.

Under 18 U.S.C. § 3553(f), in cases involving certain drug offenses, the sentencing court shall impose a sentence pursuant to the Sentencing Guidelines without regard to any statutory minimum sentence if the court finds that five criteria are satisfied.

This provision, known as the safety valve, is also set forth in the Sentencing Guidelines at § 5C1.2. It is the first criterion that is at issue in this appeal, as it requires that for Boddie to have the benefit of the safety valve, he must "not have more than 1 criminal history point, as determined under the sentencing guidelines." 18 U.S.C. § 3553(f)(1); U.S.S.G. § 5C1.2(a)(1).

The commentary to U.S.S.G. § 5C1.2 defines "more than 1 criminal history point, as determined under the sentencing guidelines" to mean "more than one criminal history point as determined under § 4A1.1 (Criminal History Category)." Under U.S.S.G. § 4A1.1, criminal history points are assigned for prior criminal convictions and the total number of points determines a defendant's criminal history category. A defendant's criminal history category is used, along with his/her offense level, to determine the applicable sentencing guideline range. Under U.S.S.G. § 4A1.3, a court may depart from the otherwise applicable guideline range and use as a reference the range for a defendant with a lower criminal history category if a defendant's criminal history category significantly over-represents the seriousness of a defendant's criminal history.

Boddie argues that because the District Court had determined that his criminal history category of II overstated the seriousness of his past criminal conduct and that his proper criminal history category was I, he should be deemed eligible for application of the safety valve. However, the safety valve provision is written in terms of criminal history points, not criminal history category.

This issue was most recently considered by the Court of Appeals for the Sixth Circuit in *United States v. Penn*, 282 F.3d 879 (6th Cir. 2002). The district court had granted the defendant a downward departure under U.S.S.G. § 4A1.3, finding that his criminal history category of II, based upon two criminal history points, did not accurately reflect the seriousness of his past criminal conduct. The district court found that the defendant should only receive one criminal history point for his prior conviction based upon the amount of time he spent in prison, and that a criminal history category of I applied. The court then applied the safety valve and sentenced the defendant below the statutory mandatory minimum.

On appeal, the court held that the district court did not have authority to alter the defendant's criminal history points based upon its conclusion that his criminal history category overstated the seriousness of his past criminal conduct. Similarly, the district court was not free to sentence the defendant below the statutory mandatory minimum where he had more than one criminal history point. The court explained that the commentary to § 5C1.2, quoted above, limits the district court's authority to apply the safety valve "to cases where a defendant has not more than one criminal history point as calculated under § 4A1.1, regardless of whether the district court determines that a downward departure in the defendant's sentence is warranted by § 4A1.3." The court further explained that the effect of a departure under § 4A1.3 is not to change the defendant's actual criminal history category or the calculation of a defendant's criminal history points.

Similarly, in *United States v. Robinson*, 158 F.3d 1291 (D.C. Cir. 1998) (per curiam), the district court had adjusted the defendant's criminal history category downward from category II (based on three criminal history points) to category I on the ground that defendant's criminal history category over-represented the seriousness of his criminal history. The court then found the defendant eligible for the safety valve provision based upon the downward departure. The Court of Appeals for the District of Columbia Circuit remanded the case for re-sentencing, explaining that

> while U.S.S.G. § 4A1.3 affords a sentencing court discretion to determine whether a criminal history category accurately reflects a defendant's criminal history, nothing in U.S.S.G. § 4A1.1 suggests that the sentencing court has any discretion with respect to the calculation of a defendant's criminal history score: Section 4A1.1 is a mechanistic provision which merely instructs the sentencing court to add points for various carefully-defined criminal history occurrences.

These cases rely on the commentary to U.S.S.G. § 5C1.2. Although Boddie recognizes that federal courts are bound by the commentary to the Sentencing Guidelines, he argues that the commentary to § 5C1.2 does not limit the courts with respect to consideration of downward departures as authorized in § 4A1.3. Rather, he contends, the commentary is silent concerning the effect of a downward departure. Boddie is correct that the commentary to § 5C1.2 does not address § 4A1.3. However, it specifically defines "more than 1 criminal history point, as determined under the sentencing guidelines" to mean "more than one criminal history point as determined under § 4A1.1."

We agree with the other courts of appeals that have addressed this issue that this definition precludes a court from applying the safety valve provision where a defendant has more than one criminal history point as determined under § 4A1.1, notwithstanding the fact that the court granted a downward departure after finding that the criminal history category is overstated.

It is no secret that the Sentencing Guidelines have been the subject of substantial controversy since their promulgation, often because of what appears to be their inflexibility in situations where equitable considerations might suggest a different outcome. In this case, for example, Boddie is sentenced to serve ten years imprisonment whereas Mabrey, his codefendant, who engaged in the same conduct and pled guilty to the same offense was sentenced to serve less than six years imprisonment, with the differential being that Boddie had more criminal history points because he committed the drug offense while on probation for driving with a suspended license. In other circumstances, the sentencing court's ability to depart downward (or upward) tempers what may be a special circumstance. Here, however, we face not only the Sentencing Guidelines but a congressional statute that is framed in terms of criminal history points. If there is to be any change in this respect, it must be by congressional action. After all, the crime that Boddie committed was a serious drug offense and if Congress chose to ameliorate the effect of some sentences in drug cases by providing a safety valve, it clearly had the option to choose the conditions for eligibility for that safety valve. Boddie is not eligible, Mabrey was.

For the reasons discussed above, we will affirm the judgment of sentence of the District Court.

3. Providing Substantial Assistance

Defendants who are able to offer "substantial assistance" to the government may also be eligible to receive a sentence below an applicable mandatory minimum. In *Wade v. United States*, the Supreme Court held that the decision of whether to file a substantial assistance motion is within the sole discretion of the prosecutor, except if there is a plea agreement to the contrary or unconstitutional action (such as racial discrimination) on the part of the prosecutor. 504 U.S. 181 (1992). As a result, a defendant who cooperates may nevertheless receive a mandatory minimum sentence, particularly if she cooperated before entering a plea agreement. In *United States v. Crickon*, for example, 66-year-old defendant Jerry Crickon was stopped by the police and confessed to transporting methamphetamine. Crickon "agreed to make a controlled delivery, thus helping the police catch Juan Carlos Delatorre, the man to whom Crickon was bringing his shipment of methamphetamine." After making the controlled delivery, the government indicted Crickon who entered a guilty plea. At sentencing, the government declined to file a substantial assistance motion and Crickon received a 151 month sentence. The United States Court of Appeals for the Seventh Circuit held this decision was within the sole discretion of the prosecutor. "Although we are understanding of [Crickon's] plight," the Court wrote, "we are constrained to affirm." 240 F. 3d 652 (7th Cir. 2001).

Even in cases where the defendant provides assistance as part of plea negotiations, the government often has nearly boundless discretion with respect to substantial assistance motions. *See, e.g.,* Ian Weinstein, *Regulating the Market for Snitches*, 47 BUFFALO L. REV. 563, 591 (1999) (observing that "the overall trend is to leave even the cooperator who complies fully with his or her agreement subject to the government's evaluation of his or her cooperation"). A handful of courts, however, have sought to provide limits on the government's decision not to file a substantial assistance motion in plea agreement cases. Some of these courts have relied on principles of contract law to impose a duty of good faith dealing on the government while others have held that the government's action should be subject to a rationality review.

United States v. Rounsavall

United States Court of Appeals for the Eighth Circuit
128 F.3d 665 (1997)

Heaney, J.

On November 9, 1995, Mary Ann Rounsavall entered into a plea agreement with the government. As part of her agreement, she pled guilty to drug and money laundering charges. Absent such an agreement, she would have faced 360 months to life with a statutory minimum of twenty years. Her agreement with the government provided that if she cooperated in the prosecution of her brother, the government would consider filing motions allowing her to receive a sentence at or below the statutory mandatory minimum. According to an affidavit submitted by Rounsavall to the district court, Assistant United States Attorney Bruce Gillan told Rounsavall that he did not want or believe that she should go to prison for the twenty years required by the statutory mandatory minimum sentence if she complied with the terms of the plea agreement. Gillan indicated Rounsavall should expect to receive somewhere between seven to ten years for her cooperation, although the decision as to the length of her sentence would be entirely up to the judge. In his affidavit, United States Attorney Thomas Monaghan stated that the government initially sought Rounsavall's assistance because the government believed that once she helped in the prosecution, Rounsavall's brother would also cooperate.

Rounsavall testified against her brother in two separate criminal proceedings. First, she testified against her brother at his drug and money laundering trial. During his trial, she testified for four days. She also testified against her brother for an additional day at a forfeiture proceeding. All told, she testified for five days, longer than any other witness, in helping the government convict her brother and secure a life sentence against him. Ultimately, the government [did not file] an 18 U.S.C. § 3553(e) motion [mandatory minimum substantial assistance motion]. Rounsavall was sentenced to twenty years, the lowest possible sentence the district court could order under the statutory mandatory minimum. Because the government withheld filing a § 3553(e) motion, the district court could not further lower Rounsavall's sentence.

According to an affidavit from United States Attorney Thomas Monaghan, the government considered but decided against filing a § 3553(e) motion for the following reasons:

> (a) the failure of the defendant to cooperate with the government until her second trial; (b) the fact that a portion of her testimony regarding money laundering given during a trial against a codefendant was not accurate or complete; (c) the fact that no other persons can be prosecuted as a result of her cooperation; and (d) the fact that she violated her plea agreement by not giving reliable and complete testimony regarding money laundering.

The district court judge strongly disagreed with the decision of the prosecutor not to file a § 3553(e) motion:

> In my opinion, Ms. Rounsavall's testimony against her brother was extremely helpful to the Government, was, in large measure, truthful and was provided to the Government at great personal cost to Ms. Rounsavall. In some ways, she's going to have to live the rest of her life knowing she contributed to her brother probably dying in prison. If the Government had filed a motion under the statute, I would likely have substantially departed below the sentence that I now must impose under the law.

Despite disagreeing with the government's decision, the district court found that there was no reason to hold an evidentiary hearing regarding Rounsavall's claim of a breach of her agreement because the government had simply agreed to consider her cooperation and nothing more. Rounsavall appeals the district court's denial of her motion to compel the government to file a § 3553(e) motion.

"A sentencing court may not grant a downward departure for substantial assistance absent a motion by the government." There are, however, limited exceptions to this rule. "Relief may be granted absent a government substantial assistance motion if a defendant shows that the government's refusal to make the motion was based on an unconstitutional motive, that the refusal was irrational, or that the motion was withheld in bad faith." A defendant is entitled to an evidentiary hearing to determine whether the government acted improperly if she is able to make a substantial threshold showing that the government acted irrationally, in bad faith, or in violation of one's constitutional rights.

We agree with the district court that United States Attorney Monaghan should have made the § 3553(e) motion for a statutory downward departure. We go a step further, however, and hold that Rounsavall made a sufficient threshold showing to require that an evidentiary hearing be held to determine whether the United States Attorney's reasons for not granting the motion were irrational and/or were made in bad faith.

No credence can be given to the United States Attorney's first reason, that the defendant failed to cooperate until her second trial. The fact is that the plea agreement was not entered into until the second trial. Thus, if the United States Attorney was going to take into consideration that Rounsavall was late in entering a plea, he should have said so at that time rather than after the fact.

Nor do we find merit in the United States Attorney's view that the testimony regarding money laundering given during the trial against a codefendant was not accurate or complete. It appears from the record that the codefendant was her brother. She testified against him for the better part of five days and he was convicted, the district court found, largely because of her testimony.

The third reason for failing to file a statutory motion, that no other person can be prosecuted as a result of her cooperation, is equally specious. If this, in fact, were a condition of her agreement, then the prosecutor should have made it clear before he accepted her plea agreement. He failed to do so.

On the basis of this record, we are unable to divine the rationale behind the [prosecutor's claim that the] money laundering [testimony] was not reliable or complete. Again, her brother was not only convicted of money laundering because of her testimony, but the district court found that she had completely cooperated post-trial in terms of her own money laundering and had voluntarily agreed to the entry of a money judgment against her in the sum of $200,000. It is difficult to imagine a higher degree of cooperation.

We then come to appellant's contention that Assistant United States Attorney Gillan told Rounsavall that she could expect to receive between seven to ten years for substantially assisting the government. At oral argument, Gillan contended that whether he made such representations to Rounsavall is outside the record. In its memorandum and order, however, the district court acknowledged that it reviewed Rounsavall's affidavit as part of the entire record before making its final determination.

Based on the alleged representations made to Rounsavall, as set forth in her affidavit, the government may have violated the plea agreement in failing to file the § 3553(e) motion. In *Wade*, the Supreme Court suggested that the decision to forego filing a § 3553(e) motion could be "superseded" by another agreement made by the prosecutor.

In this case, Gillan's representations to Rounsavall may have superseded the broad discretion prosecutors generally enjoy in determining whether to file a substantial assistance motion under § 3553(e). In her affidavit before the district court, Rounsavall alleged that Gillan said that he did not believe she deserved to go to prison for twenty years if she fully cooperated; and although it was entirely up to the judge, she should expect a seven- to ten-year sentence. As the district court found, Rounsavall clearly cooperated in providing substantial assistance to the government. The twenty-year sentence, therefore, may well have been a violation of the plea agreement between Rounsavall and the Assistant United States Attorney who prosecuted the case. This court attempted unsuccessfully to get the Assistant United States Attorney's view on this matter at oral argument. The question will have to be thoroughly addressed on remand.

The government argues that its only agreement was to consider whether Rounsavall had cooperated in determining whether it would file a § 3553(e) motion. The district court appears to have accepted this view. We do not believe the district court's authority is so limited. Notwithstanding the language of an agreement, if the government's refusal to file a § 3553(e) motion is irrational and/or in bad faith, particularly in light of representations made to a defendant, a district court may require the government to make a downward departure motion.

Additionally, it appears that the government may have based its decision to enter into a plea agreement with Rounsavall on factors other than her substantial assistance.

In this case, United States Attorney Monaghan admitted in his affidavit that the government had sought Rounsavall's "assistance because we believed that her brother would cooperate with the government once he realized that she was helping" the government. The record indicates that Rounsavall was never informed that the government wanted her assistance to get her brother to cooperate. As it turned out, Rounsavall's brother did not cooperate with the government. It appears, therefore, that when Rounsavall's brother decided not to enter into a plea agreement, the government may have acted irrationally and/or in bad faith by withholding the § 3553(e) motion.

Consistent with this opinion, we reverse and remand to the district court for an evidentiary hearing to determine whether the government acted irrationally and/or in bad faith in failing to file a § 3553(e) motion in light of Rounsavall's substantial assistance and the government's conduct, and whether the government considered factors outside of Rounsavall's substantial assistance in declining to file the § 3553(e) downward departure motion.

4. The Crack and Powder Cocaine Sentencing Disparity

The "100 to 1" sentencing disparity between federal crack and powder cocaine offenders has been one of the most hotly debated aspects of our drug laws over the past 25 years. Under this law, it took 100 times the amount of powder cocaine to result in the same mandatory minimum sentence as cocaine base (more commonly called crack cocaine). To trigger a 10-year mandatory minimum sentence, for example, a cocaine offender would need to have had 5,000 grams of cocaine (about a briefcase full) while a crack offender would only have needed 50 grams of cocaine (about the weight of a candy bar). *See* Eric E. Sterling, *Take Another Crack at That Cocaine Law*, L.A. Times, Nov. 13, 2006.

In 2010, Congress passed the Fair Sentencing Act, which reduced the disparity from 100-to-1 to 18-to-1. The Fair Sentencing Act is not retroactive, meaning that the change does not benefit defendants who were already sentenced for a federal crack cocaine offense prior to its passage. Despite this reform, the cocaine sentencing disparity remains a vitally important issue to the study of controlled substances law, particularly with respect to the relationship between race and drug policy.

Presented below is District Court Judge Clyde S. Cahill's opinion in *United States v. Clary*. In *Clary*, Judge Cahill found the 100-to-1 disparity to be unconstitutional as a violation of the Equal Protection Clause. Judge Cahill's decision was quickly reversed by the U.S. Court of Appeals for the Eighth Circuit. Other federal courts have uniformly agreed with the Eight Circuit that the 100-to-1 sentencing disparity was constitutional. Although Judge Cahill's opinion failed to carry the day in the courts, it is regarded as one of the most thorough and passionate critiques of the crack/powder cocaine sentencing disparity.

United States v. Clary
United States District Court for the Eastern District of Missouri
846 F. Supp. 786 (1994)

Cahill, J.

Defendant Edward Clary was arrested for possession with intent to distribute 67.76 grams of cocaine base. Clary pled guilty to possession with intent to distribute cocaine base ("crack cocaine"), pursuant to 21 U.S.C. § 841(b)(1)(A)(iii) (hereinafter referred to as the "crack statute"), punishable by a mandatory minimum sentence of 10 years imprisonment. Prior to sentencing, Clary, a black male, filed a motion challenging the constitutionality of the crack statute and contended that the sentence enhancement provisions contained in it and United States Sentencing Guidelines (U.S.S.G.) § 2D1.1 violated his equal protection rights guaranteed by the Fifth Amendment.

Before this Court are two different sentencing provisions contained within the same statute for possession and distribution of different forms of the same drug. The difference — the key difference — is that possession and distribution of *50* grams of crack cocaine carries the same mandatory minimum sentence of 10 years imprisonment as possession and distribution of *5000* grams of powder cocaine. Both provisions punish the *same* drug, but penalize crack cocaine 100 times more than powder cocaine!

Congress tells us that the rationale for this sentencing dichotomy which produces harsher punishment for involvement with crack cocaine is because it is so much more dangerous than powder cocaine. As "proof," Congress relied upon endless media accounts of crack's increased threat to society. While Congress may have had well-intentioned concerns, the Court is equally aware that this one provision, the crack statute, has been directly responsible for incarcerating nearly an entire generation of young black American men for very long periods, usually during the most productive time of their lives. Inasmuch as crack and powder cocaine are really the same drug (powder cocaine is "cooked" with baking soda for about a minute to make crack), it appears likely that race rather than conduct was the determining factor.

Although both statutory provisions purport to punish criminal activity for both crack and powder cocaine, the blacks using crack are punished with much longer sentences than whites using the same amount of powder cocaine. This disparity is so significantly disproportional that it shocks the conscience of the Court and invokes examination.

The Eighth Circuit Court of Appeals has rejected numerous constitutional challenges to the crack statute and the United States Sentencing Guidelines. However, the Eighth Circuit acknowledged the "extraordinary disparity in punishment between possession of cocaine powder and cocaine base." *United States v. Marshall,* 998 F.2d 634 (8th Cir. 1993).

> "With so much at stake, however, in this and other cases, we are reluctant to say that full exploration of the issues is unwarranted ... in connection with crack cocaine punishments, which continue to perplex many sentencing judges. We do not invite mere repetition of prior rejected arguments, without new facts or; legal analysis." *Id.* at 635 Fn.2.

This Court accepts the Eighth Circuit's invitation to present a novel legal analysis of the adverse disparate impact on blacks resulting from the imposition of 21 U.S.C. § 841(b)(1)(A)(iii). Here is the Court's analysis.

The Court is faced with the task of resolving whether the crack statute violated defendant Clary's equal protection rights. The equal protection component of the Fifth Amendment Due Process clause commands that similarly situated people must be treated alike. The Court's basic understanding of this constitutional rule is that when one group of people violates the same type of laws as other people similar to them, they should be punished in the same manner.

To determine whether a law treats similarly situated people in a dissimilar manner, a violation of equal protection under the U.S. Constitution, the Court must first determine the appropriate type of judicial review to apply. Judicial review is conducted under one of three different levels of scrutiny depending upon the seriousness of the constitutional violation that triggers the review.

The Court conducts the lowest level of constitutional scrutiny, a *rational basis review,* to determine whether a law that causes disparate treatment among similarly situated persons serves a rational state or governmental purpose.

The next level of review, *intermediate scrutiny,* applies when the Court must determine whether the classification scheme included in the law must "fairly be viewed as furthering a substantial interest of the state." *Plyler v. Doe,* 457 U.S. 202, 217–18 (1982). Under this standard, although a law does not involve a facially invidious classification, it will be reviewed if it gives rise to recurring constitutional difficulties."

The highest form of constitutional review that the Court evokes, *strict scrutiny,* is mandated when the legislative classification incorporates presumptively suspect factors, such as race, or fundamental individual liberties, such as religion. In such cases, once the suspect classification is revealed, the government must prove that the classification is narrowly tailored to further a compelling government interest. For example, racist statutes which on their face and in their direct language created segregated facilities such as restrooms and drinking fountains were struck down by the United States Supreme Court under strict scrutiny.

The difficult situation that a Court must face is to determine whether a statute which is facially neutral was enacted for racial reasons and would thereby have a disparate impact on a particular racial group. Whether or not racial discrimination was involved in legislative action that resulted in a law which, although facially neutral, still has a racially disparate impact "demands a sensitive inquiry into such circumstantial evidence of intent as may be available." *Arlington Heights v. Metropolitan Housing Development Corporation,* 429 U.S. 252, 266 (1977).

Under *Arlington,* the Supreme Court set forth key factors to evaluate whether a law was motivated by racial discrimination. These factors included the presence of disparate impact, the overall historical context of the legislation, the legislative history of the challenged law, and departures from the normal legislative process. Additional legal precedent has provided the Court with more criteria for its review, such as foreseeability of the consequences of the legislation; however, *Arlington* provides the Court with the major benchmark to discover the presence of racial influence in the legislative decision making process.

These various levels of constitutional review evolved as a response to the manner in which racism in America has manifested itself within the legal system. Overt racism, evidenced by such occurrences as "Jim Crow Laws," allowed legislators to enact racist laws without reprisals. As civil rights for *all* Americans became a reality, continued attempts to maintain racial barriers took on the form of more subtle, covert, facially neutral legislation. Examples of this type of legislation included zoning, voting and housing laws.

Today most legislation would not contain overtly racist referrals and, indeed, would eliminate the slightest allusion to racial factors in the words of the legislation itself. But today, despite the fact that a law may be racially neutral on its face, there still may be factors derived from unconscious racism that affect and infiltrate the legislative result.

That black people have been punished more severely for violating the same law as whites is not a new phenomenon. A dual system of criminal punishment based on racial discrimination can be traced back to the time of slavery. In order to understand the role that racism has played in enacting the penalty enhancement for using crack cocaine, one must first take note of America's history of racially tainted criminal laws, particularly drug laws. Race has often served as a significant contributing factor to the enhancement of penalties for crime.

Early in our nation's history, legislatures were motivated by racial discrimination to differentiate between crimes committed by whites and crimes committed by blacks. For example, "An Act Against Stealing Hogs" provided a penalty of 25 lashes on a bare back or a 10 pound fine for white offenders, while nonwhites (slave and free) would receive 39 lashes, with no chance of paying a fine to avoid the whipping. In 1697, Pennsylvania passed death sentence legislation for black men who raped white women[7] and castrated them for attempted rape. White men who committed the same offense would be fined, whipped, or imprisoned for one year.

During Reconstruction, Southern legislatures sought to maintain control of freed slaves by passing criminal laws directed at blacks that treated petty crimes as serious offenses. A Georgia law passed in 1875 made hog stealing a felony. A Missouri "pig law" defined the theft of property worth more than $10 as grand larceny and provided for punishment of up to five years of hard labor. As a result, Southern prisons swelled and became, for the first time, predominantly black. The prison population in Georgia alone tripled within two years.

Prior to the civil rights era, Congress repeatedly imposed severe criminal sanctions on addictive substances once they became popular with minorities. Historically, a consortium of reactionary media and a subsequently inflamed constituency have combined to influence Congress to impose more severe criminal sanctions for use of narcotics once they became popular with minorities.

Media accounts[10] and inaccurate data influenced public opinion about opium smoking. "Ambivalence and outright hostility" toward Chinese coupled with the concern that opium smoking was spreading to the upper classes, provided the foundation for the passage of the 1909 Smoking Opium Exclusion Act. "Yellow Peril" was a term used in the years between the Great Wars to express the fear that the huge population of the Far East posed a military threat to the West. This fear induced an aversion to the opium usage believed to be prevalent in Chinese communities and foisted anti-opium legislation.

The Harrison Act of 1914, the first federal law to prohibit distribution of cocaine and heroin, was passed on the heels of overblown media accounts depicting heroin-addicted black prostitutes and criminals in the cities. The author of the Act, Representative Francis Harrison, moved to include coca leaves in the bill "since [the leaves] make Coca-Cola and Pepsi-Cola and all those things are sold to Negroes all over the South." At one point the bill appeared to be facing defeat until Dr. Hamilton Wright, the American delegate to the Hague Opium Conference, 1911–1912, submitted an official report in which he warned Congress of the drug crazed blacks in the South whose drug habits "threatened to creep into the higher social ranks of the country."

In later decades cocaine became associated with exotic groups such as Hollywood entertainers and jazz musicians. It earned the moniker of the "rich man's drug." In the early 1960s and 1970s, cocaine began to move into mainstream society, and became the "drug of the eighties." Even with the widespread use of powder cocaine, no new drug laws were

---

7. Death as punishment was also reserved for slaves who were convicted three times for striking a white person, or who wounded or bruised a white person in a "grievous" manner, or who *attempted* to run away. Conversely, a white person who willfully took the life of a slave *two* times was then punished by having to pay restitution to the slave owner. Higginbotham, A. Leon, *In the Matter of Color: Race in the American Legal Process*, (1978).

10. For example, *See, San Francisco Post*, "the chinaman has impoverished our country, degraded our free labor, and hoodlumized our children. He is now destroying our young men with opium." (March 1, 1879).

enacted to further criminalize or penalize cocaine possession. The "war on drugs" with respect to powder cocaine was concentrated on impeding international import of the drug or targeted large scale financiers. The social history is clear that so long as cocaine powder was a popular amusement among young, white professionals, law enforcement policy prohibiting cocaine was weakly enforced.

Almost every major drug has been, at various times in America's history, treated as a threat to the survival of America by some minority segment of society. Panic based on media reports which incited racial fears has been used historically in this country as the catalyst for generating racially biased legislation. The association of illicit drug use with minorities and the threat of it "spreading to the higher ranks" is disturbingly similar to the events which culminated in the "100 to 1" ratio enhancement in the crack statute.[18]

Racism goes beyond prejudicial discrimination and bigotry. It arises from outlooks, stereotypes, and fears of which we are vastly unaware. Our historical experience has made racism an integral part of our culture even though society has more recently embraced an ideal that rejects racism as immoral. When an individual experiences conflict between racist ideas and the social ethic that condemns those ideas, the mind excludes his racism from his awareness.

Unconscious racism existed in some limited form during slavery. As outright discrimination against blacks became increasingly politically and socially unacceptable, and, in 1954, in some measure *illegal,* racist actions metamorphized into more subtle forms of discrimination. As more well-educated blacks flowed into America's mainstream, whites even began to differentiate between the kind of blacks who reflected white values and who were not like "those other" blacks akin to the inner city stereotype.

When counsel first argued that overt racism was really the basis for the discriminatory crack penalties, this Court rejected that approach out-of-hand, for the Court did not believe that such outrageous and outmoded ideas would affect the legislators of this day and age. But upon reflection, the Court recognizes that while intentional discrimination is unlikely today, unconscious feelings of difference and superiority still live on even in well-intentioned minds. There is a realization that most Americans have grown beyond the evils of overt racial malice, but still have not completely shed the deeply rooted cultural bias that differentiates between "them" and "us."

The illustration of unconscious racism is patently evident in the crack cocaine statutes. Had the same type of law been applied to powder cocaine, it would have sentenced droves of young whites to prison for extended terms. Before the enactment of such a law, it would have been much more carefully and deliberately considered. After all, in these days when "toughness on crime" is a political virtue, the simplest and fairest solution would have been to make the severe punishment for powder cocaine the same as for crack cocaine. But when the heavy punishment is inflicted only upon those in the weak and unpopular minority community, it is an example of benign neglect arising from unconscious racism.

The influence of "unconscious racism" on legislative decisions has never been presented to any court in this context. Constitutional redress to racial discrimination has resulted primarily from judicial vigilance directed toward correcting overt and facially discriminatory legislation forged first by slavery and followed by continuing racial animosity

---

18. All of these drug laws had one common theme: the contamination of the white population (or upper class), particularly white women, by minority drug abusers was imminent; therefore, immediate law enforcement and legislation criminalizing the use of narcotics was necessary.

toward blacks and other ethnic minorities. Remaining still is a more pernicious, albeit intangible, form of race discrimination in the individual's unconscious thoughts that influences the decision making process. As a result, "individuals ... ubiquitously attach a significance to race that is irrational and often used outside their awareness." *McCleskey v. Kemp,* 481 U.S. 279, 322 (1987) (Brennan, J. dissenting).

Consequently, the focus on "purposeful" discrimination is inadequate as a response to more subtle and deeply buried forms of racism. In 1909, the United States Supreme Court acknowledged that "[racial] bias or prejudice is such an elusive condition of the mind that it is most difficult, if not impossible, to always recognize its existence." *Crawford v. United States,* 212 U.S. 183, 196 (1909). Eighty-three years later, *Crawford* holds: the inquiry to determine racial bias is still "difficult, if not impossible." Without consideration of the influences of unconscious racism, the standard of review set forth in *Davis* is a "crippling burden of proof." *Batson v. Kentucky,* 476 U.S. 79, 92 (1985).

It is against this background that the Court considers the merits of defendant's challenge.

A current equal protection analysis must therefore take into account the unconscious predispositions of people, including legislators, who may sincerely believe that they are not making decisions on the basis of race. This predisposition is a pertinent factor in determining the existence of a racially discriminatory motive. Racial influences which unconsciously seeped into the legislative decision making process are no less injurious, reprehensible, or unconstitutional. Although intent *per se* may not have entered Congress' enactment of the crack statute, its failure to account for a foreseeable disparate impact which would effect black Americans in grossly disproportionate numbers would, nonetheless, violate the spirit and letter of equal protection.

The equal protection component of the Fifth Amendment Due Process clause commands that similarly situated people be treated alike. A criminal defendant who alleges an equal protection violation must prove that the "invidious quality" of governmental action claimed to be racially discriminatory "must ultimately be traced to a racially discriminatory purpose." *Washington v. Davis,* 426 U.S. 229, 240, 48 (1976). Absent direct evidence of intent to discriminate, the defendant can make a prima facie case "by showing [that] the totality of the relevant facts gives rise to an inference of discriminatory purpose." *Id.* In deciding whether the defendant has carried the burden of persuasion, a court must undertake a "sensitive inquiry into such circumstantial evidence of intent as may be available." *Arlington,* 429 U.S. 252, 266 (1977).

Therefore, this Court will proceed with its examination by reviewing the circumstantial evidence to determine whether race influenced the legislature's actions.

Crack cocaine eased into the mainstream of the drug culture about 1985 and immediately absorbed the media's attention. Between 1985 and 1986, over 400 reports had been broadcast by the networks. Media accounts of crack-user horror stories appeared daily on every major channel and in every major newspaper. Many of the stories were racist. Despite the statistical data that whites were prevalent among crack users, rare was the interview with a young black person who had avoided drugs and the drug culture, and even rarer was any media association with whites and crack. Images of young black men daily saturated the screens of our televisions. These distorted images branded onto the public mind and the minds of legislators that young black men were *solely* responsible for the drug crisis in America. The media created a stereotype of a crack dealer as a young black male, unemployed, gang affiliated, gun toting, and a menace to society. These stereotypical descriptions of drug dealers may be accurate, but not all young black men are drug dealers. The broad brush of uninformed public opinion paints them all as the same.

Legislators used these media accounts as informational support for the enactment of the crack statute. The Congressional Record, prior to enactment of the statute, is replete with news articles submitted by members for their colleagues' consideration which labeled crack dealers as black youths and gangs.[48] Members of Congress also introduced into the record media reports containing language that was either overtly or subtly racist, and which exacerbated white fears that the "crack problem" would spill out of the ghettos.

These stereotypical images undoubtedly served as the touchstone that influenced racial perceptions held by legislators and the public as related to the "crack epidemic." The fear of increased crime as a result of crack cocaine fed white society's fear of the black male as a crack user and as a source of social disruption. The prospect of black crack migrating to the white suburbs led the legislators to reflexively punish crack violators more harshly than their white, suburban, powder cocaine dealing counterparts. The ultimate outcome resulted in the legislators drafting the crack statute with its Draconian punishment.

The media reports associating blacks with the horrors of crack cocaine caused the Congress to react irrationally and arbitrarily. The evolution of the 100 to 1 crack to powder ratio mandatory minimum sentence was a direct result of a "frenzied" Congress that was moved to action based upon an unconscious racial animus. The "frenzied" state of Congress led members to depart from normal and substantive procedures that are *routinely* considered a part of the legislative process.

The 1986 Controlled Substances Act followed an extraordinarily hasty and truncated legislative process. As Eric Sterling, then counsel to the House Subcommittee on Crime, has summarized:

> The Controlled Substances Act sentencing provisions were initiated in the [House] Subcommittee on Crime in early August 1986 in a climate in the Congress that some have characterized as frenzied. Speaker O'Neill returned from Boston after the July 4th district work period where he had been bombarded with constituent horror and outrage about the cocaine overdose death of NCAA basketball star Len Bias after signing with the championship Boston Celtics. The Speaker announced that the House Democrats would develop an omnibus anti-drug bill, easing the reelection concerns of many Democratic members of the House by ostensibly preempting the crime and drug issue from the Republicans who had used it very effectively in the 1984 election season. The Speaker set a deadline for the conclusion of all Committee work on this bill as the start of the August recess—five weeks away.
>
>   The development of this omnibus bill was extraordinary. Typically Members introduce bills which are referred to a subcommittee, and hearings are held on the bills. Comment is invited from the Administration, the Judicial Conference, and organizations that have expertise on the issue. A markup is held on a bill, and amendments are offered to it. For this omnibus bill much of this procedure was dispensed with. The careful deliberative practices of the Congress were set aside for the drug bill.

Few hearings were held in the House on the enhanced penalties for crack offenders. Despite the lack of fact-gathering about crack, "the 100:1 cocaine to crack ratio ... was orig-

---

48. 132 Cong. Rec. S2495 (daily ed. Mar. 12, 1986) ("big city ghettos" are "infested with crack houses" and "are centers of the new cocaine trade" in crack); 132 Cong. Rec. S4670 (daily ed. April 22, 1986) ("Most of the dealers, as with past drug trends, are black or Hispanic ... whites rarely sell the cocaine rocks."); 132 Cong. Rec. S7123-25 (daily ed. June 9, 1986) (dealers "organize small cells of pushers, couriers and lookouts from the ghetto's legion of unemployed teenagers").

inally a 50:1 ratio in the Crime Subcommittee's bill, [the final law], ... arbitrarily doubled simply to symbolize redoubled Congressional seriousness."

When the Senate considered the legislation, many Senators fruitlessly cautioned against undue haste in light of the House's abbreviated consideration of the bill, to little avail. Tossing caution to the wind, the Senate conducted a single hearing between 9:40 a.m. to 1:15 p.m., including recesses. Attendance was intermittent.

Circumstantial evidence of invidious intent may include proof of disproportionate impact. *Davis,* 426 U.S. at 242. "Impact of the official action—whether it 'bears more heavily on one race than another,'" is important evidence.

Defendant's evidence that the impact of the crack statute "bears more heavily" on blacks than whites is undisputed. 98.2 percent of defendants convicted of crack cocaine charges in the Eastern District of Missouri between the years 1988 and 1992 were black. Nationally, 92.6 percent of the defendants convicted during 1992 of federal crack cocaine violations were black and 4.7 percent of the defendants were white. In comparison, 45.2 percent of defendants sentenced for powder cocaine were white, as opposed to 20.7 percent of black defendants. All of the defendants sentenced for simple possession of crack cocaine were black. The national figures comport to essentially the same percentage as the Missouri statistics.

The 1992 federal figures indicate—that blacks comprise 1.6 million of the illegal drug use population while 8.7 million whites admit to illegal drug use. Yet, blacks are four times as likely as whites to be arrested on drug charges in this country. Notably, in the Eastern District blacks are eight times as likely to be arrested.

According to the U.S. Sentencing Commission, blacks receive sentences at or above the mandatory minimum more often than whites arrested on the same charge. The disparate application appears to be related to race, and the disparity is constant even when variables such as nature of the offense and prior criminal record are considered.

Moreover, overcrowding in the Federal Bureau of Prisons reflects the disparity in a dramatic way. An estimated 90 percent increase in the prison population during the last several years is directly related to the mandatory minimum drug sentences and the sentencing guidelines. As of July 1993, 60.4 percent of the inmates in the Bureau of Prisons are there for drug related offenses.

Clary argues that the statistical disparity is overwhelming proof of discrimination, and that in cases where statistical evidence of disparity is "stark," statistics alone have been accepted as the sole source of proof of an equal protection violation. This Court agrees that the statistical evidence of disparate impact resulting from crack cocaine sentences is compelling.

Objective evidence supports the belief that racial animus was a motivating factor in enacting the crack statute. Congress' decision was based, in large part, on the racial imagery generated by the media which connected the "crack problem" with blacks in the inner city. Congress deviated from procedural patterns, departed from a thorough, rational discussion of the "crack issue" and reacted to it in a "frenzy" initiated by the media and emotionally charged constituents. Under *Arlington,* all of these factors may be considered by the Court to infer intent.

The crack statute in conjunction with the resultant mandatory minimum sentence, standing alone, may not have spawned the kind and degree of racially disparate impact that warrants judicial review but for the manner of its application by law enforcement agencies. The law enforcement practices, charging policies, and sentencing departure decisions by prosecutors constitute major contributing factors which have escalated the disparate outcome.[68]

Prosecutorial discretion as it relates to crack cocaine cases should be exercised in a manner that is responsive to Congress' expressed intent to target "kingpins" and "high level traffickers." It would seem to be economically sensible to devote scarce government resources to reducing the large ingress and wholesale distribution of powder cocaine by major traffickers which would consequently reduce the existence of crack as a derivative product. Without cocaine, there could be no crack.

However, both national and local statistical data do not show that the prosecution is targeting the upper echelons in the drug trade. Few kingpins are prosecuted. Review of the cases that have been prosecuted in this district reflects a clear pattern of disparate impact. Out of 57 convictions in the Eastern District of Missouri, 55 of the defendants were black, one was white, one was Hispanic, and not one kingpin among them. Three of the 56 defendants were jointly charged with having 944 grams, three others had 454 grams between them, and one had 451 grams. The other 50 had a total of less than 2000 grams, averaging less than 40 grams each. Eight defendants had less than 10 grams. Five of them had less than a gram, barely enough to detect or to utilize. The total amount of crack cocaine for 56 of the 57 defendants (the amount for one defendant was not determined) was less than 4,000 grams. Powder cocaine is usually imported into this country by boats, trucks, and planes, and in huge quantities. Kingpin dealers are then able to transport the drug in brick-like packages referred to as "kilos." A kilogram weighs 1,000 grams. Thus, it appears clear that the removal of this small quantity of drugs would hardly reduce the supply of crack cocaine in St. Louis or impede its flow.

The issue of prosecutorial venue is so intertwined with the racial impact flowing from the crack and mandatory minimum statute that it requires careful scrutiny. Generally, federal prosecutions are much more likely to result in conviction, with more severe punishment. In cases where there is joint jurisdiction of similar offenses, careful discernment by conscientious state and federal prosecutors can carefully select among the charges (state and federal) the ones that more nearly result in the most appropriate penalty. There would be inefficiency in double prosecutions, so a choice ought to be made. While various factors would be considered in selecting federal or state actions, certainly a decision based upon race would not be appropriate. And yet—when an examination of the crack cocaine violations in the district court is made, they are nearly all black (55 of 57). Where conviction is a certainty, harsh penalties inevitable, and nearly all defendants are black, suspicion will arise.

The Court notes that a close examination of many of the 57 files involving crack cocaine in this district shows that federal prosecution occurs with both state and federal law officers making the arrests. Generally, those arrested by state officers had very small amounts of crack cocaine. For example, nine of the 57 crack cocaine defendants were assigned to this Court and most of them had only tiny quantities of crack cocaine. All but one was black. All of them, even though arrested by state law officers, were prosecuted in the federal court. Even a disinterested inquirer would wonder why the tremendous expense of federal prosecution and subsequent incarceration should be wasted on relatively minor offenders.

---

68. Despite the conviction rates, authoritative studies show that blacks and other racial minorities are less involved in crack use than whites. According to the National Institute on Drug Abuse, over 2.4 million whites have used crack, as opposed to 990,000 blacks and 348,000 Hispanics. In other words, the NIDA statistics show that of all individuals who have ever used crack in the United States, 64.4% are white, 26.2% are black, and 9.2% are Hispanic. In the past year before the survey, 540,000 whites used crack, as opposed to 334,000 blacks and 105,000 Hispanics.

The failure by the prosecutors to explain these and other discrepancies adds a telling ingredient to the argument that the crack statute was constitutionally infirm and further exhibited the unconscious racism proffered here, generally, and as applied to this defendant. After all, while the Eastern District of Missouri includes the City of St. Louis with its large black population, it also includes St. Louis County with a white population four or five times larger. Surely if the prosecution were really free of racism, unconscious or not, there would be more than one white defendant convicted for crack violations in the federal courts of the Eastern District of Missouri in three years.

Without explanation, the logical inference to be drawn is that the prosecutors in the federal courts are selectively prosecuting black defendants who were involved with crack, no matter how trivial the amount, and ignoring or diverting whites when they do the same thing.

There may be rational explanations for these disproportionate figures. That is why this Court repeatedly requested the U.S. Attorney's Office to make available its standards or principles for the selection of crack cocaine cases. But the prosecutor refused to divulge this information (an *in camera* submission would have been sufficient), citing prosecutorial discretion. The Court is not sure that it has the authority to demand such an explanation from the prosecutor. But failure to divulge the standards used during 1989–92 raises an inference that unconscious racism may have influenced the decision to severely punish blacks for violations involving their form of cocaine while hardly touching whites who utilize another form of the same drug—both are forms of cocaine.

The focus on the prosecution of numerous low level crack dealers appears to be part of a national policy, perhaps designed to give the impression of great victories in the War on Drugs. Such a misguided approach to the elimination of drug traffic has resulted in the necessity for expensive prisons, has destroyed the lives of many young first offenders, and most importantly, has not reduced the quantity of drugs saturating the nation. In the St. Louis area there is a greater amount of cocaine available than in 1980 and it is cheaper. Small-time dealers grow like dandelions and are immediately and easily replaced, which further establishes the authority of the drug kingpins and dilutes the police resources available to curtail kingpin drug dealers.

This Court has known and respected the staff of the United States Attorney's Office for many years, and does not believe that overt racism would influence their decisions. The national statistics comport with the data from the Eastern District of Missouri. What is more likely is that the subliminal influence of unconscious racism has permeated federal prosecution throughout the nation. After all, even U.S. prosecutors are not immune from unconscious racism.

A law which burdens blacks disproportionately and whose influence has been traced to racial considerations, even if unconscious, warrants the most rigorous scrutiny. Such a law can survive only if the classification which is suspect is narrowly tailored to further a compelling governmental interest. Consistent with the history of criminalizing behavior among minority groups in this country, at the very least, the crack statute in its application has created a "de facto suspect classification" to which strict scrutiny must apply. Under this standard, the crack statute is defective.

To rebut defendant's claim that racial animus played a role in penalizing crimes involving cocaine base more severely than crimes involving powder cocaine, the Government offered evidence that members of Congress considered crack to be more dangerous because of its potency, its highly addictive nature, its affordability, and increasing prevalence. Ample evidence has been presented to this Court that contradicts many of Congress' claims.

Congress had no hard evidence before it to support the contentions that crack was 100 times more potent or dangerous than powder cocaine. Even Senator Hawkins, among the first of the members of Congress to initiate dialogue about crack cocaine, noted that "the dividing line between crack and powder cocaine is indistinct and arbitrary." Dr. Robert Byck, Professor of Psychiatry and Pharmacology of the Yale University School of Medicine, testified at the Crack Cocaine Hearing before the Senate Subcommittee on Governmental Affairs and acknowledged that there was no reliable evidence at that time that crack cocaine was more addictive or dangerous than powder cocaine. Today, there is no reliable medical evidence that crack cocaine is more addictive than powder cocaine.

There is no evidence that the use of crack makes the user physiologically or psychologically more prone to violence or other antisocial behavior than does the use of powder cocaine. Moreover, researchers have concluded that the short-term and long-term effects of crack and powder cocaine are identical.

According to the market approach, crack cocaine can be distributed in small packets at a low unit price. Crack is no cheaper than cocaine powder because cocaine is the essential product of crack. But all forms of cocaine are available today in greater quantity and at lower prices than a few years ago.

If the "100 to 1" ratio were reversed to penalize powder cocaine possession of 50 grams with a 10 year mandatory minimum, Congress would be encouraged to respond with more creative and effective ways to wage the drug war. The uproar from their constituencies would be deafening, and politicians would be moved to action much more quickly. As sad as it may sound, and as much as the Court feels discomfort in pointing it out, if young white males were being incarcerated at the same rate as young black males, the statute would have been amended long ago.

The record does not support the fact that Congress had a reasonable basis to make the harsh distinction between penalties for powder and crack cocaine. It is not difficult to understand the pressures upon Congress to react to the abundance of elements regarding the imminent arrival of crack cocaine, and the political expediency of exploiting its presumed dangers. But the frenzied, irrational response to criminalize crack at 100 times greater than powder cocaine, in a manner that would disproportionately affect blacks, is unjustified.

Even were the Congress' interests compelling, the statute was not drafted in narrow terms to accomplish those interests. Why not punish the possession and distribution of powder cocaine with equal severity as crack cocaine? COCAINE IS COCAINE. Neither should be punished less than or more than the other: they are equal in their harm to society and destruction of individual lives and the punishment should be the same for both. To impose a more severe penalty on a derivative source of an illegal narcotic while the principal source of the drug is tolerated is illogical. To the extent that the source dries up, the derivative must necessarily wither upon the vine. If any enhancement would be justified, it would be to penalize cocaine more severely. Hence, the absence of narrow tailoring corroborates the constitutional infirmity of the statute.

In the days when segregation was the order of the day and the laws all bore the unmistakable mark of discrimination, evidenced usually in the very titles of those laws, the federal courts became the refuge of hope and encouragement to the minorities who sought their protection. Unpopular though their judgments were, the courts consistently supported fairness and the Constitution, and made justice a reality for those too weak to achieve it themselves.

The Court realizes there are substantial differences between 1960 and 1990. The Court realizes that the Congress, by and large, is not bent upon discrimination and inequality today. But the Court also recognizes that the vestiges of racism so deeply imbedded in the psyche of America cannot be completely eliminated in all of their subtleties at once. Men and women of general good will are still not completely immune to the more covert forms of the disease of racism. We try, but sometimes we all fail to reach our intended goals.

The reason why we cannot wait for the congressional modification and changes that the Court believes will occur in time is that the horror of continuing is so very destructive. There are many prisoners serving 10-year sentences for possessing with intent to distribute 50 grams of crack. They are usually between 18–30 years of age and about 90 percent are black.

It must be noted that the detection, arrest, prosecution, and conviction of these petty drug peddlers consumes so much of law enforcement's time and so many of the dollars of the criminal justice system that it makes it more difficult, if not impossible, to really stop the cancerous growth of drugs. The huge numbers of young, petty drug dealers serving long mandatory minimum sentences also use precious prison bed space that would better be reserved for the use of violent repeat offenders, the class of persons that society needs to be protected from most of all.

This Court knows that its decision today will be unpopular with many and, indeed, may seem senseless to some. The Court also knows that its opinion may not be politically correct, or in keeping with the majority of opinions currently controlling the law. But just as the laws on civil rights and discrimination took many years to change (more than 50 years elapsed between *Plessy v. Ferguson* (1897) and *Brown v. Board of Education* 1954), it may take time for equality under these laws to be fully honored.

The old cliche of fools rushing in where angels fear to tread may be applicable here, but a judge's conscience must always respond to the call of the Constitution. Truth must be recognized and respected though the heavens fall.

Even if appellate review points to a different path, the evaluation and reflection that this perplexing problem has occasioned is of great value. It will not have been in vain.

The Court finds that there is no material difference between the chemical properties of crack and powder cocaine, and that they are one and the same drug. The Court further finds that this defendant has been denied equal protection of the laws when the punishment assessed against him is 100 times greater than the punishment assessed for the same violation but involving powder cocaine.

The Court further finds that the "symbolic" action of the Congress in raising the original 50 to 1 ratio to 100 to 1 is yet another indication of its irrational and arbitrary actions, and further evidences the failure of the Congress to narrowly tailor its provisions as required by law in suspect class cases.

The Court further finds that the Congress enacted this law in an arbitrary and irrational manner, without the testimony of adequate scientific and professional advice, and without providing sufficient time for subcommittee hearings and debate.

The Court further finds that the statistics offered by the defendant, both local and national, show that the disparate impact upon blacks is so great as to shock the conscience of the court. Ratios as high as 55 to 1 appear in the Eastern District of Missouri; even greater disparities are evident on the national level. These ratios are apparent in arrest levels, convictions, and the prosecutorial acts which mitigate or eliminate punishment for whites while maximizing punishment for blacks. The Court finds that the actions of

Congress and the prosecuting officials were influenced and motivated by unconscious racism, causing great harm and injury to black defendants because of their race inasmuch as whites are rarely arrested, prosecuted, or convicted for crack cocaine offenses.

The Court further finds that the Office of the U.S. Attorney for the Eastern District of Missouri only convicted one white person for crack cocaine violations during the years 1989–92 while convicting 55 blacks and one Hispanic. In the absence of explanation by the prosecutors, these disproportionate figures give rise to a strong inference that only blacks are being prosecuted in the federal courts for crack cocaine violations. Prosecution based on race is obviously discriminatory even if it is occasioned by *unconscious* racism.

Therefore, this Court concludes that the disproportionate penalties for crack cocaine as specified in all of the pertinent sections of 21 U.S.C. §841 violate the Equal Protection Clause of the U.S. Constitution generally and as applied in this case. The Court further holds that the prosecutorial selection of cases on the basis of race is constitutionally impermissible as applied to this defendant in this case.

Accordingly, the Court has sentenced the defendant to a [4 year] prison term in conformity with this memorandum.

———————

Less than a year after Judge Cahill's decision in *Clary*, the U.S. Court of Appeals for the Eighth Circuit reversed. The Eighth Circuit found that, although "the district court's painstakingly-crafted opinion demonstrates the careful consideration it gave not only to the testimony before it, but to the voluminous documents introduced by Clary," the evidence fell "short of establishing that Congress acted with a discriminatory purpose in enacting the statute." *United States v. Clary*, 34 F.3d 709 (8th Cir. 1994). "While [discriminatory] impact is an important starting point," the Court continued, the Supreme Court's decision in "*Arlington Heights* made clear that impact alone is not determinative" in most cases. "A belief that racial animus was a motivating factor, based on disproportionate impact, is simply not enough since the Equal Protection Clause is violated 'only if that impact can be traced to a discriminatory purpose.'" *Id.* For an insightful discussion of the *Clary* case and its relationship to the broader issue of race and drug policy, see Doris Marie Provine, Unequal Under the Law: Race in the War on Drugs 15–36 (2007).

Though federal constitutional challenges to the disparate treatment of crack and powder cocaine have been unsuccessful, in 1991 the Minnesota Supreme Court invalidated the state's 10 to 3 powder-to-crack ratio. *Minnesota v. Russell*, 477 N.W. 2d 886, 890 (Minn. 1991) ("Without more factual support, the three grams of crack—ten grams of powder distinction appears to be based upon an arbitrary rather than a genuine and substantial distinction.").

5. Recidivism and Drug Sentencing

Rethinking Recidivist Enhancements:
The Role of Prior Drug Convictions in Federal Sentencing
Sarah French Russell
43 U.C. Davis Law Review 1134 (2010)

Sentencing enhancements increase criminal sentences based on the details of an offense or the characteristics of a defendant. For example, assaults that seriously injure a victim or assaults motivated by race might qualify a defendant for an enhancement. Likewise, a defendant may face an enhancement for a drug offense if the defendant has a prior drug conviction. All fifty states have some form of enhancement statutes, and state sentencing guidelines regimes across the country contain enhancement provisions. Numerous statutory enhancements also exist within the federal system, and the federal sentencing guidelines contain enhancement provisions for virtually every type of federal offense.

There are two basic categories of enhancements: nonrecidivist enhancements and recidivist enhancements. Nonrecidivist enhancements stem from the particular circumstances of an offense. For example, a defendant may face a higher sentence for a bank robbery if the offense involved a gun or if someone suffered an injury during the crime. A recidivist enhancement, in contrast, increases a sentence based on a defendant's prior criminal history. Like nonrecidivist enhancements, recidivist enhancements appear in state and federal systems. A well-known example is California's three strikes law, which requires a life sentence if the defendant has three qualifying convictions. In the federal system, a felon who possesses a firearm ordinarily faces a statutory sentencing range of zero to ten years in federal court. If a defendant has three prior convictions for serious drug offenses or violent felonies, however, that defendant faces a mandatory minimum sentence of fifteen years and a maximum of life in prison.

Enhancements can appear either in statutes or in sentencing guidelines. Statutory enhancements are typically mandatory in that courts must apply them when the facts support them. Some statutory enhancements increase the maximum sentence that judges may impose, while others trigger mandatory minimum sentences. Although statutory enhancements are typically mandatory, enhancements under guideline systems are typically discretionary, as the federal guidelines—and most state guidelines regimes—are now advisory.

A defendant's prior criminal history is relevant under all guideline regimes in state and federal systems. Guidelines provide sentencing ranges based on circumstances relating to the offense and the defendant's prior criminal convictions. For example, under the federal sentencing guidelines, which provide sentencing ranges in federal cases, courts determine sentencing ranges based on a grid that contains an "adjusted offense level" on one axis and a "criminal history category" on the other axis. The offense of conviction provides a "base offense level." Courts increase this level to the "adjusted offense level" based on a variety of circumstances, such as whether the defendant possessed a gun during commission of the offense or played a leadership role in the offense. These offense-based enhancements increase the ultimate sentencing range. Judges count prior convictions to determine the defendant's criminal history category, and higher categories carry higher sentencing ranges. Some types of prior convictions, such as drug and violent offenses, can also increase the offense level for certain federal offenses. Thus, these convictions have a particularly large effect because they can increase both the criminal history category and the offense level.

Legislatures and sentencing commissions justify enhancements on several grounds. Retributive goals support offense-based enhancements; the victim's injury makes the offense more serious or the defendant more culpable. Incapacitation goals can also support the enhancements because, arguably, an offender who commits an aggravated offense is more likely to recidivate and necessitate incapacitation. Similarly, such an offender may need a harsher sentence to deter further misconduct, and the enhancement sends a message to others that the aggravated offense carries severe penalties. Moreover, the expressive theory of punishment can justify enhancements because, by enacting enhancements, legislators express moral condemnation for particular types of conduct. For example, many jurisdictions punish assaults motivated by racial or other group-based animus more harshly, and defend these enhancements in expressive terms.

Regarding recidivist enhancements, proponents justify them based on goals of deterrence, incapacitation, and retribution. As to specific deterrence, one can argue that recidivists have already proven themselves more likely to reoffend and need stiffer penalties to deter future misconduct. Likewise, some claim that enhanced penalties for recidivists serve a general deterrence purpose by preventing others from reoffending. In addition, recidivists' likelihood of reoffending can justify a longer sentence on incapacitation grounds because incarceration prevents people from committing additional crimes. Finally, regarding retributive goals, some view an offense committed by a recidivist as being itself a more serious offense, or the recidivist offender as being more culpable.

In the U.S. federal system, enhancements appear in both statutes and the federal sentencing guidelines. A common statutory enhancement is the ACCA, which requires imposition of a fifteen-year mandatory minimum sentence for felons who possess a firearm after conviction of three "serious drug offenses" or "violent felonies." Judges also frequently impose the second offender drug enhancement provision (the "851 enhancement"), which doubles the mandatory minimum sentences for drug distribution offenses committed after a prior felony drug conviction and requires a mandatory life sentence if the defendant has two prior felony drug convictions. Under the federal sentencing guidelines, courts use prior convictions to calculate a defendant's criminal history category, and higher categories result in higher recommended sentencing ranges. In addition, with regard to some offenses, prior convictions can also increase the offense level. These offense-level enhancements can lead to much lengthier sentences.

Approximately one-third of the federal criminal prosecutions are for drug offenses, and the majority of federal prisoners serve sentences for drug offenses. In the past twenty-five years, the percent of the federal prison population serving time for a drug offense has increased from twenty-five percent to fifty-five percent. The percentages are even higher for women and minorities. People convicted of federal drug offenses often receive substantially increased sentences based on prior drug convictions.

The 851 enhancement, which refers to 21 U.S.C. § 851, is a statutory provision that doubles the mandatory minimum sentences applicable in federal drug distribution offenses when the defendant committed a prior "felony drug offense." The enhancement also raises the maximum possible sentence. Under § 851, the government has discretion to seek an enhanced sentence through filing a notice. If a prosecutor seeks the 851 enhancement, the judge must apply it. The effect of this decision is staggering: it increases a five-year mandatory minimum sentence to ten years and a ten-year mandatory minimum to twenty years. The presence of two such convictions can result in a mandatory life sentence for a nonviolent drug offense.

Under the Bush Administration, the filing of 851 notices became much more common. A memorandum issued by John Ashcroft in 2003 sets forth Department of Justice policy regarding 851 enhancements. Prosecutors must file enhancements unless narrow exceptions exist. The DOJ has not revised the memorandum under the new Administration.

A wide range of prior convictions trigger the 851 enhancement. For example, a conviction for simple possession of drugs qualifies as a "prior felony drug offense," as long as it was punishable by more than one year of imprisonment. Moreover, there is no restriction on the use of old convictions. For example, a fifty-year-old defendant convicted of distributing fifty grams or more of crack cocaine faces a mandatory minimum sentence of ten years' imprisonment. Even a simple drug possession conviction from when the defendant was eighteen years old could spike the mandatory minimum sentence to twenty years. Additionally, the mandatory minimum sentence doubles only when defendants have prior drug convictions. A recent robbery or murder conviction, for example, would not trigger this doubling enhancement.

Congress provided little justification for this remarkable increase. Congress originally enacted the relevant statutory provisions as part of the Comprehensive Drug Abuse Prevention and Control Act of 1970, which attempted to provide "an overall balanced scheme of criminal penalties for offenses involving drugs." Deterrence and incapacitation rationales were central goals of the law. Under the original statute enacted in 1970, only prior federal offenses triggered enhanced penalties. Congress did not provide a specific rationale for these enhancements, but stated simply that "second offenses carry double the penalty of first offenses."

In 1984, Congress expanded the second offender provision to include state and foreign offenses as well. With the 1984 amendments, Congress responded to the concern that "illicit trafficking in drugs is one of the most serious crime problems facing the country, yet the present penalties for major drug offenses are often inconsistent or inadequate." Congress intended the amendments "to provide a more rational penalty structure for the major drug trafficking offenses." One major change was to make punishment dependent on the quantity of the controlled substance involved. Congress did not specifically address the purposes of expanding the prior conviction definition, although presumably the change was to further the general purpose of increasing penalties and providing for more consistency among sentences.

In many cases, the doubling of the mandatory minimum sentence for a recidivist drug offender does not serve the purposes of sentencing. Even accepting the view that a repeat offender has committed a more serious offense and is more culpable than a first offender, the degree of enhancement under the 851 enhancement appears greater than that necessary to provide just punishment for the later offense. In addition, overall, there is little evidence that longer sentences actually achieve specific deterrence goals, and some studies find that incarcerating drug offenders increases rather than reduces recidivism. Studies for the most part find no significant general deterrent effect from long prison sentences, and there is a strong argument that incapacitation of drug dealers does not reduce the prevalence of drug offenses.

Federal judges, who see up-close individuals facing these sentences, mostly think that the drug sentencing laws are too severe. A 2004 survey found that 73.7% of district court judges and 82.7% of circuit court judges believe that "drug punishments are greater than appropriate to reflect the seriousness of drug trafficking offenses." Indeed, federal judges have spoken out against mandatory minimum sentences, and several prominent judges have even stepped down from the bench citing their opposition to mandatory minimum sentences in drug cases.

Similar to statutory drug enhancements, application of the career offender guideline can drastically increase a defendant's sentence. Because the career offender enhancement is a guidelines provision, this enhancement is advisory for judges. The career offender guideline applies when: (1) a defendant was at least eighteen years old at the time he committed the federal offense of conviction; (2) the federal offense of conviction is a felony that is either a crime of violence or a controlled substance offense; and (3) the defendant has at least two prior felony convictions of either a crime of violence or a controlled substance offense.

Once classified as career offenders, defendants' base offense levels increase substantially and their criminal history scores increase to the maximum category: category VI.

This can have the effect of doubling, tripling, or even quadrupling a defendant's recommended guidelines range. For example, consider a defendant who has pleaded guilty to possessing with intent to distribute five grams of crack. This defendant has two prior state drug convictions, both of which resulted in a sentence of probation. If the career offender guideline does not apply (and assuming no other enhancements or reductions apply), the defendant's sentencing range will be fifty-one to sixty-three months' imprisonment. If the prior drug convictions count as "controlled substance offenses" under the guidelines, however, the guidelines classify the defendant as a career offender and increase the sentencing range to 188 to 235 months' imprisonment.

Application of the career offender provision has grown over the years. In 2008, courts applied the provision in 2,321 cases, 1,740 of which were drug cases. By contrast, in 1996, courts applied this provision in only 949 cases, and 616 of these cases were drug prosecutions.

The [Sentencing] Commission stated in a 2004 report that the career offender provision of the guidelines, at least with respect to its application to repeat drug dealers, has unwarranted adverse effects on minority defendants without clearly advancing a purpose of sentencing. The report found that although only twenty-six percent of the offenders sentenced in 2000 were African American offenders, African American offenders constituted fifty-eight percent of the offenders subject to the career offender provision. According to the report, most of these African American offenders were subject to the guideline because of the inclusion of drug crimes in the criteria qualifying offenders for the guideline. The Commission offered a possible explanation for these statistics: "Commentators have noted the relative ease of detecting and prosecuting offenses that take place in open-air drug markets, which are most often found in impoverished minority neighborhoods, which suggests that African-Americans have a higher risk of conviction for a drug trafficking crime than do similar White drug traffickers." Thus, it appears that African Americans are more likely to have prior drug convictions on their records than White offenders who engaged in the same type of prior conduct.

The Commission has also questioned whether the career offender guideline actually serves its intended purpose. In particular, the Commission reasoned that incapacitation rationales provided little support for the lengthy sentences. According to the report: "Unlike repeat violent offenders, whose incapacitation may protect the public from additional crimes by the offender, criminologists and law enforcement officials testifying before the Commission note that retail-level drug traffickers are readily replaced by new drug sellers so long as the demand for a drug remains high. Incapacitating a low-level drug seller prevents little, if any, drug selling; the crime is simply committed by someone else."

Prior drug convictions can also trigger enhancements in cases with little or no relation to drug distribution or use. For example, it is a federal crime for a person previously convicted of a felony to possess a firearm or ammunition. Cases involving firearms or ammunition are the third most-frequently prosecuted cases in federal court. A defendant's prior drug convictions may trigger statutory and guideline enhancements in these prosecutions.

The [Armed Career Criminal Act] (ACCA) provides a statutory mandatory minimum sentence for defendants convicted of possession of a firearm or ammunition with qualifying prior convictions. Under the ACCA, if defendants have three prior convictions for "violent felonies" or "serious drug offenses," they face a mandatory minimum sentence of fifteen years and a maximum of life. Without the qualifying convictions, their sentencing range is zero to ten years. The mandatory minimum sentence applies even in cases of mere possession; the government does not need to prove that the defendant used the firearm or that a threat of violence existed. Convictions qualify regardless of age. The number of ACCA sentences imposed has risen over the years. In 1996, courts applied the ACCA in 250 firearm cases nationwide. In 2008, the number was 647.

Prior drug convictions can also lead to sentencing enhancements under the guidelines in cases where a defendant receives a sentence for being a felon in possession of a firearm or ammunition. Section 2K2.1 of the guidelines, which applies to cases involving the unlawful receipt, possession, or transportation of firearms or ammunition, provides the offense level for these defendants.

As with various other guideline provisions, Section 2K2.1 sets different "base offense levels" depending on particular circumstances of the offense. The base offense level is fourteen for a defendant who possesses a firearm or ammunition after conviction for a felony. The offense level increases to twenty if the defendant has a prior conviction for a "controlled substance offense" or "crime of violence." This offense-level increase results in approximately a doubling of the sentencing range. The offense level increases to twenty-four (and triples the sentencing range) if the defendant has two prior controlled substance offenses or crimes of violence.

The firearm guidelines enhancements led to a large increase in the average sentences for firearm offenders. In 1989 — before Congress added the prior-conviction enhancements to the firearm guidelines — the average sentence for firearm offenses was approximately twenty-eight months. In 2008, firearm offense sentences averaged to approximately eighty-four months.

Immigration cases are the second most commonly prosecuted offenses in federal court. The statutory penalties for illegal reentry of a noncitizen after removal are set forth in 8 U.S.C. § 1326(b). A defendant removed after conviction for an "aggravated felony" (which includes various types of drug offenses), is subject to a maximum penalty of twenty years. The maximum sentence is ten years if removal occurs after conviction for a felony that is not an aggravated felony, or after three or more misdemeanor convictions involving drugs or crimes against the person. Otherwise, the maximum is two years.

Enacted in 1988, Congress intended § 1326 to respond to the problem of people repeatedly returning to the United States after deportation. The central purpose of § 1326 was to deter reentry of aliens after they had been deported. Congress later amended the statute to allow longer sentences for aliens deported after conviction of certain crimes. Whereas the 851 and ACCA statutory enhancements require imposition of mandatory minimum sentences, the illegal reentry statutory enhancements simply raise the maximum penalty and do not trigger mandatory minimums. Thus, judges have discretion to impose sentences well below the maximum permitted. Indeed, under the statute, they may impose no prison time at all.

The guidelines that apply in illegal reentry cases also provide for increased penalties if a defendant has prior convictions. The offense level in illegal reentry cases is determined under Section 2L1.2(a). If a defendant has a prior conviction for particular offenses, he faces a sixteen-level enhancement. Qualifying offenses include: "(i) a drug trafficking offense for which the sentence imposed exceeded 13 months; (ii) a crime of violence; (iii) a firearms offense; (iv) a child pornography offense; (v) a national security or terrorism offense; (vi) a human trafficking offense; or (vii) an alien smuggling offense." If a defendant has a "drug trafficking offense," but had a sentence imposed of thirteen months or less for the crime, that defendant faces a twelve-level increase. If the defendant's conviction is an "aggravated felony," but does not qualify for a sixteen- or twelve-level increase, an eight-level enhancement applies. If the conviction does not qualify for the other enhancements but is nonetheless a felony, a four-level enhancement applies. A four-level enhancement also applies if the defendant has three or more misdemeanor convictions for drug trafficking offenses or crimes of violence. In terms of sentencing length, the sixteen-level enhancement results in a roughly seven-fold sentencing range increase from the base offense level whereas the twelve-level enhancement increase results in a roughly four-fold sentencing range increase.

In 2008, the Commission's most recent amendments expanded the scope of the enhancements for drug convictions. In particular, the amendments provided that an "offer to sell" a controlled substance is a "drug trafficking offense." In addition, the Commission explained that cases where the conviction involved possessing or transporting a large quantity of drugs might warrant an upward departure.

Thus, the illegal reentry guideline continues to provide drastic increases in sentences for defendants with prior drug convictions. These enhancements—like those applicable to firearm cases—apply in addition to the increases to the criminal history score that the convictions cause. As observed by courts and commentators, one can put a sixteen-level increase in perspective by analyzing other guideline provisions. For example, the theft guideline calls for a sixteen-level enhancement if the defendant stole $5 million to $10 million, and the fraud guideline calls for sixteen levels if the offense caused a loss of $20 million to $40 million.

D. Drug Sentencing and the Eighth Amendment

Some drug defendants have attempted to challenge long mandatory minimum sentences based on the Eighth Amendment's prohibition against cruel and unusual punishment. Though a detailed study of Eighth Amendment jurisprudence is best left to other courses, the issue raises important questions for drug sentencing. The following case exemplifies the insurmountable burden that a drug defendant who attempts to challenge his sentence as cruel and unusual will face.

United States v. Angelos

United States District Court for the District of Utah
345 F. Supp. 2d 1227 (2004)

Cassell, J.

Defendant Weldon Angelos stands now before the court for sentencing. He is a twenty-four-year-old first offender who is a successful music executive with two young children. Because he was convicted of dealing marijuana and related offenses, both the government and the defense agree that Mr. Angelos should serve about six to eight years in prison. But there are three additional firearms offenses for which the court must also impose sentence. Two of those offenses occurred when Mr. Angelos carried a handgun to two $350 marijuana deals; the third when police found several additional handguns at his home when they executed a search warrant. For these three acts of possessing (not using or even displaying) these guns, the government insists that Mr. Angelos should essentially spend the rest of his life in prison. Specifically, the government urges the court to sentence Mr. Angelos to a prison term of no less than 61 1/2 years—six years and a half (or more) for drug dealing followed by 55 years for three counts of possessing a firearm in connection with a drug offense. In support of its position, the government relies on a statute — 18 U.S.C. § 924(c) — which requires the court to impose a sentence of five years in prison the first time a drug dealer carries a gun and twenty-five years for each subsequent time. Under § 924(c), the three counts produce 55 years of additional punishment for carrying a firearm.

The court's role in evaluating § 924(c) is quite limited. The court can set aside the statute only if it is irrational punishment without any conceivable justification or is so excessive as to constitute cruel and unusual punishment in violation of the Eighth Amendment. After careful deliberation, the court reluctantly concludes that it has no choice but to impose the 55 year sentence. While the sentence appears to be cruel, unjust, and irrational, in our system of separated powers Congress makes the final decisions as to appropriate criminal penalties. Under the controlling case law, the court must find either that a statute has no conceivable justification or is so grossly disproportionate to the crime that no reasonable argument can be made its behalf. If the court is to fairly apply these precedents in this case, it must reject Mr. Angelos' constitutional challenges. Accordingly, the court sentences Mr. Angelos to a prison term of 55 years and one day, the minimum that the law allows.

Weldon Angelos is twenty-four years old. He was born on July 16, 1979, in Salt Lake City, Utah. He was raised in the Salt Lake City area by his father, Mr. James B. Angelos, with only minimal contact with his mother. Mr. Angelos has two young children by Ms. Zandrah Uyan: six-year-old Anthony and five-year-old Jessie. Before his arrest Mr. Angelos had achieved some success in the music industry. He started Extravagant Records, a label that produces rap and hip hop music. He had worked with prominent hip hop musicians, including Snoop Dogg, on the "beats" to various songs and was preparing to record his own album.

The critical events in this case are three "controlled buys" of marijuana by a government informant from Mr. Angelos. On May 10, 2002, Mr. Angelos met with the informant, Ronnie Lazalde, and arranged a sale of marijuana. On May 21, 2002, Mr. Angelos completed a sale of eight ounces of marijuana to Lazalde for $350. Lazalde observed Mr. Angelos' Glock pistol by the center console of his car. This drug deal formed the basis for the first § 924(c) count.

During a second controlled buy with Lazalde, on June 4, 2002, Mr. Angelos lifted his pant leg to show him the Glock in an ankle holster. Lazalde again purchased approximately eight ounces of marijuana for $350. This deal formed the basis for the second § 924(c) count.

A third controlled buy occurred on June 18, 2002, with Mr. Angelos again selling Lazalde eight ounces of marijuana for $350. There was no direct evidence of a gun at this transaction, so no § 924(c) count was charged.

On November 15, 2003, police officers arrested Mr. Angelos at his apartment pursuant to a warrant. Mr. Angelos consented to a search. The search revealed a briefcase which contained $18,040, a handgun, and two opiate suckers. Officers also discovered two bags which contained approximately three pounds of marijuana. Officers also recovered two other guns in a locked safe, one of which was confirmed as stolen. Searches at other locations, including the apartment of Mr. Angelos' girlfriend, turned up several duffle bags with marijuana residue, two more guns, and additional cash.

The original indictment issued against Mr. Angelos contained three counts of distribution of marijuana, one § 924(c) count for the firearm at the first controlled buy, and two other lesser charges. Plea negotiations began between the government and Mr. Angelos. On January 20, 2003, the government told Mr. Angelos, through counsel, that if he pled guilty to the drug distribution count and the § 924(c) count, the government would agree to drop all other charges, not supersede the indictment with additional counts, and recommend a prison sentence of 15 years. The government made clear to Mr. Angelos that if he rejected the offer, the government would obtain a new superseding indictment adding several § 924(c) counts that could lead to Mr. Angelos facing more than 100 years of mandatory prison time. In short, Mr. Angelos faced the choice of accepting 15 years in prison or insisting on a trial by jury at the risk of a life sentence. Ultimately, Mr. Angelos rejected the offer and decided to go to trial. The government then obtained two superseding indictments, eventually charging twenty total counts, including five § 924(c) counts which alone carried a potential minimum mandatory sentence of 105 years. The five § 924(c) counts consisted of two counts for the Glock seen at the two controlled buys, one count for three handguns found at his home, and two more counts for the two guns found at the home of Mr. Angelos' girlfriend.

Perhaps recognizing the gravity of the situation, Mr. Angelos tried to reopen plea negotiations, offering to plea to one count of drug distribution, one § 924(c) count, and one money laundering count. The government refused his offer, and the case proceeded to trial. The jury found Mr. Angelos guilty on sixteen counts, including three § 924(c) counts: two counts for the Glock seen at the two controlled buys and a third count for the three handguns at Mr. Angelos' home. The jury found him not guilty on three counts—including the two additional § 924(c) counts for the two guns at his girlfriends' home. (The court dismissed one other minor count.)

Mr. Angelos' sentence is presumptively governed by the Federal Sentencing Guidelines. Under governing Guideline provisions, the bottom line is that all counts but the three § 924(c) counts combine to create a total offense level of 28. Because Mr. Angelos has no significant prior criminal history, he is treated as first-time offender (a criminal history category I) under the Guidelines. The prescribed Guidelines' sentence for Mr. Angelos for everything but the § 924(c) counts is 78 to 97 months.

After the Guideline sentence is imposed, however, the court must then add the § 924(c) counts. Section 924(c) prescribes a five-year mandatory minimum for a first conviction, and 25 years for each subsequent conviction. This means that Mr. Angelos is facing 55 years (660 months) of mandatory time for the § 924(c) convictions. In addition, § 924(c) mandates that these 55 years run consecutively to any other time imposed. As a consequence, the minimum sentence that the court can impose on Mr. Angelos is 61 1/2 years–6 1/2 years (78 months) for the 13 counts under the Guidelines and 55 consecutive years for the three § 924 convictions. The federal system does not provide the possibility of parole, but instead provides only a modest "good behavior" credit of approximately 15 percent of the sentence. Assuming good behavior, Mr. Angelos' sentence will be reduced to "only" 55 years, meaning he could be released when he is 78 years old.

Mr. Angelos challenges this presumptive sentence [and argues] that § 924(c) is unconstitutional as applied to him because the additional 55-year sentence is cruel and unusual punishment that violates the Cruel and Unusual Punishment Clause.

Before turning to the merits of Mr. Angelos' claims, it is important to understand the length of the sentence that the government is asking the court to impose. If Angelos serves his full 61 1/2-year sentence, he will be 85 years old upon release. Assuming the 15 percent credit for good behavior, Mr. Angelos sentence will be reduced to "only" 55 years, leading to the earliest possible release date for Mr. Angelos at 77 years of age. The average life expectancy for males in the United States is about 74 years of age. Therefore, under the best case scenario, Angelos *might* live long enough to be released from prison (assuming that the harshness of prison life does not decrease his life expectancy). Put another way, if the court imposes the sentence sought by the government, Mr. Angelos will effectively receive a sentence of life.

[T]he enhancement provided for under § 924(c) increases his sentence by 55 years, whereas were the Guidelines alone to be applied, his sentence would be enhanced by only two years. There is, of course, the possibility that the Sentencing Guidelines are too low in this case and that mandatory minimums specify the proper sentence. The more the court investigates, however, the more the court finds evidence that the § 924(c) counts here lead to unjust punishment. For starters, the court asked the twelve jurors in this case what they believed was the appropriate punishment for Mr. Angelos. Following the trial, the court sent—over the government's objection—each of the jurors the relevant information about Mr. Angelos' limited criminal history, described the abolition of parole in the federal system, and asked the jurors what they believed was the appropriate penalty for Mr. Angelos. Nine jurors responded and gave the following recommendations: (1) 5 years; (2) 5–7 years; (3) 10 years; (4) 10 years; (5) 15 years; (6) 15 years; (7) 15–20 years; (8) 32 years; and (9) 50 years. Averaging these answers, the jurors recommended a mean sentence of about 18 years and a median sentence of 15 years. Not one of the jurors recommended a sentence closely approaching the 611/2 year sentence created by § 924(c).

At oral argument, the court asked the government what it thought about the jurors' recommendations and whether it was appropriate to impose a sentence so much higher than what the jurors thought appropriate. The government's response was quite curious: "Judge, we don't know if that jury is a random representative sample of the citizens of the United States...." Of course, the whole point of the elaborate jury selection procedures used in this case was to assure that the jury was, indeed, such a fair cross section of the population so that the verdict would be accepted with confidence. It is hard to understand why the government would be willing to accept the decision of the jury as to the guilt of the defendant but not as to the length of sentence that might be imposed.

More important, the jurors' answers appear to reflect a representative of what people across the country believe. The crimes committed by Mr. Angelos are not uniquely federal crimes. They could have been prosecuted in state court in Utah or elsewhere across the country. The court asked the Probation Office to determine what the penalty would have been in Utah state court had Mr. Angelos been prosecuted there. The Probation Office reported that Mr. Angelos would likely have been paroled after serving about two to three years in prison. The government gives a substantially similar estimate, reporting that on its understanding of Utah sentencing practices Mr. Angelos would have served about five to seven years in prison. Even taking the higher figure from the government, the § 924(c) counts in this case result in punishment far beyond what Utah's citizens, through its state criminal justice system, provides as just punishment for such crimes.

The same conclusion obtains if the comparison is to the sentence that would be imposed in other states. Indeed, the government conceded that Mr. Angelos' federal sentence after application of the § 924(c) counts is more than he would have received in any of the fifty states.

In evaluating the § 924(c) counts, the court starts from the premise that Mr. Angelos committed serious crimes. Trafficking in illegal drugs runs the risk of ruining lives through addiction and the violence that the drug trade spawns. As the government properly argued, when a defendant engages in a drug-trafficking operation and "carries and possesses firearms to aid in that venture, as was the case here, the actual threat of violence always exists, even it if does not actually occur." But do any of these general rationales provide a rational basis for punishing the *potential* violence which § 924(c) is meant to deter more harshly than *actual* violence that harms a victim in its wake? In other words, is it rational to punish a person who *might* shoot someone with a gun he carried far more harshly than the person who actually *does* shoot or harm someone?

Section 924(c) imposes on Mr. Angelos a sentence 55 years or 660 months. Added to the minimum 78-month Guidelines sentence for a total sentence of 738 months, Mr. Angelos is facing a prison term which more than doubles the sentence of, for example, an aircraft hijacker (293 months), a terrorist who detonates a bomb in a public place (235 months), a racist who attacks a minority with the intent to kill and inflicts permanent or life-threatening injuries (210 months), a second-degree murderer, or a rapist.

At oral argument, to its credit, the government conceded that at least some of the[se crimes are] more serious than those committed by Mr. Angelos. Thus, the government agreed (after extensive questioning from the court) that Mr. Angelos has committed less serious crimes than a second-degree murderer, a marijuana dealer who shoots someone, or a rapist. The government maintained, however, that the court was not making the proper comparison. Because Mr. Angelos was convicted of three counts of violating § 924(c), the government argued, the proper comparison is between Mr. Angelos and a three-time hijacker, a three-time rapist, or a three-time second degree murderer. The government maintains that "the hijacker and kidnapper would serve much longer sentences if they were sentenced for committing those crimes three separate times."

The government's argument misses the whole point of the comparison. All of Mr. Angelos' crimes taken together are less serious than, for example, even a single aircraft hijacking, a single second-degree murder, or a single rape. But even adopting the government's approach, the irrationality of the scheme only becomes more apparent. Amazingly, Mr. Angelos' sentence under § 924(c) is still far more severe than criminals who committed, for example, three aircraft hijackings, three second-degree murders, three kidnappings, or three rapes. Mr. Angelos will receive a longer sentence than any three-time criminal, with the sole exception of a marijuana dealer who shoots three people. (Mr. Angelos still receives a longer sentence than a marijuana dealer who shoots two people.)

To some, this may seem like a law professor's argument—one that may have some validity in the classroom but little salience in the real world. After all, the only issue in this case is the extent of punishment for a man justly convicted of serious drug trafficking offenses. So what, some may say, if he spends more years in prison than might be theoretically justified? It is common wisdom that "if you can't do the time, don't do the crime."

The problem with this simplistic position is that it overlooks other interests that are inevitably involved in the imposition of a criminal sentence. For example, crime victims expect that the penalties the court imposes will fairly reflect the harms that they have suffered. When the sentence for actual violence inflicted on a victim is dwarfed by a sentence for carrying guns to several drug deals, the implicit message to victims is that their pain and suffering counts for less than some abstract "war on drugs."

This is no mere academic point, as a case from this court's docket will illustrate. Earlier today, shortly before Mr. Angelos' hearing, the court imposed sentence in *United States v. Visinaiz,* a second-degree murder case. There, a jury convicted Cruz Joaquin Visinaiz of second-degree murder in the death of 68-year-old Clara Jenkins. On one evening, while drinking together, the two got into an argument. Ms. Jenkins threw an empty bottle at Mr. Visinaiz, who then proceeded to beat her to death by striking her in the head at least three times with a log. Mr. Visinaiz then hid the body in a crawl space of his home, later dumping the body in a river weighted down with cement blocks. Following his conviction for second-degree murder, Mr. Visinaiz came before the court as a first-time offender for sentencing. The Sentencing Guidelines require a sentence for this brutal second-degree murder of between 210 to 262 months. The government called this an "aggravated second-degree murder" and recommended a sentence of 262 months. The court followed that recommendation. Yet on the same day, the court is to impose a sentence of 738 months for a first-time drug dealer who carried a gun to several drug deals!? The victim's family in the Visinaiz case — not to mention victims of a vast array of other violent crimes — can be forgiven if they think that the federal criminal justice system minimizes their losses. No doubt § 924(c) is motivated by the best of intentions — to prevent criminal victimization. But the statute pursues that goal in a way that effectively sends a message to victims of actual criminal violence that their suffering is not fully considered by the system.

Another reason for concern is that the unjust penalties imposed by § 924(c) can be expected to attract public notice. As shown earlier, applying § 924(c) to cases such as this one leads to sentences far in excess of what the public believes is appropriate. Perhaps in the short term, no ill effects will come from the difference between public expectations and actual sentences. But in the longer term, the federal criminal justice system will suffer. Most seriously, jurors may stop voting to convict drug dealers in federal criminal prosecutions if they are aware that unjust punishment may follow. It only takes a single juror who is worried about unjust sentencing to "hang" a jury and prevent a conviction. This is not an abstract concern. In the case of *United States v. Molina*, the jury failed to reach a verdict on a § 924(c) count which would have added 30 years to the defendant's sentence. Judge Weinstein, commenting on "the dubious state of our criminal sentencing law" noted that "jury nullification of sentences deemed too harsh is increasingly reflected in refusals to convict." In the last several drug trials before this court, jurors have privately expressed considerable concern after their verdicts about what sentences might be imposed. If federal juries are to continue to convict the guilty, those juries must have confidence that just punishment will follow from their verdicts.

Mr. Angelos argues that his 55-year sentence under § 924(c) violates the Eighth Amendment's prohibition of cruel and unusual punishment. In this argument, he is joined in an *amicus* brief filed by a distinguished group of 29 former United States District Judges, United States Circuit Court Judges, and United States Attorneys, who draw on their expertise in federal criminal law and federal sentencing issues to urge that the sentence is unconstitutional as disproportionate to the offenses at hand.

Mr. Angelos and his supporting *amici* are correct in urging that controlling Eighth Amendment case law places an outer limit on punishments that can be imposed for criminal offenses, forbidding penalties that are grossly disproportionate to any offense. This principle traces its roots to the Supreme Court's 1983 decision in *Solem v. Helm,* in which the Supreme Court seemed to modify its earlier holding in *Rummel v. Estelle* and "held as a matter of principle that a criminal sentence must be proportionate to the crime for which the defendant has been convicted." The principles of *Solem* were themselves seemingly modified by the Court's fractured 1991 decision in *Harmelin v. Michigan,* in which the Court held that imposition of a life sentence without possibility of parole for possession of 650 grams of cocaine did not violate the Eighth Amendment. Then, last year, the Supreme Court confirmed that the gross disproportionality principle — "the precise contours of which are unclear" — is applicable to sentences for terms of years; that there was a "lack of clarity" in its precedents; that it had "not established a clear or consistent path for courts to follow;" and that the proportionality principles from Justice Kennedy's *Harmelin* concurrence "guide our application of the Eighth Amendment." The Tenth Circuit, too, has instructed that "Justice Kennedy's opinion controls because it both retains proportionality and narrows *Solem.*"

In light of these controlling holdings, the court must engage in a proportionality analysis guided by factors outlined in Justice Kennedy's *Harmelin* concurrence. In particular, the court must examine (1) the nature of the crime and its relation to the punishment imposed, (2) the punishment for other offenses in this jurisdiction, and (3) the punishment for similar offenses in other jurisdictions.

The first *Harmelin* factor requires the court to compare the seriousness of the three §924(c) offenses to the harshness of the contemplated penalty to determine if the penalty would be grossly disproportionate to such offenses. In weighing the gravity of the offenses, the court should consider the offenses of conviction and the defendant's criminal history, as well as "the harm caused or threatened to the victim or society, and the culpability of the offender." Simply put, "disproportionality analysis measures the relationship between the nature and number of offenses committed and the severity of the punishment inflicted upon the offender."

The criminal history in this case is easy to describe. Mr. Angelos has no prior adult criminal convictions and is treated as a first-time offender under the Sentencing Guidelines.

The sentence-triggering criminal conduct in this case is also modest. Here, on two occasions while selling small amounts of marijuana, Mr. Angelos possessed a handgun under his clothing, but he never brandished or used the handgun. The third relevant crime occurred when the police searched his home and found handguns in his residence. These handguns had multiple purposes—including recreational activities—but because Mr. Angelos also used the gun to protect himself while dealing drugs, the possession of these handguns is also covered by §924(c).

Mr. Angelos did not engage in force or violence, or threats of force or violence, in furtherance of or in connection with the offenses for which he has been convicted. No offense involved injury to any person or the threat of injury to any person. It is well-established that crimes marked by violence or threat of violence are more serious and that the absence of direct violence affects the strength of society's interest in punishing a particular criminal.

It is relevant on this point that the Sentencing Commission has reviewed crimes like Mr. Angelos' and concluded that an appropriate penalty for all of Mr. Angelos' crimes is no more than about ten years (121 months). With respect to the firearms conduct specifically, the Commission has concluded that about 24 months is the appropriate penalty. The views of the Commission are entitled to special weight, because it is a congressionally-established expert agency which can draw on significant data and other resources in determining appropriate sentences. Comparing a recommended sentence of two years to the 55-year enhancement the court must impose strongly suggests not merely disproportionality, but gross disproportionality.

The next *Harmelin* factor requires comparing Mr. Angelos' sentence with the sentences imposed on other criminals in the federal system. Generally, "if more serious crimes are subject to the same penalty, or to less serious penalties, that is some indication that the punishment at issue may be excessive." This factor points strongly in favor of finding that the sentence in this case is excessive. As [discussed] earlier in this opinion, Mr. Angelos will receive a far longer sentence than those imposed in the federal system for such major crimes as aircraft hijacking, second-degree murder, racial beating inflicting life-threatening injuries, kidnapping, and rape. Indeed, Mr. Angelos will receive a far longer sentence than those imposed for three aircraft hijackings, three second-degree murders, three racial beatings inflicting life-threatening injuries, three kidnappings, and three rapes. Because Mr. Angelos is "treated in the same manner as, or more severely than, criminals who have committed far more serious crimes," it appears that the second factor is satisfied.

The final *Harmelin* factor requires the court to examine "sentences imposed for the same crime in other jurisdictions." Evaluating this factor is also straightforward. Mr. Angelos sentence is longer than he would receive in any of the fifty states. The government commendably concedes this point in its brief, pointing out that in Washington State Mr. Angelos would serve about nine years and in Utah would serve about five to seven years. Accordingly, the court finds that the third factor is satisfied.

Having analyzed the three *Harmelin* factors, the court believes that they lead to the conclusion that Mr. Angelos' sentence violates the Eighth Amendment. But before the court declares the sentence unconstitutional, there is one last obstacle to overcome. The court is keenly aware of its obligation to follow precedent from superior courts—specifically the Tenth Circuit and, of course, the Supreme Court. The Supreme Court has considered one case that might be regarded as quite similar to this one. In *Hutto v. Davis,* the Supreme Court held that two consecutive twenty-year sentences—totaling forty years—for possession of nine ounces of marijuana said to be worth $200 did not violate the Eighth Amendment. If *Davis* remains good law, it is hard see how the sentence in this case violates the Eighth Amendment. Here, Mr. Angelos was involved in at least two marijuana deals involving $700 and approximately sixteen ounces (one pound) of marijuana. Perhaps currency inflation could equate $700 today with $200 in the 1980s. But as a simple matter of arithmetic, if 40 years in prison for possessing nine ounces marijuana does not violate the Eighth Amendment, it is hard to see how 61 years for distributing sixteen ounces (or more) would do so.

The court is aware of an argument that the 1982 *Davis* decision has been implicitly overruled or narrowed by the 1983 *Solem* decision and other more recent pronouncements. For example, Justice Kennedy's concurring opinion in *Harmelin,* explained that "our most recent pronouncement on the subject in *Solem* appeared to apply a different analysis than in … *Davis.*" But the Court apparently continues to view *Davis* as part of the fabric of the law. Thus, Justice Kennedy's concurrence in *Harmelin,* after noting the seeming overruling of *Davis,* went on to discuss *Davis* along with other cases in distilling various "common principles" that control Eighth Amendment analysis. More recently, in reviewing California's "three strikes" legislation last year, the plurality opinion reviewed *Davis* as one of a string of cases that guide analysis of Eighth Amendment challenges.

In light of these continued references to *Davis,* the court believes it is it obligated to follow its holding here. Indeed, in *Davis* the Supreme Court pointedly reminded district court judges that "unless we wish anarchy to prevail within the federal judicial system, a precedent of this Court must be followed by the lower federal courts…." Under *Davis,* Mr. Angelos' sentence is not cruel and unusual punishment. Therefore, his Eighth Amendment challenge must be rejected.

Having disposed of the legal arguments in this case, it seems appropriate to make some concluding, personal observations. I have been on the bench for nearly two-and-half years now. During that time, I have sentenced several hundred offenders under the Sentencing Guidelines and federal mandatory minimum statutes. By and large, the sentences

I have been required to impose have been tough but fair. In a few cases, to be sure, I have felt that either the Guidelines or the mandatory minimums produced excessive punishment. But even in those cases, the sentences seemed to be within the realm of reason.

This case is different. It involves a first offender who will receive a life sentence for crimes far less serious than those committed by many other offenders—including violent offenders and even a murderer—who have been before me. For the reasons explained in my opinion, I am legally obligated to impose this sentence. But I feel ethically obligated to bring this injustice to the attention of those who are in a position to do something about it.

For all the reasons previously given, an additional 55-year sentence for Mr. Angelos under §924(c) is unjust, disproportionate to his offense, demeaning to victims of actual criminal violence—but nonetheless constitutional. While I must impose the unjust sentence, our system of separated powers provides a means of redress. The Framers were well aware that "the administration of justice ... is not necessarily always wise or certainly considerate of circumstances which may properly mitigate guilt." In my mind, this is one of those rare cases where the system has malfunctioned. "To afford a remedy, it has always been thought essential in popular governments, as well as in monarchies, to vest in some other authority than the courts power to ameliorate or avoid particular criminal judgments." Under our Constitution, the President has "the Power to grant Reprieves and Pardons for Offenses against the United States...." One of the purposes of executive clemency is "to afford relief from undue harshness."

I therefore believe that it is appropriate for me to communicate to the President, through the Office of the Pardon Attorney, my views regarding Mr. Angelos' sentence. I recommend that the President commute Mr. Angelos' sentence to a prison term of no more than 18 years, the average sentence recommended by the jury that heard this case. The court agrees with the jury that this is an appropriate sentence in this matter in light of all of the other facts discussed in this opinion. The Clerk's Office is directed to forward a copy of this opinion with its commutation recommendation to the Office of Pardon Attorney.

The 55-year sentence mandated by §924(c) in this case appears to be unjust, cruel, and irrational. But our constitutional system of government requires the court to follow the law, not its own personal views about what the law ought to be. Perhaps the court has overlooked some legal point, and that the appellate courts will find Mr. Angelos' sentence invalid. But applying the law as the court understands it, the court sentences Mr. Angelos to serve a term of imprisonment of 55 years and one day.

Following Judge Paul Cassell's 2004 decision, Weldon Angelos appealed his convictions and 55-year sentence to the U.S. Court of Appeals for the Tenth Circuit. A group of 163 former federal officials that included retired United States Circuit and District Court Judges, former United States Attorneys, and four former United States Attorneys General, among others, filed an amicus brief in support of Angelos' appeal. The Tenth Circuit upheld Angelos' convictions and 55-year sentence, in an opinion that was far more sympathetic to the government than Judge Cassell's. Judge Mary Beck Briscoe, who authored the decision, maintained that "although it is true Angelos may have had no significant adult criminal history, that appears to have been the result of good fortune rather than Angelos's lack of involvement in criminal activity." The court found that Angelos' sentence was not grossly disproportionate to his crimes, explaining "Congress 'could with reason conclude that the threat posed to the individual and society' by possessing firearms in connection with serious felonies, in particular drug-trafficking crimes, was 'momentous enough to warrant the deterrence and retribution' of lengthy consecutive sentences, such as those imposed on Angelos in this case." United States v. Angelos, 433 F.3d 738, 752 (10th Cir. 2006). Angelos' petition for certiorari was denied in December 2006.

Angelos then pursued post-conviction relief under 28 U.S.C. § 2255, arguing that "his sentence was cruel and unusual, and that he was a victim of prosecutorial vindictiveness in charging and plea bargaining, prosecutorial misconduct at trial, and ineffective assistance of counsel before and at trial." Angelos v. United States, 2008 WL 5156602 (D. Utah). The District Court denied all of Angelos' claims outright with one exception, granting him an evidentiary hearing on his claim of ineffective assistance of counsel during the plea negotiations. Following the evidentiary hearing, however, the court denied Angelos' ineffective assistance claim. Unsuccessful appeals to the Tenth Circuit and the Supreme Court followed, with the Supreme Court denying Angelos' petition for certiorari in October, 2011. Melinda Rogers, *High Court Won't Hear Case of Music Producer Sentenced to 55-Year Minimum*, SALT LAKE TRIB., Oct. 4, 2011.

As *Angelos* demonstrates, it is virtually impossible for a drug defendant to successfully challenge his sentence based on the Eighth Amendment to the federal Constitution. The same is not necessarily true when it comes to state sentences, however, as some states have adopted more robust interpretations of analogous provisions that prohibit cruel and unusual punishment in their constitutions. *See*, Julia Fong Sheketoff, Note: *State Innovations in Noncapital Proportionality Doctrine*, 85 N.Y.U. L. REV. 2209 (2010) (surveying the noncapital proportionality jurisprudence of the states).

In *Angelos*, Judge Cassell was especially troubled by the length of the sentence in relation to crimes of actual violence, like murder or rape. Some have argued that punishing crimes that create a risk of violence more seriously than crimes of actual violence is a surprisingly common feature of federal sentencing.

Indirect Harms and Proportionality: The Upside-Down World of Federal Sentencing
Mark Osler
74 Mississippi Law Journal 1 (2004)

No one seriously disputes that drug trafficking increases murder, robbery and other violent crime. No one seriously disputes that child pornography both causes and promotes the sexual abuse of children. No one seriously disputes that access to firearms increases the harmful use of guns by those who should not have them.

What must be disputed is that each of these causal factors which threaten harm is more serious than the resulting harm themselves: That drug trafficking is worse than killing, that possessing child pornography is worse than the sexual abuse of children, and that firearms possession is worse than the use of a gun to illegally hurt or kill. Yet, the United States Sentencing Guidelines makes each of these conclusions by its central process of setting proportionate periods of incarceration. In each case the causal action will very often result in a higher sentence than the resulting harm under the Guidelines. This twisted logic has skewed the justice system and established improper priorities and allocation of resources within federal criminal law, to the detriment of justice.

Nor is it an isolated phenomenon within the Guidelines. Rather, it seems to be a consistent theme.

In 1989, about the time many of the current drug laws were formulated, fifty-eight percent of Americans surveyed named drugs as the single factor most to blame for crime generally. Congress reacted to this concern, and the media reports on the crack epidemic, by passing tough new drug laws which were in large part predicated on the idea that narcotics use and sale indirectly causes other crimes, including violent crimes.

That conclusion is not disputed here. That low-level transactions for narcotics indirectly may create the conditions for violent crimes, including murder, robbery and kidnapping, is accepted for purposes of the discussion here. The question of whether or not such a link exists is not the focus of this article.

Rather, the examination here is whether low-level drug trafficking is punished more or less harshly than the directly destructive violent crimes which may be enabled, in part, by these transactions. The answer, consistent with the conclusions elsewhere in this article, is that in many cases the less serious crime which threatens a larger harm is punished more seriously than that larger harm itself under the federal Sentencing Guidelines.

Crack and methamphetamine are two controlled substances often serving as the basis of prosecution in federal courts. Below, the sentence for a small sale of each is compared with violent crimes — robbery and manslaughter. In each instance, a criminal history category of II and conviction after trial is assumed for each offender. And, in each case, the sentence for narcotics distribution, even in small amounts, is significantly more than for the violent offense which has ended or enduringly altered a life.

First, consider the defendant who is convicted of possessing with the intent to distribute twenty-five grams of crack cocaine (which is identified in the Guidelines as "cocaine base"). Even in the absence of aggravating factors such as the possession of a weapon or being labeled a leader or organizer of a conspiracy, the defendant would face a guideline range of 87–108 months after trial. Assuming that such trafficking creates violent crime, compare this sentence with one such violent crime — armed robbery. The man who uses a gun to rob a convenience store on federal or Indian land, for example, may receive a sentence of only thirty-seven to forty-six months, less than half that faced by the crack seller. Even if he stabs someone during the robbery or discharges a firearm in the store, the robber would have less exposure to prison under the guidelines than the relatively small-time drug dealer.

The methamphetamine manufacturer is likely to face a similar fate. Methamphetamine is now often made by individuals and small groups. As with crack, users of the drug are often deeply harmed by the drug use, and violent crime may be committed by either users or manufacturers of the drug in connection with their methamphetamine use. Also common as an incident to methamphetamine manufacture is the theft of materials used in the manufacturing process, such as pseudoephedrine or anhydrous ammonia.

Methamphetamine may be manufactured in one to two ounce batches, which equates to 28.35 grams to 56.70 grams. Of course, most people manufacture more than one batch, meaning that a prosecutor may easily have proof of hundreds of grams produced by a relatively small operation in a home. To be conservative, however, for the following comparison, we will consider a prosecution for manufacture of sixty grams of methamphetamine, or less than three ounces. Without aggravating factors such as environmental damage or danger to others posed by the manufacturing process, the sentence after trial for this small operator with no criminal history will be seventy to eighty-seven months.

Because methamphetamine is known to cause violent behavior and "mood disturbances," it is fair to compare this crime with the classic crime of passion, manslaughter. Even at criminal history category II, the punishment for manslaughter is sixty-three to seventy-eight months, one notch lower in the Guidelines grid than that for the methamphetamine manufacturer.

So, do we really believe, as a public value in a democratic society, that the sale of narcotics, even in small amounts, is more dangerous than intentionally killing someone? The United States Sentencing Guidelines say that we often do, consistent with the way indirect threats are dealt with elsewhere in the Guidelines.

E. Prosecutorial Discretion

Charging decisions made by prosecutors played a central role in the sentencing outcome in many of the cases included this Chapter. Consider *Angelos*, for example, where the prosecutor originally offered a deal in which the government would recommend a 15-year sentence. When Angelos refused this offer, the prosecutor "obtained two superseding indictments, eventually charging twenty total counts, including five § 924(c) counts which alone carried a potential minimum mandatory sentence of 105 years." In a portion of the opinion that was not included in the edited version of *Angelos* above, Judge Cassell highlighted the importance of the prosecutor's decisions to Angelos' sentence. With respect to the effect of plea bargaining, Cassell commented that "[s]o far as the court can determine, the superceding indictment rested not on any newly-discovered evidence but rather solely on the defendant's unwillingness to plead guilty."

Judge Cassell also examined the prosecutor's decision to charge the multiple § 924(c) counts that resulted in the 55-year mandatory minimum. He concluded that the prosecutor's approach in this regard was unusual and because of it "Mr. Angelos is probably receiving a sentence far in excess of what many other identically-situated offenders will receive for identical crimes in other federal districts. The court has been advised by judges from other parts of the county that, in their districts, an offender like Mr. Angelos would not have been charged with multiple § 924(c) counts. This is no trivial matter. The decision to pursue, for example, a third § 924 (c) count in this case makes the difference between a 36-year sentence and a 61-year sentence."

Last but not least, the decision to charge Angelos in federal as opposed to state court also significantly impacted his sentence. Angelos committed his crimes in Utah. If Angelos had been charged and convicted under Utah state law, the federal government estimated he would have served only about five to seven years in prison instead of the 55-year sentence he received in federal court.

The importance of prosecutorial discretion is, of course, not unique to drug offenses. However, there are a few characteristics of modern drug sentencing that can give prosecutors unusual power to guide sentences in drug cases. As *Angelos* demonstrates, the emergence of lengthy federal mandatory minimum drug sentences in combination with concurrent federal and state jurisdiction over drug crimes means that a prosecutor's decision to bring federal — rather than state — charges, or to bring charges that carry a mandatory minimum sentence, will often have much greater influence on a defendant's sentence than any decisions made by the Judge who imposes it.

This section considers the relationship between prosecutorial discretion and drug sentences.

Unequal Justice: The Federalization of Criminal Law
Steven D. Clymer
70 Southern California Law Review 643 (1997)

As a result of the growth of federal criminal law, much criminal conduct is now subject to federal as well as state prosecution. Although the states prosecute the majority of offenders whose conduct violates both state and federal law, federal prosecution is not uncommon. Because of differences between federal and state criminal justice systems, an offender will often fare worse if prosecuted in federal court rather than state court. He may be detained pending trial when he would have been released if charged in state court, denied discovery allowable in state court, and confronted with evidence that would have been suppressed in state court. If convicted, a federally prosecuted defendant is likely to receive a longer sentence and to serve far more of that sentence than he would if sentenced in state court.

United States v. Palmer provides a stark example of such federal/state court disparity. Palmer and Roberts were partners in a marijuana-growing operation at Palmer's residence. After police arrested the men, the federal prosecutor assigned to the case chose not to bring charges against Roberts, who, as a result, was prosecuted in state court. The state court sentenced him to a fine of $1,000—which was waived because Roberts was indigent—and assessed court costs and fees of $176. Palmer was considerably less fortunate. The federal prosecutor brought charges against him. After Palmer was convicted, the federal court sentenced him to a nonparolable ten-year term of imprisonment and an eight-year supervised release term, the most lenient sentence that federal law allowed.

Cases like Palmer, in which partners in crime receive different treatment because one is prosecuted in state court and the other in federal court, are atypical. However, comparably dramatic sentencing differentials and other disparities routinely occur when some offenders are prosecuted in state court and others, who may not be their partners but have engaged in the same criminal conduct and are otherwise similarly situated, are instead selected for federal prosecution and the often harsher treatment that it entails. Such disparate treatment occurs nationwide on a daily basis when some defendants, engaged in drug transactions, weapons offenses, or other crimes over which there is overlapping federal and state criminal jurisdiction, happen to be among the unlucky ones selected for federal prosecution.

Despite the significant ramifications of the forum selection decision, there is little administrative direction or judicial oversight to guide federal prosecutors in exercising their discretion to choose among offenders eligible for federal prosecution. Although there were valid reasons for the federal prosecutor to seek harsher treatment for Palmer than for Roberts, the prosecutor could have made the same selection decision without good reason, perhaps selecting Roberts but not Palmer. Without fear of violating Department of Justice policy or risking judicial review, the federal prosecutor could have flipped a coin to select who to prosecute in federal court and, consequently, who to subject to the possibility of a vastly more severe federal sentence. Neither the United States Attorney's Office that chose to prosecute only Palmer nor the Department of Justice has a policy requiring prosecutors to have rational reasons for determining which eligible offenders to prosecute in federal court. Similarly, although its consideration of Palmer's equal protection and due process challenges prompted the Ninth Circuit to characterize the prosecutor's charging decision as "troubling" and to conclude that "there is something basically wrong with this type of exercise of prosecutorial discretion," the court refused to review the prosecutor's decision to select only Palmer. Consistent with approaches that other courts have taken, the *Palmer* court held that "separation of powers concerns prohibit us from reviewing a prosecutor's charging decisions absent a prima facie showing that it rested on an impermissible basis, such as gender, race or denial of a constitutional right."

United States v. Elliott

United States District Court for the District of Montana
351 F. Supp. 2d 1054 (2005)

Molloy, J.

This case is about bad judgment. Dustin Elliott exercised very bad judgment on December 12, 2003 when he was stopped at Garrison Junction because he was one of three people involved in selling two pounds of marijuana to a state undercover agent. When this sale took place, according to joint drug task force Agent Steven Spanogle, federal prosecution was not warranted for the small amounts of marijuana involved. Spanogle testified that he probably told Elliott on a number of occasions that such a small amount of marijuana would not be subject to federal prosecution under the referral rules in play at the time: The assurances were necessary because Elliott would not agree to cooperate with further investigation unless he had some assurance the case was not "federal."

Elliott then exercised what turns out to be more bad judgment. He believed law enforcement officers were telling the truth and that he would not be subject to federal prosecution. So, Elliott cooperated with the state investigators. His two cohorts immediately spilled their guts to save their respective hides but they had no useful information to help the agents climb the drug distribution food chain to the real culprits in the marijuana distribution scheme. Elliott did. Based on his knowledge, and after the assurances about federal referrals, confident that he would not be charged in federal court, he cooperated fully.

Because Elliott cooperated, the police were able to identify two or more distributors, and to obtain evidence of large enough quantities of marijuana that the case finally did satisfy federal prosecution minimums. So, despite Elliott's confidence that he would not be facing the ogre of federal prosecution, once enough marijuana had been discovered through the criminal investigation based on his disclosures and cooperation, the case was presented to the federal grand jury. Elliott was indicted in federal court as a direct result of his cooperation.

In this case Agent Spanogle was being truthful when he told Elliott that two pounds was not enough marijuana to warrant federal prosecution under existing referral standards. Furthermore, Spanogle had the courage to testify at the hearing in this case that he did not believe Elliott *would* be prosecuted in federal court, and, that he did not think Elliott *should* have been prosecuted in federal court. But, here we are.

The problem presented is whether the decision to refer the case to the grand jury, and to pursue Elliott's prosecution, is so fundamentally unfair that the case should be dismissed. See *United States vs. Williams*, 780 F.2d 802, 803 (9th Cir. 1986). I have struggled in seeking a just answer to this question. However, I am convinced that while this case is more properly a state prosecution, I have no legal basis to dismiss it.

Elliott argues that the indictment should be dismissed because he performed his end of the deal by participating in a sting operation that netted the government a large marijuana supplier. He argues that instead of getting what he bargained for, a deferred imposition of sentence in the state courts, he ended up being prosecuted in federal court. That reality is what he thought he bargained away when he agreed to cooperate with the state agents. He argues that had the government upheld the bargain by deferring a two pound marijuana case to the state, he would have been able to complete his undergraduate education and attend medical school.[1]

The United States argues that even if Agent Spanogle had promised a "particular sentence," Spanogle is without authority to bind the United States. Spanogle is a state agent working on state prosecutions and at the time of Elliott's cooperation Spanogle was not assigned to any task force that included federal agents. Thus the argument goes, he could not have bound the United States to "his 'agreement' with the defendant even if he had wanted to." The United States extends the argument by asserting that even if Spanogle was a federal agent, he could not bind the United States Attorney's Office. The prosecutor does acknowledge that an exception to the "non binding" rule exists, even where the United States Attorney was not a party to the cooperation agreement, if breach of the agreement renders the prosecution fundamentally unfair.

Here the uncontroverted testimony of Agent Spanogle is as follows: 1) before Elliott's cooperation took place, Elliott would not have been prosecuted in federal court because he was caught with so little marijuana the United States Attorney would not have taken the case for referred prosecution in federal court; 2) Elliott's two cohorts had no evidence to give the investigating agents that would have allowed them to go up the drug distribution food chain; 3) Spanogle did describe to Elliott scenarios he was aware of in state marijuana prosecutions that resulted in deferred state prosecutions though he carefully avoided making a "deal" he knew he could not make for the county attorney; 4) Elliott was very specific in his concern about avoiding federal prosecution; 5) without Elliott's cooperation the state investigation could not have gone forward and upward in identifying and prosecuting the marijuana distribution network; 6) Spanogle did not think Elliott would be prosecuted in federal court; 7) Spanogle does not think Elliott should be prosecuted in federal court; and, 8) Elliott cannot be held responsible for more than two pounds of marijuana in the federal prosecution.[2] Elliott also signed an agreement stating he knew there were no binding promises regarding any state prosecution. The United States Attorney for the District of Montana considered, but refused dismissal or a deferred federal prosecution.

---

1. Elliott is a chemistry major at Carroll College who maintains between a 3.9 and 4.0 GPA. A federal conviction will likely bar him from medical school matriculation.

2. Two pounds of marijuana sets an offense level of 8 according to the federal sentencing guidelines, § 2D1.1 (At least 250 G but less than 1 KG of marijuana). With a criminal history of 1, that means the most Elliott would be looking at is 6 months of incarceration. One must question the futility of a federal felony conviction under the circumstances involved here. The question that needs to be answered is "Why is this a federal case?" If it is a federal case to deter, what will the felony conviction deter? It will deter a very bright student from becoming a doctor. It will deter an intelligent person from voting or from holding public office. It will deter a young man who made a stupid mistake from ever keeping or possessing firearms or ammunition and from ever hunting again. It will deter a smart person who made a mistaken judgment from ever being a juror or grand juror. It has a potential negative impact on Agent Spanogle's undercover law enforcement activities because his credibility is on the line. It will insert the federal government in what is clearly a state case. Ultimately, you have to ask "Why?" The fundamental issue here is "How has the federal sovereign been offended?" This prosecution is at odds with the idea that the state of Montana is a competent sovereign to prosecute drug offenses.

[In *United States v. Williams*,] Thomas Williams was convicted of theft and conspiring to sell government property. He worked as an administrator for the Veterans Administration. After his arrest, a personnel director of the VA promised him that if he resigned his job, the VA attorney would recommend dismissal of the charges to the United States Attorney. Williams resigned but the letter sent by the VA attorney did not recommend dismissal of the indictment, instead it suggested avenues of investigation to make the case. When the personnel director learned of these facts he spoke personally to the United States Attorney and recommended dismissal of the charges. The United States Attorney for the Southern District of California prosecuted anyway.

Like Elliott, Williams moved to dismiss the indictment because the VA had not honored the deal he made. The Williams court recognized that while the United States Attorney is generally not bound by a promise made by a government employee, there is an exception to the rule. When the "breach of the agreement rendered a prosecution fundamentally unfair," the district court has authority to dismiss the case.

In *Williams* the Ninth Circuit did not resolve the issue of whether the standard the district court applies is one of detrimental reliance and fundamental fairness, or whether the issue turns on the nature of the promisor. The crucial issue for the latter standard is whether the promise was made as a part of the criminal justice system of the sovereign prosecuting the case. The Williams court found under either standard the facts in Williams did not support dismissal of the case. Williams was not induced by the agreement to incriminate himself, to furnish information useful to the government in developing the case against him, or to plead guilty. Neither did he suffer any other prejudice that would render his conviction unfair.

Elliott was induced by the state agent to believe that there was little or no risk of federal prosecution because the amount of marijuana was too small to make it a "federal case." Elliott would not have talked to the state authorities if he thought the case was federal. Likewise, without Elliott's cooperation the state would not have been able to develop the proof or gather the evidence to make the conspiracy case against his more culpable co-defendants and to take the case "federal." Elliott gave information that incriminated him in the larger conspiracy, though arguably there was enough to make a two pound conspiracy case in federal court against Elliott and his two companions that were arrested at Garrison. The conspiracy that led to federal charges against Elliott could not have been made without his cooperation. Thus, it is likely that had he not talked, he would be facing state charges for distribution of two pounds of marijuana. Had he gotten a deferred prosecution or a deferred sentence for a first offense in state court he would be eligible for clearing his record in its entirety on successful completion of the deferred prosecution or sentence. The state constitution and statutes, on petition or automatically, would allow a full restoration of all of his rights, including the right to vote, the right to hold public office, the right to be a juror or a grand juror, and the right to hunt.

Elliott will suffer other prejudice that, given the referral rules in place when he began cooperating[5] give credence to his claim that the prosecution is unfair. With a felony drug conviction, he is likely to lose any chance of ever entering medical school. He will be dis-

---

5. The only evidence in the record about the federal referral rules is the testimony of Agent Spanogle. His testimony is believable because one would think the federal prosecutor has bigger fish to fry than a two pound marijuana case. In other words, common sense tells us that this is not a "federal case," it is a state case. When deciding whether to initiate or to continue a prosecution "it is the duty of the United States Attorney not to simply prosecute, but to do justice. See *U.S. vs. Weber,* 721 F.2d 266, 268 (9th Cir. 1983).

qualified from many professions because of his lack of judgment resulting in a federal felony conviction. Given his age and culpability, he will pay a pretty price for his bad judgment.

Applying the fundamental fairness and detrimental reliance test, this federal prosecution makes no sense. It is facially unjust if what we are doing is seeking a fair and just resolution concerning federal criminal conduct. Depriving a bright young person of his future because of a federal conviction that is likely to get him probation is the harsh exercise of prosecutorial power and it seems to me to be at odds with the prosecutor's duty to seek justice, not to seek convictions. Prosecuting this case *in federal court as opposed to the Montana state courts,* raises the specter of judgment caused by the bad judgment that led to the wrongdoing in the first place. At some point the federal sovereign needs to defer to the state's interest in prosecuting minor drug offenses. Federalism is still important and should not be measured by the yardstick of severe sentences, especially when that concern has no application to the case at hand.

Nonetheless, I am troubled by the idea that a court should exercise the power, except in the most egregious circumstances, to tell the prosecutor what cases to bring.[7] There is a [federal] statute that makes distributing two pounds of marijuana a federal crime. There is a [federal] statute that makes it a crime for two or more people to conspire to distribute two pounds of marijuana. So, if I impose my normative view on what cases *should* be prosecuted in federal court, I would dismiss this case and let the state prosecute it. But, such a holding would create a structural problem to say the least.

Therefore, IT IS ORDERED that Elliott's motion to dismiss is denied[.]

This case started with the bad judgment of a very bright college student who wants to be a doctor. His bad judgment continued when he believed an honest state agent who told him he would not likely be prosecuted in federal court because the amount of marijuana he had was too small for referral to make it a "federal case." The wraith of that judgment seems apparent when the case was taken to a federal grand jury against Elliott. The role of the court is to see that Elliott gets a fair trial and if he is found guilty, to fashion an appropriate sentence. Good judgment here would mean deference to the state or a deferred federal prosecution. But if there is an injustice it does not rise to the level of the "inherently unfair" standard for dismissal.

———————

The *Elliott* court appeared to be troubled by the prosecutor's charging decision in part because of the defendant's personal background. But should the fact that Elliott was "a very bright college student who wants to be a doctor" impact his punishment? Some argue prosecutors—consciously or not—allow considerations like these to factor into their charging decisions in drug cases far too often and that the result is a disparity in enforcement of the sort at issue in *Clary*, where 55 of the 57 defendants prosecuted in the Eastern District of Missouri for crack offenses over the relevant period were black. Indeed, in *Clary*, Judge Cahill intimated that if drug laws were enforced as often and as strictly against young whites as they are against young people of color, perhaps our drug laws would be different. The sentiment recalls a quotation from Abraham Lincoln: "The best way to get a bad law repealed is to enforce it strictly." *See also,* Rehavi M. Marit and

———————

7. If federal judges in Montana could exercise such power or that choice, many of the cases charged in our federal court the past few years would properly be left to the state for prosecution. Not every crime is a "federal case." The doctrine of dual sovereignty is not a license to usurp the state criminal justice system. This is particularly so when the likely sentence in federal court is probation.

Sonja B. Starr, *Racial Disparity in Federal Criminal Charging and Its Sentencing Consequences*, U. of Michigan Law & Econ. Empirical Legal Studies Center Paper No. 12-002 (May 7, 2012) (analyzing federal data and determining that "initial charging decisions can explain at least half, and perhaps substantially more, of the black-white sentencing disparities that are not otherwise explained by pre-charge observables").

Perhaps one of the most famous (and most criticized) examples of the unrestrained power that federal prosecutors enjoy in exercising their discretion was New York's "federal day," mentioned by the court in *United States v. Agilar* in Chapter 3. Under the "federal day" scheme in the 1980s, "one random day a week all drug arrests [in Manhattan were] prosecuted in Federal court" where defendants faced significantly longer sentences than they would have in state court. Stephen Labton, *Drugs and the Law; The Courts Overwhelmed*, N.Y. Times at A1, Dec. 29, 1989. *See also*, Ethan A. Brown, Snitch: Informants, Cooperators & the Corruption of Justice 19–22 (reporting on the history of "federal day").

Are critics of prosecutorial discretion in drug cases concerned about the existence of discretion or the way in which prosecutors have chosen to exercise it?

United States v. Dossie

United States District Court for the Eastern District of New York
2012 U.S. Dist. LEXIS 45691

Gleeson, J.

This case illustrates how mandatory minimum sentences in drug cases distort the sentencing process and mandate unjust sentences. In the substantial percentage of cases in which they apply, they produce a sentencing regime that is worse than the one the Sentencing Reform Act of 1984 was enacted to replace. They make opaque what that law was intended to make transparent. They strip criminal defendants of the due process rights we consider fundamental to our justice system. Most importantly, too many nonviolent, low-level, substance-abusing defendants like Jamel Dossie "lose their claim to a future" — to borrow a phrase from Attorney General Eric H. Holder, Jr. — because lengthy mandatory prison terms sweep reasonable, innovative, and promising alternatives to incarceration off the table at sentencing.

A. *The Mandatory Minimum Sentences in Drug Cases*

1. *Why They Were Enacted*

Already engaged in a fervent war on drugs, Congress was galvanized by the tragic death by overdose of University of Maryland basketball star Len Bias on June 19, 1986, and it promptly enacted the Anti-Drug Abuse Act of 1986 ("ADAA"). The ADAA created mandatory minimum sentences and enhanced maximum sentences that have now become central features of our federal sentencing landscape. Despite the speed with which the ADAA was enacted, there is ample evidence from related congressional reports of the purpose of the new enhanced minimum and maximum penalties. The ADAA's five-year minimum sentence, with a maximum enlarged from 20 to 40 years (the "5-to-40 sentence enhancement" or the "five-year mandatory minimum"), was specifically intended for the managers of drug enterprises, while the Act's ten-year minimum sentence with life as the maximum (the "ten-to-life sentence enhancement" or the "ten-year mandatory minimum") was intended for the organizers and leaders. The Sentencing Commission's recent report to the Congress on Mandatory Minimum Penalties in the Federal Criminal Justice System provided the following useful summary of that evidence:

Floor statements delivered by members in support of the [ADAA] and a committee report on a predecessor bill suggest that Congress intended to create a two-tiered penalty structure for discrete categories of drug traffickers. Specifically, Congress intended to link the five-year mandatory minimum penalties to what some called "serious" traffickers and the ten-year mandatory minimum penalties to "major" traffickers. Drug quantity would serve as a proxy for identifying the type of trafficker.

Senator Robert Byrd, then the Senate Minority Leader, summarized the intent behind the legislation:

> For the kingpins—the masterminds who are really running these operations—and they can be identified by the amount of drugs with which they are involved—we require a jail term upon conviction. If it is their first conviction, the minimum term is 10 years.... Our proposal would also provide mandatory minimum penalties for the middle-level dealers as well. Those criminals would also have to serve time in jail. The minimum sentences would be slightly less than those for the kingpins, but they nevertheless would have to go to jail—a minimum of 5 years for the first offense.

> A report issued by the House Judiciary Subcommittee on Crime following its consideration of a predecessor bill also provides evidence of Congress's intent to establish two tiered mandatory minimum penalties for serious and major traffickers. The Subcommittee determined that the five and ten-year mandatory minimum sentencing structure would encourage the Department of Justice to direct its "most intense focus" on "major traffickers" and "serious traffickers." "One of the major goals of this bill is to give greater direction to the DEA and the U.S. Attorneys on how to focus scarce law enforcement resources."

U.S. Sent'g Comm'n, *Report to the Congress: Mandatory Minimum Penalties in the Federal Criminal Justice System* 24 (2011) [hereinafter *Mandatory Minimum Report*] (second alteration in original) (quoting 132 Cong. Rec. 27, 193–94 (Sept. 30, 1986); H.R. Rep. No. 99-845, pt. 1, at 11–12 (1986)) (internal footnotes omitted).

2. *The Mistake: Using Drug Quantity as a Proxy for Role*

Most people would agree that the people who lead or manage drug-trafficking businesses deserve severe punishment. But right from the start Congress made a mistake, which is apparent in the statement of Senator Byrd quoted above: The severe sentences it mandated to punish specified *roles* in drug-trafficking offenses were triggered not by role but by drug type and quantity instead. If it wanted the statute to serve its explicitly stated purpose, Congress should have said that an offense gets the 5-to-40 sentence enhancement when the defendant is proved to be a manager of a drug business. Instead, the 5-to-40 sentence enhancement is triggered by offenses involving 28 grams of crack, 100 grams of heroin, or 500 grams of cocaine. 21 U.S.C. § 841(b)(1)(B). And instead of hinging the ten-to-life sentence enhancement on the government's proof of "kingpin" or leadership status, Congress simply used larger drug quantities: 280 grams of crack,[2] 1,000 grams of heroin, or 5,000 grams of cocaine. 21 U.S.C. § 841(b)(1)(A). So if an offense happens to

---

2. These numbers reflect the current threshold quantities for crack. Before the Fair Sentencing Act of 2010 ("FSA") was enacted, an offense involving 50 grams of crack triggered the ten-year mandatory minimum and an offense involving only five grams of crack triggered the five-year mandatory minimum.

involve a drug type and quantity that triggers an enhancement, every defendant involved in that crime, whatever his or her actual role, can be treated as a leader or manager at the option of the United States Attorney.[3]

Drug quantity is a poor proxy for culpability generally and for a defendant's role in a drug business in particular. Senator Byrd's statement that the leaders and managers of drug operations "can be identified by the amount of drugs with which they are involved" was incorrect. Compare Defendant A, who organizes a dozen teenagers into a business to distribute cocaine in a New York City housing project and adjacent high school, with Defendant B, an addict who is paid $300 to stand at the entrance to a pier and watch for the police while a boatload of cocaine is offloaded. Defendant A is more culpable, and he is the sort of defendant Congress had in mind when it enacted the ten-to-life sentence enhancement, but he will not face even the 5-to-40 sentence enhancement if the conspiracy is nipped in the bud, before it deals more than half a kilogram of cocaine. Defendant B, on the other hand, qualifies for kingpin treatment and a ten-year mandatory minimum if the prosecutor so chooses, based solely on the amount of cocaine on the boat.

Congress's mistake of equating drug quantity with a defendant's role in the offense need not continue to have the devastating consequences on display in this case. If DOJ invokes the harsh sentence enhancements only in cases in which the defendants have supervisory roles—always fewer than 10% of federal drug cases—such unintended and unjust results can be avoided in the future. However, as discussed below, in deploying the mandatory minimum penalties, DOJ has disregarded their purpose. It has turned a law that sought to impose enhanced penalties on a select few into a sentencing regime that imposes them on a great many, producing unfairly harsh consequences that Congress did not intend.

3. How DOJ Uses the Mandatory Minimum Provisions

DOJ uses mandatory minimum sentences without regard to their purpose. In fiscal year ("FY") 2011, over 74% of crack defendants faced a mandatory minimum, *see* U.S. Sent'g Comm'n, 2011 Sourcebook of Federal Sentencing Statistics tbl.44 (2011) [hereinafter 2011 Sourcebook], yet only 5.4% of them occupied an aggravating role of leader or manager of a drug business, *see id.* tbl.40. Thus, the overwhelming majority of crack defendants who feel the pain of mandatory prison terms are not the criminals Congress had in mind in creating those penalties. The "safety valve" provision that was supposed to save minor defendants from the two-by-four that a mandatory minimum becomes on sentencing day has too many conditions to be effective. Even though more than 94% of crack defendants have no leadership or managerial role, fewer than 10% of such defendants qualify for the safety valve, *see id.* tbl.44.

B. Jamel Dossie and His Offense of Conviction

Jamel Dossie is a young, small-time, street-level drug dealer's assistant. No one could reasonably characterize him as a leader or manager of anything, let alone of a drug business. Like many young men in our community, he was in the drug business because he is a drug user.

---

3. A defendant is subject to the mandatory minimum only if the charging instrument puts him on formal notice of it by alleging the requisite type and quantity of drug and citing the relevant penalty provision. *E.g., United States v. Thomas,* 274 F.3d 655, 663 (2d Cir. 2001). Thus, whether a defendant faces a mandatory minimum at all is a matter left to prosecutorial discretion. At any time during a prosecution the government can withdraw its invocation of the mandatory minimum provision, allowing the court to sentence without being bound by it.

Dossie was born in the Brownsville section of Brooklyn. His father's illegal drug use caused a split with his mother before Dossie was even born; Dossie saw his father only three times per year before his father died in 2009. Dossie's mother was (and still is) a bus driver, and she raised Dossie and his two siblings by herself.

By the time Dossie began high school, he was already abusing drugs and alcohol, which got him into trouble regularly. Finally, at age 16, a family court judge ordered him out of his home and into a residential substance abuse treatment program at Phoenix House in the Bronx. Phoenix House reports that Dossie "displayed a poor attitude and unwillingness to engage in treatment" and that he made little academic or clinical progress before his discharge a year later. He never returned to school.

Dossie has a typical criminal history for a young man with his background. A car stop in 2008 led to a simple possession (of marijuana) conviction, and in 2010 he was convicted of a misdemeanor for possessing heroin and crack. His sentences for those misdemeanors were only seven days in custody and probation, respectively, but each conviction nevertheless earned Dossie a criminal history point, terminating any chance he had for safety-valve relief even without considering the two additional points he got for committing his offense while on probation. See 18 U.S.C. §3553(f).[5] Dossie has no history of violence except as a victim; he was hit in the leg by a stray bullet while walking down the street in 2008.

Dossie on four occasions was a go-between in hand-to-hand crack sales. On April 15, 2010, when Dossie was 20 years old, a confidential informant made a recorded phone call to him and asked about buying crack. Later that day, the informant met Dossie in Brooklyn. Dossie called an unidentified supplier, who arrived by Mercedes Benz ten minutes later. The informant gave $440 to Dossie—$420 for the person in the Mercedes and $20 for Dossie. Dossie took the money into the car. When he got out, the car left, and then Dossie handed the informant 9.4 grams of crack. On April 29, 2010, they did the same thing, except this time it was $860 ($820 for the supplier, $40 for Dossie) for 15.6 grams. This was less crack than the informant had asked for; Dossie explained that the supplier didn't have enough crack and returned $120 to the informant.

On June 10, 2010, they did it again, except this time the supplier of the crack stayed in a nearby store instead of a car, and it was $1,140 ($1,100 for the supplier and $40 for Dossie) for 29.6 grams. Finally, on November 9, 2010, Dossie transferred to the informant 33.5 grams of crack for $1,225. Dossie was arrested three and one-half months later, and he subsequently pled guilty to conspiring to distribute crack.

In sum, Dossie sold a total of 88.1 grams, or 3.1 ounces, of crack. His sole function was to ferry money to the supplier and crack to the informant on four occasions for a total gain to himself of $140.[6]

Dossie's advisory Guidelines range was 57–71 months. That range is too severe for a low-level addict selling drugs on the street. [T]he drug-offense Guidelines ranges are excessively severe. In formulating those ranges, the Commission decided to jettison its pre-

5. The Sentencing Commission has recommended that Congress "consider marginally expanding the safety valve at 18 U.S.C. §3553(f) to include certain non-violent offenders who receive two, or perhaps three, criminal history points." *Mandatory Minimum Report* at xxxi; *accord id.* at 355–56. This recommendation is too tepid, given how easy it is for nonviolent offenders to rack up criminal history points, especially while under supervision, *see* U.S.S.G. §4A1.1(d).

6. The amounts paid to Dossie are detailed in the Complaint, ECF No. 1. Since the Complaint does not describe the last of the four transactions, I am assuming here that Dossie received $40 for that transaction as well, as it is comparable to the second and third sales, from which he received $40 each.

Guidelines data and instead chose to make the sentencing range in every single drug case proportional to the onerous mandatory sentences meant only for leaders and managers.

Despite the harsh Guidelines range, Dossie would have had access to justice if he had not been charged with the five-year mandatory minimum enacted for drug business managers. But he caught two bad breaks. First, as the prosecutor pointed out at his sentencing, two of his four crack sales happened to exceed the threshold quantity of 28 grams that can trigger the five-year mandatory minimum. They only barely exceeded it—sales three and four put Dossie in mandatory minimum territory by only 1.6 and 5.5 grams, respectively—but just as baseball is a game of inches, our drug-offense mandatory minimum provisions create a deadly serious game of grams. The conspiracy charge to which Dossie pled guilty also aggregates all 88.1 grams, rendering him eligible for the mandatory minimum on that basis as well.

Dossie's second bad break occurred when the government chose to cite the mandatory minimum provision in the indictment. If it hadn't, I would have been permitted, indeed obligated, to consider, among others, the facts that (1) Dossie had a very minor role in the offense; (2) the drugs he helped to sell weren't his, and he got hardly any money for his involvement; (3) Dossie got off to a very rocky start in life—there's no surer sign of a dysfunctional childhood than a family court judge ordering a 16-year-old out of his home and into a residential drug treatment program; (4) Dossie's criminal record and unsuccessful drug treatment suggest strongly that his legal problems all arose from a drug problem he developed as a child; (5) Dossie is from a very supportive family—his family made all of his court appearances—which could very well have provided the support he needs to get and remain drug-free; and (6) Dossie is genuinely remorseful. I would have considered all of these factors in sentencing Dossie, and there is no way I would have sentenced him to a prison term within the severe advisory range. I might even have given him the chance to enter our Court's Pretrial Opportunity Program, which would have given Dossie the chance to both conquer his substance abuse problem and avoid prison altogether.[8]

Instead, we had a "sentencing proceeding" that involved no written submissions, no oral advocacy, and no judging. The defense lawyer stated the obvious: The five-year mandatory minimum was more than necessary to properly punish Dossie. The prosecutor agreed that the mandatory minimum of five years should be the sentence. So that was the sentence. The proceeding had all the solemnity of a driver's license renewal and took a small fraction of the time.

C. *The Evils of Mandatory Minimum Sentencing*

When I observed at Dossie's sentencing that the five-year mandatory minimum was being used by the government to overly punish a defendant for whom it was not intended, the prosecutor assured me that there were "other factors" that justified the mandatory five-year penalty. Specifically, the colloquy went as follows:

> The Court: He's not a kingpin or a manager, he's a street-level dealer, and one
> would think that if a 60-month sentence were appropriate you'd talk the judge

---

8. The Pretrial Opportunity Program is designed for nonviolent defendants with documented substance abuse problems. Participating defendants have their sentences postponed to engage in drug treatment that involves monthly meetings with the sentencing judge and the Chief Magistrate Judge of the district. The program relies on drug court methodologies that have been proven successful in many state criminal justice systems. If the defendant successfully completes the program by, *inter alia*, staying drug-free for at least one year, the post-arrest rehabilitation is considered by the sentencing judge. For a description of the program, see U.S. Pretrial Servs. Agency, E.D.N.Y., Pretrial Opportunity Program (2012), *available at* http://www.nyed.uscourts.gov/pub/docs/local/ POPDescription01112012.pdf.

into it rather than bind the judge into it. I think it's an inappropriate exercise of discretion given the purpose of these laws.

The Prosecutor: Well, I think in terms of the exercise of discretion, I don't think that the only question from the office's perspective is what the quantity involved is. I think there are a lot of other factors and information that go into it. And because we're not relying on any of that at sentencing I wouldn't necessarily belabor it, but I think there are other factors that go into a charging decision and I can represent to the Court that there are besides just mere quantity.

As this dialogue exemplifies, the use of these mandatory minimum provisions—which were utilized in over 74% of all crack cases in FY 2011, *see* 2011 Sourcebook tbl.44—results in a sentencing process that is far more objectionable and dangerous than the regime the Guidelines were created to replace. It is true that the pre-Guidelines regime was a "wasteland" characterized by unexplained, unguided, and unreviewed sentencing discretion, Marvin E. Frankel, *Lawlessness in Sentencing*, 41 U. Cin. L. Rev. 1, 54 (1972); *see also* Kate Stith and José A. Cabranes, *Fear of Judging: Sentencing Guidelines in the Federal Courts* 172 (1998) ("What made sentencing authority truly extraordinary ... was not the broad discretion the judge exercised, but rather, the fact that his decision was virtually unreviewable on appeal."), but at least the discretion was exercised by a *judge*, whose mission was to impose a just sentence. The sentencing discretion in Dossie's case was exercised by one of the parties to the case, in furtherance of the undisclosed interests of law enforcement.

Moreover, even the harshest critics of the Guidelines acknowledge that one of their greatest accomplishments is transparency. Judges now must follow established procedures and explain the reasons for their sentences. Those procedures, together with the reasons for the sentence and the sentence itself, are all subject to appellate review. This case reveals how mandatory-minimum provisions create the ultimate opaque sentencing regime: No explanation is required for why Dossie must do five years, none of the "factors" that went into the selection of that sentence was offered, and appellate review is impossible.

When I pressed the government further, the prosecutor reluctantly implied that the decision to charge Dossie with the mandatory minimum might have related to "information that ... link[s] him to a gang." I agree that if Dossie were dealing drugs as his way of participating in a gang, that would be a relevant, aggravating sentencing consideration. I think any judge would want to know facts like what sort of gang it was, what Dossie's alleged link to it was, how long any such link lasted, and how Dossie's actions as a middleman in street-level drug deals were related to the gang. But in this respect as well, Dossie's case places in clear relief the insidious consequences of mandatory sentencing provisions. If not for the mandatory minimum, Dossie would have had the opportunity to contest the government's suggestion that his offense was gang-related, and the government would have had the obligation to prove it.

That's how our system is supposed to work; if facts material to the sentencing are in dispute, they get resolved after both sides have notice of them and an appropriate opportunity to be heard. Where the fact in dispute would aggravate the sentence, the government bears the burden of persuasion. These are basic tenets of due process.

Mandatory minimum sentencing strips all of this away. In Dossie's case, the government's unreviewable decision to invoke the mandatory sentencing provision made the actual facts irrelevant. Dossie might have denied a gang affiliation or that any such affiliation had anything to do with his offense. The government might not have been able to prove its suggestion that Dossie was linked to a gang. Dossie, for all we know, might even have been able to affirmatively disprove the link. But because a mandatory minimum was involved and everyone agreed that Dossie should not be sentenced above that minimum, none of these facts mattered. The government simply dictated a five-year sentence without even having to allege, let alone prove, the aggravating fact that it implied warranted the sentence. There is no fairness in a system that allows that to happen.

D. *The Remedy: The Attorney General Should Use the Drug-Offense Mandatory Minimum Provisions Only Against the Defendants for Whom Congress Intended Them*

Congress should get rid of mandatory minimum sentences generally, but no one expects that to happen soon. In the meantime, DOJ can and must play the leading role in bringing about needed sentencing reform. DOJ should seek mandatory minimum sentences only in the cases for which Congress intended them: in cases against leaders and managers of drug enterprises, not the low-level drug offenders like Dossie who constitute the bulk of the federal drug docket. Federal prosecutors should exercise their discretion to bring mandatory minimum charges against only the small percentage of drug defendants (less than 6% in FY 2011) who deserve the aggravating role adjustments for being leaders or managers in a drug business. Specifically, they should charge the ten-year mandatory minimum only when they intend to prove that the defendant occupied a leadership role that warrants a four-level upward enhancement under U.S.S.G. § 3B1.1(a). They should charge the five-year mandatory minimum only when they intend to prove a managerial role worthy of a three- or two-level upward enhancement under § 3B1.1(b) or (c). And if the relevant aggravating role is not proved or admitted during the sentencing proceeding, prosecutors should withdraw (or reduce, as the case may be) the mandatory minimum.

Section 3B1.1 of the Sentencing Guidelines states:

Based on the defendant's role in the offense, increase the offense level as follows:

(a) If the defendant was an organizer or leader of a criminal activity that involved five or more participants or was otherwise extensive, increase by 4 levels.

(b) If the defendant was a manager or supervisor (but not an organizer or leader) and the criminal activity involved five or more participants or was otherwise extensive, increase by 3 levels.

(c) If the defendant was an organizer, leader, manager, or supervisor in any criminal activity other than described in (a) or (b), increase by 2 levels.

The four-level adjustment under subsection (a) for organizers and leaders of drug businesses that involve five or more people (including the defendant) or are "otherwise extensive" dovetails with Senator Byrd's description of the defendants who deserve the ten-year mandatory minimum as "kingpins" and "masterminds," as well as with the House committee report's description of them as "major traffickers." The three-level adjustment under subsection (b) for managers and supervisors in such organizations similarly parallels the "middle-level dealers" or "serious traffickers" at whom the five-year mandatory minimum was directed. Finally, the two-level adjustment under subsection (c) that applies to *all* management personnel (organizers, leaders, managers, and supervisors) when the drug business involves fewer than five people and is not otherwise extensive also captures the type of defendant for whom Congress intended the five-year mandatory minimum. Even the founder and leader of a drug business that involves fewer than five people and is not extensive is not the "kingpin" or "major trafficker" Congress had in mind. Thus by following my proposal, DOJ could ensure that its use of mandatory minimum charges hews closely to Congress's intentions.

My request is also consistent with the Attorney General Holder's policy on charging and sentencing. Under that policy, a prosecutor's charging decision "must always be made in the context of an individualized assessment of the extent to which particular charges fit the specific circumstances of the case." Memorandum from Eric H. Holder, Jr., U.S. Attorney Gen., to All Fed. Prosecutors 2 (May 19, 2010) (quoting U.S. Attorneys' Manual § 9-27.300) (internal quotation marks omitted). Furthermore, the policy provides that "[i]n all cases, the charges should fairly represent the defendant's criminal conduct." *Id*. And, most importantly, the policy requires that "the decision whether to seek a statutory sentencing enhancement should be guided by these same principles." *Id*. By utilizing mandatory minimum provisions only in cases involving managerial-type drug traffickers as I propose, prosecutors can better ensure that their charging decisions fit the specific circumstances of defendants' cases and that punishments defendants receive fairly represent their criminal conduct.

I am mindful of the fact that federal prosecutors find significant value in the way that charging mandatory minimum sentences helps them solicit the cooperation of defendants. *See* Lanny A. Breuer, *The Attorney General's Sentencing and Corrections Working Group: A Progress Report*, Fed. Sent'g Rep., Dec. 2010, at 110, 112 ("We favor mandatory minimum sentences because such sentences remove dangerous offenders from society, ensure just punishment, and are an essential tool in gaining cooperation from members of violent street gangs and drug distribution networks."). I have previously written about the "enormous boost" mandatory minimum sentences give to federal law enforcement in its effort to advance investigations and obtain convictions by enlisting cooperation. John C. Jeffries, Jr. & John Gleeson, *The Federalization of Organized Crime: Advantages of Federal Prosecution*, 46 HASTINGS L.J. 1095, 1120 (1995). Federal prosecutors have gotten so inured to using severe sentences to leverage cooperation that, "[t]o an increasing degree, the Department has come to justify its requests for tougher sentencing rules, not on the ground that offenders actually deserve the higher sentences, but simply because the threat of the higher sentence provides a greater inducement for defendant cooperation." Frank O. Bowman, *Mr. Madison Meets a Time Machine: The Political Science of Federal Sentencing Reform*, 58 STANFORD L. REV. 235, 252 (2005).

An interest in pursuing cooperation justifies charging leaders and managers of drug enterprises with the corresponding mandatory minimum drug offense. Though deserving of stiff sentences, such defendants may properly be rewarded with a sentence below the mandatory minimum for providing substantial assistance to the government. The flip side is that a decision not to cooperate may effectively result in a harsher sentence, but a harsh sentence is what Congress intended for that type of drug trafficker.

That same interest in pursuing cooperation cannot justify charging a mandatory minimum when the defendant is neither a leader nor a manager. It is one thing to lower an otherwise appropriate sentence to reward a defendant's cooperation but quite another to threaten to impose an otherwise unjust sentence if he decides not to cooperate or tries but produces no law enforcement results. The latter situation essentially converts a refusal or inability to cooperate into an aggravating sentencing factor, in violation of a basic principle of our sentencing regime. See U.S.S.G. § 5K1.2 ("A defendant's refusal to assist in the investigation of other persons may not be considered as an aggravating sentencing factor.").

I have reason to believe that Attorney General Holder will be receptive to my request. In 2009 he made the following remarks to the Vera Institute of Justice:

> One specific area where I think we can do a much better job by looking beyond incarceration is in the way we deal with non-violent drug offenses. We know that people convicted of drug possession or the sales of small amounts of drugs comprise a significant portion of the prison population. Indeed, in my thirty

years in law enforcement, I have seen far too many young people lose their claim to a future by committing non-violent drug crimes.

One promising, viable solution to the devastating effect of drugs on the criminal justice system and on American communities is the implementation of more drug treatment courts. Drug court programs provide an alternative to incarceration for non-violent offenders by focusing on treatment of their underlying addiction. Program participants are placed in treatment and routinely tested for drug use—with the imposition of immediate sanctions for positive tests balanced with suitable incentives to encourage abstinence from drug use. These programs give no one a free pass. They are strict and can be extraordinarily difficult to get through. But for those who succeed, there is the real prospect of a productive future.

New York has been a leader in this area, diverting some non-violent offenders into drug court programs and away from prison, and extending early release to other non-violent offenders who participate in treatment programs. And while national prison populations have consistently increased, in New York the state prison population has dropped steadily and has 12,000 fewer inmates now than it did in 1999. And since 1999, the overall crime rate in New York has dropped 27%. Other states have followed New York's example. And most importantly, studies show significant reductions in re-arrests, from about 15 to 30 percentage points, for drug-court participants as compared to criminals simply incarcerated.

Those remarks preceded the crime in this case, but they may as well have been about Dossie, a young drug-user whose nonviolent drug offense now seriously threatens his "claim to a future" principally because the government forced me to impose a five-year jail term on him. The Attorney General was right to compliment the forward-looking approach of the state authorities here in New York. If Dossie had been prosecuted by them instead of by federal authorities he would have been given an opportunity to avoid not only time in jail but a conviction as well. The success of the Drug Treatment Alternative to Prison Program ("DTAP") in Brooklyn over the past twenty years proves the efficacy of treating defendants like Dossie rather than subjecting them to prison terms. Graduates of DTAP "have a five-year post-treatment recidivism rate that is almost half the rate for comparable offenders who served time in prison." Charles J. Hynes, Kings Cnty. Dist. Attorney, Drug Treatment Alternative-to-Prison Twentieth Annual Report at Exec. Summ. (2011).[10]

But the benefits of drug treatment and drug courts as alternatives to incarceration for nonviolent offenders are unavailable when DOJ itself *mandates* incarceration by invoking mandatory minimum sentences. Those provisions continue to be routinely invoked by DOJ against nonviolent, low-level offenders, even though it is crystal clear that Congress did not intend them to be used against such defendants. The result: Judges are removed from the sentencing process, along with transparency, appellate review, and, most importantly, justice. And young men like Jamel Dossie end up losing out on what may be their last chance to save their future.

---

10. Ironically, Dossie is such a low-level drug defendant that he would not even be eligible for admission into the DTAP Program, which requires at least one prior felony drug conviction. However, he would be "eligible to be diverted into treatment through the court-run programs in Brooklyn's three drug court parts: Misdemeanor Brooklyn Treatment Court, Brooklyn Treatment Court, and the Screening and Treatment Enhancement Part." *Id.* at 4 n.9.

E. *Conclusion*

The only reason for the five-year sentence imposed on Dossie is that the law invoked by the prosecutor required it. It was not a just sentence. To avoid similar injustices in other cases, I respectfully urge the Attorney General to lead the way forward by altering DOJ's charging policies in the manner described above.

———————

While federal prosecutors enjoy nearly unfettered discretion over whether to charge a defendant in federal court and which charges to bring, some state courts have interpreted their constitutions to require judicial oversight of some charging decisions. In *New Jersey v. Lagares*, 127 N.J. 20 (1992), for example, the Supreme Court of New Jersey held that aspects of the state's mandatory minimum drug sentencing scheme impermissibly delegated judicial sentencing powers to the prosecutor. To cure the constitutional defect, the Court held that prosecutors offices be required to adopt guidelines to govern the decision to seek enhanced sentences under the law; that prosecutors be required to state on the record the reasons for seeking an extended term; and that prosecutors' decisions be subject to judicial review under an arbitrary and capricious standard.

F. Drug Courts

Criminal drug courts provide treatment as an alternative to traditional sentences for drug defendants who meet certain criteria. Most public policy analysts have concluded that drug courts are more cost-effective than traditional modes of punishment. A systemic review of drug court research by the United States Government Accountability Office (GAO) in 2005, for example, found that the studies showed net benefits ranging from $1,000 to $15,000 per drug court participant. *See* Government Accountability Office, Report to Congressional Committees No GAO-05-219: Adult Drug Courts: Evidence Indicates Recidivism Reductions and Mixed Results for Other Outcomes 71 (2005), *available at* http://www.gao.gov/new.items/d05219.pdf.

Drug courts also seem poised to expand in the coming years. A recent survey by the National Center for State Courts reported "[e]xpanding the use of drug courts ... [was] among the leading current sentencing reform efforts in the states." Roger K. Warren, *A Tale of Two Surveys: Judicial and Public Perspectives on State Sentencing Reform*, 21 FED. SENT. REP. 276, 277 (2009). Meanwhile, the Obama Administration has made the expansion of federal funding for state and local drug court programs a cornerstone of its drug treatment strategy.

Drug courts, however, are not without their critics. This section will provide an overview of modern criminal drug courts, including how they are structured and the debate over whether they are truly a cost-effective and humane alternative to traditional forms of punishment of drug defendants.

Embracing Addiction:
Drug Courts and the False Promise of Judicial Intervention
Eric J. Miller
65 Ohio State Law Journal 1479 (2004)

Drug courts may be the most significant penal innovation in the last twenty years. Emerging as a direct response to the "severity revolution" in penal policy, they are an incredibly popular alternative to the War on Drugs. They present a vibrant counter to the stalled legislative and litigative strategies developed to stem the flow of drug users into the criminal justice system. Rather than targeting the scope or application of drug statutes, drug courts work at the level of court process and procedure to re-institutionalize the penological goals of diversion and rehabilitation.

Since its first appearance in the early 1990s, the drug court movement has sought to restructure court practice and procedure. Its goal is to use the court's sanctioning power to treat drug offenders rather than expedite the process of incarceration. Instead of challenging the drug laws, these courts operate within the current legislative framework but attempt to channel offenders away from prison and into treatment. Drug courts, therefore, constitute an alternative to the dominant liberal reaction to the War on Drugs—a reaction that either opposes the criminalization of drugs in general or seeks to end the disparate impact of drug laws on minority populations.

In 1989, the Florida Eleventh Judicial Circuit created the first drug court by administrative order of the Hon. Gerald Weatherington, the then-Chief Justice. The Miami program was set up as a diversion program, "combin[ing] treatment, including traditional treatment methods such as counseling, fellowship meetings, education, and rather nontraditional (at least then) methods like acupuncture and vocational services, with intense judicial review, including frequent reviews of urinalysis results."

The exponential growth in the numbers of drug courts is nothing short of astounding. From the first, in Dade County, there were more than eight hundred drug courts started or in the planning and implementation stages by 2000. All fifty states, as well as the District of Columbia, Guam, and Puerto Rico have founded drug courts. By now, drug courts have had a significant impact upon the lives of thousands of drug offenders. The courts' therapeutic problem-solving orientation is becoming commonplace in other areas of the legal system. Initially, however, the drug court movement developed without federal regulation or funding of the various courts. It developed as an ad hoc movement of like-minded judges and practitioners, loosely affiliated by 1993 into the National Association of Drug Court Professionals (NADCP).

A lack of uniform characteristics shared by all the courts complicates comprehensive analysis of drug court practice and procedure. In practice, there is no ideal or standard drug court; there are, rather, an immense number of local variations on the basic model.

Drug courts channel offenders into treatment at a variety of different stages of the criminal justice process. There are, however, two general channeling policies: deferred prosecution and post-adjudication diversion. Deferred prosecution drug courts require that the defendant waive his right to a speedy trial and enter treatment as soon after being charged as possible. Under the post-adjudication model, the defendant is, in fact, convicted, either after trial or after a plea bargain. In that event, an incarcerative sentence is deferred pending completion of a drug treatment program. Currently, thirty percent of drug courts divert offenders at the pretrial stage and before a plea agreement ("pretrial" and "preplea"); sixteen percent are pretrial and post-plea; twelve percent are post-conviction sentencing institutions; and the rest, forty-two percent, are some combination of the above.

Federal funding and general procedural standards ensure some degree of uniformity. These standards, promulgated initially by the NADCP, include a series of ten "key components" of the drug court and a set of guidelines governing the sanctions or rewards applicable to drug court defendants. These guidelines are tremendously influential. They embody the therapeutic practices of reward for compliance, limited tolerance of relapse, and graduated sanctions for non-compliance with the treatment program that are at the core of the drug court's methodology. In addition, the American Bar Association (ABA) has published a series of drug court standards to supplement the NADCP guidelines and ensure that defendants' procedural rights are protected.

Although neither set of standards is binding on any drug court unless adopted as the court's operating procedures, Congress has conditioned federal funding upon the adoption of the NADCP standards. Many state legislatures or judicial counsels, in formulating their local drug court procedures, clearly respond to the NADCP and ABA standards. Thus, although drug courts come in a variety of different models, in general they share certain common features.

Based on the NADCP model standards, Judge Peggy Hora has identified five features generally attributable to drug courts. First, drug courts use eligibility criteria to identify potential participants in the drug court program. These criteria generally require that the defendant be an addict who is either a nonviolent offender or an offender who poses no security risk to the community. Second, drug court procedure embodies a non-adversarial partnership among the criminal justice, correctional, and treatment systems. This partnership "work[s] together to find care for defendants and to ensure that they remain in treatment." The procedure is designed to maintain the courts' continuing jurisdiction over offenders by "delay[ing] the final disposition of cases [enabling] judges to maintain frequent ongoing contact with defendants." Third, the procedures effect a change in roles of judge, prosecutor, and defense counsel, each of whom participates as part of a treatment team. Fourth, the courts require offenders to attend a designated treatment program. Fifth, courts are able to accept and account for the potential of relapse by providing a range of prescribed and known sanctions for defendants who fail to comply with the program. Drug courts use a "system of graduated penalties.... [, which] may include more frequent contact with the court, increased urine testing, and short periods of so-called 'shock incarceration,'" to ensure compliance with their rehabilitation program.

The most striking feature of the drug court, and the feature most touted by its supporters, is its significantly reorganized court procedure premised upon therapeutic principles of justice.

Drug courts replace the predominantly punitive orientation of traditional approaches to crime control and rehabilitation with "an approach that seeks to confront and meliorate the problems associated with persons who appear in the criminal caseload." These courts eschew the due process accusatorial or adversarial model of courtroom practice. Under that form of procedure, the judge adopts a passive role that tasks the parties with investigating facts, interrogating witnesses, and developing proposals for treatment. The drug court judge no longer relies upon treatment proposals developed by a probation officer, subject to the prosecutor's and defense counsel's arguments over their propriety for the particular defendant. Instead, the drug court incorporates an invasive model of criminal procedure within the courtroom with the judge at the helm. "[J]ustice and therapy are no longer separate enterprises. Instead, they are fully merged into the common endeavor of therapeutic justice."

In drug court, the judge not only retains his authority to set the terms of treatment but now also assumes the role of regulating it. The court, rather than the treatment center, becomes the focal point of the treatment process. The other participants-prosecutor, defender, and defendant (or the drug court's "client")—are required to adopt non-traditional roles. They are supposed to form, along with the judge, a treatment team dedicated to the rehabilitation of the drug-addicted defendant. The team organization replaces the adversarial, adjudicative orientation of traditional courts with a therapeutic approach to drug addiction. The prosecutor and defender become partners collaborating in an effort to rehabilitate the addicted client. The defender must modify or mute her traditional role, "take a step back, [and] not intervene actively between the judge and the participant ... [to] allow that relationship to develop and do its work." Under the treatment team model, the offender's most direct relationships are, therefore, not with his or her counsel, but with the judge and the treatment officer.

Under the new, therapeutic orientation, the hallmarks of the drug court judge's role are, first, discretion in responding to the needs of her "clients" and, second, establishing "a personal 'on-going, working relationship' with the offender." Over the course of his or her participation in drug court, each offender engages in an intense and direct interaction with the judge directed towards "hold[ing] the defendant accountable for her actions during the course of treatment and reinforc[ing] one another in actions taken to ensure that the defendant stays in treatment whenever possible and appropriate."

The drug courts' methodology marks a dual attack on old-style criminal justice. Its strong emphasis on interventionist styles of interaction and authority reject the propriety of due process restrictions on the courts' therapeutic models. Drug courts also, however, dismiss the supposedly soft approach of prior rehabilitative regimes. They seek to bolster the safety net model of rehabilitation with tough love. Drug courts treat the addicted offender as in need of the shock and structure provided by sanctions, so long as those sanctions are consistently applied and so graduated as to recognize the role relapse plays in the therapeutic process. Rehabilitation in the drug court is not a process of "'referring, re-referring, and re-re-referring'" recalcitrant offenders to treatment regimes in hope of effecting a cure. Rather, drug courts envisage the consistent application of sanctions as part of the therapeutic process, one that imposes structure on the addicts' lives.

Generally, the court mandates supervision of drug offenders for one year and spreads treatment over a variety of phases, from intake, to counseling and drug education, to aftercare and transition issues. Each phase employs progressively less intensive supervision of the offender. The first phases are generally highly intensive and can require as much as four days per week of group and individual counseling and education or attendance at treatment providers as well as regular, often weekly, court appearances. Frequent urine testing is generally required throughout the program.

Matching offenders to particular treatment providers is central to the court's mission. In determining what treatment is appropriate, the drug court judge generally has a range of available treatment options from which to choose. Most require visits with a probation officer and a drug education component, along with the mandatory urine tests. In addition, some form of group or individual counseling is required.

Drug Courts: A Review of the Evidence
Ryan S. King and Jill Pasquarella
The Sentencing Project (2009)

The movement for an alternative court to sentence drug offenders emerged from the rapidly evolving reality that the nation's decision to address drug abuse through law enforcement mechanisms would continue to pose significant challenges for the criminal court system. In 2004, 53% of persons in state prison were identified with a drug dependence or abuse problem, but only 15% were receiving professional treatment. Drug-related crime continues to present a costly burden to American society, one that supply reduction efforts have failed to stem. In 2001, the Office of National Drug Control Policy estimated that in 1998 illegal drug use cost Americans $31.1 billion in criminal justice expenses, $30.1 billion in lost productivity and $2.9 billion in costs related to property damage and victimization.

Since 1989, drug courts have spread throughout the country; there are now over 1,600 such courts operating in all 50 states. The drug court movement reflects a desire to shift the emphasis from attempting to combat drug crimes by reducing the supply of drugs to addressing the demand for drugs through the treatment of addiction. Drug courts use the criminal justice system to address addiction through an integrated set of social and legal services instead of solely relying upon sanctions through incarceration or probation. This report surveys a range of research conducted on drug courts to date. Its aim is to outline general findings on the workings and efficacy of drug courts nationwide and to highlight potential concerns and areas where more research is needed.

Despite general indications of drug court efficacy, nearly two decades after their introduction a number of questions remain. Because drug courts are designed and operated at the local level, there are fundamental differences that make cross-jurisdictional comparisons difficult. While the general framework may be portable from program to program—a diversion program for certain categories of low-level defendants who have demonstrated a linkage between their drug abuse and criminal offending—specific selection criteria, protocols for adjudication, means of supervision and revocation procedures can differ dramatically. The localism that defines drug court design complicates efforts to identify best practices. However, we can identify specific elements from different drug courts that are critical ingredients for a successful program. The foundation of a vibrant and sustainable drug diversion program rests both on indicators of success and learning and adapting to emerging challenges.

Graduates of drug courts are, according to current evaluations, less likely to be rearrested than persons processed through traditional court mechanics. Findings from drug court evaluations show that participation in drug courts results in fewer rearrests and reconvictions, or longer periods between arrests.

A meta-analysis of 57 studies[, for example,] estimated that participation in a drug court program would produce an 8% decline in crime relative to no treatment. [And, a] Government Accountability Office report found that 13 of 17 courts reporting on post-program recidivism measured reductions between 4 and 25 percentage points in rearrests and reconvictions.

While it is generally accepted that drug courts effectively reduce rearrest rates relative to simple probation or incarceration, there is some reason to be cautious when interpreting these results. Some studies show little or no impact from drug court participation and it can be difficult to specify which components of the program or the research design may be contributing to these results.

For example, are the evaluation models appropriately specifying relevant factors that may impact outcomes, but are external to the treatment design? Gender, age, race, socioeconomic background, criminal history, and substance abuse history have all been shown to impact treatment outcomes. Many of these variables are not accounted for in analyses of drug court effectiveness. Operationalizing drug court variables can be difficult and outcome measures may be reflecting the interaction of these variables with the treatment modality.

Additionally, definitions of recidivism and the length of time that recidivism is measured differ among the studies, making an absolute comparison difficult. Some drug court evaluations have measured rearrest rates without distinguishing between participants currently under supervision and those who have completed the program. This is important because drug court participants who graduate tend to have much lower recidivism rates than drug court dropouts. Some studies suggest that among drug court dropouts, time spent in treatment had little if any effect on post-program recidivism.

Researchers have also noted that the composition of drug court participants needs to be addressed appropriately in developing a court model. For example, an evaluation of California's Proposition 36 diversion program for low-level drug offenders found that almost half of the persons who were receiving treatment for the first time had been using drugs for more than 10 years, and one in five had been using for more than 20 years.

Evaluations of the net costs and benefits of drug courts nationwide generally find that drug courts save taxpayer dollars compared to simple probation and/or incarceration, primarily due to reductions in arrests, case processing, jail occupancy and victimization costs. While not all persons diverted to drug court would have otherwise been sentenced to prison, for those individuals who are incarcerated, the average annual cost is estimated to be $23,000 per inmate, while the average annual cost of drug court participation is estimated to be $4,300 per person.

In 2005, the Government Accountability Office found that seven drug courts evaluated had net benefits of between $1,000 and $15,000 per participant due to reduced recidivism and avoided costs to potential victims.

Research to date has consistently reported that drug courts are achieving important benefits. Still largely unknown, however, are the practices which lead to success or failure of a drug court. Of great concern is the contention that drug courts could be increasing the number of people arrested for drug crimes, instead of decreasing in the long term the number of people processed in the criminal justice system. Research has not yet focused on determining whether drug court participants would have ended up in the criminal justice system if not for the drug court. Increased and uniform tracking of participants' criminal history may answer some concerns about the net-widening effects of the drug court. It would also be helpful for future research to look at the effects of a pre-plea versus a post-plea model and the use of sanctions. Research should continue to monitor the rearrest and reconviction rates of both graduates and dropouts, distinguishing between within program rates and post-program rates. It will continue to be useful to know the demographic of graduates along with the rates of recidivism in the years that follow their graduation.

Contraindicated Drug Courts
Josh Bowers
55 UCLA Law Review 783 (2008)

Drug courts have created a few enemies and a great many more supporters from all corners of political and institutional spectra. Supporters maintain that the courts effectively serve several goals: to provide second chances for nonviolent addicts, to preserve systemic resources, and to control crime by disrupting cycles of addiction and recidivism. The common refrain is that "what we were doing before simply was not working." Thus, drug courts are said to offer a necessary and fresh approach to combat drug use and drug crime. Conversely, critics principally raise institutional concerns: that these courts inappropriately convert traditional adversaries into "team players," subvert judicial function by turning historically impartial judges into therapists and interrogators, and even fail to reduce recidivism and save resources.

I wish to put to one side the broader debate over the effectiveness and institutional propriety of drug courts. My aim is to draw attention to two related, under-appreciated, and troubling facets of these courts: first, that they provide the worst results to their target populations; and, second, that this inversion of intended effect produces particularly toxic consequences in the many drug courts that subject failing participants to alternative termination sentences that exceed customary plea prices. Put concretely, drug courts are "contraindicated" for genuine addicts and for other disadvantaged groups that have traditionally filled prisons as part of the war on drugs. The consequent adverse effects may be atypically long prison sentences for the very defendants that drug courts were supposed to keep out of prison and off of drugs.

Worse still, compulsive addicts are not the only ones who face comparatively bad results in drug courts. Studies have shown that other historically disadvantaged groups — for example minorities, the poor, the uneducated, and the socially disconnected — are also more likely to fail. Accordingly, drug courts may regressively tax communities already strained by the incarceration boom, and thereby exacerbate preexisting racial and socio-economic criminal-justice "tilts."

Conversely, drug offenders who are noncompulsive or less compulsive ultimately do much better in drug courts. Even if un-addicted offenders do not want to cease drug use, they possess sufficient self-control to modify rationally their behavior in response to external carrots and sticks. Faced with the choice between incarceration and manageable programs, these offenders have every incentive to be strategic and game entry into treatment that they do not, in fact, need, in order to receive favorable dispositions that (from a retributive-justice standpoint) they do not deserve.

The root cause of this contraindication problem is the lack of theoretical coherence in drug courts. On the one hand, drug courts follow the philosophy that addiction is a compulsive disease. On the other, the courts expect addicts to be receptive rationally to external coercion. More specifically, the courts subscribe, at least rhetorically, to the purported belief that addiction is a "brain disease" — a "chronic, progressive, relapsing disorder." Under this conception, addiction is unresponsive to traditional criminal punishment, because jails and prisons lack the tools to help addicts stop, and addicts lack the volition to stop on their own. Moreover, the courts view diversion from prison and the potential reduction or dismissal of charges as retributively justified, because addicts possess diminished self-control and therefore diminished responsibility. But drug courts have not — as advertised — abandoned the "traditional criminal justice paradigm, in which drug abuse is understood as a willful choice made by an offender capable of choosing between right and wrong." They have merely relocated the old paradigm to the background. Accordingly, drug courts see addicts as sick patients and their crimes as symptomatic of illness only as long as participants respond to care. When treatment results run thin, a switch is thrown and drug courts revert to economic conceptions of motivation and to conventional punishment. Pursuant to this mixed message, addiction controls addicts' behavior at the time of the crime (at least to a degree), and addicts therefore deserve less punishment and more rehabilitation; but addicts control their addictions at the time of treatment, and they therefore deserve greater punishment if they fail to exercise control.

Drug courts operate on faith that internal motivation will follow external motivation — that carrots and sticks will jumpstart inner desire. Put differently, drug courts meet addicts' inability to exercise self-control and reason not only with therapeutic opportunities to address these deficiencies, but also with concurrent external threats to respond to reason — or else. This confidence in addicts' abilities to discover reason once in drug courts runs counter to well-established therapeutic principles that treatment works better when addicts are internally motivated. Indeed, it would be somewhat surprising if it were otherwise. After all, addicts are people for whom the everyday negative external consequences of drug use — the social, economic, legal, and physical costs — have proven insufficient to modify behavior.

Ultimately, when drug courts imprison failing participants, they punish them not for their underlying crimes, but for their inability to get with the program. In this way, drug courts bear some resemblance to early medieval trials by ordeal. These trials—in which the accused performed some onerous task as a test of God's will—measured not culpability, but rather, say, calluses on hands that enabled the accused to carry safely hot iron. Likewise, drug courts measure not culpability, but strength of will and social support in the face of addiction. In both dispositional methods, final sentences are principally reflective of innate and preexisting advantages. In one sense, drug courts may be even more problematic than trials by ordeal: Drug-court results are not just haphazard, they are predictably worst for the most addicted, the least volitional, and the neediest. As such, the expected failure of addicts to respond to external stimuli seems an odd basis from which to subject them to alternative sentences that outstrip standard pleas.

Moreover, there is little reason to hope that treatment-resistant offenders might recognize their own fallibility and consequently opt-out of treatment. The most compulsive addicts are bound to reach the least sensible decisions; the enticements of drug court are dangled before the very individuals most easily tempted. When addicts cede to that temptation they exercise effectively the same cognitive limitations and bounded willpower that saddled them with drug dependencies in the first instance. They myopically undervalue the difficulties of recovery and the weight of the distant (but heavy) stick that awaits termination. And they optimistically grasp treatment's carrots, leaving for tomorrow the question of how to master their own defective rationalities and wills. Faced with the choice between conventional pleas, risky trials, or uncertain treatment, they are prone to see drug courts as the best means of remaining at, or recapturing, liberty, even when it often is not. Ultimately, then, external motivation may prove sufficient to convince addicts to take treatment, but it is less likely to keep them there.

Almost no studies have sought to compare the sentences of failing drug-court participants with the sentences of conventionally adjudicated defendants. Two limited exceptions are a pair of federally funded studies recently completed by the Center for Court Innovation in collaboration with the New York State Unified Court System. The chief study analyzed drug courts in several New York counties, including Queens, Brooklyn, Manhattan, and the Bronx. The other study looked exclusively at the drug court in Staten Island. Accordingly, the two studies collectively examined drug courts in all New York City counties.

The studies found that the sentences for failing participants in New York City drug courts were typically two-to-five times longer than the sentences for conventionally adjudicated defendants. At the outer margin, the sentences were well over five times the standard length in Staten Island and almost four times the standard length in the Bronx. Only in Brooklyn were termination sentences anywhere close to the length of customary sentences. Significantly, the Bronx and Staten Island drug-court participants did worse on average even when graduates were included. In fact, in the Bronx, the termination sentences approximated the literal worst-case scenario: The typical failing participant was sentenced to two-to-six years in prison, which was (at the time of the relevant studies) the maximum sentence on the maximum drug-court eligible charge.

Significantly, drug court proponents could spin rosy tales from even these data. Reading quite broadly, they could claim that diversion is working: in all counties, fewer drug offenders went to prison; and, in most counties, the collective population of offenders spent less time behind bars. But at the individualized level, the positive story does not hold. Take Queens County, for example. There, drug-court defendants were incarcerated at half the rate, but those who did go to jail or prison went away for more than twice as long. Such a result sits uncomfortably with defensible notions of distributive justice and cuts against drug-court advocates' professed aim of breaking the cycle of addiction and incarceration.

America's Problem-Solving Courts:
The Criminal Costs of Treatment and the Case for Reform
National Association of Criminal Defense Lawyers (2009)

The debate over drug enforcement policy in the United States is almost always framed in stark terms premised on narrow options. Conventional thinking about criminal justice issues — prison, community corrections, probation, or possibly some sort of diversion program for minor offenses and first-time offenders — has not worked, nor has it abated the addiction problem. Drug courts have swept the nation without much debate or input from the criminal defense bar. That input is long overdue.

Policymakers, courts, and lawyers must take a step back and examine the problem being solved: drug addiction. Addiction is an illness. Illnesses should be treated through the public health system — not punished through the criminal justice system. Conditioning treatment on an arrest and entry in the criminal justice system sends a perverse message to the person who is ill and is an enormous waste of scarce public and court resources.

[The National Association of Criminal Defense Lawyers] has long believed that "addiction to any substance, whether legal or illegal, is really a health problem best treated by the medical community and others trained in the causes and treatments of addiction." Thoughtful policymakers from all points on the political spectrum have recommended the decriminalization of all drugs as the best way to combat drug addiction and make effective use of criminal justice resources. The experience of European nations provides powerful support for the soundness of this approach and belies concerns that drug use would increase. Although politicians have been unwilling to engage in a serious debate about legalizing drugs, the broader public has shown interest in the issue. It is time for a serious discussion of decriminalization.

Until decriminalization occurs, the conventional paradigm is likely to continue, and drug courts will have a role. Drug courts are largely well-intentioned efforts to offer substance abuse treatment as an alternative to lengthy prison terms and lifelong felony convictions. Much of the support for drug courts ultimately turns on their existence as the sole, or best, alternative to draconian punishment. Although drug courts may offer some positive benefits to some participants, they also cause problems and engender disparities in many areas, including the admission process, the role and ethical obligations of defense counsel, and the misguided use of limited public resources.

Most drug courts require a guilty plea as the price of admission. When guilty pleas are required before offering treatment, drug courts become little more than conviction mills. In post-adjudication courts, the defendant must plead guilty before entering drug court, and even if he or she is successful and completes the program, the conviction will never go away. In pre-adjudication courts, the defendant must plead guilty, but then, if he or she successfully completes the program there is a possibility that the plea can be withdrawn and the charge dismissed. Although procedures vary, the hoops through which participants must jump result in dismissals for relatively few defendants. Profound consequences flow from every failure.

A pre-plea, pre-adjudication program preserves due process rights, allows defendants an opportunity to seek treatment, and provides a strong incentive for successful completion. If the participant successfully completes the program, the charge is dismissed. If the participant does not succeed, the traditional court process can be pursued.

Pre-plea, pre-adjudication programs are also the only ones that permit informed, thoughtful decision-making by defendants and counsel. Conversely, in post-plea programs defendants often lack sufficient time to make informed decisions, do not have discovery, and are unable to litigate motions. This often creates impossible ethical quandaries for defense counsel.

Criteria for admission to drug court must be transparent and fully disclosed. Currently, many courts have no official criteria or have stated criteria that are backward or counterintuitive. For example, many drug courts exclude all violent offenders, including defendants charged with domestic violence. Excluding domestic violence offenses leads to the odd result of "the domestic violence offender who gets drunk and beats his wife up checking with his probation officer once every six weeks" while nonviolent offenders are appearing regularly for status hearings, giving random weekly urine samples, and attending 90 meetings in 90 days.

In many courts, whether a defendant is permitted to enter drug court is up to the prosecutor. Prosecutors are frequently hesitant to allow higher risk offenders, even those who desperately need and want the treatment and supervision, into drug court out of fear that they will be blamed for participant failure or recidivism. [W]hen prosecutors serve as gatekeepers they face the political risk of "a headline waiting to happen."

To avoid politics improperly affecting access to drug court programs, prosecutors should not be able to determine access. Admission criteria should be drafted by a panel or commission with broad representation from stakeholders in the criminal justice community, including judges, prosecutors, defense counsel, and social service providers. Admission criteria should be broad, allowing those who need and want treatment access to the program.

Drug courts seek to impose a team concept on defense lawyers, creating difficult ethical dilemmas and virtually no role for private counsel. In many situations, the current structure of drug courts requires defense attorneys to set aside their ethical obligations to further the purpose and framework of the drug court. That must change. When counsel says nothing in representing the interests of clients, defense lawyers appear headed "to an old Soviet Union model where your job as a lawyer is simply to hold your client's hand as they go off to the gallows—here's what's going to happen next."

Protecting defendants' Sixth Amendment right to competent counsel requires a process that allows defense attorneys to satisfy their ethical obligations of loyalty, confidentiality, and zealous advocacy. Doing so will not dismantle the drug court process or its objectives; rather, it will enhance the credibility of the process with both the participants and anyone who observes the court.

Too often, the criteria and process for admission into drug court are guided largely by tough-on-crime politics, focusing on first-time or nonviolent offenders, with little consideration of smart-on-crime approaches that target those most in need of intensive treatment who would otherwise spend a long time in prison.

Courts frequently select those most likely to succeed to participate in drug court—a process called skimming. [W]hen they engage in skimming, the drug courts are "sucking up all the resources that the community has to deal with this very thorny issue of addiction, and ... using it on cream puffs." In fact, drug courts, with their program of intense supervision, should be utilized for high-risk offenders for whom everything else has failed. Courts should focus on those who are facing the longest sentences and most need treatment, "where we would get the biggest bang for our buck."

Other less intensive alternatives to drug courts must be developed for low-risk offenders, who perform better without intensive judicial intervention. Communities should not "invest all of their addiction resources into one program. You can't ignore the people who don't get into drug court who are drug- and alcohol-involved. They have the same needs, the same rights, and impose the same dangers as everyone else."

As the Sentencing Project's report above discusses, the available evidence appears to indicate that drug courts are generally a cost-effective alternative to traditional sentences for drug offenders. Even if criminal drug courts produce better results than traditional criminal sentences for drug offenders, however, this does not mean that other alternatives would not be even more cost-effective. The National Association of Criminal Defense Lawyers, for example, suggests "the decriminalization of all drugs as the best way to combat drug addiction and make effective use of criminal justice resources."

In 2001, Portugal decriminalized all drugs and developed a unique and innovative approach that might best be characterized as a civil drug court system. Under Portugal's law, it is not a crime to possess small amounts of drugs for personal use. Instead, possession of drugs for personal use is a "purely administrative violation[], to be processed in a noncriminal proceeding." Glenn Greenwald, *Drug Decriminalization in Portugal: Lessons for Creating Far and Successful Drug Policies*, The Cato Institute (2009). Under this administrative system, a person who is found in possession of a small amount of drugs is given a citation and required to appear before what the law calls a "Dissuasion Commission." Portugal's Dissuasion Commissions are typically comprised of two members with an addiction treatment or medical background and one member with a legal background. If the Commission members determine that the offender is not an addict, they will typically give him a warning. Addicts can be ordered into treatment, prohibited from associating with specific people, or banned from "visiting high-risk locales (nightclubs)," among other options. *Id.* Offenders who do not meet their obligations may be fined but—consistent with the administrative nature of the program—not imprisoned. Portugal's system is examined in more detail in Chapter 9, which explores international and comparative drug control.

G. Civil Sanctions and Controls

In addition to criminal punishment, drug-involved individuals face a wide range of civil sanctions and controls. Some civil penalties result as collateral consequences of a criminal conviction. Others are wholly independent of criminal prosecution.

1. Collateral Consequences of a Drug Conviction

a. An Overview of Collateral Consequences

"Collateral Damage": No Re-Entry for Drug Offenders
Nora V. Demleitner
47 Villanova Law Review 1027 (2002)

"Punishment" for many drug offenders continues once they are released from prison. They are usually subject to so-called "collateral consequences." Many of these are virtually unknown outside the criminal justice community, and of some consequences, even judges, prosecutors and criminal defense attorneys are unaware. Federal legislation creating collateral consequences for drug offenses is frequently not part of crime legislation; it passes into law without being debated in relevant congressional committees, including the judiciary committee.

The so-called "collateral consequences" are legally classified as civil rather than criminal sanctions. For that reason they can be imposed without the protections and guarantees of the criminal justice system. This is particularly troubling since many of these "consequences" deny drug offenders fundamental social, economic and political rights. They impact the lives of ex-offenders dramatically and often also deprive their families of crucial governmental support.

Collateral consequences are justified either on punitive, deterrent or preventive grounds. The last rationale applies less to drug offenders because most collateral consequences imposed on them are not based on a risk model. On the other hand, punitive and deterrent grounds have played a dominant role in the congressional discourse surrounding drug offenders. The denial of governmental benefits to drug offenders has been justified as a measure of "user accountability." Drug users, often considered to have made a rational choice, should be held accountable and will be held out as an example.

Collateral sanctions befall all types of offenders. Although the public considers murder, rape and kidnapping more serious offenses than drug possession or distribution, the collateral consequences imposed on drug offenders tend to be more severe than those imposed on murderers, rapists and kidnappers. Drug offenders suffer from them disproportionately because many collateral consequences target them specifically. Next to sex offenders, drug felons and drug misdemeanants have borne the brunt of civil sanctions. Within the last fifteen years, the panoply of civil sanctions applicable to them has increased dramatically.

The civil sanctions most devastating to offenders are those that deprive them of the ability to reintegrate successfully. Re-entry and rehabilitation assistance are particularly crucial to offenders with two sets of characteristics, which may overlap. First, those who have served long prison terms need substantial reintegration assistance. They have lost the ability to operate as individual agents in a less structured environment, and often have difficulty adjusting to a society and job market very different than the ones in existence when they went to prison. Because of the long sentences imposed on drug traffickers, especially in the federal system, many of them fall into this category. Second, offenders who suffer from insufficient education and job training will become likely recidivists unless they receive reintegration assistance. However, it is precisely these offenders that are frequently excluded from the social safety net and from access to training and education because of collateral sanctions.

Federal law allows for the denial of a whole set of federal benefits to drug offenders. The Denial of Federal Benefits Program of 1988 empowers federal and state courts to prohibit drug offenders from accessing a broad range of benefits, excluding food stamps and other survival-type subsidies. A first drug trafficking conviction can lead to the denial of benefits for up to five years; a second conviction doubles the maximum possible ineligibility period; a third conviction mandates the court bar such benefits permanently.

Denial of survival-type welfare benefits takes collateral sanctions a step further by making critical assistance, particularly necessary after release, inaccessible. Any drug offender convicted after August 22, 1996, becomes permanently ineligible for food stamps and temporary assistance to needy families, unless the state of residence opts out. So far, twenty-four states have adopted the ban, eighteen have modified it, and eight have opted out. Modifications usually center around temporal ineligibility limitations and treatment or recovery as eligibility grounds.

Federal housing policies allow for the exclusion of drug offenders from federally subsidized or funded housing. Drug-related activity alone may result in eviction from public housing. The denial of public housing, therefore, does not result directly from a drug conviction. However, in the vast majority of cases, drug-related activity will come to the attention of housing authorities because of a conviction record. Unless an offender can demonstrate that she receives treatment, she will be banned from public housing. The public housing agency may consider proof of rehabilitation prior to issuing an eviction notice.

In many cases, the existence of an illegal drug user in a household will cause the entire household to be evicted and barred from public housing. As interpreted by the Supreme Court, the statute does not allow for an innocent owner defense. Evictions are ultimately discretionary decisions of housing agencies based on the threat drug activity constitutes.

Because private landlords often do not want to rent to ex-offenders, many of these ex-offenders find themselves on the street unless family members who do not reside in public housing are able to take them in. This creates a vicious circle for the drug offender. The lack of access to food and housing makes it frequently impossible for offenders to gain employment, and the lack of employment prevents access to food and housing.

Congress and the states have made it more difficult for ex-offenders to receive education and find employment after a drug conviction. Many of these provisions may not have been designed to limit an offender's employability, but rather were passed for punitive reasons. Only some are based on an assessment of the risk of re-offending. Nevertheless, the effect on employment is palpable while most of the restrictions are unlikely to impact public safety because they are drawn too broadly to accomplish that goal.

Some collateral consequences indirectly affect the employability of ex-offenders because they make it impossible for them to fulfill basic job requirements. [C]ongressional legislation demands the revocation or suspension of drivers' licenses for at least six months for persons convicted of drug felonies. Despite the lack of an apparent connection between drug felonies and the use of motor vehicles, Congress mandated the loss of this "privilege" as a punitive sanction. A state can avoid the imposition of this provision without penalty only if the state legislature and governor jointly express their opposition to the legislation. Unexplained non-compliance will lead to the loss of 10% of the state's highway funding.

Felony convictions lead to the automatic revocation of and bar on a wide variety of federal and state licenses. The denial of state employment licenses to felons has a long history. Throughout the 1980s many states restricted the employment opportunities of parolees and ex-offenders even further, largely to symbolize their sincerity in the "war" on crime. California, for example, prohibits parolees from working in real estate, nursing or physical therapy. Loss of such licenses means loss of employment, and in some cases a long-term, if not permanent, bar on re-employment in a profession in which the offender may have acquired certain skills and abilities. The same applies to public employment.

Federal restrictions on certain governmental programs and contracts also impact the employability of ex-offenders directly. Many of these bars, even those imposed by regulatory agencies, are virtually automatic. Drug offenders, especially, will find it difficult to obtain waivers of such bars and reinstatement of necessary licenses.

Even more problematic than the denial of specific employment opportunities are restrictions on training and education for drug offenders. Under the 1988 Denial of Federal Benefits Program, convicted drug offenders may be denied access to government benefits, including funds to finance education and job training, upon conviction. While the bar is discretionary and the decision rests with the sentencing judge in cases of first convictions, it becomes mandatory when the offender faces his third conviction for drug sales.

Education grants, loans and work assistance are now being denied automatically to all those convicted of any drug offense—a felony or misdemeanor, trafficking, or simple possession. The length of such denial depends on the number and type of convictions. One conviction for drug possession triggers a one-year denial; two convictions lead to a two-year ineligibility period; three or more convictions make the ban permanent. For drug sales, a first conviction means a two-year ban; any subsequent conviction leads to a permanent denial of aid. Only a showing of drug rehabilitation can end an indefinite loss. The denial of aid does not affect individuals convicted of offenses other than drug crimes.

Lack of an education and of marketable skills combined with the stigma of a criminal conviction make it difficult for many ex-offenders to find employment. "One year after release, as many as sixty percent of former inmates are not employed in the legitimate labor market." How much of the difficulty in finding employment can be attributed to collateral sanctions is unclear. However, they effectively close a large number of employment opportunities, skilled and unskilled, to ex-offenders, and have made it more difficult for them to get additional skills training.

Some of the most dramatic sanctions that can befall a drug offender are immigration-related. Non-U.S. citizens are inadmissible if they admit to having committed or have been convicted of a drug-related offense. Federal law also allows the immigration service to deny admission to suspected drug traffickers and their family members, even if they are not criminally convicted.

Criminal convictions make non-citizens who are in the United States removable, even if they hold permanent residency status. Any conviction of a drug offense, other than possession of thirty grams or less of marijuana for one's own use, leads to deportation. Drug users and addicts are also deportable. Since under current law a conviction for drug trafficking constitutes an "aggravated felony," the offender is disqualified from relief from removal because he cannot establish "good moral character." Two misdemeanor drug possession convictions will be treated as "aggravated felonies" which make the non-citizen automatically deportable, irrespective of his or her background.

For new permanent residents the law is even less forgiving. A single drug possession conviction can lead to mandatory deportation even if the criminal court assessed only a probationary sentence. [L]ong-term permanent resident aliens who have led law-abiding lives for many years following a minor drug conviction may also be deported to their countries of citizenship. Unless personal, familial or societal considerations weigh in favor of keeping the ex-offender in the United States, deportation will occur, even though the ex-offender may have only very limited ties or no connection to his country of citizenship.

The denial of economic, social and political benefits and rights at best delays the reintegration of ex-drug offenders into society. At worst, it leads them back to prison. The difficulties these ex-offenders face also affect their families and communities negatively, often because they create greater instability, anomie and ultimately higher crime rates.

Civil sanctions turn all offenders, especially poor, female and minority offenders, their families and their communities, into "collateral damage. For drug offenders, collateral consequences come on top of already long prison sentences and often amount to a virtual life sentence. These restrictions frequently lead to re-offending and ultimately re-imprisonment.

Arguments of "user accountability" and deterrence traditionally supported collateral consequences. They, nevertheless, impact predominantly the worst off by denying them assistance upon release from prison and creating significant obstacles to their reintegration.

The denial of basic rights affects not only the offender and her family, but also her community. Many communities to which drug offenders return suffer disproportionately from lack of cohesion, unemployment, homelessness and family instability. By increasing the number of obstacles facing ex-offenders, their chances of succeeding in this environment are further reduced, with detrimental consequences for these communities.

b. Public Housing

Department of Housing and Urban Development v. Rucker

Supreme Court of the United States
535 U.S. 125 (2002)

Chief Justice Rehnquist delivered the opinion of the Court.

With drug dealers "increasingly imposing a reign of terror on public and other federally assisted low-income housing tenants," Congress passed the Anti-Drug Abuse Act of 1988. The Act, as later amended, provides that each "public housing agency shall utilize leases which ... provide that any criminal activity that threatens the health, safety, or right to peaceful enjoyment of the premises by other tenants or any drug-related criminal activity on or off such premises, engaged in by a public housing tenant, any member of the tenant's household, or any guest or other person under the tenant's control, shall be cause for termination of tenancy." 42 U.S.C. § 1437d (l)(6). Petitioners say that this statute requires lease terms that allow a local public housing authority to evict a tenant when a member of the tenant's household or a guest engages in drug-related criminal activity, regardless of whether the tenant knew, or had reason to know, of that activity. Respondents say it does not. We agree with petitioners.

Respondents are four public housing tenants of the Oakland Housing Authority (OHA). Paragraph 9(m) of respondents' leases, tracking the language of § 1437d(l)(6), obligates the tenants to "assure that the tenant, any member of the household, a guest, or another person under the tenant's control, shall not engage in ... any drug-related criminal activity on or near the premises." Respondents also signed an agreement stating that the tenant "understands that if I or any member of my household or guests should violate this lease provision, my tenancy may be terminated and I may be evicted."

In late 1997 and early 1998, OHA instituted eviction proceedings in state court against respondents, alleging violations of this lease provision. The complaint alleged: (1) that the respective grandsons of respondents William Lee and Barbara Hill, both of whom were listed as residents on the leases, were caught in the apartment complex parking lot smoking marijuana; (2) that the daughter of respondent Pearlie Rucker, who resides with her and is listed on the lease as a resident, was found with cocaine and a crack cocaine pipe three blocks from Rucker's apartment; and (3) that on three instances within a 2-month period, respondent Herman Walker's caregiver and two others were found with cocaine in Walker's apartment. OHA had issued Walker notices of a lease violation on the first two occasions, before initiating the eviction action after the third violation.

United States Department of Housing and Urban Development (HUD) regulations administering § 1437d(l)(6) require lease terms authorizing evictions in these circumstances. The HUD regulations closely track the statutory language, and provide that "in deciding to evict for criminal activity, the [public housing authority] shall have discretion to consider all of the circumstances of the case...." 24 CFR § 966.4(l)(5)(i) (2001). The agency made clear that local public housing authorities' discretion to evict for drug-related activity includes those situations in which "[the] tenant did not know, could not foresee, or could not control behavior by other occupants of the unit."

After OHA initiated the eviction proceedings in state court, respondents commenced actions against HUD, OHA, and OHA's director in United States District Court. They challenged HUD's interpretation of the statute under the Administrative Procedure Act, 5 U.S.C. § 706(2)(A), arguing that 42 U.S.C. § 1437d(l)(6) does not require lease terms authorizing the eviction of so-called "innocent" tenants, and, in the alternative, that if it does, then the statute is unconstitutional. The District Court issued a preliminary injunction, enjoining OHA from "terminating the leases of tenants pursuant to paragraph 9(m) of the 'Tenant Lease' for drug-related criminal activity that does not occur within the tenant's apartment unit when the tenant did not know of and had no reason to know of, the drug-related criminal activity."

A panel of the Court of Appeals reversed, holding that § 1437d(l)(6) unambiguously permits the eviction of tenants who violate the lease provision, regardless of whether the tenant was personally aware of the drug activity, and that the statute is constitutional. An en banc panel of the Court of Appeals reversed and affirmed the District Court's grant of the preliminary injunction. That court held that HUD's interpretation permitting the eviction of so-called "innocent" tenants "is inconsistent with Congressional intent and must be rejected" under the first step of *Chevron U.S.A. Inc. v. Natural Resources Defense Council, Inc.,* 467 U.S. 837, 842–843 (1984).

We granted certiorari and now reverse, holding that 42 U.S.C. § 1437d(l)(6) unambiguously requires lease terms that vest local public housing authorities with the discretion to evict tenants for the drug-related activity of household members and guests whether or not the tenant knew, or should have known, about the activity.

That this is so seems evident from the plain language of the statute. It provides that "each public housing authority shall utilize leases which ... provide that ... any drug-related criminal activity on or off such premises, engaged in by a public housing tenant, any member of the tenant's household, or any guest or other person under the tenant's control, shall be cause for termination of tenancy." 42 U.S.C. § 1437d(l)(6). The en banc Court of Appeals thought the statute did not address "the level of personal knowledge or fault that is required for eviction." Yet Congress' decision not to impose any qualification in the statute, combined with its use of the term "any" to modify "drug-related criminal activity," precludes any knowledge requirement. As we have explained, "the word 'any' has an expansive meaning, that is, 'one or some indiscriminately of whatever kind.'" Thus, *any* drug-related activity engaged in by the specified persons is grounds for termination, not just drug-related activity that the tenant knew, or should have known, about.

The en banc Court of Appeals also thought it possible that "under the tenant's control" modifies not just "other person," but also "member of the tenant's household" and "guest." The court ultimately adopted this reading, concluding that the statute prohibits eviction where the tenant "for a lack of knowledge or other reason, could not realistically exercise control over the conduct of a household member or guest." But this interpretation runs counter to basic rules of grammar. The disjunctive "or" means that the qualification applies only to "other person." Indeed, the view that "under the tenant's control" modifies everything coming before it in the sentence would result in the nonsensical reading that the statute applies to "a public housing tenant ... under the tenant's control." HUD offers a convincing explanation for the grammatical imperative that "under the tenant's control" modifies only "other person": "by 'control,' the statute means control in the sense that the tenant has permitted access to the premises." Implicit in the terms "household member" or "guest" is that access to the premises has been granted by the tenant. Thus, the plain language of § 1437d(l)(6) requires leases that grant public housing authorities the discretion to terminate tenancy without regard to the tenant's knowledge of the drug-related criminal activity.

Comparing § 1437d(l)(6) to a related statutory provision reinforces the unambiguous text. The civil forfeiture statute that makes all leasehold interests subject to forfeiture when used to commit drug-related criminal activities expressly exempts tenants who had no knowledge of the activity: "No property shall be forfeited under this paragraph ... by reason of any act or omission established by that owner to have been committed or omitted without the knowledge or consent of the owner." 21 U.S.C. § 881(a)(7). Because this forfeiture provision was amended in the same Anti-Drug Abuse Act of 1988 that created 42 U.S.C. § 1437d(l)(6), the en banc Court of Appeals thought Congress "meant them to be read consistently" so that the knowledge requirement should be read into the eviction provision. But the two sections deal with distinctly different matters. The "innocent owner" defense for drug forfeiture cases was already in existence prior to 1988 as part of 21 U.S.C. § 881(a)(7). All that Congress did in the 1988 Act was to add leasehold interests to the property interests that might be forfeited under the drug statute. And if such a forfeiture action were to be brought against a leasehold interest, it would be subject to the pre-existing "innocent owner" defense. But 42 U.S.C. § 1437(d)(1)(6), with which we deal here, is a quite different measure. It is entirely reasonable to think that the Government, when seeking to transfer private property to itself in a forfeiture proceeding, should be subject to an "innocent owner defense," while it should not be when acting as a landlord in a public housing project. The forfeiture provision shows that Congress knew exactly how to provide an "innocent owner" defense. It did not provide one in § 1437d(l)(6).

The en banc Court of Appeals next resorted to legislative history. The Court of Appeals correctly recognized that reference to legislative history is inappropriate when the text of the statute is unambiguous. Given that the en banc Court of Appeals' finding of textual ambiguity is wrong there is no need to consult legislative history.

Nor was the en banc Court of Appeals correct in concluding that this plain reading of the statute leads to absurd results. The statute does not *require* the eviction of any tenant who violated the lease provision. Instead, it entrusts that decision to the local public housing authorities, who are in the best position to take account of, among other things, the degree to which the housing project suffers from "rampant drug-related or violent crime," "the seriousness of the offending action," and "the extent to which the leaseholder has ... taken all reasonable steps to prevent or mitigate the offending action[.]" It is not "absurd" that a local housing authority may sometimes evict a tenant who had no knowledge of the drug-related activity. Such "no-fault" eviction is a common "incident of tenant responsibility under normal landlord-tenant law and practice." Strict liability maximizes deterrence and eases enforcement difficulties.

And, of course, there is an obvious reason why Congress would have permitted local public housing authorities to conduct no-fault evictions: Regardless of knowledge, a tenant who "cannot control drug crime, or other criminal activities by a household member which threaten health or safety of other residents, is a threat to other residents and the project." With drugs leading to "murders, muggings, and other forms of violence against tenants," and to the "deterioration of the physical environment that requires substantial governmental expenditures," it was reasonable for Congress to permit no-fault evictions in order to "provide public and other federally assisted low-income housing that is decent, safe, and free from illegal drugs[.]"

In another effort to avoid the plain meaning of the statute, the en banc Court of Appeals invoked the canon of constitutional avoidance. But that canon "has no application in the absence of statutory ambiguity." There are, moreover, no "serious constitutional doubts" about Congress' affording local public housing authorities the discretion to conduct no-fault evictions for drug-related crime.

The en banc Court of Appeals held that HUD's interpretation "raises serious questions under the Due Process Clause of the Fourteenth Amendment," because it permits "tenants to be deprived of their property interest without any relationship to individual wrongdoing." 237 F.3d at 1124–1125 (citing *Scales v. United States*, 367 U.S. 203, 224–225 (1961); *Southwestern Telegraph & Telephone Co. v. Danaher*, 238 U.S. 482 (1915)). But both of these cases deal with the acts of government as sovereign. In *Scales*, the United States criminally charged the defendant with knowing membership in an organization that advocated the overthrow of the United States Government. In *Danaher*, an Arkansas statute forbade discrimination among customers of a telephone company. The situation in the present cases is entirely different. The government is not attempting to criminally punish or civilly regulate respondents as members of the general populace. It is instead acting as a landlord of property that it owns, invoking a clause in a lease to which respondents have agreed and which Congress has expressly required. *Scales* and *Danaher* cast no constitutional doubt on such actions.

The Court of Appeals sought to bolster its discussion of constitutional doubt by pointing to the fact that respondents have a property interest in their leasehold interest, citing *Greene v. Lindsey*, 456 U.S. 444 (1982). This is undoubtedly true, and *Greene* held that an effort to deprive a tenant of such a right without proper notice violated the Due Process Clause of the Fourteenth Amendment. But, in the present cases, such deprivation will occur in the state court where OHA brought the unlawful detainer action against respondents. There is no indication that notice has not been given by OHA in the past, or that it will not be given in the future. Any individual factual disputes about whether the lease provision was actually violated can, of course, be resolved in these proceedings.

We hold that "Congress has directly spoken to the precise question at issue." *Chevron U.S.A. Inc. v. Natural Resources Defense Council, Inc.*, 467 U.S. at 842. Section 1437d(l)(6) requires lease terms that give local public housing authorities the discretion to terminate the lease of a tenant when a member of the household or a guest engages in drug-related activity, regardless of whether the tenant knew, or should have known, of the drug-related activity.

Accordingly, the judgment of the Court of Appeals is reversed, and the cases are remanded for further proceedings consistent with this opinion.

It is so ordered.

2. Asset Forfeiture

The Forfeiture Racket
Radley Balko
Reason Magazine, February 2010

Around 3 in the morning on January 7, 2009, a 22-year-old college student named Anthony Smelley was pulled over on Interstate 70 in Putnam County, Indiana. He and two friends were en route from Detroit to visit Smelley's aunt in St. Louis. Smelley, who had recently received a $50,000 settlement from a car accident, was carrying around $17,500 in cash, according to later court documents. He claims he was bringing the money to buy a new car for his aunt.

The officer who pulled him over, Lt. Dwight Simmons of the Putnam County Sheriff's Department, said that Smelley had made an unsafe lane change and was driving with an obscured license plate. When Simmons asked for a driver's license, Smelley told him he had lost it after the accident. Simmons called in Smelley's name and discovered that his license had actually expired. The policeman asked Smelley to come out of the car, patted him down, and discovered a large roll of cash in his front pocket, in direct contradiction to Smelley's alleged statement in initial questioning that he wasn't, in fact, carrying much money.

A record check indicated that Smelley had previously been arrested (though not charged) for drug possession as a teenager, so the officer called in a K-9 unit to sniff the car for drugs. According to the police report, the dog gave two indications that narcotics might be present. So Smelley and his passengers were detained and the police seized Smelley's $17,500 cash under Indiana's asset forfeiture law.

But a subsequent hand search of the car turned up nothing except an empty glass pipe containing no drug residue in the purse of Smelley's girlfriend. Lacking any other evidence, police never charged anybody in the car with a drug-related crime. Yet not only did Putnam County continue to hold onto Smelley's money, but the authorities initiated legal proceedings to confiscate it permanently.

Smelley's case was no isolated incident. Over the past three decades, it has become routine in the United States for state, local, and federal governments to seize the property of people who were never even charged with, much less convicted of, a crime. Nearly every year, according to Justice Department statistics, the federal government sets new records for asset forfeiture. And under many state laws, the situation is even worse: State officials can seize property without a warrant and need only show "probable cause" that the booty was connected to a drug crime in order to keep it, as opposed to the criminal standard of proof "beyond a reasonable doubt." Instead of being innocent until proven guilty, owners of seized property all too often have a heavier burden of proof than the government officials who stole their stuff.

Municipalities have come to rely on confiscated property for revenue. Police and prosecutors use forfeiture proceeds to fund not only general operations but junkets, parties, and swank office equipment. A cottage industry has sprung up to offer law enforcement agencies instruction on how to take and keep property more efficiently.

Technically, civil asset forfeiture proceedings are brought against the property itself, not the owner. Hence they often have odd case titles, such as *U.S. v. Eight Thousand Eight Hundred and Fifty Dollars* or *U.S. v. One 1987 Jeep Wrangler*. The government need only demonstrate that the seized property is somehow related to a crime, generally either by showing that it was used in the commission of the act (as with a car driven to and from a drug transaction, or a house from which drugs are sold) or that it was purchased with the proceeds.

Because the property itself is on trial, the owner has the status of a third-party claimant. Once the government has shown probable cause of a property's "guilt," the onus is on the owner to prove his innocence. The parents of a drug-dealing teenager, for instance, would have to show they had no knowledge the kid was using the family car to facilitate drug transactions. Homeowners have to show they were unaware that a resident was keeping drugs on the premises. Anyone holding cash in close proximity to illicit drugs may have to document that he earned the money legitimately.

Federal asset forfeiture law dates back to the Racketeer Influenced and Corrupt Organizations (RICO) Act of 1970, a law aimed at seizing profits earned by organized crime. In 1978 Congress broadened RICO to include drug violations. But it was the Comprehensive Crime Control Act of 1984 that made forfeiture the lucrative, widely used law enforcement tool it is today.

"The Crime Control Act did a few things," says the Virginia-based defense attorney David Smith, author of the legal treatise *Prosecution and Defense of Forfeiture Cases.* "First, it corrected some poor drafting in the earlier laws. Second, it created two federal forfeiture funds, one in the Justice Department and one in the Treasury. And most important, it included an earmarking provision that gave forfeiture proceeds back to local law enforcement agencies that helped in a federal forfeiture."

This last bit was key. "The thinking was that this would motivate police agencies to use the forfeiture provisions," Smith says. "They were right. It also basically made law enforcement an interest group. They directly benefited from the law. Since it was passed, they've fought hard to keep it and strengthen it."

The 1984 law lowered the bar for civil forfeiture. To seize property, the government had only to show probable cause to believe that it was connected to drug activity, or the same standard cops use to obtain search warrants. The state was allowed to use hearsay evidence — meaning a federal agent could testify that a drug informant told him a car or home was used in a drug transaction — but property owners were barred from using hearsay, and couldn't even cross-examine some of the government's witnesses. Informants, while being protected from scrutiny, were incentivized monetarily: According to the law, snitches could receive as much as one-quarter of the bounty, up to $50,000 per case.

According to a 1992 Cato Institute study examining the early results of the Comprehensive Crime Control Act, total federal forfeiture revenues increased by 1,500 percent between 1985 and 1991. The Justice Department's forfeiture fund (which doesn't include forfeitures from customs agents) jumped from $27 million in 1985 to $644 million in 1991; by 1996 it crossed the $1 billion line, and as of 2008 assets had increased to $3.1 billion. According to the government's own data, less than 20 percent of federal seizures involved property whose owners were ever prosecuted.

More than 80 percent of federal seizures are never challenged in court, according to Smith. To supporters of forfeiture, this statistic is an indication of the owners' guilt, but opponents argue it simply reflects the fact that in many cases the property was worth less than the legal costs of trying to get it back. Under the 1984 law, forfeiture defendants can't be provided with a court-appointed attorney, meaning an innocent property owner without significant means would have to find a lawyer willing to take his case for free or in exchange for a portion of the property should he succeed in winning it back. And to even get a day in court, owners were forced to post a bond equal to 10 percent of the value of their seized property.

The average Drug Enforcement Administration (DEA) property seizure in 1998 was worth about $25,000. In 2000 a Justice Department source told the PBS series *Frontline* that this figure was also the cutoff under which most forfeiture attorneys advised clients that their cases wouldn't be worth pursuing. So a law aimed at denying drug kingpins their ill-gotten millions ended up affecting mostly those with so little loot it didn't even make sense to hire an attorney to win it back.

Police gradually came to view asset forfeiture as not just a way to minimize drug profits, or even to fill their own coffers, but as a tool to enforce maximum compliance on non-criminals. In one highly publicized example from the 1990s, Jason Brice nearly lost the motel he had bought and renovated in a high-crime area of Houston. At the request of local authorities, Brice hired private security, allowed police to patrol his property (at some cost to his business), and spent tens of thousands of dollars in other measures to prevent drug activity on the premises. But when local police asked Brice to raise his rates to deter criminals, he refused, saying it would put him out of business. Stepped up police harassment of his customers caused Brice to eventually terminate the agreement that had allowed them latitude on his property. In less than a month, local and federal officials tried to seize Brice's motel on the grounds that he was aware of drug dealing taking place there. Brice eventually won, but only after an expensive, drawn-out legal battle.

By the late 1990s, stories such as Brice's finally moved Congress to act. After a series of emotional hearings in 2000, Congress passed the Civil Asset Forfeiture Reform Act (CAFRA), authored by Rep. Henry Hyde (R-Ill.). The bill raised the federal government's burden of proof in forfeiture cases from probable cause to a preponderance of the evidence, the same standard as in other civil cases. It barred the government from using hearsay and allowed owners who won forfeiture challenges to obtain reimbursement for legal expenses.

The bill wasn't perfect. Seizures made by customs agents, as opposed to the DEA or FBI, would still be governed by the old rules. Hyde (who died in 2007) wanted an even heavier burden of proof for the government, the "beyond a reasonable doubt" standard used in criminal cases. That didn't pass. Under CAFRA, the federal government could still take your property without proving beyond a reasonable doubt that *any* crime was committed, much less that you yourself had committed one. But at least the reforms made the process a bit more difficult.

Problem was, the 1984 law had already spawned dozens of imitators on the state level, and CAFRA applied only to the feds. Forfeiture had been sending money to police departments and prosecutors' offices for 16 years, so even in the few states that passed laws to make the process more fair, officials found ways around them. Once the authorities have a license to steal, it turns out to be very difficult to revoke.

A survey of state and federal forfeiture since 2000 shows that CAFRA hasn't stopped the exponential growth of government asset seizure. Adjusted for inflation, the Justice Department's asset forfeiture fund, which includes proceeds from forfeitures carried out by all federal agencies except Immigration and Customs Enforcement, grew from $1.3 billion in 2001 to $3.1 billion in 2008. (The total includes some money left over from previous years, but according to Smith, almost all of the money is doled out to local and federal agencies on an annual basis.) National Public Radio has reported that between 2003 and 2007, the amount of money seized by local law enforcement agencies enrolled in the federal forfeiture program tripled from $567 million to $1.6 billion. That doesn't include property seized by local law enforcement agencies without involving federal authorities.

In addition to raising questions of fairness, forfeiture has warped the priorities of law enforcement agencies. In 2008 the Bureau of Alcohol, Tobacco, Firearms, and Explosives asked for bids from private contractors on 2,000 Leatherman pocket knives for its agents, to be inscribed with the phrase "Always Think Forfeiture," a play on the agency's traditional "ATF" initials. The agency rescinded the order after it was reported in the *Idaho Statesman*, but critics said it betrayed the ethic of an organization more interested in taking people's property than in fighting crime.

Some police agencies come to view forfeiture not just as an occasional windfall for buying guns, police cars, or better equipment, but as a source of funding for basic operations. This is especially true with multijurisdictional drug task forces, some of which have become financially independent of the states, counties, and cities in which they operate, thanks to forfeiture and federal anti-drug grants.

In a 2001 study published in the *Journal of Criminal Justice*, the University of Texas at Dallas criminologist John Worral surveyed 1,400 police departments around the country on their use of forfeiture and the way they incorporated seized assets into their budgets. Worral, who describes himself as agnostic on the issue, concluded that "a substantial proportion of law enforcement agencies are dependent on civil asset forfeiture" and that "forfeiture is coming to be viewed not only as a budgetary supplement, but as a necessary source of income." Almost half of surveyed police departments with more than 100 law enforcement personnel said forfeiture proceeds were "necessary as a budget supplement" for department operations.

Such widespread use of forfeiture has created an industry of facilitators. Organizations such as the International Association for Asset Recovery sponsor conferences where law enforcement officials learn how to maximize their asset-seizing potential. They also offer certifications in forfeiture expertise. Advertising a Florida conference on its website in 2009, an outfit called Asset Recovery Watch (slogan: "Make the bad guys pay!") assures budget-conscious police departments that federal law permits them to use forfeiture funds to send police officers away to forfeiture conferences for training.

Forfeiture may also undermine actual enforcement of the law. In a 1994 study reported in *Justice Quarterly*, criminologists J. Mitchell Miller and Lance H. Selva observed several police agencies that identified drug supplies but delayed making busts to maximize the cash they could seize, since seized cash is more lucrative for police departments than seized drugs. This strategy allowed untold amounts of illicit drugs to be sold and moved into the streets, contrary to the official aims of drug enforcement.

In other states, the problem isn't so much the strict provisions on the books, but rather the relevant law's ambiguity, which can give police and prosecutors too much leeway. Tiny Tenaha, Texas, population 1,046, made national news in 2008 after a series of reports alleged that the town's police force was targeting black and Latino motorists along Highway 84, a busy regional artery that connects Houston to Louisiana's casinos, ensuring a reliable harvest of cash-heavy motorists. The *Chicago Tribune* reported that in just the three years between 2006 and 2008, Tenaha police stopped 140 drivers and asked them to sign waivers agreeing to hand over their cash, cars, jewelry, and other property to avoid arrest and prosecution on drug charges. If the drivers agreed, police took their property and waved them down the highway. If they refused, even innocent motorists faced months of legal hassles and thousands of dollars in attorney fees, usually amounting to far more than the value of the amount seized. One local attorney found court records of 200 cases in which Tenaha police had seized assets from drivers; only 50 were ever criminally charged.

National Public Radio reported in 2008 that in Kingsville, Texas, a town of 25,000, "Police officers drive high-performance Dodge Chargers and use $40,000 digital ticket writers. They'll soon carry military-style assault rifles, and the SWAT team recently acquired sniper rifles." All this equipment was funded with proceeds from highway forfeitures.

Texas prosecutors benefited too. Former Kimble County, Texas, District Attorney Ron Sutton used forfeiture money to pay the travel expenses for him and 198th District Judge Emil Karl Pohl to attend a conference in Hawaii. It was OK, the prosecutor told NPR, because Pohl approved the trip. (The judge later resigned over the incident.) Shelby County, Texas, District Attorney Lynda Kay Russell, whose district includes Tenaha, used forfeiture money to pay for tickets to a motorcycle rally and a Christmas parade. Russell is also attempting to use money from the forfeiture fund to pay for her defense against a civil rights lawsuit brought by several motorists whose property she helped take. In 2005, the district attorney in Montgomery County, Texas, had to admit that his office spent forfeiture money on an office margarita machine. The purchase got attention when the office won first place in a margarita competition at the county fair.

Not every state has kept its old laws intact. Kessler, the New York attorney and forfeiture expert, says 27 states have adopted CAFRA-style reforms. Some go even further, requiring that the proceeds from forfeited property go directly to the state general fund or to a fund earmarked for a specific purpose, such as education.

But here, too, things aren't always as they seem. In Missouri, for example, forfeited property is supposed to go to the state's public schools. But in 1999 a series of reports in *The Kansas City Star* showed how Missouri police agencies were circumventing state law. After seizing property, local police departments would turn it over to the DEA or another federal agency. Under federal law, the federal agency can keep 20 percent or more of the money; the rest, up to 80 percent, goes back to the local police department that conducted the investigation. None of the money in these cases goes to the schools.

The *Kansas City Star* investigation made national news at the time, but Kessler says the practice of circumventing earmarking through federal "adoption" is now common all over the country. "It happens a lot," he says. "It clearly goes against the intent of the state legislatures that passed these laws, but I don't know of any state that has made a serious effort to prevent it from happening."

As for Anthony Smelley: As of this writing, more than a year after the police took $17,500 of his money, he has yet to have his day in court.

Policing for Profit: The Drug War's Hidden Economic Agenda
Eric Blumenson and Eva Nilsen
65 University of Chicago Law Review 35 (1998)

The forfeiture laws were designed to combat drug crime by attacking the economic viability of drug trafficking enterprises, and they continue to be billed as the weapon of choice in the Drug War. The Director of the Department of Justice's forfeiture unit testified to a congressional subcommittee that "asset forfeiture can be to modern law enforcement what air power is to modern warfare." But in fact the aggressive use of forfeiture laws in the last decade has never produced this intended benefit. The $730 million in 1994 federal forfeitures was surely inadequate to stifle a $50 billion drug trade, although it was more than enough to reward police and government officials for their efforts.

What forfeiture does do well is raise money. Police and prosecutors argue that 21 USC § 881 enables them to carry out ordinary law enforcement business and raise money at the same time—to do well by doing good. Unfortunately, the real impact of forfeiture has not been so benign. In practice, forfeiture laws have not simply enhanced the ability of law enforcement to do its job, but rather have changed the nature of the job itself. Both the crime prevention and due process goals of our criminal justice system are compromised when salaries, continued tenure, equipment, modernization, and departmental budgets depend on how much money can be generated by forfeitures.

The most intuitively obvious problem presented by the forfeiture and equitable sharing laws is the conflict of interest created when law enforcement agencies are authorized to keep the assets they seize. It takes no special sophistication to recognize that this incentive constitutes a compelling invitation to police departments to stray from legitimate law enforcement goals in order to maximize funding for their operations.

Consider first police investigations. The shift in law enforcement priorities, from crime control to funding raids, is perhaps best revealed by the advent of the "reverse sting," a now common police tactic that rarely was used before the law began channeling forfeited assets to those who seized them. The reverse sting is an apparently lawful version of police drug dealing in which police pose as dealers and sell drugs to an unwitting buyer. The chief attraction of the reverse sting is that it allows police to seize a buyer's cash rather than a seller's drugs (which have no legal value to the seizing agency). According to one reverse-sting participant, "This strategy was preferred by every agency and department with which I was associated because it allowed agents to gauge potential profit before investing a great deal of time and effort. [Reverse stings] occurred so regularly that the term reverse became synonymous with the word deal." Whether the suspects were engaged in major or trivial drug activity, and whether the strategy actually placed more drugs on the street, were of little, if any, importance. Even if a sting targeted a drug dealer, the police might defer the operation until the dealer sold some of the drugs to other buyers in order to make the seizure incident to arrest more profitable. Alternatively, law enforcement agencies might select their targets according to the funding they could provide rather than the threat they posed to the community. A Department of Justice report proposed precisely this approach to multijurisdictional task force commanders, suggesting that as asset seizures become more important, "it will be useful for task force members to know the major sources of these assets and whether it is more efficient to target major dealers or numerous smaller ones."

A similar motivation may underlie the otherwise baffling policy adopted in 1986 by both the New York City and Washington, D.C. police departments. Invoking 21 USC § 881(a)(4), the policy directed police to seize the cash and cars of persons coming into the city to buy drugs. The consequence of this strategy was that the drugs that would have been purchased continued to circulate freely. Patrick Murphy, formerly the Police Commissioner of New York City, explained the origin of this policy to Congress. Police, he said, have "a financial incentive to impose roadblocks on the southbound lanes of I-95, which carry the cash to make drug buys, rather than the northbound lanes, which carry the drugs. After all, seized cash will end up forfeited to the police department, while seized drugs can only be destroyed."

Consider also forfeiture's corrupting influence on the disposition of criminal cases. Ironically, as the Drug War was escalating during the 1980s and 1990s, major efforts were underway to remove corrupt influences and unjust disparities from criminal sentences. The federal government and many states sought to accomplish this by rewriting their sentencing laws to specify the sentence that fit each crime and the criminal history of each offender. But these sentencing reform laws have been largely undone in the drug area. Forfeiture laws promote unfair, disparate sentences by providing an avenue for affluent drug "kingpins" to buy their freedom. This is one reason why state and federal prisons now confine large numbers of men and women who had relatively minor roles in drug distribution networks, but few of their bosses.

As investigations in several jurisdictions have documented, criminal defendants with the most assets to forfeit routinely serve shorter prison sentences and sometimes no prison sentence at all. In New Jersey, for example, a defendant facing a "drug kingpin" indictment (twenty-five years to life) obtained a dismissal of that charge and parole eligibility in five years on a lesser conviction, by agreeing to forfeit over $1 million in assets. In Massachusetts, a recent investigation by journalists found that on average a "payment of $50,000 in drug profits won a 6.3 year reduction in a sentence for dealers," while agreements to forfeit $10,000 or more bought elimination or reduction of trafficking charges in almost three-fourths of such cases. The Massachusetts prosecutors who were investigated have a compelling reason to recalibrate the scales of justice in this way because 12 percent of their budgets are financed through forfeiture income. And the Supreme Court has facilitated this practice by finding no right to a judicial inquiry as to whether property relinquished pursuant to a guilty plea is properly subject to forfeiture. As Justice Stevens noted in dissent, "it is not unthinkable that a wealthy defendant might bargain for a light sentence by voluntarily 'forfeiting' property to which the Government had no statutory entitlement." But these distorted, disparate plea offers remain untested under the due process right to an impartial prosecutor, and the most hopeful challenge may come from the asset-poor defendants who suffer the most in plea bargaining from the government's conflict of interest.

To illustrate the extent of a suspect's stake in uncorrupted law enforcement, we present a final example: the enlightening and appalling case of Donald Scott. Scott was a sixty-one year-old wealthy recluse who owned a two hundred acre ranch in Malibu, California adjacent to a large recreational area maintained by the National Park Service. In 1992, the Los Angeles County Sheriff's Department ("LASD") received an informant's report that Scott was growing several thousand marijuana plants on his land. The LASD assembled a team—including agents from the Los Angeles Police Department, the DEA, the Forest Service, the California Air National Guard, the Border Patrol, and the California Bureau of Narcotic Enforcement—to investigate the tip, largely through the use of air and ground surveillance missions. Despite several unsuccessful efforts to corroborate the informant's claim, and despite advice that Scott posed little threat of violence, the LASD dispatched a multijurisdictional team of thirty law enforcement officers to conduct a military-style raid. On October 2, 1992 at 8:30 am, the officers descended upon the Scott ranch to execute their search warrant. After knocking and announcing their presence, they kicked in the door and rushed through the house. There they saw Scott, armed with a gun in response to his wife's screams. With Scott's wife watching in horror, they shot and killed him. There were no marijuana plants anywhere on the land, and no drugs or paraphernalia in the house.

Following Scott's death, the Ventura County District Attorney's Office conducted a five-month investigation of the raid. The seventy-page report found no credible evidence of present or past marijuana cultivation on Donald Scott's property. As for the search warrant, the report found that much of the information supporting the warrant was false, that exculpatory surveillance evidence was withheld from the judge, and that the LASD knowingly sought the warrant on legally insufficient information. The search warrant "became Donald Scott's death warrant," the report concluded, and Scott was unjustifiably, needlessly killed.

The targeting of Donald Scott, with its massive multijurisdictional police presence, cannot be explained as any kind of crime control strategy. Rather, as the Ventura County District Attorney's report concluded, a purpose of this operation was to garner the proceeds from the forfeiture of Scott's $5 million ranch. Among the documents distributed to some of the officers at the pre-raid briefing were a property appraisal of Scott's ranch, a parcel map of the ranch with a reference to the sales price of a nearby property, and a statement that the ranch would be seized if fourteen marijuana plants were found.

United States v. $124,700, in U.S. Currency
United States Court of Appeals for the Eighth Circuit
458 F. 3d 822 (2006)

Colloton, J.

The United States initiated civil forfeiture proceedings against $124,700 in United States currency, alleging that the money was subject to forfeiture as the proceeds of a drug transaction or as property used to facilitate the possession, transportation, sale, concealment, receipt, or distribution of a controlled substance. Three individuals filed claims opposing the forfeiture, and after a bench trial, the district court entered judgment in favor of the claimants. The government appeals, and we reverse and remand for further proceedings.

The defendant currency was seized on May 28, 2003, from one of the claimants, Emiliano Gomez Gonzolez. According to testimony adduced at trial, Gonzolez was driving west on Interstate 80 in a rented Ford Taurus when a Nebraska State Patrol Trooper, Chris Bigsby, stopped Gonzolez for exceeding the posted speed limit. Trooper Bigsby testified that he asked Gonzolez to sit in the front passenger side of his patrol vehicle during the stop. At Bigsby's request, Gonzolez presented a Nevada driver's license and a rental contract for the car, but the rental contract was not in Gonzolez's name and did not list Gonzolez as an additional driver.

Trooper Bigsby did not speak fluent Spanish, but he testified that Gonzolez responded to his questions, which were mostly in English, in a combination of English and Spanish. Bigsby asked Gonzolez where he was going, and Gonzolez responded that he had been in Chicago for three days. Gonzolez indicated that a person named "Luis" had rented the car for him, but the name "Luis" did not match the name on the rental agreement that he presented to Trooper Bigsby. Trooper Bigsby also twice inquired whether Gonzolez had ever been arrested or placed on probation or parole, and Gonzolez said that he had not.

Before Trooper Bigsby had completed the traffic stop, another officer, Jason Brownell, stopped to ask if Bigsby needed any assistance. When Trooper Bigsby found out that Trooper Brownell had some Spanish-speaking ability, Bigsby asked if Brownell would stay and assist. Trooper Bigsby testified that with Brownell's assistance, he completed a warning citation and returned Gonzolez's license and paperwork. Having learned through his dispatcher that Gonzolez had been arrested in 2003 for driving while intoxicated, Bigsby then asked, through Trooper Brownell, if he could "ask a few more questions," and Gonzolez answered yes. Again through Trooper Brownell, Bigsby asked if Gonzolez had ever been arrested for driving while intoxicated, and Gonzolez answered that he had. Bigsby and Brownell also inquired whether any alcohol, guns, marijuana, methamphetamine, heroin, or large amounts of cash were in the car, and Gonzolez answered no. Brownell then asked for, and received, consent to search the car. Trooper Bigsby went directly to the rear passenger side of the vehicle and opened a cooler that was in the back seat, where he found a large plastic bag that contained seven bundles wrapped in rubber bands inside aluminum foil packaging. These bundles contained a total of $124,700 in currency. Gonzolez and the vehicle were then taken to the Nebraska State Patrol office in Lincoln.

In Lincoln, Trooper Bigsby continued his investigation with the help of another trooper, Sean Caradori, and Trooper Caradori's police canine, Rico. Rico was deployed to sniff the exterior of the car, and the dog alerted to the rear passenger side of the vehicle. Trooper Caradori testified that he conducted a test of the money that was found within the vehicle by hiding both the currency taken from Gonzolez's car and a separate stack of seven bills borrowed from other troopers in the troopers' break room. Caradori testified that Rico alerted to the defendant currency but not to the money borrowed from the troopers.

At trial, the government argued that the dog's alert, along with the large amount of cash that was seized, the circumstances of Gonzolez's travel, and Gonzolez's initial false denials that he was carrying cash or that he had a criminal history, showed that the currency was substantially connected to a drug transaction. The claimants, however, argued that the cash was acquired legitimately. Manuel Gomez testified that he had given Gonzolez $65,000 in cash, which was a combination of money that he had borrowed from his father-in-law and his own personal cash savings, with the expectation that Gonzolez would help him buy a refrigerated truck for the produce business. Gonzolez testified that he gave $40,000 of his own money, plus $20,000 from a friend, Andres Madrigal Morgan, as an investment in Gomez's truck. Consistent with Gonzolez's account, Andres Madrigal Morgan testified that he contributed $20,000 in proceeds from a vehicle sale to Gonzolez's investment in the truck.

Gonzolez testified that after he had pooled the cash from Madrigal Morgan and Gomez with his own cash, he heard from a friend in Chicago that a truck might be available there from a friend of the friend, and he set out for Chicago by plane, taking the cash with him in a small carry-on bag. Gonzolez said, however, that when he arrived in Chicago and his friend picked him up from the airport, he learned that the truck had been sold. In addition, the unidentified friend alerted Gonzolez that it was "bad" to carry more than $10,000 in cash on your person. Newly fearful of carrying his cash back to California by plane, Gonzolez testified that he decided to rent a car rather than fly, but because neither he nor his friend had a credit card, a third individual rented the car for him.

Gonzolez also testified that he hid the money in a cooler because he was afraid that he might be assaulted or have the money stolen if it was readily observable. He also explained that he was "scared" when the troopers began questioning him about whether he was carrying drugs or currency. He said that he lied about the money and about the names of other parties involved, because he believed that carrying large amounts of cash might be illegal, and he did not want to get his friends in trouble. With respect to Trooper Bigsby's question about whether he had ever been arrested, Gonzolez testified that Bigsby asked whether he "had any crimes" or "had been a prisoner." Gonzolez said he answered "no," despite his arrest for driving under the influence, because he "didn't think that that was a crime."

The district court concluded that the government had not established, by a preponderance of the evidence, that there was a substantial connection between the money and a drug trafficking offense. The court noted that large sums of unexplained currency can be evidence of drug trafficking, and that in this case the money was bundled in an unusual manner. The court also concluded, however, that the claimants had given a "plausible and consistent explanation for [the money's] origin and intended use," and that "the bundling is consistent with an attempt to sort the currency by contributor and conceal the currency from would-be thieves," and not just to evade law enforcement. In addition, the court observed that the government had not presented any expert testimony about "whether the manner the bundles were wrapped either increased or decreased the likelihood of the currency's use or connection with a drug trafficking offense."

With respect to the canine alert, the court agreed that the alert provided some, but only slight, evidence that the money was connected to drug trafficking. The court also considered the circumstances and route of Gonzolez's travel, and the fact that Gonzolez had lied about the names of his friends and other details, but did not believe that this evidence taken together with the other circumstances, including all the claimants' lack of significant criminal history, established a substantial connection to drug activity. Because the court determined that the money was not subject to forfeiture, it did not reach the question whether the claimants were innocent owners.

Since the enactment of the Civil Asset Forfeiture Reform Act of 2000, the burden is on the government to establish, by a preponderance of the evidence, that seized property is subject to forfeiture. Forfeiture is warranted under 21 U.S.C. § 881 when the government establishes a "'substantial connection' between the property" and a controlled substance offense. We review any predicate factual findings for clear error, but the ultimate conclusion as to whether those facts establish a "substantial connection" between seized currency and a narcotics transaction is a mixed question of law and fact that we review *de novo*.

The district court's opinion includes no finding as to the credibility of Gonzolez and the other two claimants. The court did observe that the explanations of the claimants were "plausible and consistent," but this is different from a finding that the court actually *believed* the testimony. "Plausible" means "apparently acceptable or trustworthy (sometimes with the implication of mere appearance)," and we thus read the district court's opinion to hold that given a "plausible and consistent" explanation from the claimants on one side of the balance, the government's countervailing proof was not strong enough to meet its burden of showing a substantial connection by a preponderance of the evidence.

On *de novo* review, we respectfully disagree and reach a different conclusion. We believe that the evidence as a whole demonstrates by a preponderance of the evidence that there was a substantial connection between the currency and a drug trafficking offense. Possession of a large sum of cash is "strong evidence" of a connection to drug activity and Gonzolez was carrying the very large sum of $124,700. The currency was concealed in aluminum foil inside a cooler, and while an innocent traveler might theoretically carry more than $100,000 in cash across country and seek to conceal funds from would-be thieves on the highway, we have adopted the common-sense view that bundling and concealment of large amounts of currency, combined with other suspicious circumstances, supports a connection between money and drug trafficking. The canine alert also supports the connection.

The route and circumstances of Gonzolez's travel were highly suspicious. Gonzolez had flown on a one-way ticket, which we have previously acknowledged is evidence in favor of forfeiture and he gave a vague explanation, attributed to advice from an unidentified third person, about why he elected to return by car. Gonzolez purportedly carried $125,000 in cash with him on his flight, for the purpose of buying a truck that he had never seen, from a third party whom he had never met, with the help of a friend whose name he could not recall at trial. This testimony does not inspire confidence in the innocence of the conduct. When he was stopped by the Nebraska State Patrol, Gonzolez was driving a rental car that was leased in the name of another person who was not present, another circumstance that gives rise to suspicion. Then, when Gonzolez was questioned by officers, he lied about having money in the car and about the names of his friends, thus giving further reason to question the legitimacy of the currency's presence. The totality of these circumstances — the large amount of concealed currency, the strange travel pattern, the inability to identify a key party in the purported innocent transaction, the unusual rental car papers, the canine alert, and the false statements to law enforcement officers — leads most naturally to the inference that Gonzolez was involved in illegal drug activity, and that the currency was substantially connected to it.

While the claimants' explanation for these circumstances may be "plausible," we think it is unlikely. We therefore conclude that the government proved by a preponderance of the evidence that the defendant currency was substantially connected to a narcotics offense. Accordingly, we reverse the judgment of the district court and remand for further proceedings.

Lay, dissenting.

I respectfully dissent. Although the circumstantial evidence offered by the government provides some indication that the money seized in this case may be related to criminal activity, I cannot agree that the government has proven, by a preponderance of the evidence, the requisite *substantial* connection between the currency and a *controlled substance offense*.

Notwithstanding the fact that claimants seemingly suspicious activities were reasoned away with plausible, and thus presumptively trustworthy, explanations which the government failed to contradict or rebut, I note that no drugs, drug paraphernalia, or drug records were recovered in connection with the seized money. There is no evidence claimants were ever convicted of any drug-related crime, nor is there any indication the manner in which the currency was bundled was indicative of drug use or distribution. At most, the evidence presented suggests the money seized may have been involved in some illegal activity — activity that is incapable of being ascertained on the record before us.

The law of our circuit makes clear that the possession of a large amount of cash provides strong evidence of a connection between the *res* and illegal drug activity. Yet this fact is not dispositive. A faithful reading of the cases cited by the majority from our court reveal that we have required some additional nexus between the property seized and drug activity to support forfeiture. In *United States v. U.S. Currency, in the Amount of $150,660.00,* 980 F.2d 1200 (8th Cir. 1992), we recognized such a nexus where the investigating officer immediately smelled marijuana upon inspecting the currency. In *United States v. $84,615 in U.S. Currency,* 379 F.3d 496 (8th Cir. 2004), we concluded forfeiture was proper where the owner of the seized currency "undisputedly possessed illegal drugs at the time" the currency was discovered. Most recently, in *United States v. $117,920.00 in United States Currency,* 413 F.3d 826 (8th Cir. 2005), we determined that forfeiture was warranted where materials known to be used to package and conceal drugs were recovered in close physical proximity to the seized currency, and where the investigating officer detected the smell of marijuana on some of these materials.

Here, the only evidence linking the seized money to illegal drug activity is a canine sniff that alerted officers to the presence of narcotics on the currency itself and the exterior of the rear passenger side of the rental car where the currency was discovered. However, as Justice Souter recently recognized, a large percentage of currency presently in circulation contains trace amounts of narcotics. See *Illinois v. Caballes,* 543 U.S. 405, 410–12 (2005) (Souter, J. dissenting). As a result, this fact is virtually "meaningless and likely quite prejudicial." *United States v. Carr,* 25 F.3d 1194, 1216 (3d Cir. 1994) (Becker, J., concurring). Our decision in *$84,615 in U.S. Currency* to afford this evidence only "slight" weight is thus well-founded, and this factor, taken in conjunction with the large amount of currency seized, does not favor forfeiture. Finally, the mere fact that the canine alerted officers to the presence of drug residue in a *rental car*, no doubt driven by dozens, perhaps scores, of patrons during the course of a given year, coupled with the fact that the alert came from the same location where the currency was discovered, does little to connect the money to a controlled substance offense. Therefore, I respectfully dissent.

———————

As Radley Balko's article notes, state asset forfeiture laws do not always follow the federal approach. For an assessment of every state's asset forfeiture law, see Marian R. Williams, Jefferson E. Holcomb, Tomislav V. Kovandzic, and Scott Bullock, *Policing for Profit: The Abuse of Civil Asset Forfeiture*, Institute for Justice 41–102 (2010) (grading state asset forfeiture laws).

Chapter 5

Investigating Drug Crimes

A. Investigating Victimless Crimes

As discussed in Chapter 2, the question of whether drug crimes are "victimless" and undeserving of punishment is an important part of the drug policy debate. Some argue that drug users and distributors are engaged in consensual transactions and it is inappropriate to use the criminal law just to protect drug users from themselves. Others believe that drug users can be properly understood as victims in need of the criminal law's protection and that communities and families are also victimized by the negative consequences associated with drug addiction. We will not return to this debate here.

Instead, this chapter uses "victimless crime" in a much narrower sense related to the investigation of drug offenses: drug crimes lack a complaining witness. In the case of a robbery, the victim will generally report the crime to the police. The same is not true of the manufacture or sale of controlled substances where all of the parties to the transaction are willing participants who have an incentive to keep their activities hidden from the police. Similarly, whether or not one regards drug users as victims in a moral sense, they are exceedingly unlikely to report their drug purchases to the police. As one book designed as an investigative resource for drug enforcement officers puts it, "[f]requently ... drug enforcement agents must initiate their own cases with few initial leads." Michael D. Lyman, PRACTICAL DRUG ENFORCEMENT at 2 (3rd ed. 2007). Though many of the law enforcement techniques considered in this section are used in the policing of all crimes, the victimless nature of drug offenses makes these techniques uniquely important to drug investigations.

1. Police Participation in Drug Crimes

Breaking the Law to Enforce It:
Undercover Police Participation in Crime
Elizabeth E. Joh
62 Stanford Law Review 155 (2009)

Covert policing necessarily involves deception, which in turn often leads to participation in activity that appears to be criminal. In undercover operations, the police have introduced drugs into prison, undertaken assignments from Latin American drug cartels to launder money, established fencing businesses that paid cash for stolen goods and for "referrals," printed counterfeit bills, and committed perjury, to cite a few examples.

In each of these instances, undercover police engaged in seemingly illegal activity to gather evidence or to maintain their fictitious identities. Yet unless these acts are committed by "rogue cops" not authorized to participate in illegal activity, these activities aren't considered crimes. Indeed, they are considered a justifiable and sometimes necessary aspect of undercover policing.

At first glance, it may seem that the key distinction between undercover work and all other kinds of policing is deception. Deception is used, however, in many aspects of policing. The detective may lie to the defendant in order to gain a confession. A uniformed officer might con an armed and barricaded suspect into providing entry by promising no arrest. And so the fact is that petty deceptions pervade the craft of effective policing. The difference between these deceptions and those of undercover work may be a matter of a degree, but it is a significant one. A detective may lie in the interrogation room about the status of a case to encourage a confession: a deception of purpose. In undercover work, suspects are unaware of both the purpose and the identity of the police. Indeed, the objective of undercover policing is to capture criminals in their "natural" state, although of course the irony is that the observers are duplicitous, or, in the cases of bait-sales and street crime decoys, are part of the circumstances of the crime.

Investigative deception is a firmly entrenched aspect of contemporary American policing. Even critics of undercover work generally acknowledge that its elimination is neither feasible nor desirable.

Unlike an impulsive or opportunistic crime, some crimes involve secretive, complex, and consensual activities. The manufacture of methamphetamine, the bribery of local officials, food stamp fraud, prostitution, [and] dogfighting rings are examples of such offenses, and they are difficult, if not impossible, to investigate if the police must wait for victim complaints, witness statements, or physical evidence. If these crimes are to be prosecuted successfully, then the police must infiltrate criminal ranks or play willing victims.

Such undercover operations are not the specialty of a few departments, but are instead used widely among police departments of varied sizes. Likewise, undercover operations are usually used as an initial course of action rather than as a means used when others have failed.

Undercover officers participate in authorized crimes for a number of different reasons. Two of the most important are: (1) to provide opportunities for the suspects to engage in the target crime, and (2) to maintain a false identity or to facilitate access to the suspect. These needs are at their greatest in facilitative operations, when police must both maintain their covert identities as well as encourage the commission of crime (short of entrapment).

In facilitative operations, the police furnish a simulated environment that can be as elaborate as the establishment of a false business or as simple as the presentation of a false identity as an especially vulnerable victim. Many of these facilitative activities would constitute crimes had the police agents not been given the authorization to commit them.

In the most commonplace stings, the police may pretend to be drug users or illegal gun buyers looking for a willing seller. In variations of "reverse stings," undercover officers may provide the illegal drugs themselves, the chemicals necessary for drug manufacture, or the "buy" money to the suspects.

The isolation, stress, and psychological toll of undercover work sometimes lead undercover investigators to exceed the bounds of authorized criminality altogether, and participate in offenses as ordinary criminals. It is not entirely uncommon for undercover cops to "go native" and believe in the truth of their own fictive identities.

The practice of authorized criminality may contribute directly to this problem. The conceptual line between authorized and unauthorized criminality is clear: unauthorized crimes further no law enforcement purpose. In the trenches, however, the difference between pretending to use drugs to maintain cover and using drugs to socialize with "friends" in the criminal underworld may be a difficult distinction to draw, particularly for those investigators who are asked to assume "deep cover" roles in which true identities must remain deeply suppressed for long periods of time. In these situations, the costs and visibility of unauthorized criminal participation are low, while opportunities are pervasive.

Although courts and commentators have acknowledged that the practice of authorized criminality is troubling but necessary, the conditions under which undercover police officers may participate in crime have seldom been the subject of regulatory oversight. Instead, what exists is a patchwork of applicable state and federal constitutional law restraints that loosely regulates undercover operations and generally accepts that undercover officers "violate the letter of the law in order to catch criminals."

Missouri v. Torphy

Court of Appeals of Missouri, Kansas City
78 Mo. App. 206 (1899)

Gill, J.

Defendant has appealed from a judgment of the lower court adjudging him guilty of the statutory crime of gambling. The case was submitted to the trial judge on an agreed statement of facts, the substance of which was, that while defendant was a member of the city council of Carthage and as such one of the committee on police, he undertook, under the instruction and direction of the mayor, to ferret out and secure evidence against certain parties suspected of violating the law relating to gambling. With this in view, and for this purpose only, the defendant visited the suspected room in Carthage; and there finding certain parties, he entered with them into a game of poker, betting a small sum of money on the result. The agreed case concedes that defendant's sole object and purpose in engaging in the game was to disarm suspicion and enable him to secure evidence to convict these habitual violators of the law.

On the facts above stated, it seems to me that defendant ought not to have been convicted; there was clearly no criminal intent. The general proposition is, that without a criminal intent there ought not to be criminal punishment. In the late work of McClain on Criminal Law, section 117, the learned author says:

"Another illustration of the doctrine that the intent determines criminality is found in the rule that a detective who joins with persons in the commission of a crime for the purpose of securing their arrest and conviction is not punishable, although he so far cooperates as to be guilty if his intention had been the same as theirs. Thus a detective who has cooperated with a criminal in committing an offense is not to be deemed an accomplice whose evidence must be corroborated." The cases cited in notes by the author fully sustain the text.

In view of the rule above stated and as announced in the foregoing authorities, the defendant ought not to be held. The other judges concurring the judgment will be reversed and defendant discharged.

Ellison, J., dissenting.

A detective, or a decoy, may seemingly take part with others in the commission of a crime or misdemeanor, for the purpose of bringing such others to justice. I think that is all the cases cited by Judge Gill will be found to sustain. But the detective can not actually commit the crime himself and escape punishment, on the ground that his object was to apprehend others. It was decided in Pennsylvania that a detective did not become the accomplice of those who murdered a man by reason of joining the conspiracy and urging the crime, his intention being to have them apprehended before the murder, though in this he failed. *Campbell v. Commonwealth,* 84 Pa. 187.

He may become a member of a band of murderers for the purpose of exposing them to justice, but he, himself, could not be excused for killing the man selected for assassination. For there he would do the act which makes up the whole crime. There are many instances where detectives, for the purpose of apprehending burglars or other thieves, join them in *their* perpetration of this offense, and such detectives, seemingly, do commit the offense, but in reality they do not convert the goods to their own use, and have no intention of doing so, and therefore the main ingredient of the crime does not attach to them. But if they joined such criminals, and though acting as detectives, they not only seemingly but did actually convert and secrete the property, they would be thieves of course, and would be punished as such.

So it has been decided that one may purchase liquor of another engaged in its illegal sale and he is not an accomplice; and this, whether he is acting as a detective or otherwise. But it would not be contended that for the purpose of discovering the illegal vendor of the liquor, a detective could engage as his clerk, or partner, and himself make the illegal sale and not be held guilty. In some jurisdictions it is a misdemeanor and in some, a felony, to commit adultery. It would scarcely be pretended that one could escape punishment when he actually committed the act, on the plea that he did it for the purpose of discovering the adultress. The reason for all this is, that the detective has *purposely* committed *all* of the act which makes up the thing forbidden by law.

So in the case before us, the misdemeanor prohibited by law was playing at cards for money. Defendant did this: He did the thing prohibited by the statute, and he did it purposely, that is, intentionally. It will not do to say that he had no intention to gamble, for he *did* gamble, but said he did so with the view of detecting others. That was merely his motive, as distinguished from his intention. His intention was to do the act prohibited and his motive was to catch others. But one's motive, however sincere, will not excuse his violation of the penal statute. "That ultimate good was the transgressor's leading motive, while yet he intended to do what the law forbade, or that in fact good attended or followed the doing, will not avail him." 1 Bishop's Crim. Law, sec. 341. The motive to murder might be to rid the community of a bad man; or to theft or forgery, to obtain money for the payment of debts or to relieve necessities, yet these do not excuse. 1 Wharton's Crim. Law, sec. 119. In my opinion the defendant was properly convicted.

a. Entrapment

United States v. Russell
Supreme Court of the United States
411 U.S. 423 (1973)

Mr. Justice Rehnquist delivered the opinion of the Court.

Respondent Richard Russell was charged in three counts of a five-count indictment returned against him and codefendants John and Patrick Connolly. After a jury trial in the District Court, in which his sole defense was entrapment, respondent was convicted on all three counts of having unlawfully manufactured and processed methamphetamine ("speed") and of having unlawfully sold and delivered that drug. He was sentenced to concurrent terms of two years in prison for each offense, the terms to be suspended on the condition that he spend six months in prison and be placed on probation for the following three years. On appeal, the United States Court of Appeals for the Ninth Circuit, one judge dissenting, reversed the conviction solely for the reason that an undercover agent supplied an essential chemical for manufacturing the methamphetamine which formed the basis of respondent's conviction. The court concluded that as a matter of law "a defense to a criminal charge may be founded upon an intolerable degree of governmental participation in the criminal enterprise." We granted certiorari and now reverse that judgment.

There is little dispute concerning the essential facts in this case. On December 7, 1969, Joe Shapiro, an undercover agent for the Federal Bureau of Narcotics and Dangerous Drugs, went to respondent's home on Whidbey Island in the State of Washington where he met with respondent and his two codefendants, John and Patrick Connolly. Shapiro's assignment was to locate a laboratory where it was believed that methamphetamine was being manufactured illicitly. He told the respondent and the Connollys that he represented an organization in the Pacific Northwest that was interested in controlling the manufacture and distribution of methamphetamine. He then made an offer to supply the defendants with the chemical phenyl-2-propanone, an essential ingredient in the manufacture of methamphetamine, in return for one-half of the drug produced. This offer was made on the condition that Agent Shapiro be shown a sample of the drug which they were making and the laboratory where it was being produced.

During the conversation, Patrick Connolly revealed that he had been making the drug since May 1969 and since then had produced three pounds of it. John Connolly gave the agent a bag containing a quantity of methamphetamine that he represented as being from "the last batch that we made." Shortly thereafter, Shapiro and Patrick Connolly left respondent's house to view the laboratory which was located in the Connolly house on Whidbey Island. At the house, Shapiro observed an empty bottle bearing the chemical label phenyl-2-propanone.

By prearrangement, Shapiro returned to the Connolly house on December 9, 1969, to supply 100 grams of propanone and observe the manufacturing process. When he arrived he observed Patrick Connolly and the respondent cutting up pieces of aluminum foil and placing them in a large flask. There was testimony that some of the foil pieces accidentally fell on the floor and were picked up by the respondent and Shapiro and put into the flask.[3] Thereafter, Patrick Connolly added all of the necessary chemicals, including the propanone brought by Shapiro, to make two batches of methamphetamine. The manufacturing process having been completed the following morning, Shapiro was given one-half of the drug and respondent kept the remainder. Shapiro offered to buy, and the respondent agreed to sell, part of the remainder for $60.

About a month later, Shapiro returned to the Connolly house and met with Patrick Connolly to ask if he was still interested in their "business arrangement." Connolly replied that he was interested but that he had recently obtained two additional bottles of phenyl-2-propanone and would not be finished with them for a couple of days. He provided some additional methamphetamine to Shapiro at that time. Three days later Shapiro returned to the Connolly house with a search warrant and, among other items, seized an empty 500-gram bottle of propanone and a 100-gram bottle, not the one he had provided, that was partially filled with the chemical.

---

3. Agent Shapiro did not otherwise participate in the manufacture of the drug or direct any of the work.

There was testimony at the trial of respondent and Patrick Connolly that phenyl-2-propanone was generally difficult to obtain. At the request of the Bureau of Narcotics and Dangerous Drugs, some chemical supply firms had voluntarily ceased selling the chemical.

At the close of the evidence, and after receiving the District Judge's standard entrapment instruction,[4] the jury found the respondent guilty on all counts charged. On appeal, the respondent conceded that the jury could have found him predisposed to commit the offenses but argued that on the facts presented there was entrapment as a matter of law. The Court of Appeals agreed, although it did not find the District Court had misconstrued or misapplied the traditional standards governing the entrapment defense. Rather, the court in effect expanded the traditional notion of entrapment, which focuses on the predisposition of the defendant, to mandate dismissal of a criminal prosecution whenever the court determines that there has been "an intolerable degree of governmental participation in the criminal enterprise." In this case the court decided that the conduct of the agent in supplying a scarce ingredient essential for the manufacture of a controlled substance established that defense.

This new defense was held to rest on either of two alternative theories. One theory is based on two lower court decisions which have found entrapment, regardless of predisposition, whenever the government supplies contraband to the defendants. The second theory, a nonentrapment rationale, is based on a recent Ninth Circuit decision that reversed a conviction because a government investigator was so enmeshed in the criminal activity that the prosecution of the defendants was held to be repugnant to the American criminal justice system. The court below held that these two rationales constitute the same defense, and that only the label distinguishes them. In any event, it held that "both theories are premised on fundamental concepts of due process and evince the reluctance of the judiciary to countenance 'overzealous law enforcement.'"

This Court first recognized and applied the entrapment defense in *Sorrells v. United States,* 287 U.S. 435 (1932). In *Sorrells,* a federal prohibition agent visited the defendant while posing as a tourist and engaged him in conversation about their common war experiences. After gaining the defendant's confidence, the agent asked for some liquor, was twice refused, but upon asking a third time the defendant finally capitulated, and was subsequently prosecuted for violating the National Prohibition Act.

Mr. Chief Justice Hughes, speaking for the Court, held that as a matter of statutory construction the defense of entrapment should have been available to the defendant. Under the theory propounded by the Chief Justice, the entrapment defense prohibits law enforcement officers from instigating a criminal act by persons "otherwise innocent in order to lure them to its commission and to punish them." Thus, the thrust of the entrapment defense was held to focus on the intent or predisposition of the defendant to commit the crime. "If the defendant seeks acquittal by reason of entrapment he cannot complain of an appropriate and searching inquiry into his own conduct and predisposition as bearing upon that issue."

Mr. Justice Roberts concurred but was of the view "that courts must be closed to the trial of a crime instigated by the government's own agents." The difference in the view of

---

4. The District Judge stated the governing law on entrapment as follows: "Where a person already has the willingness and the readiness to break the law, the mere fact that the government agent provides what appears to be a favorable opportunity is not entrapment." He then instructed the jury to acquit respondent if it had a "reasonable doubt whether the defendant had the previous intent or purpose to commit the offense ... and did so only because he was induced or persuaded by some officer or agent of the government." No exception was taken by respondent to this instruction.

the majority and the concurring opinions is that in the former the inquiry focuses on the predisposition of the defendant, whereas in the latter the inquiry focuses on whether the government "instigated the crime."

In 1958[, in *Sherman v. United States*,] the Court again considered the theory underlying the entrapment defense and expressly reaffirmed the view expressed by the *Sorrells* majority. In *Sherman* the defendant was convicted of selling narcotics to a Government informer. As in *Sorrells*, it appears that the Government agent gained the confidence of the defendant and, despite initial reluctance, the defendant finally acceded to the repeated importunings of the agent to commit the criminal act. On the basis of *Sorrells*, this Court reversed the affirmance of the defendant's conviction.

In affirming the theory underlying *Sorrells*, Mr. Chief Justice Warren for the Court, held that "to determine whether entrapment has been established, a line must be drawn between the trap for the unwary innocent and the trap for the unwary criminal."

In the instant case, respondent asks us to reconsider the theory of the entrapment defense as it is set forth in the majority opinions in *Sorrells* and *Sherman*. His principal contention is that the defense should rest on constitutional grounds. He argues that the level of Shapiro's involvement in the manufacture of the methamphetamine was so high that a criminal prosecution for the drug's manufacture violates the fundamental principles of due process. The respondent contends that the same factors that led this Court to apply the exclusionary rule to illegal searches and seizures, *Weeks v. United States*, 232 U.S. 383 (1914); *Mapp v. Ohio*, 367 U.S. 643 (1961), and confessions, *Miranda v. Arizona*, 384 U.S. 436 (1966), should be considered here. But he would have the Court go further in deterring undesirable official conduct by requiring that any prosecution be barred absolutely because of the police involvement in criminal activity. The analogy is imperfect in any event, for the principal reason behind the adoption of the exclusionary rule was the Government's "failure to observe its own laws." *Mapp v. Ohio, supra*, at 659. Unlike the situations giving rise to the holdings in *Mapp* and *Miranda*, the Government's conduct here violated no independent constitutional right of the respondent. Nor did Shapiro violate any federal statute or rule or commit any crime in infiltrating the respondent's drug enterprise.

Respondent would overcome this basic weakness in his analogy to the exclusionary rule cases by having the Court adopt a rigid constitutional rule that would preclude any prosecution when it is shown that the criminal conduct would not have been possible had not an undercover agent "supplied an indispensable means to the commission of the crime that could not have been obtained otherwise, through legal or illegal channels." Even if we were to surmount the difficulties attending the notion that due process of law can be embodied in fixed rules, and those attending respondent's particular formulation, the rule he proposes would not appear to be of significant benefit to him. For, on the record presented, it appears that he cannot fit within the terms of the very rule he proposes.

The record discloses that although the propanone was difficult to obtain, it was by no means impossible. The defendants admitted making the drug both before and after those batches made with the propanone supplied by Shapiro. Shapiro testified that he saw an empty bottle labeled phenyl-2-propanone on his first visit to the laboratory on December 7, 1969. And when the laboratory was searched pursuant to a search warrant on January 10, 1970, two additional bottles labeled phenyl-2-propanone were seized. Thus, the facts in the record amply demonstrate that the propanone used in the illicit manufacture of methamphetamine not only *could* have been obtained without the intervention of Shapiro but was in fact obtained by these defendants.

While we may some day be presented with a situation in which the conduct of law enforcement agents is so outrageous that due process principles would absolutely bar the government from invoking judicial processes to obtain a conviction, the instant case is distinctly not of that breed. Shapiro's contribution of propanone to the criminal enterprise already in process was scarcely objectionable. The chemical is by itself a harmless substance and its possession is legal. While the Government may have been seeking to make it more difficult for drug rings, such as that of which respondent was a member, to obtain the chemical, the evidence described above shows that it nonetheless was obtainable. The law enforcement conduct here stops far short of violating that "fundamental fairness, shocking to the universal sense of justice," mandated by the Due Process Clause of the Fifth Amendment.

The illicit manufacture of drugs is not a sporadic, isolated criminal incident, but a continuing, though illegal, business enterprise. In order to obtain convictions for illegally manufacturing drugs, the gathering of evidence of past unlawful conduct frequently proves to be an all but impossible task. Thus in drug-related offenses law enforcement personnel have turned to one of the only practicable means of detection: the infiltration of drug rings and a limited participation in their unlawful present practices. Such infiltration is a recognized and permissible means of investigation; if that be so, then the supply of some item of value that the drug ring requires must, as a general rule, also be permissible. For an agent will not be taken into the confidence of the illegal entrepreneurs unless he has something of value to offer them. Law enforcement tactics such as this can hardly be said to violate "fundamental fairness" or "shocking to the universal sense of justice[.]"

Respondent also urges, as an alternative to his constitutional argument, that we broaden the nonconstitutional defense of entrapment in order to sustain the judgment of the Court of Appeals. This Court's opinions in *Sorrells v. United States* and *Sherman v. United States* held that the principal element in the defense of entrapment was the defendant's predisposition to commit the crime. Respondent conceded in the Court of Appeals, as well he might, "that he may have harbored a predisposition to commit the charged offenses." Yet he argues that the jury's refusal to find entrapment under the charge submitted to it by the trial court should be overturned and the view[] of Justice[] Roberts in *Sorrells*, which [would] make the essential element of the defense turn on the type and degree of governmental conduct, be adopted as the law.

We decline to overrule these cases. *Sorrells* is a precedent of long standing that has already been once reexamined in *Sherman* and implicitly there reaffirmed. Since the defense is not of a constitutional dimension, Congress may address itself to the question and adopt any substantive definition of the defense that it may find desirable.

Critics of the rule laid down in *Sorrells* and *Sherman* have suggested that its basis in the implied intent of Congress is largely fictitious, and have pointed to what they conceive to be the anomalous difference between the treatment of a defendant who is solicited by a private individual and one who is entrapped by a government agent. Questions have been likewise raised as to whether "predisposition" can be factually established with the requisite degree of certainty. Arguments such as these, while not devoid of appeal, have been twice previously made to this Court, and twice rejected by it, first in *Sorrells* and then in *Sherman*.

We believe that at least equally cogent criticism has been made of the concurring views in these cases. Commenting in *Sherman* on Mr. Justice Roberts' position in *Sorrells* that "although the defendant could claim that the Government had induced him to commit the crime, the Government could not reply by showing that the defendant's criminal conduct was due to his own readiness and not to the persuasion of government agents," Mr. Chief Justice Warren quoted the observation of Judge Learned Hand in an earlier stage of that proceeding: "'Indeed, it would seem probable that, if there were no reply [to the claim of inducement], it would be impossible ever to secure convictions of any offences which consist of transactions that are carried on in secret.'"

Nor does it seem particularly desirable for the law to grant complete immunity from prosecution to one who himself planned to commit a crime, and then committed it, simply because government undercover agents subjected him to inducements which might have seduced a hypothetical individual who was not so predisposed. We are content to leave the matter where it was left by the Court in *Sherman*:

> "The function of law enforcement is the prevention of crime and the apprehension of criminals. Manifestly, that function does not include the manufacturing of crime. Criminal activity is such that stealth and strategy are necessary weapons in the arsenal of the police officer. However, 'A different question is presented when the criminal design originates with the officials of the Government, and they implant in the mind of an innocent person the disposition to commit the alleged offense and induce its commission in order that they may prosecute.'"

Those cases establish that entrapment is a relatively limited defense. It is rooted, not in any authority of the Judicial Branch to dismiss prosecutions for what it feels to have been "overzealous law enforcement," but instead in the notion that Congress could not have intended criminal punishment for a defendant who has committed all the elements of a proscribed offense, but was induced to commit them by the Government.

Sorrells and *Sherman* both recognize "that the fact that officers or employees of the Government merely afford opportunities or facilities for the commission of the offense does not defeat the prosecution". Nor will the mere fact of deceit defeat a prosecution, for there are circumstances when the use of deceit is the only practicable law enforcement technique available. It is only when the Government's deception actually implants the criminal design in the mind of the defendant that the defense of entrapment comes into play.

Respondent's concession in the Court of Appeals that the jury finding as to predisposition was supported by the evidence is, therefore, fatal to his claim of entrapment. He was an active participant in an illegal drug manufacturing enterprise which began before the Government agent appeared on the scene, and continued after the Government agent had left the scene. He was, in the words of *Sherman,* not an "unwary innocent" but an "unwary criminal." The Court of Appeals was wrong, we believe, when it sought to broaden the principle laid down in *Sorrells* and *Sherman*. Its judgment is therefore

Reversed.

Mr. Justice Douglas, with whom Mr. Justice Brennan concurs, dissenting.

A federal agent supplied the accused with one chemical ingredient of the drug known as methamphetamine ("speed") which the accused manufactured and for which act he was sentenced to prison. His defense was entrapment, which the Court of Appeals sustained and which the Court today disallows. Since I have an opposed view of entrapment, I dissent.

In my view, the fact that the chemical ingredient supplied by the federal agent might have been obtained from other sources is quite irrelevant. Supplying the chemical ingredient used in the manufacture of this batch of "speed" made the United States an active participant in the unlawful activity. As stated by Mr. Justice Brandeis, dissenting in *Casey v. United States*:

> "I am aware that courts — mistaking relative social values and forgetting that a desirable end cannot justify foul means — have, in their zeal to punish, sanctioned the use of evidence obtained through criminal violation of property and personal rights or by other practices of detectives even more revolting. But the objection here is of a different nature. It does not rest merely upon the character of the evidence or upon the fact that the evidence was illegally obtained. The obstacle to the prosecution lies in the fact that the alleged crime was instigated by officers of the Government; that the act for which the Government seeks to punish the defendant is the fruit of their criminal conspiracy to induce its commission. The Government may set decoys to entrap criminals. But it may not provoke or create a crime and then punish the criminal, its creature."

Mr. Justice Roberts in *Sorrells* put the idea in the following words:

> "The applicable principle is that courts must be closed to the trial of a crime instigated by the government's own agents. No other issue, no comparison of equities as between the guilty official and the guilty defendant, has any place in the enforcement of this overruling principle of public policy."

Federal agents play a debased role when they become the instigators of the crime, or partners in its commission, or the creative brain behind the illegal scheme. That is what the federal agent did here when he furnished the accused with one of the chemical ingredients needed to manufacture the unlawful drug.

Mr. Justice Stewart, with whom Mr. Justice Brennan and Mr. Justice Marshall join, dissenting.

In *Sorrells v. United States* and *Sherman v. United States* the Court took what might be called a "subjective" approach to the defense of entrapment. In that view, the defense is predicated on an unexpressed intent of Congress to exclude from its criminal statutes the prosecution and conviction of persons, "otherwise innocent," who have been lured to the commission of the prohibited act through the Government's instigation. The key phrase in this formulation is "otherwise innocent," for the entrapment defense is available under this approach only to those who would not have committed the crime but for the Government's inducements. Thus, the subjective approach focuses on the conduct and propensities of the particular defendant in each individual case: if he is "otherwise innocent," he may avail himself of the defense; but if he had the "predisposition" to commit the crime, or if the "criminal design" originated with him, then — regardless of the nature and extent of the Government's participation — there has been no entrapment. And, in the absence of a conclusive showing one way or the other, the question of the defendant's "predisposition" to the crime is a question of fact for the jury. The Court today adheres to this approach.

The concurring opinion of Mr. Justice Roberts in the *Sorrells* case, and that of Mr. Justice Frankfurter in the *Sherman* case, took a different view of the entrapment defense. In their concept, the defense is not grounded on some unexpressed intent of Congress to exclude from punishment under its statutes those otherwise innocent persons tempted into crime by the Government, but rather on the belief that "the methods employed on behalf of the Government to bring about conviction cannot be countenanced." Thus, the focus of this approach is not on the propensities and predisposition of a specific defendant, but on "whether the police conduct revealed in the particular case falls below standards, to which common feelings respond, for the proper use of governmental power." Phrased another way, the question is whether—regardless of the predisposition to crime of the particular defendant involved—the governmental agents have acted in such a way as is likely to instigate or create a criminal offense. Under this approach, the determination of the lawfulness of the Government's conduct must be made—as it is on all questions involving the legality of law enforcement methods—by the trial judge, not the jury.

In my view, this objective approach to entrapment advanced by the Roberts opinion in *Sorrells* and the Frankfurter opinion in *Sherman* is the only one truly consistent with the underlying rationale of the defense. Indeed, the very basis of the entrapment defense itself demands adherence to an approach that focuses on the conduct of the governmental agents, rather than on whether the defendant was "predisposed" or "otherwise innocent." I find it impossible to believe that the purpose of the defense is to effectuate some unexpressed congressional intent to exclude from its criminal statutes persons who committed a prohibited act, but would not have done so except for the Government's inducements. For, as Mr. Justice Frankfurter put it, "the only legislative intention that can with any show of reason be extracted from the statute is the intention to make criminal precisely the conduct in which the defendant has engaged." Since, by definition, the entrapment defense cannot arise unless the defendant actually committed the proscribed act, that defendant is manifestly covered by the terms of the criminal statute involved.

Furthermore, to say that such a defendant is "otherwise innocent" or not "predisposed" to commit the crime is misleading, at best. The very fact that he has committed an act that Congress has determined to be illegal demonstrates conclusively that he is not innocent of the offense. He may not have originated the precise plan or the precise details, but he was "predisposed" in the sense that he has proved to be quite capable of committing the crime. That he was induced, provoked, or tempted to do so by government agents does not make him any more innocent or any less predisposed than he would be if he had been induced, provoked, or tempted by a private person—which, of course, would not entitle him to cry "entrapment." Since the only difference between these situations is the identity of the tempter, it follows that the significant focus must be on the conduct of the government agents, and not on the predisposition of the defendant.

The purpose of the entrapment defense, then, cannot be to protect persons who are "otherwise innocent." Rather, it must be to prohibit unlawful governmental activity in instigating crime. As Mr. Justice Brandeis stated in *Casey v. United States*: "This prosecution should be stopped, not because some right of Casey's has been denied, but in order to protect the Government. To protect it from illegal conduct of its officers. To preserve the purity of its courts." If that is so, then whether the particular defendant was "predisposed" or "otherwise innocent" is irrelevant; and the important question becomes whether the Government's conduct in inducing the crime was beyond judicial toleration.

This does not mean, of course, that the Government's use of undercover activity, strategy, or deception is necessarily unlawful. Indeed, many crimes, especially so-called victimless crimes, could not otherwise be detected. Thus, government agents may engage in conduct that is likely, when objectively considered, to afford a person ready and willing to commit the crime an opportunity to do so.

But when the agents' involvement in criminal activities goes beyond the mere offering of such an opportunity, and when their conduct is of a kind that could induce or instigate the commission of a crime by one not ready and willing to commit it, then—regardless of the character or propensities of the particular person induced—I think entrapment has occurred. For in that situation, the Government has engaged in the impermissible manufacturing of crime, and the federal courts should bar the prosecution in order to preserve the institutional integrity of the system of federal criminal justice.

Since, in my view, it does not matter whether the respondent was predisposed to commit the offense of which he was convicted, the focus must be, rather, on the conduct of the undercover government agent. What the agent did here was to meet with a group of suspected producers of methamphetamine, including the respondent; to request the drug; to offer to supply the chemical phenyl-2-propanone in exchange for one-half of the methamphetamine to be manufactured therewith; and, when that offer was accepted, to provide the needed chemical ingredient, and to purchase some of the drug from the respondent.

It is undisputed that phenyl-2-propanone is an essential ingredient in the manufacture of methamphetamine; that it is not used for any other purpose; and that, while its sale is not illegal, it is difficult to obtain, because a manufacturer's license is needed to purchase it, and because many suppliers, at the request of the Federal Bureau of Narcotics and Dangerous Drugs, do not sell it at all. It is also undisputed that the methamphetamine which the respondent was prosecuted for manufacturing and selling was all produced on December 10, 1969, and that all the phenyl-2-propanone used in the manufacture of that batch of the drug was provided by the government agent. In these circumstances, the agent's undertaking to supply this ingredient to the respondent, thus making it possible for the Government to prosecute him for manufacturing an illicit drug with it, was, I think, precisely the type of governmental conduct that the entrapment defense is meant to prevent.

[A]ssuming in this case that the phenyl-2-propanone was obtainable through independent sources, the fact remains that that used for the particular batch of methamphetamine involved in all three counts of the indictment with which the respondent was charged—*i e.*, that produced on December 10, 1969—was supplied by the Government. This essential ingredient was indisputably difficult to obtain, and yet what was used in committing the offenses of which the respondent was convicted was offered to the respondent by the Government agent, on the agent's own initiative, and was readily supplied to the respondent in needed amounts. If the chemical was so easily available elsewhere, then why did not the agent simply wait until the respondent had himself obtained the ingredients and produced the drug, and then buy it from him? The very fact that the agent felt it incumbent upon him to offer to supply phenyl-2-propanone in return for the drug casts considerable doubt on the theory that the chemical could easily have been procured without the agent's intervention, and that therefore the agent merely afforded an opportunity for the commission of a criminal offense.

In this case, the chemical ingredient was available only to licensed persons, and the Government itself had requested suppliers not to sell that ingredient even to people with a license. Yet the Government agent readily offered, and supplied, that ingredient to an unlicensed person and asked him to make a certain illegal drug with it. The Government then prosecuted that person for making the drug produced *with the very ingredient* which its agent had so helpfully supplied. This strikes me as the very pattern of conduct that should be held to constitute entrapment as a matter of law.

It is the Government's duty to prevent crime, not to promote it. Here, the Government's agent asked that the illegal drug be produced for him, solved his quarry's practical problems with the assurance that he could provide the one essential ingredient that was difficult to obtain, furnished that element as he had promised, and bought the finished product from the respondent—all so that the respondent could be prosecuted for producing and selling the very drug for which the agent had asked and for which he had provided the necessary component. Under the objective approach that I would follow, this respondent was entrapped, regardless of his predisposition or "innocence."

In the words of Mr. Justice Roberts:

"The applicable principle is that courts must be closed to the trial of a crime instigated by the government's own agents. No other issue, no comparison of equities as between the guilty official and the guilty defendant, has any place in the enforcement of this overruling principle of public policy."

I would affirm the judgment of the Court of Appeals.

––––––––––

Justice Rehnquist's opinion explains the rationale for the "subjective" test for entrapment. The subjective test considers the defendant's state of mind to determine whether he was "predisposed" to commit the offense. In dissent, Justice Stewart made the case for the "objective" test for entrapment, which focuses on the government's conduct rather than the defendant's predisposition and asks whether the government's actions were "of a kind that could induce or instigate the commission of a crime by one not ready and willing to commit it."

Though most states have followed the federal approach and adopted the subjective test, a sizeable minority employ the objective test. *See*, Derrick Augustus Carter, *To Catch the Lion, Tether the Goat: Entrapment, Conspiracy, and Sentencing Manipulation*, 42 Akron L. Rev. 135, 145–151 (2009) (providing an overview of the subjective, objective, and hybrid approaches to entrapment).

Utah v. J.D.W.

Court of Appeals of Utah
910 P.2d 1242 (1995)

Bench, J.

Appellant J.D.W., a seventeen-year-old minor, appeals from the trial court's determination that J.D.W. was not entrapped into committing a drug offense.

J.D.W. and a friend went to the Layton Hills Mall to buy a musical compact disc. While there, they were approached by officer Dave Wakefield of the Davis Metro Narcotics Strike Force. Wakefield asked if they were interested in a smoke. J.D.W.'s friend asked "smoke what?" and Wakefield made a gesture simulating smoking marijuana. Wakefield told them that he had some marijuana and hashish and that if they were interested they could go outside and look at it. J.D.W. and his friend thereupon followed Wakefield outside. Once outside, J.D.W.'s friend stopped while J.D.W. and Wakefield continued on a short distance further. Wakefield presented J.D.W. a baggy containing marijuana. J.D.W. took the baggy, "separated the buds from the shake" and smelled the contents. Wakefield also offered J.D.W. the hashish, but J.D.W. refused it. J.D.W. asked how much the marijuana cost. Wakefield told him that it was $35. J.D.W. only had a $100 bill and offered to go get change. Wakefield told J.D.W. that he could make change, whereupon J.D.W. paid Wakefield, who then gave J.D.W. the marijuana and the change. Wakefield then arrested J.D.W. for possession of a controlled substance.

J.D.W. was charged in a juvenile court petition with one count of possession of a controlled substance, a class B misdemeanor, in violation of Utah Code Ann. § 58-37-8(2)(a)(i). J.D.W. filed a motion to dismiss based on a claim of entrapment. After an evidentiary hearing on J.D.W.'s motion to dismiss, the trial court issued a memorandum decision in which it determined, based on the facts, that J.D.W. was not entrapped.

J.D.W. entered a conditional guilty plea in which he preserved his right to challenge the trial court's denial of his motion to dismiss. The issue on appeal is whether J.D.W. was entrapped, as a matter of law, when he purchased marijuana from an undercover police officer.

J.D.W. asks this court to adopt the entrapment per se rule, that is, anytime the police or their agents provide drugs for sale, then that action automatically constitutes entrapment. *See State v. Kummer,* 481 N.W.2d 437 (N.D. 1992). In Utah, however, the entrapment per se rule has never been adopted. Utah Code Ann. §76-2-303(1) (1994) provides, in pertinent part:

> Entrapment occurs when a law enforcement officer or a person directed by or acting in cooperation with the officer induces the commission of an offense in order to obtain evidence of the commission … creating a substantial risk that the offense would be committed by one not otherwise ready to commit it. Conduct merely affording a person an opportunity to commit an offense does not constitute entrapment.

Several factors must be considered in determining whether government action induces criminal activity or, conversely, if it merely affords a person the opportunity to participate in criminal activity. "The transactions leading up to the offense, the interaction between the agent and the defendant, and the response to the inducements of the agent" must all be evaluated. Moreover, "extreme pleas of desperate illness or appeals based primarily on sympathy, pity, or close personal friendship, or offers of inordinate sums of money, are examples, depending on an evaluation of circumstances in each case, of what might constitute prohibited police conduct." Additionally, excessive pressure or goading by an undercover officer might constitute entrapment. Because entrapment is such a highly fact-intensive defense, we defer to the fact-finder's determination, unless we hold it to be erroneous, as a matter of law.

The facts in the record support the trial court's determination that, by merely providing the opportunity for a drug purchase, Wakefield did not engage in any activity that "would be effective to persuade an average person … to commit the offense."[2] Wakefield did not rely on any type of close, personal relationship to induce J.D.W. to buy the marijuana. Wakefield did not offer J.D.W. inordinate amounts of money, or large quantities of marijuana for an extremely low price. Rather, Wakefield used the market rate to determine the price of the marijuana. Furthermore, Wakefield did not make repeated requests or badger J.D.W. to buy the marijuana. J.D.W. immediately responded positively to Wakefield's offer. Despite the trial court's discomfort about some of Wakefield's actions, the trial court determined that Wakefield did not entrap J.D.W. under the standards set forth by the Utah Legislature.[3] We cannot say, as a matter of law, that J.D.W. was entrapped. We therefore defer to the trial court's resolution of the issue.

---

2. On the day of J.D.W.'s drug purchase, Wakefield approached over one hundred people in the mall. No one but J.D.W. made a purchase.

3. The trial court was concerned by the fact that Officer Wakefield sold drugs to a juvenile in a "drug-free zone." There is nothing, however, in the statute that precludes such activity as a matter of law. Officers are specifically exempted from the provisions of the statute establishing "drug-free zones" so long as the officers are acting within the scope of their employment. J.D.W. did not argue below, that Wakefield was acting outside the scope of his employment. J.D.W. also made no claim that Wakefield had entrapped J.D.W. because he sold drugs to a person that was not previously suspected of drug activity. Based on the facts and arguments presented at the evidentiary hearing, the trial court ruled that J.D.W. was not entrapped as the defense has been outlined by the legislature. It is not the prerogative of courts to modify the statutory scheme established by the legislature. The courts can only give construction to statutes as provided by the legislature. Any attempt to change the statutory scheme

Affirmed.

Orme, J (concurring in the result).

Given clear and apparently controlling case law in Utah, I must reluctantly concur in this court's judgment affirming the trial court's ruling on this troublesome entrapment issue. In so doing, I must also note that, like the trial court, I am very concerned about the incident which led to charges in this case.

We have the situation in which an officer, newly assigned to drug enforcement responsibilities, takes marijuana from the police evidence room and goes to a nearby shopping mall where, for a period of some hours, he bothers innocent passers-by, many of whom are in the company of young children, and none of whom has been previously suspected of using drugs or has expressed to the officer any interest in procuring illegal drugs prior to his solicitation. Many of the shoppers were predictably annoyed that an apparent drug dealer would be openly purveying his wares in the common area of the local mall and several complained to mall management.

In what the Legislature has taken pains to characterize as a "drug-free zone," the drug-selling officer was not only making a nuisance of himself, but was—but for the cloak of statutory immunity—engaged in a course of trespass, soliciting illegal drug sales, and contributing to the delinquency of minors. It is reprehensible to me that someone charged with upholding the law would set about in this fashion to see if a randomly targeted minor, presented with adequate temptation, is willing to break the law.

I think what the officer did is indefensible. The overall societal cost of such methods is simply too great to justify the arrest of a single juvenile purchaser. I regret that the current state of the law is such that I can do nothing more than fuss about it. My hope is that the Supreme Court will grant certiorari in this case and consider the advisability of adopting some kind of per se entrapment doctrine, see, e.g., *State v. Kummer,* 481 N.W.2d 437, 441–44 (N.D. 1992), or consider whether "the conduct of the law enforcement agents is so outrageous that due process principles would absolutely bar the government from invoking judicial processes to obtain a conviction." *United States v. Russell,* 411 U.S. 423, 431–32 (1973). Alternatively, perhaps the Legislature will see fit to tighten up the "drug-free zone" concept so that such zones are completely drug free rather than only free of drugs except those introduced by the "good guys," or, at least, to limit police solicitations of this sort to individuals who have previously been identified as suspected drug users or traffickers.

Subjecting the general public to unwelcome and unsolicited offers to buy drugs is simply not a police method which our society should embrace as a tactic in the war on drugs.

In *J.D.W.*, the concurring judge laments the "cloak of statutory immunity" that allowed a police officer to sell marijuana to a minor in a school zone. What limitations should the law place on immunity for police participation in crime? If police officers can sell marijuana to a minor, as in *J.D.W.*, should they also be allowed to commit a robbery or a homicide while working undercover?

As Elizabeth E. Joh notes in the excerpt above, "the conditions under which undercover police officers may participate in crime have seldom been the subject of regulatory oversight" and are instead governed by a "patchwork of applicable state and federal con-

---

that allows law enforcement officers to sell drugs to a juvenile in a "drug-free zone" should therefore be addressed to the legislature.

stitutional law restraints that loosely regulates undercover operations[.]" Elizabeth E. Joh, *Breaking the Law to Enforce It: Undercover Police Participation in Crime*, 62 Stan. L. Rev. 155, 168 (2009). *See also*, Jacqueline E. Ross, *The Place of Covert Surveillance in Democratic Societies: A Comparative Study of the United States and Germany*, 55 Am. J. Comp. L. 493, 540 (2007) ("The blanket immunity for authorized acts of law-breaking is further backed up by prosecutorial discretion in deciding whether to bring charges.").

In the case of drug crimes, there is a federal statute that directly immunizes law enforcement officials who violate the Controlled Substances Act. 21 U.S.C. § 885(d) provides that "no civil or criminal liability shall be imposed … upon any duly authorized Federal officer lawfully engaged in the enforcement of this title, or upon any duly authorized officer of any State, territory, political subdivision thereof, the District of Columbia, of any possession of the United States, who shall be lawfully engaged in the enforcement of any law or municipal ordinance relating to controlled substances." This immunity provision has been at issue in only a handful of published decisions. In one case that stands out for its unusual set of facts, Frank Fuller, the mayor of the small town Vance, South Carolina, was prosecuted after being videotaped selling crack cocaine outside of a convenience store on four separate occasions. "Fuller freely testified at trial and acknowledged his role in the transactions but rested his defense on his claim that he was conducting a police-style undercover investigation into employee misconduct at Angler's Mini-Mart. He asserted that he had the authority as mayor to engage in such activities." The jury, as well as the United States Court of Appeals for the Fourth Circuit, was not convinced, however. *United States v. Fuller*, 162 F.3d 256 (4th Cir. 1998) ("Since we conclude, however, that Fuller was not authorized under South Carolina law to engage in illegal drug transactions as part of his investigation, the immunity conferred by 21 U.S.C. § 885(d) does not apply."). *See also*, Chapter 7, *infra* (discussing 21 U.S.C. § 885(d) in the context of state medical marijuana laws).

b. Police Corruption

The Harmful Side Effects of Drug Prohibition
Randy Barnett

2009 Utah Law Review 11

To appreciate the hidden costs of drug law enforcement, it is not necessary to claim that the sale and use of drugs are "victimless" in the moral sense—that is, to claim that such activity harms only consenting parties and therefore that it violates no one's rights and may not justly be prohibited. For this limited purpose it is not necessary to question the contentions that drug users and sellers "harm society" or that drug use violates "the rights of society."

Nevertheless, to understand the hidden costs of drug laws, it is vitally important to note that drug laws attempt to prohibit conduct that is "victimless" in a strictly nonmoral or descriptive sense: there is no victim to complain to the police and to testify at trial.

When a person is robbed, the crime is usually reported to the police by the victim. When the robber is caught, the victim is the principal witness in any trial that might be held. As a practical matter, if the crime is never reported, there will normally not be a prosecution because the police will never pursue and catch the robber. From the perspective of the legal system, it will be as though the robbery never took place. So too, if the victim refuses to cooperate with the prosecution after a suspect has been charged, the prosecution of the robber will usually not go forward. What special law enforcement problems result from an attempt to prosecute crimes in the absence of a "complaining witness" who will assist law enforcement officials?

Because drug use takes place in private and drug users and sellers conspire to keep their activities away from the prying eyes of the police, law enforcement surveillance must be extremely intrusive to be effective. The police must somehow gain access to private areas to watch for this activity.

One way to accomplish this is for a police officer, or more likely an informant, to pose as a buyer or seller. This means that the police must initiate the illegal transaction and run the risk that the crime being prosecuted was one that would not have occurred but for the police instigation. And, since possession alone is also illegal, searches of persons without probable cause might also be necessary to find contraband.

Such illegal conduct by police is to be expected when one seeks to prohibit activity that is deliberately kept away from normal police scrutiny by the efforts of both parties to the transaction, thereby requiring police intrusion into private areas if they are to detect these acts. It is impossible for police to establish probable cause for every search for illicit drugs, no matter how small the quantity. Where no constitutional grounds exist for such an intrusion, a police department and its officers are forced to decide which is more important: the protection of constitutional rights or the political consequences of failing to get results.

The fact that such privacy-invading conduct by police may be unconstitutional and therefore illegal does not prevent it from occurring. Some of those who are most concerned about the harm caused by drug laws are lawyers who have confronted the massive violations of constitutional rights that drug laws have engendered. Such unconstitutional behavior is particularly likely, given our bizarre approach to policing the police.

At present we attempt to rectify police misconduct mainly by preventing the prosecution from using any illegally seized evidence at trial. In most instances, the success of a suppression motion depends on whether the police tell the truth about their constitutional mistake in their report and at trial. They may not do so if they think that their conduct is illegal. "There is substantial evidence to suggest that police often lie in order to bring their conduct within the limits of the practices sanctioned by judicial decisions." The only person who can usually contradict the police version of the incident is the defendant, and a defendant's credibility does not generally compare favorably with that of police officers.

Those who have committed no crime—who possess no contraband—will have no effective recourse at all. Because no evidence was seized, there is no evidence to exclude from a trial. As a practical matter, then, the police only have to worry about unconstitutional searches if something illicit turns up; but if they can confiscate whatever turns up and make an arrest, they may be better off than if they respect constitutional rights and do nothing at all. Moreover, by encouraging such frequent constitutional violations, the enforcement of drug laws desensitizes the police to constitutional safeguards in other areas as well.

The constitutional rights of the general public are therefore threatened in at least two ways. First, the burden placed on law enforcement officials to enforce possessory laws without complaining witnesses virtually compels them to engage in wholesale violations of constitutional prohibitions against unreasonable searches and seizures. For every search that produces contraband there are untold scores of searches that do not. Given our present method of deterring police misconduct by excluding evidence of guilt, there is little effective recourse against the police available to those who are innocent of any crime.

Second, the widespread efforts of police and prosecutors to stretch the outer boundaries of legal searches can be expected, over time, to contribute to the eventual loosening up of the rules by the courts. In drug prosecutions, the evidence being suppressed strongly supports the conclusion that the defendants are guilty. The more cases that police bring against obviously guilty defendants, the more opportunities and incentives appellate courts will have to find a small exception here or there. And instead of prosecuting the police for illegal conduct, the prosecutor's office becomes an insidious and publicly financed source of political and legal agitation in the defense of such illegal conduct. As I have said elsewhere, "the arm of the government whose function is to prosecute illegal conduct is called upon, in the name of law enforcement, systematically to justify police irregularities. If these arguments are successful, the definition of illegal conduct will be altered." Refusing to consider these long run effects on the stability of constitutional protections is both dangerous and unrealistic.

One point should be made clear. The police are not the heavies in this tale. They are only doing what drug-law advocates have asked them to do by the only means such a task can be done effectively.

While most people have read about corrupt law enforcement officials who are supposed to be enforcing drug laws, few people are fully aware how this corruption is caused by the type of laws being enforced. Drug laws allow the police to use force to prevent voluntary activities. Unavoidably, the power to prohibit also gives the police a de facto power to franchise the manufacture and sale of drugs, in return for a franchise fee.

The corruption caused by prohibiting consensual activity is increased still further by the ease with which law enforcement officers can assist criminals when there is no complaining witness. [W]ithout a victim to file an official complaint, it is easier for police to overlook a crime that they might see being committed. When there is no victim to contradict the police version of events, it is much easier for police to tailor their testimony to achieve the outcome they desire, for example by describing circumstances of a bad search that would lead to the evidence beings suppressed and the charges dropped. When it is the word of the police against the defendant's, the defendant usually loses. With no victim pressing for a successful prosecution, the police, prosecutor, or judge may scuttle a prosecution with little fear of public exposure.

When compared to a victim crime like robbery, the victimless character of drug offenses (in the descriptive sense discussed above), and the fact that drug users are willing to pay for drugs, creates perverse incentives. When robbery is made illegal, robbers who take anything but cash must sell their booty at a tremendous discount. In other words, laws against robbery reduce the profit that sellers of illegally obtained goods receive and thereby discourage both robbery and the potential for corruption.

Drug laws have the opposite effect. Drug law enforcement creates an artificial scarcity of a desired product resulting in sellers receiving a higher price than they would without such laws. While it is true that drug prohibition makes it more costly to engage in the activity, this cost is partially or wholly offset by an increased return in the form of higher prices and by attracting criminal types who are less risk-averse—that is, individuals who are less likely to discount their realized cash receipts by their risk of being caught. For such persons, the subjective costs of providing illicit drugs are actually less than they are for more honest persons.

The extremely lucrative nature of the illicit drug trade makes the increased corruption of police, prosecutors, and judges all but inevitable.

The fact that law enforcement personnel are corrupted by drug laws should be no more surprising than the fact that many people decide to get high by ingesting certain chemicals. Among the many tragic ironies of drug prohibition is that by attempting to prevent the latter, they make the former far more prevalent. Yet drug-law advocates typically avoid the question of whether the increased systemic corruption that their favored policies unavoidably cause is simply too high a price to pay for whatever reduction in the numbers of drug users is achieved.

United States v. Reese

United States Court of Appeals for the Ninth Circuit
2 F.3d 870 (1992)

O'Scannlain, J.

A jury convicted appellants of federal civil rights crimes stemming from their actions as Oakland Housing Authority police officers. Their appeals raise a number of difficult questions, among them certain matters of first impression. We are required to decide what the government must prove to convict a law enforcement officer of depriving an individual of his federal constitutional right to be free of excessive force during detention or arrest. We also must decide whether criminal liability may be imposed on a commanding police officer who fails to prevent the use of excessive force by officers under his command.

The Oakland Housing Authority (the "OHA") is a municipal agency that provides housing to low income residents in Oakland, California. The Oakland Housing Authority Police Department (the "OHAPD") provides security and police services to the residents of OHA properties. Prior to the events with which we are here concerned, the OHAPD consisted of some two dozen officers, including one chief, three sergeants, and one corporal.

Among the properties administered by the OHA were large public housing developments plagued by high levels of drug activity, much of it involving crack cocaine. In April 1989, a special drug suppression task force (the "Task Force") was created within the OHAPD using funds provided by a federal grant. Six new officers were hired to man the Task Force, among them appellants Reese, Dwyer, and Houston. Officers Garden, Barryer, and Yee were the remaining members. Appellant Broussard, already an OHAPD sergeant, was chosen to command them.

The Task Force operated as an independent unit within the department. The group was not assigned responsibility for patrolling any particular area, but was left free to deal with narcotics problems wherever they arose on OHA property. It held its daily group meetings apart from the regular OHAPD patrol officers. Its members worked on a single shift.

At Broussard's direction, the Task Force officers acted together virtually at all times while in the field. Typically, they would go out in two or three vehicles, drive up to an area on or near OHA property where they suspected drug activity, jump out of the vehicles, and, in the words of Officer Barryer, "just take anything and everything we saw on the street corner ... more or less like a wolf pack."

Broussard offered guidance to the men under his command in a number of respects around the time when the Task Force was first assembled. He told them, for example, that a lot of "dirty" drug money would be passing through their hands, and that it would not really matter if they kept some of it for themselves. The suspects, he noted, would be in no position to complain if some of their money came up missing. He also regularly exhorted Task Force officers to keep their arrest numbers up. All the officers were aware that the federal grant that funded their unit, and on which their jobs depended, was good for only eighteen to twenty-four months. Broussard warned that they would need statistics to show that the federal money was well spent and thus to secure another grant. On more than one occasion, he sent the Task Force out to begin a shift with comments like, "Let's go out and kick ass," and "Everybody goes to jail tonight for everything, all right?"

We turn now to the various incidents that were part of the government's case at trial, whether charged as individual substantive violations or as overt acts in furtherance of appellants' alleged conspiracy.

On May 8, 1989, during the Task Force's first night on patrol, Dwyer and Garden chased and caught a fleeing suspect in a parking lot. The two officers had the suspect on the ground and were beating him when other Task Force members stepped in; he did not appear to be resisting. Dwyer then walked the suspect over to one of the patrol cars and slammed him against it abruptly, so that his face and chest came down on the hood, even though the suspect was under control and in handcuffs at the time. Yee then pulled the suspect away from Dwyer, and the suspect was arrested for loitering. At the Task Force's briefing the next day, Dwyer told Yee he did not appreciate having his "investigation" interfered with.

Garden received a cut on his face during this incident. In response, Broussard told his assembled officers that any suspect who injured a Task Force member had better end up going to the hospital himself. On other occasions, Broussard admonished his men that, if a suspect were to run from them, they should "catch him [and] whip his ass." "No one runs," Broussard told another OHAPD sergeant. "Those who run will pay."

On May 16, 1989, at about 2:00 p.m., Jackie Dailey was helping to fix the car of an OHA resident, across the street from his own residence. Task Force members arrived on the scene and ordered Dailey and the other individuals present to stand spread-eagled against the car while they were searched and their names checked for outstanding warrants. No such warrants were found, and the search revealed no contraband. Reese then approached Dailey and told him that he found the hat Dailey was wearing offensive. The hat had the words "One Pimp, six holes" written on it. Reese took the hat off Dailey's head, ripped it, and threw it on the ground. He then seized Dailey by the neck and the back of the pants and threw him against the police car, then lifted him and threw him to the ground twice in succession. Houston then arrested Dailey for loitering. Broussard, the supervisor in charge at the time, was present at this incident and watched it develop, but took no steps to intercede.

After his release from jail, Dailey went to a hospital emergency room, where an x-ray was taken. He was later diagnosed as having sustained a fracture of his right elbow. Pain medication was prescribed and his arm was placed in a sling, which prevented him from filling out the complaint form he wished to file with the OHA — a friend had to write out the complaint for him.

On May 19, 1989, Dwyer attempted to place a suspect in the back seat of a patrol car. He found himself unable to do so because another suspect, Bryan Kiel, already in custody and handcuffed, had fallen asleep there. Dwyer twice told Kiel to move, then, receiving no response, kicked him hard in the chest.

A meeting involving the members of the Task Force and the chief of the OHAPD was held in the wake of this incident. The chief told the officers that the use of unnecessary or excessive force would not be tolerated, that Dwyer had come close to being terminated, and that any officer guilty of using excessive force in the future would be. After the chief left, Dwyer confronted Yee, saying he would hold him directly responsible if he were fired. Houston then told Yee that he was not a team player and was not aggressive enough. Reese added that, while he had no problems with Yee personally, he "felt he had to watch his back and look over his shoulder when [Yee] was around, because he was afraid [Yee would] say something." Both Reese and Houston told Yee he should consider leaving the Task Force.

Broussard, who had said little to that point in the meeting, then stated that "team business should remain team business," that matters involving Task Force members were the Task Force's own affair, and that no one else need know about them. On this and other occasions, Broussard told his officers that "team business" was not to be discussed with OHA patrol officers. Any Task Force member who had a problem with this, he added, would be "severely dealt with" by Broussard himself.

On May 23, 1989, Barryer conducted a pat search of Demetrius Findley. Barryer found nothing, and was prepared to release the suspect, but Broussard told him to continue the search. Barryer eventually discovered a plastic baggie containing suspected rock cocaine underneath Findley's testicles.

Barryer believed, however, that he had not had probable cause to conduct such an extensive search. He and Broussard discussed the problem of how to write up the arrest report in such a way as to make the search appear valid. Barryer proposed saying that he had felt something like a weapon in Findley's pants, but Broussard rejected this idea on the grounds that it would not provide a strong enough case. Barryer then indicated that he would simply say that he had seen Findley throw the cocaine on the ground. "Yeah, that'll work," Broussard said. Barryer wrote up his report in these terms, and Broussard read and approved the report.

The following month, Barryer was subpoenaed to testify in court in connection with the Findley arrest. Upon meeting with the deputy district attorney, however, Barryer indicated that he would be unable to testify to what he had said in his arrest report because it was false. He was then released from his subpoena.

Barryer returned to the OHAPD where he related these events first to the chief and then to Broussard. Broussard insisted that Barryer should have testified to what he had written in the report, saying, "Who do you think they're going to believe, you or the dirt bag?" Barryer was fired two weeks later for having falsified his report.

On the night of June 1, 1989, a Task Force patrol car carrying Barryer, Dwyer, and Reese crashed into a backstop while pursuing David McClendon across a baseball field. Barryer, the driver of the car, chased McClendon on foot up an adjacent street, then caught him and threw him to the ground. Dwyer arrived promptly thereafter. Barryer had McClendon under control and was preparing to handcuff him when Garden's voice came through over his radio saying that Reese had been injured in the crash. Dwyer then hit McClendon on the top of the head with his flashlight, causing a wound that required twenty-five stitches to close.

McClendon was brought back to the ball field, where Broussard's attention was drawn to the bloody wound on his head. Broussard then stated that McClendon would have to be arrested for something in order to justify his injury and his trip to the hospital. Garden wrote a false report stating that he had seen McClendon discard rock cocaine while running from Task Force officers, and that he had dropped a package of narcotics while being transferred from one patrol car to another.

On June 2, 1989, Task Force members stopped Edward Jackson, a juvenile, walking across a parking lot. Reese searched Jackson, including his underwear, but found nothing and told him to go. Broussard then produced a plastic bag of rock cocaine from a nearby hole in the ground. Jackson denied the drugs were his, but was arrested anyway. Reese wrote a report stating that he and Garden had observed Jackson for some fifteen minutes, and had seen him return frequently to the hole in the ground, where he inspected a plastic bag and removed things from it. The report was false.

Later that month, Jackson came up for trial in juvenile court. Garden, reading the report Reese had written for the first time on the day of the trial, told Reese they were going to have to get their stories together. They met during breaks in the trial, and visited the scene of the arrest during the lunch recess, agreeing upon the content of their testimony. Jackson was found guilty of possessing cocaine for sale. On returning to OHAPD headquarters, Garden and Reese told Dwyer that they had "lied [their] asses off in court" that day.

On the evening of June 29, 1989, Glen Losh was sitting with his girlfriend in his pickup truck, parked near OHA property. The Task Force, with all appellants present, pulled up behind them. Reese removed Losh from the truck and frisked him, then directed him to cross the sidewalk and to place his hands above his head against a fence. Reese then asked Losh what he was doing in the area. When Losh replied that he was there to sell an extra car battery he had acquired, Reese accused him of lying, and struck him with the heel or palm of his hand in the ribs on both sides of his body, knocking the wind out of him and causing him to fall to his knees.

Reese then frisked Losh again and removed his billfold and $30 in cash. He asked again why Losh was in the area, and what he, a white person, was doing in a black neighborhood. Reese then held up Losh's money — a twenty-dollar bill and two five-dollar bills — and said, "It looks like you have ten dollars." Reese threw the two fives on the ground, and put the twenty in his pocket. Losh never received the money back.

Garden and Broussard searched Losh's truck. Garden found a mirror, a gold razor blade, and a gold straw, items that he considered to be cocaine paraphernalia, which he smashed in the street. Garden confronted Losh about these items, pulling his beard and backhanding him across the mouth to get his attention. Houston, meanwhile, came over and questioned Losh further regarding his presence in the area, striking him in the lower back near the kidneys more than once. Losh was not arrested.

During this same shift, early on the morning of June 30, 1989, the same Task Force officers encountered Rosie Verduzco and her husband Salvador. The two were sitting in their car, parked near OHA property in front of the home of Salvador's parents; Salvador was talking to his brother David Verduzco and his cousin Michael Guzman, who stood on the sidewalk. Arriving on the scene, the officers ordered Rosie and Salvador to get out of their car and to place their hands on the roof, which they did.

Rosie was searched and her identification was taken by one of the officers. She then asked Houston, who was standing to her left, what the problem was. He responded by saying, "Shut up, bitch." Rosie kept asking questions, and Houston repeatedly responded with the same phrase. Eventually, Houston grabbed Rosie's hair, then yanked her head back over her shoulder so that she was looking at him. He did this several times. At no time did Rosie take her hands off the roof of the car or make any moves toward Houston. Finally, Houston shoved Rosie against the side of the car and struck her on the head with his flashlight. The laceration bled profusely and later required two staples to close. Rosie was arrested for resisting arrest and for having an open container in her car. Broussard was standing five to ten feet behind Houston as this incident unfolded.

Meanwhile, Salvador stood spread-eagled on the opposite side of the car, his legs apart and his hands on the roof. When he protested against Houston's treatment of his wife, Dwyer kicked him in the testicles from behind, telling him to shut up, and adding, "How do you like that, wetback"? Salvador was not arrested.

The OHA received numerous citizen complaints regarding the conduct of OHAPD officers during the period between May and July 1989. On one occasion, OHAPD Sergeant Watson spoke to Broussard about complaints alleging the use of excessive force. Broussard said he was not aware of any such problems involving the members of the Task Force, but he would bring the matter to the attention of his men. Watson also spoke to Dwyer, Houston, and Reese about the complaints, and told them not to use more force than was necessary, and to document properly any incident in which they resorted to force.

When the other OHA sergeant, Sergeant Santiago, spoke to Broussard about the increased number of citizen complaints, he was told: "Don't worry about it. They're just dope dealers and … they don't have any complaint." Asked specifically about the complaints filed by Glen Losh and his girlfriend, Broussard said, "Oh, they were just out there to buy dope." On one occasion, when Broussard was delayed in arriving at work, Santiago convened a special joint briefing session of the Task Force and regular patrol officers. He discussed the influx of internal affairs complaints about excessive force and the theft of money and property, and warned the officers that such conduct would not be condoned, and could lead to an investigation by an outside agency.

On August 13, 1989, Task Force officers encountered a group of black males. Searching the area across the street from the group, Garden found a box containing baggies of marijuana. Reese and Broussard conferred, and Reese then asked whose box it was. When no one stepped forward, Reese announced that whoever was carrying the most money would go to jail. That person proved to be David Lyles, a juvenile, and he was promptly arrested. Reese wrote up an arrest report in which he stated that he and Garden had seen Lyles holding the box, and that Lyles had dropped the box and crossed the street when he saw the officers' vehicle pull up. This was untrue. Nonetheless, Reese and Garden both testified in court to what Reese had written, and Lyles was found guilty.

On August 25, 1989, acting on the basis of information received earlier that day, Reese and Houston stopped a car driven by Cliofus Soluno, a suspected drug supplier. Broussard, Garden, and Dwyer joined them, and Soluno's trunk was searched. A large amount of marijuana and $2000 in cash was found in the trunk. Observing that Soluno, an undocumented alien from Mexico, would not miss the money, the five officers divided the cash among themselves.

On or about September 23, 1989, Task Force members chased and caught a suspect in a field. No drugs were found on his person or anywhere near him. Dwyer went to the trunk of his patrol car, and retrieved a baggie containing three pieces of rock cocaine. Dwyer then wrote an arrest report stating that these drugs had been taken from the suspect. Houston and Garden, as well as Dwyer, maintained "stashes" of narcotics which they used against suspects at various times.

On the night of October 7, 1989, Jerry Watkins was walking down the street in a neighborhood known as a "heavy drug area," looking for his stepson. Dwyer jumped out of a civilian car, and, without identifying himself as a police officer, yelled at Watkins, "Come here, you son of a bitch, [or I'll] kill you." Frightened, Watkins attempted to escape through a backyard. Dwyer, however, caught up with him and struck him in the head with his flashlight as he attempted to climb through a hole in a fence. The wound Watkins received later required eight to ten stitches. Dwyer wrote a report stating that Watkins had dropped a piece of rock cocaine while attempting to flee; he submitted what he said was this cocaine into evidence. This report was false.

On October 26, 1989, the Task Force stopped Keith Rogers. Dwyer began to search him for drugs and found a small baggie of marijuana. Dwyer continued the search, but Rogers grew belligerent when Dwyer moved to search his underwear. In response, Dwyer tried to rip Rogers' underwear off him, then used a buck knife to cut it off, saying, "Fuck your rights. What about your rights now?" Broussard then directed the officers to drive Rogers to an area outside a closed OHA complex. Arriving there, the officers bent Rogers over the front of a patrol vehicle and held him there. Dwyer put on a pair rubber gloves and said, "The doctor is in," then proceeded to perform a rectal search on Rogers. Rogers was visible from the street during this search. No drugs were found.

On November 1, 1989, Task Force officers on patrol observed two black males looking into a brown paper bag. When the men saw the officers' vehicle, they fled. The bag turned out to contain a large amount of rock cocaine, and Sherman Gay was arrested for its possession by Task Force Officer Williamson. Broussard explained to Williamson and Garden that Gay was a big time drug dealer and that he "definitely" needed to go to jail in connection with the drugs. A discussion ensued among the three officers regarding what Williamson should write in his arrest report, and Williamson suggested that he could write up the arrest as an observed hand-to-hand drug transaction. Williamson wrote the report accordingly, even though he had observed no such transaction.

By November 1989, the activities of the Task Force had prompted an investigation by the Oakland Police Department and the Alameda County District Attorney's Office. As part of the investigation, several videotaped undercover operations were conducted. Generally these operations involved an undercover officer, carrying a pager and a predetermined sum of money, standing on the sidewalk near OHA property with drugs placed somewhere nearby. The investigating officers would then call the OHA dispatcher to complain about the "drug dealer" who was working in that area, giving the undercover agent's description. The jury viewed a number of these videotapes as evidence in appellants' trial.

On November 14, 1989, Officer Robert Pursley was working undercover in one of these operations. The drugs had been placed in a cigarette package; Pursley stood near the package, and once sat down next to it. Meanwhile, across the street from Pursley, genuine drug deals were being conducted by one Billy Cooley.

The Task Force was dispatched to the scene. Garden told Pursley to get on the ground, then went across the street to Cooley. Dwyer then approached Pursley, straddled him and told him to roll over onto his back. Pursley rolled over with his arms extended, whereupon Dwyer hit Pursley in the hands with his flashlight and told him never to raise his hands to him again. Dwyer then kicked Pursley in the ribs, and grabbed him by the throat and started choking him, without provocation.

On November 21, 1989, Officer George Elzie assumed the role of the undercover agent in this operation, and was arrested by Reese. Elzie had been given $630 prior to being placed in the field. Together, Reese and Houston removed all of this money from Elzie's pockets. However, Reese turned in just $280, and claimed in his arrest report that this was all that had been recovered from Elzie. The rest of the money was never accounted for.[14]

On the basis of these incidents among others, appellants were tried by jury under a nineteen count indictment. The first count charged all four appellants with a criminal conspiracy whose object was the deprivation of constitutional rights, in violation of 18 U.S.C.

---

14. During the undercover operation staged on November 22, 1989, the Task Force learned that it was under surveillance when a suspect revealed the presence of video cameras at the surveillance location. The operation therefore had to be terminated.

§ 241. The jury returned a verdict of guilty on the conspiracy count. The other counts delineated the specific substantive violations of these rights committed by the individual officers, in violation of 18 U.S.C. § 242. The jury voted to convict on most of these counts. In particular, each appellant was convicted for his role in one or more episodes involving excessive force.

Appellants were sentenced under the Guidelines to terms ranging from thirty-six to ninety-six months. They filed timely notices of appeal. A panel of this court subsequently granted their motions for bail pending appeal.

[The Appellants raised various challenges to the district court's jury instructions and to its application of the Sentencing Guidelines. The Court of Appeals rejected each of Appellants' arguments and affirmed their convictions and sentences.]

2. Informants

a. The Importance of Informants in Drug Investigations

Deregulating Guilt:
The Information Culture of the Criminal System
Alexandra Natapoff
30 Cardozo Law Review 965 (2008)

Nearly every drug case involves a snitch, and drug cases represent an ever larger proportion of both state and federal dockets. As U.S. District Judge Marvin Shoob once complained, "I can't tell you the last time I heard a drug case of any substance in which the government did not have at least one informant.... Most of the time, there are two or three informants, and sometimes they are worse criminals than the defendant on trial." As the use of informants becomes an increasingly common investigative and case management tool, the impact of the official practice of trading information for liability with criminals becomes of central importance for understanding the system's changing information culture.

Criminal informants—i.e., criminal offenders who receive lenient treatment because of their cooperation with the government—are a longstanding and important part of the criminal system. Certain kinds of cases—drug conspiracies, antitrust, corporate fraud, terrorism—are difficult to investigate or prosecute without them, as the government is in a poor position to obtain incriminating information without inside help. Some kinds of information, for example, are only possessed by participants. Moreover, informants are procedurally simple and cheap. For example, while the government can apply for a wiretap order under Title III, it needs to show probable cause, and the resulting order will include time and other limitations. Alternatively, the government can skip the warrant process altogether and get an informant to wear a wire, without having to show probable cause and without temporal or spatial restrictions. Their usefulness and ease have thus made informants a staple of drug and other investigations.

Notwithstanding their investigative value, informants pose significant challenges. The informant deal is the antithesis of the trial-centric, regulated, due process information model. It proceeds in secret, with almost no constraints on the parties' ability to use information or to bargain. Police have nearly unfettered discretion both to seek information from suspects and to decline to arrest them in exchange, while prosecutors have similarly unfettered discretion to trade charging and sentencing concessions for cooperation. The secrecy surrounding the practice enables the government to use almost any information it wants to pressure a deal, including illegal evidence, racial profiling, and personal information about the suspect or his/her intimate relationships.

One reason for these developments is that the use of criminal informants falls squarely between the gaps of informational doctrine. Street-corner interactions between police officer and informant are largely unaffected by search and seizure or self-incrimination law. Many seminal criminal procedure cases turn on the inapplicability of the Bill of Rights to interactions with informants. Even in more regulated settings, a defendant's decision to cooperate will eviscerate many constitutional restraints on governmental information gathering, not only against the informant himself but also against third parties. Perhaps the most dramatic consequence is the ability of the government to evade Fourth, Fifth and Sixth Amendment restrictions by persuading an informant to obtain information that government agents could not obtain on their own. The gaps in information doctrine thus create a zone of procedural permissiveness that naturally promotes the use of informants.

Once the deal is struck, the information obtained from informants is problematic in its own right. Not only is it famously unreliable, but it is colored by the choices made by informants themselves, who may identify others in order to further their own criminal or personal desires. For example, a suspected drug dealer who told Atlanta police that they would find a kilogram of cocaine at Kathryn Johnston's address was released in exchange for that tip, even though the tip was inaccurate and led to the death of the 92-year-old grandmother.

Despite these flaws and biases, informant information drives a great deal of official decision-making. Police design investigations and prosecutors select targets based on their informant sources. The kinds of information that informants tend to give become an important determinant shaping law enforcement. The symbiosis between source and handler, moreover, becomes an informational force to be reckoned with.

There are numerous examples of productive informant deals. From Sammy the Bull to Edward Partin to Jack Abramoff, using informants often produces important investigations and convictions. The fact that approximately fifteen percent of all federal defendants — and one-quarter of drug defendants — receive sentencing credit for "substantial assistance" indicates that federal prosecutors and courts believe that cooperating defendants provide valuable investigative resources.

The costs and dangers of informant use are more difficult to document, in part because there are few mechanisms for recording cases where informants give bad information, or commit new crimes, or lead to corruption. Anecdotal evidence, however, suggests the nature of some of the problems.

For example:

Ann Colomb and her three sons were federally indicted for allegedly running the largest crack ring in Louisiana out of their home. They were convicted in jury trials and served four months in prison before they were released and all charges dismissed. Their wrongful convictions were based on fabricated information obtained from a ring of jailhouse informants who bought and sold information about the Colomb family so that inmates could offer testimony and reduce their own sentences. The government identified 31 informants that it planned to use in this way, before the scheme was revealed. The presiding judge, U.S. District Judge Tucker Melancon, said afterwards: "It was like revolving-door inmate testimony. The allegation was that there was in the federal justice system a network of folks trying to get relief from long sentences by ginning up information on folks being tried in drug cases. I'd heard about it before. But it all culminated in the Colomb trial."

Amy Gepfert was suspected of participating in a conspiracy to deal cocaine. The police told her that she was facing a forty year sentence, although in fact her maximum sentence would have been ten years. Police also discouraged her from calling a lawyer. In exchange for avoiding prosecution, the police required her to engage in oral sex with another suspect and to ask him for money. That suspect was then charged with soliciting a prostitute.

In Dallas, police made an arrangement with a group of informants in which the informants planted fake drugs on Mexican immigrants. The police then arrested the immigrants and fabricated or failed to conduct the drug tests that would have revealed that the alleged cocaine was actually gypsum, the substance found in wallboard. The informants were paid thousands of dollars, while the police used the arrests to inflate their drug-bust statistics. Numerous immigrants pleaded guilty and were deported before the scheme was discovered.

In New York, Brooklyn police officers paid informants with drugs taken from dealers who were arrested after the informants pointed them out. One officer bragged about the practice on tape, explaining that officers would seize drugs but report a lesser amount, keeping the unreported drugs to give to informants later on.

Such examples—which represent just the tip of the iceberg—illustrate the myriad potential influences of informant use on the criminal process. They reveal not only the potential unreliability of the practice, but the often corrupting personal relationships established between police and snitches, particularly the power inequalities that characterize this method of gathering information. They demonstrate the reversal of means and ends implicit in the trading of information for liability, and the potential increase in crime and violence that can accompany it. Finally, they suggest the impact of the practice on the meaning of guilt itself.

The most infamous and best documented hallmark of snitching is its unreliability. Both in theory and practice, information obtained from criminal informants who are compensated for their information is often wrong. According to one recent report, nearly half of all wrongful capital convictions are a result of a lying informant witness. Numerous cases and media stories reveal the extent to which informants lie in exchange for lenience, and the extent to which police and prosecutors rely on their information knowing it to be problematic or outright false.

Informant unreliability is exacerbated by secrecy, making mistakes harder to discern and errors easier to conceal after the fact. Nevertheless, the pressure to keep informant identity and information secret has been a powerful force in criminal procedure

b. Reliability of Informants

One of the biggest challenges police and prosecutors face when dealing with informants is ensuring the information they provide is reliable. Most informants do not give information to the government out of the kindness of their hearts. They provide information in exchange for a benefit, such as a reduced sentence or money. Because of mandatory minimum sentencing, drug defendants can often have an especially strong incentive to cooperate with the police. Moreover, as discussed in Chapter 4, prosecutors may often have the final say over whether a defendant's information was useful enough to qualify as substantial assistance and yield a reduced sentence. These factors may, in some cases, give even scrupulous defendants a strong incentive to provide false information to the government if they come to view it as the only way to reduce a lengthy sentence.

Concern about the veracity of informants who are induced to testify against others by promises of leniency influenced one panel of the United States Court of Appeals for the Tenth Circuit in the late 1990s to issue a decision barring the practice. *United States v. Singleton*, 144 F.3d 1343 (10th Cir. 1998). The panel's decision was quickly overturned in the opinion below by the court sitting *en banc*.

United States v. Singleton

United States Court of Appeals for the Tenth Circuit
165 F.3d 1297 (1999)

Porfilio, J.

Sonya Singleton was convicted of money laundering and conspiring to distribute cocaine. A panel of this court reversed that conviction on the ground the prosecuting attorney violated 18 U.S.C. § 201(c)(2) when he offered leniency to a co-defendant in exchange for truthful testimony. The panel held the testimony of the co-defendant should have been suppressed and that the failure to do so was not harmless error. The en banc court vacated the panel decision and has now reheard the appeal. We now hold 18 U.S.C. § 201(c)(2) does not apply to the United States or an Assistant United States Attorney functioning within the official scope of the office.

The conspiracy forming the basis of Ms. Singleton's conviction required her to send and receive drug proceeds by Western Union wires. Her co-conspirator Napoleon Douglas entered into a plea agreement in which he agreed to testify truthfully in return for the government's promise not to prosecute him for related offenses, to advise the sentencing court of his cooperation, and to advise a state parole board of the "nature and extent" of his cooperation.

Before trial, Ms. Singleton moved to suppress the testimony of Mr. Douglas on the ground the government had violated 18 U.S.C. § 201(c)(2), the so-called "anti-gratuity statute," by promising him leniency in exchange for his testimony. The district court denied the motion and Mr. Douglas testified, acknowledging the benefits he would receive in exchange for his testimony and implicating Ms. Singleton in the charged offenses. Ms. Singleton asks us to review the court's denial of her motion.

The question before us is whether section 201(c)(2) applies to the government in the prosecution of criminal offenses. Ms. Singleton argues the plain language of the statute permits no answer but that it does. As expected, the government counters such a reading is beyond the intent of Congress and clearly wrong. We review this issue of law de novo and begin our analysis with the pertinent portions of 18 U.S.C. § 201(c)(2) itself:

> (c) Whoever—
>
>   ....
>
>   (2) directly or indirectly, gives, offers, or promises anything of value to any person, for or because of the testimony under oath or affirmation given or to be given by such person as a witness upon a trial ... before any court ... shall be fined under this title or imprisoned for not more than two years, or both.

Ms. Singleton takes the position that when Mr. Douglas testified after receiving the government's promise of lenient treatment in exchange for his truthful testimony, he became a "paid 'occurrence' witness," and testimony from those of such ilk is contrary to the fundamental precepts of American justice because the payment of something of value would give the witness a strong motivation to lie. She reasons section 201(c)(2) was enacted to deter that result, and we need only apply plain meaning to the word "whoever" contained in the statute to conclude it must apply broadly and encompass the government and its representatives.

In contrast, the United States argues to allow section 201(c)(2) to sweep so broadly would not only be a radical departure from the ingrained legal culture of our criminal justice system but would also result in criminalizing historic practice and established law. The government maintains Congress did not intend to hinder the sovereign's authority to prosecute violations against the United States in this fashion.

Viewing the statute on its face, it is apparent the dispute revolves about the word "whoever." Indeed, the significance of the remaining parts of the statute is not seriously controverted. However, like many words chosen by the legislative branch to convey its intent, this one word evokes more meaning than an innocent first reading of it would portend.

As correctly argued by Ms. Singleton, "whoever" is a broad term which by its ordinary definition would exclude no one. Indeed, if one were to take the word at face value, defendant's argument becomes colorable, at least. However, the defendant's approach, while facially logical, ignores a crucial point that must be considered in any attempt to apply the statute to the issues of this case. She argues the breadth of the word "'whoever' includes within its scope the assistant United States attorney who offered Douglas something of value in exchange for his testimony." To begin the parsing of the statute with this assumption, however, ignores a fundamental fact: the capacity in which the government's lawyer appears in the courts.

The prosecutor, functioning within the scope of his or her office, is not simply a lawyer advocating the government's perspective of the case. Indeed, the prosecutor's function is far more significant. Only officers of the Department of Justice or the United States Attorney can represent the United States in the prosecution of a criminal case. Indeed, a federal court cannot even assert jurisdiction over a criminal case unless it is filed and prosecuted by the United States Attorney or a properly appointed assistant. Therefore, the government's sovereign authority to prosecute and conduct a prosecution is vested solely in the United States Attorney and his or her properly appointed assistants. Of course, it cannot be otherwise because the government of the United States is not capable of exercising its powers on its own; the government functions only through its officers and agents. We thus infer in criminal cases that an Assistant United States Attorney, acting within the scope of authority conferred upon that office, is the alter ego of the United States exercising its sovereign power of prosecution. Hence, in the attempt to apply section 201(c)(2), the United States and the Assistant United States Attorney cannot be separated. Indeed, the alter ego role of the prosecutor is not unusual, for in a similar case, the Sixth Circuit has noted:

> When an assistant United States Attorney (AUSA) enters into a plea agreement with a defendant, that plea agreement is between the United States government and the defendant. When an AUSA uses at trial testimony obtained through a plea agreement or an agreement not to prosecute, he does so as the government. An AUSA who, pursuant to the provisions of the United States Sentencing Guidelines, moves for a downward departure under § 5K1.1, does so as the government.

Put into proper context, then, the defendant's argument is: in a criminal prosecution, the word "whoever" in the statute includes within its scope the United States acting in its sovereign capacity. Extending that premise to its logical conclusion, the defendant implies Congress must have intended to subject the United States to the provisions of section 201(c)(2), and, consequently, like any other violator, to criminal prosecution. Reduced to this logical conclusion, the basic argument of the defendant is patently absurd.

There is even a more fundamental reason for arriving at the same conclusion, however. Although Congress may, by legislative act, add to or redefine the meaning of any word, it did not do so in the passage of section 201(c)(2). Therefore, we must presume it intended to employ the common meaning of the word. The word "whoever" connotes a being. The United States is an inanimate entity, not a being. Therefore, construing "whoever" to include the government is semantically anomalous. Looking beyond definitions, though, there are rules of statutory construction that will lead to the same conclusion.

Statutes of general purport do not apply to the United States unless Congress makes the application clear and indisputable. In *The Dollar Savings Bank v. United States*, 86 U.S. 227 (1873), the [United States Supreme] Court instructed:

> It is a familiar principle that the King is not bound by any act of Parliament unless he be named therein by special and particular words. The most general words that can be devised (for example, any person or persons, bodies politic or corporate) affect not him in the least, if they may tend to restrain or diminish any of his rights and interests.... The rule thus settled respecting the British Crown is equally applicable to this government, and it has been applied frequently in the different States, and practically in the Federal courts. It may be considered as settled that so much of the royal prerogatives as belonged to the King in his capacity of *parens patriae*, or universal trustee, enters as much into our political state as it does into the principles of the British constitution.

The Court revisited the concept in *Nardone v. United States*, 302 U.S. 379, 383–84 (1937), when it held this canon of construction generally applies when failure to limit the application of a statute would "deprive the sovereign of a recognized or established prerogative title or interest" or "where a reading which would include [the government] would work obvious absurdity."

The next question, then, is whether applying the statute to the government would deprive the sovereign of a recognized or established prerogative, title, or interest. The answer to that question is, inescapably yes.

From the common law, we have drawn a longstanding practice sanctioning the testimony of accomplices against their confederates in exchange for leniency. Indeed,

> no practice is more ingrained in our criminal justice system than the practice of the government calling a witness who is an accessory to the crime for which the defendant is charged and having that witness testify under a plea bargain that promises him a reduced sentence.

United States v. Cervantes-Pacheco, 826 F.2d 310, 315 (5th Cir. 1987).

This ingrained practice of granting lenience in exchange for testimony has created a vested sovereign prerogative in the government. It follows that if the practice can be traced to the common law, it has acquired stature akin to the special privilege of kings. However, in an American criminal prosecution, the granting of lenience is an authority that can only be exercised by the United States through its prosecutor; therefore, any reading of section 201(c)(2) that would restrict the exercise of this power is surely a diminution of sovereignty not countenanced in our jurisprudence.

Moreover, in light of the longstanding practice of leniency for testimony, we must presume if Congress had intended that section 201(c)(2) overturn this ingrained aspect of

American legal culture, it would have done so in clear, unmistakable, and unarguable language.

Our conclusion in no way permits an agent of the government to step beyond the limits of his or her office to make an offer to a witness other than one traditionally exercised by the sovereign. A prosecutor who offers something other than a concession normally granted by the government in exchange for testimony is no longer the alter ego of the sovereign and is divested of the protective mantle of the government. Thus, fears our decision would permit improper use or abuse of prosecutorial authority simply have no foundation.[2] It is noteworthy, then, that defendant's premise relies upon the shibboleth "the government is not above the law." While we agree with that notion, we simply believe this particular statute does not exist for the government. Accordingly, we AFFIRM the district court's denial of the motion to suppress on 18 U.S.C. § 201(c)(2) grounds. We adopt the ruling of the panel that the evidence in the record was sufficient to sustain the judgment of conviction, notwithstanding the panel's conclusion the testimony of Mr. Douglas should have been suppressed.

Lucero, J., with whom Henry, J. joins, concurring.

I concur in the judgment that the United States and its agent, an Assistant United States Attorney, did not violate 18 U.S.C. § 201(c)(2) by offering in a plea agreement to exchange leniency for the testimony of Singleton's co-conspirator. But I write separately to state my disagreement with the majority's holding that the word "whoever" in 18 U.S.C. § 201(c)(2), as it is used to define the class of persons who can violate the statute, cannot include the government or its agents. The majority's interpretation would permit the conclusion that consistent with the provisions of § 201, a United States Attorney may pay a prosecution witness for false testimony.

I cannot join the dissent, however, because § 201(c)(2) operates in conjunction with other statutes to allow the government, upon proper disclosure and/or with court approval, to trade certain items of value for testimony. These statutes include 18 U.S.C. § 3553(e) and 28 U.S.C. § 994(n), passed as part of the Sentencing Reform Act of 1984, which allow courts, acting pursuant to the Sentencing Guidelines and upon motion of the government, to reduce sentences for individuals who provide "substantial assistance in the investigation or prosecution of another"; the federal immunity statutes, 18 U.S.C. §§ 6001–6005, passed as part of the Organized Crime Control Act of 1970, which require courts, upon the request of the government, to confer immunity upon witnesses for their testimony in aid of the prosecution; and the Witness Relocation and Protection Act, 18 U.S.C. §§ 3521–3528, passed as part of the Comprehensive Crime Control Act of 1974, which allows the government to bestow various benefits for the protection of cooperating witnesses. Because these specific statutes are in conflict with the general prohibitions of § 201(c)(2), the specific statutes control, and permit the prosecution's actions in this case.

Congress has developed an extensive and detailed statutory framework authorizing sentence reductions and recommendations, immunity, and other incentives for cooper-

---

2. The concurrence expresses a concern our disposition would "permit the conclusion that consistent with the provisions of § 201, a United States Attorney may pay a prosecution witness for false testimony." We believe the concern is misplaced. It is inconceivable that any court would hold that a prosecutor who pays for the *false* testimony of a witness is carrying out an official function of the government. Our disposition protects only those prosecutorial acts of the government which have been recognized in common law or authorized by statute. A prosecutor who goes beyond those limitations is clearly not performing a governmental function.

ating witnesses. Federal immunity statutes, for example, which authorize prosecutors to request immunity for cooperating witnesses "reflect[] the importance of testimony, and the fact that many offenses are of such a character that the only persons capable of giving useful testimony are those implicated in the crime." *Kastigar v. United States,* 406 U.S. 441, 446 (1972). The Supreme Court has characterized the immunity statutes as "essential to the effective enforcement of various criminal statutes" and "so familiar that they have become part of our 'constitutional fabric,'" *United States v. Mandujano,* 425 U.S. 564, 575–76 (1976).

Although, as the Singleton panel noted, the government moves the court to grant immunity rather than bestowing immunity directly upon a cooperating witness the government's role in the process is more important than that of the court. See *United States v. Doe,* 465 U.S. 605 (1984) (noting that the immunity statutes grant government authorities "exclusive authority to grant immunities" and that the courts play "only a minor role in the immunizing process"). Indeed, the statutory language itself requires the court, "upon the request of the United States attorney," to "issue ... an order requiring [a witness] to give testimony or provide other information which he refuses to give or provide on the basis of his privilege against self-incrimination."

When granted statutory immunity, the potential witness is given something of value by the government in that his immunized testimony cannot be used to prosecute him. By the same token, the government plainly gains something of value from immunizing the testimony—the testimony itself. The immunity statutes give the government leverage with which to obtain testimony from recalcitrant witnesses, and the power to grant immunity serves as one of the bargaining tools in the prosecutorial process.

Dispositive in this case is the Sentencing Reform Act of 1984, which, as amended, authorizes courts, upon motion of the government, to reduce sentences for individuals who provide "substantial assistance in the investigation or prosecution of another." There can be little doubt that Congress intended to include the provision of cooperative testimony under the rubric of "substantial assistance." Both 18 U.S.C. § 3553(e) and 28 U.S.C. § 994(n) define such assistance in terms of "the investigation or prosecution of another person who has committed an offense." Although there are some forms of assistance in prosecution that are neither testimonial nor duplicative of investigatory assistance, it stretches credulity to suppose that Congress intended to exclude cooperative testimony from "substantial assistance" as used in these statutes.

By allowing prosecutors to reward testimony with sentencing benefits, the statutes must also be read to authorize prosecutors to inform a defendant and potential witness of the possibility of such reward. Barring a prosecutor from discussing leniency prior to testimony would seriously inhibit the intended effect of these statutes by reducing the pool of defendants willing to testify against their co-conspirators to those informed by their counsel of the potential benefits of cooperation.

Pursuant to these grants of statutory authority, the Sentencing Commission has issued a policy statement entitled "Substantial Assistance to Authorities," *see* U.S.S.G. § 5K1.1, which allows a downward departure in consideration of "the truthfulness, completeness, and reliability of any information or testimony provided by the defendant." Courts have upheld the exchange of testimony for leniency under this authority.

In totality, these various statutes create both a substantive and procedural framework for bargaining between government agents and potential witnesses. They limit the "something of value" that the government may offer, and detail the roles of both the prosecution and the courts in determining sentences, providing immunity, and granting other forms of assistance. The result is a coherent, narrowly defined set of laws that operate in the same field as the more general prohibitions of § 201(c)(2). Under long-established principles of statutory construction, where specific statutes overlap with a general statute, the latter must give way, insofar as it would prohibit that which the narrow statutes would allow. It is for this reason that I concur with the majority's result.

This analysis has several advantages over that of the majority. It provides both a roadmap for the bargaining process and a clearly articulated criminal statute with which to punish straying prosecutors. The majority's reading of § 201(c)(2), on the other hand, creates a conceptually messy legal regime for handling the case of the errant United States Attorney "who offers something other than a concession normally granted by the government," such as bribing a witness to provide false testimony.

Kelly, J, with whom Seymour, CJ., and Ebel, J., join, dissenting.

The court holds that 18 U.S.C. § 201(c)(2) does not apply to the government because government prosecutors are inseparable from the sovereign, and that its application would deprive the sovereign of its power to grant leniency in exchange for testimony and would conflict with various statutory provisions. Because courts must apply unambiguous statutes as they are written and § 201(c) does not admit of an exception for the government or its prosecutors, I respectfully dissent.

As an initial observation, since the panel issued its opinion in this case, prosecutors from coast to coast have attempted to portray it as the death knell for the criminal justice system as we know it. These are the same grave forecasts made by prosecutors after the Supreme Court's decision in *Miranda v. Arizona*, 384 U.S. 436 (1966), and the advent of the exclusionary rule. But experience has proven that the government, just like the private citizens it regulates and prosecutes, can live within the rules. No one would suggest that the criminal justice system has ceased to function because the Court or Congress has effectuated constitutional or statutory guarantees designed to promote a more reliable outcome in criminal proceedings.

In holding that § 201(c)(2) simply does not apply to the government, the court does not hold that leniency in exchange for testimony does not constitute "anything of value." To be sure, the investigation and prosecution of criminal wrongdoing is an important societal function. Yet, largely missing from the debate since the panel opinion was issued is any concern for the other deeply held values that § 201(c) was intended to protect and which, I believe, the panel opinion honored by applying § 201(c) as Congress wrote it. Those concerns center on maintaining the integrity, fairness, and credibility of our system of criminal justice. Criminal judgments are accepted by society at large, and even by individual defendants, only because our system of justice is painstakingly fair. An additional core value honored by the panel opinion is the preservation of the separation of powers carefully articulated in the Constitution between the legislative and judicial branches, and the proper role of the judiciary as the law-interpreting, rather than lawmaking, branch of the federal government.

Contrary to the concerns expressed by some commentators and courts a straightforward interpretation of § 201(c), which encompasses a prohibition against the government buying witness testimony with leniency, actually aids the search for truth. In theory, the leniency is only in exchange for "truthful" testimony. But as the Supreme Court has recognized: "Common sense would suggest that [an accused accomplice] often has a greater interest in lying in favor of the prosecution rather than against it, especially if he is still awaiting his own trial or sentencing. To think that criminals will lie to save their fellows but not to obtain favors from the prosecution for themselves is indeed to clothe

the criminal class with more nobility than one might expect to find in the public at large." *Washington v. Texas,* 388 U.S. 14, 22–23 (1967); see also Yvette A. Beeman, Note, Accomplice Testimony Under Contingent Plea Agreements, 72 Cornell L. Rev. 800, 802 (1987) ("Accomplice plea agreements tend to produce unreliable testimony because they create an incentive for the accomplice to shift blame to the defendant or other co-conspirators. Further, an accomplice may wish to please the prosecutor to ensure lenient prosecution in his own case."). To be sure, there are devices that partially ameliorate the problem. The government is required to disclose exculpatory information, including impeachment information, to a defendant. Testifying accomplices may be cross-examined. Their credibility may be impeached, and the jury is instructed that it may regard such testimony with caution. However, all of these devices have limitations. In the real world of trial and uncertain proof, and in view of § 201(c), a witness's demeanor and actual testimony are simply too important to hinge upon promises of leniency. Although the court notes that a prosecutor who procures false testimony could be prosecuted for subornation of perjury, such a remedy offers little practical advantage to a defendant facing trial. By barring an exchange of leniency for testimony, Congress in § 201(c) has sought to eliminate, at the source, the most obvious incentive for false testimony.

On the other side of the ledger is my concern for the institutional role of Article III courts. Much of this case has been about policy. I accept the government's position that accomplices can provide important information and interpreting § 201(c) to include prosecutors might require some changes to elicit testimony of some witnesses. While it would be up to the Department of Justice to devise ways of compliance, the government is not precluded from offering leniency in exchange for information and assistance short of actual testimony at trial. Likewise, the government could prosecute accomplices first, then compel their testimony by subpoena against co-conspirators. Finally, the government could request that the district court order an accomplice to testify under a grant of immunity. Surely the Department has the ability and resources to come up with effective and lawful means for procuring necessary accomplice testimony. However, I also accept the defense attorneys' position that government leniency in exchange for testimony can create a powerful incentive to lie and derail the truth-seeking purpose of the criminal justice system. The very nature and complexity of this policy debate reinforces my initial belief that this is an argument better left to Congress. This court must perform its constitutional duties and no more. Ours is not to explore the farthest meanings that the term "whoever" can bear so as to effectuate the policy we think best. Our duty is to interpret the plain meaning of the statute. I continue to believe that meaning is clear: § 201(c), as written, applies to prosecutors and criminal defendants alike. If the balance struck by § 201 is to be reweighed, that reweighing should be done by the policymaking branch of government—the Congress, and not the courts. In that regard, it bears repeating that the panel's original opinion was purely a matter of statutory construction, not constitutional analysis, and it remains completely open for Congress to reweigh the conflicting values sought to be addressed in § 201.

The government argues that construing the word "whoever" to include the government is semantically anomalous because "whoever" connotes a being. As a textual and contextual matter, this is wrong. Textually, "whoever" clearly connotes more than a being and in fact denotes inanimate entities. The Dictionary Act, 1 U.S.C. § 1, definition of "whoever" includes, but is not limited to, corporations, companies, associations, firms, partnerships, societies, and joint stock companies—all inanimate entities. Contextually, the government concedes that "whoever" in § 201(b) applies to the government and it acknowledges that § 201(c) applies to the government if the government pays an informant money to testify. It makes absolutely no sense to give "whoever" one meaning in § 201(b) (and in § 201(c) when the inducement offered by the government is money) and to give the very same word a completely different meaning in § 201(c) when the inducement offered is leniency or some other promise to improve the informant's position. Bought testimony is so fraught with the potential for perjury that Congress imposed a blanket prohibition that also applies to the government, just as hearsay testimony is so fraught with the potential for unreliability that the Federal Rules of Evidence generally prohibit its admission, whether offered by the government or private litigants.

Beyond Unreliable:
How Snitches Contribute to Wrongful Convictions
Alexandra Natapoff
37 Golden Gate University Law Review 107 (2006)

[I]nformants do not generate wrongful convictions merely because they lie. After all, lying hardly distinguishes informants from other sorts of witnesses. Rather, it is how and why they lie, and how the government depends on lying informants, that makes snitching a troubling distortion of the truth-seeking process. Informants lie primarily in exchange for lenience for their own crimes, although sometimes they lie for money. In order to obtain the benefit of these lies, informants must persuade the government that their lies are true. Police and prosecutors, in turn, often do not and cannot check these lies because the snitch's information may be all the government has. Additionally, police and prosecutors are heavily invested in using informants to conduct investigations and to make their cases. As a result, they often lack the objectivity and the information that would permit them to discern when informants are lying. This gives rise to a disturbing marriage of convenience: both snitches and the government benefit from inculpatory information while neither has a strong incentive to challenge it. The usual protections against false evidence, particularly prosecutorial ethics and discovery, may thus be unavailing to protect the system from informant falsehoods precisely because prosecutors themselves have limited means and incentives to ferret out the truth.

In 2000, the groundbreaking book Actual Innocence estimated that twenty-one percent of wrongful capital convictions are influenced by snitch testimony. Four years later, a study by the Center on Wrongful Convictions doubled that number. Another recent report estimates that twenty percent of all California wrongful convictions, capital or otherwise, result from false snitch testimony.

Behind these general statistics lie numerous stories of informant crime, deceit, secret deals and government duplicity. In Los Angeles, DEA informant Essam Magid not only avoided jail for his many crimes but earned hundreds of thousands of dollars by serving as an informant. During this time, he framed dozens of innocent people before one person he targeted finally refused to plead guilty and revealed the arrangement.

Although such horror stories provoke outcry, little has been done to cabin the law enforcement discretion that makes such informant operations possible, or to impose greater transparency and oversight onto the process in order to curtail such abuses.

Informants have become law enforcement's investigative tool of choice, particularly in the ever-expanding world of drug enforcement. Informants are part of a thriving market for information. In this market, snitches trade information with police and prosecutors in exchange for lenience, the dismissal of charges, reduced sentences, or even the avoidance of arrest. It is a highly informal, robust market that is rarely scrutinized by courts or the public. And it is growing. While data is hard to come by, federal statistics indicate that sixty percent of drug defendants cooperate in some fashion. Informants permeate all aspects of law enforcement, from investigations to plea-bargaining to trial.

The growth in the sheer number of informants reflects the increasing dependence of police and prosecutors on informants. Professor Ellen Yaroshefsky describes prosecutors' own complaints: "These [drug] cases are not very well investigated.... Our cases are developed through cooperators and their recitation of the facts. Often, in DEA, you have agents who do little or no follow up so when a cooperator comes and begins to give you information outside of the particular incident, you have no clue if what he says is true."

Because investigations and cases rely so heavily on informants, protecting and rewarding informants has become an important part of law enforcement. Police and prosecutors are well known for protecting their snitches: all too often, when defendants or courts seek the identity of informants, cases are dismissed or warrant applications are dropped. More fundamentally, police and prosecutors become invested in their informants' stories, and therefore may lack the objectivity to know when their sources are lying.

Informants are thus punished for silence and rewarded for producing inculpatory information, even when that information is inaccurate. The system protects them from the consequences of their inaccuracies by guarding their identities and making their information the centerpiece of the government's cases. The front line officials who handle informants — police and prosecutors — are ill equipped to screen that information, and once they incorporate it into their cases, they acquire a stake in its validity. This phenomenon explains in part why snitch testimony generates so many wrongful convictions: it permeates the criminal system and there are few safeguards against it.

––––––––––

Although, as Alexandra Natapoff argues, police and prosecutors can "become invested in their informants' stories, and therefore may lack the objectivity to know when their sources are lying," defense attorneys have a strong incentive to challenge an informant's credibility. Because defense attorneys do not have the same investigative tools as the state, however, gathering information about an informant's credibility can sometimes be difficult. In one recent and unusual case, an Indiana criminal defense attorney investigated an informant who had allegedly purchased methamphetamine from his client while working for the police. The attorney, David Schalk, came to believe that the informant was himself continuing to sell drugs while the police looked the other way. In an effort to confirm his suspicions, Schalk gave new meaning to the phrase zealous representation by attempting a private sting operation against the informant. The informant sold marijuana to Shalk's hired investigators and Shalk contacted the police to report the informant's crime. Unfortunately for Schalk, the police did not react to the news as he had expected.

Schalk v. Indiana
Court of Appeals of Indiana
943 N.E.2d 427 (2011)

Najam, J.

In June 2007, Schalk was representing Chad Pemberton, who had been charged with dealing in methamphetamine, as a Class A felony. Pemberton's charge stemmed from a sale of methamphetamine he had made to a confidential informant working with police. Schalk learned that Brandon Hyde was the confidential informant. Because Pemberton believed that Hyde continued to deal drugs while working with police, Schalk sought to obtain proof of his dealing in order to impeach his credibility at trial.

Schalk discussed with Pemberton's mother the idea of proving that Hyde was still dealing drugs. Schalk then asked Pemberton's sister, a minor, whether she or someone she knew might purchase marijuana from Hyde and record the transaction. Schalk recommended purchasing a large quantity of drugs to make the impeachment evidence more "reliable." When Pemberton's sister declined to help, Pemberton suggested that his friends Lisa Edwards and Roger Grubb might be willing to participate in a drug buy with Hyde.

Leslie spoke with Edwards about the plan, and Pemberton spoke with Edwards and Grubb to convince them to talk with Schalk. Edwards then spoke with Schalk several times, and Schalk assured her that the plan for Edwards and Grubb to buy marijuana from Hyde was "legit" and that none of them would get into trouble. On June 25, Schalk telephoned Edwards and Grubb, and the three subsequently met at a restaurant in Ellettsville. Schalk gave Edwards a voice recorder to use during the buy, and he told her to buy a "felony amount" of marijuana from Hyde. Schalk wrote down the serial numbers from $200 in bills and gave the buy money to Edwards.

Shortly after the meeting in Ellettsville, Edwards left Schalk a voice mail message that the drug buy had been completed. However, instead of buying $200 worth of marijuana, Edwards and Grubb bought only $50 worth of marijuana from Hyde, and the pair spent the rest of the money on gas and food. And before Edwards and Grubb met with Schalk to deliver the marijuana and return the voice recorder, Grubb decided to keep the marijuana. Edwards also deleted the recording of the drug transaction with Hyde.

When Edwards and Grubb met with Schalk, they brought a rolled up newspaper and represented that the marijuana they had purchased from Hyde was inside the newspaper. Schalk refused to take possession of the newspaper alleged to contain marijuana, and he instructed Edwards and Grubb to keep it until he could find a law enforcement officer to take possession of it. Edwards and Grubb subsequently smoked all of the marijuana they had purchased from Hyde.

In the meantime, Schalk attempted to contact six or seven law enforcement officers in an effort to find someone who would take possession of the marijuana that Edwards and Grubb had purchased from Hyde. Schalk was unsuccessful in those attempts. He eventually reached Chief Deputy Prosecutor Robert Miller at home and reported that he had arranged the drug buy, had provided the buy money, and that the transaction was complete. Schalk asked Miller for "advice on how he should deal with the disposition" of the marijuana, and Miller advised Schalk to contact Sheriff's Deputy Jerry Reed "to make a report." But Schalk was unable to reach Deputy Reed by telephone.

The day following the drug buy, Schalk obtained reimbursement from Pemberton's mother for the buy money, which she thought was for the cost of depositions. The same day, Schalk also "petitioned the Court [in Pemberton's criminal proceeding] to take custody" of the marijuana Edwards and Grubb had purchased from Hyde for use "in the upcoming Pemberton trial."[1] Apparently, Schalk believed that if the contraband was turned over to law enforcement or to the court, a crime would not have been committed. On June 26 or 27, Miller contacted the Monroe County Sheriff's Department to report Schalk's involvement in the scheme to buy marijuana from Hyde. After an investigation, Detec-

---

1. After a hearing, the trial court in Pemberton's criminal proceeding removed Schalk as Pemberton's counsel.

tive Shawn Karr filed an affidavit of probable cause, and the State charged Schalk with conspiracy to possess marijuana, a Class D felony.

Schalk filed various motions to dismiss the charge against him, which the trial court denied. The State ultimately amended the charge to attempted possession of marijuana, a Class A misdemeanor, after Schalk waived his right to a trial by jury. Following a bench trial, the trial court found Schalk guilty as charged, entered a judgment of conviction, and sentenced Schalk to three months, all suspended to non-supervised probation. This appeal ensued.

Schalk summarizes his argument on appeal as follows: "David Schalk's providing cash for the purchase of marijuana was never in dispute, and that is the basis of his conviction for attempted possession of marijuana. The issues presented pertain to the legality—or lack thereof—of Schalk's actions." Schalk's primary contention is that, as a defense attorney, he is "on the same legal footing as the prosecuting attorneys, other police officers, and confidential informants planning and executing controlled buys." Thus, he reasons that his conduct did not constitute a criminal offense. We think not.

To prove attempted possession of marijuana, as a Class A misdemeanor, the State was required to prove that Schalk knowingly or intentionally took a substantial step toward possessing marijuana. Schalk admitted to the trial court that he provided Edwards with money and a recording device to use in purchasing marijuana from Hyde. But Schalk asks that we recognize an exception to culpability under a criminal statute for a defense attorney who arranges a drug buy to discredit a witness against his client at trial. This we cannot do.

The Legislature has defined "law enforcement officer" as

(1) a police officer (including a correctional police officer), sheriff, constable, marshal, prosecuting attorney, special prosecuting attorney, special deputy prosecuting attorney, the securities commissioner, or the inspector general;

(2) a deputy of any of those persons;

(3) an investigator for a prosecuting attorney or for the inspector general;

(4) a conservation officer;

(5) an enforcement officer of the alcohol and tobacco commission; or

(6) an enforcement officer of the securities division of the office of the secretary of state.

The Legislature has not included defense attorneys in the definition of law enforcement officers.

Further, Schalk's assertion that ... his conduct was legal given his intent to turn the marijuana from the drug buy over to police is not well taken. Intent is a mental state. Therefore, the trier of fact is entitled to make reasonable inferences based upon an examination of the surrounding circumstances and, here, the trial court did so adversely to Schalk. [W]e will not reweigh the evidence. The evidence supports the trial court's determination that Schalk knowingly or intentionally attempted to possess marijuana. While Schalk contends that his only intent was to deliver the marijuana to law enforcement or the court for use in defending his client at trial, such a purpose does not immunize him from prosecution.

Schalk next asks that we "hold that the Indiana State Legislature did not intend to prohibit Hoosiers from taking prohibited drugs away from dealers so the drugs could be kept in police custody, used as evidence in court, and destroyed." In support of that contention,

Schalk directs us to Indiana['s law authorizing a citizen arrest.] But no reasonable interpretation of the statute could support Schalk's contention on this issue. Schalk does not suggest, and there is no evidence, that he ever tried to "arrest" Hyde. Rather, Schalk arranged an illegal drug buy. Schalk's contention on this issue is without merit.

Schalk also alleges that "[t]he constitutional right of people accused of crimes to defend themselves is under attack. Chad Pemberton is not a party to this appeal, but David Schalk has standing to assert his right to defend his clients as part of the guarantees of the Sixth Amendment to the Constitution of the United States of America and Article I, Section 13 of the Constitution of Indiana."

We agree that Schalk's client has a right to legal representation guaranteed by both the federal and state constitutions. But we reject Schalk's contention that an attorney, an officer of the court, who has given an oath to support the Constitution of the United States and the Constitution of the State of Indiana is authorized to engage in criminal activity in defense of his client under either the Sixth Amendment or Article I, Section 13.

In sum, Schalk asks this court to grant him the same "legal footing" as law enforcement officers for the purpose of conducting an illegal drug buy in an effort to discredit a witness against his client. The legislature has clearly identified those persons legally authorized to engage in law enforcement, and defense attorneys are not included. An attorney is not exempt from the criminal law even if his only purpose is the defense of his client. "Under the Code of Professional Responsibility an attorney is charged with defending and advancing the interests of his clients within the framework of our legal system." *Matter of Mann,* 270 Ind. 358, 385 N.E.2d 1139, 1143 (1979). "It should be abundantly clear that an attorney cannot resort to illegal means in order to obtain a favorable disposition for his client." *Id.* This is not a close case. The material facts are undisputed and fully support the trial court's judgment of conviction. Schalk has not shown reversible error.

———

At least seventeen states have enacted laws to help address concerns about informant reliability by requiring corroboration of informant testimony for a conviction in certain circumstances. In 2011, for example, California adopted an informant corroboration law that provides: "A jury or judge may not convict a defendant, find a special circumstance true, or use a fact in aggravation based on uncorroborated testimony of an in-custody informant." The law defines an in-custody informant as "a person, other than a codefendant, percipient witness, accomplice, or coconspirator, whose testimony is based on statements allegedly made by the defendant while both the defendant and the informant were held within a city or county jail, state penal institution, or correctional institution." Cal. Pen. Code § 1111.5.

While many corroboration laws are aimed exclusively at jailhouse informants, Nebraska has a long-standing corroboration statute for controlled substances offenses specifically.

Nebraska v. Johnson

Supreme Court of Nebraska
261 Neb. 1001 (2001)

Miller-Lerman, J.

Johnson was convicted of two counts of distribution of a controlled substance, marijuana, in violation of Neb. Rev. Stat. § 28-416(1)(a). The charges arose out of incidents which were alleged to have occurred on January 14 and 15, 1999. Count I pertains to January 14, and count II pertains to January 15. The direct testimonial evidence against Johnson consisted primarily of the testimony of a confidential informant who assisted the city of Hastings and Adams County by participating in controlled drug transactions for which she was compensated by the drug task force. Johnson testified in his own defense. The confidential informant's and Johnson's versions of events differed.

The confidential informant's testimony regarding two alleged controlled buys on January 14 and 15, 1999, was as follows: As to the January 14 incident, the confidential informant testified that she contacted Johnson and arranged to meet him at the Olive Saloon in Hastings. Prior to the meeting, the confidential informant was searched by a police officer, given a transmitter disguised as a pager, and given "buy money." At the bar, the confidential informant told Johnson she needed to buy an ounce of marijuana. Johnson replied that he did not have that much with him, and the two arranged to meet later at the Reno Bar. The two met at the Reno Bar, then went outside to Johnson's car where Johnson gave the confidential informant two baggies of marijuana in exchange for $75. Four law enforcement personnel testified at trial that they had seen Johnson and the confidential informant leave the bar together and go to Johnson's car on January 14.

As to the January 15, 1999, incident, the confidential informant testified that she again contacted Johnson to make another purchase. As on January 14, she was searched and given a transmitter and "buy money" prior to the meeting. The confidential informant testified that she and Johnson met again at the Reno Bar where Johnson gave her three baggies of marijuana in exchange for $90. No law enforcement personnel or any other witness testified as to having seen Johnson at the Reno Bar or to having observed Johnson meeting with the confidential informant on January 15.

After each purchase, the confidential informant delivered the marijuana to the police officers with whom she was working. On cross-examination, the confidential informant testified that she was being compensated for each occasion. Johnson was ultimately arrested and charged with two counts of distribution on July 16, 1999. He pled not guilty, and the case went to trial.

In addition to the testimony of the confidential informant and law enforcement personnel as outlined above, Johnson testified at trial. Johnson denied having sold marijuana to the confidential informant on either January 14 or 15, 1999. Johnson, however, recalled an incident which he thought may have occurred on January 14. Johnson testified he met the confidential informant at the bar and went to his car with her at her invitation to smoke marijuana which she, rather than Johnson, provided. According to Johnson, the confidential informant handed him a small amount of marijuana which he placed in a pipe. Before he could light it, the confidential informant said she had to go and left the car. Johnson thought her behavior was strange because they had smoked marijuana together in the past. Johnson returned to the bar without smoking any marijuana.

With respect to the January 15, 1999, incident, Johnson testified that although he frequented the bar, he did not specifically recall being there on January 15 and did not recall any conversation or incident involving marijuana on that date.

During the course of the trial, Johnson requested that the jury be instructed on the lesser-included charge of possession. The request was denied by the district court. The jury convicted Johnson of two counts of distribution of a controlled substance.

Johnson appealed his convictions and sentences to the Court of Appeals. The Court of Appeals, in an unpublished decision, rejected Johnson's assignments of error and affirmed his convictions and sentences. Johnson petitioned this court for further review. We granted his petition.

Johnson ... asserts that the Court of Appeals erred in affirming the district court's denial of Johnson's motion for directed verdict at the close of all the evidence and in concluding that his convictions were supported by sufficient evidence. In a criminal case, a court can direct a verdict only when there is a complete failure of evidence to establish an essential element of the crime charged or the evidence is so doubtful in character, lacking probative value, that a finding of guilt based on such evidence cannot be sustained. If there is any evidence which will sustain a finding for the party against whom a motion for directed verdict is made, the case may not be decided as a matter of law. We conclude that the evidence was sufficient to submit count I to the jury but that count II should not have been submitted to the jury due to the lack of evidence corroborating the cooperating individual's testimony.

In connection with our consideration of the sufficiency of evidence in this case, we note that Neb. Rev. Stat. §28-1439.01 provides: "No conviction for an offense punishable under any provision of the Uniform Controlled Substances Act shall be based solely upon the uncorroborated testimony of a cooperating individual." We agree with the conclusion of the Court of Appeals that there was sufficient evidence to submit count I regarding the January 14, 1999, incident to the jury where properly instructed. However, with regard to count II involving the incident on January 15, we conclude that the testimony of the confidential informant regarding the critical events of January 15 is uncorroborated and, therefore, insufficient under §28-1439.01. Johnson's motion for a directed verdict on count II should have been sustained, and such count should have been dismissed.

"Cooperating individual" is defined for purposes of the Uniform Controlled Substances Act as "any person, other than a commissioned law enforcement officer, who acts on behalf of, at the request of, or as agent for a law enforcement agency for the purpose of gathering or obtaining evidence of offenses punishable under the Uniform Controlled Substances Act." Neb. Rev. Stat. §28-401(32). The confidential informant in this case is a "cooperating individual" under §28-1439.01. We further note that Johnson was charged with two counts of distribution of a controlled substance, marijuana, in violation of §28-416(1)(a), which is a provision of the Uniform Controlled Substances Act. Therefore, pursuant to §28-1439.01, neither of Johnson's convictions in this case may be based solely upon the uncorroborated testimony of the confidential informant serving as a cooperating individual.

We have held that corroboration is sufficient to meet the requirement of §28-1439.01 if the witness is corroborated as to material facts and circumstances which tend to support the testimony as to the principal fact in issue. We have further held that corroboration may be supplied by observation that a meeting between the subject and a cooperating individual actually took place, coupled with searches of the cooperating individual both before and within a reasonable time after the drug purchase took place. We have held, however, that the evidence is legally insufficient to sustain a conviction when the State has failed to corroborate the testimony of a cooperating individual which identifies the defendant as the person involved in a distribution.

Although the Court of Appeals did not directly address the corroboration issue, it did note that the confidential informant testified that she was searched for drugs prior to both her meetings with Johnson on January 14 and 15, 1999. Although not mentioned by the Court of Appeals, law enforcement personnel involved in the operation testified that the confidential informant had been searched prior to both meetings with Johnson; that the confidential informant was wired for both meetings; and that on January 14, they saw Johnson enter the bar and later exit the bar with the confidential informant and go to Johnson's vehicle, where according to the confidential informant, the actual distribution took place. However, aside from the confidential informant, no one testified as to having seen Johnson enter or exit the bar or meet with the confidential informant on January 15.

As to count I involving the incident on January 14, 1999, there is sufficient corroborating evidence because the police officers searched the confidential informant prior to and after the meeting with Johnson and because police officers observed Johnson going into the bar and later leaving the bar with the confidential informant and going to his car where, according to the confidential informant's testimony, the distribution occurred. The fact of Johnson's having met with the confidential informant on January 14 is further corroborated by Johnson's testimony regarding the events of January 14, about which he testified that he met the confidential informant in the bar and that the two of them went to his car.

However, as to count II involving the January 15, 1999, incident, the record lacks sufficient evidence corroborating the testimony of the confidential informant serving as a cooperating individual. Although there was evidence that the confidential informant was searched by police prior to and after her alleged meeting with Johnson on January 15, the police officers did not testify that they observed Johnson on January 15, nor did they testify that they observed the confidential informant and Johnson meet on January 15. There was no testimony by police officers or anyone other than the confidential informant that Johnson was actually at the bar on January 15 or that he met with the confidential informant on that date.

We have previously identified the objectives of the predecessor statute to § 28-1439.01 by referring to the legislative history. The introducer of the bill, Senator Fowler, indicated the concerns sought to be addressed by the legislation. Senator Fowler noted that cooperating individuals "often have ulterior motives in accusing others of drug offenses ... such as monetary gain or relieving themselves of criminal liability from drug offenses they themselves have committed." Judiciary Committee Hearing, L.B. 276, 85th Leg., 1st Sess. 66 (Feb. 22, 1977). Senator Fowler also noted: "Arrests for delivery of controlled substances violations often do not occur until weeks and often months after the date upon which the violation was alleged to have occurred. This means that even ... innocent persons charged with such ... violations [have] little if any effective means of defending [themselves] against the unjust charges unless they can succeed in establishing their innocence by the often difficult if not impossible task of establishing that they could not have been in the place at that time the offense was alleged to have occurred."

Both concerns noted by Senator Fowler were present in the instant case because the confidential informant was paid for her work and because Johnson was not arrested until July 1999 for the violation alleged to have occurred on January 15, 1999. Regarding the January 15 incident, there was no evidence to corroborate the confidential informant's testimony that she met with Johnson at the Reno Bar or any evidence other than her testimony that Johnson was at the bar on that date. As noted by the introducer, testimony to corroborate a defendant's presence at the time and place of the alleged violation is especially vital when a period of months exists between the alleged violation and the defendant's arrest.

The State argues that the evidence is sufficient as to count II because the testimony by Johnson and the law enforcement officers specifically corroborating the confidential informant's testimony regarding the January 14, 1999, incident also corroborates her testimony regarding the January 15 incident. We reject this argument. Although both counts were charged in the same information, each count represents a separate offense. Because § 28-1439.01 requires that "no conviction for *an offense* punishable under any provision of the Uniform Controlled Substances Act shall be based solely upon the uncorroborated testimony of a cooperating individual," we conclude that each count represents a separate offense and that the evidence supporting each count must independently satisfy the requirements of § 28-1439.01.

We conclude that Johnson's conviction on count II was not based on sufficient evidence because it was based solely on the uncorroborated testimony of the confidential informant who was serving as a cooperating individual. In enacting § 28-1439.01, the Legislature has indicated that such uncorroborated testimony cannot be the sole basis for a conviction under the Uniform Controlled Substances Act. Accordingly, Johnson's motion for directed verdict at the close of all the evidence should have been granted as to count II. The district court erred in denying this motion as to count II, and the Court of Appeals erred in affirming the district court's denial of Johnson's motion for a directed verdict as to count II made at the close of the evidence.

c. Informant Safety and Sanctioned Criminality

In some cases, the lack of judicial oversight over the use of informants can lead police and prosecutors to provide them with too many rewards, thereby increasing the risk informants will give inaccurate information. In other cases, however, the lack of judicial oversight can put informants themselves in danger.

Consider, for example, the case of Bianca Hervey, a 20-year-old college student from Attica, New York. In 2009, Hervey was driving home to her apartment one afternoon after her classes when she was stopped by the police and arrested for driving without a license, which had been suspended for failure to pay traffic tickets. At the police station, Hervey was handcuffed to a bench and told she would spend the night in jail unless she signed an agreement to become a confidential informant for the Wyoming County Drug Task Force. Hervey told the police she didn't use drugs and didn't know anyone who used or sold drugs. Even though Hervey's arrest had nothing to do with drugs and despite her insistence that she did not have any connections to the drug world, the police insisted she would spend the night in jail unless she signed up to become an informant for the drug task force. Hervey eventually agreed and signed the confidential informant contract. After she was released, Hervey told her father—an attorney who represents police unions—about the incident. Hervey's father complained to local officials that pressuring individuals without drug involvement to become drug informants might put them in danger. The Wyoming County Sheriff and District Attorney, however, refused to release any information about the department's informant policy and said they stood by the effort to enlist Hervey as an informant. "'I think if you talk to people who have task forces anywhere,' the sheriff said, 'the policy would be similar.'" *See* Michael Beebe, *Would-be Informant Says Police Coerced Her Into Cooperation*, THE BUFFALO NEWS, Nov. 8, 2009.

What problems, if any, do you think might arise from engaging individuals like Hervey to work as informants? What legal protections, if any, do you think should be established to regulate the use of informants?

Coerced Informants and Thirteenth Amendment Limitations on the Police-Informant Relationship
Michael L. Rich
50 Santa Clara Law Review 681 (2010)

On May 7, 2008, Rachel Morningstar Hoffman, a twenty-three-year-old Tallahassee resident and recent graduate of Florida State University, disappeared while trying to purchase 1500 pills of ecstasy, two-and-a-half ounces of cocaine, and a handgun for $13,000 from two suspected drug dealers. Two days later, the Tallahassee Police Department ("TPD") arrested the dealers, Andrea Green and Deneilo Bradshaw, who led police to Hoffman's body. Hoffman had been shot and her body dumped in a rural area outside of the city.

The swift apprehension of Bradshaw and Green might, at first glance, appear to be an example of efficient police work. But in fact, the TPD were intimately involved in the events that led to her death, as Hoffman was a confidential informant who set up the deal at the TPD's express direction and under threat of criminal prosecution. Three weeks before her death, the TPD searched Hoffman's apartment and found approximately five ounces of marijuana, six ecstasy pills, and other drug paraphernalia. The next day, officers met with Hoffman and gave her a choice: she could help the TPD apprehend other drug dealers or face prosecution on multiple felony charges. The decision no doubt seemed simple to Hoffman. The TPD told her that she only had to provide "substantial assistance" or do "one big deal" to avoid charges and promised that they would keep her safe. But if she refused to cooperate, they threatened significant prison time on multiple felony charges, and these new charges would have made her ineligible for drug court disposition of earlier marijuana possession charges. Given her options, she agreed to cooperate with the TPD.

Hoffman's situation is typical of those faced by an increasing number of civilians who assist police in exchange for leniency. She decided to cooperate alone, without an opportunity to consult her attorney. She lacked a meaningful understanding of the charges she could face as a result of the drugs found in her apartment, or what she had to do in order to receive leniency. Once recruited, she risked injury and death to cooperate with the government and did so with no training in conducting undercover police operations or protecting herself from harm.

Given the importance of informants in many areas of law enforcement, police officers are encouraged to pursue all available avenues to grow their informant networks. At the state level, guidelines for determining whether a civilian is a good informant candidate are at best scattershot, and generally involve little oversight. At the federal level, the Department of Justice has established guidelines requiring that a case agent consider seventeen factors to determine a potential informant's suitability, including her age, motivation, relationship with the target of the investigation, reliability, and history of drug abuse. Though the guidelines provide no direction as to how these factors should be weighed or applied in making the ultimate suitability determination, they do require a supervisor's approval of the decision to recruit an informant. Nonetheless, even when guidelines do exist, they often give way to the government's constant need for more informants.

While informants can come from any walk of life, officers are encouraged to target those civilians who are engaged in criminal activity, live or work in close proximity to criminals or crime, or associate with criminals, because they are most likely to possess useful information and connections. Among law-abiding citizens, professions that place individuals in a position to interact with criminals and surreptitiously obtain information, such as barbers, bartenders, hotel clerks, postal workers, doormen, and waiters, are considered to be excellent sources of useful informants.

Non-criminals can be useful informants, but the most productive, long-term informants tend to be criminals themselves. Criminals rarely volunteer to become informants without any police encouragement, so efforts to "flip" a suspected criminal typically begin immediately following her arrest. A civilian's uncertainty about her future is highest in the hours after being arrested, thus making her most likely to agree to cooperate at that time. One former officer who trains police in informant recruitment recommends that "all individuals arrested should be interviewed for becoming potential informants," because "informants who have initiated significant cases or provided information for an investigation have been known to be developed following an arrest for a minor offense."

While the agreement to cooperate is superficially similar to a plea agreement, it lacks the safeguards that attach to a formal plea, including specificity, judicial review, and, in most cases, the participation of defense counsel. When promising leniency, police are instructed to avoid making specific promises about what amount of assistance will be sufficient to earn leniency or exactly what form that leniency will take. As a result, the police frequently tell an informant only that "substantial assistance" is expected of her, and promise nothing more than to share the fact of the informant's cooperation with the prosecutor or the court. Additionally, while a court must ensure that a defendant's waiver of his constitutional rights is knowing, voluntary, and intelligent before a plea is valid, the active informant agrees to cooperate without judicial oversight of, acquiescence in, or even awareness of the deal. Finally, the negotiation of the cooperation agreement often occurs outside the presence and without the knowledge of the informant's attorney.

Shortly after an arrest, police maximize the arrestee's fear of a long sentence by emphasizing the maximum penalties for the crimes with which she might be charged and suggesting that the only easy way out is for her to cooperate. At least one expert suggests that even when there is insufficient evidence to bring charges against an individual, police should claim that charges will soon be filed to encourage an arrestee to assist the police. Alternatively, he suggests filing criminal charges against uncooperative individuals for the sole purpose of encouraging them to become informants.

Following Rachel Hoffman's death, Florida enacted legislation known as "Rachel's Law" to regulate police interactions with informants in the state. The law is "the first of its kind to be passed by a state legislature" and "requires law enforcement agencies to establish policies and procedures, including recordkeeping rules to guide police when they turn a suspect into an informant." Under the law, "[p]olice must consider an informant's suitability—including their age, maturity, and risk of physical harm—before entering into an agreement." The law does not, however, require that would-be informants consult with an attorney before agreeing to cooperate and "also leaves open what sort of information the police must collect and keep about their informants." Alexandra Natapoff argues that "Rachel's Law illustrates just how secretive and unregulated law enforcement practices are. In any other legal context, it would be uncontroversial to require the government to have written procedures to guide and keep track of its important decisions.... Every year, thousands of drug suspects secretly become informants, and they do it without lawyers, judicial oversight, or documentation." Alexandra Natapoff, *Regulating Criminal Snitching,* Los Angeles Daily Journal (reporting on the enactment of Rachel's law). *See also,* Andrea L. Dennis, *Collateral Damage? Juvenile Snitches in America's "Wars" on Drugs, Crime, and Gangs,* 46 AM. CRIM. L. REV. 1145, 1147 (2009) ("As a result of their informant activities, some children have been killed.... Even children who were simply suspected of being snitches have been killed."); Ian Leson, Note, *Toward Efficiency and Equity in Law Enforcement: "Rachel's Law" and the Protection of Drug Informants,* 32 B.C.J.L. & SOC. JUST. 391 (2012).

The absence of oversight for the use of informants can also allow law enforcement to formally or informally sanction criminal behavior in exchange for information. In some cases, this might mean informants are allowed to continue committing relatively petty crimes without facing punishment. In other instances, law enforcement officials might become so focused on obtaining information that is helpful to their own investigation that they allow their informant to commit serious crimes whose costs outweigh any public safety benefit their cooperation could conceivably provide. In one recent case, a United States Attorney along with the acting director of the Bureau of Alcohol, Tobacco, Firearms and Explosives (ATF) resigned their positions following a scandal in the gun control setting. In a program known as "Operation Fast and Furious," the ATF instructed "cooperating gun dealers to sell to people they suspected were straw purchasers [buying weapons on behalf of Mexican drug cartels] in the hopes of building cases against major arms smugglers." Susan Crabtree, *ATF Director 'Sick To His Stomach' When He Learned Details of Fast and Furious*, TPMMUCKRAKER, July 6, 2011. The ATF planned to monitor the weapons as they were taken across the border into Mexico but the program "lacked adequate controls" and agents "lost track of hundreds" of weapons. "Many later turned up at crime scenes in Mexico, and two were revealed at a site in Arizona where a United States Border Patrol agent was killed." Charlie Savage, *Gun Inquiry Costs Officials Their Jobs*, N.Y. TIMES, Aug. 30, 2011. *See also, e.g.,* Evan Ratliff, *The Mark: The F.B.I. Needs Informants, But What Happens When They Go Too Far?*, THE NEW YORKER, May 2, 2011 ("In 1999, it was revealed that two F.B.I. agents had for many years helped the Boston gangster Whitey Bulger, who was working as an informant, cover up crimes and avoid arrest."); Ginger Thompson, *D.E.A. Launders Mexican Profits of Drug Cartels*, N.Y. TIMES, Dec. 3, 2011 (reporting that D.E.A. agents had "laundered or smuggled millions of dollars in drug proceeds" as part of undercover investigations and that "[a]s it launders drug money, the agency often allows cartels to continue their operations over months or even years before making seizures or arrests").

d. The Public Authority and Innocent Intent Defenses

Because confidential informant agreements do not always precisely memorialize the work the informant will be performing for the government, there is a risk the informant might misunderstand the nature of his agreement and engage in criminal behavior on the mistaken belief that it is part of his work for the authorities. A defendant who is prosecuted for criminal activity he committed while working as an informant may attempt to rely on a public authority or an innocent intent defense.* These two closely related defenses are discussed in the following case.

United States v. Fulcher

United States Court of Appeals for the Fourth Circuit
250 F.3d 244 (2001)

Luttig, J.

Defendants Ethel, Michael, and Rosanna Fulcher were convicted by a jury of various money laundering and drug violations. Following trial, a government agent wrote an *ex parte* letter to the district court explaining that he may have led the defendants to believe

---

* A third defense—entrapment by estoppel—can often arise in these cases as well. Because all three defenses are so similar and the precise relationship between them remains unsettled, coverage of the entrapment by estoppel defense is not included here. For a discussion of entrapment by estoppel as compared to the public authority defense, see United States v. Giffin, 473 F.3d 30 (2nd Cir. 2006).

that they were authorized to conduct the entire operation on behalf of the government. The district court granted a new trial to the defendants pursuant to Fed. R. Crim. P. 33, holding that the newly discovered evidence satisfied every requisite element for a new trial. For the reasons that follow, we affirm.

This case arises out of the pervasive presence of drugs at Bland Correctional Center ("BCC"), an institution operated by the Virginia Department of Corrections. The network of drug distribution at BCC was extensive, involving inmates, prison officials, and even the relatives and girlfriends of inmates. The drug operation managed by Michael Fulcher ("Michael") was no exception.

Michael purchased his supply of marijuana from various prison officials, including prison guards and counselors. He would then divide the drugs he received into smaller quantities—most often teaspoon-sized servings—for distribution to inmates at BCC. Since his customers were prohibited from using cash while incarcerated, inmates purchased the drugs with money orders written on their inmate trust accounts, remitting payment to a number of individuals located outside the prison, including Rosanna Fulcher ("Rosanna"), Michael's wife, and Ethel Fulcher ("Ethel"), Michael's mother. The funds collected would then be used to purchase additional marijuana from prison officials, beginning the cycle anew.

The appellants, Michael and Rosanna, were charged in a 47-count indictment—along with 22 other defendants—with engaging in drug and money laundering conspiracies, as well as substantive counts of the same. The jury convicted Rosanna of a money laundering conspiracy and ten substantive counts of money laundering. Michael was convicted of drug and money laundering conspiracies, a continuing criminal enterprise offense ("CCE"), and 17 substantive money laundering counts.

On the eve of sentencing, the district court received an *ex parte* letter from Special Agent Donald O. Lincoln, Jr., of the Drug Enforcement Administration ("DEA"). In the letter, Lincoln explained that he rejected Michael's request to formally investigate the distribution of drugs at BCC for two reasons: (1) it would be impossible to ensure his safety from other inmates and prison guards while he was incarcerated; and (2) the amount of marijuana was "so minuscule that I advised him that there was no way that we could justify a Federal investigation on what would at best be misdemeanor level quantities."

Although Lincoln never formally granted permission for Michael to initiate a formal drug investigation, Lincoln nonetheless stated his concern that he, along with state law enforcement officers working with the DEA, may have provided Michael with the mistaken impression that he had tacit approval to investigate drug dealing at BCC. Specifically, Lincoln explained:

> It has come to my attention that in my absence Mr. Fulcher would periodically talk to Deputy Kenny Parker of the Botetourt County Sheriff's Office, who was working in the DEA Office, serving as a DEA Task Force Officer at that time. In these conversations Mr. Fulcher told Deputy Parker what he was working on. Deputy Parker, believing that the operation had already been approved by me, discussed a number of options with Mr. Fulcher. One of these involved arranging for one or more of the guards who were involved to make an attempted pickup of marijuana from Deputy Parker, in an undercover capacity, in Botetourt County. Under those circumstances the case could have been taken to State Court in Botetourt or, if it developed into something interstate or substantial it could be brought to Federal Court. Deputy Parker discussed this potential operation with Sheriff Reed Kelly, and both of them recall the conversations. In

addition Deputy Parker reminded me of a conversation he had with me concerning setting up a potential sting operation against a prison guard, to go down at a Botetourt County truck stop.

Lincoln also stated in the letter that during his numerous telephone conversations with Michael over a three-year period,

> there were indeed times when I was in a hurry to get him off the phone due to other commitments. If I said anything in haste which led him to believe he was "covered" it may be the proximate cause of all of this. I honestly do not recall ever saying anything to that effect, but if Task Force Agent Parker and Sheriff Kelly also believe that I did, then I must lend credibility to the possibility. I don't know what if any consideration can be given to all that I have related here, your Honor, but I felt it incumbent on me to state the facts as I now know them.

On the basis of the letter, appellants filed a motion, asserting that they were entitled to a new trial on the basis of newly discovered evidence pursuant to Fed. R. Crim. P. 33. The district court held an evidentiary hearing, in which both Lincoln and Deputy Parker testified. Lincoln stated that David Fulcher, Michael's father, told him that Michael and Parker had spoken on several occasions concerning a possible sting operation. According to Lincoln, Parker told him that he had talked with Michael several times regarding a possible drug operation, and that Parker had discussed a number of options with Michael about how to set up a sting operation involving prison officials. On redirect, Lincoln acknowledged that, since his testimony at the pretrial hearing, his opinion regarding whether the Fulchers may have believed that they were authorized to conduct the operation had changed:

> Q: All right. Now during your July testimony, June testimony (sic) in the courtroom, I asked you a question about, "Did you ever do anything that in your estimation could have been construed as permission to conduct this investigation?" And do you recollect your answer as being, "No"?
>
> A: I probably did say that, and I guess that's—...
>
> Q: Are you now of the opinion that you could have been communicating to him and his mother that if the case was bigger it would be prosecuted and he could get his sentence reduced?
>
> A: I don't know, but, yes, that's my primary concern at this point.
>
> Q: Do you believe you might have?
>
> A: Yes. And if not me, then the fact that he talked to the other people in my office or to other people in my office (sic) and he felt that they somehow blessed it, then there is the very real possibility, especially from the part of Mrs. Fulcher.

On the basis of the letter and the testimony adduced at the evidentiary hearing, the district court granted the motion for a new trial, holding that the newly discovered evidence was material because it was directly related to the public authority defense and to whether the defendants possessed the requisite *mens rea* for their crimes.

The government argues on appeal that the district court erred in granting a new trial to defendants on the basis of newly discovered evidence.

Under Fed. R. Crim. P. 33, "on a defendant's motion, the court may grant a new trial to that defendant if the interests of justice so require." In determining whether a new trial should be granted under Rule 33 for newly discovered evidence, this court utilizes a five-part test:

(a) the evidence must be, in fact, newly discovered, i.e., discovered since the trial; (b) facts must be alleged from which the court may infer diligence on the part of the movant; (c) the evidence relied on must not be merely cumulative or impeaching; (d) it must be material to the issues involved; and (e) it must be such, and of such nature, as that, on a new trial, the newly discovered evidence would probably produce an acquittal.

Without ruling out the possibility that a rare example might exist, we have never allowed a new trial unless all five elements were established.

The district court made extensive findings on each of the elements of the *Custis* test and, of course, we review for an abuse of discretion the district court's decision to grant a new trial based on those findings.

[The court then applied the first, second, and third elements of the five-part test and found that each had been met by the defendant.]

The fourth element of *Custis* is whether the newly discovered evidence is "material to the issues involved." The government's principal argument on appeal is that the district court misapplied the defenses of public authority and mistake of fact and, in doing so, granted a new trial when the newly discovered evidence is not material.

At the post-trial evidentiary hearing, the following colloquy took place between Lincoln and Assistant United States Attorney Mott regarding whether Lincoln had actual authority to authorize money laundering activities:

> Q: If you were conducting a money laundering investigation, would you expect to document where the money went?
>
> A: Yes. And first and foremost I would expect to have to get an attorney's general's exemption to do it.
>
> Q: *And in a money laundering case you've got to go to the AG to get an exemption?*
>
> A: *You have to go to the AG.* That's why I would never have authorized him to do that without permission.

Lincoln further testified to the following when asked about his authority to authorize a drug operation of the type managed by Michael:

> Q: And kind of a paramount rule in drug investigations is that you don't let the drugs walk?
>
> A: Correct.
>
> Q: And that means you would never allow Mr. Fulcher to sell marijuana to someone without recovering it very shortly thereafter?
>
> A: That's correct.
>
> Q: *You would never authorize him to conduct drug sales on behalf of the DEA?*
>
> A: *That's true, and he knows that.*

On the basis of Lincoln's testimony, the government argues that Lincoln and his colleagues possessed, at most, apparent authority to approve the operation undertaken by the Fulchers, and that such authority was insufficient to either negate intent or to support the defense of public authority. Though we agree with the legal arguments advanced by the government, we nonetheless conclude that there is insufficient evidence in the record regarding the extent of Lincoln's authority (or that of his colleagues at the DEA).

Thus, we ultimately hold that the district court did not abuse its discretion when it concluded that the newly discovered evidence was material.

The defendants first seek to introduce Lincoln's testimony for the purpose of negating criminal intent. "The defendant may allege that he lacked criminal intent because he honestly believed he was performing the otherwise-criminal acts in cooperation with the government. Innocent intent is not a defense *per se*, but a defense strategy aimed at negating the *mens rea* for the crime, an essential element of the prosecution's case."

While an honest belief that a defendant is acting in cooperation with the government is a necessary element of establishing innocent intent, it is not alone sufficient. That is, evidence that defendants "honestly believed" that they acted in concert with a government official could abrogate the criminal intent necessary to prove the particular crimes with which the defendants were charged, but, as we have recognized previously, any such abrogation *also* depends upon the nature of that official's authority.

For instance, if a government official possessed *actual* authority to authorize the defendants' activity, then criminal intent certainly would be negated by the defendant's honest belief that he was cooperating with such an official. However, if the official possessed *neither* actual nor apparent authority to authorize the otherwise criminal activity, then criminal intent would not be negated.

The question most readily presented by Lincoln's testimony, and a question we have not heretofore addressed, is neither whether intent is negated when a defendant acts in concert with an official who does not possess either actual or apparent authority nor whether criminal intent is negated when a defendant acts in cooperation with an official with actual authority but, rather, whether the criminal intent for the crimes with which these defendants were charged is negated if they were acting in conjunction with an official who possesses only apparent authority. We hold, consistent with our sister circuits that have considered the question, that intent is not negated when a defendant cooperates with an official who possesses only *apparent* authority.

Essentially, defendants argue that, if they acted at the direction of an official who possessed apparent authority, they would lack the requisite *mens rea* for the crimes with which they were charged. According to defendants, under such a circumstance, they would have made only a mistake of fact — a cognizable defense negating intent when the *mens rea* requirement for a crime is at least knowledge — regarding whether DEA officials possessed actual authority to authorize their drug and money laundering activities.

Any such defense is foreclosed, however, by our reasoning in *Kelly*. There, the defendant relied on a government informant who enlisted his help to assist in a government operation. The defendant argued that if he acted at the invitation of the informant, he could not have possessed the requisite criminal intent for conspiracy to distribute drugs. We disagreed, explaining that defendant's mistake arose not from "a mistake of fact as to the informant's status, but resulted from a misconception of the legal prerogatives attached to that status." We thus held that if the defendant "indeed acted on the basis of a mistake ... it was a mistake of law, not a mistake of fact." Of course, since defendant's error was a mistake of law, his belief did not constitute a defense to his criminal act.

Though we did not address in *Kelly* whether a defendant's intent may be negated when he acts pursuant to an official's apparent authority, the reasoning of that case compels us to now answer that question in the negative. For, reliance on the apparent authority of a government official is nothing more than a mistake about "the legal prerogatives attached" to such status and thus constitutes a mistake of law. *See United States v. Rosenthal,* 793 F.2d 1214, 1235–36 (11th Cir. 1986) (stating that a "defendant may only be exonerated on the basis of his reliance on real and not merely apparent authority."); *Duggan,* 743 F.2d at 83 ("The mistake that defendants advance here as an excuse for their criminal activities—their reliance on Hanratty's purported authority—is an error based upon a mistaken view of legal requirements and therefore constitutes a mistake of law.").

Therefore, we hold that criminal intent is negated if two elements are met: (1) the defendant honestly believed that he was acting in cooperation with the government, and (2) the government official or officials upon whose authority the defendant relied possessed actual authority to authorize his otherwise criminal acts.

Defendants also seek to introduce Lincoln's testimony to support their defense of public authority. The public authority defense allows "the defendant to seek exoneration based on the fact that he reasonably relied on the authority of a government official to engage him in a covert activity." Thus, in contrast to the innocent intent doctrine, this affirmative defense allows a defendant to seek exoneration based upon his *objectively reasonable reliance* on the authority of a government official.

We have never addressed the scope of the public authority defense, and, in particular, we have never explained whether such a defense entitles a defendant to rely on the apparent authority of a government official or whether actual authority is necessarily required. However, we again find *Kelly* persuasive in answering this question. As explained above, *Kelly* stands for the proposition that any mistake about "the legal prerogatives" attached to a person's status is not a defense to a criminal act. Our recognition of an apparent public authority defense would contravene *Kelly* by creating an affirmative defense in precisely such circumstances.

Accordingly, we adopt the unanimous view of our sister circuits that the defense of public authority requires reasonable reliance upon the actual authority of a government official to engage him in a covert activity.

The government requests that we decide as a matter of law that the newly discovered evidence is not material despite the deferential standard of review we employ in reviewing a district court's decision to grant a new trial. We decline to reach that conclusion because neither party has been furnished with an opportunity to introduce any evidence regarding whether Lincoln or his colleagues at the DEA possessed actual authority to sanction defendants' money laundering and drug activities. Furthermore, while Lincoln's testimony certainly suggests that these officials did not possess such authority, his testimony does not conclusively establish that this is so, especially with regard to Michael's drug activities.

Therefore, if defendants can establish at a new trial that DEA officials authorized them to conduct the operation and that such officials had the actual authority to do so, defendants would be entitled to appropriate jury instructions on the defenses of public authority and innocent intent. Since the jury would then be entitled to acquit the defendants if it concluded that defendants' activities were legitimately authorized, we hold that the district court did not abuse its discretion in concluding that the newly discovered evidence is "material to the issues involved."

The fifth element of *Custis* is whether the evidence is "such, and of such nature, as that, on a new trial, the newly discovered evidence would probably produce an acquittal." Much of our analysis on the third and fourth elements of *Custis* is equally applicable here. In particular, we again note that the persuasive value of Lincoln's testimony cannot be underestimated due to his status as a DEA agent who participated in the investigation of this case. Furthermore, as the district court observed, if the jury credits

Lincoln's testimony that DEA officials may have led defendants to believe that they were acting pursuant to governmental authority, "it would certainly create a record more favorable for the Fulchers." Therefore, we cannot say that the district court abused its discretion in concluding that the newly discovered evidence "would probably produce an acquittal."

For the foregoing reasons, the district court's decision to grant a new trial to defendants is affirmed and the case is remanded for further proceedings consistent with this opinion.

Fulcher holds that for a defendant to succeed, the government agent upon whom she relied must have had the actual authority to empower her to engage in the conduct in question. This approach is not universally followed, however. The Ninth Circuit, for example, requires only that "the defendant reasonably believed that a government agent authorized her to engage in illegal acts." *United States v. Bear*, 439 F.3d 565, 568 (9th Cir. 2006). *See also*, *United States v. Jumah*, 493 F.3d 868, 877 (7th Cir. 2007) ("A defendant acts under public authority if, one, the defendant is affirmatively told that his conduct would be lawful; two, the defendant is told this by an official of the government; three, the defendant actually relies on what the official tells him in taking the action; and, four, the defendant's reliance on what he was told by the official is reasonable in light of the circumstances.").

3. Wiretaps

Wiretaps are another important tool for investigating drug crimes, though they are not as commonly employed as one might assume. According to the Administrative Office of the United States Courts, only 3,194 domestic wiretaps were authorized in 2010, 1,207 by federal judges and 1,987 by state judges. This figure does not include intercepts pursuant to the Foreign Intelligence Surveillance Act of 1978 (FISA) or recordings made with the consent of one of the principal parties to the conversation. Though wiretaps are not widespread, drug investigations are responsible for the great majority of them. In 2010, 84 percent of all wiretap applications cited illegal drugs as the most serious offense under investigation.

The high cost of wiretaps may explain why they are not used more often. The average cost of a wiretap in 2010 was $50,085. As a text written as a resource for law enforcement officers on drug investigations explains: because wiretaps require "a considerable amount of time and manpower; many departments often cannot justify [their] use." Michael D. Lyman, PRACTICAL DRUG ENFORCEMENT at 120 (3rd ed. 2007). *See also*, Max Minzer, *Putting Probability Back Into Probable Cause*, 87 TEX. L. REV. 913, 926–29 (2009) (discussing a study concluding the high cost of wiretaps are a greater constraint on their use than the probable cause requirement).

In addition to the cost associated with employing and monitoring a wiretap, law enforcement officers must meet special statutory requirements before a wiretap is authorized. Though wiretaps are considered to be "searches" under the Fourth Amendment, the federal and state statutory requirements for wiretaps are stricter than the constitutional requirements. *See*, *United States v. Gaines*, 2011 WL 1662363 (8th Cir. 2011) (comparing Title III's particularity requirement with the Fourth Amendment's particularity requirement). The case that follows provides an overview of some of the legal issues that can arise in the context of a wiretap investigation.

United States v. Meléndez-Santiago

United States Court of Appeals for the First Circuit
644 F.3d 54 (2011)

Lynch, J.

After a twenty-eight-day trial in 2007 a jury found Elkin Meléndez-Santiago, one of twelve indicted co-conspirators, guilty of conspiracy to import five or more kilograms of cocaine and one or more kilograms of heroin, as well as actual importation of five or more kilograms of cocaine, as part of a massive cocaine and heroin importation organization. Only one other defendant went to trial and he was also convicted. The remainder pled guilty.

In the conspiracy, Meléndez provided cash to co-conspirators to cover expenses for some drug smuggling operations and purchased cocaine and heroin imported into Puerto Rico for further distribution. Millions of dollars worth of drugs were imported. During one importation attempt in 2004, federal officers who had been tipped off to the drugs' arrival seized the drugs after a shootout with some of Meléndez's co-conspirators. The district court found it was known or foreseeable that firearms were being carried in furtherance of the conspiracy, justifying a sentence enhancement.

Meléndez was a cocaine addict who used cocaine daily, but he had no prior criminal record. He was sentenced to 360 months' imprisonment, which was less than the life sentence advised by the U.S. Sentencing Guidelines.

His appeal argues ... the district court committed reversible error in not suppressing evidence of conversations recorded in two Title III wiretaps because the affidavits in support of the wiretaps did not sufficiently explain why traditional investigative procedures were inadequate, necessitating wiretaps, see 18 U.S.C. § 2518(1)(c), (3)(c), and because the affidavits contained misleading information. He argues that the district court should have held a *Franks* hearing to permit him to establish that the affidavits included misleading information and that without such information, the affidavits would not have sufficed to establish probable cause for the wiretaps. See *Franks v. Delaware*, 438 U.S. 154, 155–56 (1978).

The initial determination as to compliance with the stringent standards for issuing a wiretap authorization is made by the judge to whom the application is made. At this later stage, appellate review of that authorization is not de novo, but deferential. We "decide if the facts set forth in the application were minimally adequate to support the determination that was made."

Here, two wiretap authorizations resulted from applications dated November 23 and December 9, 2004, both supported by sworn affidavits by FBI agent Jose Mena. Both applications targeted certain cell phone numbers and were approved by a district court judge. These cell phone numbers were used by the conspiracy leader, Luis Alfredo De La Rosa-Montero, also known as "Luis Viagra" or "El Compadre," to coordinate the drug conspiracy.

In order to be approved, the applications needed to show what is commonly referred to as the "necessity" of resort to wiretaps. To make this showing, wiretap applications must provide "a full and complete statement as to whether or not other investigative procedures have been tried and failed or why they reasonably appear to be unlikely to succeed if tried or to be too dangerous." 18 U.S.C. § 2518(1)(c). In *United States v. Villarman-Oviedo,* we interpreted § 2518(1)(c) "to mean that the statement should demonstrate that the government has made 'a reasonable, good faith effort to run the gamut of normal investigative procedures before resorting to means so intrusive as electronic interception of telephone calls.'" In such a statement, "[i]t is not necessary ... to show that other methods have been entirely unsuccessful."

Our reading of the affidavits disproves Meléndez's contentions that they were insufficient to support issuance of the wiretap authorizations. Indeed, they were better than minimally adequate. The November 23 affidavit contained the available identifying information known about the conspirators, all Dominican or Puerto Rican nationals. The affidavit also described how three confidential sources and one confidential informant had at times aided the investigation, providing information about those who were working in the conspiracy and about particular prior shipments, information that had led to successful arrests and drug seizures. The affidavit described in twenty-five detailed pages the conversations and interactions the sources and informant had with De La Rosa, some of which were recorded by the sources and some of which were verified when transactions were interrupted and smugglers arrested by federal officials. The affidavit also described what information had been gleaned from existing pen register and trap and trace analysis of De La Rosa's phone numbers.

The November 23 affidavit also described the limited success of efforts to conduct physical surveillance of the conspiracy leader De La Rosa. Physical surveillance was especially difficult in St. Thomas, where De La Rosa lived, because the streets were narrow and foreigners easily spotted. De La Rosa and other conspirators stayed in areas frequented by other Dominican nationals who were part of the same criminal subculture. The conspirators were wary of surveillance and they, in fact, mounted vigilant counter-surveillance. The conspirators did not use their real names and distrusted others not like them. Federal agents either mounting surveillance or attempting to infiltrate the organization undercover who were not members of that subculture would be easily spotted, would not be trusted by other members of the conspiracy, and would consequently be at great risk. Importantly, at the time of the wiretap application, one of the confidential sources had been missing for five months and was presumed dead; another had been threatened with death and was no longer trusted by members of the organization.

The information from sources other than surveillance was also constrained. The affidavit explained why traditional investigative techniques that had not been used—a grand jury investigation, interviews with co-conspirators or their associates, or execution of search warrants—were, particularly given the limited information known about the co-conspirators' identities and roles, likely to tip off the co-conspirators as to the developing investigation without yielding much helpful information. Pen registers and trap and trace records were already being used and would continue to be used, but gleaned only limited information about the cell phones being used.

The December 9 application sought wiretap authorization for another, new cell phone number used by De La Rosa. The supporting affidavit was similar in its level of detail to the first, related affidavit.

The affidavits' exhaustive explanation of what facts were known, what details remained unknown, what investigative techniques had been used and what techniques were likely to be unhelpful in the specific context of this particular conspiracy clearly constituted "a full and complete statement as to whether or not other investigative procedures have been tried and failed or why they reasonably appear to be unlikely to succeed if tried or to be too dangerous." 18 U.S.C. §2518(1)(c). The affidavits certainly supported the determination to authorize the wiretaps.

Meléndez argues that the affidavits failed to disclose that the agent who signed them was himself of Dominican origin, as was one of the confidential sources, and that they understated the scope of that source's knowledge about the internal workings of the criminal conspiracy. These arguments are in service of Meléndez's hypothesis that someone of Dominican origin could easily have been slipped into the organization as an undercover agent, and that alternatively, the confidential source must already have had sufficient knowledge about the conspiracy's organization, both facts obviating any need for wiretaps.

Meléndez takes it one step further and argues that because these facts were so obviously material, the affidavit misled the district court judges who authorized the wiretaps into authorizations they would not otherwise have granted. See *Franks*, 438 U.S. at 171–72 (holding that if "deliberate falsity or reckless disregard" for the truth in a warrant affidavit are specifically and reliably alleged, and if there is no longer sufficient material to support a finding of probable cause when the material in question "is set to one side," the court must grant the defendant a hearing to prove the allegations).

This house of cards is too flimsy to stand. To be of Dominican origin does not make one a natural undercover agent (or inconspicuous as part of a criminal sub-culture); nor does it mitigate the likelihood of an agent or confidential source being murdered by the conspiracy upon discovery.[1] Meléndez's speculation that the confidential source must already have known and shared with the investigators the details of the conspiracy's inner workings before the wiretap application is equally illogical and unsupported. No inference of falsity or reckless disregard of the truth can be drawn from the non-disclosure of these irrelevant bits of information. For that reason no hearing was required. Nor did the ample probable cause set forth in the affidavit for tapping the phones depend in any way on these alleged omissions, also obviating the need for a Franks hearing.

The judgment of conviction is affirmed.

B. Drug Investigations and the Fourth Amendment

The Fourth Amendment, which is studied in detail in Criminal Procedure courses, provides rules for when and how the police may gather evidence and detain suspects. Many (if not most) of the cases assigned in a Criminal Procedure course today involved drug investigations. This section does not attempt to duplicate the material covered in Criminal Procedure courses. Instead, it focuses on Fourth Amendment problems that are uniquely related to the enforcement and investigation of drug offenses.

The Fourth Amendment provides in full: "The right of the people to be secure in their persons, houses, papers, and effects, against unreasonable searches and seizures, shall not be violated, and no Warrants shall issue, but upon probable cause, supported by Oath or affirmation, and particularly describing the place to be searched, and the persons or things to be seized." The prohibition against "unreasonable searches and seizures" means that the police typically must develop probable cause and then obtain a warrant from a neutral magistrate before conducting a search or a seizure. There are, however, many situations where the police will not need a warrant or even probable cause to search or seize someone. For example, the police may conduct a stop (seizure) and frisk (search) based on reasonable suspicion, a lower standard than probable cause.

---

1. Indeed, as the affidavit explained, the confidential source Meléndez refers to was in custody at the time of the application because members of the conspiracy already distrusted him and had threatened his life.

1. Searches Following an Observed Drug Sale

One recurring Fourth Amendment issue that arises in drug cases is the observed sale in a so-called "high crime area." In these cases, a police officer observes individuals exchange money for small objects in an area the officer claims is known for drug trafficking. Is this observed transaction, without more, enough to give the officer reasonable suspicion or probable cause that a drug transaction has occurred?

New Jersey v. Pineiro
Supreme Court of New Jersey
181 N.J. 13 (2004)

Justice Wallace delivered the opinion of the Court.

In this search and seizure case, following the denial of his motion to suppress evidence, defendant pled guilty to possession of drugs based on evidence seized after a warrantless arrest. As in *State v. Moore*, [a companion case] also decided today, we review whether the State had reasonable suspicion to make an investigatory stop and whether the State had probable cause to search defendant. The trial court and the Appellate Division both answered that question in the affirmative. We disagree in part. We conclude that although there was a reasonable and articulable suspicion to stop defendant and investigate, the totality of the circumstances failed to support a finding of probable cause to search defendant without a warrant.

Wildwood Police Officer Elias Aboud was the sole witness at the suppression hearing. On December 8, 2000, around 6:15 p.m., he was on routine patrol in the area of Roberts and Pacific Avenues in Wildwood, New Jersey. Aboud characterized this area as a high drug, high crime area. While in his patrol vehicle Aboud observed defendant Jose R. Pineiro and codefendant Jorge Rodriguez standing on the corner of Roberts and Pacific Avenues. There was a bicycle nearby.

Aboud recognized both individuals. He previously had encountered defendant "while clearing the corners" in that same area, and he had received intelligence reports indicating defendant was a suspected drug dealer. Aboud knew Rodriguez, having arrested him for child support and possibly for possession of a controlled dangerous substance (CDS). He also was aware that Rodriguez was a drug user.

The overhead lights in the area allowed Aboud to observe defendant give Rodriguez a pack of cigarettes. Aboud was aware that a cigarette pack sometimes is used to transport drugs. Neither man was smoking at the time. Immediately after the transfer, the two men noticed Aboud. They looked at him with shock and surprise and turned to leave the area. Defendant walked down Pacific Avenue while Rodriguez mounted the bicycle and pedaled westbound on Roberts Avenue. Aboud called for assistance to detain defendant while he pursued Rodriguez. He overtook Rodriguez and detained him. Aboud informed Rodriguez that he believed he had just purchased drugs. Rodriguez began to cry and denied any drug involvement. Aboud asked Rodriguez for the cigarette pack, and upon receipt of it, looked inside and found a baggie containing three smaller light blue baggies of suspected heroin.

Concurrently, other Wildwood police officers stopped and arrested defendant. The record does not reveal that any evidence was seized from defendant.

The trial court found there was probable cause to arrest Rodriguez and defendant for their involvement in a drug transaction. The Appellate Division agreed, finding that

Aboud's specialized knowledge that cigarette packs are used to conceal drugs, his knowledge of Rodriguez's drug involvement, the officer's prior observation of defendant in that same high crime area, and the men's reaction upon seeing the officer established probable cause. We granted defendant's petition for certification and now reverse.

We recently reviewed the constitutionally permissible forms of police encounters with citizens. A "field inquiry" is the least intrusive encounter, and occurs when a police officer approaches an individual and asks "if [the person] is willing to answer some questions." A field inquiry is permissible so long as the questions "[are] not harassing, overbearing, or accusatory in nature." "The person approached, however, need not answer any question put to him; indeed, he may decline to listen to the questions at all and may go on his way."

The next type of encounter, an investigatory stop, sometimes referred to as a *Terry* stop, is valid "if it is based on specific and articulable facts which, taken together with rational inferences from those facts, give rise to a reasonable suspicion of criminal activity." The suspicion need not rise to the "probable cause necessary to justify an arrest."

The last type of encounter is that occasioned by the probable cause standard. Probable cause is not easily defined. In *Moore,* we stated:

> [T]he probable cause standard "'is a well-grounded suspicion that a crime has been or is being committed.'" "Probable cause exists where the facts and circumstances within ... [the officers'] knowledge and of which they had reasonably trustworthy information [are] sufficient in themselves to warrant a [person] of reasonable caution in the belief that an offense has been or is being committed."

Turning to the case at hand, the State seeks to justify the initial stop of defendant as an investigatory stop.

As noted, there must be a showing of reasonable and articulable suspicion for courts to sanction a brief investigatory stop. In *State v. Stovall*, the Court reaffirmed the United States Supreme Court definition of reasonable suspicion as "'a particularized and objective basis for suspecting the person stopped of criminal activity.'"

In [a previous New Jersey Supreme Court case] *Arthur,* the police observed a woman in a high drug traffic area get into the defendant's car, remain with the defendant for about five minutes, leave with a brown paper bag under her arm, and look around in a suspicious manner. Based on the woman's conduct and their knowledge that paper bags were often used to transport drugs, the police stopped the woman, seized the bag, looked inside, and discovered between 100 and 200 glass vials containing a white residue. The police stopped the defendant's car, and when he was ordered to exit the car he blurted out that he had "bottles" (slang for cocaine). The Court held that the stop of the woman was lawful, but that the officers' observations did not justify a search of her bag in the absence of any belief that she was armed or dangerous. The Court determined that the search of the woman was merely an attempt to look for evidence of drugs. Nevertheless, the Court upheld the investigatory stop of the defendant's car because the totality of the circumstances supported a reasonable and articulable suspicion that the defendant was engaged in illegal drug activity and his admission that he had "bottles" gave the police probable cause to search his person.

Here, Aboud observed defendant give Rodriguez a pack of cigarettes. Based on his experience, Aboud was aware that drugs sometimes are transported in cigarette packs. While the transfer of the cigarette pack may have been purely innocent, *Arthur* support[s] the proposition that the police may rely on behavior that is consistent with innocence as well as guilt in finding reasonable and articulable suspicion to conduct an investigatory stop. "The fact that purely innocent connotations can be ascribed to a person's actions does not mean that an officer cannot base a finding of reasonable suspicion on those actions as long as 'a reasonable person would find the actions are consistent with guilt.'"

Aboud was familiar with defendant from having "cleared him off the corners" in the same area. Furthermore, Aboud had received intelligence reports that identified defendant as a suspected drug dealer. Regarding Rodriguez, Aboud was aware that he had been involved with illicit drugs and that Aboud previously had arrested him. Additionally, both defendant and Rodriguez immediately departed the area upon seeing Aboud. Based on his knowledge that drugs were sometimes carried in cigarette packs, that he had not observed either of the men smoking, and his familiarity with both men, Aboud decided to stop Rodriguez and defendant. We are satisfied that, even though standing alone each factor may not have been sufficient, the totality of the circumstances, as viewed by a reasonable officer with Aboud's knowledge and experience, established a reasonable and articulable suspicion of criminal activity, justifying an investigatory stop.

Our concurring colleague urges that the police should not consider an area's reputation for or history of crime, or even the transfer of a cigarette pack, to aid in the determination of reasonable and articulable suspicion. In support of his view, our concurring colleague references a few decisions from other jurisdictions, but he fails to account for either our jurisprudence, or that of other jurisdictions, that considers the reputation or history of an area and an officer's experience with and knowledge of the suspected transfer of narcotics as relevant factors to determine the validity of a *Terry* stop. *See, e.g., State v. Cooper,* 830 So.2d 440, 445 (La.App.2002) (holding that officer's experience, training, and common sense may be considered in determining reasonable inferences for investigatory stop; reputation of area is relevant, articulable fact on which officer can rely in determination of reasonable suspicion for investigatory stop).

We next consider whether the facts supported probable cause to seize and search Rodriguez. Both courts below found probable cause to seize the cigarette pack from Rodriguez and to arrest him. The State contends that once drugs were discovered on Rodriguez, there was probable cause to arrest both him and defendant for suspected drug activity. Thus, we must consider whether the cigarette pack was lawfully seized from Rodriguez.

As we noted above, warrantless searches are presumed invalid. Unless the warrantless search comes within one of the prescribed exceptions, the search is not permissible. Similar to its position in *Moore,* the State argues that based on the information available to Aboud, there was probable cause to arrest Rodriguez for possession of drugs.

Today in *Moore* we found probable cause based on the law enforcement officers' observations in a high crime area, which included observing the defendant and a companion walk away from a group of people to the back of a vacant lot, and hand a third man currency in exchange for small unknown objects believed to be drugs. Here, unlike in *Moore,* there was no observation of currency or anything else exchanged, rather, there was merely a transfer of a cigarette pack under circumstances that had both innocent and suspected criminal connotations. Moreover, there was no proof of "regularized police experience that objects such as [hard cigarette packs] are the probable containers of drugs." The sum of the evidence was merely the officer's prior general narcotics training and experience, and his conclusory testimony that he knew that cigarette packs are used to transport drugs because he had seen that type of activity before. The evidence did not even include the number of times the officer had encountered the use of cigarette packs to exchange drugs or what percentage of observed cigarette packs held drugs.

Although we recognize that this is a close case, in our view the totality of the circumstances here fall short of probable cause.[2] The activity observed by Aboud was the passing of a cigarette pack in a high crime area between a known felon and a suspected drug dealer. Aboud apprehended Rodriguez and accused him of having been involved in a drug transaction. After Rodriguez began to cry and denied he had any drugs, Aboud asked if he would voluntarily surrender the cigarette pack and Rodriguez did so. We conclude that the observations by Aboud raised a reasonable and articulable suspicion that criminal activity was occurring, but more is required to support a fair probability that contraband or evidence of a crime would be found in the cigarette pack. After all, the passing of the cigarette pack just as easily could have been nothing more than the transfer of a cigarette pack between two adults. Although nervousness and crying by Rodriguez may have raised the officer's suspicions, we do not find that those factors, even when considered with the other circumstances, reached the level of the elusive concept of probable cause.

In summary, we hold that under a totality of the circumstances analysis, the State failed to meet its burden to show probable cause to seize the cigarette pack and arrest the individuals. Consequently, it was error to deny defendant's motion to suppress the evidence.

The judgment of the Appellate Division is reversed.

Justice Albin, concurring.

The mere passing of a cigarette pack between two individuals is an unremarkable occurrence that does not suggest criminal activity, whether in a high crime area or any other locale. Such ordinary behavior does not lose its innocent character, in my estimation, even if engaged in by a paroled drug offender. For that reason, I cannot agree with my colleagues that the passing of a cigarette pack from one person to another without the exchange of money in a high crime area by people with suspected drug backgrounds gave the police officers a reasonable and articulable suspicion to stop and detain the individuals.

The handing of a cigarette pack from one person to another at a Starbucks in Westfield or outside the Bridgewater Commons Mall would not attract anyone's attention or give a police officer cause for a second thought because such conduct, standing alone, does not suggest that criminal activity is afoot. Such innocuous conduct is not transformed into a criminal enterprise, justifying a *Terry*-type detention and questioning, merely because it occurs in a police-designated high crime area. The police officer's possession of vague "intelligence reports"—of unknown reliability—"indicating defendant was a suspected drug dealer" and his recollection that he "possibly" arrested the other individual for a drug offense should not alter the calculus.

There are tens of thousands of previous drug offenders in this state who are on parole, probation, or who have completed the terms of their sentences. Many of those people live in communities that are designated high crime areas. In my opinion, the Court's holding goes too far and subjects those individuals to a *Terry* stop whenever they hand a cigarette pack to another person.

Although the detective stated at the suppression motion that cigarette packs are sometimes used to conceal drug transactions, there was no testimony concerning the percentage of times a packet of cigarettes is used for such illicit purposes.

---

2. The State does not seek to justify the search under the consent exception, recognizing that Aboud did not inform Rodriguez of his right to refuse consent. *See State v. Johnson*, 120 N.J. 263, 288 (1990).

The words "high crime area" should not be invoked talismanically by police officers to justify a *Terry* stop that would not pass constitutional muster in any other location. *See State v. Carter,* 69 Ohio St. 3d 57 (1994) (finding that high crime area alone was not sufficient to warrant investigative stop, and noting that "[t]o hold otherwise would result in the wholesale loss of personal liberty of those with the misfortune of living in high crime areas"); Margaret Raymond, *Down on the Corner, Out in the Street: Considering the Character of the Neighborhood in Evaluating Reasonable Suspicion,* 60 Ohio St. L.J. 99, 143 (1999) (arguing that "the character of the neighborhood for criminality should be considered only where the behavior that is relied upon to establish reasonable suspicion is behavior not commonly observed among law-abiding persons at the time and place observed").

Whether they have drug backgrounds or not, those who live in high crime areas—a geographical designation that may include a whole neighborhood in an urban area—should not be subject to a lesser expectation of privacy under the State and Federal Constitutions. This is not a case in which the police over a period of time observed singularly suspicious activity, such as an individual handing out a number of cigarette packs to others or accepting money for individual cigarettes or packs of cigarettes. In this case, a police officer merely happened onto a scene in which he made the mundane observation of one individual passing a pack of cigarettes to another. That alone, regardless of the backgrounds of the individuals involved, did not warrant a stop and detention. Vigorous enforcement of the law through a heightened police presence in a high crime area does not require the sacrifice of constitutional protections under the Fourth Amendment.

The analysis of the majority has not departed from, but merely followed, a set of precedents on the boundary line of our Fourth Amendment jurisprudence.

In the war against drugs, the justification of one questionable search as the basis for the next questionable search, and the next one, is slowly leading to the erosion of our Fourth Amendment protections. This process occurs almost imperceptibly in much the same way that light fades into dusk and dusk into darkness. It is in this twilight period when changes are barely discernable that we must be most vigilant to guard against the unintended surrender of our valued rights. I am concerned that the incremental extension of precedents on the outer perimeter of our Fourth Amendment jurisprudence will sanction unreasonable searches.

I would not extend *Arthur* to permit a finding of a reasonable and articulable suspicion of criminal activity on the basis of the seemingly innocent passing of a cigarette pack from one individual to another without any exchange of money—even if the cigarette pack passes between individuals with suspected drug backgrounds in a high crime area. I concur with the majority that the actual seizure of the cigarette pack was not supported by probable cause and, therefore, I join the judgment of the Court.

Justice LaVecchia, concurring in part and dissenting in part.

Based on the totality of the circumstances here, I am satisfied that Officer Aboud had reasonable suspicion to stop Rodriguez, and that probable cause and exigent circumstances justified Officer Aboud's search of the cigarette pack handed to him by Rodriguez.

Officer Aboud had considerable experience in narcotics investigations; he was on patrol in a high drug-trafficking area; he had previously encountered defendant "clearing corners" in that location and identified defendant as a drug dealer; defendant received a known container for illegal narcotics from Rodrigues; when Aboud approached, defendant appeared shocked and surprised; defendant and his cohort immediately fled; and when later confronted by Aboud, defendant began to cry, and seemed nervous and defensive in his responses. I simply cannot agree that the totality of those circumstances do not give rise to probable cause sufficient to justify the search. The majority notes Aboud's failure to witness an exchange of currency, finding that omission as significant in forming its conclusion that these circumstances do not amount to probable cause that a crime was being committed. That reasoning, however, divorces the "omitted fact" from context. The alleged "failure" to witness an exchange of currency for drugs should be recognized for what it was: an interrupted drug transaction caused by the participants' realization that Aboud was virtually next to them in his patrol car. And, Aboud, as a trained professional, had every reason to perceive what he was observing as such, and to act thereupon by following the evidence of the crime he had just witnessed. Given the circumstances, Officer Aboud reasonably concluded that he had probable cause to stop and search Rodriguez. The lower courts credited his practical and common-sense decision to pursue that evidence, and so would I. I believe that, by holding as it does, the Court creates a constitutionally unnecessary barrier to the ability of law enforcement authorities to effectuate searches and seizures in respect of consummated, albeit also ongoing, criminal activities. I therefore respectfully dissent.

In *Pineiro*, the Court debates whether an area's reputation for a history of drug trafficking or other crime should factor into the calculus when determining whether there is reasonable suspicion or probable cause under the Fourth Amendment. But what exactly is a "high crime" neighborhood? College and university students often experiment with drugs. Should colleges and universities be classified as "high drug crime" areas?

Can't You See What I'm Saying?
Making Expressive Conduct a Crime in High-Crime Areas
Lenese C. Herbet

9 Georgetown Journal of Poverty Law and Policy 135 (2002)

As an eager young Assistant United States Attorney who "papered" countless complaints, conducted numerous hearings, and tried a substantial number of cases, I learned how to decode police officer jargon and law enforcement terminology. One of the most commonly used—yet seldom defined—phrases was "high-crime area." Rarely did law enforcement officers explain why certain areas and not others were classified as inherently dangerous, deadly, or lawless; yet, the police seemed confident in their ability to assert the existence of these areas and define their boundaries. Before court appearances, I would often question police officers about this characterization. In court, however, judges rarely challenged the proffered label or required its definition. Judges never asked officers for data to support assertions that an area was high-crime. Even defense counsel seldom explored what this classification meant, the bases for it, or its relevance. Nor did counsel challenge the way this label simultaneously tarred clients and prompted judges—who happily deferred to the officers' superior knowledge of the jurisdiction's "mean streets"—to absolve the police for their use of questionable law enforcement tactics.

I began to suspect that when officers used the term high-crime area, they were not describing particular locations. A high-crime area is a misnomer: areas do not commit crimes; people do. Still, despite varying levels of police training, officers seemed to identify areas as "criminal" based on fixed, incontrovertible, and fairly obvious traits.

I suspected that the police were using a code language to suggest that their actions were justified because they were directed at "high-crime people": poor, undereducated, black and brown males who live in or frequent depressed (e.g., culturally, educationally, socially, economically) inner-city neighborhoods or who look as if they do. In practice, police have the implicit authorization to create and apply an inferior set of rights to individuals in high-crime areas, presumably because those individuals are regarded as being less worthy than other citizens. The erosion of individual rights leaves people in high-crime areas unprotected and often requires a sub-citizen level of obeisance to those who patrol their streets.

Crime Mapping and the Fourth Amendment: Redrawing "High-Crime Areas"
Andrew Guthrie Ferguson
63 Hastings Law Journal 179 (2011)

On a map of a city, an irregular rectangle is marked off in gray. It is a "high-crime area," a "hotspot" of crime. The chief of police has duly designated the north, south, east, and west boundaries. It is official, documented, and legal. The shaded area means there existed a statistically disproportionate amount of crime during a given time period. Depending on the jurisdiction, this map may result in an increased police presence or targeted police activities in an area. As a strictly administrative matter, a "high-crime area" designation may be a good example of data-driven policing—responding to crime-ridden areas with increased police presence. As a legal matter, however, this designation may have Fourth Amendment implications. More fundamentally, for the thousands of citizens living inside this shaded area, this official designation has the potential to alter the liberty protections they enjoy: because these people live in a high-crime area, they may receive less protection under the Fourth Amendment and it may be more reasonable for police to stop or search them on suspicion of criminal activity.

In the past few years, the ability of police administrators to identify and officially label high-crime areas has rapidly expanded. [Graphic Information Systems ("GIS")] crime-mapping technology has simplified the collection and analysis of crime statistics. Sophisticated computer programs, databases, and algorithms have made it easier empirically to designate certain areas as having a disproportionately higher level of crime.

Simply stated, these GIS crime-mapping technologies can produce almost perfect information about the frequency and geographic location of crimes in any given area. The crime data can be broken down and analyzed by location, crime, and time period. Some jurisdictions have almost real-time data collection and daily reports of problematic areas to officers in the field. There is no longer a statistical question about which areas, in fact, have higher levels of crime. Maps can be created detailing the last twenty auto thefts in a given neighborhood, the last three months of drug arrests within a city, or the locations of all of the homicides committed in a given year. Typically, the data collection, storage, and analysis are done by police administrators to determine staffing needs or allocate resources. However, these technologies can now be used officially to label areas as having an empirically higher level of crime.

While these technologies serve as effective policing tools, they also present unexamined constitutional questions. Under existing Supreme Court precedent, *Illinois v. Wardlow*, the fact that an area is designated a high-crime area has Fourth Amendment implications. Such a finding in a suppression hearing can affect a court's determination about whether police officers had "reasonable suspicion" to stop an individual suspected of a crime. After *Wardlow*, the fact that the stop occurred in a "'high crime area' [is] among the relevant contextual considerations in a *Terry [v. Ohio]* analysis." The result in

Wardlow was a finding of reasonable suspicion based on the "totality of circumstances" of only two factors—a high-crime area plus an unprovoked flight from police. In thousands of post-*Wardlow* cases, the designation of an area as a high-crime area has had not only constitutional effects on the liberty interests of individuals in those areas, but also practical effects on courts analyzing the reasonableness of a Fourth Amendment stop.

What a "high-crime area" is, however, has not been defined by courts, legislatures, or police administrators in any consistent fashion.

The Fourth Amendment "impose[s] a standard of 'reasonableness' upon the exercise of discretion by government officials, including law enforcement agents, in order to safeguard the privacy and security of individuals against arbitrary invasions." Three types of police-citizen encounters can occur: (1) consensual encounters, which require no objective level of suspicion; (2) investigative detentions, or stops, which must be preceded by reasonable, articulable suspicion of criminal activity; and (3) full searches and arrests, which must be supported by probable cause.

The high-crime area analysis generally arises only in the second type of encounter. Following the well-known *Terry v. Ohio* framework, a police officer may briefly detain a suspect if the officer has a reasonable suspicion, supported by particularized and articulable facts, that criminal activity is afoot. Reasonable suspicion is an objective standard, and reviewing courts assess reasonable suspicion based on the "totality of circumstances," including, when relevant, the crime level of the area. While the character of the area can influence the totality analysis, the same objective standard of reasonable suspicion is assumed to apply in all neighborhoods and to all people. In other words, the reasonable suspicion legal standard in a high-crime area should be the same as in a non high-crime area.

For almost forty years, the Supreme Court has relied on an understanding that the crime level of an area can influence the reasonable suspicion determination. Yet only rarely has the Court been presented with crime statistics generated from crime-mapping programs or official designations labeling a certain area. In no case has the Supreme Court analyzed crime data or the implications of crime-mapping technologies. However, a comparison of two cases provides some guidance as to how the Court might approach this issue in the future.

In *Illinois v. Wardlow*, the high-crime area designation of a stop became one of only two factors the Supreme Court used in its totality of circumstances analysis. The Court held that "unprovoked flight" in a high-crime area justified the reasonable suspicion of the officers conducting the stop of Mr. Wardlow. The finding that the area was a high-crime area was based on an officer's testimony that he was part of a special operations division focusing on "heavy narcotics trafficking." Officer Nolan testified that he was part of a four-car caravan driving through Chicago's 11th Police District when he observed Mr. Wardlow holding a white plastic bag near 4035 West Van Buren Street.

The issue of whether the area surrounding this location was, in fact, a high-crime area or an "area known for heavy narcotics trafficking" had been contested during the state court proceedings. The Appellate Court of Illinois found the record too vague to determine whether the area was a high-crime area:

> From the record before us, we cannot discern the precise location of the area known by the officers to have a high incidence of narcotics trafficking. After he testified that he noticed defendant at 4035 West Van Buren, Officer Nolan was asked why he went to that area. He responded that it was one of the areas in the 11th District that had "high narcotics traffic." His testimony indicates only that the officers were headed somewhere in the general area. There was no evidence

that the officers were investigating the specific area where defendant had been standing or that any of the police cars had stopped at that location or that defendant
had any basis for believing that police were interested in his activity.

Officer Nolan testified that he was "caravaning" down West Van Buren when
he noticed defendant. He did not testify that the officers were targeting 4035
West Van Buren because it was known to be a location where drugs were sold.
From the evidence elicited at the hearing on the motion to suppress, it appears
that the officers were simply driving by, on their way to some unidentified location, when they noticed defendant standing at 4035 West Van Buren. The record
here is simply too vague to support the inference that defendant was in a location with a high incidence of narcotics trafficking or, for that matter, that defendant's flight was related to his expectation of police focus on him.

The Supreme Court of Illinois disagreed with this determination, concluding that Officer Nolan's "uncontradicted and undisputed testimony, which was accepted by the trial
court, was sufficient to establish that the incident occurred in a high-crime area."

Wardlow thus presented the Supreme Court with the opportunity to address how to
define "high-crime areas" in a Fourth Amendment case. Crime statistics and crime-
mapping techniques were introduced by the parties. As one amicus brief stated:

The reputation of an area for having substantial criminal activity can be based,
not only on the objective knowledge and experience of police officers, but on
verifiable and quantifiable data. Sophisticated data collection, geographical computer and other mapping, and detailed geographical analysis systems have all
become an essential part of crime prevention.

The use of geographical factors in policing is the subject of extensive ongoing studies. In conducting these studies, researchers rely on computer mapping
as a fundamental tool when working with geographical data. Aided by ad-
vancements in technology, computer mapping, which can encompass the production of a simple pin map or the complex interactive mapping for detailed
geographical analysis, has become an essential part of crime prevention in larger
cities.

But despite the invitation to embrace GIS crime-mapping technologies, the Supreme
Court declined to address the issue.

One reason why the Court might have avoided the issue is that the crime data did not
necessarily support its ultimate conclusion. [T]he data presents a more complicated picture of crime in the area of Mr. Wardlow's stop. For example, while the majority opinion relies on testimony that the area was in a high narcotics trafficking area, there were
no statistics on drug arrests presented to the Supreme Court. Further, nothing Mr. Wardlow was doing at 12:35 pm holding a white plastic bag necessarily indicated narcotics trafficking. The crime statistics presented to the Court demonstrated that District 11 had the
highest murder rate of Chicago's twenty-five districts, and a quite high rate for sexual assault and robberies, but was ranked right in the middle of the twenty-five districts for
crime overall. The relevance of the number of murders or sexual assaults to an officer's
observation of a man holding a plastic bag is not obvious. Finally, while crime statistics
were presented on a district level—a district that encompassed 98,000 people—there
was no specific information about the 4035 West Van Buren address or any particularized
complaints about that location. There appears, thus, to be a substantial disconnect between the existing crime data and any argument for how that data should have affected
the reasonable suspicion of the officer observing Mr. Wardlow.

The Court addressed a similar issue in *Pennsylvania v. Dunlap*, in which Chief Justice John Roberts and Justice Anthony Kennedy dissented from a denial of a writ of certiorari. In a homage to the noir fiction genre, the Chief Justice highlighted the importance of the character of the neighborhood in justifying a police stop:

> North Philly, May 4, 2001. Officer Sean Devlin, Narcotics Strike Force, was working the morning shift. Undercover surveillance. The neighborhood? Tough as a three-dollar steak. Devlin knew. Five years on the beat, nine months with the Strike Force. He'd made fifteen, twenty drug busts in the neighborhood.
>
> Devlin spotted him: a lone man on the corner. Another approached. Quick exchange of words. Cash handed over; small objects handed back. Each man then quickly on his own way. Devlin knew the guy wasn't buying bus tokens. He radioed a description and Officer Stein picked up the buyer. Sure enough: three bags of crack in the guy's pocket. Head downtown and book him. Just another day in the office.

In dissenting from the denial of certiorari, Chief Justice Roberts signaled his disapproval of the Supreme Court of Pennsylvania's holding that a single, isolated drug transaction in a high-crime area was insufficient to justify a stop of the suspect. Relying in part on the officer's specific knowledge of the area as well as the officer's specific experience in making arrests in the area, Chief Justice Roberts reasoned that such information should constitute probable cause to arrest.

While there remains an open question whether fifteen or twenty arrests in the general vicinity of an area is sufficiently particularized to make suspicious what Officer Devlin observed, there is in fact a closer nexus between what he knew about the area and what he saw. Relevantly, Officer Devlin's purpose for being there was that the Philadelphia Police Department's Narcotics Strike Force had authorized a "plain-clothes surveillance" for a particular corner. Unlike in *Wardlow*, in which the Narcotics Strike Force was driving through the streets and happened to see Mr. Wardlow on West Van Buren, Officer Devlin had staked out a particularized location with a particularized crime problem because of an official decision of his police administrators. Further, the expected type of criminal activity matched what Officer Devlin actually saw—suspected narcotics dealing.

In *Dunlap*, as opposed to *Wardlow*, an understanding of crime patterns made the officer's observations more reasonable because the particularized knowledge of the area was tied to the particularized suspicion of the observed person. These two cases help frame the federal and state court approaches to the issue.

Most federal and state courts that have addressed the high-crime area issue post-Wardlow employ the term without much sustained analysis. In many cases, the "area" is not defined by geographic location or connected to a particular type of crime. Only a handful of courts have referenced any statistical data for crime patterns in an area. A few courts have narrowed the area to a more particularized address or location, usually in keeping with the initial justifications for police suspicion. While some courts have expressed concern or confusion about what exactly a high-crime area is or how it should be weighed in the totality of circumstances, only a few federal courts of appeals have explicitly addressed the empirical basis for and constitutional problems with the term. Unsurprisingly, courts have developed different standards and different solutions to resolve the issue.

The reasonable suspicion analysis is elastic enough for certain police departments to announce targeted "stop and frisk" tactics, whereby officers are encouraged to make contact with citizens in the hopes of creating justification for a full seizure or frisk. The legal standard is the same, but in practice, citizens in targeted high-crime areas have less robust Fourth Amendment protections.

A vivid example of such a tactic took place in Brownsville, Brooklyn, an eight-square-block high-crime area. From 2006 to 2010, police officers conducted 52,000 stop and frisks among a population of 14,000. That means one stop per year for each of the residents in the area. One man, a twenty-six-year-old legal assistant, had been stopped over thirty times. Out of those stops, only about one percent of the suspects were arrested. However, Brownsville is statistically a higher-crime area—one that deservedly has drawn the attention of police administrators.

How did the designation of the neighborhood as a high-crime area affect the liberty interests of its citizens? First, it has to be acknowledged that from a traditional Fourth Amendment perspective, there is no protection from heightened police presence in public. Additional police on the street, additional surveillance techniques, and even additional consensual police contacts do not infringe upon a reasonable expectation of privacy, because what one knowingly exposes to the public, including one's presence, is not protected. While the Court did acknowledge in *Katz v. United States* that the Fourth Amendment may protect information that we "seek[] to preserve as private, even in an area accessible to the public," most denizens of higher crime areas cannot take measures to signal such an expectation of privacy.

Yet, while there may not be a Fourth Amendment violation, broader Fourth Amendment values affecting the expectation of privacy need to be evaluated in considering the effect of predesignating high-crime areas. An intensive and visible police presence affects behavior. Police walking on the street, inquiring about the reason for being in a certain area, or monitoring the travel of residents will regulate freedom of movement. Some of this is explicit, such as when individuals are ordered not to congregate together. In Washington, D.C.'s "drug free zones," more than two people may not walk or talk together after being ordered to disperse. Such associational rights may be significantly impacted in high-crime areas. Citizens may be concerned about retaining informational privacy, revealing intimate facts, or a loss of autonomy, even in a public space. Police regulation and self-regulation can have an effect on individual expression, creativity, and freedom to travel.

An increased police presence also means an increased likelihood of interpersonal police-citizen encounters. For example, a high percentage of the stop and frisks in New York City turned out to be mistaken (meaning no contraband was recovered), resulting in an unnecessary infringement on personal liberty. Scholars have recognized that these largely negative police-citizen encounters may affect dignity rights of citizens, may involve a stigmatic harm, and may be interpreted as a lack of respect that can itself undermine core constitutional principles. This restructuring of power undercuts the "right to be let alone" that informs our Fourth Amendment protections. Whether they embrace it as a positive protective presence or reject it as an unnecessary interference, residents in these areas are forced to think about police surveillance as an ever-present reality.

Finally, citizens may perceive inequality in the application of the law based on class or race. The correlation between high-crime areas and low income communities is strong. The correlation between low-income communities and communities of color is similarly strong. Neighborhoods may become a proxy for racially biased law enforcement. Residents in those neighborhoods may believe that different rules apply because of race. This perceived discriminatory treatment both undermines the belief that the legal system is fair, and disrupts other social organizing structures in a community.

2. Profiling and Pretextual Stops

Florida v. Johnson

Supreme Court of Florida
561 So. 2d 1139 (1990)

Barkett, J.

We have for review *State v. Johnson*, which certified the following question of great public importance:

> May a profile of similarities of drug couriers, which is developed by a law enforcement officer and which, in light of his experience, suggests the likelihood of drug trafficking, be relied upon by him to form an articulable or founded suspicion which will justify a brief investigatory traffic stop on highways known to the officer to be frequently used for the transport of drugs?

On June 4, 1985, Florida Highway Patrol Trooper Robert Vogel was assigned to a special drug detail working on Interstate 95 in Volusia County. At about 4:15 am., he spotted a large luxury car driving north, bearing Maryland license plates and traveling at exactly 55 m.p.h., the legal speed limit.

Vogel decided to make an "investigatory" stop because the following facts fit a personal drug courier profile Vogel had developed: (1) the car was driving at 4:15 am.; (2) the driver was alone; (3) the driver was about thirty years of age; (4) the car had out-of-state tags; (5) the car was of a large model type,; (6) the driver was male; (7) the driver was wearing casual clothes; (8) the driver was being "overly cautious" by driving at precisely the speed limit; (9) the car was driving on a known drug corridor, Interstate 95. Based solely on these factors, Vogel stopped and detained Johnson. After making the stop, Vogel discovered marijuana in the trunk of the vehicle, seized it, and arrested Johnson.

At trial, Vogel testified that he had thirteen and one-half years' experience in identifying and arresting persons transporting illegal drugs. Between March 5, 1984, and April 18, 1985, Vogel compiled his own drug courier profile based on elements common to each of thirty arrests made during this period. However, he testified that he does not keep records of all the vehicles that fit the "profile" which he stops and does not search, or stops and searches but finds no contraband. Testimony at trial indicated that the Florida Highway Patrol had its own drug courier profile, which included the presence of air shocks on a car, blacked-out glass and evidence the vehicle was heavily loaded. However, Vogel testified he did not rely on the Patrol's profile.

Based on these facts, the trial court suppressed the evidence seized from the vehicle. The trial judge concluded that the factors given by Vogel did not constitute founded suspicion that Johnson had engaged in criminal conduct.

On appeal, the Fifth District agreed based partly on its prior rejection of Vogel's profile in *In re Forfeiture of $6,003.00*, 505 So.2d 668 (Fla. 5th DCA), *review denied*, 511 So.2d 998 (Fla.), *cert. denied*, 484 U.S. 965 (1987). It found that the factors given by Vogel in their totality did not create founded suspicion of criminal activity.

The state's sole basis for supporting the validity of the stop is Vogel's personal profile. Thus, the question presented is whether a late model out-of-state car driven by a thirty-year-old male at 4:15 in the morning, in accordance with all traffic laws and regulations, gives rise to founded suspicion of criminal conduct. We find that it does not.

Indeed, this conclusion is supported by at least three other cases that have considered similar "profiles" used by this same officer, Trooper Vogel, in other similar automobile stops. In the case of *In re Forfeiture of $6.003.00*, the Fifth District concluded that Trooper Vogel's profile was "too general and unparticularized." It reached this conclusion based on a profile consisting of factors similar to those at bar, which differed only in that the stopped automobile bore Florida rental tags and had two occupants.

Previously, the Eleventh Circuit Court of Appeals had occasion to review Trooper Vogel's profile. In *United States v. Smith,* the court condemned Vogel's profile as "a classic example of those inarticulate hunches' that are insufficient to justify a seizure under the fourth amendment." Indeed, the Eleventh Circuit termed Trooper Vogel's list of factors as nothing but "nondistinguishing characteristics." In the context of *Smith*, these characteristics consisted of out-of-state car tags on a car traveling fifty miles per hour, containing two occupants, with a driver about thirty years of age who appeared to be overly cautious.

Trooper Vogel's profile again came before the federal bench in *United States v. Miller,* and again was rejected. In *Miller*, the Eleventh Circuit made a telling comment:

> In this case, Trooper Vogel pulled over at 9:40 at night a car that was obeying the speed limit, that was being driven cautiously, and that was from out-of-state. During the Florida tourist season, that description likely describes a high percentage of cars on Interstate 95.... The record does not reveal how many unsuccessful searches Trooper Vogel has conducted or how many innocent travelers the officer has detained. Common sense suggests that those numbers may be significant.

We agree with these observations, and find that they apply equally to the instant case. Accordingly, we conclude that article I, section 12 of the Florida Constitution,[3] prohibits the police conduct that occurred in this instance.

We have little doubt that individual police officers may exercise a degree of discretion in choosing to make a stop after observing a situation indicating a likelihood of criminal wrongdoing. A "profile" thus is permissible precisely to the degree that it reasonably describes behavior likely to indicate crime. That is, the officer, prior to the stop, must observe some activity that links a particular person to some specific, articulable evidence of criminal wrongdoing. However, Florida law does not permit a profile based on factors that are little more than mundane or unremarkable descriptions of everyday law-abiding activities.

We are mindful of the concerns raised in Chief Justice Ehrlich's dissent. However, we find that the authority on which he relies, even if applied to this case, would fully support our views. For instance, in *United States v. Brignoni-Ponce,* 422 U.S. 873 (1975), the Court held that founded suspicion of an immigration law violation cannot be based solely

---

3. Article I, section 12, provides: Searches and seizures. — The right of the people to be secure in their persons, houses, papers and effects against unreasonable searches and seizures, and against the unreasonable interception of private communications by any means, shall not be violated. No warrant shall be issued except upon probable cause, supported by affidavit, particularly describing the place or places to be searched, the person or persons, thing or things to be seized, the communication to be intercepted, and the nature of evidence to be obtained. This right shall be construed in conformity with the 4th Amendment to the United States Constitution, as interpreted by the United States Supreme Court. Articles or information obtained in violation of this right shall not be admissible in evidence if such articles or information would be inadmissible under decisions of the United States Supreme Court construing the 4th Amendment to the United States Constitution.

on the fact that the occupants of a car appear to be Mexican. In that context, the Court went on to say that it was unwilling to "dispense entirely with the requirement that officers must have a reasonable suspicion to justify roving-patrol stops" even in the context of a search for illegal aliens.

If this standard applies to federal efforts to detect illegal aliens, then the same standard *at the very least* applies to roving stops of state citizens by state police, such as occurred in the present case. And in that regard, we cannot agree that the characteristics constituting Trooper Vogel's profile support a "rational inference" of criminal wrongdoing. Indeed, we find that the United States Supreme Court's recent decision in *United States v. Sokolow,* 490 U.S. 1 (1989), upon which the dissent relies, would support the same conclusion even if the instant case did not implicate state constitutional concerns. Unlike the inadequate "profile" in *Brignoni-Ponce* and the present case, the facts in unmistakably support a rational inference of wrongdoing.

In *Sokolow,* the United States Supreme Court upheld an airport search based on a profile when the defendant (1) had bought two airline tickets totalling $2,100 using twenty-dollar bills that he peeled from a much larger roll of cash; (2) had traveled under an assumed name; (3) had traveled to Miami, a city that is a common source of illicit drugs; (4) had planned to stay in Miami only about twenty-eight hours; (5) had appeared nervous throughout his trip; and (6) had checked no luggage. Thus, the profile in *Sokolow* justified a stop precisely because it described *unusual* conduct that set the defendant apart from other travelers and that strongly suggested concealed criminal conduct.

In the present case, there was nothing at all unusual or out of the ordinary about the conduct that constituted Trooper Vogel's "profile." It described conduct that was entirely unremarkable and completely lawful, just as the appearance of being Mexican was unremarkable and completely lawful in *Brignoni-Ponce*. The elements of Trooper Vogel's profile do not suggest concealed criminal conduct, as did the facts in *Sokolow*. Men of a certain age who drive certain kinds of cars in the evening hours, traveling at or below the speed limit on interstate corridors, simply cannot be described as an inherently "suspicious" bunch.

Indeed, the class of persons described by Trooper Vogel's profile is enormous. This profile literally would permit police to stop tens of thousands of law-abiding tourists, businessmen or commuters, just as the "profile" in *Brignoni-Ponce* would have authorized unrestrained stops of law-abiding Mexican-Americans. The resulting intrusion upon the privacy rights of the innocent is too great for a democratic society to bear. Were we to approve this profile, we might just as well approve a profile based on racial or ethnic characteristics, religious background, sex or any other completely innocent trait.

By contrast, the profile used in *Sokolow* manifestly would apply to only a few individuals who exhibit highly suspicious behavior in making airline travel arrangements. The intrusion upon privacy rights of the innocent in *Sokolow* is likely to be minimal. We thus cannot equate the *Sokolow* profile with that of Trooper Vogel, nor can we say that any of the other case law cited in the dissent would support a result contrary to the one we reach. The *Sokolow* profile is closely tailored to rationally describe concealed criminal conduct, whereas the profiles in *Brignoni-Ponce* and in the present case are not.

Finally, we do not agree with Justice Ehrlich's assessment that our opinion limits law enforcement to stopping only those who have violated traffic laws. Nor are we requiring a level of suspicion equal to probable cause in vehicle-stop cases. To the contrary, we find that even a sequence of lawful acts not rising to the level of probable cause may, in appropriate circumstances, so strongly suggest *concealed* criminal conduct as to justify a stop, as was the case in *Sokolow*. What we require today is that there must be a strong and articulable link— a "rational inference"—between the sequence of acts observed by the police and the concealed criminal conduct believed to exist, whether or not this sequence is described as a "profile." Such a link simply does not exist in the record before us.

The opinion of the district court below is approved.

It is so ordered.

McDonald, J., dissenting.

Vogel's profile, which included an accumulation of factors, was reasonable; reasonable profile stops of an automobile on a state highway should be contemplated by users of the highway, whose expectation of privacy should be considerably less than normal under the circumstances existing in this case.

We have a huge drug problem in Florida, particularly in South Florida, a major distribution center of drugs. It is known that I-95 and the Florida Turnpike are major avenues for this distribution. Vogel is a trained police officer and evidence in the instant case established that one-third to one-half of his vehicle stops resulted in major drug arrests. Thus it cannot be said that he is indiscriminate in his arrests. The stops themselves are relatively unobtrusive and short in duration. Balancing the interests of the state against the minimal intrusion of motorists who should anticipate some occasional stops for one reason or another, I conclude that the stop was reasonable and violated neither Florida nor United States constitutional provisions.

How, if at all, does a drug courier profile differ from a profile of a would-be bank robber? By design, innocent conduct can give rise to reasonable suspicion or probable cause. After all, reasonable suspicion and probable cause are both standards to guide police investigation of *suspected* criminal activity. This structure contemplates that while some investigations will confirm the officer's suspicion that criminal activity is afoot, in others the suspicious conduct will have an innocent explanation.

Morgan Cloud argues that drug courier profiles differ from other settings. First, in drug investigations, "the investigating officers generally do not possess any advance information suggesting that a specific crime has been committed nor even that any passenger on a particular flight is carrying drugs. Instead, they operate on the assumption that illegal drugs are carried by some members of the general population of air travelers. Relying on this assumption, the officers observe boarding or deplaning air passengers and attempt to identify drug couriers on the basis of characteristics not unique to the suspects but displayed by many travelers." Second, "[u]nlike cases where the suspect's conduct is the source of individualized suspicion satisfying fourth amendment standards, investigations based on the drug courier profile are justified by the assumption that the suspect's conduct conforms to the behavior of the class of airport drug couriers. The profile's focus is literally not upon an individual's unique conduct, but upon that conduct's alleged similarity to the behaviors of others." Morgan Cloud, *Search and Seizure By the Numbers: The Drug Courier Profile and Judicial Review of Investigative Formulas*, 65 B.U. L. Rev. 843 (1985).

Does the use of profiles to target suspects play a role in racial disparities in drug enforcement? Samuel R. Gross and Katherine Y. Barnes explain the link between racial profiling and drug enforcement as follows: "Racial profiling depends on police discretion in choosing suspects. At one end of the continuum, racial profiling is impossible once the police are looking for a particular person—the victim's partner, the woman in the surveillance video, Osama bin Laden—although it may be a factor at an earlier stage, in determining who to look for. At the other extreme, racial profiling can flourish in proactive investigations in which the police scan large numbers of people in search of culprits in crimes that have not been reported or have not yet occurred." Samuel R. Gross and Katherine Y. Barnes, *Road Work: Racial Profiling and Drug Interdiction on the Highway*, 101 Mich. L. Rev. 651, 654 (2002).

The Impact of the War on Drugs on Procedural Fairness and Racial Equality
David Rudovsky
1994 University of Chicago Legal Forum 237

Law enforcement authorities have used drug courier profile encounters as a weapon in the War on Drugs for the past twenty years. Law enforcement authorities use drug courier profiles to select which persons to stop and investigate as suspected drug couriers in areas where large numbers of persons travel. The profile model is conceptually quite different from the model of police investigation that relies upon individualized suspicion based on specific information and observations as a predicate for stops or searches. The profile model relies on factors that are not criminal in nature and that are usually characteristic of the activities of law-abiding persons.

Drug courier profiles are remarkably vague, indeterminate, and overbroad. Judge George C. Pratt of the United States Court of Appeals for the Second Circuit has correctly compared the use of drug courier profiles to Alice-in-Wonderland logic. In a case upholding a stop based on several of the drug courier profile characteristics, Judge Pratt, in dissent, demonstrated the fluidity of each factor. Judge Pratt began with the disputed "source city" concept:

> To justify their seizure of Hooper's bag the agents testified he had come from a "source city" and fit the DEA's "drug courier profile". Yet the government conceded at oral argument that a "source city" for drug traffic was virtually any city with a major airport, a concession that was met with deserved laughter in the court-room.

Judge Pratt went on to discuss the "chameleon-like" nature of the other profile factors. It is apparently significant if the suspect: arrived late at night or early in the morning; was one of the first to deplane or one of the last to deplane; used a one-way ticket or a round-trip ticket; carried brand-new luggage or a small gym bag; travelled alone or with a companion; acted nervously; wore expensive clothing and gold jewelry, or dressed in black corduroys, a white pullover shirt, and loafers without socks, or in dark slacks, a work shirt, and a hat, or in a brown leather aviator jacket, gold chain, with hair down to the shoulders, or in a loose-fitting sweatshirt and denim jacket; and walked rapidly through the airport, or walked aimlessly through the airport.

Given these imprecise and fluid characteristics, it is not surprising that profile stops are extraordinarily overinclusive. Profiles encourage stops based on non-criminal behavior and personal appearance and include characteristics shared by a large number of innocent people. In the operations at the Buffalo Airport discussed by Judge Pratt, the police were "correct" in their stops in fewer than 2 percent of their profile encounters: of the six hundred people stopped, only ten were carrying drugs. Similar results typify other profile investigations. Yet the courts continue to credit these stops, rarely even considering the empirical evidence to the contrary.

In part, the approval of profile stops is a predictable consequence of the kinds of cases that actually reach the courts. For the most part, judges see only those cases in which drugs or other contraband are seized. In these cases, enormous pressure exists to ignore constitutional violations, thereby preventing suppression of the evidence. In the thousands of cases where the individual stopped is completely innocent, even if that person was detained and searched illegally, it is unlikely that she will pursue legal remedies. Thus, the case law develops on a highly skewed notion of reality, subject to the distorting effect of the discovery of contraband in the specific case.

It is true that merely approaching someone to obtain information is not a seizure under the Fourth Amendment unless it would appear to a reasonable person that she was not free to leave or to refuse to answer police inquiries. But the profile encounter is just the first step in the process. What often follows is questioning designed to obtain "consent" or cause for a full search. A disturbing example of the Court's willingness to overlook coercive tactics is *Florida v Bostick*. *Bostick* involved a search conducted by police officers who boarded a bus at an intermediate stop on an interstate trip and, without any cause or suspicion, selected Bostick and another passenger, both seated in the back of the bus, as investigative targets. One officer asked Bostick for identification while another stood nearby, carrying a pistol in a zipper pouch, the equivalent of carrying a gun in a holster. After Bostick produced identification and his ticket (which matched), the police requested permission to search his luggage. "Permission" was granted, and the search disclosed narcotics in one of his suitcases.

The Supreme Court ruled that this police tactic ("working the buses") was not *per se* unconstitutional. The Court found no Fourth Amendment violation in police boarding buses and targeting individuals without any cause or suspicion, because one would not necessarily feel constrained by the police in this situation. It is on this latter point that the Court's opinion, driven by the exigencies of the War on Drugs, departs from reality. Bostick, a black man, was confronted by armed police officers. He was seated in the back of an interstate bus, at a stop in a remote area, and could only leave by breaking the barrier created by the officers. His choices were indeed limited. If he left the bus, he would be stranded at that stop without his luggage. He was faced with armed officers in a crowded area of the bus seeking to search his belongings. To find that he was not seized (i.e., that he reasonably believed he could leave) or that his permission was fully voluntary and consensual is to drain those terms of any meaning.

The authorization to conduct sweeps of buses, airports, and train stations is seemingly unlimited. As long as the initial encounter is not a "seizure" of the person, the basis for the stop is immaterial. Theoretically, it cannot be based solely on race, but as a practical matter racial motivation is very difficult to prove. For example, in *United States v Taylor*, the defendant, who was "poorly attired," was the only black to emerge in the initial group of passengers exiting from a plane that arrived in Memphis from Miami. The Sixth Circuit decided that because the encounter that led to his arrest and conviction on cocaine charges was "consensual," it did not need to consider whether Taylor was stopped because of his race or whether the incorporation of a racial component into the Drug Enforcement Administration's ("DEA") drug courier profile would violate equal protection and due process guarantees. The court did state that if the defendant could show that he was targeted for a consensual stop "because he was an African-American," or if the police "implemented a general practice or pattern that primarily targets minorities," equal protection would be implicated. But as the dissent demonstrated, the failure of the court to find racial motivation on this record revealed an inadequate equal protection standard.

There is yet another police tactic—the pretextual stop of automobiles—that is based on a rationale similar to that which animates drug courier profile stops. Police use traffic violation stops as a way to gain consent, plain view, or other justification for a search or seizure. Highway officers are encouraged to stop cars on alleged traffic or motor vehicle offenses to establish the requisite cause to search for drugs. In many instances, the stop is based on "profile" characteristics or is otherwise pretextual, done with the expectation that in a certain number of cases the stop will enable the officer to obtain consent, observe contraband in plain view, or develop other cause for a search.

Having stopped an automobile for an alleged traffic violation, the police may, without any cause or suspicion, use dogs to sniff the occupants and the vehicle to determine whether drugs are present. Moreover, as in the bus, rail station, and airport scenarios, the police are free to attempt to secure consent for the search. The problem here, of course, is determining after the fact whether the police coerced the permission or whether it was gained voluntarily. And, where drugs are found and the issue must be determined in a suppression context, the pressures to credit the police version are significant.

Defendants' claims that they were targeted because of race or alienage, that consent was coerced, or that the search was made with no consent are, as noted above, not always treated fairly in the criminal prosecution context. Occasionally, however, litigation offers a larger perspective of the practices involved. A federal district court has certified a class action on the issues of whether police are stopping motorists on Interstate 95 near Philadelphia without cause, on the basis of race, and whether searches of the cars are being conducted by coerced consent. Civil discovery rules have enabled the plaintiffs to obtain records of stops of motorists by the township's police department. These documents and follow-up interviews with persons subjected to these stops reveal several problematic characteristics of these stops. First, the interdiction program is based on the power to make a pretextual traffic stop. Numerous vehicles have been stopped, for example, for having small items tied to their rearview mirrors, for outdated inspection stickers, or for other minor violations, all supposedly observed as the car passed the police at sixty miles per hour. Second, the stops are racially disproportionate. Third, claims of consent are rebutted by numerous innocent individuals who give consistent accounts of being told that they would have to wait for a police dog, have their car towed, or suffer other types of roadside detention unless they consented to a search. Finally, a significant number of those stopped claim that the police searched without any permission whatsoever.

These discovery results are not unique. In Volusia County, Florida, videotapes and other documents relating to stops on Interstate 95, made by the Sheriff's drug squad, disclosed that highway stops were based in large measure on the race of the driver. Seventy percent of the motorists stopped were black or Hispanic; 80 percent of the cars that were searched were driven by blacks or Hispanics; only 1 percent of those stopped received a traffic citation; and over five hundred motorists were subjected to searches and frisks without any cause or suspicion. By comparison, only 5 percent of the drivers on this stretch of Interstate 95 were black or Hispanic, and only 15 percent of all persons convicted in Florida for traffic violations during this period were of a minority race.

The practice of using pretextual stops has been validated by most federal courts, thus giving the police a largely unreviewable way to avoid Fourth Amendment scrutiny. The courts justify this approach by citing the objective reasonableness of the stops: as long as there was cause for the police action, it does not matter that the police were using their powers as a pretext to conduct a drug investigation that was at the time unsupported by cause or suspicion. The Supreme Court's acceptance of pretextual stops, searches, and detentions pretermits most challenges to the highly random and, in many circumstances, arbitrary targeting of persons. It does not matter that the ultimate purpose of the police action has nothing to do with the "legal" reason for the intrusion and everything to do with the search for drugs. Whatever the correct doctrinal interpretation of the Fourth Amendment on this issue, it must at least be recognized that the pretext doctrine, as currently interpreted, sanctions search and seizure practices that can be conducted without individualized suspicion or cause.

The Fourth Amendment has always allowed law enforcement officials substantial discretion in the investigation of criminal activity. The requirements of cause and judicial warrants place important, but not onerous, limitations on police power. The Court's enthusiastic embrace of the tactics that police have developed in the War on Drugs — profile and pretextual stops, sweeps of buses, drug testing without suspicion — abruptly upsets the balance previously struck. No longer is individualized cause or suspicion the hallmark of the Fourth Amendment. Today, simply fitting the vague contour of profiles or police hunches justifies intrusions on personal privacy.

How Racial Profiling in America Became the Law of the Land: United States v. Brignoni-Ponce *and* Whren v. United States *and the Need for Truly Rebellious Lawyering*
Kevin R. Johnson
98 Georgetown Law Journal 1005 (2010)

For all of recent memory, police across the United States have aggressively pursued the "war on drugs," which began many years before the so-called war on terror after September 11, 2001. For more than two decades, Congress and state legislatures stiffened criminal penalties for drug crimes and increased law enforcement budgets, as politicians from a diversity of political persuasions embraced "tough on crime" measures. State and federal governments spent millions of dollars to build new prisons. Not coincidentally, the U.S. prison population increased sixfold from 1972 to 2000, with about 1.3 million men incarcerated in state and federal prisons at the beginning of the new millennium. As of 1997, a whopping 60% of federal prisoners and 20% of state prisoners had been convicted of drug crimes.

In the early 1990s, the perception among the general public was that crime was out of control on the streets of urban America. This parallels the perceived loss of control of the U.S. border with Mexico in the 1970s and 1980s. Legislators and law enforcement officers aggressively responded to this widespread public perception. In 1994, for example, President Bill Clinton, a "New" Democrat who supported a firm anti-crime platform, signed into law a comprehensive crime bill that was filled with anti-drug measures and authorized the imposition of the death penalty for certain federal criminal offenses.

A critical fact often lost in the public debate over the propriety of the nation's "war on drugs" is that the available statistical data suggests that Whites, Latina/os, Blacks, and Asian-Americans have roughly similar rates of illicit drug use. Nonetheless, the "war on drugs" as it has been enforced has had devastating impacts on minority communities across the United States. One particularly egregious example occurred in the small rural town of Tulia, Texas, where an undercover narcotics officer framed more than twenty percent of the adult African-American population. Some have labeled the drug war as the "new" Jim Crow, tapping into memories of a long period in U.S. history when criminal laws buttressed racial segregation and served as a bulwark of white supremacy.

In fighting the drug war, federal, state, and local law enforcement agencies developed profiles to identify likely offenders. Police in their investigatory activities commonly employed drug courier and gang member profiles, which almost invariably directed law enforcement attention toward African-American and Latino youth. Racial profiling of young African-American and Latino men in traffic stops on the American roads and highways emerged as a central law enforcement tool in the "war on drugs." Police regularly stop and search Blacks and Latina/os in larger numbers than their percentage of the general population. A much-publicized study by the New Jersey Attorney General, for example, found that these minority groups represented the overwhelming majority of searches (77.2%). In cities across the country, minorities persistently complain of being stopped for nothing more than driving while Black and driving while Brown.

Racially disparate policing has had dramatic and severe—and racially disparate—consequences. Blacks and Latina/os today are disproportionately represented among prison populations across the country—one of the few institutions in modern America in which these groups are over-represented as compared to their percentage of the general U.S. population.

The impacts of the drug war were so racially disproportionate that one law professor, and former federal prosecutor, advocated that jurors, as a matter of principle, should acquit Black defendants on drug charges because of the harms imposed on the African-American community by their mass imprisonment. As the radical call for jury nullification of the drug laws suggests, minority communities deeply distrust the criminal justice system in the United States. Profiling has contributed to this distrust by singling out Blacks and Latina/os, law-abiding citizens as well as lawbreakers, for the humiliation, distress, and danger of race-based traffic stops. Ironically, evidence suggests that profiling is not even an effective law enforcement tool.

As previously alluded to, the "war on drugs" is not the first time that the criminal laws in the United States have had racial impacts. From the days of the slave codes, the criminal justice systems throughout the nation have had racially disparate impacts on African-Americans. *Brown v. Board of Education* and the civil rights movement helped begin the process of removing explicit racism from the law. The laws that comprise the "war on drugs," despite their disparate impacts, are facially neutral and do not expressly discriminate on the basis of race; their stated purpose is to eradicate the drug trade as well as illicit drug use in the United States, not to target and punish racial minorities.

Despite the official claims of neutrality, racial profiling in the enforcement of the law intuitively strikes many observers as contrary to the law. Law enforcement measures based on alleged group propensities for criminal conduct appear to run afoul of the U.S. Constitution, which is generally premised on the view that *individualized*, not *group*, suspicion of criminal wrongdoing is necessary for police action. Racial profiling also runs counter to the Fourteenth Amendment's guarantee of equal protection of the law.

So far, the constitutional concerns described here do not appear to have played significant roles in the decisions of the U.S. Supreme Court. Since at least 1970, the Court has played a central role in the "war on drugs." With relatively few exceptions, it has consistently refused to interfere with aggressive police practices in fighting crime and has steadily expanded the discretion afforded police officers.

Some commentators bitterly complain that the Supreme Court has developed a jurisprudence of drug exceptionalism in which the Bill of Rights gives way when the Court reviews the exercise of police power in the "war on drugs." None other than Justice John Paul Stevens boldly observed that "[n]o impartial observer could criticize [the] Court for hindering the progress of the war on drugs. On the contrary, decisions like the one [in *California v. Acevedo*, which found that the search of a closed container in an automobile did not violate the Fourth Amendment,] will support the conclusion that *this Court has become a loyal foot soldier in the Executive's fight against crime.*"

United States v. Lamour

United States Court of Appeals for the Sixth Circuit
16 F.3d 109 (1994)

Batchelder, J.

Marcus Harvey appeals from the judgment of conviction entered on his conditional plea of guilty following the district court's denial of his motion to suppress the evidence obtained from a warrantless search of the vehicle in which he was a passenger. For the reasons that follow, we affirm the conviction.

Briefly stated the facts are these. On May 22, 1990, on I-475 in Genesee County, Michigan, the defendant was a passenger in a 1978 Chevrolet automobile that had no front bumper or right front headlight and that was clocked by police officers exceeding the speed limit by several miles per hour. The officers stopped the vehicle for speeding and equipment violations and because, as one officer later testified at the suppression hearing, "the vehicle that I observed with the defective equipment was very similar in appearance and profile to several other vehicles that I have stopped which ultimately ended in arrests of drug traffickers." When the driver of the car was unable to produce a driver's license, he was asked to step out of the car. He admitted then that his license was suspended; he was placed under arrest for driving with a suspended license; and, while being searched incident to the arrest, he was found to have a rock of crack cocaine in his jacket pocket. The driver gave conflicting stories about who owned the car, but the vehicle registration that he produced showed defendant Marcus Harvey to be the owner. Neither Harvey nor the other passenger could produce a driver's license (Harvey's license had been suspended also and the other passenger had never obtained a license), or any other form of identification. Both passengers were asked to get out of the vehicle and were patted down for weapons by the officers; no weapons were found. Following the policy of their police department, the officers impounded the car because there was no licensed driver to drive it away, and conducted an inventory search of the car. Because none of the occupants had the key to the vehicle's trunk, the officers removed the back seat in order to inventory the trunk and found there a pair of men's sweat pants whose pockets contained 78 rocks of crack cocaine and six live .357 magnum revolver cartridges. Also in the trunk was a bulletproof vest. At this point the officers pried open the trunk of the car to more carefully search it and found a .357 magnum six-shot revolver.

Defendant Harvey was arrested for possession with intent to distribute cocaine and possession of a firearm during the commission of a felony. Defendant was subsequently indicted for possession with intent to distribute cocaine, conspiracy to distribute cocaine, and use of a firearm during a drug trafficking offense. The trial court denied defendant's motion to suppress the evidence seized during the search of the vehicle ... and defendant entered this conditional plea.

Defendant's first assignment of error is foreclosed by this court's recent en banc decision in *United States v. Ferguson*, 8 F.3d 385 (6th Cir. 1993). Defendant does not dispute that the automobile in which he was riding was exceeding the speed limit at the time it was stopped, or that it was in violation of the applicable state laws because of its equipment deficiencies. Defendant concedes that had the officers stopped the car solely because of either or both of those violations, the stop would have been lawful. Rather, defendant argues that no reasonable police officer would have stopped the car for those violations absent some other motive, and that the actual reason for the stop in this instance was not the obvious violations of the law but the fact that the car and its occupants fit the officer's notion of a "drug profile." In *Ferguson*, we held that

> so long as the officer has probable cause to believe that a traffic violation has occurred or was occurring, the resulting stop is not unlawful and does not violate the Fourth Amendment. We focus not on whether a reasonable officer "would" have stopped the suspect (even though he had probable cause to believe that a traffic violation had occurred), or whether any officer "could" have stopped the suspect (because a traffic violation had in fact occurred), but on whether this particular officer in fact had probable cause to believe that a traffic offense had occurred, regardless of whether this was the only basis or merely one basis for the stop. The stop is reasonable if there was probable cause, and it is irrelevant what else the officer knew or suspected about the traffic violator at the time of the stop. It is also irrelevant whether the stop in question is sufficiently ordinary or routine according to the general practice of the police department or the particular officer making the stop.

There is no dispute about the fact that the traffic violations occurred, and the district court found that those violations would have been obvious to any officer observing the car. Because that finding is not clearly erroneous, we hold that, under *Ferguson*, the stop of the car was not pretextual and was lawful.

Nor did the district court err in determining that the search of the vehicle in which Harvey was a passenger was lawful. In fact, the district court found that the warrantless search of the automobile was permissible under either the "automobile exception" or as an inventory search. A review of the record of the suppression hearing persuades us that the district court's findings of fact cannot be said to be clearly erroneous, either as to the facts upon which it based its determination that the officers had probable cause to believe that the car contained drugs or other contraband, or as to the fact that the officers' impounding of the car and the subsequent inventory search were pursuant to departmental policy and not for the purposes of a "fishing expedition."

Having held that both the stop and the search of the vehicle were lawful, we hold that the district court did not err in refusing to suppress the evidence obtained in the search. The judgment of conviction is affirmed.[3]

---

3. We are constrained to respond briefly to the dissent. The dissent makes much — indeed, everything — of the fact that Officer Collardey testified that one of the reasons this vehicle caught his attention was that it fit his own empirically justified profile of drug couriers, which included a racial factor. And as the dissent's quotations from the record indicate, Collardey did indeed say that he took note of occupants' race. But the dissent entirely mischaracterizes this testimony when it says repeatedly that Collardey testified that he stopped the vehicle because the occupants were African-Americans; when it says that "Collardey testified [that] if the occupants had not been African-Americans, he would not have stopped the car"; and when it says that Collardey had a "primary race-based motivation" for the stop. There is no such testimony in the record; the dissent quotes the testimony that most supports its view of this case, and nowhere in that testimony is there any suggestion that Collardey's use of race was a "but for" cause of the stop. Nor is such an inference justified based on this record. It does not follow from the fact that Collardey testified that race was a factor in his "why I stopped the vehicle" calculus that the suspects' race was a "necessary" cause of the stop.

Keith, J., dissenting.

Because I strongly disagree with the majority's conclusion that the district court correctly denied Harvey's motion to suppress evidence, I respectfully dissent.

The Sixth Circuit recently discussed pretextual stops and held the correct inquiry is "whether this particular officer in fact had probable cause to believe that a traffic offense had occurred, regardless of whether this was the only basis or merely one basis for the stop." *United States v. Ferguson*, 8 F.3d 385 (6th Cir. 1993). I dissented in *Ferguson* because I believe this test is ripe for abuse. Today, although I am bound by the law of this circuit, I write separately to emphasize how the instant case illustrates the abuses of which I warned in *Ferguson* and to insist that egregious circumstances, such as in this case, warrant an exception to the *Ferguson* test.

In the instant case, Officer Collardey admits repeatedly he stopped the vehicle because the occupants were African-Americans. On redirect he testified:

> Q: Officer Collardey, you gave the Prosecutor two reasons for your effecting a traffic stop. One was the traffic infraction, speeding and equipment violation, and then you referred to something that I hadn't heard yet today, that was, fitting the general description of some sort of a profile?
>
> A: It did, yeah, it did fit.
>
> Q: Was it a certain way that the damage had been on this car that made it look like it fit a profile for you?
>
> A: No, I made that statement on the basis of my experience on that highway, and drug traffickers that I have arrested coming to the Flint area.

Officer Collardey continued:

> Q: What else was it that made you think this fits some sort of a profile?
>
> A: There were three young black male occupants in an old vehicle.
>
> Q: Three young black male occupants in a car?
>
> A: Yes, sir.
>
> Q: And that was the basis or part of the basis for your stopping that car?
>
> A: The age of the vehicle and the appearance of the occupants.

Under oath, Officer Collardey stated he stopped the vehicle because there were three African-American males in an old car. Recognizing Officer Collardey's use of the minor traffic violations as pretext for stopping the vehicle, the district judge improperly rehabilitated Officer Collardey's testimony:

> Q (district judge): What was it about the appearance of the occupants that got your attention?
>
> A: It wasn't so much the appearance. *Almost every time that we have arrested drug traffickers from Detroit, they're usually young black males driving old cars.*
>
> Q (district judge): Was that why you stopped the car, or did you stop the car for traffic violations?
>
> A: I stopped them for traffic violations.

(emphasis added). Only after the court gave Officer Collardey an either/or question did he give the appropriate response.

My dissent in *United States v. Ferguson* emphasized that the test, as adopted by the majority, provides officers with unlimited discretion to determine whom they will stop for minor traffic violations. As a result, the court renders meaningless the Fourth Amendment's prohibition of unwarranted searches and seizures.

The Fourth Amendment imposes "a standard of 'reasonableness' upon the exercise of discretion by government officials." Under the *Ferguson* test, the court's failure to limit an officer's discretion to stop motorists once a traffic offense establishes probable cause negates any reasonableness inquiry. In essence, the absence of limitations allows pretext to serve as probable cause thus undermining the guarantees of the Fourth Amendment.

The instant case clearly pinpoints the abuses to which the *Ferguson* test is subject. By myopically focusing on whether probable cause exists to believe a motorist committed a traffic offense, the majority waived any meaningful review of the seizure and its legality, and allowed pretext (the traffic violations) to serve as probable cause. Here, Harvey and his companions committed minor traffic violations. They drove three miles over the speed limit in a car which was missing a bumper and a headlight. Indisputably, probable cause existed to believe a traffic offense occurred. The problem, however, is the officer said he stopped the vehicle because the occupants were African-Americans. Officer Collardey testified if the occupants had not been African-Americans, he would not have stopped the car. Officer Collardey's improper motivation for the stop inserted an unconstitutional illegality into the stop. Applying the *Ferguson* test, because a minor traffic violation was present, the majority concludes Collardey's primary race-based motivation, although illegal, is irrelevant.

Equal Protection principles absolutely and categorically prohibit state actors from using race to differentiate between motorists. Yet, the majority acquiesces to an officer's substitution of race for probable cause and essentially licenses the state to discriminate. Moreover, the majority states race-based motivation is irrelevant under these or any circumstances. Not only is the officer's race-based motivation relevant, it is patently unconstitutional.

The Fourteenth Amendment of the United States Constitution prohibits state actors from denying persons equal protection of the laws. In *Samaad v. City of Dallas*, the Fifth Circuit stated: "The heart of the *equal protection clause* is its prohibition of discriminatory treatment. If a governmental actor has imposed unequal burdens based upon race, it has violated the clause." Traditionally, courts review state action singling a person out solely on the basis of race with the strictest scrutiny, and generally condemn the action.

In my twenty-six years as a federal judge, although I have suspected discrimination by police officers, I have never heard an officer admit he stopped an individual based on the color of his skin. This case presents blatantly egregious circumstances and warrants an exception to the *Ferguson* test. Such an exception does not grant special treatment to African-Americans, but merely ensures equal treatment as guaranteed by the Equal Protection Clause. The majority's willful disregard of the flagrant discriminatory treatment in this case endorses a system where one set of traffic regulations exist for African-Americans, like myself, and a more lenient set exists for white Americans. For the same minor traffic infraction, a white motorist remains an unimpeded violator, whereas an African-American motorist automatically becomes a suspected felon and menace to society. Such disparate treatment alienates and ostracizes African-Americans, fortifying their badge of second-class citizenship.

As the old adage warns, the more things change, the more they remain the same. In Montgomery, Alabama, on January 26, 1956, police officers arrested and jailed Dr. Martin Luther King, Jr. for allegedly driving thirty miles per hour in a twenty-five mile per hour zone. *See* Randall Kennedy, *Martin Luther King's Constitution: A Legal History of the Montgomery Bus Boycott*, 98 Yale L.J. 999, 1028 (1989). Today, everyone readily acknowledges the police officers stopped, arrested, jailed and harassed Dr. King because he was an African-American and because he actively and vigorously sought equal protection and equal treatment for African-Americans. Today, almost thirty years later, the majority's actions in this case again allow police officers to stop individuals based on their race under the guise of an insignificant traffic violation. It is a sad commentary that this court not only approves disparate treatment based on race but legitimizes a "legal" basis for disparate treatment. Certainly this circuit cannot in good faith state that the decisions in *Ferguson* and in this case represent equal justice under law.

Unfortunately, the present case is not unique; rather, it eloquently illustrates the plight of many African-Americans. News reports detail unreasonable stops of African Americans by police motivated solely by irrational and illogical racial stereotypes. For example, a national newspaper reported "the same percentage of whites and blacks use drugs." Sam Meddis, *Suburbs 'Have Gotten Off Easy,' Whites' Drug Activity Often Better Hidden*, USA Today, (July 26, 1993), at 6A. Blacks, however, are four times as likely to be arrested for drugs in central cities, six times as likely in suburbs, and three times as likely in rural areas. *Id.* In Michigan, the ratios are much worse. For example:

Detroit	2:1
Warren	32:1
Royal Oak	27:1
Livonia	43:1
Dearborn Heights	40:1
Lincoln Park	46:1

Id. African-Americans are more likely to be arrested because drug courier profiles reflect the erroneous assumption that one's race has a direct correlation to drug activity. *See United States v. Taylor*, 956 F.2d 572, 580 (6th Cir. 1992) (*en banc*) (Keith dissenting) (citing Sheri Lynn Johnson, *Race and the Decision to Detain a Suspect*, 93 Yale L.J. 214, 234 (1983)); *see also* Morgan Cloud, *Search and Seizure by the Numbers: The Drug Courier Profile and Judicial Review of Investigative Formulas*, 65 B.U.L. Rev. 843 (1985) (discussing the historical use of drug profiles).

The deprivation of Defendant Harvey's constitutional rights in this case demonstrates the victimization of African-Americans by a flawed and stereotypical system. His case presents clear and articulated racial discrimination. National statistics illustrate how the insulation of the use of illegitimate, illegal and illogical stereotypes disproportionately impacts African-Americans. Concededly, disproportionate impact alone does not constitute a violation of the Equal Protection Clause; intentional discrimination, however, does. Here, Officer Collardey testified he stopped the vehicle because it contained three young African-Americans. The majority, however, blindly refuses to recognize this glaring constitutional violation and suppress the evidence that flowed from it.

This court's application of the *Ferguson* test to this case is repugnant to our Constitution and national conscience and does not reflect due regard for the integrity of our justice system. Courts exist to promote justice and judges have the duty to support and protect the Constitution as well as to observe its fundamental guarantees. Unfortunately, in this case, the Sixth Circuit abdicates that sacred duty.

Two years after the Sixth Circuit's decision in *Lamour*, the United States Supreme Court addressed the question of pretextual traffic stops in *Whren v. United States*, 517 U.S. 806

(1996). In *Whren,* the Supreme Court followed the *Lamour* majority's approach and held that a police officer may constitutionally stop an individual for a traffic violation any time the officer has sufficient cause to believe a traffic violation has occurred. The officer's subjective intent is irrelevant to the Fourth Amendment inquiry. With respect to racially motivated pretextual stops, the *Whren* Court explained: "We of course agree with petitioners that the Constitution prohibits selective enforcement of the law based on considerations such as race. But the constitutional basis for objecting to intentionally discriminatory application of laws is the Equal Protection Clause, not the Fourth Amendment. Subjective intentions play no role in ordinary, probable-cause Fourth Amendment analysis."

3. Drug Dog Sniffs

As the material on profiling indicates, pretextual traffic stops are a common drug enforcement tactic. In these scenarios, the police will stop a driver for a minor traffic violation in order to question him. While issuing the traffic citation, the officer will ask the driver's permission to search the vehicle for drugs. In many cases, the driver will grant the police permission to search. *See, e.g.,* Robert H. Whorf, *Consent Searches Following Routine Traffic Stops: The Troubled Jurisprudence of a Doomed Drug Interdiction Technique,* 28 Ohio N.U.L. Rev. 1 (2001); Timothy P. O'Neill, *Vagrants in Volvos: Ending Pretextual Traffic Stops and Consent Searches of Vehicles in Illinois,* 40 Loy. U. Chi. L.J. 745 (2009).

In cases where the driver refuses to allow a search of her vehicle, however, the police may employ "drug dogs" to sniff around the car while the citation is being issued. In *Canine Sniffs: The Search That Isn't,* criminal defense attorney Ken Lammers describes the widespread use of drug dogs in pre-textual traffic stops: "I practice criminal defense in a jurisdiction where the local drug interdiction unit uses drug-sniffing dogs extensively. Generally, one officer performs a blatant pretext stop, such as pulling someone over for having an air freshener hanging from the rear view mirror. Sometimes the police operate as a team and preposition the dog in anticipation of the stop. Sometimes the officer with the dog operates in a particular area and responds to nearby stops. In either case, the officers run the dog past both the stopped vehicle and its occupants." 1 N.Y.U. J.L. & Liberty 844 (2005).*

In *Illinois v. Caballes,* the United States Supreme Court held that the use of a drug dog to sniff a vehicle does not amount to a "search" under the Fourth Amendment. As a result, the police do not need any suspicion in order to conduct a drug dog sniff of a vehicle.

Illinois v. Caballes
Supreme Court of the United States
543 U.S. 405 (2005)

Justice Stevens delivered the opinion of the Court.

Illinois State Trooper Daniel Gillette stopped respondent for speeding on an interstate highway. When Gillette radioed the police dispatcher to report the stop, a second trooper,

---

* At the beginning of his article, Lammers recounts the following exchange about the reliability of drug dogs:

"[Defense attorney]: Do you keep records as to the effectiveness of your dog?

[Police officer]: Yes, sir, I do?"

[Defense attorney]: Do you know how often your dog gives false positives?

[Police officer]: He doesn't give any false positives. We're just unable to verify the alerts at that time"

Craig Graham, a member of the Illinois State Police Drug Interdiction Team, overheard the transmission and immediately headed for the scene with his narcotics-detection dog. When they arrived, respondent's car was on the shoulder of the road and respondent was in Gillette's vehicle. While Gillette was in the process of writing a warning ticket, Graham walked his dog around respondent's car. The dog alerted at the trunk. Based on that alert, the officers searched the trunk, found marijuana, and arrested respondent. The entire incident lasted less than 10 minutes.

Respondent was convicted of a narcotics offense and sentenced to 12 years' imprisonment and a $256,136 fine. The trial judge denied his motion to suppress the seized evidence and to quash his arrest. He held that the officers had not unnecessarily prolonged the stop and that the dog alert was sufficiently reliable to provide probable cause to conduct the search. Although the Appellate Court affirmed, the Illinois Supreme Court reversed, concluding that because the canine sniff was performed without any "'specific and articulable facts'" to suggest drug activity, the use of the dog "unjustifiably enlarg[ed] the scope of a routine traffic stop into a drug investigation."

The question on which we granted certiorari is narrow: "Whether the Fourth Amendment requires reasonable, articulable suspicion to justify using a drug-detection dog to sniff a vehicle during a legitimate traffic stop." Thus, we proceed on the assumption that the officer conducting the dog sniff had no information about respondent except that he had been stopped for speeding.

Here, the initial seizure of respondent when he was stopped on the highway was based on probable cause and was concededly lawful. It is nevertheless clear that a seizure that is lawful at its inception can violate the Fourth Amendment if its manner of execution unreasonably infringes interests protected by the Constitution. A seizure that is justified solely by the interest in issuing a warning ticket to the driver can become unlawful if it is prolonged beyond the time reasonably required to complete that mission. In an earlier case involving a dog sniff that occurred during an unreasonably prolonged traffic stop, the Illinois Supreme Court held that use of the dog and the subsequent discovery of contraband were the product of an unconstitutional seizure. We may assume that a similar result would be warranted in this case if the dog sniff had been conducted while respondent was being unlawfully detained.

In the state-court proceedings, however, the judges carefully reviewed the details of Officer Gillette's conversations with respondent and the precise timing of his radio transmissions to the dispatcher to determine whether he had improperly extended the duration of the stop to enable the dog sniff to occur. We have not recounted those details because we accept the state court's conclusion that the duration of the stop in this case was entirely justified by the traffic offense and the ordinary inquiries incident to such a stop.

Despite this conclusion, the Illinois Supreme Court held that the initially lawful traffic stop became an unlawful seizure solely as a result of the canine sniff that occurred outside respondent's stopped car. That is, the court characterized the dog sniff as the cause rather than the consequence of a constitutional violation. In its view, the use of the dog converted the citizen-police encounter from a lawful traffic stop into a drug investigation, and because the shift in purpose was not supported by any reasonable suspicion that respondent possessed narcotics, it was unlawful. In our view, conducting a dog sniff would not change the character of a traffic stop that is lawful at its inception and otherwise executed in a reasonable manner, unless the dog sniff itself infringed respondent's constitutionally protected interest in privacy. Our cases hold that it did not.

Official conduct that does not "compromise any legitimate interest in privacy" is not a search subject to the Fourth Amendment. We have held that any interest in possessing contraband cannot be deemed "legitimate," and thus, governmental conduct that *only* reveals the possession of contraband "compromises no legitimate privacy interest." This is because the expectation "that certain facts will not come to the attention of the authorities" is not the same as an interest in "privacy that society is prepared to consider reasonable." In *United States v. Place,* 462 U.S. 696 (1983), we treated a canine sniff by a well-trained narcotics-detection dog as "*sui generis*" because it "discloses only the presence or absence of narcotics, a contraband item." Respondent likewise concedes that "drug sniffs are designed, and if properly conducted are generally likely, to reveal only the presence of contraband." Although respondent argues that the error rates, particularly the existence of false positives, call into question the premise that drug-detection dogs alert only to contraband, the record contains no evidence or findings that support his argument. Moreover, respondent does not suggest that an erroneous alert, in and of itself, reveals any legitimate private information, and, in this case, the trial judge found that the dog sniff was sufficiently reliable to establish probable cause to conduct a full-blown search of the trunk.

Accordingly, the use of a well-trained narcotics-detection dog—one that "does not expose noncontraband items that otherwise would remain hidden from public view"—during a lawful traffic stop, generally does not implicate legitimate privacy interests. In this case, the dog sniff was performed on the exterior of respondent's car while he was lawfully seized for a traffic violation. Any intrusion on respondent's privacy expectations does not rise to the level of a constitutionally cognizable infringement.

The judgment of the Illinois Supreme Court is vacated, and the case is remanded for further proceedings not inconsistent with this opinion.

It is so ordered.

Justice Souter, dissenting.

I would hold that using the dog for the purposes of determining the presence of marijuana in the car's trunk was a search unauthorized as an incident of the speeding stop and unjustified on any other ground. I would accordingly affirm the judgment of the Supreme Court of Illinois, and I respectfully dissent.

In *United States v. Place,* we categorized the sniff of the narcotics-seeking dog as "*sui generis*" under the Fourth Amendment and held it was not a search. The classification rests not only upon the limited nature of the intrusion, but on a further premise that experience has shown to be untenable, the assumption that trained sniffing dogs do not err. What we have learned about the fallibility of dogs in the years since *Place* was decided would itself be reason to call for reconsidering *Place*'s decision against treating the intentional use of a trained dog as a search. The portent of this very case, however, adds insistence to the call, for an uncritical adherence to *Place* would render the Fourth Amendment indifferent to suspicionless and indiscriminate sweeps of cars in parking garages and pedestrians on sidewalks; if a sniff is not preceded by a seizure subject to Fourth Amendment notice, it escapes Fourth Amendment review entirely unless it is treated as a search. We should not wait for these developments to occur before rethinking *Place*'s analysis, which invites such untoward consequences.

At the heart both of *Place* and the Court's opinion today is the proposition that sniffs by a trained dog are *sui generis* because a reaction by the dog in going alert is a response to nothing but the presence of contraband. Hence, the argument goes, because the sniff can only reveal the presence of items devoid of any legal use, the sniff "does not implicate legitimate privacy interests" and is not to be treated as a search.

The infallible dog, however, is a creature of legal fiction. Although the Supreme Court of Illinois did not get into the sniffing averages of drug dogs, their supposed infallibility is belied by judicial opinions describing well-trained animals sniffing and alerting with less than perfect accuracy, whether owing to errors by their handlers, the limitations of the dogs themselves, or even the pervasive contamination of currency by cocaine. See, *e.g.,* *United States v. Scarborough,* 128 F.3d 1373, 1378, n. 3 (CA10 1997) (describing a dog that erroneously alerted 4 times out of 19 while working for the postal service and 8% of the time over its entire career); *United States v. $242,484.00,* 351 F.3d 499, 511 (CA11 2003) (noting that because as much as 80% of all currency in circulation contains drug residue, a dog alert "is of little value"). Indeed, a study cited by Illinois in this case for the proposition that dog sniffs are "generally reliable" shows that dogs in artificial testing situations return false positives anywhere from 12.55 to 60% of the time, depending on the length of the search. In practical terms, the evidence is clear that the dog that alerts hundreds of times will be wrong dozens of times.

Once the dog's fallibility is recognized, however, that ends the justification claimed in *Place* for treating the sniff as *sui generis* under the Fourth Amendment: the sniff alert does not necessarily signal hidden contraband, and opening the container or enclosed space whose emanations the dog has sensed will not necessarily reveal contraband or any other evidence of crime. This is not, of course, to deny that a dog's reaction may provide reasonable suspicion, or probable cause, to search the container or enclosure; the Fourth Amendment does not demand certainty of success to justify a search for evidence or contraband. The point is simply that the sniff and alert cannot claim the certainty that *Place* assumed, both in treating the deliberate use of sniffing dogs as *sui generis* and then taking that characterization as a reason to say they are not searches subject to Fourth Amendment scrutiny. And when that aura of uniqueness disappears, there is no basis in *Place*'s reasoning, and no good reason otherwise, to ignore the actual function that dog sniffs perform. They are conducted to obtain information about the contents of private spaces beyond anything that human senses could perceive, even when conventionally enhanced. The information is not provided by independent third parties beyond the reach of constitutional limitations, but gathered by the government's own officers in order to justify searches of the traditional sort, which may or may not reveal evidence of crime but will disclose anything meant to be kept private in the area searched. Thus in practice the government's use of a trained narcotics dog functions as a limited search to reveal undisclosed facts about private enclosures, to be used to justify a further and complete search of the enclosed area.

I would treat the dog sniff as the familiar search it is in fact, subject to scrutiny under the Fourth Amendment.

––––––––––

Some State Constitutions provide for greater protection than the federal Constitution when it comes to drug dogs. In *New York v. Devone,* for example, the Court of Appeals of New York held that "a canine sniff of the exterior of an automobile constitutes a search under article I, § 12" of the New York Constitution and that the police need to demonstrate a "founded suspicion" before conducting a canine sniff of an automobile. 15 N.Y. 3d 106 (2010).

In the federal system, a number of important questions remain unresolved with respect to drug dogs. At the time this book was going to press, the United States Supreme Court had granted *certiorari* to hear two drug dog sniff cases during the October 2012 Term. The first case, *Florida v. Jardines,* raises the question of whether *Caballes* and *Place* apply to dog sniffs of the exterior of a home. Though the Court has held that it is not a search for a drug dog to sniff a vehicle or a piece of luggage, the Fourth Amendment typically provides greater protection to the home than in other areas. *See, e.g., Kyllo v. United States,* 533 U.S. 27 (2001).

In the second case, *Florida v. Harris,* the Supreme Court will consider what level of training and record of field performance is sufficient for a drug dog's alert to establish probable cause. In *Harris,* the Florida Supreme Court held "the fact that a drug detection dog has been trained and certified to detect narcotics, standing alone, is not sufficient to demonstrate the reliability of the dog. To demonstrate that an officer has a reasonable basis for believing that an alert by a drug-detection dog is sufficiently reliable to provide probable cause to search, the State must present evidence of the dog's training and certification records, an explanation of the meaning of the particular training and certification, field performance records (including any unverified alerts), and evidence concerning the experience and training of the officer handling the dog, as well as any other objective evidence known to the officer about the dog's reliability." 71 So. 3d 756, 775 (2011). *See also,* Jeff Weiner, *Police K-9's and the Constitution: What Every Lawyer and Judge Should Know,* THE CHAMPION 22, May 2012 (discussing *Harris* and *Jardines*). For a different approach to this issue, see *South Dakota v. Nguyen,* 726 N.W. 2d 871 (2007).

The relationship between a drug dog's reliability and probable cause has been a frequently litigated issue in the lower courts since *Caballes.* As a result, *Harris* is likely to be particularly closely watched by criminal practitioners.

Those Doggone Sniffs Are Often Wrong: The Fourth Amendment Has Gone to the Dogs
Jeffrey S. Weiner and Kimberly Homan
30 The Champion 12 (2006)

Dogs can be trained to distinguish various odors with some degree of accuracy, but they are far from infallible, and their responses are often only as reliable as the interpretations placed upon them by their handlers. In fact, one commentator has reported that on most occasions on which no drugs are found as the result of a search based on a canine alert, the fault is not that of the dog but rather that of the handler in misinterpreting the dog's behavior. While a dog can be initially trained in a few weeks, training the human handler requires more time and effort. In some circuits, an affidavit in support of an application for a search warrant based in whole or in part upon a positive canine alert need do no more to establish the dog's reliability than to state that the dog is "trained" and/or "certified." This is, however, only half the equation. The focus must be redirected to the reliability and integrity of the dog/handler *team.* The amount of training the handler has had and the length of time the handler and dog have worked together are important factors, and the reported cases indicate that handler training runs the gamut from two weeks to hundreds of hours.

The amount of training and experience which the handler has had with the dog is a critical element, as, contrary to the way in which courts have tended to view the process, the dog does not announce to the handler that, if he searches, he will find drugs in a particular location. Rather, each dog behaves in a particular manner, which the handler then "interprets" as an "alert," indicating the presence of drugs. An alert is not the objective proof as which it has generally been regarded by the courts; instead, it has a large—and sometime *very* large—subjective component. Some courts have expressed an appreciation of the role which handler interpretation plays in the process, although, with rare exception, that appreciation has not led to any less deference to the handler's testimony that the dog alerted. Repeated stress upon the subjective and interpretive aspects of the canine in-spection, bolstered by expert testimony should dislodge the unshakable faith which courts have placed in the objective veracity of canine alerts.

Another too-little examined aspect of alert-based searches is the question of just what is an "alert." Dogs are trained to give a particular response when they smell certain ille-gal drugs and, during training, are rewarded when they correctly give that response in the presence of drug odor. In general, dogs are trained to alert "aggressively" or "pas-sively," responses which have very different physical manifestations. When the handler testifies that the dog alerted in something other than the manner in which it was trained to respond to the presence of drugs, there is cause to question whether the dog actually did alert, *i.e.*, give the final response which it was trained to make when it was certain that the odor it had been trained to detect was present and, concomitantly, reason to de-cline to base a finding of probable cause to search on the alert alone. As Dr. Daniel Craig, a noted expert in canine training and performance, who has on a number of occasions testified as a defense expert witness in dog-sniff cases, has explained:

> Detector dog handlers have been known to say things like "I can read my dog," "My dog knows it's there," "My dog's behavior tells me it's in there," "I can read my dog's behavioral change and I know the odor is there," "I am the only one who can read my dog," "I know what my dog is thinking," "I know when he is in the scent cone," et cetera. Are they just repeating what they were taught? If not, where do they get this notion? In initial training and subsequent training the only time they reward (reinforce) their dog is when the dog makes the definitive defined final response. Then and only then can the trainer verify that the dog has de-tected and responded to a specific target odor. The dog is rewarded for that re-sponse and no other.

> Educated guesses based upon the handler's knowledge of their dog's training and past performance are nothing more than educated guesses when their dog fails to make the defined final response during a specific search....

Thus, it is not enough that the handler testifies at the suppression hearing that the dog "alerted," and defense counsel should hesitate before stipulating that the dog alerted and should refrain from conceding that an "alert" is a reliable indicator of anything. Instead, the handler should be examined at the suppression hearing or, where permitted, in pre-hearing deposition, to elicit a precise description of the definitive final response which the dog was trained to give upon identifying the odor of narcotics. If the dog gave any other response, then it was not doing what it was trained to do, and there is sound reason to question whether an alert did in fact take place. There may be videotapes of the dog's training exercises available to assist in this process, just as there may be a videotape of the stop during which the canine sniff was conducted, both of which may provide cru-cial evidence, at least if the "alert" appears on the videotape, which — unsurprisingly — it sometimes does not. Unfortunately, and incredibly, most courts have blindly credited testimony from handlers of the "I know it when I see it" variety.

A few courts have, however, wisely been skeptical of reliance upon canine behavior which differed from the dog's trained final response and depended entirely upon the han-dler's interpretation of equivocal behavior. In *United States v. Heir*, for example, the dog was trained to alert by scratching, but had not done so in this case. Instead, the dog sniffed intently around certain areas of the car, which the handler testified constituted an alert, ac-knowledging, however, that such alert behavior was "subtle" and might only be recognized by himself or another person familiar with the dog's tendencies. Defense experts testified that they saw nothing on the videotape of the stop to indicate that the dog had alerted. The court adopted the magistrate judge's conclusion that an alert had not occurred, as well as the conclusion that even if the alert behavior described by the handler occurred, it was too subjective a standard to establish probable cause. Instead, the court ruled, an "objectively observable 'indication' by the dog of the presence of drugs" was required.

"Reliability" is generally regarded by the courts as the measure of how likely an alert by the dog in question is to be an accurate indicator of the presence of drugs (or of whatever the dog has been trained to detect). Dogs are not scientific machines. A number of courts have recognized—or at least paid lip service to—the concept that a particular dog/handler team may be insufficiently reliable to support a finding of probable cause. As one court has stated:

> The possibility of error exists and, in limited circumstances, the error may be of such magnitude that a canine alert is not sufficient to establish probable cause. For instance, it stretches the bounds of jurisprudential imagination to believe that a positive alert by an untrained dog or by a dog with an extensive history of false positive alerts could be relied upon to establish probable cause without raising Fourth Amendment concerns.

In challenging the reliability of the dog/handler team, access to the dog's training, certification, and field performance records is essential. Some courts have recognized the importance of discovery regarding the dog's training, certification, and performance records, but others continue to regard exploration of the documentary record of the dog's performance as largely a waste of time, holding that the government need only present the testimony of the handler and need not produce the underlying records. The more thoroughly courts can be persuaded to regard alerts by dogs which simply have been "trained" and "certified" as something less than automatic probable cause, the more likely courts will come to regard discovery requests for the historical records of the dog's training and field performance as an essential component of the litigation of motions to suppress where probable cause for the search was predicated in whole or in part on a canine alert.

Access to the records of the dog's performance in training and in the field is essential to challenging predictable handler testimony regarding the always "excellent reliability" of their dogs—as well as to convincing courts that handler testimony alone should not be considered sufficient to establish the reliability of the dog. For example, handlers will sometimes report very high—even perfect—accuracy rates, even where drugs have not been found following the dog's alert, based on the unprovable assumption that, if the dog alerted, it must mean that drugs had been present in the location to which the dog alerted. Only with the dog's training records can it potentially be determined how often this occurred. Unfortunately, courts have, by and large, been only too ready to accept the premise that "residual odor" provides a valid explanation for a false alert or to admit canine alert evidence as evidence that drugs were, at some time, present at the location to which the dog alerted.

4. "No-Knock" Drug Raids

In *Wilson v. Arkansas*, 514 U.S. 927 (1995) and *Richards v. Wisconsin*, 520 U.S. 385 (1997), the United States Supreme Court held that the police must typically knock and announce their presence before searching a residence pursuant to a warrant. In *Richards*, the Court described the circumstances in which the police may search a residence without knocking as follows: "In order to justify a 'no-knock' entry, the police must have a reasonable suspicion that knocking and announcing their presence, under the particular circumstances, would be dangerous or futile, or that it would inhibit the effective investigation of crime by, for example, allowing the destruction of evidence." 520 U.S. 385, 594 (1997). In the 2006 case *Hudson v. Michigan*, 547 U.S. 586 (2006), however, the Court held that the exclusionary rule does not forbid the use of evidence obtained after a violation of the knock and announce requirement. *Wilson, Richards,* and *Hudson* are addressed in detail in most Criminal Procedure courses. This section focuses on the link between no-knock searches and drug enforcement. The following excerpt from a 2006 report on paramilitary style raids in domestic law enforcement provides an overview of their history and relationship to drug enforcement.

Overkill: The Rise of Paramilitary Police Raids in America
Radley Balko
The Cato Institute 2006

"They [police officers] made a mistake. There's no one to blame for a mistake. The way these people were treated has to be judged in the context of a war." — *Hallandale, Florida, attorney Richard Kane, after police officers conducted a late night drug raid on the home of Edwin and Catherine Bernhardt. Police broke into the couple's home and threw Catherine Bernhardt to the floor at gunpoint. Edwin Bernhardt, who had come down from his bedroom in the nude after hearing the commotion, was also subdued and handcuffed at gunpoint. Police forced him to wear a pair of his wife's under-wear, then took him to the police station, where he spent several hours in jail. Police later discovered they had raided the wrong address.*

The typical SWAT team carries out its missions in battle fatigues: Lace-up, combat-style boots; black, camouflage, or olive-colored pants and shirts, sometimes with "ninja-style" or balaclava hoods; Kevlar helmets and vests; gas masks, knee pads, gloves, communication devices, and boot knives; and military-grade weapons, such as the Heckler and Koch MP5 submachine gun, the preferred model of the U.S. Navy Seals. Other standard SWAT-team weaponry includes battering rams, ballistic shields, "flashbang" grenades, smoke grenades, pepper spray, and tear gas. Many squads are now ferried to raid sites by military-issue armored personnel carriers. Some units have helicopters. Others boast grenade launchers, tanks (with and without gun turrets), rappelling equipment, and bayonets.

Paramilitary raids are generally carried out late at night, or just before dawn. Police are technically bound by law to "knock and announce" themselves, and give occupants time to answer the door before forcing entry. But ... that requirement is today commonly either circumvented through court-sanctioned loopholes, ignored completely with little consequence, or only ceremoniously observed, with a knock and announcement unlikely to be noticed by anyone inside.

Police generally break open doors with a battering ram, or blow them off their hinges with explosives. Absent either, police have pried doors open with sledgehammers or screwdrivers, ripped them off by attaching them to the back ends of trucks, or entered by crashing through windows or balconies. After an entryway is cleared, police sometimes detonate a flashbang grenade or a similar device designed to disorient the occupants in the targeted house. They then enter the home under its cover. SWAT teams have entered homes through fire escapes, by rappelling down from police helicopters, and by crashing through second-story windows. Once police are inside, the occupants are quickly and forcefully incapacitated. They're instructed to remain in the prone position, generally at gunpoint, while police carry out the search warrant. Any perceived noncompliance is typically met with force, which can potentially be lethal, depending on the nature of the noncompliance.

Once rare, these procedures are now performed dozens of times per day in cities and towns all across the country.

Longtime Los Angeles police chief Daryl F. Gates is widely credited with inventing the SWAT team in early 1966, though there's some evidence that the idea was brought to Gates a year earlier, when he was inspector general, by Los Angeles Police Department officer John Nelson. The inspiration for the modern SWAT team was a specialized force in Delano, California, made up of crowd control officers, riot police, and snipers, assembled to counter the farm worker uprisings led by Cesar Chavez. In search of new methods to counter the snipers and guerrilla tactics used against L.A. police during the Watts riots, Gates and other L.A. police officials quickly embraced the idea of an elite, military-trained cadre of law enforcement officers who could react quickly, accurately, and with overwhelming force to particularly dangerous situations. Gates brought in a team of ex-Marines to train a small group of police officers Gates handpicked for the new endeavor. Gates called his unit the Special Weapons Attack Team, or SWAT. City officials liked the idea, including the acronym, but balked at the word "attack." They persuaded Gates to change the units name to Special Weapons and Tactics, though the new moniker was purely cosmetic — no change in training or mission accompanied the name change.

SWAT quickly gained favor with public officials, politicians, and the public. In August 1966, former Marine Charles Whitman barricaded himself at the top of a clock tower at the University of Texas and opened fire on the campus below. Whitman shot 46 people and killed 15. Police struggled for more than 90 minutes to remove Whitman from his tower perch. Public horror at Whitman's slaughter quickly turned into support for Gates's idea of training elite teams to complement city policing in dangerous situations like the Whitman massacre. SWAT teams subsequently began to pop up in larger urban areas across the country.

Three years later, the L.A. SWAT team engaged in a highly publicized shootout with the city's Black Panther militia. Publicity from the standoff won the L.A. SWAT team and the concept of SWAT teams in general widespread public acclaim.

Gates's experiment soon became a celebrated part of American pop culture. A SWAT-themed television show debuted in 1975, and the show's theme song hit the Billboard Top Forty. In 1995, Gates launched a SWAT video game franchise with Sierra Entertainment. The SWAT series spawned several award winning "first-person" style shooter games, the most recent version of which was released in early 2005. In January 2006, cable television channel A&E debuted a new reality television show called Dallas SWAT, which follows the lives of the members of a Dallas, Texas, SWAT team. Court TV now carries the show Texas SWAT, in which seasoned war journalist Jeff Chagrin tags along with several SWAT teams across the state.

But despite the American public's fascination with SWAT, until the 1980s, actual deployments of the paramilitary units were still largely confined to extraordinary, emergency situations such as hostage takings, barricades, hijackings, or prison escapes. Though the total number of SWAT teams gradually increased throughout the 1970s, they were mostly limited to larger, more urbanized areas, and the terms surrounding their deployment were still for the most part narrowly and appropriately defined. That changed in the 1980s.

The election of Ronald Reagan in 1980 brought new funding, equipment, and a more active drug-policing role for paramilitary police units across the country. Reagan's new offensive in the War on Drugs involved a more confrontational, militaristic approach to combating the drug supply, a policy enthusiastically embraced by Congress. During the next 10 years, with prodding from the White House, Congress paved the way to widespread military-style policing by carving yawning drug war exceptions to the Posse Comitatus Act, the Civil War-era law prohibiting the use of the military for civilian policing. These new exceptions allowed nearly unlimited sharing of drug interdiction intelligence, training, tactics, technology, and weaponry between the Pentagon and federal, state, and local police departments.

The first of these exemptions was the Military Cooperation with Law Enforcement Act, passed in 1981. This wide-reaching legislation encouraged the military to give local, state, and federal police access to military bases, research, and equipment for drug interdiction. It also authorized the military to train civilian police officers to use the newly available equipment, and not only encouraged the military to share drug-war-related information with civilian police but authorized the military to take an active role in preventing drugs from entering the country.

In a 1999 paper for the Cato Institute on the militarization of American policing, Diane Cecilia Weber outlined ensuing laws passed in the 1980s and 1990s that further eroded the clear demarcation between military and civilian drug enforcement set forth by Posse Comitatus. Among the laws cited by Weber are the following:

• In 1986, President Reagan issued a National Security Decision Directive, which declared drugs a threat to U.S. "national security." The directive allowed for yet more cooperation between local, state, and federal law enforcement and the military.

• In 1988, Congress ordered the National Guard to assist state drug enforcement efforts. Because of this order, National Guard troops today patrol for marijuana plants and assist in large-scale anti-drug operations in every state in the country.

• In 1989, President Bush created a series of regional task forces within the Department of Defense, charged with facilitating cooperation between the military and domestic police forces.

• In 1994, the Department of Defense issued a memorandum authorizing the transfer of equipment and technology to state and local police. The same year, Congress created a "reutilization program" to facilitate handing military gear over to civilian police agencies.

Despite the fact that these laws were a significant departure from longstanding domestic policy, most were passed without much media attention or public debate. What debate there was muted by assurances from politicians and drug war supporters that (a) the scourge of drugs was too threatening and too pervasive to be fought with traditional policing and (b) critics who feared for the civil liberties of American civilians under a more militarized system were alarmist and overstating their case. Rep. Charles Bennett (D-FL), for example, called the century-old Posse Comitatus Act—a law whose principles can be traced directly to concerns expressed by the Founding Fathers—a "sinful, evil law." In 1989, Drug Enforcement Agency administrator Francis Mullen forthrightly asserted that Congress should green-light the use of the U.S. military in law enforcement because "there is sufficient oversight on the part of Congress and others to deter infringement on individual liberties." Also in 1989, then-secretary of defense Dick Cheney declared, "The detection and countering of the production, trafficking and use of illegal drugs is a high priority national security mission of the Department of Defense."

After each of these policies was enacted, police departments across the country helped themselves to the newly available equipment, training, and funding. By the late 1990s, the various laws, orders, and directives softening Posse Comitatus had added a significant military component to state and local police forces. The National Defense Authorization Security Act of 1997, commonly called "1033" for the section of the U.S. Code assigned to it, created the Law Enforcement Support Program, an agency headquartered in Ft. Belvoir, Virginia. The new agency was charged with streamlining the transfer of military equipment to civilian police departments. It worked. Transfers of equipment took off at an even greater clip than before. The National Journal reports that between January 1997 and October 1999, the agency handled 3.4 million orders of Pentagon equipment from over 11,000 domestic police agencies in all 50 states. By December 2005, the number was up to 17,000. The purchase value of the equipment comes to more than $727 million. The National Journal reported that included in the bounty were 253 aircraft (including six- and seven-passenger airplanes, and UH-60 Blackhawk and UH-1 Huey helicopters), 7,856 M-16 rifles, 181 grenade launchers, 8,131 bulletproof helmets, and 1,161 pairs of night-vision goggles.

Civilian police departments suddenly found themselves flush with military arms. The Los Angeles Police Department was offered bayonets. The city of St. Petersburg, Florida, bought an armored personnel carrier from the Pentagon for just $1,000. The seven police officers of Jasper, Florida — which has all of 2,000 people and hasn't had a murder in 14 years — were each given a military-grade M-16 machine gun, leading one Florida paper to run the headline, "Three Stoplights, Seven M-16s." The sheriff's office in landlocked Boone County, Indiana, was given an amphibious armored personnel carrier.

In a 1997 60 Minutes segment on the trend toward militarization, the CBS news magazine profiled the Sheriff's Department of Marion County, Florida, a rural, agricultural area known for its horse farms. Courtesy of the various Pentagon giveaway programs, the county sheriff proudly showed reporter Lesley Stahl the department's 23 military helicopters, two C-12 luxury executive aircraft (often called the "Rolls Royce with wings"), a motor home, several trucks and trailers, a tank, and a "bomb robot." This, in addition to an arsenal of military-grade assault weapons.

With all of this funding and free or discounted equipment and training from the federal government, police departments across the country needed something to do with it. So they formed SWAT teams — thousands of them. SWAT teams have since multiplied and spread across the country at a furious clip.

In a widely cited survey, criminologist Peter Kraska found that as of 1997, 90 percent of cities with populations of 50,000 or more had at least one paramilitary police unit, twice as many as in the mid-1980s. The increase has been even more pronounced in smaller towns: In a separate study, Kraska found that the number of SWAT teams serving towns with populations between 25,000 and 50,000 increased 157 percent between 1985 and 1996. They've popped up in college towns like South Bend, Indiana, and Champaign, Illinois, where they're increasingly used for routine marijuana policing. The University of Central Florida's campus police department actually has its own, separate SWAT team, independent of the city and county. As of 1996, 65 percent of towns within the 25,000–50,000-population range had a SWAT team, with another 8 percent planning to form one. Given that the trends giving rise to SWAT proliferation in the 1990s haven't gone away, it's safe to assume that all of these numbers have continued to rise and are significantly higher today. In fact, SWAT teams are increasingly popping up in even smaller towns.

In 2002, ... the Miami Herald ran a prophetic report about the SWAT teams proliferating across small-town Florida, including in Broward County suburbs like Miramar (population 101,000), Pembroke Pines (150,000), and Davie (82,579). "Police say they want [SWAT teams] in case of a hostage situation or a Columbine-type incident," the paper reported, "But in practice, the teams are used mainly to serve search warrants on suspected drug dealers. Some of these searches yield as little as few grams of cocaine or marijuana."

A subsequent investigation by the St. Petersburg Times found that many Florida police departments even fudged crime statistics and exaggerated local drug crimes in an effort to get more military weaponry. The "panhandle town of Lynn Haven (pop. 12,451) reported a 900 percent rise in armed robberies," the paper wrote, "without telling regulators that the raw number of robberies rose from one to 10, then fell to one again just as quickly." The investigation also found that without the military's sophisticated anti-theft system tracking the weapons once they reached the police departments, many went missing or were stolen, meaning many officers could potentially later encounter the same weapons in the hands of criminals.

As the Miami Herald reported was happening in Florida, it's commonplace for police officials who want a SWAT team to attempt to assuage community concerns by arguing the units are necessary to thwart the possibility of terrorism, school shootings, or violent crime. Once in place, however, SWAT teams are inevitably used far more frequently, mostly in the service of drug warrants.

In 2001, Madison, Wisconsin's Capital Times reported that as of 2001, 65 of the state's 83 local SWAT teams had come into being since 1980, 28 since 1996, and 16 since 2000. Many of those newly established teams had popped up in absurdly small towns like Forest County (population 9,950), Mukwonago (7,519), and Rice Lake (8,320).

Like the Miami Herald ... the Capital Times investigation found that though paramilitary units are often justified to town councils and skeptical citizens as essential to fight terrorism, deal with hostage situations, and diffuse similarly rare but volatile situations; once established, they're rarely deployed for those reasons. Instead, they're almost always sent to serve routine search warrants, make drug arrests, and conduct similar drug-related proactive policing.

One sheriff, for example, convinced his county to give him a SWAT team after one of his deputies was killed in a shootout. Now, he told the Capital Times, he uses the unit primarily for "drug searches and stuff." A police captain in Green Bay noted that armed barricades are happening "less and less," and so the SWAT team instead "assists the drug task force on a regular basis." The Jackson County, Wisconsin, SWAT captain likewise told the paper that the most common use of the teams is for "drug search warrants." Columbia County, Wisconsin, put its $1.75 million Pentagon bounty to use at "Weedstock" in nearby Saulk County, where cops in full SWAT attire stood guard to intimidate while, as the Times reports, "hundreds of young people gather[ed] peacefully to smoke marijuana and listen to music."

The Capital Times also found that in addition to free equipment, the federal government gave money to the states for drug control, primarily through the Byrne Justice Assistance Grant program, as well as various federal law enforcement block grants. The states then disbursed the money to local police departments on the basis of each department's number of drug arrests. The extra funding was only tied to anti-drug policing. In some cases, the funding could offset the entire cost of establishing and maintaining a SWAT team, with funds left over. The paper found that the size of the disbursements was directly tied to the number of city or county drug arrests, noting that each arrest in theory would net a given city or county about $153 in state and federal funding. Jackson County, Wisconsin, for example, quadrupled its drug arrests between 1999 and 2000. Correspondingly, the county's federal subsidy quadrupled, too.

Thanks to the federal subsidies for drug arrests, then, not only did the number of SWAT teams soar through the 1980s and 1990s, so too did the frequency with which they were deployed. In 1972, there were just a few hundred paramilitary drug raids per year in the United States. According to Kraska, by the early 1980s there were 3,000 annual SWAT deployments, by 1996 there were 30,000, and by 2001 there were 40,000. The average city police department deployed its paramilitary police unit about once a month in the early 1980s. By 1995, that number had risen to seven. To give one example, the city of Minneapolis, Minnesota, deployed its SWAT team on no-knock warrants 35 times in 1987. By 1996, the same unit had been deployed for drug raids more than 700 times that year alone.

In small-to medium-sized cities, Kraska estimates that 80 percent of SWAT callouts are now for warrant service. In large cities, it's about 75 percent. These numbers, too, have been on the rise since the early 1980s. Orange County, Florida, deployed its SWAT team 619 times during one five-year period in the 1990s. Ninety-four percent of those callouts were to serve search warrants, not for hostage situations or police standoffs.

For several years, the heavily armed Fresno SWAT team mentioned earlier was used for routine, full-time patrolling in high-crime areas. The Violent Crime Suppression Unit, as it was called, was given carte blanche to enter residences and apprehend and search occupants in high-crime, mostly minority neighborhoods. The unit routinely stopped pedestrians without probable cause, searched them, interrogated them, and entered their personal information into a computer. "It's a war," one SWAT officer told a reporter from the Nation. Said another, "If you're 21, male, living in one of these neighborhoods, and you're not in our computer, then there's something definitely wrong." The VCSU was disbanded in 2001 after a series of lawsuits alleging police brutality and wrongful shootings, though officials claim the unit was dissolved because it had "fulfilled its goals."

The deployment of SWAT teams for routine police work, even independent of the drug war, has reaped unfortunate—though predictable—results, from general police overreaction to mass raids on entire neighborhoods, to the deaths of innocent people. In January 1999, for example, a SWAT team in Chester, Pennsylvania, outraged the local community when it raided Chester High School in full tactical gear to break up a half dozen students who had been loitering outside the school in the early afternoon. An incident like that is troubling enough. But the use of heavily armed police tactics in response to nonviolent offenses can have far more tragic consequences. In 1998, the Virginia Beach SWAT team shot and killed security guard Edward C. Reed in a 3 a.m. gambling raid on a private club. Police say they approached the tinted car where Reed was working security, knocked, and identified themselves, at which point Reed refused to drop his handgun. Reed's family insists that the police version of events is unlikely, given that Reed was a security guard and had no criminal record. More likely, they say, Reed mistakenly believed the raiding officers were there to do harm, particularly given that the club had been robbed not long before. According to police, Reed's last words were, "Why did you shoot me? I was reading a book." Club owner Darrin Hyman actually shot back at the SWAT team. Prosecutors would later decline to press felony charges against Hyman, concluding he had good reason to believe he was under attack. Hyman was convicted of a misdemeanor gambling offense (playing a game of dice with friends) and of discharging a firearm.

The most obvious problem with the militarization of civilian policing is that the military and the police have two distinctly different tasks. The military's job is to seek out, overpower, and destroy an enemy. Though soldiers attempt to avoid them, collateral casualties are accepted as inevitable. Police, on the other hand, are charged with "keeping the peace," or "to protect and serve."

Given that civilian police now tote military equipment, get military training, and embrace military culture and values, it shouldn't be surprising when officers begin to act like soldiers, treat civilians like combatants, and tread on private property as if it were part of a battlefield. Of course, it's hard to overlook the fact that the soldiering-up of civilian police forces is taking place as part of the larger War on Drugs, which grows more saturated with war imagery, tactics, and phraseology every day.

War imagery and the endorsement of indiscriminate, military battle tactics for the War on Drugs has become common in political discourse. For example, the nation's first Drug Czar, William Bennett, recommended in 1989 that the United States abolish habeas corpus for drug offenders. "It's a funny war when the 'enemy' is entitled to due process of law and a fair trial," Bennett later told Fortune magazine. On the Larry King Show Bennett suggested that drug dealers be publicly beheaded.

Given such rhetoric, it isn't all that surprising when civilian agencies police drug crimes like soldiers instead of peacekeepers and treat civilians like combatants instead of citizens with rights.

The most obvious criticism of paramilitary drug raids is that, contrary to assertions from proponents that they minimize the risk of violence, they actually escalate provocation and bring unnecessary violence to what would otherwise be a routine, nonviolent police procedure. SWAT teams typically serve drug warrants just before dawn, or late at night. They enter residences unannounced, or just seconds after announcing. Targets, then, are suddenly awoken from sleep, and confronted with the prospect that their homes are being invaded. Police sometimes deploy diversionary devices such as flashbang grenades, designed to cause temporary blindness and deafness, intentionally compounding the confusion.

It isn't difficult to see why a gun owner's first instinct upon waking under such conditions would be to disregard whatever the intruders may be screaming at him, and reach for a weapon to defend himself. Even public officials have expressed that sentiment. In 1992, police in Venice, Illinois, mistakenly raided the wrong home on a paramilitary narcotics raid. Fortunately, no one was home. But the house turned out to be the home of Tyrone Echols, Venice's mayor. "To tell the truth, I don't remember what they said because I was furious," Echols told the St. Louis Post-Dispatch. "If I'd been here and heard that going on I probably would have taken my pistol and shot through the door. I'd probably be dead. And some of the officers would probably be dead, too."

Even former police officers have instinctively reached for their weapons when SWAT teams have mistakenly entered their homes on faulty, no-knock search warrants. So have many civilians—some guilty of drug crimes, some completely innocent—who were then shot and killed by police officers who understandably mistook an otherwise nonviolent suspect's attempt to defend himself as an act of aggression. Should a suspect or any occupant of the residence be asleep in a room far away from the point of entry, or perhaps on another floor, it's not difficult to see how he might be awoken by the commotion but not hear the announcement that the intruders are police (assuming such an announcement was made in the first place).

Another problem with military-style, late-night drug raids is that there's good reason for civilians to suspect late night intruders aren't police. Spurred on in part by the frequent nature and popularization of surprise drug raids, it is not uncommon for criminals to disguise themselves as raiding police to gain entry into homes and businesses.

One infamous example took place in 1994, when a group of men entered the home of Lisa Renee and abducted her as retribution for a drug deal, which they'd conducted with her brothers, gone wrong. In a chilling 911 call, as Renee pleads with the operator to send help, one of the men announces through the door that he's the "FBI." Renee says to the operator, "Oh, they're the FBI." One intruder then says, "Open the door and we'll talk." Renee says again, "They're the FBI. They say they're the FBI, ma'am," and opens the door. The call ends with screaming. The men kidnapped Renee, raped and beat her over the next several days, then buried her alive in a shallow grave. Given its sensational elements, the Renee case is perhaps the most famous case of armed intruders posing as police. But it's by no means the only example. New York City alone reports more than 1,000 cases each year of people pretending to be police officers, many of them in attempts to rob homes and businesses.

An overwhelming number of mistaken raids take place because police relied on information from confidential informants. Police routinely secure warrants for paramilitary drug raids on the basis of a tip from a single, confidential informant, many of whom are paid, or rewarded with leniency in their own criminal cases. Back in 1995, National Law Journal estimated that money paid to informants jumped from $25 million in 1985 to about $97 million in 1993. It's safe to assume that number is significantly higher now. Those figures also don't include money seized by police from drug suspects, a portion of which often gets filtered back to informants.

One of the more egregious examples of how the informant system can lead to tragedy is the case of Pedro Oregon Navarro. In the summer of 1998, two police officers in Houston pulled over a car with three men inside. One of them was subsequently arrested for public intoxication. Already on probation, the suspect came up with a bargain for the arresting officers. He'd give them a tip on a drug dealer if they'd let him off. They agreed. The man made up a story and gave police Navarro's address. At 1:40 a.m., six police from the city's anti-gang task force raided Navarro's house. The informant knocked on the door, and Navarro's brother-in-law answered. At that point, the officers stormed Navarro's bedroom, where the man awoke, startled and frightened, and reached for his gun. Police opened fire. They shot Navarro 12 times, killing him. Navarro never fired his gun.

There isn't much data available on just how often judges or prosecutors turn down search warrants because of the untrustworthiness of a confidential informant or on how often they turn down drug search warrants in general. But most criminal justice experts agree that it's rare.

A 2000 Denver Post investigation found that judges exercise almost no discretion at all when it comes to issuing no-knock warrants. The Post found that Denver judges had denied just five of 163 no-knock applications over a 12-month period (local defense attorneys were surprised to learn there were even five). "No-knock search warrants appear to be approved so routinely that some Denver judges have issued them even though police asked only for a regular warrant," the Post wrote. "In fact, more than one of every 10 no-knock warrants issued over the past seven months was transformed from a regular warrant with just a judge's signature." Among the paper's other findings: In 8 of 10 raids, police assertions in affidavits that weapons would be present turned out to be wrong.

Judge Robert Patterson, the presiding judge for Denver's criminal court system provided an astonishing defense. "We are not the fact gatherers," he said. "It's pretty formulaic how it's done. If you sign your name 100 times, you can look away and sign in the wrong place. We read a lot of documents. We may, just like anyone else, sign something and realize later that it's the wrong place or the wrong thing. Is it wrong not to be paying attention? No. It's just that we're doing things over and over again."

Perhaps what's most troubling about the use of no-knock and quick-knock raids is that for all the peril and confrontation associated with them, the little evidence available suggests they aren't even all that effective. The public scrutiny that followed [a] botched no-knock raid in Denver that killed immigrant Ismael Mena in 2000, for example, enabled Denver's Rocky Mountain News to get access to warrants and court records for all of the no-knock raids conducted in the city in 1999. The paper's findings were alarming: Of 146 no-knock raids conducted in the city that year, only 49 produced charges of any kind. And of those, just 2 resulted in prison time for the targets of the raids. In comparison, the paper noted that while 21 percent of the city's felony defendants on average are sent to prison, just 4 percent of its no-knock defendants were. One former prosecutor said of the results, "When you have that violent intrusion on people's homes with so little results, you have to ask why." The Rocky Mountain News continued: "Almost all of the 1999 no-knock cases were targeted at people suspected of being drug dealers.... Often the tips went unsubstantiated, and little in the way of narcotics was recovered. The problem doesn't stem only from the work of inexperienced street cops, which city officials have maintained. Even veteran narcotics detectives sometimes seek no-knock warrants based on the word of an informant and without conducting undercover buys to verify the tips."

A 1997 investigation by the Palm Beach Post found that in a sampling of 50 of the 309 arrests made by Palm Beach County's 12 SWAT teams, the longest jail sentence meted out from any of the raids was five years. The vast majority produced sentences of less than six months, parole, or no sentence at all. Of the defendants actually found guilty, most were sentenced to less than six months in jail, suggesting they were hardly the hardened, violent, dangerous criminals police and prosecutors say require the use of a heavily fortified paramilitary team.

After [a] New York City raid that [resulted in the death of the suspect], Police Chief Raymond Kelly estimated that at least 10 percent of the city's 450+ monthly no-knock drug raids were served on the wrong address, under bad information, or otherwise didn't produce enough evidence for an arrest. Kelly conceded, however, that NYPD didn't keep careful track of botched raids, leading one city council member to speculate the problem could be even worse.

Supporters of the increased use of paramilitary tactics often say that such aggressive tactics are necessary because drug dealers are increasingly arming themselves with heavier and more sophisticated weaponry. The only way to counter that trend, they say, is to keep police well ahead in the arms race, and to show overwhelming force when serving drug search and arrest warrants.

[However], there's simply not much evidence that criminals are arming themselves with heavy weaponry. In a paper by David Kopel and Eric Morgan published by the Independence Institute in 1991, about a decade into the militarization of civilian policing that began in 1980, the authors point to a number of statistics showing that high-powered weapons, which are often cumbersome and difficult to conceal, simply aren't favored by criminals, including drug peddlers. The authors surveyed dozens of cities and found that, in general, less than 1 percent of weapons seized by police fit the definition of an "assault weapon." Nationally, they found that fewer than 4 percent of homicides across the United States involved rifles of any kind. And fewer than one-eighth of 1 percent involved weapons of military caliber.

The massive increase in SWAT callouts over the last two decades ought to be of concern for reasons other than the fact that it presents more opportunities for a botched raid on an innocent person to end in gunfire. It represents the needless terrorizing of American citizens and an increased perception that the drug war is just that: a war. It suggests that in terms of civil liberties, American citizens are given little more consideration than the citizens of a country with which the United Sates is at war: No real rights or protections against unwarranted searches, and in some neighborhoods, the real possibility that lives and homes could become collateral damage. It's striking how many police and government officials have responded to paramilitary raids on the homes of innocents by dismissing them as regrettable, but inevitable and acceptable, consequences of the War on Drugs.

5. Drug Testing

The United States Supreme Court has held that the government may not conduct suspicionless drug testing for law enforcement purposes. *See Ferguson v. City of Charleston*, 532 U.S. 67 (2001) (holding that suspicionless drug testing of pregnant women for law enforcement purposes violates the Fourth Amendment). Though drug testing is not commonly used to investigate drug crimes, it is nevertheless a part of daily life for many Americans. Employees—including government employees—are often asked to take a drug test in order to obtain or keep a job. *See, e.g.,* Mark A. Rothstein, *Workplace Drug Testing: A Case Study in the Misapplication of Technology*, 5 HARV. J. L. & TECH. 65 (1991) ("In less than a decade drug testing has become a way of life in public and private employment."). Many schools drug test their students as a condition of participating in extracurricular activities. Probationers, parolees, and drug court participants are also frequently drug tested. Indeed, based on the number of individuals who take (or have taken) a drug test, one could argue that no aspect of the drug war directly impacts more Americans than drug testing.

The materials below provide an overview of some of the legal and policy issues raised by drug testing.

Testing Drugs versus Testing for Drug Use:
Private Risk Management in the Shadow of Criminal Law
Robert J. MacCoun
56 DePaul Law Review 507 (2007)

Workplace drug testing is now fairly common, as exhibited in the 1994 and 1997 versions of the National Household Survey on Drug Abuse (NHSDA). These surveys show that 49% of workers in 1997, and 44% in 1994, reported that their workplaces conducted drug testing; testing was more common in large firms (74%) than in medium (58%) or small (28%) firms. According to the American Management Association, the proportion of its members using drug testing rose from 21% to 81% between 1987 and 1996. The NHSDA study found that pre-employment testing was more common (39%) than either testing for cause (30%) or random testing (25%). Similarly, a National Institute on Drug Abuse (NIDA) survey of workplace drug testing data in the early 1990s found that pre-employment testing was more common (44% of testing firms) than random testing (27% of testing firms).

In the NHSDA study, about 8% of full-time workers reported using illicit drugs during the month; a similar share reported heavy alcohol use. Full-time workers accounted for 70% of current illicit drug users aged 18 to 49. Because the household survey likely excluded a sizeable fraction of the addicted population, the true employment rate among current drug users is surely lower. Nevertheless, this suggests an upper-bound estimate that a third ... of current adult drug users are subject to drug-testing surveillance.

In the 1998 Monitoring the Future survey of high school seniors, 14% of schools and 16% of students reported having some form of drug testing. Similar testing rates (16% of schools and 16% of students) were found in 2001. A somewhat lower rate was reported by the National Study of Delinquency Prevention in Schools (NSDPS), which relied on administrative rather than student respondents. It found that from 1997 to 1998, "approximately 9 percent of secondary schools conducted some sort of testing program, presumably focused on athletes." This estimate covers a time period just after the Supreme Court held in *Vernonia School District 47J v. Acton* that mandatory drug testing of student athletes is legal under the Fourth and Fourteenth Amendments. A later opinion by Justice Clarence Thomas in *Board of Education of Independent School District No. 92 of Pottawatomie County v. Earls* further established student drug testing by holding that it "is a reasonably effective means of addressing the School District's legitimate concerns in preventing, deterring, and detecting drug use" among schoolchildren.

Most of what we know about drug use among arrestees comes from urinalyses conducted for research purposes, rather than for criminal processing. Drug testing of arrestees is rare, except in Washington, D.C. and jurisdictions participating in the Treatment Alternatives for Special Clients (TASC) program or the recently cancelled Arrestee Drug Abuse Monitoring (ADAM) program. Most probationers and parolees are technically subject to testing, but it is very infrequent. Based on his recent study in Los Angeles, San Diego, and Santa Cruz Counties, Professor Mark Kleiman and his colleagues argue that testing of probationers is an inadequate means of surveillance and monitoring: "Once-a-week testing produces about a 35% chance of detecting any given incident of drug use; twice a week pushes that figure above 80%. By contrast, a probationer tested once a month—a far more typical pattern in the three departments studied—has less than one chance in ten of being detected for any given incident of use."

One might assume that the criminal justice system occupies the most intrusive and punitive end of the drug testing spectrum, but Eric Wish and Bernard Gropper of the National Institute of Justice note that in such settings "a single positive test result will seldom have the drastic consequences it can have in the employment setting." They argue that "the level of recent drug use in the offender population is so high that it would be counterproductive to attempt to revoke probation or parole or incarcerate all persons who tested positive." Instead, a positive test is usually "used to trigger more assessment, testing, or supervision and not to punish people or deprive them of their liberty."

Quest Diagnostics, "the leading provider of employer drug testing services in the United States," publishes a regular Drug Testing Index summarizing its results. Between January 2005 and June 2005, Quest conducted over 3.6 million drug tests; the positivity rate was 5% for the general U.S. workforce and 2% for federal workers in safety-sensitive positions. The results show a general decline in positivity rates in recent years, particularly for marijuana. An early 1990s NIDA survey of workplace drug testing found that almost 4% of samples were positive for an illicit substance: 2% for marijuana, 1% for cocaine, and less than 1% for opiates and benzodiazepines. Positive rates were highest in the construction sector at 6%, compared to only 3% for the retail sector and 2% for both the manufacturing and transportation sectors.

Not surprisingly, positive drug test rates are dramatically higher among criminal justice arrestees. The National Institute of Justice began collecting systematic drug testing data from arrestees with its Drug Use Forecasting (DUF) program in 1988. An improved methodology, the ADAM program, was implemented in 2000. The most recent data available are from 2000. In that year, more than half of thirty-five sites reported that 64% or more of their male arrestees tested positive for either cocaine, opiates, marijuana, methamphetamine, or PCP (the NIDA-5). The most common drugs present were marijuana (40%) and cocaine (30%).

Any consideration of drug test results should be qualified by the serious limitations of existing testing methods. Blood testing is the most accurate method for identifying drug influences at the moment of testing, but it is intrusive, expensive, and rare. Urine testing, which is also intrusive, is far more common. But it is a poor indicator of immediate drug status because drugs cannot be detected in urine until they have been metabolized, often many hours after consumption. Urine testing is particularly sensitive to cannabis use, and can detect use dating back several months for a heavy user, but it is far less likely to detect other "hard" drugs. Saliva and hair testing are less intrusive and are becoming more common. In fact, hair testing can detect use dating back two to three months, and can even date the use with some accuracy.

Use testing is vulnerable to false positives due to contaminants (for urine testing), as well as false negatives due to temporary abstention (for blood, urine, and saliva testing), "water loading" (for urine testing), and even a haircut (for hair testing). Detailed advice on defeating a drug test is available on various websites. For example, false positives for marijuana can be triggered by many different prescription and over-the-counter medications.

Another reason to be wary of the accuracy of use testing results is problems with sampling. "Random testing" may sound a lot like "random sampling," but there is selection into and out of the sample, because users and others who object to testing may avoid the testing organization altogether—whether it be the military, a workplace, or a school sports program.

From a deterrence perspective, use testing should be an effective way to reduce drug use. Use testing increases the certainty of sanctioning, and even when it does not lead to arrest, the consequences of a positive test are effectively punitive, because it damages one's reputation with family, friends, and colleagues. Nevertheless, support for a general deterrent effect of drug testing is mixed.

The available studies are correlational and hence subject to a variety of inferential problems. It is astonishing that such an intrusive intervention is being implemented so widely in the absence of a carefully controlled experiment group, with random assignment to testing condition either at the individual, site, or organizational level.

On the basis of the special workplace modules, the NHSDA 1994/1997 project noted the effect of information availability in the workplace: "There is evidence that workplace policies matter. Employees in three of the four occupations with the lowest rates of drug use (protective service, extraction and precision production, and administration support) were also among employees in the four occupations with the highest rates of drug information and policies in the workplace."

In 1981, the U.S. military implemented a tough "zero-tolerance" drug policy, which imposed mandatory drug testing and threatened job termination for violations. Two studies have examined the effects of the policy. Professor Jerald Bachman and his colleagues used the Monitoring the Future cohort data from young adults who graduated from high school between 1976 and 1995. They found declining rates of drug use among active duty military personnel and nonmilitary cohort members in the two years after graduation, but beginning in 1981, the rate of decline was steeper for the military group, at least for illicit drugs. This is a pattern "strongly suggestive of causal relationships." In a separate study, economists Stephen Mehay and Rosalie Pacula compared NHSDA and Department of Defense health survey data collected before and after the military adopted the zero-tolerance policy. They estimated a 16% drop in the prevalence of past-year drug use in the military, with a lower bound estimate of 4%.

Dr. W. Robert Lange and his colleagues examined the effects of a decision at Johns Hopkins hospital to shift from "for cause" employee testing in 1989 to universal pre-employment testing in 1991. In 1989, 10.8% of 593 specimens were positive — 55% of them for marijuana — and there were seven "walkouts" who refused to be tested. In 1991, 5.8% of 365 specimens tested positive — 28% for marijuana — with no walkouts. The authors interpreted these results as evidence of the deterrent effect of drug testing. But Professors M.R. Levine and W.P. Rennie offer a variety of alternative explanations, including the fact that in 1991 users had advance warning of the test and could abstain, water load, or ingest legal substances that would confound the test.

The most comprehensive study of the effects of school testing on student drug use comes from analyses of data from the Monitoring the Future survey. This analysis found no measurable association between either random or "for cause" drug testing and students' self-reported drug use. The study is cross-sectional, rather than prospective, and is somewhat limited by the relative rarity of exposure to testing.

At present, the evidence suggests that the military's testing program had a deterrent effect, but no such effect was found in workplaces or in schools. Still, the absence of evidence is not evidence of absence. There are very few rigorous studies; low statistical power, noisy measurement, and other factors may hide genuine effects. Alternatively, the military program may be more effective as a deterrent due to differences in its implementation, its target population, its consequences for users, or its institutional setting.

Proponents of use testing see both use reduction (deterrence) and harm reduction (safety) benefits of testing. In the courts, the harm reduction rationale has generally trumped the use reduction rationale. For example, in *Vernonia*, the Court held that the importance of deterring drug use among schoolchildren "can hardly be doubted." But the Court focused on the harm reduction benefits of use testing: "It must not be lost sight of that this program is directed more narrowly to drug use by school athletes, where the risk of immediate physical harm to the drug user or those with whom he is playing his sport is particularly high." The D.C. Circuit has ruled that random testing is an unreasonable invasion of employee privacy except for safety-sensitive positions. Based on its reading of three Supreme Court decisions, the Substance Abuse and Mental Health Services Administration has identified four classes of presumptive testing — employees who carry firearms, motor vehicle operators carrying passengers, aviation flight crew members and air traffic controllers, and railroad operating crews — "that are to be included in every plan if such positions exist in the agency."

The National Research Council (NRC) took a comprehensive look at the evidence for a safety-promoting benefit of drug testing in the workplace. They concluded that the evidence linking alcohol and drug use to workplace accidents was largely inconclusive, partly because both workplace accidents and workplace intoxication were relatively rare events: "Despite the wide variety of research in the studies reviewed above, few definitive statements can be made about the impact of using alcohol and other drugs on job performance. The abundance of evidence presented here indicates that the relationship between use and job behaviors and outcomes is clearly negative. However, the magnitude of the relationships found is generally small, and causal spuriousness and direction are problems that have not been adequately addressed in the literature."

The intuition that drug testing might prevent accidents involves an implicit causal chain: drug use impairs psychomotor functioning, which in turn enhances accident risk. Drug testing is designed to detect drug use, the earliest link in the chain, and hopefully to deter or prevent it. But the model also explicitly demonstrates some of the drawbacks of relying on drug use to prevent accidents. This point is illustrated by the statistical logic of "path analysis," first articulated by mathematician Sewall Wright in 1934. In a causal chain (for example, A—>B—>C) where the effect of a variable at one end (A) on the other end (C) is "mediated" by a variable in the middle (B), the distal A—>C correlation equals the product of the two intermediate correlations, and will thus be smaller than either one. The percentage of variance in accident risk due to drug use will drop rapidly with less than perfect correlation in the two intermediate links in the chain.

From a prediction standpoint, one might argue that drug tests can serve as a double proxy for drug use and low self-control. But psychometrically, a better strategy would be to directly assess low self-control and psychomotor functioning. Psychologists and ergonomic specialists have developed a wide variety of valid psychomotor tests, and many are already in use in the military and other "mission-critical" organizations. The private sector has also begun to recognize the potential advantages of directly testing impaired psychomotor performance. There are a variety of psychometrically reliable and valid measures of impulsivity, sensation-seeking, and self-control. More controversially, there are paper-and-pencil "integrity tests" that allow corporations to assess drug and alcohol use, honesty, and other behavioral factors.

A preference for drug testing over psychomotor testing suggests that use testing is really about drug control rather than safety. This is also shown by the fact that drug testing is more common than alcohol testing, even though the link between alcohol and accidents is better established. Granted, it may be easier to consume alcohol without intoxication than cannabis or other drugs. And alcohol is far more prevalent, meaning far more positive test results—though from a safety perspective that is not much of an argument at all.

Use testing may also have some unintended consequences. Theoretically, it could encourage users to substitute less detectable intoxicants. In 1995, 20% of worksites tested for illicit drugs but not for alcohol. The most commonly tested substances are the NIDA-5: marijuana, cocaine, PCP, opiates, and amphetamines. Thus, users might shift from the NIDA-5 to other illicit drugs like MDMA (Ecstasy) and barbiturates, or from illicit drugs to alcohol. I am unaware of studies examining such substitution effects, but these effects have been linked to other policies. There is some evidence that users substitute marijuana for hard drugs when marijuana is decriminalized, and that users substitute marijuana for alcohol when the legal drinking age is raised or beer prices increase. Because marijuana has the longest window of detectability in urinalysis, one might see a shift toward less readily detectable substances like MDMA, amphetamines, and barbiturates.

A related concern is that use testing will drive users away from testing organizations—workplaces, schools, sports teams, and the military. This might make those particular organizations safer, but it displaces the harm to other settings where use might even escalate.

A similar argument is suggested by "labeling theory" in criminology. Labeling theory predicts that legal controls can actually enhance the likelihood of future offenses if the stigma associated with criminal sanctioning alienates the individual from conventional society. Alienation encourages contact with criminally involved referent groups, and weakens the reputational costs that may restrain deviance—thus creating a self-fulfilling prophecy.

Evidence supports this prediction, but the results are not conclusive. Neither Mehay and Pacula nor Bachman found any evidence linking past drug use to self-selection into the military. On the other hand, using the 1994 NHSDA survey, John Hoffmann and Cindy Larison of the National Opinion Research Center found that those using marijuana or cocaine at least weekly were more likely to work for companies that had no testing program. And the NHSDA 1994/1997 workplace analysis suggested that current users were more likely than nonusers to say they would avoid working for an employer who conducts pre-employment screening (22% versus 4%), random drug testing (29% versus 6%), or "for cause" testing (24% versus 10%).

National Treasury Employees Union v. Von Raab

Supreme Court of the United States

489 U.S. 656 (1989)

Justice Kennedy delivered the opinion of the Court.

The United States Customs Service, a bureau of the Department: of the Treasury, is the federal agency responsible for processing persons, carriers, cargo, and mail into the United States, collecting revenue from imports, and enforcing customs and related laws. An important responsibility of the Service is the interdiction and seizure of contraband, including illegal drugs. In 1987 alone, Customs agents seized drugs with a retail value of nearly $9 billion. In the routine discharge of their duties, many Customs employees have direct contact with those who traffic in drugs for profit. Drug import operations, often directed by sophisticated criminal syndicates may be effected by violence or its threat. As a necessary response, many Customs operatives carry and use firearms in connection with their official duties.

In December 1985, respondent, the Commissioner of Customs, established a Drug Screening Task Force to explore the possibility of implementing a drug-screening program within the Service. After extensive research and consultation with experts in the field, the task force concluded that "drug screening through urinalysis is technologically reliable, valid and accurate." Citing this conclusion, the Commissioner announced his intention to require drug tests of employees who applied for, or occupied, certain positions within the Service. The Commissioner stated his belief that "Customs is largely drug-free," but noted also that "unfortunately no segment of society is immune from the threat of illegal drug use." Drug interdiction has become the agency's primary enforcement mission, and the Commissioner stressed that "there is no room in the Customs Service for those who break the laws prohibiting the possession and use of illegal drugs."

In May 1986, the Commissioner announced implementation of the drug-testing program. Drug tests were made a condition of placement or employment for positions that meet one or more of three criteria. The first is direct involvement in drug interdiction or enforcement of related laws, an activity the Commissioner deemed fraught with obvious dangers to the mission of the agency and the lives of Customs agents. The second criterion is a requirement that the incumbent carry firearms, as the Commissioner concluded that "public safety demands that employees who carry deadly arms and are prepared to make instant life or death decisions be drug free." The third criterion is a requirement for the incumbent to handle "classified" material, which the Commissioner determined might fall into the hands of smugglers if accessible to employees who, by reason of their own illegal drug use, are susceptible to bribery or blackmail.

After an employee qualifies for a position covered by the Customs testing program, the Service advises him by letter that his final selection is contingent upon successful completion of drug screening. An independent contractor contacts the employee to fix the time and place for collecting the sample. On reporting for the test, the employee must produce photographic identification and remove any outer garments, such as a coat or a jacket, and personal belongings. The employee may produce the sample behind a partition, or in the privacy of a bathroom stall if he so chooses. To ensure against adulteration of the specimen, or substitution of a sample from another person, a monitor of the same sex as the employee remains close at hand to listen for the normal sounds of urination. Dye is added to the toilet water to prevent the employee from using the water to adulterate the sample.

Upon receiving the specimen, the monitor inspects it to ensure its proper temperature and color, places a tamper-proof custody seal over the container, and affixes an identification label indicating the date and the individual's specimen number. The employee signs a chain-of-custody form, which is initialed by the monitor, and the urine sample is placed in a plastic bag, sealed, and submitted to a laboratory.

The laboratory tests the sample for the presence of marijuana, cocaine, opiates, amphetamines, and phencyclidine.

Customs employees who test positive for drugs and who can offer no satisfactory explanation are subject to dismissal from the Service. Test results may not, however, be turned over to any other agency, including criminal prosecutors, without the employee's written consent.

Petitioners, a union of federal employees and a union official, commenced this suit in the United States District Court for the Eastern District of Louisiana on behalf of current Customs Service employees who seek covered positions. Petitioners alleged that the Custom Service drug-testing program violated the Fourth Amendment.

In *Skinner* v. *Railway Labor Executives' Assn,* [also] decided today, we held that federal regulations requiring employees of private railroads to produce urine samples for chemical testing implicate the Fourth Amendment, as those tests invade reasonable expectations of privacy. Our earlier cases have settled that the Fourth Amendment protects individuals from unreasonable searches conducted by the Government, even when the Government acts as an employer and, in view of our holding in *Railway Labor Executives* that urine tests are searches, it follows that the Customs Service's drug-testing program must meet the reasonableness requirement of the Fourth Amendment.

While we have often emphasized, and reiterate today, that a search must be supported, as a general matter, by a warrant issued upon probable cause our decision in *Railway Labor Executives* reaffirms the longstanding principle that neither a warrant nor probable cause, nor, indeed, any measure of individualized suspicion, is an indispensable component of reasonableness in every circumstance. As we note in *Railway Labor Executives,* our cases establish that where a Fourth Amendment intrusion serves special governmental needs, beyond the normal need for law enforcement, it is necessary to balance the individual's privacy expectations against the Government's interests to determine whether it is impractical to require a warrant or some level of individualized suspicion in the particular context.

It is clear that the Customs Service's drug-testing program is not designed to serve the ordinary needs of law enforcement. Test results may not be used in a criminal prosecution of the employee without the employee's consent. The purposes of the program are to deter drug use among those eligible for promotion to sensitive positions within the Service and to prevent the promotion of drug users to those positions. These substantial interests, no less than the Government's concern for safe rail transportation at issue in *Railway Labor Executives,* present a special need that may justify departure from the ordinary warrant and probable-cause requirements.

Petitioners do not contend that a warrant is required by the balance of privacy and governmental interests in this context, nor could any such contention withstand scrutiny.

We have recognized before that requiring the Government to procure a warrant for every work-related intrusion "would conflict with 'the common-sense realization that government offices could not function if every employment decision became a constitutional matter.'"

Even where it is reasonable to dispense with the warrant requirement in the particular circumstances, a search ordinarily must be based on probable cause. Our cases teach, however, that the probable-cause standard "'is peculiarly related to criminal investigations.'" In particular, the traditional probable-cause standard may be unhelpful in analyzing the reasonableness of routine administrative functions, especially where the Government seeks to *prevent* the development of hazardous conditions or to detect violations that rarely generate articulable grounds for searching any particular place or person. Cf. *Camara v. Municipal Court of San Francisco,* (noting that building code inspections, unlike searches conducted pursuant to a criminal investigation, are designed "to prevent even the unintentional development of conditions which are hazardous to public health and safety"). Our precedents have settled that, in certain limited circumstances, the Government's need to discover such latent or hidden conditions, or to prevent their development, is sufficiently compelling to justify the intrusion on privacy entailed by conducting such searches without any measure of individualized suspicion. We think the Government's need to conduct the suspicionless searches required by the Customs program outweighs the privacy interests of employees engaged directly in drug interdiction, and of those who otherwise are required to carry firearms.

The Customs Service is our Nation's first line of defense against one of the greatest problems affecting the health and welfare of our population. We have adverted before to "the veritable national crisis in law enforcement caused by smuggling of illicit narcotics." Our cases also reflect the traffickers' seemingly inexhaustible repertoire of deceptive practices and elaborate schemes for importing narcotics. The record in this case confirms that, through the adroit selection of source locations, smuggling routes, and increasingly elaborate methods of concealment, drug traffickers have managed to bring into this country increasingly large quantities of illegal drugs. The record also indicates, and it is well known, that drug smugglers do not hesitate to use violence to protect their lucrative trade and avoid apprehension.

Many of the Service's employees are often exposed to this criminal element and to the controlled substances it seeks to smuggle into the country. The physical safety of these employees may be threatened, and many may be tempted not only by bribes from the traffickers with whom they deal, but also by their own access to vast sources of valuable contraband seized and controlled by the Service. The Commissioner indicated below that "Customs officers have been shot, stabbed, run over, dragged by automobiles, and assaulted with blunt objects while performing their duties." At least nine officers have died in the line of duty since 1974. He also noted that Customs officers have been the targets of bribery by drug smugglers on numerous occasions, and several have been removed from the Service for accepting bribes and for other integrity violations.

It is readily apparent that the Government has a compelling interest in ensuring that front-line interdiction personnel are physically fit, and have unimpeachable integrity and judgment. Indeed, the Government's interest here is at least as important as its interest in searching travelers entering the country. We have long held that travelers seeking to enter the country may be stopped and required to submit to a routine search without probable cause, or even founded suspicion, "because of national self protection reasonably requiring one entering the country to identify himself as entitled to come in, and his belongings as effects which may be lawfully brought in." *Carroll v. United States,* 267

U.S. 132 (1925). This national interest in self-protection could be irreparably damaged if those charged with safeguarding it were, because of their own drug use, unsympathetic to their mission of interdicting narcotics. A drug user's indifference to the Service's basic mission or, even worse, his active complicity with the malefactors, can facilitate importation of sizable drug shipments or block apprehension of dangerous criminals. The public interest demands effective measures to bar drug users from positions directly involving the interdiction of illegal drugs.

The public interest likewise demands effective measures to prevent the promotion of drug users to positions that require the incumbent to carry a firearm, even if the incumbent is not engaged directly in the interdiction of drugs. Customs employees who may use deadly force plainly "discharge duties fraught with such risks of injury to others that even a momentary lapse of attention can have disastrous consequences." We agree with the Government that the public should not bear the risk that employees who may suffer from impaired perception and judgment will be promoted to positions where they may need to employ deadly force. Indeed, ensuring against the creation of this dangerous risk will itself further Fourth Amendment values, as the use of deadly force may violate the Fourth Amendment in certain circumstances.

Against these valid public interests we must weigh the interference with individual liberty that results from requiring these classes of employees to undergo a urine test. The interference with individual privacy that results from the collection of a urine sample for subsequent chemical analysis could be substantial in some circumstances. We have recognized, however, that the "operational realities of the workplace" may render entirely reasonable certain work-related intrusions by supervisors and co-workers that might be viewed as unreasonable in other contexts. While these operational realities will rarely affect an employee's expectations of privacy with respect to searches of his person, or of personal effects that the employee may bring to the workplace, it is plain that certain forms of public employment may diminish privacy expectations even with respect to such personal searches. Employees of the United States Mint, for example, should expect to be subject to certain routine personal searches when they leave the workplace every day. Similarly, those who join our military or intelligence services may not only be required to give what in other contexts might be viewed as extraordinary assurances of trustworthiness and probity, but also may expect intrusive inquiries into their physical fitness for those special positions.

We think Customs employees who are directly involved in the interdiction of illegal drugs or who are required to carry firearms in the line of duty likewise have a diminished expectation of privacy in respect to the intrusions occasioned by a urine test. Unlike most private citizens or government employees in general, employees involved in drug interdiction reasonably should expect effective inquiry into their fitness and probity. Much the same is true of employees who are required to carry firearms. Because successful performance of their duties depends uniquely on their judgment and dexterity, these employees cannot reasonably expect to keep from the Service personal information that bears directly on their fitness. While reasonable tests designed to elicit this information doubtless infringe some privacy expectations, we do not believe these expectations outweigh the Government's compelling interests in safety and in the integrity of our borders.

Without disparaging the importance of the governmental interests that support the suspicionless searches of these employees, petitioners nevertheless contend that the Service's drug-testing program is unreasonable in two particulars. First, petitioners argue that the program is unjustified because it is not based on a belief that testing will reveal any drug use by covered employees. In pressing this argument, petitioners point out that the Service's testing scheme was not implemented in response to any perceived drug problem among Customs employees, and that the program actually has not led to the discovery of a significant number of drug users. Counsel for petitioners informed us at oral argument that no more than 5 employees out of 3,600 have tested positive for drugs. Second, petitioners contend that the Service's scheme is not a "sufficiently productive mechanism to justify [its] intrusion upon Fourth Amendment interests," because illegal drug users can avoid detection with ease by temporary abstinence or by surreptitious adulteration of their urine specimens. These contentions are unpersuasive.

Petitioners' first contention evinces an unduly narrow view of the context in which the Service's testing program was implemented. Petitioners do not dispute, nor can there be doubt, that drug abuse is one of the most serious problems confronting our society today. There is little reason to believe that American workplaces are immune from this pervasive social problem, as is amply illustrated by our decision in *Railway Labor Executives.* Detecting drug impairment on the part of employees can be a difficult task, especially where, as here, it is not feasible to subject employees and their work product to the kind of day-to-day scrutiny that is the norm in more traditional office environments. Indeed, the almost unique mission of the Service gives the Government a compelling interest in ensuring that many of these covered employees do not use drugs even off duty, for such use creates risks of bribery and blackmail against which the Government is entitled to guard. In light of the extraordinary safety and national security hazards that would attend the promotion of drug users to positions that require the carrying of firearms or the interdiction of controlled substances, the Service's policy of deterring drug users from seeking such promotions cannot be deemed unreasonable.

The mere circumstance that all but a few of the employees tested are entirely innocent of wrongdoing does not impugn the program's validity. The same is likely to be true of householders who are required to submit to suspicionless housing code inspections and of motorists who are stopped at the checkpoints we approved in *United States v. Martinez-Fuerte,* 428 U.S. 543 (1976). The Service's program is designed to prevent the promotion of drug users to sensitive positions as much as it is designed to detect those employees who use drugs. Where, as here, the possible harm against which the Government seeks to guard is substantial, the need to prevent its occurrence furnishes an ample justification for reasonable searches calculated to advance the Government's goal.

We think petitioners' second argument—that the Service's testing program is ineffective because employees may attempt to deceive the test by a brief abstention before the test date, or by adulterating their urine specimens—overstates the case. As the Court of Appeals noted, addicts may be unable to abstain even for a limited period of time, or may be unaware of the "fade-away effect" of certain drugs. More importantly, the avoidance techniques suggested by petitioners are fraught with uncertainty and risks for those employees who venture to attempt them. A particular employee's pattern of elimination for a given drug cannot be predicted with perfect accuracy, and, in any event, this information is not likely to be known or available to the employee.

In sum, we believe the Government has demonstrated that its compelling interests in safeguarding our borders and the public safety outweigh the privacy expectations of employees who seek to be promoted to positions that directly involve the interdiction of illegal drugs or that require the incumbent to carry a firearm. We hold that the testing of these employees is reasonable under the Fourth Amendment.

We are unable, on the present record, to assess the reasonableness of the Government's testing program insofar as it covers employees who are required "to handle classified material." We readily agree that the Government has a compelling interest in protecting truly sensitive information from those who, "under compulsion of circumstances or for other reasons, … might compromise [such] information." We also agree that employees who seek promotions to positions where they would handle sensitive information can be required to submit to a urine test under the Service's screening program, especially if the positions covered under this category require background investigations, medical examinations, or other intrusions that may be expected to diminish their expectations of privacy in respect of a urinalysis test.

It is not clear, however, whether the category defined by the Service's testing directive encompasses only those Customs employees likely to gain access to sensitive information. Employees who are tested under the Service's scheme include those holding such diverse positions as "Accountant," "Accounting Technician," "Animal Caretaker," "Attorney (All)," "Baggage Clerk," "Co-op Student (All)," "Electric Equipment Repairer," "Mail Clerk/Assistant," and "Messenger."

We cannot resolve this ambiguity on the basis of the record before us, and we think it is appropriate to remand the case to the Court of Appeals for such proceedings as may be necessary to clarify the scope of this category of employees subject to testing. Upon remand the Court of Appeals should examine the criteria used by the Service in determining what materials are classified and in deciding whom to test under this rubric. In assessing the reasonableness of requiring tests of these employees, the court should also consider pertinent information bearing upon the employees' privacy expectations, as well as the supervision to which these employees are already subject.

The judgment of the Court of Appeals for the Fifth Circuit is affirmed in part and vacated in part, and the case is remanded for further proceedings consistent with this opinion.

It is so ordered.

[The dissenting opinion of Justice Marshall, joined by Justice Brennan, has been omitted.]

Justice Scalia, with whom Justice Stevens joins, dissenting.

The issue in this case is not whether Customs Service employees can constitutionally be denied promotion, or even dismissed, for a single instance of unlawful drug use, at home or at work. They assuredly can. The issue here is what steps can constitutionally be taken to *detect* such drug use. The Government asserts it can demand that employees perform "an excretory function traditionally shielded by great privacy," while "a monitor of the same sex … remains close at hand to listen for the normal sounds," and that the excretion thus produced be turned over to the Government for chemical analysis. The Court agrees that this constitutes a search for purposes of the Fourth Amendment — and I think it obvious that it is a type of search particularly destructive of privacy and offensive to personal dignity.

Until today this Court had upheld a bodily search separate from arrest and without individualized suspicion of wrongdoing only with respect to prison inmates, relying upon the uniquely dangerous nature of that environment. Today, in *Skinner*, we allow a less intrusive bodily search of railroad employees involved in train accidents. I joined the Court's opinion there because the demonstrated frequency of drug and alcohol use by the targeted class of employees, and the demonstrated connection between such use and grave harm, rendered the search a reasonable means of protecting society. I decline to join the Court's opinion in the present case because neither frequency of use nor connection to harm is demonstrated or even likely. In my view the Customs Service rules are a kind of immolation of privacy and human dignity in symbolic opposition to drug use.

[T]he substantive analysis of our opinion today in *Skinner* begins, "the problem of alcohol use on American railroads is as old as the industry itself," and goes on to cite statistics concerning that problem and the accidents it causes, including a 1979 study finding that "23% of the operating personnel were 'problem drinkers.'"

The Court's opinion in the present case, however, will be searched in vain for real evidence of a real problem that will be solved by urine testing of Customs Service employees. Instead, there are assurances that "the Customs Service is our Nation's first line of defense against one of the greatest problems affecting the health and welfare of our population"; that "many of the Service's employees are often exposed to [drug smugglers] and to the controlled substances [they seek] to smuggle into the country"; that "Customs officers have been the targets of bribery by drug smugglers on numerous occasions, and several have been removed from the Service for accepting bribes and other integrity violations"; that "the Government has a compelling interest in ensuring that front-line interdiction personnel are physically fit, and have unimpeachable integrity and judgment"; that the "national interest in self-protection could be irreparably damaged if those charged with safeguarding it were, because of their own drug use, unsympathetic to their mission of interdicting narcotics"; and that "the public should not bear the risk that employees who may suffer from impaired perception and judgment will be promoted to positions where they may need to employ deadly force." To paraphrase Churchill, all this contains much that is obviously true, and much that is relevant; unfortunately, what is obviously true is not relevant, and what is relevant is not obviously true. The only pertinent points, it seems to me, are supported by nothing but speculation, and not very plausible speculation at that. It is not apparent to me that a Customs Service employee who uses drugs is significantly more likely to be bribed by a drug smuggler, any more than a Customs Service employee who wears diamonds is significantly more likely to be bribed by a diamond smuggler—unless. perhaps, the addiction to drugs is so severe, and requires so much money to maintain, that it would be detectable even without benefit of a urine test. Nor is it apparent to me that Customs officers who use drugs will be appreciably less "sympathetic" to their drug-interdiction mission, any more than police officers who exceed the speed limit in their private cars are appreciably less sympathetic to their mission of enforcing the traffic laws. (The only difference is that the Customs officer's individual efforts, if they are irreplaceable, can theoretically affect the availability of his own drug supply—a prospect so remote as to be an absurd basis of motivation.) Nor, finally, is it apparent to me that urine tests will be even marginally more effective in preventing gun-carrying agents from risking "impaired perception and judgment" than is their current knowledge that, if impaired, they may be shot dead in unequal combat with unimpaired smugglers—unless, again, their addiction is so severe that no urine test is needed for detection.

What is absent in the Government's justifications—notably absent, revealingly absent, and as far as I am concerned dispositively absent—is the recitation of *even a single instance* in which any of the speculated horribles actually occurred: an instance, that is, in which the cause of bribetaking, or of poor aim, or of unsympathetic law enforcement, or of compromise of classified information, was drug use. Although the Court points out that several employees have in the past been removed from the Service for accepting bribes and other integrity violations, and that at least nine officers have died in the line of duty since 1974 there is no indication whatever that these incidents were related to drug use by Service employees. Perhaps concrete evidence of the severity of a problem is unnecessary when it is so well known that courts can almost take judicial notice of it; but that is surely not the case here. The Commissioner of Customs himself has stated that he "believe[s] that Customs is largely drug-free," that "the extent of illegal drug use by Customs employees was not the reason for establishing this program," and that he "hope[s] and expect[s] to receive reports of very few positive findings through drug screening." The test results have fulfilled those hopes and expectations. According to the Service's counsel, out of 3,600 employees tested, no more than 5 tested positive for drugs.

The Court's response to this lack of evidence is that "there is little reason to believe that American workplaces are immune from [the] pervasive social problem" of drug abuse. Perhaps such a generalization would suffice if the workplace at issue could produce such catastrophic social harm that no risk whatever is tolerable—the secured areas of a nuclear power plant, for example. But if such a generalization suffices to justify demeaning bodily searches, without particularized suspicion, to guard against the bribing or blackmailing of a law enforcement agent, or the careless use of a firearm, then the Fourth Amendment has become frail protection indeed.

Today's decision would be wrong, but at least of more limited effect, if its approval of drug testing were confined to that category of employees assigned specifically to drug interdiction duties. Relatively few public employees fit that description. But in extending approval of drug testing to that category consisting of employees who carry firearms, the Court exposes vast numbers of public employees to this needless indignity. Logically, of course, if those who carry guns can be treated in this fashion, so can all others whose work, if performed under the influence of drugs may endanger others—automobile drivers, operators of other potentially dangerous equipment, construction workers, school crossing guards. A similarly broad scope attaches to the Court's approval of drug testing for those with access to "sensitive information."

There is only one apparent basis that sets the testing at issue here apart from all these other situations—but it is not a basis upon which the Court is willing to rely. I do not believe for a minute that the driving force behind these drug-testing rules was any of the feeble justifications put forward by counsel here and accepted by the Court. The only plausible explanation, in my view, is what the Commissioner himself offered in the concluding sentence of his memorandum to Customs Service employees announcing the program: "Implementation of the drug screening program would set an important example in our country's struggle with this most serious threat to our national health and security." Or as respondent's brief to this Court asserted: "If a law enforcement agency and its employees do not take the law seriously, neither will the public on which the agency's effectiveness depends." What better way to show that the Government is serious about its "war on drugs" than to subject its employees on the front line of that war to this invasion of their privacy and affront to their dignity? To be sure, there is only a slight chance that it will prevent some serious public harm resulting from Service employee drug use, but it will show to the world that the Service is "clean," and—most important of all—will demonstrate the determination of the Government to eliminate this scourge of our society! I think it obvious that this justification is unacceptable; that the impairment of individual liberties cannot be the means of making a point; that symbolism, even symbolism for so worthy a cause as the abolition of unlawful drugs, cannot validate an otherwise unreasonable search.

There is irony in the Government's citation, in support of its position, of Justice Brandeis' statement in *Olmstead v. United States,* 277 U.S. 438, 485 (1928) that "for good or for ill, [our Government] teaches the whole people by its example." Brief for Respondent 36. Brandeis was there *dissenting* from the Court's admission of evidence obtained through an unlawful Government wiretap. He was not praising the Government's example of vigor and enthusiasm in combatting crime, but condemning its example that "the end justifies the means." An even more apt quotation from that famous Brandeis dissent would have been the following:

> "It is ... immaterial that the intrusion was in aid of law enforcement. Experience should teach us to be most on our guard to protect liberty when the Government's purposes are beneficent. Men born to freedom are naturally alert to repel invasion of their liberty by evil-minded rulers. The greatest dangers to liberty lurk in insidious encroachment by men of zeal, well-meaning but without understanding."

Those who lose because of the lack of understanding that begot the present exercise in symbolism are not just the Customs Service employees, whose dignity is thus offended, but all of us—who suffer a coarsening of our national manners that ultimately give the Fourth Amendment its content, and who become subject to the administration of federal officials whose respect for our privacy can hardly be greater than the small respect they have been taught to have for their own.

In addition to testing for current drug use, some government agencies refuse to hire applicants based on their past drug use. The Federal Bureau of Investigation, for example, requires candidates for some positions to "swear that they have not used any illegal substances recently—three years for marijuana and 10 years for other drugs." Prior to 2007, the hiring restrictions were even more stringent, "barr[ing] FBI employment to anyone who had used marijuana more than 15 times in their lives or who had tried other illegal narcotics more than five times." Dan Eggen, *FBI Bows to Modern Realities, Eases Rules on Past Drug Use*, WASH. POST, Aug. 7, 2007. The Department of Justice won't hire an applicant who has used an illegal drug less than one year prior to their application for employment and has an "absolute post-bar [exam] prohibition on any drug use, including marijuana" for attorney applicants. "Any other drug use is reviewed on a case-by-case basis." Loyola University of Chicago School of Law, Government Security Clearance Information, http://www.luc.edu/law/career/govt_security.html (last visited July 6, 2012). Needless to say, neither agency's policy bars past or present alcohol users from employment.

Drug testing of students in public schools has been a topic of ongoing debate in both courts and communities. The United States Supreme Court has heard two student drug testing cases. In *Vernonia School Dist. 47J v. Acton*, 515 U.S. 646 (1995), the Court upheld the suspicionless drug testing of school athletes. Seven years later, in *Board of Education v. Earls*, 536 U.S. 822 (2002), five Justices found constitutional a high school drug testing program that applied to all students engaged in extracurricular activities. The reasoning of the lead opinion in *Earls* gives the impression that the Court would be likely to find a high school testing program that applied to *all* students to be constitutional. In a concurring opinion, however, Justice Breyer indicated that his vote was contingent on leaving students the choice to opt-out of drug testing programs by foregoing extracurricular activities. "[T]he testing program avoids subjecting the entire school to testing[,]" Breyer wrote in *Earls*. "And it preserves an option for a conscientious objector. He can refuse testing while paying a price (nonparticipation) that is serious, but less severe than expulsion from the school." Perhaps because of Breyer's opinion, it appears that few public high schools have adopted school-wide drug testing programs for all students.

Today, between one quarter and one fifth of public school students report that their school has a drug testing program. During the Bush administration, federal funding for student drug testing programs increased dramatically, climbing from $2 million to $10 million between 2004 and 2006 alone. Yet studies indicate student drug testing programs have a negligible impact on student drug use. An author of one recent study advised that their findings should "send[] a cautionary note to the estimated 20% or more of high schools that have joined the drug testing bandwagon. We find little evidence that this approach to minimizing teen drug use is having the deterrent effect its proponents claim." Shari Roan, *Student Drug Testing May Have Only Small Effect in Reducing Use*, L.A. TIMES, Aug. 17, 2011. *See also*, Ryoko Yamaguchi, et al., *Drug Testing in Schools: Policies, Practices, and Association with Student Drug Use*, Youth, Education & Society Occasional Paper 2, Inst. For Social Research, Univ. of Mich., 2003 (finding that student drug testing did not appear to be effective at reducing drug use).

Though the Supreme Court sanctioned both of the student drug testing programs it considered, students still retain some of their Fourth Amendment protections at school even in the context of drug searches. In *Safford Unified School District v. Redding*, the Court considered the constitutionality of a strip search of a 13-year old girl for prescription-strength ibuprofen and an over-the-counter pain reliever. 129 S. Ct. 2633 (2009). The Court found school officials had reasonable suspicion to believe that the student, Savanna Redding, had ibuprofen pills. The Court held more was needed, however, in order to conduct a strip search of a student:

> Here, the content of the suspicion failed to match the degree of intrusion. Wilson knew beforehand that the pills were prescription-strength ibuprofen and over-the-counter naproxen, common pain relievers equivalent to two Advil, or one Aleve. He must have been aware of the nature and limited threat of the specific drugs he was searching for, and while just about anything can be taken in quantities that will do real harm, Wilson had no reason to suspect that large amounts of the drugs were being passed around, or that individual students were receiving great numbers of pills.

> Nor could Wilson have suspected that Savana was hiding common painkillers in her underwear. Petitioners suggest, as a truth universally acknowledged, that "students ... hid[e] contraband in or under their clothing" and cite a smattering of cases of students with contraband in their underwear. But when the categorically extreme intrusiveness of a search down to the body of an adolescent requires some justification in suspected facts, general background possibilities fall short; a reasonable search that extensive calls for suspicion that it will pay off. But non-dangerous school contraband does not raise the specter of stashes in intimate places, and there is no evidence in the record of any general practice among Safford Middle School students of hiding that sort of thing in underwear; neither Jordan nor Marissa suggested to Wilson that Savana was doing that, and the preceding search of Marissa that Wilson ordered yielded nothing. Wilson never even determined when Marissa had received the pills from Savana; if it had been a few days before, that would weigh heavily against any reasonable conclusion that Savana presently had the pills on her person, much less in her underwear.

> In sum, what was missing from the suspected facts that pointed to Savana was any indication of danger to the students from the power of the drugs or their quantity, and any reason to suppose that Savana was carrying pills in her underwear. We think that the combination of these deficiencies was fatal to finding the search reasonable.

In recent years, an increasing number of states have considered proposals to drug test recipients of public benefits. *See*, A.G. Sulzberger, *States Adding Drug Test as Hurdle for Welfare*, N.Y. TIMES, Oct. 10, 2011. Though controversial, the idea of subjecting recipients of public benefits to suspicionless drug testing has caught on among some politicians who argue that it might save cash-strapped states money. In 2011, Florida Governor Rick Scott cited this rationale when he signed a law requiring welfare recipients pass an annual drug test to receive benefits. However, preliminary results from the state's first round of testing found the program is unlikely to save Florida any money. The results showed only 2 percent of welfare applicants had tested positive for drugs. Based on that number, Florida would keep approximately $32,200 to $48,200 that would otherwise have gone to rejected recipients. Because it costs Florida an estimated $28,800 to $43,200 every month to administer the drug tests, however, the law would save the state at most a negligible amount of money. *See* Catherine Whittenburg, *Welfare Drug-Testing Yields 2% Positive Results*, TAMPA TRIBUNE, Aug. 25, 2011; Jordan C. Budd, *Pledge Your Body for Your Bread: Welfare, Drug Testing, and the Inferior Fourth Amendment*, 19 WM. & MARY BILL OF RTS. J. 751 (2011) (arguing that "[c]onsidering the absence of any data to suggest that the incidence of drug abuse among the poor is appreciably greater than in the general population" the drug testing of welfare recipients "evidently seeks to vindicate little more than the familiar impulse to stigmatize and stereotype the impoverished").

Putting the policy wisdom of welfare drug testing programs aside, are they constitutional? Only one federal appellate court has addressed the issue. In 2002, a panel of the Sixth Circuit reversed a district court decision blocking a Michigan law to drug test recipients of state aid. The full court, sitting *en banc*, reversed the panel's decision by an equally divided vote in a four sentence order. *Marchwinski v. Howard*, 319 F.3d 258 (6th Cir. 2003). In October 2011, a federal district court judge granted a preliminary injunction blocking the implementation of Florida's public benefits testing law. *Lebron v. Welkins*, 820 F. Supp. 2d 1273, 1292 (M.D. Fla. 2011) (finding that the Plaintiff had shown a substantial likelihood of success on the merits because Florida "failed to demonstrate a special need for its suspicionless drug testing statute"). The case was still being litigated at the time this book went to press. *See also*, Jeffrey Widelitz, *Florida's Suspicionless Drug Testing of Welfare Applicants*, 36 NOVA L. REV. 253 (2011) (discussing Florida's drug resting law); Walker Newell, *Tax Dollars Earmarked for Drugs? The Policy and Constitutionality of Drug Testing Welfare Recipients*, 43 COLUM. HUM. RTS. L. REV. 215 (2011).

C. Other Constitutional Issues

1. Is There a "Drug Exception" to the Constitution?

Some commentators—and even some judges—have argued that courts have developed an implicit "drug exception" to the Constitution. *See, e.g.,* Steven Wisotsky, *Crackdown: The Emerging 'Drug Exception' to the Bill of Rights*, 38 HASTINGS L. J. 889 (1987). How, if at all, has the drug war impacted the scope of constitutional protections?

Drug Exceptionalism
Erik Luna
47 Villanova Law Review 753 (2002)

A particularly powerful illustration of both macro- and micro-level exceptionalism is provided by America's second war on drugs—the ongoing ban on the sale, possession and use of illegal narcotics. Like alcohol Prohibition, the modern drug war pits deeply held ideological values against one another: individualism, which would limit government interference with a person's choice to ingest a substance, versus moralism, which would demand state involvement to prevent self-destructive and anti-social behavior from unraveling the moral fabric of society. As was true at the height of the Temperance Movement, morality has won out over privacy and autonomy in society's current drug war. This is evidenced by, among other things, the very use of the term war — a state-sponsored metaphor intended to emphasize the seriousness of the underlying threat, as well as the righteous and unyielding efforts of government to enforce drug laws. "To endorse a war," Seymour Martin Lipset suggests in his book on exceptionalism, "Americans must define their role in a conflict as being on God's side against Satan — for morality, against evil." And in the war on drugs, God and the good society are with the prohibitionists.

Criminal procedure is independent of substantive criminal law, or so we are led to believe. On their face, the relevant constitutional provisions do not discriminate among the various categories of crime, as the texts specify general methods for administering justice rather than drawing lines between suspects entitled to procedural protections and those who receive process only as a matter of grace. Pickpockets and bank robbers alike are supposed to be informed of their *Miranda* warnings prior to custodial interrogation, while the ban on unreasonable searches and seizures is not subject to a "murder scene" exception. And for the most part, the courts have outwardly refused to incorporate a substantive variable into constitutional criminal procedure.

This substantive neutrality allegedly applies to narcotics offenses as well. "Those suspected of drug offenses," the Court has argued, "are no less entitled to [constitutional] protection than those suspected of non-drug offenses." Yet scholars and jurists have recognized that the Constitution seems to bend when the criminal procedure rights of drug offenders are at stake. They are accorded, for instance, lesser expectations of privacy in their homes, cars, personal effects and so on. What has emerged from the case law, as just mentioned, is drug exceptionalism in constitutional interpretation — although no majority opinion of any court in the land would dare admit as much.

As these scholars have noted, drug exceptionalism in judicial decisionmaking is wide-ranging and can be seen in a number of areas of constitutional jurisprudence, including the Court's interpretation of First Amendment religious freedom, the Sixth Amendment right to counsel, Eighth Amendment limitations on detention and punishment and the Fourteenth Amendment's guarantee of equal protection. Nonetheless, this [discussion] will focus on the "hors de combat of the government's so-called War on Drugs" — the Fourth Amendment.

Since its 1967 decision in *Katz v. United States*, the Supreme Court's search and seizure jurisprudence has been based on notions of privacy rather than property, holding that "the Fourth Amendment protects people, not places," and, in particular, expectations of privacy that society is prepared to consider reasonable. The *Katz* formula was clearly intended to provide individuals with a higher level of security against government surveillance, but in an ironic twist, the decision has frequently been used to constrict constitutional rights rather than expand them. As Fourth Amendment scholars have noted, "reasonableness" may well be the law's favorite weasel word, beyond hard definition, simple in application and sufficiently elastic to reach nearly any result. Nowhere does this seem more evident than in the Court's drug-related cases testing reasonable expectations of privacy.

Consider a series of decisions during the mid-to late-1980s on drug enforcement activities around private dwellings. Police can ignore "no trespassing" signs and jump over locked fences to sneak onto the property surrounding homes. They may snoop into the buildings adjacent to a residence, peering at whatever activity is occurring in private sheds or barns. Narcotics agents may parse through garbage bags to uncover what a citizen is doing in the privacy of his own home. And law enforcement may fly over houses in planes or helicopters, spying on an individual's otherwise private backyard activities. According to the Supreme Court, no reasonable expectation of privacy is implicated in any of these cases, meaning that such drug war-driven intrusions can be undertaken without judicial oversight and in the absence of a warrant or probable cause.

Each of these decisions appeared doctrinally and logically suspect. In the first case, *Oliver v. United States*, the Supreme Court decided that narcotics agents could ignore a "no trespassing" sign, enter onto a private farm and thereby violate state trespassing laws in search of marijuana—all without a warrant or probable cause. Dissenting Justice Thurgood Marshall and scholars such as Stephen Saltzburg dissected the majority's tortured reasoning on a number of fronts: The Court utilized a strict form of textualism that was impossible to square with nearly two decades of prior precedents and the majority's own holding; it misused the common law and stretched a sixty-year-old case to create a sweeping limitation on the Fourth Amendment, despite the fact that the hoary precedent likely did not survive Katz; the Court's analysis of land use and "our societal understanding" of constitutional protection demonstrated only conclusory, result-oriented reasoning; and it left undefined legally dispositive terms for future police searches while simultaneously rejecting a case-by-case approach as too ambiguous for law enforcement.

The apparent distortion of Fourth Amendment doctrine is further demonstrated by a pair of Supreme Court decisions on the search and seizure rights of houseguests. In *Minnesota v. Olson*, the police entered the home where a suspected robber and murderer had been spending the night as a guest and arrested him without a warrant or any exigency. In *Minnesota v. Carter*, a police officer peered through a small gap in an apartment's drawn window blind and witnessed the resident bagging up cocaine with her house guests. Despite the fact that in both cases the defendants were neither the homeowners nor long-term occupants but instead were solely present with the permission of their respective hosts, only the robber-murderer maintained a legitimate expectation of privacy that had been violated by the state. According to the Carter Court, the drug dealers had no Fourth Amendment protection because they were engaged in a "purely commercial" transaction, were in the home for a relatively short period of time and had no previous association with the resident.

As with *Oliver* and its descendants, Carter presents a troubled opinion. The case largely ignores the special solicitude given to private dwellings, while, in turn, encouraging law enforcement to bust into homes on the chance that someone inside is not an overnight guest. The decision also seems doctrinally jarring when placed along side prior case law: Apparently, an individual has greater Fourth Amendment protection when executing a business deal by public phone (for example, placing an illegal bet in *Katz*) than when performing a commercial transaction in a residence (bagging up drugs in *Carter*).

2. Drug Policy and the First Amendment

The Second Casualty of War: Civil Liberties and the War on Drugs
Paul Finkelman
66 Southern California Law Review 1389 (1993)

There is an old saying that truth is the first casualty of war. In the United States it seems safe to add that the Bill of Rights is the second casualty of war. In most of our wars the Bill of Rights has suffered as individual liberties were subordinated to the needs of "national security." This seems to be true as well in the war on drugs.

Law enforcement activities, government policies, legislative innovations, and court decisions related to the drug war threaten to diminish the First, Fourth, Fifth, Sixth, Seventh, and Eighth Amendments of the Constitution. Depending on how one understands the meaning of the Second and Ninth amendments, they too are under assault. More importantly, the very philosophy behind the Bill of Rights is in danger.

At first glance it would seem that the First Amendment has been untouched by the war on drugs. Unlike in other wars, there seem to be no limitations on the free speech of those who oppose this war. Sessions at a national meeting of academics—and entire academic conferences—criticizing the war on drugs seem to attest that our free speech has not been harmed by this war. It is unlikely that comparable sessions and conferences decrying American involvement in World War I would have been possible after April, 1917. Similarly, only the bravest of academics dared speak out against McCarthyism at its peak.

Despite the ability of scholars, politicians, judges, lawyers, and scientists to speak out against current drug policy, the war on drugs has led to the suppression of ideas and speech. It has also led to a contraction of religious liberty.

In 1990 High Times, a monthly magazine with a circulation of about 250,000, was under investigation by federal prosecutors. High Times is one of the nation's few magazines devoted to the legalization of marijuana, and editors there believed the government was trying to silence their investigative reports on the value of marijuana and hemp. The executive director of the Reporters Committee for Freedom of the Press noted at the time that "this is the first instance ... where the war on drugs has been directed at a publishing organization ... where it has gone right into the newsroom."

In May 1990 High Times sought to quash grand jury subpoenas issued to its editors. The motion to quash noted that the manner in which the United States Attorney in New Orleans issued the subpoenas violated Justice Department regulations on investigation of the press. The motion argued that "by intimidating High Times advertisers and subscribers the government is attempting to exercise unlawful prior restraint and self-censorship by intimidation" and that "the forms of harassment currently being applied towards High Times magazine have a substantial effect on its ability to disseminate information to the public."

Canada, with its weak protection of a free press, already prohibits the sale of High Times. In the United States an outright ban of the magazine would probably not withstand a court challenge. But law enforcement officials at the state and federal level have found other, less reviewable, ways to suppress the magazine. A Montana police chief has tried to convince newsstands not to carry High Times. Such behavior by a high ranking public official is bound to have a chilling effect on the First Amendment. This sort of pressure borders on a new form of seditious libel. The Montana police chief argued, "The point of the magazine is, "Hey, let's make pot legal.'" In other words, at least some police officials are interested in suppressing the magazine because it promotes ideas which undermine the war effort against drugs and challenge the scientific and cultural basis for the war itself.

Besides articles on drugs, the magazine contains discussions of politics, music, and culture. The government pressure on the magazine thus threatens a broad range of expression. While a Montana police chief honestly says he would ban High Times because it advocates legalizing marijuana, the federal government's crusade against the magazine is more shrewd, and is couched in terms that do not focus on the ideas for which the magazine stands. Federal officials claim that High Times is part of a national conspiracy to distribute drugs. The federal prosecutors claim that their subpoenas are "demands for purely commercial or financial information unrelated to the news-gathering function." The government is arguing that High Times has violated the law by running advertisements for a Dutch seed catalogue which sells marijuana seeds. The government does not allege that High Times has advertised to sell the seeds themselves, but only that the magazine has printed advertisements for catalogues from the Dutch company that sells the seeds. It is worth noting that in Holland it is not illegal to possess or sell marijuana seeds. Because the magazine's advertisers sell drug paraphernalia, equipment to grow indoor plants, and marijuana seeds, federal prosecutors claim that the magazine may be a "continuing criminal enterprise," a status which would subject it to the severe penalties of the federal RICO statute.

The DEA and state authorities have also raided numerous stores and mail-order houses which sell horticultural equipment because these businesses have advertised in High Times. The agents have confiscated business records in an attempt to discover who is growing marijuana in their homes. In one case, police officials from the North Carolina State Bureau of Investigation conducted a warrantless search on a man's home because he had ordered three light meters from a firm which advertised in High Times. The man grew orchids.

The raids on advertisers and consumers of perfectly legal products raise serious questions about the protection of a free press. Harassing a magazine's advertisers is an effective form of censorship. After raids on businesses that advertised in High Times in October 1989, the magazine initially lost two-thirds of its advertisers. Over a six month period following the raids the magazine's total advertising revenue dropped by a third. If this type of government behavior continues the magazine may be forced out of business.

Drying up a source of talent in journalism is a second way drug warriors can silence a magazine that they find annoying. As part of its investigation, federal prosecutors have also asked for the names, addresses, and phone numbers of every "current and past" employee of the magazine. Such an investigation is likely to intimidate any current or potential High Times employee.

––––––––––

In 2007, the Supreme Court appeared to establish a free speech exception for some drug-related speech in public schools. In *Morse v. Frederick*, Juneau, Alaska high school senior Joseph Frederick unfurled a 14-foot banner emblazoned with the inscrutable phrase "BONG HiTS 4 JESUS" at a school event connected with the 2002 Olympic Torch Relay. The school's principle, Deborah Morse, "told Frederick to take the banner down because she thought it encouraged illegal drug use" in violation of a Juneau School Board Policy prohibiting "any assembly or public expression that ... advocates the use of substances that are illegal to minors[.]" Frederick refused and he was ultimately suspended from school for 10 days. Frederick sued the school board, alleging that his First Amendment rights had been violated. Five members of the Supreme Court disagreed, holding that " '[t]he special characteristics of the school environment' and the governmental interest in stopping student drug abuse ... allows schools to restrict student expression that they reasonably regard as promoting illegal drug use." Justices Alito and Kennedy filed a concurrence to caution that they joined the majority opinion "on the understanding that ... it provides no support for any restriction of speech that can plausibly be interpreted as commenting on a political or social issue, including speech on issues such as 'the wisdom of the war on drugs or of legalizing marijuana for medicinal use." *Morse v. Frederick*, 551 U.S. 393 (2007). Is this distinction tenable? Isn't a statement in favor of marijuana use also, by implication, a statement against marijuana prohibition? How would statements that contain both explicitly political and pro-drug use messages be treated? For example, would *Morse* allow a public school to ban a t-shirt in favor of a marijuana legalization ballot measure if it read: "Vote Yes on Measure X because marijuana is fun to use"?

Writing in dissent in *Morse*, Justice Stevens worried that the majority's holding will permit "the censorship of any student speech that mentions drugs, at least so long as someone could perceive that speech to contain a latent pro-drug message." He argued that "it would be profoundly unwise to create special rules for speech about drug and alcohol use," citing his personal recollection from the era of alcohol prohibition. "[T]he current dominant opinion supporting the war on drugs in general, and our antimarijuana laws in particular, is reminiscent of the opinion that supported the nationwide ban on alcohol consumption when I was a student. While alcoholic beverages are now regarded as ordinary articles of commerce, their use was then condemned with the same moral fervor that now supports the war on drugs.... But just as prohibition in the 1920s and early 1930s was secretly questioned by thousands of otherwise law-abiding patrons of bootleggers and speakeasies, today the actions of literally millions of otherwise law-abiding users of marijuana, and the majority of voters in each of the several States that tolerate medicinal uses of the product, lead me to wonder whether the fear of disapproval by those in the majority is silencing opponents of the war on drugs. Surely our national experience with alcohol should make us wary of dampening speech suggesting — however inarticulately — that it would be better to tax and regulate marijuana than to persevere in a futile effort to ban its use entirely." *Id.* (Stevens, J., dissenting). For more on *Morse v. Frederick*, see JAMES C. FOSTER, BONG HITS 4 JESUS: A PERFECT CONSTITUTIONAL STORM IN ALASKA'S CAPITAL (2010).

Allegations of government censorship of statements in favor of drug policy reform have also recently emerged in the law enforcement setting. In late 2011, for example, former Border Patrol agent Bryan Gonzalez said he was fired after remarking to a fellow agent that "[i]f marijuana were legalized ... the drug-related violence across the border in Mexico would cease" and continuing on to discuss "an organization called Law Enforcement Against Prohibition that favors ending the war on drugs.... After an investigation, a termination letter arrived that said Mr. Gonzalez held 'personal views that were contrary to the core characteristics of Border Patrol Agents, which are patriotism, dedication and esprit de corps.'" Marc Lacey, *Police Officers Find That Dissent on Drug Laws May Come With a Price*, N.Y. TIMES, Dec. 3, 2011 at A11.

In addition to cases concerning speech rights, a number of individuals have attempted to bring First Amendment challenges to drug laws based on freedom of religion. Courts have nearly universally rejected these challenges, finding drug laws may be constitutionally applied to religious users because the burden on religion is "merely the incidental effect of a generally applicable and otherwise valid" law and not the object of the law. *See Employment Division v. Smith*, 494 U.S. 872, 878 (1990). Though the First Amendment does not grant a religious exception to generally applicable drug laws, the Religious Freedom Restoration Act of 1993 (RFRA) provides statutory protection to religiously motivated activities beyond what is constitutionally required. In *Gonzales v. O Centro Espirita Beneficente Uniao Do Vegetal*, 546 U.S. 418 (2006), the United States Supreme Court applied RFRA in the context of the religious use of a hallucinogenic controlled substance.

Gonzales v. O Centro Espirita Beneficente Uniao Do Vegetal

Supreme Court of the United States

546 U.S. 418 (2006)

Chief Justice Roberts delivered the opinion of the Court.

In *Employment Div., Dept. of Human Resources of Ore. v. Smith,* 494 U.S. 872 (1990), this Court held that the Free Exercise Clause of the First Amendment does not prohibit governments from burdening religious practices through generally applicable laws. In *Smith,* we rejected a challenge to an Oregon statute that denied unemployment benefits to drug users, including Native Americans engaged in the sacramental use of peyote. In so doing, we rejected the interpretation of the Free Exercise Clause announced in *Sherbert v. Verner,* 374 U.S. 398 (1963), and, in accord with earlier cases held that the Constitution does not require judges to engage in a case-by-case assessment of the religious burdens imposed by facially constitutional laws.

Congress responded by enacting the Religious Freedom Restoration Act of 1993 (RFRA), which adopts a statutory rule comparable to the constitutional rule rejected in *Smith.* Under RFRA, the Federal Government may not, as a statutory matter, substantially burden a person's exercise of religion, "even if the burden results from a rule of general applicability." § 2000bb-1(a). The only exception recognized by the statute requires the Government to satisfy the compelling interest test—to "demonstrate that application of the burden to the person—(1) is in furtherance of a compelling governmental interest; and (2) is the least restrictive means of furthering that compelling governmental interest." A person whose religious practices are burdened in violation of RFRA "may assert that violation as a claim or defense in a judicial proceeding and obtain appropriate relief."

The Controlled Substances Act regulates the importation, manufacture, distribution, and use of psychotropic substances. The Act classifies substances into five schedules based on their potential for abuse, the extent to which they have an accepted medical use, and their safety. Substances listed in Schedule I of the Act are subject to the most comprehensive restrictions, including an outright ban on all importation and use, except pursuant to strictly regulated research projects. The Act authorizes the imposition of a criminal sentence for simple possession of Schedule I substances and mandates the imposition of a criminal sentence for possession "with intent to manufacture, distribute, or dispense" such substances.

O Centro Espirita Beneficente Uniao do Vegetal (UDV) is a Christian Spiritist sect based in Brazil, with an American branch of approximately 130 individuals. Central to the UDV's faith is receiving communion through *hoasca* (pronounced "wass-ca"), a sacramental tea made from two plants unique to the Amazon region. One of the plants, *psychotria viridis,* contains dimethyltryptamine (DMT), a hallucinogen whose effects are enhanced by alkaloids from the other plant, *banisteriopsis caapi.* DMT, as well as "any material, compound, mixture, or preparation, which contains any quantity of [DMT]," is listed in Schedule I of the Controlled Substances Act.

In 1999, United States Customs inspectors intercepted a shipment to the American UDV containing three drums of *hoasca.* A subsequent investigation revealed that the UDV had received 14 prior shipments of *hoasca.* The inspectors seized the intercepted shipment and threatened the UDV with prosecution.

The UDV filed suit against the Attorney General and other federal law enforcement officials, seeking declaratory and injunctive relief. The complaint alleged that applying the Controlled Substances Act to the UDV's sacramental use of *hoasca* violates RFRA.

The Government contends that the Act's description of Schedule I substances as having "a high potential for abuse," "no currently accepted medical use in treatment in the United States," and "a lack of accepted safety for use ... under medical supervision," by itself precludes any consideration of individualized exceptions such as that sought by the UDV. The Government goes on to argue that the regulatory regime established by the Act—a "closed" system that prohibits all use of controlled substances except as authorized by the Act itself—"cannot function with its necessary rigor and comprehensiveness if subjected to judicial exemptions." According to the Government, there would be no way to cabin religious exceptions once recognized, and "the public will misread" such exceptions as signaling that the substance at issue is not harmful after all. Under the Government's view, there is no need to assess the particulars of the UDV's use or weigh the impact of an exemption for that specific use, because the Controlled Substances Act serves a compelling purpose and simply admits of no exceptions.

RFRA, and the strict scrutiny test it adopted, contemplate an inquiry more focused than the Government's categorical approach. RFRA requires the Government to demonstrate that the compelling interest test is satisfied through application of the challenged law "to the person"—the particular claimant whose sincere exercise of religion is being substantially burdened.

Under the more focused inquiry required by RFRA and the compelling interest test, the Government's mere invocation of the general characteristics of Schedule I substances, as set forth in the Controlled Substances Act, cannot carry the day. It is true, of course, that Schedule I substances such as DMT are exceptionally dangerous. Nevertheless, there is no indication that Congress, in classifying DMT, considered the harms posed by the particular use at issue here—the circumscribed, sacramental use of *hoasca* by the UDV. Congress' determination that DMT should be listed under *Schedule I* simply does not provide a categorical answer that relieves the Government of the obligation to shoulder its burden under RFRA.

This conclusion is reinforced by the Controlled Substances Act itself. The Act contains a provision authorizing the Attorney General to "waive the requirement for registration of certain manufacturers, distributors, or dispensers if he finds it consistent with the public health and safety." 21 U.S.C. §822(d). The fact that the Act itself contemplates that exempting certain people from its requirements would be "consistent with the public health and safety" indicates that congressional findings with respect to Schedule I substances should not carry the determinative weight, for RFRA purposes, that the Government would ascribe to them.

And in fact an exception has been made to the Schedule I ban for religious use. For the past 35 years, there has been a regulatory exemption for use of peyote—a Schedule I substance—by the Native American Church. In 1994, Congress extended that exemption to all members of every recognized Indian Tribe. Everything the Government says about the DMT in *hoasca*—that, as a *Schedule I* substance, Congress has determined that it "has a high potential for abuse," "has no currently accepted medical use," and has "a lack of accepted safety for use ... under medical supervision"—applies in equal measure to the mescaline in peyote, yet both the Executive and Congress itself have decreed an exception from the Controlled Substances Act for Native American religious use of peyote. If such use is permitted in the face of the congressional findings in §812(b)(1) for hundreds of thousands of Native Americans practicing their faith, it is difficult to see how those same findings alone can preclude any consideration of a similar exception for the 130 or so American members of the UDV who want to practice theirs.

The Government argues that the existence of a *congressional* exemption for peyote does not indicate that the Controlled Substances Act is amenable to *judicially crafted* exceptions. RFRA, however, plainly contemplates that *courts* would recognize exceptions— that is how the law works. See 42 U.S.C. § 2000bb-1(c) ("A person whose religious exercise has been burdened in violation of this section may assert that violation as a claim or defense in a judicial proceeding and obtain appropriate relief against a government").

We do not doubt that there may be instances in which a need for uniformity precludes the recognition of exceptions to generally applicable laws under RFRA. But it would have been surprising to find that this was such a case, given the longstanding exemption from the Controlled Substances Act for religious use of peyote, and the fact that the very reason Congress enacted RFRA was to respond to a decision denying a claimed right to sacramental use of a controlled substance. And in fact the Government has not offered evidence demonstrating that granting the UDV an exemption would cause the kind of administrative harm recognized as a compelling interest in [other cases]. The Government failed to convince the District Court at the preliminary injunction hearing that health or diversion concerns provide a compelling interest in banning the UDV's sacramental use of *hoasca*. It cannot compensate for that failure now with the bold argument that there can be no RFRA exceptions at all to the Controlled Substances Act.

We have no cause to pretend that the task assigned by Congress to the courts under RFRA is an easy one. Indeed, the very sort of difficulties highlighted by the Government here were cited by this Court in deciding that the approach later mandated by Congress under RFRA was not required as a matter of constitutional law under the Free Exercise Clause. But Congress has determined that courts should strike sensible balances, pursuant to a compelling interest test that requires the Government to address the particular practice at issue. Applying that test, we conclude that the courts below did not err in determining that the Government failed to demonstrate, at the preliminary injunction stage, a compelling interest in barring the UDV's sacramental use of *hoasca*.

Part III

Chapter 6

The Controlled Substances Act

A. The Controlled Substances Act: Overview and Constitutionality

The previous chapters have focused on the criminalization of controlled substances, examining the wisdom of prohibition, the elements of a variety of controlled substances offenses, sentencing of drug offenders and the investigation of drug crimes. The foundation for these criminal laws is a complex regulatory scheme that raises a range of policy questions and legal issues in its own right.

The federal Controlled Substances Act of 1970 (CSA), which is administered primarily by the Drug Enforcement Administration (DEA), aims to provide a comprehensive and uniform structure for classifying drugs of abuse and regulating their manufacture, distribution, and use in medical studies. Under the CSA, controlled substances are divided into five "schedules" based on their potential for abuse, medicinal value, and addictiveness. The following chart illustrates the factors for each of the five schedules.

Classification under the Controlled Substances Act, 21 U.S.C. §812(b)

	Abuse Potential	Medical Use	Safety and Dependence
Schedule I	High potential for abuse	No currently accepted medical use	Lack of accepted safety for use under medical supervision
Schedule II	High potential for abuse	Has a currently accepted medical use	Abuse may lead to severe dependence
Schedule III	Potential for abuse less than Schedules I and II	Has a currently accepted medical use	Abuse may lead to moderate or low physical dependence or high psychological dependence
Schedule IV	Low potential for abuse relative to Schedule III	Has a currently accepted medical use	Abuse may lead to limited dependence relative to Schedule III
Schedule V	Low potential for abuse relative to Schedule IV	Has a currently accepted medical use	Abuse may lead to limited dependence relative to Schedule IV

Looking over the chart, can you spot any regulatory gaps? How would a substance determined to have a "low potential for abuse" relative to the substances in Schedules I and II but "no currently medical use" be classified under this scheme?

The federal Controlled Substances Act only governs the classification and control of drugs under federal law. States are free to adopt their own regulatory schemes for controlled substances, just as they have the authority to make their own determinations on the definition drug crimes and sentencing of drug offenders. Over the past decade and a half, for example, some states have enacted medical marijuana laws notwithstanding the federal CSA's characterization of the substance as one without a currently accepted medical use.

By and large, however, the state regulatory structure governing controlled substances mirrors federal law. This is because of the Uniform Controlled Substances Act (UCSA), which was originally drafted in 1970 by the National Conference of Commissioners on Uniform State Laws. The UCSA was designed to maintain consistency between state and federal law and the Commissioners have promulgated revisions to the UCSA in 1990 and 1994 to account for changes in federal law. The vast majority of states have adopted a version of the UCSA, as has the District of Columbia, Puerto Rico, and the Virgin Islands. While the UCSA serves as the foundation for controlled substances laws across the country, each state has modified the UCSA in various ways. For example, while many states follow the UCSA in making distribution and possession with the intent to distribute a crime, others criminalize "sale" or possession for "sale." *See* Elaine M. Chiu, *The Challenge of Motive in the Criminal Law*, 8 Buff. Crim. L. R. 653, 699–700 (2005). The UCSA has intentionally left some issues to the discretion of the states. Perhaps most notably, the UCSA does not prescribe specific sentences for drug offenders. As a result, sentences between states for the same offense can vary widely. *See, e.g.,* Michael M. O'Hear, *National Uniformity/Local Uniformity: Reconsidering the Use of Departures to Reduce Federal-State Sentencing Disparities*, 87 Iowa L. Rev. 721, 749 (2002) ("A cocaine dealer, for instance, is subject to a two to four year term in California state court, but faces a minimum of five years and a maximum of life in Oklahoma."). And, of course, local court practices might lead a criminal case to "progress quite differently depending on the jurisdiction" even if the law on the books is similar. *See, e.g.,* Jenny Roberts, *Why Misdemeanors Matter: Effective Advocacy in the Lower Criminal Courts*, 45 U.C. Davis L. Rev. 277, 349–50 (2011) (describing how a hypothetical misdemeanor drug possession case would proceed in three different jurisdictions).

With respect to the classification of controlled substances, the UCSA has been especially influential. The UCSA is built around the same five-schedule structure as the federal CSA, classifying substances on the basis of their potential for abuse (and addiction) and usefulness in medical treatment. But, because the classification of substances under the CSA and UCSA changes over time based on federal and state administrative action, uniformity in the classification scheme does not always translate into uniformity as to whether a specific substance has been scheduled (and, if so, which schedule it falls under) at any given time. *See, e.g., Ruiz-Vidal v. Gonzales*, 473 F.3d 1072, 1078 (9th Cir. 2007) ("We note that California law regulates the possession and sale of numerous substances that are not regulated by the CSA. For instance, the possession of apomorphine is specifically excluded from Schedule II of the CSA, but California's Schedule II specifically includes it."); *California v. Davis*, 200 Cal. App. 4th 205 (2011) (acknowledging that MDMA is not named as a controlled substance under California law but upholding an MDMA conviction on the theory that MDMA "contains some quantity of methamphetamine or amphetamine").

To account for this problem, the UCSA provides for a "short-form" scheduling process in addition to the standard scheduling procedure. The short form method allows states to incorporate scheduling decisions under the federal CSA into their own regulatory scheme in a streamlined fashion. A number of state courts have struck down this aspect of the UCSA, however, on the grounds that their legislatures cannot delegate "legislative power to a federal agency, nor to Congress." *Louisiana v. Rodriguez*, 379 So. 2d 1084, 1087 (1980). *See also*, F. Scott Boyd, *Looking Glass Law: Legislative Reference in the States*, 68 La. L. Rev. 1201, 1267–69 (describing the split between states that have upheld this aspect of the UCSA and those that have struck it down); Richard L. Braun, *Uniform Controlled Substances Act of 1990*, 13 Campbell L. Rev. 365, 368 (1990) (noting that some states "even prohibit delegation to *state* administrative agencies of the power to add to or delete from statutorily created schedules"). As a result, the process for scheduling or rescheduling a substance can vary from state to state. But the UCSA's substantive criteria for scheduling decisions and the five-schedule classification scheme are followed in almost every state.

Because the essential regulatory features of state controlled substances laws and the federal CSA are so similar, this book does not consider the state classification of controlled substances separately, with the exception of areas where some states have taken a dramatically different approach than the federal government such as medical marijuana. This Chapter focuses on the federal CSA with the understanding that in most states the law is likely to be substantially similar to the CSA.

Though the CSA is primarily responsible for the classification and regulation of illegal recreational drugs, there are a number of other statutes and agencies that regulate medications and legal recreational drugs (like tobacco and alcohol). The excerpt below provides additional insight into drug regulation generally and raises questions about whether the CSA achieves its stated goals of consistently classifying drugs of abuse based on science or whether non-scientific factors motivate how the law regulates drugs.

Making Sense of Drug Regulation:
A Theory of Law for Drug Control Policy
Kimani Paul-Emile

19 Cornell Journal of Law and Public Policy 691 (2010)

The United States is a nation of drug users. The prevalence of drug use in the United States is astounding: from senior citizens who receive Medicare coverage, the largest group of drug users, to people convicted of drug offenses, who constitute a substantial portion of the state and federal prison populace. Today, drugs are consumed by members of nearly every segment of society and affect every aspect of modern life. Due to the sheer ubiquity of drug use today, many Americans may feel confident that they have a reasonable understanding of how drugs are, or should be, regulated. Readers may imagine that in a liberal democratic society, drugs are regulated according to scientific or medical evidence regarding their dangers and benefits.

In fact, however, drug regulatory decision-making in the United States over the past 150 years has often borne very little relationship to science. Many drugs are regulated in ways that belie scientific or medical evidence regarding their pharmacological characteristics. Tobacco products, for example, are the leading cause of preventable death in the United States, yet they can be bought and sold legally by adults, while marijuana—a significantly safer substance—is a Schedule I controlled drug and its use is therefore strictly prohibited. Similarly, although all forms of cocaine share the same active ingredients and produce the same psychotropic effects, simple possession of one particular form of cocaine—crack—renders one subject to some of the most severe sanctions available for any drug. Anabolic steroids are controlled substances; however, their distribution to some people seeking to enhance virility (particularly elderly men) is permissible, while sale to other healthy people seeking the same effects is not.

The health effects of drug use do not appear to determine how a particular drug will be regulated. And this raises two questions: how are regulators able to treat drugs differently, irrespective of the dangers they may pose, and what processes do they follow to achieve this phenomenon? The state, at all levels of government, has at its disposal many regulatory mechanisms to control drug production, consumption and sale, including: drug scheduling by the U.S. Drug Enforcement Administration (DEA); imposition of state criminal and civil laws and penalties; market-based strategies, such as production subsidies and taxation; and the U.S. Food and Drug Administration (FDA) drug approval process and corresponding intellectual property laws, among others. The choice among these various mechanisms, however, has often not been based on empirical evidence grounded in science or medicine. Although some drugs carry substantial health risks and others do not, the amount of risk posed is not accurately reflected in the regulatory processes selected to govern each drug. Equally confounding is the fact that the use of these divergent regulatory mechanisms does not appear to have arisen from one overarching goal; nor is it based upon universal principles of public health or even a unified moral or ethical ideal.

This Article posits a model for making sense of this dissonance. Although much has been written on the topic of licit and illicit drug regulation, none of the scholarship in this vast literature has attempted to explain through an examination of pharmaceutical, illicit, and over-the-counter drugs how the apparent inconsistencies and incoherence of the U.S. system of drug control have been achieved and sustained. This Article fills the gap in this literature by proposing an innovative and comprehensive theoretical model for understanding how drugs become "medicalized," "criminalized," or deemed appropriate for recreational use, irrespective of any danger the drugs may pose.

The analytical framework this Article proposes, the "Regulatory Regime/Norms" model, posits that drugs begin as blank slates onto which meaning is conferred. Prior to regulatory intervention, the way any particular drug is perceived or understood is indeterminate and amorphous. As a result, the project of regulating drugs is about allocating specific meaning and significance to a drug in order to prompt individuals to think about the drug in a way that allows for state intervention. This is accomplished by regulatory regimes.

The Regulatory Regime/Norms model identifies three primary regulatory regimes used to control drug consumption and sale: the market regime, public health regime, and criminal regime. Each regime creates and reinforces specific norms with respect to the drugs it regulates: moral norms in the criminal regime, disclosure norms in the public health regime, and assumption of risk and rational choice norms in the market regime. These norms shape public understanding of drugs and the regulatory enterprise undertaken by the regime.

Broadly defined, a drug is a substance other than food that, when absorbed into the body of a living organism, affects the structure or function of the body. Virtually every society and culture in human history has embraced the use of some sort of drug and developed norms governing its consumption. Only the early inhabitants of arctic climates lacked indigenous drugs due to the inhospitable nature of their environment, which did not allow for the cultivation of such substances. Once introduced by outside groups, however, drugs were readily adopted into these cultures. The types of substances consumed and their effects are as varied as the cultures that use them. Some drugs are taken to cure or ameliorate the symptoms of a disease or illness, while others, such as opiates and cannabis, are taken to relieve pain. There are drugs like coffee, tobacco, coca, tea, and khat that are taken for their stimulant effects. Still other drugs induce relaxation, provoke aggression, remove inhibitions, relieve tension, arouse or suppress the libido, or alter one's temporal experience. While some drugs are taken to help people cope with depression, hardship or tragedy, others are consumed simply as recreational activity to ameliorate the monotony of daily life. Psychotropic plants—organic substances that have the capacity to change the way one experiences time and space—are almost universally the most heavily regulated.

In order to address the prevalence of drug use, government—at the federal, state and local levels—promulgates and enforces laws to control production, consumption, and sale. Thus, today, individuals of all income levels, from rural, suburban, and urban areas, and from virtually every age, racial, and ethnic group are subject to a dizzying array of drug laws and regulations. These drug control measures differ in many critical respects, as do their social and demographic effects; from the highly touted "war on drugs" and the increased policing of tobacco use in public spaces, to regulations that have allowed for the unprecedented proliferation of prescription drugs.

The state justifies these laws as efforts to protect personal and public health, and to curb the social disorganization that may result from unregulated drug use. The specific aims and regulatory mechanisms used by the policy-making bodies that are granted jurisdiction over drug use differ sharply; from the lofty stated goals of the FDA to the punitive powers of the DEA. For example, one regulatory mechanism is drug scheduling. Pursuant to the Controlled Substances Act, the DEA and FDA administer five categories or "schedules" established to classify controlled substances according to their potential for abuse, therapeutic value, and possible addictiveness. Schedule I is the most restrictive classification and includes drugs such as heroin, LSD, and marijuana; while Schedule V is the least restrictive and includes codeine, a commonly prescribed painkiller. The drug regulations enacted according to these schedules are enforced by the DEA.

Another mechanism for drug control is the FDA drug approval process, which involves drug research, testing, and clinical trials undertaken by scientists, including academic researchers who often work in concert with the pharmaceutical companies that will ultimately manufacture and market the drug. Patent and intellectual property laws create financial incentives for innovation.

Other regulatory mechanisms are: state criminal laws and penalties; production subsidies that allow government to encourage the cultivation of certain drugs; regulation that occurs at the point of sale, such as age restrictions on the sale of alcohol and nicotine; taxation that allows the government to discourage, or levy a cost on, certain types of drug use; and the dictates of private associations as with anabolic steroids. An additional regulatory mechanism is litigation, which has increasingly become a dominant means by which drug use, production, and distribution are regulated, particularly when policy-makers are unwilling or unable to act legislatively. Finally, there is the option to not regulate, thereby leaving the issue to be resolved by market forces.

Before the government may regulate drugs or engage in any significant intervention into people's private affairs, it needs legitimating circumstances or a stated justification, such as a show of harm or a substantial state interest. While the specific types of "threats" that drug regulators deem in need of remedy have differed over time, the most often stated justifications for intervention are harm to self, harm to others, and moral and ethical concerns.

These broad justifications tend to revolve around a few common themes, principally: ensuring the safety and efficacy of commercially manufactured pharmaceutical drugs; protecting children from the direct or indirect effects of drug use; fighting addiction; and reducing the secondary effects of drug use, such as criminal activity. The underlying rationale is that the government can properly intervene when (1) vulnerable populations that may be limited in their ability to make independent, rational decisions about drug use are at risk, such as children; (2) individuals infringe upon the rights and freedoms of others, such as those who engage in secondary criminal activity, etc.; or (3) drug activity conflicts with state expectations about what constitutes appropriate, moral, responsible, and virtuous behavior. Thus, the state must demonstrate whom it is protecting and why. Once the rationale has been stated, the issue then becomes which regulatory regime is the most suitable: the criminal regime, the public health regime, or the market regulatory regime.

Drug regulatory regimes, as operative today, did not exist a century ago. They have taken shape over time and expanded their sphere of influence into areas of social life previously deemed "private" or beyond the proper reach of government. In so doing, they developed specific areas of specialization that enabled them to establish their legitimacy and command authority. Regulatory regimes have evolved into increasingly differentiated and autonomous systems. Each is comprised of specific actors and institutions. And each regime is largely distinct from the others and maintains its own logic, training, and language. Each is bound by its own rules, values, ethics, and culture; employs different regulatory methods; relies upon distinct forms of knowledge; embodies unique preferences, expectations, and commitments; and serves different, although occasionally overlapping, political, commercial, and governmental interests. Each produces discourses that articulate regime norms, philosophies, and agendas. These discourses are deployed strategically and persuasively by the actors who administer and enforce the different regimes. For example, phrases such as "war on drugs," "harm reduction," and "personal responsibility" are not only constitutive parts of the criminal, public health, and market regimes, respectively, but they also work to influence public perceptions of drugs and drug users. The operation of this complex internal matrix allows each regime to erect its own institutional barriers. Thus, while drug regulatory regimes remain sensitive to outside norms and pressures, each regime exhibits a self-referential closure that enables it to reproduce itself as a distinct entity.

The governing principles that structure each regime are assumption of risk and rational choice principles in the market regime, disclosure principles in the public health regime, and moral principles in the criminal regulatory regime.

Regulation through the market regime is the default position in a liberal, capitalist democratic society. Within this regime, drugs are understood as consumer goods that are normalized through advertising and the respectability of their distribution through over-the-counter sales. The lack of stigma associated with drugs regulated through this regime allows the users to be deemed rational consumers who have assumed the risks attendant to their drug use. This risk allocation, according to the market ethos, promotes efficiency by ensuring that the costs and burdens of drug use are borne by those best able to take appropriate measures to reduce injury. Tobacco, alcohol, and caffeine are examples of drugs governed primarily by the market regime.

Corporations are the primary players in this regime. Drug companies (e.g., tobacco, alcohol, etc.) are driven by the self-reinforcing need to maximize profits by increasing their share of the market of potential drug users through the creation of consumers and the generation of sales. Drug companies have become a formidable economic and political force, capable of thwarting most significant governmental attempts to intervene in the market regime to regulate drugs. This is due largely to the fact that the governing principles that structure the market regime reflect the orthodoxy of liberalism: the prevailing social arrangement of contemporary U.S. society. These corporate actors, therefore, work hard to frame their drugs in ways that resonate with the dominant principles of the market regime: rational choice and assumption of risk. This is accomplished primarily through advertising, which normalizes drug consumption by shaping popular understanding of certain drug use as normal, healthy, pleasurable and, indeed, necessary. Advertising is so critical to the operation of the market regulatory regime that corporations spend billions of dollars to carefully engineer advertisements for strategically targeted populations of potential consumers.

The so-called "free market," however, is by no means unfettered by government interference. Rather than reflecting a Hobbesian or natural state, the market is instead a socially conditioned and legally structured entity. It is the laissez-faire state that enforces liberal prescription in the market regime as government plays a much smaller role in this regime than in the others. Thus, many drugs in the market regime are subject to some, albeit minimal, regulation (e.g., alcohol and tobacco as opposed to caffeine or salvia divinorum, a powerful yet unregulated hallucinogen). Because the market regime is the original position in a liberal, capitalist, democratic society, regulators must justify their decisions to intervene in this regime.

The public health regulatory regime governs through science, which is more than just a metaphor; it is, rather, a specific and penetrating form of governance. From the FDA and National Institute on Drug Abuse to the Office of National Drug Control Policy and the National Institutes of Health, the missions of public health institutions and agencies with respect to drug regulation are vast, encompassing, broad-based efforts to: evaluate population health; prevent addiction, reduce the harms attendant to drug use (e.g., diseases passed through shared needles, etc.), assure the safety and efficacy of commercially manufactured drugs, evaluate the quality of and ensure access to drug treatment services, oversee and finance research, and encourage healthy behavior.

The institutes and actors that constitute the public health regime operate under principles of disclosure. These principles have emerged from the creation, evaluation, and dissemination of scientific knowledge, which requires an open, collaborative process, where transparency is paramount, and data is shared freely among those engaged in its research and evaluation. Disclosure, therefore, is essential to the fundamental authority of regulatory decision-making in the public health regime as this authority is based entirely upon the independence, accuracy, and integrity of the procedures and protocols used to arrive at medical, scientific, and public health policy conclusions.

Disclosure principles also enable the FDA to effectively evaluate drug safety and efficacy during all phases of the drug approval process including requiring commercial drug manufacturers to release research data on drug properties and possible negative side effects, in order to ensure that drugs function according to manufacturers' claims. The disclosure of such health data from drug makers is essential to enabling medical practitioners to make informed professional decisions affecting patient care and for consumers to select the appropriate drugs to address their health needs.

The criminal drug regulatory regime focuses on the investigation, interdiction, arrest, prosecution and incarceration of those involved with illicit drug consumption, distribution, trafficking, and manufacture with the goal of punishing those who have transgressed the boundaries of civilized society. In the criminal regulatory regime, drug regulation is not only a practice of government, a means of shaping conduct, and an exercise of power and authority; it is also an aspirational endeavor to the extent that it seeks to forge notions of whom and what we should be individually and collectively. Thus, for a drug to be moved from the market or public health regimes to the criminal regulatory regime, it must do more than pose an ostensible threat to public health or safety; use of the drug must be perceived to violate fundamental moral values.

The criminal regime creates and reinforces principles derived from moral prescriptives. In addition to its regulatory and juridical functions, the criminal regulatory regime creates and reaffirms the moral principles of the collective consciousness writ large. Understood as such, this type of regulation is preconditioned upon notions of morality; both in terms of how regulators influence values, behavior, and beliefs with regard to that which constitutes good, just, appropriate, and responsible behavior; as well as how individuals perceive and respond to government.

If a group is able to persuasively frame a drug in a way that is consonant with the norms of the regime that suits the group's preferences, then the drug may be placed in that regime, regardless of whether the designation decision is supported by empirical evidence grounded in science or medicine. For example, tobacco was regulated for over a century in the market regime because its manufacturers successfully used advertising to painstakingly shape the meaning of smoking to reflect the prevailing norms of the market regulatory regime: rational choice and assumption of risk.

Despite tobacco's undisputed negative health effects and staggeringly high mortality rate, the tobacco industry has effectively used advertising to portray tobacco consumption as synonymous with freedom, independence, masculinity, sophistication, and cosmopolitanism. This characterization shaped public opinion and drove public acceptance, which was reflected back and popularized through positive media representations of smokers as young, healthy, and attractive. The tobacco industry's success in framing the drug in a way that is consistent with market regime norms has enabled it to not only defeat numerous attempts to shift tobacco into the public health regime, but has made it the second most popular recreational drug in the United States after alcohol.

In the case of marijuana, by contrast, no corporation bankrolled the fight to keep the drug in the market regime, where marijuana had been widely available as a commonly used appetite stimulant, muscle relaxant, analgesic, hypnotic, and anticonvulsant. Instead, marijuana was moved to the criminal regulatory regime due to the success of a grassroots movement in the Southwestern United States to frame marijuana use in a way that resonated with the moral norms of the criminal regime. This movement, later joined by the Federal Bureau of Narcotics, and assisted by the media, successfully labeled marijuana in the public mind as "Mexican opium," a drug that turned Mexican field hands violent and high school students insane. Indeed, at the turn of the twentieth century, marijuana consumption in southwestern states was limited almost exclusively to the Mexican population, which was perceived by many in the region as posing an economic threat to the domestic labor force. Before long, racist and xenophobic fears about Mexican immigrants, fueled by claims of a causal relationship between marijuana and criminality, prompted southwestern states with large Mexican populations to begin passing legislation outlawing the drug. By 1937, forty-six states had passed such legislation, often with little debate.

Similarly, cocaine was a popular recreational and therapeutic drug found in everything from alcoholic beverages, cigarettes, cough suppressants, baby elixirs and, most famously, Coca-Cola, until Southern whites, during the early twentieth century, success-fully characterized cocaine as a drug that incited criminality, sexual deviance, and defi-ant behavior in African-Americans. This framing of cocaine in moral terms prompted its movement from the market regime to the criminal regulatory regime. So persuasive was this characterization of cocaine that in the ensuing hysteria, Southern police de-partments switched from .32 to .38 caliber bullets due to widespread reports that cocaine-endowed African-Americans with extraordinary cunning and strength thus rendering them virtually invincible to conventional weaponry. Despite whites' fears that cocaine would provoke an African-American-led revolt and crime spree, none ever materialized. Nevertheless, the fear that these myths and fantasies evoked was enough to ease the pas-sage of several laws restricting cocaine use, including the nation's first criminal drug con-trol law, the Harrison Act of 1914.

The regulation of anabolic androgenic steroids (AAS), a commercially manufactured pharmaceutical drug, is also illustrative of the Regulatory Regime/Norms Model. For nearly half a century, AAS had been classified as prescription drugs and the FDA had reg-ulated them in the public health regime. The sale of AAS for other than medicinal pur-poses, however, was criminalized with passage of the Anabolic Steroid Control Act of 1990, which added the drug to Schedule III of the Controlled Substances Act. AAS were not relegated to the criminal regime because of their alleged health effects or concerns about illicit trafficking. Rather, AAS were criminalized because of their place at the cen-ter of a cheating scandal at the 1988 Seoul Summer Olympic Games and the subsequent dramatic coverage of AAS use in a series of articles published in Sports Illustrated.

On November 18, 1988, scarcely a month after Canadian sprinter Ben Johnson was stripped of his Olympic gold medal having tested positive for AAS after beating Ameri-can rival Carl Lewis in a world record setting race, President Ronald Reagan signed into law the Anti-Drug Abuse Act of 1988. This law amended the Food, Drug, and Cosmet-ics Act by establishing a new criminal provision that significantly increased the penalties for AAS distribution.

Within months, Congress held a series of hearings on whether to add AAS to the sched-ule of controlled substances. At these hearings, scant evidence was presented that AAS use posed a significant threat to healthy adult men. Furthermore, just months before the 1988 Olympics, the Drug Enforcement Agency (DEA) and the U.S. Department of Health and Human Services (HHS) recommended against scheduling AAS. Legislators, never-theless, emerged victorious in their efforts to frame AAS to fit the moral norms of the criminal regime. The morally charged issue of cheating in sports had specific resonance in the criminal regulatory regime that was not present in the public health or market regimes. This enabled Congress to criminalize nonmedical AAS sales legislatively, over objections from the American Medical Association, FDA, and DEA. In so doing, Congress circumvented the forty-year-old administrative drug scheduling process and thereby set a drug regulatory precedent.

The Regulatory Regime/Norms model also explains passage of the historic Pure Food and Drug Act of 1906. Drugs sold prior to 1906 ran the gamut from well-intentioned but ineffective medicines to patently phony nostrums. The quality of these drugs was gener-ally unreliable and of questionable purity because many drugs, including "soothing syrups" for infants, contained inert substances and often some quantity of cocaine, opium, alco-hol, arsenic, mercury, or other narcotic, addictive, or lethal drug. Estimations at the time put the death toll from such drugs in the tens of thousands. Despite the obvious need for regulation, the ethos of the market regime was that it was up to the consumer to take ap-propriate precautions against adulterated and fake drugs. Thus, there was little protection for drug consumers because assumption of risk and rational choice principles dominated the market regime.

In 1905, however, those who championed drug control legislation — primarily women and physicians — successfully characterized the issue in a way that resonated with the norms of the public health regime. Rather than highlight the immorality of selling toxic, addictive, or lethal drugs — which would have moved dangerous drugs into the criminal regulatory regime — these reformers instead argued that the contents of hazardous drugs should be disclosed because individuals cannot make safe decisions about drug consumption if they are unaware of what is in their drugs. Pointing to high profile exposes of the drug industry to advance their claims, these reformers persuasively characterized the problem in a way that resonated with the disclosure norms of the nascent public health regime and, in so doing, forced passage of the Pure Food and Drug Act of 1906. The unprecedented legislation did not criminalize or ban the manufacture or sale of dangerous drugs, but rather centered public health concerns. The Act prohibited misrepresentation in drug labeling and mandated that manufacturers disclose the presence and amount of certain drugs, including alcohol, opium, cocaine, heroin, morphine, chloroform, or acetanilide, although it did not prohibit inclusion of such substances. Thus, although the Pure Food and Drug Act predated regulatory regimes as we know them today, by disrupting the norms of the market regime and characterizing drugs in a way that was consistent with the disclosure norms of the burgeoning public health regime, reformers were able to pave the way for passage of the first federal law to regulate drugs in the name of public health.

As we have seen with marijuana, cocaine, AAS, and the passage of the Pure Food and Drug Act, specific social events can create opportunities for those who engage in drug designation contests to succeed in characterizing a drug in a way that penetrates public thinking and makes regulatory regime changes possible. As the Regulatory Regime/Norms model makes clear, there is a contingency as to how a drug becomes vulnerable to the framing contests that lead to drug regulatory regime change. Anabolic steroids demonstrate this contingency. It is quite conceivable that had it not been for the Olympic cheating scandal, anabolic steroids could have become over-the-counter drugs regulated with age restrictions, much like tobacco and alcohol. Likewise, based on its broad social appeal, if marijuana were discovered today it might not be criminalized. Similarly, widely published exposes of the drug industry allowed drug regulation advocates, at the turn of the century, to focus public attention on their argument that drug makers should be required to disclose the contents of their drugs. However, these contingencies of historical context and physical place do not drive regulatory outcomes, but simply create opportunities for interested parties to characterize a drug in a way that shapes its popular understanding.

———————

Kimani Paul-Emile argues that drug classification in the United States cannot be explained solely, or even primarily, by objective markers grounded in science and medicine. In the following case, the National Organization for the Reform of Marijuana Laws argued the CSA's classification of marijuana as a Schedule I substance was so irrational that it should be declared unconstitutional. The court applied the familiar rational basis test to reject NORML's constitutional challenge. As a matter of constitutional law, the decision is unexceptional. The chief value of the case for purposes of studying the CSA is the policy questions it raises about how substances of abuse *should* be classified.

The National Organization for the Reform of Marijuana Laws (NORML) v. Bell

United States District Court for the District of Columbia
488 F. Supp. 123 (1980)

Tamm, J.

In this action, the National Organization for The Reform of Marijuana Laws (NORML or plaintiff) challenges the provisions of the Controlled Substances Act, 21 U.S.C. §§ 801–904 (CSA or Act), that prohibit the private possession and use of marijuana.

NORML filed this action October 10, 1973, seeking a declaratory judgment that the CSA and District of Columbia Uniform Narcotic Drug Act are unconstitutional in prohibiting the private possession and use of marijuana and requesting a permanent injunction enjoining enforcement of those statutes. This court stayed the proceedings for a year while NORML tried to obtain administrative relief through a proceeding to reclassify marijuana.[3] After the stay was vacated, the parties battled over preliminary motions for two years. Finally, in June 1978, this court heard five days of evidentiary hearings. Both sides presented live and documentary evidence concerning the effects of marijuana. Shortly thereafter, the parties submitted proposed findings of fact on the effects of marijuana and legal arguments for the court's consideration.

Congress passed the Comprehensive Drug Abuse Prevention and Control Act of 1970 (DAPCA), 21 U.S.C. §§ 801–966 (1976), to fight this nation's growing drug problem. The act was designed to "deal in a comprehensive fashion with the growing menace of drug abuse in the United States (1) through providing authority for increased efforts in drug abuse prevention and rehabilitation of users, (2) through providing more effective means for law enforcement aspects of drug abuse prevention and control, and (3) by providing for an overall balanced scheme of criminal penalties for offenses involving drugs." H.R. Rep. No. 1444, 91st Cong., 2d Sess. 1 (hereinafter cited as 1970 House Report). It ended the patchwork federal effort against drug abuse and signaled a national commitment to deal with this problem by committing federal funds for rehabilitation programs.[4]

In addition to the rehabilitation programs, DAPCA also revised completely the federal drug laws dealing with drug control.[5] Title II, called the Controlled Substances Act (CSA), establishes five schedules for classifying controlled substances according to specified cri-

---

3. On May 18, 1972, NORML filed an application with the Attorney General to remove marijuana from control under the CSA or, in the alternative, to reclassify the drug in a different schedule. This endeavor continues today. The Drug Enforcement Administration (DEA) twice rejected these efforts at reclassification, citing American treaty obligations under the Single Convention on Narcotic Drugs. The United States Court of Appeals for the District of Columbia Circuit reversed these determinations. *NORML v. DEA,* 559 F.2d 735 (D.C. Cir. 1977); *NORML v. Ingersoll,* 497 F.2d 654 (D.C. Cir. 1974). In the DEA case, the court directed the DEA to "refer the NORML petition to the Secretary of HEW for medical and scientific findings and recommendations for rescheduling, consistent with the requirements of the Single Convention." On remand the DEA again declined to reclassify marijuana. The Administrator of the DEA followed the recommendation of the Secretary of HEW that marijuana remain in Schedule I. NORML is appealing this ruling to the District of Columbia Circuit. NORML v. DEA, No. 79-1660 (D.C.Cir., filed June 27, 1979).

4. Title I of DAPCA deals with the rehabilitation of drug abusers and authorizes federal funds for treatment centers and drug abuse programs. Title II establishes controls and registration requirements for drugs, while Title III regulates the import and export of controlled substances.

5. Previous federal laws dealing with drug abuse included the Harrison Act, ch. 1, 38 Stat. 785 (1914) (repealed 1970), and the Marihuana Tax Act, ch. 553, 50 Stat. 551 (1937) (repealed 1970). For a discussion of federal efforts against drug abuse before passage of DAPCA, see Bonnie and White-

teria. Two criteria—the potential for abuse and the medical applications of a drug—are the major bases for classification, along with certain social and medical information. Congress, on the basis of information gathered from extensive hearings, made the initial classifications. Recognizing that scientific information concerning controlled substances would change, Congress empowered the Attorney General to hear petitions for the reclassification or removal of drugs from the schedules.

Marijuana (cannabis sativa L.) is a psychoactive drug made of the leaves, flowers, and stems the Indian Hemp plant. It derives its psychoactive properties from delta-9-tetrahydrocannabinol (THC), which exists in varying concentrations in the plant, depending on its origin, growing conditions, and cultivation. The concentration of THC within the sections of the plant also varies widely. The resin contains the greatest concentration of THC; smaller amounts are found, respectively, in the flowers, the leaves, and the stems. The most potent form of the drug, hashish, is prepared from the resins of the flowers and contains 5–12% THC. Marijuana generally found in the United States is weaker, with around 1% THC.

The drug produces a number of physiological and psychological effects. The short-term physiological effects have been well documented. They are reddening of the whites of the eye, dryness in the mouth, increased pulse rate, and impaired motor responses. The short-term psychological effects are equally well known:

> At low, usual "social" doses, the intoxicated individual may experience an increased sense of well-being; initial restlessness and hilarity followed by a dreamy, carefree state of relaxation; alteration of sensory perceptions including expansion of space and time; and a more vivid sense of touch, sight, smell, taste, and sound; a feeling of hunger, especially a craving for sweets; and subtle changes in thought formation and expression. To an unknowing observer, an individual in this state of consciousness would not appear noticeably different from his normal state.

> At higher, moderate doses, these same reactions are intensified.... The individual may experience rapidly changing emotions, changing sensory imagery, dulling of attention, more altered thought formation and expression such as fragmented thought, flight of ideas, impaired immediate memory, disturbed associations, altered sense of self-identity and, to some, a perceived feeling of enhanced insight.

> At very high doses, psychotomimetic phenomena may be experienced. These include distortions of body image, loss of personal identity, sensory and mental illusions, fantasies and hallucinations.

The intensity of these reactions depends on dosage, method of use, metabolism, attitude and setting, tolerance, duration of use, and pattern of use.

Experiences under marijuana intoxication are usually pleasurable, but negative reactions are not infrequent. These negative reactions include distortion of body image, depersonalization, acute panic anxiety reaction, nausea, and, more rarely, psychosis. These reactions may be caused or exaggerated by pre-existing psychological problems.

---

bread, The Forbidden Fruit and the Tree of Knowledge: An Inquiry into the Legal History of American Marijuana Prohibition, 56 Va.L.Rev. 976 (1970).

Studies have dispelled many of the myths about the drug: marijuana is not a narcotic, not addictive,[15] and generally not a stepping-stone to other, more serious drugs.[16] Furthermore, it causes neither aggressive behavior nor insanity.

Despite these findings, questions about long-term use remain. Studies have indicated that marijuana may affect adversely the lungs and the endocrine, the immunity, and the cardiovascular systems. Some of these studies are disputed, but an examination of these adverse findings illustrates the important questions still remaining about marijuana use.

In addition to these problems, other tests have found negative aspects to marijuana use. Amotivational difficulties and changes in brain cells, chromosomes, and cell metabolism have been noted in various studies. These findings have not been corroborated, however, and other research has reached contradictory conclusions. As with the other areas, these questions demand further scientific study to determine conclusively the long-term effects of marijuana. Although we now know that marijuana is not the "killer" drug, as branded in the past, its long-term effects are still an open question and must be approached as unresolved. These lingering questions must be kept in mind in considering the legal issues.

NORML contends that the CSA violates the equal protection component of the due process clause. First, it argues that the classification of marijuana, a relatively harmless drug, as a controlled substance violates equal protection. Second, NORML believes that, even if marijuana may be controlled, its classification as a Schedule I drug is infirm: placement in Schedule I is both underinclusive in failing to include as a controlled substance drugs such as alcohol and nicotine, which satisfy Schedule I criteria, and overinclusive for establishing the same penalties for possession of marijuana as for all other controlled substances and for including marijuana in Schedule I with the more dangerous narcotics and opiates. For the reasons stated below, this court rejects these contentions.

Legislation that does not affect a "fundamental" right or a "suspect" class need only bear a rational relationship to a legitimate state interest. This standard of judicial review gives legislatures wide discretion and permits them to attack problems in any rational manner. The classification will be upheld unless "the varying treatment of different groups or persons is so unrelated to the achievement of any combination of legitimate purposes that (a court) can only conclude that the legislature's actions were irrational."

The inclusion of marijuana as a controlled substance under the CSA easily satisfies this deferential rationality standard. Congress gave the CSA provisions concerning marijuana considerable attention. It recognized that much of the information regarding marijuana was inaccurate and that bias and ignorance had perpetuated many myths about the consequences and dangers of marijuana use. Despite all the concern over the drug, few

---

15. Marijuana is not physically addictive, but some studies have found that long-term users develop a psychological addiction.

16. Clinical studies have failed to discover a relationship between use of marijuana and use of more addictive drugs such as heroin. These laboratory studies may fail to take account of the social and psychological pressures confronting marijuana users "on the street." Testifying before Congress, Doctor Robert W. Baird, director of the Haven Clinic, a narcotics rehabilitation center in Harlem, stated that use of marijuana provided youngsters a pleasurable introduction to the "drug culture"; after initial experimentation with marijuana, young marijuana users were more willing to try stronger, more dangerous, substances. Decriminalization of Marihuana: Hearings Before the House Select Committee on Narcotics Abuse and Control, 95th Cong., 1st Sess. 423–38 (1977) (testimony of Dr. Robert W. Baird).

reliable scientific studies existed that could give accurate information to the legislators. Representative Cohelan acknowledged this lack of accurate information on marijuana during the House discussion of the bill: "Much remains to be done to find out the effects of marijuana. Assertions from both sides are not hard to find, but there is precious little hard clinical data on this subject." Unsure of marijuana's effects, Congress placed marijuana in Schedule I, with its program of strict controls, until it could obtain more scientific information on the drug's effects. In so doing, Congress followed the recommendation of the Department of Health, Education, and Welfare, which had suggested classification in Schedule I until further tests could be completed.[32]

Inclusion of marijuana as a controlled substance in 1970 certainly was rational. The information then available indicated that marijuana might well have substantial detrimental effects, and Congress thus reasonably could decide to include the drug as a controlled substance rather than leave it unregulated. NORML argues that, although classification of marijuana as a controlled substance in 1970 might have been rational, the scientific evidence available today establishes that "private possession and use of marijuana by adults (do) not pose any significant danger to the public health, safety or welfare." NORML therefore asserts the classification of marijuana as a controlled substance is no longer rational and invokes *United States v. Carolene Products Co.*, 304 U.S. 144, 153 (1938): "the constitutionality of a statute predicated upon a particular state of facts may be challenged by a showing to the court that those facts have ceased to exist."

The record, however, is not so clear as NORML contends. Experts still strongly disagree about the safety of marijuana, and its long-term effects remain an open question. Studies indicate that marijuana may impair the circulatory, the endocrine, and the immunity systems of the body, alter chromosomes, and change cell metabolism. Although many dispute these findings, this contradictory evidence demonstrates that important questions about marijuana use persist.

Given the continuing debate over marijuana, this court must defer to the legislature's judgments on disputed factual issues. The classification need not change continually as more information becomes available. Congressional action must be upheld as long as a rational basis still exists for the classification. The continuing questions about marijuana and its effects make the classification rational.

In a related equal protection challenge, NORML argues that classification of marijuana in Schedule I is irrational as being both underinclusive and overinclusive. The CSA does not regulate alcohol and tobacco, which are more harmful than marijuana, and it places marijuana in the same schedule with such dangerous substances as heroin and other narcotics. Thus, even if the classification of marijuana as a controlled substance is rational, the plaintiff believes that the legislation nonetheless is unconstitutional because marijuana's treatment within the Act is irrational in relation to other controlled substances.

"Underinclusive classifications do not include all who are similarly situated with respect to a rule, and thereby burden less than would be logical to achieve the intended government end." L. Tribe, American Constitutional Law, § 16-4, at 997 (1978). To be successful in a challenge based on underinclusiveness, plaintiff must show that the governmental choice is "clearly wrong, a display of arbitrary power, not an exercise of judgment[.]"

---

32. In an effort to secure more information about marijuana, Congress established the Commission on Marihuana and Drug Abuse to study marijuana use and its effects. The Commission, headed by Governor Raymond P. Shafer, issued its report, Marihuana: A Signal of Misunderstanding, in 1972. The Commission recommended that federal and state penalties for private possession of marijuana be eliminated and that governmental efforts should focus on discouraging marijuana use.

Mathews v. de Castro, 429 U.S. 181, 185 (1976). Few challengers can sustain such a heavy burden of proof. Courts have recognized the very real difficulties under which legislatures operate difficulties that arise due to the nature of the legislative process and the society that legislation attempts to reshape. As Professor Tribe has explained: "underinclusive" or "piecemeal legislation is a pragmatic means of effecting needed reforms, where a demand for completeness may lead to total paralysis...."

Legislatures have wide discretion in attacking social ills. "A State may direct its law against what it deems the evil as it actually exists without covering the whole field of possible abuses, and it may do so none the less that the forbidden act does not differ in kind from those that are allowed." *Hughes v. Superior Court,* 339 U.S. 460, 468 (1950). Failure to address a certain problem in an otherwise comprehensive legislative scheme is not fatal to the legislative plan.

Given this policy of legislative freedom in confronting social problems, the exclusion of alcohol and tobacco from the CSA does not render the scheme unconstitutional. Different legislative schemes control the sale and distribution of alcohol and tobacco. The specific exemption of alcohol and tobacco from the provisions of the CSA, 21 U.S.C. § 802(6), reflects Congress's view that other regulatory schemes are more appropriate for alcohol and tobacco.[36] That alcohol and tobacco may have adverse effects on health does not mean the CSA is the only proper means of regulating these drugs, nor does it mean that marijuana should be treated identically. As a Presidential commission on drug abuse pointed out, "While alcoholism constitutes a major social problem, surely it is not valid to justify the adoption of a new abuse on the basis that it is no worse than a presently existing one. The result could only be added social damage from a new source." Congress, having the power to deal with drug abuse in any reasonable manner, decided to exclude alcohol and tobacco from the CSA. This court will not disturb that judgment.

A law also may be challenged for including within a prohibited class an item that does not rationally belong with the other members of that class. NORML once again draws its support from the *Carolene Products* decision: "[T]he constitutionality of a statute, valid on its face, may be assailed by proof of facts tending to show that the statute as applied to a particular article is without support in reason because the article, although within the (particular) class, is so different from others of the class as to be without the reason for the prohibition." *United States v. Carolene Products Co.,* 304 U.S. at 153–54. The plaintiff here argues marijuana's classification in Schedule I is impermissible because the drug does not fit the statutory criteria for placement in that schedule.

NORML argues that marijuana does not belong in Schedule I, for it does not satisfy that schedule's statutory criteria high potential for abuse, no medically accepted use, and no safe use of the drug even under medical supervision. The Government disagrees and contends that all three criteria are met. It claims the drug has a "high potential for abuse," in that millions of Americans use marijuana on their own initiative rather than on the basis of medical advice. While tests have indicated that marijuana may have therapeutic uses in the treatment of glaucoma and cancer, the Food and Drug Administration does not currently accept it for any form of medical treatment. Finally, the Government claims that marijuana cannot be used safely due to the differing concentrations of THC in cannabis.

---

36. In discussing the regulation of alcohol and tobacco, one district court observed: "The legislative judgment concerning alcohol and nicotine may well have taken into account the degree to which their dangers are known, the adverse consequences of prohibition, and the economic significance of their production. Whether such factors should lead to similar judgments concerning marijuana is within legislative discretion." *United States v. Maiden,* 355 F. Supp. 743, 747–48 (D.Conn.1973).

Even assuming, arguendo, that marijuana does not fall within a literal reading of Schedule I, the classification still is rational. Placing marijuana in Schedule I furthered the regulatory purposes of Congress. The statutory criteria of section 812(b)(1) are guides in determining the schedule to which a drug belongs, but they are not dispositive. Indeed, the classifications at times cannot be followed consistently, and some conflict exists as to the main factor in classifying a drug potential for abuse or possible medical use.[40] The district court in *United States v. Maiden,* 355 F. Supp. 743 (D.Conn.1973), discussed this problem in rejecting the identical claim raised here by NORML:

> [The statutory classifications] cannot logically be read as cumulative in all situations. For example finding (B) for Schedule I requires that "The drug or other substance has no currently accepted medical use in treatment in the United States." Finding (B) for the other four schedules specifies that the drug has a currently accepted medical use. At the same time, finding (A) requires that the drug has a "high potential for abuse" for placement in Schedule I, but a "potential for abuse less than the drugs or other substances in Schedules I and II" for placement in Schedule III. If the findings are really cumulative, where would one place a drug that has no accepted medical use but also has a potential for abuse less than the drugs in Schedules I and II? According to finding (A) for Schedule III it belongs in Schedule III, but finding (B) for that schedule precludes Schedule III; according to finding (B) for Schedule I it belongs in Schedule I, but finding (A) for that schedule appears to preclude Schedule I.

The legislative history also indicates the statutory criteria are not intended to be exclusive. The House report states that "[a]side from the criterion of actual or relative potential for abuse, subsection (c) of section 201 (21 U.S.C. §811(c)) lists seven other criteria ... which must be considered in determining whether a substance meets the specific requirements specified in section 202(b) (21 U.S.C. §812(b)) for inclusion in particular schedules...." 1970 House Report, *supra* at 35, reprinted in (1970) U.S. Code Cong. & Admin. News at 4602. The criteria listed in section 811(c)[41] include the state of current knowledge, the current pattern of abuse, the risk to public health, and the significance of abuse. These more

---

40. According to the House Report, "(a) key criterion for controlling a substance, and the one which will be used most often, is the substance's potential for abuse." Senator Hughes, on the other hand, believed the existence of an accepted medical use was the primary factor in a drug's classification. Discussing the penalties for possession of marijuana and heroin, he noted: "Classification in the bill depends primarily upon whether there is an accepted medical use for the drug. Because heroin and marijuana have no recognized medical use, they are classified in the same category.... If there is no valid use for a drug, there is a sound reason to impose the strictest recordkeeping controls. But criminal sanctions for illegal distribution and use should be based upon the danger to society and the individual, not upon whether there is any valid medical use."

Other members of Congress indicated the two criteria were equally important.

41. This section states: "In making any finding under subsection (a) of this section or under subsection (b) of section 202 (21 U.S.C. §812(b)), the Attorney General shall consider the following factors with respect to each drug or other substance proposed to be controlled or removed from the schedules:

(1) Its actual or relative potential for abuse.

(2) Scientific evidence of its pharmacological effect, if known.

(3) The state of current scientific knowledge regarding the drug or other substance.

(4) Its history and current pattern of abuse.

(5) The scope, duration, and significance of abuse.

(6) What, if any, risk there is to the public health.

(7) Its psychic or physiological dependence liability.

(8) Whether the substance is an immediate precursor of a substance already controlled under this title. 21 U.S.C. §811(c).

subjective factors significantly broaden the scope of issues to be considered in classifying a drug. Given these other concerns, Congress might well want marijuana in Schedule I for regulatory purposes. Such a classification carries heavier penalties for sale, distribution, and importation, thus aiding law enforcement officials in their effort to reduce the supply of marijuana.

In addition, Congress itself made the initial classifications and established a procedure for reclassifying drugs and controlled substances: "Schedules I, II, III, IV, and V shall, unless and until amended pursuant to section 811 of this title, consist of the following drugs and other substances...." 21 U.S.C. §812(c). In making the initial determination, Congress placed marijuana in Schedule I. The clear meaning of section 812(c) is that Congress intended marijuana to remain in Schedule I until such time as it might be reclassified by the Attorney General on the basis of more complete scientific information about the drug. In such a reclassification hearing, the statutory criteria would be the guides to determining the most appropriate schedule for marijuana. By providing for periodic review and constant revision of drug classifications, Congress enacted a sensible mechanism for scrutinizing the classification of marijuana. As Judge Feinberg stated in *United States v. Kiffer*:

> [T]he very existence of the statutory scheme indicates that, in dealing with the "drug" problem, Congress intended flexibility and receptivity to the latest scientific information to be the hallmarks of its approach. This ... is the very antithesis of the irrationality (plaintiff) attributes to Congress.

The legislative scheme under section 811 offers a flexible means of reclassifying controlled substances, and the Attorney General may reclassify marijuana pursuant to that scheme. The propriety of any administrative determination on the reclassification of marijuana is not before this court. The constitutional legitimacy of the classification of marijuana in Schedule I is challenged, however, and this court concludes that the classification is constitutionally permissible. Thus, plaintiff's equal protection challenge must be rejected.

In this case, NORML has asked this court to overturn the CSA prohibition on private possession of marijuana. In so doing, NORML misdirects its efforts. This challenge presents the difficult social questions that legislatures are especially adept at resolving, and we do not sit to second-guess their judgments. Under our system of checks and balances, it is the court's duty to examine legislation and to determine the legality or illegality of that legislation within the confines of the law. The legislative system may not always work efficiently, or fairly, but we have staked our fortunes on it, and our history would support the wisdom of our forefathers' judgment.

NORML's efforts have seared the conscience of many representatives. Eleven states have decriminalized possession of marijuana and efforts to decriminalize are continuing in many others. The legislative branch, and not the judicial, is the proper battleground for the fight to decriminalize the possession of marijuana. The people, and not the courts, must decide whether the battle will be won or lost.

The court in *NORML v. Bell* suggests that advocates for marijuana law reform should pursue their arguments through the legislative process or the Controlled Substances Act's administrative procedure for rescheduling controlled substances. But was it constitutional for Congress to delegate the power to criminalize substances under the CSA to the same administrative entity responsible for enforcing the CSA? In *Touby v. United States,* 500 U.S. 160 (1991), defendants who had been convicted of manufacturing "Euphoria" argued that the CSA's delegation of scheduling power to the Attorney General conflicted with Article I of the Constitution, which provides that "all legislative Powers herein granted shall be vested in a Congress of the United States." The Supreme Court rejected the challenge, concluding that the CSA "place[s] multiple specific restrictions on the Attorney General's discretion to define criminal conduct. These restrictions satisfy the constitutional requirements of the nondelegation doctrine." In *Touby*, the Court also upheld the Attorney General's subdelegation of scheduling authority to the Drug Enforcement Administration.

B. Classifying Substances under the Controlled Substances Act

Representative List of Drugs Classifications Under the CSA, 21 CFR § 1308

Schedule I	Schedule II	Schedule III	Schedule IV	Schedule V
Heroin, LSD, marijuana, MDMA	Cocaine, Codeine, Methadone, Methamphetamine, Oxycodone	Anabolic steroids, Tylenol with Codeine, Marinol (synthetic THC), Ketamine	Xanax, Valium, Rohypnol, Modafinil, Ambien	Robitussin A-C, Lyrica

Note: In some cases a brand or street name has been substituted for the chemical name of the substance as it identified under the CSA.

Literally hundreds of substances are scheduled under the CSA. *See* 21 CFR § 1308 (providing the current list of controlled substances). The chart above provides a short representative list, showing where some of the more well known substances are classified. It is important always to remember that the scheduling system dictates the controls a substance is subject to, not the sentence one would receive for illegally possessing or distributing the substance. For example, although cocaine is in Schedule II and marijuana is in Schedule I, sentences for cocaine offenses are typically longer than for comparable marijuana offenses. While it is useful to have a sense of where different substances fall under the CSA, it is more important to understand the procedures and criteria that drive the classification system.

In the 1980 case *NORML v. Bell*, the court described the Controlled Substances Act's scheduling factors as "guides in determining the schedule to which a drug belongs, but they are not dispositive. Indeed, the classifications at times cannot be followed consistently, and some conflict exists as to the main factor in classifying a drug['s] potential for abuse and possible medical use." 488 F. Supp. 123, 140 (D.D.C. 1980).

In the cases that follow, courts and administrative decision makers apply the CSA's scheduling criteria to classify substances. When reading these cases, consider whether the conflicts and inconsistencies described in *NORML v. Bell* have been resolved and whether you believe the Controlled Substances Act achieves its aim of facilitating consistent, predictable, and science-based classifications of substances of abuse. Is the term "accepted medical use," for example, sufficiently well defined? Are you able to discern from the cases how much weight each of the scheduling criteria is to be given in scheduling decisions?

If a substance were found to have a negligible potential for abuse and no currently accepted medical use, in what schedule would it fall?

Before you continue, be sure to take a moment to refer back to the chart at the beginning of this Chapter outlining the factors for each of the five schedules so that you have the CSA's basic classification structure in mind while reading the material that follows.

Grinspoon v. Drug Enforcement Administration

United States Court of Appeals for the First Circuit
828 F.2d 881 (1987)

Coffin, J.

On November 13, 1986, the Administrator of the Drug Enforcement Administration ("DEA") issued a final rule placing the substance 3,4-methylenedioxymethamphetamine ("MDMA")* into Schedule I of the Controlled Substances Act ("CSA"). In reaching this decision, the Administrator found that MDMA met all three of the statutory requirements for classification as a Schedule I substance, namely, (A) The drug or other substance has a high potential for abuse. (B) The drug or other substance has no currently accepted medical use in treatment in the United States. (C) There is a lack of accepted safety for use of the drug or other substance under medical supervision. 21 U.S.C. § 812(b)(1).

Dr. Lester Grinspoon, a psychiatrist and faculty member of the Harvard Medical School, petitions this court to review the final rule. Dr. Grinspoon seeks to conduct research on the therapeutic use of MDMA and believes that the imposition of Schedule I controls will effectively foreclose such research. He cites four reasons for vacating the Administrator's scheduling determination. The first reason advanced is that the Administrator applied the wrong legal standards for "currently accepted medical use in treatment in the United States" and for "accepted safety for use ... under medical supervision" in 21 U.S.C. § 812(b)(1). The other three reasons contained in Dr. Grinspoon's petition challenge the scheduling determination as arbitrary and capricious because (a) the Administrator's determination that MDMA had a "high" potential for abuse was flawed by his failure to articulate a legal standard and his reliance on insufficient record evidence; (b) the Administrator failed to give adequate weight to the evidence showing that placing MDMA into Schedule I would create a barrier to medical research on the drug; and (c) the rule is based upon incomplete and arbitrary recommendations from the Secretary of Health and Human Services. Petitioner urges this court to remand the case to the DEA with instructions to place the substance MDMA into Schedule III.

Although we are satisfied that these final three claims do not require us to overturn the rule, we believe that Dr. Grinspoon's first claim has considerable merit and requires us to remand the scheduling determination for reconsideration by the Administrator.

In January of 1984, the DEA prepared a document entitled "Schedule I Control Recommendation Under the CSA for 3,4-Methylenedioxymethamphetamine (MDMA)." The control recommendation, which was based upon information compiled from various DEA data sources and scientific and medical literature, considered all three Schedule I criteria listed in section 812(b)(1) and concluded that (1) MDMA has a high potential for abuse; (2) MDMA has no known legitimate medical use for treatment in the United States; and (3) there is a lack of accepted safety for the use of MDMA under medical supervision. Based upon these findings, the DEA recommended that MDMA be placed into Schedule I of the CSA.

---

* MDMA is also commonly referred to as "ecstasy." [*Footnote by casebook author.*]

In March of 1984, pursuant to the procedures set out in the CSA, 28 U.S.C. 811(b),[2] the Administrator submitted the DEA's control recommendation to the Assistant Secretary for Health of the Department of Health and Human Services ("HHS") for scientific and medical evaluation and for an HHS recommendation as to whether MDMA should be controlled. The HHS evaluation was conducted by Dr. Charles Tocus, Chief of the Drug Abuse Staff of the Food and Drug Administration ("FDA"). Dr. Tocus stated in his affidavit that he searched the FDA files and found no reference to MDMA. Based upon this absence of information in the FDA files and a review of the information contained in the DEA control recommendation carried out by Dr. Tocus, HHS responded by making minor (typographical) corrections in the DEA's eight-factor analysis[3] and concurring in the recommendation that MDMA be placed into Schedule I.

Upon receiving the HHS evaluation and recommendation, the Administrator issued a Notice of Proposed Rulemaking with regard to placing MDMA into Schedule I of the CSA. Later, following the receipt of several comments and requests for a hearing, the Administrator referred the matter to an Administrative Law Judge ("ALJ") with instructions to "conduct a hearing for the purpose of receiving factual evidence and expert opinion regarding the proposed scheduling of MDMA." During the course of the hearing, the ALJ heard 33 witnesses and received 95 exhibits into evidence.[4] On May 22, 1986, the ALJ issued a comprehensive opinion finding that MDMA fit none of the three criteria prerequisite to placement in Schedule I. Relying on the hearing testimony of experts in the health care community, the ALJ concluded that MDMA had an accepted medical use for treatment in the United States, and an accepted safety for use under medical supervision. The ALJ also found that the record did not establish that MDMA had a "high" potential for abuse. The ALJ therefore recommended that MDMA be placed into Schedule III of the CSA.

The Administrator, however, declined to accept the reasoning and scheduling recommendation of the ALJ. In his October 13, 1986, decision, the Administrator held that the phrases "currently accepted medical use in treatment in the United States" and "accepted safety for use ... under medical supervision" as used in the CSA both mean that the FDA has evaluated the substance for safety and approved it for interstate marketing in the United States pursuant to the Federal Food, Drug, and Cosmetic Act of 1938 ("FDCA"), 21 U.S.C. § 355. From these premises, the Administrator reasoned that because the FDA has not approved a new drug application ("NDA") or investigational new drug application ("IND") authorizing interstate marketing of MDMA under the FDCA, MDMA cannot be lawfully marketed and has neither a currently accepted medical use in treatment

---

2. 21 U.S.C. § 811(b) provides that[:] "The Attorney General shall, before initiating proceedings under subsection (a) of this section to control a drug or other substance..., and after gathering the necessary data, request from the Secretary a scientific and medical evaluation, and his recommendations, as to whether such drug or other substance should be so controlled."

3. Section 811(c) requires the Administrator to consider the following eight factors for each drug proposed to be controlled under the CSA: "(1) [The drug's] actual or relative potential for abuse. (2) Scientific evidence of its pharmacological effect, if known. (3) The state of current scientific knowledge regarding the drug or other substance. (4) Its history and current pattern of abuse. (5) The scope, duration, and significance of abuse. (6) What, if any, risk there is to the public health. (7) Its psychic or physiological dependence liability. (8) Whether the substance is an immediate precursor of a substance already controlled under this subchapter." 21 U.S.C. § 811(c).

4. On July 1, 1985, while the hearing was proceeding, the Administrator placed MDMA into Schedule I of the Controlled Substances Act pursuant to the emergency scheduling provisions of the Act, 21 U.S.C. § 811(h)(1). The Administrator determined that this action was necessary to avoid an imminent hazard to the public safety.

in the United States nor an accepted safety for use under medical supervision. Finally, the Administrator found that the DEA had sustained its burden of proving that MDMA has a high potential for abuse. The Administrator's final rule, effective November 13, 1986, placed MDMA into Schedule I. Dr. Grinspoon appeals from this final rule under the CSA.

We turn first to petitioner's claim that the Administrator erred in interpreting the phrases "accepted medical use in treatment in the United States" and "accepted safety for use ... under medical supervision" in section 812(b)(1) to mean, in essence, "approved for interstate marketing by the FDA under the FDCA." Before embarking on an analysis of that issue, however, we begin by explaining the appropriate standard of review in a case, such as this, where a court must assess an agency's interpretation of a statute it administers.

The Administrator argues correctly that we must review his interpretation of the CSA in light of the guidelines set forth by the Supreme Court in *Chevron U.S.A., Inc. v. Natural Resources Defense Council, Inc.,* 467 U.S. 837 (1984). In *Chevron* the Court explained that a reviewing court must employ a two-step analysis that focuses initially on the intentions of Congress:

> First, always, is the question whether Congress had directly spoken to the precise question at issue. If *the intent of Congress is clear*, that is the end of the matter; for the court, as well as the agency, must give effect to the unambiguously expressed intent of Congress.

In the absence of congressional intent, however, the court must proceed to a second inquiry:

> If ... the court determines Congress has not directly addressed the precise question at issue, the court does not simply impose its own construction on the statute, as would be necessary in the absence of an administrative interpretation. Rather, if the statute is silent or ambiguous with respect to the specific issue, the question for the court is whether the agency's answer is based on a *permissible construction of the statute.*

It is undisputed that Congress has not directly spoken to the question at issue here, namely, the proper means of interpreting the second and third criteria of section 812(b)(1). The absence of express intent, however, does not compel us to proceed to the deferential second step of the *Chevron* scheme. As the Supreme Court indicated in a footnote to its *Chevron* opinion, "if a court, employing traditional tools of statutory construction, ascertains that Congress had an intention on the precise question at issue, that intention is law and must be given effect."

The Administrator contends that congressional intent favoring his interpretation of the CSA can be gleaned from the language of the statute, its legislative history, and the language and history of subsequent legislative enactments designed to enhance the regulatory system established by the CSA in 1970. In the alternative, he argues that if the intent of Congress is ambiguous, then his construction of the statute is permissible in view of the statutory scheme. Our review of the sources identified by the litigants convinces us that Congress neither expressed nor implied an affirmative intent regarding how the second and third Schedule I criteria should be interpreted. Nevertheless, these same sources—the language and structure of the CSA and FDCA, the legislative history of the CSA, and the subsequent handiwork of Congress in the area of controlled substance regulation—lead us to conclude that the Administrator's construction is contrary to congressional intent.

The Administrator begins by arguing that the language of the CSA itself is evidence of congressional intent favoring his construction of the statute. His argument is based on the definitions of terms chosen by Congress in drafting the relevant provisions of the CSA. He first cites the definition of the term "United States" as used in "accepted medical use in treatment in the United States." This term is the only portion of the Schedule I criteria that Congress has expressly defined in the CSA, providing that "the term 'United States,' when used in a geographic sense, means *all places* ... subject to the jurisdiction of the United States." Coupling this statutory definition of "United States" with the dictionary definition of "accepted"—which means "generally approved" or "generally agreed upon"—the Administrator argues that the phrase "*accepted* medical use in treatment in the *United States*," must contemplate an administrative determination that the substance has been "generally approved" for use in treatment in "all places" subject to United States jurisdiction. In other words, FDA interstate marketing approval is necessary to satisfy this criterion because, otherwise, the substance could not be deemed to be "generally approved" *everywhere* in the United States.[7]

We find this argument to be strained and unpersuasive. The CSA's definition of "United States" plainly does not require the conclusion asserted by the Administrator simply because section 802(28) defines "United States" as "*all places* subject to the jurisdiction of the United States." Congress surely intended the reference to "all places" in section 802(28) to delineate the broad jurisdictional scope of the CSA and to clarify that the CSA regulates conduct occurring *any place*, as opposed to *every place*, within the United States. As petitioner aptly notes, a defendant charged with violating the CSA by selling controlled substances in only two states would not have a defense based on section 802(28) if he contended that his activity had not occurred in "all places" subject to United States jurisdiction.

Nor does the dictionary definition of "accepted" offered by the Administrator convince us that Congress intended FDA approval to be the equivalent of the second and third Schedule I criteria. Use of the term "accepted" in sections 812(b)(1)(B) and 812(b)(1)(C) may indicate that Congress intended the medical use or safety of the substance to be "generally agreed upon," but this alone does not inform us as to *who* must generally be in agreement. The Administrator reads "accepted" to mean that *the FDA* must have approved the drug for interstate marketing. Dr. Grinspoon, on the other hand, prefers to interpret "accepted" as meaning that the *medical community* generally agrees that the drug in question has a medical use and can be used safely under medical supervision. Our conclusion is that the term "accepted" does not cure the statute's ambiguity. We are simply unable to extrapolate from the drafters' choice of the word "accepted" and thereby ascertain a general congressional intention favoring the interpretation advanced by the Administrator.

In another argument focusing upon the language of the statute, the Administrator urges us to adopt his interpretation of the CSA because it is entirely consistent with the interpretation of the phrase "accepted medical use in treatment in the United States" employed in the Commissioners' Notes to the Uniform Controlled Substances Act ("Uniform CSA").[8] At first glance, this argument appears to have considerable merit. The

---

7. The Administrator does not confine this argument to section 812(b)(1)(B), but also states that "*accepted* Safety for use ... under medical supervision, 21 U.S.C. §812(b)(1)(C), is equivalent to FDA approval because, otherwise, the safety of the substance could never be "generally agreed upon."

8. "Experimental substances found to have a potential for abuse in early testing will also be included in Schedule I. When those substances are accepted by the Federal Food and Drug Administration as being safe and effective, they will then be considered to have an accepted medical use for treatment in the United States, and thus, will be eligible to be shifted to an appropriate schedule based upon the criteria set out in Sections 205, 207, 209, and 211." 9 U.L.A. at 221.

Uniform CSA, like its federal counterpart, creates five schedules of controlled substances and, indeed, was modeled on the federal CSA.[9] But, while we agree that the Uniform CSA offers an interesting comparison, we fail to see how the interpretation of the Uniform CSA offered by the Commissioners has any bearing at all on the intent of Congress, which enacted the federal CSA *prior to* the creation of the Uniform CSA. We can only conclude, therefore, that this argument, despite its facial appeal, has no bearing on the claim that the language of the federal CSA evidences congressional intent to adopt the construction of the statute favored by the Administrator.

While the Administrator's arguments fail to persuade us that Congress affirmatively intended his construction of the CSA, we believe nevertheless that the language and structure of the two relevant statutes, the CSA and the FDCA, are helpful in determining whether the Administrator's interpretation squares with congressional intent. Although, as the District of Columbia Circuit has stated, "the interrelationship between the two Acts [CSA and FDCA] is far from clear," we are persuaded that this interrelationship precludes the Administrator's reliance on the absence of FDA approval as a substitute for the second and third Schedule I criteria under the CSA.

The CSA clearly provides that a substance may not be placed in Schedule I unless it lacks *both* a "currently accepted medical use in treatment in the United States" *and* "accepted safety for use ... under medical supervision." The FDCA, on the other hand, provides that a substance may fail to obtain FDA interstate marketing approval (or exemption) for any of seven specific reasons. 21 U.S.C. § 355(d)(1)–(7). Although approval may be withheld because the substance lacks both "safety", and "efficacy" for a particular use, it is equally possible for a substance to be disapproved for interstate marketing because it lacks only *one* of these attributes, or because the application fails to contain relevant patent information, or even because the labeling proposed for the drug "is false or misleading in any particular." Thus, we find no necessary linkage between failure to obtain FDA interstate marketing approval and a determination that the substance in question is unsafe *and* has no medical use. Indeed, the FDCA does not even mention the term "medical use." In short, it is plainly possible that a substance may fail to obtain interstate marketing approval even if it has an accepted medical use.

Another possible reason for failure to obtain FDA new drug approval is that the manufacture, distribution, and use of a substance might not involve interstate marketing. Unlike the CSA scheduling restrictions, the FDCA interstate marketing provisions do not apply to drugs manufactured and marketed wholly intrastate. Thus, it is possible that a substance may have both an accepted medical use and safety for use under medical supervision, even though no one has deemed it necessary to seek approval for interstate marketing. Indeed, as Dr. Grinspoon argues, there is no economic or other incentive to seek interstate marketing approval for a drug like MDMA because it cannot be patented and exploited commercially. The prospect of commercial development, of course, is irrelevant to one who, like Grinspoon, seeks only to do research.

These considerations tend to indicate that the absence of FDA approval for interstate commerce does not foreclose the possibility that a substance might still possess an accepted medical use or even be considered safe for use under medical supervision. It appears, instead, that blind reliance on the lack of FDA interstate marketing approval could cause a substance to be placed in Schedule I, even though one or two of the three re-

---

9. The Uniform CSA was approved for adoption by the states in 1970. To date, 48 states, the District of Columbia, Guam, and the Virgin Islands have adopted the Uniform CSA. 9 U.L.A. Supp. 123–24 (1986).

quirements prescribed by Congress for placement of a drug in Schedule I have not been proven. Based solely on the language of the CSA and the FDCA, therefore, we find it unlikely that substituting the lack of FDA interstate marketing approval for the statutory requirements that a substance lack both an "accepted medical use" and "accepted safety for use ... under medical supervision" is consistent with the intent of Congress in enacting the CSA. We turn now to consider whether the legislative history of the CSA confirms or rebuts this tentative conclusion.

The Administrator purports to have identified portions of the CSA's legislative history that support his construction of the statutory language. [H]e cites a passage from the House Committee Report that states:

> Under Reorganization Plan No. 1 of 1968 a Bureau of Narcotics and Dangerous Drugs has been established in the Department of Justice to regulate all these drugs (including legitimate importation, exportation, manufacture, and distribution) to prevent diversion from legitimate channels. Safety and efficacy will continue to be regulated under the Federal Food, Drug, and Cosmetic Act by [HHS].

From this, the Administrator draws the proposition that "Congress clearly intended that the 'safety and efficacy' of narcotic and dangerous drugs (*e.g.*, whether such drugs are acceptable for medical use and safe for such use) be determined by [HHS] under the [FDCA]." The Administrator's conclusion is objectionable, however, because his parenthetical comment—equating a finding of "safety and efficacy" by the FDA with a finding of "accepted medical use" and "accepted safety for use ... under medical supervision"—is totally unsupported by the quoted passage from the House Committee Report. Nowhere does Congress equate "safety and efficacy" under the FDCA with the second and third Schedule I criteria contained in section 812(b)(1). This, indeed, is the point at issue in this litigation, and we are loath to accept such a disingenuous argument.

The Administrator has cited subsequent legislative enactments as support for his position that Congress has approved his construction of the second and third criteria for Schedule I substances. Our review of these legislative enactments, however, leads us to find that the subsequent legislation tends to weaken, not strengthen, the position espoused by the Administrator in this litigation.

[I]n 1984, Congress amended the CSA to include an "emergency scheduling" provision. This provision allows the Attorney General to place certain substances into Schedule I on a temporary basis without regard to the regular scheduling criteria and procedures if such emergency scheduling is "necessary to avoid an imminent hazard to the public safety." This amendment to the CSA, however, expressly states that the Attorney General's authority to schedule substances in this expedited manner does not apply where an "exemption or approval is in effect for the substance under section 355 of this title,"[11] *i.e.*, where the FDA has permitted the substance to be marketed in interstate commerce. The fact that Congress expressly authorized the Attorney General to use expedited procedures and rely upon the absence of FDA interstate marketing approval, rather than the usual Schedule I criteria, only in temporary emergency situations suggests to us that these shorthand methods are not appropriate in routine (i.e., nonemergency) situations such as the one before us in the instant case. We do not interpret the explicit reference to FDA approval in the "emergency scheduling" provision to mean, as the Administrator would have us believe, that Congress sought to permit blind reliance on FDA standards as a legitimate shortcut in the general run of cases.

---

11. 21 U.S.C. § 355 is the section of the FDCA describing the standards and procedures for FDA interstate marketing approvals and exemptions.

We believe there is yet one additional policy reason, no doubt related to some of the other factors already discussed, for rejecting the construction of the CSA advanced by the Administrator as contrary to congressional intent. Under the statutory scheme set up by Congress, the Attorney General may not schedule a substance under the CSA without first obtaining the recommendation of the FDA, through its parent agency, HHS, and providing an "opportunity for a hearing pursuant to the rulemaking procedures prescribed by [the Administrative Procedure Act]." It is plain, therefore, that while Congress intended the recommendation of HHS to have significant weight in the decisionmaking process, it also intended that there be an opportunity for a meaningful hearing *after* receipt of the HHS report. It would surely be anomalous if the FDA's recommendation, based solely on the absence of approval for interstate marketing, sufficed to determine the ultimate conclusion prior to the hearing.

If we were to accept the Administrator's construction of section 812(b)(1) in this case, the opportunity for a meaningful hearing would be lost, and satisfaction of the "accepted medical use" and "accepted safety" criteria would turn solely on the existence of FDA approval for interstate marketing. A hearing on issues of the sort required by the statute—Does the substance have an accepted medical use in treatment in the United States? Is the substance safe for use under medical supervision?—would be reduced to an empty formality and, for participants like Dr. Grinspoon, would amount to an exercise in futility. We hesitate to interpret the CSA in a manner that would cause its important provision requiring a[n] administrative hearing to be meaningless as to two of the three requirements for scheduling a substance in Schedule I. We believe instead that, for the hearing opportunity to be a significant one on these issues, the agency must remain flexible enough to weigh and consider claims raised at the administrative hearing to the effect that a substance has an accepted use and is accepted as safe even though it is not approved for distribution in interstate commerce.

For the reasons listed above, we conclude that the Administrator erroneously applied an interpretation of the "accepted medical use in treatment in the United States" and "accepted safety for use ... under medical supervision" criteria of section 812(b)(1) that directly conflicts with congressional intent. We therefore vacate the Administrator's determination that MDMA should be placed in Schedule I of the CSA and remand the rule for further consideration by the DEA. On remand, the Administrator will not be permitted to treat the absence of FDA interstate marketing approval as conclusive evidence that MDMA has no currently accepted medical use and lacks accepted safety for use under medical supervision.

Petitioner Grinspoon has offered his own theory concerning the type of inquiry the Administrator must make under the statute. He urges us to adopt a standard for the second and third criteria that is based upon the opinion of members of the medical community. He contends that Congress drafted the CSA with this type of standard in mind. To support this contention, Grinspoon cites the testimony of two representatives of the Bureau of Narcotics and Dangerous Drugs ("BNDD"), DEA's predecessor agency, during legislative consideration of the Comprehensive Drug Abuse Prevention and Control Act of 1970. Michael R. Sonnenreich, Deputy Chief Counsel of the BNDD, testified that drugs in Schedule I would "have no medical use as determined by the medical community," and that "the medical community" would decide "whether or not the drug has [a] medical use...." Likewise, John Ingersoll, Director of the BNDD, testified that substances placed in Schedule I would be those drugs that "the medical profession has already determined to have no legitimate medical use in the United States."

While we acknowledge that the statements by the BNDD witnesses before the House Subcommittee tend to support Dr. Grinspoon's position, we do not believe they are entitled to much weight as indicia of congressional intent in fashioning the "accepted medical use" and "accepted safety for use ... under medical supervision" criteria. This is especially true where, as here, there is no indication whatsoever in either the legislative history or the history of any subsequent amendments that Congress concurred with the views expressed by the witnesses. In short, we do not find Grinspoon's evidence to be persuasive on the issue of affirmative congressional intent to have certain members of the medical community determine whether a substance has an "accepted medical use in treatment in the United States" or "accepted safety for use ... under medical supervision."

The nature of our review further constrains us from requiring the Administrator to adopt Dr. Grinspoon's proposed construction of section 812(b)(1). Although we find that the Administrator's present interpretation of the second and third Schedule I criteria contravenes congressional intent, we are unable to ascertain with any certainty what Congress intended to be the proper interpretation of subsections (B) and (C). In other words, while we are satisfied that Congress intended to preclude reliance on the absence of FDA approval in assessing whether a substance has an "accepted medical use" and "accepted safety for use ... under medical supervision," we have found nothing to indicate how Congress affirmatively intended these two ambiguous statutory phrases to be construed and applied. It appears to us that Congress has implicitly delegated to the Administrator the authority to interpret these portions of the CSA, and we must therefore refrain from imposing our own statutory interpretation upon the agency. Hence, to avoid unduly infringing upon the Administrator's legitimate discretion to develop a legally acceptable standard—i.e., one that does not conflict with the intentions of Congress, and makes sense in light of the statutory language, the legislative history, and the purposes of the entire legislative scheme—we remand the rule to the Administrator for reconsideration and for further proceedings not inconsistent with this opinion.

Although a remand is necessary due to our above holding, we nonetheless feel compelled to address the other issues raised in Dr. Grinspoon's petition because they are likely to arise again when the Administrator reconsiders the rule.

In addition to the "accepted medical use" and "accepted safety" criteria discussed above, the CSA also requires substances identified for placement in Schedule I to have a "high potential for abuse." Dr. Grinspoon contends that the Administrator's placement of MDMA in Schedule I is arbitrary and capricious because the Administrator failed to articulate a legal standard for assessing MDMA's potential for abuse and because the evidence in the record is insufficient to support a finding that MDMA has a "high" potential for abuse. While conceding that MDMA has some potential for abuse, and therefore should be scheduled under the CSA, Dr. Grinspoon insists that the Administrator has not proved, as he must for a Schedule I substance, that MDMA's potential for abuse is high.

The CSA provides no definition of the phrase "high potential for abuse," but both parties agree that the legislative history of the statute provides guidance in this regard. Specifically, the report of the House Committee on Interstate and Foreign Commerce accompanying the bill that eventually became the CSA sets forth four alternative legal standards for determining when a substance possesses a "potential for abuse." Borrowing from regulations promulgated under the FDCA, the House Committee Report provides that the Administrator may determine a substance has potential for abuse if:

(1) There is evidence that individuals are taking the drug or drugs containing such a substance in amounts sufficient to create a hazard to their health or to the safety of other individuals or of the community; *or*

(2) There is significant diversion of the drug or drugs containing such a substance from legitimate drug channels; *or*

(3) Individuals are taking the drug or drugs containing such a substance on their own initiative rather than on the basis of medical advice from a practitioner licensed by law to administer such drugs in the course of his professional practice; *or*

(4) The drug or drugs containing such a substance are new drugs so related in their action to a drug or drugs already listed as having a potential for abuse to make it likely that the drug will have the same potentiality for abuse as such drugs, thus making it reasonable to assume that there may be significant diversions from legitimate channels, significant use contrary to or without medical advice, or that it has a substantial capability of creating hazards to the health of the user or to the safety of the community.

The Committee Report goes on to state that "potential for abuse" exists only when there is "a substantial potential for the occurrence of significant diversions from legitimate channels, significant use by individuals contrary to professional advice, or substantial capability of creating hazards to the health of the user or the safety of the community."

The Administrator argues that he applied the standards expressly approved by Congress, but Dr. Grinspoon complains that the Administrator articulated no standard for showing that MDMA had a *relative* potential for abuse sufficient to warrant placement in Schedule I. As Grinspoon notes, the passage from the legislative history quoted above provides guidance only as to the minimum needed to show *any* potential for abuse, in other words, enough to justify a level of CSA control as low as placement in Schedule V. It offers no guidance for assessing whether a substance should be subject to Schedule I controls, the strictest imposed under the CSA, which require a "high" potential for abuse. For this, argues Grinspoon, the Administrator must prove that MDMA has a high potential for abuse *relative* to other scheduled substances and must base its proof on existing levels of actual abuse "on the streets."

While we acknowledge that the Administrator's final rule is silent with respect to the legal standard required for a finding of "high" potential for abuse, we do not find the Administrator's action to be arbitrary and capricious. The fourth standard contained in the segment of the Committee Report quoted above makes it quite clear that the Administrator can permissibly reach a conclusion regarding a substance's level of potential for abuse by comparing the substance to drugs already scheduled under the CSA. Here the Administrator has done just that, offering several findings concerning the evidence of close structural and pharmacological similarity between MDMA and other substances, such as MDA, which already have been found to have a high potential for abuse and have been placed in Schedule I or II. The Administrator also cited animal studies, human behavioral studies, and a survey of MDMA users which suggest that MDMA is related in its effects to Schedule I and II substances such as LSD, cocaine, mescaline, and MDA. We believe this approach to ascertaining MDMA's potential for abuse is entirely consistent with the statutory scheme developed by Congress and therefore hold that the Administrator's method is not arbitrary and capricious.[12] The question remains, of course, whether the

---

12. While we appreciate Dr. Grinspoon's point that MDMA abuse is low relative to other drugs that seem to be more popular "on the street," we do not believe that this fact precludes the Administrator from finding that MDMA has a high *potential* for abuse. Grinspoon's argument overlooks the importance of the term "potential" in section 812(b)(1)(A) and runs contrary to the explicit intent

evidence collected by the Administrator is sufficient to justify his conclusion that MDMA has a high potential for abuse. Since Dr. Grinspoon has also challenged this aspect of the scheduling determination as arbitrary and capricious, we turn next to a discussion of this issue.

In reviewing the Administrator's conclusion regarding MDMA's potential for abuse, we must determine whether it is based on "substantial evidence," a term the Supreme Court has defined as "'such relevant evidence as a reasonable mind might accept as adequate to support a conclusion.'"

The question before us, therefore, is whether there is substantial evidence in the administrative record to support the Administrator's determination that MDMA is "so related in [its] action to a drug or drugs already listed as having a [high] potential for abuse" that it is likely MDMA "will have the same potentiality for abuse as such drugs." In support of his conclusion, the Administrator made 46 numbered findings related to MDMA's similarity to other drugs with a high potential for abuse. These findings were based on scientific evidence concerning the chemical structural similarity between MDMA and other Schedule I and II drugs; the similar pharmacological effects of MDMA and these other drugs; animal drug discrimination studies; animal self-administration studies; and recent studies of the neurotoxic effects of MDMA and related drugs on rats.

Dr. Grinspoon, in an item-by-item analysis contained in the proposed findings of fact and conclusions of law he submitted to the DEA, calls into question many of the Administrator's findings concerning MDMA's similarity to other drugs with a high potential for abuse. For instance, Grinspoon agrees that MDMA is a member of a family of psychoactive drugs, but disputes the validity of the inference drawn from the similarity by the Administrator. According to Grinspoon, "chemical similarity is not necessarily a good guide to the actual effects of a compound in the human body." Grinspoon notes that of the 28 known phenethylamines, 17 were not scheduled under the CSA as late as December 1983. Even a subsequent review of these 17 substances by the World Health Organization's Expert Committee on Drug Dependence resulted in a recommendation that only nine of the substances be scheduled by member nations. Eight were thought harmless enough to remain unscheduled.

We have reviewed Dr. Grinspoon's item-by-item analysis closely, but find no basis sufficient to overturn the Administrator's decision. Grinspoon's reinterpretation of the scientific evidence before the agency surely demonstrates that the available evidence does not inexorably lead to a conclusion that MDMA is similar to drugs possessing a high potential for abuse. But, faced with such uncertainty, we must defer to the conclusion reached by the Administrator, even if we may have favored Dr. Grinspoon's approach had we studied the evidence in a *de novo* fashion. In reaching this conclusion, we follow the well-established maxim that "where the agency presents scientifically respectable evidence which the petitioner can continually dispute with rival, and we will assume, equally respectable evidence, the court must not second-guess the particular way the agency chooses to weigh the conflicting evidence or resolve the dispute." We find this maxim to have particular force in a case such as this because, as one court has explained, "appellate courts have neither the expertise nor the resources to evaluate complex scientific claims."

---

of Congress that the Administrator "not be required to wait until a number of lives have been destroyed or substantial problems have already arisen before designating a drug as subject to the controls of the bill." So long as the Administrator can marshal substantial evidence to demonstrate that MDMA is sufficiently similar to scheduled drugs with a "high potential for abuse," we will sustain his determination regardless of existing levels of actual abuse.

Dr. Grinspoon also takes issue with the Administrator's alleged failure to consider evidence tending to show that placement of MDMA in Schedule I would strongly discourage medical research on the drug. Grinspoon contends that failure to consider the impact of a scheduling decision on legitimate research amounts to arbitrary and capricious action on the part of the Administrator because he did not weigh all relevant factors in making his decision. To buttress his contention, Grinspoon recites a litany of legal, administrative, and practical obstacles that hinder researchers seeking to conduct experiments with Schedule I drugs. These obstacles include mandatory FDA approval of research involving Schedule I substances; mandatory special registration with the DEA; mandatory reporting and security procedures beyond those required for drugs placed in Schedules II through V; unavoidable bureaucratic delays; and other adverse impacts due to the grave concern caused by a substance's placement in Schedule I, such as difficulty in obtaining volunteers for clinical studies and, for academic researchers, difficulty in securing approval from institutional review boards.

Again, we do not doubt that Dr. Grinspoon has correctly identified several ways in which the placement of MDMA in Schedule I will impede his research and the efforts of other researchers interested in exploring the possibility of clinical uses for MDMA. We must conclude, nevertheless, that the existence of such hurdles does not render the Administrator's scheduling decision arbitrary and capricious.

Dr. Grinspoon has identified nothing in the CSA, its legislative history, or its implementing regulations that can be read to require the Administrator to consider the impact of a scheduling determination upon legitimate scientific research. From our review of the CSA, we can only conclude that Congress has already weighed the costs and benefits of legitimate research on dangerous drugs and has determined, in a categorical manner, that if the three Schedule I criteria are satisfied, then the substance should be subject to Schedule I controls even if this action will create administrative and other burdens for researchers. Here there is no dispute that the Administrator *considered* all of the section 812(b)(1) criteria in arriving at his final rule, so we are left with a situation in which there can be no complaint that the Administrator failed to consider any relevant factor.

Dr. Grinspoon's final dissatisfaction with the final rule is the Administrator's alleged reliance on the conclusions recommended by HHS on the criteria enumerated in section 812(b)(1). Grinspoon argues that the determination by the Secretary of HHS was arbitrary and capricious and not in accordance with law, and that all relevant scientific and medical evidence was not before the Secretary at the time of the determination. The record, in fact, reveals that HHS performed in a less than admirable fashion in making its recommendation to the Administrator. The record indicates that HHS failed to look beyond its own files upon receiving the Administrator's section 811(b) request for a scientific and medical evaluation; neglected to consult any organization of medical professionals or even the FDA's own panel of experts, the Drug Abuse Advisory Committee; and simply rubber-stamped the Administrator's conclusion by adopting the section 811(c) eight-factor analysis already performed by the DEA. There is also evidence that FDA analysts failed to forward a letter received from the National Institute of Drug Abuse, which stated that the evidence cited by the DEA did not support the existence of abuse potential in animals, to either the FDA Commissioner or the Assistant Secretary of HHS prior to the issuance of the HHS recommendation to the Administrator.

Despite these alleged procedural shortcomings, we fail to see how the procedure followed by HHS tainted the Administrator's determination. The CSA does not specify the steps to be taken by HHS; it simply requires the Administrator to request from the Secretary of HHS a scientific and medical evaluation. Moreover, the HHS recommendation to schedule a substance is not binding[18] and, indeed, serves to trigger an administrative hearing at which interested persons may introduce evidence to rebut the Secretary's scheduling recommendation. Ultimately, of course, responsibility rests with the Administrator, not HHS, to ensure that the final rule rests on permissible legal standards and substantial evidence. It is true that the Administrator twice mentioned the HHS recommendation in his final rule, once in relation to the "accepted medical use" criterion and once in relation to the "high potential for abuse" criterion. With regard to the first mention, however, we have already determined that this aspect of the case must be remanded and reconsidered because the Administrator interpreted the statutory language in a manner that is contrary to the intent of Congress. Because, on remand, the Administrator will not be able to rely on lack of FDA approval to demonstrate the absence of an accepted medical use, we need not discuss any possible reliance on the HHS recommendation regarding the absence of an accepted medical use. With regard to the second mention, we believe that the Administrator's conclusion that MDMA has a high potential for abuse is amply supported by a substantial amount of independent evidence. Because we believe that the Administrator's finding with regard to MDMA's potential for abuse is justified even in the absence of the HHS recommendation to place MDMA in Schedule I, we hold that any reliance on the HHS evaluation by the Administrator constitutes, at most, harmless error.

For the foregoing reasons, the rule is vacated and remanded to the Administrator for further proceedings consistent with this opinion.

The *Grinspoon* Court observes that the term "United States" is "the only portion of the Schedule I criteria that Congress has expressly defined in the CSA[.]" Why do you think Congress chose not to define any of the other terms in the CSA's classification scheme?

On remand in *Grinspoon*, the Administrator concluded, once again, that MDMA should be placed in Schedule I. The Administrator declined to hold a new hearing and, instead, reached his determination by applying the following definition of "accepted medical use" to the existing evidentiary record: "The characteristics of a drug or other substance with an accepted medical use in treatment include scientifically determined and accepted knowledge of its chemistry; the toxicology and pharmacology of the substance in animals; establishment of its effectiveness in humans through scientifically designed clinical trials; general availability of the substance and information regarding its use; recognition of its clinical use in generally accepted pharmacopia, medical references, journals or textbooks; specific indications for the treatment of recognized disorders; recognition of the use of the substance by organizations or associations of physicians; and recognition and use of the substance by a substantial segment of the medical practitioners in the United States." 53 Fed. Reg. 5156 (1988).

While *Grinspoon* provides a revealing introduction to many of the key questions raised by the CSA's scheduling provisions, no scheduling issue has generated as much interest (or litigation) as marijuana's classification as a Schedule I substance. In 1972, the National Organization for the Reform of Marijuana Laws (NORML) filed a petition seeking to reschedule marijuana. The matter worked its way through the administrative process and the courts for 22 years before it was finally resolved in 1994. During that time, the

---

18. According to section 811(b), the HHS recommendation is binding as to "scientific and medical" matters, but not with respect to the appropriate schedule in which to place a particular substance. The exception to this rule is that, "if the Secretary recommends that a drug or other substance *not* be controlled, the Attorney General shall not control the drug or other substance." 21 U.S.C. § 812(b) (emphasis supplied).

United States Court of Appeals for the District of Columbia considered appeals related to NORML's petition on five separate occasions. NORML's effort proved unsuccessful and marijuana remains classified as a Schedule I substance.

Though other organizations and individuals have filed marijuana rescheduling petitions after the conclusion of NORML's case, the final series of administrative and court decisions in response to NORML's petition provide a particularly illuminating look at the CSA's classification scheme. Presented below are three decisions from the NORML petition: a 1988 opinion by Administrative Law Judge Francis Young recommending marijuana be transferred to Schedule II; the Drug Enforcement Administrator's 1989 order rejecting Young's recommendation; and a 1991 decision by the District of Columbia Court of Appeals that addresses the Administrator's order. As you read these decisions, pay particular attention to how each defines "currently accepted medical use" and "accepted safety for use of the drug or other substance under medical supervision."

In the Matter of Marijuana Rescheduling Petition
September 6, 1988

Opinion and Recommended Ruling, Findings of Fact, Conclusions of Law and Decision of Administrative Law Judge Francis L. Young.

This is a rulemaking pursuant to the Administrative Procedure Act to determine whether the marijuana plant (Cannabis sativa L) considered as a whole may lawfully be transferred from Schedule I to Schedule II of the schedules established by the Controlled Substances Act (the Act). None of the parties is seeking to "legalize" marijuana generally or for recreational purposes. Placement in Schedule II would mean, essentially, that physicians in the United States would not violate Federal law by prescribing marijuana for their patients for legitimate therapeutic purposes. It is contrary to Federal law for physicians to do this as long as marijuana remains in Schedule I. This proceeding had its origins on May 18, 1972 when the National Organization for the Reform of Marijuana Laws (NORML) and two other groups submitted a petition to the Bureau of Narcotics and Dangerous Drugs (BNDD), predecessor agency to the Drug Enforcement Administration (DEA or the Agency), asking that marijuana be removed from Schedule I and freed of all controls entirely, or be transferred from Schedule I to Schedule V where it would be subject to only minimal controls. The Act by its terms had placed marijuana in Schedule I thereby declaring, as a matter of law that it had no legitimate use in therapy in the United States and subjecting the substance to the strictest level of controls. The Act had been in effect for just over one year when NORML submitted its 1972 petition.

On September 1, 1972 the Director of BNDD announced his refusal to accept the petition for filing, stating that he was not authorized to institute proceedings for the action requested because of the provisions of the Single Convention on Narcotic Drugs, 1961. NORML appealed this action to the United States Court of Appeals for the District of Columbia Circuit. The court held that the Director had erred in rejecting the petition without "a reflective consideration and analysis," observing that the Director's refusal "was not the kind of agency action that promoted the kind of interchange and refinement of views that is the lifeblood of a sound administrative process." The court remanded the matter in January 1974 for further proceedings not inconsistent with its opinion, "to be denominated a consideration on the merits."

A three-day hearing was held at DEA by Administrative Law Judge Lewis Parker in January 1975. The judge found in NORML's favor on several issues but the Acting Administrator of DEA entered a final order denying NORML's petition "in all respects." NORML again petitioned the court for review. Finding fault with DEA's final order the court again remanded for further proceedings not inconsistent with its opinion. The Court directed the then-Acting Administrator of DEA to refer NORML's petition to the Secretary of the Department of Health, Education and Welfare (HEW) for findings and, thereafter, to comply with the rulemaking procedures outlined in the Act at 21 U.S.C. § 811 (a) and (b).

On remand the Administrator of DEA referred NORML's petition to HEW for scientific and medical evaluation. On June 4, 1979 the Secretary of HEW advised the Administrator of the results of the HEW evaluation and recommended that marijuana remain in Schedule I. Without holding any further hearing the Administrator of DEA proceeded to issue a final order ten days later denying NORML's petition and declining to initiate proceedings to transfer marijuana from Schedule I. NORML went back to the Court of Appeals.

When the case was called for oral argument there was discussion of the then-present status of the matter. DEA had moved for a partial remand. The court found that "reconsideration of all the issues in this case would be appropriate" and again remanded it to DEA, observing: "We regrettably find it necessary to remind respondents [DEA and HEW] of an agency's obligation on remand not to 'do anything which is contrary to either the letter or spirit of the mandate construed in the light of the opinion of [the] court deciding the case.'" DEA was directed to refer all the substances at issue to the Department of Health and Human Services (HHS), successor agency to HEW, for scientific and medical findings and recommendations on scheduling. DEA did so and HHS has responded. In a letter dated April 1, 1986 the then-Acting Deputy Administrator of DEA requested this administrative law judge to commence hearing procedures as to the proposed rescheduling of marijuana and its components.

After the Judge conferred with counsel for NORML and DEA, a notice was published in the Federal Register on June 24, 1986 announcing that hearings would be held on NORML's petition for the rescheduling of marijuana and its components commencing on August 21, 1986 and giving any interested person who desired to participate the opportunity to do so.

Of the three original petitioning organizations in 1972 only NORML is a party to the present proceeding. In addition the following entities responded to the Federal Register notice and have become parties, participating to varying degrees: the Alliance for Cannabis Therapeutics (ACT), Cannabis Corporation of America (CCA) and Carl Eric Olsen, all seeking transfer of marijuana to Schedule II; the Agency, National Federation of Parents for Drug-Free Youth (NFP) and the International Association of Chiefs of Police (IACP), all contending that marijuana should remain in Schedule I.

Preliminary pre-hearing sessions were held on August 21 and December 5, 1986 and on February 20, 1987. During the preliminary stages, on January 20, 1987, NORML filed an amended petition for rescheduling. This new petition abandoned NORML's previous requests for the complete descheduling of marijuana or rescheduling to Schedule V. It asks only that marijuana be placed in Schedule II.

All Parties present stipulated, for the purpose of this proceeding, that marijuana has a high potential for abuse and that abuse of the marijuana plant may lead to severe psychological or physical dependence.

During the Spring and Summer of 1987 the parties identified their witnesses and put the direct examination testimony of each witness in writing in affidavit form. Copies of these affidavits were exchanged. Similarly, the parties assembled their proposed exhibits and exchanged copies. Opportunity was provided for each party to submit objections to the direct examination testimony and exhibits proffered by the others. The objections submitted were considered by the administrative law judge and ruled on. The testimony and exhibits not excluded were admitted into the record. Thereafter hearing sessions were held at which witnesses were subjected to cross-examination. These sessions were held in New Orleans, Louisiana on November 18 and 19, 1987; in San Francisco, California on December 8 and 9, 1987; and in Washington, D.C. on January 5 through 8 and 26 through 29, and on February 2, 4 and 5, 1988. The parties have submitted proposed findings and conclusions and briefs. Oral arguments were heard by the judge on June 10, 1988 in Washington.

The Act provides (21 U.S.C. § 812(b)) that a drug or other substance may not be placed in any schedule unless certain specified findings are made with respect to it. The findings required for Schedule I and Schedule II are as follows:

Schedule I. (A) The drug or other substance has a high potential for abuse. (B) The drug or other substance has no currently accepted medical use in treatment in the United States. (C) There is a lack of accepted safety for use of the drug or other substance under medical supervision.

Schedule II. (A) The drug or other substance has a high potential for abuse. (B) The drug or other substance has a currently accepted medical use in treatment in the United States or a currently accepted medical use with severe restrictions. (C) Abuse of the drug or other substances [sic] may lead to severe psychological or physical dependence.

As noted above the parties have stipulated, for the purpose of this proceeding, that marijuana has a high potential for abuse and that abuse of it may lead to severe psychological or physical dependence. Thus the dispute between the two sides in this proceeding is narrowed to whether or not marijuana has a currently accepted medical use in treatment in the United States, and whether or not there is a lack of accepted safety for use of marijuana under medical supervision.

With respect to whether or not marijuana has a "currently accepted medical use in treatment in the United States" for chemotherapy patients, the record shows the following facts to be uncontroverted.

One of the most serious problems experienced by cancer patients undergoing chemotherapy for their cancer is severe nausea and vomiting caused by their reaction to the toxic (poisonous) chemicals administered to them in the course of this treatment. This nausea and vomiting at times becomes life threatening. The therapy itself creates a tremendous strain on the body. Some patients cannot tolerate the severe nausea and vomiting and discontinue treatment. Beginning in the 1970s there was considerable doctor-to-doctor communication in the United States concerning patients known by their doctors to be surreptitiously using marijuana with notable success to overcome or lessen their nausea and vomiting.

Many physicians, some engaged in medical practice and some teaching in medical schools, have accepted smoking marijuana as effective in controlling or reducing the severe nausea and vomiting (emesis) experienced by some cancer patients undergoing chemotherapy for cancer.

Such physicians include board-certified internists, oncologists and psychiatrists. (Oncology is the treatment of cancer through the use of highly toxic chemicals, or chemotherapy.) Doctors who have come to accept the usefulness of marijuana in controlling or reducing emesis resulting from chemotherapy have done so as the result of reading reports of studies and anecdotal reports in their professional literature, and as the result of observing patients and listening to reports directly from patients.

In many cases doctors have found that, in addition to suppressing nausea and vomiting, smoking marijuana is a highly successful appetite stimulant. The importance of appetite stimulation in cancer therapy cannot be overstated. Patients receiving chemotherapy often lose tremendous amounts of weight. They endanger their lives because they lose interest in food and in eating. The resulting sharp reduction in weight may well affect their prognosis. Marijuana smoking induces some patients to eat. The benefits are obvious, doctors have found. There is no significant loss of weight. Some patients will gain weight. This allows them to retain strength and makes them better able to fight the cancer. Psychologically, patients who can continue to eat even while receiving chemotherapy maintain a balanced outlook and are better able to cope with their disease and its treatment, doctors have found.

The vomiting induced by chemotherapeutic drugs may last up to four days following the chemotherapy treatment. The vomiting can be intense, protracted and, in some instances, is unendurable. The nausea which follows such vomiting is also deep and prolonged. Nausea may prevent a patient from taking regular food or even much water for periods of weeks at a time.

The State of New Mexico set up a program in 1978 to make marijuana available to cancer patients pursuant to an act of the State legislature. The legislature had accepted marijuana as having medical use in treatment. It overwhelmingly passed this legislation so as to make marijuana available for use in therapy, not just for research. Marijuana and synthetic THC were given to patients, administered under medical supervision, to control or reduce emesis. The marijuana was in the form of cigarettes obtained from the Federal government. The program operated from 1979 until 1986, when funding for it was terminated by the State. During those seven years about 250 cancer patients in New Mexico received either marijuana cigarettes or THC. Twenty or 25 physicians in New Mexico sought and obtained marijuana cigarettes or THC for their cancer patients during that period. All of the oncologists in New Mexico accepted marijuana as effective for some of their patients. At least ten hospitals [were] involved in this program in New Mexico, in which cancer patients smoked their marijuana cigarettes. The hospitals accepted this medicinal marijuana smoking by patients. Voluminous reports filed by the participating physicians make it clear that marijuana is a highly effective anti-emetic substance. It was found in the New Mexico program to be far superior to the best available conventional anti-emetic drug, compazine, and clearly superior to synthetic THC pills. More than 90% of the patients who received marijuana within the New Mexico program reported significant or total relief from nausea and vomiting. Before the program began cancer patients were surreptitiously smoking marijuana in New Mexico to lessen or control their emesis resulting from chemotherapy treatments. They reported to physicians that it was successful for this purpose. Physicians were aware that this was going on.

Certain law enforcement authorities have been outspoken in their acceptance of marijuana as an antiemetic agent. Robert T. Stephan, Attorney General of the State of Kansas, and himself a former cancer patient, said of chemotherapy in his affidavit in this record: "The treatment becomes a terror." His cancer is now in remission. He came to know a number of health care professionals whose medical judgment he respected. They had accepted marijuana as having medical use in treatment. He was elected Vice President of the National Association of Attorneys General (NAAG) in 1983. He was instrumental in the adoption by that body in June 1983 of a resolution acknowledging the efficacy of marijuana for cancer and glaucoma patients. The resolution expressed the support of NAAG for legislation then pending in the Congress to make marijuana available on prescription to cancer and glaucoma patients. The resolution was adopted by an overwhelming margin. NAAG's President, the Attorney General of Montana, issued a statement that marijuana does have accepted medical uses and is improperly classified at present. The Chairman of NAAG's Criminal Law and Law Enforcement Committee, the Attorney General of Pennsylvania, issued a statement emphasizing that the proposed rescheduling of marijuana would in no way affect or impede existing efforts by law enforcement authorities to crack down on illegal drug trafficking.

[The Administrative Law Judge then recounted a number of additional stories of patients and doctors who had concluded that marijuana had medicinal value.]

From the foregoing uncontroverted facts it is clear beyond any question that many people find marijuana to have, in the words of the Act, an "accepted medical use in treatment in the United States" in effecting relief for cancer patients. Oncologists, physicians treating cancer patients, accept this. Other medical practitioners and researchers accept this. Medical faculty professors accept it. Nurses performing hands-on patient care accept it. Patients accept it.

Of relevance, also, is the acceptance of marijuana by state attorneys-general, officials whose primary concern is law enforcement. A large number of them have no fear that placing marijuana in Schedule II, thus making it available for legitimate therapy, will in any way impede existing efforts of law enforcement authorities to crack down on illegal drug trafficking.

The Act does not specify by whom a drug or substance must be "accepted [for] medical use in treatment" in order to meet the Act's "accepted" requirement for placement in Schedule II. Department of Justice witnesses told the Congress during hearings in 1970 preceding passage of the Act that "the medical Profession" would make this determination, that the matter would be "determined by the medical community." The Deputy Chief Counsel of BNDD, whose office had written the bill with this language in it, told the House subcommittee that "this basic determination ... is not made by any part of the federal government. It is made by the medical community as to whether or not the drug has medical use or doesn't".

No one would seriously contend that these Justice Department witnesses meant that the entire medical community would have to be in agreement on the usefulness of a drug or substance. Seldom, if ever, do all lawyers agree on a point of law. Seldom, if ever, do all doctors agree on a medical question. How many are required here? A majority of 51%? It would be unrealistic to attempt a plebiscite of all doctors in the country on such a question every time it arises, to obtain a majority vote.

In determining whether a medical procedure utilized by a doctor is actionable as malpractice the courts have adopted the rule what it is acceptable for a doctor to employ a method of treatment supported by a respectable minority of physicians.

As noted above, there is no question but that this record shows a great many physicians, and others, to have "accepted" marijuana as having a medical use in the treatment of cancer patients' emesis. True, all physicians have not "accepted" it. But to require universal, 100% acceptance would be unreasonable. Acceptance by "a respectable minority" of physicians is all that can reasonably be required. The record here establishes conclusively that at least "a respectable minority" of physicians has "accepted" marijuana as having a "medical use in treatment in the United States." That others may not makes no difference.

It is not for [the DEA] to tell doctors whether they should or should not accept a drug or substance for medical use. The statute directs the Administrator merely to ascertain whether, in fact, doctors have done so.

The overwhelming preponderance of the evidence in this record establishes that marijuana has a currently accepted medical use in treatment in the United States for nausea and vomiting resulting from chemotherapy treatments in some cancer patients. To conclude otherwise, on this record, would be unreasonable, arbitrary and capricious.

[The Administrative Law Judge then analyzed other claimed medical uses of marijuana and concluded that marijuana also had an accepted medical use in treatment in the United States for spasticity resulting from multiple sclerosis and for hyperparathyroidism. The Judge found, however, that marijuana did not have an accepted medical use in treatment in the United States for glaucoma because the record "fail[ed] to show that the preponderance of the evidence that a respectable minority of physicians accepts marijuana as being useful in the treatment of glaucoma in the United States."]

With respect to whether or not there is "a lack of accepted safety for use of [marijuana] under medical supervision", the record shows the following facts to be uncontroverted.

The most obvious concern when dealing with drug safety is the possibility of lethal effects. Can the drug cause death?

Nearly all medicines have toxic, potentially lethal effects. But marijuana is not such a substance. There is no record in the extensive medical literature describing a proven, documented cannabis-induced fatality.

This is a remarkable statement. First, the record on marijuana encompasses 5,000 years of human experience. Second, marijuana is now used daily by enormous numbers of people throughout the world. Estimates suggest that from twenty million to fifty million Americans routinely, albeit illegally, smoke marijuana without the benefit of direct medical supervision. Yet, despite this long history of use and the extraordinarily high numbers of social smokers, there are simply no credible medical reports to suggest that consuming marijuana has caused a single death.

By contrast aspirin, a commonly used, over-the-counter medicine, causes hundreds of deaths each year.

Drugs used in medicine are routinely given what is called an LD-50. The LD-50 rating indicates at what dosage fifty percent of test animals receiving a drug will die as a result of drug induced toxicity. A number of researchers have attempted to determine marijuana's LD-50 rating in test animals, without success. Simply stated, researchers have been unable to give animals enough marijuana to induce death.

At present it is estimated that marijuana's LD-50 is around 1:20,000 or 1:40,000. In layman terms this means that in order to induce death a marijuana smoker would have to consume 20,000 to 40,000 times as much marijuana as is contained in one marijuana cigarette. A smoker would theoretically have to consume nearly 1,500 pounds of marijuana within about fifteen minutes to induce a lethal response.

Another common medical way to determine drug safety is called the therapeutic ratio. This ratio defines the difference between a therapeutically effective dose and a dose which is capable of inducing adverse effects.

A commonly used over-the-counter product like aspirin has a therapeutic ratio of around 1:20. Two aspirins are the recommended dose for adult patients. Twenty times this dose, forty aspirins, may cause a lethal reaction in some patients, and will almost certainly cause gross injury to the digestive system, including extensive internal bleeding.

The therapeutic ratio for prescribed drugs is commonly around 1:10 or lower. Valium, a commonly used prescriptive drug, may cause very serious biological damage if patients use ten times the recommended (therapeutic) dose.

There are, of course, prescriptive drugs which have much lower therapeutic ratios. Many of the drugs used to treat patients with cancer, glaucoma and multiple sclerosis are highly toxic. The therapeutic ratio of some of the drugs used in antineoplastic therapies, for example, are regarded as extremely toxic poisons with therapeutic ratios that may fall below 1:1.5. These drugs also have very low LD-50 ratios and can result in toxic, even lethal reactions, while being properly employed.

By contrast, marijuana's therapeutic ratio, like its LD-50, is impossible to quantify because it is so high.

In strict medical terms marijuana is far safer than many foods we commonly consume. For example, eating ten raw potatoes can result in a toxic response. By comparison, it is physically impossible to eat enough marijuana to induce death.

Marijuana, in its natural form, is one of the safest therapeutically active substances known to man. By any measure of rational analysis marijuana can be safely used within a supervised routine of medical care.

[By contrast, for example,] Cisplatin, one of the most powerful chemo-therapeutic agents used on humans may cause deafness; may lead to life-threatening kidney difficulties and kidney failure; adversely affects the body's immune system, suppressing the patient's ability to fight a host of common infections.

[Many currently used cancer treatment] agents cause a number of disturbing adverse effects. Most of these drugs cause hair loss. Studies increasingly indicate all of these drugs may cause other forms of cancer. Death due to kidney, heart or respiratory failure is a very real possibility with all of these agents and the margin for error is minimal. Similarly, there is a danger of overdosing a patient weakened by his cancer. Put simply, there is very great risk associated with the medical use of these chemicals agents. Despite these high risks, all of these drugs are considered "safe" for use under medical supervision and are regularly administered to patients on doctor's orders in the United States today.

There have been occasional instances of panic reaction in patients who have smoked marijuana. Such persons have responded to simple person-to-person communication with a doctor and have sustained no long term mental or physical damage. If marijuana could be legally obtained, and administered in an open, medically-supervised session rather than surreptitiously, the few instances of such adverse reaction doubtless would be reduced in number and severity.

Other reported side effects of marijuana have been minimal. Sedation often results. Sometimes mild euphoria is experienced. Short periods of increased pulse rate and of dizziness are occasionally experienced. Marijuana should not be used by persons anxious or depressed or psychotic or with certain other health problems. Physicians could readily screen out such patients if marijuana were being employed as an agent under medical supervision.

All drugs have "side effects" and all drugs used in medicine for their therapeutic benefits have unwanted, unintended, sometimes adverse effects.

The [Controlled Substances] Act, at 21 U.S.C. §812(b)(1)(C), requires that marijuana be retained in Schedule I if "[t]here is a lack of accepted safety for use of [it] under medical supervision." If there is no lack of such safety, if it is accepted that this substance can be used with safety under medical supervision, then it is unreasonable to keep it in Schedule I.

Again we must ask[:] "accepted" by whom?

The gist of the Agency's case against recognizing marijuana's acceptance as safe is to assert that more studies, more tests are needed. The Agency has presented highly qualified and respected experts, researchers and others, who hold that view. But, as demonstrated in the discussion above, it is unrealistic and unreasonable to require unanimity of opinion on the question confronting us. For the reasons there indicated, acceptance by a significant minority of doctors is all that can reasonably be required. This record makes it abundantly clear that such acceptance exists in the United States.

Based upon the facts established in this record and set out above one must reasonably conclude that there is accepted safety for use of marijuana under medical supervision. To conclude otherwise, on this record, would be unreasonable, arbitrary and capricious.

Based upon the foregoing facts and reasoning, the administrative law judge concludes that the provisions of the Act permit and require the transfer of marijuana from Schedule I to Schedule II. The Judge realizes that strong emotions are aroused on both sides of any discussion concerning the use of marijuana. Nonetheless it is essential for this Agency, and its Administrator, calmly and dispassionately to review the evidence of record, correctly apply the law, and act accordingly.

Marijuana can be harmful. Marijuana is abused. But the same is true of dozens of drugs or substances which are listed in Schedule II so that they can be employed in treatment by physicians in proper cases, despite their abuse potential.

Transferring marijuana from Schedule I to Schedule II will not, of course, make it immediately available in pharmacies throughout the country for legitimate use in treatment. Other government authorities, Federal and State, will doubtless have to act before that might occur. But this Agency is not charged with responsibility, or given authority, over the myriad other regulatory decisions that may be required before marijuana can actually be legally available. This Agency is charged merely with determining the placement of marijuana pursuant to the provisions of the Act. Under our system of laws the responsibilities of other regulatory bodies are the concerns of those bodies, not of this Agency.

There are those who, in all sincerity, argue that the transfer of Marijuana to Schedule II will "send a signal" that marijuana is "OK" generally for recreational use. This argument is specious. It presents no valid reason for refraining from taking an action required by law in light of the evidence. If marijuana should be placed in Schedule II, in obedience to the law, then that is where marijuana should be placed, regardless of misinterpretation of the placement by some. The reasons for the placement can, and should, be clearly explained at the time the action is taken. The fear of sending such a signal cannot be permitted to override the legitimate need, amply demonstrated in this record, of countless suffers for the relief marijuana can provide when prescribed by a physician in a legitimate case.

The evidence in this record clearly shows that marijuana has been accepted as capable of relieving the distress of great numbers of very ill people, and doing so with safety under medical supervision. It would be unreasonable, arbitrary and capricious for DEA to continue to stand between those sufferers and the benefits of this substance in light of the evidence in this record.

The administrative law judge recommends that the Administrator conclude that the marijuana plant considered as a whole has a currently accepted medical use in treatment in the United States, that there is no lack of accepted safety for use of it under medical supervision and that it may lawfully be transferred from Schedule I to Schedule II. The judge recommends that the Administrator transfer marijuana from Schedule I to Schedule II.

Marijuana Scheduling Petition; Denial of Petition
Drug Enforcement Administration
54 F.R. 53767
December 29, 1989

John C. Lawn, Administrator.

This is a final order of the Administrator of the Drug Enforcement Administration (DEA) denying the petition of the National Organization for Reform of Marijuana Laws (NORML) to reschedule the plant material marijuana from Schedule I to Schedule II of the Controlled Substances Act. This order follows a rulemaking on the record as prescribed by the Controlled Substances Act and the Administrative Procedures Act. There are seven parties in the rulemaking proceeding. Four parties, NORML, the Alliance for Cannabis Therapeutics (ACT), the Cannabis Corporation of America (CCA), and Carl Eric Olsen, comprised the pro-marijuana parties, those advocating the rescheduling of marijuana from Schedule I to Schedule II. The three remaining parties, who advocated that marijuana remain in Schedule I, were DEA, the National Federation of Parents for a Drug-Free Youth, and the International Association of Chiefs of Police (IACP).

The two issues involved in a determination of whether marijuana should be rescheduled from Schedule I to Schedule II are whether marijuana plant material has a currently accepted medical use in treatment in the United States, or a currently accepted medical use with severe restrictions; and whether there is a lack of accepted safety for use of marijuana plant material under medical supervision. After a thorough review of the record in this matter, the Administrator rejects the recommendation of the administrative law judge to reschedule marijuana into Schedule II and finds that the evidence in the record mandates a finding that the marijuana plant material remain in Schedule I of the Controlled Substances Act.

The pro-marijuana parties advocate the placement of marijuana plant material into Schedule II for medical use in the treatment of a wide variety of ailments, including nausea and vomiting associated with chemotherapy, glaucoma, spasticity in amputees and those with multiple sclerosis, epilepsy, poor appetite, addiction to drugs and alcohol, pain, and asthma. The evidence presented by the pro-marijuana parties includes outdated and limited scientific studies; chronicles of individuals, their families and friends who have used marijuana; opinions from over a dozen psychiatrists and physicians; court opinions involving medical necessity as a defense to criminal charges for illegal possession of marijuana; state statutes which made marijuana available for research; newspaper articles; and the opinions of laypersons, including lawyers and associations of lawyers. The Administrator does not find such evidence convincing in light of the lack of reliable, credible, and relevant scientific studies documenting marijuana's medical utility; the opinions of highly respected, credentialed experts that marijuana does not have an accepted medical use; and statements from the American Medical Association, the American Cancer Society, the American Academy of Ophthalmology, the National Multiple Sclerosis Society, and the Federal Food and Drug Administration that marijuana has not been demonstrated as suitable for use as a medicine.

The record contains many research studies which have been published in scientific journals and many unpublished studies conducted by individual states. In order to evaluate the validity of any research study many factors must be considered. Certain scientific practices have been generally accepted by the scientific community which are designed to increase the validity of experimental studies. Studies or research projects which do not follow these accepted scientific practices have very limited, if any, credibility. A review of such studies must first examine the degree to which researchers control, or hold constant, all the variables which could affect the results, except the variable being studied. For example, if you wish to evaluate the effectiveness of marijuana on a group of glaucoma patients, you must control any other medication which the patient is taking. Otherwise, it is impossible to conclude that the results are attributable to the marijuana.

The second factor, or aspect of the design of a research project which must be evaluated, is the placebo effect. This is the tendency of research subjects to act and respond in a manner they believe is expected of them. To eliminate this factor, research subjects are usually "blinded," or not informed, of what drug they are receiving. Results of non-blind studies are questionable since they could be attributable, in large part, to psychological reactions of subjects rather than any real effects from the experimental drug. The next factor which must be minimized or eliminated for a research study to be valid is the expectation of the researcher. This is especially true where the effect being measured is subjective and not objective. For example, if the researcher is evaluating if the patient is nauseated, that is very subjective. If the researcher knows which patients are receiving the experimental drug, his perception of the results could be significantly altered.

Other factors to be considered when evaluating the validity of research include the number of subjects in the study, how the subjects are selected for the study, the length of the study, or how many times the experimental drug is administered, and the measurement of results in quantifiable, objective terms. The fewer the subjects in a research study, the less valid the results. If the sample of subjects is not statistically significant, the chances of the same results being duplicated in other individuals is reduced. Subjects for a research study should be randomly selected and representative of the population that is targeted to use the drug. Testing of marijuana in cancer patients for relief of nausea and vomiting should not be limited to those who have previously used marijuana recreationally and request its use in the study. The length of a study is particularly significant when the drug is to be used to treat a chronic condition such as glaucoma or spasticity. Studies based upon acute or one-time administration of the drug must be viewed with caution when the goal is treatment of a chronic condition. The effectiveness of the drug for long-time administration and the existence of side effects resulting from chronic use will not be revealed in acute studies.

In addition to factors related to the design and execution of a research study, there are two other factors which must be reviewed in evaluation of a research study. Research results are always considered tentative or preliminary until they have been replicated or confirmed by another researcher. The research study must be reported in sufficient detail to permit others to repeat it. Finally, publication of a study in a scientific journal, especially a journal which subjects an article to review prior to publication, adds validity to a study. Journal publication subjects a study to review and scrutiny by the scientific community and opens the door to replication of the studies. Unpublished studies are inherently suspect.

While research studies with the limitations mentioned above may provide useful and preliminary data which will be valuable in designing further studies, research studies with substantial limitations are not sufficient to support a determination that a drug has an accepted medical use. Both the published and unpublished research studies submitted by the pro-marijuana parties in this proceeding to support marijuana's medical use suffer from many deficiencies. They are, in essence, preliminary studies. None of these studies has risen to the level of demonstrating that marijuana has an accepted medical use for treatment of any medical condition.

Five studies were presented by the pro-marijuana parties to support the medical use of marijuana [to treat nausea and vomiting associated with chemotherapy.] [One] study compared a combination of pure THC and marijuana to placebo cigarettes. This study by Chang, et al., *Delta-9-Tetrahydrocannabinol as an Antiemetic in Cancer Patients Receiving High-Dose Methotrexate,* 91 Annals of Internal Medicine, 819–824 (1979), was randomized, double-blind, and placebo controlled. The study concluded, "that a combination of oral and smoked THC is a highly effective antiemetic compared to placebo[.]" This study was limited to 15 subjects, some of whom received both marijuana and THC at the same time. The validity of the results of this study is severely limited by its small size and administration of the mixture of the two drugs, THC and marijuana. The study is not helpful in determining the therapeutic utility of marijuana alone in treating nausea and vomiting.

[Another] study conducted by Dr. Thomas J. Ungerleider, a psychiatrist, involved the administration of marijuana to 16 bone marrow transplant patients suffering from severe nausea and vomiting from radiation therapy. The results of this study are of little value due to the limited number of patients, the subjective nature of the data, and the fact that the results of the study were never published. The conclusion that there was less nausea and vomiting with use of marijuana was based upon the subjects' and researcher's subjective determination. There were no objective measurements, such as number of incidents or frequency of vomiting. During cross-examination, Dr. Ungerleider indicated that the results of the study were not published because there was not enough hard data.

[One of the claimed] stud[ies] presented by the pro-marijuana parties is actually a group of programs, collectively labeled "Controlled Substances Therapeutic Research Programs," conducted by six states in the 1970s and 1980s. These programs involved the use of both marijuana cigarettes and synthetic THC capsules. The programs were given Investigational New Drug (IND) approval by the Food and Drug Administration (FDA) and the marijuana and THC were supplied by the Federal Government. The protocols of these programs were very loosely constructed. There were no controls. That is, there were no individuals who did not take the experimental drugs to compare with those who did. The studies were not blind or double-blind. Every research subject knew what drug they were receiving and, in many cases, were permitted to request either marijuana or THC. The studies were not randomized. In most instances, the results were measured by the subject's subjective evaluation of the drug's effectiveness. This is even more of a problem where the drug in question is a psychotropic or mind-altering substance like marijuana, which by its very nature makes some individuals feel "high," and may distort their perception of physical symptoms. There were no objectively measured results. The results were not published in scientific journals and, in some cases, data were lost or not recorded. The number of individuals who actually smoked marijuana in these studies was relatively small. These state studies were born of compassion and frustration. They abandoned traditional scientific methods in favor of dispensing marijuana to as many individuals as possible on the chance that it might help them. Though well-intentioned, these studies have little scientific value.

The research studies presented by the pro-marijuana parties in this proceeding do not support a conclusion that marijuana has a therapeutic use for treatment of nausea and vomiting associated with chemotherapy.

The pro-marijuana parties presented many testimonials from cancer patients, their families, and friends about the use of marijuana to alleviate nausea and vomiting associated with chemotherapy. These stories of individuals who treat themselves with a mind-altering drug, such as marijuana, must be viewed with great skepticism. There is no scientific merit to any of these accounts. In many cases the individuals were taking a variety of other medications and were using anything which might help treat the cancer as well as the nausea. They were using marijuana purchased on the street, and were unaware of the strength of the drug. They were not using the drug under medical supervision. Many of these individuals had been recreational users of marijuana prior to becoming ill. These individuals' desire for the drug to relieve their symptoms, as well as a desire to rationalize their marijuana use, removes any scientific value from their accounts of marijuana use. There is no doubt that these individuals and their loved-ones believed that marijuana was beneficial. The accounts of these individuals' suffering and illnesses are very moving and tragic; they are not, however, reliable scientific evidence, nor do they provide a basis to conclude that marijuana has an accepted medical use as an antiemetic.

There were many physicians and other medical experts who testified in this proceeding. In reviewing the weight to be given to an expert's opinion, the facts relied upon to reach that opinion and the credentials and experience of the expert must be carefully examined. The experts presented by the pro-marijuana parties were unable to provide a strong scientific or factual basis to support their opinions. In addition, many of the experts presented by the pro-marijuana parties did not have any expertise in the area of research in the specific medical area being addressed. The pro-marijuana parties presented the testimony of five psychiatrists to support the use of marijuana as an antiemetic. None of these individuals is an oncologist, nor have they treated cancer patients. Three of the psychiatrists, Drs. Grinspoon, Ungerleider and Zinberg are current or former board members of NORML or ACT. All these physicians indicated that they relied on scientific studies which they had read, their experience with cancer patients, or stories from others, to reach their conclusions. When questioned on cross-examination as to which studies they relied upon, most were unable to list one study. A review of the available literature has already demonstrated the unreliability of the studies that exist. The testimonials upon which these psychiatrists relied are also scientifically suspect. The opinions of these psychiatrists are, therefore, of little value in determining whether marijuana is therapeutically useful as an antiemetic.

Two general practitioners, Drs. Weil and Kaufman, also provided testimony on behalf of the pro-marijuana parties. Neither are oncologists, nor do they treat cancer patients. Dr. Weil is a wellness counselor at a health spa, and Dr. Kaufman is an officer of a company that audits hospital quality control programs. Dr. Weil has written a number of books on drugs and admitted that he has personally used every mind-altering, illicit drug he has written about. Dr. Kaufman stopped practicing medicine in 1974, and was unable to provide any information on cross-examination regarding the basis for his opinion that marijuana has an accepted medical use. Neither Dr. Weil nor Dr. Kaufman has a credible basis for their opinions regarding marijuana, and, therefore, their testimony will be disregarded.

Four oncologists presented testimony on behalf of the pro-marijuana parties. They were Drs. Goldberg, Silverberg, Bickers, and Stephens. Dr. Goldberg is a board certified oncologist, but practices primarily internal medicine. She only administers chemotherapy to one or two patients a year. In her career, she has administered chemotherapy to no more than ten patients whom she believed to be using marijuana. On cross-examination, she could not recall any studies regarding marijuana. Dr. Goldberg was a member and financial contributor to NORML. Dr. Silverberg has practiced oncology for 20 years. He is a Professor of Clinical Oncology at the University of California at San Francisco, but is not a board certified oncologist. In his testimony, Dr. Silverberg indicated that there was voluminous medical research regarding marijuana's effectiveness in treating nausea and vomiting. On cross-examination, Dr. Silverberg could not identify any studies, and was forced to admit that he had been incorrect and that there were, in fact, very few studies conducted using marijuana as an antiemetic. Although Dr. Silverberg has advised patients to use marijuana to control nausea and vomiting associated with chemotherapy, he has never been involved in any research nor has he documented any of his observations. Dr. Bickers is an oncologist in New Orleans and is a Professor of Medicine at the Louisiana University School of Medicine. Although Dr. Bickers claims that young patients have better control over nausea and vomiting after using marijuana, he has never documented this claim. Dr. Bickers was unable to identify any scientific information which he relied upon in reaching his conclusion regarding marijuana. Dr. Stephens, an oncologist, Professor of Medicine and Director of Clinical Oncology at the University of Kansas, characterized marijuana as a "highly effective, and in some cases, critical drug in the reduction of chemotherapeutically-induced emesis." During cross-examination, Dr. Stephens stated that he was unaware of any scientific studies which had been done with marijuana, and that he had never done research or treated patients with marijuana. He indicated that he received his information about the patient's use of marijuana from the nursing staff or the patient's family. None of these oncologists based their opinions about marijuana on scientific studies or their own research. Most did not base their opinions on their direct observations, but on the opinions of others. In light of lack of scientific basis for these opinions, they will be given little regard.

The agency presented the testimony of nationally recognized experts in oncology. Dr. Ettinger, a Professor of Oncology at Johns Hopkins School of Medicine, is the author of over 100 published articles on cancer treatment. Dr. Ettinger testified: "There is no indication that marijuana is effective in treating nausea and vomiting resulting from radiation treatment or other causes. No legitimate studies have been conducted which make such conclusions."

Dr. Laszlo, currently Vice President of Research for the American Cancer Society, is an expert who has devoted the majority of his over 30 years in medicine to the treatment of cancer. During his career, he spent eleven years as the Director of Clinical Programs at the Duke University Comprehensive Cancer Center. Dr. Laszlo has authored numerous scientific articles about cancer research and treatment and has written a book titled, *Antiemetics and Cancer Chemotherapy*. In his testimony for this proceeding, Dr. Laszlo stated that he does not advocate the use of marijuana as an antiemetic, in part, because there has not been sufficient testing of marijuana to show that it is a safe and effective drug. He also indicated that because there are other available, highly effective antiemetics, a physician does not need to resort to a crude drug such as marijuana. Dr. Laszlo concluded that marijuana does not have a currently accepted medical use in the United States for treatment of nausea and vomiting resulting from cancer chemotherapy.

The American Cancer Society provided DEA with its policy statements regarding medical use of marijuana. The American Cancer Society has, and continues to, support research with substances which may provide relief to cancer patients, including marijuana. It states, however, that the results of clinical investigations are insufficient to warrant the decontrol of marijuana for medical use. The American Medical Association has expressed a similar opinion.

The Food and Drug Administration has provided DEA with a scientific and medical evaluation of marijuana, as well as testimony from one of its leading pharmacologists. Evaluating marijuana against its criteria for safety and effectiveness, FDA has concluded that there is inadequate scientific evidence to support a finding that marijuana is safe and effective for treating nausea and vomiting experienced by patients undergoing chemotherapy.

The numerous testimonials and opinions of lay persons which were presented in this proceeding by the pro-marijuana parties are not useful in determining whether marijuana has a medical use. While experiences of individuals with medical conditions who use marijuana may provide a basis for research, they cannot be substituted for reliable scientific evidence. For the many reasons stated in the previous discussion of scientific evidence, these statements can be given little weight. Similarly, endorsements by such organizations as the National Association of Attorneys General, that marijuana has a medical use as an antiemetic, are of little persuasive value when compared with statements from the American Cancer Society and the American Medical Association.

[The Administrator then discussed the evidence related to the use of marijuana as a medicine to treat glaucoma and spasticity.]

In order to be effective, a drug's therapeutic benefits must be balanced against, and outweigh, its negative or adverse effects. This has not been established with marijuana. As the previously discussed evidence has demonstrated, there is as yet no reliable scientific evidence to support marijuana's therapeutic benefit. It is, therefore, impossible to balance the benefit against the negative effects. The negative effects of marijuana use are well-documented in the record. Marijuana smoking, the route of administration advocated by many witnesses presented by the pro-marijuana parties, causes many well-known and scientifically documented side effects. These include decreased blood pressure, rapid heart rate, drowsiness, euphoria, disphoria and impairment of motor function, not to mention various negative effects on the respiratory and pulmonary systems. Therefore, the only conclusion is that marijuana is not safe for use under medical supervision, because its safety has not been established by reliable scientific evidence.

In summary, the Administrator finds that there is insufficient, and in many instances no, reliable, credible, scientific evidence, supported by properly conducted scientific research, to support a conclusion that marijuana has a medical use to treat any ailment or disease. In addition, there is a lack of scientific evidence to support a conclusion that marijuana is safe for use under medical supervision. This agency, and the Government as a whole, would be doing the public a disservice by concluding that this complex psychoactive drug with serious adverse effects has a medical use based upon anecdotal and unreliable evidence. The evidence presented by the pro-marijuana parties in this proceeding consisted of a few published scientific studies involving marijuana and THC, testimony of general practice physicians and psychiatrists, and testimony of individuals who have used marijuana for various medical conditions. The majority of these individuals did not use marijuana under medical supervision and used "street" marijuana. In contrast, recognized, credentialed specialists in the fields of oncology, glaucoma and multiple sclerosis, and organizations involved in medical research in these areas, have concluded that marijuana does not have an accepted medical use in treatment in the United States. The Administrator would be abdicating his responsibility to the public if he concluded that marijuana has a medical use and is safe for use under medical supervision.

The Administrator finds that the administrative law judge failed to act as an impartial judge in this matter. He appears to have ignored the scientific evidence, ignored the testimony of highly-credible and recognized medical experts and, instead, relied on the testimony of psychiatrists and individuals who used marijuana.

The Administrator rejects the administrative law judge's findings and conclusions. They were erroneous; they were not based upon credible evidence; nor were they based upon evidence in the record as a whole. Therefore, in this case, they carry no weight and do not represent the position of the agency or its Administrator. The inadequacy of Judge Young's analysis of the case is exemplified by his acceptance of, and reliance upon, irresponsible and irrational statements propounded by the pro-marijuana parties. Such statements include the following: "marijuana is far safer than many of the foods we commonly consume. For example, eating ten raw potatoes can result in a toxic response. By comparison, it is physically impossible to eat enough marijuana to induce death." That such a statement would come from the proponents of marijuana is understandable. To give it the weight of an administrative law judge's finding is appalling.

The Administrator has accepted the agency's findings of fact as his own. In order to conclude that these facts support a conclusion that marijuana remain in Schedule I, they must be applied to the criteria set forth in the Controlled Substances Act for substances in Schedule I.

The three criteria are found at 21 U.S.C. 812(b)(1) and are as follows:

(a) The drug or other substance has a high potential for abuse.

(b) The drug or other substance has no currently accepted medical use in treatment in the United States.

(c) There is lack of accepted safety for use of the drug or other substance under medical supervision.

For purposes of this proceeding, the parties stipulated that marijuana has a high potential for abuse. The criteria for substances listed in Schedule II also includes that the drug has a high potential for abuse.

The issue of what "currently accepted medical use in treatment in the United States," and "accepted safety for use ... under medical supervision" mean, has been the subject of a previous scheduling proceeding involving the drug MDMA. In that proceeding, the Administrator did not adopt Judge Young's recommendation and defined both phrases to mean approved for marketing as safe and effective pursuant to the Food, Drug, and Cosmetic Act. The Administrator's decision was reviewed by the United States Court of Appeals for the First Circuit in *Grinspoon v. DEA*, 828 F.2d 881 (1987). The Court remanded the matter to the Administrator finding that his standard was too restrictive. The Court did not suggest a standard to be adopted and, instead, stated that "Congress has implicitly delegated to the Administrator the authority to interpret these portions of the CSA[.]" The Administrator then published a revised final rule in which he listed several characteristics of a drug or other substance which has an "accepted medical use in treatment in the United States." These characteristics are:

1. Scientifically determined and accepted knowledge of its chemistry;

2. The toxicology and pharmacology of the substance in animals;

3. Establishment of its effectiveness in humans through scientifically designed clinical trials;

4. General availability of the substance and information regarding the substance and its use;

5. Recognition of its clinical use in generally accepted pharmacopeia, medical references, journals or textbooks;

6. Specific indications for the treatment of recognized disorders;

7. Recognition of the use of the substance by organizations or associations of physicians; and

8. Recognition and use of the substance by a substantial segment of the medical practitioners in the United States.

These characteristics rely heavily on verifiable scientific data and acceptance by the medical community. These two areas go hand-in-hand, as aptly demonstrated by the record in this proceeding. Most physicians and organizations of physicians rely on scientific data in formulating their opinions regarding the safety and effectiveness of a drug and whether they will provide it for their patients. Many of the experts and organizations who concluded that marijuana did not have an "accepted medical use in treatment in the United States," stated that they reached this conclusion because of the lack of adequate scientific data to support the safety and efficacy of marijuana. The Administrator also notes that the Controlled Substances Act and its legislative history require him to consider scientific evidence in determining the schedule in which a drug should be placed. For example, the Controlled Substances Act at 21 U.S.C. 811(c) lists eight factors to be considered in evaluating the three scheduling criteria. Included among those factors are "scientific evidence of its pharmacological effect, if known" and "the state of current scientific knowledge regarding the drug or other substance." In addition, the Controlled Substances Act requires the Administrator to request a scientific and medical evaluation from the Secretary of Health and Human Services. The Administrator is then bound by the Secretary's recommendation as to scientific and medical matters. In this proceeding, the Assistant Secretary for Health has provided the Administrator with an extensive scientific and medical evaluation in which it was recommended that marijuana remain in Schedule I because there is insufficient scientific and medical evidence to conclude that marijuana is a safe and effective drug.

It is clear from the evidence presented in this proceeding that marijuana does not have the characteristics of a drug which has an "accepted medical use in treatment in the United States." Because of the complex composition of marijuana, containing over 400 separate constituents (many of which have not been tested) varying from plant to plant, the chemistry, toxicology and pharmacology of marijuana is not established. As discussed previously, the effectiveness of marijuana has not been documented in humans with scientifically-designed clinical trials. While many individuals have used marijuana and claim that it is effective in treating their ailments, these testimonials do not rise to the level of scientific evidence. Marijuana is available from the Federal Government to those researchers who obtain proper licensure. However, the evidence suggests that only small numbers of researchers and physicians have obtained marijuana for this purpose, and that some research programs sponsored by states had trouble getting physicians to participate. The vast majority of physicians do not accept marijuana as having a medical use. Marijuana is not recognized as medicine in generally accepted pharmacopeia, medical references, journals or textbooks. As evidenced by expert physician testimony and the statements of many professional medical and research organizations, marijuana is not accepted by organized medicine or a substantial segment of the physician population.

The administrative law judge's conclusion that a "respectable minority" of physicians is all that is necessary to establish accepted medical use in treatment in the United States is preposterous. By placing a substance in Schedule II, the Administrator, and through him, the Federal Government, establishes a national standard for drug use. Using the same criteria as medical malpractice cases to determine a national standard of medical acceptance is untenable. It must be recognized that in every profession, including the medical and scientific community, there are those that deviate from the accepted practices of the profession. These deviations may be the beginning of new revolutionary treatments or they may be rejected as quackery. The opinions of those few physicians and scientists are not sufficient to create a finding of national acceptance. The Administrator feels that, in light of the potential risks of declaring a drug has an accepted medical use in treatment in the United States, he must adhere to the strict standard that was established in the MDMA proceeding. It is clear that the evidence conclusively demonstrates that marijuana does not have an accepted medical use in treatment in the United States or an accepted medical use with severe restrictions.

The Administrator's standard for "accepted safety for use ... under medical supervision" was also stated in the second MDMA final rule published on February 22, 1988. The tests for determining accepted safety of a drug were stated as follows: "The first requirement in determining safety of a substance is that the chemistry of the substance must be known and reproducible. The next step is to conduct animal toxicity studies to show that the substance will not produce irreversible harm to organs at proposed human doses. Limited clinical trials may then be initiated, but they must be carefully controlled so that adverse effects can be monitored and studies terminated if necessary ... safety in humans is evaluated as a risk/benefit ratio for a specific use."

It is clear that marijuana cannot meet the criteria set forth above for safety under medical supervision. The chemistry of marijuana is not known and reproducible. The record supports a finding that marijuana plant material is variable from plant to plant. The quantities of the active constituents, the cannabinoids, vary considerably. In addition, the actions and potential risks of several of the cannabinoids have not been studied. Animal toxicity studies with marijuana show several potential risks or hazards of marijuana use, especially when the marijuana is smoked. These hazards have not been evaluated against the benefit or effectiveness of the drug. This is due, in great part, to the fact that marijuana's effectiveness in treating specific medical conditions has not been established by reliable scientific studies. Since a proper risk/benefit ratio cannot be made, the safety of marijuana for medical use cannot be demonstrated. Such lack of information is the basis for the majority of the medical and scientific community, and the Food and Drug Administration, concluding that marijuana does not have "accepted safety for use ... under medical supervision." The Administrator, therefore, concludes that marijuana lacks "accepted safety for use ... under medical supervision."

As a final note, the Administrator expresses his displeasure at the misleading accusations and conclusions leveled at the Government and communicated to the public by the pro-marijuana parties, specifically NORML and ACT. These two organizations have falsely raised the expectations of many seriously ill persons by claiming that marijuana has medical usefulness in treating emesis, glaucoma, spasticity and other illnesses. These statements have probably caused many people with serious diseases to experiment with marijuana to the detriment of their own health, without proper medical supervision, and without knowing about the serious side effects which smoking or ingesting marijuana may cause. These are not the Dark Ages. The Congress, as well as the medical community, has accepted that drugs should not be available to the public unless they are found by scientific studies to be effective and safe. To do otherwise is to jeopardize the American public, and take advantage of desperately ill people who will try anything to alleviate their suffering. The Administrator strongly urges the American public not to experiment with a potentially dangerous, mind-altering drug such as marijuana in an attempt to treat a serious illness or condition. Scientific and medical researchers are working tirelessly to develop treatments and drugs to treat these diseases and conditions. As expressed in the record, treatments for emesis (nausea and vomiting) associated with cancer chemotherapy have advanced significantly in the last ten years. Recent studies have shown an over 90 percent rate of effectiveness for the new antiemetic drugs and therapies. NORML and ACT have attempted to perpetrate a dangerous and cruel hoax on the American public by claiming marijuana has currently accepted medical uses. The Administrator again emphasizes that there is insufficient medical and scientific evidence to support a conclusion that marijuana has an accepted medical use for treatment of any condition, or that it is safe for use, even under medical supervision.

Based upon the evidence in the record and the conclusions discussed previously, the Administrator, under the authority vested in the Attorney General by section 201(a) of the Controlled Substances Act and delegated to the Administrator of the Drug Enforcement Administration by regulations of the Department of Justice, 28 CFR 0.100(b), hereby orders that marijuana remain a Schedule I controlled substance as listed in 21 CFR 1308.11(d)(14).

Alliance for Cannabis Therapeutics v. Drug Enforcement Administration

United States Court of Appeals for the District of Columbia
930 F.2d 936 (1991)

Silberman, J.

This is a petition for review of a final order of the Administrator of the Drug Enforcement Administration (DEA). The order maintains the classification of marijuana as a narcotic drug under Schedule I of the Controlled Substances Act. Petitioners, Alliance for Cannabis Therapeutics (ACT) and National Organization for the Reform of Marijuana Laws (NORML), who claim that marijuana should be reclassified in Schedule II, argue that the DEA Administrator's decision rests on an improper application of the statutory standards and an incorrect determination that petitioners failed to meet them. We think that the Administrator's interpretation of the statute was in the main acceptable, but he appears to have relied on several factors that are unreasonable because logically impossible to satisfy; therefore, we remand.

The Controlled Substances Act (CSA) is a comprehensive regulatory measure that divides the universe of hazardous drugs into five different categories of substances (so-called schedules), which determine the severity of restrictions on doctors' and patients' access to controlled drugs.[1] Drugs can be "re-scheduled" or "de-scheduled" only if the DEA makes certain statutorily-mandated findings. Schedule I drugs are subject to the most severe controls and give rise to the harshest penalties for violations of these controls; they are deemed to be the most dangerous substances, possessing no redeeming value as medicines.

---

1. When it enacted the CSA in 1970, Congress placed marijuana in Schedule I. From that time, petitioners have indefatigably sought to obtain a change in marijuana's classification. The long and checkered history of this proceeding and an explanation of the complex statutory scheme are detailed in *National Org. for the Reform of Marijuana Laws v. Ingersoll*, 497 F.2d 654 (D.C. Cir. 1974); *National Org. for the Reform of Marijuana Laws v. Drug Enforcement Admin.*, 559 F.2d 735 (D.C. Cir. 1977).

[O]ne salient concept distinguishing the two schedules is whether a drug has "no currently accepted medical use in treatment in the United States." This case turns on the appropriate definition and application of that phrase.

The Administrator is guided by a set of statutory factors in making a classification decision as to which schedule is appropriate. And two of those factors bear on the Administrator's definition of generally accepted medical use — the "scientific evidence of [the drug's] pharmacological effect, if known" and "the state of current scientific knowledge regarding the drug or other substance."

Petitioners argued below that marijuana has medical uses for the treatment of cancer, glaucoma, and other diseases and therefore it cannot properly be maintained in Schedule I. The ALJ agreed with petitioners and found, based on testimony of a number of physicians and patients, that a "respectable minority" of American physicians accept those uses, which was sufficient, according to the ALJ, to say that marijuana had a currently accepted medical use. The Administrator rejected the ALJ's recommendation, however, determining that the phrase "currently accepted medical use" required a greater showing than that a minority — even a respectable minority — of physicians accept the usefulness of a given drug.

In a prior proceeding, the Administrator had employed an additional eight factor test to further elaborate the characteristics of a drug that he thought had a "currently accepted medical use": "(1) Scientifically determined and accepted knowledge of its chemistry; (2) The toxicology and pharmacology of the substance in animals; (3) Establishment of its effectiveness in humans through scientifically designed clinical trials; (4) General availability of the substance and information regarding the substance and its use; (5) Recognition of its clinical use in generally accepted pharmacopeia, medical references, journals or textbooks; (6) Specific indications for the treatment of recognized disorders; (7) Recognition of the use of the substance by organizations or associations of physicians; and (8) Recognition and use of the substance by a substantial segment of the medical practitioners in the United States."

The Administrator, in his opinion in this proceeding, reaffirmed this eight factor test. Most important to the Administrator was his conclusion that "the chemistry, toxicology, and pharmacology of marijuana is not established" and its effectiveness has not been documented in humans with scientifically-designed clinical trials (such as double-blind studies where neither the patient nor the observer knows who received the placebo and who received the actual substance). Therefore, "the vast majority of physicians do not accept marijuana as having a medical use" and it is "not recognized as medicine in generally accepted pharmacopoeia, medical references, journals, or textbooks." The Administrator exercised with a vengeance his prerogative under *Universal Camera Corp. v. NLRB,* 340 U.S. 474 (1951), to reject the ALJ's recommended decision, labelling the ALJ's standard for "currently accepted medical use" as use by a "respectable minority" of physicians as "preposterous."

The petitioners renew their argument that the Administrator unreasonably rejected the evidence they presented (largely anecdotal) that a number of physicians believe marijuana is medically useful and, instead, improperly predicated his determination on the absence of demonstrated scientific evidence that the drug is medically useful and safe. The difficulty we find in petitioners' argument is that neither the statute nor its legislative history precisely defines the term "currently accepted medical use"; therefore, we are obliged to defer to the Administrator's interpretation of that phrase if reasonable. And since Congress required the Administrator, in making scheduling determinations with respect to any drug, to consider the "scientific evidence of [the drug's] pharmacological effect" and the "state of current scientific knowledge regarding the drug," we do not see how it can be thought an unreasonable application of the statutory phrase to emphasize the lack of exact scientific knowledge as to the chemical effects of the drug's elements. Perhaps if virtually all doctors in the United States were vociferous in their espousal of marijuana for medical treatment — notwithstanding scientific uncertainties — the Administrator's position would be more vulnerable. But that is not the case; the ALJ's finding (not contested by the petitioners) is only that a "respectable minority" take that position. The determination as to how much weight to place on scientific uncertainties as opposed to anecdotal evidence in applying the statutory phrase "currently accepted medical uses," then, is very much a policy judgment which we have no authority to challenge. We certainly have no grounds, on this record, to dispute the Administrator's premise that without much more complete scientific data American physicians will not "accept" marijuana.

Petitioners, however, mount something of a flanking attack on that premise. They assert that the Administrator's eight factor test, which emphasizes, in factors 1, 2 and 3, scientific knowledge of the chemistry of the drug and its effectiveness in humans established through scientifically-designed clinical trials, is improperly drawn from the Food, Drug and Cosmetic Act (administered by the Food and Drug Administration) and not the Controlled Substances Act which the Administrator is authorized to apply. The First Circuit in *Grinspoon v. Drug Enforcement Administration*, 828 F.2d 881, 891–92 (1st Cir. 1987), upon which petitioners rely, had held that earlier criteria the Administrator had employed to define "currently accepted medical use" were contrary to the statute because they were a carbon copy of those used by the FDA in licensing new drugs. The present criteria, it is argued, duplicate a number of those original criteria. But the criteria challenged in *Grinspoon* included several elements, such as the availability of patent information or FDA-required labelling, which were necessary only to market the drug in interstate commerce. These criteria are clearly relevant to the FDA's mission, but not to the DEA's. The First Circuit never suggested the DEA Administrator was foreclosed from incorporating and relying on those standards employed by the FDA that are relevant to the pharmaceutical qualities of the drug. The court merely held that while FDA approval is sufficient to establish the existence of an accepted medical use, the converse is not true — that absent FDA approval, commonly accepted medical use cannot be proven. Nor can we conceive of a reason the Administrator should be barred from employing notions developed by a sister agency insofar as those notions serve the missions of both agencies.

Which brings us to the most troubling part of the Administrator's decision — the part which we think obliges us to order a remand. Petitioners, almost in passing, point out that three of the factors in the Administrator's eight-factor test appear impossible to fulfill and thus must be regarded as arbitrary and capricious. Impossible requirements imposed by an agency are perforce unreasonable[.] These three factors are: "(4) General availability of the substance and information regarding the substance and its use; (5) Recognition of its clinical use in generally accepted pharmacopeia, medical references, journals or textbooks; (8) Recognition and use of the substance by a substantial segment of the medical practitioners in the United States."

Petitioners argue that one cannot logically show that a drug enjoys general "availability" or "use" by a substantial segment of medical practitioners if the drug remains in Schedule I. One of the very purposes in placing a drug in Schedule I is to raise significant barriers to prevent doctors from obtaining the drugs too easily. DEA regulations require doctors who wish to use such drugs to submit a scientific research protocol to the FDA for approval and permit use only in accordance with the protocol. And the FDA insists that a developed scientific study program be presented in order to gain approval of the protocol. The DEA regulations further impose mandatory registration with the DEA and mandatory record-keeping and safe-keeping requirements, presenting additional barriers to widespread use. We are therefore hard-pressed to understand how one could show that *any* Schedule I drug was in general use or generally available. We are also concerned that the fifth factor "recognition of [a drug's] clinical use in generally accepted pharmacopeia, medical references, journals, or textbooks" might be subject to the same objection. Petitioners assert that if a drug is not widely prescribed—regardless of its safety or use—it will not appear in a pharmaceutical listing of medically useful drugs. Since the government did not respond clearly to the argument, we are left in doubt as to the argument's validity. Under these circumstances, we think the appropriate course is to remand to the agency for an explanation as to how all three of these factors were utilized by the Administrator in reaching his decision.

To be sure, the Administrator did not explicitly rely on factors (4) and (8) in the analytical portion of his opinion (he did say "marijuana is not recognized as a medicine in generally accepted pharmacopeia, medical references, and textbooks," indicating his reliance on factor (5)). But since he did reaffirm the eight criteria's applicability to this case, we simply cannot be certain what role, if any, factors (4) and (8) played in his decision. Under our governing cases, we must remand for the requisite explanation.

For the foregoing reasons, the case is remanded.

It is so ordered.

On remand, the Administrator discarded the eight-part test in favor of a new five-part test for determining whether a controlled substance has a currently accepted medical use. The new test provided that "(1) The drug's chemistry must be known and reproducible; (2) there must be adequate safety studies; (3) there must be adequate and well-controlled studies proving efficacy; (4) the drug must be accepted by qualified experts; and (5) the scientific evidence must be widely available." *Alliance for Cannabis Therapeutics v. Drug Enforcement Administration*, 15 F.3d 1131, 1135 (1994). The Administrator applied this test and again determined that marijuana did not have a currently accepted medical use.

This time on appeal, the D.C. Circuit Court of Appeals upheld the Administrator's order, finding that the new five-part test was a permissible one. NORML raised an additional challenge to the Administrator's determination, arguing "the Administrator's ruling was not the product of reasoned decisionmaking because he was biased and ignored the record." *Id*. In support of this argument, NORML pointed to "what they describe as a long history of the Drug Enforcement Administration's anti-marijuana prejudice as evidenced by this court's need to remand their petition on four occasions and what they describe as the Administrator's 'unusually strident decision' rejecting the administrative law judge's recommendation that the drug be rescheduled." *Id*. at 136–37. The D.C. Circuit disagreed and concluded that the Administrator's findings were "supported by substantial evidence" and were "consistent with the view that only rigorous scientific proof can satisfy the CSA's 'currently accepted medical use' requirement." *Id*. at 137.

By the time NORML's rescheduling petition was before the Administrative Law Judge, the group had dropped its request to move marijuana below Schedule II and stipulated that marijuana has a "high potential for abuse and that abuse of the marijuana plant may lead to severe psychological or physical dependence." As a result, the decisions above only considered two of the three scheduling criteria. What would happen, however, if it was determined that marijuana (or some other substance) had a "low potential for abuse" relative to the substances in Schedules I and II and yet did not have "a currently accepted medical use"? As a substance with a low "potential for abuse," it would not satisfy the "high potential for abuse" criteria of Schedule I. But, without a "currently accepted medical use," the substance would also fail to meet one of the requirements for Schedules II through V. The Drug Enforcement Administration has taken the position that, in this circumstance, the substance should be placed in Schedule I. *See*, Notice of Denial of Petition, 66 F.R. 20038, 20039 (2001) (concluding that "even if one were to assume" that "marijuana had some potential for abuse but less than the 'high potential for abuse' commensurate with schedules I and II ... marijuana would not meet the criteria for placement in schedules III through V since it has no currently accepted medical use in treatment in the United States").

Attempts to reclassify marijuana continue. Two recent rescheduling efforts were stymied when the parties seeking rescheduling in each case were determined to lack standing under Article III of the Constitution to appeal the denial of their petitions. *See, Gettman v. Drug Enforcement Administration*, 290 F.3d 430 (D.C. Cir. 2002); *Olsen v. Drug Enforcement Administration*, 2009 U.S. App. LEXIS 19137 (8th Cir. 2009). A third rescheduling petition was filed in 2002 by the Coalition for Rescheduling Cannabis, an association that includes the National Organization for the Reform of Marijuana Laws and Americans for Safe Access. In 2011, the Drug Enforcement Administration denied the petition. At the time this book went to press, the DEA's denial was on appeal before the D.C. Circuit Court of Appeals.

The CSA's classification of marijuana as a Schedule I substance also encompasses industrial hemp. This feature of the CSA has been particularly controversial. Industrial hemp has a variety of uses, including in paper, textiles, clothing, and health food. Hemp is legally grown in more than thirty countries today, including China, Germany and Russia. It is also legal to import hemp and hemp products into the United States. "Given hemp's wide-ranging utility, supporters of domestic cultivation estimate that it would create a $300 million industry. However, its legal status, as interpreted by the DEA, has thwarted the attempts of farmers to grow hemp domestically." Christine A. Kolosov, Comment: *Evaluating the Public Interest: Regulation of Industrial Hemp Under the Controlled Substances Act*, 57 UCLA L. REV. 237, 244 (2009).

Monson v. Drug Enforcement Administration

United States District Court for the District of North Dakota
522 F. Supp. 2d 1188 (2007)

Hovland, J.

In this case, two North Dakota farmers seeking to cultivate industrial hemp have sought a declaration that they cannot be criminally prosecuted under the federal Controlled Substances Act. The issue before the Court is a question of law, namely, whether the Controlled Substances Act applies to the proposed cultivation of industrial hemp pursuant to North Dakota's new state regulatory regime.

Marijuana and industrial hemp have similar characteristics but far different applications. The industrial hemp plant is of the same species of plant as marijuana — Cannabis sativa L. — but one that has been bred to a low concentration of the psychoactive element of marijuana: tetrahydrocannabinol or THC. THC is the compound that causes the "high" associated with the recreational use of the street drug marijuana. The stalk, fiber, sterilized seed, and oil of the industrial hemp plant, and their derivatives, are legal under federal law, and those parts of the plant are expressly excluded from the definition of "marijuana" under the Controlled Substances Act, 21 U.S.C. § 802(16). This statutory exclusion has allowed for the widespread use and trade of hemp stalk, fiber, and sterilized hemp seed and seed oil. These hemp commodities are sold throughout the world.

In 1999, the State of North Dakota enacted a law authorizing the cultivation of industrial hemp so that its farmers could supply the legal parts of the plant—stalk, fiber, seed and oil—that would otherwise have to be imported from other countries. The state regulatory regime provides for the licensing of farmers to cultivate industrial hemp; imposes strict THC limits precluding any possible use of the hemp as the street drug marijuana; and attempts to ensure that no part of the hemp plant will leave the farmer's property other than those parts already exempt under federal law. The plaintiffs are two North Dakota farmers who have received state licenses, have an economic need to begin cultivation of industrial hemp, and apparently stand ready to do so but are unwilling to risk federal prosecution of possession for manufacture or sale of a controlled substance. The farmers seek a declaratory judgment that the Controlled Substances Act does not prohibit their cultivation of industrial hemp pursuant to their state licenses.

The Controlled Substances Act ("CSA") establishes a comprehensive federal scheme to regulate controlled substances.

A controlled substance is listed in Schedule I, the most restrictive schedule, if it has "a high potential for abuse," "no currently accepted medical use in treatment in the United States," and "a lack of accepted safety for use … under medical supervision." 21 U.S.C. § 812(b)(1). Under the CSA, any person who seeks to manufacture, distribute, or possess a Schedule I controlled substance must apply for and obtain a certificate of registration from the Drug Enforcement Agency (DEA). When evaluating an application to manufacture a Schedule I substance, the DEA is required to consider such factors as the applicant's "maintenance of effective controls against diversion," "past experience in the manufacture of controlled substances," and criminal history.

Since Congress enacted the CSA in 1970, "marijuana" (or "marihuana") and tetrahydrocannabinols (THC) have been classified as Schedule I controlled substances. "Marijuana" is defined under the CSA to include "all parts of the plant Cannabis sativa L." except certain components of the plant such as mature stalks, fiber produced from the stalks, sterilized seeds, and oil from the seeds.

The plaintiffs, David Monson and Wayne Hauge, are North Dakota farmers. Monson is also a member of the House of Representatives of the North Dakota Legislative Assembly. In 1999, the Legislative Assembly passed a bill, introduced by Monson and others, legalizing the growth, possession, and sale of "industrial hemp" under North Dakota law. The statute defines "industrial hemp" as any Cannabis plant "having no more than three-tenths of one percent tetrahydrocannabinol [THC]." THC is the primary psychoactive chemical constituent of the Cannabis plant. Contrary to the federal Controlled Substances Act, the North Dakota statute regulates Cannabis based on THC concentration.

In December 2006, the North Dakota Department of Agriculture finalized regulations governing the growth of "industrial hemp" pursuant to the new statute. Recognizing that "industrial hemp" is regulated under federal law as "marijuana," a Schedule I controlled substance, the Department of Agriculture regulations originally provided that any person seeking to grow "industrial hemp" must, in addition to complying with North Dakota regulations, obtain a certificate of registration from the DEA. However, on December 26, 2006, the Commissioner of Agriculture asked the DEA to waive the registration requirement for all farmers seeking to grow Cannabis pursuant to the new North Dakota law. In essence, the North Dakota Commissioner of Agriculture asked the federal government to forego all regulation of marijuana that meets North Dakota's definition of "industrial hemp."

The DEA denied the Commissioner's request: "Congress expressly commanded the United States Department of Justice to take the lead in controlling licit and illicit drug activity through enforcement of the CSA.... [F]or DEA to simply turn over to any state the agency's authority and responsibility to enforce the CSA ... would be directly at odds with the Act." The DEA also said that, because "[f]ederal law uses the terms 'marihuana' and 'cannabis' and defines marihuana without distinction based on THC content," the CSA requires a DEA registration for the cultivation of marijuana for industrial purposes, regardless of the THC content.

On or about February 12, 2007, the North Dakota Department of Agriculture submitted registration applications on behalf of Plaintiffs Monson and Hauge and, on March 5, 2007, demanded resolution of those applications by April 1, 2007. The DEA responded that registration applications require substantial time to process as they require a notice of application in the Federal Register, a sixty-day response period for comments, a background investigation of the applicant, and an onsite investigation of the manufacturing facilities. The DEA informed the Department of Agriculture that a decision within seven weeks, as requested, was unrealistic. In response, the North Dakota Legislative Assembly struck the DEA registration requirement from the new industrial hemp law. The revised statute now provides that "[a] license required by this section is not conditioned on or subject to review or approval by the United States drug enforcement agency [sic]."

The DEA contends that it continues to process the plaintiffs' registration applications. On June 1, 2007, it published notice of the plaintiffs' applications in the Federal Register. On June 15, 2007, the DEA sent letters to both of the plaintiffs seeking additional information about their intended cultivation of marijuana. The plaintiffs responded by filing this lawsuit. They claim that the DEA has misconstrued the Controlled Substances Act by requiring that persons who seek to grow marijuana for industrial purposes obtain DEA registrations. Oral arguments were presented at a hearing held on November 14, 2007.

The defendants have moved to dismiss the complaint pursuant to Fed. R. Civ. P. 12(b)(6) and the plaintiffs have cross-moved for summary judgment pursuant to Fed. R. Civ. P. 56(a).

The DEA ... contends that the claim is not ripe for adjudication because ... the plaintiffs cannot demonstrate any hardship "justifying judicial review prior to DEA's resolution of their registration applications," and that if, "as Plaintiffs speculate, the DEA denies their registration applications, the plaintiffs may seek judicial review of that denial" in the Court of Appeals.

It should be noted that the only reason the plaintiffs applied to the DEA for a certificate of registration is that formerly under North Dakota law, a farmer needed to obtain a DEA registration prior to obtaining a state license. During the 2007 Legislative Session, and in response to the DEA's correspondence with state officials indicating the DEA's intention to review such license requests as if the plaintiffs were simply planning to grow the street drug marijuana, the state law was amended to eliminate the requirement that a DEA license be obtained prior to planting industrial hemp.

It is apparent from the record that the DEA has, arguably, prejudged the merits of the registration applications by characterizing them as requests being submitted by "manufacturers of marijuana—which is the most widely abused controlled substance in the United States...." And as made clear by the Affidavit of Burton Johnson, it is unlikely the

DEA will act promptly on the pending applications. Professor Johnson states that North Dakota State University (NDSU) was directed, by N.D.C.C. §4-05.1-05, to "collect feral hemp seed stock and develop appropriate adapted strains of industrial hemp containing less than 3/10 of one percent THC in the dried flowering tops." He further explains that:

> Pursuant to this legislative mandate, NDSU submitted its own application to DEA for a registration for cultivation of industrial hemp for research purposes, on September 28, 1999.... NDSU proposed to plant 160,000 viable seeds to produce 144,000 hemp plants in the field, and to evaluate characteristics including emergence, growth and development, phenology, pest incidence, seed and biomass yield and seed and biomass quantity.

Professor Johnson confirms that to date—nearly eight (8) years after its filing—the DEA has not acted on NDSU's pending application. There appears from the record to be no legitimate excuse for this unreasonable delay.

It is clear that the issue presented by the plaintiffs in this action may never be addressed and resolved by the DEA through the registration and application process. As a practical matter, there is no realistic prospect that the plaintiffs will ever be issued a license by the DEA to grow industrial hemp. The futility of waiting until a registration application submitted to the DEA is acted upon is apparent. The legal argument that administrative remedies have not been exhausted is meritless. The issue presented is a legal issue which is ripe for adjudication and fit for immediate judicial resolution.

The plaintiffs argue that any Cannabis plant that falls within the definition of "industrial hemp" under North Dakota law is not a controlled substance under the Controlled Substances Act and, consequently, anyone seeking to grow such Cannabis plants need not obtain a DEA registration. However, the Eighth Circuit Court of Appeals has recently confirmed that the Controlled Substances Act unambiguously designates the Cannabis plant as a controlled substance and prohibits the growth of that plant without a DEA registration.

Under the Controlled Substances Act, marijuana is designated as a Schedule I controlled substance. The CSA defines "marijuana" as follows:

> [A]ll parts of the plant Cannabis sativa L., whether growing or not; the seeds thereof; the resin extracted from any part of such plant; and every compound, manufacture, salt, derivative, mixture, or preparation of such plant, its seeds or resin. Such term does not include the mature stalks of such plant, fiber produced from such stalks, oil or cake made from the seeds of such plant, any other compound, manufacture, salt, derivative, mixture, or preparation of such mature stalks (except the resin extracted therefrom), fiber, oil, or cake, or the sterilized seed of such plant which is incapable of germination.

This definition of "marijuana" unambiguously includes the Cannabis sativa L. plant and does not in any manner differentiate between Cannabis plants based on their THC concentrations. Although the definition does exclude certain components of the plant, it is clear that a growing Cannabis plant falls within the definition of "marijuana."

In addition, the CSA designates "any material ... which contains any quantity of ... [t]etrahydrocannabinol[] [THC]" as a Schedule I controlled substance. The plaintiffs concede that the plant they intend to grow is Cannabis sativa L. The plaintiffs also concede that the plant they seek to grow will contain some quantity of THC. Whether viewed as marijuana or as THC-containing material, the plant the plaintiffs seek to grow is clearly a Schedule I controlled substance under the plain language of the Controlled Substances Act. The language of the statue is unambiguous. The proper venue to amend the statute is Congress and not the courts.

The federal courts that have considered this issue agree that Cannabis plants grown for industrial purposes and containing lower THC concentrations are "marijuana" within the meaning of the Controlled Substances Act. *Hemp Indus. Ass'n v. Drug Enforcement Admin.*, 333 F.3d 1082, 1085 n.2 (9th Cir. 2003) ("The industrial hemp plant itself, which falls under the definition of marijuana, may not be grown in the United States. Therefore, the seeds and oil must be imported.").

The Eighth Circuit Court of Appeals in *United States v. White Plume* recognized that the growing of industrial hemp may be a viable agricultural commodity and that there may be "countless numbers of beneficial products which utilize hemp in some fashion." There seems to be little dispute that the retail hemp market is significant, growing, and has real economic potential for North Dakota. Nevertheless, ... the federal Controlled Substances Act does not distinguish between marijuana and industrial hemp in its regulation.

Industrial hemp may not be the terrible menace the DEA makes it out to be, but industrial hemp is still considered to be a Schedule I controlled substance under the current state of the law in this circuit and throughout the country. Marijuana and industrial hemp are members of the Cannabis sativa L. plant species for which the Controlled Substances Act presently makes no distinction. The Court recognizes that at some stage in the process the plant may contain such low levels of THC that it would be impractical to use as a recreational street drug. However, perceived problems relating to detection and enforcement seem to remain as does the current ban imposed by Congress and the Drug Enforcement Administration.

The policy arguments raised by the plaintiffs are best suited for Congress rather than a federal courtroom in North Dakota. The undersigned is aware of recent efforts in Congress to exclude industrial hemp from the definition of "marijuana" as defined under the Controlled Substances Act. The Industrial Hemp Farming Act of 2007 was introduced in the House of Representatives on February 13, 2007, and was specifically designed to address the current dilemma. Congress can best address this problem and passage of the Industrial Hemp Farming Act of 2007 would accomplish what the plaintiffs seek in this lawsuit. Whether efforts to amend the law will prevail, and whether North Dakota farmers will be permitted to grow industrial hemp in the future, are issues that should ultimately rest in the hands of Congress rather than in the hands of a federal judge.

C. Research of Controlled Substances

In explaining his rejection of NORML's rescheduling petition, the Drug Enforcement Administrator emphasized the absence of "scientifically-designed clinical trials" documenting marijuana's value as a medicine. The Administrator's order even seemed to imply that researchers were not conducting clinical trials because they thought the idea that marijuana could have medicinal uses was not plausible enough to be worth their attention: "Marijuana is available from the Federal Government to those researchers who obtain proper licensure," the Administrator wrote. "However, the evidence suggests that only small numbers of researchers and physicians have obtained marijuana for this purpose, and that some research programs sponsored by states had trouble getting physicians to participate."

But if clinical trials of Schedule I controlled substances are rare, it may say more about the bureaucratic hurdles that await researchers who seek to study them than anything else. Even though accepted medical use is one of the three scheduling criteria under the

Controlled Substances Act, the CSA does not require that any research into the potential medical value of a substance actually be performed before it is scheduled. And once a substance has been placed in Schedule I, it becomes significantly more difficult for researchers to study it.

Indeed, as discussed in *Grinspoon v. Drug Enforcement Administration*, Dr. Grinspoon objected to the placement of MDMA in Schedule I on precisely this basis, arguing that it "would strongly discourage medical research on the drug" and that the "failure to consider the impact of a scheduling decision on legitimate research" was "arbitrary and capricious on the part of the Administrator." The court in *Grinspoon* summarized some of the obstacles facing researchers who wish to study Schedule I substances, noting that they "include mandatory FDA approval of research involving Schedule I substances; mandatory special registration with the DEA; mandatory reporting and security procedures beyond those required for drugs placed in Schedules II through V; unavoidable bureaucratic delays; and other adverse impacts due to the grave concern caused by a substance's placement in Schedule I, such as difficulty in obtaining volunteers for clinical studies and, for academic researchers, difficulty in securing approval from institutional review boards." In addition to administrative hurdles, there is often little financial incentive for private companies to fund studies into the potential medicinal effects of Schedule I controlled substances. Many of the substances are not patent-protected. In addition, even if studies were to reveal that a Schedule I substance has medicinal value, the procedure for rescheduling it under the CSA is time-consuming and uncertain.

Though obtaining the necessary permission and funding to research Schedule I substances can be difficult, it is not impossible. Recently, researchers have undertaken studies into potential medicinal uses of psychedelic substances, including MDMA and psilocybin (the psychoactive ingredient found in hallucinogenic mushrooms). *See* John Tierney, *Hallucinogens Have Doctors Tuning in Again*, N.Y. TIMES, Apr. 11, 2010. In 2010, researchers released a study on the use of MDMA to combat posttraumatic stress disorder (PTSD). The paper, which was published in the *Journal of Psychopharmacology*, "showed that ecstasy is not only safe when administered in controlled settings but also remarkably effective in treating PTSD in conjunction with psychotherapy." John Cloud, *Ecstasy Shows Promise in Relieving PTSD*, TIME, July 20, 2010. It took researchers more than a decade to get approval for the study, however, and "[b]ecause of budget and time restraints, only 20 participants could be recruited." *Id.*

The article below describes some of the requirements researchers must meet in order to conduct studies using Schedule I substances. In reading it, consider what purposes these restrictions serve. Are they in place to prevent Schedule I substances used in research from being diverted to the black market? Were they designed with the health and safety of the participants who would be using Schedule I substances during clinical trials in mind? Do the restrictions have any drawbacks? If so, do you think the current approach strikes the proper balance between the risks and benefits of studying Schedule I drugs?

Medical Marijuana: The Conflict between Scientific Evidence and Political Ideology
Peter J. Cohen
2009 Utah Law Review 35

[T]he first objective study of the safety and efficacy of smoked marijuana was published less than two years ago. Why did it take so long for this study to appear in the peer-reviewed scientific literature? Why did the pharmaceutical industry fail to show any interest in this promising compound?

In 1992, Dr. Donald Abrams, a clinical pharmacologist, Professor of Medicine at the University of California San Francisco, and Chair of the Bay Area's Community Consortium on HIV research, proposed a study "designed to provide objective data about whether or not smoked marijuana could ease subjective symptoms of AIDS wasting and produce objective gains in body weight." The University of California planned to fund the study, the FDA approved the I[nvestigational] N[ew] D[rug application], and the ethics of the study protocol were approved by the University Hospital's Institutional Review Board. However, Dr. Abrams was denied permission to import marijuana from the Netherlands as he had originally planned or to use illegal marijuana that had been seized by the DEA.

Since the National Institute on Drug Abuse (NIDA) grows marijuana and is the only domestic source for scientific investigators, Dr. Abrams requested their assistance, a request that would have involved only a minimal expense to NIDA. However, it was then the policy of the NIH to restrict its provision of marijuana only to investigators who had received a peer-reviewed NIH grant to conduct a study. Because Abrams's funding had originated at his university, and not the National Institutes of Health (NIH) of which NIDA is a part, he was refused access to NIH's marijuana.

In May of 1996, hoping that the NIH had changed its policies, Dr. Abrams resubmitted his study proposal to the NIH. At that time, the study had again been approved and funded at the university level; thus, NIH approval was required not for funding, but to allow him to obtain federally grown marijuana. In October 1996, four years after he had first initiated requests to obtain marijuana legally, he was again informed that the NIH would not supply it.

In 1998, after six years of frustrating attempts to obtain marijuana either in the United States or abroad, the NIH finally approved Dr. Abrams's request and he was able to obtain marijuana legally. Abrams then initiated the first federally funded effort to study the effects of marijuana on patients with AIDS, an investigation that was eventually published in the peer-reviewed scientific literature.

This was not the only instance in which the federal government appeared to place significant roadblocks in the way of university-sponsored research directed toward obtaining information about the possible medical uses of marijuana. Because of difficulties in obtaining marijuana from NIDA's "marijuana farm," Lyle E. Craker, PhD, a professor in the Department of Plant and Soil Sciences at the University of Massachusetts Amherst, petitioned the Drug Enforcement Agency (DEA) in 2003 for permission to cultivate marijuana to use in university-approved clinical studies that would evaluate marijuana's ability to provide pain relief and control nausea in patients with cancer, as well as to alleviate some of the symptoms of multiple sclerosis in other patients. His petition was denied by the DEA in spite of DEA Administrative Law Judge Mary Ellen Bittner's nonbinding opinion that it would be in the public interest to grant it. She stated in that opinion that the federal government's system for evaluating requests for marijuana for clinical study had hindered investigation of the drug's safety and effectiveness. As of mid-2008, the case is still pending. Four years after the petition was filed, DEA spokesman Steve Robertson told the American Medical News that the agency was reviewing the decision but he declined to comment other than to declare that "the government maintains that no sound scientific studies exist to support marijuana's medical value."

The federal government's stance regarding scientific investigation of medical marijuana has, however, been far from monolithic. While those individuals within the NIH who acted on Dr. Abrams's request appeared to reject even minimal support of scientific study of the medical use of marijuana, other NIH personnel appeared to take an opposite stance. After considerable "wide-ranging public discussion on the potential medical use of marijuana, particularly smoked marijuana," the National Institutes of Health convened a conference "to review the scientific data concerning the potential therapeutic uses for marijuana and the need for and feasibility of additional research" in February 1997.

At this forum, a group of experts in anesthesiology, internal medicine, neurology, oncology, ophthalmology, pharmacology and psychiatry maintained that there was a need for accurate and nonbiased scientific investigation of medical marijuana. The participants suggested that although [DELTA] 9-tetrahydrocannabinol, the major psychoactive component of marijuana, is currently available as a separate and approved medication, this should not obviate the need to study the efficacy of smoked marijuana itself. They noted the plant may also contain other compounds with important therapeutic properties. Moreover, "the bioavailability and pharmacokinetics of THC from smoked marijuana are substantially different than those of the oral dosage form."

The expert group proposed that the possibly beneficial (or even superior) role of smoked marijuana cannot be delineated without proper investigation. They maintained that studies of marijuana should not be precluded because effective approved therapy was currently available for the diseases in which it might also be efficacious.

This was not the only expert discussion suggesting that the use of medical marijuana should not be dismissed out of hand. A meeting sponsored by the National Academies of Sciences-Institute of Medicine to discuss the medical use of marijuana (Workshop on Prospects for Cannabinoid Drug Development, National Academies of Sciences-Institute of Medicine) was held in February 1998; the proceedings were published in 1999. Discussion at this meeting centered on both the adverse effects and potential benefits of smoked marijuana. Participants indicated that smoked marijuana could be a valuable agent in the treatment of chemotherapy-induced nausea and vomiting, HIV-related gastrointestinal disorders, AIDS wasting, severe pain, and some forms of spasticity. Some participants stressed—as had those at the NIH conference held the preceding year—that since the whole marijuana plant contains many possibly active cannabinoids besides THC, its possible efficacy may not be replicated by medications containing only THC.

Nonetheless, the suggestion by an impartial conference of experts that marijuana might have some medical utility that should be discussed and that its properties should be subjected to scientific investigation evoked a forceful but inaccurate response from the federal government[, which released the following statement shortly after the Institute of Medicine report]: "A past evaluation by several Department of Health and Human Services (HHS) agencies, including the Food and Drug Administration (FDA), Substance Abuse and Mental Health Services Administration (SAMHSA) and National Institute for Drug Abuse (NIDA), concluded that no sound scientific studies supported medical use of marijuana for treatment in the United States, and no animal or human data supported the safety or efficacy of marijuana for general medical use."

This "authoritative" statement did not go unnoticed by the media. A reporter for the New York Times observed that: "The Food and Drug Administration said Thursday that 'no sound scientific studies' supported the medical use of marijuana, contradicting a 1999 review by a panel of highly regarded scientists. [It] directly contradicts a 1999 review by the Institute of Medicine [IOM], a part of the National Academy of Sciences, the nation's most prestigious scientific advisory agency. That review found marijuana to be 'moderately well suited for particular conditions, such as chemotherapy-induced nausea and vomiting and AIDS wasting.'"

Dr. John Benson, cochairman of the IOM committee and professor of internal medicine at the University of Nebraska Medical Center, whose report had suggested that smoked marijuana could have therapeutic value, strongly disputed the FDA's stance. "The federal government loves to ignore our report," said Dr. Benson, "They would rather it never happened." Dr. Jerry Avorn, a medical professor at Harvard Medical School, declared, "Unfortunately, this is yet another example of the F.D.A. making pronouncements that seem to be driven more by ideology than by science."

The account above describes some of the regulatory obstacles researchers who seek to conduct clinical trials for Schedule I controlled substances can face. A 2010 New York Times article reported that study into the potential medical uses of smoked marijuana seems to be particularly discouraged by the federal government. *See*, Gardiner Harris, *Researchers Find Study of Medical Marijuana Discouraged*, N.Y. TIMES, Jan. 19, 2010. Although researchers must apply to the National Institute on Drug Abuse (NIDA) to obtain marijuana from the nation's only federally licensed marijuana supplier, the University of Mississippi, a NIDA spokeswoman told the *Times* that NIDA's "focus is primarily on the negative consequences of marijuana use[, w]e generally do not fund research focused on the potential beneficial medical effects of marijuana." *Id.*

As Peter J. Cohen describes above, perceived difficulty in obtaining marijuana from the University of Mississippi led University of Massachusetts Amherst professor Lyle E. Craker to apply for permission to cultivate marijuana for use in research. In 2007, Administrative Law Judge Mary Ellen Bittner recommended the application be granted, finding that there was "currently an inadequate supply of marijuana available for research purposes" and that "the competition in the provision of marijuana for such purposes is inadequate." *In the Matter of Lyle E. Craker,* Opinion and Recommended Ruling, Dep't of Justice Docket No. 05-16, Feb. 12, 2007, at 87. In the opinion, Judge Bittner quoted from a letter that leading AIDS researcher Donald Abrams sent to NIDA after NIDA denied his application to purchase marijuana for research: "As an AIDS investigator who has worked closely with [the] National Institutes of Health and the U.S. Food and Drug Administration for the past 14 years of this [AIDS] epidemic, I must tell you that dealing with your Institute has been the worst experience of my career! The lack of any official communication for nine months is unheard of, even in the most cumbersome of government bureaucracics." *Id.* at 41. Two years later, however, the DEA declined to adopt Administrative Law Judge Bittner's recommendation. Craker then filed a motion for reconsideration, which was rejected in late 2011. At the time this book went to press, Craker's appeal of the DEA's denial was before the United States Court of Appeals for the First Circuit.

Chapter 7

Controlled Substances as Medicines

A. The Relationship Between the Controlled Substances Act and the Food, Drug, and Cosmetic Act

As Kimani Paul-Emile explains in the article excerpted at the beginning of the last Chapter, the "aims and regulatory mechanisms" of the Food and Drug Administration and the Drug Enforcement Administration "differ sharply." Kimani Paul-Emile, *Making Sense of Drug Regulation: A Theory of Law for Drug Control Policy*, 19 CORNELL J. L. & PUB. POL'Y 691 (2010). When it comes to drug control, the FDA is principally concerned with ensuring drug safety and efficacy while the DEA's website states that its mission is to "bring to the criminal and civil justice system of the United States, or any other competent jurisdiction, those organizations and principal members of organizations, involved in the growing, manufacture, or distribution of controlled substances appearing in or destined for illicit traffic in the United States." As we have seen already, however, there is sometimes regulatory overlap between the FDA and DEA and the federal laws they administer—the Food, Drug, and Cosmetic Act and the Controlled Substances Act. Recall, for example, that in *Grinspoon v. Drug Enforcement Administration*, the DEA unsuccessfully argued that a drug could not have an "accepted medical use" under the Controlled Substances Act unless "the FDA ha[d] evaluated the substance for safety and approved it for interstate marketing in the United States pursuant to the Federal Food, Drug, and Cosmetic Act [FDCA.]" The *Grinspoon* court began its analysis of that argument by citing an earlier case that described "the interrelationship between" the CSA and FDCA as "far from clear."

Though a detailed examination of the FDA and the FDCA is the domain of courses on Food and Drug Law, an understanding of how the FDA and FDCA relate to the DEA and the CSA helps to illuminate some of the issues that can arise in the regulation of substances that have both medicinal and recreational uses.

American Pharmaceutical Association v. Weinberger
United States District Court for the District of Columbia
377 F. Supp. 824 (1974)

Pratt, J.

This is an action for judicial review of a regulation of the Food and Drug Administration (FDA) which restricts the distribution of methadone to certain specified outlets as set forth in the regulation. In effect, it prohibits virtually all licensed pharmacies from dispensing this drug when lawfully prescribed by a physician, despite the fact that methadone was invented and was first used as a safe, useful and effective agent in the treatment of severe pain and for antitussive purposes. Decision is not made easier by the fact that in recent years methadone has become a widely known maintenance agent in the treatment of heroin addicts and there is evidence of serious abuses in the distribution of this drug. In their efforts to control improper distribution of methadone, there are strong public policy arguments on the side of defendants. At the same time, the popularity of methadone for use as a pain killer has declined because of the introduction of effective new drugs, and as recently as 1972 the plaintiff Association formally recommended that FDA withdraw its approval of methadone for its indications as an analgesic and antitussive and expressed its philosophic non-disagreement with a course of regulation which would restrict the distribution and use of methadone to approved methadone treatment programs.

The challenged regulation, while ruling out most so-called community pharmacies in the dispensing of methadone for any purpose, still permits approved hospital pharmacies to dispense methadone for analgesic and antitussive purposes. Stripped of the rhetoric which abounds in the papers before us, this appears to be the basis of plaintiffs' complaint. Whether the FDA has the authority to enact the challenged regulation depends on the interplay and connection between two complementary but distinct statutes, the Food, Drug and Cosmetic Act of 1938 and the Comprehensive Drug Abuse Prevention & Control Act of 1970 and the respective roles assigned by Congress to the agencies which administer these Acts. With this brief background, we proceed to the issues presented.

This cause came on for hearing on defendants' motion to dismiss, or in the alternative, for summary judgment and plaintiffs' cross-motion for summary judgment on May 8, 1974. Plaintiffs challenge the validity of certain provisions of the Food and Drug Administration's methadone regulations, 21 C.F.R. § 130.44 ("Conditions for use of methadone") and § 130.48 ("Drugs that are subjects of approved new-drug applications and that require special studies, records and reports.") Specifically, plaintiffs object to those parts of the regulations which purport to restrict the distribution of methadone to direct shipments from the manufacturer to (a) approved maintenance treatment programs, (b) approved hospital pharmacies, and (c) in cases where hospital pharmacies are unavailable in a particular area, to selected community pharmacies.

Plaintiffs include the American Pharmaceutical Association (APhA), a professional association of pharmacists with a membership in excess of 50,000, three individual professional pharmacists and an individual physician. They argue that the restrictions imposed on the channels of distribution exceed the limits of FDA's authority. Plaintiffs seek declaratory relief holding said restrictions invalid and enjoining defendants from enforcing them.

Defendants are the Secretary of Health, Education and Welfare, the Commissioner of Food and Drugs, the Attorney General and the Acting Administrator of the Drug Enforcement Administration. They counter plaintiffs' contentions by citing FDA's authority under the Federal Food, Drug and Cosmetic Act (the Act) to control access to the public market of all new drugs and to promulgate regulations for the efficient enforcement of the Act and their authority under the Comprehensive Drug Abuse Prevention & Control Act of 1970 "[to] determine the appropriate methods of professional practice in the medical treatment of ... narcotic addicts...."

The drug methadone, a synthetic substitute for morphine, is a "new" drug within the meaning of section 201(p) of the Federal, Food, Drug and Cosmetic Act and, as a new drug, requires FDA's approval of a NDA, filed with the Commissioner of Food and Drugs pursuant to section 505(b) of the Act. The drug was first approved by FDA in the 1950s as safe for use as an analgesic and antitussive agent as well as for short-term detoxification of persons addicted to heroin. Subsequently, investigation of methadone for use in long-term maintenance of narcotic addicts (methadone maintenance) was approved by FDA pursuant to its authority under 21 U.S.C. § 355(i), the investigational new-drug (IND) exemption. Section 355(i) of the Act empowers FDA to exempt from NDA approval requirements those new drugs "intended solely for investigational use by experts qualified by scientific training and experience to investigate the safety and effectiveness of drugs." Final guidelines for long-term maintenance programs were promulgated by FDA in 1971. A year later FDA determined that "retention of the drug [methadone] solely on an investigational status appears to be no longer warranted" and published a notice of proposed rulemaking which resulted, with certain modifications, in the regulations now in question.

The final regulation gave notice that pursuant to FDA's authority under 21 U.S.C. § 355(c), the Commissioner was withdrawing approval of all outstanding NDA's because of "a lack of substantial evidence that methadone is safe and effective for detoxification, analgesia, or antitussive use *under the conditions of use that presently exist*."[5] Having withdrawn all approved NDA's, the Commission's new regulatory scheme is presently the exclusive means of distribution for the drug methadone. The Commissioner has thereby created an admittedly unique classification for methadone since on the one hand he has determined that methadone should not be limited solely to investigational status while at the same time concluding that the drug is inappropriate for regular NDA approval. As statutory support for this novel solution to the methadone dilemma, defendants rely on an expansive interpretation of the Commissioner's NDA authority under § 355 of the Act.

Under the Federal Food, Drug and Cosmetic Act, the FDA (through the Secretary of HEW) has the responsibility of passing on the merits of NDA's. The grounds upon which an NDA can be denied approval are explicitly stated in subsection (d) of § 355 and the NDA shall be approved "if [FDA] ... finds that none of the grounds for denying approval ... applies." The NDA must be supported by "substantial evidence" defined to mean "evidence consisting of adequate and well-controlled investigations, including clinical investigations, by experts qualified by scientific training and experience to evaluate the effectiveness of the drug involved, on the basis of which it could be fairly and responsibly concluded by such experts that the drug will have the effect it purports or is represented to have under the conditions of use prescribed, recommended, or suggested in the labeling or proposed labeling thereof."

One of the six enumerated grounds for refusing approval of a new drug application (NDA) specifically deals with the "methods" or "controls" used in connection with the proffered drug. Subsection (d)(3) of § 355 reads as follows: "(d) If the Secretary finds ... (3) the methods used in, and the facilities and controls used for, the *manufacture, processing*, and *packing* of such drug are inadequate to preserve its identity, strength, quality, and purity; ... he shall issue an order refusing to approve the application." (emphasis added.)

This is the only provision of § 355 which speaks of the Secretary's authority with respect to "controls." The Congress apparently intended that the Secretary, or his delegate, FDA, be responsible for the adequacy of premarketing methods and controls inasmuch as the provision delineates the scope of the provision to the manufacturing, processing and packaging stage of a drug's genesis.

---

5. Although the Commissioner notes a lack of evidence with respect to methadone's effectiveness for the enumerated uses, defendants have relied exclusively on the drug's alleged safety hazard in attempting to justify the challenged restrictions on distributions.

The defendants point out, however, that § 355(d) also gives the Secretary the authority to refuse to approve an NDA where the reports of the investigations submitted do not include adequate tests showing whether the new drug is "safe for use under the conditions prescribed, recommended, or suggested in the proposed labeling thereof." Defendants argue that the term "safe" should be interpreted with reference not only to the inherent qualities of the drug under consideration but also in the sense of the drug's being secure from possible misuse. Such a broad interpretation would, according to defendants' theory, serve as the statutory foundation for FDA's exercise of authority in restricting methadone's channels of distribution because FDA's principal rationale for restricting distribution was "to help reduce the likelihood of diversion."

As a general proposition of statutory construction, a general term should not be construed in isolation but should be interpreted according to the context of the statute within which it is found. As noted above, the term "safe" is used in conjunction with the phrase "for use under the conditions prescribed, recommended, or suggested in the proposed labeling thereof." When taken in this context, a determination of whether a drug is "safe" is premised on the drug's use in the "prescribed, recommended, or suggested" manner. Thus the context of the statute indicates that the term "safe" was intended to include only the inherent safety of the drug when used in the manner intended. Moreover, as also noted above, the subject of "controls" is specifically covered in provision (3) of the same subsection (d) wherein the term "safe" appears. Provision (3) extends the Secretary's authority to pass on the adequacy of methods, facilities and *controls* only with respect to *manufacturing, processing* and *packaging*. Under the doctrine of "expressio unius est exclusio alterius" any stage of the drug's genesis not specifically mentioned in provision (3) was presumably intended to be excluded from the Secretary's authority. Thus by examining the term "safe" in the context of those provisions of the Act in which it appears as well as in relationship to the provision of the Act which specifically deals with controls, the Court concludes that the term "safe" was intended to refer to a determination of the inherent safety or lack thereof of the drug under consideration when used for its intended purpose.

Finally, the legislative history of the Act fully supports this conclusion. In enacting the Comprehensive Drug Abuse Prevention and Control Act of 1970, Congress was presented with a conscious decision as to how the lines of authority should be drawn with respect to the regulation of dangerous drugs. Congress decided to continue all control authority over the distribution of dangerous drugs in the Justice Department despite a recommendation of the Prettyman Commission that this function be transferred to HEW. The House Committee on Interstate and Foreign Commerce in their report on the Comprehensive Drug Abuse Prevention and Control Act of 1970 indicated that Title II of that Act, known as the Controlled Substances Act, was designed to "provide authority for the Department of Justice to keep track of all drugs subject to abuse manufactured or distributed in the United States in order to prevent diversion of these drugs from legitimate channels of commerce." Although it is nowhere specifically stated that Congress contemplated that the Justice Department would have exclusive authority to prevent diversion, this result would appear logically to follow from a comparison of the functions delegated to the Secretary of HEW with those assigned to the Attorney General.

In addition to being a "new" drug and thus within the jurisdiction of the FDA, methadone is a controlled substance within Schedule II of the Controlled Substances Act. Under this Act the Attorney General is made responsible for the registration of any person who manufactures, distributes or dispenses any controlled substance. An applicant may be refused registration if the Attorney General makes a determination that registering the applicant would be inconsistent with the public interest. Congress has also provided the specific means for revoking or suspending the authority of a registrant to distribute controlled substances. In addition, Congress has specified the precise procedure to be followed by the Attorney General in attempting to revoke or suspend a registration.

The Court concludes that Congress intended to create two complementary institutional checks on the production and marketing of new drugs. At the production or pre-marketing stage, the FDA is given the primary responsibility in determining which new drugs should be permitted to enter the flow of commerce. The Commissioner must approve or deny every NDA, or he may determine that a particular new drug qualifies for IND status in order to permit additional experimentation. When an IND exemption is approved, the Commissioner may, of course, severely restrict the distribution of the exempted drug to bona fide researchers and clinicians. But once a drug is cleared for marketing by way of a NDA-approval, for whatever uses the Commissioner deems appropriate, the question of permissible distribution of the drug, when that drug is a controlled substance, is one clearly within the jurisdiction of the Justice Department. The diversion of the particular drug to a use not approved by the Commissioner would be grounds for revocation of the offending distributor's registration. FDA attempts to accomplish peremptorily by way of its challenged regulation, that which could only be accomplished, according to the scheme of the Controlled Substances Act, by way of show-cause proceedings initiated by the Attorney General, i.e., revoking the authority of otherwise duly-registered distributors with respect to the drug methadone. To allow the challenged portions of the methadone regulations to stand, therefore, would be to abrogate the collective judgment of Congress with regard to the appropriate means of controlling unlawful drug diversion.

This is particularly true of the regulations' denial of authority to the plaintiffs at bar. Although the Attorney General generally has discretion to register applicants wishing to distribute or dispense controlled substances [under the Controlled Substances Act] in the case of "practitioners" the Attorney General *must* register them "if they are authorized to dispense under the law of the State in which they regularly conduct business." Congress has thereby specifically sanctioned the registration of all State-licensed practitioners with the clear intent of permitting them to dispense controlled substances on an equal basis with all other approved distributors. In the face of such clear-cut Congressional intent, it would be anomalous to suggest that an agency, by the mere issuance of a regulation, could modify these mandated channels of distribution. Accordingly, the Court concludes that FDA has overstepped the bounds of its authority in purporting to limit the distribution of methadone in the manner contemplated by its regulations.

It is undoubtedly true that methadone poses unique problems of medical judgment, law enforcement and public policy but this fact alone cannot justify a federal agency of specifically delimited jurisdiction from implementing equally unique control solutions not authorized by Congress. The problem of unlawful diversion is one presently consigned by Congress to the Drug Enforcement Administration (DEA, formerly the Bureau of Narcotics and Dangerous Drugs) of the Department of Justice. FDA, on the other hand, has the responsibility of making the initial decision, based on all available medical and scientific data, as to whether a particular new drug is safe and effective for its intended use. While the functions of FDA and DEA are not entirely exclusive of one another,[16] a certain division of authority and responsibility was clearly intended by Congress and must

---

16. For example, the Attorney General, in exercising his authority under 21 U.S.C. § 811(a) to add or remove drugs from the schedules of controlled substances established by the Controlled Substances Act, must first call upon FDA for its recommendation. The recommendations of FDA, inso-

be recognized by this Court in order to preserve the integrity of the legislative scheme. Under these circumstances, the relative merits of FDA's plan to control the distribution of methadone, a controlled substance, must first be passed upon by Congress.

Wherefore, for all the foregoing reasons, ... plaintiffs' motion for summary judgment ... is, granted[.]

The D.C. Circuit Court affirmed *American Pharmaceutical Association v. Weinberger* in a *per curiam* opinion "on the basis of the opinion of the District Court." *American Pharmaceutical Association v. Matthews*, 530 F. 2d 1054 (1976). The decision included a brief concurring opinion by Judge McGowan describing the distinction between the FDA's authority to authorize the distribution of a drug on a prescription-only basis and its effort to place restrictions on the distribution of methadone out of concern that the drug would be misused:

> The pivotal provision of the Federal Food, Drug and Cosmetic Act [in this case] is 21 U.S.C. §355(d), which prohibits the approval of a new drug application unless there are adequate data to establish that the "drug is safe for use under the conditions prescribed, recommended, or suggested in the proposed labeling thereof...." The FDA contends that where there exists a documented pattern of drug misuse contrary to the intended uses specified in the labelling, the drug is unsafe for approval unless controls over distribution are imposed. As a corollary, it asserts that for a drug such as methadone, for which there is substantial evidence of misuse, the FDA must have the power to restrict distribution to avoid the dilemma of either disapproving a drug with important therapeutic benefits or of placing on the market a drug likely to be misused. The FDA claims that section 355(d) authorized restricting distribution to a prescription-only basis before the FDA was explicitly granted that authority in 1951, and that the regulations at issue differ only in degree from a prescription-only restriction.
>
> Although these arguments have some weight, I do not find them ultimately convincing. The word "safe" in section 355(d) is, to my mind, best interpreted as requiring the labelling to include the evidence from drug testing, and the inferences therefrom, indicating the therapeutic benefits, possible dangers, and uncertainties involved in use of a drug, as an aid to a conscientious physician in determining appropriate medical treatment. That view seems to me to accord with both the most reasonable interpretation of the statutory language and the common understanding of the FDA's mission. Thus, methadone is safe for its intended use notwithstanding the possibility that it will be employed in unintended fashions.
>
> The controls on distribution here are different in kind from prescription-only restrictions. The latter restrictions prevent self-diagnosis by the layman. If such restrictions had not been permitted before 1951, drug labelling would have had to include both specific medical evidence about a drug and all the general medical knowledge that a physician must possess in order to decide, after reading a labelling, whether to administer a drug. Although one might contend in theory that any drug is safe for its intended use if the labelling contains enough information, it is evident that a layman cannot be expected to digest a mass of complicated medical information and bring to bear upon it the medical judgment of a prac-

---

far as they concern "scientific and medical matters" relating to the "appropriate schedule, if any, under which such drug or substance should be listed" are binding on the Attorney General. 21 U.S.C. §811(b).

ticing physician. Thus, restrictions to a prescription-only basis are necessary to ensure that persons intending to use drugs in accordance with the implications of medical evidence gathered by the FDA and contained in a drug labelling can do so. The restrictions on methadone involved here are quite different. Without them an informed and sound medical judgment about medical safety and effectiveness can still be made. They are designed instead to control drug misuse by persons who have no intent to try to use drugs for medical purposes.

There would be almost no limit to the FDA's authority were its view adopted. If, for example, it had concluded before 1970 that without restrictions on methadone of the sort now contained in the Controlled Substances Act, the possibility of drug misuse remained high, there would be no barrier under its argument to its having established a regulatory scheme of the complexity of that ultimately adopted in that Act. Thus, under the authority of section 355(d) (and the general power to promulgate implementing regulations in section 371(a)), the FDA might have established a comprehensive registration scheme, complete with detailed record-keeping, security, and inspection requirements. I do not believe that the current grant of statutory authority contemplates such activity by the FDA, but accepting the FDA's view would require upholding far-ranging regulation of that sort.

The extent of the FDA's authority to restrict the distribution of drugs remain unclear in some respects. As Lars Noah described in an article on regulatory issues surrounding the abortifacient drug mifepristone, the FDA has taken the position that it can place distribution restrictions on a drug where its purpose in doing so is to ensure safety in its use and administration rather than to prevent abuse of the substance. Based on this theory, the FDA "suggested a variety of unusual distribution restrictions [on mifepristone] such as making the drug available only through physicians who performed surgical abortions and would agree to register with the manufacturer. This degree of oversight resembles some of the restrictions imposed on Schedule II controlled substances such as methadone, but no one has suggested that mifepristone qualifies as a narcotic subject to the Controlled Substances Act, and nothing in the FDA's enabling statute explicitly authorized the imposition of such controls on access to the drug. Indeed, when the agency once attempted to restrict the distribution of methadone, the courts concluded that it had overstepped its jurisdiction. Notwithstanding its apparent lack of broader statutory authority, the FDA has managed to place controls on the distribution of drugs that do not qualify as controlled substances. For instance, when it approved thalidomide for the treatment of leprosy patients, the agency conditioned approval on extremely strict controls because of the serious risk of birth defects: distribution only through specially-registered physicians and pharmacists, and tracking of patients who must agree to use two forms of contraception and undergo frequent pregnancy tests. Even so, the FDA's power to impose such restrictions remains very much in doubt." Lars Noah, *A Miscarriage in the Drug Approval Process?: Mifepristone Embroils the FDA in Abortion Politics*, 36 Wake Forest L. Rev. 571 (2001).

B. The Controlled Substances Act and Prescription Drugs

The 2010 National Drug Control Strategy calls prescription drug abuse "the fastest-growing drug problem in the United States" and notes that "data show that among young people, 7 of the top 10 abused substances are pharmaceuticals." THE WHITE HOUSE NA-TIONAL DRUG CONTROL STRATEGY 30 (2010). The recreational use of prescription medications presents particularly difficult legal and policy challenges. In addition to the policy issues explored at the beginning of this casebook—such as whether it is legitimate for the government to criminalize the distribution or use of a substance for recreational purposes—the regulation of prescription drugs raises the question of how to balance a patient's interest in having convenient and affordable access to their medication with the government's desire to stop recreational use. This is because every administrative and criminal control aimed at preventing the diversion of prescription drugs to recreational users will inevitably add an additional cost or hurdle that may be borne by patients. Unlike FDA regulations which, as discussed in *American Pharmaceutical Association v. Weinberger,* are promulgated with the aim of furthering the interest of patients (e.g., by ensuring that a drug is properly labeled and its side effects identified and disclosed), the Controlled Substances Act's provisions related to pharmaceuticals exist in order to try and prevent recreational use and abuse. When reading the materials that follow, consider whether you think the law has struck the proper balance between these interests.

Challenges in the Federal Regulation of Pain Management Technologies
Lars Noah
31 Journal of Law, Medicine & Ethics 55 (2003)

The modern pharmaceutical industry traces its origins back more than a century, around the time that the German company Bayer first synthesized aspirin (acetylsalicylic acid) and began marketing it as an analgesic. Federal regulation of drug products in the United States began shortly thereafter, and it has evolved alongside the growing sophistication of the pharmaceutical industry. Although not specifically geared toward the control of pain management technologies, these various laws have had important consequences for the availability and use of analgesic products, at least in part because of certain peculiar aspects of these pharmaceuticals. In parallel, Congress has imposed special requirements on narcotics often used for analgesia because of concerns about addiction and abuse.

Whether a company wishes to market an over-the-counter pain reliever containing a well-known active ingredient, a prescription drug containing a novel analgesic compound, or a medical device intended for the treatment of pain, it must satisfy a number of requirements designed to ensure the safety and effectiveness of the product. In addition, if a drug product contains a narcotic or other controlled substance, its availability will depend on the manner in which the DEA has classified that substance. Although implemented by two quite dissimilar agencies—the former preoccupied with medical and scientific questions, while the latter focuses on law enforcement matters—these two regulatory regimes operate in tandem and overlap in potentially important ways.

If federal agencies become excessively concerned about misuse, they may deprive patients of valuable new analgesic agents. Indeed, depending on the stringency of the restrictions imposed, companies may be unable or unwilling to develop such products in the first place, or health care professionals may fail to make full use of them. Already hesitant to approve powerful analgesics, the FDA and the DEA may be forced to revisit their original clearance decisions due to the growing problems with the theft and diversion of currently marketed painkillers containing ingredients such as oxycodone and fentanyl. Any such regulatory actions—whether expressed as a refusal to allow an analgesic product to enter the market initially or the withdrawal of such a product in the face of rampant abuse—would have to grapple with the classic difficulty of choosing between the medical needs of individual patients and the broader societal hazards associated with the availability of such products. These questions do not admit of any simple answers, of course, but they cannot be avoided.

Before pain management technologies can reach patients, the Food and Drug Administration must assess their safety and effectiveness. If a product has not received marketing approval (or an exemption) from the agency, then it cannot be sold. Even if a company has surmounted the often difficult hurdle of proving that a product serves a therapeutic purpose without posing an undue risk, the FDA's decisions about appropriate labeling may affect how readily patients will be able to access it.

Over the course of the last century, federal regulation of medical technologies has shifted from an emphasis on policing against economic frauds to a premarket approval system mandating proof to support therapeutic claims. The FDA has, for example, expressed long-standing and largely justified skepticism about "quack" medical devices, including products indicated for pain relief. As a result, legitimate articles used for analgesia may encounter significant regulatory obstacles originally fashioned to protect consumers from wasting their resources on worthless remedies.

In particular, the FDA's insistence on placebo-controlled clinical trials when evaluating the effectiveness of pharmaceuticals and medical devices means that firms seeking to market pain management technologies shoulder a particularly challenging evidentiary burden given the pronounced placebo effect that researchers encounter in this context. Moreover, because of difficulties in measuring a largely subjective condition such as pain, coupled with the significant variability in patient response, the agency may struggle to interpret placebo-controlled clinical trials submitted as part of an application for new drug approval (NDA).

Even if persuaded that a drug works, the agency will have to decide whether or not the inevitable side-effects pose too great a hazard to justify granting product approval. In making these risk-benefit judgments, "the FDA takes into account the significance of a targeted health condition, or the status of that condition as a treatable disease." Interventions such as analgesics that provide *only* symptomatic relief may not fare as well in this process, though some experts maintain that pain should qualify as a serious disease process in its own right. A similar dichotomy, between curative and palliative care, may account for the persistent undertreatment of pain by health care professionals.

Notwithstanding this pair of potential obstacles—namely, the heightened difficulty of establishing efficacy and the presumption that symptomatic relief represents a less compelling clinical endpoint for purposes of making risk-benefit judgments—no one has accused the FDA of overcaution in reviewing new analgesics. On the contrary, some observers have criticized the agency for approving too many new non-steroidal antiinflammatory drugs (NSAIDs) that offer no particular advantage over existing, and typically less expensive, drugs in the class. The FDA usually does not, however, make judgments about comparative efficacy, preferring to leave that task for physicians and patients based on the information supplied in the labeling dictated by agency reviewers.

One fundamental labeling question is whether to make a product available only upon a prescription from—or through direct administration by—a licensed health care professional. Because analgesics relieve symptoms and do not purport to treat any underlying disease process, they would seem to represent natural candidates for nonprescription or over-the-counter (OTC) marketing. Even if most consumers would not need a physician's diagnostic skills in order to decide whether to select a particular pain reliever, however, the safety profile of a product may justify some restriction on access. At least initially, most new ingredients are available only by prescription while the FDA collects additional adverse event data. In addition, the risk of abuse has, from the outset, represented one of the primary rationales for limiting drugs to prescription-only sale.

The FDA may decide to authorize OTC marketing for drugs that do not require the supervision of a physician, have a history of safe use, and present no abuse potential. This may happen in a couple of different ways. First, a company may sell an OTC drug if it abides by the terms of the applicable "monograph," which specifies for particular categories of products the active ingredients and dosages that the FDA has determined to be safe and effective, along with the precise labeling necessary to facilitate appropriate consumer use.

The second route to OTC marketing requires that a company secure supplemental NDA for a reformulation (including revised labeling) of a product previously approved for prescription use. Among its most prominent Rx to OTC switches, the FDA authorized nonprescription sale of a lower dose product containing ibuprofen (e.g., Motrin(R)). It later switched a number of other NSAIDs, including ketoprofen and naproxen, from prescription to OTC status. Of course, it did not take long for consumers to realize that they could self-medicate with a prescription strength simply by exceeding the dose recommended in the OTC labeling.

Nonprescription marketing does not mean that a drug product entails no serious risks, as again revealed by the FDA's experience with analgesics. For instance, in the early 1980s, the agency became aware of a link between Reye syndrome and the use of aspirin by children suffering from viral infections. The labels of OTC drug products containing aspirin now must include the following statement: "WARNING: Children and teenagers should not use this medicine for chicken pox or flu symptoms before a doctor is consulted about Reye syndrome, a rare but serious illness reported to be associated with aspirin." Notably, the FDA rejected suggestions urging "more drastic measures such as banning use of aspirin in products for individuals under 21 years of age or limiting such products to prescription use." More recently, after it received reports of an association between acetaminophen and liver toxicity, the agency imposed special warning requirements.

Although NSAIDs dominate both the prescription and OTC markets in terms of volume, most of the truly significant pain management technologies used by physicians qualify as "controlled substances," primarily opioid analgesics. (Less frequently, health care professionals may try behavioral therapy, surgical interventions such as nerve blocks, or medical devices such as transcutaneous electrical nerve stimulators.) Unlike peripherally acting drugs, opioids relieve pain by acting directly on the central nervous system, binding with the receptors that are involved in the transmission of pain signals to the brain. These drugs must undergo the same FDA premarket review process as any other pharmaceutical product, but special authority over controlled substances resides with a separate agency, the Drug Enforcement Administration of the U.S. Department of Justice.

In 1970, Congress enacted the Controlled Substances Act (CSA), which establishes different "schedules" of narcotics and other substances prone to abuse or diversion. By way of illustration, Schedule I includes substances such as heroin (diacetylmorphine) and marijuana (cannabis). Schedule II includes, for instance, drugs containing synthetic forms of morphine sold as Dilaudid (hydromorphone hydrochloride) and Demerol (meperidine hydrochloride). Schedule III includes products such as Tylenol (acetaminophen) with codeine. Schedule IV includes products such as Darvon (propoxyphene hydrochloride). Schedule V includes products such as Robitussin, a cough syrup which contains a limited amount of codeine.

Congress understood that "many of the drugs included within this subchapter have a useful and legitimate medical purpose and are necessary to maintain the health and general welfare of the American people." This explains the central role, for purposes of distinguishing Schedule I from all other controlled substances, of the criterion that asks whether the drug has "a currently accepted medical use in treatment in the United States."

Under the statute, the DEA supervises the manufacturing and distribution of legal narcotics. For Schedule II drugs, manufacturers must register their operations, and the DEA assigns aggregate and individual production quotas. Schedule II drugs must be produced in a secure facility, transported with care, stored in a vault, tracked using a precise inventory system, supplied in response to an order form completed by a registered practitioner, and dispensed only upon a written prescription and without refills. Progressively weaker restrictions apply to Schedule III, IV, and V drugs. Physicians wishing to prescribe controlled substances first must register with the DEA, which enjoys sweeping authority to suspend or revoke certificates of registration.

A [...] controversy arose in the early 1980s in connection with the ultimately unsuccessful efforts by some in Congress to reschedule heroin. Unlike marijuana, which may have multiple therapeutic applications and an arguably exaggerated abuse potential, no one seriously doubts that heroin causes addiction, but, in common with the Schedule II drugs cocaine and morphine, it also offers a powerful analgesic effect. In fact, some have argued that it has unique properties as a pain reliever for terminally ill patients or, at the very least, offers an alternative for those who do not respond well to approved opioids. For this reason, the United Kingdom continues to recognize the medical usefulness of heroin; however, the CSA requires that a controlled substance have a currently accepted use *in the United States* in order to avoid classification in Schedule I. In the end, fears of diversion and confidence in the effectiveness of already available opioid analgesics—coupled with the understandable political imperative against appearing to be soft on drugs—scuttled the effort to reschedule heroin.

In another instance, Congress decided to reclassify a drug as Schedule I even though it clearly enjoyed a currently accepted medical use. The FDA previously had approved methaqualone for treating insomnia, which concededly gave the drug a currently accepted use in treatment, but Congress concluded that methaqualone offered no advantages over other products that posed less of a risk of abuse. For that reason, Congress directed the DEA to reschedule the drug and the FDA to withdraw its NDA. Although this did not alter the statutory criteria generally applicable to scheduling decisions, the legislative rescheduling of methaqualone arguably set a troublesome precedent.[91] In effect, Congress adopted a "one size fits all" approach, which fails to account for the possibility that this drug might provide some unique benefit to a small group of patients who are refractory to the drug of choice, whether because of their physiologic or genetic deviation from the norm, progression of disease, heightened susceptibility to side-effects, co-morbid factors, or concomitant use of other medications. If aggregate risk-benefit balancing of this sort becomes the standard for future scheduling decisions, then the needs of individual patients will compete against the consequences of the irresponsible behavior of abusers, and the DEA may opt to sacrifice products that offer insufficiently dramatic advantages over existing alternative treatments.

In the case of newly synthesized chemicals, or in response to new information about previously scheduled controlled substances, the DEA may have to make its own sched-

---

91. Congress may have set a similar precedent when it originally decided to classify cocaine as a Schedule II "narcotic" even though pharmacologically the substance does not qualify as a narcotic. See *United States v. Whitley,* 734 F.2d 1129, 1140–41 (6th Cir. 1984) (upholding the classification as rational in order to promote law enforcement purposes).

uling decisions. Congress mandated that the agency first consult with HHS, which has sub-delegated that task to the FDA, and then abide by any recommendations that the DEA receives from the Department. In this way, Congress hoped to "strike[] a balance between the extent to which control decisions should be based upon law enforcement criteria, and the extent to which such decisions should be based on medical and scientific determinations." Given the long-running "war on drugs" in this country, it is difficult to maintain this sort of balance.

Such cooperative arrangements between agencies or "split enforcement" models have posed challenges in other contexts. Apart from questions of efficiency, these organizational choices can have significant impacts on substance, especially if two agencies have different sorts of expertise and missions, and respond to different constituencies. Without meaning to exaggerate the cultural explanations for their contrasting approaches to pain management technologies, the FDA probably would have implemented the Controlled Substances Act differently than the DEA has done.

This distribution of regulatory authority, between a traditional law enforcement agency and one that focuses on patient health, can generate incongruities. In some instances, the DEA's desire to facilitate prosecution of drug abusers by placing a substance into Schedule I or II conflicts with the FDA's effort to promote the development of a drug potentially valuable in the treatment of a legitimate class of users. In other instances, at least where it has not already approved a drug proposed for inclusion in Schedule I, the FDA has done little more than "rubber stamp" DEA scheduling recommendations. Once placed in Schedule I, of course, it becomes exceedingly difficult to conduct the sort of research necessary to secure FDA approval and subsequent down-scheduling by the DEA.

The DEA has overlaid another "currently accepted medical use" requirement in regulating prescriptions for narcotics. Physicians may prescribe controlled substances only for "a legitimate medical purpose." In turn, pharmacists may dispense controlled substances only pursuant to a valid prescription, which might require a comparison between the indications appearing in the FDA-approved labeling and the patient's condition.

In contrast, the FDA has long recognized the legitimacy of "off-label" drug prescribing, an outgrowth of Congress's admonition against federal interference with the practice of medicine. As the agency has explained, "once a drug product has been approved for marketing, a physician may, in treating patients, prescribe the drug for uses not included in the drug's approved labeling." Apart from deferring to the congressional decision against undue interference with the practice of medicine, this policy acknowledges the inevitability of incomplete information, the lag time before widely accepted new uses appear in revised labeling (if they ever do), and patient variability. Thus, physicians routinely, and often appropriately, deviate from the directions contained in approved prescription drug labeling.

In the case of controlled substances, however, physicians may not have the freedom to engage in such off-label prescribing. In contrast to the FDA, which focuses its attention on the activities of commercial entities, the DEA enjoys the power to supervise the activity of individual physicians by virtue of its registration requirements. The agency also has shown less deference to medical practitioners and the regulatory prerogative of the states, instead seeming to regard them with some suspicion. For example, when it down-scheduled [the drug dronabinol which contains synthetic] THC, the DEA formally announced a policy threatening to revoke (as inconsistent with the public interest) the registration of anyone "who engages in the distribution or dispensing of dronabinol for medical indications outside the [FDA] approved [antiemetic] use associated with cancer treatment."

For a variety of reasons, patients respond variably to opioids, which explains the need for a range of alternatives and the interest in using powerful analgesics in different combinations. For instance, a certain genetic polymorphism found in more than 5 percent of patients makes them poor metabolizers of codeine. In addition, patients may develop tolerance from chronic treatment. Would a physician or pharmacist face DEA sanctions for prescribing or dispensing a Schedule II drug approved only for nonanalgesic indications to a patient with severe pain refractory to the other available drugs? In recent testimony before Congress, the DEA Administrator seemed to imply otherwise, but the agency's position remains unclear.

For the most part, scheduling decisions relate to the intrinsic characteristics of active ingredients, paying little attention to product formulation and dosage,[131] though the DEA's differential treatment of smoked marijuana and THC encapsulated for ingestion may represent an exception. In contrast, the FDA routinely addresses precisely these sorts of issues when it reviews an NDA application, and the choices that it makes may have important repercussions for the threat of abuse and diversion.

Fentanyl citrate is a Schedule II controlled substance. During the last decade, the FDA approved products containing this opioid analgesic in unusual dosage forms. First, it authorized the marketing of a transdermal fentanyl patch (Duragesic). Within a couple of years, the misuse of these patches—for instance, a few individuals died after sucking on them—led the agency to demand stronger warnings to physicians and patients. More controversially, in 1994, the FDA approved a transmucosal form of fentanyl—a lollipop intended for use by children (Oralet)—notwithstanding objections that it had received from the DEA and others that this would promote abuse. In 1997, another manufacturer received approval to market a lollipop form of fentanyl (Actiq), though this time intended only for use by cancer patients experiencing breakthrough pain and with special packaging designed to minimize the risk of accidental poisoning by children.

Recent years have seen widespread misuse of other opioid analgesics, especially OxyContin (oxycodone hydrochloride). Introduced in 1996, shortly after securing FDA approval, OxyContin quickly became the most widely prescribed narcotic painkiller, recording more than $1 billion in sales last year. The drug's active ingredient is a synthetic form of morphine regulated as a Schedule II controlled substance. Older painkillers such as Percocet(R) and Percodan(R) also contain oxycodone, but OxyContin uses a time-released formulation designed to offer sustained relief over a 12-hour period to patients with chronic moderate-to-severe pain. In contrast, the older drug products in this class (including the related hydrocodone drugs such as Vicodin and Lortab) may offer uneven relief over just a 3–4 hour period.

It is difficult trying to quantify the benefits of this drug. Anecdotal reports from physicians testify to the effectiveness of OxyContin in particular patients, but these give no sense for the drug's aggregate utility. One could use the number of prescriptions written each year—now in excess of 6 million—as a rough proxy. Even if some number of physicians prescribed the drug to patients who did not actually suffer from severe pain or to those for whom the older opioids had offered satisfactory relief, the high volume of prescribing suggests that OxyContin has helped to fill a significant unmet need and that many "thousands" of patients have benefited from its availability. If nothing else, the

---

131. In the less stringent schedules, some of the listed substances refer to particular formulations and dosage strengths. See 21 U.S.C. § 812(c)(III)(d) & (V); see also *id.* § 811(g)(1) (calling for the descheduling of any nonnarcotic substance used in an FDA-approved OTC drug product); *United States v. Martinez*, 950 F.2d 222, 223–24 (5th Cir. 1991) (construing this provision).

slow-release feature made OxyContin more convenient than older opioids, which patients with severe pain would have to take every 4 hours throughout the day and night.

The time-released formulation also seemed to make OxyContin less prone to abuse because it would not provide a quick euphoric effect upon initial ingestion. As a result, Purdue Pharma and Abbott Labs promoted their drug to a broader group of physicians and as presenting a lower risk of abuse and diversion. The companies apparently failed to appreciate the creativity of drug abusers. To defeat the slow-release feature, these individuals chewed, crushed, dissolved, or scraped the coating off of the tablets, leaving stronger dosages of oxycodone than found in individual Percocet or Percodan tablets. They would then ingest, snort, or inject the substance. Reports indicate that hundreds of people have died after overdosing in this fashion, usually as a result of acute pulmonary edema.

Diversion occurs in several ways. Individuals might feign pain and shop for doctors willing to prescribe the drug, or they might engage in prescription fraud and theft. These individuals then might use the drugs themselves or sell their supplies to others. A few desperate addicts have committed armed robberies at pharmacies, demanding OxyContin rather than cash. Most of the deaths and other injuries linked to the drug have occurred in persons other than legitimate patients.

Although deaths resulting from OxyContin have received significant publicity, they should be put in context: The diversion of other prescription controlled substances over the years has resulted in numerous deaths among drug abusers, and the toll pales in comparison to the injuries associated with the lawful use of nonnarcotic drugs. NSAIDs may represent a far more serious public health menace, contributing to thousands of patient deaths each year. The volume of use is also higher, but these comparative statistics raise an interesting policy question: Should injuries to third parties who misuse prescription drugs attract greater concern from public officials than injuries suffered by legitimate patients?

Purdue recently announced plans to investigate the possibility of including another ingredient (naltrexone) that might counteract efforts to defeat the slow-release mechanism, but it will have to conduct trials to determine the safety and efficacy of this combination and then await FDA approval of a supplemental NDA, which could take several years. What if naltrexone reduces the effectiveness of OxyContin, as happened during clinical trials using a similar ingredient (naloxone), or else causes adverse reactions in some subset of users? From the perspective of the patient with cancer or other type of intractable pain, such a new form of the drug definitely would not represent an improvement.

Just as happens with formulation issues, the abuse potential of a drug may extend beyond the intrinsic characteristics of the active ingredient to include how the manufacturer promotes the drug product to health care professionals. Some critics have alleged that Purdue Pharma overpromoted OxyContin for the treatment of temporary or less serious pain, arguing that this led to excessive prescribing and created a larger supply for potential diversion. Even though the DEA does not regulate the marketing of controlled substances (leaving that task to the FDA), it has castigated the manufacturer for its aggressive promotion of OxyContin to physicians.

Critics also object that Purdue and Abbott made OxyContin generally available for prescribing by any physician and dispensing by any pharmacy. The companies might have decided to supply the drug only to hospital pharmacies for dispensing, and only in response to a prescription by a pain management (or similar) specialist, but such a restricted distribution network would have been unprecedented and perhaps even unlawful. The FDA generally does not have the authority to restrict the distribution of drugs that it approves. Although the DEA clearly enjoys the power to limit the channels of distribution for controlled substances by virtue of its scheduling decisions, it does not usually impose more precise restrictions tailored to a particular drug. Either agency could attempt to persuade a manufacturer to accept nominally voluntary limitations that they could not mandate directly, but that did not happen at the time of OxyContin's approval.

In whatever manner achieved, distribution restrictions would have important practical consequences for patients. Although more stringent limitations may reduce the threat of diversion and abuse, they also may complicate access for legitimate users of these drugs. For instance, with just over 1,000 pain management specialists practicing in the United States, patients would have difficulty getting prescriptions for needed drugs if only such specialists were permitted to prescribe them. Similarly, patients would find it inconvenient if they regularly had to fill their prescriptions at a hospital pharmacy. Even without distribution restrictions, of course, physicians hesitate before prescribing controlled substances, and local pharmacists may fail to stock them. One should not lose sight of the fact that the FDA's decision to restrict access to some analgesics on prescription-only creates an important barrier, both because physicians have ethical and legal obligations designed to limit inappropriate prescribing and because of the practical (especially financial) hurdles involved in visiting a physician. Schedule II, by further restricting physician flexibility and by insisting on repeat office visits (through the no-refill rule), enhances these barriers to patient access.

The experience with antibiotics may offer an instructive contrast. Physicians continue to overprescribe these often powerful prescription drugs with attendant risks to their patients' health. Patients also may abuse antibiotics, whether by disregarding dosage and duration of use instructions or by passing them along to family members and friends. Unlike the abuse and diversion of controlled substances, none of this unwise behavior violates federal law. The same problems may, of course, arise with any pharmaceutical product, but antibiotic misuse carries a societal risk as well—widespread overuse has created drug-resistant strains of infectious agents. As with analgesics, this explains the need to continue developing new and improved antimicrobial agents even though the old stand-bys usually work well enough for most patients with simple bacterial infections. So far, public health agencies have responded by pleading with physicians to exercise restraint in prescribing, but some commentators would go further and restrict access to the latest compounds. Because individual physicians and patients do not directly bear the diffuse societal risks associated with the spread of resistance, and because they do not face any real legal consequences for misusing antibiotics, a paternalistic strategy of limiting access has much to recommend it. Because law enforcement tools already exist to deal with the abuse and diversion of controlled substances, however, federal access restrictions that may interfere with legitimate use seem far less defensible.

Perhaps the central lesson from this brief discussion of antibiotics is that neither the FDA nor the DEA has approached pain management issues from the proper perspective. Traditionally, the FDA has adopted a clinical (or individualistic) mindset, leaving most of the difficult risk-benefit judgments in the hands of health care professionals and patients. Although such an attitude has much to commend it, the agency may have placed excessive faith in the good sense of physicians and the power of labeling to encourage proper use and to limit the occasions for inappropriate prescribing. Conversely, the DEA's law enforcement mindset goes to the opposite extreme, giving perhaps undue weight to the negative externalities associated with access to narcotics and not trusting health care professionals. A public health perspective, which the Centers for Disease Control and Prevention (CDC) has expressed in connection with antibiotics as well as vaccine programs, might help to mediate between these two potentially incompatible perspectives.

1. Regulation and Prosecution of Physicians

United States v. Moore
Supreme Court of the United States
423 U.S. 122 (1975)

Mr. Justice Powell delivered the opinion of the Court.

Dr. Moore was charged, in a 639-count indictment, with the knowing and unlawful distribution and dispensation of methadone (Dolophine), a Schedule II controlled substance, in violation of 21 U.S.C. §841(a)(1). That subsection provides:

"Except as authorized by this subchapter, it shall be unlawful for any person knowingly or intentionally—

"(1) to manufacture, distribute, or dispense, or possess with intent to manufacture, distribute, or dispense, a controlled substance...."

The indictment covered a 5 1/2-month period from late August 1971 to early February 1972. It was reduced before trial to 40 counts, and the jury convicted respondent on 22 counts. He was sentenced to concurrent terms of five to 15 years' imprisonment on 14 counts, and to concurrent terms of 10 to 30 years on the remaining eight counts. The second set of sentences was to be consecutive with the first. Fines totaling $150,000 were also imposed.[2]

Methadone is an addictive drug used in the treatment of heroin addicts. If taken without controls it can, like heroin, create euphoric "highs," but if properly administered it eliminates the addict's craving for heroin without providing a "high." The two principal methods of treating heroin addicts with methadone are "detoxification" and "maintenance." Under a maintenance program, the addict is given a fixed dose once a day for an indefinite period to keep him from using heroin. In detoxification the addict is given a large dose of methadone during the first few days of treatment to keep him free of withdrawal symptoms. Then the dose is gradually reduced until total abstinence is reached.

Maintenance is the more controversial method of treatment. During the period covered by the indictment, registration under §822, in itself, did not entitle a physician to conduct a maintenance program. In addition to a §822 registration, the physician who wished to conduct such a program was required to obtain authorization from the Food and Drug Administration for investigation of a new drug. Dr. Moore's authorization by the FDA was revoked in the summer of 1971, and he does not claim that he was conducting an authorized maintenance program. Instead, his defense at trial was that he had devised a new method of detoxification based on the work of a British practitioner. He testified that he prescribed large quantities of methadone to achieve a "blockade" condition, in which the addict was so saturated with methadone that heroin would have no effect, and to instill a strong psychological desire for detoxification. The Government's position is that the evidence established that Dr. Moore's conduct was inconsistent with all accepted methods of treating addicts, that in fact he operated as a "pusher."

Respondent concedes in his brief that he did not observe generally accepted medical practices. He conducted a large-scale operation. Between September 1971 and mid-February 1972 three District of Columbia pharmacies filled 11,169 prescriptions written by Dr. Moore. These covered some 800,000 methadone tablets. On 54 days during that

---

2. In addition, Dr. Moore's license to practice medicine was revoked pursuant to D.C. Code Ann. §2-131 (1973), which authorizes revocation upon the conviction of "any felony." An appeal from the conviction acts "as a supersedeas to the judgment ... revoking his license...."

period respondent wrote over 100 prescriptions a day. In billing his patients he used a "sliding-fee scale" pegged solely to the quantity prescribed, rather than to the medical services performed. The fees ranged from $15 for a 50-pill prescription to $50 for 150 pills. In five and one-half months Dr. Moore's receipts totaled at least $260,000.

When a patient entered the office he was given only the most perfunctory examination. Typically this included a request to see the patient's needle marks (which in more than one instance were simulated) and an unsupervised urinalysis (the results of which were regularly ignored). A prescription was then written for the amount requested by the patient. On return visits — for which appointments were never scheduled — no physical examination was performed and the patient again received a prescription for whatever quantity he requested. Accurate records were not kept, and in some cases the quantity prescribed was not recorded. There was no supervision of the administration of the drug. Dr. Moore's instructions consisted entirely of a label on the drugs reading: "Take as directed for detoxification." Some patients used the tablets to get "high"; others sold them or gave them to friends or relatives. Several patients testified that their use of methadone increased dramatically while they were under respondent's care.

The Court of Appeals, with one judge dissenting, assumed that respondent acted wrongfully but held that he could not be prosecuted under § 841. The court found that Congress intended to subject registered physicians to prosecution only under §§ 842 and 843, which prescribe less severe penalties than § 841.[6] The court reasoned:

> "… Congress intended to deal with registrants primarily through a system of administrative controls, relying on modest penalty provisions to enforce those controls, and reserving the severe penalties provided for in § 841 for those seeking to avoid regulation entirely by not registering."

It said, further, that §§ 842 and 843 were enacted to enforce that scheme, while § 841 was reserved for prosecution of those outside the "legitimate distribution chain." Persons registered under the Act were "authorized by [the] subchapter" within the meaning of § 841 and thus were thought to be immunized against prosecution under that section.

Respondent advances two basic arguments, contending that each requires affirmance of the Court of Appeals: (i) as that court held, registered physicians may be prosecuted only under §§ 842 and 843; and (ii) in any event, respondent cannot be prosecuted under § 841 because his conduct was "authorized by [the] subchapter" in question. We now consider each of these arguments.

Section 841(a)(1) makes distribution and dispensing of drugs unlawful "[e]xcept as authorized by this subchapter. …" Relying on this language, the Court of Appeals held that a physician registered under the Act is *per se* exempted from prosecution under § 841 because of his status as a registrant. We take a different view, and hold that only the lawful acts of registrants are exempted. By its terms § 841 reaches "any person." It does not exempt (as it could have) "all registrants" or "all persons registered under this Act."

---

6. Violations of § 841, under which respondent was convicted, carry sentences of up to 15 years, fines as high as $25,000, or both. Knowing violators of § 842 are subject at most to imprisonment for one year, a fine of $25,000, or both. There also may be a civil penalty of $25,000 for violation of § 842. The penalties for violation of § 843 are imprisonment for not more than four years, a fine of not more than $30,000, or both. All three sections impose higher penalties for violations after the first conviction.

The Court of Appeals relied also on § 822 (b), which provides: "Persons registered ... under this subchapter to distribute, or dispense controlled substances are authorized to possess, ... distribute, or dispense such substances ... to the extent authorized by their registration and in conformity with the other provisions of this subchapter." This is a qualified authorization of certain activities, not a blanket authorization of all acts by certain persons. We think the statutory language cannot fairly be read to support the view that all activities of registered physicians are exempted from the reach of § 841 simply because of their status.

If § 822 (b) were construed to authorize all such activities, thereby exempting them from other constraints, it would constitute a sharp departure from prior laws. But there is no indication that Congress had any such intent. Physicians who stepped outside the bounds of professional practice could be prosecuted under the Harrison Act (Narcotics) of 1914, the predecessor of the CSA. In *Jin Fuey Moy v. United States,* 254 U.S. 189 (1920), the Court affirmed the conviction of a physician on facts remarkably similar to those before us (*e.g.,* no adequate physical examination, the dispensing of large quantities of drugs without specific directions for use, and fees graduated according to the amount of drugs prescribed). A similar conviction was upheld in *United States v. Behrman,* 258 U.S. 280 (1922), where the defendant-doctor had prescribed heroin, morphine, and cocaine to a person whom he knew to be an addict.

In enacting the CSA Congress attempted to devise a more flexible penalty structure than that used in the Harrison Act. Penalties were geared to the nature of the violation, including the character of the drug involved. But the Act was intended to "strengthen," rather than to weaken, "existing law enforcement authority in the field of drug abuse."

Section 822 (b) was added to the original bill at a late date to "make it clear that persons registered under this title are authorized to deal in or handle controlled substances." It is unlikely that Congress would seek, in this oblique way, to carve out a major new exemption, not found in the Harrison Act, for physicians and other registrants. Rather, § 822 (b) was added merely to ensure that persons engaged in lawful activities could not be prosecuted.

Respondent nonetheless contends that §§ 841 and 822 (b) must be interpreted in light of a congressional intent to set up two separate and distinct penalty systems: Persons not registered under the Act are to be punished under § 841, while those who are registered are to be subject only to the sanctions of §§ 842 and 843. The latter two sections, the argument goes, establish modest penalties which are the sole sanctions in a system of strict administrative regulation of registrants.

The operative language of those sections provides no real support for the proposition that Congress intended to establish two mutually exclusive systems. It is true that the term "registrants" is used in §§ 842 and 843, and not in § 841. But this is of limited significance. All three sections provide that "[i]t shall be unlawful for any person ... [to commit the proscribed acts]." Two of the eight subsections of § 842 (a), one of the five subsections of § 843 (a), and § 842 (b) further qualify "any person" with "who is a registrant." The other subsections of §§ 842 and 843 are not so limited. In context, "registrant" is merely a limiting term, indicating that the only "persons" who are subject to these subsections are "registrants."[10] There is no indication that "persons" means "nonregistrants" when introducing the other subsections.

_____

10. This represents a commonsense recognition by Congress that only a registrant could, for example, distribute drugs "not authorized by his registration," § 842 (a)(2), or manufacture substances "not expressly authorized by his registration" or "in excess of [his] quota." §§ 842 (b)(1), (2). Nor would there be any reason to apply to nonregistrants the penalties for distributing drugs without

There are other indications that § 841, and §§ 842 and 843, do not constitute two discrete systems. Section 843 (b), for example, makes it unlawful for any person to use a communication facility in committing a felony under any provision of the subchapter. But violations of both § 841 and § 843 lead to felony convictions; criminal violations of § 842 are misdemeanors. And counsel for respondent agreed at oral argument that registrants can be prosecuted under § 841 (a)(2), which prohibits the creation, distribution, dispensing, or possession with intent to distribute or dispense of a "counterfeit substance."

The legislative history indicates that Congress was concerned with the nature of the drug transaction, rather than with the status of the defendant. The penalties now embodied in §§ 841–843 originated in §§ 501–503 of the Controlled Dangerous Substances Act of 1969. The Report of the Senate Judiciary Committee on that bill described § 501 (the counterpart of § 841) as applying to "traffickers." Section 502 provided "[a]dditional penalties ... for those involved in the legitimate drug trade," and "[f]urther penalties ... for registrants" were specified in § 503. The House Committee Report on the bill that was to become the CSA explains: "The bill provides for control ... of problems related to drug abuse through registration of manufacturers, wholesalers, retailers, and all others in the legitimate distribution chain, and makes transactions outside the legitimate distribution chain illegal." Although this language is ambiguous, the most sensible interpretation is that the penalty to be imposed for a violation was intended to turn on whether the "transaction" falls within or without legitimate channels. All persons who engage in legitimate transactions must be registered and are subject to penalties under §§ 842 and 843 for "[m]ore or less technical violations." But "severe criminal penalties" were imposed on those, like respondent, who sold drugs, not for legitimate purposes, but "primarily for the profits to be derived therefrom."

Congress was particularly concerned with the diversion of drugs from legitimate channels to illegitimate channels. It was aware that registrants, who have the greatest access to controlled substances and therefore the greatest opportunity for diversion, were responsible for a large part of the illegal drug traffic.

Recognizing this concern the Court of Appeals suggested that Dr. Moore could be prosecuted under § 842 (a)(1) for having violated the provisions of § 829 with respect to the issuing of prescriptions.[12] Whether Dr. Moore could have been so prosecuted is not

---

complying with the labeling and order-form requirements of the Act, §§ 842 (a)(3), 843 (a)(1), for nonregistrants are barred from making any distributions whatsoever.

12. Section 829 provides, in part: "Except when dispensed directly by a practitioner, other than a pharmacist, to an ultimate user, no controlled substance in schedule II, which is a prescription drug as determined under the Federal Food, Drug, and Cosmetic Act, may be dispensed without the written prescription of a practitioner, except that in emergency situations, as prescribed by the Secretary by regulation after consultation with the Attorney General, such drug may be dispensed upon oral prescription in accordance with section 353 (b) of this title. Prescriptions shall be retained in conformity with the requirements of section 827 of this title. No prescription for a controlled substance in schedule II may be refilled."

The Attorney General's regulations enacted pursuant to § 829 required "A prescription for a controlled substance to be effective must be issued for a legitimate medical purpose by an individual practitioner acting in the usual course of his professional practice. The responsibility for the proper prescribing and dispensing of controlled substances is upon the prescribing practitioner, but a corresponding responsibility rests with the pharmacist who fills the prescription. An order purporting to be a prescription issued not in the usual course of professional treatment or in legitimate and authorized research is not a prescription within the meaning and intent of section 309 of the Act (21 U.S.C. 829) and the person knowingly filling such a purported prescription, as well as the person issuing it, shall be subject to the penalties provided for violations of the provisions of law relating to controlled substances." 21 CFR § 306.04 (a) (1973) (redesignated as 21 CFR § 1306.04 (a) (1975)).

before the Court.[13] We note, however, that the penalties for such a violation could hardly have been deemed by Congress to be an appropriate sanction for drug trafficking by a registered physician. Indeed, the penalty for conviction under § 842 would be significantly lighter than, for example, that applicable to a registrant convicted under § 843 for using a suspended registration number. Moreover, a physician who wished to traffic in drugs without threat of criminal prosecution could, if violation of § 829 were the sole basis for prosecution, simply dispense drugs directly without the formality of issuing a prescription. Direct dispensing is exempt from § 829 and thus is not reached by any subsection of § 842 or § 843 so long as the technical requirements are complied with.

But we think it immaterial whether Dr. Moore also could have been prosecuted for his violation of statutory provisions relating to dispensing procedures. There is nothing in the statutory scheme or the legislative history that justifies a conclusion that a registrant who may be prosecuted for the relatively minor offense of violating § 829 is thereby exempted from prosecution under § 841 for the significantly greater offense of acting as a drug "pusher."

Respondent argues that even if Congress did not intend to exempt registrants from all prosecutions under § 841, he cannot be prosecuted under that section because the specific conduct for which he was prosecuted was "authorized by [the] subchapter" and thus falls within the express exemption of the section.

The trial judge assumed that a physician's activities are authorized only if they are within the usual course of professional practice. He instructed the jury that it had to find

> "beyond a reasonable doubt that a physician, who knowingly or intentionally, did dispense or distribute [methadone] by prescription, did so other than in good faith for detoxification in the usual course of a professional practice and in accordance with a standard of medical practice generally recognized and accepted in the United States."

The Court of Appeals did not address this argument because it concluded that registrants could not be prosecuted under § 841 under any circumstances. But it suggested that if a registrant could be reached under § 841 he could not be prosecuted merely because his activities fall outside the "usual course of practice."

Under the Harrison Act physicians who departed from the usual course of medical practice were subject to the same penalties as street pushers with no claim to legitimacy. Section 2 of that Act required all persons who sold or prescribed certain drugs to register and to deliver drugs only to persons with federal order forms. The latter requirement did not apply to "the dispensing or distribution of any of the aforesaid drugs to a patient by a physician ... registered under this Act in the course of his professional practice only." As noted above, Congress intended the CSA to strengthen rather than to weaken the prior drug laws. There is no indication that Congress intended to eliminate the existing limitation on the exemption given to doctors.[16] The difficulty arises because the CSA, unlike the Harrison Act, does not spell out this limitation in unambiguous terms.

---

13. On its face § 829 addresses only the form that a prescription must take. A written prescription is required for Schedule II substances. § 829 (a). Either a written or an oral prescription is adequate for drugs in Schedules III and IV. § 829 (b). The only limitation on the distribution or dispensing of Schedule V drugs is that it be "for a medical purpose." The medical purpose requirement explicit in subsection (c) could be implicit in subsections (a) and (b). Regulation § 306.04 makes it explicit. But § 829 by its terms does not limit the authority of a practitioner.

16. The Narcotic Addict Treatment Act of 1974 (NATA) modified the registration and revocation procedures provided in the CSA in order to facilitate "more expeditious" criminal prosecutions by making revocation easier.

There was no indication that Congress thought that trafficking doctors could escape felony pros-

Instead of expressly removing from the protection of the Act those physicians who operate beyond the bounds of professional practice, the CSA uses the concept of "registration." Section 822 (b) defines the scope of authorization under the Act in circular terms: "Persons registered ... under this subchapter ... are authorized [to dispense controlled substances] ... to the extent authorized by their registration and in conformity with the other provisions of this subchapter." But the scheme of the statute, viewed against the background of the legislative history, reveals an intent to limit a registered physician's dispensing authority to the course of his "professional practice."

Registration of physicians and other practitioners is mandatory if the applicant is authorized to dispense drugs or conduct research under the law of the State in which he practices. In the case of a physician this scheme contemplates that he is authorized by the State to practice medicine and to dispense drugs in connection with his professional practice. The federal registration, which follows automatically, extends no farther. It authorizes transactions within "the legitimate distribution chain" and makes all others illegal. Implicit in the registration of a physician is the understanding that he is authorized only to act "as a physician."

This is made explicit in § 802 (20), which provides that "practitioner" means one who is "registered ... by the United States or the jurisdiction in which he practices or does research, to distribute, dispense, conduct research with respect to, administer, or use in teaching or chemical analysis, a controlled substance in the course of professional practice or research." This section defines the term "practitioner" for purposes of the Act. It also describes the type of registration contemplated by the Act. That registration is limited to the dispensing and use of drugs "in the course of professional practice or research."

The evidence presented at trial was sufficient for the jury to find that respondent's conduct exceeded the bounds of "professional practice."[20] As detailed above, he gave inadequate physical examinations or none at all. He ignored the results of the tests he did make. He did not give methadone at the clinic and took no precautions against its misuse and diversion. He did not regulate the dosage at all, prescribing as much and as frequently as the patient demanded. He did not charge for medical services rendered, but graduated his fee according to the number of tablets desired. In practical effect, he acted as a large-scale "pusher"—not as a physician.

Respondent further contended at trial that he was experimenting with a new "blockade" theory of detoxification. The jury did not believe him. Congress understandably was concerned that the drug laws not impede legitimate research and that physicians be allowed reasonable discretion in treating patients and testing new theories. But respondent's interpretation of the Act would go far beyond authorizing legitimate research and experimentation by physicians.

In enacting the Comprehensive Drug Abuse Prevention and Control Act of 1970, Title II of which is the CSA, Congress faced the problem directly. Because of the potential for

---

ecution altogether under pre-NATA law. Rather, it sought to "cure the present difficulty in such prosecutions because of the intricate and nearly impossible burden of establishing what is beyond 'the course of professional practice' for criminal law purposes when such a practitioner speciously claims that the practices in question were ethical and humanitarian in nature." Dr. Moore's conviction was cited to illustrate that successful criminal actions could be brought only "in the most aggravated of circumstances ... after prolonged effort to make undercover penetrations."

20. The jury was instructed that Dr. Moore could not be convicted if he merely made "an honest effort" to prescribe for detoxification in compliance with an accepted standard of medical practice.

abuse it decided that some limits on free experimentation with drugs were necessary. But it was also aware of the concern expressed by the Prettyman Commission:*

> "[A] controversy has existed for fifty years over the extent to which narcotic drugs may be administered to an addict solely because he is an addict.

> "The practicing physician has ... been confused as to when he may prescribe narcotic drugs for an addict. Out of a fear of prosecution many physicians refuse to use narcotics in the treatment of addicts except occasionally in a withdrawal regimen lasting no longer than a few weeks. In most instances they shun addicts as patients."

Congress' solution to this problem is found in §4 of Title I of the 1970 Act. That section requires the Secretary of Health, Education, and Welfare, after consultation with the Attorney General and national addict treatment organizations, to "determine the appropriate methods of professional practice in the medical treatment of ... narcotic addiction...." It was designed "to clarify for the medical profession ... the extent to which they may safely go in treating narcotic addicts as patients." Congress pointed out that "criminal prosecutions" in the past had turned on the opinions of federal prosecutors. Under the new Act, "[t]hose physicians who comply with the recommendations made by the Secretary will no longer jeopardize their professional careers...." The negative implication is that physicians who go beyond approved practice remain subject to serious criminal penalties.

In the case of methadone treatment the limits of approved practice are particularly clear. As Dr. Moore admitted at trial, he was authorized only to dispense methadone for detoxification purposes. His authorization by the FDA to engage in a methadone maintenance program had been revoked. Nor was respondent unfamiliar with the procedures for conducting a legitimate detoxification program. Charges arising out of his 1969 treatment program, which involved a combination of "long term" and "short term" detoxification, were dropped after he testified before a grand jury and agreed to abide by certain medical procedures in future methadone programs. These included obtaining a medical history of each patient, conducting a reasonably thorough physical examination, abiding by the results of urine tests, recording times and amounts of dosages, and either administering the methadone in his office or prescribing no more than a daily dosage. At trial respondent admitted that he had failed to follow these procedures.

The judgment of the Court of Appeals is reversed.

So ordered.

The majority of states follow *Moore* and hold that physicians can be prosecuted under the same criminal provisions that apply to non-physicians engaged in the distribution of controlled substances. In some states, however, doctors accused of prescribing controlled substances for illegitimate purposes can only under be prosecuted under statutes that pertain specifically to registered practitioners, which generally carry significantly lower penalties. *See* State v. Young, 185 W. Va. 327, 338–40 (1991) (collecting cases). *Moore* distinguishes between physicians who dispense controlled substances for legitimate medical purposes and those who operate, in the words of the Court, as "pushers." Not surprisingly, this issue can present particularly difficult line-drawing problems.

---

* The Prettyman Commission, was established by President John F. Kennedy to advise the President on drug policy. [*Footnote by casebook author.*]

Treating Pain v. Reducing Drug Diversion and Abuse: Recalibrating the Balance in Our Drug Control Laws and Policies
Diane E. Hoffmann

18 Saint Louis University Journal of Health Law and Policy 231 (2008)

The exact number of physicians who have been investigated, arrested, and/or prosecuted over the last decade for inappropriately prescribing opioids is difficult to determine. Investigations, arrests, and charges are not compiled in a central, publicly available database. Therefore, estimates must be pieced together from reports, news articles, DEA statements, and Web sites that track some of these cases. In 2001, DEA statistics indicate that there were 3,097 diversion investigations, 861 of which were investigations of doctors. In 2003, there were 736 DEA investigations and 51 arrests of physicians for diversion of controlled substances. Focusing only on OxyContin, between October 1999 and March 2002, DEA reported investigating 247 OxyContin diversion cases, which led to 328 arrests. DEA also has its own Web site that lists "investigations of physician registrants in which DEA was involved that resulted in the arrest and prosecution of the registrant." The list, covering arrests from January 2003 through February 2008, includes 117 physicians, at least 47 of whom were arrested for prescribing pain medication outside the scope of professional practice or without a legitimate medical purpose. This figure is based solely on selected federal arrests announced by the DEA. Therefore, it underestimates the total of such law enforcement actions, which also include arrests by state law enforcement personnel.

While many of these arrests and prosecutions were appropriate, a number were not. For example, in many of the cases, (1) the physicians treated a large number of chronic pain patients and prescribed large volumes of opioids; (2) there was no evidence that the physicians benefited financially from their prescribing (other than for the office visit); (3) experts disputed the "reasonableness" of the physician's prescribing practices; and (4) the physician's patients often included drug addicts who lied to the physician to obtain their drugs.

In September 2003, Dr. William Hurwitz was arrested on a forty-nine count federal indictment charging him with "drug trafficking resulting in death and serious injury, engaging in a criminal enterprise, conspiracy and health care fraud." He was visiting his children on the eve of Rosh Hashanah when federal agents took him away in handcuffs. The indictment was a result of a "wide-ranging federal investigation into doctors, pharmacists and patients suspected of selling potent and addictive painkillers on a lucrative black market." More than forty people were convicted in the comprehensive probe. According to a news account of the arrest, "[t]he indictment signal[ed] an aggressive push by federal prosecutors to hold doctors accountable for what happens to the drugs they prescribe" and "highlight[ed] the complexities of proving criminal culpability in cases of licensed and reputable physicians prescribing a legal painkiller." Hurwitz ... was one of the first physicians to be charged with conspiracy related to his prescribing of opioids. According to the grand jury, "Hurwitz prescribed 'countless prescriptions for excessive doses' of controlled drugs with the goal of hooking his patients, getting them to pay him a monthly fee and encouraging illegal sales." Of the forty-nine charges, the most serious were that in two cases the conspiracy caused fatal overdoses. Furthermore, "[t]he indictment allege[d] that Hurwitz prescribed medications in as many as [thirty-nine] states, issuing the prescriptions with little or no physical examination and sometimes over the phone, fax, or the Internet."

Hurwitz received his medical degree from Stanford University in 1971 and law degree from George Mason University School of Law in 1996. Prior to his criminal arrest, Hurwitz was prosecuted by the Virginia Board of Medicine and, in August 1996, had his license to practice in Virginia revoked based on excessive prescribing and inadequate supervision of his patients. The Board initiated its action after two of his patients died in January 1996. Hurwitz argued that one of the patients committed suicide by taking multiple times the recommended dose of a drug that he prescribed and that the other died as a result of gastric bleeding, not an overdose. The Board took action despite the fact that "expert testimony had essentially disproven the state's allegation that Hurwitz was at fault." Based on the evidence, the Board dropped its initial allegations against Hurwitz, recognizing that individuals with chronic pain often require high dosages of narcotics, but pursued action against him based on "prescribing without adequate medical records." The Board argued that Hurwitz prescribed hundreds and thousands of doses to patients without appropriately monitoring their progress or status. Hurwitz stated that "most of his pain patients came to him with well-established problems" and that his main purpose in doing a physical exam was to ensure that the patient's complaint was well founded. He saw patients who lived in the area once a month but saw those who lived out of state only once or twice a year. He supplemented out-of-state patients' visits with "a monthly written report and telephone calls."

Hurwitz's license was suspended for three months and then restored on a probationary basis. He also lost his DEA privileges to prescribe narcotics for a year. Dr. Hurwitz appealed the Virginia Board's decision, arguing, in part, that the safe harbor provisions of the state's Intractable Pain Act limit the Board's authority to take action against a medical doctor based on the dosages of pain medicine prescribed. The Virginia Circuit Court, however, affirmed the Board's decision, finding that it acted in accordance with the law, did not make a procedural error resulting in harm, and had sufficient evidentiary support for its findings of facts.

During the disciplinary proceedings, a number of pain experts supported Hurwitz's practices. Dr. James Campbell, professor of neurosurgery and director of the Blaustein Pain Treatment Center at Johns Hopkins University in Baltimore, stated that at Hopkins, they have a national practice: "We have great difficulty finding physicians ... that will take over medications that work in these patients and take over their programs. I think (Dr. Hurwitz) is doing heroic things for his patients. I think what he is doing involves an enormous sacrifice. There are a lot of bad doctors but he is not one of them. If we suspend the license of all doctors ... because one patient committed suicide, the pain field would be out of business."

In the summer of 1998, after his license was reinstated and before his arrest, Hurwitz was able to prescribe controlled substances and began to treat pain again.

Dr. Hurwitz's criminal trial began in November 2004. During the six-week trial, the prosecution called more than sixty witnesses and played tapes of Hurwitz talking to patients who he did not realize were government informants. Also during the trial, several past presidents of the American Pain Society sent a letter to Hurwitz's lawyer expressing their dismay at how the case was being handled. In particular, they cited "misrepresentations" by one of the Justice Department's expert witnesses. A similar letter was subsequently presented to the presiding judge.

On December 15, 2004, a federal jury convicted Hurwitz on fifty counts, including drug trafficking, which led to the death of one patient and seriously injured two other patients. The jury acquitted him of nine other counts and deadlocked on three counts. The prosecution sought a life sentence without parole, but the district court sentenced Hurwitz to twenty-five years in prison.

The outcome sent chills through the pain treatment community and was criticized by a number of prominent journalists. Hurwitz appealed the convictions on three grounds, one of which was that the court instructed the jury that it could not consider Hurwitz's "good faith" in his prescribing. Hurwitz argued that "his good faith in issuing the challenged prescriptions was relevant to his intent when treating his patients and thus relevant to the jury's determination of whether he acted outside the bounds of accepted medical practice or without a legitimate medical purpose."

The court of appeals "agree[d] with Hurwitz that a doctor's good faith generally is relevant to a jury's determination of whether the doctor acted outside the bounds of medical practice or with a legitimate medical purpose when prescribing narcotics." The case was retried at the district court level with the appropriate instruction in April 2007. After deliberating for seven days, on April 27th, a jury found Hurwitz guilty on 16 counts of drug trafficking, acquitted him on 17 counts, and was unable to reach a verdict on the remaining 12 counts. On July 13, 2007, the district court judge sentenced Hurwitz to fifty-seven months in prison. The two and a half years he had already served would count toward this term and he would be given time off for good behavior. While the judge had some sympathy for Hurwitz, she felt that the sentence was warranted because Hurwitz was "willfully blind" to the actions of his patients who were diverting their drugs.

The scrutiny and prosecution of these physicians is a useful foundation for an examination of the clash between a medical view regarding appropriate prescribing of opioids for pain treatment and a law enforcement perspective that such drugs are dangerous and have the potential for abuse and diversion. But, these prosecutions also represent a more deep-seated adversariness, akin to animosity, between the two groups. This animosity is evident in the language used by each side when describing the other. War and terrorism are major themes in the rhetoric of both sides. While government prosecutors have long referred to their activities against drug diversion as part of a "war on drugs," they have also likened doctors who prescribe large doses of opioids to terrorists, stating that they will "root [them] out like the Taliban." Pain advocates have responded in kind, referring to the government's efforts as "a war on pain doctors," "a government jihad," and "state-sponsored terrorism." Media reports add fuel to this rhetoric, describing the DEA as using "hardball tactics," including "storming clinics in SWAT-style gear, ransacking offices, and hauling off doctors in handcuffs."

State and federal prosecutors have also used the language of organized crime. They have referred to arrested doctors as "being no different than drug kingpins or crack dealers" and call their patients drug addicts. Pain advocates, in contrast, refer to these doctors as pioneers and even heroes, and patients as vulnerable and suffering human beings. The two sides also characterize the drugs that are the focus of regulation very differently. OxyContin, for example, is characterized by drug enforcement officials as "a seductive, deadly menace," whereas pain physicians and patients refer to it as "a miracle drug."

Opium was regarded as a virtual panacea by the medical profession throughout much of the nineteenth century. The drug had many uses, but "it was particularly prized for its analgesic properties because of the lack of alternative pain-relieving agents at this time."

While opioids were used regularly in hospitals to relieve acute pain due to injury or surgery, they were not used for pain of longer duration until relatively recently. The modern use of opioids for pain treatment arising from disease grew out of the hospice movement of the 1960s, when it was established that opioids were highly effective in treating cancer pain. This movement was largely limited to terminally ill patients, but the use of opioids outside the hospice setting began to permeate more traditional medical practices as evidence began to mount that people in pain who received opioids did not become addicted to them. In the late 1980s, opioids had become the standard of care for treatment of moderate to severe cancer pain. It was not until 1990, however, when the World Health Organization published guidelines on cancer pain treatment, that the standard was more widely acknowledged. Subsequently, in 1992, the American Pain Society published *Principles on Analgesic Medication for Acute Pain and Cancer Pain*, and in 1994, the Agency for Health Care Policy and Research (now the Agency for Healthcare Research and Quality (AHRQ)), established that opioids, in combination with other medications, were the appropriate treatment for chronic malignant pain.

While the 1990s became the decade in which the medical profession began to recognize the benefits of opioids for the treatment of chronic pain and developed guidelines for their use, it was also a decade in which great public attention was brought to bear on the fact that pain, both cancer-related and non-malignant chronic pain, was being woefully undertreated in the United States. Between 1999 and 2004, in line with the "sea change" in attitudes toward pain treatment, two state medical boards disciplined physicians for failure to adequately prescribe pain medication for their patients. On the heels of the second disciplinary action, in 2004, the [Federation of State Medical Boards] FMSM provided physicians with an additional incentive to adequately treat pain by updating its Guidelines and issuing a *Model Policy for the Use of Controlled Substances for the Treatment of Pain*. The new policy went "beyond attempting to reassure physicians that they [would] not be sanctioned for prescribing large doses of pain medication if appropriate" and sent "a message that undertreatment of pain [could] be considered substandard care."

Many pain experts now assert that there is no upper limit of safety for opioid dosages. They believe that "[a]s long as the dose is [started] low and increased gradually, large doses [may] be taken [and are] limited only by adverse [side] effects." Unlike non-opioid analgesics, opioids do not cause damage to major organs. The correct amount, they argue, is what reduces or eliminates the patient's pain without unacceptable side effects.

Law enforcement officials appear to believe that patients complaining of pain who need large volumes of medication often are either addicts or diverters and, therefore, prescribing to them is not a legitimate medical purpose.

The debate, in large part, appears to turn on the actual risk of opioid addiction. As long as doctors have administered narcotics, they have been worried about their patients becoming addicted to the drugs. Their worries were often due to a misunderstanding of the differences between addiction, tolerance, and dependence. Tolerance results when exposure to a drug leads to a reduction in one or more of the drug's intended effects over time so that an increased dose may be required to maintain the same physiological effects. Physical dependence is a condition manifested by withdrawal symptoms when a drug is abruptly terminated or reduced in dose. Addiction, in contrast, is a condition resulting in "impaired control over drug use, compulsive use, continued use despite harm, and craving."

While most individuals receiving opioid therapy do develop physical dependence, a number of studies have confirmed that "patients treated with narcotics rarely become addicts."

In the midst of the debate over the addictive potential of long-term and high doses of opioids, a renewed concern about drug diversion, in light of the availability and abuse associated with OxyContin, appeared in the late 90s and has continued through the present. OxyContin "is a 12-hour, timed-release form of oxycodone, a synthetic opioid that has long been available in products such as Percocet, Percodan, and Tylox." By the early 2000s, the drug had become the most prescribed Schedule II narcotic in the country. As the DEA and state drug enforcement officials found evidence of diversion of the drug from legitimate users to addicts, they began to scrutinize physicians and pharmacists who prescribed and dispensed large doses of the drug. They were able to link OxyContin to a number of overdose deaths, pharmacy robberies, and other criminal activities.

The recent arrests and prosecutions of physicians described in this paper have coincided with a series of "campaigns" initiated by the DEA to pursue physicians prescribing opioids. In 2001, the DEA announced a new anti-drug campaign that it called the Oxy-Contin Action Plan. DEA Administrator Asa Hutchinson testified that the initiative was necessary to combat what has been called "a deadly drug epidemic spreading throughout rural America" and that the DEA would reallocate its resources to address this threat. The DEA targeted doctors, pharmacists, and dentists in this crackdown on illegal prescription diversion.

While the DEA was ramping up its enforcement efforts, it came under intense criticism by physician groups for the chilling effects of its high profile arrests and prosecutions of physicians. In response to the DEA actions, thirty attorneys general wrote a letter to DEA Administrator Karen Tandy arguing that "the agency was not properly balancing the need for stopping drug diversion with the need to treat legitimate pain."

At issue in many of the cases brought against physicians prescribing opioids is what constitutes "legitimate medical practice," which is not defined in the law or regulations. While this definitional issue is often at the heart of the relevant court cases, the more significant question may be whether the current standard for violation of the law, i.e., failure to prescribe within "the usual course of ... professional practice" and "for a legitimate medical purpose," is appropriate. Arguably, the standard draws the line too far on the side of prosecutions and does not adequately take into account the range of patients seen by physicians treating pain.

At this point in time, "[t]here is no objective test for pain." Neither is there an easy test to determine whether the patient is telling the truth. The determination of whether or not a patient is lying is a judgment call a physician must make by observing the patient's behavior.

In response to prosecutor claims that doctors should know when individuals are feigning pain solely to obtain prescriptions for opioids, Drs. Jung and Reidenberg did a study to determine how readily physicians can tell when patients lie. They found that physicians correctly identified patients who were lying (pretending to be patients when they were not) only 10% of the time. The authors attributed this result to an observation that doctors operate with a "truth bias," i.e., they "assume that patients come to see them because they have a problem for which they want treatment." Given this bias, second guessing a physician's judgment in these matters, after the fact, seems patently unfair.

Additionally, physicians may see patients who are diverting or abusing narcotics but who are also legitimately in pain. Arguably, prosecuting a physician who prescribes opioids to such patients is unfair if he or she is attempting to relieve the patient's pain, even if the physician knows, based on past behavior, that the patient may abuse or divert the drugs. Despite the possibility for abuse or diversion, "in the absence of some kickback or tangible benefit..., or incontrovertible evidence that the doctor has simply exercised no medical judgment at all, it is difficult to justify criminal prosecution of a doctor for his prescribing or dispensing" of opioids for patients complaining of chronic pain.

Clearly, focusing on volume and dosage is not an appropriate basis for arrest when expert medical opinion is that no consistent upper limit to prescribing for pain across all patients exists. Rather, it is the quantity of medication that eliminates the patient's pain without serious adverse side effects that is appropriate. That dosage is unique for each patient. Nevertheless, it appears from both news accounts and DEA literature that many doctors have been investigated because of the large volumes of opioids they prescribe and because they are seeing patients from outside of the state where they practice. In part, these prescribing practices result from non-pain experts referring to these doctors out of fear of regulatory scrutiny. Therefore, a small number of doctors are becoming saddled with treating a large number of patients in pain.

The competing policy goals of eliminating drug diversion and abuse and appropriately treating pain are brought into stark relief by the government's policies and practices regarding drug enforcement. With most regulations, the government may either overreach with its regulatory net, capturing too many innocent individuals (false positives), or underreach, failing to capture guilty individuals (false negatives). Scientists refer to these errors inherent in virtually all regulatory schemes respectively as Type I and Type II errors. The question is whether we should be depriving patients in pain of needed opioids (a result of Type I errors) in order to prevent their use for non-medical purposes (a result of Type II errors). While the DEA has recognized the importance of pain treatment through official statements, its practices do not give adequate weight to this policy goal. Arguably, state and federal drug enforcement agents are grossly overreaching with regard to drug policy enforcement, resulting in too many false positives. If regulators and prosecutors must err in their enforcement and prosecution with respect to this issue, it would be more appropriate as a policy matter to underreach than overreach.

In this context, *overreaching* means arresting and prosecuting physicians who are legitimately treating pain patients. The costs of such erroneous actions are sweeping. Not only does the innocent physician bear the costs of the harm, including loss of livelihood that may impact the individual and his/her family or dependents, the humiliation, embarrassment, and physical stress of public arrest and prosecution, and the cost of a legal defense, but others also suffer from the prosecution's ripple effect. This ripple effect includes harms to the physician's current pain patients who may not be able to find another physician who will treat their pain, as well as to other current and future chronic pain patients who may not be able to find a pain treatment practitioner because of the chilling effect such criminal actions have on physicians' general willingness to treat chronic pain. The DEA's view is that these high-profile cases "'have been a learning lesson to other physicians'"—that other physicians are much more cautious now of how they prescribe narcotics. Unfortunately, it appears that many are so cautious they will no longer prescribe narcotics as pain treatment or treat pain patients at all. They fear that prescribing "opium-based drugs for pain is becoming criminalized by aggressive drug agents and zealous prosecutors."

At the time of Dr. Hurwitz's medical board hearing, Russell Portenoy, then co-chief of Palliative Care at Memorial Sloan Kettering Cancer Center in New York, stated that "most physicians are reluctant to treat pain with narcotics, fearing they will face criminal or regulatory investigations." Hurwitz was one of the few physicians at the time who was willing to prescribe large doses of narcotics to non-terminally ill pain patients. Many of his patients "spoke of living in agony before finding pain relief from narcotics." But the evidence is more than anecdotal. Several studies have confirmed the chilling impact of potential legal sanctions for prescribing of narcotics for pain treatment.

According to some, few enough physicians in the country are willing to prescribe narcotics for chronic pain that patients might travel hundreds of miles to see them. One physician used the term "the Painful Underground Railroad" to describe the system now in play for patients with chronic pain to find physicians who will treat them. Others have labeled doctors' fear of prescribing medications for their patient's pain as "opiophobia." News stories have reported that some doctors display signs in their offices that say "Don't ask for OxyContin" or "No OxyContin prescribed here" and that medical schools are advising "students not to choose pain management as a career because the field is too fraught with potential legal dangers."

The American Academy of Pain Management estimates that "about 50 million Americans live with chronic pain, caused by cancer, other diseases and disorders, and accidents [and that] [a]nother 25 million live with acute pain caused by surgery or accidents." Moreover, "[t]he majority of those with the most severe pain do not have it under control and suffer substantially in their enjoyment of life, their social relations, and their economic productivity."

Estimates of costs associated with loss of productivity due to pain have been as high as $100 billion per year. A study published in 2003 on lost work time and costs due to pain conditions concluded that "[p]ain is an inordinately common and disabling condition in the US workforce," costing employers an "estimated $61.2 billion per year in pain-related lost productive time." But in addition to work related costs, "pain [also] has a tremendous physiologic, sociologic, psychological and existential impact on the individual and society;" it affects marriages, families, and friendships as well as careers.

Costs to individuals with untreated pain may defy quantification. Pain patients say "[t]heir pain ... [is] like being on fire[,] ... like having an electrode shoot juice up your neck all day[,] ... like having a car parked on your face. So intense [is] their torment ... that suicide often seem[s] the better alternative." In some cases, before they found relief from opioid analgesics these individuals were bedridden for years. Their problems ranged from "crushed vertebrae and damaged jaws, [to] congenital bowel inflammations and disintegrating hips, [to] terrible burns and monstrous migraines." Individuals with this type of intense and enduring pain may also suffer depression and/or commit suicide. One of Dr. Hurwitz's patients, a forty-two-year-old resident from upstate New York, did, in fact, commit suicide when Hurwitz was unable to find another physician who would treat him.

[A]s a policy matter, we must ask whether the law enforcement strategy of targeting physicians is the most effective means of reducing narcotic abuse and addiction. The government's decision to target physicians in their war on prescription drug abuse seems inherently misguided. The most common means of opioid drug diversion have been described by DEA as "fraudulent prescriptions, doctor shopping, over-prescribing, and pharmacy theft." Physicians are arguably responsible only for "over-prescribing," and it is debatable how much over-prescribing is actually taking place and whether this is the source of most opiate drug diversion. For example, individuals may obtain some drugs, including opioids, illegally over the Internet.

United States v. Hurwitz

United States Court of Appeals for the Fourth Circuit
459 F.3d 463 (2006)

Traxler, J.

A jury convicted Dr. William E. Hurwitz of multiple counts of drug trafficking for prescribing narcotic pain medicine in violation of 21 U.S.C.A. §§ 841(a)(1) and 846.

Hurwitz is a medical doctor who operated a practice in McLean, Virginia, dedicated to the treatment of patients suffering from pain. Hurwitz's approach to pain management involved the use of opioids, including methadone, oxycodone (typically Oxycontin, a brand-name version of a time-release form of oxycodone), and hydromorphone (usually the brand-name Dilaudid). Many of Hurwitz's patients were on a protocol that used very high doses of opioids to control their pain.

Hurwitz came to the attention of federal authorities in 2002, after several of his patients were arrested for attempting to sell illicit and prescription drugs. The patients identified Hurwitz as the source of their prescription drugs, and they began cooperating with the investigators. The information these patients provided eventually led to Hurwitz's indictment on numerous drug-related charges—one count of conspiracy to engage in drug trafficking; one count of engaging in a continuing criminal enterprise; two counts of healthcare fraud; and 58 counts of drug trafficking, including two counts each of drug-trafficking resulting in serious bodily injury and drug-trafficking resulting in death.

The government's evidence at trial painted a picture of a doctor who operated well outside the boundaries of usual medical practice. The government contended that Hurwitz was little more than a common drug dealer who operated out of a medical office rather than on a street corner. The government's expert witnesses testified that a doctor who knowingly prescribed opioids to an addict or to a patient the doctor knew was selling the drugs on the street was acting outside the bounds of legitimate medical practice, and the government presented compelling evidence suggesting that Hurwitz did just that—continued to prescribe large quantities of opioids to patients that he knew were selling the drugs or abusing them (for example, by injecting drugs that were directed to be taken orally).

Several of the patients who were cooperating with the authorities tape-recorded their appointments with Hurwitz. In one recording, Hurwitz indicated that it was "not inconceivable" to him that some patients were "selling part of their medicines so they could buy the rest." In another recording Hurwitz stated, "so I have kind of a huge conspiracy of silence because I, in fact, even, even knowing what I'll call the suspicious nature of you guys, assumed that you weren't stupid enough to—to not protect my practice and preserve your own … access to medications." Hurwitz told another patient to get an x-ray or an MRI "for the files to cover our butts."

The government presented evidence of what seemed to be extraordinarily high doses of opioids prescribed by Hurwitz. An expert witness for the government testified that high-dose opioid therapy typically involved doses of the equivalent of approximately 195 milligrams of morphine a day, although there had been a study involving doses of 350 milligrams a day and another involving doses of up to two grams a day.

The doses prescribed by Hurwitz, however, vastly exceeded those quantities. Hurwitz often wrote prescriptions calling for a patient to take thirty 80-milligram Oxycontins per day. For Hurwitz's patients in the high-dose program, a prescribed opioid dosage of 100 pills per day was not uncommon. Hurwitz testified that between 1998 and 2002, the median daily dosage for his patients was approximately 2000 milligrams (2 grams) of morphine or its equivalent. (Because Oxycontin is stronger than morphine, Hurwitz testified that 2000 milligrams of morphine would translate to about 1000 milligrams of Oxycontin.) Between July 1999 and October 2002, Hurwitz prescribed to one patient a total of more than 500,000 pills, which amounted to more than 400 pills per day. Towards the end of the time that Hurwitz treated the patient, the prescribed dosage included 1,600 5-milligram Roxicodones (a non-timed release version of Oxycontin) per day.[1] Still another patient was prescribed 10,000 Roxicodones as a one-month supply. Patients with limited visible sources of income spent tens of thousands of dollars a month on narcotics prescribed by Hurwitz.

---

1. At trial, Hurwitz contended that the 1,600 pills per day dosage was the product of a clerical error.

The government also presented evidence showing that Hurwitz had previously been disciplined for improper prescribing practices. In 1992, the District of Columbia Board of Medicine had reprimanded Hurwitz and placed him on probation for prescribing drugs when not authorized to do so and for failing to conform to the prevailing standards of acceptable medical practice. In 1996, the Virginia Board of Medicine revoked his license upon finding that he had prescribed excessive amounts of controlled substances. The Virginia Board also required Hurwitz to attend classes on proper prescription practices and how to detect when patients were trying to use him as a source for prescription drugs rather than a doctor to treat pain.

Not surprisingly, the defense painted an entirely different picture. Hurwitz and his witnesses contended that the high-dose protocol was a proper medical procedure for treating patients with intractable pain. They testified that the body quickly develops resistance to the dangerous side-effects of opioids (such as respiratory depression), which then permits an escalation of the dosage until pain relief is obtained. One expert testified that once a patient becomes tolerant of the side-effects, there is effectively "no ceiling" on the quantity of opioids that can be prescribed if necessary to control pain. That expert also testified that many patients over time will require an increase in their opioid dosage in order to maintain control of their pain. Hurwitz's experts also testified that there is no medical reason to stop treating a patient for pain simply because that patient may be abusing illicit drugs and that, in some cases, stopping such treatment may even be more problematic.

Hurwitz testified about his practices and the patients he treated. He discussed how patients were generally asked to fill out questionnaires and submit medical records before receiving treatment and how he often included patients' family members during visits as a part of his approach to treating pain. Hurwitz participated in an e-mail discussion group with other professionals about how to approach various situations in pain treatment, and he would confer with other physicians concerning the treatment of certain patients. Hurwitz also discussed how he based his pain-management approach on what he learned at pain management conferences and what he understood other doctors would do.

Some of Hurwitz's patients testified on his behalf, explaining that Hurwitz was the only physician who had managed to relieve their debilitating pain. Molly Shaw, for example, discussed her futile attempts to treat what the Mayo Clinic had diagnosed as neuropathic pain, a pain so severe that it forced her to retire at age 47 and remain almost completely bedridden. She testified that Hurwitz's treatments allowed her to regain her life and live in considerably less pain. The patients' testimony, as well as the testimony of Hurwitz's staff, portrayed Hurwitz as a caring physician whose sole focus was providing pain relief for his patients.

Hurwitz was convicted of one count of drug trafficking conspiracy, one count of drug trafficking resulting in death, two counts of drug trafficking resulting in serious bodily injury, and forty-six counts of drug trafficking. The jury acquitted Hurwitz of six counts of drug trafficking, as well as one count of engaging in a continuing criminal enterprise and two counts of healthcare fraud. The jury failed to reach a decision on the remaining drug trafficking counts. The district court sentenced Hurwitz to 25 years in prison. This appeal followed.

Section 841 provides that, "[e]xcept as authorized by this subchapter, it shall be unlawful for any person knowingly or intentionally ... to ... distribute, or dispense, or possess with intent to ... distribute, or dispense, a controlled substance." Doctors who are "registered" by the Attorney General are authorized to write prescriptions for or to otherwise dispense controlled substances, so long as they comply with the requirements of their registration.

As authorized by the Controlled Substances Act, the Attorney General has promulgated regulations addressing the conditions under which registrants are authorized to dispense controlled substances. The regulations provide that a prescription for a controlled substance is effective only if it is "issued for a legitimate medical purpose by an individual practitioner acting in the usual course of his professional practice." 21 C.F.R. § 1306.04(a) (2006). The regulation further provides that:

> An order purporting to be a prescription issued not in the usual course of professional treatment or in legitimate and authorized research is not a prescription within the meaning and intent of section 309 of the Act (21 U.S.C. 829) and the person knowingly ... issuing [such a purported prescription] shall be subject to the penalties provided for violations of the provisions of law relating to controlled substances.

Synthesizing the requirements of the relevant statutes and regulations, we have held that to convict a doctor for violating § 841, the government must prove: (1) "that the defendant distributed or dispensed a controlled substance"; (2) that the defendant "acted knowingly and intentionally"; and (3) "that the defendant's actions were not for legitimate medical purposes in the usual course of his professional medical practice or were beyond the bounds of medical practice." *United States v. Tran Trong Cuong,* 18 F.3d 1132, 1141 (4th Cir. 1994).[7]

Hurwitz contends that the district court erred by rejecting his request for a "good faith" instruction. Hurwitz argues that his good faith in issuing the challenged prescriptions was relevant to his intent when treating his patients and thus relevant to the jury's determination of whether he acted outside the bounds of accepted medical practice or without a legitimate medical purpose.

The district court agreed with the government's position that Hurwitz's good faith was legally irrelevant to the drug-trafficking charges, and the court declined to include Hurwitz's requested instruction. However, as to the two healthcare fraud charges, the district court agreed to give a good-faith instruction. As to those counts, the district court instructed the jury that it could not convict Dr. Hurwitz if he "acted in good faith in dispensing any of the prescriptions alleged to constitute the crime of healthcare fraud." The court defined "good faith" to mean "good intentions in the honest exercise of best professional judgment as to a patient's needs. It means the doctor acted according to what he believed to be proper medical practice." The district court instructed the jury that "good faith applies only" to the healthcare fraud counts. Thus, the district court not only declined to give a good-faith instruction with regard to the drug counts, but also informed the jury that it *could not* consider good faith when deciding whether to convict Hurwitz of drug trafficking under § 841.[8]

As an initial premise, we agree with Hurwitz that a doctor's good faith generally is relevant to a jury's determination of whether the doctor acted outside the bounds of medical practice or with a legitimate medical purpose when prescribing narcotics.

---

7. Other circuits have concluded that whether the defendant's actions were for legitimate medical purposes or were beyond the bounds of medical practice is not an essential element of a § 841 charge against a doctor. *See, e.g., United States v. Steele,* 147 F.3d 1316, 1318 (11th Cir. 1998) (en banc); *United States v. Polan,* 970 F.2d 1280, 1282 (3d Cir. 1992); *United States v. Seelig,* 622 F.2d 207, 211–12 (6th Cir. 1980).

8. The jury acquitted Hurwitz of the healthcare fraud charges.

In *United States v. Moore,* 423 U.S. 122 (1975), the seminal case addressing the prosecution of physicians under § 841, the Supreme Court concluded that "registered physicians can be prosecuted under § 841 when their activities fall outside the usual course of professional practice." In the course of concluding that the evidence was sufficient to support the jury's conclusion that the defendant acted beyond the bounds of professional practice, the Court noted two good-faith instructions that had been given to the jury. The district court had instructed the jury that the defendant could be convicted if the jury found that he knowingly distributed controlled substances "other than in good faith for detoxification in the usual course of a professional practice and in accordance with a standard of medical practice generally recognized and accepted in the United States," and that the defendant "could not be convicted if he merely made 'an honest effort' to prescribe ... in compliance with an accepted standard of medical practice."

Building on the Supreme Court's approach in *Moore,* lower courts have concluded that when resolving the ultimate question in a § 841 prosecution against a doctor — whether the doctor acted without a legitimate medical purpose or beyond the bounds of accepted medical practice — some latitude must be given to doctors trying to determine the current boundaries of acceptable medical practice. Thus, courts have consistently concluded that it is proper to instruct juries that a doctor should not be held criminally liable if the doctor acted in good faith when treating his patients. Accordingly, the district court erred by concluding that good faith is not relevant when a registered physician is charged with violating § 841.

The question we must next consider is Hurwitz's argument that the district court erred by refusing his proffered good-faith charge. While the government objected below to any suggestion that a good-faith instruction was appropriate, the government on appeal does not contend that a good-faith instruction is never warranted in a case where a registered physician is prosecuted under § 841. Instead, the government argues that Hurwitz is not entitled to reversal on this point because the good-faith instruction Hurwitz offered below was an incorrect statement of the law. We agree with the government that the good-faith instruction offered by Hurwitz was not an accurate statement of the law.

The good-faith instruction offered by Hurwitz at trial stated that: "If a doctor dispenses a drug in good faith to medically treat a patient, then the doctor has dispensed the drug for a legitimate medical purpose and in the course of medical practice. That is, he has dispensed the drug lawfully. 'Good faith' in this context means good intentions in the honest exercise of best professional judgment as to a patient's needs. It means the doctor acted according to what *he believed to be proper medical practice.*" This proposed instruction clearly sets forth a subjective standard, permitting Hurwitz to decide for himself what constitutes proper medical treatment. As the government contends, however, allowing criminal liability to turn on whether the defendant-doctor complied with his own idiosyncratic view of proper medical practices is inconsistent with the Supreme Court's decision in *Moore.*

In *Moore,* the Supreme Court discussed the circumstances under which doctors could be prosecuted under § 841 using language that strongly suggests the inquiry is an objective one. For example, the Court held that "registered physicians can be prosecuted under § 841 when their activities fall outside the *usual course of professional practice.*" The Court also noted that, when passing the Controlled Substances Act, Congress intended to "confine authorized medical practice within *accepted limits,*" and that "physicians who go beyond *approved practice* remain subject to serious criminal penalties." And as discussed above, the Supreme Court when concluding that the evidence was sufficient to support the defendant's conviction noted two good-faith instructions that had been given to the jury. Those instructions clearly set forth an objective standard.

Hurwitz, however, contends that his proffered good-faith instruction was proper because it was derived from our opinion in *United States v. Tran Trong Cuong*, 18 F.3d 1132 (4th Cir. 1994). In that case, the defendant argued that the district "court and the prosecution used a medical malpractice standard rather than a criminal standard to judge his actions." In the course of addressing the defendant's arguments, we reviewed the jury instructions given by the district court and concluded that the instructions correctly set forth a criminal standard of liability.

The jury instructions in *Tran Trong Cuong* included the following language: "[If a] doctor dispenses a drug in good faith in medically treating a patient, then the doctor has dispensed the drug for a legitimate medical purpose in the usual course of medical practice. That is, he has dispensed the drug lawfully. Good faith in this context means good intentions in the honest exercise of best professional judgment as to a patient's need. It means the doctor acted in accordance with what he believed to be proper medical practice." This charge is essentially identical to the good-faith instruction proffered by Hurwitz. Since we described the instructions in *Tran Trong Cuong* as correctly establishing a criminal standard of liability, Hurwitz argues that we approved of the good-faith portion of those instructions. We disagree.

No issue was raised by the defendant in *Tran Trong Cuong* that required us to consider the precise contours of a good-faith instruction. Instead, the only challenge to the jury instructions was the defendant's claim that the instructions set forth a civil rather than criminal liability standard. Because in *Tran Trong Cuong* we were not called on to consider the defendant's good faith ... it simply cannot be said that in *Tran Trong Cuong* we *approved* the good-faith instruction sought by Hurwitz.

In this case, however, we are squarely presented with the question of whether, in a § 841 prosecution against a doctor, the inquiry into the doctor's good faith in treating his patients is a subjective or objective one. We believe that the inquiry must be an objective one, a conclusion that has been reached by every court to specifically consider the question. As the Second Circuit explained,

> "[P]rofessional practice" [as used in 21 C.F.R. § 1306.04(a)] refers to generally accepted medical practice; a practitioner is not free deliberately to disregard prevailing standards of treatment....
>
>   ....
>
> To permit a practitioner to substitute his or her views of what is good medical practice for standards generally recognized and accepted in the United States would be to weaken the enforcement of our drug laws in a critical area.

Vamos, 797 F.2d at 1151, 1153; *see also* 3 Leonard B. Sand et al., *Modern Federal Jury Instructions*, Instruction 56-19, comment (2003) ("Every court to examine the issue has held that the objective standard that the doctor acted in accordance with what he *reasonably* believed to be proper medical practice should apply.").

Because the instruction proffered by Hurwitz set forth a subjective standard for measuring his good faith, the instruction was not a correct statement of the law. Accordingly, although we conclude that good faith generally is relevant in a § 841 case against a registered physician, we nonetheless conclude that the district court did not err by refusing the particular charge sought by Hurwitz.

Though the district court did not err by refusing Hurwitz's good-faith charge, there remains a separate issue regarding the court's good-faith instructions. As mentioned above, the district court gave a good-faith instruction with regard to the healthcare fraud charges and then specifically instructed the jury that good faith was relevant *only* to the fraud charges. As we have explained, however, a doctor's good faith in treating his patients is relevant to the jury's determination of whether the doctor acted beyond the bounds of legitimate medical practice.

The government contends that because Hurwitz's proposed instruction was not a correct statement of the law, any errors in the district court's good-faith instructions cannot justify a new trial. We disagree. The government's argument confuses two separate issues — whether the district court erred by refusing to use the good-faith charge proposed by Hurwitz, and whether the district court erred by affirmatively informing the jury that good faith was relevant only to the fraud charges. Hurwitz timely objected to that instruction, thus preserving that error of commission as a separate issue for review on appeal. The district court's incorrect instruction on good faith is not insulated from review on appeal simply because Hurwitz's proposed good-faith instruction was incorrect.

The government also contends that any error with regard to the good-faith instruction is harmless, because a good-faith instruction was not warranted in this case.

The government first suggests that any error is harmless because Hurwitz's attorney admitted during closing argument that Hurwitz's actions were beyond the bounds of accepted medical practice. The government argues that this admission is binding on Hurwitz and amounts to a concession that the jury could not reasonably have concluded that Hurwitz acted in good faith. We disagree.

Although counsel stated that Hurwitz "did practice outside the bounds of medicine," the statement referred to Hurwitz's dealings with various state medical boards. Given counsel's statement that the medical boards "were back in the Stone Age," the statement could be understood as meaning only that Hurwitz in the past acted outside the bounds of what *those boards* believed to be proper medical practice. That Hurwitz practiced outside the bounds of an out-of-step medical board's view of proper medical practices does not necessarily mean that his actions were beyond the bounds of *generally accepted* medical practices. The attorney's statement therefore cannot be viewed as a clear and unambiguous admission that Hurwitz knowingly acted outside the bounds of accepted medical practice.

A more difficult question, however, is presented by the government's contention that the evidence presented at trial so overwhelmingly demonstrated that Hurwitz was acting well beyond the bounds of accepted medical practice that the jury could not reasonably have found that he acted in good faith. *See Mathews v. United States,* 485 U.S. 58, 63 (1988) ("As a general proposition a defendant is entitled to an instruction as to any recognized defense for which there exists evidence sufficient for a reasonable jury to find in his favor."). Under the government's view, then, any error in the instructions was necessarily harmless, because Hurwitz was not entitled to a good-faith instruction under the evidence presented at trial.

While the government's evidence was powerful and strongly indicative of a doctor acting outside the bounds of accepted medical practice, we cannot say that no reasonable juror could have concluded that Hurwitz's conduct fell within an objectively-defined good-faith standard. Hurwitz presented expert testimony showing that it was proper to use opioids when treating addicts who suffered from pain. Hurwitz's experts testified that his high-dose opioid therapy was a medically appropriate way to treat intractable pain and that the quantities of opioids he prescribed were appropriate. Even as to the patients whose dosages appeared extraordinarily high, such as the patient who was prescribed over 500,000 pills during the course of his treatment, the record contains expert testimony showing that Hurwitz's treatment and the quantities of opioids prescribed was medically proper. In addition, the testimony of Hurwitz and his staff indicated that he ran a legitimate medical practice, requiring patients to submit medical records and questionnaires before visits, conferring with other physicians outside of his practice about proper procedures, and relying on information from professional conferences when determining proper treatment practices. Thus, the record reveals a sufficient evidentiary basis for a good-faith instruction.

Good faith was at the heart of Hurwitz's defense. Hurwitz did not dispute the bulk of the government's factual evidence—that is, he did not argue that he did not prescribe the narcotics that were the basis for the charges against him. Instead, Hurwitz argued that the manner in which he used narcotics to treat chronic and debilitating pain was a medically proper approach to a difficult medical issue. By concluding that good faith was not applicable to the § 841 charges and affirmatively instructing the jury that good faith was not relevant to those charges, the district court effectively deprived the jury of the opportunity to consider Hurwitz's defense. Thus, while we recognize that the government's evidence was strong, we simply cannot conclude that the district court's error in removing good faith from the jury's consideration was harmless.

Accordingly, we conclude that Hurwitz was prejudiced by the district court's error in instructing the jury that Hurwitz's good faith was relevant only to the fraud charges.

To summarize, we conclude that good faith is relevant to § 841 charges against a registered physician and that the district court erred by incorrectly instructing the jury that Hurwitz's good faith was relevant only to the healthcare fraud charges. This error in the court's instructions to the jury cannot be considered harmless, and a new trial is therefore required. On remand, the district court shall include a good-faith instruction (if requested by Hurwitz and if supported by the evidence presented at re-trial), but that instruction must reflect an objective rather than subjective standard for measuring Hurwitz's good faith.

Accordingly, for the foregoing reasons, we vacate Hurwitz's convictions under 21 U.S.C.A. §§ 841 and 846, and we remand for a new trial in accordance with this opinion.

––––––––––––

Criminal prosecutions of physicians under the Controlled Substances Act have been especially controversial and commanded the attention of policy groups, legal commentators and the media alike. Though the DEA's administrative power over doctors has not generated as many headlines, it is likely of greater practical relevance for the average physician. The following excerpt briefly describes the DEA's physician registration system.

Did You Forget to Say You're Sorry? Litigating a Show Cause Hearing for a Physician's DEA Registration
Douglas J. Behr
9 Quinnipiac Health Law Journal 99 (2005)

A physician must be registered with the DEA in order to purchase, prescribe, administer, or dispense controlled substances. As of November 27, 2005, more than a million practitioners held such registrations.

The registration process requires only the completion of an application listing the doctor's name, address, identification of the schedules for which the doctor seeks to be registered, and payment of the required fee. A separate registration is required for each "principal place of professional practice." Pursuant to statute, the DEA "shall register an applicant" unless it "determines that the issuance of such registration is inconsistent with the public interest." An application for registration can be denied only if the DEA finds, after providing notice and, if requested, a hearing, that the registration is not in the public interest. This process applies, even if the prospective registrant has previously lost a registration.

Registration, once obtained, can be lost only by being voluntarily surrendered to the DEA or by revocation through notice and, if requested, a hearing. In order to revoke an existing registration, the DEA must determine that continued registration is no longer in the public interest.

Under 21 U.S.C. 824, a registration application may be denied or revoked upon a finding that the registrant: "(1) has materially falsified any application ... ; (2) has been convicted of a felony under federal or state law relating to controlled substances or a list I chemical; (3) has had his State license or registration suspended, revoked, or denied and is no longer authorized to handle controlled substances in the State in which he maintains a DEA registration (4) has committed acts that would render his registration inconsistent with the public interest as determined pursuant to 21 U.S.C. 823(f); or (5) has been excluded from participation in a program pursuant to 42 U.S.C. 1320a-7(a) of Title 42."

Violation of any one of the statutory factors justifies revocation/denial of registration.

The fourth statutory factor, acts inconsistent with the public interest, was added to the statute in 1984. The "public interest" factor invests the Administrator with discretion to consider any relevant information. Oftentimes, the "public interest" basis is cited in conjunction with another statutory factor or as encompassing it. However, the Administrator has found violations of the "public interest" factor based primarily on conduct that does not fit within any of the other statutory factors. The Administrator examines the factors set out in 21 U.S.C. 823(f) in determining the "public interest" and has found that a registration was not in the public interest in cases where the physician had been prescribing controlled substances without a legitimate medical need, or engaged in other abusive practices, including illegally obtaining drugs for his own use even though no criminal charges had been brought. On one occasion, the public interest factor was the basis for the revocation of the registration of a physician who prescribed large quantities of narcotics to three individuals who were either drug addicts or were diverting the drugs, where the doctor's medical license had been placed on probation, and the doctor had been ordered not to prescribe Schedule II controlled substances even though no criminal charges had been filed. Additionally, this public interest factor was cited when a physician had issued prescriptions for controlled substances that he did not have the authority to write as well as when a physician was arrested and charged with possession with intent to distribute street cocaine but no conviction had yet occurred.

According to the DEA, the public interest, consistent with section 823(f), is evaluated using the following criteria, "1. The recommendation of the appropriate State licensing board or professional disciplinary authority; 2. The applicant's experience in dispensing, or conducting research with respect to controlled substances; 3. The applicant's conviction record under Federal or State laws relating to manufacture, distribution, or dispensing of controlled substances 4. Compliance with applicable State, Federal, or local laws relating to controlled substances; and, 5. Such other factors which may threaten the public health and safety." These factors are considered in the disjunctive. "The Deputy Administrator may properly rely on any one or any combination of these factors, and may give each factor the weight he deems appropriate...." While any of the specifically defined criteria can support a revocation or denial of an application, no one criteria requires revocation or denial.

In determining whether to grant or continue a registration, the DEA generally evaluates each of the five "public interest" factors set out above. In determining whether registration is in the public interest, the Administrator looks at the totality of the circumstances. The governing statute is discretionary. The Administrator gives each factor the weight she deems appropriate in the exercise of her discretion. While the factors to be considered are varied ... a review of the decisions leaves the clear impression that whether the applicant has recognized the error of his ways and dealt with the motivations and causes that brought about those errors is of particular importance. The Respondent must demonstrate that he can "be entrusted with the authority to prescribe and dispense controlled substances ..." that a DEA registration represents. "Poor medical judgment, and the dispensing of controlled substances that resulted from such judgment, is sufficient to establish that Respondent cannot be trusted to responsibly handle such substances...." The failure to "admit to the full extent of his involvement in documented misconduct involving controlled substances [has led] the Deputy Administrator [to doubt] such a Respondent's commitment to compliance with the Controlled Substances Act...." Thus, "[t]he revocation of a DEA Certificate of Registration is not a penalty or a punitive measure. It is a remedial measure, based upon the public interest and the necessity to protect the public from those individuals who have misused controlled substances or their DEA Certificate of Registration, and who have not presented sufficient mitigating evidence to assure the Administrator that they can be trusted with the responsibility carried by such a registration."

———

While the prosecution and registration of doctors may deter them from prescribing controlled substances for non-medical purposes, these measures do not address the phenomenon of "doctor shopping" whereby an individual may seek to obtain prescriptions from multiple doctors. Federal law largely leaves this issue to the states, forty of which have adopted prescription drug monitoring programs (though not all are operational). *See* THE WHITE HOUSE NATIONAL DRUG CONTROL STRATEGY 31 (2010). The majority of states with prescription drug monitoring programs have adopted them within the past decade. Though prescription drug monitoring programs differ from state to state, in general they have physicians and pharmacists log prescriptions into a database in order to prevent people from obtaining multiple prescriptions for the same medication and to help medical professionals avoid adverse medication interactions. The Office of National Drug Control Policy has recently announced that it will convene interested agencies, state officials and other organizations with the goal of developing a "standardized and compatible system" that "can be easily used by all parties." *See also, e.g.,* David B. Brushwood, *Maximizing the Value of Electronic Prescription Monitoring Programs,* 31 J. L. MEDICINE & ETHICS 41 (2003) (providing an overview of prescription drug monitoring programs); *Whalen v. Roe,* 429 U.S. 589, 605–06 (1977) (finding an early New York State prescription monitoring law constitutional though cautioning that the outcome may be different in cases involving "unwarranted disclosure of accumulated private data—whether intentional or unintentional—or ... a [prescription monitoring] system that did not contain comparable security provisions").

2. Regulation and Prosecution of Pharmacies

Searching for Safety: Addressing Search Engine, Website, and Provider Accountability for Illicit Online Drug Sales
Bryan A. Liang and Tim Mackey
35 American Journal of Law and Medicine 125 (2009)

The business of selling prescription pharmaceuticals over the Internet has fueled an industry that analysts estimate generated from $15–20 billion in sales in 2004. Yet the illicit nature of online drug sales is apparent. For example, a detailed study of online drug sellers indicated that fully eighty five percent of websites offering drugs for sale required no prescription from a patient's physician. To make matters worse, of the fifteen percent of sites offering drugs online that "require" a prescription, only half ask that the prescription be faxed, introducing tremendous opportunities for fraud and circumvention of legitimate and important physician oversight.

The exact number of Internet drug sale sites on the web is difficult to determine accurately due to the fact that illegitimate or "rogue" Internet drug sellers, which open and close with high frequency, often have several URLs for one company, and may only be transiently listed on select search engines. As a reflection of this reality, a simple Google search at any given time using "Internet pharmacy" as the search term will reveal millions of results. As might be expected, government officials trying to regulate these online sellers have had little success due to the sheer volume of sellers.

These Internet drug sellers are of great concern with respect to consumer safety. Many are of international origin, advertise purchasing drugs without a prescription, and purport to have been approved by U.S. federal agencies such as the Food and Drug Administration ("FDA"). These Internet drug sellers represent the highest risk category for consumers given the inability of U.S. regulators to ensure quality and safety. As noted by Joseph Califano, Jr., director of the National Center on Addiction and Substance Abuse, "anyone of any age can obtain dangerous and addictive prescription drugs with the click of a mouse."

The dangers these websites pose are numerous and rather self-evident. All implicate consumer safety as well as financial security. These dangers include: the delivery of drugs or active pharmaceutical ingredients without a valid prescription; lack of professional oversight; the risk of questionable quality, counterfeit or substandard product; poor or lack of medication instructions; failure to provide adequate independent information to patients on possible adverse reaction and drug interactions; fraud; inability for consumers to be reimbursed by health insurance programs; and lack of confidentiality of personal medical data.

Importantly, the uninsured and underinsured populations represent a significant at-risk group purchasing from these sites. These patients do not have access to or often cannot afford to see a physician and may instead elect to purchase drugs and seek treatment online.

There is a high degree of variability in quality and safety among Internet drug sellers. Four major types of online drug sellers exist: (1) traditional, established chain pharmacies with a web presence; (2) independent community pharmacies with a web presence; (3) stand-alone, exclusively online pharmacy sites; and (4) rogue or illegal sites. Internet sellers which are in the latter two groups, and which are by far the most numerous, pose the highest risk to consumers.

The risk of ordering through Internet drug sellers is often directly related to the manner of order, delivery, and the type of pharmacy the patient does business with. The spectrum of ordering methods demonstrates an increasing distance from legitimacy and oversight that increases risks associated with the purchase, sale, and use of the product. Ordering methods include consumers: (a) mailing in a legitimate prescription; (b) having their physicians submit prescriptions by phone, fax or mail to an online distributor; and (c) obtaining a prescription from the website itself through an online "survey."

The latter ordering method is of particular concern. The use of "cyber doctors" through which consumers may fill a prescription simply by responding to a scripted online questionnaire eliminates physician oversight of potential adverse reactions, allows purchasers to provide inaccurate and/or false information, and results in situations where patients forego needed treatment. Physicians who participate in such a scheme are contravening standards of the Federation of State Medical Boards, the American Medical Association, the National Association of Boards of Pharmacy, and the Drug Enforcement Administration.

As might be evident from a cursory assessment, the potential for fraud and inappropriate sales of drugs over the Internet is high, particularly in the latter circumstances. Any system of drug purchasing without a substantive physician-patient relationship and a valid prescription is dangerous. Of course, as noted previously, many websites simply do not require a prescription at all, allowing the unfettered purchase of drug materials over the Internet. Clearly, greater risk of harm is associated with transactions that result in fake or substandard materials being ingested by patients.

The United States Food and Drug Administration ("FDA") is the primary federal agency tasked with addressing the issue of online drug sales. The FDA regulates this industry through enforcement of the Federal Food, Drug, and Cosmetic Act ("FDCA") and the Internet Drug Sales Action Plan ("IDSAP") adopted in July 1999. The FDA has broad authority to regulate the practice of selling prescription drugs when the sale is done without the supervision of a licensed professional, when connected with health care fraud, and when it involves unapproved, counterfeit, adulterated, or illegal drugs. The FDA's plan primarily seeks to reduce illegal Internet sales of prescription drugs by: (1) expanding enforcement efforts through increasing monitoring and criminal or civil enforcement actions; (2) partnering with other state and federal agencies and other organizations such as the National Association of Boards of Pharmacy ("NABP") and Federation of State Medical Boards to more effectively enforce federal and state laws against illegal online sales; and (3) engaging in public outreach to better inform consumers about the dangers of Internet drug sellers.

In testimony in front of Congress, the FDA reported only 372 Internet-related criminal investigations, 150 Internet-related arrests and 92 convictions, 100 open Internet criminal investigations, 200 cyber warning letters, and a handful of injunctions, seizures, product recalls and voluntary product destruction. In the context of billions of dollars of sales, proliferation of Internet sales and marketing of drugs, and limited international cooperation, the FDA's efforts have been severely challenged. Indeed, "U.S. Food and Drug Administration officials say they are unable to stop the illegal flow of drugs sold on the Internet."

The Drug Enforcement Administration ("DEA") acts as the enforcement agency for the Department of Justice ("DOJ") concerning the dispensing and sale of controlled substances, including transactions via the Internet as promulgated in the Controlled Substances Act. In a guidance document issued in April 2001, the DEA emphasized and clarified that controlled substances may only be dispensed by licensed practitioners acting in the usual course of their professional practice and requires them to be registered with the DEA, including those who sell online. Further, this guidance addresses websites that dispense drugs without a prescription by providing specific requirements for ensuring that only legitimate prescriptions are written and filled, and requirements for the importation of controlled substances.

These rules require Internet drug sellers to register their physical location with the DEA and maintain all relevant state licenses required for the operation of their website. A bona fide physician-patient relationship must also theoretically exist in order for prescriptions to be filled. The DEA addresses the illegality and possible criminal consequence for consumers who purchase and import controlled substances from foreign Internet sites. It also regulates attempts to provide consumer information on how to identify illegal sites, the reporting of illegal drug sales, and the risks inherent to Internet drug sellers. The DEA has followed up its initial 2001 guidance with additional consumer alerts aimed at reinforcing the illegality and possible criminal consequences for purchasing controlled substances, such as narcotic pain relievers, sedatives, stimulants and anabolic steroids, without a valid prescription. As the agency directly responsible for narcotic drugs of abuse, the DEA emphasizes that illegal Internet drug sellers represent not only a public health risk, but also the evolution of traditional illicit drug dealers to the distribution and sale of drugs via cyberspace.

In April 2005, the DEA, FDA, and CBP announced the results of the year-long Operation Cyber Chase, which the DEA had implemented with the help of several foreign governments, to crack down on illegal online drug sellers distributing controlled substances without a prescription. As a result of this operation, twenty individuals in eight U.S. cities and four foreign countries, who were members of an Internet drug trafficking organization that used 200 websites to sell millions of pills globally, forfeited over $6 million of illicit proceeds.

Although Operation Cyber Chase has been touted as a significant step against illegal online distribution of drugs and a successful collaboration between U.S. and international law enforcement agencies, analysis of the operation's results rebut this conclusion. The difficulty of locating and prosecuting criminals in international jurisdictions, a failure to address systemic problems such as the high cost of pharmaceuticals, and questions regarding the cost-benefit of attempting to locate undetectable and advanced criminals using traditional law enforcement techniques, all raise the important issue of whether enforcement alone can truly make an impact on the potential dangers of international Internet drug sellers.

In fact, despite the notable efforts of Operation Cyber Chase, other operations such as Operation CyberX, as well as recent additional efforts, are also having little impact on illegal online drug sales. The proceeds collected from major inter-agency operations do not come close to sales of suspect online drug sellers. For example, one suspect Internet drug seller, MyCanadianPharmacy.com, which has been linked to a major worldwide criminal spamming operation, is estimated to have sales of $150 million annually. Indeed, it is estimated that eighty percent of spam advertises illegal and suspect online drug sales, which completely dwarfs any agency efforts to control these illicit activities.

DEA enforcement efforts are limited by the practicalities of the Internet, particularly offshore where many of the problems arise. A website's anonymous Internet presence and easy removal make it difficult for law enforcement to identify, track, monitor, and shut down foreign-based Internet drug sellers. Further, globalization has created havens for online sellers such as free trade zones (areas specifically designated by several countries to promote trade by providing low or waived tariffs and reduced regulatory oversight) in order to conceal, manufacture, and market counterfeit drugs. These free trade zones are often in countries that do not have the expertise, resources, awareness, or desire to detect and deal with the complex issues surrounding online sales of illegal pharmaceuticals.

In situations where identified online sellers are not within U.S. boundaries and thus are not easily subjected to the U.S. law enforcement jurisdictional authority, investigators and agents have little recourse other than to request the applicable foreign government to take action against the website. Since drug laws vary by country, however, enforcement efforts against Internet drug sellers on foreign soil are often thwarted because foreign governments may be reluctant to share information or develop mechanisms to cooperate with U.S. law enforcement efforts. Thus, the Internet creates a virtually impenetrable cloak that allows illegal online sales to go unchecked and unregulated despite extensive efforts to limit this practice and the dangers inherent therein.

United States v. Quinones
United States Court of Appeals for the Second Circuit
635 F.3d 590 (2011)

Katzmann, J.

The facts of this case are largely undisputed. The evidence at trial showed that Antonio entered the Internet pharmacy business in 2002, when he purchased Prescriptions & Travel, a pharmacy that filled prescriptions for an Internet pharmacy known as RX Networks. Vincent Chhabra, an Internet pharmacy entrepreneur, owned RX Networks. Antonio later hired Steven Mahana, a website developer, to copy Chhabra's website design and the system that Chhabra used to manage medication orders.

Antonio's operation worked as follows: An Internet user who searched for a prescription medication would be directed by a search engine to Antonio's website. Once at the website, the customer would select his drug and provide payment information and delivery instructions. The customer would also fill out a brief medical questionnaire, which asked the customer for his name, gender, weight, allergies, current medications, reason for requesting the medication, and known medical conditions. The questionnaire was the same regardless of whether a drug required a prescription. The customer's order then would be transmitted to a so-called "Doctor's Module," whereby the questionnaire would be reviewed by a doctor who would approve or disapprove the order. Antonio selected the doctors who reviewed the questionnaires and approved orders made on his websites. The doctors, who were paid per questionnaire reviewed, often reviewed over a hundred applications per day. Once a doctor approved an order, it would be transmitted to a licensed physical pharmacy controlled by Antonio that filled the prescription. Antonio's pharmacies typically filled one thousand orders per day and shipped the ordered medications to customers by Federal Express.

Antonio's system permitted no interaction whatsoever between a doctor and a customer. In fact, Mahana placed a disclaimer on his invoices to Antonio stating that the system did not provide a sufficient basis to establish a relationship between a doctor and a patient in order to prescribe medication. Moreover, the system provided few safeguards against substance abuse. For example, some customers were able to obtain excessive amounts of medications by placing orders to the same address using different names. Others were able to receive drugs even though they did not provide all of the information required by the questionnaire.

Mahana, who built twenty-five to thirty websites for Antonio, referred to Antonio's network of websites as the "administrative back-end"—a "piece of software that is designed to control all aspects of the website or multiple websites." Through the "back-end," Antonio controlled, among other things, the approval of prescription medication orders even without the involvement of physicians. As administrator of the system, he had access to detailed reports about operation of his websites and the manner in which prescriptions were filled. Antonio used the "back-end" also to charge a filling fee for each prescription, a referral fee for access to doctors, and a "per accepted order" fee for each order received by an affiliate of his network. Antonio's son, Herman, filled orders for his father's websites and ran his father's Internet pharmacy customer service call center. Eventually, Herman obtained his own website, 888meds.com, which was connected to the back-end.

Moreover, Antonio used corporations, owned by relatives and friends, to buy medicine from wholesalers, receive payments from affiliated websites, and manage the customer service call center for his Internet pharmacies. He used a company known as My Rainbow Marketing ("My Rainbow"), which was nominally owned by his sister-in-law, Susana Mendez, to buy medicine from wholesale pharmaceutical distributors and to bill websites for medications that Antonio supplied and the filling fees that he charged. Defense counsel conceded in summation that My Rainbow was in fact controlled by Antonio. In addition, Thundergames, a corporation owned by Antonio's long-time friend, was the legal entity that ran the customer call center for Antonio's websites.

In November 2003, Chhabra was arrested and charged with illegal distribution of controlled substances. Immediately following Chhabra's arrest, Antonio stopped using Prescriptions & Travel to fill orders for his websites and took steps to liquidate its assets. He began using a new filling pharmacy, Innovative Remedies, which was located in Florida. In the following months, however, Antonio learned that a proposed change in Florida law would require face-to-face contact between a physician and patient, so he moved his filling pharmacy to Queens. Antonio continued to move his operations to new locations as law enforcement raided or shuttered his filling pharmacies. In all, Antonio used approximately a dozen different pharmacies to fill prescription orders.

In December 2007, Antonio and Herman were indicted on three counts: (1) conspiracy to distribute and possess with intent to distribute Schedule III and IV controlled substances without valid prescriptions through the Internet in violation of 21 U.S.C. §§ 841(a)(1) and 846, (2) distribution of Schedule III and IV controlled substances in violation of 21 U.S.C. § 841(a)(1), and (3) money laundering conspiracy. Over defense counsel's objection, the court instructed the jury on a conscious avoidance theory in connection with the knowledge requirement of the unlawful distribution of controlled substances counts. The jury found Antonio guilty on all counts. It found Herman guilty of distribution of controlled substances. The district court sentenced Antonio and Herman principally to terms of imprisonment of ninety-seven and eighteen months, respectively. This appeal followed.

We turn first to the defendants' argument that the conscious avoidance charge was improper. "A conscious avoidance instruction permits a jury to find that a defendant had culpable knowledge of a fact when the evidence shows that the defendant intentionally avoided confirming the fact."

Our analysis begins with the knowledge requirement of the controlled-substance distribution crime. A doctor may be convicted of unlawful distribution and dispensation of a controlled substance if his "activities fall outside the usual course of professional practice." A lay defendant likewise may be convicted of unlawful distribution of a controlled substance where the defendant relies upon a doctor's prescription that he knows or reasonably should have known was invalid. *See United States v. Vamos*, 797 F.2d 1146,

1153 (2d Cir. 1986) ("[W]hile those who assist practitioners in distributing controlled drugs clearly cannot be held to the standard of a reasonable practitioner, they are not free to unreasonably rely on the judgment of their employers."). Thus, to convict the defendants of unlawful distribution of controlled substances, the jury must have found that they knew or reasonably should have known that the doctors and pharmacists were distributing controlled substances outside the usual course of professional practice and without a legitimate medical purpose—or, in other words, that these professionals acted in "bad faith."

At oral argument, the defendants indeed conceded that because they claim to have relied upon the determinations of doctors and pharmacists, they could be convicted if the jury found that they were aware, or reasonably should have been aware, that the doctors and pharmacists were acting in bad faith. The district court therefore correctly charged the jury that "you must find the defendant not guilty unless the government proves beyond a reasonable doubt that the defendant knew *or reasonably should have known* that the doctors and pharmacists were not acting in good faith."

On appeal, the defendants argue that they are entitled to a new trial because there was an insufficient factual predicate for a conscious avoidance instruction and, in any event, the instruction was improperly worded. Even if their contentions have merit, however, the salient question is whether any error would have been prejudicial to the defendants. Any error in giving a conscious avoidance instruction is harmless where there is "overwhelming evidence" that the defendants possessed the requisite knowledge.

Accordingly, the fundamental question here is whether the government adduced overwhelming evidence that the defendants knew or reasonably should have known that the doctors and pharmacists on whom they relied were acting in bad faith. Upon our review of the record, we find overwhelming evidence that the defendants possessed the requisite knowledge in this case.

First of all, there is no dispute that the defendants were aware that their online pharmacy permitted no interaction whatsoever between a customer and a doctor. In fact, Mahana placed a disclaimer on his invoices to Antonio stating that the system did not provide a sufficient basis to establish a relationship between a doctor and a patient in order to prescribe medication. Antonio, who controlled and monitored all aspects of his business through the back-end, selected the doctors who reviewed customers' questionnaires and approved orders made on his websites. The doctors, who were paid per questionnaire reviewed, often reviewed over a hundred applications per day, and Antonio's pharmacies typically filled one thousand orders per day. A pharmacist at one of Antonio's filling pharmacies testified that she was able to review only about 140 of the one thousand orders that were filled daily and that she was the only pharmacist on duty.[3]

Moreover, Antonio discussed with Dr. Jack Tomas, the owner of Innovative Remedies, a change in Florida law prohibiting Florida doctors from writing prescriptions without face-to-face consultations with their patients. Only days after the Florida law was passed, Antonio moved his filling pharmacy to Queens. In the next three years, Antonio moved his operations to more than ten different locations as law enforcement raided or shuttered his filling pharmacies. When law enforcement shut down one of Antonio's phar-

---

3. Although the dissent makes much of Antonio's consultation with attorneys, there is no evidence that Antonio disclosed to any attorney any facts relevant to whether the doctors and pharmacists were acting outside the usual course of professional practice, including that the doctors and pharmacists were issuing prescriptions based only upon their review of a generic medical questionnaire and without any contact with patients.

macies in Maryland, for example, an employee was directed to "shred paper" relating to its orders. Two weeks later, Antonio abandoned the pharmacy for a new location after firing much of its staff. On another occasion, Antonio instructed Tomas to use an unlicensed location, the basement of a 99-cent store known as the "Cave," as a temporary pharmacy after a local inspector visited one of Antonio's pharmacies. At trial, Antonio testified that he instructed one of his pharmacists to lie to the authorities about how his operation was being conducted.

In 2003, the government subpoenaed Antonio for documents relating to the approximately 90,000 orders he had filled for Vincent Chhabra's website through Prescription & Travel. When Chhabra was arrested later that year for unlawful distribution of controlled substance medications, Antonio emailed Mahana a link to the news story. Following Chhabra's arrest, Antonio stopped using Prescriptions & Travel to fill orders for his websites and took steps to liquidate its assets. At trial, Antonio conceded that he used the same questionnaire and sold the same medications as Chhabra.

Between 2004 and 2006, government agents advised certain people working for Antonio that Internet pharmacies like the defendants' were illegal, and that information was relayed to Antonio. In December 2004, for example, Tomas informed Antonio that DEA agents had provided him a notice stating "that the online sale of prescription drugs was illegal." In January 2006, DEA agents informed Donald Cooper, one of Antonio's associates, that it was illegal to sell controlled substances through an Internet pharmacy. Cooper relayed that information to Antonio, who replied that "[i]f anybody would get into trouble, it would be the pharmacists and the doctors."

Several months later, in May 2006, DEA agents visited Thundergames, which ran the call center for Antonio's websites, and advised two of Antonio's employees that Internet pharmacies were illegal because they lacked a legitimate doctor-patient relationship. One of those employees, Arianne Pelegrin, relayed this information to Antonio, who responded that "there was nothing to worry about." Antonio, however, thereafter moved Thundergames' accounting department to an office at a car dealership. A short time later, Herman began running the customer service operation for his own pharmacy from the car dealership office space.

In these circumstances, we conclude that the government has adduced overwhelming evidence that the defendants knew or reasonably should have known that the doctors and pharmacists upon whom they purportedly relied were acting in bad faith. Any actual belief to the contrary would have been unreasonable. Thus, any error in giving a conscious avoidance instruction was not prejudicial to the defendants.

Straub, J., dissenting in part, concurring in part.

With today's decision the majority blurs the once distinct and enforced parameters of our conscious avoidance jurisprudence. The Quinoneses raised two issues regarding the conscious avoidance jury instruction on appeal: (1) whether it should have been included in the jury charge at all and (2) whether its language violated our precedent ... because it did not account for their actual beliefs. While I agree that because the Quinoneses asserted "the lack of some specific aspect of knowledge required for conviction, and ... the appropriate factual predicate for the charge exist[ed]," the instruction was properly before the jury, I disagree with the majority's conclusion that the error found in the instruction's language was harmless. Because it is my opinion that the conscious avoidance instruction was fundamentally flawed and that the error was plain and prejudicial, I respectfully dissent and would vacate the judgment against the Quinoneses and grant them a new trial. I concur in the majority opinion in all other respects.

The doctrine of conscious avoidance stands for the principle "that a person who deliberately shuts his eyes to an obvious means of knowledge has sufficient *mens rea* for an offense based on such words as 'permitting,' 'allowing,' 'suffering' and 'knowingly.'"[2] In our Circuit, "a conscious avoidance charge must communicate two points: (1) that a jury may infer knowledge of the existence of a particular fact if the defendant is aware of a high probability of its existence, (2) unless the defendant actually believes that it does not exist." While other circuits rarely have authorized the use of the instruction, we have authorized it "somewhat more readily."

Since adopting the conscious avoidance doctrine from English common law, American courts have balanced its application with a concern for defendants' actual beliefs. In *Spurr v. United States,* 174 U.S. 728 (1899), the Supreme Court first tacitly acknowledged the doctrine's legitimacy, but also recognized the improper usage of the conscious avoidance instruction deprived the defendant of his defense of honest belief. Later, this concern for defendants' actual beliefs was incorporated into the Model Penal Code's directive on conscious avoidance: "When knowledge of the existence of a particular fact is an element of an offense, such knowledge is established if a person is aware of a high probability of its existence, unless he actually believes that it does not exist." The Supreme Court expressed its approval of this formulation in *Leary v. United States,* 395 U.S. 6, 46 n.93 (1969), and we require substantially similar language for a proper conscious avoidance jury instruction in our Circuit. District courts and prosecutors have been on notice for over three decades that the "actual belief" language must be "incorporated into every conscious avoidance charge."

The "actual belief" prong is critical to ensure a proper conscious avoidance jury instruction. The risk of the language's exclusion is dire because "[f]ailure to include that proviso improperly permits the jury to convict a defendant who honestly believed that he was not engaging in illegal activity." Moreover, as the proviso goes to what a defendant believes, and not what he knows or should know, the belief held by the defendant need not be reasonable in order for it to defeat a conscious avoidance theory of actual knowledge. *See United States v. Catano-Alzate,* 62 F.3d 41, 43 (2d Cir. 1995) (per curiam) ("[T]he doctrine of conscious avoidance does not permit a finding of guilty knowledge if the defendant actually did not believe that he or she was involved in the transportation of drugs, however irrational that belief may have been."). In cases like this one, where a defendant relies on his lack of knowledge of a crucial fact as a central element of his defense, the "actual belief" language is "particularly appropriate."

Because the Quinoneses did not specifically object to the language of the conscious avoidance jury instruction, we review for plain error. FED. R. CRIM. P. 30(d). Under this standard, the Quinoneses must demonstrate that any error "(1) is clear or obvious, rather than subject to reasonable dispute; (2) affected [their] substantial rights — i.e., that there is a reasonable probability that the error affected the outcome of the trial; and (3) seriously affects the fairness, integrity or public reputation of judicial proceedings."

The District Court charged the jury: "In determining what the defendant knew or reasonably should have known, you may consider whether the defendant deliberately closed his eyes to what otherwise would have been obvious. This does not mean that the defendant acted carelessly, negligently or even foolishly. One may not, however, avoid criminal liability by wilfully and intentionally remaining ignorant of a fact material and important to his or her conduct. Thus, even if you find beyond a reasonable doubt that

---

2. In various American and English cases, the doctrine is also referred to as willful blindness, deliberate ignorance, connivance, and the deliberate closing of one's eyes.

the defendant was aware that there was a high probability that the doctors and pharmacists were acting outside the usual course of professional practice and not for a legitimate medical purpose, but deliberately and consciously avoided learning this fact, then you may treat this deliberate avoidance of knowledge as the equivalent of knowledge."

This instruction is completely silent on the Quinoneses' actual beliefs, and thus it is wholly deficient and clearly erroneous.

The majority is wrong that "the defendants' actual but unreasonable belief in the existence of a fact—here, the doctors' and pharmacists' good faith—could not absolve the defendants of culpability." Our conscious avoidance cases say the opposite: If the jury found that the Quinoneses actually believed that the doctors and pharmacists were acting in good faith, it could not have convicted them under the doctrine of conscious avoidance. Because the jury was not presented with the "actual belief" proviso, however, it had almost no alternative but to find the Quinoneses guilty when it combined the flawed conscious avoidance instruction with the *should have known* knowledge element.

[T]he majority opinion holds that even if the instruction was improperly worded, the error was non-prejudicial and, thus, harmless because (1) the government presented overwhelming evidence that the Quinoneses actually knew or should have known that the doctors and pharmacists were acting in bad faith and (2) the Quinoneses' actual beliefs were unreasonable and consequently would not absolve their crimes. I find the majority's first rationale unpersuasive and I believe the second misapplies the law.

The majority's opinion rests on its finding that there was overwhelming evidence of "actual knowledge." Upon completing the harmless error inquiry ... I come to the opposite conclusion. The evidence tends to indicate that the Quinoneses honestly believed their business was legal; it is certainly not "essentially uncontroverted" that they knew the practitioners were acting in bad faith. Moreover, when considering whether there was overwhelming evidence that they *should* have known, we must account for the jury instruction that the Quinoneses were "entitled to reasonably rely on the determinations of doctors and pharmacists."

The Quinoneses' defense ... was predicated on their lack of knowledge of a key fact—in this case, that the doctors and pharmacists involved in their internet pharmacy operation were acting outside the usual course of professional practice. The jury heard ample testimony from Antonio on the steps he took to ensure that his business was legal and on his actual belief that the doctors and pharmacists were operating in good faith. He consulted with an attorney, who visited the pharmacy, reviewed the business in operation, checked the prescriptions, and concluded that the business was legal. He also spoke with at least one doctor in Puerto Rico to ensure that the doctors were licensed and the internet pharmacies in compliance with the law. He paid an additional attorney to research and explain a telemedicine law enacted in Puerto Rico that he believed allowed him to operate his internet pharmacies legally. Furthermore, as the majority discussed, Antonio moved his business out of Florida when a new law was enacted prohibiting Florida doctors from writing prescriptions without face-to-face consultations. He also maintained a "block list" to prevent drug abusing customers from repeatedly purchasing pills. This evidence, along with Antonio's uncontroverted testimony that he honestly believed that his business was in compliance with the law would allow a rational juror to conclude (1) that the Quinoneses actually believed that the doctors and pharmacists were operating in good faith and (2) that they did not have actual knowledge to the contrary.

The majority claims that ... the Quinoneses would still have been convicted if they reasonably *should have* known that the doctors and pharmacists were acting in bad faith.

The majority contends that there was overwhelming evidence that they should have known this fact. This reasoning ignores the good-faith reliance instruction included in the jury charge. The District Court's statement on "good faith" immediately preceded the conscious avoidance instruction: "The defendant is entitled to reasonably rely on the determinations of doctors and pharmacists. This means that even if you find that the doctors and pharmacists who allegedly wrote and filled the prescriptions at issue in this case were not, in fact, acting in good faith, as I previously defined the phrase of good faith to you, you must find the defendant not guilty unless the government proves beyond a reasonable doubt that the defendant knew or reasonably should have known that the doctors and pharmacists were not acting in good faith and if you find that to be the case, then the defendants will be guilty."

Accounting for this instruction, the government needed to prove that after speaking with doctors, who assured him that the drugs were being prescribed in good faith, Antonio nonetheless should have known that these doctors were not telling the truth.

Just as with "actual knowledge," I do not think that the evidence before our Court allows for a finding that there was overwhelming evidence that the Quinoneses should have known the practitioners were acting in bad faith. As the record contains conflicting testimony as to what the Quinoneses knew and believed, as well as clear evidence that Antonio consulted with both the doctors as well as attorneys about whether his business was legal, a jury should determine whether the Quinoneses are guilty after hearing a proper jury charge. Again, as the conscious avoidance jury instruction was employed as an alternative means of proving the Quinoneses' knowledge, it is possible that the juxtaposition of the good faith and conscious avoidance instructions left the jury confused as to the proper standard. The jurors may have thought they had little choice but to convict the Quinoneses considering the interplay between the reasonably should have known standard and the flawed conscious avoidance language. It is unclear from the record whether the jury convicted the Quinoneses under an actual knowledge or a conscious avoidance theory. "[N]o matter how often the jury was instructed that it could not convict unless it found that the defendant acted knowingly, this was undermined by the charge that the jury could find '[the Quinoneses] acted knowingly if you find that [they] deliberately ... closed [their] eyes to what otherwise would have been obvious to [them],' without the necessary [actual belief] proviso." *Sicignano,* 78 F.3d at 72 (internal alterations omitted).

Whether the Quinoneses' beliefs were reasonable does not change our analysis. If the jury intended to convict the Quinoneses under the conscious avoidance doctrine, but found that they actually believed that the doctors and pharmacists were operating in good faith, then it would have been required, using the correct standard, to acquit, regardless of whether it found the Quinoneses' beliefs were reasonable. While it is true that the jury would still be free to convict the Quinoneses under the "reasonably should have known" standard found in the jury instructions, I think there is "a reasonable probability that the jury convicted [the Quinoneses] on a conscious avoidance theory and that the jury would not have done so but for the instructional error." Thus, the jury instructions were fundamentally flawed and the error was not harmless.

3. Regulation and Prosecution of Manufacturers

Manufacturers of controlled substances with medical uses are also subject to a wide range of regulations, the violation of which may lead to civil or criminal liability. In contrast to physicians and pharmacies, however, manufacturers of pain medications like Oxycontin that are accused of wrongdoing have generally been prosecuted under the Food, Drug, and Cosmetic Act rather than the Controlled Substances Act.

"There's Danger Here, Cherie!": Liability for the Promotion and Marketing of Drugs and Medical Devices for Off-Label Uses
Richard C. Ausness
73 Brooklyn Law Review 1253

Physicians often prescribe prescription drugs and other medications for uses that are not approved by the Food and Drug Administration ("FDA"), and such "off label" prescription is widely accepted within the medical community as a legitimate form of treatment. However, the federal government discourages off-label prescription and use in various ways. For example, the FDA restricts the dissemination of information by drug companies about potential off-label therapies.

An off-label use is one that is not provided for on the product's FDA-approved labeling. A doctor makes an off-label prescription when he or she prescribes a drug or medical device to treat a medical condition other than the one the drug or device was approved to treat. Off-label prescription also involves using a different method of applying the treatment as well as prescribing a drug or device to patient groups other than those for whom the FDA approved it. In addition, off-label use includes prescriptions for drug dosages that are different from the recommended dosage or for periods that exceed the recommended use in the labeling.

Off-label uses are not necessarily unusual or experimental. In fact, they are widely accepted within the medical community and may sometimes be the most effective treatment for certain types of medical conditions. It is estimated that between twenty and sixty percent of all prescriptions are for off-label uses. For example, a large percentage of prescriptions for pediatric use are off-label because many drugs are not tested or approved for use by children. Off-label uses are also common in cancer therapy and are often considered to be among the most effective treatments.

Courts have repeatedly held that certain off-label uses are legitimate forms of therapy. The FDA has also tacitly recognized that off-label uses are legitimate. Nevertheless, the FDA severely restricts the ability of drug manufacturers to promote off-label uses for their products. Thus, drug companies are forced to circumvent, or even violate, the law if they wish to inform physicians about beneficial off-label therapies (and make money from the increased sales of their products). The drug companies that cross the line and get caught face substantial civil and criminal liability.

The recent experience of Purdue Pharma, manufacturer of the prescription pain medication OxyContin, illustrates the perils of misbranding and other violations of the FDCA. The company was accused of encouraging physicians to prescribe OxyContin for use every eight hours instead of the twelve-hour dosage approved by the FDA. It eventually agreed to pay $19.5 million to twenty-six states and the District of Columbia to settle a civil suit based on its alleged promotion of off-label use of the painkiller. This led Connecticut Attorney General Richard Blumenthal to declare, "We are raising the bar on off-label marketing—and other promotion tactics—that lead to abuse and diversion of prescription drugs." However, Purdue Pharma suffered an even more serious blow when the U.S. Department of Justice brought criminal charges against the company and three of its top executives. Federal prosecutors contended that Purdue Pharma had engaged in a fraudulent and deceptive marketing campaign that falsely claimed that OxyContin, because of its timed-release formula, was more resistant to abuse and less likely to cause addiction than competing products such as Percocet. The federal government also charged some company sales representatives with giving doctors misleading scientific data to support their fraudulent claims.

Pursuant to an agreement, Purdue Pharma and the three corporate officers pleaded guilty to these criminal charges. As part of the plea bargain deal, Purdue Pharma acknowledged that it had made false statements, and it agreed to pay $470 million in fines and payments to various state and federal agencies as well as $130 million to settle civil lawsuits brought against the company by former patients who claimed to have become addicted to OxyContin. According to federal prosecutors, the $600 million in fines and civil penalties that Purdue Pharma agreed to pay amounted to ninety percent of the profits that it initially made from OxyContin sales. Furthermore, as part of the plea bargain deal, the court sentenced the company to five years' probation.

Three company executives also pleaded guilty to misdemeanor charges of misbranding OxyContin, a violation of the FDCA that does not require proof that the defendants intended to defraud doctors or consumers or that they knew about the wrongdoing of others. These officials agreed to pay a total of $34.5 million in fines. At a "lengthy and highly emotional hearing" in federal district court, parents of those who had died from overdoses of OxyContin condemned the company officials and urged the court to reject the plea agreements and sentence the officials to jail terms. However, the court accepted the plea agreements and only sentenced the three officials to three years' probation and 400 hours each of community service in drug treatment programs. Nevertheless, the judge expressed disappointment that he was unable to send the defendants to prison because federal prosecutors had not produced evidence that the company officials were aware of the wrongdoing at Purdue Pharma.

Though the FDA has taken the lead in investigating drug manufacturers in cases like Purdue's, the DEA also closely regulates the manufacture of controlled substances. The following case relates to the procedure for registering as an importer of narcotic raw materials under the Controlled Substances Act.

Penick Corporation v. Drug Enforcement Administration

United States Court of Appeals for the District of Columbia
491 F.3d 483 (2007)

Henderson, J.

Chattem Chemicals, Inc. (Chattem) applied to the Drug Enforcement Administration (DEA) for registration as an importer of narcotic raw materials (NRMs) pursuant to the Controlled Substances Act and the Controlled Substances Import and Export Act (collectively referred to as CSA). Penick Corp. (Penick) opposed the application and requested a hearing before the DEA, arguing that Chattem's registration as a NRM importer would increase the danger of NRM diversion to illicit use and thereby undermine the public interest. The Deputy Administrator of the DEA granted the application, concluding that Chattem "met its burden of proof to show that it is in the public interest ... to grant its application to be registered as an importer of NRMs." Penick petitions for review of the Deputy Administrator's decision and, as detailed below, we deny the petition.

The CSA requires that the importation of NRMs and the manufacture of their alkaloids—the most prominent of which are morphine and codeine—remain tightly controlled in order to prevent their diversion to illicit use. Accordingly, the CSA prohibits the importation of NRMs into the United States unless the importing company is registered by the DEA and importation is limited to "such amounts of [NRMs] ... as the Attorney General finds to be necessary to provide for medical, scientific, or other legitimate purposes." The Attorney General "register[s] an applicant to import or export [NRMs] if he determines that such registration is consistent with the public interest and with United States obligations under international treaties, conventions, or protocols."

Pursuant to these provisions, on February 9, 2001, Chattem applied to the DEA for registration as an importer of NRMs and bulk manufacturer of their alkaloids.

On December 18, 2001, the DEA approved Chattem's application for registration as a bulk manufacturer. Its concurrent application to import NRMs was opposed, however, by Penick, Noramco of Delaware, Inc. (Noramco) and Mallinckrodt, Inc. (Mallinckrodt), all of which requested a hearing on Chattem's application. At the time of Chattem's application, Noramco and Mallinckrodt were the only registered importers of NRMs, a group that Penick joined in 2004. Because of these potential competitors' opposition, then, the administrative law judge (ALJ) conducted hearings on Chattem's application in September and October 2002 at which all parties—as well as the government—"called witnesses to testify and introduced documentary evidence" relating to the impact on the public interest of Chattem's registration. The ALJ ultimately recommended that Chattem's application be granted.

On February 17, 2006, the Deputy Administrator heeded that recommendation and decided "to grant [Chattem's] application to be registered as an importer of NRMs." The Deputy Administrator, applying 21 U.S.C. §958(a), first determined that Chattem's registration would not violate any international obligations of the United States because the registration "would not likely cause significant increased diversion" and thus it was not "'essential' to deny Chattem's application" in order to prevent global diversion of NRMs. Regarding Chattem's potential impact on diversion, the Deputy Administrator recognized that diversion "at the retail level has greatly increased in recent years, and is an extremely serious problem," but nonetheless concluded that "Chattem ha[d] met its burden of proof in showing that its registration as an importer of NRMs will not significantly interfere with the maintenance of effective controls against diversion." The Deputy Administrator noted the unchallenged adequacy of Chattem's internal security measures to prevent diversion of narcotics to illicit use, the complete lack of "documented cases of diversion of NRMs imported into the United States," the "DEA['s] continued ... regist[ration of] bulk manufacturers" during the pendency of Chattem's application and the fact that the DEA already conducts regular inspections of Chattem as a registered bulk manufacturer of alkaloids.

The Deputy Administrator further determined that ... "[t]here is no significant evidence that Chattem has failed to comply with applicable State and local law" or violated state or federal narcotics regulations. She also determined that "the evidence showed that Chattem possesses sufficient technology to process NRMs with efficiency" because "Chattem introduced credible evidence ... that the processing of NRMs is not complicated, and that Chattem has sufficient facilities to carry out the process," facilities already approved by the DEA for bulk manufacture of NRM alkaloids. In light of these considerations, the Deputy Administrator concluded that "Chattem ... met its burden of proof to show that it is in the public interest ... to grant its application to be registered as an importer of NRMs." Penick now petitions for review.

Section 823(a)(1) requires the Deputy Administrator to consider "maintenance of effective controls against diversion of particular controlled substances ... into other than legitimate medical, scientific, research, or industrial channels" in determining whether registration is consistent with the public interest. Penick argues that, in section 823(a)(1), the Congress has "directly spoken" and "requires the applicant to establish the systemic impact of its registration throughout the chain of distribution, including the registration's impact on" diversion at the retail level. Instead, Penick claims, the Deputy Administrator misinterpreted this requirement and rendered the factor superfluous by focusing her diversion discussion solely on Chattem's internal security measures, a factor properly covered by section 823(a)(5)'s mandate to consider "the existence in the establishment of effective control against diversion." Yet this claim fails for a simple reason: the Deputy Administrator plainly considered and rejected the contention that Chattem's registration would increase retail-level diversion.

Before the Deputy Administrator, "[t]he Government argued that registering another importer could lead to increase[d] diversion at the retail level because of the potential of increased importation, increased manufacturing ... and greater availability of narcotic medication." Indeed, the Deputy Administrator found "that the diversion of ... narcotics at the retail level has greatly increased in recent years, and is an extremely serious problem." She nonetheless concluded that Chattem's registration would not increase retail-level diversion because "there [was] little evidence in the record that Chattem's registration as an importer would have any greater effect on diversion downstream than DEA's continued registration of bulk manufacturers." Moreover, the Deputy Administrator noted the DEA's ability to control the level of NRM importation and diversion through quotas and inspections, both of which already included Chattem in its capacity as a registered bulk manufacturer of controlled substances. Accordingly, we reject Penick's challenge to the DEA's interpretation of section 823(a)(1).

Still, an agency's action will be overturned if its findings are not "supported by substantial evidence," or its reasoning is "arbitrary, capricious, an abuse of discretion, or otherwise not in accordance with law." Penick asserts that the DEA's registration of Chattem fails both of these standards because the Deputy Administrator arbitrarily and "improperly shift[ed] the burden of proof from Chattem to the objectors." We disagree.

Here, the Deputy Administrator recognized that the ultimate burden of proof rested with Chattem and relied on Chattem's evidence with respect to each of the enumerated public interest factors. For instance, ... the Deputy Administrator concluded that the risk of diversion at the retail level would not be significantly increased by Chattem's registration in light of Chattem's evidence that the DEA continued to register additional bulk manufacturers of opium alkaloids even though those manufacturers present comparable diversion dangers. Finally, the Deputy Administrator relied on the existence of DEA quotas and inspections to control diversion as well as testimony that "there were no documented cases of diversion of NRMs imported into the United States, and no significant diversion at the bulk manufacturing level." Given all of this evidence, the Deputy Administrator concluded that "Chattem ... met its burden of proof in showing that its registration as an importer of NRMs will not significantly interfere with the maintenance of effective controls against diversion."

Given the significant evidence Chattem supplied, the Deputy Administrator's decision was neither based on insubstantial evidence nor arbitrary or capricious. We "will not disturb the decision of an agency that has 'examine[d] the relevant data and articulate[d] a satisfactory explanation for its action including a rational connection between the facts found and the choice made.'"

Penick raises an additional challenge to Chattem's registration which we also reject. The DEA may register an importer only if "it determines that such registration is consistent ... with United States obligations under international treaties, conventions, or protocols." Penick asserts that Chattem's registration is inconsistent with the United Nations Single Convention on Narcotic Drugs of 1961 (Single Convention), which obligates the United States "to take all necessary measures to ensure that the international movement of narcotics is limited to legitimate medical and scientific needs." The Single Convention's commentary notes that "it may be advisable or even essential to keep to a minimum the number of ... manufacturers and international traders (importers as well as exporters) ... engaged in these activities." Although the Deputy Administrator found Chattem's registration consistent with the Single Convention, Penick argues that (1) the Single Convention requires the DEA to control diversion by "*first* ... restricting the registration of importers." and (2) the Deputy Administrator improperly ignored the danger of increased foreign diversion from Chattem's registration. Penick's contentions ignore the requirements of the Single Convention, the Deputy Administrator's opinion and our precedent.

First, the Single Convention does not, as Penick asserts, require that the number of importers be limited as the first step in preventing diversion. Instead, the commentary merely suggests "it *may* be advisable or even essential to keep to a *minimum* the number of ... importers" without defining the "minimum" that would be "advisable" and the Deputy Administrator found "that the evidence did not show that it would be 'advisable' or 'essential' to deny Chattem's application for registration." Indeed, the Deputy Administrator considered Chattem's registration's potential effect on downstream diversion and the potential "contribution of foreign diversion to diversion in the United States," specifically referencing this diversion discussion in finding that Chattem's registration would not circumvent the Single Convention.

Moreover, while the Deputy Administrator considered evidence of foreign diversion only to the extent such diversion might "contribut[e] ... to diversion in the United States," her decision is consistent with our holding that, in enacting the CSA, "the Congress was concerned with preventing diversion in this country rather than abroad." In light of the speculative nature of any increased foreign diversion stemming from Chattem's registration and the existence of alternative means of controlling diversion, such as quotas, "the Deputy Administrator f[ound] no substantial evidence in the record that Chattem's registration as an importer would result in a significant increase in foreign diversion of NRMs, or that such diversion, if it were to occur, would significantly increase diversion of controlled substances in this country." Because the Deputy Administrator's conclusion under 21 U.S.C. § 958(a) is consistent with the Single Convention, the evidence and our precedent, we reject Penick's challenge.

For the foregoing reasons, Penick's petition for review is denied.

4. What Constitutes Legitimate Medical Use of a Prescription Drug?

Restrictions on the distribution of controlled substances in Schedules II through V are designed to limit the market for these substances to medical uses and prevent against diversion to recreational users. But what constitutes a legitimate medical use?

Shortly after passage of the Harrison Narcotics Act in 1914, a series of cases made their way to the United States Supreme Court in which physicians argued that prescribing narcotics for addiction maintenance—in other words, to keep addicted patients from suffering withdrawal symptoms—was a legitimate medical use. *See, e.g.,* Alfred R. Linde-smith, The Addict and the Law 3–17 (1967) (discussing these early cases). United States law does not generally view the prescription of recreational-use drugs for addiction maintenance as a legitimate medical use, though the Controlled Substances Act does allow for maintenance treatment with some substances such as methadone. *See* Jessica G. Katz, Note, *Heroin Maintenance Treatment: Its Effectiveness and the Legislative Changes Necessary to Implement it in the U.S.*, 26 J. CONTEMP. HEALTH L. & POL'Y 300, 305–08 (2010) (describing methadone treatment in the United States).

A handful of other countries have taken a different approach, however. Switzerland, for example, operates a heroin assisted treatment program in which heroin is given to addicts in a controlled environment. The program includes twenty-three centers that serve nearly 1,300 patients and provide them with psychiatric and social counseling. Some studies have suggested that these programs may improve the medical and employment status of addicted patients in the program and help to reduce heroin addiction-related crime. In 2008, sixty-eight percent of Swiss voters approved a measure to permanently incorporate the program into the country's national health policy.

Should prescribing heroin to addicts through an addiction maintenance program like the one in Switzerland be considered a legitimate medical use?

Failure of Physicians to Prescribe Pharmacotherapies for Addiction: Regulatory Restrictions and Physician Resistance
Ellen M. Weber
13 Journal of Health Care Law and Policy 49 (2010)

Federal regulation of physician prescription practices for narcotics treatment over the past century has shaped current medical practice.* This regulation has essentially removed physicians from the delivery of addiction treatment, resulting in the development of specialized facilities that provide such care. As the following brief history of the federal regulatory framework demonstrates, beginning around 1914 and running through most of the late-twentieth century, federal law prohibited the prescription of controlled substances for the treatment of narcotic addiction except by physicians working in highly regulated clinics. These standards stigmatized medication-assisted treatment as well as the patients who received such care, and left generations of physicians unprepared to diagnose and treat patients with alcoholism and drug addiction.

In the early twentieth century, the medical community viewed addiction as a medical problem, and physicians prescribed opioid medications for the care of addicted patients without legal restrictions. Throughout the mid-to late-nineteenth century, physicians regularly prescribed patent medicines that contained morphine, cocaine and heroin. Medicines used as possible "cures" for morphine, opium, and alcohol addiction also contained opiates, cocaine, and heroin, and physicians prescribed such medications for the treatment and maintenance of addiction. According to historian David Musto, the medical community was slow to recognize that physicians were overusing morphine, that addic-

---

* Ellen M. Weber wishes to acknowledge the sources that informed and have been quoted in this article, including David Musto's *The American Disease: Origins of Narcotic Control* (3d ed. 1999), the Institute of Medicine's *Federal Regulation of Methadone Treatment* (Rettig and Yarmolinsky eds., 1995), and Jerome Jaffe and Charles O'Keeffe's *From Morphone Clinics to Buprenorphine: Regulating Opiod Agonist Treatment of Addiction in the United States*, 70 Drug & Alcohol Dependence (Supp. 1) S3 (2001). [*Footnote by casebook author in consultation with Ellen M. Weber.*]

tion to heroin, morphine and cocaine was possible, and that these substances should be reduced or removed from patent medicines. Public health officers involved in the treatment of addiction at the turn of the century believed that physicians were indeed responsible for the majority of individuals who developed drug addictions.

Responding to the development of a relatively large population of addicts and "a fear of addiction and addicting drugs," Congress enacted the Harrison Narcotics Act of 1914. The Harrison Act was a revenue bill that required physicians who prescribed preparations containing opium, cocaine, or their derivatives, to register, pay an annual tax, write prescriptions for such medicines, and maintain records of the patient and quantity of drugs dispensed. The Act also established restrictions on the quantity of opiates and cocaine that could be contained in patent medicines. The Act did not directly prohibit physicians from prescribing medicines containing opiates and cocaine, but it required prescriptions to be issued "in the course of his professional practice only" and limited a patient's possession of these drugs to those that had been prescribed in "good faith" by a registered physician. The primary goal of federal narcotics control officials, however, was to use the Harrison Act to stop physicians from both prescribing opiates and cocaine to individuals with addictions and maintaining such individuals on these drugs.

Although federal enforcement efforts to halt the prescription of narcotics to persons with addictions under the Harrison Act were rejected initially by the Supreme Court, subsequent amendments to the Act strengthened the ability of the government to regulate physician practices and curtail addiction maintenance. Social and cultural change, fueled by the war effort and intense nationalism following World War I, also increased public intolerance for alcohol and narcotic use and cast addiction as immoral. According to Musto, by 1919, the country had denounced the maintenance of both alcoholics, via the ratification of the Eighteenth Amendment, and narcotic addicts, via robust enforcement of the Harrison Act.

A series of Supreme Court decisions, starting in 1919, barred physicians from prescribing heroin and cocaine to patients with addictions, putting an end to medication maintenance of addiction. In *Webb v. United States*, the Supreme Court ruled that a physician's prescription for morphine that was given to "an habitual user" to "keep him comfortable by maintaining his customary use" rather than for purposes of attempting to "cure ... the habit" was not a "prescription" within the protection of the Harrison Act. In *United States v. Doremus*, issued the same day as Webb, the Supreme Court upheld the indictment of a registered physician who had sold a large quantity of heroin to a patient who was addicted to narcotics without using the required prescription. The Court also upheld the constitutionality of the Harrison Act as a tax measure that was intended to, among other things, prevent a non-registered patient from reselling narcotics without payment of the required tax. In *United States v. Behrman*, the Supreme Court ruled that a physician's prescription of large quantities of heroin, cocaine, and morphine to a patient who was known to be addicted did not fall into the physician's regular course of professional practice. Although the Court recognized that physicians should be able to exercise their judgment in prescribing different doses of medication in individual cases, it concluded that the "enormous number of doses" prescribed to one patient "could only result in the gratification of a diseased appetite for these pernicious drugs or result in an unlawful parting with them to others in violation of the act...."

As a result of these decisions, a physician was not permitted to prescribe such drugs, at least in large quantities, if drug addiction was the only disease being treated. The heightened threat of prosecution deterred most physicians from providing care to patients with addictions, even if they prescribed within the legal limits.

The model for contemporary specialized medication-assisted treatment programs also originated during the first quarter of the twentieth century. Initially sympathetic to the health concerns of persons who had developed addictions, federal and state health officials and local law enforcement, beginning around 1912, created maintenance clinics in a dozen states that would prescribe medication in an effort to prevent suffering related to addiction and wean individuals from their drug use through the gradual reduction of dosage. In Jacksonville, Florida, for example, the City health officer established a clinic in which persons with addictions could receive free narcotics prescriptions. In Tennessee, persons with addictions were registered and given refillable opiate prescriptions to minimize suffering and reduce illegal drug trafficking. In New York, a series of laws and policy directives enforced between 1913 and 1920 permitted maintenance of persons with addictions by private physicians; these measures also provided for increased regulation of physician practices, patient registration requirements, and the establishment of state-run narcotics clinics for both the maintenance and treatment of addiction. With a narcotics clinic system in place, state narcotic control officials intended to revoke the prescribing authority of physicians who refused to adhere to prescription limitations or dosages deemed to be consistent with "curing" addiction. Federal and State officials also promoted institutionalized care to help patients withdraw from drugs, even though that care proved relatively ineffective as patients could resume use by attending a narcotics clinic.

By 1920, federal officials had resolved to close maintenance clinics. The operation of clinics by local health departments was a continuing source of "legal" drug maintenance, which, by this time, was unlawful under *Webb* and *Doremus*. Maintenance clinics also made enforcement of the Harrison Act against private physicians who abused prescription standards difficult, since both provided essentially the same care. Discouraged by the failure of maintenance clinics and hospitals to cure addiction, some public health officials had come to believe that elimination of drug availability was the best hope of a successful cure. Although not supported by evidence from the treatment provided in hospitals, some of the most ardent supporters of a medical model began to endorse abrupt withdrawal from narcotics. The American Medical Association issued a resolution in 1920 opposing ambulatory maintenance clinics and condemning the use of heroin, which sanctioned the further prosecution of physicians who continued to prescribe maintenance medication.

Federal and state initiatives to address addiction as a disease ended by the mid-1920s. All maintenance clinics were shuttered by 1925, and the federal government adopted a supply-side strategy to eliminate drug addiction through strict law enforcement and international treaties. Opiate and cocaine dependence were no longer considered a medical problem but rather a criminal justice issue. This history "became part of the 'lore' that affected medical practice and research for almost 50 years and had a profound influence on government officials when the issue of narcotic maintenance again emerged in relation to methadone."

The current regulatory scheme for medications that are approved to treat opiate addiction continues to restrict physician practice and impose federal oversight that is unprecedented for the prescription of FDA-approved medications, including Schedule II drugs. The regulatory framework dates back to the 1960s when research conducted by Drs. Vincent Dole and Marie Nyswander determined that methadone, a synthetic opiate that had been used in the late 1950s for detoxification treatment for heroin dependence, could be used as a maintenance medication to effectively treat heroin dependence. Treatment centers, operating under Investigational New Drug applications issued by the FDA, began prescribing methadone for addiction treatment under the disguise of research and claimed exemption from the Federal Bureau of Narcotics' policies that still rendered the dispensing of opioids to addicts illegal. In 1972, in response to the dramatic expansion of methadone treatment and concerns about the abuse and diversion of this medication, the FDA, in collaboration with the Special Action Office for Drug Abuse Prevention and the Bureau of Narcotics and Dangerous Drugs (the predecessor to the DEA), promulgated regulations that authorized the use of methadone maintenance treatment under strict and close control to ensure safe distribution, administration, and dispensing.

The regulatory framework itself was antithetical to the integration of addiction treatment into mainstream medical practice: it restricted the availability of methadone to approved programs and hospital pharmacies, and precluded private physicians from prescribing medication for addiction treatment unless they were approved as a "program" and met all requirements of the regulation including staffing requirements. The regulations also dictated who would be eligible for methadone treatment (based on an individual's age and duration of drug dependence), maximum initial doses, minimum amount of counseling, urinalysis testing, and the factors used to determine a patient's eligibility for non-supervised administration of ("take-home") medication. These standards not only usurped individualized medical determinations for patient care but also institutionalized a stigma surrounding patients in methadone treatment. Patients were required to obtain care in separate, free-standing programs and to take their medication on a daily basis under directly observed administration for substantial periods of time. States were also authorized to impose additional restrictions on patients who participated in methadone treatment.

Two years later, Congress enacted the Narcotic Addict Treatment Act of 1974, which was intended to complement the FDA regulations and clamp down further on what Congress considered to be inappropriate prescribing practices by physicians. This Act amended the Controlled Substances Act to require annual registration of practitioners and treatment sites with the Drug Enforcement Administration (DEA) and authorized the DEA to regulate the storage and security of drugs used to treat addiction.

This federal regulatory framework for methadone maintenance treatment remained in place for thirty years, notwithstanding recommendations to dramatically revamp the standards so that patients would have greater access to this effective medication for opiate addiction. In 1995, the Institute of Medicine (IOM) concluded that "no compelling medical reason [exists] for regulating the therapeutic use of methadone differently from any other Schedule II controlled substance." It found that the regulations had deprived society of reaping the full benefit of methadone as an effective treatment for addiction and preventative measure for other public health problems and crime. According to the IOM, the extraordinary regulatory controls had prevented some individuals from obtaining treatment tailored to their needs; prevented doctors from exercising professional judgment in treating patients; and resulted in the isolation of treatment programs from mainstream medical practice. The IOM recommended, among other things, that the regulations be reduced in scope, supplemented by clinical practice guidelines that shift responsibility for treatment decisions from regulators to clinicians, and provide for maintenance treatment outside of a licensed treatment program.

Long-overdue revisions to the federal methadone regulations, promulgated in 2001, have moved in the direction of a clinical practice model by instituting an accreditation and certification scheme for programs, but do little to encourage or enable physicians to establish an office-based model for dispensing methadone. The Department of Health and Human Services (HHS) rejected recommendations to develop standards that would permit physicians to prescribe methadone in office-based settings without affiliation with an opioid treatment program (OTP), citing "the lack of trained and experienced practitioners to diagnose, admit, and treat opiate addicts who are not sufficiently stabilized without the support of an OTP." Although a physician could theoretically seek accreditation and certification for an office-based practice, the cost associated with satisfying these requirements make it impractical for a physician who is not associated with an existing program to do so. The regulations instead seek to gradually increase treatment capacity in office-based practices by authorizing "medical maintenance" of stabilized patients who, after two years of continuous treatment, may be permitted to have a one-month supply of medication and may be referred to physicians who maintain formal arrangements with OTPs. Apart from this limited expansion, the current regulations reduce, albeit not substantially, the restrictions on patient attendance requirements and take-home (unsupervised) medication privileges. The federal regulations continue to weight the risk of diversion as more salient than clinical judgment, individualized patient care, and strategies to encourage patients to enter treatment earlier in the course of their addiction.

Nearly a decade later, modification of federal regulatory standards to reduce barriers to office-based methadone practice seems unlikely. A sharp increase in methadone-related overdose deaths, dating from 2002, linked to the increased availability of methadone for pain management from private physicians, has resulted in a call by some in Congress for increased regulation of prescription practices for methadone. Addiction treatment experts, undoubtedly wary of a backlash to advances in office-based care for individuals with histories of opiate dependence, have urged caution in imposing new regulations, which would deter the use of beneficial medications. They instead recommend that private physicians follow patient-centered practices that include understanding a patient's history of alcohol and drug use, adjusting care management for patients with substance use histories, and implementing practices to ensure that patients store medications securely, use prescribed medications appropriately, and are monitored for diversion.

The enactment of the Drug Addiction Treatment Act of 2000 (hereinafter DATA 2000) created, for the first time in nearly a century, a real opportunity to integrate pharmacotherapy addiction treatment into an office-based medical practice in the United States. Under DATA 2000, physicians who receive training and certification are permitted to prescribe buprenorphine—a Schedule III Controlled Substance approved by the Food and Drug Administration (FDA) in 2002 for the treatment of opioid dependence. Since 2001, more than 24,000 physicians have been trained in the use of buprenorphine, and over 18,000 have received certification. More than one million patients have been prescribed buprenorphine since 2002, the majority of whom were new to substance abuse treatment and dependent on non-heroin (prescription) opioids.

The enactment of DATA 2000 and the FDA's approval of buprenorphine for office-based practices in 2002 have increased access to opioid addiction treatment in a range of health care settings. Keenly aware of the history regarding addiction maintenance in the 1920s, the limited scope of medical education related to addiction treatment, and the regulatory strictures and stigma associated with methadone maintenance treatment, the federal government and the manufacturer of buprenorphine have taken important steps to ensure appropriate prescription practices while expanding access to office-based care. They have developed clinical practice guidelines, risk management strategies, and physician education and on-going clinical support with a cadre of physician-leaders. Anticipating reluctance among physicians to prescribe buprenorphine for addiction treatment out of fear of disciplinary actions, the federal government has encouraged the Federation of State Medical Boards to develop a model policy guideline that recommends physicians assess all patients for substance abuse and sets out guidelines for prescribing buprenorphine consistent with legitimate medical purposes. The federal government publicizes the growing number of certified physicians and maintains a web-based physician locater to aid individuals who are seeking care. It has also funded a range of demonstration projects to evaluate best practices in providing office-based care. Finally, whenever evidence of diversion of buprenorphine has emerged, federal and state officials have responded quickly to prevent the most drastic of regulatory solutions—rescheduling buprenorphine as a Schedule II controlled substance—that would reverse the gains that have been achieved through office-based practice.

Regulatory and non-regulatory obstacles—some of which are the collateral consequences of the past century's restrictions on medical practice—continue to limit access to buprenorphine in an office-based practice. In late 2009, speculation surfaced about the DEA's desire to suppress the number of physicians who prescribe buprenorphine when the enforcement agency informed DATA 2000 waiver practitioners of its plans to inspect their practices. For many, the DEA's action reflected its "reputation among some doctors for choosing heavy-handed enforcement over patient needs—along with a perceived hostility toward buprenorphine and other opiate-replacement therapies...." Treatment experts observed that DEA's actions could have a chilling effect on family practitioners and internal medicine specialists who have been encouraged to embrace the treatment, but may grow tired of "all of the challenges one needs to surmount to prescribe buprenorphine."

Although the buprenorphine experience is promising, it may be too early to tell whether the "use of buprenorphine in office based settings will ... lead the United States to a more pragmatic attitude towards dealing with the consequences of heroin addiction—and [whether] that ... pragmatism will be long lasting...."

Because the Controlled Substances Act does not consider the distribution of a Schedule I substance for purposes of addiction maintenance to be a legitimate medical use, a maintenance program like Switzerland's—in which heroin is dispensed directly to patients—would be illegal under federal law. This has led some proponents of maintenance programs within the U.S. to suggest that cities consider establishing supervised injection facilities, where drug users would be allowed to self-administer heroin that they obtain on their own in an environment supervised by medical professionals. Though federal law would present fewer legal hurdles for safe injection facilities than it does for heroin maintenance programs, their legal status is still uncertain. *See* Scott Burris, Evan D. Anderson, Leo Beletsky and Corey S. Davis, *Federalism, Policy Learning, and Local Innovation in Public Health: The Case of the Supervised Injection Facility*, 52 St. Louis L.J. 1089 (2009) (analyzing the legality of safe injection facilities).

The question of what constitutes a legitimate medical use can occasionally arise outside the context of addiction maintenance treatment as well. In 2006, the United States Supreme Court considered the applicability of the Controlled Substances Act to physicians in Oregon who sought to prescribe controlled substances as part of the State's assisted suicide law. The case concerned an Interpretive Rule issued by the Attorney General in 2001 that determined "using controlled substances to assist suicide is not a legitimate medical practice and that dispensing or prescribing them for this purpose is unlawful under the CSA." The Supreme Court struck down the Attorney General's rule, reasoning that the CSA's prescription requirement was designed to "ensure[] patients use controlled substances under the supervision of a doctor so as to prevent addiction and recreational abuse. As a corollary, the provision also bars doctors from peddling to patients who crave the drugs for those prohibited uses. To read prescriptions for assisted suicide as constituting 'drug abuse' under the CSA is discordant with the phrase's consistent use throughout the statute, not to mention its ordinary meaning." *Gonzales v. Oregon*, 546 U.S. 243 (2006).

C. State Medical Marijuana Laws

1. State Medical Marijuana Laws: An Overview

Although federal law continues to classify marijuana as a Schedule I controlled substance with no currently accepted medical use, since 1996 eighteen states and the District of Columbia have adopted laws that legalize or decriminalize medical marijuana. The details of these laws can vary significantly. For example, Colorado's medical marijuana law permits businesses to cultivate and sell marijuana to qualified patients on a for-profit basis. By contrast, Maryland's medical marijuana law does not even make it legal for a patient to possess marijuana. In Maryland, a patient who possesses less than one ounce of marijuana and can prove she uses it out of medical necessity with a doctor's recommendation will have a partial defense in a criminal prosecution. But even if she succeeds in this defense, she can still be fined up to $100. The following report, produced by a marijuana law reform advocacy organization, provides an overview of state medical marijuana laws.

State-by-State Medical Marijuana Laws
Marijuana Policy Project (2011)

States have been trying to give patients legal access to marijuana since 1978. By 1991, favorable laws had been passed in 34 states and the District of Columbia. (The 35th state, Hawaii, enacted its law in 2000, Maryland, the 36th state, enacted its law in 2003, and Delaware, the 37th state, enacted its law in 2011.) Unfortunately, because of numerous federal restrictions, most of these laws have been largely symbolic, with little or no practical effect. For example, several states passed laws stating that doctors may "prescribe" marijuana. However, federal law prohibits doctors from writing "prescriptions" for marijuana, so doctors are unwilling to risk federal sanctions for doing so. Furthermore, even if a doctor were to give a patient an official "prescription" for marijuana, the states did not account for the fact that it is a federal crime for pharmacies to distribute it, so patients would have no way to legally fill their marijuana prescriptions.

The tide began to turn in 1996 with the passage of a California ballot initiative. California became the first state to effectively remove criminal penalties for qualifying patients who possess and use medical marijuana. California's law, like the initial wave of effective state laws, provided access by allowing patients to cultivate their own medicine or to designate a caregiver to do so. California's law specifies that qualifying patients need a doctor to "recommend" marijuana. By avoiding issuing a prescription, doctors are not violating federal law in order to certify their patients. (Of note, Arizona voters also passed a medical marijuana initiative in 1996, but it turned out to be only symbolic because it required a prescription—an order to dispense a medication—rather than a recommendation—a statement of a doctor's professional opinion.)

Over the next four years, seven states and the District of Columbia followed in California's footsteps. Alaska, Oregon, Washington, and the District of Columbia passed similar initiatives in 1998. (Until 2010, Congress was able to prevent the D.C. initiative from taking effect because D.C. is a district, not a state, and is therefore subject to strict federal oversight.) Maine passed an initiative in 1999, and Colorado and Nevada followed suit in 2000.

Also in 2000, Hawaii broke new ground, when it became the first state to enact a law to remove criminal penalties for medical marijuana users via a state legislature. Gov. Ben Cayetano (D), who submitted the original bill in 1999 and signed the final measure into law on June 14, 2000, said, "The idea of using marijuana for medical purposes is one that's going to sweep the country."

On May 22, 2003, Gov. Robert Ehrlich of Maryland became the first Republican governor to sign workable medical marijuana legislation into law. Gov. Ehrlich signed H.B. 702, the Darrell Putman Compassionate Use Act, in the face of staunch opposition from White House drug czar John Walters. This law was a very limited sentencing mitigation—patients still faced arrest, a fine of $100 and possible related court costs, and had no means of accessing their medicine.

In fall 2003, California's legislature and Gov. Gray Davis (D) expanded the state's existing law to allow patients and caregivers to collectively or cooperatively cultivate marijuana as long as it was not done for "profit." The improved law forms the legal basis for dispensaries operating in the state, but it does not explicitly allow them, and it does not include any state regulation or registration.

Vermont became the ninth state to pass an effective medical marijuana law on May 26, 2004, when Gov. James Douglas (R) allowed S. 76, An Act Relating to Marijuana Use by Persons with Severe Illness, to become law without his signature. Gov. Douglas, too, was pressured by the White House drug czar to reject the bill, but due to the high profile of the medical marijuana bill in the media and overwhelming public support by Vermonters, he decided against a veto.

In November 2004, 62% of Montana voters approved an initiative to allow qualified patients to use and cultivate marijuana for their medical use.

Rhode Island became the 11th state to pass an effective medical marijuana law in 2006—and the first state to enact a medical marijuana law since the U.S. Supreme Court's decision in *Gonzales v. Raich.*

Beginning in 2007, some states began to include state-regulated dispensaries in their laws. In 2007, Gov. Bill Richardson (D) signed SB 523, making New Mexico the 12th state to protect medical marijuana patients from arrest. New Mexico's law was the first to allow state-regulated and state-licensed larger-scale providers. In addition, patients are allowed to obtain a cultivation license to grow their own medicine.

On November 4, 2008, 63% of Michigan voters approved a medical marijuana initiative, making Michigan the 13th state with an effective medical marijuana law, and the first in the Midwest. Michigan's was the last effective state medical marijuana law enacted that relied only on home cultivation and caregivers, without providing for state-regulated dispensaries.

In 2009, the Rhode Island General Assembly broke new ground by becoming the first state to add regulated non-profit dispensaries, called compassion centers, to its existing law. Like the state's initial law, this was enacted over Gov. Carcieri's veto. Maine's voters followed suit in November 2009, approving an initiative that added non-profit dispensaries, a patient and caregiver registry, and additional qualifying conditions to the state's medical marijuana law.

On January 18, 2010, New Jersey became the 14th medical marijuana state and the first to enact a medical marijuana law that relied solely on dispensaries, without providing for home cultivation. Gov. Jon Corzine (D) signed the bill into law during his last week in office, one week after the legislature approved it.

In spring 2010, the D.C. Council put the initiative voters had approved in 1998 on hold, while it significantly revised the law Congress had finally allowed to go into effect. The revisions significantly restricted the law, by removing the option of home cultivation and eliminating most of the qualifying conditions. The law allows five to eight dispensaries and up to 10 cultivation centers.

Also in spring 2010, Colorado's legislature approved a bill that expanded the state's existing medical marijuana law by explicitly allowing, regulating, and licensing dispensaries (called "medical marijuana centers") and infused product manufacturers.

In November 2010, Arizona voters approved an initiative that made their state the 15th with an effective medical marijuana law. Unlike the state's 1996 measure, this law used "certification" instead of "prescription" to ensure it would be effective. The law allows about 125 non-profit dispensaries and for patients or their caregivers to cultivate if they do not live near dispensaries. However, in May 2011, Gov. Jan Brewer suspended the dispensary portion of the law and announced a federal lawsuit questioning the validity of the state's law.

In May 2011, the Delaware Legislature passed and Gov. Jack Markell (D) signed legislation making Delaware the 16th medical marijuana state. Like many of the more recent laws, Delaware's new law allows for a limited number of non-profit dispensaries, three of which will be chosen based on a competitive process by January 1, 2013.

Also in 2011, Vermont's legislature and Gov. Peter Shumlin (D) enacted legislation that added four non-profit dispensaries to the state's existing medical marijuana law. The state's Department of Public Safety must issue four dispensary registrations by June 2, 2012.

In addition, in spring 2011, Maryland's legislature and Gov. Martin O'Malley (D) approved legislation that expanded the state's very limited law and established a medical marijuana work group. The new law provides an affirmative defense that can prevent a conviction—but not an arrest or prosecution—for simple marijuana possession. The law still does not allow a safe means of access, such as by cultivation or dispensaries.

More than 90 million Americans—about 29% of the U.S. population—now live in the 16 states, or the federal district, where medical marijuana users are protected from criminal penalties under state law.

The 11 initiative-created laws and the six laws created by state legislatures are similar in what they accomplish. Each of the 16 states and the District of Columbia allow patients to possess and use medical marijuana if approved by a medical doctor. Depending on the state, patients may cultivate their own marijuana, designate a caregiver to do so, and/or obtain marijuana from a dispensary.

Fourteen of the laws allow patients to cultivate a modest amount of marijuana in their homes—all but Delaware, New Jersey, and the District of Columbia. In Arizona, patient cultivation is only allowed if the patient lives more than 25 miles away from a dispensary.

Eight states' and the District of Columbia's laws allow for state-regulated dispensing, though some of the laws are so new that their dispensaries are not yet up and running, and the dispensing programs in Arizona and Rhode Island are currently on hold. The states with laws providing for state-registered dispensaries are Arizona, Delaware, Colorado, New Mexico, Maine, New Jersey, Rhode Island, and Vermont. In addition, California has hundreds, or even thousands, of dispensaries, many of which are regulated at the local level, but there is no statewide licensing or regulation of them.

In addition, under each of the state laws, physicians are immune from liability for discussing or recommending medical marijuana in accordance with the law.

To qualify for protection under the law, patients must have documentation verifying they have been diagnosed with a specified serious illness. The conditions are not specified in California, although in most states there is a defined list of medical conditions.

States generally require a statement of approval signed by the patient's physician. To help law enforcement identify qualifying patients, all but one of the states (Washington) have implemented formal state registry programs that issue identification cards to registered patients and their caregivers, though the ID cards are voluntary in California and Maine.

Patients' marijuana possession and cultivation limits are generally restricted to a concrete number: one to 24 ounces of usable marijuana and six to 24 plants, sometimes limiting the number that can be mature. (California's 1996 medical marijuana law permits enough marijuana "for the personal medical purposes of the patient." A 2003 addition to the law, S.B. 420, guarantees protection from arrest for patients who possess state-issued ID cards and up to eight ounces of usable marijuana and six mature plants or 12 immature plants.)

In many states, regardless of whether patients grow their own, get it from a caregiver or dispensary, or buy it from the criminal market, a patient in possession of an allowable quantity of marijuana and otherwise in compliance with the law is protected from arrest and/or conviction. However, New Jersey and Washington, D.C. only allow patients to possess marijuana that was obtained from dispensaries.

The 11 medical marijuana initiatives that voters approved have been described as the first wave of activity to protect medical marijuana patients nationwide. Not only do they provide legal protection for patients in states that collectively contain almost 25% of the U.S. population, they also verify Americans' strong support for favorable medical marijuana laws.

In turn, the successes in Hawaii and five subsequent legislatures are the second wave, whereby state legislatures are enacting effective laws to protect medical marijuana patients. In the 2011 legislative session, Delaware's legislature enacted medical marijuana legislation, and 17 other state legislatures considered bills to allow medical marijuana under state law.

In addition, many medical marijuana states are considering adding dispensaries or collective cultivation to existing laws, or regulating existing dispensaries or producers. Eight state laws and the District of Columbia's now provide for state-regulated, state-registered larger-scale providers. Six additional states saw the introduction of proposals to add dispensaries or collectives to existing laws in 2011. Many of these proposals, as well as the new medical marijuana laws, call for competitive licensing of dispensary operators to ensure best practices in the industry.

The role of state legislatures in the movement to protect medical marijuana patients cannot be overstated. Only 23 states and the District of Columbia have the initiative process, which means that citizens in 27 states cannot directly enact their own laws. They must rely on their state legislatures to enact favorable medical marijuana laws, and the number of future legislative victories will depend on how many people effectively lobby their state officials. Moreover, legislation is much more cost-effective than ballot initiatives, which can be very expensive endeavors.

The third and final wave will be a change in federal law. While it is unlikely that federal law will change in the immediate future, the more states act, the sooner federal law will change.

2. The Federal Response to State Medical Marijuana Laws

Shortly after California voters approved the first modern state medical marijuana law in 1996, the federal government began a vigorous effort to block its implementation. Then-director of the Office of National Drug Control Policy Barry McCaffrey announced that the Drug Enforcement Administration would seek to revoke the DEA registrations of physicians who recommended medical marijuana to their patients, thereby leaving them unable to prescribe other controlled substances. This prompted a group of California patients and doctors to file suit. The case made its way to the United States Court of Appeals for the Ninth Circuit, which held that the DEA's plan was an unconstitutional infringement on physicians' first amendment rights. *Conant v. Walters*, 309 F.3d 629 (2002). While the DEA may have the authority to regulate the prescription of controlled substances, California's law functions on the basis of a less formal recommendation system. The Court found that "[b]eing a member of a regulated profession does not, as the government suggests, result in a surrender of First Amendment Rights." In the Court's view, preventing physicians from recommending medical marijuana to their patients would "strike at the core of First Amendment interests of doctors and patients. An integral component of the practice of medicine is the communication between a doctor and a patient. Physicians must be able to speak frankly and openly to patients."

Contemporaneous with its effort to prevent California physicians from recommending medical marijuana to their patients, the federal government filed suit against six medical marijuana cooperatives. Relying on the federal Controlled Substances Act, the government sought to enjoin the cooperatives from dispensing marijuana. The medical marijuana cooperatives successfully argued before the Ninth Circuit that a medical necessity defense would likely apply to their activities. The Supreme Court, however, granted *certiorari* and reversed. The Court found that under the terms of the Controlled Substances Act, "the balance already has been struck against a medical necessity exception." *United States v. Oakland Cannabis Buyers' Coop.*, 532 U.S. 483 (2001).

United States v. Oakland Cannabis Buyers' Cooperative
Supreme Court of the United States
532 U.S. 483 (2001)

Justice Thomas delivered the opinion of the Court.

In November 1996, California voters enacted an initiative measure entitled the Compassionate Use Act of 1996. Attempting "to ensure that seriously ill Californians have the right to obtain and use marijuana for medical purposes," the statute creates an exception to California laws prohibiting the possession and cultivation of marijuana. These prohibitions no longer apply to a patient or his primary caregiver who possesses or cultivates marijuana for the patient's medical purposes upon the recommendation or approval of a physician. In the wake of this voter initiative, several groups organized "medical cannabis dispensaries" to meet the needs of qualified patients. Respondent Oakland Cannabis Buyers' Cooperative is one of these groups.

The Cooperative is a not-for-profit organization that operates in downtown Oakland. A physician serves as medical director, and registered nurses staff the Cooperative during business hours. To become a member, a patient must provide a written statement from a treating physician assenting to marijuana therapy and must submit to a screening interview. If accepted as a member, the patient receives an identification card entitling him to obtain marijuana from the Cooperative.

In January 1998, the United States sued the Cooperative and its executive director, respondent Jeffrey Jones (together, the Cooperative), in the United States District Court for the Northern District of California. Seeking to enjoin the Cooperative from distributing and manufacturing marijuana, the United States argued that, whether or not the Cooperative's activities are legal under California law, they violate federal law. Specifically, the Government argued that the Cooperative violated the Controlled Substances Act's prohibitions on distributing, manufacturing, and possessing with the intent to distribute or manufacture a controlled substance. Concluding that the Government had established a probability of success on the merits, the District Court granted a preliminary injunction.

The Cooperative did not appeal the injunction but instead openly violated it by distributing marijuana to numerous persons. To terminate these violations, the Government initiated contempt proceedings. In defense, the Cooperative contended that any distributions were medically necessary. Marijuana is the only drug, according to the Cooperative, that can alleviate the severe pain and other debilitating symptoms of the Cooperative's patients. The District Court rejected this defense, however, after determining there was insufficient evidence that each recipient of marijuana was in actual danger of imminent harm without the drug. The District Court found the Cooperative in contempt and, at the Government's request, modified the preliminary injunction to empower the United States Marshal to seize the Cooperative's premises. Although recognizing that "human suffering" could result, the District Court reasoned that a court's "equitable powers [do] not permit it to ignore federal law." Three days later, the District Court summarily rejected a motion by the Cooperative to modify the injunction to permit distributions that are medically necessary.

[A panel of the Ninth Circuit Court of Appeals] reversed and remanded. According to the Court of Appeals, the medical necessity defense was a "legally cognizable defense" that likely would apply in the circumstances.

The United States petitioned for certiorari to review the Court of Appeals' decision that medical necessity is a legally cognizable defense to violations of the Controlled Substances Act.

According to the Cooperative, because necessity was a defense at common law, medical necessity should be read into the Controlled Substances Act. We disagree.

As an initial matter, we note that it is an open question whether federal courts ever have authority to recognize a necessity defense not provided by statute. A necessity defense "traditionally covered the situation where physical forces beyond the actor's control rendered illegal conduct the lesser of two evils." Even at common law, the defense of necessity was somewhat controversial. And under our constitutional system, in which federal crimes are defined by statute rather than by common law, it is especially so.

We need not decide, however, whether necessity can ever be a defense when the federal statute does not expressly provide for it. In this case, to resolve the question presented, we need only recognize that a medical necessity exception for marijuana is at odds with the terms of the Controlled Substances Act. The statute, to be sure, does not explicitly abrogate the defense. But its provisions leave no doubt that the defense is unavailable.

Under any conception of legal necessity, one principle is clear: The defense cannot succeed when the legislature itself has made a "determination of values." In the case of the Controlled Substances Act, the statute reflects a determination that marijuana has no medical benefits worthy of an exception (outside the confines of a Government-approved research project). Whereas some other drugs can be dispensed and prescribed for medical use, the same is not true for marijuana. Indeed, for purposes of the Controlled Substances Act, marijuana has "no currently accepted medical use" at all.

Under the statute, the Attorney General could not put marijuana into schedule I if marijuana had any accepted medical use.

The Cooperative points out, however, that the Attorney General did not place marijuana into schedule I. Congress put it there, and Congress was not required to find that a drug lacks an accepted medical use before including the drug in schedule I. We are not persuaded that this distinction has any significance to our inquiry. Under the Cooperative's logic, drugs that Congress places in schedule I could be distributed when medically necessary whereas drugs that the Attorney General places in schedule I could not. Nothing in the statute, however, suggests that there are two tiers of schedule I narcotics, with drugs in one tier more readily available than drugs in the other. On the contrary, the statute consistently treats all schedule I drugs alike.

The Cooperative further argues that use of schedule I drugs generally—whether placed in schedule I by Congress or the Attorney General—can be medically necessary, notwithstanding that they have "no currently accepted medical use." According to the Cooperative, a drug may not yet have achieved general acceptance as a medical treatment but may nonetheless have medical benefits to a particular patient or class of patients. We decline to parse the statute in this manner. It is clear from the text of the Act that Congress has made a determination that marijuana has no medical benefits worthy of an exception. The statute expressly contemplates that many drugs "have a useful and legitimate medical purpose and are necessary to maintain the health and general welfare of the American people," but it includes no exception at all for any medical use of marijuana. Unwilling to view this omission as an accident, and unable in any event to override a legislative determination manifest in a statute, we reject the Cooperative's argument.

Finally, the Cooperative contends that we should construe the Controlled Substances Act to include a medical necessity defense in order to avoid what it considers to be difficult constitutional questions. In particular, the Cooperative asserts that, shorn of a medical necessity defense, the statute exceeds Congress' Commerce Clause powers, violates the substantive due process rights of patients, and offends the fundamental liberties of the people under the Fifth, Ninth, and Tenth Amendments. As the Cooperative acknowledges, however, the canon of constitutional avoidance has no application in the absence of statutory ambiguity. Because we have no doubt that the Controlled Substances Act cannot bear a medical necessity defense to distributions of marijuana, we do not find guidance in this avoidance principle. Nor do we consider the underlying constitutional issues today. Because the Court of Appeals did not address these claims, we decline to do so in the first instance.

For these reasons, we hold that medical necessity is not a defense to manufacturing and distributing marijuana.[7] The Court of Appeals erred when it held that medical necessity is a "legally cognizable defense."

---

7. Lest there be any confusion, we clarify that nothing in our analysis, or the statute, suggests that a distinction should be drawn between the prohibitions on manufacturing and distributing and the other prohibitions in the Controlled Substances Act. Furthermore, the very point of our holding is that there is no medical necessity exception to the prohibitions at issue, even when the patient is "seriously ill" and lacks alternative avenues for relief.

Justice Stevens, with whom Justice Souter and Justice Ginsburg join, concurring in the judgment.

Lest the Court's narrow holding be lost in its broad dicta, let me restate it here: "We hold that medical necessity is not a defense to *manufacturing* and *distributing* marijuana." This confined holding is consistent with our grant of certiorari, which was limited to the question "whether the Controlled Substances Act forecloses a medical necessity defense to the Act's prohibition against *manufacturing* and *distributing* marijuana, a Schedule I controlled substance."

Congress' classification of marijuana as a schedule I controlled substance — that is, one that cannot be distributed outside of approved research projects — makes it clear that "the Controlled Substances Act cannot bear a medical necessity defense to *distributions* of marijuana."

[T]he Court reaches beyond its holding, and beyond the facts of the case, by suggesting that the defense of necessity is unavailable for anyone under the Controlled Substances Act. Because necessity was raised in this case as a defense to distribution, the Court need not venture an opinion on whether the defense is available to anyone other than distributors. Most notably, whether the defense might be available to a seriously ill patient for whom there is no alternative means of avoiding starvation or extraordinary suffering is a difficult issue that is not presented here.

The overbroad language of the Court's opinion is especially unfortunate given the importance of showing respect for the sovereign States that comprise our Federal Union. That respect imposes a duty on federal courts, whenever possible, to avoid or minimize conflict between federal and state law, particularly in situations in which the citizens of a State have chosen to "serve as a laboratory" in the trial of "novel social and economic experiments without risk to the rest of the country." In my view, this is such a case. By passing Proposition 215, California voters have decided that seriously ill patients and their primary caregivers should be exempt from prosecution under state laws for cultivating and possessing marijuana if the patient's physician recommends using the drug for treatment. This case does not call upon the Court to deprive *all* such patients of the benefit of the necessity defense to federal prosecution, when the case itself does not involve *any* such patients.

I join the Court's judgment of reversal because I agree that a distributor of marijuana does not have a medical necessity defense under the Controlled Substances Act. I do not, however, join the dicta in the Court's opinion.

Just four years after *Oakland Cannabis Buyers' Cooperative*, California's medical marijuana law was before the Supreme Court again, this time in the context of a federalism-based challenge. In *Gonzales v. Raich*, 545 U.S. 1 (2005), a case that is read in most Constitutional Law courses, the Supreme Court considered the scope of Congress's power to regulate medical marijuana under the Commerce Clause. In 2002, DEA agents raided the home of Dianne Monson, a California medical marijuana patient, and seized six marijuana plants. Although the government did not bring charges against her, Monson, along

---

Finally, we share Justice Stevens' concern for "showing respect for the sovereign States that comprise our Federal Union." However, we are "construing an Act of Congress, not drafting it." Because federal courts interpret, rather than author, the federal criminal code, we are not at liberty to rewrite it. Nor are we passing today on a constitutional question, such as whether the Controlled Substances Act exceeds Congress' power under the Commerce Clause.

with fellow patient Angel Raich and her two caregivers, filed suit to enjoin the DEA from enforcing the Controlled Substances Act against them for cultivating medical marijuana. The *Raich* plaintiffs relied on two Supreme Court decisions, *United States v. Lopez*, 514 U.S. 549 (1995), and *United States v. Morrison*, 529 U.S. 598 (2000), which had restricted the federal government's authority under the Commerce Clause. In essence, *Lopez* and *Morrison* had held that the commerce power did not extend to "noncommercial" activity, placing such activity beyond the reach of federal law. Thus, for example, the Court in *Lopez* struck down a provision of the Gun Free School Zones Act of 1990 that made possession of a gun in a school zone a federal crime on the grounds that it was not commercial activity. Raich and Monson argued that, like possession of a gun in a school zone, the cultivation and possession of marijuana for personal medical use was the sort of noncommercial activity that fell outside the federal government's authority under the Commerce Clause.

In a 6–3 decision, the Supreme Court held the federal government could reach Monson and Raich's activities under the commerce power. The Court reasoned that the regulation of the possession and noncommercial cultivation of marijuana was a necessary part of Congress' efforts to criminalize the interstate market for the drug under the Controlled Substances Act. This distinguished *Raich* from *Lopez* and *Morrison*, according to the majority, because the regulation of the noncommercial possession and cultivation of marijuana was an "essential part of a larger regulation of economic activity, in which the regulatory scheme could be undercut unless the intrastate activity were regulated."

On remand in the Ninth Circuit, Raich argued that application of the Controlled Substances Act based on her medicinal use of marijuana would infringe on her "fundamental right to 'mak[e] life-shaping medical decisions that are necessary to preserve the integrity of her body, avoid intolerable pain, and preserve her life.'" *Raich v. Gonzales*, 500 F.3d 850 (9th Cir. 2007). The Ninth Circuit rejected this argument, finding that "legal recognition" of medical marijuana "has not yet reached the point where a conclusion can be drawn that the right to use medical marijuana is 'fundamental' and 'implicit in the concept of ordered liberty.'" The Court continued:

> Justice Anthony Kennedy told us that "times can blind us to certain truths and later generations can see that laws once thought necessary and proper in fact serve only to oppress." For now, federal law is blind to the wisdom of a future day when the right to use medical marijuana to alleviate excruciating pain may be deemed fundamental. Although that day has not yet dawned, considering that during the last ten years eleven states have legalized the use of medical marijuana, that day may be upon us sooner than expected. Until that day arrives, federal law does not recognize a fundamental right to use medical marijuana prescribed by a licensed physician to alleviate excruciating pain and human suffering.

Raich has left no doubt that the federal government can prosecute individuals whose conduct is in compliance with state medical marijuana laws, including even individual patients for possession of personal use-amounts of marijuana. In her dissent in *Raich*, Justice O'Connor lamented that the Court's decision had "sanction[ed] an application of the federal Controlled Substances Act that extinguishes" California's medical marijuana laws. Yet in the years following *Raich*, so-called medical marijuana dispensaries—stores that provide marijuana to qualified patients—opened at a faster rate than prior to the decision. Indeed, by the time President George W. Bush left office in 2009, it was estimated that more than 700 medical marijuana dispensaries were operating in California alone. Thus, despite the federal government's legal authority to prosecute medical marijuana patients and providers, it has been unable to shut down state medical marijuana laws.

What accounts for this dynamic? And, if the federal government has been unable to block state medical marijuana laws, what impact (if any) has the federal prosecution of medical marijuana patients and providers had on those laws?

Beyond the Prohibition Debate: Thoughts on Federal Drug Laws in an Age of State Reforms
Alex Kreit
13 Chapman Law Review 555 (2010)

In 2008, and again in 2009, Congressman Barney Frank introduced bills to "decriminalize" marijuana, saying that the government should allow people to "make their own choices as long as they are not impinging on the rights, freedom or property of others[.]" And, when President Barack Obama held an online town-hall meeting to answer questions submitted and voted on by voters through a White House website, reformers worked to help push a question about marijuana legalization to the top of the list. President Obama offered only a brief response to the question that garnered the most votes, joking, "I don't know what this says about the online audience," before dismissing the idea. Meanwhile, when faced with questions about proposals to tax and regulate marijuana like alcohol, President Obama's "drug czar" Gil Kerlikowske has taken to saying that "legalization isn't in the President's vocabulary, and it certainly isn't in mine."

Kerlikowske's "vocabulary" line has been a source of frustration among marijuana legalization advocates and has been viewed as a sign that the administration is not willing to engage the question with a serious response, even if it were to ultimately remain opposed to the idea. The criticism is certainly understandable. After all, President Obama gave serious and substantive responses to all of the other questions he received in his online town hall meeting, but only a one-sentence humor-based reply to the question about marijuana policy.

In an important sense, however, the debate about legalizing or decriminalizing marijuana truly is misplaced in the context of federal drug laws. Indeed, to ask if the federal government should legalize marijuana is to ask an essentially irrelevant question—irrelevant not because it is unimportant or on the political fringe (certainly, if the polling is to be believed, it is not), but because it misunderstands the role of the federal law in shaping drug policy. Whether or not legalizing or decriminalizing marijuana is a good idea, the federal government simply does not have the power to effect such a change.

Imagine, for example, that every federal elected official decided tomorrow that marijuana should be taxed and regulated like alcohol. Even if they were to pass legislation that removed all federal criminal penalties for possessing, manufacturing, or selling marijuana, the drug would still be illegal everywhere in the country because all fifty states have their own laws criminalizing the sale of marijuana. To be sure, if the federal government were to remove criminal penalties for the cultivation and distribution of marijuana, it would have a substantial impact on the enforcement of marijuana laws in the United States. That impact, however, would not be "legalization" of the drug inasmuch as marijuana would not be legal to buy and sell in any state unless and until that state also changed its laws. In short, unless the federal government decided to preempt state law, it could not unilaterally "legalize" a controlled substance even if it wanted to.

To see why this point has important implications for thinking about federal drug laws, consider Congressman Frank's proposed legislation. Congressman Frank and the media framed the bill, dubbed the "Act to Remove Federal Penalties for Personal Use of Marijuana by Responsible Adults," as a proposal to decriminalize marijuana nationwide. But, if we think a bit more about what the bill would actually do, we find that the question of whether or not our country should decriminalize marijuana is not particularly relevant to assessing the merits of Congressman Frank's proposal.

The Personal Use of Marijuana by Responsible Adults Act would enact a simple change in federal law by eliminating federal penalties for "the possession of marijuana for personal use," defined as 100 grams or less of marijuana, "or for the not-for-profit transfer between adults of marijuana for personal use." How would this change in the law impact marijuana enforcement in the United States? A quick look at the data for federal prosecutions reveals that the actual effect of the legislation would be quite minimal. In 2008 there were a total of only 626 simple marijuana possession cases disposed of in federal court. To put this number in perspective, there were approximately 754,223 arrests for marijuana possession nationwide in 2008. In other words, the bill would impact about 0.0008 percent of all individuals arrested for marijuana possession.

It is also worth noting that the 626 figure is almost certainly larger than the number of individuals who would have been charged with a federal crime based on simple possession of a personal use amount of marijuana alone. This is because, in all likelihood, a number of the 626 defendants were initially charged with a more severe offense but were convicted of marijuana possession as part of a plea deal. Indeed, of the 370 defendants convicted of federal marijuana possession in 2008, 367 were based on guilty pleas. And, though data is not available on the number of individuals who were federally charged based on the not-for-profit transfer of personal use amounts of marijuana, there is no reason to believe that it is significantly larger than the number of individuals charged with simple possession.

With this in mind, to say that the Personal Use of Marijuana by Responsible Adults Act would have a negligible impact on marijuana arrests and prosecutions would be an understatement, particularly when one considers that individuals who might avoid federal prosecution under the legislation would not necessarily escape punishment, as they could still be prosecuted at the state level. Far from "decriminalizing" marijuana, then, the direct impact of Congressman Frank's proposal would be to remove a few hundred defendants from the federal system and leave their cases to local prosecutors. Indeed, even if the proposal were expanded beyond marijuana to take the federal government out of the business of prosecuting simple possession for all drugs, the real-world effect would still be surprisingly trivial, as there were only 394 prosecutions for simple possession for all drugs other than marijuana in 2008.

When viewed in this light, it becomes clear that to discuss a proposal like the Personal Use of Marijuana by Responsible Adults Act primarily by reference to terms like decriminalization and prohibition is really to misstate the relevant issue. A debate over whether to remove federal penalties for small amounts of marijuana or other drugs is not a debate about decriminalization, but about the best use of federal resources and the most sensible role for federal law in addressing the problem of drug abuse. In other words, the policy question posed by Congressman Frank's bill is not whether to criminalize possession of small amounts of marijuana, but rather who is best able to enforce criminal laws against possession of small amounts of marijuana, and whether the activity is one that the federal government can or should concern itself with.

The case for moving beyond the legalization debate when thinking about federal drug laws becomes even stronger when we consider the sort of changes to state drug laws that we are most likely to see over the coming five to ten years. Among the most prominent and viable state reforms that appear to be on the horizon are the continued enactment of state medical marijuana laws and the probability that one or more states will legalize marijuana for recreational purposes. [S]ince 1996, fourteen states have legalized the use and, in some instances, distribution of marijuana for medicinal purposes. Similar proposals have already been introduced in the legislatures of other states and, unless there is a sudden reversal in public opinion on the issue, it is very likely we will continue to see more states enacting medical marijuana laws. Moreover, with proposals to tax and regulate marijuana like alcohol, and polls showing support for doing so at above fifty percent in parts of the country, a number of political observers believe we may see marijuana legalized for recreational use in one or more states within the near future.

As in the case of the Congressman Frank's Personal Use of Marijuana by Responsible Adults Act, we find that the debate over prohibition and legalization is only tangentially relevant to how federal law should address these proposed state reforms. A review of the federal response to state medical marijuana laws is particularly useful to help see why this is so.

Perhaps the most significant, though largely underappreciated, lesson to be learned from fourteen years of state medical marijuana laws is that the ability of the federal government to override or interfere with state drug laws is actually quite limited. As Robert A. Mikos persuasively argues in his insightful article, *On the Limits of Supremacy: Medical Marijuana and the States' Overlooked Power to Legalize Federal Crime*, "states [have] retained both de jure and de facto power to exempt medical marijuana from criminal sanctions, in spite of Congress' uncompromising—and clearly constitutional—ban on the drug." In other words, just as the federal government does not have the power unilaterally to legalize or decriminalize a controlled substance, it also appears unable to prevent states from doing so.

Between them, *OCBC* and *Raich* left little doubt that federal officials could constitutionally prosecute medical marijuana growers, providers, and even patients themselves. And, throughout the past decade, the federal government enthusiastically exercised this authority, at least in California. It has raided at least 190 medical marijuana collectives and brought criminal charges against medical marijuana growers and collective operators, many of whom were operating in strict compliance with California's law. In one high profile prosecution, for example, the federal government obtained a conviction against Charlie Lynch, who operated a medical marijuana collective in Morro Bay, California. Lynch had the backing of town officials and even held a ribbon-cutting ceremony attended by the mayor and members of the city council when he opened up shop. At his sentencing, District Court Judge George H. Wu indicated some displeasure with having to impose a one-year jail sentence for Lynch. The New York Times reported that Wu "talked at length about what he said were Mr. Lynch's many efforts to follow California's laws on marijuana dispensaries" before concluding: "I find I cannot get around the one-year sentence[.]" The DEA has even gone after landlords who have knowingly rented their property to medical marijuana collective operators and growers through asset forfeiture proceedings.

Despite all of these efforts, however, the federal government has not succeeded in blocking California's medical marijuana law. By 2009, there were an estimated 300,000 to 400,000 qualified patients under California's medical marijuana laws. Even more telling, there were over 700 medical marijuana collectives openly distributing the medicine via storefronts. The majority of these stores, which are organized pursuant to a California statute that permits patients to associate "collectively or cooperatively to cultivate marijuana for medical purposes," have been operating with the acceptance or even active support of city and county governments. Indeed, over three dozen cities and counties in the state have adopted ordinances to regulate the zoning and land-use permitting of medical marijuana collectives.

Perhaps because it is one of the few medical marijuana states that has allowed a distribution system to develop, California has drawn more attention from the federal government than most of the others. But, despite a dedicated and sustained effort, the federal government has been unable to impede California's medical marijuana law. Federal officials have been no more successful in stopping other states from implementing their own medical marijuana laws.

As Robert Mikos explains, the federal government's inability to block state medical marijuana laws results from a few different factors. First, the federal government's limited law enforcement resources mean that it cannot arrest and prosecute more than a small fraction of collective operators and growers, let alone patients. Thus, although federal law may make marijuana possession, cultivation, and distribution illegal for any and all purposes, that fact has little deterrent power in states with medical marijuana laws. Unless the federal government was to radically increase both the federal drug control budget as well as the percentage of the budget devoted specifically to the prosecution of medical marijuana cases in states where the drug is legal, it can do little to change this dynamic. Similarly, Mikos argues that state laws hold greater sway over social norms and personal preferences than federal laws, at least in the area of drug policy. As a result, the existence of a federal ban does little to alter people's personal beliefs about medical marijuana. Finally, the federal government is unable to resort to preemption to try to block state medical marijuana laws. This is because Congress does not have the authority to tell a state what activity to make criminal — indeed, doing so would violate the anti-commandeering principle. As a result, a state's decision to remove its own sanctions for medical marijuana-related activity cannot be preempted by the federal government.

Though the federal government has not succeeded in preventing states from legalizing marijuana for medicinal use, its effort to do so has not been entirely without effect. First, federal enforcement efforts have resulted in rifts between state and federal officials that, in at least some cases, have undermined existing drug enforcement partnerships focused on issues that all would agree are far more pressing than medical marijuana. Second, every federal enforcement dollar that has been put toward interfering with state medical marijuana laws is one less dollar available for other uses. Finally, to the extent that federal arrests and prosecutions of individuals in compliance with state medical marijuana laws has had an influence on state policy, it has been to make the laws less controlled than they might otherwise be.

[I]n light of the fact that the federal government is unable to stop state medical marijuana laws, it is difficult to view its effort to do so as anything other than a waste of law enforcement resources. Of course, some would argue that arresting and prosecuting medical marijuana patients and providers is a poor use of law enforcement resources under any circumstance. My point here, however, is different, and should hold regardless of one's personal views on the wisdom of state laws that permit the medical use of marijuana. Unless the federal government is prepared to marshal enough resources to block, or at least significantly weaken, state medical marijuana laws, it makes little sense to engage in a scattershot series of raids and prosecutions. Because medical marijuana collectives already operate openly and without fear of state prosecution in the states where they are legal, the remote possibility that they will face federal prosecution likely has at best an insignificant impact on the price of the marijuana that they dispense. Joseph Russoniello, the United States Attorney for the Northern District of California, announced in 2008 that even though he was personally opposed to medical marijuana his office would not be targeting medical marijuana providers for this very reason. "We could spend a lifetime closing dispensaries," he said, but "it would be terribly unproductive and probably not an efficient use of precious federal resources[.]"

[T]o the extent that federal interference with state medical marijuana laws has created uncertainty and risk, it has only made the state laws harder to control and easier to abuse. For example, states and localities are likely to refrain from physically inspecting collectives to make sure they are run properly, or testing medical marijuana to guard against adulterants and provide dosage and potency information, out of concern that doing so would run afoul of federal law. Since the federal government is unable to stop the implementation of state medical marijuana laws, maintaining barriers to state controls only serves to make it easier for black market profiteers and recreational users to abuse the system.

States and cities that have considered adopting government-run medical marijuana programs provide an especially illuminating example here. New Mexico, Maine, and San Francisco have all publicly discussed the idea of adopting a government-run medical marijuana cultivation and distribution model, though none of them have done so. In the case of Maine, at least, the fear that the state officials who implemented the program could be federally prosecuted and the potential loss of federal grant money was central to the decision not to adopt a state-run system. While a state-run medical marijuana program might be a tough pill for medical marijuana opponents to swallow, it would seem to be preferable to the alternative system of privately run collectives. A state-run system would be much more closely supervised and monitored than a private system. It could provide certainty that the medical marijuana used in the program was grown by state officials and was not lining the pockets of black-market producers. A state-run system would also likely be much more effective at guarding against diversion of marijuana to recreational users. Though medical marijuana opponents would surely prefer not to have medical marijuana collectives at all, in light of the federal government's inability to stop the implementation of state medical marijuana laws, that does not appear to be an option. And, if the choice is between a state-run system or a private system, a state-run system would appear to be far better from the perspective of those who favor the strictest possible control.

As a presidential candidate, Barack Obama said that he did not think it was a good use of federal resources to interfere with state medical marijuana laws, explaining: "I'm not going to be using Justice Department resources to try to circumvent state laws on this issue." Tim Dickinson, *Obama's War on Pot*, ROLLING STONE, Feb. 16, 2012. Not long after being confirmed as Obama's Attorney General, Eric Holder was asked about medical marijuana prosecutions and replied: "What the president said during the campaign, you'll be surprised to know, will be consistent with what we'll be doing in law enforcement." Rob Egelko, *U.S. to Yield Marijuana Jurisdiction to the States*, S.F. CHRON., Feb. 27, 2009. Consistent with that position, Holder announced that "[t]he policy is to go after those people who violate both federal and state law." Josh Meyer and Scott Glover, *Medical Marijuana Dispensaries Will no Longer be Prosecuted, U.S. Attorney General Says*, L.A. TIMES, March 19, 2009.

A few months after Attorney General Holder's comments to the press, Deputy Attorney General David Ogden issued a memo to all United States Attorneys that advised federal prosecutors "not [to] focus federal resources in [their] States on individuals whose actions are in clear and unambiguous compliance with existing state laws providing for the medical use of marijuana." Memorandum from David W. Ogden, Deputy Attorney Gen., to Selected U.S. Attorneys (Oct 19, 2009).

Ogden's memo was thought to be the realization of Obama's statements as a candidate that he would end federal interference with state medical marijuana laws. Indeed, it was widely reported that the memo meant an end to federal raids of medical marijuana dispensaries, so long as they were operating lawfully under relevant state law. The *New York Times* ran a front-page article about the memo under the headline "U.S. Won't Prosecute in States That Allow Medical Marijuana," reporting that "[p]eople who use marijuana for medical purposes and those who distribute it to them should not face federal prosecution, provided they act according to state law, the Justice Department said Monday in a directive with far-reaching political and legal implications." David Stout and Solomon Moore, *U.S. Won't Prosecute in States That Allow Medical Marijuana*, N.Y. TIMES, Oct. 19, 2009 at A1.

Consistent with the Ogden memo, federal raids and prosecutions of medical marijuana dispensaries slowed for a short period but did not stop. Even as the Ogden memo was released, United States Attorneys continued prosecuting medical marijuana operators, without much clarity as to whether they believed the operators were out of compliance with state law or whether they were simply choosing to exercise their discretion in how to use resources differently from what the memo counseled. One of these prosecutions took place in San Diego against James Stacy, who operated a medical marijuana collective called Movement in Action and had taken "great care to make sure that his cooperative was formed and operated in compliance with California law." Stacy became a federal defendant just ten weeks after opening his collective in the late summer of 2009. During a joint-investigation involving the DEA and the San Diego County Sheriff's Office, a local undercover agent obtained a medical marijuana recommendation under false pretenses and then purchased medicine from Movement in Action. Not surprisingly, Stacy sought to rely on the Ogden memo to block his prosecution, filing a motion to dismiss the indictment based on an entrapment by estoppel theory. Stacy argued that public statements by Attorney General Holder had led him to believe his conduct was lawful under federal law and that the Ogden memo meant he could not be prosecuted if he was operating in compliance with California law. The court held that the memo gave him no legal protection, however. "Even if Defendant's prosecution were contrary to the guidance set forth in the Memorandum," the Court explained, there is no legal basis "for dismissing an indictment because it is contrary to internal Department of Justice guidelines." *United States v. Stacy*, 696 F. Supp. 2d 1141, 1143 (2010). Because Stacy's compliance with California law and his reliance on the widely reported Obama policy would not provide him with a defense in federal court, he ultimately accepted a plea deal and was sentenced to two years of probation.

Perhaps sensing that there would be no internal repercussions for ignoring the Ogden memo, the number of federal medical marijuana raids, prosecutions, and threats of prosecution slowly began to increase throughout 2010. By the end of that year, claims that federal anti-medical marijuana efforts exclusively targeted individuals who were in violation of both state and federal law were losing credibility and began to fall by the wayside. It was becoming clear that the federal approach to medical marijuana under President Obama was not much different than it had been under President Bush. In June 2011, likely in recognition of the fact that many prosecutors had decided not to follow the Ogden memo in good faith, Deputy Attorney General James M. Cole issued a second memo. Memorandum from James M. Cole, Deputy Attorney Gen., to Selected U.S. Attorneys (June 29, 2011).

Ostensibly, the Cole memo was issued to provide "additional guidance" regarding the Ogden memo but, in reality, it directly contradicted it. Notwithstanding the Ogden memo's instruction not to "focus federal resources in your States on individuals whose actions are in clear and unambiguous compliance with existing state laws providing for the medical use of marijuana," Cole's memo advised that "[t]he Ogden Memorandum was never intended to shield" medical marijuana dispensaries "even where those activities purport to comply with state law."

By the beginning of 2012, the Obama administration had largely abandoned any pretense of taking a more deferential approach than previous administrations to state medical marijuana laws. The more than 100 raids on dispensaries during Obama's first three years in office is on pace to exceed the number under Bush. In a 2012 article overviewing the Obama administration's approach to medical marijuana, *Rolling Stone* writer Tim Dickinson argued "over the past year, the Obama administration has quietly unleashed a multi-agency crackdown on medical cannabis that goes far beyond anything undertaken by George W. Bush." Tim Dickinson, *Obama's War on Pot*, ROLLING STONE, Feb. 16, 2012.

Why didn't Ogden's memorandum have a bigger impact on federal prosecutions of medical marijuana providers?

A Critical Appraisal of the Department of Justice's New Approach to Medical Marijuana
Robert A. Mikos
22 Stanford Law and Policy Review 633 (2011)

The Obama Administration has embarked upon a much-heralded shift in federal policy toward medical marijuana. Eschewing the hard-ball tactics favored by earlier Administrations, Attorney General Eric Holder announced in October 2009 that the Department of Justice (DOJ) would stop enforcing the federal marijuana ban against persons who comply with state medical marijuana laws.

On the surface, the Non-Enforcement Policy (NEP) signals a welcome reprieve for the more than 400,000 people now using marijuana legally under state law and the thousands more who supply them. Under the Clinton and Bush II Administrations, the DOJ had campaigned vigorously against medical marijuana programs. For example, the Drug Enforcement Administration (DEA) raided hundreds of medical marijuana dispensaries and it threatened to derail the careers of physicians who recommended marijuana to their patients. Under the new Administration, it would seem, patients, physicians, and dispensaries can breathe a lot easier.

What is more, the NEP appears to cede an important policy domain to the states. Medical marijuana has been one of the most salient and contentious federalism battlegrounds of the past fifteen years. Federal officials have railed against the intransigence of the states; state officials have protested overreaching by the national government; and the Supreme Court has twice weighed in to settle jurisdictional disputes over the drug. The NEP seemingly calls a truce in this war, but its impact could extend more broadly. The states' pioneering efforts regarding medical marijuana have already fueled calls for even more ambitious drug law reforms, including proposals to legalize marijuana outright. The NEP could bolster calls for reform and accelerate the pace of change.

[T]h[is] Article suggests that early enthusiasm for the NEP is misguided; on close inspection, the NEP represents at most a very modest change in federal policy. To begin, ... the NEP won't necessarily stop federal law enforcement agents from pursuing criminal prosecutions. In a twist of irony, the non-enforcement policy itself is not enforceable. It doesn't create any legal rights a court could invoke to dismiss a criminal case. Even the DOJ will have a difficult time ensuring that federal prosecutors comply with the agency's own stated policy.

I do not mean to overstate the threat federal law poses to the medical marijuana movement. As I've argued elsewhere, the federal government lost the war against medical marijuana long before the NEP. It never had enough law enforcement resources to quash medical marijuana on its own; and it couldn't compel the states' assistance. Medical marijuana use survived and indeed thrived in the shadow of the federal ban. The question now is whether the federal government will allow the states to construct a sensible regulatory regime free of federal interference or whether it will instead wage an ongoing guerilla-style campaign against medical marijuana—one with many casualties, but with no real victory possible.

The ... NEP was formally promulgated in an October 2009 memorandum to United States Attorneys from Deputy Attorney General David Ogden. The memorandum urged federal prosecutors not to enforce the federal marijuana ban against persons who act in "clear and unambiguous compliance" with state medical marijuana laws. Ogden simultaneously affirmed the Administration's commitment to the war on drugs; the memorandum, for example, urges United States Attorneys to continue to target "significant traffickers" of illegal narcotics and "manufacturing and distribution networks." But he suggested that prosecuting medical marijuana defendants was not the most efficient use of the federal government's scarce capacity to wage that war.

The NEP doesn't create a legal defense to a CSA violation. No defendant could cite the policy as the basis for dismissing a criminal prosecution brought by the United States.

First, by its own terms, the NEP doesn't create any legally enforceable rights. Indeed, an entire paragraph of the NEP Memorandum is devoted to debunking any claim to a legal defense based on the NEP. It reads, in relevant part:

> This guidance regarding resource allocation does not "legalize" marijuana or provide a legal defense to a violation of federal law, nor is it intended to create any privileges, benefits, or rights, substantive or procedural, enforceable by any individual, party or witness in any administrative, civil, or criminal matter. Nor does clear and unambiguous compliance with state law ... create a legal defense to a violation of the Controlled Substances Act. Rather, this memorandum is intended solely as a guide to the exercise of investigative and prosecutorial discretion.

To be sure, a handful of defendants facing federal charges have sought to dismiss their prosecutions by invoking the NEP Memorandum and related statements made by Attorney General Holder and President (or candidate) Obama. But the lower federal courts have uniformly rejected NEP-based defenses, at least in part by invoking the language of the NEP itself.

Second, even assuming the NEP more plainly and forcefully sought to foreclose prosecutions—i.e., that it was less wishy-washy—there's arguably nothing that a federal court (or criminal defendant) could do to enforce it against the DOJ. In fact, one court has already ruled that the NEP would be unenforceable on separation of powers grounds, even assuming that its language had more plainly sought to bar the prosecution of the defendant at hand.

Of course, one might expect the DOJ to heed its own policy, in which case judicial enforcement of the NEP would be unnecessary. In reality, however, the DOJ is a fragmented agency, one in which several autonomous decision-makers help shape enforcement policy. The United States Attorneys (USAs) in particular have tremendous power over federal criminal law enforcement and a great deal of independence from the DOJ in Washington. As a formal matter, it is the USAs—and not the DOJ in Washington—that decide what charges (if any) to bring in criminal cases. And not all USAs necessarily support the decrees emanating from Washington.

To be sure, the DOJ wields some practical influence over charging decisions, and, in theory, it could use that influence to encourage United States Attorneys to abide by the NEP. Perhaps most importantly, USAs are nominated by the President and are thus likely to share the President's vision of federal criminal justice, including the President's views concerning the wisdom of criminally prosecuting medical marijuana cases. In any event, the President may always remove a USA who disregards DOJ policy. Indeed, as the Office of Inspector General recently explained, "U.S. Attorneys are Presidential appointees who may be dismissed for any reason or for no reason." The Attorney General can also encourage compliance, for example, by removing Assistant United States Attorneys (AUSAs) who disregard DOJ policy or by slashing the budgets of non-conforming Districts. She can even (arguably) move to vacate convictions she believes were obtained in violation of DOJ policy.

Generally speaking, these tools give the DOJ some leverage over charging decisions. For purposes of enforcing the NEP, however, they are largely unavailing, because the DOJ cannot easily monitor compliance with that policy. The NEP discourages employees from prosecuting defendants who have complied with state law, but determining whether any given defendant has actually done so proves remarkably difficult, for several reasons. First, some defendants operate in a legal vacuum. Many states have neglected to address such rudimentary issues as how patients are supposed to obtain marijuana legally and who may supply it to them. Hence, it may be an open question whether a particular defendant (say, a dispensary) is operating in compliance with state law. Second, even if an authoritative regulation exists, it could prove extremely difficult to find. State medical marijuana laws are a mash-up of referenda approved by the voters, statutes passed by state legislatures, regulations issued by state agencies, ordinances passed by local governments, and judicial interpretations of all of the above. Third, complicating matters, some state and local laws are of dubious legal status. The California Supreme Court, for example, has invalidated portions of a state statute (S.B. 420) that imposed modest restrictions on medical marijuana (e.g., limits on the quantity of marijuana patients could legally possess). Similarly, lower state courts have recently enjoined enforcement of local ordinances that restricted the number and location of medical marijuana dispensaries. Given the uncertain status of such regulations, the DOJ cannot easily discern whether the prosecution of someone who violated one of them constitutes a breach of the NEP. Fourth, even when the legal rules are clear, determining whether a given defendant has complied with them may be impractical. For example, a state might criminalize the sale of marijuana to anyone other than a qualified patient, but there may be no easy, reliable way to determine who is a qualified patient. In states like California, where patients are not required to register or even obtain a physician's recommendation in writing, judging whether a dispensary has complied with such restrictions in any given transaction could be enormously time-consuming.

These factors make it unlikely that the DOJ can accurately gauge whether any given medical marijuana prosecution brought by a United States Attorney was warranted by the NEP. Indeed, for similar reasons, the United States Attorney would find it a challenge to follow the policy in good faith. And if the DOJ is unable to gauge compliance with the NEP, it cannot credibly pressure USAs to adhere to the policy.

Moreover, even if President Obama is able to constrain USAs from pursuing medical marijuana cases during his Administration, nothing about the NEP bars the next Presidential Administration from reviving such prosecutions, *even if the charged violations took place during the Obama Administration.* As explained above, no defendant could cite the NEP to block prosecution. If, for example, President Obama is defeated by a more hawkish Republican contender in 2012, any drug offense committed during his four-year Administration could be prosecuted by the new President's USAs—the statute of limitations on federal drug charges is five-years long.

In sum, the NEP may not have much influence over criminal prosecutions brought by USAs. It is not a legally enforceable policy. No court would block a federal criminal prosecution on its account. The NEP might pressure USAs to curtail medical marijuana prosecutions. But it is too anemic to stop them altogether. Indeed, perhaps most tellingly, it appears that federal agents continue to raid medical marijuana dispensaries and prosecute medical marijuana cases, much as they did before non-enforcement became the DOJ's official policy.

In a previous article, I analyzed the preemptive reach of the CSA in some depth. Here, suffice to say that the CSA preempts state laws that positively conflict with the federal statute. Such a conflict arises only when a state engages in, requires, or otherwise aids and abets conduct that violates the CSA. Importantly, the CSA does not (and indeed, *could not*) preempt state laws that merely allow residents to cultivate, distribute, or possess marijuana.

To date, states have successfully skirted most preemption challenges by adopting a purely passive approach to regulating the supply of marijuana. At most, they merely allow private parties to grow and distribute the drug. They have not directed state officials to participate in violations of the CSA. This passive approach is not preempted because the federal government can't compel the states to criminalize the cultivation, possession, or distribution of marijuana by private citizens.

Some states, however, are proposing to assert direct control over the supply of medical marijuana. Under one type of proposal, introduced in Colorado, New Jersey, New Mexico, and Oregon, a state agency would grow and/or distribute marijuana directly to qualified patients, essentially replacing private dispensaries. Under a second proposal, introduced in Maine and Vermont, state law enforcement agents would redistribute marijuana seized from drug dealers through state-operated or -licensed dispensaries.

No state has yet created a state dispensary, but it appears the NEP has rekindled interest in such plans. Before the NEP, it appears some states were deterred from opening state dispensaries by the threat of incurring federal criminal liability. In 2007, for example, New Mexico scuttled plans for a state-run marijuana farm and dispensary, at least in part out of concerns that its employees could be criminally prosecuted by the federal government. Not surprisingly, the NEP has seemingly assuaged such concerns. In fact, in the wake of the NEP announcement, lawmakers in at least two states—Colorado and Oregon—proposed legislation to create state dispensaries and lawmakers in two more states—Hawaii and New Hampshire—commenced studies to examine the option.

Giving the state direct control—and perhaps even a monopoly—over the supply of medical marijuana has obvious advantages. The state could more easily prevent diversion of medical marijuana, and state police could more easily distinguish legal from illegal sales, if the state held exclusive license to grow and/or distribute the drug. Cash-strapped states could also generate new revenues by monopolizing the lucrative market for medical marijuana. Indeed, many states employed a similar tactic to control and profit from the sale of alcohol following the repeal of Prohibition in the 1930s. Even today, a handful of states continue to operate state liquor stores.

The problem is that state dispensaries are clearly preempted by the CSA. State agents may look askance when private citizens grow, distribute, or possess marijuana. However, they may not grow, distribute, or possess marijuana themselves; doing so creates a positive conflict with CSA. This means that federal and state courts could enjoin state agents from growing or distributing marijuana.

In short, if a state were to participate directly in supply of marijuana—by growing, distributing, redistributing, or even subsidizing purchases of the drug—its program could be challenged as preempted and enjoined.

While this preemption threat is fairly narrow—only laws that require state agents to violate the CSA are preempted by it—it could derail important measures that some states are now considering to augment their core medical marijuana exemptions. The viability of preemption lawsuits—and thus, the reforms they challenge—would be unaffected by the NEP.

In many respects, the NEP is an empty gesture. It doesn't necessarily prevent medical marijuana users or dispensaries from being criminally prosecuted, even if they comply with state law. No court would enforce the NEP and even the DOJ can't guarantee compliance.

One could say that if the goal of the NEP is to economize federal law enforcement resources, the mission has been accomplished. The NEP has probably reduced the number of medical marijuana cases brought, even if it hasn't eliminated them entirely. The gains of such a policy shift, however, hardly seem noteworthy. Medical marijuana cases probably consumed no more than a sliver of the DOJ's budget, even at the heights of enforcement. Even a more drastic cut in enforcement actions against medical marijuana seems unlikely to change the landscape of federal criminal law.

However, if the goal was to empower states to regulate medical marijuana according to local preferences—and to grant reprieve to patients and dispensaries operating pursuant to state law—the NEP falls far short. Federal law continues to impede the development of rational state medical marijuana programs. Users, suppliers, and caregivers remain vulnerable to a host of federal civil sanctions and private sanctions against which the states are currently unable to provide shelter.

I remain agnostic on the ultimate question whether this drug should be made legal. I am convinced, however, that the present system of regulation—combining a confusing and conflicting set of rules—is seriously flawed. The NEP, unfortunately, has not improved that assessment.

———————

As Robert Mikos explains, although the federal government may prosecute medical marijuana patients and caregivers under federal law, the Controlled Substances Act "does not (and indeed, *could not*) preempt state laws that merely allow residents to cultivate, distribute, or possess marijuana." This is because the federal government cannot commandeer state resources by, for example, requiring states to make the use of marijuana for medical purposes illegal. The following case sheds additional light on the relationship between the federal CSA and state medical marijuana laws.

County of San Diego v. San Diego NORML

Court of Appeal of California, Fourth Appellate District
165 Cal. App. 4th 798 (2008)

McDonald, J.

In this action, plaintiffs County of San Diego (San Diego) and County of San Bernardino (San Bernardino) contend that, because the federal Controlled Substances Act (hereafter

CSA) prohibits possessing or using marijuana for any purpose, certain provisions of California's statutory scheme [related to medical marijuana] are unconstitutional under the supremacy clause of the United States Constitution. San Diego and San Bernardino (together Counties) did not claim below, and do not assert on appeal, that the exemption from state criminal prosecution for possession or cultivation of marijuana provided by California's Compassionate Use Act of 1996 (hereafter CUA) is unconstitutional under the preemption clause. Instead, Counties argue the [Medical Marijuana Program Act, hereafter] MMP is invalid under preemption principles, arguing the MMP poses an obstacle to the congressional intent embodied in the CSA.

In California, marijuana is classified as a schedule I controlled substance and its possession is generally prohibited. However, when California voters adopted the CUA, California adopted an exemption from state law sanctions for medical users of marijuana. The CUA, codified in section 11362.5, provides [in part]: "Section 11357, relating to the possession of marijuana, and Section 11358, relating to the cultivation of marijuana, shall not apply to a patient, or to a patient's primary caregiver, who possesses or cultivates marijuana for the personal medical purposes of the patient upon the written or oral recommendation or approval of a physician."

In 2003, the Legislature enacted the MMP to "address issues not included in the CUA." Among the MMP's purposes was to "'facilitate the prompt identification of qualified patients and their designated primary caregivers in order to avoid unnecessary arrest and prosecution of these individuals and provide needed guidance to law enforcement officers.'" To that end, the MMP included provisions establishing a voluntary program for the issuance of identification cards to persons qualified to claim the exemptions provided under California's medical marijuana laws. Participation in the identification card program, although not mandatory, provides a significant benefit to its participants: they are not subject to arrest for violating California's laws relating to the possession, transportation, delivery or cultivation of marijuana, provided they meet the conditions outlined in the MMP.

Although the bulk of the provisions of the MMP confer no rights and impose no duties on counties,[2] one set of provisions under the MMP—the program for issuing identification cards to qualified patients and primary caregivers—does impose certain obligations on counties. Under the identification card program, the California Department of Health Services is required to establish and maintain a program under which qualified applicants may voluntarily apply for a California identification card identifying them as qualified for the exemptions; the program is also to provide law enforcement a 24-hour a day center to verify the validity of the state identification card. The MMP requires counties to provide applications to applicants, to receive and process the applications, verify the accuracy of the information contained on the applications, approve the applications of persons meeting the state qualifications and issue the state identification cards to qualified persons, and maintain the records of the program.

---

2. For example, the MMP's exemptions encompass a broad list of specified drug offenses from which qualified patients and primary caregivers would be immune. The MMP provides that exempt persons would not "'be subject, on that sole basis, to criminal liability under Section 11357 [possession of marijuana], 11358 [cultivation of marijuana], 11359 [possession for sale], 11360 [transportation], 11366 [maintaining a place for the sale, giving away or use of marijuana], 11366.5 [making available premises for the manufacture, storage or distribution of controlled substances], or 11570 [abatement of nuisance created by premises used for manufacture, storage or distribution of controlled substance].'" The MMP also contains definitional provisions for those entitled to the protections of the MMP, imposes obligations on applicants and holders of identification cards, and contains several other miscellaneous provisions.

The identification card program is voluntary and a person need not obtain an identification card to be entitled to the exemptions provided by state law.

The [federal Controlled Substances Act] CSA provides it is "unlawful for any person knowingly or intentionally to possess a controlled substance unless such substance was obtained directly, or pursuant to a valid prescription or order, from a practitioner, while acting in the course of his professional practice." The exception regarding a doctor's prescription or order does not apply to any controlled substance Congress has classified as a schedule I drug, including marijuana.

Possession of marijuana for personal use is a federal misdemeanor. The legislative intent of Congress to preclude the use of marijuana for medicinal purposes is reflected in the statutory scheme of the CSA: "By classifying marijuana as a Schedule I drug, as opposed to listing it on a lesser schedule, the manufacture, distribution, or possession of marijuana became a criminal offense, with the sole exception being use of the drug as part of a Food and Drug Administration preapproved research study."

Although the use of marijuana for medical purposes has found growing acceptance among the states, marijuana remains generally prohibited under the CSA.

In 2006 San Diego filed a complaint against the State of California and Sandra Shewry, in her former capacity as Director of the California Department of Health Services (together State), as well as the San Diego chapter of the National Organization for the Reform of Marijuana Laws (NORML). San Diego's complaint alleged it had declined to comply with its obligations under the MMP and NORML had threatened to file suit against San Diego for its noncompliance. Accordingly, San Diego sought a judicial declaration that it was not required to comply with the MMP, arguing the entirety of the MMP and the CUA (except for [California Health and Safety Code] § 11362.5, subd. (d))* was preempted by federal law. San Bernardino filed its suit raising the same preemption claims, and its complaint was subsequently consolidated with that of San Diego. Additional parties, composed of medical marijuana patients and others qualified for exemptions under the CUA and MMP, intervened in the action.

The parties subsequently filed cross-motions for judgment on the pleadings, which were consolidated for hearing in November 2006. The court ruled the CUA and MMP were not preempted by federal law and the MMP was not invalid under the California Constitution, and entered judgment accordingly. Counties appeal.

Principles of preemption have been articulated by numerous courts. "The supremacy clause of article VI of the United States Constitution grants Congress the power to preempt state law. State law that conflicts with a federal statute is without effect." It is equally well established that "[c]onsideration of issues arising under the Supremacy Clause 'start[s] with the assumption that the historic police powers of the States [are] not to be superseded by ... Federal Act unless that [is] the clear and manifest purpose of Congress.'" Thus, "[t]he purpose of Congress is the ultimate touchstone of pre-emption analysis."

The California Supreme court has identified "four species of federal preemption: express, conflict, obstacle, and field. First, express preemption arises when Congress 'define[s] explicitly the extent to which its enactments pre-empt state law. Pre-emption funda-

---

* Section 11362.5(d), the portion of the Compassionate Use Act quoted above, provides: "Section 11357, relating to the possession of marijuana, and Section 11358, relating to the cultivation of marijuana, shall not apply to a patient, or to a patient's primary caregiver, who possesses or cultivates marijuana for the personal medical purposes of the patient upon the written or oral recommendation or approval of a physician." [*Footnote by casebook author.*]

mentally is a question of congressional intent and when Congress has made its intent known through explicit statutory language, the courts' task is an easy one.' Second, conflict preemption will be found when simultaneous compliance with both state and federal directives is impossible. Third, obstacle preemption arises when 'under the circumstances of [a] particular case, [the challenged state law] stands as an obstacle to the accomplishment and execution of the full purposes and objectives of Congress.' Finally, field preemption, i.e., 'Congress' intent to pre-empt all state law in a particular area,' applies 'where the scheme of federal regulation is sufficiently comprehensive to make reasonable the inference that Congress left no room for supplementary state regulation.'"

The parties agree, and numerous courts have concluded, that Congress's statement in the CSA that "[n]o provision of this subchapter shall be construed as indicating an intent on the part of the Congress to occupy the field in which that provision operates, including criminal penalties, to the exclusion of any State law on the same subject matter" (21 U.S.C.§ 903) demonstrates Congress intended to reject express and field preemption of state laws concerning controlled substances. When Congress has expressly described the scope of the state laws it intended to preempt, the courts "infer Congress intended to preempt no more than that absent sound contrary evidence."

Although the parties agree that neither express nor field preemption apply in this case, they dispute whether title 21 United States Code section 903 signified a congressional intent to displace only those state laws that positively conflict with the provisions of the CSA, or also signified a congressional intent to preempt any laws posing an obstacle to the fulfillment of purposes underlying the CSA.

Conflict preemption will be found when "simultaneous compliance with both state and federal directives is impossible."

Congress has the power to permit state laws that, although posing some obstacle to congressional goals, may be adhered to without requiring a person affirmatively to violate federal laws. In *Gonzales v. Oregon*, 546 U.S. 243, the court considered whether the CSA, by regulating controlled substances and making some substances available only pursuant to a prescription by a physician "issued for a legitimate medical purpose", permitted the federal government to effectively bar Oregon's doctors from prescribing drugs pursuant to Oregon's assisted suicide law by issuing a federal administrative rule (the Directive) that use of controlled substances to assist suicide is not a legitimate medical practice and dispensing or prescribing them for this purpose is unlawful under the CSA. The majority concluded the CSA's preemption clause showed Congress "explicitly contemplates a role for the States in regulating controlled substances", including permitting the states latitude to continue their historic role of regulating medical practices. In dissent, Justice Scalia concluded title 21 United States Code section 903 was "embarrassingly inapplicable" to the majority's preemption analysis because the preemptive impact of section 903 reached only state laws that affirmatively mandated conduct violating federal laws.[10] Thus, it appears Justice Scalia's interpretation suggests a state law is preempted by a federal "positive conflict" clause only when the state law affirmatively requires acts violating the federal proscription.

---

10. Justice Scalia explained that title 21 United States Code section 903 only "affirmatively *prescrib[ed]* federal pre-emption whenever state law creates a conflict. In any event, the Directive does not purport to pre-empt state law in any way, not even by conflict pre-emption—unless the Court is under the misimpression that some States *require* assisted suicide. The Directive merely interprets the CSA to prohibit, like countless other federal criminal provisions, conduct that happens not to be forbidden under state law (or at least the law of the State of Oregon)." (*Gonzales v. Oregon, supra,* 546 U.S. at pp. 289–290 (dis. opn. of Scalia, J.).)

Obstacle preemption will invalidate a state law when "under the circumstances of [a] particular case, [the challenged state law] stands as an obstacle to the accomplishment and execution of the full purposes and objectives of Congress." Under obstacle preemption[:] "If the purpose of the [federal] act cannot otherwise be accomplished — if its operation within its chosen field else must be frustrated and its provisions be refused their natural effect — the state law must yield to the regulation of Congress within the sphere of its delegated power."

The intent of Congress when it enacted the CSA is the touchstone of our preemption analysis. When Congress legislates in a "field which the States have traditionally occupied[,] … we start with the assumption that the historic police powers of the States were not to be superseded by the Federal Act unless that was the clear and manifest purpose of Congress." Because the MMP and CUA address fields historically occupied by the states — medical practices and state criminal sanctions for drug possession — the presumption against preemption informs our resolution of the scope to which Congress intended the CSA to supplant state laws, and cautions us to narrowly interpret the scope of Congress's intended invalidation of state law.

The language of 21 United States Code section 903 expressly limits preemption to only those state laws in which there "is a *positive conflict* between [the federal and state law] *so that the two cannot consistently stand together.*" When construing a statute, the courts seek to attribute significance to every word and phrase in accordance with their usual and ordinary meaning. The phrase "positive conflict," particularly as refined by the phrase that "the two [laws] cannot consistently stand together," suggests that Congress did not intend to supplant all laws posing some conceivable obstacle to the purposes of the CSA, but instead intended to supplant only state laws that could not be adhered to without violating the CSA. Because 21 United States Code section 903 preserves state laws except where there exists such a *positive* conflict that the two laws *cannot* consistently stand together, the *implied* conflict analysis of obstacle preemption appears beyond the intended scope of 21 United States Code section 903.

Counties argue this construction is too narrow, and we should construe Congress's use of the term "conflict" in 21 United States Code section 903 as signifying an intent to incorporate both positive and implied conflict principles into the scope of state laws preempted by the CSA. Certainly, the United States Supreme Court has concluded that federal legislation containing an express preemption clause and a savings clause does not necessarily preclude application of implied preemption principles. However, none of Counties' cited cases examined preemption clauses containing the "positive conflict" language included in 21 United States Code section 903, and thus provide little guidance here. Indeed, Counties' proffered construction effectively reads the term "positive" out of section 903, which transgresses the interpretative canon that we should accord meaning to every term and phrase employed by Congress. Moreover, when Congress has intended to craft an express preemption clause signifying that *both* positive and obstacle conflict preemption will invalidate state laws, Congress has so structured the express preemption clause. Where statutes involving similar issues contain language demonstrating the Legislature knows how to express its intent, "the omission of such provision from a similar statute concerning a related subject is significant to show that a different legislative intent existed with reference to the different statutes."

Because Congress provided that the CSA preempted only laws positively conflicting with the CSA so that the two sets of laws could not consistently stand together, and omitted any reference to an intent to preempt laws posing an obstacle to the CSA, we interpret 21 United States Code section 903 as preempting only those state laws that positively conflict with the CSA so that simultaneous compliance with both sets of laws is impossible.

Counties do not identify any provision of the CSA necessarily violated when a county complies with its obligations under the state identification laws.[13] The identification laws obligate a county only to process applications for, maintain records of, and issue cards to, those individuals entitled to claim the exemption. The CSA is entirely silent on the ability of states to provide identification cards to their citizenry, and an entity that issues identification cards does not engage in conduct banned by the CSA.

Counties appear to argue there is a positive conflict between the identification laws and the CSA because the card issued by a county confirms that its bearer may violate or is immunized from federal laws. However, the applications for the card expressly state the card will not insulate the bearer from federal laws, and the card itself does not imply the holder is immune from prosecution for federal offenses; instead, the card merely identifies those persons California has elected to exempt from California's sanctions. (Cf. *U.S. v. Cannabis Cultivators Club* (N.D.Cal. 1998) 5 F.Supp.2d 1086, 1100 [California's CUA "does not conflict with federal law because on its face it does not purport to make legal any conduct prohibited by federal law; it merely exempts certain conduct by certain persons from the California drug laws"].) Because the CSA law does not compel the states to impose criminal penalties for marijuana possession, the requirement that counties issue cards identifying those against whom California has opted not to impose criminal penalties does not positively conflict with the CSA.

Accordingly, we reject Counties' claim that positive conflict preemption invalidates the identification laws because Counties' compliance with those laws can "consistently stand together" with adherence to the provisions of the CSA.

Although we conclude 21 United States Code section 903 signifies Congress's intent to maintain the power of states to elect "to 'serve as a laboratory' in the trial of 'novel social and economic experiments without risk to the rest of the country'" by preserving all state laws that do not positively conflict with the CSA, we also conclude the identification laws are not preempted even if Congress had intended to preempt laws posing an obstacle to the CSA. Although state laws may be preempted under obstacle preemption when the law "stands as an obstacle to the accomplishment and execution of the full purposes and objectives of Congress" not every state law posing some de minimus impediment will be preempted. To the contrary, "[d]isplacement will occur only where, as we have variously described, a '*significant conflict*' exists between an identifiable 'federal policy or interest and the [operation] of state law,' or the application of state law would 'frustrate specific objectives.'"

We conclude the identification card laws do not pose a significant impediment to specific federal objectives embodied in the CSA. The purpose of the CSA is to combat recreational drug use, not to regulate a state's medical practices. (*Gonzales v. Oregon*, 546 U.S. 270–272 [holding Oregon's assisted suicide law fell outside the preemptive reach of the CSA].) The identification card laws merely provide a mechanism allowing qualified California citizens, if they so elect, to obtain a form of identification that informs state law enforcement officers and others that they are medically exempted from the state's criminal sanctions for marijuana possession and use.

---

13. San Bernardino concedes on appeal that compliance with California law "may not require a violation of the CSA," although it then asserts it "encourages if not facilitates the CSA's violation." However, the *Garden Grove* court has already concluded, and we agree, that governmental entities do not incur aider and abettor liability by complying with their obligations under the MMP (*City of Garden Grove v. Superior Court*, 157 Cal. App. 4th at 389–392), and we therefore reject San Bernardino's implicit argument that requiring a county to issue identification cards renders that county an aider and abettor to create a positive conflict with the CSA.

Counties also appear to assert the identification card laws present a significant obstacle to the CSA because the bearer of an identification card will not be arrested by California's law enforcement officers despite being in violation of the CSA. However, the unstated predicate of this argument is that the federal government is entitled to conscript a state's law enforcement officers into enforcing federal enactments, over the objection of that state, and this entitlement will be obstructed to the extent the identification card precludes California's law enforcement officers from arresting medical marijuana users. The argument falters on its own predicate because Congress does not have the authority to compel the states to direct their law enforcement personnel to enforce federal laws. In *Printz v. United States* (1997) 521 U.S. 898, the federal Brady Act purported to compel local law enforcement officials to conduct background checks on prospective handgun purchasers. The United States Supreme Court held the 10th Amendment to the United States Constitution deprived Congress of the authority to enact that legislation, concluding that "Congress cannot compel the States to enact or enforce a federal regulatory program. Today we hold that Congress cannot circumvent that prohibition by conscripting the State's officers directly. The Federal Government may neither issue directives requiring the States to address particular problems, nor command the States' officers, or those of their political subdivisions, to administer or enforce a federal regulatory program." Accordingly, we conclude the fact that California has decided to exempt the bearer of an identification card from arrest by state law enforcement for state law violations does not invalidate the identification laws under obstacle preemption. (Cf. *Conant v. Walters,* 309 F.3d at 646 (conc. opn. of Kozinski, J.) ["That patients may be more likely to violate federal law if the additional deterrent of state liability is removed may worry the federal government, but the proper response — according to *New York* and *Printz* — is to ratchet up the federal regulatory regime, *not* to commandeer that of the state."].)

We conclude that even if Congress intended to preempt state laws that present a significant obstacle to the CSA, the MMP identification card laws are not preempted.

Though state laws that permit their residents to possess, cultivate, or distribute marijuana for medical use are not preempted by the CSA, state laws that go further may be. For example, as Robert Mikos discusses above, a law that sought to establish a state-run medical marijuana dispensary would be preempted by the CSA because it would require state employees to engage in conduct that the CSA prohibits, thereby creating a positive conflict with federal law. State laws that grant medical marijuana users rights against sanctions by private actors — such as laws barring housing or employment discrimination against medical marijuana users — present a closer question. *See* Robert A. Mikos, *On the Limits of Supremacy: Medical Marijuana and the States' Overlooked Power to Legalize Federal Crime*, 62 VAND. L. REV. 1421 1456–57 (2009) (arguing that laws in this category may be preempted to the extent they would aid and abet violations of federal law and concluding that the answer would likely depend on the particulars of the law at issue). The Supreme Court of Oregon recently held that federal law preempted aspects of its state medical marijuana law in the context of an employment discrimination claim, though the Court indicated that Oregon might be able to shield medical marijuana patients from employment discrimination under a revised law. *See, Emerald Steel Fabricators, Inc. v. Bureau of Labor and Industries,* 348 Ore. 159, 172 n.12 (2010) (holding that the CSA preempted the portion of Oregon's medical marijuana law that protected medical marijuana users from employment discrimination but noting that the Court "express[ed] no opinion on whether the legislature, if it chose to do so and worded Oregon's disability law differently, could require employers to reasonably accommodate disabled employees who use medical marijuana to treat their disability").

Federalism concerns have also been at issue in cases where patients sought the return of medical marijuana improperly seized by state law enforcement officials. In *Oregon v. Kama*, police officers seized a small amount of marijuana from Kama who was then charged with possession of a controlled substance. 178 Ore. App. 561 (2002). The State dismissed the charges because Kama was a qualified medical marijuana patient under Oregon Law. Kama then filed a return of property motion for the marijuana that had been seized. The government argued that returning the marijuana to Kama would require them to commit a federal crime, namely distribution of a controlled substance. The Court ordered the return of the marijuana to Kama, finding that the Controlled Substances Act's immunity provision applied to the return of medical marijuana required by state law. The Court explained:

> The federal Controlled Substances Act confers immunity on all state and federal law enforcement officers engaged in the enforcement of the Act or of any state or municipal law relating to controlled substances: "No civil or criminal liability shall be imposed by virtue of this subchapter upon ... any duly authorized officer of any State ... who shall be lawfully engaged in the enforcement of any law or municipal ordinance relating to controlled substances." 21 USC § 885(d). Thus, for example, the statute confers immunity on law enforcement personnel engaged in undercover drug operations.

> In this case, there is no debate that defendant is entitled to possession of the marijuana under [Oregon law.] Even assuming that returning the marijuana otherwise might constitute delivery of a controlled substance, the city does not explain—and we do not understand—why police officers would not be immune from any federal criminal liability that otherwise might arise from doing so.

The City of Oakland, California attempted to use the federal immunity statute cited in *Kama* to shield private medical marijuana providers from federal prosecution. Oakland deputized Edward Rosenthal for purposes of cultivating and distributing medical marijuana to the Oakland Cannabis Buyers' Cooperative. Rosenthal was later prosecuted by the federal government and convicted of violating provisions of the federal Controlled Substances Act. Rosenthal argued that, having been deputized by the City of Oakland, he was immunized by Section 885(d). The United States Court of Appeals for the Ninth Circuit disagreed, finding that "cultivating marijuana for medical use does not constitute 'enforcement' within the meaning of § 885(d)." *United States v. Rosenthal*, 454 F.3d 943 (9th Cir. 2006). The Court compared Rosenthal's circumstances to those in *Kama*, explaining that "[i]n that case, the state law *mandated* the return of marijuana to the individual from whom the marijuana had been seized, and therefore the officers in question were 'enforcing' the state law that *required* them to deliver the marijuana to that individual because he had a state-law right to its return." (emphasis in original). *See also, City of Garden Grove v. Superior Court*, 157 Cal. App. 4th 355, 368–69 (2007) (discussing *Kama* and *Rosenthal* and ordering the City to return marijuana that it had seized from a medical marijuana patient).

Chapter 8

The Regulation of Substances That Are Legal for Recreational Use

As the court in *NORML v. Bell, supra* discussed, Congress has exempted alcohol and tobacco from regulation under the Controlled Substances Act. 21 U.S.C. 812(6) ("The term 'controlled substance'... does not include distilled spirits, wine, malt beverages, or tobacco[.]"). This does not mean the substances are unregulated, of course. Far from it, alcohol and tobacco are both subject to a wide variety of federal, state and local laws. A study of alcohol or tobacco law could easily occupy its own course. Indeed, there is a casebook devoted to just one subset of alcohol control—wine law. *See*, RICHARD MENDELSON, WINE IN AMERICA: LAW AND POLICY (2011). Even caffeine, while not as strictly controlled as alcohol or tobacco, is also regulated by a fairly robust set of laws.

Though the particulars of how alcohol, tobacco, and caffeine are controlled vary significantly, one fact sets them apart from nearly every other drug: it is legal to buy and sell them for recreational use. Because this book is focused on the law governing substances whose recreational use is prohibited, a detailed account of alcohol, tobacco, and caffeine regulation falls outside of its scope. A basic understanding of how alcohol, tobacco, and caffeine are controlled, however, is useful to the study of controlled substances law. As you read the material that follows, consider whether you believe permitting the recreational use of alcohol, tobacco and caffeine while criminalizing the recreational use of other drugs is justified.

A. Alcohol

Federalism, Positive Law, and the Emergence of the American Administrative State: Prohibition in the Taft Court Era
Robert Post
48 William and Mary Law Review 1 (2006)

If one were forced to identify the single issue that most dominated political attention and debate during the 1920s, prohibition would certainly be a strong candidate. It was "the largest political issue ... since the Civil War." In his 1922 State of the Union Address, President Harding was moved to complain "that many voters are disposed to make all political decisions with reference to this single question. It is distracting the public mind and prejudicing the judgment of the electorate." In contrast to the enforcement of state and local prohibition laws that predated prohibition, federal efforts to enforce the Eighteenth Amendment were so conspicuously ineffectual that widespread violation of prohibition became, in Harding's words, a "nation-wide scandal" that was "the most demoralizing factor in our public life."

"Conspicuous and flagrant violations" of prohibition provoked a vigorous discussion about the extent to which federal law could be used "to effect a radical change in the personal habits of a large part of the population, under the compulsion of the combined executive and judicial branches of the government of the United States." Prohibition provoked this debate because the Eighteenth Amendment was a truly astonishing and disorienting social innovation. Contemporaries of all political stripes recognized the Eighteenth Amendment as "the most radical political and social experiment of our day," and prohibition as "one of the most extensive and sweeping efforts to change the social habits of an entire nation recorded in history."

The radical reach of prohibition was made possible by the "frenzy" of World War I. The ratification of the Eighteenth Amendment was "attributed in large measure to the influence of the war," and prohibition was seen as "an outgrowth of the reforming and religious enthusiasm engendered during the war." Throughout the 1920s prohibition stood as the avatar of the anomalous desire of Americans during World War I to endow the federal government with comprehensive police powers. Although in the immediate aftermath of the war the nation scrambled frantically to return to "normalcy" by dismantling the extensive emergency authorities that had been allocated to the national government, prohibition endured because it had been constitutionally entrenched. In the Republican and conservative environment of the 1920s, prohibition was a striking reminder of the excesses of the war; it was "something out of the normal."

The "abnormal" circumstances of prohibition's ratification set it athwart the ordinary lines that divided liberals from conservatives. The roots of prohibition lay in evangelical protestant moralism, so much so that Richard Hofstadter could dismiss it as "a pseudo-reform" produced by a "rural-evangelical virus" capable of transmuting "the reforming energies of the country ... into mere peevishness." But prohibition, at least as it matured in the second decade of the twentieth century, was also "one of the reforms of the Progressive Movement." Prohibition expressed "middle-class" aspirations to use "government action to protect or advance the public interest." It was advocated to promote health, workplace effectiveness, "war efficiency," crime reduction, the Americanization of new immigrants, and the control of southern blacks.

The anomalous political status of prohibition was rooted in its unique capacity to serve as a "bridge between the old and the new, between those who wanted to reform individuals and those who wanted to reform society." Conservatives supported prohibition because of its pietistic moralism, its hostility to large unruly urban populations, its nativism, and its commitment to authoritarian social control. Progressives supported prohibition because of its association with moral uplift, its affirmation of efficiency, and its use of social engineering to achieve social mastery.

For both conservatives and progressives, however, prohibition came at a price. For conservatives the price was commitment to a social reform that unabashedly sought to use state compulsion to improve society. Prohibition was in many ways the apotheosis of the administrative state, for it deployed a vast governmental apparatus to control intimate details of personal consumption. Even if this control were acceptable when exercised at the local level by individual states, the Eighteenth Amendment located responsibility in the national government, which was required to issue uniform regulations preempting all local variation. Conservatives could support prohibition only by advocating "an experiment in federal centralization, which, if successful, would radically alter the customary and the appropriate distribution of responsibility for social welfare between Washington and the state capitals."

For progressives the price was more subtle. Progressives had long aspired to endow the federal government with the democratic legitimacy necessary to sustain the kind of extensive social regulation required by prohibition. But progressives in the 1920s were highly ambivalent about prohibition, because the Eighteenth Amendment was a legal cataclysm of such unimaginable proportions that it undermined basic progressive assumptions about the desirability of the national administrative state. As the New Republic reported, "[n]ational prohibition" had been ratified "on the supposition that the American people would on the whole support its enforcement," but "this calculation ... prove[d] to be entirely false."

It was almost immediately evident that prohibition could succeed only if it were sustained by the kind of focused national coercive power that risked making the federal government "feared, disliked and suspected by many millions of American citizens." To the extent that enforcing prohibition "brought [the national government] into suspicion, disrepute and even contempt," it contradicted "[t]he first condition of a progressive revival," which was "the restoration of the federal government in the esteem, the loyalty and the obedience of the American people." Prohibition thus provoked progressives to rethink the normative foundations of American federalism. It forced liberals to consider whether certain forms of "social behavior" should "in any well balanced federal system ... be treated at least partly as a matter of local rather than of national responsibility."

Prohibition also required progressives to question the proper boundaries of the administrative state. The "volume, the stubbornness and the unscrupulousness of the existing resistance to the law" by millions of citizens who were "in other respects law-abiding," and who included "all the business, artistic, professional, labor and political leaders of the larger cities," raised for progressives the "totally new question" of whether law could "exterminate a habit of popular conduct to which people are so stubbornly attached." To the extent that progressivism aspired to express "the collective conscience of the community in its effort to make for more and better human life," prohibition required progressives to think anew about the relationship between traditional values and positive law.

The New Republic, for example, concluded that government "must expect to have its authority flouted" when "it forbids its citizens to perform innocent and inoffensive acts of private conduct." This dependence of legal legitimacy on the brute facts of popular custom carried with it the startling idea that progressives may previously have "over-emphasized the importance of government as the instrument of human amelioration," because the "moral authority of the government does not rest on its legal right to issue commands." Prohibition exposed the many ways in which legal legitimacy was dependent upon custom, even as progressives sought to use positive law to reform traditional mores.

Prohibition put enormous strain on the ideals of federalism to which the country was committed in the years before World War I. Most constitutional grants of federal power simply authorize the national government to regulate in a particular domain, such as interstate commerce. But the Eighteenth Amendment was different because, like the Thirteenth Amendment, it imposed a particular rule of conduct that forbade "the manufacture, sale, or transportation of intoxicating liquors ... for beverage purposes." The Volstead Act, passed on October 28, 1919, over Woodrow Wilson's veto, used a strict 0.5 percent alcohol content standard to define "intoxicating liquors." With the passage of the Act, the federal government suddenly found itself responsible for suppressing all trade and manufacture of liquor in the United States, a task for which it was utterly unprepared.

Over the opposition of the Secretary of the Treasury and the Commissioner of Internal Revenue, Congress specified in the Volstead Act that prohibition be enforced by the Bureau of Internal Revenue. But compliance with the draconian provisions of the Volstead Act could be ensured only by "an army of enforcement agents far larger than it would be practicable to assemble or obtain an appropriation for." The Commissioner therefore promptly announced that the Bureau could fulfill its responsibility only by securing "the closest cooperation between the Federal officers and all other law-enforcing officers—State, county, and municipal."

The striking fact about prohibition was that this cooperation was not forthcoming, even though virtually every state eventually passed its own version of a prohibition statute. By 1923 President Harding was complaining that although "the Federal government is not equipped with the instrumentalities to make enforcement locally effective" because "it does not maintain either a police or a judicial establishment adequate or designed for such a task[.]"

Without the active and willing assistance of state police, the only option for federal prohibition enforcement would be, as Taft had pointed out in 1915, a "horde of Federal officials" who would constitute "a direct blow at local self-government and at the integrity of our Federal system, which depended on preserving the control by the States of parochial and local matters."

Whether for this or for some other reason, Congress throughout the 1920s refused to fund federal prohibition enforcement at anything close to the levels that would have been required to ensure full compliance with the law. National prohibition enforcement was understaffed, with agents who were underpaid and unprofessional. The federal judicial system was completely unprepared to deal with the huge influx of cases generated by prohibition. H.L. Mencken famously quipped that "[p]erhaps the chief victims of Prohibition, in the long run, will turn out to be the Federal judges," whose "typical job today, as a majority of the plain people see it, especially in the big cities, is simply to punish men who have refused or been unable to pay the bribes demanded by Prohibition enforcement officers." The massive numbers of prohibition prosecutions forced federal courts "to perform the function of petty police courts."

It is no wonder that Coolidge sought to solve the problem of prohibition enforcement by arguing that the Eighteenth Amendment "puts a concurrent duty on the States. We need their active and energetic cooperation, the vigilant action of their police, and the jurisdiction of their courts to assist in enforcement." Coolidge appealed to the enigmatic second section of the Eighteenth Amendment, which provided that "[t]he Congress and the several States shall have concurrent power to enforce this article by appropriate legislation." Section 2 of the Eighteenth Amendment raised a deep question about the constitutional structure of American federalism, for it forced contemporaries to theorize the relationship between independent state sovereignty and the affirmative constitutional requirement of prohibition.

The idea that states were obligated independently to enforce the Eighteenth Amendment would seem to imply that states were constitutionally required to enact statutes prohibiting the sale and transportation of liquor. But in 1923 New York repealed its antiliquor statute, the Mullan-Gage law. In discussing his decision not to veto the repeal, Governor Smith ... asserted that he was "entirely unwilling to admit the contention that there was put upon the State, either by the Eighteenth Amendment [or] the Volstead act ... any obligation to pass any law adopting into the State law the provisions of the Volstead act." The Eighteenth Amendment was "not a command but an option. It does not create a duty"; any other conclusion, Smith contended, would be inconsistent with "the supremacy of the Federal Government in its own sphere and the sovereignty of the several States in theirs," which is "one of the great elements in the strength of our democracy."

The Prohibition Hangover:
Why We Are Still Feeling the Effects of Prohibition
Marcia Yablon

13 Virginia Journal of Social Policy and the Law 552 (2006)

Over time, the purpose behind the ratification and then repeal of National Prohibition has been forgotten by the majority of Americans. Currently, Prohibition is most often referred to as a "failed experiment" or a "strange aberration" in our country's history. However, although Prohibition was the culmination of the temperance movement's goals, the temperance movement itself was nothing new. This movement had been an important and accepted part of American society since the early Nineteenth Century. Consequently, in 1933, when the Twenty-First Amendment was passed, it was not at all clear that the Amendment's ratification signified the end of the temperance movement. The temperance movement had faced other, nearly as great, setbacks before, and the Twenty-First Amendment was seen only as the end of National Prohibition, not necessarily, or even likely, the end of the temperance movement. As Historian Norman Clark explained, "repeal was by no means the very end; it was not a social fluke or a moral retrogression." Instead, after repeal, there was an enduring struggle for many people "to define how much or how little liquor control was consistent with the circumstances of life in the second half of the twentieth century."

Although National Prohibition ended with the ratification of the Twenty-First Amendment, state and local Prohibition was expected to, and did, continue long after its passage. Similarly, liquor regulation did not conclude with the repeal of the Eighteenth Amendment. Instead, after repeal the country returned to a system of liquor regulation very similar to the system in place immediately before Prohibition. "Although the new system of state alcohol regulation was more uniform in practice and more efficient in enforcement, it nevertheless resembled the basic forms of liquor control practiced at the turn of the century...."

[T]o Americans living in the pre-Prohibition era..., alcohol was seen as a serious threat to the family precisely because it was so often consumed away from the family. Saloons were places that men went by themselves, separate from their wives and children. In the Nineteenth Century, women were exceedingly unwelcome in saloons. At this time, a woman's place was in the home, but many men felt most at home in the neighborhood saloon. "The saloon thereby served to effectively divorce husbands from wives" and "posed a serious threat to ... family values."

This separation caused great anxiety in a society which placed extreme importance on the home and the family. There was a widespread belief that "alcohol could disintegrate social and family loyalties and that this disintegration would be followed by poverty and crime and a frightful depth of conjugal squalor." These fears were especially felt by women, who were expected to protect the home and family, and as a result, women became the driving force behind the push towards Prohibition. "Women were culturally positioned to feel such threats most keenly. The ideals of domesticity already encouraged women to act as moral guardians for their families and to tutor their children in the duties of virtuous citizenship." Nineteenth Century women "had identified drunkenness as an affront

to middle-class survival, a threat to the health and harmony of families, and a peril awaiting every boy as he grew to manhood."

The perceived threat to the family posed by the saloon was further enhanced by the tremendous wave of immigrants from drinking cultures, particularly Irish immigrants, who
came to America during this period. Irish families were structured differently than most
middle class American families who found this difference extremely disconcerting. These
Irish families lived "lives that did not conform to the middle-class model of the family."
For example, unlike American women, Irish women "had a long tradition of working
outside the home," and therefore they did not fit the "ideology of women's separate spheres
and delicate natures." In addition, Irish children frequently worked, and they often earned
nearly half their family's income. The common employment of women and children in
Irish families contradicted the Nineteenth Century "ideology of domesticity."

The temperance movement, with its strong nativist undertones was simply another
way of alleviating the perceived threat posed by these "deviant" immigrant families. "In
the culture of the Irish ... use of whisky or beer was customary and often a stable part of
the diet." The Irish immigrants' acceptance of alcohol was considered one of the main
reasons for their poverty, and it was their excessive poverty that made it necessary for
Irish women and children to work and therefore violate Victorian family values. In addition, unemployed Irish men helped fuel the increasingly worrisome male drinking culture that was separating men from their families.

One of the main goals of temperance movement was to reverse this trend towards family separation. The temperance movement hoped to revitalize the family, and temperance advocates believed that temperance would help "to support and protect the family,
and to return the husband ... to the home."

The temperance advocates' fear of the saloon and its impact on the family was not unfounded. The saloon was a threat to more than just the idealized vision of the family. The
perception that the saloon destroyed families was based on reality. "The nineteenth-
century drunkard's reputation as a wife beater, child abuser, and sodden, irresponsible non-
provider was not undeserved." "Temperance workers ... who were well aware of the social
problems that stemmed from alcohol and drunkenness and their aim was broader than
simply regulating moral behavior." They were "fighting against the rape and battering of
victims of all ages, against deprivation of needed food, drink, clothing, not to mention
respect, kindness, health, independence." The push for Prohibition was in part recognition of the seriousness of these dangers as well as an acknowledgement that earlier legislative measures had been inadequate to deal with the problem.

State legislative attempts to deal with the threat to the family posed by intemperate
husbands in terms of both physical and financial harm can be seen in statutes such as
New York's "Dram Shop Act," which "gave to every person injured in person, property, or
means of support by any intoxicated person or in consequence of the intoxication of any
person a right of action against any person who by selling intoxicating liquors has caused
the intoxication in whole or in part." In other states, Dram Shop statutes were even more
explicit in their concern for families of drunken men. For example, the Alabama Dram
Shop Act specifically delineated this right first and foremost as the right of a drunkard's
"wife," "child" or "parent." The purpose of dram shop laws was to give the family of the
injured drunkard or the family injured by the drunkard a right of action against the saloon keeper who got him drunk. Although such legislation strained the legal definition
of proximate cause, the danger that male drinking posed to families was seen as overriding such concerns.

Interestingly, although most temperance advocates spoke out against the evils of alcohol, they did not actually view the primary threat to the family as one caused by alcohol per se. Instead, they believed the disintegration of the family was caused the culture of the saloon, which was at least as big a draw as was the actual alcohol being served. The urban working-class saloon was "the poor man's club." It offered men a welcome escape from the harsh realities of their everyday lives. These men had "no access to the well-appointed hotel bars and exclusive clubs that offered recreation to the salaried and professional men." "For men who worked in sweaty often dangerous jobs and lived in crowed, stuffy tenements, the saloon beckoned as a warm, well-lit, pleasant refuge for relaxation and masculine companionships."

The unique threat posed by the saloon, as distinct from alcohol alone, is demonstrated by the relative unconcern with which other types of drinking establishments were viewed in the pre-Prohibition period. Although not as numerous, there were exceptions to the masculine saloon such as ethnic bars, clubs and beer gardens that invited families. These drinking establishments, though by far in the minority, never had the worrisome connotations of the saloon because they were places that encouraged family activity and togetherness.

The perceived difference in the threat between family friendly alcohol establishments and male dominated saloons did not end with repeal. The continued recognition of this distinction can be seen in post-Prohibition legislation such as The Michigan Beer Bill, passed immediately after the Repeal of Prohibition, which prohibited bars, but permitted the operation of establishments such as beer gardens. Such legislation demonstrates that even after repeal there was a continuing desire to eliminate the drinking culture of the saloon. At the same time, it also shows that this concern did not extend to drinking establishments like beer gardens, which have traditionally been family oriented. The Michigan Beer Bill was passed only to prevent the return of the saloon; it specifically allowed the return of other types of drinking establishments.

The Michigan Beer Bill was not unique. Similar legislation was passed by numerous other states after the repeal of Prohibition and in many instances such statutes remained good law until it was quite certain that the old time saloon could never return. For instance, post-repeal legislation in Texas prohibited "open saloons," until 1971. It was only then "that 'liquor by the drink,' was legalized finally by constitutional amendment."

Today, alcohol regulation is governed by a complex set of interrelated federal, state, and local laws. The unusual relationship between federal and state laws in this area has been driven in part by the Twenty First Amendment which, in addition to repealing alcohol prohibition, vests states with special regulatory authority over alcohol. Specifically, Section 2 of the Amendment provides that "[t]he transportation or importation into any State, Territory, or possession of the United States for delivery or use therein of intoxicating liquors, in violation of the laws thereof, is hereby prohibited." This provision of the Twenty First Amendment has resulted in some particularly tricky legal questions in relation to the so-called "dormant" Commerce Clause, which restricts states from passing laws that burden or discriminate against interstate commerce. The Supreme Court most recently addressed the relationship between the Twenty First Amendment and the dormant Commerce Clause in *Granholm v. Heald*, presented below. Before turning to *Granholm*, however, it is helpful to have a sense of the general contours of modern alcohol regulation.

Although the Twenty First Amendment leaves alcohol control largely in the hands of the states, the federal government also plays an important role in alcohol regulation. Two years after the repeal of prohibition, Congress passed the Federal Alcohol Administration Act in 1935 (FAA Act). 27 U.S.C. § 201, *et seq.* Among other things, the FAA Act regulates the labeling and marketing of alcohol and provides for the licensing of alcohol producers, wholesalers, and importers. The FAA Act is administered by the Alcohol and Tobacco Tax and Trade Bureau (TTB), which is housed within the U.S. Treasury Department, though the TTB often consults with other agencies that have expertise in relevant areas. *See, e.g.,* Elaine T. Byszewski, *What's in the Wine? A History of the FDA's Role*, 57 FOOD DRUG L. J. 545 (2002) (discussing the Food and Drug Administration's role in the regulation of alcohol).

While federal law is involved in regulating the production, importation and exportation of alcohol, states and localities retain exclusive jurisdiction over retail sales. After the repeal of national prohibition, a number of states continued to follow a policy of statewide prohibition and many more enacted local option laws that allow counties or cities to ban the sale of alcohol at the local level. The last state to ban the sale of alcohol entirely was Mississippi, which remained dry until 1966. Marcia Yablon, *The Prohibition Hangover: Why We Are Still Feeling the Effects of Prohibition*, 13 VA. J. SOC. POL'Y & L. 552, 595 (2006). However, many states have retained local option laws and about half of all states currently have at least one dry county or municipality. *See,* RICHARD MENDELSON, WINE IN AMERICA: LAW AND POLICY 34–39 (2011) (providing an overview of dry municipalities in the United States).

States typically follow a three-tier alcohol licensing structure that separates manufacturers, wholesalers, and retailers from one another. Under this system, for example, a company that holds an alcohol wholesale license cannot also manufacture alcohol or sell it at the retail level. Many states have adopted limited exceptions, however, that allow for "brewpubs" and wineries to both produce and sell alcohol directly to consumers. *See,* Andrew Tamayo, Comment, *What's Brewing in the Old North State: An Analysis of the Beer Distribution Laws Regulating North Carolina's Craft Breweries*, 88 N.C.L. Rev. 2198, 2205 (2010) (discussing the laws regulating brewpubs and reporting that thirty-four states currently allow for brewpubs). A number of other states let alcohol manufacturers ship their product directly to consumers, at least in certain circumstances. Most states do not participate directly in the market and instead license private businesses at each of the three tiers. But in 18 so-called "control states," the state itself acts as an alcohol wholesaler and/or retailer, often with a monopoly over the function it engages in.

Granholm v. Heald

Supreme Court of the United States
544 U.S. 460 (2005)

Justice Kennedy delivered the opinion of the Court.

Like many other States, Michigan and New York regulate the sale and importation of alcoholic beverages, including wine, through a three-tier distribution system. Separate licenses are required for producers, wholesalers, and retailers. The three-tier scheme is preserved by a complex set of overlapping state and federal regulations. For example, both state and federal laws limit vertical integration between tiers. We have held previously that States can mandate a three-tier distribution scheme in the exercise of their authority under the Twenty-first Amendment. As relevant to today's cases, though, the three-tier system is, in broad terms and with refinements to be discussed, mandated by Michigan and New York only for sales from out-of-state wineries. In-state wineries, by contrast, can obtain a license for direct sales to consumers. The differential treatment between in-state and out-of-state wineries constitutes explicit discrimination against interstate commerce.

This discrimination substantially limits the direct sale of wine to consumers, an otherwise emerging and significant business. From 1994 to 1999, consumer spending on direct wine shipments doubled, reaching $500 million per year, or three percent of all wine sales. The expansion has been influenced by several related trends. First, the number of small wineries in the United States has significantly increased. By some estimates there are over 3,000 wineries in the country, more than three times the number 30 years ago. At the same time, the wholesale market has consolidated. Between 1984 and 2002, the number of licensed wholesalers dropped from 1,600 to 600. The increasing winery-to-wholesaler ratio means that many small wineries do not produce enough wine or have sufficient consumer demand for their wine to make it economical for wholesalers to carry their products. This has led many small wineries to rely on direct shipping to reach new markets. Technological improvements, in particular the ability of wineries to sell wine over the Internet, have helped make direct shipments an attractive sales channel.

Approximately 26 States allow some direct shipping of wine, with various restrictions. Thirteen of these States have reciprocity laws, which allow direct shipment from wineries outside the State, provided the State of origin affords similar nondiscriminatory treatment. In many parts of the country, however, state laws that prohibit or severely restrict direct shipments deprive consumers of access to the direct market. According to the Federal Trade Commission (FTC), "[s]tate bans on interstate direct shipping represent the single largest regulatory barrier to expanded e-commerce in wine."

The wine producers in the cases before us are small wineries that rely on direct consumer sales as an important part of their businesses. Domaine Alfred, one of the plaintiffs in the Michigan suit, is a small winery located in San Luis Obispo, California. It produces 3,000 cases of wine per year. Domaine Alfred has received requests for its wine from Michigan consumers but cannot fill the orders because of the State's direct-shipment ban. Even if the winery could find a Michigan wholesaler to distribute its wine, the wholesaler's markup would render shipment through the three-tier system economically infeasible.

Most alcoholic beverages in Michigan are distributed through the State's three-tier system. Producers or distillers of alcoholic beverages, whether located in state or out of state, generally may sell only to licensed in-state wholesalers. Wholesalers, in turn, may sell only to in-state retailers. Licensed retailers are the final link in the chain, selling alcoholic beverages to consumers at retail locations and, subject to certain restrictions, through home delivery.

Under Michigan law, wine producers, as a general matter, must distribute their wine through wholesalers. There is, however, an exception for Michigan's approximately 40 in-state wineries, which are eligible for "wine maker" licenses that allow direct shipment to in-state consumers. The cost of the license varies with the size of the winery. For a small winery, the license is $25. Out-of-state wineries can apply for a $300 "outside seller of wine" license, but this license only allows them to sell to in-state wholesalers.

Some Michigan residents brought suit against various state officials in the United States District Court for the Eastern District of Michigan. Domaine Alfred, the San Luis Obispo winery, joined in the suit. The plaintiffs contended that Michigan's direct-shipment laws discriminated against interstate commerce in violation of the Commerce Clause. The trade association Michigan Beer & Wine Wholesalers intervened as a defendant. Both the State and the wholesalers argued that the ban on direct shipment from out-of-state wineries is a valid exercise of Michigan's power under § 2 of the Twenty-first Amendment.

Time and again this Court has held that, in all but the narrowest circumstances, state laws violate the Commerce Clause if they mandate "differential treatment of in-state and out-of-state economic interests that benefits the former and burdens the latter." This rule is essential to the foundations of the Union. The mere fact of nonresidence should not foreclose a producer in one State from access to markets in other States. States may not enact laws that burden out-of-state producers or shippers simply to give a competitive advantage to in-state businesses. This mandate "reflect[s] a central concern of the Framers that was an immediate reason for calling the Constitutional Convention: the conviction that in order to succeed, the new Union would have to avoid the tendencies toward economic Balkanization that had plagued relations among the Colonies and later among the States under the Articles of Confederation."

Laws of the type at issue in the instant cases contradict these principles. They deprive citizens of their right to have access to the markets of other States on equal terms. The perceived necessity for reciprocal sale privileges risks generating the trade rivalries and animosities, the alliances and exclusivity, that the Constitution and, in particular, the Commerce Clause were designed to avoid.

The discriminatory character of the Michigan system is obvious. Michigan allows in-state wineries to ship directly to consumers, subject only to a licensing requirement. Out-of-state wineries, whether licensed or not, face a complete ban on direct shipment. The differential treatment requires all out-of-state wine, but not all in-state wine, to pass through an in-state wholesaler and retailer before reaching consumers. These two extra layers of overhead increase the cost of out-of-state wines to Michigan consumers. The cost differential, and in some cases the inability to secure a wholesaler for small shipments, can effectively bar small wineries from the Michigan market.

State laws that discriminate against interstate commerce face "a virtually *per se* rule of invalidity." The Michigan and New York laws by their own terms violate this proscription. The two States, however, contend their statutes are saved by § 2 of the Twenty-first Amendment, which provides:

"The transportation or importation into any State, Territory, or possession of the United States for delivery or use therein of intoxicating liquors, in violation of the laws thereof, is hereby prohibited."

The States' position is inconsistent with our precedents and with the Twenty-first Amendment's history. Section 2 does not allow States to regulate the direct shipment of wine on terms that discriminate in favor of in-state producers.

Before 1919, the temperance movement fought to curb the sale of alcoholic beverages one State at a time. The movement made progress, and many States passed laws restricting or prohibiting the sale of alcohol. This Court upheld state laws banning the production and sale of alcoholic beverages, but was less solicitous of laws aimed at imports. In a series of cases before ratification of the Eighteenth Amendment the Court, relying on the Commerce Clause, invalidated a number of state liquor regulations.

These cases advanced two distinct principles. First, the Court held that the Commerce Clause prevented States from discriminating against imported liquor. *Walling v. Michigan,* 116 U.S. 446 (1886). In *Walling,* for example, the Court invalidated a Michigan tax that discriminated against liquor imports by exempting sales of local products.

Second, the Court held that the Commerce Clause prevented States from passing facially neutral laws that placed an impermissible burden on interstate commerce. *Bowman v. Chicago & Northwestern R. Co.,* 125 U.S. 465 (1888). For example, in *Bowman,* the

Court struck down an Iowa statute that required all liquor importers to have a permit. *Bowman* and its progeny rested in part on the since-rejected original-package doctrine. Under this doctrine goods shipped in interstate commerce were immune from state regulation while in their original package. As the Court explained in *Vance*:

> "The power to ship merchandise from one State into another carries with it, as an incident, the right in the receiver of the goods to sell them in the original packages, any state regulation to the contrary notwithstanding; that is to say, that the goods received by Interstate Commerce remain under the shelter of the Interstate Commerce clause of the Constitution, until by a sale in the original package they have been commingled with the general mass of property in the State."

Bowman reserved the question whether a State could ban the sale of imported liquor altogether. Iowa responded to *Bowman* by doing just that but was thwarted once again. In *Leisy,* the Court held that Iowa could not ban the sale of imported liquor in its original package.

Leisy left the States in a bind. They could ban the production of domestic liquor, but these laws were ineffective because out-of-state liquor was immune from any state regulation as long as it remained in its original package. To resolve the matter, Congress passed the Wilson Act (so named for Senator Wilson of Iowa), which empowered the States to regulate imported liquor on the same terms as domestic liquor[.]

By its own terms, the Wilson Act did not allow States to discriminate against out-of-state liquor; rather, it allowed States to regulate imported liquor only "to the same extent and in the same manner" as domestic liquor.

Although the Wilson Act increased the States' authority to police liquor imports, it did not solve all their problems. In *Vance* and *Rhodes* ... the Court made clear that the Wilson Act did not authorize States to prohibit direct shipments for personal use.

[In *Vance*, the Court held] that consumers had the right to receive alcoholic beverages shipped in interstate commerce for personal use[.] The Court expanded on this point ... in *Rhodes. Rhodes* construed the Wilson Act narrowly to avoid interference with this right. The Act, the Court said, authorized States to regulate only the resale of imported liquor, not direct shipment to consumers for personal use. Without a clear indication from Congress that it intended to allow States to ban such shipments, the *Rhodes* Court read the words "upon arrival" in the Wilson Act as authorizing "the power of the State to attach to an interstate commerce shipment," only after its arrival at the point of destination and delivery there to the consignee. The right to regulate did not attach until the liquor was in the hands of the customer. As a result, the mail-order liquor trade continued to thrive.

After considering a series of bills in response to the Court's reading of the Wilson Act, Congress responded to the direct-shipment loophole in 1913 by enacting the Webb-Kenyon Act, 27 U.S.C. § 122. The Act, entitled "An Act Divesting intoxicating liquors of their interstate character in certain cases," provides:

> "That the shipment or transportation ... of any spirituous, vinous, malted, fermented, or other intoxicating liquor of any kind, from one State ... into any other State ... which said spirituous, vinous, malted, fermented, or other intoxicating liquor is intended, by any person interested therein, to be received, possessed, sold, or in any manner used, either in the original package or otherwise, in violation of any law of such State ... is hereby prohibited."

The constitutionality of the Webb-Kenyon Act itself was in doubt. *Vance* and *Rhodes* implied that any law authorizing the States to regulate direct shipments for personal use would be an unlawful delegation of Congress' Commerce Clause powers. Indeed, President Taft, acting on the advice of Attorney General Wickersham, vetoed the Act for this specific reason. Congress overrode the veto and in *Clark Distilling Co. v. Western Maryland R. Co.*, 242 U.S. 311 (1917), a divided Court upheld the Webb-Kenyon Act against a constitutional challenge.

The Court construed the Act to close the direct-shipment gap left open by the Wilson Act. States were now empowered to forbid shipments of alcohol to consumers for personal use, provided that the States treated in-state and out-of-state liquor on the same terms. The Court understood that the Webb-Kenyon Act "was enacted simply to extend that which was done by the Wilson Act." The Act's purpose "was to prevent the immunity characteristic of interstate commerce from being used to permit the receipt of liquor through such commerce in States contrary to their laws, and thus in effect afford a means by subterfuge and indirection to set such laws at naught." The Court thus recognized that the Act was an attempt to eliminate the regulatory advantage, *i.e.*, its immunity characteristic, afforded imported liquor under *Bowman* and *Rhodes*.

The ratification of the Eighteenth Amendment in 1919 provided a brief respite from the legal battles over the validity of state liquor regulations. With the ratification of the Twenty-first Amendment 14 years later, however, nationwide Prohibition came to an end. Section 1 of the Twenty-first Amendment repealed the Eighteenth Amendment. Section 2 of the Twenty-first Amendment is at issue here.

Michigan and New York say the provision grants to the States the authority to discriminate against out-of-state goods. The history we have recited does not support this position. To the contrary, it provides strong support for the view that § 2 restored to the States the powers they had under the Wilson and Webb-Kenyon Acts. "The wording of § 2 of the Twenty-first Amendment closely follows the Webb-Kenyon and Wilson Acts, expressing the framers' clear intention of constitutionalizing the Commerce Clause framework established under those statutes."

The aim of the Twenty-first Amendment was to allow States to maintain an effective and uniform system for controlling liquor by regulating its transportation, importation, and use. The Amendment did not give States the authority to pass nonuniform laws in order to discriminate against out-of-state goods, a privilege they had not enjoyed at any earlier time.

Some of the cases decided soon after ratification of the Twenty-first Amendment did not take account of this history and were inconsistent with this view. In *State Bd. of Equalization of Cal. v. Young's Market Co.*, 299 U.S. 59 (1936), for example, the Court rejected the argument that the Amendment did not authorize discrimination:

> "The plaintiffs ask us to limit this broad command [of § 2]. They request us to construe the Amendment as saying, in effect: The State may prohibit the importation of intoxicating liquors provided it prohibits the manufacture and sale within its borders; but if it permits such manufacture and sale, it must let imported liquors compete with the domestic on equal terms. To say that, would involve not a construction of the Amendment, but a rewriting of it."

The Court reaffirmed the States' broad powers under § 2 in a series of cases and unsurprisingly many States used the authority bestowed on them by the Court to expand trade barriers.

It is unclear whether the broad language in *Young's Market* was necessary to the result because the Court also stated that "the case [did] not present a question of discrimination prohibited by the commerce clause." The Court also declined, contrary to the approach we take today, to consider the history underlying the Twenty-first Amendment. This reluctance did not, however, reflect a consensus that such evidence was irrelevant or that prior history was unsupportive of the principle that the Amendment did not authorize discrimination against out-of-state liquors. There was ample opinion to the contrary.

Our more recent cases, furthermore, confirm that the Twenty-first Amendment does not supersede other provisions of the Constitution and, in particular, does not displace the rule that States may not give a discriminatory preference to their own producers.

The modern § 2 cases fall into three categories.

First, the Court has held that state laws that violate other provisions of the Constitution are not saved by the Twenty-first Amendment. The Court has applied this rule in the context of the First Amendment, the Establishment Clause, the Equal Protection Clause, the Due Process Clause, and the Import-Export Clause.

Second, the Court has held that § 2 does not abrogate Congress' Commerce Clause powers with regard to liquor. The argument that "the Twenty-first Amendment has somehow operated to 'repeal' the Commerce Clause" for alcoholic beverages has been rejected.

Finally, and most relevant to the issue at hand, the Court has held that state regulation of alcohol is limited by the nondiscrimination principle of the Commerce Clause. "When a state statute directly regulates or discriminates against interstate commerce, or when its effect is to favor in-state economic interests over out-of-state interests, we have generally struck down the statute without further inquiry."

Bacchus provides a particularly telling example of this proposition. At issue was an excise tax enacted by Hawaii that exempted certain alcoholic beverages produced in that State. The Court rejected the argument that Hawaii's discrimination against out-of-state liquor was authorized by the Twenty-first Amendment. "The central purpose of the [Amendment] was not to empower States to favor local liquor industries by erecting barriers to competition." Despite attempts to distinguish it in the instant cases, *Bacchus* forecloses any contention that § 2 of the Twenty-first Amendment immunizes discriminatory direct-shipment laws from Commerce Clause scrutiny.

Recognizing that *Bacchus* is fatal to their position, the States suggest it should be overruled or limited to its facts. As the foregoing analysis makes clear, we decline their invitation.

The States argue that any decision invalidating their direct-shipment laws would call into question the constitutionality of the three-tier system. This does not follow from our holding. "The Twenty-first Amendment grants the States virtually complete control over whether to permit importation or sale of liquor and how to structure the liquor distribution system." A State which chooses to ban the sale and consumption of alcohol altogether could bar its importation; and, as our history shows, it would have to do so to make its laws effective. States may also assume direct control of liquor distribution through state-run outlets or funnel sales through the three-tier system. We have previously recognized that the three-tier system itself is "unquestionably legitimate." State policies are protected under the Twenty-first Amendment when they treat liquor produced out of state the same as its domestic equivalent. The instant cases, in contrast, involve straightforward attempts to discriminate in favor of local producers. The discrimination is contrary to the Commerce Clause and is not saved by the Twenty-first Amendment.

States have broad power to regulate liquor under § 2 of the Twenty-first Amendment. This power, however, does not allow States to ban, or severely limit, the direct shipment of out-of-state wine while simultaneously authorizing direct shipment by in-state producers. If a State chooses to allow direct shipment of wine, it must do so on evenhanded terms. Without demonstrating the need for discrimination, New York and Michigan have enacted regulations that disadvantage out-of-state wine producers. Under our Commerce Clause jurisprudence, these regulations cannot stand.

Justice Stevens, with whom Justice O'Connor joins, dissenting.

The New York and Michigan laws challenged in these cases would be patently invalid under well-settled dormant Commerce Clause principles if they regulated sales of an ordinary article of commerce rather than wine. But ever since the adoption of the Eighteenth Amendment and the Twenty-first Amendment, our Constitution has placed commerce in alcoholic beverages in a special category. Section 2 of the Twenty-first Amendment expressly provides that "[t]he transportation or importation into any State, Territory, or possession of the United States for delivery or use therein of intoxicating liquors, in violation of the laws thereof, is hereby prohibited."

Today many Americans, particularly those members of the younger generations who make policy decisions, regard alcohol as an ordinary article of commerce, subject to substantially the same market and legal controls as other consumer products. That was definitely not the view of the generations that made policy in 1919 when the Eighteenth Amendment was ratified or in 1933 when it was repealed by the Twenty-first Amendment.[1] On the contrary, the moral condemnation of the use of alcohol as a beverage represented not merely the convictions of our religious leaders, but the views of a sufficiently large majority of the population to warrant the rare exercise of the power to amend the Constitution on two occasions. The Eighteenth Amendment entirely prohibited commerce in "intoxicating liquors" for beverage purposes throughout the United States and the territories subject to its jurisdiction. While § 1 of the Twenty-first Amendment repealed the nationwide prohibition, § 2 gave the States the option to maintain equally comprehensive prohibitions in their respective jurisdictions.

The views of judges who lived through the debates that led to the ratification of those Amendments are entitled to special deference. Foremost among them was Justice Brandeis, whose understanding of a State's right to discriminate in its regulation of out-of-state alcohol could not have been clearer:

> "The plaintiffs ask us to limit [§ 2's] broad command. They request us to construe the Amendment as saying, in effect: The State may prohibit the importation of intoxicating liquors provided it prohibits the manufacture and sale within its borders; but if it permits such manufacture and sale, it must let imported liquors compete with the domestic on equal terms. To say that, would involve not a construction of the Amendment, but a rewriting of it.... Can it be doubted that a State might establish a state monopoly of the manufacture and sale of beer, and either prohibit all competing importations, or discourage importation by laying a heavy impost, or channelize desired importations by confining them to

---

1. In the words of Justice Jackson: "The people of the United States knew that liquor is a lawlessness unto itself. They determined that it should be governed by a specific and particular Constitutional provision. They did not leave it to the courts to devise special distortions of the general rules as to interstate commerce to curb liquor's 'tendency to get out of legal bounds.' It was their unsatisfactory experience with that method that resulted in giving liquor an exclusive place in constitutional law as a commodity whose transportation is governed by a special, constitutional provision." *Duckworth v. Arkansas,* 314 U.S. 390, 398–399 (1941) (opinion concurring in result).

a single consignee?"[2] *State Bd. of Equalization of Cal. v. Young's Market Co.,* 299 U.S. 59, 62–63 (1936).

In the years following the ratification of the Twenty-first Amendment, States adopted manifold laws regulating commerce in alcohol, and many of these laws were discriminatory. So-called "dry states" entirely prohibited such commerce; others prohibited the sale of alcohol on Sundays; others permitted the sale of beer and wine but not hard liquor; most created either state monopolies or distribution systems that gave discriminatory preferences to local retailers and distributors. The notion that discriminatory state laws violated the unwritten prohibition against balkanizing the American economy — while persuasive in contemporary times when alcohol is viewed as an ordinary article of commerce — would have seemed strange indeed to the millions of Americans who condemned the use of the "demon rum" in the 1920s and 1930s. Indeed, they expressly authorized the "balkanization" that today's decision condemns. Today's decision may represent sound economic policy and may be consistent with the policy choices of the contemporaries of Adam Smith who drafted our original Constitution; it is not, however, consistent with the policy choices made by those who amended our Constitution in 1919 and 1933.

My understanding (and recollection) of the historical context reinforces my conviction that the text of § 2 should be "broadly and colloquially interpreted." Indeed, the fact that the Twenty-first Amendment was the only Amendment in our history to have been ratified by the people in state conventions, rather than by state legislatures, provides further reason to give its terms their ordinary meaning. Because the New York and Michigan laws regulate the "transportation or importation" of "intoxicating liquors" for "delivery or use therein," they are exempt from dormant Commerce Clause scrutiny.

[Justice Thomas filed a dissenting opinion, joined by the Chief Justice and Justices Stevens and O'Connor, in which he argued that the Webb-Kenyon Act and Twenty-First Amendment "displaced the negative Commerce Clause as applied to regulation of liquor imports into a State."]

B. Tobacco

Smoking Out the Impact of Tobacco-Related Decisions on Public Health Law
Micah L. Berman
75 Brooklyn Law Review 1 (2009)

Tobacco is a product — and public health problem — unlike any other. No other legal consumable product is nearly as addictive or as deadly as the cigarette, which kills approximately 440,000 Americans every year. Moreover, tobacco products have exerted an unparalleled influence over American society and culture. As Allan Brandt wrote in *The Cigarette Century*, cigarettes have "deeply penetrated American culture," leaving "few, if any, central aspects of American society that are truly smoke-free." These and other char-

---

2. According to Justice Black, who participated in the passage of the Twenty-first Amendment in the Senate, § 2 was intended to return "'absolute control' of liquor traffic to the States, free of all restrictions which the Commerce Clause might before that time have imposed." *Hostetter v. Idlewild Bon Voyage Liquor Corp.,* 377 U.S. 324, 338 (1964) (dissenting opinion).

acteristics make tobacco use a highly unusual public health issue, and therefore courts have often distorted precedents and shaped their decisions to accommodate the unique exigencies of tobacco-related cases. In turn, these decisions have significantly reshaped public health law doctrine, affecting a wide variety of health-related concerns outside the tobacco context.

Although many people assume that cigarettes have been popular for centuries, it was not until the early Twentieth Century that the cigarette rolling machine was invented, allowing tobacco companies to mass produce and mass market cigarettes. Cigarettes soon became hugely popular, helped in part by the distribution of free cigarettes to U.S. soldiers in World War II. By the early 1950s, when the first credible reports of the link between smoking and cancer were published in medical journals, "nearly one out of two Americans could be counted as a regular smoker."

The rapid growth of the industry was impressive, but it was the industry's response to revelations of the cigarette's dangers that set its history on a unique course. Instead of removing the product from the market or providing explicit warnings to consumers, the tobacco companies chose a third option—a cover-up. With the help of a public relations firm, Hill & Knowlton, the industry began its fifty-year campaign to deceive the public about the health effects of smoking.

Although manufacturers of other products have delayed reporting known dangers of their products, the scope and duration of the tobacco industry's campaign of deception stands alone. The success of this fraudulent campaign had substantial legal implications, as the tobacco companies were able to successfully argue in court for decades that cigarettes did not cause cancer (or, in each specific case, that cigarettes had not caused the plaintiff's cancer). By the time that defense was no longer tenable, the tobacco companies were able to pivot—amazingly, without conceding the connection between smoking and disease—to the defense that the plaintiff's own decision to smoke (in light of the "common knowledge" that smoking causes disease) should absolve the companies of any responsibility.

The tobacco companies, however, were not able to fully escape legal liability. Most notably, the tobacco companies signed the Master Settlement Agreement (MSA) in 1998, committing themselves to paying more than $200 billion to state governments. Although the MSA (and the avalanche of document disclosures that both preceded and followed the agreement) wounded the tobacco industry's reputation, it permitted the industry to continue operating and it provided a measure of immunity from state-initiated lawsuits. It also provided some amount of protection from private lawsuits, as the industry was later able to argue in court that the MSA had forced it to fully account for its past misdeeds and reform its conduct.

Looking at this history as a whole, the continued existence of tobacco in the marketplace can be seen as a historical accident. As Thomas Merrill has written, "If cigarettes were introduced today, knowing what we know about them as a product, there is little doubt that they would be banned." (This is in contrast to other public health concerns such as firearms and alcohol, where the risk/benefit trade-off has been more or less apparent for centuries.) However, because the cigarette became so deeply engrained in American society before its dangers were acknowledged—and because roughly 45 million Americans remain addicted to cigarettes—prohibition is not seen as an attractive or realistic policy option. Thus, tobacco remains a legal product, but one that poses unique challenges for the courts and public health regulators because of its entrenchment in society and the massive number of people addicted to this highly dangerous product.

Smoking Abroad and Smokeless at Home:
Holding the Tobacco Industry Accountable in a New Era
Karen C. Sokol

13 New York University Journal of Legislation and Public Policy 81 (2010)

Over four decades ago, the U.S. Surgeon General issued a landmark report stating that cigarette smoking causes cancer and other deadly diseases and "substantially contributes … to the overall death rate" in this country.

In the 1964 Report, the Surgeon General announced the U.S. Public Health Service's determination that "cigarette smoking is a health hazard of sufficient importance in the United States to warrant appropriate remedial action" by the federal government.

Shortly after the issuance of the 1964 Report on cigarette smoking and health, the Federal Trade Commission (FTC) responded to the Surgeon General's call for remedial action by promulgating a rule that would have required cigarette manufacturers to disclose that "cigarette smoking is dangerous to health and may cause death from cancer and other diseases" in all cigarette advertising and on all cigarette packaging. To market cigarettes without such a disclosure, the FTC determined, would be "an unfair or deceptive act or practice" in violation of the Federal Trade Commission Act.

However, tobacco companies responded quickly and convinced Congress to suspend the FTC's rule and to instead enact legislation that required health warnings only on product packaging. This law—the Federal Cigarette Labeling and Advertising Act of 1965 (FCLAA)—weakened the required warning statement by mandating only a statement that "cigarette smoking may be hazardous to your health" and required no reference to the risk of death from smoking-related diseases. Furthermore, the 1965 FCLAA provided that companies could not be required to include any statements "relating to smoking and health" on product packaging other than that required by the Act and could not be required to include any warnings in cigarette advertising until the Act's preemption provision regarding the regulation of cigarette advertising terminated in four years.

Since 1965, the federal government has subjected tobacco companies to greater—but still quite limited—marketing regulation. In 1969, Congress amended the FCLAA to strengthen the warning requirements for cigarette packaging, reinstate the FTC's authority to issue the rule requiring disclosure of the health risks of smoking in cigarette advertising, and ban broadcast advertising of cigarettes. The FTC issued what was in effect the equivalent of the advertising rule the following year in an order based on the agency's determination that the six major U.S. tobacco companies had systematically represented in their cigarette advertisements that smoking is "desirable" without making "clear and conspicuous disclosures that cigarette smoking is dangerous to health." Such representations were, the agency concluded, deceptive acts and unfair practices in violation of the Federal Trade Commission Act because the companies thereby intentionally misled the public regarding the dangers of smoking. In this decision, the FTC required that the companies include in their advertising the new warning statement required on cigarette packaging under the recent amendment to the FCLAA. A decade later, Congress codified the FTC's order by again amending the FCLAA to extend the health-warning requirements to cigarette advertising. Congress also amended the Act's warning provisions, requiring rotation of the four now familiar, more specific warning statements (such as "SURGEON GENERAL'S WARNING: Smoking Causes Lung Cancer, Heart Diseases, Emphysema, and May Complicate Pregnancy").

While tobacco companies have thus been subject to some marketing regulation since the 1960s, their manufacturing processes historically have been almost entirely unregulated. Unlike most consumer product industries whose manufacturing processes are governed by regulatory regimes such as that established by the Consumer Product Safety Act, tobacco companies have not been required to adhere to any standards in manufacturing their products. In fact, tobacco products and guns are the only products exempted from the Consumer Product Safety Act that are not subject to manufacturing regulation by other, product-specific statutes. The FCLAA and the Smokeless Tobacco Act required merely that tobacco companies submit "a list of the ingredients added to tobacco in the manufacture of" their products to the Department of Health and Human Services (HHS). The HHS had no authority to require anything further of tobacco companies based on the ingredient lists; indeed, the companies submitted the lists anonymously and without identifying the particular product brand containing the ingredients. In short, tobacco companies have essentially been permitted to manufacture their products entirely behind closed doors.

Notwithstanding the increasing prevalence of information about the health threats presented by smoking, cigarette sales continually rose for about two decades after the 1964 Report, and cigarette smoking became — and remains — the leading cause of preventable death and disease in the United States. In the late 1980s and early 1990s, the reasons for this increase in cigarette use were finally laid bare.

In light of these developments in public knowledge about the nature of tobacco products and of the industry that designed and marketed them, many governmental officials recognized the urgent need for much greater regulation of the tobacco industry, regulation beyond the traditional information provision approach. Shortly after Representative Waxman's 1994 hearings on tobacco products, the FDA issued a proposed rule regulating all tobacco products as drug delivery devices. In light of the industry's knowledge and practices relating to nicotine, the FDA determined that tobacco products fell within the statutory definition that triggered its regulatory authority: "Based on the evidence now before the agency, cigarettes and smokeless tobacco products are drug delivery systems whose purpose is to deliver nicotine to the body in a manner in which it can be most readily absorbed by the consumer." The FDA rule subjected the industry to much greater marketing regulation than mere information provision. Specifically, the rule aimed to prevent tobacco companies from marketing to children and adolescents by, inter alia, prohibiting the giving out of free samples of tobacco products, promotion of tobacco product brands on non-tobacco items (such as clothing and accessories), brand name sponsorship of sport and musical events, and by restricting advertising to black text on white background in publications with significant underage readership.

The potential borne by the FDA's rule for curbing the tobacco epidemic was unfortunately never realized: the industry mounted a successful judicial challenge to the regulation, derailing the federal government's attempt to begin providing public health protections that would meaningfully respond to the industry's strategy. In 2000, the U.S. Supreme Court held in *FDA v. Brown & Williamson Tobacco Corp.* that Congress had not given the FDA authority to regulate tobacco, and therefore struck down the FDA's rule. As a result, the Supreme Court's decision required that Congress enact specific legislation authorizing the FDA to regulate tobacco before the FDA could take action. The Court therefore put the tobacco regulatory ball back into Congress's court, where the industry has continued to wield tremendous influence.

Over the course of the last few decades..., state and localities did succeed in implementing some significant tobacco-control measures that went beyond the provision of information about the health dangers of smoking. Initially, documents produced in litigation brought against the industry in state court by private plaintiffs and state attorneys general brought to light much of the companies' longstanding misconduct. In the wake of the resulting widespread awareness of the nature of the industry's practices, indoor smoking bans have swept across the country, despite strong industry opposition. These bans—extending to offices, restaurants, and even quintessential "smoking" environments such as bars and casinos—would not have been possible without the dramatic reversal that has occurred in societal perceptions about the acceptability of smoking and the nature of the industry, a reversal undoubtedly driven in large part by the revelations of the industry's systematic public deception uncovered in the state lawsuits. These bans have, in turn, further increased the stigma associated with smoking.

The state litigation against the tobacco industry has further aided the battle against smoking by diminishing the industry's ability to maintain its strategy vis-a-vis cigarette sales. The Master Settlement Agreement (MSA) that concluded the litigation restricts the industry's ability to market to children and adolescents. Because the MSA is between the major cigarette manufacturers and forty-six states, the District of Columbia, and five other U.S. jurisdictions, the agreement created a nearly nationwide set of restrictions on the industry's marketing toward children, including, for example, the banning of cartoons and of advertising on billboards. For example, thirty-eight state attorneys general recently invoked the youth-marketing restrictions of the MSA in launching an investigation into Reynolds American's marketing of cigarettes in a large array of flavors such as "Twista Lime" and "Mocha Taboo." In response, the company reached an agreement with the states under which it is obligated "to stop identifying cigarettes with candy, fruit, desserts or alcoholic beverage names, imagery or ads."

This confluence of increased public awareness of the industry's deceptive business strategies as a result of the state litigation, of marketing restrictions imposed by the MSA, and of the numerous indoor smoking bans across the nation, appears to have been bad for cigarette business in the United States. In 2005, cigarette sales dropped to a fifty-five-year low, the culmination of a sharp decline that began in the late 1990s. In fact, by that year, cigarette sales had fallen by more than twenty-one percent since the execution of the MSA in 1998. In the FTC's most recent report on cigarette sales and the major companies' advertising and promotion expenditures, the agency found "that the total number of cigarettes sold or given away decreased by 4.2 billion cigarettes (1.1 percent) from 2003 to 2004, and then by 8.8 billion (2.4 percent) from 2004 to 2005."

On June 22, 2009, President Obama signed into law the Family Smoking Prevention and Tobacco Control Act (TCA).

Like the 1996 FDA rule that was struck down by the Supreme Court in *Brown & Williamson*, the TCA is based on the two major developments in knowledge that are relevant to tobacco control policy in this country, and yet did not inform the previous tobacco regulatory regime: knowledge of the highly addictive nature of nicotine and of the industry's misconduct in manufacturing and marketing its products. However, the TCA is different from the FDA rule in two key respects. First, the Act amends the Federal Food, Drug, and Cosmetic Act (FDCA) by providing the FDA with sui generis authority to regulate tobacco products, including any marketing of the "modified risk" variety of tobacco products. Tobacco products are not regulated as "drugs" or "devices" under the FDCA as they were in the 1996 rule; rather, Congress has created a new regulatory regime specifically designed for tobacco products by adding a new subchapter to the FDCA that is devoted to tobacco products. Second, the TCA is much more comprehensive than the 1996 rule. Like the FDA rule, prohibitions of marketing to the young are a principal part of the TCA. But the Act also provides for much needed further marketing regulation, such as establishing controls on modified risk marketing and granting the FDA broad authority to regulate the sale and distribution of tobacco products.

Regarding modified risk marketing—industry claims that a given product presents less health risks than other tobacco products—the TCA defines the parameters of the tobacco harm reduction issue much more broadly than does the industry. The Act requires companies to obtain permission from the FDA before marketing any product as "modified risk." In evaluating a company's "modified risk" marketing application, the FDA must consider not only whether the individual user will benefit from using the product, but also whether use of the product "benefits the health of the population as a whole." This public health analysis includes the likelihood that current tobacco users will use the modified risk product rather than quit tobacco use, the likelihood that non-users will start using the product, and the risks and benefits of using the product in comparison to using a product approved for the purpose of treating nicotine dependence. The TCA specifies that such modified risk marketing can include not only claims made in product labeling and advertising, but also any other "action" taken by tobacco product manufacturers "directed to consumers through the media or otherwise ... respecting the product that would be reasonably expected to result in consumers believing that the tobacco product ... may present a lower risk of disease or is less harmful than one or more commercially marketed tobacco products."

In addition to subjecting the industry to this increased marketing regulation, the Act for the first time in the country's history provides for governmental oversight of tobacco product manufacturing. Notably, the Act requires the non-anonymous submission of ingredient lists by manufacturers. More specifically, they must submit a list of the ingredients in, and the nicotine content of, each tobacco product brand and must inform the agency of any changes in the additive content of a product.

The TCA provides the FDA with other important means of overseeing the tobacco industry's manufacturing practices, including: (1) the authority to inspect manufacturing facilities; (2) the authority to require manufacturers to submit "any or all documents (including underlying scientific information) relating to research activities, and research findings, conducted, supported, or possessed by the manufacturer ... on the health, toxicological, behavioral, or physiologic effects of tobacco products and their constituents..., ingredients, components, and additives;" and (3) a pre-market review process under which manufacturers must apply to the FDA for permission to market a new tobacco product by submitting extensive information on the proposed product and demonstrating its compliance with any applicable product standards. The Act grants the FDA broad authority to respond to the information it gathers from the manufacturers, facility inspections, and elsewhere by establishing standards for both manufacturing processes and the composition of the final product that the agency determines to be necessary to protect the health of "the population as a whole."

C. Caffeine

The Consumable Vice: Caffeine, Public Health, and the Law
James G. Hodge, Jr., Megan Scanlon, Alicia Corbett and Andrew Sorensen
27 Journal of Contemporary Health Law and Policy 76 (2010)

Among Americans' many consumable vices (e.g., illicit drugs, tobacco, alcohol, sugars, salt, high fat foods), caffeine represents a unique and popular ingredient that infiltrates multiple product lines, directly impacts individual and communal health (especially among children and adolescents), and yet enjoys relatively little regulation. Caffeine is pervasive in our beverages, foods, and medicines. Americans may find it difficult, even impossible, to completely eliminate caffeine from their diets. Caffeine is a natural ingredient in coffees, chocolates, and teas. It is intentionally added to products ranging from sodas, sports drinks, "high-performance" dietary supplements, alcoholic beverages, headache medicines, and even drinking water. Routine, extensive ingestion of "America's favorite drug" reflects our societal acquiescence in addiction. A "caffeine high" is an innocent pleasure that millions undertake one or more times each day to stimulate their minds and bodies to perform at peak levels. Caffeine provides a daily, inexpensive boost of energy that makes life better for many Americans, regardless of their social class, ethnicity, or status.

Caffeine, it seems, is the perfect drug. It is widely-available, cheap, and fast-acting. For many adult users, its ingestion presents relatively few short- or long-term health effects. Research studies have shown that moderate levels of caffeine can improve intellectual and athletic performance and help treat or prevent some physical and mental health conditions. Caffeine may even boost one's personal confidence and self-esteem. However, the collective impact of caffeine on public health is notable. When taken in multiple doses or in extreme amounts over prolonged periods, caffeine use contributes directly to multiple physical and mental health conditions, especially among children and adolescents. Early addiction to caffeine can be a precursor to experimentation and use of more serious, illicit drugs. Caffeine may be tied to the national obesity epidemic because (1) its use leads people to intake more calories and (2) many high-calorie foods and drinks include it to stimulate individuals to consistently consume them. Widespread caffeine use may also negatively affect national productivity as employees' constant drive for caffeine to quell caffeine "headaches" contributes to lost hours of work and potentially reduces on-the-job performance.

Perhaps the potential downsides of extensive caffeine use seem relatively minor for a substance that is otherwise harmless and may even be beneficial for millions of consumers. It is hard to vilify consumers or manufacturers for their use or inclusion of caffeine in foods, drinks, supplements, and medications. Unlike second-hand tobacco smoke, there is no readily identifiable "caffeine industry" to attack, no direct impact of caffeine use on others, and few deaths are directly attributable to the use of caffeine. These facts may help explain why caffeine is relatively unregulated. Largely treated as a food additive or a dietary supplement, like sugar or salt, caffeine is included in a panoply of consumable products available anywhere foods or beverages are sold and marketed extensively to people of all ages, including children and adolescents. Except for select state-based regulations, there are relatively few prohibitions of the sale and marketing of even highly-caffeinated products to minors of any age. A seven-year old child cannot lawfully purchase cigarettes, alcohol, or illicit drugs, but she can buy a can of Red Bull energy drink, a Starbucks coffee, and over-the-counter caffeinated medications. While a retailer may refuse to sell any product to a minor, they have no more legal reason to deny minors the purchase of a caffeinated Vitamin Water than an avocado. Many parents or caretakers of children may cringe at the sight of their child gulping down a can of Pepsi Max (with sixty-nine milligrams of caffeine), but parents, retailers, and manufacturers are not legally barred from allowing children to purchase or consume these and other caffeinated products.

The availability and consumption of caffeinated products are prevalent in the United States. Adult consumers are largely aware of the presence of caffeine in consumables like coffees, teas, soft drinks, medications, energy drinks, and certain alcoholic beverages.

Many adults and minors, however, may not know about the gamut of additional food and medicinal products that contain caffeine. Especially popular among children and adolescents are food products combining caffeine, sugars, and sweeteners, such as candies, gum, mints, lollipops, marshmallows, cookies, and brownie mixes. Health conscious consumers may be surprised to know that some brands of oatmeal, yogurt, cereal, sunflower seeds, beef jerky, and bottled water contain caffeine. Even certain brands of soap, such as Shower Shock and Bath Buzz, are designed to provide caffeine by absorption through the skin.

Caffeine, however, is not added to foods to enhance flavor. As a natural ingredient, caffeine, which serves as a natural pest deterrent in coffee, tea, and cocoa plants, has a bitter, unpalatable taste. One study by Johns Hopkins University School of Medicine concluded that caffeine is added to soft drinks not for taste, but for its addictive qualities and ultimately to boost consumption. Pepsi, for example, started including caffeine in 1919 to boost declining sales.

With the widespread availability of inexpensive products containing caffeine, it is not surprising that over eighty percent of American adults consume caffeinated products daily. An average adult who consumes caffeine ingests approximately 200 milligrams a day. This is roughly the equivalent of the amount of caffeine contained in four twelve-ounce cans of soda, one ten-ounce cup of coffee, three Excedrin Extra Strength(R) tablets, or six Anacin Max Strength(R) tablets. The average daily caffeine intake of Americans who drink coffee may be considerably higher.

Caffeine consumption among children and adolescents nationally is not well-documented and may vary by region. Nevertheless, studies show that caffeine consumption among minors increased at least seventy percent from 1977 to 1999. Carbonated soft drinks, with little or no nutritional value, have replaced milk as the primary beverage consumed in the U.S. for all age groups. For children, milk consumption declines as soft drink consumption increases. One recent study reported that ninety-eight percent of children and adolescents between five and eighteen years old consume caffeine weekly. In one dietary survey conducted in 2003, children who reported eating fast food consumed only 260 grams of milk, but drank 358 grams of carbonated soft drinks per day. A 2008 study involving 191 students in seventh to ninth grade revealed their caffeine intake over a two-week period ranged from 0 and 800 milligrams per day.

National consumption of caffeinated products is propelled by extensive marketing efforts to promote their use among consumers, especially minors. Marketing of caffeinated products, particularly soft drinks, is long-standing, extensive, and at times impressionable. Until 1920, advertisements for caffeinated soft drinks emphasized their stimulant qualities. Such marketing claims ceased only after the federal government investigated the use of caffeine in soft drinks.

Historically, soft drink manufacturers have aggressively promoted their caffeinated products to all age groups, including children as young as nine years old. Of the ten top-selling carbonated soft drinks in the United States in 2009, eight are caffeinated. Before the voluntary withdrawal of sugar-containing soft drinks from many schools, soft drink manufacturers used numerous methods to target children at school, including passing out free samples (which one U.S. Senator assimilated to tobacco companies handing out free cigarettes to children) and giving away coupons for fast food. Many younger consumers consume soft drinks and fast food in combination. Correspondingly, soft drink manufacturers use promotions involving major fast food chains to market their products. Following the threat of lawsuits and to counter numerous critics, Coca-Cola and

PepsiCo announced in March 2008 that they would eliminate soft drink marketing aimed toward children under twelve years of age. Despite this pledge, indirect marketing to children and adolescents continues in non-school forums. For instance, Coca-Cola spends millions each year to co-sponsor the *American Idol* program and, in a practice also employed by other soda manufacturers, disseminates text messages offering prizes and coupons directly to cell phones, including those used by minors.

Some manufacturers of highly caffeinated products have been criticized for marketing campaigns aimed at children and adolescents. KickStart SPARK Smart(R), for example, is an energy drink made specifically for children "ages four and older." The manufacturer of Monster recommends its product is only for those over the age of thirteen. Marketing of caffeinated products mixed with alcohol to youthful audiences has led some large companies to voluntarily drop such products due to public outcry, potential health risks, and ongoing criminal and civil litigation. In the Fall of 2010, a recent spate of hospitalizations of consumers of the caffeinated alcohol drink Four Loko(R) led the state of Washington and other jurisdictions to ban its sale.

While research on caffeine's effect on individual health is inconclusive, moderate, routine use of caffeine does not generally lead to long-term negative impacts on individual adult health. In fact, regular caffeine consumption, even at higher than average levels, can positively improve adult health. A 1999 study concluded that people who regularly drank at least two cups of coffee halved their risk for gallstone disease and reduced the risk of colorectal cancer by one-quarter. Additional research supports the role of caffeine in delaying the onset of Alzheimer's disease, preventing death due to heart failure, increasing energy expenditure, and preventing the onset of type 2 diabetes.

Despite the positive effects of moderate caffeine use, there are extensive negative health impacts of caffeine consumption, especially among minors and adults who consume high levels of caffeine. Adverse impacts of caffeine among adults include headaches, nausea, irritability, palpitations, and sleep disorders, particularly for those consuming in excess of 400 mg of caffeine a day. Caffeine can negatively impact fertility. Pregnant women are urged to limit their caffeine consumption, as high, daily consumption increases the risk of spontaneous abortion and impaired fetal growth. Breastfeeding mothers are expressly warned against consuming large amounts of caffeine because caffeine can enter the breast milk ingested by their babies.

The negative effects of over-ingestion of caffeine for millions of children and adolescents vary depending on their age and weight, but some common effects include jitteriness, nervousness, stomachaches, nausea, dependence/withdrawal, and increased risks of sleep disturbances. A 2003 study correlated caffeine with poor sleep habits in seventh to ninth graders. Excessive caffeine intake in children can mimic or contribute to a number of psychiatric and behavioral disorders, including poor attention span, anxiety neuroses, anger, ADHD, eating disorders, and serotonin syndrome. High caffeine consumption and cycles of caffeine withdrawal among children can negatively impact their academic performance.

Caffeine can be a dangerous drug, even lethal, when taken in extreme quantities. In exceptional cases, ingestion of highly-caffeinated diet pills or other medications can kill users. The death of a British man in October 2010 was attributed to his over-ingestion of a caffeine powder that he had purchased online. Poison control centers and emergency rooms report increasing numbers of people suffering from symptoms of caffeine overdose, as well as deaths—including suicides—from caffeine overdoses (i.e., ingesting caffeine pills). Caffeine toxicity can occur among persons who consume high levels of caffeine or are particularly sensitive to its effects. One survey suggested that seven percent of caffeine users met criteria for caffeine intoxication.

FDA has determined that regular consumption of large amounts of caffeine can lead to "habituation," a mild form of addiction. The social acceptance of caffeine use can cause the addiction to be treated differently than other addictions. Individuals attempting to quit their caffeine habit may experience withdrawal symptoms such as headaches, fatigue, difficulty concentrating, depression, irritability, nausea, and muscle aches that peak between twenty and forty-eight hours after the last consumption of caffeine.

Despite historic and current evidence of potential negative individual and population-based health effects of widespread caffeine consumption, particularly among children and adolescents, caffeinated products are relatively unregulated by federal, state, or local governments. Caffeine is primarily regulated on the federal level by the FDA under the Food Drug and Cosmetic Act (FDCA). The Dietary Supplement Health and Education Act (DSHEA) of 1994 provides a loophole for caffeinated beverages and other products marketed as dietary supplements.

Federal regulatory requirements for caffeine differ considerably depending on whether the caffeinated product is classified as a food, dietary supplement, or drug. How a product is classified is driven in part by how it is marketed and consumed. In general, drugs are regulated more closely by the FDA than foods and dietary supplements, presumably because prescription and over-the-counter drugs entail more risks for consumers. The FDA's tripartite classification scheme for caffeinated foods, drugs, and dietary supplements can obfuscate potential harms that these products may pose to the public.

The FDA defines "food" broadly to include any article (or components of such articles) "used for food or drink" including caffeine when added as an ingredient to existing products, such as sodas. In this context, caffeine as an additive is classified as a food, as are foods and beverages that contain caffeine naturally (*e.g.*, coffee, tea, and chocolate). Under the FDCA, caffeine is "generally recognized as safe when used in cola-type beverages in accordance with good manufacturing practice." The FDA has established that the acceptable amount of caffeine in beverages is 0.02% of the total content (or no more than 71 milligrams of caffeine in a twelve ounce beverage). This determination resulted from a court approved settlement in *United States v. Forty Barrels and Twenty Kegs of Coca-Cola* in which the FDA approved the amount of caffeine in cola-type beverages at a level similar to the amount traditionally added to Coca Cola. Although the FDA noted its long-standing knowledge and approval of the inclusion of caffeine in Coca-Cola in settling *Forty Barrels*, in 1980, the FDA actually proposed eliminating caffeine from soft drinks due to health concerns. The FDA continues to classify caffeine as a food product that is generally regarded as a safe ingredient instead of as a psychoactive ingredient (which would have potentially subjected soft drinks to more rigorous regulations related to the inclusion of drugs in products).

Unlike foods in which caffeine is a natural component, the FDA requires that solids or beverages to which caffeine is intentionally and artificially added, list caffeine as an ingredient, but the agency does not require the amount of caffeine to be labeled. The FDA's mandatory Nutritional Panel label on foods must only list recommended dietary information for "nutrients." Some manufacturers voluntarily provide the amount of caffeine artificially added to their foods for the benefit of consumers. While the FDA also does not require food manufacturers to provide warning labels on their caffeinated products, it may require such warnings if future health data demonstrate that caffeine poses a public hazard.

The FDA may defer to the intent of the manufacturer in determining whether or not to classify a product as a food. Manufacturers can effectively evade FDA regulations concerning the inclusion of caffeine in foods by marketing products as dietary supplements, which are regulated by [The Dietary Supplements Health and Education Act of 1994]. DSHEA classifies products that are derived from natural sources *e.g.*, vitamins, minerals, herbs as dietary supplements, and not food or drugs. High-caffeine energy drinks commonly avoid the FDA's limitations on caffeine content in soft drinks and food labeling requirements, because they are often sold as nutritional supplements. One of the first energy drinks to be marketed in the United States, Red Bull, emerged shortly after DSHEA was enacted. When DSHEA was originally passed, federal legislators expressed concerns that manufacturers of these and other products might characterize their products as nutritional supplements to avoid FDA requirements. Subsequently amended in part to assuage these concerns, DSHEA still allows energy drinks and other nutritional supplements to avoid comparatively stricter limitations on caffeine content and labeling requirements than food or drugs.

FDA defines a drug as any article "intended for use in the diagnosis, cure, mitigation, treatment, or prevention of disease." Products that contain caffeine, and are classified as a drug, are subject to more comprehensive regulation than those classified as food or dietary supplements. For example, FDA limits caffeine in over-the-counter (OTC) pain medicines to no more than sixty-five milligrams per dose. FDA requires lengthy warning labels on OTC drugs containing caffeine and labeling of stimulant products, such as caffeine. Manufacturers of OTC stimulants, including caffeine, are required to provide consumers with a statement of identity, indications, warnings, and directions. Warnings include the appropriate dosage, related health risks, and guidance against children taking such stimulant.

The discrepancies inherent in the FDA's tripartite regulatory scheme for products containing caffeine are striking. For example, a consumer may choose a two ounce candy bar that has little to no caffeine content, or a Snickers Charged(R) bar with sixty milligrams of caffeine which is not required to have caffeine listed on the label. While a carbonated beverage sold as food is limited to no more than 71 milligrams of caffeine per twelve ounces, the same size carbonated energy drink sold by the same manufacturer and retailer, and often found in the same refrigerated unit, may contain over 150 milligrams of caffeine. Even though a pain medication containing sixty-five milligrams of caffeine is required by the FDA to indicate the amount of caffeine, related health risks, and dosage limitations on its label, Pepsi Max (with its sixty-nine milligrams of caffeine) is not subject to the same requirements. In addition, while an OTC drug with more than 100 milligrams of caffeine must carry a warning label specifically related to the inclusion of caffeine as an ingredient, Rockstar energy drink, which contains 160 milligrams of caffeine, is not required to display any warning.

One of the more profound facets of regulation of the sale and consumption of caffeinated products is that there are few restrictions on how children and adolescents access these goods. Caffeinated products, whether food, dietary supplements, or drugs, may be purchased by adults, adolescents, and children at nearly every grocery, convenience store, or pharmacy in the United States. There are no national limitations on the sale or consumption of most caffeine or caffeinated products to children. Recently, however, a handful of states have introduced legislation to prohibit the sale of energy drinks or other highly-caffeinated beverages to minors. In 2008, for example, Kentucky State Representative Danny Ford introduced House Bill 374 to prohibit the sale of energy drinks to minors. The bill targeted carbonated beverages with a "caffeine content of 71 milligrams per 12 ounce serving" that also contain taurine and glucuronolactone. Michigan lawmakers proposed a similar bill that same year. Both bills failed to pass in their respective state legislatures.

While state-wide bans of energy drink sales to minors have failed, some jurisdictions are focused on preventing the sale of energy drinks in schools. In 2007, [the Institute of Medicine] opined that beverages with added levels of caffeine should be eliminated from school lunches. However, adoption of this guidance has been relatively unsuccessful/limited. Rhode Island's legislature failed in its attempt to ban the sale of energy drinks from all schools. But a 2004 county-wide ban in Fairfax County, Virginia, prohibiting high school student-athletes from consuming energy drinks at school succeeded. Another high school in New Jersey also prohibited energy drinks in 2008. In Texas, state Attorney General Greg Abbott targeted the energy drink, Cocaine, instead of attempting to ban all energy drinks. Cocaine, now renamed "Censured" by its manufacturer, Redux, contains nearly 300 milligrams of caffeine in a single eight-ounce serving. Its manufacturer claims the beverage is like "speed in a can" and a "legal alternative" to street drugs. Abbott criticized the product by stating, "Texans have zero tolerance for those who peddle products meant to mimic illegal drugs. This advertising campaign enticed young people with illegal drug references and false claims of health benefits."

Part IV

Chapter 9

International and Comparative Drug Control

A. The International Market for Controlled Substances

Disciplining Globalization: International Law, Illegal Trade, and the Case of Narcotics
Chantal Thomas
24 Michigan Journal of International Law 549 (2003)

While the omni-term "globalization" can mean many (probably too many) different things, from a purely material standpoint the term refers to the dramatic increase in contemporary times of international production and consumption.

After World War II, world trade in goods "grew at a rate twice as fast as the overall world economy." For the United States, "trade volume multiplied nearly twenty-fold" during the same time frame. In the globalized economy, intricate chains of manufacture, assembly, distribution, and retail link together an ever greater number of countries. Lan Cao's description of modern automobile production is classic: "A Chevy may be built in Mexico from imported parts and then re-imported into the United States; a Ford built in German plants by Turkish workers and sold in Hong Kong and Nigeria; a Toyota Camry designed by an American designer at Toyota's Newport Beach California Calty Design Research Center, assembled at the Georgetown, Kentucky plant from American-made parts (except that the engine and drive trains are still Japanese) and then test driven at Toyota's Arizona proving ground."

Car production seems a typical facet of the global production. Illegal drug production, however, exceeds car production as a proportion of the global economy. The United Nations Office for Drug Control and Crime Prevention (UNODCCP) reports that the last two decades have witnessed "the global spread of drug trafficking," rendering it "now truly a global phenomenon." The complexity of narcotics trade rivals that of multinational corporations. The United States Bureau for International Narcotics and Law has observed that "the relatively simple charts of drug flows" of previous eras "now resemble schematic drawings of intricate ... networks tying nearly every country in the world to the ... drug production and trafficking countries."

In addition to sharing the same characteristics, the globalization of licit goods and illicit narcotics share many of the same causes. Advances in communications technology constitute one such cause; for example, the telecommunications network that facilitates international capital investment also facilitates money laundering for the illicit narcotics trade. In addition, modern transportation (such as air, rail, road, and even national mail and commercial courier services) facilitates the production and distribution of narcotics. Further, because narcotics are so frequently smuggled in otherwise legal distribution chains, often it is not only the same types of technology, but the same actual shipment, that drives trade in both licit goods and illicit narcotics.

There is one final connection between the globalization of licit and illicit trade, found in international trade law itself. The primary multilateral trade agreements name the expansion of world trade as their central objective. Most believe that these agreements have largely achieved their objective: John Jackson, for example, has asserted that "to a great extent, contemporary international economic interdependence can be attributed to the success" of the multilateral trade regime in expanding global trade. The expansion in communications, transportation, and trade volume also facilitates trafficking, so that the institutionalized expansion of legal trade has generated "spillover effects" expanding illegal trade.

In the twentieth century, the licit international trade regime progressed from a relatively antagonistic approach to imports to an ever more liberal one. In the period after World War I and before World War II, the governments of Europe and the United States engaged in unabashed protectionism. The United States, for example, adopted tariff levels under its Smoot-Hawley Tariff Act of 1930 that resulted in the highest average tariff imposed on dutiable goods in U.S. history. Following World War II, most economists and statesmen concluded that the ills of the interwar period—both the economic decline and the political hostilities—had been exacerbated by the protectionist policies of the world's major powers. Consequently, the leading governments after World War II sought to construct a trade regime that would prevent a return to such widespread protectionism. The resulting General Agreement on Tariffs and Trade (hereinafter GATT) established basic principles of non-discrimination and a mechanism through which governments could negotiate the gradual reduction of trade barriers.

At the same time that the international regime for governing trade in licit goods was slowly shifting from a protectionist to a liberal approach, the international narcotics regime was effecting a shift in the opposite direction.

For most of the nineteenth century, the British championed the expansion of international trade in narcotics. Indeed, through its production stronghold in India, the narcotics trade provided a significant source of revenue for the British Empire. So dear was the opium market that Britain went to war with China over the latter's refusal to admit British imports of opium. Of course, the preference for liberalization was not total—the British trade in opium traveled through monopolies—but the British unquestionably favored the minimization of import restrictions on narcotics at this time. At the turn of the twentieth century, both opium and cocaine were widely used by consumers in the developed world in a variety of over-the-counter food and medicine products.

Between the conclusion of the Opium War and the first modern multilateral agreement regulating trade in narcotics—the Hague Convention of 1912—the prevalent attitude in the West toward narcotics shifted considerably. The Hague Convention of 1912 obliged signatories to "confine to medical and legitimate purposes the manufacture, sale and use of" opium, heroin, morphine, and cocaine. The next several agreements built on this model of medical control. The Geneva Convention of 1925 required Member States to furnish statistics supporting their estimates of "medical and legitimate" narcotics imports and exports. The Geneva Convention of 1931 required Member States to extend their export control schemes to all States, not just other members. Finally, the 1948 Paris Protocol required Member States to report information about any "medical and scientific" drugs not listed in the 1931 Convention that could have harmful effects or could be subject to abuse. The Protocol also provided for the application of the 1931 Convention's controls to any drug deemed harmful by the World Health Organization.

Thus, the agreements in the first half of the twentieth century gradually strengthened the medical controls narcotics trade. In doing so, the agreements evinced an "administrative" approach — neither liberal, nor prohibitive — that sought to circumscribe, but not to prevent, narcotics production and trade. These early agreements sought neither to expand nor to eliminate narcotics production and trade, but rather to control it in accordance with "medical and scientific" concerns.

The second half of the twentieth century saw the U.N. narcotics regime shift from an administrative model toward an increasingly prohibitionist one. The 1961 United Nations Single Convention on Narcotic Drugs marked the beginning of this shift. On the one hand, the 1961 Convention retained the administrative focus, though it tightened controls on members' ability to produce and trade narcotics for medical purposes. On the other, it sowed the seeds of a punitive approach by requiring Member States to establish as criminal offenses the production or trade of narcotics. The 1961 Convention also required States to establish conspiracy as a crime.

The 1961 Convention's intermingling of the medical-administrative and punitive approaches is perhaps best found in an important exception to the criminalization provisions: where unauthorized narcotics production or trade occurred at the hands of "abusers of drugs," a signatory could adopt measures of "treatment, education, after-care, rehabilitation and social reintegration" as an alternative response.

The medical, rehabilitative tone of the 1961 Convention shifted to a more punitive register in the 1988 Convention on Narcotic Drugs and Psychotropic Substances. The 1961 Convention's "drug abuser" exception narrowed in 1988 to production only "for personal consumption," or otherwise to "cases of a minor nature." Moreover, the 1988 Convention multiplied the number of offenses deemed criminal: Now not only were production, trade and conspiracy criminal, but knowing acquisition, possession, use, conversion or transfer of property derived the reform. By expanding the scope of the criminal and reducing the reach of the rehabilitative, the 1988 Convention shifted away from the administrative and toward the prohibitive mode.

The latest U.N. agreement, the Convention on Transnational Organized Crime of 2000, expands the range of criminal offenses even further. In addition to the offenses identified by the 1961 and 1988 Conventions, the 2000 Convention adds anti-racketeering type provisions, criminalizing "participation in an organized criminal group" and "laundering of the proceeds of crime." The 2000 Convention also makes criminal both the promise, offer, or gift of reward to, and the solicitation or acceptance of reward by, a public official to facilitate criminal activity.

Comparing the development of the international trade regime to the international narcotics regime reveals opposing trends. The regime governing general trade in goods has shifted from a protectionist regulatory model, to an administrative model, and finally toward a liberalized model. The regime governing trade in narcotics, however, has moved from a liberalized model to an administrative model, to an expansively prohibitionist model.

The GATT/WTO system operates on the foundational belief that liberalization of international trade in goods will maximize world welfare. The international narcotics regime operates on the belief that prohibition of trade in narcotic drugs will do the same. Why should liberalization of one set of goods be desirable, but liberalization in another set of goods be undesirable?

Like any species of market control, the criminalization of the international narcotics trade betrays the ambivalent impulses of "liberal governance." On the one hand, the market provides a grand theater for individual choice that is the *sine qua non* of prevailing liberal theory. On the other hand, governments maintain an infinite array of controls on the choices available to individuals in the market.

The tension between principles of liberalism and practices of market control emerges in both the trade regimes for legal goods and for illegal narcotics. In the GATT/WTO system, the principles of free trade are offset by exceptions allowing for trade restrictions. In the international narcotics regime, the backdrop of a liberalized international economic order contrasts with the foreground of narcotics prohibitionism.

Such puzzles should not be dismissed as unrelated idiosyncrasies of modern international governance. These conflicting regimes do relate to each other in an underlying framework, in which the discrepancy between liberalization and prohibition is mediated through the concept of normalcy in international trade: liberalization for "normal" international trade; restriction and prohibition for "abnormal" international trade. The normalcy concept organizes the apparent contradiction along parallel sides of a dichotomy.

World Drug Report, 2011
United Nations Office on Drugs and Crime

Globally, [the United Nations Office on Drugs and Crime (UNODC)] estimates that, in 2009, between 149 and 272 million people, or 3.3% to 6.1% of the population aged 15–64, used illicit substances at least once in the previous year. About half that number are estimated to have been current drug users, that is, having used illicit drugs at least once during the past month prior to the date of assessment. While the total number of illicit drug users has increased since the late 1990s, the prevalence rates have remained largely stable, as has the number of problem drug users, which is estimated at between 15 and 39 million.

Cannabis is by far the most widely used illicit drug type, consumed by between 125 and 203 million people worldwide in 2009. This corresponds to an annual prevalence rate of 2.8%–4.5%. In terms of annual prevalence, cannabis is followed by ATS (amphetamine-type stimulants; mainly methamphetamine, amphetamine and ecstasy), opioids (including opium, heroin and prescription opioids) and cocaine. Lack of information regarding use of illicit drugs—particularly ATS—in populous countries such as China and India, as well as in emerging regions of consumption such as Africa, generate uncertainty when estimating the global number of users. This is reflected in the wide ranges of the estimates.

While there are stable or downward trends for heroin and cocaine use in major regions of consumption, this is being offset by increases in the use of synthetic and prescription drugs. Non-medical use of prescription drugs is reportedly a growing health problem in a number of developed and developing countries.

Moreover, in recent years, several new synthetic compounds have emerged in established illicit drug markets. Many of these substances are marketed as 'legal highs' and substitutes for illicit stimulant drugs such as cocaine or 'ecstasy.' Two examples are piperazines and mephedrone, which are not under international control. A similar development has been observed with regard to cannabis, where demand for synthetic cannabinoids ('spice') has increased in some countries. Sold on the internet and in specialized shops, synthetic cannabinoids have been referred to as 'legal alternatives' to cannabis, as they are not under international control. The control status of these compounds differs significantly from country to country.

In terms of the health consequences of drug use, the global average prevalence of HIV among injecting drug users is estimated at 17.9%, or equivalently, 2.8 million people who inject drugs are HIV positive. This means that nearly one in five injecting drug users is living with HIV. The prevalence of Hepatitis C among injecting drug users at the global level is estimated at 50% (range: 45.2%–55.3%), suggesting that there are 8.0 million (range: 7.2–8.8 million) injecting drug users world-wide who are also infected with HIV. Deaths related to or associated with the use of illicit drugs are estimated between 104,000 and 263,000 deaths each year, equivalent to a range of 23.1 to 58.7 deaths per one million inhabitants aged 15–64. Over half of the deaths are estimated to be fatal overdose cases.

Global opium poppy cultivation amounted to some 195,700 [hectares] in 2010, a small increase from 2009. The vast bulk — some 123,000 [hectares] — were cultivated in Afghanistan, where the cultivation trend remained stable. The global trend was mainly driven by increases in Myanmar, where cultivation rose by some 20% from 2009. There was a significant reduction in global opium production in 2010, however, as a result of disease in opium poppy plants in Afghanistan.

The global area under coca cultivation continued to shrink to 149,100 [hectares] in 2010, falling by 18% from 2007 to 2010. There was also a significant decline in potential cocaine manufacture, reflecting falling cocaine production in Colombia which offset increases identified in both Peru and the Plurinational State of Bolivia.

While it is difficult to estimate total global amphetamine-type stimulants manufacture, it has spread, and more than 60 Member States from all regions of the world have reported such activity to date. The manufacture of amphetamines-group substances is larger than that of ecstasy. Methamphetamine — which belongs to the amphetamines-group — is the most widely manufactured ATS, with the United States of America reporting a large number of detected illicit laboratories.

Cannabis herb cultivation occurs in most countries worldwide. Although there was insufficient data available to update the global cultivation estimate, the relatively stable seizure trend suggests a stable level of production. Indoor cultivation of cannabis herb is still largely limited to the developed countries of North America, Europe and Oceania. Cannabis resin production estimates were not updated this year, but based on ARQ replies to UNODC, Afghanistan and Morocco were major producers.

Trafficking flows vary according to the drug type involved. The most commonly seized drug type, cannabis herb, is often locally produced and thus, international trafficking is limited. Cocaine and heroin are trafficked both intra- and inter-regionally, though considerable amounts are consumed quite far from the countries of cultivation and production. Most ATS manufacture occurs in the region of consumption, whereas their precursor chemicals are trafficked inter-regionally.

The long-term trends show increased seizures for all the major drug types. Between 1998 and 2009, seizures of cocaine, heroin and morphine, and cannabis almost doubled. ATS seizures more than tripled over the same period.

Though it is still the most commonly seized drug, by far, the relative importance of cannabis in total illicit drug seizures has declined, rendering the other drug types — particularly ATS — increasingly prominent.

Looking at recent trends, global seizures of ATS rose to a record high in 2009, driven by increases in methamphetamine seizures. Ecstasy seizures, on the other hand, decreased. The predominant type of ATS seized varies according to region, with methamphetamine dominating in Oceania, Africa, North America and much of Asia.

Seizures of opiates remained stable in 2009, with the Islamic Republic of Iran and Turkey continuing to account for the largest national seizure totals. Cocaine seizures also remained largely stable, at a high level. For cannabis, seizures of cannabis herb—the most widely consumed variety—increased, whereas resin seizures decreased.

For cocaine and cannabis resin, seizures are shifting away from the main consumer markets to source regions. Both North America and West and Central Europe account for declining shares of global cocaine seizures, while South America is seizing more. Similarly, cannabis resin seizures decreased significantly in Europe but increased in North Africa from 2008 to 2009.

A Report on Global Illicit Drugs Markets 1998–2007: Assessing the Operation of the Global Drug Market, Report 1
Peter H. Reuter

RAND Corporation, Prepared for the European Commission (2009)

Illicit drugs, predominantly cocaine and heroin, now generate a substantial international and domestic trade. For these two drugs, production is concentrated in poor nations and the bulk of revenues, though not of consumption, is generated by users in wealthy countries. Earnings have an odd shape; most of the money goes to a very large number of low level retailers in wealthy countries while the fortunes are made by a small number of entrepreneurs, many of whom come from the producing countries. Actual producers and refiners receive one or two percent of the total; almost all the rest is payment for distribution labour. The industry is in general competitive, though some sectors in some countries have small numbers of competing organisations.

It is not difficult to explain why cocaine heroin production occurs primarily in poor countries and only a little harder to understand why the accounting profits are downstream. Almost everything else about the trade presents a challenge, both descriptively and analytically. Why is the production of cocaine and heroin concentrated in such a small number of poor countries? How are the different sectors organized, in terms of enterprise size and internal structure? What is the relationship of drug trafficking and distribution to other transnational and organized criminal activities?

Cannabis and [Amphetamine Type Stimulants (ATS)] provide a contrast in several dimensions. For cannabis a high percentage is produced in rich consuming countries and a larger share goes to the growers. ATS is produced in both rich and poor countries and traded in both directions.

A small number of nations account for the vast bulk of production of coca and opium. According to official estimates (e.g. U.S. Department of State, 2008; UNODC, 2008), Myanmar and Afghanistan have accounted for over 80 percent of global production of opium since the mid-1980s. Since the turn of the century, Afghanistan has increasingly dominated, so that in 2007 it was estimated to account for 93% of the total (8,200 tons out of 8,870 tons). A total of six countries account for 98% of world production.

Bolivia, Colombia and Peru account for all of coca production. The distribution of production among them has changed over time. In the 1980s, when the illegal market in

Table 1. Prices of Cocaine and Heroin through the Distribution System ca. 2000 (per pure kilogram equivalent)

Stage	Cocaine	Heroin
Farm gate	$650 (Leaf in Colombia)	$550 (Opium in Afghanistan)
Export	$1,000 (Colombia)	$2,000–$4,000 (Afghanistan)
Import	$15–20,000 (Miami)	$35,000
Wholesale (Kilo)	$33,000 (Chicago)	$50,000 (London)
Wholesale (Ounce)	$52,000 (Chicago)	$65,000
Retail (100 mg. pure)	$120,000 (Chicago)	$135,000 (London)

Source: Drug Enforcement Administration; EMCDDA; UNODC; Matrix, 2007.

the U.S. first emerged, it was produced primarily in Peru, Bolivia was second and Colombia a distant third. Since the mid-1990s this has changed markedly, with Colombia responsible for about two thirds of total production. Though other nations in the Andes, particularly Ecuador, are always rumoured to be about to enter the coca growing sector, none has so far done so.

There is no technical reason for not producing cocaine or heroin in the United States or Western Europe. Hydroponic techniques could be used for both coca and opium poppies. However the enforcement risks faced by producers in the U.S. or Western Europe are substantial and the risk compensation costs sufficiently high, that even with transportation costs and associated interdiction risks, local production of coca and opium poppies have never developed; indeed, these drugs are not even refined in the Western world.

Francisco Thoumi contrasts the distribution of coca and opium production across nations with that for legitimate agricultural products. Coffee can be grown in many countries; in fact, a large number of those countries do have coffee producing and exporting industries. Many countries are capable of producing opium or coca; very few of them do. For example, opium has at various times been grown in China, Lebanon, Macedonia and Turkey. However none of these are currently active producers for the illicit market.

It is useful to contrast this configuration with that for cannabis. One hundred and thirty four countries report to UNODC that cannabis is produced in their territory. U.S. production accounts for a substantial (though unknown) share of U.S. consumption, apparently much of it grown indoors. The Netherlands estimates domestic production that approximately 18,000 "cannabis farms" produced between 130 and 300 tons of cannabis in the early part of this decade, far more than might be consumed by Dutch users and the coffee shop visitors (less than 80 tons). Some of this is exported to other Western European nations.

Mexico and Morocco are the only nations identified as major exporters, Mexico exclusively to the United States and Morocco to Europe. There are no estimates of what share of consumption in these markets are accounted for by imports from these producers. However it is unlikely that the total international trade component of the cannabis trade is large.

Cannabis' exceptional status in terms of disbursed production probably rests on four factors: the bulkiness per unit value,[2] which raises smuggling costs substantially; the high yields per square meter, which allow a grower to produce substantial revenues from a small area; and the existence of a boutique market of user/growers interested in developing better breeds of the plant; and the ease of entry, since the seeds are widely available and there are probably few economies of scale beyond quite a small number of plants.

ATS production is scattered around the world but not in many countries and not always in developing countries. It is useful to consider the three component drugs (amphetamine, ecstasy and methamphetamine) separately.

Amphetamine is primarily consumed in Europe and that is the locus of production as well. Manufacturing requires neither highly specialized skills nor sophisticated facilities. The United Kingdom was for some years the principal production centre but other Western and Eastern European nations (notably Belgium, the Netherlands and Poland) have become more prominent in recent years.

Methamphetamine is produced mostly in East Asia and North America. In Asia the UNODC (2008) reports substantial methamphetamine production in China, Indonesia, Myanmar and the Philippines; these countries service both large domestic markets and markets in other Asian countries such as Japan and Korea. However methamphetamine is also produced in Australia, where a substantial domestic market has developed. Mexico produces for the U.S. market; however tough enforcement at the border and perhaps effective precursor controls in Mexico itself have led to the development of a U.S. based production capacity.

For ecstasy on the other hand, rich nations (such as the Netherlands and the U.K.) are major exporters to many countries, including developing countries such as Brazil. The production process requires considerable sophistication both of technicians and equipment; this may explain the location of the producers in the developed world.

Risks and the costs of bearing them provide a plausible, though still untested, explanation for all these observations. Coca and opium are grown in countries characterized by labour and land that have low prices relative to those in Europe and North America. The comparative advantage of these countries is reinforced by the reluctance or inability of governments in Bolivia, Colombia and Peru (for coca) and Afghanistan and Myanmar (for opium/heroin) to act aggressively against growers or early stage refiners. Low opportunity cost for factors of production plus low enforcement risks produce very modest prices for the refined product and also ensure that production does not move upstream geographically.

It is also useful to consider why neighbouring countries, involved in transhipment, have not been major producers. Consider for example Thailand. In the early 1970s it was a major producer of opium. It also has had a substantial addict population (predominantly heroin using). It continues to suffer from high levels of corruption, both in the powerful military and in the civilian government. It would seem to be a strong candidate for a large opium production sector.

Yet Thailand now produces little and serves primarily as a consuming and transhipment country for Myanmar. The explanation can probably be found in economic factors. Over the past thirty years Thailand has had high rates of growth, raising the

---

2. A kilogram of cocaine might have a border price of 10,000 Euros entering Europe; a kilogram of cannabis would be only a few hundred Euros.

opportunity cost of land and labour relative to impoverished Myanmar. Thus, Thai farmers have not been able to compete in the opium growing sector, particularly since the illegality of the product has inhibited the development of more technologically advanced growing methods. Targeted alternative development programs, sponsored by the Thai king, may also have contributed to the decline of production in Thailand. The Thai government, despite the corruption of its border drug controls, has also been more willing to act aggressively against growers.

Until the mid-1990s Colombia was the other anomaly, a nation that would have been expected to dominate coca growing, given that coca grew readily there and domestic production would reduce the risk of interdiction. Though the principal source of refined exports to the United States, and an important source for Western Europe, it was a distant third in coca production until the mid-1990s. The subsequent and rather sudden expansion of coca growing in Colombia, which has accompanied a decline in Peruvian and, to a lesser extent, Bolivian production may be the result of specific political factors and developments in the other two producers. The upturn in political violence in Colombia has led to a large internal migration from more settled agricultural regions, where the paramilitary are most active, to unsettled areas in which there are few economic opportunities other than coca growing and in which the guerrillas can provide effective protection. The decline in Peruvian production may also be the consequence of an extended blight, the first to hit the coca crop in recent decades, and a period of intense enforcement against air traffic of coca base between Peru and Colombia. In Bolivia a broad program of developmental support in the principal producing area (the Chapare) and perhaps actions of the governments prior to the 2006 election of Evo Morales as president led to sharp decline in production. If peace and stability ever return to rural Colombia, the coca trade may shift back to the poorer Bolivia; the recent loss of leadership and membership in the FARC, along with the demilitarisation of the paramilitary, may allow a test of that proposition.

Both in the Andes and in Afghanistan the growers are small producers and there is no suggestion that they have any collective power in bargaining. Mansfield, in a series of studies over the last decade has shown that opium is just another crop that farmers choose to grow with the amount grown depending on access to water, availability of infrastructure, prices of other agricultural commodities, availability of family labour etc. At that level, it is a typical agricultural product, produced by many independent decision makers. Even at the level of traders, the market appears to be competitive. Only at the highest level of the domestic Afghanistan trade is there any indication of possible market power. While there are no similarly detailed studies of the coca producing and cocaine refining sectors in Colombia, there is little indication of any control.

There is an emerging literature on cannabis production in wealthy countries. For example, Bouchard provides a fine-grained description of marijuana growing in Quebec, an important supplier to the U.S. market according to his careful estimates. Again what emerges is an industry of many small producers with minimal co-ordination, often employing teenagers as workers. Less is available on production in poor countries that serve as suppliers to the West. In Morocco, cannabis growing is a major agricultural activity in some regions, again involving small farmers who sell to numerous middle-men. There are no published studies of cannabis production in Mexico.

The modest share of retail price associated with international cocaine and heroin smuggling is easily explained. First, consider cocaine, which travels in large bundles at that stage; seizures suggest that shipments of 250–500 kilograms are quite common. Though large sums may be paid to pilots for flying small planes carrying cocaine or to Honduran colonels in return for ignoring their landing, these costs are defrayed over a large quantity. A pilot who demands $500,000 for flying a plane with 250 kilograms is generating costs of only $2,000 per kilogram, about 2 percent of the retail price in the United States. Even if the plane has to be abandoned after one flight, that adds only another $2,000 to the kilogram price. For Europe, where courier smuggling may be more important, since it is remote from production areas for both cocaine and heroin, payments to the couriers again amount to only a few thousand Euros per kilo. For shipments in container cargo, seizure constitutes little more than random tax collection; replacement cost of the seized drugs is substantially less than the landed price, so high seizure rates have modest effect even on wholesale prices.

A large share of cocaine in the 1980s was smuggled to the United States in dedicated vessels, either small boats or planes. Intense interdiction has changed both routes and patterns. Small (and sometimes not so small) planes are still used to carry a substantial fraction of cocaine to Mexico, from where it enters the U.S. in regular cargo, either by truck or cargo vessel. Patterns of seizure also suggest that in recent years even shipments direct from Colombia have tended to travel in commercial traffic, both air and sea. The drug is found concealed in an enormous variety of cargoes; frozen fruit pulp containers, wooden furniture and suspended in other liquids. European smuggling patterns are influenced by the simple distance from Colombia to Western Europe; dedicated small planes and boats are less feasible. An increasing share is now coming through West African transit countries, such as Ghana and Guinea-Bissau.

Heroin smuggling appears to be less efficient, at least as measured in dollars per kilogram. Heroin that exits Myanmar at $1,000 per kilogram (in bundles of ten kilograms or more) sells on arrival in the United States for $50,000 per kilogram. There have been a few multi-hundred kilogram shipments of heroin but they are very rare compared to those for cocaine. The drug often travels in small bundles carried internally by individual couriers. "Body-packing" where the couriers are low wage earners, produces per kilogram smuggling costs of less than $10,000. A body-packer can apparently carry about 3/4 of a kilogram. A payment of $5,000 for incurring a 1 in 10 risk in prison (perhaps acceptable for couriers whose legitimate wages are only about $2,000 per annum), along with $3,000 in travel expenses, produces a kilogram cost of just over $11,000 compared to a retail price of $1 million. The remainder of the smugglers' margin is for assuming other kinds of risk. Body packing is also a common mode of smuggling from Central Asia, particularly Tajikistan, into Russia. The payments to couriers there are much lower, perhaps as little as $200, reflecting both the greater poverty of that region compared to Mexico (a Middle Income country now by World Bank standards) and the lower risk of apprehension.

Nigeria is an interesting anomaly, a nation that seems to have little potential role in the international drug trade. It is isolated from any of the principal producer or consumer countries and lacks a significant base of traditional domestic production or consumption. Nonetheless, Nigerian traffickers have come to play a significant role in the shipping of heroin between Southeast Asia and the U.S. and also to Europe. They have even been identified as important figures in the early stages of heroin trafficking in Central Asia. More recently Nigerian traffickers have even entered the cocaine business, though the production centres are still more remote from their home country.

The explanation is probably to be found in a complex of factors. Nigerians are highly entrepreneurial, have been misruled by corrupt governments over a long time, have large overseas populations, weak civil society, very low domestic wages and moderately good commercial links to the rest of the world. Thus it is relatively easy to buy protection for transactions in Nigerian airports (corruption and a weak governmental tradition), to establish connections in both the source and consumption nations (large overseas populations) and to use existing commercial transportation; smuggling labour is cheap (low domestic wages) and the entrepreneurial tradition produces many competent and enthusiastic smuggling organizers. Nigeria is not unique in most of these dimensions (except for size and connections with the rest of the world) and there is perhaps an accidental quality to its initiation into the trade, but these other factors plausibly play a major role. The country of Nigeria may have been supplanted by other West African states as a transit location in recent years, as indicated by the origin of seizures at London's Heathrow Airport, but it is less clear that Nigerians have been supplanted as smugglers.

Immigrants have advantages in exporting, with better knowledge of potential sellers and corruption opportunities. Few potential US importers speak any of the languages of the Golden Triangle (Myanmar, Laos and Thailand); English has more currency in Pakistan but not much in Afghanistan. Corrupt officials may be much more at ease in dealing with traffickers whose families they can hold in mutual hostage. Moreover, non-native traffickers are likely to be conspicuous in the growing regions. Nor are the exporters merely agents for wealthy country nations, in sharp contrast to the international trade in refined agricultural products. Khun Sa, an exotic figure associated with irredentist ethnic groups on the periphery of Myanmar was the dominant figure in opium exports from the Golden Triangle for many years. The Colombian cocaine trade has spawned some spectacular figures, such as Pablo Escobar and Carlos Lehder, all of them of Colombian descent. If there are major US or European exporters in the source countries, they have managed to escape detection.

The smuggling sector is where great fortunes appear to be made. Most prominent have been the Colombian entrepreneurs such as Carlos Lehder and Pablo Escobar whose extravagant lifestyles provided an important part of the imagery of the failure of the state to prevent their accumulation of power and wealth. Though there are no documented estimates of their actual earnings, there is no doubt that they accumulated many hundreds of millions of Euros during their careers. Khun Sa, the dominant figure in Myanmar's heroin industry (both production and exporting) also became extraordinarily wealthy and was able to negotiate with the national government an exit from the trade that may well have involved payment of large sums. The principal figures in the Mexican drug trade, which is mostly smuggling to the U.S., are also reputed to have very large fortunes.

Though for a long time it was assumed that illegal drug markets were typically monopolized in fact monopoly control is rare. Prior to 1980, it was widely believed that the Mafia had dominated the major illegal markets such as those for bookmaking and loan sharking, and even for heroin importation into New York City until the late 1960s. Despite finding that some dealers within the U.S. have enormous incomes and traffic in large quantities, no researcher has found evidence, except on the most local basis (e.g., a few blocks), that a dealer organisation has the ability to exclude others or to set prices, the hallmarks of market power.

Even at the trafficker level, market power seems elusive. Notwithstanding references to the Medellin and Cali "cartels", these groups seem to have been only loose syndicates of independent entrepreneurs, who sometimes collabourated but also had to compete with other, smaller, Colombian smuggling enterprises. The small share of the retail price accounted for by all activities up to import is strong, but not conclusive, evidence of competition at this level. The continuing decline of prices over an almost twenty year period at all levels of the market suggests that, if market power ever existed, it has now been dissipated.

Some characteristics of smuggling organisations seem quite general. For example, smuggling is rarely integrated with downstream distribution activities. Organisations which import 250 kilogram shipments of cocaine do not distribute beyond the initial transaction, selling in loads of 10 kilograms or more. The explanation for this probably lies in risk management; lower level transactions are more visible and the purchasers less reliable. Integration thus increases risk of arrest. Only very small scale importers are likely to operate close to the retail level.

Markets for smuggling services contain many forms and sizes of organisation. A credible case can be made that the 1990s US cocaine market has been dominated by a few large organisations. For other eras, countries and drugs, smaller and more ephemeral organisations may account for a significant share of the total.

If drugs travel in legitimate commerce and traffic, then transportation companies, as well as financial institutions, may be active accomplices. For example, American Airlines has paid substantial fines in the past for inadequate monitoring; its planes were importing clandestine cocaine shipments. Revelations at the Miami International Airport in the late 1990s showed that employees of the airline have continued to find opportunities for large scale smuggling; these ones involved baggage handlers at the U.S. landing point.

Corruption in the consuming countries seems to be less central to the business, an assertion that arouses considerable scepticism in producer countries. Corruption, like scientific hypotheses, presents a problem of epistemological asymmetry. Scientific hypotheses can only be disproved, not proven; corruption can be found but its existence never disproved. Nonetheless, U.S. prosecutors pursue corrupt agents with considerable zeal when they find them; at the same time the overlapping authority of enforcement agencies creates a situation in which any corrupt agent, no matter how well protected in her own department, has to be concerned with possible investigation by another agency. The market for corruption will shrink in such an environment. In many Western European countries with large drug markets, such as the United Kingdom and Switzerland, there simply is a dearth of credible corruption allegations beyond the occasional individual police officer who takes drugs or money.

The final sale of drugs to users is the sector accounting for most of the enforcement effort, participants and revenues. It is the easiest and best studied sector of the market, resulting in studies in many Western countries.

The large fraction of sellers operating at the retail level is simply a consequence of the incentives for concealment, which lead to a very tiered distribution system. High level dealers will seek to sell to small numbers of customers in order to reduce the number of potential informants against them. It is plausible, though empirically untested, that the number of customers a dealer is willing to transact with will rise as the drug moves down the distribution system; since the higher level dealers earn more and face higher penalties if caught, they are likely to be more cautious than those further down the distribution system. If each high level dealer will transaction with, say, only five customers (themselves dealers) and there are just three distribution levels in the market, retailers will account for almost five sixths of sellers. Thus is it hardly surprising that most of those who are incarcerated for drug selling operate at the bottom of the system.

The low level of earnings of participants in the retail markets is shown in a number of studies. Levitt and Venkatesh used the financial records of a cocaine dealing organisation in Chicago to show that most participants earned less than the minimum wage; they worked in the organisation in the hope of rising to the top, where earnings were very large indeed. Reuter, MacCoun and Murphy, collecting data ten years earlier when the crack and cocaine markets in Washington, D.C. were near their peak, found that street level dealers earned more than the minimum wage but still quite modest sums, in part because they were able to work profitably only for a few hours each week.

The high share of the retail price accounted for by low level distributors is easily explained in the standard risk compensation model used by economists. Assume that a higher level trafficker sells 1 kilogram of cocaine and has a 1 percent probability of being imprisoned for one year as a result of the transaction; the rich trafficker values a year in prison at 100,000 Euros. Assume a retailer sells 1 gram of cocaine and has only a 1 in 1,000 chance of the same imprisonment; he values a year in prison at 25,000 Euros. The trafficker will charge 1 Euro per gram to cover the risk, while the retailer, even though he has a lower chance of being jailed and values that less highly, needs 25 Euros to cover the risk associated with one gram. The figures are intended to be illustrative only.

Drug markets lend themselves to mythologising, because they are difficult to study and because the effects of the drugs themselves create a good deal of glamour to what is in fact a banal and grubby business. The common view that drug markets are lucrative, violent and monopolistic is, for most drugs, places and time exactly wrong. Mostly participants earn low incomes from engaging in routine activities in the context of small organisations with no capacity to control their customers. There are important exceptions at the higher levels of the markets, particularly for cocaine and heroin, in which a few individuals earn large incomes and control great violence. These constitute a specific social problem which needs to be dealt with but nothing is gained by generalising the exceptional few to the mass market in which millions of participants are engaged on a daily basis.

———————

Peter Reuter suggests that "[c]orruption in [drug] consuming countries"—like the United States—"seems to be less central to the [drug] business" than in drug producing countries. The recent experiences of Mexico and the United States are consistent with this view. Though drug consumption is much higher in the United States than in Mexico, to say that drug prohibition-related violence and corruption is worse in Mexico than in the United States would be an understatement. Mexican drug cartels have become so powerful that former U.S. drug czar Barry McCaffrey has said he believes the country is at risk of becoming a failed "narco-state." David Luhnow and José de Cordoba, *The Perilous State of Mexico*, WALL ST. J., Feb. 21, 2009. Former Mexican President Vicente Fox, who once "declared the 'mother of all battles' against drug cartels while in office, has reversed course and now favors legalization, saying that because of the drug war Mexico is 'losing in many things: tourism is stagnant, trade on the border, nightclubs, hotels are all stuck. We don't deserve to pay this price.'" Ioan Grillo and San Francisco del Rincon, *Mexico's Ex-President Vicente Fox: Legalize Drugs*, TIME, Jan. 19, 2011. The idea that drug consumption in the U.S. is fueling drug cartel violence across the border has become a common refrain but shouldn't logic dictate that the country with the greater amount of use and accompanying retail sales also have more violence and corruption? What might explain this imbalance? Was there a similar imbalance in the costs and benefits of prohibition among countries during alcohol prohibition? If not, what accounts for the difference?

Note: *Globalization of the U.S. Black Market: Prohibition, the War on Drugs, and the Case of Mexico*
Seth Harp
85 New York University Law Review 1661 (2010)

On Valentine's Day, 1929, seven members and hangers-on of the Bugs Moran gang arrived at a garage in the Lincoln Park neighborhood of Chicago, supposedly to receive a shipment of hijacked whiskey at a discount. It was a set-up. Members of the rival Capone gang, some dressed as police officers, led the seven underground, lined them up against a brick wall, and machine-gunned them to death. The uniformed killers led the plain-clothed killers outside at gunpoint to mislead bystanders into believing the shooting was under official control.

The hit had targeted Bugs Moran, Al Capone's chief rival for control of the illegal alcohol market, but Moran was either late or saw the "police" car in time and eluded assassination. However, Moran's evasion was not the primary failure of the attempted hit. The murders were at that time the most heinous offenses associated with the high-profile world of larger-than-life bootleggers and the crime syndicates they controlled, and the media backlash was severe. The murders were, in Capone's words, "lousy public relations." "MURDER COPS HUNTED IN MASSACRE" shouted the headline of *the Daily Mirror*, which devoted its entire front page to the story, including a large, gruesome photo of the crime scene and mug shots of each victim. "The viciousness of the killing and the powerlessness of police were both part of the abiding image of Prohibition." Public opinion had reached an inflection point, and it was not long before Prohibition was abandoned.

On September 2, 2009, hitmen working for the Sinaloa Cartel, a powerful Mexican drug-trafficking organization, broke into an addiction rehabilitation center in a northern sector of Juarez, Mexico, within view of the U.S. border, pushed eighteen people up against a wall, and machine-gunned them to death. The mass-murder was not directed at a rival cartel, but at a few recovering addicts regarded by the Sinaloa Cartel as potential informants.

Juarez and El Paso, Texas, are essentially one city split by the Rio Grande, an international border; the metropolis is home to more than two million people, making it the world's most populous binational area. Despite the depravity of the killings and the fact that Juarez is geographically contiguous with the United States, CNN declined to cover the event in lieu of such topics as President Obama's speech to schoolchildren, a football coach charged with homicide, Michael Jackson's funeral, the weather phenomenon El Nino, environmental terrorism, the sale of human body parts, Twitter, and the kidnapping of Jaycee Dugard.

The editorial decision was partly understandable, as the killings were nothing new: From January 2008 to the date of the killings described above, more than 1800 people had been murdered in Juarez, the most violent place in the world. It is in no sense metaphorical to describe the city as a war zone, as rival cartels have for years been engaged in open battle with one another, the federal army, the local police (ambiguously allied), and American agents, in a multifaceted, overlapping, and perpetually mutating conflict.

It is more likely that the lack of attention to the bloodshed in Juarez was due to the understandable human tendency to care less about what happens to people in other countries. But the war in Mexico does not properly belong to Mexico. It is caused by exactly the same phenomenon that caused the Saint Valentine's Day Massacre: competition between outlaw organizations that supply the American black market for recreational drugs.

The United States consumes more drugs and alcohol than any other country in the world. The U.S. legal strategy for reducing recreational drug consumption has long emphasized outright criminalization of possession and police interdiction of supply. "Prohibition," the ban on the drug alcohol from 1919 to 1933, is a dramatic example of such a policy. The "War on Drugs," the current campaign against a number of drugs, but especially cocaine, heroin, marijuana, and methamphetamine, is another. The similarities between the two are many, and the subject of much literature. Most notably, both failed or are failing to eliminate consumption of the targeted drug(s) while generating secondary costs that outweigh the problems caused by the drugs themselves, and both failed or are failing for the same reason: the futility of trying to eliminate, by fiat, flourishing markets for highly demanded goods.

This much has been well argued by many authors, but this Note explores the most salient difference between the two regimes, namely that Prohibition was met with a decisive backlash and repeal, while the War on Drugs manages to retain popular support, even though it has created violence on a scale beyond anything seen during Prohibition. This Note argues that the divergence in public choice is substantially explained by drug production taking place outside the United States, a fact that lowers the visibility of corruption and murder to those who support the War on Drugs. Simply because drugs are produced abroad, much of the human misery immanent in black markets of every kind has been offloaded onto people in third world countries. By contrast, black market alcohol was mostly produced in the United States, where Prohibition's bad effects were concentrated. The visibility of local costs led to relatively quick repeal of the 18th Amendment.

Reducing consumption of drugs and alcohol is a social goal with widespread support. How effective are prohibitions at achieving this goal? In general, they probably reduce consumption by a small to moderate margin. This is the primary benefit of a drug prohibition regime.

There is now tentative consensus among historians that Prohibition probably decreased alcohol consumption by a small to moderate margin that diminished over time.

[I]t is reasonable to conclude that the War on Drugs has decreased consumption by an unknown but almost certainly small margin. So the principal benefit of prohibitions, whether of alcohol or other drugs, is a slight or moderate reduction in consumption.

If it were as simple as that, if banning drugs were like banning, say, lead paint—that is, if taxpayers paid no more than the dollar price of administering the newly prohibited substance's removal from the market and the disutility, if any, of its absence—drug prohibitions might be reasonable or even good laws. But that is not how it works in practice.

When the sale of a popular recreational drug is banned, wealth and power flowing from productive capital are amplified and transferred from the arena of competition between legitimate firms to the monopoly control of entrepreneurs whose competitive advantage is a willingness to break the law. The government then invests in thwarting the criminals, who counterinvest in resistance and subterfuge. Meanwhile, large numbers of transactions take place without recourse to private property rights or the civil courts, leaving violence as the only mechanism for adjudicating contractual disputes and enforcing industry norms. Violence is used to take over and hold supply routes and distribution territory, with each gangster knowing that to succeed he must be more brutal than the gangster whom he has just supplanted. Over time, violence and expenditures ratchet upward, making it increasingly more expensive to bring the good to market, exacerbating the cycle. Meanwhile, consumers whose demand for drugs is inelastic (in some cases due to addiction) resort to theft to pay for artificially priced drugs they can no longer afford. The only constant in this uncontrollable spiral is a steady supply. The only change to consumers is increased price and reduced quality. Instead of champagne or powder cocaine, they get moonshine or crack, the latter substances being cheaper to produce clandestinely, more compact for transportation, and providing greater per-unit intoxication to consumers wishing to minimize their transactions with criminal suppliers.

[Alcohol p]rohibition is generally regarded to have been a disastrous experience because it was much more costly than expected. The murder rate rose sharply following the passage of the Eighteenth Amendment, remained high for fourteen years, and then, after repeal and passage of the Twenty-First Amendment, declined for eleven straight years. Once regulated alcohol was removed from the market, death and severe illnesses from adulterated homemade liquor became epidemic. Meanwhile, judicial criminal dockets were overwhelmed, and, given the difficulty of securing convictions against participants in voluntary transactions, prosecutors resorted to disproportionate punishments against bootleggers, up to life in prison in some cases. In fact, the origins of the American mass prison system trace to the Prohibition era, when the number of federal prisons had to be doubled. Yet illegal alcohol production and consumption was a "respectable crime." Like the presence of women in saloons, it became socially acceptable, for the first time, to be seen intoxicated in public. Most infamously, corruption among law enforcement became rampant, due in part to the large number of officials at every level of the executive branch, including the White House, who themselves were "ready to drink anything that burns, at the same time giving thanks to God." These unintended effects bent public opinion against Prohibition and produced a reexamination of policy at a national level.

Like Prohibition, the War on Drugs is expensive, even when the measurement is confined to U.S. borders. "The War on Drugs [costs the government] more ... than the Commerce, Interior, and State Departments put together." To American taxpayers, the cost of the War on Drugs, including the opportunity cost of drug peace, is estimated to be more than eighty billion dollars annually. How does enforcing bans on a few rudimentary chemicals come to be so expensive?

First, the War on Drugs causes violence. Violent conflict arises from competition between gangs that buy drugs wholesale and distribute them to consumers.

In addition to causing violence, the War on Drugs increases property crime. It is estimated that users seeking to finance purchases of drugs, some of which are 50 to 100 times more expensive than the predicted free market equilibrium price, commit around forty percent of all property crime in the United States.

In addition to causing violence and property crime, the War on Drugs increases official corruption. Bribery and graft are the result of a surfeit of drug profits, the lack of real moral revulsion directed against the use of drugs (compared to crimes that immediately cause tangible harm to others), and police fatigue with the Sisyphean struggle. Over the last half century the War on Drugs has led to serious and widespread corruption, especially in the police departments of high-crime cities and in the federal agencies tasked with controlling the southern border.

Because the U.S. War on Drugs pits large costs against moderate benefits, the criminalization of drugs has long been a controversial legal policy, but not as controversial as it should be: Despite the similarities between Prohibition and the War on Drugs, pressure to end the latter is clearly lower than pressure to end the former was at the height of Prohibition. This must be in substantial part because most of the violence caused by the War on Drugs is realized outside the United States.

As discussed, the War on Drugs causes violence in the United States. Yet that violence, mostly inner-city shootings, is trivial compared to the mayhem caused in illegal-drug-producing countries, like Mexico, the primary supplier of U.S. demand. Were these effects manifested in the United States, even if confined to marginalized and impoverished communities, the War on Drugs would probably go the same way as Prohibition—written off as a social experiment that proved too costly.

Mexico is currently embroiled in a major national conflict with a 2009 body count that surpassed the body count in Iraq and Afghanistan combined. Steadily enriched by the constant flow of money from American drug sales, the cartels have infiltrated every layer of society in Mexico.

Al Capone's thugs were farmboys and immigrants with sawed-off shotguns and tommyguns. Retail gangs in American cities wield pistols, knives, and fists. The armed wings of Mexico's cartels, by contrast, are manned by disciplined soldiers well equipped with increasingly sophisticated arsenals now reported to go beyond mere assault rifles, machine guns, and grenades, to include such military materiel as anti-aircraft guns and semisubmersible submarines. Cartel operatives coordinate their operations from sophisticated command centers using cell phones, two-way radios, scanner devices, Voice Over Internet Protocol, broadband satellite instant messaging, and encrypted text messages. Street battles between them and the federal army are sustained infantry engagements that can last hours and leave dozens dead.

Los Zetas, a private army that rose to prominence as the enforcement branch of the Gulf Cartel, originated out of the Grupo Aeromovil de Fuerzas Especiales, the special forces branch of the Mexican army. Its defection to entrepreneurial endeavors was a stark testament to the ability of the drug trade to compete with the Mexican state.

As of 2010, large swaths of the country are under cartel control. As much as thirty percent of Mexico's arable land is under drug crop cultivation. Every political party takes drug money, the Federal Investigative Agency has been corrupted, and one-fifth of the Attorney General's office is under investigation. Vigilantism is rampant. The Central Intelligence Agency (CIA) and Department of Defense are preparing for the possibility of the failure of the Mexican state. The cartels are believed to be actively trying to kill the head of state, and some business leaders have even called for the U.N. to occupy the country.

In short, Mexico is a country pushed to the brink of a particularly awful kind of failure, the cause of which is its status as the leading producer and transporter of drugs bound for the U.S. black market.

Imagine instead, however implausibly, that the United States produced all of the drugs it consumes. To be sure, eradication efforts would be more efficient, because the United States is wealthier and more developed. But the resulting scarcity would drive the price of drugs higher, making them an even more lucrative product. The higher price commanded by drugs would induce more determined, better-financed criminals to enter the illegal market. This would increase production, again spurring an increase in corresponding antinarcotics efforts, making drugs even more costly. Those increased costs would in turn be passed on to drug consumers, again raising the price of drugs, again exacerbating the cycle, until an equilibrium were reached at which the price of drugs would be much higher than at the outset but the total quantity supplied would have changed little or not at all. All the while counternarcotics efforts would be increasing, and domestic criminal syndicates would be gaining money, power, and reputational capital. Eventually, with the two upward trajectories pitted against one another, the conflict would approach an outright war.

In response to such a pointless conflagration, the country would likely seek an alternative means to regulate drugs other than a criminal ban. That is precisely what happened at the end of Prohibition. Nowadays, by contrast, the violence inherent in the War on Drugs is out of sight and out of mind of the average voter.

But how did the violence come to be outsourced in the first place?

In the absence of some barrier, production of a commodity will take place where it is cheapest. During Prohibition, it was cheapest to produce alcohol in the United States because significant productive capital already existed, and alcohol was easy to make at home and expensive to warehouse and transport. Although a significant amount of marijuana is produced in the United States, most illegal drugs are produced abroad.

It is cheapest to produce drugs for the American market abroad for a number of reasons.

To begin with, when marijuana, cocaine, and heroin were made illegal there was little demand for any of them, so there was not much productive capital to eliminate. Unlike the Eighteenth Amendment and the Volstead Act, the bans on these drugs were not in response to a perceived problem of widespread use among the general population; rather, they were directed most particularly at blacks and immigrants.

But the illegality of these drugs did not stop them from becoming popular among the middle classes. Indeed, to 1960s counterculturists, that very illegality was part of the attraction, illustrating another counterproductive tendency of prohibition. By the 1970s, demand for opium, cannabis, and cocaine was substantial.

When alcohol was banned, the de facto tax of illegality was insufficient to drive production abroad wherever sunken investment outweighed the cost of subterfuge. But entrants to the rapidly expanding drug market in the second half of the twentieth century faced a different cost structure. For them, investment in productive capacity anywhere in the United States necessarily entailed a high risk of detection, seizure, fines, and imprisonment. At the outset, then, not only did suppliers face the usual pressure to locate production where conventional inputs—e.g., land and labor—were cheapest, they also had an incentive to invest in countries that had not banned the substance to be produced, or where law enforcement was lax or the central state weak.

Some of the plants from which drugs are made are highly particular to certain regions. Varietals of the coca plant containing the cocaine alkaloid are essentially confined to Bolivia, Colombia, and Peru. Cocaine, once in demand, was bound to be produced there—and other drugs as well—due to economies of scope.

Sometimes a climate amenable to indigenous narcotic botanicals combines with a forbidding terrain and social factors of the kind already discussed (a weak state, lax enforcement, cheap labor) to give a country a near monopoly over a specific drug crop. The Andean-Amazonian region, for example, has a near monopoly on coca, not only because of its traditional use there and the coca plant's poor survival elsewhere, but also because of the protection provided by high mountain ranges, dense jungles, and low population density. In the United States, California and federal police fight a losing battle to eradicate cannabis plots in a handful of national forests. Consider, then, the impossibility for Latin American security forces, who have their own policing priorities, of eradicating millions of acres of plants hidden high in the Andes or deep in the Amazon rain forest amongst recalcitrant campesinos to whom the opportunity cost of growing such crops approaches zero, the alternative being sustenance farming. To take another example, poppy grows well throughout much of Europe, South America, and Asia, yet Afghanistan produces approximately 94 percent of the global heroin supply. Afghanistan's arid climate and long history of poppy cultivation explain less of its dominance than the country's lawlessness, tribal balkanization, lack of available economic alternatives for laborers, and a rugged terrain that is arguably impossible to police.

The comparative advantage enjoyed by overseas drug producers outlined above is lessened, however, by the necessity of international transportation. Drugs produced in Latin

America, or elsewhere, have to be shipped to the United States in order to be sold. But because of the rapid growth of international transportation and communications networks in the twentieth and twenty-first centuries, globalization, and the implementation of international free trade accords like the WTO, GATT, and NAFTA, these exportation costs are declining rapidly.

International liberalization—opening markets and freeing the movement of goods and services—is at odds with efforts to control the international drug trade. First, expansion of neoliberal free trade policies tends to reduce the price of precursor commodities, such as land, labor, and chemicals, used to make saleable narcotics and makes legally controlled chemical precursors more difficult to restrict. A global reduction in the price commanded by more mundane agricultural commodities also makes drug crops more attractive to peasant farmers. Second, international economic liberalization lowers the price of transportation, improves international infrastructure, and enhances distribution networks, all of which make transportation of drugs across long distances more affordable. Third, by increasing the overall volume in world trade, globalization gives smugglers more hiding places for drugs. Fourth, streamlined customs procedures lower the probability of seizures. Finally, financial deregulation, the proliferation of offshore banking, and increasingly rapid capital flows across borders make money laundering easier.

For all these reasons, globalized criminal networks concentrate drug production in about a dozen countries—including Mexico, Colombia, Bolivia, Peru, Afghanistan, Pakistan, Kazakhstan, Myanmar, Thailand, Morocco, Jamaica, and Laos—countries that are generally large, fertile, mountainous or jungly, and underdeveloped, with a weak or war-hobbled central state. These countries supply the developed world with drugs. Currently, Mexico has a lock on the U.S. drug market, but, in the past, Colombia has held that position (making use of maritime rather than overland importation channels), and in the future it could be any one of them. As global trade grows more laissez-faire, competition increases: In an industry that operates outside law, this translates directly to more violence.

Three decades of campaigning by the United States and the security forces of client regimes have done little to dislodge this arrangement, and there is little reason to expect change soon.

The externalization of War on Drugs costs described above would be a boon to the United States if the country received the benefits of a moderate reduction in drug consumption without paying the concomitant price in blood, unless it were conceded that the value of a human life does not depend on nationality. Even though governments clearly owe the greatest duty of consideration to their own citizens, it is unreasonable, not to mention uncompassionate, in a globally interconnected and interdependent world to knowingly sacrifice tens of thousands of foreign lives for a marginal reduction in the amount of recreational drugs consumed by Americans. Taking into account the suffering borne by noncitizens, it is necessary to search for some other method of regulating drugs: a regulatory framework the costs of which are as moderate as its benefits.

Seth Harp argues that "Mexico is a country pushed to the brink of a particularly awful kind of failure, the cause of which is its status as the leading producer and transporter of drugs bound for the U.S. black market." Another commentator recently contended that the drug war in Mexico is "a de jure armed conflict, thus triggering the portions of international humanitarian law ... that accompany a non-international armed conflict classification." Carina Bergal, Note: *The Mexican Drug War: The Case for a Non-International*

Armed Conflict Classification, 34 FORDHAM INT'L L. J. 1042, 1048 (2011). The following excerpt examines the state of drug war-related violence in Mexico in more detail.

Drug Violence in Mexico: Data and Analysis through 2010
Viridiana Ríos and David A. Shirk
University of San Diego Trans-Border Institute

Measuring drug related violence in Mexico is inherently challenging. First and foremost is the problem of definitions. "Drug violence" and "drug related homicide" are not formal categories in Mexican criminal law, and there is some disagreement among scholars and analysts over the appropriate terminology used to describe the phenomenon. Certainly, like many other ill-defined social phenomena, most people recognize drug related violence when they see it. Mass-casualty shoot-outs in the public square, bodies hanging from bridges, decapitated heads placed in front of public buildings, mass grave sites, and birthday party massacres are among the worst examples of such violence.

However, establishing a verifiable connection to drug trafficking activities requires proper police investigation and due process of law, all of which can be very time consuming in the best of circumstances. In Mexico, such investigations are often slowed by the resource limitations of police agencies, particularly at the state and local level. As a result, numerically counting "drug related" murders has thus far been a highly subjective exercise, prone to substantial guesswork even when done by government authorities. In part for this reason, Mexican authorities have been exceedingly cautious in reporting statistics on the number of drug related homicides. Indeed, over the last few years, the Mexican government regularly denied requests by the Trans-Border Institute (TBI) and other organizations for a full accounting of civilian deaths in Mexico's drug war.

On January 2011, growing public scrutiny and pressure led the Mexican government to release a comprehensive online database with a wealth of new information. A clearer picture of the patterns of Mexican drug violence thus emerges by combining data from several sources: figures on drug-related homicides from 2000–2008 gathered by Mexico's National Human Rights Commission (CNDH) from the Mexican Attorney General's Office (PGR); data from 2006 to 2010 gathered by the Trans-Border Institute from estimates compiled by the Mexico City-based *Reforma* newspaper; and recently released official statistics on organized crime-related homicides from December 2006 to 2010 compiled by the PGR for the National Public Security System (SNSP) under Mexican President Felipe Calderón.

Regardless what measure is used, the most immediately observable trend regarding recent violence in Mexico is simply the large and increasing number of intentional homicides associated with organized crime. [A]ccording to PGR figures reported by the CNDH, there were a total of 6,680 drug-related killings from 2001–2005. With 1,776 officially designated organized crime killings in 2005 and 2,221 in 2006, the rate of violence increased by 36% and 25%, respectively, during these years.

During the period from 2007 to 2010, however, the total number of organized crime related homicides identified by the Mexican government reached 34,550. In other words, the number of organized crime homicides reported during the first four years of the Calderón administration was four times greater than the total of 8,901 such killings identified during the entire Fox administration (2001–2006). With an estimated 76,131 intentional homicides in Mexico since 2007, killings related to organized crime accounted for about 45% of all murders in the country. While the upward trend in violence dates back to 2005, the major increase in violence came after a dramatic spike in 2008, as organized crime related homicides jumped to 6,837 killings, a 142% increase from 2007. After another increase of more than 40% to 9,614 killings in 2009, the number of killings linked to organized crime jumped by 59% in 2010, reaching a new record total of 15,273 deaths.

According to the government's recently released statistics, roughly 40% of organized crime killings since December 2006 occurred in just ten of the country's roughly 2,450 municipalities. Combined, the next 90 most violent municipalities accounted for another 32% of the violence, while the rest of the country accounted for only 28%. The top five most violent cities in 2010—Ciudad Juárez, Culiacán, Tijuana, Chihuahua, and Acapulco—accounted for 31.7% of the violence for the year.

Increases in violence tend to vary over time in certain states and municipalities. Tijuana, in the state of Baja California, is the most widely cited example; in 2008, violence from organized crime increased by over 270% before dropping to moderately higher levels than in the past. Ciudad Juárez, in the state of Chihuahua, presents the worst case scenario, since violence increased more than tenfold that same year, and has persisted at ever higher levels since then.

Qualitatively, violence has become more extreme and widely targeted over time. Indeed, statistics utterly fail to convey the ghastly nature of many killings, many of which are accompanied by beheadings, dismemberment, torture, and other acts of extraordinary cruelty. In addition, organized crime groups have resorted to more aggressive tactics, including the use of explosive devices and traffic blockades, that have wide-ranging effects on the civilian population. On multiple occasions in 2010, drug traffickers commandeered buses and dragged citizens from their vehicles to blockade major streets, paralyzing traffic and policing in Monterrey, Mexico's third largest city. Furthermore, to amplify their message of fear and intimidation, ever more brazen organized crime groups often take great pains to advertise their handiwork using handwritten banners, viral internet videos, and even popular ballads, or *narcocorridos*. In this sense, the tone of violence has become increasingly ominous over recent years.

Meanwhile, the number of high-profile victims—such as elected officials, police, soldiers, and journalists—has increased in recent years. For example, in 2010 alone, 14 of the country's roughly 2,450 mayors were assassinated, an unprecedented number in Mexico's history. From 2004 to 2010, there were 27 mayors killed, largely as a result of aggression by organized crime groups, though in a small number of cases this was not clear from the circumstances. The killing of mayors has been concentrated in Durango (eight mayors), Michoacán (four), Chihuahua (three), Guerrero (two), and Oaxaca (two). In addition, Silverio Cabazos, former governor of Colima from 2005 to 2009, was assassinated by gunmen outside his home in November 2010.

There were also signs of violence and intimidation in Mexico's July 4, 2010 elections, which put into play 12 governorships nationwide. DTOs [Drug Trafficking Organizations] assassinated thirteen candidates, including the PRI-candidate for governor of Tamaulipas, Rodolfo Torre Cantú. His assassination, just a few days before the election in which he was the clear frontrunner, was the highest-profile murder of a political candidate since 1994 when presidential candidate Luis Donaldo Colosio was assassinated in Tijuana. In Tamaulipas and other states, violence significantly reduced electoral turnout and citizen participation in the organization of elections.

In addition, according to the Committee to Protect Journalists (CPJ), an average of seven journalists were killed annually in Mexico since 2006. While not all of these killings involved organized crime, many exhibited clear signs of DTO involvement. The first murder of a journalist in 2010 came in early January when Valentín Valdés Espinosa, a newspaper reporter in Coahuila, was found dead a day after he and a colleague were kidnapped. Subsequently, at least 10 more journalists were assassinated, and many others were threatened, resulting in domestic and international calls for stronger protections for the press in Mexico.

Politicians and journalists were not the only victims. Indeed, the direct targeting of civilians by organized crime also increased significantly during 2010. Particularly relevant was the case of Villas de Salvárcar, a working class neighborhood in Ciudad Juárez, where in late January, armed gunmen stormed into a birthday celebration and massacred 15 people — mostly college students and one 13 year old girl — evidently mistaken to be traffickers. The action brought enormous civil protests and became a symbol of the failure of the government's heavy-handed approach to combating organized crime. The event resulted in the launch of a new, federal security strategy named "Todos Somos Juárez" (We are all Juárez), personally endorsed by President Calderon. The new strategy included a broad set of social policies meant to reduce violence in both the short and long term, with a strong emphasis on prevention via education, labor opportunities, and social development.

Another critical moment came in March, when two U.S. consular employees (and one of their spouses) were assassinated by gunmen while returning from a Sunday afternoon birthday party in Ciudad Juárez. In the aftermath, a delegation of high level U.S. authorities led by Hillary Clinton traveled to Mexico to unveil a new framework for the Mérida Initiative, a three year $1.4 billion assistance package to help Mexico fight drug trafficking started under President George Bush. Like "Todos Somos Juárez," the next phase of this initiative will focus more on social spending with the purpose of improving justice sector performance, reducing criminality, and improving general social conditions in communities affected by violence. In recent years, Mexico has not been a major recipient of U.S. economic assistance, particularly compared to other countries — like Colombia — where the United States has tried to improve security through social development spending.

In short, Mexico's violence demonstrates substantial increases over time, exhibits a significant degree of geographic concentration in production and trafficking zones, and presents a growing threat to the Mexican state and civil society. Although 2010 was the most violent year on record, the last half of the year demonstrated a significant downward trend. This has raised hope among some authorities and analysts that Mexico has finally turned a corner, and violence will return to more manageable levels in the coming years. Below we discuss the underlying factors and sequence of events that have contributed to Mexico's violence.

Why has there been so much violence in Mexico? One explanation, advanced by Mexican officials, is that drug violence is an unfortunate side effect of government counterdrug efforts. The arrests of top cartel bosses disrupt their operations and contribute to greater infighting between and within competing organized crime groups. This is surely at least part of the explanation. The determination of government officials to aggressively combat drug trafficking during recent presidential administrations represents a sea change in political will in Mexico. Yet this newfound resolve also points to another part of the explanation for the growth in violence: the reformulation of political-bureaucratic corruption that has accompanied Mexico's transformation from a single-party state into a more competitive democratic system.

During the 1980s, many of today's top cartel operatives, virtually all of them with roots in Sinaloa, helped to construct a loosely knit criminal network to smuggle drugs into the United States. Criminals within this network obtained their "commissions" (or "plazas") to control specific territories and distribution routes with the support of corrupt officials at very high levels who were paid substantial bribes. Because governmental authority was highly centralized—thanks to single party rule by the Institutional Revolutionary Party (PRI)—this arrangement provided drug traffickers with a tremendously profitable scope of operations, an enormous degree of impunity, and even certain degree of harmony among competing organizations.

Over the last thirty years, Mexico experienced a dramatic political transformation that significantly altered the domestic regulatory environment affecting drug trafficking organizations (DTOs). As single party rule gave way to state and local opposition victories during the 1990s, previously established agreements were rejected or renegotiated by new political actors, sometimes to the disadvantage of criminal networks once favored by state protection. Over the long term, in this context of political diversity and uncertainty—among other factors—the state no longer served as an effective broker and criminal organizations began to splinter and battle each other for turf.

That said, corruption remains a pervasive problem, as illustrated by several examples in 2010. In late May, Quintana Roo's gubernatorial candidate and the former mayor of Cancun, Gregorio Sánchez, was detained on drug charges and accused of having ties to the Beltrán Leyva and Zeta DTOs. Sánchez's arrest took place weeks after Mario Villanueva, the former governor of the same state (1993–1999), was extradited to the United States on similar charges. In October, Chihuahua state Attorney General, Patricia González Rodriguez, was accused by her own brother of having ties to the Juárez Cartel. The accusation was made in a widely disseminated YouTube video confession—with her brother, Mario González, surrounded by gunmen and showing signs of duress—days before he was found dead. Also, after avoiding authorities for 15 months as a fugitive and infiltrating the offices of the Mexican Congress to take his oath of office, Julio Cesar Godoy was formally impeached and is now under investigation for allegedly accepting $2 million in bribes, based on his recorded telephone conversations with drug traffickers. Finally, over 300 inmates escaped from Mexico's troubled federal prisons in 2010, often abetted by officials who allowed prisoners to walk out the front door; as when prison officials granted inmates an unofficial furlough in order to murder a group of 17 people in July.

Such examples suggest several new dynamics regarding drug trafficking and corruption in Mexico today. First, corruption is pervasive at all levels. Second, drug corruption is not limited to any particular political party, though it remains associated with certain geographic areas in states that still tend to favor the PRI. Third, allegations of corruption are often difficult to prove, and can be engineered to target upstanding public officials who present an obstacle to organized crime. Finally, while it may appear that Mexico has more corruption today than in the past, it is likely that corruption is simply more clearly visible. Today, there is both greater transparency and—importantly—competition has emboldened DTOs to expose the corruption networks of their rivals, either through public accusations or as informants for the government upon arrest.

In addition to the factors mentioned above, some analysts believe that increased competition among traffickers has been fueled by volatility in U.S. drug consumption (shrinking demand), increased border interdiction (greater costs for traffickers), fluctuating drug prices (lower profits), growing domestic demand in Mexico (new markets), and efforts to crack down on organized crime (government intervention). However, what stands out about Mexico's security crisis in recent years is the extent to which recent violence has been driven by competition among Mexican DTOs. The first major schisms among Mexican DTOs started in the early 1990s, as four main groups emerged as the country's predominant wholesale traffickers of drugs: the Juárez Cartel, the Tijuana Cartel, the Sinaloa Cartel, and the Gulf Cartel. In recent years, the Sinaloa Cartel's efforts to encroach on the territories of its rivals (and some of its former allies) have contributed to conflicts and schisms that have greatly increased drug violence.

It is not clear how accurately the Mexican government is able to discern the specific drug trafficking organizations that are tied to a particular killing. However, in August 2010, Mexican authorities reported that the Sinaloa organization's conflict with the Juárez Cartel alone accounted for nearly a quarter of Mexico's recent drug-related violence. Meanwhile, accounting for another 30% of the violence are the Sinaloa Cartel's clashes with their former allies in the Beltran Leyva Organization (BLO), which broke away in 2008, and its battles with the Tijuana and Gulf Cartels.

The balance of power and dynamics of competition among these organizations was also affected by tactical operations and arrests by the Mexican government. Over the course of 2010, at least 13 of the country's most wanted criminals were either captured or killed, including Ignacio 'Nacho' Coronel (killed), Teodoro "El Teo" García Simental (arrested), Edgar "The Barbie" Valdez (arrested), Ezequiel "Tony Tormenta" Cárdenas Guillén (arrested), and Nazario "El Chayo" Moreno (killed). These blows were especially damaging to the BLO, the LFM organization, and the Zetas, leading to some speculation as to whether the government's tactical strategy was biased in favor of the Sinaloa Cartel or simply followed the pragmatic goal of targeting the most vulnerable DTOs.

Mexican officials have long insisted that such arrests are part of a comprehensive strategy to break the cartels into smaller, more manageable pieces. They want to downsize drug traffickers from a national security threat to a local security problem. For the time being, the result appears to be a much more chaotic and unpredictable pattern of violent conflict among drug trafficking groups than in the past. Indeed, Calderón's critics point to recent data as evidence that the government's strategy of direct confrontation has actually exacerbated the violence. As drug trafficking organizations have fought and splintered, their targets have increasingly included officials and ordinary civilians and their illegal activities have become more diversified. With no end in sight, some analysts and civic groups have called for a drastic change in strategy. Nonetheless, the Calderón administration remains steadfast that the government should continue its direct confrontation of Mexican DTOs—along with the continued deployment of the armed forces—until the country's civilian public security agencies can be strengthened to manage the task.

To this end, in the effort to reduce crime, violence, and corruption, Mexican authorities have begun to implement major reforms to the criminal justice system. Specifically, a series of reforms has introduced new provisions to strengthen due process, increase transparency, and improve efficiency in criminal procedure. Also, the Mexican government has established new professional standards and procedures for police throughout the country, as well as federal grants for training, technology, and equipment. Some of these changes may have destabilizing effects in the short term. For example, the removal of corrupt officers from a police force may harm one organized crime group while allowing another new entry to operate in the same territory. Likewise, as court procedures are modified to strengthen due process, the failures of ill prepared or incompetent judges, prosecutors, and public defenders may allow some criminals to walk free. In short, because systems of professional recruitment, training, and oversight (such as internal investigations and citizen councils) in the criminal justice system are currently inadequate, the current battle against organized crime will most likely be long and protracted, with significant and costly setbacks.

Mexico is presently confronted by a significant challenge. Clashes among drug cartels with highly sophisticated operations present a growing threat to Mexican government and society. In 2010, Mexico saw a dramatic increase in violence in many parts of the country, largely due to spikes in areas that previously had low or moderate levels of violence. Still, it is important to keep Mexico's recent violence in perspective. In a country of more than 100 million people, the odds of being killed in a drug-related homicide in 2010 were one in 6,667, about the same as the odds of being killed in an automobile accident in the United States (about one in 6,500). The odds of being killed in Mexico's drug violence decrease dramatically if a person is not a drug trafficker, mayor, or police officer in a disputed trafficking region.

With this perspective, it is important not to exaggerate the magnitude of recent violence in Mexico. Still, it is clear that recent violence presents a vexing and persistent problem for the Mexican state, and a source of serious concern for ordinary Mexicans. Drawing on recent developments, it is worth considering the best- and worst-case scenarios for Mexico's near term future. In the best case scenario, Mexico's drug-related violence will soon reach a turning point at which—due to a shift in the balance of power that produces a new equilibrium among DTOs—violence will die down significantly. This appears to be what has happened in Baja California, where the weakening of the Tijuana Cartel has allowed the Sinaloa Cartel to make new inroads. While it is difficult to know whether a similar shift could occur after recent blows against the BLO, LFM, and the Zetas, government efforts targeting these breakaway organizations will almost certainly have a significant impact on the course of events in 2011.

In the worst case scenario, the number of drug related homicides will continue to increase over the coming year, with continued spikes in locations previously unaffected by drug violence and a growing number of officials and ordinary citizens caught in the crossfire. It is not likely that such an increase in violence would necessarily lead to the collapse of the Mexican government, widespread political insurgency, or a sudden military takeover. Despite even higher levels of violence than currently found in Mexico, the governments of Brazil, Colombia, and Guatemala remain intact. Even so, any further increases in violence could result in more severe damage to the Mexican economy, internal population displacement, and negative impacts for neighboring countries in Central America, where Mexican DTO operations and violent clashes have already spread. Moreover, given evidence of significant political penetration by DTOs, there are real risks for democratic governance that could increase with the approach of the country's 2012 presidential elections.

Most likely, the proximate future lies somewhere in between these two scenarios. With no sign of surrender on the part of the government or the DTOs, Mexico's drug war is far from over. Nor is it even clear that the worst has passed. Indeed, the start of 2011 seems to herald a continuation or increase in violence in the coming year. In the first three weeks of January 2011, *Reforma* reported 245 drug-related killings per week, 41 more than during the same period a year ago and 20 more than the average for 2010. At the same time, with the presidential elections looming, the Calderón administration needs to shift to a strategy that will help build political support for his party in 2012. This may lead the federal government to focus on regions that are easily controllable and efforts that will yield high-impact results. However, this may leave the most difficult cases, such as Ciudad Juárez, in turmoil, with violence keeping the same high but steady trend that occurred in 2010.

Continuing drug prohibition-related violence has led a number of prominent international political figures to call for a dramatic reassessment of international drug control strategy in recent years. As noted above, former Mexican President Vicente Fox raised the prospect of ending drug prohibition in late 2010. But the trend began in 2009, when the Latin American Commission on Drugs and Democracy issued a striking report criticizing the United States-led drug war. The Commission was comprised of a blue-ribbon panel of experts from throughout Latin America and headed by three former Latin American Presidents: Fernando Henrique Cardoso of Brazil, César Gaviria of Colombia and Ernesto Zedillo of Mexico. The Commission concluded that the war on drugs is a "failed war" that has led to an increase in organized crime and drug-related violence without reducing drug use or availability. The group called for a paradigm shift in drug policy toward an approach that focuses on demand reduction and "[c]hanges the status of addicts from drug buyers in the illegal market to that of patients cared for in the public health system." THE LATIN AM. COMM'N ON DRUGS AND DEMOCRACY, DRUGS AND DEMOCRACY: TOWARD A PARADIGM SHIFT 1 (2009) (noting that after a decades-long war "[w]e are farther than ever from the announced goal of eradicating drugs").

In June 2011, the Global Commission on Drug Policy released a report that was perhaps even more critical of the war on drugs. The Global Commission on Drug Policy, which included the three former Presidents who had convened the Latin American Commission on Drugs and Democracy among its 19 members, was formed to "build on" the Latin American Commission's work. The Global Commission also featured former Secretary General of the United Nations, Kofi Annan, and former U.S. Secretary of State under President Ronald Reagan, George P. Shultz.

War on Drugs
Report of The Global Commission on Drug Policy (2011)

The global war on drugs has failed. When the United Nations Single Convention on Narcotic Drugs came into being 50 years ago, and when President Nixon launched the US government's war on drugs 40 years ago, policymakers believed that harsh law enforcement action against those involved in drug production, distribution and use would lead to an ever-diminishing market in controlled drugs such as heroin, cocaine and cannabis, and the eventual achievement of a 'drug free world'. In practice, the global scale of illegal drug markets—largely controlled by organized crime—has grown dramatically over this period. While accurate estimates of global consumption across the entire 50-year period are not available, an analysis of the last 10 years alone shows a large and growing market.

In spite of the increasing evidence that current policies are not achieving their objectives, most policymaking bodies at the national and international level have tended to avoid open scrutiny or debate on alternatives.

This lack of leadership on drug policy has prompted the establishment of our Commission, and leads us to our view that the time is now right for a serious, comprehensive and wide-ranging review of strategies to respond to the drug phenomenon. The starting point for this review is the recognition of the global drug problem as a set of interlinked health and social challenges to be managed, rather than a war to be won.

Commission members have agreed on four core principles that should guide national and international drug policies and strategies, and have made eleven recommendations for action.

PRINCIPLES

> 1. Drug policies must be based on solid empirical and scientific evidence. The primary measure of success should be the reduction of harm to the health, security and welfare of individuals and society.

In the 50 years since the United Nations initiated a truly global drug prohibition system, we have learned much about the nature and patterns of drug production, distribution, use and dependence, and the effectiveness of our attempts to reduce these problems. It might have been understandable that the architects of the system would place faith in the concept of eradicating drug production and use (in the light of the limited evidence available at the time). There is no excuse, however, for ignoring the evidence and experience accumulated since then. Drug policies and strategies at all levels too often continue to be driven by ideological perspectives, or political convenience, and pay too little attention to the complexities of the drug market, drug use and drug addiction.

Effective policymaking requires a clear articulation of the policy's objectives. The 1961 UN Single Convention on Narcotic Drugs made it clear that the ultimate objective of the system was the improvement of the 'health and welfare of mankind'.

This reminds us that drug policies were initially developed and implemented in the hope of achieving outcomes in terms of a reduction in harms to individuals and society—less crime, better health, and more economic and social development. However, we have primarily been measuring our success in the war on drugs by entirely different measures—those that report on processes, such as the number of arrests, the amounts seized, or the harshness of punishments. These indicators may tell us how tough we are being, but they do not tell us how successful we are in improving the 'health and welfare of mankind'.

> 2. Drug policies must be based on human rights and public health principles. We should end the stigmatization and marginalization of people who use certain drugs and those involved in the lower levels of cultivation, production and distribution, and treat people dependent on drugs as patients, not criminals.

Certain fundamental principles underpin all aspects of national and international policy. These are enshrined in the Universal Declaration of Human Rights and many international treaties that have followed. Of particular relevance to drug policy are the rights to life, to health, to due process and a fair trial, to be free from torture or cruel, inhuman or degrading treatment, from slavery, and from discrimination. These rights are inalienable, and commitment to them takes precedence over other international agreements, including the drug control conventions. As the UN High Commissioner for Human Rights, Navanethem Pillay, has stated, "Individuals who use drugs do not forfeit their human rights. Too often, drug users suffer discrimination, are forced to accept treatment, marginalized and often harmed by approaches which over-emphasize criminalization and punishment while under-emphasizing harm reduction and respect for human rights."

A number of well-established and proven public health measures (generally referred to as *harm reduction,* an approach that includes syringe access and treatment using the proven medications methadone or buprenorphine) can minimize the risk of drug overdose deaths and the transmission of HIV and other blood-borne infections. However, governments often do not fully implement these interventions, concerned that by improving the health of people who use drugs, they are undermining a 'tough on drugs' message. This is illogical—sacrificing the health and welfare of one group of citizens when effective health protection measures are available is unacceptable, and increases the risks faced by the wider community.

An indiscriminate approach to 'drug trafficking' is similarly problematic. Many people taking part in the drug market are themselves the victims of violence and intimidation, or are dependent on drugs. An example of this phenomenon are the drug 'mules' who take the most visible and risky roles in the supply and delivery chain. Unlike those in charge of drug trafficking organizations, these individuals do not usually have an extensive and violent criminal history, and some engage in the drug trade primarily to get money for their own drug dependence. We should not treat all those arrested for trafficking as equally culpable—many are coerced into their actions, or are driven to desperate measures through their own addiction or economic situation. It is not appropriate to punish such individuals in the same way as the members of violent organized crime groups who control the market.

Finally, many countries still react to people dependent on drugs with punishment and stigmatization. In reality, drug dependence is a complex health condition that has a mixture of causes—social, psychological and physical (including, for example, harsh living conditions, or a history of personal trauma or emotional problems). Trying to manage this complex condition through punishment is ineffective—much greater success can be achieved by providing a range of evidence-based drug treatment services. Countries that have treated citizens dependent on drugs as patients in need of treatment, instead of criminals deserving of punishment, have demonstrated extremely positive results in crime reduction, health improvement, and overcoming dependence.

> 3. The development and implementation of drug policies should be a global shared responsibility, but also needs to take into consideration diverse political, social and cultural realities. Policies should respect the rights and needs of people affected by production, trafficking and consumption, as explicitly acknowledged in the 1988 Convention on Drug Trafficking.

The UN drug control system is built on the idea that all governments should work together to tackle drug markets and related problems. This is a reasonable starting point, and there is certainly a responsibility to be shared between producing, transit and consuming countries (although the distinction is increasingly blurred, as many countries now experience elements of all three).

However, the idea of shared responsibility has too often become a straitjacket that inhibits policy development and experimentation. The UN (through the International Narcotics Control Board), and in particular the US (notably through its 'certification' process), have worked strenuously over the last 50 years to ensure that all countries adopt the same rigid approach to drug policy—the same laws, and the same tough approach to their enforcement. As national governments have become more aware of the complexities of the problems, and options for policy responses in their own territories, many have opted to use the flexibilities within the Conventions to try new strategies and programs, such as decriminalization initiatives or harm reduction programs. When these involve a more tolerant approach to drug use, governments have faced international diplomatic pressure to 'protect the integrity of the Conventions', even when the policy is legal, successful and supported in the country.

A current example of this process (what may be described as 'drug control imperialism'), can be observed with the proposal by the Bolivian government to remove the practice of coca leaf chewing from the sections of the 1961 Convention that prohibit all non-medical uses. Despite the fact that successive studies have shown that the indigenous practice of coca leaf chewing is associated with none of the harms of international cocaine markets, and that a clear majority of the Bolivian population (and neighboring countries) support this change, many of the rich 'cocaine consumer' countries (led by the US) have formally objected to the amendment.

The idea that the international drug control system is immutable, and that any amendment—however reasonable or slight—is a threat to the integrity of the entire system, is short-sighted. As with all multilateral agreements, the drug conventions need to be subject to constant review and modernization in light of changing and variable circumstances. Specifically, national governments must be enabled to exercise the freedom to experiment with responses more suited to their circumstances. This analysis and exchange of experiences is a crucial element of the process of learning about the relative effectiveness of different approaches, but the belief that we all need to have exactly the same laws, restrictions and programs has been an unhelpful restriction.

> 4. Drug policies must be pursued in a comprehensive manner, involving families, schools, public health specialists, development practitioners and civil society leaders, in partnership with law enforcement agencies and other relevant governmental bodies.

With their strong focus on law enforcement and punishment, it is not surprising that the leading institutions in the implementation of the drug control system have been the police, border control and military authorities directed by Ministries of Justice, Security or Interior. At the multilateral level, regional or United Nations structures are also dominated by these interests.

Although governments have increasingly recognized that law enforcement strategies for drug control need to be integrated into a broader approach with social and public health programs, the structures for policymaking, budget allocation, and implementation have not modernized at the same pace.

These institutional dynamics obstruct objective and evidence-based policymaking. This is more than a theoretical problem—repeated studies have demonstrated that governments achieve much greater financial and social benefit for their communities by investing in health and social programs, rather than investing in supply reduction and law enforcement activities. However, in most countries, the vast majority of available resources are spent on the enforcement of drug laws and the punishment of people who use drugs.

The lack of coherence is even more marked at the United Nations. The development of the global drug control regime involved the creation of three bodies to oversee the implementation of the conventions—the UN Office on Drugs and Crime (UNODC), the International Narcotics Control Board (INCB), and the Commission on Narcotic Drugs (CND). This structure is premised on the notion that international drug control is primarily a fight against crime and criminals. Unsurprisingly, there is a built-in vested interest in maintaining the law enforcement focus and the senior decisionmakers in these bodies have traditionally been most familiar with this framework.

Now that the nature of the drug policy challenge has changed, the institutions must follow. Global drug policy should be created from the shared strategies of all interested multilateral agencies—UNODC of course, but also UNAIDS, WHO, UNDP, UNICEF, UN Women, the World Bank, and the Office of the High Commissioner on Human Rights. The marginalization of the World Health Organization is particularly worrisome given the fact that it has been given a specific mandate under the drug control treaties.

While national governments have considerable discretion to move away from repressive policies, the UN drug control system continues to act largely as a straitjacket, limiting the proper review and modernization of policy. For most of the last century, it has been the US government that has led calls for the development and maintenance of repressive drug policies. We therefore welcome the change of tone emerging from the current administration—with President Obama himself acknowledging the futility of a 'war on drugs' and the validity of a debate on alternatives. It will be necessary, though, for the US to follow up this new rhetoric with real reform, by reducing its reliance on incarceration and punishment of drug users, and by using its considerable diplomatic influence to foster reform in other countries.

———————

Although the Global Commission on Drug Policy's report speaks positively of "the change of tone emerging from" President Barack Obama's administration, the White House Office of National Drug Control Policy (ONDCP) did not respond favorably to the Commission's report. An ONDCP spokesperson criticized the report, saying that "[m]aking more drugs available—as this report suggests—will make it harder to keep our communities healthy and safe." Ken Ellingwood and Brian Bennett, *High-profile Panel Urges Non-criminal Approach to World Drug Policy*, L.A. TIMES, June 1, 2011. Former U.S. President Jimmy Carter was much more receptive to the report and wrote an editorial in support of the Commission's recommendations in the *New York Times*. Carter praised the report for "describ[ing] the total failure of the present global antidrug effort, and in particular America's 'war on drugs'" and argued that "to make drug policies more humane and more effective, the American government should support and enact the reforms laid out by the Global Commission on Drug Policy." Jimmy Carter, *Call Off the Global Drug War*, N.Y. TIMES, June 17, 2011 at A35.

In contrast to the Global Commission's belief that increased drug-war violence weighs in favor of abandoning the war on drugs, many proponents of Mexico's strategy argue the violence is a sign that the approach is working. Those who adopt this interpretation argue that as the drug cartels are weakened by heavy-handed enforcement, they turn on each other, which causes violence to spike in the short-term. Head of the U.S. Drug Enforcement Administration Michele Leonhart, for example, has compared the drug cartels to "caged animals, attacking one another." In response to a report that nearly 1,000 Mexican children were killed in drug war violence between 2006 and 2010, Leonhart argued: "It may seem contradictory, but the unfortunate level of violence is a sign of success in the fight against drugs." Anne-Marie O'Connor and William Booth, *Mexican Drug Cartels Targeting and Killing Children*, WASH. POST, Apr. 9, 2011.

The phrase global war on drugs has taken on a new dimension in recent years, as drug trafficking organizations and terrorist groups have become increasingly intertwined. *See, e.g.,* Vanda Felbab-Brown, Shooting Up: Counterinsurgency and the War on Drugs (2009). The Global Commission on Drug Policy pointed to this development to critique the drug war, arguing "it is the illicit nature of the market that creates much of the marker-related violence … and, in some cases, fund[s] insurgency and terrorism." However, others believe that the link between terrorism and the illegal drug market means we should prosecute the drug war even more vigorously. Which conclusion do you think is correct? Consider the following remarks by former U.S. Secretary of Homeland Security, Michael Chertoff, from a speech he gave at a recent law review symposium.

The Nexus between Drug Trafficking, Terrorism and Organized Crime
Michael Chertoff
13 Chapman Law Review 681 (2010)

We have a tendency to say everything is war, the war on poverty, the war on drugs, the war on this—but some of these areas really do have a war. There's repeated violence and destruction, and when we look at the intersection between terrorism and international drug trafficking, I think we really do have a war. So, what I thought I'd do is give you a little bit of a sense of change from the beginning of this decade through the next decade. I'll tell you right up front, I'm not recommending legalizing drugs. I think that would be a major mistake.

I first looked at the nexus between drug trafficking and terrorism when I was head of the Criminal Division at the Department of Justice. Some of you may remember that the FARC, the Revolutionary Army in Colombia, which was a left wing political organization, was very strong in the 1990s and the early part of this decade. It has lost a considerable amount of ground since then, partly because of our work with President Uribe of Colombia and his people in really reforming the military and pushing back against the FARC. But certainly they remain a potent force, and they were very potent in the late 1990s and the early 2000s.

We brought a series of indictments against the FARC for various terrorism-related violations which included, among other things, kidnapping people—including Americans—and holding them for ransom. But one of the things that emerged as we investigated was that the FARC had begun to migrate toward becoming a classic drug organization. What happened first was they began to encounter drug traffickers in the areas of Columbia that they controlled, and then they began to charge them a tax or a protection fee. This is similar to what organized crime often does in the United States. They don't directly engage in the sale of drugs, but they essentially reap the benefits by extorting money from the drug dealers, or taxing them and protecting them against being ripped off.

So the FARC began to move into the protection racket, but pretty soon that migrated into something a little bit more enabling. They'd be involved in managing staging areas, helping load airplanes, and ultimately they became full-fledged partners in drug trafficking. And, in fact, we had indictments issued against the FARC that included both terrorism and drug trafficking charges. In many ways, that was the first concrete example of the intersection between a global criminal organization involved in the drug trade— one that has access to the modern tools of money, movement, communications, and travel—with terrorist organizations who benefit from the money and the enabling capabilities of the drug organizations, and who can provide violence and the support of violence, which of course is important for the drug organizations.

We've now seen this problem migrate from Colombia around the world. It's no secret in Afghanistan, for example, where the cultivation of poppies creates a major source for heroin. It's no secret that the Taliban has protected and, in fact, is cooperating with drug dealers, because they receive money from the drug dealing and the drug trafficking. That money enables them to buy arms and, not coincidentally, the drug activity winds up also hurting the West and the enemies of the Taliban, so they get a double bang for their buck. They have the ability both, in some general sense, to strike at their enemies and, in a more specific, narrow sense, to get the kinds of financing that they need in order to acquire the weapons and trading capabilities which allow them to be such lethal adversaries.

What we've now seen, however, is that this is moving into South America, as well in places apart from Colombia. For example, recent information tells us that there has been an increase in the movement of cocaine from South America into Europe. That's partly a reflection of some of the progress we've made in making it more difficult to bring drugs into the United States. Partly, it's a rise in demand in Europe, but what's interesting, for the purpose of my talk, is how it's getting there. And the way a lot of it is getting there is via North Africa. The cocaine moves out of South America, often through Venezuela, where, of course, Hugo Chavez is really a dedicated enemy of the United States and the West and, therefore, very happy to be in a neighborhood of drug trafficking. It then moves from Venezuela into North Africa, where it is staged and ultimately sent into Europe to be sold.

What we have learned is that in North Africa, groups affiliated with terrorism, including Al-Qaeda in the Maghreb (which is a North African group that is sympathetic and, in fact, formally linked with the core Al-Qaeda in Pakistan and Afghanistan), have become involved in protecting the loads when they arrive and while they're being held in staging to be ultimately shipped into Europe. And the reason for that, again, is perfectly obvious, because it's a source of money which enables them to recruit and buy arms and further their own political goals. So, once again, we begin to see the capabilities of drug organizations, and the money they generate, to create an attractive partner for terrorist organizations. Terrorist organizations also have the ability to provide the violence and the security that is very important to the drug traffickers.

What I predict is going to happen is, at some point, some trafficker is going to look in the mirror and say: "You know, I'm not a drug trafficker. I'm a political insurgent." We're very close to having that cross-over of political ideology, no matter how far-fetched it is, beginning to engraft itself into the violence and the mayhem that is part of the drug trade. That, of course, is going to bring two dangerous adversaries together in a way which is only going to multiply the problems for those of us around the world who are trying to protect society.

Where this might touch this country most seriously is in Northern Mexico. I know people in California know this, but it's not that well-known in other parts of the country—there's currently nothing less than a war going on in Northern Mexico for the control and governance of the country. It is underway because the President of Mexico has done a courageous thing—he has recognized that tolerating the rule of drug organizations in various cities in Northern Mexico is not an acceptable alternative for a modern democracy. You cannot surrender parts of your country to organized crime or narcotics trafficking gangs. And so he made it his top priority when he came into office several years ago to take these groups on.

Not surprisingly, when you strike at organized criminal groups, they strike back. And the tactics that they've adopted in many of the cartels in Northern Mexico are directly derived from what they have seen on television or over the Internet in Iraq and Afghanistan. We have beheadings. We have kidnappings. We have bombings. We have torture. All the things that Al-Qaeda and the Taliban have done are now being used by these organized crime cartels.

The reason is quite explicit. It is to terrorize the population of Mexico so that either this President at some point will be forced to pull back, or when the next election comes, it is more likely to go to somebody who is either tacitly or overtly willing to make peace with the cartels. That would be a disaster for the United States. It would be the equivalent of putting Waziristan on our southern border. It's one of the reasons that, when I was Secretary, we put into effect a process of contingency planning against the remote—but nevertheless certainly not unthinkable—possibility that we might have an increase in cross-border violence coming from Mexico into the United States.

The short answer here, of course, is to support President Calderon in his effort. It's one of the reasons that President Bush pushed very hard for an initiative to send not only money but weapons, training, and modern technology to Mexico to help the Mexicans ramp up their own ability to fight the drug gangs. This policy is continuing into the current administration, which is also firmly committed to supporting Mexico in this endeavor. But, again, I want to put before you the notion that if one of these drug leaders one day decides that rather than thinking of himself as a thug, he'd rather think of himself as a political leader, we will have completed that merger between terrorism and organized criminality, which I think we've seen in its incipient phases in various places of the world.

Tracking Narco-Terrorist Networks: The Money Trail
Michael Jacobson and Matthew Levitt
34 Fletcher Forum of World Affairs 117 (2010)

In October 2008, after a two-year joint investigation by U.S. and Colombian authorities, the Colombian government arrested thirty-six individuals on money laundering and drug charges. According to authorities, this network—comprised of Lebanese expatriates—was more than a traditional criminal syndicate, and was shipping a portion of its profits back to Hizbollah in Lebanon.

These types of cases—where terrorist groups and organized crime networks are closely intertwined—are growing far more common. These "hybrid" organizations—part terrorist group, part organized crime network—are "meaner and uglier than anything law enforcement or militaries have ever faced" in the view of senior U.S. Drug Enforcement Agency (DEA) officials.

While this growing linkage is certainly a dangerous trend from the U.S. perspective, it also presents opportunities for policymakers. As the nexus of terrorism and criminal activity intensifies, targeting terrorist groups' criminal activities becomes an increasingly effective strategy. Terrorist networks are becoming increasingly transnational and a key challenge in confronting them is achieving international cooperation in counterterrorism initiatives. By capitalizing on terrorists' increasing criminal activity, the Obama administration could leverage its strategy of international cooperation and diplomatic engagement to gain broader support against illicit financing of transnational threats.

The terrorist threat is not static. Terrorists adapt and evolve, partly in response to the very countermeasures we enact. As the terrorist threat has evolved, the means by which terrorist groups raise, store, and move funds have also changed and have often hindered government efforts to thwart terrorist activities. Studies show that terrorist groups learn from one another, exchange information on new technologies, and share innovations. This is particularly evident in the financing and resourcing of terrorist activities.

Before September 11, 2001, al-Qaeda funded and controlled operations from its base in Afghanistan. Al-Qaeda provided funding for the East Africa embassy bombings in 1998, the 2000 attack on the *USS Cole* in Yemen, and the 2001 World Trade Center attacks. Today, the terrorist threat is more decentralized, with the al-Qaeda core no longer funding other terrorist groups, cells, or operations as they did in the past. Local cells are being increasingly left to fund their own activities. While many fundraising techniques remain popular, including abuse of charities and otherwise legitimate businesses, terrorist cells increasingly engage in criminal activity to fund their actions. For example, Al-Jemaah al-Islamiyah, an al-Qaeda affiliate in Southeast Asia, helped to finance the jewelry stores. Another example is the 2002 Bali bombings by robbing 2005 attacks in London, which were partially financed by credit card fraud.

Terrorist groups are involved in a wide variety of criminal activities, from cigarette smuggling to selling counterfeit products, but the nexus of drugs and terror is particularly glaring. According to the DEA, nineteen of the forty-three designated foreign terrorist organizations are linked definitively to the global drug trade, and up to 60 percent of terrorist organizations are connected to the illegal narcotics industry. For example, the 2004 Madrid train bombings, which killed 191 people, were partially bankrolled by hashish sales.

Indeed, the drug trade's financial benefits are acutely alluring. The United Nations estimates that the international drug trade generates $322 billion per year, making drugs by far the most lucrative illicit activity. Beyond mere sales, drugs provide diverse revenue sources, including taxes on farmers and local cartels, and necessitate security detail for all aspects of production, trade, and distribution. Groups like the Afghan Taliban, the Revolutionary Armed Forces of Colombia, the Kurdistan Workers' Party, and Lebanon's Hizbollah generate significant revenue from extortion fees collected from drug cartels and poppy or coca farmers operating in their territory.

It may seem hypocritical for supposedly religious terrorist groups to pursue criminal activity; however, many of these groups acknowledge the contradiction and seek to justify their actions. For instance, in 2006, Taliban member Khan Mohammed, who was sentenced to life in prison for drug trafficking and narco-terrorism, described his participation in the Afghan drug trade as stemming from a desire to see "God turn all the infidels into corpses." He added, "Whether it is by opium or by shooting, this is our common goal." A leader of the Lebanon-based Fatah al-Islam, a group with ties to al-Qaeda, justified Fatah al-Islam's bank robberies by positing that stealing money from the "infidels" and their institutions is something that Allah "has permitted us to do," noting that this money is instead "directed towards jihad."

In Afghanistan, an independent Taliban militia controls its own territory, maintains bases and training camps, facilitates weapons smuggling, and engages in every aspect of the narcotics production pipeline. Naturally, the Taliban seeks to maintain control over its own territory. Indeed, an increasing number of DEA arrests in recent years have targeted drug kingpins closely tied to the Taliban, such as Baz Mohammad and Haji Juma Ka Khan. In October 2005, the U.S. government formally extradited Mohammad from Afghanistan to New York. According to the DEA, Mohammad was a "Taliban-linked narco-terrorist" who had conspired to import more than $25 million worth of heroin from Afghanistan into the United States and other countries. Khan, the first defendant prosecuted under the 2006 Federal Narco-Terrorism statute, trafficked massive quantities of drugs "with the intent to support a terrorist organization."

All things considered, the growing nexus between international terrorism and organized crime may actually be a positive development. For one, tracking terrorists for their illicit activities, rather than their terrorism-based endeavors, is less complicated. Also, while countries may adhere to dissimilar definitions of terrorism or hold divergent lists of designated terrorist organizations, there is more of a consensus on the need to fight crime.

Some countries are more willing to coordinate with the United States on criminal law enforcement than on counterterrorism efforts, for a variety of reasons. Many countries do not want to acknowledge that they have a terrorist problem that they are not dealing with effectively. Others are reluctant to be seen cooperating with the United States in the unpopular "War on Terror." The governments in the Tri-Border Area (TBA) of Argentina, Paraguay, and Brazil, where Hizbollah, Hamas, and other terrorist organizations have had a long-standing presence, is a good example of the former. For instance, in December 2006, the U.S. Treasury designated several prominent Lebanese expatriates in the TBA as terrorists because of their Hizbollah ties. In response, the Argentine, Paraguayan, and

Brazilian governments issued a joint statement exonerating these individuals and rejecting American claims of terrorist activity in the TBA.

However, the 2007 State Department annual report on terrorism reveals that these three governments take a markedly more aggressive approach to other criminal activities: "The governments of the TBA have long been concerned with arms and drugs smuggling, document fraud, money laundering, and the manufacture and movement of contraband goods through this region." Thus, the United States would be wise to work with the TBA governments through crime enforcement and drug-related channels rather than by ineffectively promoting collaboration on counterterrorism measures.

This approach is appealing because it would require neither changes to domestic legal structures nor a reorganization of government bodies or legal, administrative, and regulatory authorities. Drug laws are comprehensive and ubiquitous; governments must simply enforce existing laws and hold terrorists accountable for their transgressions. Enforcing domestic laws is not a political statement, but merely a function of law and order and of national sovereignty.

This approach of targeting terrorist organizations for their criminal activity could pay especially large dividends when it comes to Hizbollah. The United States and many of its allies, particularly the Europeans, disagree on whether or not Hizbollah is a terrorist organization. There is far more agreement, however, that Hizbollah's global criminal activities and infrastructure pose a serious problem and need to be addressed.

To date, the European Union has not designated any part of Hizbollah as a terrorist organization, although the EU included Hizbollah members involved in specific acts of terrorism, such as Imad Mughniyeh, on its terrorism list. Even the United States' closest ally, the United Kingdom, has been reluctant to treat Hizbollah as a terrorist group. In March 2009, the United Kingdom announced that it was reviving dialogue with the political wing of Hizbollah. Unlike the United States, which has blacklisted the entire Hizbollah organization, the United Kingdom has banned only Hizbollah's terrorist (External Security Organization) and military wings. The ban on the terrorist wing began in 2000, while the ban on the military wing followed Hizbollah's June 2008 decision to increase its support to Iraqi and Palestinian militants.

The inherent challenge in developing an international consensus on the definition of terrorism is highlighted by enduring debates at the United Nations, which tend to devolve into semantic arguments over the distinction between "terrorist" and "freedom fighter." Even the United States and its European allies encounter disagreement. For example, Europe has yet to designate Hizbollah as a terrorist group because of the organization's activity in the Lebanese political arena. Many European officials argue that Hizbollah, which is a part of the Lebanese government, is now on the path to becoming a legitimate political party, and that the designation would backfire and reverse this progress.

Despite the differences between U.S. and European perceptions of and policies toward Hizbollah, there is one critical area where all parties' interests converge: law enforcement. The United States and its European counterparts have a particularly strong interest in combating Hizbollah's burgeoning role in illicit drug trafficking. Regardless of divergent political considerations or varying definitions of terrorism, combating crime and enforcing sovereign laws are straight-forward issues. Of all Islamic groups, Hizbollah has the longest record of engaging in criminal activity to support its activities. While Hizbollah is involved in a wide variety of criminal activities, its role in the production and trafficking of narcotics is particularly salient. Hizbollah has capitalized on the vast Lebanese

Shi'a expatriate population, mainly located in South America and Africa. With its strong presence in Africa, Hizbollah has been able to utilize the continent as a strategic location from which to raise and transfer funds and to engage in such criminal enterprises as diamond smuggling.

In early 2009, Admiral James G. Stavridis, the supreme allied commander, Europe, testified before the House Armed Services Committee about the nexus of illicit drug trafficking. He testified that in August 2008, the U.S. Southern Command and the DEA coordinated with host nations to target a Hizbollah drug trafficking ring in the TBA of Argentina, Brazil, and Paraguay. According to Michael Braun, the former assistant administrator and chief of operations at the DEA, "both Hamas and Hizbollah are active in this [Tri-Border] region, where it is possible to make a profit of 1 million dollars from the sale of fourteen or fifteen kilos of drugs, an amount that could be transported in a single suitcase." As discussed above, in late 2008, U.S. and Colombian investigators identified and dismantled an international cocaine smuggling and money-laundering ring based in Colombia. This operation, which was composed of a Colombian drug cartel and Lebanese members of Hizbollah, used portions of its profits—allegedly hundreds of millions of dollars per year—to finance Hizbollah.

Terrorism and criminal activity are likely to overlap even further in the coming years with terrorist organizations' marked turn to drug trafficking. As former DEA operations chief Michael Braun explained in a July 2008 speech, "terrorist organizations and drug cartels often rely on the same money launderers" and shadow facilitation networks. Targeting the full range of money launderers, drug traffickers, document forgers and other facilitators could prove instrumental in the struggle to combat today's terrorism threat.

B. International Drug Treaties and Control Organizations

The International Control of Illegal Drugs and the U.N. Treaty Regime: Preventing or Causing Human Rights Violations?
Daniel Heilmann
19 Cardozo Journal of International and Comparative Law 217 (2011)

International drug control, administered under the auspices of the United Nations, rests on three pillars: The [1961] Single Convention on Narcotic Drugs as amended by the Protocol (1972) (Single Convention), the Convention on Psychotropic Substances (1971 Convention), and the United Nations Convention Against Illicit Traffic in Narcotic Drugs and Psychotropic Substances (1988 Convention).

The status of the international drug control regime in international law is noteworthy because the system is almost universally recognized. Almost every State in the world is a party to at least one of the conventions, including: 184 State parties to the Single Convention, 183 State parties to the 1971 Convention, and 184 State parties to the 1988 Convention.... Alcohol, despite its psychoactive effect, is not included in the conventions and therefore falls outside the scope of international drug control.

By defining control measures to be maintained within each State party's jurisdiction and by prescribing rules to be obeyed by the parties in their relations with each other, the system provides a legal framework for drug control. The rules focus on commodity control on one hand (regulation of licit production, supply and consumption of drugs) and sanctions on the other (suppression of illicit production, supply and possession mainly through criminal law). Thus, the control system has been developed on the premise that a reduction in the illicit drug markets will be achieved predominantly through prohibition-oriented measures.

Concerted drug control efforts have evolved over a period of more than 100 years. At the end of the nineteenth century, the increased consumption of psychoactive substances such as morphine, heroin and cocaine, and the globally unregulated market for these substances led to serious concerns in the United States. However, for the other colonial powers, such as the United Kingdom or the Netherlands, narcotic drugs, especially opium, were a commodity of enormous economic significance. For example, the export of Indian opium to China created significant revenues and ultimately led to the two Opium Wars between Britain and China (1839–42 and 1857–60) in which Britain defended the interests of British merchants in the region.

Opium consumption was at a record level when the United States convened an international opium conference in Shanghai in 1909. Due to its relative lack of overseas possessions and slight trading presence in Asia, the United States had no genuine interest in maintaining the global opium market. Therefore, the US approach emphasized that the prohibition of opium was a moral question. However, other countries were not ready to concede a total ban on the opium trade. They preferred controlled trade over a complete prohibition. Due to these discrepancies in strategic interest, no final agreement (besides a set of non-binding resolutions) was reached at the Shanghai conference. But, in retrospect, the conference proved to be crucial because it paved the way for a follow-up conference in The Hague in 1911. These follow-up negotiations resulted in the 1912 International Opium Convention. In addition to opium and morphine, cocaine and heroin were also included as controlled substances. The main principles stipulated in the convention are still valid today. For example, the axiom that the manufacture, trade and use of narcotic drugs should be limited to medical and scientific purposes governs the control system to this day. Under the 1912 Opium Convention, national governments were required to enact laws to control the production and distribution of narcotic drugs.

Nevertheless, due to the aforementioned differences in strategic interests between the participating governments, the 1912 Opium Convention was only ratified by China, Norway, the Netherlands, the United States and Honduras before the outbreak of World War I. This changed when the Convention was imposed on the losing parties of the war by linking the ratification of the Opium Convention to the Versailles Peace Treaty of 1919. Thus, by the mid-1920s close to sixty States were party to the 1912 Opium Convention. Furthermore, in the aftermath of World War I the League of Nations assumed responsibility for overseeing the Opium Convention, and specialized bodies, in particular the Advisory Committee on the Traffic in Opium and Other Dangerous Drugs, were created under its auspices. This proved to be a strong foundation for the successful establishment of a comprehensive international drug control system.

A further cornerstone of the international drug control system was established a few years later by the 1925 Geneva Opium Convention and the Agreement Concerning the Manufacture of, Trade in, and Use of Prepared Opium. Now States were required to annually submit statistics on the production of opium and coca leaves to the newly established Permanent Central Opium Board (PCOB). The obligatory control system included mandatory import certification and export authorization by government. Unfortunately, the system failed to prevent legally manufactured drugs from seeping into the illegal market.

One more major drug control treaty was adopted in the period between the First World War and the Second World War: the Convention for the Suppression of the Illicit Traffic in Dangerous Drugs. It emphasized the importance of agreement by States on the implementation of provisions into their domestic laws on severe punishment, for, *inter alia*, the production, trafficking, and sale of illicit substances. Articles 7 to 10 were novel in that they dealt in great detail with extradition for drug related crimes. Overall, the inter-war drug control system achieved considerable success in limiting and screening the production and trade of narcotic drugs.

After World War II, the administration of the drug control regime was transferred from the defunct League of Nations to the United Nations by the Protocol amending the Agreements, Conventions and Protocols on Narcotic Drugs (Protocol of Lake Success). The Commission on Narcotic Drugs (CND), which replaced the Opium Advisory Committee, was established by the Economic and Social Council (ECOSOC) at its first session. From then on it has been the main body advising ECOSOC on all drug-related matters.

In 1948, the Paris Protocol supplemented the 1931 Convention and provided for bringing under international control the drugs outside the scope of the 1931 Convention. This measure was much needed because of the rise of "designer drugs" (in particular opiate derivatives with harmful effects, such as methadone or pethidine), which had been developed to evade international restrictions. A new opium protocol was signed in New York in 1953 (1953 Opium Protocol). The intention behind the protocol was to eliminate the overproduction of opium by authorizing only seven states to produce opium for export (Bulgaria, India, Iran, Greece, the Soviet Union, Turkey and Yugoslavia).

Despite the passage of the 1953 Opium Protocol and its predecessors—due to the increasing complexity of the drug control system—the international community felt an increasing need to consolidate the numerous conventions introduced since the initial Opium Convention of 1912 into one treaty. The resultant efforts led to the drug control regime in force today.

The main underlying objectives of the [1961] Single Convention, besides the codification of the existing laws into one multilateral treaty, were the streamlining of the control mechanisms and the extension of existing controls. The Single Convention was intended to be the final and definitive document that supersedes all previous treaties, i.e. terminates and replaces them. Covered by the Single Convention are ... the definitions of controlled substances; the framework for the operations of the drug control bodies; reporting obligations of Member States regarding manufacture, trade and consumption of controlled substances; and penal provisions and actions to be taken against illicit trafficking. The scope of the Single Convention includes the classic plant-based drugs, such as opium, heroin, cocaine, and cannabis. It consists of fifty-one articles and four schedules: over one-hundred illicit substances are listed in the four schedules, with drugs grouped according to their perceived dependence-creating properties.

The Preamble stipulates that "addiction to narcotic drugs constitutes a serious evil for the individual and is fraught with social and economic danger to mankind." Article 4(c), the central operational provision of the Convention, manifests a prohibitionist approach by stipulating that "the parties shall take such legislative and administrative measures ... to limit exclusively to medical and scientific purposes the production, manufacture, export, import distribution of, trade in, use and possession of drugs." However, it must be noted that medical purposes include veterinary and dental purposes and that the meaning of the term "medical purpose" may change and is not exclusive to the use permitted under the system of "western medicine."

Article 2 of the Single Convention addresses control measures for the respective substances; the action of two agencies, the WHO and the CND, is required to put a narcotic drug under control. First, the WHO must determine whether a substance has dangerous properties and should therefore be listed on one of the schedules. Then the CND can either act in accordance with the recommendation of the WHO, or take no action at all.

Countries allowing for the cultivation of coca bushes and opium poppies were required to establish national monopolies and subsequently centralize and phase out their cultivation and production. The ultimate goal of these efforts is a universal international prohibition of the non-medical use of these substances. In regard to manufacturing, trade and distribution, and international trade of controlled narcotic drugs, a strict licensing system and extensive control measures are prescribed to the parties. Under Article 39, parties are allowed to adopt laws with stricter measures of control than those provided by the Single Convention if they deem them desirable or necessary.

The Single Convention of 1961 was amended by a Protocol in 1972 (1972 Protocol). The objective of the adoption of the 1972 Protocol was to further strengthen the international drug control system. This objective was furthered by introducing provisions on technical and financial assistance and the establishment of regional centers for scientific research and education to combat illegal use and traffic in drugs. Article 22(2) of the 1972 Protocol provided for the seizure and destruction of illegally cultivated opium poppies and cannabis. In addition, the 1972 Protocol modified the penal provisions of the Single Convention by providing extradition provisions similar to those in the 1936 Convention for the Suppression of the Illicit Traffic in Dangerous Drugs.

In the late 1960s, the technical advances in the manufacture of synthetic drugs led to an unregulated global market for psychotropic substances, (such as amphetamines, barbiturates and hallucinogens). After careful analysis, the CND concluded that the existing drug control system was limited to narcotic drugs and that the Single Convention was not applicable to psychotropic substances. Nonetheless, the international community felt that a control mechanism over those substances was urgently needed, and the CND was called upon to draft a convention, which would bring those substances under control.

The result of the CND's efforts was the 1971 Convention, which consists of thirty-three articles and four schedules. It can fairly be described as being based on the Single Convention, and its general purpose to limit the manufacture, trade, and use of psychotropic substances to medical and scientific purposes is similar to Article 4 of the Single Convention in respect to narcotic drugs. Any substance included in the schedules must be licensed by the government for manufacture, trade, and distribution. However, compared with the strict controls imposed on plant-based drugs under the Single Convention, the 1971 Convention imposes a somewhat weaker control mechanism. Similar to the control mechanism of the Single Convention, the WHO recommends whether a drug should be controlled. But, the CND is not bound by the recommendation of the WHO. It may, (provided that the WHO has made and communicated its findings on control measures), place the substance concerned under a control regime, change the control regime, or free a substance from a control regime—contrary to the recommendations of the WHO. This obviously gives the CND much wider discretion under the 1971 Convention than under the Single Convention.

Detailed provisions deal with licences, prescriptions, and warnings on packages and advertisements. Concerning prescriptions, the main difference between the Single Convention and the 1971 Convention is that under the 1971 Convention a medical prescription is, in general, required for individual use of all psychotropic substances or preparations, whereas under the Single Convention a medical prescription is only required for certain drugs in its Schedule I. According to Article 10 of the 1971 Convention, directions for use, including cautions and warnings, need to be given only if they are necessary for the safety of the patients using them. What is necessary for the safety of the user is left to the judgment of the party concerned. Advertisements to the general public for psychotropic substances are prohibited under the 1971 Convention; this includes newspapers, television and radio, but not announcements in technical journals, e.g. published specifically for medical practitioners.

Article 20 of the 1971 Convention also addresses measures to be taken against the abuse of psychotropic substances, including treatment, education, rehabilitation and social reintegration. Article 20 acknowledges that a system of penal sanctions and administrative control alone is not sufficient to keep drugs from the users and should therefore not form the sole subject of international cooperation against drug abuse. However, the penal provisions are similar to those in the Single Convention, (but without the extradition provisions which were added to the Single Convention by the 1972 Protocol).

Although the international drug control system satisfactory regulated the lawful production of narcotic drugs and psychotropic substances, the situation regarding illicit production did not noticeably improve. By the mid-1980s it was apparent that global drug abuse had reached unprecedented dimensions. Of special concern was the growing illegal opium production in Asia and the illegal cocaine production in the Andean countries. Against this background, the CND was requested by the General Assembly to prepare a draft convention against illicit traffic in narcotic drugs. Three years of deliberations by expert and review groups resulted in the 1988 United Nations Convention Against Illicit Traffic in Narcotic Drugs and Psychotropic Substances.

The main accomplishment of the 1988 Convention is that it extends controls to the entire market chain, including precursors at the beginning of the chain, to anti-money laundering measures at the end of the chain. The Convention consists of thirty-four articles (together with an annex containing two lists of substances frequently used in the illicit manufacture of narcotic drugs and psychotropic substances) and aims at strengthening compliance with the established drug control system. Member States are required to cooperate and to coordinate their efforts to prevent global drug trafficking. However, some States were worried that the Convention could be misused for other political objectives, i.e. be used to undermine their sovereign rights. Article 2(2) therefore clarifies that "the parties shall carry out their obligations under this Convention in a manner consistent with the principles of sovereign equality and territorial integrity of States and that of non-intervention in the domestic affairs of other States."

While under the Single Convention, Member States are obliged to make trafficking in drugs "punishable offenses," Article 3 of the 1988 Convention goes a step further and obliges Parties to make them "criminal offenses." According to Article 3(2) this includes the possession, purchase, or cultivation of drugs for personal consumption. Nevertheless, States are allowed to provide for alternatives to punishment (e.g. treatment, education, or rehabilitation) in cases of a minor nature and personal consumption. Furthermore, States are called upon to introduce domestic legislation to prevent drug related money laundering. Although money laundering was in principle already a punishable offense under the Single Convention, the provisions of the 1988 Convention are much more precise.

Article 3(1)(b) establishes drug related money laundering as a criminal offense, and, in targeting criminal proceeds, the 1988 Convention asks State Parties to confiscate proceeds from drug related offenses and to empower courts to seize bank and financial records.

As previously mentioned, the establishment of a control system for precursor chemicals was a novelty to the drug control regime. According to Article 12, the manufacture, transport or distribution of precursor chemicals should be deemed criminal offenses. This is reflected in the extension of criminal offenses for which extradition can be sought: they include the offenses of drug related money laundering and the manufacture, transport, and distribution of equipment and precursor chemicals.

Some confusion was created by Article 14(2), which stipulates that measures adopted to prevent illicit cultivation of narcotic plants "shall respect fundamental human rights and take due account of traditional licit uses, where there is a historic evidence of such use." Some States tried to interpret this as an acknowledgement that traditional licit uses still existed and had to be taken into account. However, the Single Convention had already outlawed the traditional habits of [coca] chewing and opium smoking. The maximum transitional period granted by the Single Convention ended for opium in 1979 and for cannabis and the [coca]-leaf in 1989. Thus, it is clear that the drug conventions, including the 1988 Convention, do not provide for the production of these controlled drugs for licit traditional use. Such a conclusion is underpinned by Article 14(1) of the 1988 Convention, which points out that "any measures taken pursuant to this Convention by Parties shall not be less stringent than the provisions applicable to the eradication of illicit cultivation of plants containing narcotic and psychotropic substances ... under the provisions of the 1961 Convention."

Although during the 1990s law enforcement measures based on the international drug control system had been successfully employed in the dismantling of some of the most notorious drug cartels (e.g. the Cali and Medellin cartels), global drug abuse did not, as had been hoped for, decrease. A remarkable initiative to refocus international attention on the global drug problem was therefore taken by the UN General Assembly in 1998 when a Special Session (UNGASS) was convened. UNGASS focused on a number of measures to enhance international cooperation, and the UN General Assembly adopted a Declaration on the Guiding Principles of Drug Demand Reduction, a Political Declaration, and various action plans to this end.

The Political Declaration is notable for various reasons, but particularly so for linking, for the first time, the illicit production and trafficking of drugs with terrorism and arms trafficking. States were called upon to consider the documents agreed on at UNGASS when formulating national drug strategies. Moreover, they were encouraged to report biennially to the CND on their efforts to meet the goals of the action plans. However, in contrast to the three drug conventions, the Political Declaration does not set up a system for monitoring compliance with the Declaration and the accompanying action plans. Article 20 of the Political Declaration solely declares that the CND will analyze the reports that it obtains from member States and use them for the enhancement of cooperation, but there is no formal sanction system foreseen in the Political Declaration. It thus remains a soft instrument.

The year 2008 was envisaged as a target date by which measurable results of the implementation of the action plans were to be achieved, and indeed, considerable success was achieved in reducing the cultivation of coca in South America and opium in some regions of Southeast Asia. But these achievements were overshadowed by the rapid expansion of opium production in Afghanistan. Overall the problem of global drug abuse did not improve significantly during the UNGASS period. Based on the review, the CND at its fifty-second session in 2009 considered further action and adopted a new political declaration and action plan. The new action plan addresses novel trends in drug trafficking, such as the use of information technology, and calls for better regulation of online pharmacies and enhanced intelligence exchange and judicial cooperation.

In order to complete the overview of the functioning of the admittedly complex control regime, some remarks are warranted on the agencies coordinating and developing international drug policies. Compliance with the drug control system outlined in the preceding chapter is managed (rather than enforced) by the United Nations. Three bodies carry out the UN's main activities in this area: the Commission on Narcotic Drugs (CND), the International Narcotics Control Board (INCB), and the UN Office on Drugs and Crime (UNODC). Other UN related agencies are also involved, on the periphery, in administering the global drug control effort, most notably the World Health Organization (WHO) and the United Nations Educational, Scientific, and Cultural Organization (UNESCO).

The CND is a functional commission of ECOSOC and the central policy-making body concerning all drug related matters in the UN. It was created by ECOSOC at its first session in 1946 and although initially composed of fifteen States, membership increased over time to fifty-three States.

Summed up, the main task of the CND is to analyze the global situation on drug control and, when necessary, advise ECOSOC on changes to enhance the drug control system. In this context, the CND acts as guardian of the three international drug conventions. For example, according to Article 8 of the Single Convention, the CND is authorized to consider all matters pertaining to the aims of the Single Convention. Similar blanket clauses can be found in Article 17 of the Convention on Psychotropic Substances and Article 21 of the Convention Against the Illicit Traffic in Narcotic Drugs and Psychotropic Substances.

Furthermore, special functions are assigned to the CND under the drug control conventions. Most important in the catalogue of competencies is the CND's supervision of the classification of controlled substances. The CND's authority to decide — on the basis of recommendations by the WHO — whether a drug is listed on, deleted from, or transferred to the schedules, is powerful. Similarly, the CND decides pursuant to the 1988 Convention on the recommendation of the INCB, on placing precursor chemicals on the Convention's list of controlled substances. Whereas general decisions of the CND — as those of any other functional commission of the UN system — remain subject to approval by the ECOSOC or the General Assembly, this is not the case when the CND decides on amending the schedules annexed to the conventions. Although a decision on amending the schedules is not subject to an initial review by ECOSOC or the General Assembly, the CND's powers are restricted by the right of any party to file an appeal against such a decision. ECOSOC may then confirm, alter or reverse the decision of the CND. Recently the position of the CND has been strengthened by the mandate to receive reports on States' efforts to meet the goals agreed upon at the UNGASS.

The INCB differs from the CND and UNODC in that it is an independent treaty body rather than a UN agency. Notably, it is not purely an inter-governmental body, as the members are elected by ECOSOC from candidates proposed by governments and the WHO. However, the elected members do not represent governments, but act in their personal capacity as experts on drug related matters.

The INCB was established in 1968 as the monitoring body for the implementation of the Single Convention. Today it monitors the implementation of all three drug conventions and is concerned with the monitoring and screening of the production, trade, and use of licit and illicit drugs. To this end it works closely with national governments to ensure that adequate supplies of drugs are available for medical and scientific uses, and that weaknesses in national approaches to combating the production, trafficking, and use of illicit drugs are identified. The INCB collects and administers the statistical data for drug production, trade, and consumption; a measure aimed at helping governments to establish a balance between (licit) supply and demand. The main task in this regard is the administration of the estimates and statistical returns systems. States have an obligation to report their statistical data at certain deadlines, and, if they fail to submit estimates, the INCB might establish the estimates for them. If the INCB has objective reason to believe that the aims of the Convention are being seriously endangered by a party (e.g. if a State is under the risk of becoming a centre of the illicit cultivation or production of narcotic drugs), the INCB may request the State to explain the condition, and it may propose the opening of consultations or the initiation of a study. The mandate of the INCB includes entering into a continuing dialogue with governments relating to their obligations under the drug control conventions, and ultimately, if all measures of cooperation with the respective government fail, the INCB may recommend that other States stop the import and export of drugs to and from a country that fails to explain properly its activities. However, the authority is much weaker than that of the INCB's predecessor, the Permanent Central Board, which actually could impose sanctions on States. Although the INCB does not have the power to administer sanctions, it may well censure States which it judges not to be in compliance; such censure may have a positive effect in and of itself on compliance with the control regime.

The set-up of the UN programs and initiatives on drug control has changed frequently in recent decades. In 1991, the secretariat of the INCB (but not the Board itself), the functions of the Division of Narcotic Drugs (DND), and the UN Fund for Drug Abuse Control (UNFDAC) were integrated into the UN Drug Control Programme (UNDCP). A further streamlining took place in 1997, when UNDCP was merged with the Centre for International Crime Prevention to form the UN Office for Drug Control and Crime Prevention (UNODCCP). This agency finally became the UN Office on Drugs and Crime (UNODC) in 2002. With a staff of about five hundred worldwide, UNODC is a rather small office, but carries out important activities.

Besides providing secretarial services for the other drug control bodies, UNODC is also responsible for the coordination of the UN anti-drug programs. Its mission involves close cooperation and assistance to national governments on the domestic and regional level. A variety of programs, mainly in developing and transitional countries, are executed under the supervision of UNODC. One of the most prominent initiatives is the Global Programme on Monitoring Illicit Crops, which covers the cultivation of illegal crops in the most troubled countries, such as Myanmar, Laos, Afghanistan in Asia, and Bolivia, Colombia, and Peru in South America. In pursuing its mandate UNODC follows a twofold approach: on the one side research and awareness-raising by publishing material on global trends in drug cultivation and trafficking (e.g., the annual World Drug Report, which is the most cited document on the state of the global drug problem), and on the other side programs on drug abuse prevention and drug dependence treatment/rehabilitation.

The UN-guided international drug control effort must be put into perspective by acknowledging that it does not operate in a vacuum. In fact, it is interdependent with unilateral efforts at the domestic level and with numerous bilateral initiatives (for example between the United States and various Latin American countries). Additionally, regional and sub-regional cooperation on drug control takes place on all continents. To a considerable extent these multilateral efforts are also supervised by the United Nations through the CND. Five subsidiary bodies have been established, in which the Heads of National Drug Law Enforcement Agencies (HONLEA) coordinate and strengthen their efforts in drug law enforcement activities. The HONLEA bodies meet annually to identify policy and enforcement issues and to establish respective working groups.

But, regional organizations and action plans have also been launched outside of the UN system. Although these initiatives oftentimes cooperate with UNODC on some level, they are not directly affiliated with the United Nations. For example, the European Council, in December 2004, endorsed a European Union Drugs Strategy. This was followed by two successive Drugs Action Plans, which aimed at strengthening cross-border cooperation with third countries and international organizations. In Asia, members of The Association of Southeast Asian Nations (ASEAN) and China endorsed an action plan called Drug Free ASEAN 2015, under which the respective States plan to improve their bilateral and regional cooperation. In South America, the Inter-American Drug Abuse Control Commission (CICAD) was established in 1986 under the framework of the Organization of American States (OAS). Furthermore, a Permanent Commission for the Eradication of the Illicit Production, Trafficking, Consumption and Use of Illicit Narcotic Drugs and Psychotropic Substances was established for Central America in 1993. Also the African Union has recently taken action by adopting in 2008 the Plan of Action on Drug Control and Crime Prevention. An important inter-regional drug control initiative worth mentioning is the Paris Pact Initiative. It is a partnership of more than fifty countries and international organizations aimed at combating the trafficking and consumption of Afghan opiates and focuses on enhanced border control and law enforcement on the drug trafficking routes from Central Asia to Europe. In addition to the aforementioned high-level institutions and programs, various other regional and bilateral initiatives have been created, e.g., in the field of intelligence sharing, joint investigations, and the establishment of permanent task forces.

The application of the Single Convention to the traditional practice of chewing coca leaves among indigenous people in Bolivia has generated significant controversy in recent years. As Daniel Heilmann discusses above, the Single Convention has been interpreted to encompass traditional uses of coca and opium. The coca leaf is "an everyday part of Bolivian life" where it is used to "calm upset stomachs," "stave[] off hunger and thirst," and combat the effects of altitude sickness. It also "plays a key role in the religious ceremonies of many of the country's indigenous people, who constitute more than 60 percent of the population." Recently, Bolivia sought to amend the Single Convention to recognize these uses but its effort was opposed by a number of countries, including the United States. This led Bolivia to withdraw from the Single Convention effective January 1, 2012, with its Foreign Minister David Choquehuanca citing "the need to guarantee respect for the human rights of indigenous peoples, and all who chew coca as a traditional cultural practice." Bolivia has already applied to rejoin the Single Convention with "the reservation that it does not recognize language that bans chewing the coca leaf." Other parties to the Convention will have until the end of 2012 to object to the reservation. Sara Shahriari, *Bolivia Drops Out of UN Drug Pact to Protect Its Coca Chewers*, THE CHRISTIAN SCIENCE MONITOR, July 18, 2011. *See also, e.g.,* Martin Jelsma, *Lifting the Ban on Coca Chewing: Bolivia's Proposal to Amend the 1961 Single Convention*, THE TRANSNATIONAL INSTITUTE SERIES ON INTERNATIONAL REFORM OF DRUG POLICY, No. 11 (2011) (describing the dispute surrounding Bolivia's proposed amendment); Will Reisinger, *The*

Unintended Revolution: U.S. Anti-Drug Policy and the Socialist Movement in Bolivia, 39 CAL. W. INT'L L. J. 237 (2009) (providing an overview of the traditional use and cultivation of coca in Bolivia).

Though the Single Convention has included an obligation to abolish coca chewing since its adoption in 1961, Bolivia did not adhere to this mandate even before its decision to withdraw from the treaty. The country's domestic law has always allowed for some legal use and production of the plant. How did Bolivia's coca policies and the Single Convention coexist prior to 2012?

The answer may lie, in part, on the process for ensuring compliance with the treaty. The International Narcotics Control Board (INCB) is tasked with overseeing domestic application of the three drug conventions, but "while often vocal in its criticism of national policy, the INCB ... has no formal power to enforce implementation of the Convention provisions. Nor has the Board the formal power to punish parties for non-compliance." David R. Bewley-Taylor, *Challenging the UN Drug Control Conventions: Problems and Possibilities,* 14 INT'L J. DRUG POL'Y 171 (2003). This does not mean the treaties are toothless. The INCB has mechanisms for applying "informal pressure in its attempts to encourage what it perceives to be treaty compliance" including recommending to other convention parties "that they 'stop the import of drugs, the export of drugs, or both, from or to the country or territory concerned' for a designated period or until [the INCB] is satisfied with the situation within the country or territory." David R. Bewley-Taylor and Mike Trace, *The International Narcotics Control Board: Watchdog or Guardian of the UN Drug Control Conventions?,* THE BECKLEY FOUNDATION DRUG POLICY PROGRAMME (2006). Moreover, even in the absence of external pressure, nations commit to interpret and implement treaties to which they are a party in good faith.

Nevertheless, the relationship between international drug treaties, international control bodies, and domestic drug law and enforcement is both complex and imprecise. For a detailed history of international drug treaties and control bodies, see William B. McAllister, *Drug Diplomacy in the Twentieth Century: An International History* (2000).

How Well Do International Drug Conventions Protect Public Health?
Robin Room and Peter Reuter
379 The Lancet 84 (2012)

The management and enforcement of the drug treaties are done by several international agencies that have overlapping responsibilities and different mandates and sometimes work at cross-purposes. The international political body that governs drug issues is the Commission on Narcotic Drugs, which operates under the remit of the UN Economic and Social Council. The commission is composed of representatives from 53 states chosen by the Economic and Social Council on the basis of geography and interest, and it meets every year in Vienna to negotiate, adopt resolutions, and approve the system's budget. The commission operates on a consensus basis, which makes change very difficult.

The UN Office on Drugs and Crime (UNODC) is the specialised UN agency on drug issues that serves as the secretariat for the Commission on Narcotic Drugs. It advises governments on effective law enforcement and treatment systems and methods of estimation of illicit drug production and consumption. UNODC is a small agency (about 500 employees) whose work is largely influenced by the governments that contribute most of its funding. In 2009, UNODC's core funding was estimated at US$13.1 million, whereas funding earmarked by donor governments for particular purposes was $197.9 million.

The International Narcotics Control Board comprises 13 experts elected by the UN Economic and Social Council. The board is responsible for overseeing the operation of the international drug treaties, management of international markets in medicines controlled by the treaties, and ensuring the supply of opioids for pain and other medical uses. The board deems itself the guardian of the treaties and often publishes interpretations of their provisions and names countries judged to have violated treaty provisions.

Under the 1961 and 1971 international drug conventions, [the World Health Organization] WHO provides medical and scientific advice on which drugs should be under international control and to what extent. According to the 1971 convention, WHO expert committees' assessments "shall be determinative as to medical and scientific matters". WHO provides advice and nominates five candidates for membership of the International Narcotics Control Board (from which the Economic and Social Council chooses three), but the Commission on Narcotic Drugs makes the final decisions about scheduling drugs, subject to review by the council.

The international system has two aims: to suppress the production, distribution, and use of all drugs under its control for all but medical and scientific purposes; and to ensure that controlled drugs (especially the opioids) are made available for medical purposes — eg, pain control.

Informally, the USA has long had a leading role in the international system. The USA has strongly opposed harm reduction approaches to illicit drug problems (eg, needle and syringe programmes, supervised injecting centres, and heroin maintenance treatment), with support from other nations such as Japan and Russia. The USA now accepts needle and syringe programmes but still objects to use of harm reduction wording in UN documents. UNODC used to share this objection, but has become more accepting of measures such as needle and syringe programmes.

Since harm reduction is a core principle of public health, the embargo on the use of this term is symbolic of the marginalisation of the role of WHO in the UN drug control system. At the end of the 1990s, WHO moved projects on reduction of HIV infection among drug users to the UN agency on AIDS, which had some protection from direct pressure from individual countries.

WHO's advice has on occasion been ignored by the UNODC and the Commission on Narcotic Drugs. In 2002, the WHO Director General, under pressure from the UNODC, declined to transmit to Vienna a recommendation by the 33rd expert committee that pharmaceutical delta-9-tetrahydrocannabinol (the main psychoactive constituent of cannabis) should be reclassified from schedule 2 to the lowest schedule of the 1971 Convention. A similar recommendation by the 2006 expert committee was rejected by the Commission on Narcotic Drugs.

Despite the substantial uniformity in legal frameworks required by the international drug control system, national drug policies differ in priorities. Some nations (eg, China and the USA) treat drugs primarily as a problem for law enforcement and so prioritise the suppression of trafficking, whereas others (eg, the Netherlands and Portugal) focus on help for drug users and reduction of the adverse consequences of drug use. These variations show national attitudes towards drug use, individual rights, and the role of government; the nature and history of national drug problems; and the different ways in which drug use affects a nation. For some nations, the drug problem is primarily a domestic one, but for others (eg, Mexico and Nigeria) the greatest damage to public health and safety arises from trafficking to the USA and Europe. For example, in Mexico drug trafficking to the US market has led to 35,000 homicides between 2007 and 2010. By contrast, much less violence is associated with drug markets in many European countries.

Assessments of drug programmes have had a marginal role in the formulation of policy even in developed countries that have heavily invested in research (eg, Australia, Canada, the UK, and the USA). The US National Institute on Drug Abuse dominates worldwide funding of scientific research on drugs, but does not fund research on drug policy. The greatest inconsistency between US policy and evidence is the mass incarceration of drug offenders (about 500,000 individuals in 2005). A ten-times increase in the number of individuals imprisoned for drug offences has occurred since 1980 despite declines in drug quantities sold, in the number of drug users, and in estimated illicit revenues. The evidence is clear that incarceration is an ineffective way to increase the price and reduce the availability of drugs.

The international conventions severely restrict the ability of national governments to experiment with alternative drug control systems by requiring all signatories to criminalise non-medical drug use. This constraint has had different effects on policies for injected drugs like heroin and cocaine and policies for the most widely used illicit drug, cannabis.

In the case of injected drugs, public health advocates in many developed countries have successfully campaigned to provide clean injecting equipment to prevent HIV transmission. Eight countries (Australia, Canada, Germany, Luxembourg, the Netherlands, Norway, Spain, and Switzerland) have provided supervised injecting centres to reduce blood-borne virus transmission and overdose and to increase drug users' contact with treatment services. These changes, which have largely been made without legislation to remove criminal penalties for use, have been criticised by UNODC and the International Narcotics Control Board as contrary to the treaties. UNODC has now accepted that needle and syringe programmes and treatment diversion programmes comply with the treaties, but the International Narcotics Control Board continues to argue that the status of supervised injection centres is unclear.

In the case of cannabis, the main legislative experiments in the past 50 years have been to reduce or eliminate criminal penalties, or to substitute civil penalties (eg, fines) for the use or possession of the drug. This policy has been extended to all illicit drugs in Brazil, Colombia, the Czech Republic, Mexico, and Portugal. Often a statutory criminal penalty is retained to avoid conflict with the international treaties.

The International Narcotics Control Board has argued that decriminalisation of drug use and toleration of drug sales violates the 1988 convention. Governments that have changed penalties and some scholars disagree. The UNODC has issued a discussion paper in which it argues that diversion of illicit drug users into treatment is consistent with international treaties, as long as criminal penalties are retained in law.

No evidence is available on whether the presence or absence of criminal penalties for use and possession of cannabis substantially affects the prevalence of use or levels of health-related harm. Criminal penalties are frequently enforced in a discriminatory way against socially excluded minorities. Therefore to justify the criminalisation of cannabis use as a strategy to reduce use is difficult.

The reduction of penalties for cannabis possession and use while the international treaties are complied with has often had the converse consequence of so-called net widening. Because the implementation of offences with reduced or non-criminal penalties is not time-consuming for police, more young people might receive police records for failure to pay fines than if criminal penalties had been retained. Studies in North America and many European countries show that arrests for cannabis use have risen substantially in recent years, alongside reductions in the severity of penalties for use.

The Netherlands has moved the furthest away from criminal penalties by de facto (but not de jure) legalising retail sales of small amounts of cannabis in coffee shops. Evidence that this form of legalisation has affected rates of use or harm is scarce, although commercialisation could have done so. The prevalence of cannabis use in the Netherlands is less than in countries such as the UK, France, and the USA, which have retained criminal penalties.

No developed nation has formally legalised cannabis supply to address what is known in the Netherlands as the back door problem — ie, that although front door sales of cannabis are de facto legal, the back door supply of the drug is not. In parts of India, however, cannabis shops operate under state government licences, a practice that has so far escaped censure from the International Narcotics Control Board.

The liberal definition of medical marijuana use in California is arguably a form of de-facto legalisation of cannabis sales. The Californian and local authorities have partly addressed the back door issue by allowing non-profit cooperatives to supply cannabis to medical dispensaries. To legally access medical marijuana, a patient must have a doctor's letter specifying that he or she has a health disorder that could benefit from cannabis use. Over 200,000 patients are claimed to have such letters (8% of the estimated 2,500,000 past-month cannabis users in the state). Doctors in California advertise provision of these letters for under $100, often for disorders (eg, anxiety, sleeplessness, and pain) for which evidence of benefit from controlled trials is scarce.

How successfully has the international system achieved its goals?

The international system has ensured supplies of opioids for medical need in developed countries, but WHO has estimated that 80% of the world's population has either no or inadequate access to effective pain medication. The International Narcotics Control Board acknowledges that such difficulty with access "continues to be a matter of concern". One factor seems to be that the international system's emphasis on policing has encouraged nations to give a greater priority to prevention of diversion of prescribed opioids to the black market than to provision for pain control.

The system has failed to achieve its original goals of elimination of illicit markets and the non-medical use of controlled drugs. In 1998, the UN system set the more restricted but still ambitious goal of "eliminating or significantly reducing the illicit cultivation of coca bush, the cannabis plant, and the opium poppy by the year 2008". However, by 2009, this goal was as distant as it was in 1998. Between 1998 and 2009, the production of synthetic drugs such as 3,4-methylenedioxymethylamfetamine (MDMA) and [methamphetamine] increased, as did domestic cannabis cultivation in many developed and developing countries.

According to the UNODC, between 172 million and 250 million people worldwide were estimated to have used an illicit drug in 2007. Cannabis is the most commonly used prohibited drug and accounts for nearly three-quarters of users. Mass markets for cocaine, heroin, and some other prohibited drugs exist in many developed and some low-income and middle-income countries. Injecting drug use has become a worldwide issue that has contributed to the spread of HIV/AIDS. The non-medical use of prescription opioids, benzodiazepines, and stimulant drugs has also increased since the early 2000s, particularly in North America and Australasia.

The goal of increasing health and wellbeing by eliminating drug-related harm has also not been met.

The spread of non-medical drug use has been accompanied by steady reductions in illicit drug prices and increases in drug purity in many countries. This situation has occurred despite increased expenditure on law enforcement in most developed countries (most notably in the USA, which has the best time series data on price and purity).

Neither international nor national systems of drug control are based on estimations of risks from drug use, or on the consequences of different control mechanisms. Conspicuously, few international controls are in place on the two most harmful substances in the comparative risk analysis of global burden of disease: alcohol and tobacco. No international agreement exists for alcohol and the provisions of the Framework Convention on Tobacco Control are far weaker than those of the international drug treaties. Prohibition of the non-medical use of substances covered by the treaties precludes regulation via market and availability controls. That which is prohibited cannot easily be regulated.

Cannabis is the drug whose inclusion in the international system is most often seen as anomalous because it is widely used by young adults in many countries, and its health effects are much less harmful than those of the opioids and stimulants. However, the treaties prevent any experimentation with alternative policies for reduction of harm associated with this drug.

The international drug conventions allow for their amendment, but the conditions that have to be met to do so make change difficult. Nonetheless, without amendment, other ways for a country, or group of countries, to move forward are possible in principle. The least disruptive way would be for countries to reassert their authority to adopt a regulatory rather than prohibitory system domestically for one or more drugs, while continuing to meet their obligations under the treaties to control international trade in drugs.

The most feasible way for an individual country to do so would be to withdraw from one or more of the treaties and then re-accede with specified reservations. For example, Switzerland and the Netherlands ratified the 1988 treaty with a reservation against the provision that required the criminalisation of use and possession. Bolivia is using the strategy of withdrawal and re-accession to allow internal legalisation of coca leaf chewing.

Alternatively, a group of like-minded countries could agree on a new international treaty which would then take precedence with respect to their internal markets and their dealings with each other.

National experimentation in approaches to prevention and reduction of drug-related harm should be allowed. The international drug treaties in their present form seriously constrain governments' capacities to engage in such policy experiments. Countries that wish to experiment with different ways of regulating drug use and reducing drug-related harm will need to consider opting out of provisions of the existing drug control treaties.

The cultural positions of different drugs vary enough to preclude universal policies on how to deal with all illicit or indeed licit drugs. From the perspective of public health, we need to move towards a control system that is more aligned with the risks that different drugs pose to users and shows an understanding of the effects of different regulatory approaches on drug use and harm.

––––––––––

Though the international drug control regime is built on domestic enforcement of treaty-based laws, some commentators have proposed granting an international court the power to hear serious drug trafficking cases directly. *See, e.g.,* Faiza Patel, *Crime Without Frontiers: A Proposal for an International Narcotics Court,* 22 N.Y.U. J. INT'L L. & POL., 709 (1990). By and large, supporters of this approach argue that the International Criminal Court (ICC) should be given jurisdiction over drug cases. Molly McConville, for example, contends that a system of international prosecution before the ICC is needed because "too many countries simply refuse to prosecute or extradite drug traffickers." Molly McConville, Note: *A Global War on Drugs: Why the United States Should Support the Prosecution of Drug Traffickers in the International Criminal Court*, 37 Am. Crim. L. Rev. 75, 81 (2000). Others argue that the ICC's jurisdiction should be reserved for more serious offenses.

Explaining State Commitment to the International Criminal Court: Strong Enforcement Mechanisms as a Credible Threat
Yvonne M. Dutton
10 Washington University Global Studies Law Review 477 (2011)

Situated in The Hague, Netherlands, the ICC is the first permanent, treaty-based international criminal court established to help end impunity for perpetrators of genocide, crimes against humanity, and war crimes. Although the United Nations first began considering the prospect of an international criminal court after World War II, it was not until 1990, following a request submitted by Trinidad and Tobago, that work again commenced in earnest towards drafting a statute for the creation of such a court. The United Nations General Assembly tasked the ILC with drafting a statute for the establishment of an international criminal court. In July 1994, an ILC draft statute was adopted and recommended to the General Assembly. The General Assembly thereafter adopted a resolution to establish an Ad Hoc Committee to address the core issue of the viability of actually creating an international criminal court, and in light of that issue, the possibility of convening a diplomatic conference of states. A Preparatory Committee ("Prep Comm") took over with the objective of negotiating the precise statutory language governing the court and its functions. The Prep Comm met in 1996, 1997, and 1998. The draft statute approved during the April 1998 Prep Comm meeting—which contained 116 articles, many of which included bracketed optional provisions—formed the basis of negotiations at the Rome Conference during the summer of 1998.

The statute creating the court—the Rome Statute—was finally adopted at the conclusion of the Rome Conference. Attending the conference were 160 states, 33 international governmental coalitions, and a coalition of more than 200 non-governmental organizations (NGOs). Of the states in attendance, 120 voted in favor of adopting the statute, 7 voted against, and 21 abstained. In July 2002 after the required 60 states had ratified the statute, the ICC came into existence.

As of August 2010, some 139 countries had signed the Rome Statute, and 113 had actually become States Parties to it. Of the States Parties, 20 are from Western Europe, 17 are from Eastern Europe, 31 are from Africa, 14 are from Asia, and 25 are from Latin America and the Caribbean. The United States, Israel, China, Russia, Indonesia, and India are notable powerful states that have declined to ratify the treaty. Also not parties to the treaty are a number of Islamic and African states, including: Bahrain, Iran, Iraq, Kuwait, Pakistan, Qatar, Syria, Turkey, United Arab Emirates, Yemen, Algeria, Angola, Cameroon, Cape Verde, Cote d'Ivoire, Egypt, Morocco, Sudan, and Zimbabwe. In June 2010, Bangladesh became the first country from southern Asia to join the court.

The adoption of the Rome Statute—particularly in its current form—was anything but a foregone conclusion. Indeed, a handful of core issues concerning ICC jurisdiction over crimes, the mechanism for triggering prosecution, and the role of the United Nations Security Council were the subject of much negotiation. Although a number of states favored an independent prosecutor with power to initiate proceedings and no Security Council veto on prosecutions, some powerful states, such as the United States, pushed for granting the Security Council a greater role in determining which cases to pursue. Nevertheless, at the conclusion of negotiations, the Rome Statute states voted to adopt was one that envisioned a powerful and independent court.

Indeed, the ICC that these states joined differs substantially from any preceding international criminal tribunal. Unlike the ad hoc international criminal tribunals such as those established to deal with crimes committed in Rwanda and the former Yugoslavia, the ICC's jurisdiction is not circumscribed to dealing with particular atrocities in particular states. Nor can states decide whether or not to accede to the court's jurisdiction on a case-by-case basis. Rather, by committing to the treaty creating the ICC, states agree that investigations may be commenced against the state's own nationals for the covered crimes of genocide, crimes against humanity, or war crimes, as long as those crimes were committed after the court came into existence or after the state ratified the treaty, whichever is later. Furthermore, the ICC treaty is not only backward-looking; by joining the court, states agree that the court can prosecute any future atrocities in the event the state itself does not prosecute those atrocities domestically. Moreover, the treaty does not recognize any immunity that states may otherwise grant to heads of state who engage in criminal activities.

The treaty creating the ICC also has stronger enforcement mechanisms than those traditionally associated with international human rights treaties. According to the terms and provisions of the Rome Statute, an independent ICC prosecutor may initiate investigations against nationals of States Parties for the covered crimes on his own with the approval of the court, or based on referrals from a State Party or the United Nations Security Council. The prosecutor and the court operate without direct Security Council oversight, with the Council having no veto power over what situations are investigated or prosecuted. Not only have States Parties to the ICC delegated authority to independent decision makers, but they have also given those decision makers power to enforce those decisions. Most importantly, the ICC is empowered to issue arrest warrants to bring those who have committed mass atrocities to stand trial for their crimes in The Hague.

In sum, the treaty states enacted to create the ICC envisions a powerful and independent prosecutor and court that can significantly invade in the realm of state sovereignty: states committing to the ICC face the possibility that if government officials or any of its nationals commit atrocities, they will be prosecuted at the ICC unless the state prosecutes those atrocities domestically.

Just Say No: The Case against Expanding the International Criminal Court's Jurisdiction to Include Drug Trafficking
Heather L. Kiefer
31 Loyola of Los Angeles International and
Comparative Law Review 157 (2008)

Currently, those who are responsible for drug trafficking and related offenses cannot be prosecuted in the International Criminal Court (ICC). The ICC is not a court of general jurisdiction; it has jurisdiction only over the offenses enumerated in the Rome Statute. Because drug trafficking is not among the offenses included in the Statute, it falls outside the Court's subject matter jurisdiction. But the contents of the Rome Statute are not set in stone. The Statute, including its jurisdictional provisions, may be amended at any time "[a]fter the expiry of seven years from the [Statute's] entry into force...." That date—July 2, 2008—has now arrived. Any state party to the Statute may now propose an amendment. If the Assembly chooses to consider the proposal, it can either "deal with the proposal directly or convene a Review Conference if the issue involved so warrants."

Indeed, sometime in the first half of 2010, the Assembly will convene a Review Conference in Kampala, Uganda to consider amendments to the Statute. The Conference will likely consider, among other things, proposals to expand the Court's jurisdiction to include terrorism and drug trafficking offenses.

Although there are numerous multilateral treaties addressing the issue of drug trafficking, it is debatable whether the global issue of drug trafficking is sufficiently addressed through the current regime or if it should also be incorporated into another multilateral treaty that contains a stronger enforcement mechanism, namely the ICC.

Currently, the jurisdiction of the International Criminal Court encompasses genocide, crimes against humanity, war crimes, and crimes of aggression. Given the present contents of the Rome Statute, the origins and motivation of the effort to establish the International Criminal Court are somewhat surprising. While international tribunals of various sorts existed prior to the creation of the ICC, the ICC itself was initially conceived as a means to combat a crime not previously within the jurisdiction of any international tribunal: drug trafficking. Led by Arthur Robinson, the Prime Minister of Trinidad and Tobago, [in 1989] seventeen Caribbean and Latin American states proposed the idea of an international court with subject matter jurisdiction covering drug trafficking offenses—a proposal the UN General Assembly quickly embraced.

In 1994, the International Law Commission (ILC) prepared a Draft Statute for an International Court. The Draft Statute created a court with broader jurisdiction than the original proponents of the ICC had envisioned, but the Court's function as an international tribunal to try drug trafficking offenses was nevertheless preserved.

Following the release of the Draft Statute, the General Assembly created the Preparatory Committee on the Establishment of an International Criminal Court. The Committee's main function was to consider and resolve the more controversial points of the Draft Statute. During the Committee's proceedings, two schools of thought emerged regarding the question of whether to include drug trafficking crimes within the subject matter jurisdiction of the ICC. On one hand, some delegations argued: "[D]rug trafficking should not be included because these crimes were not of the same nature as those listed in other paragraphs of Article 20 and were of such a quantity as to flood the court; the court would not have the necessary resources to conduct lengthy and complex investigations required to prosecute the crimes; the investigation of the crimes often involved highly sensitive information and confidential strategies; and the crimes could be more effectively investigated and prosecuted by national authorities under existing international cooperation arrangements."

The last point was one made emphatically by Kazakhstan, whose delegation expressed the view that the inclusion of trafficking violated the fundamental principle of complementarity. On the other hand, another group of delegations to the Preparatory Committee "expressed the view that particularly serious drug trafficking offenses which involved an international dimension should be included" because the current regime of controlling and punishing trafficking had serious shortcomings.

The literature predating the convening of the Committee also helps to illuminate the reasons for supporting the creation of an international court with subject matter jurisdiction over drug trafficking offenses. To proponents of the inclusion of such offenses within the jurisdiction of an international court, drug trafficking was viewed as international in character, having very serious and harmful effects, and requiring international cooperation. These characteristics supported the notion that drug trafficking was an international crime even in the absence of positive law ... establishing its criminality. Given the magnitude of the trafficking problem, its perceived status as an international crime, and great discrepancies in the willingness and ability of states to prosecute traffickers, proponents urged the creation of an international court to handle the prosecution of drug crimes. Proponents believed that such a court was not only eminently desirable, but also feasible.

By 1998, states came to a consensus regarding the subject matter jurisdiction of the ICC. The consensus was on the side of a narrower, more limited jurisdiction that did not include drug trafficking offenses. Despite that consensus, however, the second version of the Draft Statute, finalized in 1998, still included drug trafficking among the offenses within the Court's jurisdiction. Although the second Draft Statute was transmitted to the Rome Conference, the final product of the Rome Conference, the Rome Statute of the International Criminal Court, contained no mention of drug trafficking—neither explicitly nor by incorporation—because there were problems with defining the scope of the offense with an acceptable degree of precision. There is some measure of irony in this result: the impetus for the movement to create the ICC was the desire to create an international court to try drug traffickers, and yet, the result of that movement, the Rome Statute, deprived the Court of jurisdiction over drug trafficking offenses.

This irony was not lost on those who had started the movement. Trinidad and Tobago, widely cited as the state behind the movement to create the ICC, abstained from voting to adopt the Rome Statute. It abstained for two reasons. First, as discussed above, the Rome Statute did not expressly provide for jurisdiction over drug trafficking—the very reason Trinidad and Tobago had pushed for an international criminal court. Second, some delegations, including Trinidad and Tobago, wanted the Rome Statute to provide for capital punishment, and the final version of the treaty did not allow for that penalty. Despite the abstention, however, Trinidad and Tobago became the second state to ratify the Statute.

Once the Rome Statute entered into force, states that found themselves on the losing end of the jurisdictional battle were still left ... [to] wait for the Review Conference, at which point the states could push to amend the Statute to include drug trafficking as an offense within the Court's jurisdiction. The making of this proposal is widely anticipated.

[A] myriad of political and administrative problems that would arise if we were to create a more expansive and more ambitious ICC. These concerns are discussed in greater detail below.

Drugs have been used throughout history by various cultures for various purposes. Archaeological evidence suggests that as far back as 2000 B.C., opium was used in Cyprus, Crete, and Greece for various ritualistic purposes. In Colombia, indigenous cultures such as the Muisca have used the coca leaf, the main ingredient in producing cocaine, for many rituals and as a means of healing various ailments. Although these examples may suggest that cultural uses of drugs are a thing of the past, the Netherlands provides a prime example of how drugs, specifically marijuana, have become a part of modern cultures as well. Since 1976, Amsterdam has been notable for its relaxed restrictions on marijuana possession within its coffee shops and coffee-shop culture. Portugal provides another example of liberal drug laws. Portugal decriminalized drug use, possession, and acquisition for both "casual users" and addicts as of July 1, 2001. Even states that do not accept cultural uses of drugs permit certain drugs for medicinal uses. Parts of Europe and certain American states, such as California, allow for the medicinal use of marijuana.

These differences in drug policies between states underscore the problems that arise when trying to determine which drugs should be illegal and under what circumstances. Different states have different views about how each substance ought to be regulated, and these different views imply discrepancies concerning the severity of drug trafficking offenses, if such activities are criminalized at all. This could severely impinge on the consensus that is needed to create treaties and regulations on drug trafficking. The problem is exaggerated with respect to the ICC because so much more is at stake. States may feel compelled not to be a party—or opt out of a previous commitment—to the Rome Statute because of disagreements over drug trafficking provisions, despite their agreement with other provisions of the Statute. Lack of consensus on drug trafficking could jeopardize the prosecution of crimes against humanity, genocide, war crimes, and crimes of aggression currently under the jurisdiction of the ICC.

Another complication created by the proposal to add the offense of drug trafficking to the Rome Statute as a separate jurisdictional category stems from the concept of complementarity. Some have argued that ICC jurisdiction over drug trafficking would support the principle of complementarity, articulated in the preamble and Article 1 of the Rome Statute. Article 1 states: "[The Court] shall be a permanent institution and shall have the power to exercise its jurisdiction over persons for the most serious crimes of international concern, as referred to in this Statute, and shall be complementary to national criminal jurisdictions." With respect to drug trafficking, if a country did not prosecute or extradite an offender, the ICC could prosecute that offender. The principle of complementarity when applied to drug trafficking, however, presents numerous problems.

First, the jurisdiction of the ICC does not extend to nationals of non-signatory states as long as those persons remain in the territory. As a result, offenders from some countries would not be prosecuted while offenders from other, signatory states are held responsible. This sends an inconsistent notion of justice to the international community and weakens the argument that ICC jurisdiction will provide a strong deterrent for drug traffickers.

The second complication is the possible infringement of state sovereignty. The United States provides an apt example of this complication. In the United States, the intelligence community, which is responsible for investigating drug trafficking, has a responsibility to protect its sources and methods used to gather intelligence. In order for the ICC to determine if a state is "unwilling or unable genuinely to carry out the investigation or prosecution," a requirement for complementarity, the United States might have to provide information likely to compromise the intelligence community's sources and methods. In so doing, it would be giving up its sovereign right and self-imposed responsibility to protect its sources and methods of gathering intelligence.

One of the most persuasive arguments for not allowing the ICC to have jurisdiction over drug trafficking cases is the lack of ICC resources.

Cannabis alone is cultivated in 172 countries and territories. In order to collect the evidence needed for prosecution, the ICC would have to undertake the expensive and time-consuming task of sending investigators around the globe. Mahnoush Arsanjani, the Director of the Codification Division of the UN's Office of Legal Affairs, points out that the evidence-gathering obstacles shaped the development of the Rome Statute's jurisdictional provisions: "The opposition [to including drug trafficking] was based on the fact that the nature of investigating the crimes of drug trafficking and terrorism, which requires long-term planning, infiltration into the organizations involved ... makes them better suited for national prosecution."

There are good reasons to think these perceptions were, and are correct. In 2005, the ICC budget totaled approximately €69,564,000 or $86,634,310 at then-prevailing exchange rates. In contrast, the United States appropriated $2.141 billion dollars to its Drug Enforcement Agency in 2005 alone. Some might argue that this demonstrates that states need to dedicate more resources to the ICC as well as other international institutions. But the gap between the investigative expenditures of international institutions and states is so large that it is hard to imagine that the latter would be willing, or could even afford, to dedicate similar resources to the ICC. Moreover, if states completely ceded their investigative role to the ICC, it would render the principle of complementarity irrelevant.

The problem of drug trafficking is dealt with in part through the comprehensive treaty regime currently in place. Under the Rome Statute, however, the existence of a wide-scale problem is not sufficient to vest in the ICC jurisdiction over the offense. Specific provisions must instead provide for the Court's jurisdiction over particular categories of offenses.

Despite the superficial attraction of including additional offenses within Article 5, however, the Review Conference should refrain from doing so. Debates over the Statute itself and the Draft Code show that there is no real consensus over whether drug trafficking offenses rise to the same level of severity as the other offenses currently included in Article 5. With no consensus on the subject, the inclusion of the offense would ignore the significant differences in cultural attitudes toward drug use and trafficking, as well as the appropriate punishment for such offenses. Moreover, the investigation of drug trafficking is complex and expensive. Beyond these practical challenges, the inclusion of drug trafficking threatens to devalue one of the Court's fundamental principles: complementarity. These problems, taken together, could create insurmountable obstacles for a court trying to establish its institutional competence and legitimacy.

As anticipated, Trinidad and Tobago put forward a proposal at the 2010 Review Conference in Uganda to add drug trafficking to the list of crimes over which the ICC has jurisdiction. However, the proposal was not adopted.

Though the ICC does not have jurisdiction over drug crimes, Mexican human rights lawyer Netzai Sandoval recently filed a complaint before the ICC asking it to investigate whether war crimes and crimes against humanity have been committed in connection with Mexico's war against drugs. The complaint, signed by 23,000 Mexican citizens, alleges that "President Filepe Calderón, other top officials and the country's most-wanted drug trafficker" have "allow[ed] subordinates to kill, torture and kidnap victims." The ICC prosecutor is reviewing the complaint to determine whether the allegations fall under the Court's jurisdiction, a process that may take months or years to complete. Sara Webb and Manuel Rueda, *Activists Seek International Probe of Mexican Drug War*, CHICAGO TRIB., Nov. 27, 2011. Though it is unusual to see drug enforcement-centered allegations before the ICC, concerns about human rights violations and drug policy are by no means unique to Mexico. *See, e.g.*, THE BECKLEY FOUNDATION, RECALIBRATING THE REGIME: THE NEED FOR A HUMAN RIGHTS-BASED APPROACH TO INTERNATIONAL DRUG POLICY (2008) (discussing the relationship between drug policy and human rights and reporting, for example, that in 2003, Thailand "launched a violent and murderous 'war on drugs,' the initial three-month phase of which resulted in some 2,275 extrajudicial killings"); Spencer Thomas, Note: *A Complementarity Co-nundrum: International Criminal Enforcement in the Mexican Drug War*, 45 VAND. J. TRANSNATIONAL L. 599 (2012) (analyzing "Los Zetas leader Heriberto Lazcano's potential ICC liability stemming from a mass execution of seventy-two migrants by Los Zetas in August 2010").

Whether or not the alleged abuses in the complaint qualify as crimes against humanity or war crimes as defined by the ICC, recent reports about human rights and the drug war in Mexico paint a troubling picture. Shortly before the ICC complaint, Human Rights Watch released a report detailing findings from a two-year investigation into Mexico's drug war. The organization concluded that Mexico's strategy "has not succeeded in reducing violence. Instead, it has resulted in a dramatic increase in grave human rights violations, virtually none of which appear to be adequately investigated. In sum, rather than strengthening public security in Mexico, Calderón's 'war' has exacerbated a climate of violence, lawlessness, and fear in many parts of the country." *Neither Rights Nor Security: Killings, Torture and Disappearances in Mexico's "War on Drugs,"* Human Rights Watch (2011).

C. U.S. Influence on International Drug Control

The United States has been a driving force behind drug prohibition efforts internationally, pursuing drug enforcement with war-like intensity both at home and abroad. As William B. McAllister observes in his authoritative history of international drug control, "in the late twentieth-century the United States promoted adoption of American-style drug control laws in other countries as vigorously as any commercial export, often threatening the domestic stability of other states in the process." WILLIAM B. MCALLISTER, DRUG DIPLOMACY IN THE TWENTIETH CENTURY 254 (2000). This section considers the role of the United States and its "war on drugs" strategy in international drug control.

1. Extraterritorial Application of U.S. Drug Laws

As discussed above, although there is a significant amount of international cooperation among nations in drug control, there is no international body that has jurisdiction over drug investigations or prosecutions. As a result, drug law enforcement remains a fundamentally national task. Inevitably, however, some domestic drug prosecutions will involve international conduct. Imagine, for example, a drug business operator living in Mexico whose organization sends marijuana into the United States. Should the U.S. be allowed to prosecute the drug operator, even if he has never stepped foot on U.S. soil?

There are five accepted principles of jurisdiction under international law that guide the reach of domestic criminal statutes: (1) the territorial principle; (2) the nationality principle; (3) the protective principle; (4) the passive personality principle; and (5) the universality principle. *See generally*, RESTATEMENT (THIRD) OF FOREIGN RELATIONS LAW OF THE UNITED STATES §§ 401–404. The territorial principle grants nations jurisdiction over crimes committed within their own territory. This principle includes typical domestic crimes as well as crimes that produce an effect within the country exercising jurisdiction, even though the conduct occurred in a different country. This is referred to as "objective territorial jurisdiction." The nationality principle allows states to exercise jurisdiction over their own nationals. The protective principle "recognizes the right of a state to punish ... offenses directed against the security of the state or other offenses threatening the integrity of governmental functions[.]" *Id.* at §402 cmt. f. Under the passive personality principle, nations may exercise jurisdictions over crimes committed against their nationals. Finally, the universality principle gives states the "jurisdiction to define and prescribe punishment for certain offenses recognized by the community of nations as of universal concern, such as piracy, slave trade, attacks on or hijacking of aircraft, genocide, war crimes, and perhaps certain acts of terrorism, even where none of the [other] bases of jurisdiction ... is present." *Id.* at §404.

Though the basic principles of the extraterritorial application of domestic law are easily stated, determining whether a specific statute should be applied extraterritorially in a particular case can be a much more difficult task. As one scholar recently observed, "[t]he increasing phenomenon of U.S. extraterritoriality, or extension of federal law to activity outside U.S. borders, embroils a complex tangle of multifaceted and often overlapping legal doctrines." Anthony J. Colangelo, *A Unified Approach to Extraterritoriality*, 97 Va. L. Rev. 1019, 1020–21 (2011).

Over the past few decades, the U.S. has increasingly sought to prosecute international drug crimes in its courts. Some of the resulting cases have presented courts with particularly controversial and challenging questions about the extraterritorial reach of U.S. drug laws.

a. Prosecution of Foreign Drug Producers and Distributors

United States v. Noriega

United States District Court for the Southern District of Florida
746 F. Supp. 1506 (1990)

Hoeveler, J.

The case at bar presents the Court with a drama of international proportions, considering the status of the principal defendant and the difficult circumstances under which he was brought before this Court. The pertinent facts are as follows:

On February 14, 1988, a federal grand jury sitting in Miami, Florida returned a twelve-count indictment charging General Manuel Antonio Noriega with participating in an international conspiracy to import cocaine and materials used in producing cocaine into and out of the United States. Noriega is alleged to have exploited his official position as head of the intelligence branch of the Panamanian National Guard, and then as Commander-in-Chief of the Panamanian Defense Forces, to receive payoffs in return for assisting and protecting international drug traffickers, including various members of the Medellin Cartel, in conducting narcotics and money laundering operations in Panama.

Specifically, the indictment charges that General Noriega protected cocaine shipments from Columbia through Panama to the United States; arranged for the transshipment and sale to the Medellin Cartel of ether and acetone, including such chemicals previously seized by the Panamanian Defense Forces; provided refuge and a base for continued operations for the members of the Medellin Cartel after the Columbian government's crackdown on drug traffickers following the murder of the Columbian Minister of Justice, Rodrigo Lara-Bonilla; agreed to protect a cocaine laboratory in Darien Province, Panama;

and assured the safe passage of millions of dollars of narcotic proceeds from the United States into Panamanian banks. Noriega also allegedly traveled to Havana, Cuba and met with Cuban president Fidel Castro, who, according to the indictment, mediated a dispute between Noriega and the Cartel caused by the Panamanian troops' seizure of a drug laboratory that Noriega was paid to protect. All of these activities were allegedly undertaken for General Noriega's own personal profit. Defendant [Lt. Col. Luis] Del Cid, in addition to being an officer in the Panamanian Defense Forces, was General Noriega's personal secretary. He is charged with acting as liaison, courier, and emissary for Noriega in his transactions with Cartel members and other drug traffickers.

Because of the activities alleged, Defendants are charged with engaging in a pattern of racketeering activity, in violation of the RICO statutes, 18 U.S.C. §§ 1962(c) and 1962(d); conspiracy to distribute and import cocaine into the United States, in violation of 21 U.S.C. § 963; and distributing and aiding and abetting the distribution of cocaine, intending that it be imported into the United States, in violation of 21 U.S.C. § 959 and 18 U.S.C. § 2. Defendant Noriega is further charged with aiding and abetting the manufacture of cocaine destined for the United States, in violation of 21 U.S.C. § 959 and 18 U.S.C. § 2; conspiring to manufacture cocaine intending that it be imported into the United States, in violation of 21 U.S.C. § 963; and causing interstate travel and use of facilities in interstate commerce to promote an unlawful activity, in violation of 18 U.S.C. § 1952(a)(3) and 18 U.S.C. § 2.

Subsequent to the indictment, the Court granted General Noriega's motion to allow special appearance of counsel, despite the fact that Noriega was a fugitive and not before the Court at that time. Noriega's counsel then moved to dismiss the indictment on the ground that United States laws could not be applied to a foreign leader whose alleged illegal activities all occurred outside the territorial bounds of the United States. Counsel further argued that Noriega was immune from prosecution as a head of state and diplomat, and that his alleged narcotics offenses constituted acts of state not properly reviewable by this Court.

Upon hearing arguments of counsel, and after due consideration of the memoranda filed, the Court denied Defendant's motion, for reasons fully set forth below. At that time, the Court noted that this case was fraught with political overtones, but that it was nonetheless unlikely that General Noriega would ever be brought to the United States to answer the charges against him. The former observation proved to be considerably more correct than the latter, in light of subsequent events.

In the interval between the time the indictment was issued and Defendants were arrested, relations between the United States and General Noriega deteriorated considerably. Shortly after charges against Noriega were brought, the General delivered a widely publicized speech in which he brought a machete crashing down on a podium while denouncing the United States. On December 15, 1989, Noriega declared that a "state of war" existed between Panama and the United States. Tensions between the two countries further increased the next day, when U.S. military forces in Panama were put on alert after Panamanian troops shot and killed an American soldier, wounded another, and beat a Navy couple. Three days later, on December 20, 1989, President Bush ordered U.S. troops into combat in Panama City on a mission whose stated goals were to safeguard American lives, restore democracy, preserve the Panama Canal treaties, and seize General Noriega to face federal drug charges in the United States. Before U.S. troops were engaged, American officials arranged a ceremony in which Guillermo Endara was sworn in as president and recognized by the United States as the legitimate head of the government of Panama. Endara was reported to have won the Panamanian presidential election held several months earlier, the results of which were nullified and disregarded by General Noriega.

Not long after the invasion commenced, Defendant Del Cid, the commander of about two thousand Panamanian troops located in the Chiriqui Province, surrendered to American forces. He was then transferred into the custody of agents from the United States Drug Enforcement Agency, who thereupon arrested Del Cid for the offenses for which he is under indictment in this Court. The apprehension of General Noriega was not quite so easy. He successfully eluded American forces for several days, prompting the United States government to offer a one million dollar bounty for his capture. Eventually, the General took sanctuary in the Papal Nunciature in Panama City, where he apparently hoped to be granted political asylum. Noriega's presence in the Papal Nunciature touched off a diplomatic impasse and a round of intense negotiations involving several countries. Vatican officials initially refused to turn Noriega over to the United States. While he was still ensconced in the nunciature, American troops stationed outside pelted the building with loud rock-and-roll music blasted through loudspeakers. The music was played continuously for three days until church authorities protested the action as offensive. After an eleven-day standoff, Noriega finally surrendered to American forces, apparently under pressure from the papal nuncio and influenced by a threatening crowd of about 15,000 angry Panamanian citizens who had gathered outside the residence. On January 3, 1990, two weeks after the invasion began, Noriega walked out of the Papal Nunciature and surrendered himself to U.S. military officials waiting outside. He was flown by helicopter to Howard Air Force Base, where he was ushered into a plane bound for Florida and formally arrested by agents of the Drug Enforcement Agency. During the course of this litigation, which has included several hearings, no evidence was presented nor suggestion made that Noriega was in any way physically mistreated.

As is evident from the unusual factual background underlying this case, the Court is presented with several issues of first impression. This is the first time that a leader or de facto leader of a sovereign nation has been forcibly brought to the United States to face criminal charges. The fact that General Noriega's apprehension occurred in the course of a military action only further underscores the complexity of the issues involved. In addition to Defendant Noriega's motion to dismiss based on lack of jurisdiction over the offense and sovereign immunity, Defendants Noriega and Del Cid argue that they are prisoners of war pursuant to the Geneva Convention. This status, Defendants maintain, deprives the Court of jurisdiction to proceed with the case. Additionally, Noriega contends that the military action which brought about his arrest is "shocking to the conscience", and that due process considerations require the Court to divest itself of jurisdiction over his person. Noriega also asserts that the invasion occurred in violation of international law. Finally, Noriega argues that, even in the absence of constitutional or treaty violations, the Court should dismiss the indictment pursuant to its supervisory powers so as to prevent the judicial system from being party to and tainted by the government's alleged misconduct in arresting Noriega. The Court examines each of these issues, in turn, below.

The first issue confronting the Court is whether the United States may exercise jurisdiction over Noriega's alleged criminal activities. Noriega maintains that "the extraterritorial application of the criminal law is unreasonable under the unique facts of this case, and cannot be relied upon to secure jurisdiction over a leader of a sovereign nation who has personally performed no illegal acts within the borders of the United States." Although the defendant attempts to weave his asserted status as a foreign leader into his challenge to the extraterritorial application of this country's criminal laws, the question of whether the United States may proscribe conduct which occurs beyond its borders is separate from the question of whether Noriega is immune from prosecution as a head of state. The Court therefore reserves analysis of Noriega's claim to head of state immunity and confines its discussion here to the ability of the United States to reach and prosecute acts committed by aliens outside its territorial borders. While the indictment cites specific instances of conduct occurring within the United States, including the shipment of cocaine from Panama to Miami and several flights to and from Miami by Noriega's alleged co-conspirators, the activity ascribed to Noriega occurred solely in Panama with the exception of the one trip to Cuba. Noriega is charged with providing safe haven to international narcotic traffickers by allowing Panama to be used as a location for the manufacture and shipment of cocaine destined for this country's shores.

Where a court is faced with the issue of extraterritorial jurisdiction, the analysis to be applied is 1) whether the United States has the power to reach the conduct in question under traditional principles of international law; and 2) whether the statutes under which the defendant is charged are intended to have extraterritorial effect. As Noriega concedes, the United States has long possessed the ability to attach criminal consequences to acts occurring outside this country which produce effects within the United States. For example, the United States would unquestionably have authority to prosecute a person standing in Canada who fires a bullet across the border which strikes a second person standing in the United States. *See* Restatement (Third) [of the Foreign Relations Laws of the United States] §402, Comment d. "All the nations of the world recognize 'the principle that a man who outside of a country willfully puts in motion a force to take effect in it is answerable at the place where the evil is done....'" The objective territorial theory of jurisdiction, which focuses on the effects or intended effects of conduct, can be traced to Justice Holmes' statement that "acts done outside a jurisdiction, but intended to produce or producing effects within it, justify a State in punishing the cause of the harm as if he had been present at the effect, if the State should succeed in getting him within its power." *Strassheim v. Daily,* 221 U.S. at 285. Even if the extraterritorial conduct produces no effect within the United States, a defendant may still be reached if he was part of a conspiracy in which some co-conspirator's activities took place within United States territory. The former Fifth Circuit, whose decisions establish precedent for this Court, has on numerous occasions upheld jurisdiction over foreigners who conspired to import narcotics into the United States but never entered this country nor personally performed any acts within its territorial limits, as long as there was proof of an overt act committed within the United States by a co-conspirator.

More recently, international law principles have expanded to permit jurisdiction upon a mere showing of *intent* to produce effects in this country, without requiring proof of an overt act or effect within the United States. According to the Restatement (Third):

> Cases involving intended but unrealized effect are rare, but international law does not preclude jurisdiction in such instances, subject to the principle of reasonableness. When the intent to commit the proscribed act is clear and demonstrated by some activity, and the effect to be produced by the activity is substantial and foreseeable, the fact that a plan or conspiracy was thwarted does not deprive the target state of jurisdiction to make its law applicable.

In the drug smuggling context, the 'intent doctrine' has resulted in jurisdiction over persons who attempted to import narcotics into the United States but never actually succeeded in entering the United States or delivering drugs within its borders. The fact that no act was committed and no repercussions were felt within the United States did not preclude jurisdiction over conduct that was clearly directed at the United States. *United States v. Wright-Barker, supra* ("The purpose of these [narcotics laws] is to halt smugglers *before* they introduce their dangerous wares into and distribute them in this country.") (emphasis in original).

These principles unequivocally support jurisdiction in this case. The indictment charges Noriega with conspiracy to import cocaine into the United States and alleges several overt acts performed within the United States in furtherance of the conspiracy. Specifically, the indictment alleges that co-conspirators of Noriega purchased a Lear jet in Miami, which was then used to transport drug proceeds from Miami to Panama. Moreover, Noriega's activities in Panama, if true, undoubtedly produced effects within this country as deleterious as the hypothetical bullet fired across the border. The indictment alleges that, as a result of Noriega's facilitation of narcotics activity in Panama, 2,141 pounds of cocaine were illegally brought into Miami from Panama. While the ability of the United States to reach and proscribe extraterritorial conduct having effects in this country does not depend on the amount of narcotics imported into the United States or the magnitude of the consequences, the importation of over 2,000 pounds of cocaine clearly has a harmful impact and merits jurisdiction. Finally, even if no overt acts or effects occurred within the territorial borders, the object of the alleged conspiracy was to import cocaine into the United States and therefore an intent to produce effects is present.

The defendant's argument that the exercise of jurisdiction over his alleged activities in Panama is unreasonable is simply unsupportable in light of established principles of international law and the overwhelming case law in this Circuit upholding jurisdiction under similar circumstances. Other than asserting his status as a foreign leader, which presents a different question from the one posed here, Noriega does not distinguish this case from those cited above. He cites the principle of reasonableness recently articulated in the Restatement (Third) § 403, but fails to say how extending jurisdiction over his conduct would be unreasonable. In fact, the defendant's invocation of a reasonableness requirement supports rather than undermines the application of jurisdiction in the present case. Thus, for example, Noriega quotes the following language from the Restatement:

> In applying the principle of reasonableness, the exercise of criminal (as distinguished from civil) jurisdiction in relation to acts committed in another state may be perceived as particularly intrusive.... It is generally accepted by enforcement agencies of the United States government that criminal jurisdiction over activity with substantial foreign elements should be exercised more sparingly than civil jurisdiction over the same activity, and only upon strong justification.

However, the same section of the Restatement establishes that narcotics offenses provide the strong justification meriting criminal jurisdiction: "Prosecution for activities committed in a foreign state have generally been limited to serious and universally condemned offenses, such as treason or traffic in narcotics, and to offenses by and against military forces. In such cases the state in whose territory the act occurs is not likely to object to regulation by the state concerned." The Restatement therefore explicitly recognizes the reasonableness of extending jurisdiction to narcotics activity such as that alleged here. *See also United States v. Wright-Barker,* 784 F.2d at 168 (construing § 403 to permit jurisdiction over extraterritorial narcotics trafficking). Even if another state were likely to object to jurisdiction here, the United States has a strong interest in halting the flow of illicit drugs across its borders. In assessing the reasonableness of extraterritorial jurisdiction, one of the factors to be considered is the character of the activity to be regulated, including the importance of regulation to the regulating state and the degree to which the desire to regulate is generally accepted. Restatement (Third) § 403(1)(c). The consensus of the American public on the need to stem the flow of drugs into this country is well publicized and need not be elaborated upon in detail. Further, the Court notes that the United States has an affirmative duty to enact and enforce legislation to curb illicit drug trafficking under the Single Convention on Narcotics Drugs. Given the serious nature of the drug epidemic in this country, certainly the efforts of the United States to combat the problem by prosecuting conduct directed against itself cannot be subject to the protests of a foreign government profiting at its expense. In any case, the Court is not made aware of any instance in which the Republic of Panama objected to the regulation of drug trafficking by the United States. In sum, because Noriega's conduct in Panama is alleged to have resulted in a direct effect within the United States, the Court concludes that extraterritorial jurisdiction is appropriate as a matter of international law.

This conclusion does not end the Court's analysis, however, since a further requirement is that the criminal statutes under which the defendant is charged be intended to apply to conduct outside the United States. Noriega is charged with violations of 21 U.S.C. § 959 (distributing a controlled substance with the knowledge that it would be unlawfully imported into the United States); 21 U.S.C. § 952 (importing a controlled substance into the United States from a place outside thereof); 21 U.S.C. § 963 (conspiring to commit the above offenses); and 18 U.S.C. § 2 (aiding and abetting the violation of § 959). The indictment also alleges that Noriega participated in a pattern of racketeering activity consisting of the above crimes, in violation of the Racketeer Influenced and Corrupt Organizations Act (RICO), §§ 1962(c) and 1962(d), and caused the travel and use of facilities in interstate and foreign commerce in furtherance of a narcotics conspiracy, in violation of 18 U.S.C. § 1952 (a)(3).

Section 959, prohibiting the distribution of narcotics intending that they be imported into the United States, is clearly meant to apply extraterritorially. The statute expressly states that it is "intended to reach acts of manufacture or distribution committed outside the territorial jurisdiction of the United States." 21 U.S.C. § 959(c). The remaining statutes, by contrast, do not on their face indicate an express intention that they be given extraterritorial effect. Where a statute is silent as to its extraterritorial reach, a presumption against such application normally applies. However, "such statutes may be given extraterritorial effect if the nature of the law permits it and Congress intends it. Absent an express intention on the face of the statutes to do so, the exercise of that power may be inferred from the nature of the offenses and Congress' other legislative efforts to eliminate the type of crime involved."

With respect to 21 U.S.C. § 952, it is apparent from the very nature of the offense that the statute was intended to reach extraterritorial acts. Section 952 makes it unlawful to import narcotics "into the United States from *any place outside* thereof …" (emphasis added). Because importation by definition involves acts originating outside of the territorial limits of the United States, the Court can only infer that § 952 applies to conduct which begins abroad; any interpretation to the contrary would render the statute virtually meaningless. With jurisdiction over the substantive violations of §§ 959 and 952 established, jurisdiction over the conspiracy and aiding and abetting counts likewise follows. Since a conspiracy to commit an offense is closely related to the offense itself, courts have regularly inferred the extraterritorial reach of the § 963 conspiracy statute on the basis of a finding that the substantive statutes apply abroad. The same must be said for an aiding and abetting charge; if anything, the act of aiding and abetting is even more intimately connected to the underlying crime. In short, the Court perceives no sound jurisdictional reason for distinguishing the conspiracy and aiding and abetting charges from the substantive offense for purposes of extraterritorial application. Section 963 and 18 U.S.C. § 2 must therefore be given extraterritorial effect as well.

Whether the RICO and Travel Act statutes reach conduct abroad is a more difficult question. None of the cases cited by the parties address this point and the Court is unaware of any case reaching the issue. The question of these statutes' extraterritorial effect is therefore a matter of apparent first impression.

Section 1962(c) makes it unlawful for "*any* person associated with *any* enterprise engaged in, or the activities of which affect, interstate or foreign commerce, to conduct or participate. in the conduct of such enterprise's affairs through a pattern of racketeering activity. . . ." 18 U.S.C. § 1962(c) (emphasis added). Section 1962(d) similarly makes it illegal for "*any* person to conspire to violate" Section 1962(c). These prohibitions are on their face all-inclusive and do not suggest parochial application. Indeed, if any statute reaches far and wide, it is RICO.

When Congress passed RICO, it was primarily concerned with eradicating the destructive influence of organized crime on our society[.] Though its emphasis is on economic effects, RICO itself is not so limited; its history demonstrates concern with our domestic security and welfare as well as our gross national product.

Given the Act's broad construction and equally broad goal of eliminating the harmful consequences of organized crime, it is apparent that Congress was concerned with the effects and not the locus of racketeering activities. The Act thus permits no inference that it was intended to apply only to conduct within the United States. Such a narrow construction would frustrate RICO's purpose by allowing persons engaged in racketeering activities directed at the United States to escape RICO's bite simply by moving their operations abroad. Yet in the context of narcotics activities, perhaps the greatest threat to this country's welfare comes from enterprises outside the United States such as the Columbian cocaine cartels. Keeping in mind Congress' specific instruction that RICO be applied liberally to effect its remedial purpose, the Court cannot suppose that RICO does not reach such harmful conduct simply because it is extraterritorial in nature. As long as the racketeering activities produce effects or are intended to produce effects in this country, RICO applies.

Noriega is also charged with violating the Travel Act, 18 U.S.C. § 1952(a)(3), by causing foreign travel and the use of facilities in foreign and interstate commerce to promote an unlawful activity. The indictment alleges that, on two separate occasions, co-conspirators of Noriega used an airplane to transport drug proceeds from Miami to Panama.

Like RICO, the Travel Act was originally designed to combat organized crime. Specifically, "the purpose of the Travel Act was to aid local law enforcement officials. In many instances, the 'top men' of a given criminal enterprise resided in one State but conducted their illegal activities in another; by creating a federal interest in limiting the interstate movement necessary to such operations, criminal conduct beyond the reach of local officials could be controlled." *United States v. Nardello,* 393 U.S. 286, 290 (1969). The Act was thus an attempt to reach criminal activities uniquely broad and transitory in scope, i.e., those whose influence extend beyond state and national borders and therefore require federal assistance. While courts have sometimes, as above, referred to persons "residing in one state," the Act itself indicates no such territorial limitation; the reference is therefore more properly understood as calling attention to the interstate character of the activity rather than the defendant's location. Stated more broadly, the Act "constitutes an effort to deny individuals who act for criminal purposes access to the channels of commerce."

In this case, the defendant allegedly participated in a criminal syndicate which utilized the channels of commerce to carry out illegal drug activities in the United States. His location may have differed from the typical defendant charged under the Travel Act but the nature and effect of the alleged activity is the same, and implicates the same congressional desire to reach conduct which transcends state lines both physically and symbolically.

Jurisdiction over Defendant's extraterritorial conduct is therefore appropriate both as a matter of international law and statutory construction.

[The Court went on to reject Noriega's additional arguments that (1) he was immune from prosecution based on head of state immunity, the act of state doctrine, and diplomatic immunity; (2) the Court did not have jurisdiction to proceed with the case because Noriega was a prisoner of war within the meaning of the Geneva Convention; and (3) the Court should divest itself of jurisdiction because he was illegally arrests.]

In view of the above findings and observations, it is the Order of this Court that the several motions presented by Defendants relating to this Court's jurisdiction as well as that suggesting dismissal under supervisory authority be and each is DENIED.

Manuel Noriega was tried and convicted in 1992. Though Noriega completed his sentence in 2007, he was not released from custody. Instead, Noriega was extradited to France where he received a seven-year prison sentence for money laundering offenses. *See* Geoffrey S. Corn and Sharon C. Finegan, *America's Longest Held Prisoner of War: Lessons Learned from the Capture, Prosecution, and Extradition of General Manuel Noriega*, 71 L. L. REV. 1111 (2011). Interestingly, before Noriega became a target of the United States, he spent decades as a paid informant for the United States. According to one former DEA officer, the US suspected Noriega of involvement in drug trafficking "[a]s early as 1972" but "the State Department told the [DEA] in no uncertain terms that Noriega and his boss, Panamanian strongman Omar Torrijos, were too important to be touched [because t]hey provided critical intelligence on Soviet influence on Latin American countries." *See, e.g.,* ROBERT M. STUTMAN AND RICHARD ESPOSITO, DEAD ON DELIVERY: INSIDE THE DRUG WARS, STRAIGHT FROM THE STREET 98–99 1992.

In *Noriega*, the Court found that the objective territorial principle of international law gave U.S. court jurisdiction over cases "upon a mere showing of *intent* to produce effects in" the United States. But is an intent to produce effects in the United States necessary for the extraterritorial application of federal drug laws? Or, can federal courts exercise jurisdiction over drug cases with a weaker connection to the United States?

United States v. Manuel

United States District Court for the Southern District of New York
371 F. Supp. 2d 404 (2005)

Lynch, J.

Defendant Virgilio Martinus Manuel was charged, along with six other defendants, in two different conspiracy counts. Count One charged defendants with conspiring to import over 300,000 ecstasy pills into the United States, in violation of 21 U.S.C. §§ 963, 812, 952(a)(2) and 960(b)(3). Count Two charged them with conspiring to distribute or possess with intent to distribute ecstasy, in violation of 21 U.S.C. §§ 846, 841(a)(1), and 841(b)(1)(C). Manuel was tried before a jury from March 23 through March 30, 2005. At the close of the Government's case, the Court dismissed Count One, holding that the evidence was insufficient to prove beyond a reasonable doubt that Manuel knew that the drugs were destined for the United States. However, the Court ruled at that time that this insufficiency did not require acquittal on Count Two. The jury subsequently found Manuel guilty on that count. Manuel now renews his motion for acquittal on that charge, arguing that the evidence was insufficient to permit his conviction and that the court lacks subject matter jurisdiction over the offense. The motion will be denied.

Manuel does not contest that the Government's evidence was sufficient to establish the following facts. Beginning in the spring of 2001, a skillful German undercover police officer insinuated himself into a group of conspirators in the Netherlands, who hoped to export large quantities of ecstasy (a controlled substance whose distribution is illegal in the Netherlands, Germany, and the United States) from Europe to the United States. The undercover officer persuaded the chief conspirators, Beatriz Henao, Armando Enano, Valderama Ruiz, and Victor deBoer, that, for a fee, he could safely transport large quantities of pills to the United States.

The conspirators decided to try an initial test run of 47,000 pills in June 2001. DeBoer delivered the pills to the undercover officer in Germany, for transportation to America. From the criminals' perspective, the test went off almost without a hitch: The pills were delivered undetected (so far as they knew) to their courier in New York, Ricardo Quintero. Through a clever ruse, by making it appear that the drugs were discovered by accident after a successful delivery to the courier, the investigators were able to arrest Quintero and seize the drugs without bringing the undercover officer under suspicion. Writing that seizure off to bad luck and the incompetence of their New York courier, the leaders of the enterprise decided to go ahead with a larger shipment in August 2001.

Because deBoer was in Colombia at that time, the conspirators arranged to use a different courier to deliver the second shipment, of 301,000 pills, to the undercover officer at a highway rest stop in Germany. The conspirators advised the undercover officer that the courier would be driving a white car and wearing a white hat. That courier was Manuel, who arrived at the designated location in a white car wearing a white cap, made contact with the undercover, and delivered the drugs. On September 29, 2001, the undercover delivered the pills, as instructed by the conspiracy's leaders, to Carlos Ruiz in New York. Ruiz was arrested and the drugs seized.

So far as the evidence at trial revealed, Manuel's sole role in the conspiracy was to deliver the pills from Holland to Germany on August 7, 2001. For purposes of this motion, he does not dispute that a reasonable jury could infer that he knew that he was delivering illegal drugs, since (among other reasons) professional drug dealers would hardly entrust an unwitting dupe to carry drugs worth over $1,000,000 wholesale in Europe (and $6,000,000 to $9,000,000 retail at their eventual destination in the streets and clubs of New York) across an international border. There was no evidence whatsoever, on the other hand, suggesting that Manuel knew the eventual destination of the pills.[2]

---

2. The Government halfheartedly argues in a footnote that the jury could have found, by the same process of inference, that Manuel must have had a high enough rank in the conspiracy to be privy to the details of the conspiracy. This claim is without merit. It is reasonable to assume that a courier entrusted the task of transporting valuable illegal commodities across an international border would be aware of the nature of his cargo; the conspirators would be foolish to run the risk that an unwitting courier would steal or neglect the cargo, attract police attention by violating traffic laws, or fail to take action to evade customs patrols. There is no reason to assume, however, that a mere courier, albeit one with criminal intent, would be advised of the business plans of the leaders. On the contrary, it would presumably be advisable to keep subordinates in the dark. Moreover, as evidence in the record indicates that the Netherlands is the leading source country for ecstasy, and that there is a thriving market for ecstasy in Germany, there is no reason why a courier would assume that the drugs were destined for further transshipment.

The point of departure for analysis of Manuel's claims is *United States v. Londono-Villa*, 930 F.2d 994 (2d Cir. 1991). In Londono-Villa, as in this case, an undercover narcotics officer negotiated with foreign drug dealers (in that case, cocaine smugglers in Panama, rather than ecstasy sellers in the Netherlands) regarding drugs to be shipped to the United States. The negotiations having been successfully concluded, the undercover agent was advised that his pilot could pick up the drugs at a hidden airfield in Colombia and bring them back to Panama for eventual transshipment to the United States. Londono, an experienced pilot who had frequently used that airfield, was recruited by the conspirators to guide the undercover agent's plane to the secret landing strip; Londono would then remain in Colombia while the plane returned to Panama with the drugs. Londono unquestionably knew of the illegal purpose of the flight; indeed, he inspected the cocaine at the landing field, and was sufficiently intimate with the drug sellers that when the shipment turned out to be short, the parties relied on him to verify the amount of cocaine actually delivered to the plane. The cocaine was eventually transported to the United States.

Nevertheless, the Second Circuit held that the evidence was insufficient to convict Londono of conspiracy to import the drugs into the United States. The Court held that in order to be guilty of this offense, an individual must by definition have knowledge that the illegal drugs are intended to enter the United States. This holding is rooted in the language of the statute. The very definition of the offense that is the object of the conspiracy requires that the defendant "knowingly or intentionally import[]" a controlled substance in violation of § 952. 21 U.S.C. § 960(a)(1). Section 952 is even more explicit, making it illegal "to import [a controlled substance] into the United States from any place outside thereof." 21 U.S.C. § 952. In order to conspire to "import [cocaine] into the United States," in violation of 21 U.S.C. § 963, one would necessarily have to agree not merely to possess the drug or to distribute it to others, but specifically to bring the drugs into the United States. Absent knowledge that the United States was the destination for the drug, one could not so agree.

This precedent compelled the dismissal of Count One of the present indictment. Manuel, like Londono, was directly involved in smuggling illegal drugs across an international border. There was no evidence, however that Manuel, a mere courier so far as the evidence shows, was aware of the larger goal of the conspiracy. As in Londono-Villa, Manuel "was not involved in any of the lengthy negotiations for the sale of the [ecstasy]; he was not present at most of the meetings but rather came into the picture only at the end, in order to serve as a [courier] who was to pick up the [ecstasy] in [the Netherlands] and take it [to Germany]. There was no evidence that [Manuel] had been told that the United States was to be the ultimate destination of the cocaine, and no evidence that the United States was ever mentioned in his presence."

Count Two, however, charges a different offense. The definition of the crime that is the object of the conspiracy charged in Count Two does not refer to importation, nor does it refer to the United States. Instead, the statute in question merely makes it a crime to "distribute, ... or possess with intent to ... distribute ... a controlled substance." 21 U.S.C. § 841(a)(1). It is not questioned, for purposes of this motion, that Manuel conspired with others to do exactly that: by agreeing to undertake, by prearrangement with others, the delivery of over 300,000 ecstasy pills to the undercover in Germany, he joined a conspiracy whose object was the retail distribution of that controlled substance.

It is beyond dispute, as Manuel points out, that this offense requires a jurisdictional nexus to the United States. Congress did not intend to prohibit every act of distributing drugs anywhere in the world, but only distribution within the United States. See *United*

States v. Hayes, 653 F.2d 8, 15–16 (1st Cir. 1981) (declining to "impute to Congress an intent to punish all whom its courts can catch, for conduct which has no consequences in the United States" by applying §841(a)(1) to possession of a controlled substance outside the United States with intent to distribute, unless the "intent to distribute" is an intent to distribute within the United States) (quoting *United States v. Aluminum Co. of America,* 148 F.2d 416, 443 (2d Cir. 1945) (Hand, J.)). But the distribution of ecstasy that was the object of this conspiracy was indeed to occur in the United States. That was the very purpose of the conspiracy, which enlisted the undercover officer precisely for his supposed prowess in smuggling goods into the United States. Nor was this intention purely hypothetical: the conspirators arranged for colleagues in the Southern District of New York to receive the drugs, and both shipments were accepted by those co-conspirators here in New York. The quantity of drugs in both shipments makes plain that the importation was for the purpose of further distribution here.

These facts doom Manuel's argument that "the court lacks subject matter jurisdiction over the defendant for the offenses charged." In the first place, the argument misstates the question. A court has subject matter jurisdiction over a case, not over a person, and the Court plainly has jurisdiction over the case, because the indictment charged a violation of federal law. What Manuel means to argue is either that Congress lacked legislative jurisdiction to prohibit his actions, or that he is not guilty of the offense charged because Congress did not intend the law to have extraterritorial application to his acts.

But however defined, Manuel's argument fails on the merits. Any challenge to the legislative jurisdiction of Congress must fail, since there is no constitutional bar to the extraterritorial application of penal laws. Whether a statute has such extraterritorial application is solely a question of legislative intent. *United States v. Bowman,* 260 U.S. 94, 97–98 (1922).[4] The Supreme Court has specifically upheld the exercise of jurisdiction over conspirators who have never entered the United States, where the conspiracy "was directed to violation of the United States law within the United States." *Ford v. United States,* 273 U.S. 593, 620 (1927). Where, as here, the object of a conspiracy is the violation of American law, and co-conspirators committed extensive overt acts within American territory, there can be no serious question of the jurisdiction of the United States to punish all members of the conspiracy.

The sole remaining question is whether Congress intended to do so in enacting the statutes at issue in this case. Although there is a presumption that Congress does not intend a statute to apply to conduct outside the United States, that presumption can be overcome if Congress clearly expresses its intent. It is well-established that Congress intended to give extraterritorial reach to the statutes at issue here. Thus, the Second Circuit has held that jurisdiction to prosecute violations of §841(a)(1) exists both where defendants possess drugs outside the United States with intent to distribute them in the United States, or possess drugs inside the United States with intent to distribute them elsewhere. *United States v. Muench,* 694 F.2d 28, 32–33 (2d Cir. 1982).

There is no question that *both* bases of jurisdiction applied here. The heads of the conspiracy possessed ecstasy in the Netherlands with intent to distribute it in the United States, and the conspirators in New York actually possessed the drug here with the intent

---

4. While international law standards of national jurisdiction are not binding on the Congress, it should be noted that extraterritorial application of United States law to Manuel is entirely in keeping with international law, since international law permits a country to exercise jurisdiction over acts committed outside it that have harmful effects within it. See Restatement (Third) of the Foreign Relations Law of the United States §§402–403.

to distribute it. Thus, the crime that was the object of the conspiracy Manuel joined was a violation of United States law.

Where a crime is within the jurisdiction of the United States, it is not necessary that the offender be aware of the facts that establish jurisdiction. Thus, for example, a defendant need not know that the person he is assaulting is a federal officer in order to be guilty of violating 18 U.S.C. § 111, *United States v. Feola,* 420 U.S. 671, 684 (1975); a defendant need not know that securities were transported across a state line to be guilty of interstate transportation of stolen securities under 18 U.S.C. § 2314, *United States v. Eisenberg,* 596 F.2d 522, 526 (2d Cir. 1979); and a defendant need not know he was stealing from an interstate shipment to be guilty of violating 18 U.S.C. § 659, *United States v. Green,* 523 F.2d 229, 233–34 (2d Cir. 1975). If the defendant knowingly commits the acts that cause the harm that the legislature intended to prevent (here, the distribution of narcotics), and jurisdiction exists (because, objectively speaking, the crime satisfies the condition that creates jurisdiction), the statute has been violated. Had the defendants in *Muench* inadvertently wandered into United States territory from Canada, rather than being carried (unwillingly, but knowingly) into the United States by a diverted flight, it could have made no difference: in either case, they committed the crime of possessing narcotics with intent to distribute, and their actions in doing so came within the legislative jurisdiction of the United States in a manner that Congress intended to reach.

Nor does the fact that the crime charged is a conspiracy, and thus requires an intentional agreement to violate the statute, alter the result. Conviction for conspiracy requires no greater *mens rea* than that required to violate the underlying statute. Indeed, ordinary doctrines of conspiracy law confirm the conclusion that Manuel is guilty of the conspiracy charged in Count Two. It is axiomatic that a conspirator does not need to know all of the details of a conspiracy in order to be guilty of joining the agreement and it is equally axiomatic that a conspirator is responsible for the overt acts of co-conspirators, including those necessary to establish venue. Here, it is unquestioned for purposes of this motion that Manuel and his co-conspirators were in "agreement on the essential nature of the plan, and on the kind of criminal conduct ... in fact contemplated." His co-conspirators committed acts on American soil, and other acts abroad with the specific intention of having effects in the United States. Under basic conspiracy law, he is guilty of joining their conspiracy, and is brought under American jurisdiction by their acts.

There is nothing unfair about this conclusion. Like the defendants in *Feola,* Manuel clearly "knew from the very outset that his planned course of conduct [was] wrongful. The situation is not one where legitimate conduct becomes unlawful solely because of the identity of the [country] affected.... The concept of criminal intent does not extend so far as to require that the actor understand not only the nature of his act but also its consequence for the choice of a judicial forum." Unlike *Londono-Villa,* and Count One of this indictment, in which the object of the conspiracy by its nature required an intention to cross the American border, and in which the defendant did not share in the plan to send drugs into the United States that was the very essence of the conspiracy charged, the effect on the United States in Count Two is a mere jurisdictional element, which does not require knowledge or intent on the part of Manuel.

It was established beyond a reasonable doubt at trial that the conspiracy here was to possess a controlled substance with intent to distribute; that Manuel joined the conspiracy, with full knowledge that its goal was to possess and distribute ecstasy; and that that conspiracy came under the jurisdiction of the United States because co-conspirators both possessed the drugs in the United States and intended to distribute them here. Nothing more is required to convict Manuel of the charge in Count Two.

For these reasons, defendant's motion for acquittal under Federal Rule of Criminal Procedure 29(c) is denied.

———————

In a footnote in *Manuel*, Judge Lynch suggests that a drug courier is likely to "be aware of the nature of his cargo" because "the conspirators would be foolish to run the risk that an unwitting courier would steal or neglect the cargo, attract police attention by violating traffic laws, or fail to take action to evade customs patrols." Is this really the case? In spring 2012, the federal government revealed that Mexican drug trafficking groups have been using "unwitting courier[s]" — so called "blind mules" — near the San Diego border. The traffickers place classified advertisements for seemingly legitimate jobs that require travel into the United States, such as work as a housecleaner or furniture mover. The driver is not told that the company vehicle is loaded with drugs, however. *See* Elliot Spagat, *Drug Smugglers Placing Job Ads In Mexican Newspapers*, Associated Press, April 11, 2012. Why might a drug trafficker use a "blind mule" in light of the considerations outlined by Judge Lynch?

In *Manuel*, Judge Lynch also noted that the intent to distribute ecstasy was not "purely hypothetical: the conspirators arranged for colleagues in the Southern District of New York to receive the drugs, and both shipments were accepted by those co-conspirators in New York." Could a defendant like Manuel be prosecuted in the United States even if the intent to send drugs into the country was "purely hypothetical"?

A recent series of federal drug prosecutions has presented courts with this question. The Drug Enforcement Administration has increasingly sought to bring overseas drug operators into United States courts through the use of informants. Though the details vary, DEA agents typically pose as drug traffickers as part of elaborate sting operations in which drugs are shipped between two countries outside of the United States — for example, from Colombia to Africa. "In order to establish U.S. jurisdiction, [the under cover agent or informant will] tell suspects that some of the drugs will be sold in the United States[.]" Chris Hawley, *Swede Charged in NYC With Guns-for-Coke Scheme*, Associated Press, May 10, 2011. None of the actual traffickers plan to bring drugs into the United States. The only link to the United States is the undercover agent's stated intention. *See also, e.g.,* Jeralyn E. Merritt, *Trial Starts Monday in "DEA African Adventures" Case*, TalkLeft, April 3, 2011, http://www.talkleft.com/story/2011/4/3/0940/05256 (describing the increasing use of this investigative tactic). Is this manufactured connection to the U.S. sufficient to ground jurisdiction?

In one case, four defendants — a Nigerian, a Russian, and two Ghanaians — faced charges based on drug shipments between South America and West Africa. A DEA informant participating in the scheme "stated clearly to the defendants he planned to import cocaine from them to the United States." Colin Moynihan, *Jury Convicts 2 and Acquits 2 in Scheme to Funnel Cocaine into U.S.*, N.Y. Times, April 28, 2011 at A25. Of course, the informant never actually intended to send drugs to the United States; the story was devised as a tool to give U.S. courts jurisdiction over the case. At least one of the defendants moved to dismiss the indictment, arguing that the U.S. had improperly "manufactured jurisdiction." The Judge denied the motion, however, finding that the indictment alleged the defendant had taken "affirmative, voluntary actions implicating federal jurisdiction" because he allegedly "understood that from Liberia, portions of this cocaine would subsequently be imported into the United States" by the informant. *United States v. Umeh*, 762 F. Supp. 2d 658, 665 (2011). At trial, three of the defendants conceded that they were involved in international drug trafficking but argued that they had no knowledge of the informant's statements that he planned to send some of the drugs into the U.S. The jury convicted two of the four defendants and acquitted the other two.

The "manufactured jurisdiction" cases have drawn criticism both inside and outside of the United States. Commenting on the *Umeh* case, for example, Russian Prime Minister Vladamir Putin argued that the U.S. was overreaching in asserting jurisdictions in the case. "How do the U.S. state interests come into the Picture? No one can say exactly," Putin said. Chris Hawley, *Swede Charged in NYC With Guns-for-Coke Scheme*, ASSOCIATED PRESS, May 10, 2011.

United States v. Lopez-Vanegas

United States Court of Appeals for the Eleventh Circuit
493 F.3d 1305 (2007)

Walter, J.

Doris Mangeri Salazar ("Salazar") and Ivan Lopez-Vanegas ("Lopez") appeal their convictions on one count each of conspiracy to possess with the intent to distribute five kilograms or more of a mixture and substance containing cocaine, in violation of 21 U.S.C. §§ 841(a)(1) and (b)(1)(A)(ii), and 21 U.S.C. § 846. The Government alleged that Salazar and Lopez brokered a deal between a Colombian drug trafficking organization headed by Juan Gabriel Usuga ("Usuga") and a Saudi Arabian Prince, Nayef Al-Shaalan (the "Prince"), to transport cocaine on the Prince's airplane from Caracas, Venezuela to Paris, France, for distribution in Europe.

On appeal, Lopez and Salazar assert, inter alia, that the conduct of which they were accused, and for which they have been convicted, does not violate 21 U.S.C. §§ 841 and 846. Finding that Salazar and Lopez have committed no crime against the United States, the judgments of conviction and sentences issued by the district court are VACATED.

By 1998, Usuga, Carlos Ramon ("Ramon"), Oscar Campuzano ("Campuzano") and Bernard Sanchez ("Sanchez") (collectively, the "Usuga Group") had become partners in a large-scale Colombian cocaine trafficking organization out of Medellin, Colombia. Usuga was the leader; Campuzano was in charge of collecting money; Sanchez was responsible for transporting, packaging, warehousing and labeling the cocaine in South America; Ramon handled transportation abroad, including the receipt and delivery of cocaine at its destination. Clemente, a Spaniard, was also closely affiliated with the group, though not a member, and specialized in laundering the Usuga Group's drug money.

Evidence at trial showed that the Usuga Group exported at least 50 tons of cocaine during the 1990s throughout Europe and North America. The Group also provided transportation services to other traffickers. The Usuga Group's trademark transportation method was to hide cocaine within isotanks containing petro chemicals.

By January 2000, all four members of the Usuga Group had been indicted in Miami and elsewhere in connection with, among other investigations, Operation Millennium, which targeted high-level narcotics traffickers for extradition. All four members of the Usuga Group surrendered, entered into plea agreements and cooperated with the Government. In particular, Usuga and Campuzano pleaded guilty only to money laundering in connection with Operation Millennium, and each received a reduced sentence of 34 months. Their sentences were later reduced to 22 and 23 months, respectively. Both Usuga and Campuzano had served their time before testifying at trial.

Sanchez pleaded guilty to drug trafficking and received a reduced sentence of 156 months[.] Ramon pleaded guilty to drug trafficking and received a reduced sentence of six years, with the hope of an additional sentence reduction.

Usuga testified at trial that the plans behind the Paris Load began in 1998, when Lopez approached Usuga in Medellin and told him about a "friend of a woman friend of mine" with whom they could engage in financial transactions or deals in Europe. Usuga later learned that Salazar was Lopez's "woman friend," and that the Prince was Salazar's friend. Over the course of a year, the Usuga Group, Clemente, Lopez, the Prince and Salazar had meetings across the globe[5] where, according to the Government, the group conspired to purchase cocaine in Colombia, to be shipped from Venezuela to Paris, France, for distribution in Europe. For purposes of this appeal, the Court will assume that all facts alleged by the Government are uncontested. With that in mind, the following meetings took place in Miami, Florida:

a. Miami, Florida ("Porto Fino") — Mid-September 1998. In mid-September, 1998, Usuga, Ramon and Campuzano met at the "Porto Fino," Ramon's South-Beach condominium. Neither Lopez nor Salazar was present. At this meeting, the group discussed "the way we were going to set up this organization." "Various tasks" were assigned after Usuga told his cohorts that "he had been able to confirm that in fact ... [the Prince] had a bank in Geneva and that [the Prince] was who he said he was." Usuga told the group that he would soon be traveling to Saudi Arabia for further discussions. Campuzano confirmed Usuga's account of this Miami meeting.

At this meeting, it was agreed that "there would be two groups ... [the Prince's] group would consist of [the Prince] and [Salazar] ... [Salazar would] receive a commission from [the Prince]." Lopez would receive his commission from the Usuga Group for each kilogram transported. Usuga would handle direct communications with the Prince; Ramon would be responsible for the movement of the cocaine; and Campuzano "would be responsible for setting up the straw corporations abroad."

Usuga presented two proposals: one possibility involved the shipment of ten or twenty tons of cocaine using isotanks from Venezuela to Saudi Arabia for re-export to New York;[6]

---

5. Meetings were held in Marbella, Spain, Geneva, Switzerland, Saudi Arabia, Aruba, Colombia and Miami. The Court will focus on the Miami meetings as they are the only events related to the charged conspiracy that took place in the United States.

6. There is no dispute that Usuga, not the Prince, wanted to send the shipment to New York. Further, the Government has not asserted that shipment to New York was anything more than a one-sided fleeting thought.

In its appellate brief, the Government relies solely upon the "domestic conspiratorial conduct" of Lopez and Salazar to support its argument that the district court had jurisdiction, or as is discussed below, that a crime was actually committed under 21 U.S.C. §§ 841(a)(1) and 846. Further, the Government's subsequent arguments presume that there was no agreement to distribute illegal narcotics in the United States, e.g., "[t]he law does not impose upon §§ 846 and 841(a)(1) any requirement that the object of such a conspiracy must be to possess or distribute cocaine in the United States"; "[b]ecause a defendant may be convicted of a substantive offense under § 841(a)(1) without intending to distribute narcotics in the United States, it follows that defendants like Salazar and Lopez may be guilty of conspiracy to possess with intent to distribute cocaine, in violation of § 846, as long as they or others have engaged in conspiratorial activities to violate that statute in the United States." Brief for the United States, pp. 29–30. Further, as noted above, in response to Salazar's motion for judgment of acquittal, the Government argued that "the drug conspiracy touches here" because the conspirators held meetings in Miami.

In other words, the Government does not rely upon Usuga's statement that he initially wanted to ship cocaine to New York rather than Paris. Thus, this Court finds that the Government has abandoned any such argument. See *Sepulveda v. United States Attorney General*, 401 F.3d 1226, 1228 n. 2 (11th the second proposal was to transport cocaine in the Prince's airplane from Venezuela to Saudi Arabia.

b. Miami, Florida (Dinner at The Forge Restaurant) — November/December 1998. In November or December of 1998, Ramon, Salazar, Clemente, Lopez, Usuga and Pepe Gugliatto met for dinner at The Forge. There, Lopez and Salazar introduced Gugliatto to Usuga. Salazar assured Usuga that Gugliatto was a close friend akin to a relative "with whom [Usuga] could comfortably talk." According to Ramon, Gugliatto was Lopez's personal friend and came with good references from Lopez and Salazar. Two matters were discussed at this Miami meeting: the Brazil shoe deal,[7] and Gugliatto's potential for "partnership" with the Prince. Salazar sat with the group at the Forge; "she gave her opinions" though Ramon could not recall her exact words.

Ramon testified that another meeting occurred at the Biltmore Hotel in Miami, involving Usuga, Ramon, Clemente, Salazar and Gugliatto. At that meeting, "some comments were made" about the potential Prince deal, but nothing specific. Usuga, however, testified that they did not discuss the deal at this meeting.

c. Miami, Florida (Don Shula Hotel) — March 5, 1999. On March 5, 1999, Usuga met Salazar, Lopez and Gugliatto at the Don Shula Hotel in Miami. The brief discussion at this meeting centered on the upcoming arrival of the Prince in Caracas, Venezuela for which "everything was ready." Lopez stated that he would notify Usuga of the Prince's arrival date, a few days prior to that date. Usuga replied "that we would be waiting for that."

d. Miami, Florida (Tides Hotel) — July 1999. After the Paris Load was successfully purchased in Colombia, transported to Caracas, Venezuela, and shipped to Paris, France on May 16, 1999, most of the load was distributed, but 804 kilograms of cocaine were seized by French law enforcement on June 3, 1999. In July 1999, Usuga, Campuzano, Clemente and Salazar met at the Tides Hotel in Miami Beach to discuss the amount of money owed to the Prince, who had already been paid $5,000,000 from Lopez's sale of 250 kilograms of cocaine. According to Usuga and Campuzano, Salazar demanded payment of her commission "for the Paris operation" and an additional $10,000,000 owed the Prince, but Usuga refused. Salazar insisted "that the money was owed to the Prince and it had to be paid." Salazar further insisted that Usuga was "responsible for the incident" and, thus, was responsible for her commission.

e. Recorded Conversations With Lopez. After Usuga was arrested and was cooperating with the Government, he recorded a number of conversations with Lopez between April 2000 and March 2001. After Campuzano surrendered and agreed to cooperate with the Government, Lopez called and Campuzano also recorded their conversation. Lopez's conversations with Campuzano and Usuga centered on the debts owed to the Prince, and those owed by and to Lopez as a result of the Paris Load.

Whether a criminal statute reaches a defendant's conduct is reviewed de novo.

Appellants assert that the agreement to ship cocaine from Colombia to Venezuela to Saudi Arabia to France for distribution throughout Europe does not violate 21 U.S.C.

Cir. 2002) (concluding that the petitioners abandoned an issue by failing to raise it in their initial appellate brief).

7. Gugliatto proposed sending cocaine from Brazil to the Port of Miami; the cocaine would be hidden in a commercial cargo container of shoes where Gugliatto could access them "before Customs could touch them." Lopez contributed $350,000 to be part of the Brazil shoe deal, which would have involved "a ton of units," but that deal never materialized. The Government conceded, and the district court acknowledged and *instructed the jury*, that the Brazil shoe deal was a separate *uncharged* conspiracy that was offered simply to explain the relationship among the participants.

§ 846 because the object of the conspiracy—the possession and distribution of cocaine on foreign soil—is not a violation of 21 U.S.C. § 841(a)(1). Thus, the district court should have granted defendants' motion for acquittal at the close of the Government's case. The Government asserts that the defendants' conduct was encompassed by the prohibitions of 21 U.S.C. § 846 and § 841(a)(1), forbidding conspiracy to possess with intent to distribute cocaine. The issue of whether discussions occurring in the United States related to possession of controlled substances outside of the United States with intent to distribute those substances outside of the United States is a crime in the United States is *res nova* in the Eleventh Circuit. We squarely address that issue now.

Title 21 U.S.C. § 841(a)(1), in conjunction with § 846, makes it unlawful for any person to conspire to possess with the intent to distribute a controlled substance, such as cocaine. Neither statute expressly requires that possession, distribution nor an act in furtherance of the conspiracy occur in the United States. A silent statute is presumed to apply only domestically. *Small v. United States,* 544 U.S. 385, 388 (2005). Such statutes may be given extraterritorial application if the nature of the law permits it *and* Congress intends it. "Absent an express intention on the face of the statutes to do so, the exercise of that power may be inferred from the nature of the offenses and Congress' other legislative efforts to eliminate the type of crime involved." The United States Supreme Court explained the issues involved with a statute silent as to its extraterritorial application:

> The necessary locus, when not specially defined, depends upon the purpose of Congress as evinced by the description and nature of the crime and upon the territorial limitations upon the power and jurisdiction of a government to punish crime under the law of nations. Crimes against private individuals or their property, like assaults, murder, burglary, larceny, robbery, arson, embezzlement, and frauds of all kinds, which affect the peace and good order of the community must, of course, be committed within the territorial jurisdiction of the government where it may properly exercise it. If punishment of them is to be extended to include those committed out side {*sic*} of the strict territorial jurisdiction, it is natural for Congress to say so in the statute, and failure to do so will negative the purpose of Congress in this regard.

> But the same rule of interpretation should not be applied to criminal statutes which are, as a class, not logically dependent on their locality for the government's jurisdiction, but are enacted because of the right of the government to defend itself against obstruction, or fraud wherever perpetrated, especially if committed by its own citizens, officers, or agents. Some such offenses can only be committed within the territorial jurisdiction of the government because of the local acts required to constitute them. Others are such that to limit their locus to the strictly territorial jurisdiction would be greatly to curtail the scope and usefulness of the statute and leave open a large immunity for frauds as easily committed by citizens on the high seas and in foreign countries as at home. In such cases, Congress has not thought it necessary to make specific provision in the law that the locus shall include the high seas and foreign countries, but allows it to be inferred from the nature of the offense. *United States v. Bowman,* 260 U.S. 94, 97–98 (1922).

Our case law, and that of our sister circuits, has applied § 841(a)(1) and § 846 extraterritorially in certain circumstances, even though Congress has not specifically expressed its intent on the matter. See *United States v. Baker,* 609 F.2d 134, 139 (5th Cir. 1980). However, in each of those cases some other nexus to the United States allowed for extraterritorial application of § 841(a)(1): defendants either possessed or conspired to possess controlled substances within the United States, or intended to distribute controlled substances within the United States. Our predecessor Court made clear in *Baker* that § 841(a)(1) does not apply to possession outside United States territory unless the possessor intends to distribute the contraband within the United States. *[S]ee Muench*, 694 F.2d at 33 (discussing Baker and Hayes). Furthermore, there can be no violation of § 846 if the object of the conspiracy is not a violation of the substantive offense. 21 U.S.C. § 846 ("Any person who ... conspires to commit any offense defined in this subchapter...."). Accordingly, where, as here, the object of the conspiracy was to possess controlled substances outside the United States with the intent to distribute outside the United States, there is no violation of § 841(a)(1) or § 846.

Further, Congress has shown it is capable of addressing acts involving controlled substances occurring outside of the United States, and has shown it thinks it necessary to make specific provisions in the law that allow the locus to include acts of manufacture or distribution of controlled substances on foreign soil when there is an intent to unlawfully import such substances or chemicals into the United States. In 21 U.S.C. § 959, Congress specifically stated that the statute "is intended to reach acts of manufacture or distribution committed outside the territorial jurisdiction of the United States." Under 21 U.S.C. §§ 841 and 846, Congress has not stated its intent to reach discussions held in the United States in furtherance of a conspiracy to *possess* controlled substances *outside* the territorial jurisdiction of the United States, with intent to *distribute* those controlled substances *outside* of the territorial jurisdiction of the United States.

Because the Court holds that 21 U.S.C. §§ 841 and 846 do not apply extraterritorially, the conduct of Lopez and Salazar does not violate those statutes. The judgments of conviction and sentences issued by the district court are VACATED.

––––––––––

Lopez-Vanegas highlights the distinction between the two key questions involved in the extraterritorial application of the law. In *Lopez-Vanegas*, there is no doubt that application of U.S. drug laws would have been consistent with accepted international principles of jurisdiction. For example, the territorial principle would have permitted jurisdiction because meetings at which the conspiracy was planned occurred in the United States. *Cf, e.g., Kauthar SDN BHD v. Sternberg*, 149 F.3d 659 (7th Cir. 1998) (upholding the extraterritorial application of U.S. securities laws where "the conduct occurring in the United States directly cause[d] the plaintiff's alleged loss in that the conduct form[ed] a substantial part of the alleged fraud and [was] material to its success"). But, the fact that international law would allow for jurisdiction says nothing about whether the statute at issue does, in fact, apply extraterritorially. As *Lopez-Vanegas* indicates, to determine extraterritorial reach of a particular law, courts are guided by Congressional intent.

Are you persuaded by the *Lopez-Vanegas* court's conclusion with respect to Congressional intent? Is there a reason that Congress would intend for 21 U.S.C. § 841 and 21 U.S.C. § 846 to apply to a defendant like Virgilio Martinus Manuel (who delivered drugs from Holland to Germany without knowing that the recipient planned to send the cargo to the United States) but not Lopez-Vanegas and Salazar (who planned their drug conspiracy on U.S. soil)?

The extraterritorial application of drug laws typically involves the prosecution of foreign nationals engaged in drug trafficking abroad. But the nationality principle allows states to exercise jurisdiction over their own nationals for conduct committed overseas, even if the conduct itself has no connection to the prosecuting nation. Singapore's Misuse of Drugs Act (Chapter 185 § 8a), for example, criminalizes the "consumption of drug outside Singapore by [a] citizen or permanent resident." In late 2011, the U.S. House of Representatives considered a bill that would have had a similar effect. The proposed law, titled the "Drug Trafficking Safe Harbor Elimination Act of 2011," would have made it a crime for U.S. citizens to plan to "engage in conduct at any place outside the United States that would constitute a violation of" federal drug laws "if committed within the United States"—even if the planned activity were legal in the country where it occurred. The legislation was introduced in response to the holding in *Lopez-Vanegas* but, contrary to the law's name, the law would not have been limited to traffickers. The law was written so broadly that it would have made it a federal crime for a U.S. citizen to plan to use marijuana while vacationing in Amsterdam. Though the bill passed the U.S. House Judiciary Committee, it had not advanced any further in the legislative process at the time this book went to press. *See,* Radley Balko, *U.S. Drug Policy Would Be Imposed Globally By New House Bill*, HUFFINGTON POST, Oct. 7, 2011.

b. Prosecution of Drug Possession on the High Seas

Lopez-Vanegas held that 21 U.S.C. § 841 and 21 U.S.C. § 846 did not apply where the defendants, while in the United States, facilitated a drug deal to transport cocaine from Venezuela to France for distribution in Europe. Can the United States exercise jurisdiction over drug traffickers even when there is no evidence the defendants intended to bring drugs into the United States? Two federal laws—the Drug Trafficking Vessel Interdiction Act, 18 U.S.C. § 2285, and the Maritime Drug Law Enforcement Act, 46 U.S.C. app. § 1901—target ships transporting drugs on the high seas seemingly without regard to where they set sail or where they are headed. In some cases, these ships have no direct connection to the U.S. but courts have consistently upheld extraterritorial application of the laws, citing the protective principle of jurisdiction and (less frequently) the universal principle of jurisdiction. Is the application of U.S. law to drug shipments with no direct connection to the United States consistent with principles of international law?

Beyond the Article I Horizon: Congress's Enumerated Powers and Universal Jurisdiction Over Drug Crimes
Eugene Kontorovich
93 Minnesota Law Review 1191 (2009)

In March 2007, the United States Coast Guard boarded a suspicious Panamanian vessel that had been spotted by a surveillance plane. The boarding resulted in the largest maritime cocaine seizure to date: over forty-two thousand pounds uncut. Fourteen crewmembers were arrested, and the eleven non-Panamanian detainees were brought to Florida for prosecution.

Yet the seizure did not take place in U.S. waters. It took place in Panamanian territorial waters, approximately one thousand nautical miles from Miami. Moreover, none of the crew—now facing decades or life in U.S. jails—were Americans. Finally, the Drug Enforcement Administration (DEA) conceded the drugs were not bound for the United States.

This case, while exceptional in the amount seized, is otherwise not unusual. It repeats itself dozens of times each year, as the United States enforces its own drug laws in foreign territory.

The international law doctrine of universal jurisdiction (UJ) holds that a nation can prosecute certain serious international offenses even though it has no connection to the conduct or participants. It has increasingly been used by European national courts and international tribunals to prosecute alleged human rights violations around the world. The United States, however, has been wary of these developments.

However, under a little-known statute, America uses UJ far more than any other nation, and perhaps even more than all other nations combined. For two decades, the United States has been punishing drug crimes (including possession) committed entirely by foreigners outside U.S. territory, with no demonstrable connection to the United States. Under the Maritime Drug Law Enforcement Act (MDLEA), the U.S. Coast Guard apprehends vessels carrying drugs on the high seas, often thousands of miles from American waters; the crews of these vessels are prosecuted in U.S. courts for violating U.S. drug law, and are sentenced to terms in U.S. jails. In none of these cases is there any evidence the drugs were destined for the United States. While European UJ prosecutions in war crimes and genocide cases attract a great deal of attention because they involve major wars and high government officials, the MDLEA cases have gone almost unnoticed—perhaps because the defendants are undistinguished members of the Latin American drug trade.

The MDLEA's UJ provisions raise fundamental questions about the source and extent of Congress's constitutional power to regulate purely foreign conduct. Courts have said the MDLEA fits under Congress's power to "define and punish Piracies and Felonies committed on the high Seas." This raises the unexplored question of whether that provision has any jurisdictional limits.

The increasing flow of drugs from Central and South America into the United States— first marijuana in the 1970s and then the more profitable cocaine in the 1980s—and the increasing sophistication of the smugglers led Congress to gradually expand the scope of its extraterritorial lawmaking. Because of the difficulty of catching traffickers in the relatively short time they are in U.S. waters, the United States began projecting its enforcement increasingly far from its shores. Today the Coast Guard patrols the oceans thousands of miles away—and often just off the coasts of other states—as part of U.S. anti-drug efforts. And to ensure the Coast Guard's ability to catch those with drugs bound for the United States, Congress cast a net that pulls in—and makes subject to U.S. law—even those foreign vessels whose cargo is not demonstrably destined here.

The MDLEA built on and expanded the jurisdictional provisions of its predecessor, the Marijuana on the High Seas Act (MHSA), passed in 1980. Drug importation had significantly increased in the 1970s, and Coast Guard interdiction efforts became an important part of the War on Drugs. Smugglers adopted a "mothership" strategy, where a large drug-laden ship would hover on the high seas, just outside of U.S. customs waters, and bring the contraband to shore via many small and difficult to detect boats. When the motherships were seized on the high seas, successful prosecution proved elusive. The motherships themselves were generally foreign-flagged and foreign-crewed, and proving a conspiracy to import was apparently difficult. The House Report on the bill complained that the impunity of the foreign drug traffickers hurt Coast Guard morale.

The main relevant innovation of the MHSA was to extend U.S. jurisdiction on the high seas not just to "U.S. vessels," but also to a new category, "vessels subject to the jurisdiction of the United States." This latter category was defined as stateless vessels, meaning a vessel flying no flag, or bearing fraudulent or multiple registries. Earlier drafts of the legislation sought to extend jurisdiction to genuinely foreign vessels whenever the flag state consents. However, the Committee on Merchant Marine and Fisheries reported "various jurisdictional and constitutional" objections to using a state's "prior consent as a basis for ... domestic criminal jurisdiction." The constitutional concerns were not made explicit, and the chief worry seemed to be about international law, which was understood to require a nexus for prosecution. The statute's authors seemed to think that as a matter of international law, flag state consent would still be an inadequate basis given that drug trafficking "is not generally accepted as an international crime." However, under the MHSA, a "purported flag state" could reject a vessel's claim of nationality. Thus the Marijuana on the High Seas Act swept in cases involving foreigners on the high seas, on non-American vessels, without proof that the vessel or cargo was destined for America. Moreover, the alleged flag state's ability to deny claims of registry at its discretion could function as an informal version of consent jurisdiction.

The MHSA proved anachronistic almost as soon as it was adopted. The cocaine boom of the 1980s lead to a vast increase in drug smuggling and a correlate demand for more aggressive action. The 1980 statute, designed for the marijuana era, now seemed weak. Thus, in 1986, Congress expanded the jurisdictional provisions of its maritime drug laws once again.

The Senate Report claimed the MHSA was troublesome to enforce. Extraterritorial jurisdiction over foreign vessels turned on defects in registry. However, evidence of a vessel's nationality took several days to obtain from the defendant's home state. It could be hard to prove whether a vessel was stateless. Obtaining such evidence that would be "sufficient to withstand evidentiary objections in a U.S. courtroom can take months." The MDLEA sought to avoid such problems by expanding jurisdiction far beyond stateless vessels.

First, the MDLEA extended jurisdiction to any vessel with some U.S. connection. This included anyone aboard vessels registered in the United States, owned or formerly owned, in whole or part by U.S. nationals or corporations; U.S. nationals and resident aliens aboard any vessels; as well as any vessel in U.S. territorial or customs waters. However, the statute also applied U.S. drug laws (not just importation laws) to vessels that fall outside this broad description, and even to foreign-crewed vessels in foreign waters. Indeed, the MDLEA expanded on the MHSA by extending U.S. jurisdiction to any foreign vessels on the high seas, or even in foreign territorial waters, so long as the relevant foreign nation consents.

This consent is broadly defined—it may be "oral"—and not subject to challenge in court: it "may be verified or denied by radio, telephone, or similar oral or electronic means." Moreover, the MDLEA expanded the definition of stateless vessels to include those that do not produce evidence of their registry when requested by the Coast Guard— a request which, on the high seas or in foreign territorial waters, they may feel fully entitled to reject—as well as those whose registry is not "affirmatively and unequivocally" confirmed by the foreign state. Given that the Senate Report makes clear that obtaining any kind of registry confirmation from foreign states is slow, difficult, and confusing, this provision would sweep in many genuinely foreign (not actually lacking a legitimate registry) vessels.

Because these vessels are classified as "vessels subject to the jurisdiction of the United States," no conspiracy to import need be proven; they are treated exactly as if they were U.S. ships, which fall within Congress's broad admiralty powers. Thus, the statute criminalizes mere "possession" on the foreign vessels in foreign or international waters. Moreover, the statute brushes aside any presumptions against extraterritoriality, and bars any jurisdictional or substantive defenses based on the United States' "failure to comply with international law." Indeed, a 1996 amendment sought to keep all questions of statelessness away from a jury by providing that "jurisdiction of the United States with respect to vessels subject to this chapter is not an element of any offense ... [and instead] are preliminary questions of law to be determined solely by the trial judge." With the cocaine epidemic raging, the "constitutional objections" that had dissuaded Congress from adopting a state-consent model of jurisdiction for the MHSA were absent from the discussion of the MDLEA.

Congress did not specify which head of Article I authority it exercised when enacting the MDLEA or its predecessor. However, courts have consistently seen the law as authorized by the Define and Punish Clause because "that clause is the only specific grant of power to be found in the Constitution for the punishment of offenses outside the territorial limits of the United States." A few courts have implied that the act must be an exercise of the felonies power in particular, though most have mistakenly spoke of "Piracies and Felonies" as if they are synonymous or interchangeable. Since this clause speaks directly to criminal legislation for the high seas, it seems to be the natural place to seek authority for the MDLEA.

Under standard rules of international law, the Coast Guard cannot stop or board foreign vessels on the high seas or in foreign waters. Thus, the United States has negotiated "bilateral maritime agreements" with twenty-six Caribbean and Latin American states since the enactment of the MDLEA. These agreements have been negotiated country by country over the past twenty years. They set out frameworks for the United States to stop, search, and sometimes board the other state's vessels if they are suspected of drug trafficking. The agreements coordinate numerous technical and tactical aspects of joint counter-narcotics enforcement, including the "shiprider" program, where a law enforcement officer from one country embarks on the other's vessels, carrying the authority to board and make arrests in the name of his home state. The agreements generally follow a standard six-part form apparently drafted by U.S. officials. However, the particular arrangement with each country often varies somewhat from the basic template, depending on particular local concern.

The MDLEA has quietly become the largest font of universal jurisdiction in U.S. courts, dwarfing the more high-profile Alien Tort Statute litigation. Indeed, the MDLEA appears to be the only statute under which the United States asserts universal criminal jurisdiction. The practical consequences are significant. Prosecutions under the MDLEA often involve a vessel's entire crew. Given the large quantities of drugs on these vessels, these foreigners, captured on foreign vessels in international waters, can face decades in federal prison. This is despite the fact that these individuals potentially never have set foot in, or directed their activities towards, the United States.

The MDLEA has been subject to a wide variety of largely unsuccessful legal challenges.

Constitutional challenges to the MDLEA have focused on due process. Defendants argue that the Fifth Amendment requires they have some "nexus" or factual connection with the prosecuting forum. This would rule out UJ, which is defined by the lack of such a nexus. But this nexus argument is framed in terms of individual rights rather than the Article I limits. Most courts of appeals (including the Eleventh Circuit, which gets most MDLEA cases) have held that the Fifth Amendment requires no nexus. The Ninth Circuit, on the other hand, requires some nexus with the United States. Courts that do not require a nexus argue that any due process requirement is waived by the consent given by the defendant's home state, which is routine in MDLEA cases. This highlights an important difference in whether a nexus requirement is located in the Fifth Amendment or in Article I limits on Congress's legislative power. Structural limits — unlike personal rights — cannot be waived by individual defendants, to say nothing of foreign nations.

The question of whether the MDLEA exceeds Congress's Article I limits has not been fully addressed by any court. However, in the past few years some defendants have begun to point to a pair of early nineteenth-century Supreme Court cases — *United States v. Palmer* and *United States v. Furlong* as indicating limits on UJ under the Felonies power. These arguments have usually been raised in a cursory manner, usually for the first time on appeal and thus have faced an uphill battle under a plain error standard. The Eleventh Circuit has denied such appeals with almost no discussion, simply noting that other courts have found the MDLEA to be an exercise of the Piracies and Felonies power. However, those cases simply cited the clause, and did not discuss the issue of its limits.

To the extent courts have considered arguments from the Piracies and Felonies Clause, they misread *Palmer* and *Furlong* as purely statutory cases about the scope of the 1790 Crimes Act, or as based on international rather than constitutional law principles. Furthermore, litigants only began to mention the Define and Punish Clause after most courts had ruled that the Fifth Amendment does not require a nexus in MDLEA cases. Thus judges mistakenly saw the Felonies argument as simply a repleading of the oft-rejected nexus argument, and treated it is as a matter of *stare decisis*. This conflates inquiries based on two totally different provisions — the Fifth Amendment and the Define and Punish Clause. That the Fifth Amendment does not require a nexus says nothing about the logically prior question of whether Congress has the power to legislate absent a nexus.

[T]here is good reason to believe that much of the MDLEA's UJ application exceeds Congress's Article I limits. This was indeed recognized by the Marshall Court in *Palmer* and *Furlong*, as a close reading of those cases suggests. It is also corroborated by a wide range of other evidence not yet considered by any court in an MDLEA case: strong statements made by Justices James Wilson and Joseph Story in their grand jury instructions, John Marshall's famous House of Representatives speech in the Thomas Nash affair, and Congress's decision that it could not extend UJ to the slave trade before it had become universally cognizable in international law. Nor have courts considered the lessons that might be learned from the drafting history and purposes of the clause.

Indeed, judicial discussions of the Piracies and Felonies power treat these "parallel provisions within the same constitutional clause" as having the same scope. This renders "Piracies" entirely redundant: all piracies are felonies. [P]iracy was different from all other felonies in one crucial way: it was universally cognizable. The separate enumeration of piracy suggests that its unique jurisdictional trait applies only to it, and not to other felonies on the high seas.

Some might view the grant to Congress of a power to "define ... Piracies and ... Offences" as giving it the final say on what is a non-UJ felony and what is not. Thus before considering whether modern [customary international law, or] CIL provides some basis for the MDLEA, this section shows that Congress does not get the first and last word on the content of CIL.

The Define and Punish Clause raises questions about how much flexibility Congress has in "defining." Can courts look to the law of nations to determine whether Congress has defined a crime that is actually recognized by international law? Conversely, is whether something violates the law of nations itself a question left entirely to Congress through its power to "define"? The word "define" may suggest some latitude for Congress that it is not entirely bound by some external, objectively determinable body of international law.

Few decisions address the question directly. However, the Court has, from the time of the early Republic, acted as if it can review Congress's definition against the external standard of the "Law of Nations." In a similar vein to Marshall's 1800 House speech, n201 the Court in Furlong, strongly insisted that Congress cannot arbitrarily classify something as a felony or piracy (i.e., universally cognizable).

The purposes of the Offenses Clause and precedents interpreting it provide no support for the view that Congress can entirely invent offenses, or that courts cannot measure exercises of the Offenses Clause against the "Law of Nations" as they understand it. According to Justice Story, the word "define" means an "express enumeration of all the particulars included in that term." This suggests that Congress can fill in interstitial questions or resolve particular disputes and uncertainties about the elements of an offense, but it cannot punish primary conduct that is not an international crime.

Because the Offenses Clause refers to an external legal standard to limit Congress, it suggests a particularly strong role for judicial review. If the law of nations cannot be used to establish judicially reviewable limits on Congress's action, Congress could use the Offenses power to legislate regarding anything. The obscure Offenses Clause would overshadow all other regulatory powers, even the Commerce Clause. It would be odd that such a vast grant of authority over individuals, unchecked by any limiting principle, would exist in the Constitution, or that it would have gone unnoted at the convention and ratification debates. Thus, the most extensive examination of the question has found that courts have consistently looked for substantial state practice to establish the existence of a CIL norm.

Because UJ is only available for a subset of international crimes, the question of whether drug smuggling has become modern piracy merges with the question of whether it falls under the "Offences against the Law of Nations" that Congress can punish under the Define and Punish Clause. The major sources of international law are treaties and customary (unwritten) international law. When a treaty is in the picture, the terms of the treaty itself govern the scope of Congress's jurisdictional power. The Offenses Clause is implicated when there is no treaty basis for the law, and so one must determine whether Congress's offense roughly corresponds to CIL.

Drug trafficking is not recognized in CIL as a universally cognizable offense. While there is no firm agreement on the precise set of crimes subject to UJ, there is a general consensus that they are egregious, violent human rights abuses. Not a single UJ offense, or indeed widely recognized international crime, is a so-called victimless offense. All U.S. courts that have considered the issue have held that narcotics traffic falls outside UJ. The most respected lists of UJ offenses do not mention drugs at all. There appears to be no state practice establishing UJ over drug trafficking (aside from the MLDEA, of course).

The common denominator of UJ offenses is their extraordinary heinousness. An offense must be regarded as so inhumane, so shocking to the conscience, that it makes all jurisdictional limitations moot. Indeed, the Second Circuit has recently held that terrorism has not attained the status of a universal jurisdiction offense, and thus U.S. courts cannot put it on the same jurisdictional footing as piracy.

The Senate Report on the MDLEA described drug smuggling as "universally recognized criminal behavior." Yet there is a vast difference between conduct that all nations criminalize and international crimes. Uniform condemnation and criminalization does not make something an international crime. Murder and rape, and indeed, most *malum in se* offenses, are also universally condemned, and all fall outside of international law. Presumably Congress cannot legislate the punishment of purely foreign rapes despite it being "universally recognized criminal behavior." Indeed, the Senate Report makes no findings that would be relevant to the offense's being universally cognizable, such as the offense being extremely heinous. Indeed, different nations' drug laws and attitudes vary far more than those for murder. There simply is no state practice, and a palpable lack of support in relevant legal sources, for treating drug trafficking as a universally cognizable crime.

United States v. Saac

United States Court of Appeals for the Eleventh Circuit
632 F.3d 1203 (2011)

Martin, J.

This case consolidates criminal appeals by four co-defendants challenging the constitutionality of the Drug Trafficking Vessel Interdiction Act of 2008 ("DTVIA"), 18 U.S.C. § 2285.

On January 6, 2009, a United States helicopter crew observed defendants on board a self-propelled, semi-submersible vessel that was dead in the international waters of the eastern Pacific Ocean. Defendants' semi-submersible vessel lacked a flag, registration number, homeport, or navigational lights. The next day, as the United States Coast Guard approached defendants' vessel, a helicopter crew saw the four defendants, three of whom were wearing life vests, emerge from the vessel's hatch and jump into the water. The vessel sank within minutes. The Coast Guard recovered all four defendants the same day. Mr. Rodriguez Renegifo identified himself as the master of the vessel but claimed no nationality for it. Defendants asserted that they were Colombian citizens.

The government filed a two-count indictment in federal district court. The first count charged defendants with knowingly conspiring to operate a semi-submersible vessel without nationality and with the intent to evade detection in violation of 18 U.S.C. §§ 2285(a) and (b). The second charged defendants with knowingly and intentionally, while aiding and abetting each other, operating and embarking in a semi-submersible vessel without nationality, with the intent to evade detection in violation of 18 U.S.C. § 2285(a) and (b).

The DTVIA provides that: "[w]hoever knowingly operates, or attempts or conspires to operate, by any means, or embarks in any submersible vessel or semi-submersible vessel that is without nationality and that is navigating or has navigated into, through, or from waters beyond the outer limit of the territorial sea of a single country or a lateral limit of that country's territorial sea with an adjacent country, with the intent to evade detection, shall be fined under this title, imprisoned not more than 15 years, or both."

A submersible vessel is one that "is capable of operating completely below the surface of the water, including both manned and unmanned watercraft." A semi-submersible vessel is "any watercraft constructed or adapted to be capable of operating with most of its hull and bulk under the surface of the water, including both manned and unmanned watercraft."

Defendants pleaded not-guilty at arraignment. Mr. Rodriguez Renegifo filed a motion to dismiss the indictment, arguing that 18 U.S.C. § 2285 is unconstitutional. The other defendants each filed a "motion to adopt co-defendant Rodriguez Renegifo's motion to dismiss indictment," and the district court considered Mr. Rodriguez Renegifo's motion as to all defendants. The district court denied the motion to dismiss the indictment, concluding that § 2285 is not unconstitutionally vague, does not violate the Due Process Clause, and does not exceed Congress's power under Article I, Section 8, Clause 10 of the Constitution.

After the district court denied the motion to dismiss, defendants entered unconditional guilty pleas, without plea agreements, as to both counts of the indictment. At the change of plea hearing, defendants informed the district court that, based on binding precedent, they understood that their guilty pleas would not preclude them from contesting the constitutionality of the DTVIA on appeal. The district court agreed with defendants' reading of the relevant precedent. The government made no argument to the contrary.

The court sentenced each defendant to 108 months imprisonment and 3 years of supervised release for each count, all to run concurrently. The court assessed each defendant $100 per count. Defendants each filed separate, timely notices of appeal.

Defendants challenge the constitutionality of the DTVIA on two grounds, only one of which is properly before us. Defendants first argue that the DTVIA violates their procedural due process rights because it shifts to the defendant the burden of disproving essential elements of the offense and creates a presumption of guilt. Defendants lack standing to raise that argument because "[a] guilty plea serves as an admission of all the elements of a formal criminal charge.... [A] defendant may not challenge the statute where the facts admitted by the guilty plea render the statute's alleged unconstitutionality moot as to the defendant." Because defendants voluntarily pleaded guilty, thereby admitting guilt, the government never made use of any presumption, assuming that one exists, nor shifted the burden of proof to defendants.

We turn to defendants' argument that in enacting the DTVIA Congress exceeded its power under the High Seas Clause of the Constitution, Article I, §8, cl. 10. The High Seas Clause enables Congress "[t]o define and punish Piracies and Felonies committed on the high Seas, and Offences against the Law of Nations." U.S. Const., art. I, §8, cl. 10. While there is a dearth of authority interpreting the scope of Congress's power under the High Seas Clause, early Supreme Court opinions intimate that statutes passed under the High Seas Clause may properly criminalize conduct that lacks a connection to the United States. For instance, in *United States v. Palmer,* 16 U.S. (3 Wheat.) 610, 630 (1818), the Court explained that "[t]he constitution having conferred on congress the power of defining and punishing piracy, there can be no doubt of the right of the legislature to enact laws punishing pirates, although they may be foreigners, and may have committed no particular offence against the United States."

Defendants argue that for Congress to criminalize conduct by statute under the High Seas Clause, the conduct must have a nexus with the United States. We first observe that the text of the clause makes no mention of such a jurisdictional nexus requirement. The clause gives Congress the power "[t]o define and punish Piracies and Felonies committed on the high Seas, and Offences against the Law of Nations." The clause's text does not limit that power to only those piracies and felonies committed in waters within the territorial jurisdiction of the United States. Neither does the clause expressly limit Congress's power to only those offenses committed on or by United States citizens.

Defendants rely on *United States v. Furlong,* 18 U.S. (5 Wheat.) 184, 185 (1820), as support for the proposition that the High Seas Clause allows Congress to reach only conduct with a connection to the United States. But in Furlong the Supreme Court examined the scope of a statute Congress passed pursuant to the High Seas Clause, rather than the scope of Congress's power under the High Seas Clause itself. The Court held that because the particular statute at issue included the phrase "out of the jurisdiction of any particular *State*" its scope was limited to murders committed "out of any *one of the United States.*" *Id.* at 200 (emphasis added). The Court reasoned that "[b]y examining the context, it will be seen that *particular State* is uniformly used in contradistinction to *United States* [within the statute]." Thus, the Court's analysis is a textual one, confined to an interpretation of the language and structure of the statute before it. *Furlong*, a statutory interpretation case, therefore, does not resolve the parties' debate over the scope of Congress's constitutional authority.

When analyzing a constitutional challenge to the Maritime Drug Law Enforcement Act ("MDLEA"), 46 U.S.C. app. §1901 et seq., we rejected the same argument that defendants make here — that Congress exceeded its constitutional authority under the High Seas Clause in passing a statute that punishes conduct without a nexus to the United States. See *United States v. Estupinan,* 453 F.3d 1336, 1338 (11th Cir. 2006). In doing so, we explained that "this circuit and other circuits have not embellished the MDLEA with the requirement of a nexus between a defendant's criminal conduct and the United States." *Id.* (quotation marks omitted). In the MDLEA cases, the appellants argued that offenses other than piracies may not be punished under Congress's High Seas Clause power when there is no nexus to the United States. In each case, the court concluded, however, that Congress's High Seas Clause power includes the authority to punish offenses other than piracies outside the territorial limits of the United States. This Court, and our sister circuits, have refused to read a jurisdictional nexus requirement into the clause.

In examining the constitutionality of the MDLEA, we concluded that the statute's extraterritorial reach was justified under the universal principle of international law. *Estupinan,* 453 F.3d at 1339. According to this principle, a nation may pass laws to define and punish certain crimes considered to be of "universal concern." We adopted the reasoning of the Third Circuit, which opined that "[i]nasmuch as the trafficking of narcotics is condemned universally by law-abiding nations, we see no reason to conclude that it is 'fundamentally unfair' for Congress to provide for the punishment of persons apprehended with narcotics on the high seas." *Estupinan,* 453 F.3d at 1339 (citing *Martinez-Hidalgo,* 993 F.2d at 1056). Thus, we reasoned that because the MDLEA criminalizes conduct that is condemned universally, the statute's extraterritorial reach was permissible.

We now conclude that the DTVIA is also justified under the universal principle and thus a constitutional exercise of Congress's power under the High Seas Clause. In passing the DTVIA, Congress reported that it: "finds and declares that operating or embarking in a submersible vessel or semi-submersible vessel without nationality and on an international voyage is a serious international problem, facilitates transnational crime, including drug trafficking, and terrorism, and presents a specific threat to the safety of maritime navigation and the security of the United States."[3] Congress's findings show that the DTVIA targets criminal conduct that facilitates drug trafficking, which is "condemned universally by law-abiding nations." *Estupinan,* 453 F.3d at 1339 (citing *Martinez-Hidalgo,* 993 F.2d at 1056).

Given Congress's findings, the "protective principle" of international law provides an equally compelling reason to uphold the DTVIA. Under that principle, a nation may "assert jurisdiction over a person whose conduct outside the nation's territory threatens the nation's security or could potentially interfere with the operation of its governmental functions." *United States v. Gonzalez,* 776 F.2d 931, 938 (11th Cir. 1985). "The protective principle does not require that there be proof of an actual or intended effect inside the United States." *Id. at 939.* Those who engage in conduct the DTVIA targets threaten our nation's security by evading detection while using submersible vessels to smuggle illegal drugs or other contraband, such as illegal weapons, from one country to another, and often into the United States.

---

3. Vessels without nationality include: "(A) a vessel aboard which the master or individual in charge makes a claim of registry that is denied by the nation whose registry is claimed; (B) a vessel aboard which the master or individual in charge fails, on request of an officer of the United States authorized to enforce applicable provisions of United States law, to make a claim of nationality or registry for that vessel; and (C) a vessel aboard which the master or individual in charge makes a claim of registry and for which the claimed nation of registry does not affirmatively and unequivocally assert that the vessel is of its nationality."

The United States Coast Guard reported to Congress that semi-submersible vessels present "one of the emerging and most significant threats we face in maritime law enforcement today." These vessels pose a formidable security threat because they are difficult to detect and easy to scuttle or sink. These vessels therefore facilitate the destruction of evidence and hinder prosecution of smuggling offenses.

Based on the foregoing, we conclude that Congress acted properly within its constitutional authority under the High Seas Clause in passing the DTVIA. The fact that defendants are challenging the constitutionality of a statute other than the MDLEA does not alter our conclusion about the scope of Congress's power under the High Seas Clause. We declined to embellish one statute passed under the High Seas Clause with a nexus requirement. We now decline defendants' invitation to rewrite the Constitution to create one.

Notice what the Drug Trafficking Vessel Interdiction Act of 2008 criminalizes: "operat[ing] ... or embark[ing] in any submersible vessel or semi-submersible vessel that is without nationality and that is navigating or has navigated into, through, or from waters beyond the outer limit of the territorial sea of a single country ... with the intent to evade detection." 18 U.S.C. §2285. In *United States v. Ibarguen-Mosquera*, the defendants argued that the law was unconstitutional "because it effectively redefines the offense of drug trafficking, eliminating the requirement of drug possession." In rejecting the challenge, the court explained that despite the law's title, "Congress determined to criminalize *not only* the underlying conduct ... but also traveling on the vessel itself.... Even if Appellants proved that they were not trafficking drugs, they would still be guilty of violating the DTVIA if the government proved, beyond a reasonable doubt, all of the elements of the crime." The court continued that "[t]here is no defense if a defendant is found not to be trafficking in narcotics." 634 F.3d 1370 (11th Cir. 2011).

Not all federal judges agree with the expansive application of U.S. drug laws on the high seas. In *United States v. Cardales-Luna*, the court upheld a MDLEA conviction of a Colombian national who was serving as a crew member on a Bolivian flag vessel found in international waters with 400 kilograms of cocaine and 25 kilograms of heroin. In dissent, Judge Torruella argued that the MDLEA "is an unconstitutional exercise of power beyond the authority granted to Congress under Article I of the Constitution. Except for piracy, slave trading, and stateless vessels, the United States lacks UJ to apprehend and try foreigners for conduct on foreign vessels on the high seas for violation of United States criminal laws where there is no nexus to the United States." 632 F.3d 731 (2011) (Torruella, J., dissenting).

2. Extradition of Drug Offenders

The extraterritorial application of U.S. drug laws typically begins with an extradition request. Extradition cases can present challenging and esoteric legal problems. *See, e.g.,* Ann Powers, *Justice Denied? The Adjudication of Extradition Applications*, 37 Tex. Int'l L. J. 277 (2002) (noting that "[e]ven counsel who deal regularly with immigration and deportation matters rarely deal with extradition, and they may be unaware of its unusual elements"); David Aronofsky and Jie Qin, *U.S. International Narcotics Extradition Cases: Legal Trends and Developments with Implications for U.S.-China Drug Enforcement Activities*, 19 Mich. St. J. Int'l L. 279 (2011) (surveying some of the difficult legal issues that have been raised in drug extradition cases). The excerpt that follows provides an overview of the role of extradition in U.S. prosecutions of international drug cases.

Traffic Circles: The Legal Logic of Drug Extraditions
Edward M. Morgan

31 University of Pennsylvania Journal of International Law 373 (2009)

[E]xtradition, as opposed to domestic prosecution, has become the law enforcement vehicle of choice for governments willing to engage with the United States in the anti-drug campaign.

Despite the plethora of U.N.-sponsored, multilateral conventions relating to narcotics trafficking, drugs have not been the focus of much adjudication by international judicial organs. The negotiations culminating in the Statute of the International Criminal Court raised the possibility of categorizing drug trafficking as an international offense; however, the sessions concluded only with a resolution that the state parties consider including it at a future review conference. Although drug policy plays a central role in international legal discourse and the United Nations monitors narcotics treaty implementation by its member states, actual enforcement and prosecution has been left to the unilateral and coordinated actions of domestic legal systems.

The vision of nationals as a cog in the societal wheel and that of the citizen as a self-standing force in opposition to state action have met directly, and clashed, in the law of extradition. As a starting point, international theorists have long perceived the community of nations to operate under a natural duty to extradite offenders from neighboring states. This duty is most frequently translated into an interstate obligation to ensure that no one jurisdiction stands as a safe haven or refuge for serious offenders fleeing another jurisdiction. Some early theorists limited the sphere of operation of extradition only to those international relations backed by an enforceable treaty. However, Grotius' maxim: "extradite or prosecute," has long placed the international exchange of fugitives between nations at the epicenter of the contest between the national as owing duties and allegiance to the state community of which he is a member, and the citizen as holding rights to be asserted against any combination of sovereign states.

The compromise followed by most civil law jurisdictions, and a number of common law countries, has been to extradite only third-party nationals, protecting citizens of the requested state from being the subject of an international exchange. In contrast, the United States has, since its first extradition agreements with England, France, and Switzerland, been prepared to extradite its own citizens on the same basis as nationals of the treaty partners or of third countries. While it is possible for a treaty to preclude the extradition of nationals, U.S. policy has generally been antagonistic to the idea. In fact, in 1913, the Supreme Court ruled that reciprocity is not a necessary ingredient to extradition treaty enforcement, and American fugitives can be sent by the United States to countries which refuse to send their own nationals in return.

While the blanket exemption of nationals from the extradition process has been condemned as a matter of international law theory, several prominent civil law countries in Western Europe continue to refuse extradition of their own citizens. Among Latin American countries, the practice has also tended to exempt nationals, despite substantial American pressure to change policies to accommodate the war on drugs. Thus, for example, Colombia agreed in 1982 in a revised extradition treaty to send fugitive citizens to the United States, but the treaty was declared unenforceable by the Colombia

Supreme Court in 1986 in a decision widely perceived to be a capitulation to the power of narcotics cartels. Extraditions were reinstated for Colombians, without judicial review, by executive order of the President in 1989, but were permanently eliminated in 1991 when extradition of citizens was rendered unconstitutional by means of a specific constitutional amendment.

The extradition treaty between the United States and Mexico has likewise proved to be a highly contentious instrument in terms of the two-way flow of nationals. In the first place, although the treaty was negotiated in terms meant to grant each of the signing governments the discretionary power to extradite its own nationals, the governing clause is stated in the negative: "neither contracting parties shall be bound to deliver up its own nationals...." For its part, the United States government has been willing to extradite U.S. citizens even in the face of a credible claim that the evidence supporting the Mexican allegations were obtained through torture. Moreover, the Courts of Appeals have specifically rejected the argument that the United States should put a moratorium on extraditions of U.S. citizens to Mexico until such time as Mexico determines that it will extradite its nationals for trial in the United States.

By contrast, the Mexican legal system has traditionally barred extradition of citizens, although it has reserved for the executive branch the discretion to determine case by case whether exceptional circumstances warranting extradition of a Mexican citizen exist. This has typically been justified on the ground that the Mexican courts have inherent jurisdiction over and are competent to try all crimes, wherever committed, that are perpetrated by Mexican nationals. Despite assurances to the contrary, through most of the twentieth century Mexican officials so rarely acted on extradition warrants aimed at their citizens that the U.S. Drug Enforcement Agency developed a practice of bypassing the extradition process altogether by kidnapping fugitives and smuggling them into U.S. territory for trial. In recent years, in response to increased pressure to follow U.S. law enforcement policies, Mexico has been more willing to deem drug traffickers as falling under the "exceptional circumstances" category denying selected Mexican nationals from the exemption otherwise applicable to all Mexican nationals. That said, the Mexican policy has been enforced inconsistently, with protection from extradition frequently applied even to fugitives accused of crimes of extreme violence.

The controversy over extraditing nationals strikes the dual chords of which the international and constitutional norms surrounding nationality and citizenship are composed. On one hand, the image of citizens as non-extraditable parts of the nation stands opposite that of citizens as rights holder as against her nation, although both lead to the same result. By contrast, the image of fugitives as extraditable individuals imbued with personal stature and responsibility stands opposite that of accused persons wedded to the society and locale in which their crime was committed, although again both lead to the same result. Whether the state in question chooses to extradite its nationals or to keep them at home, the dual strands of nationality law are inevitably in play. Persons are both part of society and apart from it, and their citizenship can potentially stand for both positions.

Among U.S. policymakers and critics, it has often been debated whether the anti-narcotics campaign of the past several decades is a product of law enforcement necessity or cynical politics; likewise, it has been debated whether the global drug prohibition has been a winning or a losing endeavor. Additionally, in U.S. legal commentary, it has frequently been debated whether the Constitution supports the fight against drug use and trafficking or is contrary to the "war" effort. Whatever side one prefers in these debates, it is clear from the U.S. interventions in the Colombian and Mexican drug wars that international politics cannot be factored out of the debates over extraditing nationals.

Running parallel with the explicit linkage of drug law enforcement to foreign policy goals, are the judicial politics that underscore recent judgments. The dual nature of nationality, as an identity marker that affiliates persons with sovereign states and as a rights emblem that sets persons apart from state power, has given rise to a set of cases that reflect a confusion of ideological motifs. The nationality cases in extradition law bring to the surface the fact that courts appear unable to determine whether due process is owed by states to persons or to each other. This dilemma, in turn, has led adjudicators to confuse the civil libertarianism of criminal law with state self-interest, and the authoritarianism of law enforcement with international cooperation.

Three contemporary extradition cases, each sending a suspected drug fugitive to the United States, will illustrate the phenomenon.

In December of 2000, a federal grand jury in Florida indicted Samuel "Ninety" Knowles—a colorful Bahamian national who, as reported by the local press, "got his nickname by blowing $90,000 in one day"—on several counts of conspiracy to possess, distribute, and import cocaine and marijuana into the United States. The indictment formed the basis of an extradition request from the U.S. government to the Republic of Bahamas, which was in turn challenged in *habeas corpus* proceedings on the grounds that the statutory conditions for extradition had not been met. During the course of lengthy appeal and review proceedings, and well before the signing of an extradition order by the Bahamian Foreign Minister, the President of the United States exercised his statutory authority to designate Knowles as a foreign drug "kingpin," thereby seizing his U.S. assets and barring him from using the U.S. financial system prior to any judicial finding of guilt.

In one of his two trips to the Privy Council, Knowles challenged the extradition to the United States on the grounds that the "kingpin" designation was widely published, notorious, and tantamount to a public declaration of his guilt. As the defense put it, once in the United States, "the jurors at his trial might well know or learn of his designation ... [and] his trial would not be fair if a juror were prejudiced by such knowledge." Moreover, the U.S. statute triggered a citizenship issue, the other half of Knowles' challenge being that the prejudice against his fair trial "derived from his nationality, since the [Foreign Narcotics Kingpin Designation] Act did not apply to U.S. citizens." Thus, although the terms of the U.S.-Bahamas Extradition Treaty specify that "extradition shall not be refused on the grounds that the fugitive is a citizen or national of the Requested State", the citizenship question played a central role in the fairness/discrimination argument both in court and in the public discourse that accompanied the Bahamian proceedings.

The "kingpin" issue barely got off the ground when "Ninety" was sent fifty miles across the Gulf Stream to face the federal charges in Miami. Indeed, the Bahamas Court of Appeal ruled after his departure that the government had acted prematurely in sending him to stand trial. The identical question of prejudice to foreign extraditees, however, had in the meantime been considered by the Privy Council in yet another drug extradition from yet another Caribbean jurisdiction, the islands of St. Kitts and Nevis. Two cocaine co-conspirators, Noel Heath and Glenroy Mathews, had been designated as foreign drug "kingpins" on June 1, 2000, and, according to the Privy Council, had been announced as such on a U.S. government website despite provisions in the legislation for non-disclosure of the designee's name if such disclosure could jeopardize the integrity of the ongoing criminal trial.

In a relatively brief judgment, Lord Brown of Eaton-under-Heywood gave the kingpin argument relatively short shrift. Analogizing the problem to one of ordinary domestic publicity, the law lords were willing to leave it to the ultimate trial judge to determine an appropriate remedy. Turning to the particular problem of foreign proceedings, and the fact that the domestic extradition court cannot predict the remedies that a foreign trial court will invoke, the court fell back on a presumption of judicial innocence. Lord Brown cited the 1987 judgment of the Supreme Court of Canada in *Argentina v. Mellino* in order to invoke what he found to be the commonplace principle that "our courts must assume that [the defendant] will be given a fair trial in the foreign country."

In September of 2004, a grand jury in southern Florida indicted Ze'ev Rosenstein — a stocky, domineering figure in the Tel Aviv underworld referred to as "The Fat Man" by undercover U.S. investigators in taped telephone conversations — on charges of heading an international conspiracy to traffic in the drug methylenedioxy-methamphetamine ("MDMA," more generally known as "ecstasy"). The indictment formed the basis of an extradition request from the government of the United States to the State of Israel. That request, in turn, prompted a challenge by the defense in the Jerusalem District Court on the grounds that extradition would violate Israeli constitutional safeguards.

In his appeal to Israel's Supreme Court, Rosenstein presented a long list of legal arguments, the crux of which contended that since he is "an Israeli citizen and resident, and the alleged offense was committed entirely in Israel, extradition to another country deviates from the balance required by Basic Law: Human Dignity and Freedom, and by fundamental principles of penal law." Although by the time of his arrest Israel had revised its law to permit the extradition of Israeli citizens under certain circumstances, the defense argued that for a person whose center of life is in the territory of the State, "the prosecution's policy on drug offenses has long been to conduct trials in Israel, even if the act was committed outside of Israel." Under the circumstances, the due process demanded by the alleged ecstasy financier was presented as a counterweight to the lead prosecutor's assertion that extradition "is good for the country and good for the cooperation between countries against international crime."

In rejecting the defendant's challenges and arriving at its conclusion that Rosenstein can be sent to the United States, the court relied heavily on American investigatory evidence. [T]his appears to be part of an ongoing law enforcement strategy by Israeli authorities to contract large drug prosecutions out to the United States[.]

[I]n *Lake v. Canada* (Minister of Justice)[,] Talib Steven Lake was caught selling roughly 100 grams of crack cocaine in a series of transactions in Windsor, Ontario, and across the bridge in Detroit, Michigan, with an undercover officer of the Ontario Provincial Police. He was tried and convicted for the Canadian transactions. After serving a relatively light sentence of three years in prison, he was processed for extradition to the United States where an indictment had been issued in the U.S. District Court for the Eastern District of Michigan relating to the Detroit transaction. Upon losing his committal battle in the Ontario courts, Lake requested that the Minister of Justice exercise his discretion not to order him extradited, but the Minister decided against him and ordered him sent back to Michigan in February 2005.

The Minister incorrectly determined that Canada had no jurisdiction to try Lake on the Michigan charge, and thus, the extradition did not infringe his mobility rights under the Charter. The Minister also considered the prospect of Lake facing a mandatory minimum sentence of ten years under U.S. law — a far more severe punishment than would be meted out by the Canadian judicial system. However, the Minister rejected Lake's potential punishment under U.S. law as grounds for exercising his discretion in the fugitive's favor because the minimum incarceration term was not seen to shock the conscience of Canadians. Lake sought judicial review of the Minister's discretionary decision, and on appeal the Supreme Court of Canada determined that, whatever its failings, the ministerial decision deserved a level of deference with which the court should not interfere. Although he argued heatedly that "the Minister is required to respect a fugitive's constitutional rights in deciding whether to exercise his or her discretion...," the court effectively threw cold water on Lake.

The case law reveals that when the United States calls for drug extraditions, the fugitives tend to come; or, more accurately, tend to be sent.

Drugs have reintroduced the national to the sovereign nation, removing the protections afforded by a sovereign law. The American insistence on policing the worlds of narcotics trade, and the changes wrought by that insistence on the character of global society, has had this transformative effect on extradition policy around the world. Although the "war on drugs" has been a failure if measured by the goal of eradication it has set for itself, it has had remarkable impact on judicial opinions among neighbors and allies of the United States.

3. Extraterritorial Drug Investigation and Enforcement by U.S. Officials

Though the United States increasingly has been successful at convincing other countries to extradite their nationals, some countries remain hesitant to send their citizens abroad for prosecution. If a country does not wish to extradite one of its citizens, can the U.S. send its own agents into that country to arrest him or pay a third party to kidnap him and bring him into the U.S.? The question implicates a distinct aspect of extraterritorial jurisdiction: the jurisdiction to enforce. *See* RESTATEMENT (THIRD) OF THE LAW OF FOREIGN RELATIONS OF THE UNITED STATES §401 (1986) (explaining the distinction between the jurisdiction to prescribe, the jurisdiction to adjudicate, and the jurisdiction to enforce).

United States v. Alvarez-Machain

Supreme Court of the United States
504 U.S. 655 (1992)

Chief Justice Rehnquist delivered the opinion of the Court.

The issue in this case is whether a criminal defendant, abducted to the United States from a nation with which it has an extradition treaty, thereby acquires a defense to the jurisdiction of this country's courts. We hold that he does not, and that he may be tried in federal district court for violations of the criminal law of the United States.

Respondent, Humberto Alvarez-Machain, is a citizen and resident of Mexico. He was indicted for participating in the kidnap and murder of United States Drug Enforcement Administration (DEA) special agent Enrique Camarena-Salazar and a Mexican pilot working with Camarena, Alfredo Zavala-Avelar. The DEA believes that respondent, a medical doctor, participated in the murder by prolonging Agent Camarena's life so that others could further torture and interrogate him. On April 2, 1990, respondent was forcibly kidnaped from his medical office in Guadalajara, Mexico, to be flown by private plane to El Paso, Texas, where he was arrested by DEA officials. The District Court concluded that DEA agents were responsible for respondent's abduction, although they were not personally involved in it.[2]

---

2. Apparently, DEA officials had attempted to gain respondent's presence in the United States through informal negotiations with Mexican officials, but were unsuccessful. DEA officials then,

Respondent moved to dismiss the indictment, claiming that his abduction constituted outrageous governmental conduct, and that the District Court lacked jurisdiction to try him because he was abducted in violation of the extradition treaty between the United States and Mexico. The District Court rejected the outrageous governmental conduct claim, but held that it lacked jurisdiction to try respondent because his abduction violated the Extradition Treaty. The District Court discharged respondent and ordered that he be repatriated to Mexico

[T]he Court of Appeals affirmed the District Court's finding that the United States had authorized the abduction of respondent, and that letters from the Mexican Government to the United States Government served as an official protest of the Treaty violation. Therefore, the Court of Appeals ordered that the indictment against respondent be dismissed and that respondent be repatriated to Mexico. We granted certiorari and now reverse.

Although we have never before addressed the precise issue raised in the present case, we have previously considered proceedings in claimed violation of an extradition treaty and proceedings against a defendant brought before a court by means of a forcible abduction. We addressed the former issue in *United States v. Rauscher,* 119 U.S. 407 (1886); more precisely, the issue whether the Webster-Ashburton Treaty of 1842, 8 Stat. 576, which governed extraditions between England and the United States, prohibited the prosecution of defendant Rauscher for a crime other than the crime for which he had been extradited. Whether this prohibition, known as the doctrine of specialty, was an intended part of the treaty had been disputed between the two nations for some time. Justice Miller delivered the opinion of the Court, which carefully examined the terms and history of the treaty; the practice of nations in regards to extradition treaties; the case law from the States; and the writings of commentators, and reached the following conclusion: "[A] person who has been brought within the jurisdiction of the court *by virtue of proceedings under an extradition treaty*, can only be tried for one of the offences described in that treaty, and for the offence with which he is charged in the proceedings for his extradition, until a reasonable time and opportunity have been given him, after his release or trial upon such charge, to return to the country from whose asylum he had been forcibly taken under those proceedings." *Id.,* at 430 (emphasis added). Unlike the case before us today, the defendant in *Rauscher* had been brought to the United States by way of an extradition treaty; there was no issue of a forcible abduction.

In *Ker v. Illinois,* 119 U.S. 436 (1886), also written by Justice Miller and decided the same day as *Rauscher*, we addressed the issue of a defendant brought before the court by way of a forcible abduction. Frederick Ker had been tried and convicted in an Illinois court for larceny; his presence before the court was procured by means of forcible abduction from Peru. A messenger was sent to Lima with the proper warrant to demand Ker by virtue of the extradition treaty between Peru and the United States. The messenger, however, disdained reliance on the treaty processes, and instead forcibly kidnaped Ker and brought him to the United States. We distinguished Ker's case from *Rauscher*, on the basis that Ker was not brought into the United States by virtue of the extradition treaty between the United States and Peru, and rejected Ker's argument that he had a right under the extradition treaty to be returned to this country only in accordance with its terms. We rejected Ker's due process argument more broadly, holding in line with "the highest authorities" that "such forcible abduction is no sufficient reason why the party should not

---

through a contact in Mexico, offered to pay a reward and expenses in return for the delivery of respondent to the United States.

answer when brought within the jurisdiction of the court which has the right to try him for such an offence, and presents no valid objection to his trial in such court."

In *Frisbie v. Collins,* 342 U.S. 519 (1952), we applied the rule in *Ker* to a case in which the defendant had been kidnaped in Chicago by Michigan officers and brought to trial in Michigan. We upheld the conviction over objections based on the Due Process Clause and the federal Kidnaping Act and stated: "This Court has never departed from the rule announced in [*Ker*] that the power of a court to try a person for crime is not impaired by the fact that he had been brought within the court's jurisdiction by reason of a 'forcible abduction.'"

The only differences between *Ker* and the present case are that *Ker* was decided on the premise that there was no governmental involvement in the abduction and Peru, from which Ker was abducted, did not object to his prosecution. Respondent finds these differences to be dispositive, as did the Court of Appeals[.] The Government, on the other hand, argues that *Rauscher* stands as an "exception" to the rule in *Ker* only when an extradition treaty is invoked, and the terms of the treaty provide that its breach will limit the jurisdiction of a court. Therefore, our first inquiry must be whether the abduction of respondent from Mexico violated the Extradition Treaty between the United States and Mexico. If we conclude that the Treaty does not prohibit respondent's abduction, the rule in *Ker* applies, and the court need not inquire as to how respondent came before it.

In construing a treaty, as in construing a statute, we first look to its terms to determine its meaning. The Treaty says nothing about the obligations of the United States and Mexico to refrain from forcible abductions of people from the territory of the other nation, or the consequences under the Treaty if such an abduction occurs. Respondent submits that Article 22(1) of the Treaty, which states that it "shall apply to offenses specified in Article 2 [including murder] committed before and after this Treaty enters into force" evidences an intent to make application of the Treaty mandatory for those offenses. However, the more natural conclusion is that Article 22 was included to ensure that the Treaty was applied to extraditions requested after the Treaty went into force, regardless of when the crime of extradition occurred.

More critical to respondent's argument is Article 9 of the Treaty, which provides:

"1. Neither Contracting Party shall be bound to deliver up its own nationals, but the executive authority of the requested Party shall, if not prevented by the laws of that Party, have the power to deliver them up if, in its discretion, it be deemed proper to do so.

"2. If extradition is not granted pursuant to paragraph 1 of this Article, the requested Party shall submit the case to its competent authorities for the purpose of prosecution, provided that Party has jurisdiction over the offense."

According to respondent, Article 9 embodies the terms of the bargain which the United States struck: If the United States wishes to prosecute a Mexican national, it may request that individual's extradition. Upon a request from the United States, Mexico may either extradite the individual or submit the case to the proper authorities for prosecution in Mexico. In this way, respondent reasons, each nation preserved its right to choose whether its nationals would be tried in its own courts or by the courts of the other nation. This preservation of rights would be frustrated if either nation were free to abduct nationals of the other nation for the purposes of prosecution. More broadly, respondent reasons, as did the Court of Appeals, that all the processes and restrictions on the obligation to extradite established by the Treaty would make no sense if either nation were free to resort to forcible kidnaping to gain the presence of an individual for prosecution in a manner not contemplated by the Treaty.

We do not read the Treaty in such a fashion. Article 9 does not purport to specify the only way in which one country may gain custody of a national of the other country for the purposes of prosecution. In the absence of an extradition treaty, nations are under no obligation to surrender those in their country to foreign authorities for prosecution. Extradition treaties exist so as to impose mutual obligations to surrender individuals in certain defined sets of circumstances, following established procedures. The Treaty thus provides a mechanism which would not otherwise exist, requiring, under certain circumstances, the United States and Mexico to extradite individuals to the other country, and establishing the procedures to be followed when the Treaty is invoked.

The history of negotiation and practice under the Treaty also fails to show that abductions outside of the Treaty constitute a violation of the Treaty. As the Solicitor General notes, the Mexican Government was made aware, as early as 1906, of the *Ker* doctrine, and the United States' position that it applied to forcible abductions made outside of the terms of the United States-Mexico Extradition Treaty.[11] Nonetheless, the current version of the Treaty, signed in 1978, does not attempt to establish a rule that would in any way curtail the effect of *Ker*. Moreover, although language which would grant individuals exactly the right sought by respondent had been considered and drafted as early as 1935 by a prominent group of legal scholars sponsored by the faculty of Harvard Law School, no such clause appears in the current Treaty.

Thus, the language of the Treaty, in the context of its history, does not support the proposition that the Treaty prohibits abductions outside of its terms. The remaining question, therefore, is whether the Treaty should be interpreted so as to include an implied term prohibiting prosecution where the defendant's presence is obtained by means other than those established by the Treaty.

Respondent contends that the Treaty must be interpreted against the backdrop of customary international law, and that international abductions are "so clearly prohibited in international law" that there was no reason to include such a clause in the Treaty itself. The international censure of international abductions is further evidenced, according to respondent, by the United Nations Charter and the Charter of the Organization of American States. Respondent does not argue that these sources of international law provide an independent basis for the right respondent asserts not to be tried in the United States, but rather that they should inform the interpretation of the Treaty terms.

[T]he difficulty with the support respondent garners from international law is that none of it relates to the practice of nations in relation to extradition treaties. In *Rauscher*, we implied a term in the Webster-Ashburton Treaty because of the practice of nations with regard to extradition treaties. In the instant case, respondent would imply terms in the Extradition Treaty from the practice of nations with regards to international law more generally. Respondent would have us find that the Treaty acts as a prohibition against a violation of the general principle of international law that one government may not "ex-

---

11. In correspondence between the United States and Mexico growing out of the 1905 Martinez incident, in which a Mexican national was abducted from Mexico and brought to the United States for trial, the Mexican Charge wrote to the Secretary of State protesting that as Martinez' arrest was made outside of the procedures established in the extradition treaty, "the action pending against the man can not rest [on] any legal foundation." Letter of Balbino Davalos to Secretary of State, *reprinted in* Papers Relating to the Foreign Relations of the United States, H. R. Doc. No. 1, 59th Cong., 2d Sess., pt. 2, p. 1121 (1906). The Secretary of State responded that the exact issue raised by the Martinez incident had been decided by *Ker*, and that the remedy open to the Mexican Government, namely, a request to the United States for extradition of Martinez' abductor, had been granted by the United States.

ercise its police power in the territory of another state." There are many actions which could be taken by a nation that would violate this principle, including waging war, but it cannot seriously be contended that an invasion of the United States by Mexico would violate the terms of the Extradition Treaty between the two nations.

In sum, to infer from this Treaty and its terms that it prohibits all means of gaining the presence of an individual outside of its terms goes beyond established precedent and practice. In *Rauscher*, the implication of a doctrine of specialty into the terms of the Webster-Ashburton Treaty, which, by its terms, required the presentation of evidence establishing probable cause of the crime of extradition before extradition was required, was a small step to take. By contrast, to imply from the terms of this Treaty that it prohibits obtaining the presence of an individual by means outside of the procedures the Treaty establishes requires a much larger inferential leap, with only the most general of international law principles to support it. The general principles cited by respondent simply fail to persuade us that we should imply in the United States-Mexico Extradition Treaty a term prohibiting international abductions.

Respondent and his *amici* may be correct that respondent's abduction was "shocking" and that it may be in violation of general international law principles. Mexico has protested the abduction of respondent through diplomatic notes and the decision of whether respondent should be returned to Mexico, as a matter outside of the Treaty, is a matter for the Executive Branch.[16] We conclude, however, that respondent's abduction was not in violation of the Extradition Treaty between the United States and Mexico, and therefore the rule of *Ker* v. *Illinois* is fully applicable to this case. The fact of respondent's forcible abduction does not therefore prohibit his trial in a court in the United States for violations of the criminal laws of the United States.

The judgment of the Court of Appeals is therefore reversed, and the case is remanded for further proceedings consistent with this opinion.

Justice Stevens, with whom Justice Blackmun and Justice O'Connor join, dissenting.

The Court correctly observes that this case raises a question of first impression. The case is unique for several reasons. It does not involve an ordinary abduction by a private kidnaper, or bounty hunter, as in *Ker v. Illinois,* 119 U.S. 436 (1886); nor does it involve the apprehension of an American fugitive who committed a crime in one State and sought asylum in another, as in *Frisbie v. Collins,* 342 U.S. 519 (1952). Rather, it involves this country's abduction of another country's citizen; it also involves a violation of the terri-

---

16. The Mexican Government has also requested from the United States the extradition of two individuals it suspects of having abducted respondent in Mexico, on charges of kidnaping.

The advantage of the diplomatic approach to the resolution of difficulties between two sovereign nations, as opposed to unilateral action by the courts of one nation, is illustrated by the history of the negotiations leading to the treaty discussed in *Cook v. United States.* The United States was interested in being able to search British vessels that hovered beyond the 3-mile limit and served as supply ships for motor launches, which took intoxicating liquor from them into ports for further distribution in violation of prohibition laws. The United States initially proposed that both nations agree to searches of the other's vessels beyond the 3-mile limit; Great Britain rejected such an approach, since it had no prohibition laws and therefore no problem with United States vessels hovering just beyond its territorial waters. The parties appeared to be at loggerheads; then this Court decided *Cunard S. S. Co. v. Mellon,* 262 U.S. 100 (1923), holding that our prohibition laws applied to foreign merchant vessels as well as domestic within the territorial waters of the United States, and that therefore the carrying of intoxicating liquors by foreign passenger ships violated those laws. A treaty was then successfully negotiated, giving the United States the right to seizure beyond the 3-mile limit (which it desired), and giving British passenger ships the right to bring liquor into United States waters so long as the liquor supply was sealed while in those waters (which Great Britain desired).

torial integrity of that other country, with which this country has signed an extradition treaty.

A Mexican citizen was kidnaped in Mexico and charged with a crime committed in Mexico; his offense allegedly violated both Mexican and American law. Mexico has formally demanded on at least two separate occasions[1] that he be returned to Mexico and has represented that he will be prosecuted and, if convicted, punished for his offense.[2] It is clear that Mexico's demand must be honored if this official abduction violated the 1978 Extradition Treaty between the United States and Mexico. In my opinion, a fair reading of the treaty in light of our decision in *United States v. Rauscher*, 119 U.S. 407 (1886), and applicable principles of international law, leads inexorably to the conclusion that the District Court and the Court of Appeals for the Ninth Circuit correctly construed that instrument.

The extradition treaty with Mexico is a comprehensive document containing 23 articles and an appendix listing the extraditable offenses covered by the agreement. The parties announced their purpose in the preamble: The two governments desire "to cooperate more closely in the fight against crime and, to this end, to mutually render better assistance in matters of extradition." From the preamble, through the description of the parties' obligations with respect to offenses committed within as well as beyond the territory of a requesting party, the delineation of the procedures and evidentiary requirements for extradition, the special provisions for political offenses and capital punishment, and other details, the Treaty appears to have been designed to cover the entire subject of extradition. Thus, Article 22, entitled "Scope of Application," states that the "Treaty shall apply to offenses specified in Article 2 committed before and after this Treaty enters into force," and Article 2 directs that "extradition shall take place, subject to this Treaty, for willful acts which fall within any of [the extraditable offenses listed in] the clauses of the Appendix." Moreover, as noted by the Court, Article 9 expressly provides that neither contracting party is bound to deliver up its own nationals, although it may do so in its discretion, but if it does not do so, it "shall submit the case to its competent authorities for purposes of prosecution."

The Government's claim that the Treaty is not exclusive, but permits forcible governmental kidnaping, would transform these, and other, provisions into little more than verbiage. For example, provisions requiring "sufficient" evidence to grant extradition, withholding extradition for political or military offenses, withholding extradition when the person sought has already been tried, withholding extradition when the statute of limitations for the crime has lapsed, and granting the requested country discretion to refuse to extradite an individual who would face the death penalty in the requesting country, would serve little purpose if the requesting country could simply kidnap the person. As the Court of Appeals for the Ninth Circuit recognized in a related case, "each of these provisions would be utterly frustrated if a kidnapping were held to be a permissible course of

---

1. The abduction of respondent occurred on April 2, 1990. Mexico responded quickly and unequivocally. On April 18, 1990, Mexico requested an official report on the role of the United States in the abduction, and on May 16, 1990, and July 19, 1990, it sent diplomatic notes of protest from the Embassy of Mexico to the United States Department of State. In the May 16th note, Mexico said that it believed that the abduction was "carried out with the knowledge of persons working for the U.S. government, in violation of the procedure established in the extradition treaty in force between the two countries" and in the July 19th note, it requested the provisional arrest and extradition of the law enforcement agents allegedly involved in the abduction.

2. Mexico has already tried a number of members involved in the conspiracy that resulted in the murder of the Drug Enforcement Administration agent. For example, Rafael Caro-Quintero, a co-conspirator of Alvarez-Machain in this case, has already been imprisoned in Mexico on a 40-year sentence.

governmental conduct." In addition, all of these provisions "only make sense if they are understood as *requiring* each treaty signatory to comply with those procedures whenever it wishes to obtain jurisdiction over an individual who is located in another treaty nation."

It is true, as the Court notes, that there is no express promise by either party to refrain from forcible abductions in the territory of the other nation. Relying on that omission, the Court, in effect, concludes that the Treaty merely creates an optional method of obtaining jurisdiction over alleged offenders, and that the parties silently reserved the right to resort to self-help whenever they deem force more expeditious than legal process.[11] If the United States, for example, thought it more expedient to torture or simply to execute a person rather than to attempt extradition, these options would be equally available because they, too, were not explicitly prohibited by the Treaty.[12] That, however, is a highly improbable interpretation of a consensual agreement, which on its face appears to have been intended to set forth comprehensive and exclusive rules concerning the subject of extradition. In my opinion, "the manifest scope and object of the treaty itself" plainly imply a mutual undertaking to respect the territorial integrity of the other contracting party.

In *Rauscher*, the Court construed an extradition treaty that was far less comprehensive than the 1978 Treaty with Mexico. The 1842 treaty with Great Britain determined the boundary between the United States and Canada, provided for the suppression of the African slave trade, and also contained one paragraph authorizing the extradition of fugitives "in certain cases." In Article X, each nation agreed to "deliver up to justice all persons" properly charged with any one of seven specific crimes, including murder. After Rauscher had been extradited for murder, he was charged with the lesser offense of inflicting cruel and unusual punishment on a member of the crew of a vessel on the high seas. Although the treaty did not purport to place any limit on the jurisdiction of the demanding state after acquiring custody of the fugitive, this Court held that he could not be tried for any offense other than murder. Thus, the treaty constituted the exclusive means by which the United States could obtain jurisdiction over a defendant within the territorial jurisdiction of Great Britain.

The Court noted that the treaty included several specific provisions, such as the crimes for which one could be extradited, the process by which the extradition was to be carried out, and even the evidence that was to be produced, and concluded that "the fair purpose of the treaty is, that the person shall be delivered up to be tried for that offence and for no other." The Court reasoned that it did not make sense for the treaty to provide such specifics only to have the person "pas[s] into the hands of the country which charges him with the offence, free from all the positive requirements and just implications of the treaty under which the transfer of his person takes place." To interpret the treaty in a contrary way would mean that a country could request extradition of a person for one of the seven crimes covered by the treaty, and then try the person for another crime, such as a political crime, which was clearly not covered by the treaty; this result, the Court concluded, was clearly contrary to the intent of the parties and the purpose of the treaty.

---

11. To make the point more starkly, the Court has, in effect, written into Article 9 a new provision, which says: "Notwithstanding paragraphs 1 and 2 of this Article, either Contracting Party can, without the consent of the other, abduct nationals from the territory of one Party to be tried in the territory of the other."

12. It is ironic that the United States has attempted to justify its unilateral action based on the kidnaping, torture, and murder of a federal agent by authorizing the kidnaping of respondent, for which the American law enforcement agents who participated have now been charged by Mexico. This goes to my earlier point that extradition treaties promote harmonious relations by providing for the orderly surrender of a person by one state to another, and without such treaties, resort to force often followed.

Thus, the Extradition Treaty, as understood in the context of cases that have addressed similar issues, suffices to protect the defendant from prosecution despite the absence of any express language in the Treaty itself purporting to limit this Nation's power to prosecute a defendant over whom it had lawfully acquired jurisdiction.

Although the Court's conclusion in *Rauscher* was supported by a number of judicial precedents, the holdings in these cases were not nearly as uniform[19] as the consensus of international opinion that condemns one nation's violation of the territorial integrity of a friendly neighbor. It is shocking that a party to an extradition treaty might believe that it has secretly reserved the right to make seizures of citizens in the other party's territory.[21] Justice Story found it shocking enough that the United States would attempt to justify an American seizure of a foreign vessel in a Spanish port: "But, even supposing, for a moment, that our laws had required an entry of The Apollon, in her transit, does it follow that the power to arrest her was meant to be given, after she had passed into the exclusive territory of a foreign nation? We think not. *It would be monstrous* to suppose that our revenue officers were authorized to enter into foreign ports and territories, for the purpose of seizing vessels which had offended against our laws. It cannot be presumed that congress would voluntarily justify such a clear violation of the laws of nations." *The Apollon*, 22 U.S. 362 (1824) (emphasis added).

The law of nations, as understood by Justice Story in 1824, has not changed. Thus, a leading treatise explains: "A State must not perform acts of sovereignty in the territory of another State.... It is ... a breach of International Law for a State to send its agents to the territory of another State to apprehend persons accused of having committed a crime. Apart from other satisfaction, the first duty of the offending State is to hand over the person in question to the State in whose territory he was apprehended." 1 Oppenheim's International Law 295, and n. 1 (H. Lauterpacht 8th ed. 1955).[23]

In the *Rauscher* case, the legal background that supported the decision to imply a covenant not to prosecute for an offense different from that for which extradition had been granted was far less clear than the rule against invading the territorial integrity of a treaty partner that supports Mexico's position in this case. If *Rauscher* was correctly decided—and I am convinced that it was—its rationale clearly dictates a comparable result in this case.

A critical flaw pervades the Court's entire opinion. It fails to differentiate between the conduct of private citizens, which does not violate any treaty obligation, and conduct expressly authorized by the Executive Branch of the Government, which unquestionably constitutes a flagrant violation of international law, and in my opinion, also constitutes a breach of our treaty obligations. Thus, at the outset of its opinion, the Court states the issue as "whether a criminal defendant, abducted to the United States from a nation with which it has an extradition treaty, thereby acquires a defense to the jurisdiction of this coun-

---

19. In fact, both parties noted in their respective briefs several authorities that had held that a person could be tried for an offense other than the one for which he had been extradited.

21. When Abraham Sofaer, Legal Adviser of the State Department, was questioned at a congressional hearing, he resisted the notion that such seizures were acceptable: "'Can you imagine us going into Paris and seizing some person we regard as a terrorist ... ? How would we feel if some foreign nation—let us take the United Kingdom—came over here and seized some terrorist suspect in New York City, or Boston, or Philadelphia, ... because we refused through the normal channels of international, legal communications, to extradite that individual?'"

23. *See* Restatement § 432, Comment c ("If the unauthorized action includes abduction of a person, the state from which the person was abducted may demand return of the person, and international law requires that he be returned").

try's courts." That, of course, is the question decided in *Ker v. Illinois*, 119 U.S. 436 (1886); it is not, however, the question presented for decision today.

The importance of the distinction between a court's exercise of jurisdiction over either a person or property that has been wrongfully seized by a private citizen, or even by a state law enforcement agent, on the one hand, and the attempted exercise of jurisdiction predicated on a seizure by federal officers acting beyond the authority conferred by treaty, on the other hand, is explained by Justice Brandeis in his opinion for the Court in *Cook v. United States*, 288 U.S. 102 (1933). That case involved a construction of a Prohibition Era treaty with Great Britain that authorized American agents to board certain British vessels to ascertain whether they were engaged in importing alcoholic beverages. A British vessel was boarded 11 1/2 miles off the coast of Massachusetts, found to be carrying unmanifested alcoholic beverages, and taken into port. The Collector of Customs assessed a penalty which he attempted to collect by means of libels against both the cargo and the seized vessel.

The Court held that the seizure was not authorized by the treaty because it occurred more than 10 miles off shore. The Government argued that the illegality of the seizure was immaterial because, as in *Ker*, the court's jurisdiction was supported by possession even if the seizure was wrongful. Justice Brandeis acknowledged that the argument would succeed if the seizure had been made by a private party without authority to act for the Government, but that a different rule prevails when the Government itself lacks the power to seize.

The same reasoning was employed by Justice Miller to explain why the holding in *Rauscher* did not apply to the *Ker* case. The arresting officer in *Ker* did not pretend to be acting in any official capacity when he kidnaped Ker. As Justice Miller noted, "the facts show that it was a clear case of kidnapping within the dominions of Peru, without any pretence of authority under the treaty *or from the government of the United States.*" *Ker v. Illinois*, 119 U.S. at 443 (emphasis added). The exact opposite is true in this case, as it was in *Cook*.

As the Court observes at the outset of its opinion, there is reason to believe that respondent participated in an especially brutal murder of an American law enforcement agent. That fact, if true, may explain the Executive's intense interest in punishing respondent in our courts. Such an explanation, however, provides no justification for disregarding the Rule of Law that this Court has a duty to uphold.[33] That the Executive may wish to reinterpret[34] the Treaty to allow for an action that the Treaty in no way authorizes should not influence this Court's interpretation. Indeed, the desire for revenge exerts "a kind of hydraulic

---

33. As Justice Brandeis so wisely urged: "In a government of laws, existence of the government will be imperilled if it fails to observe the law scrupulously. Our Government is the potent, the omnipresent teacher. For good or for ill, it teaches the whole people by its example. Crime is contagious. If the Government becomes a law-breaker, it breeds contempt for law; it invites every man to become a law unto himself; it invites anarchy. To declare that in the administration of the criminal law the end justifies the means — to declare that the Government may commit crimes in order to secure the conviction of a private criminal — would bring terrible retribution. Against that pernicious doctrine this Court should resolutely set its face." *Olmstead v. United States*, 277 U.S. 438, 485, (1928) (dissenting opinion).

34. Certainly, the Executive's view has changed over time. At one point, the Office of Legal Counsel advised the administration that such seizures were contrary to international law because they compromised the territorial integrity of the other nation and were only to be undertaken with the consent of that nation. 4B Op. Off. Legal Counsel 549, 556 (1980). More recently, that opinion was revised, and the new opinion concluded that the President did have the authority to override customary international law. Hearing before the Subcommittee on Civil and Constitutional Rights of the House Committee on the Judiciary, 101st Cong., 1st Sess., 4–5 (1989) (statement of William P. Barr, Assistant Attorney General, Office of Legal Counsel, U.S. Department of Justice).

pressure ... before which even well settled principles of law will bend" but it is precisely at such moments that we should remember and be guided by our duty "to render judgment evenly and dispassionately according to law, as each is given understanding to ascertain and apply it." The way that we perform that duty in a case of this kind sets an example that other tribunals in other countries are sure to emulate.

The significance of this Court's precedents is illustrated by a recent decision of the Court of Appeal of the Republic of South Africa. Based largely on its understanding of the import of this Court's cases—including our decision in *Ker*—that court held that the prosecution of a defendant kidnaped by agents of South Africa in another country must be dismissed. *S v. Ebrahim*, S. Afr. L. Rep. (Apr.–June 1991). The Court of Appeal of South Africa—indeed, I suspect most courts throughout the civilized world—will be deeply disturbed by the "monstrous" decision the Court announces today. For every nation that has an interest in preserving the Rule of Law is affected, directly or indirectly, by a decision of this character.[37] As Thomas Paine warned, an "avidity to punish is always dangerous to liberty" because it leads a nation "to stretch, to misinterpret, and to misapply even the best of laws." To counter that tendency, he reminds us: "He that would make his own liberty secure must guard even his enemy from oppression; for if he violates this duty he establishes a precedent that will reach to himself."

I respectfully dissent.

———————

Following the Supreme Court's decision, Humberto Alvarez-Machain was tried and acquitted. In 1993, he returned to Mexico and filed a civil action in the United States under the Federal Tort Claims Act, 28 U.S.C. §§ 1346(b)(1), and the Alien Tort Statute, 28 U.S.C. § 1350. Alvarez-Machain sued the United States for false arrest and sued the individuals (including four DEA agents) who were involved in his abduction for "a violation of the law of nations." The civil suit also made its way to the United States Supreme Court, where the Justices unanimously held against Alvarez-Machain, albeit with some disagreement as to the legal rationale. *Sosa v. Alvarez-Machain*, 542 U.S. 692 (2004).

Not surprisingly, the U.S. practice of kidnapping Mexican citizens for drug prosecutions only contributed to Mexico's reluctance to extradite its nationals to the United States. *See, e.g.,* María Celia Toro, *The Internationalization of Police: The DEA in Mexico*, 86 J. Am. Hist. 623, 636 (1999) ("The kidnapping of Alvarez Macháin, for instance, had an immediate effect on Mexico's laws regarding DEA agents in its territory."). In recent years, however, "Mexico's long-standing reluctance to extradite has vanished." Devin C. McNulty, *The Changing Face of Extraditions Between Mexico and the United States*, 31 Champion 32 (2007) (describing how a number of developments, including the U.S. drug enforcement certification program, has led Mexico to begin extraditing its nationals to the U.S. for prosecution).

The DEA's involvement in kidnappings is a particularly striking example of the scope of the agency's drug enforcement efforts outside of the U.S. Since its creation in 1973, the DEA has been "transformed into a global intelligence organization with a reach that extends far beyond narcotics, and an eavesdropping operation so expansive it has to fend off foreign politicians who want to use it against their political enemies[.]" Today, the DEA has 87 offices in 63 countries and "has steadily built its international turf, an expansion primarily driven by the multinational nature of the drug trade, but also by forces

———————

37. As Judge Mansfield presciently observed in a case not unlike the one before us today: "Society is the ultimate loser when, in order to convict the guilty, it uses methods that lead to decreased respect for the law." *United States v. Toscanino,* 500 F.2d 267, 274 (CA2 1974).

within the agency seeking a larger mandate." Ginger Thompson and Scott Shane, *Cables Portray Expanded Reach of Drug Agency*, N.Y. Times, Dec. 26, 2010 at A1. *See also, e.g.,* Peter Andreas and Ethan Nadelmann, Policing the Globe: Criminalization and Crime Control in International Relations 129 (2006) (noting that in 1967 the U.S. drug enforcement budget was approximately $3 million and only 12 U.S. drug agents were stationed outside of the U.S.); Drug Enforcement Administration: A Tradition of Excellence, 1973–2003 (describing the history of the DEA).

Do constitutional constraints on police investigations within the U.S. apply to investigations by U.S. drug enforcement agents abroad?

United States v. Verdugo-Urquidez
Supreme Court of the United States
494 U.S. 259 (1990)

Chief Justice Rehnquist delivered the opinion of the Court.

The question presented by this case is whether the Fourth Amendment applies to the search and seizure by United States agents of property that is owned by a nonresident alien and located in a foreign country. We hold that it does not.

Respondent Rene Martin Verdugo-Urquidez is a citizen and resident of Mexico. He is believed by the United States Drug Enforcement Agency (DEA) to be one of the leaders of a large and violent organization in Mexico that smuggles narcotics into the United States. Based on a complaint charging respondent with various narcotics-related offenses, the Government obtained a warrant for his arrest on August 3, 1985. In January 1986, Mexican police officers, after discussions with United States marshals, apprehended Verdugo-Urquidez in Mexico and transported him to the United States Border Patrol station in Calexico, California. There, United States marshals arrested respondent and eventually moved him to a correctional center in San Diego, California, where he remains incarcerated pending trial.

Following respondent's arrest, Terry Bowen, a DEA agent assigned to the Calexico DEA office, decided to arrange for searches of Verdugo-Urquidez's Mexican residences located in Mexicali and San Felipe. Bowen believed that the searches would reveal evidence related to respondent's alleged narcotics trafficking activities and his involvement in the kidnaping and torture-murder of DEA Special Agent Enrique Camarena Salazar (for which respondent subsequently has been convicted in a separate prosecution. Bowen telephoned Walter White, the Assistant Special Agent in charge of the DEA office in Mexico City, and asked him to seek authorization for the search from the Director General of the Mexican Federal Judicial Police (MFJP). After several attempts to reach high ranking Mexican officials, White eventually contacted the Director General, who authorized the searches and promised the cooperation of Mexican authorities. Thereafter, DEA agents working in concert with officers of the MFJP searched respondent's properties in Mexicali and San Felipe and seized certain documents. In particular, the search of the Mexicali residence uncovered a tally sheet, which the Government believes reflects the quantities of marijuana smuggled by Verdugo-Urquidez into the United States.

The District Court granted respondent's motion to suppress evidence seized during the searches, concluding that the Fourth Amendment applied to the searches and that the DEA agents had failed to justify searching respondent's premises without a warrant. A divided panel of the Court of Appeals for the Ninth Circuit affirmed. It cited this Court's decision in *Reid v. Covert*, 354 U.S. 1 (1957), which held that American citizens tried by United States military authorities in a foreign country were entitled to the protections of the Fifth and Sixth Amendments, and concluded that "The Constitution imposes substantive constraints on the federal government, even when it operates abroad." Relying on our decision in *INS v. Lopez-Mendoza,* 468 U.S. 1032 (1984), where a majority of Justices assumed that illegal aliens in the United States have Fourth Amendment rights, the Ninth Circuit majority found it "difficult to conclude that Verdugo-Urquidez lacks these same protections." It also observed that persons in respondent's position enjoy certain trial-related rights, and reasoned that "it would be odd indeed to acknowledge that Verdugo-Urquidez is entitled to due process under the fifth amendment, and to a fair trial under the sixth amendment, ... and deny him the protection from unreasonable searches and seizures afforded under the fourth amendment." Having concluded that the Fourth Amendment applied to the searches of respondent's properties, the court went on to decide that the searches violated the Constitution because the DEA agents failed to procure a search warrant. Although recognizing that "an American search warrant would be of no legal validity in Mexico," the majority deemed it sufficient that a warrant would have "substantial constitutional value in this country," because it would reflect a magistrate's determination that there existed probable cause to search and would define the scope of the search.

The dissenting judge argued that this Court's statement in *United States v. Curtiss-Wright Export Corp.,* 299 U.S. 304, 318 (1936), that "neither the Constitution nor the laws passed in pursuance of it have any force in foreign territory unless in respect of our own citizens," foreclosed any claim by respondent to Fourth Amendment rights. More broadly, he viewed the Constitution as a "compact" among the people of the United States, and the protections of the Fourth Amendment were expressly limited to "the people." We granted certiorari.

Before analyzing the scope of the Fourth Amendment, we think it significant to note that it operates in a different manner than the Fifth Amendment, which is not at issue in this case. The privilege against self-incrimination guaranteed by the Fifth Amendment is a fundamental trial right of criminal defendants. Although conduct by law enforcement officials prior to trial may ultimately impair that right, a constitutional violation occurs only at trial. The Fourth Amendment functions differently. It prohibits "unreasonable searches and seizures" whether or not the evidence is sought to be used in a criminal trial, and a violation of the Amendment is "fully accomplished" at the time of an unreasonable governmental intrusion. For purposes of this case, therefore, if there were a constitutional violation, it occurred solely in Mexico. Whether evidence obtained from respondent's Mexican residences should be excluded at trial in the United States is a remedial question separate from the existence *vel non* of the constitutional violation.

The Fourth Amendment provides: "The right of the people to be secure in their persons, houses, papers, and effects, against unreasonable searches and seizures, shall not be violated, and no Warrants shall issue, but upon probable cause, supported by Oath or affirmation, and particularly describing the place to be searched, and the persons or things to be seized."

That text, by contrast with the Fifth and Sixth Amendments, extends its reach only to "the people." Contrary to the suggestion of *amici curiae* that the Framers used this phrase "simply to avoid [an] awkward rhetorical redundancy," "the people" seems to have been a term of art employed in select parts of the Constitution. The Preamble declares that the Constitution is ordained and established by "the People of the United States." The Second Amendment protects "the right of the people to keep and bear Arms," and the Ninth and Tenth Amendments provide that certain rights and powers are retained by and reserved to "the people." While this textual exegesis is by no means conclusive, it suggests that "the people" protected by the Fourth Amendment, and by the First and Second Amendments, and to whom rights and powers are reserved in the Ninth and Tenth Amendments, refers to a class of persons who are part of a national community or who have otherwise developed sufficient connection with this country to be considered part of that community. See *United States ex rel. Turner v. Williams*, 194 U.S. 279, 292 (1904) (Excludable alien is not entitled to First Amendment rights, because "he does not become one of the people to whom these things are secured by our Constitution by an attempt to enter forbidden by law"). The language of these Amendments contrasts with the words "person" and "accused" used in the Fifth and Sixth Amendments regulating procedure in criminal cases.

What we know of the history of the drafting of the Fourth Amendment also suggests that its purpose was to restrict searches and seizures which might be conducted by the United States in domestic matters. The Framers originally decided not to include a provision like the Fourth Amendment, because they believed the National Government lacked power to conduct searches and seizures. Many disputed the original view that the Federal Government possessed only narrow delegated powers over domestic affairs, however, and ultimately felt an Amendment prohibiting unreasonable searches and seizures was necessary. Madison, for example, argued that "there is a clause granting to Congress the power to make all laws which shall be necessary and proper for carrying into execution all of the powers vested in the Government of the United States," and that general warrants might be considered "necessary" for the purpose of collecting revenue. The driving force behind the adoption of the Amendment, as suggested by Madison's advocacy, was widespread hostility among the former colonists to the issuance of writs of assistance empowering revenue officers to search suspected places for smuggled goods, and general search warrants permitting the search of private houses, often to uncover papers that might be used to convict persons of libel. The available historical data show, therefore, that the purpose of the Fourth Amendment was to protect the people of the United States against arbitrary action by their own Government; it was never suggested that the provision was intended to restrain the actions of the Federal Government against aliens outside of the United States territory.

There is likewise no indication that the Fourth Amendment was understood by contemporaries of the Framers to apply to activities of the United States directed against aliens in foreign territory or in international waters. Only seven years after the ratification of the Amendment, French interference with American commercial vessels engaged in neutral trade triggered what came to be known as the "undeclared war" with France. In an Act to "protect the Commerce of the United States" in 1798, Congress authorized President Adams to "instruct the commanders of the public armed vessels which are, or which shall be employed in the service of the United States, to subdue, seize and take any armed French vessel, which shall be found within the jurisdictional limits of the United States, or elsewhere, on the high seas." This public naval force consisted of only 45 vessels, so Congress also gave the President power to grant to the owners of private armed ships and vessels of the United States "special commissions," which would allow them "the same license and authority for the subduing, seizing and capturing any armed French vessel, and for the recapture of the vessels, goods and effects of the people of the United States, as the public armed vessels of the United States may by law have." Under the latter provision, 365 private armed vessels were commissioned before March 1, 1799; together, these enactments resulted in scores of seizures of foreign vessels under congressional authority. Some commanders were held liable by this Court for unlawful seizures because their actions were beyond the scope of the congressional grant of authority, but it was never suggested that the Fourth Amendment restrained the authority of congress or of United States agents to conduct operations such as this.

The global view taken by the Court of Appeals of the application of the Constitution is also contrary to this Court's decisions in the *Insular Cases*, which held that not every constitutional provision applies to governmental activity even where the United States has sovereign power. See, *e. g., Balzac v. Porto Rico,* 258 U.S. 298 (1922) (Sixth Amendment right to jury trial inapplicable in Puerto Rico); *Dorr v. United States,* 195 U.S. 138 (1904) (jury trial provision inapplicable in Philippines). In *Dorr,* we declared the general rule that in an unincorporated territory—one not clearly destined for statehood—Congress was not required to adopt "a system of laws which shall include the right of trial by jury, and that *the Constitution does not, without legislation and of its own force, carry such right to territory so situated.*" 195 U.S., at 149 (emphasis added). Only "fundamental" constitutional rights are guaranteed to inhabitants of those territories. If that is true with respect to territories ultimately governed by Congress, respondent's claim that the protections of the Fourth Amendment extend to aliens in foreign nations is even weaker. And certainly, it is not open to us in light of the *Insular Cases* to endorse the view that every constitutional provision applies wherever the United States Government exercises its power.

To support his all-encompassing view of the Fourth Amendment, respondent points to language from the plurality opinion in *Reid v. Covert,* 354 U.S. 1 (1957). *Reid* involved an attempt by Congress to subject the wives of American servicemen to trial by military tribunals without the protection of the Fifth and Sixth Amendments. The Court held that it was unconstitutional to apply the Uniform Code of Military Justice to the trials of the American women for capital crimes. Four Justices "rejected the idea that when the United States acts *against citizens* abroad it can do so free of the Bill of Rights." *Id., at 5* (emphasis added).

Respondent urges that we interpret this discussion to mean that federal officials are constrained by the Fourth Amendment wherever and against whomever they act. But the holding of *Reid* stands for no such sweeping proposition: it decided that United States citizens stationed abroad could invoke the protection of the Fifth and Sixth Amendments. The concurring opinions by Justices Frankfurter and Harlan in *Reid* resolved the case on much narrower grounds than the plurality and declined even to hold that United States citizens were entitled to the full range of constitutional protections in all overseas criminal prosecutions. Since respondent is not a United States citizen, he can derive no comfort from the *Reid* holding.

Verdugo-Urquidez also relies on a series of cases in which we have held that aliens enjoy certain constitutional rights. See, *e. g., Plyler v. Doe,* 457 U.S. 202, 211–212 (1982) (illegal aliens protected by Equal Protection Clause); *Kwong Hai Chew v. Colding, 344 U.S. 590, 596 (1953)* (resident alien is a "person" within the meaning of the Fifth Amendment). These cases, however, establish only that aliens receive constitutional protections when they have come within the territory of the United States and developed substantial connections with the country. See, *e.g., Plyler, supra,* at 212 (The provisions of the Fourteenth Amendment "'are universal in their application, *to all persons within the territorial jurisdiction …*'"). Respondent is an alien who has had no previous significant voluntary connection with the United States, so these cases avail him not.

Justice Stevens' concurrence in the judgment takes the view that even though the search took place in Mexico, it is nonetheless governed by the requirements of the Fourth Amendment because respondent was "lawfully present in the United States … even though he was brought and held here against his will." But this sort of presence—lawful but involuntary—is not of the sort to indicate any substantial connection with our country. The extent to which respondent might claim the protection of the Fourth Amendment if the duration of his stay in the United States were to be prolonged—by a prison sentence, for example—we need not decide. When the search of his house in Mexico took place, he had been present in the United States for only a matter of days. We do not think the applicability of the Fourth Amendment to the search of premises in Mexico should turn on the fortuitous circumstance of whether the custodian of its nonresident alien owner had or had not transported him to the United States at the time the search was made.

The Court of Appeals found some support for its holding in our decision in *INS v. Lopez-Mendoza,* 468 U.S. 1032 (1984), where a majority of Justices assumed that the Fourth Amendment applied to illegal aliens in the United States. We cannot fault the Court of Appeals for placing some reliance on the case, but our decision did not expressly address the proposition gleaned by the court below. The question presented for decision in *Lopez-Mendoza* was limited to whether the Fourth Amendment's exclusionary rule should be extended to civil deportation proceedings; it did not encompass whether the protections of the Fourth Amendment extend to illegal aliens in this country. The Court often grants certiorari to decide particular legal issues while assuming without deciding the validity of antecedent propositions and such assumptions—even on jurisdictional issues—are not binding in future cases that directly raise the questions. Our statements in *Lopez-Mendoza* are therefore not dispositive of how the Court would rule on a Fourth Amendment claim by illegal aliens in the United States if such a claim were squarely before us. Even assuming such aliens would be entitled to Fourth Amendment protections, their situation is different from respondent's. The illegal aliens in *Lopez-Mendoza* were in the United States voluntarily and presumably had accepted some societal obligations; but respondent had no voluntary connection with this country that might place him among "the people" of the United States.

Not only are history and case law against respondent, but as pointed out in *Johnson v. Eisentrager,* 393 U.S. 763 (1950), the result of accepting his claim would have significant and deleterious consequences for the United States in conducting activities beyond its boundaries. The rule adopted by the Court of Appeals would apply not only to law enforcement operations abroad, but also to other foreign policy operations which might result in "searches or seizures." The United States frequently employs armed forces outside this country—over 200 times in our history—for the protection of American citizens or national security. Application of the Fourth Amendment to those circumstances could significantly disrupt the ability of the political branches to respond to foreign situations involving our national interest. Were respondent to prevail, aliens with no attachment to this country might well bring actions for damages to remedy claimed violations of the Fourth Amendment in foreign countries or in international waters.

We think that the text of the Fourth Amendment, its history, and our cases discussing the application of the Constitution to aliens and extraterritorially require rejection of respondent's claim. At the time of the search, he was a citizen and resident of Mexico with no voluntary attachment to the United States, and the place searched was located in Mexico. Under these circumstances, the Fourth Amendment has no application.

For better or for worse, we live in a world of nation-states in which our Government must be able to "function effectively in the company of sovereign nations." Some who violate our laws may live outside our borders under a regime quite different from that which obtains in this country. Situations threatening to important American interests may arise halfway around the globe, situations which in the view of the political branches of our Government require an American response with armed force. If there are to be restrictions on searches and seizures which occur incident to such American action, they must be imposed by the political branches through diplomatic understanding, treaty, or legislation.

The judgment of the Court of Appeals is accordingly

Reversed.

Justice Kennedy, concurring.

I agree that no violation of the Fourth Amendment has occurred and that we must reverse the judgment of the Court of Appeals. Although some explanation of my views is appropriate given the difficulties of this case, I do not believe they depart in fundamental respects from the opinion of the Court, which I join.

I cannot place any weight on the reference to "the people" in the Fourth Amendment as a source of restricting its protections. With respect, I submit these words do not detract from its force or its reach. Given the history of our Nation's concern over warrantless and unreasonable searches, explicit recognition of "the right of the people" to Fourth Amendment protection may be interpreted to underscore the importance of the right, rather than to restrict the category of persons who may assert it. The restrictions that the United States must observe with reference to aliens beyond its territory or jurisdiction depend, as a consequence, on general principles of interpretation, not on an inquiry as to who formed the Constitution or a construction that some rights are mentioned as being those of "the people."

I take it to be correct, as the plurality opinion in *Reid* v. *Covert* sets forth, that the Government may act only as the Constitution authorizes, whether the actions in question are foreign or domestic. But this principle is only a first step in resolving this case. The question before us then becomes what constitutional standards apply when the Government acts, in reference to an alien, within its sphere of foreign operations. [W]e must interpret constitutional protections in light of the undoubted power of the United States to take actions to assert its legitimate power and authority abroad.

The conditions and considerations of this case would make adherence to the Fourth Amendment's warrant requirement impracticable and anomalous. Just as the Constitution in the *Insular Cases* did not require Congress to implement all constitutional guarantees in its territories because of their "wholly dissimilar traditions and institutions," the Constitution does not require United States agents to obtain a warrant when searching the foreign home of a nonresident alien. If the search had occurred in a residence within the United States, I have little doubt that the full protections of the Fourth Amendment would apply. But that is not this case. The absence of local judges or magistrates available to issue warrants, the differing and perhaps unascertainable conceptions of reasonableness and privacy that prevail abroad, and the need to cooperate with foreign officials all indicate that the Fourth Amendment's warrant requirement should not apply in Mexico as it does in this country. For this reason, in addition to the other persuasive justifications stated by the Court, I agree that no violation of the Fourth Amendment has occurred in the case before us. The rights of a citizen, as to whom the United States has continuing obligations, are not presented by this case.

I do not mean to imply, and the Court has not decided, that persons in the position of the respondent have no constitutional protection. The United States is prosecuting a foreign national in a court established under Article III, and all of the trial proceedings are governed by the Constitution. All would agree, for instance, that the dictates of the Due Process Clause of the Fifth Amendment protect the defendant. Indeed, as Justice Harlan put it, "the question of which specific safeguards ... are appropriately to be applied in a particular context ... can be reduced to the issue of what process is 'due' a defendant in the particular circumstances of a particular case." Nothing approaching a violation of due process has occurred in this case.

Justice Stevens, concurring in the judgment.

In my opinion aliens who are lawfully present in the United States are among those "people" who are entitled to the protection of the Bill of Rights, including the Fourth Amendment. Respondent is surely such a person even though he was brought and held here against his will. I therefore cannot join the Court's sweeping opinion. I do agree, however, with the Government's submission that the search conducted by the United States agents with the approval and cooperation of the Mexican authorities was not "unreasonable" as that term is used in the first Clause of the Amendment. I do not believe the Warrant Clause has any application to searches of noncitizens' homes in foreign jurisdictions because American magistrates have no power to authorize such searches. I therefore concur in the Court's judgment.

Justice Brennan, with whom Justice Marshall joins, dissenting.

Today the Court holds that although foreign nationals must abide by our laws even when in their own countries, our Government need not abide by the Fourth Amendment when it investigates them for violations of our laws. I respectfully dissent.

Particularly in the past decade, our Government has sought, successfully, to hold foreign nationals criminally liable under federal laws for conduct committed entirely beyond the territorial limits of the United States that nevertheless has effects in this country. Foreign nationals must now take care not to violate our drug laws,[1] our antitrust laws, our securities laws, and a host of other federal criminal statutes. The enormous expansion of federal criminal jurisdiction outside our Nation's boundaries has led one commentator to suggest that our country's three largest exports are now "rock music, blue jeans, and United States law." Grundman, *The New Imperialism: The Extraterritorial Application of United States Law*, 14 Int'l Law. 257, 257 (1980).

The Constitution is the source of Congress' authority to criminalize conduct, whether here or abroad, and of the Executive's authority to investigate and prosecute such conduct. But the same Constitution also prescribes limits on our Government's authority to investigate, prosecute, and punish criminal conduct, whether foreign or domestic. As a plurality of the Court noted in *Reid v. Covert,* 354 U.S. 1, 5–6 (1957): "The United States is entirely a creature of the Constitution. Its power and authority have no other source. It can only act in accordance with all the limitations imposed by the Constitution."

The Court today creates an antilogy: the Constitution authorizes our Government to enforce our criminal laws abroad, but when Government agents exercise this authority, the Fourth Amendment does not travel with them. This cannot be. At the very least, the Fourth Amendment is an unavoidable correlative of the Government's power to enforce the criminal law.

The Fourth Amendment guarantees the right of "the people" to be free from unreasonable searches and seizures and provides that a warrant shall issue only upon presentation of an oath or affirmation demonstrating probable cause and particularly describing the place to be searched and the persons or things to be seized. According to the majority, the term "the people" refers to "a class of persons who are part of a national community or who have otherwise developed sufficient connection with this country to be considered part of that community." The Court admits that "the people" extends beyond

---

1. Federal drug enforcement statutes written broadly enough to permit extraterritorial application include laws proscribing the manufacture, distribution, or possession with intent to manufacture or distribute of controlled substances on board vessels, see 46 U.S.C. App. § 1903(h) (1982 ed., Supp. V) ("This section is intended to reach acts ... committed outside the territorial jurisdiction of the United States"), the possession, manufacture, or distribution of a controlled substance for purposes of unlawful importation, see 21 U.S.C. § 959(c) (same), and conspiracy to violate federal narcotics laws, see *Chua Han Mow v. United States,* 730 F.2d 1308, 1311–1312 (CA9 1984) (applying 21 U.S.C. §§ 846 and 963 to conduct by a Malaysian citizen in Malaysia).

the citizenry, but leaves the precise contours of its "sufficient connection" test unclear. At one point the majority hints that aliens are protected by the Fourth Amendment only when they come within the United States and develop "substantial connections" with our country. At other junctures, the Court suggests that an alien's presence in the United States must be voluntary and that the alien must have "accepted some societal obligations." At yet other points, the majority implies that respondent would be protected by the Fourth Amendment if the place searched were in the United States.

What the majority ignores, however, is the most obvious connection between Verdugo-Urquidez and the United States: he was investigated and is being prosecuted for violations of United States law and may well spend the rest of his life in a United States prison. The "sufficient connection" is supplied not by Verdugo-Urquidez, but by the Government. Respondent is entitled to the protections of the Fourth Amendment because our Government, by investigating him and attempting to hold him accountable under United States criminal laws, has treated him as a member of our community for purposes of enforcing our laws. He has become, quite literally, one of the governed. Fundamental fairness and the ideals underlying our Bill of Rights compel the conclusion that when we impose "societal obligations," such as the obligation to comply with our criminal laws, on foreign nationals, we in turn are obliged to respect certain correlative rights, among them the Fourth Amendment.

By concluding that respondent is not one of "the people" protected by the Fourth Amendment, the majority disregards basic notions of mutuality. If we expect aliens to obey our laws, aliens should be able to expect that we will obey our Constitution when we investigate, prosecute, and punish them. We have recognized this fundamental principle of mutuality since the time of the Framers. James Madison, universally recognized as the primary architect of the Bill of Rights, emphasized the importance of mutuality when he spoke out against the Alien and Sedition Acts less than a decade after the adoption of the Fourth Amendment: "It does not follow, because aliens are not parties to the Constitution, as citizens are parties to it, that, whilst they actually conform to it, they have no right to its protection. Aliens are not more parties to the laws than they are parties to the Constitution; yet it will not be disputed that, as they owe, on one hand, a temporary obedience, they are entitled, in return, to their protection and advantage." Madison's Report on the Virginia Resolutions (1800), reprinted in 4 Elliot's Debates 556 (2d ed. 1836).

Mutuality is essential to ensure the fundamental fairness that underlies our Bill of Rights. Foreign nationals investigated and prosecuted for alleged violations of United States criminal laws are just as vulnerable to oppressive Government behavior as are United States citizens investigated and prosecuted for the same alleged violations. Indeed, in a case such as this where the Government claims the existence of an international criminal conspiracy, citizens and foreign nationals may be codefendants, charged under the same statutes for the same conduct and facing the same penalties if convicted. They may have been investigated by the same agents pursuant to the same enforcement authority. When our Government holds these codefendants to the same standards of conduct, the Fourth Amendment, which protects the citizen from unreasonable searches and seizures, should protect the foreign national as well.

Mutuality also serves to inculcate the values of law and order. By respecting the rights of foreign nationals, we encourage other nations to respect the rights of our citizens. Moreover, as our Nation becomes increasingly concerned about the domestic effects of international crime, we cannot forget that the behavior of our law enforcement agents abroad sends a powerful message about the rule of law to individuals everywhere.

If we seek respect for law and order, we must observe these principles ourselves. Lawlessness breeds lawlessness.

Finally, when United States agents conduct unreasonable searches, whether at home or abroad, they disregard our Nation's values. For over 200 years, our country has considered itself the world's foremost protector of liberties. The privacy and sanctity of the home have been primary tenets of our moral, philosophical, and judicial beliefs. Our national interest is defined by those values and by the need to preserve our own just institutions. We take pride in our commitment to a Government that cannot, on mere whim, break down doors and invade the most personal of places. We exhort other nations to follow our example. How can we explain to others—and to ourselves—that these long cherished ideals are suddenly of no consequence when the door being broken belongs to a foreigner?

In its effort to establish that respondent does not have sufficient connection to the United States to be considered one of "the people" protected by the *Fourth Amendment*, the Court relies on the text of the Amendment, historical evidence, and cases refusing to apply certain constitutional provisions outside the United States. None of these, however, justifies the majority's cramped interpretation of the *Fourth Amendment's* applicability.

The majority looks to various constitutional provisions and suggests that "'the people' seems to have been a term of art." But the majority admits that its "textual exegesis is by no means conclusive." The majority suggests a restrictive interpretation of those with "sufficient connection" to this country to be considered among "the people," but the term "the people" is better understood as a rhetorical counterpoint to "the Government," such that rights that were reserved to the "the people" were to protect all those subject to "the Government." "The people" are "the governed."

In drafting both the Constitution and the Bill of Rights, the Framers strove to create a form of Government decidedly different from their British heritage. Whereas the British Parliament was unconstrained, the Framers intended to create a Government of limited powers. The colonists considered the British government dangerously omnipotent. After all, the British declaration of rights in 1688 had been enacted not by the people, but by Parliament. Americans vehemently attacked the notion that rights were matters of "'favor and grace,'" given to the people from the Government.

Thus, the Framers of the Bill of Rights did not purport to "create" rights. Rather, they designed the Bill of Rights to prohibit our Government from infringing rights and liberties presumed to be pre-existing. See, e.g., U.S. Const., Amdt. 9 ("The enumeration in the Constitution of certain rights, shall not be construed to deny or disparage others retained by the people"). The Fourth Amendment, for example, does not create a new right of security against unreasonable searches and seizures. It states that "[t]he right of the people to be secure in their persons, houses, papers, and effects, against unreasonable searches and seizures, shall not be violated. . . ." The focus of the Fourth Amendment is on what the Government can and cannot do, and how it may act, not on against whom these actions may be taken. Bestowing rights and delineating protected groups would have been inconsistent with the drafters' fundamental conception of a Bill of Rights as a limitation on the Government's conduct with respect to all whom it seeks to govern. It is thus extremely unlikely that the Framers intended the narrow construction of the term "the people" presented today by the majority.

The Court also relies on a series of cases dealing with the application of criminal procedural protections outside of the United States to conclude that "not every constitutional provision applies to governmental activity even where the United States has sovereign power." None of these cases, however, purports to read the phrase "the people" as limiting the protections of the Fourth Amendment to those with "sufficient connection" to the United States, and thus none gives content to the majority's analysis. The cases shed no light on the question whether respondent—a citizen of a nonenemy nation being tried in a United States federal court—is one of "the people" protected by the Fourth Amendment.

The majority's rejection of respondent's claim to Fourth Amendment protection is apparently motivated by its fear that application of the Amendment to law enforcement searches against foreign nationals overseas "could significantly disrupt the ability of the political branches to respond to foreign situations involving our national interest." The majority's doomsday scenario—that American Armed Forces conducting a mission to protect our national security with no law enforcement objective "would have to articulate specific facts giving them probable cause to undertake a search or seizure"—is fanciful. Verdugo-Urquidez is protected by the Fourth Amendment because our Government, by investigating and prosecuting him, has made him one of "the governed." Accepting respondent as one of "the governed," however, hardly requires the Court to accept enemy aliens in wartime as among "the governed" entitled to invoke the protection of the Fourth Amendment.

Moreover, with respect to non-law-enforcement activities not directed against enemy aliens in wartime but nevertheless implicating national security, doctrinal exceptions to the general requirements of a warrant and probable cause likely would be applicable more frequently abroad, thus lessening the purported tension between the Fourth Amendment's strictures and the Executive's foreign affairs power. Many situations involving sensitive operations abroad likely would involve exigent circumstances such that the warrant requirement would be excused. Therefore, the Government's conduct would be assessed only under the reasonableness standard, the application of which depends on context.

In addition, where the precise contours of a "reasonable" search and seizure are unclear, the Executive Branch will not be "plunge[d] ... into a sea of uncertainty" that will impair materially its ability to conduct foreign affairs. Doctrines such as official immunity have long protected Government agents from any undue chill on the exercise of lawful discretion. Similarly, the Court has recognized that there may be certain situations in which the offensive use of constitutional rights should be limited. In most cases implicating foreign policy concerns in which the reasonableness of an over-seas search or seizure in unclear, application of the Fourth Amendment will not interfere with the Executive's traditional prerogative in foreign affairs because a court will have occasion to decide the constitutionality of such a search only if the Executive decides to bring a criminal prosecution and introduce evidence seized abroad. When the Executive decides to conduct a search as part of an ongoing criminal investigation, fails to get a warrant, and then seeks to introduce the fruits of that search at trial, however, the courts must enforce the Constitution.

Because the Fourth Amendment governs the search of respondent's Mexican residences, the District Court suppressed the evidence found in that search because the officers conducting the search did not obtain a warrant. I cannot agree with Justice Blackmun and Justice Stevens that the Warrant Clause has no application to searches of noncitizens' homes in foreign jurisdictions because American magistrates lack the power to authorize such searches. The Warrant Clause would serve the same primary functions abroad as it does domestically, and I see no reason to distinguish between foreign and domestic searches.

The primary purpose of the warrant requirement is its assurance of neutrality. As Justice Jackson stated for the Court in *Johnson v. United States,* 333 U.S. 10, 13–14 (1948):

"The point of the Fourth Amendment, which often is not grasped by zealous officers, is not that it denies law enforcement the support of the usual inferences which reasonable men draw from evidence. Its protection consists in requiring that those inferences be drawn by a neutral and detached magistrate instead of being judged by the officer engaged in the often competitive enterprise of ferreting out crime. When the right of privacy must reasonably yield to the right of search is, as a rule, to be decided by a judicial officer, not by a policeman or government enforcement agent." A warrant also defines the scope of a search and limits the discretion of the inspecting officers. These purposes would be served no less in the foreign than in the domestic context.

The Warrant Clause cannot be ignored simply because Congress has not given any United States magistrate authority to issue search warrants for foreign searches. Congress cannot define the contours of the Constitution. If the Warrant Clause applies, Congress cannot excise the Clause from the Constitution by failing to provide a means for United States agents to obtain a warrant.

Nor is the Warrant Clause inapplicable merely because a warrant from a United States magistrate could not "authorize" a search in a foreign country. Although this may be true as a matter of international law, it is irrelevant to our interpretation of the Fourth Amendment. As a matter of United States constitutional law, a warrant serves the same primary function overseas as it does domestically; it assures that a neutral magistrate has authorized the search and limited its scope. The need to protect those suspected of criminal activity from the unbridled discretion of investigating officers is no less important abroad than at home.

When our Government conducts a law enforcement search against a foreign national outside of the United States and its territories, it must comply with the Fourth Amendment. Absent exigent circumstance or consent, it must obtain a search warrant from a United States court. When we tell the world that we expect all people, wherever they may be, to abide by our laws, we cannot in the same breath tell the world that our law enforcement officers need not do the same. Because we cannot expect others to respect our laws until we respect our Constitution, I respectfully dissent.

Justice Blackmun, dissenting.

I cannot accept the Court of Appeals' conclusion, echoed in some portions of Justice Brennan's dissent, that the Fourth Amendment governs every action by an American official that can be characterized as a search or seizure. American agents acting abroad generally do not purport to exercise sovereign authority over the foreign nationals with whom they come in contact.

I am inclined to agree with Justice Brennan, however, that when a foreign national is held accountable for purported violations of United States criminal laws, he has effectively been treated as one of "the governed" and therefore us entitled to Fourth Amendment protections. Although the Government's exercise of power abroad does not ordinarily implicate the Fourth Amendment, the enforcement of domestic criminal law seems to me to be the paradigmatic exercise of sovereignty over those who are compelled to obey. In any event, as Justice Stevens notes, respondent was lawfully (though involuntarily) within this country at the time the search occurred. Under these circumstances I believe that respondent is entitled to invoke protections of the Fourth Amendment. I agree with the Government, however, that an American magistrate's lack of power to authorize a search abroad renders the Warrant Clause inapplicable to the search of a noncitizen's residence outside this country.

The Fourth Amendment nevertheless requires that the search be "reasonable." And when the purpose of a search is the procurement of evidence for a criminal prosecution, we have consistently held that the search, to be reasonable, must be based upon probable cause. Neither the District Court not the Court of Appeals addressed the issue of probable cause, and I do not believe that a reliable determination could be made on the basis of the record before us. I therefore would vacate the judgment of the Court of Appeals and remand the case for further proceedings.

———————

The increased presence of U.S. drug enforcement abroad extends beyond the DEA. Throughout the 1980s, the Reagan and Bush Administrations worked to integrate the nation's military into the "war on drugs." *See, e.g.,* MARK BOWDEN, KILLING PABLO: THE HUNT FOR THE WORLD'S GREATEST OUTLAW 140 (2001) (reporting that in 1989, then-Defense Secretary Dick Cheney "sent a memo to all top military commanders directing them to define counterdrug efforts as 'a high priority mission' and requesting them to submit plans for increased military involvement" in drug enforcement); Sean J. Kealy, *Reexamining the Possee Comitatus Act: Toward a Right to Civil Law Enforcement,* 21 YALE L. & POL'Y REV. 383 (2003). Today, both the U.S. military and private military contractors are involved in international drug enforcement work.

Comment: *War for Sale! Battlefield Contractors in Latin America & the 'Corporatization' of America's War on Drugs*
Kristen McCallion
36 University of Miami Inter-American Law Review 317 (2005)

The Pentagon's efforts to increase efficiency by utilizing troops for purely military missions, combined with the incredible technological development in aircraft and military equipment, have resulted in a largely accepted, yet hardly understood phenomenon— the outsourcing of military work to private military companies. Private military companies ("PMCs") are business organizations which provide professional services inexorably linked to warfare. PMCs deliver military services, conduct military and combat training, provide security services, and supply technical expertise and intelligence to the United States government all over the world.

It is estimated that PMCs generate at least $100 billion in revenue annually from the U.S. government. In fact, many of these private military companies ranked in the 2004 Fortune Global 500 List. A leading contractor exemplifying the camaraderie between PMCs and the current Bush Administration is Kellogg Brown & Root, a unit of Vice President Richard Cheney's oil powerhouse Halliburton, which was awarded a $16 million contract for constructing the military prison at Guantanamo Bay. Despite these high-priced contracts, government officials maintain that privatization saves taxpayers money, yet this claim is still up for debate. Additionally, the U.S. Department of State asserts that PMCs, such as Arlington-based Military Professional Resources Incorporated ("MPRI"), are capable of providing advanced training more effectively and at a lower cost than the United States Army. As a result, the Pentagon compensates PMCs with more than $4 billion a year for training American troops alone.

In addition to training, civilian contractors, as PMC employees, act as technical experts for sophisticated weaponry, and are stationed on or near battlefields to be available for emergency repairs and maintenance. In some instances, contractors identify potential enemy targets in a combat zone, as well as rescue and salvage downed aircraft. As a result, contractors have become heavily involved in overseas conflicts.

Today, civilian contractors battle Colombian guerilla rebel groups, man armed helicopters, and train the Colombian Army. Their employment, commenced as assistance to aid the

United States in its 'War on Drugs,' has grown out of proportion to what their original contracts provided. As a result, critics have characterized U.S. activity in Colombia "as a small, undeclared war[.]"

As civilian contractors perform virtually every function essential to a successful military operation, it comes as no surprise that they have been characterized as modern day mercenaries. The overwhelming number of civilian contractors, combined with the sheer breadth of military operations in which they are engaged, results in a distortion of the boundary between military and civilian roles. Additionally, the employment of civilian contractors by the government raises issues regarding government liability, responsibility, and deniability for civilian action, as Congressional troop cap mandates are circumvented and profit maximizing procedures are implemented to the detriment of these civilian warfighters.

Both the Clinton and Bush Administrations have hired PMCs to diminish coca crops in Latin American countries, particularly in the Andean Region. PMCs such as DynCorp, MPRI, and Northrop Grumman receive over $1 billion a year to fly fumigation spray planes to eradicate coca fields in Colombia and monitor drug traffickers from remote radar sites.

Colombia, Bolivia, and Peru produce virtually all of the world's cocaine and 60% of the heroin seized in the United States. In fact, "Peru is the second largest cocaine producer in the world...." Brazil is not categorized as a drug-producing country, but acts as a conduit for cocaine from Colombia to the United States. Brazil implemented "a $1.4 billion sensor and radar project called the Amazon Vigilance System ("SIVAM")" to monitor and control drug trafficking. The country shares this monitoring data with the United States.

Venezuela and Ecuador are both major oil producing countries, members of the Organization of Petroleum Exporting Countries ("OPEC"), and supply considerable quantities of oil to the United States.

In 1999, the United States and Ecuador signed a ten year agreement for a 'forward operating location' ("FOL"), which serves as a U.S. drug monitoring operation and aerial detection center. This was a consequence of Panama's unwillingness "to allow the United States to retain a formal military presence" for drug surveillance within its borders. As such, FOLs in Ecuador, El Salvador, and Aruba act as substitute locations for this activity.

In addition to the role that commerce and oil play in elucidating U.S. involvement in Latin America, the amplified role of civilian contractors in Latin America is due largely to the increased focus of the Bush Administration on global terrorism as a result of the September 11 attacks on the United States. Consequently, the war on drugs in Latin America now encompasses the war on terrorism as well. Both wars have become intertwined elements that comprise "narcoterrorism." Accordingly, civilian contractors are engaged in not only anti-drug efforts, but counter-insurgency and anti-terrorism operations in this region for the United States government. As a result, civilian contractors who were first contracted to fumigate drug crops are now engaged in battling terrorists in this "small, undeclared war[.]"

Perhaps more troubling than the continual increase in contractor presence is the high level of secrecy regarding the range of militaristic activities in which private contractors are involved. Although government activities are by law open to examination by the Freedom of Information Act, private company contracts are protected by proprietary law. Internal company policies may prohibit directors, employees, and agents from disclosing or using confidential or proprietary information outside the company. Therefore, most contracts between PMCs and the government provide non-disclosure agreements, and are deemed confidential by both the contracting PMC as well as the Pentagon. The confidential nature of contracted work may perhaps constitute the main reason behind the hiring of private contractors.

Obviously, this policy of accepted secrecy creates a breeding ground for unanswered questions and misinformation. The ability to 'contract out' jobs like spraying coca leaf, patrolling the skies, and providing intelligence services provides the U.S. government with "'plausible deniability[.]'" For instance, U.S. troops may be legally prohibited by Congress from entering into combat in Latin America, but PMC employees constitute civilians under U.S. contract, and therefore, may not be bound by the same restrictions.

Plausible deniability is further exemplified as contractors take on more expansive roles than what is specified in their contracts. The expansion of duties is illustrated by Dyn-Corp's training and support responsibilities for the Colombian National Police. [T]he firm's contract with the government provides for contractors to engage in pilot training and technical support to Colombian police units involved in drug crop eradication. However, it has also been reported that DynCorp employees are employed in aerial reconnaissance and combat. Specifically, contractors are reportedly engaged in fighting narco-terrorists and Colombian guerillas. DynCorp employees have in fact, admitted to engaging in high risk operations. It is obvious that DynCorp's employees are involved in more dangerous missions than were initially anticipated by Congress.

Unsurprisingly, PMCs are also secretive about their participation in Latin America. When asked about the expanded role of its contractors in fighting the war on drugs, Dyn-Corp executives generally decline to comment. Apparently, DynCorp employees are bound by strict confidentiality agreements and are prohibited from talking to media. Furthermore, when DynCorp employees are killed in operations, DynCorp executives claim that the deaths are the result of 'accidents' rather than military engagements. It is important to note that the death of an American soldier in this context would result in an investigation, with a report released by the U.S. Embassy regarding the deceased's identity and background information. Simply because a contractor is a private civilian as opposed to a military recruit, the government is not bound to concede responsibility or provide release information regarding the incident.

The accepted oversight and deniability which the government and PMCs share regarding the events in Colombia paint a grave picture of the war on drugs.

4. Crop Eradication Initiatives

U.S. efforts to try to reduce the supply of drugs extend beyond interdiction. One particularly controversial supply reduction measure has been the fumigation of coca and opium crops. Critics of crop eradication policies argue that they cause environmental damage and displace farmers in developing countries without resulting in an overall decrease in drug production. A 2008 report by the Brookings Institute's Partnership for the America's Commission found that "[e]radication efforts have not delivered sustained reductions in drug production. Total coca leaf and cocaine production in the Andean region is currently at historic highs, with Colombia still the dominant producer." According to the report, eradication programs are not successful because they simply cause drug production to shift elsewhere. "Though policymakers can point to pockets of success at specific times in particular countries, counternarcotics policies have simply displaced cultivation and trafficking from one country or region to another, without reducing the overall supply of drugs." The report concludes that "[t]he only long-run solution to the problem of illegal narcotics is to reduce the demand for drugs in the major consuming countries, including the United States." *Rethinking U.S.-Latin American Relations: A Hemispheric Partnership for a Turbulent World, Report of the Partnership for the Americas Commission*, The Brookings Institution, 25–26 (2008).

Note: *A New Approach to Extraterritorial Application of Environmental Statutes?: Uncovering the Effects of Plan Colombia* Joanne Sum-Ping

31 Colombia Journal of Environmental Law 139 (2006)

The drug trade creates problems extending much further than the drugs themselves. In Colombia, both paramilitaries and insurgents admit to funding their operations through "taxes" levied on farmers of illicit crops and have been accused of direct involvement in drug production and trafficking. Referred to as the "Hobbesian Trinity," narco-traffickers, paramilitaries, and insurgents wage violent battles. This violence, which the Colombian government has been unable to control, has created a brutal society rife with kidnappings, tortures, murders, and other human rights abuses. These brutal conditions threaten democracy in Colombia and surrounding countries.

Despite the destructive nature of the drug trade, poor farmers in southern Colombia turn to drug crops because it is their best option to make a living—a farmer with a 3-acre cocaine field earns almost ten times the minimum wage of 1200 dollars a year. Further, while narco-traffickers pick up drug crops directly from farmers' fields, the roads, markets, and other infrastructural elements necessary to support legitimate crops do not exist in Colombia. As one opium farmer in southern Colombia explains, "Opium is bad for people, but what am I going to do? If there was something else to grow, I wouldn't touch it."

To address these problems, the U.S. Congress approved 1.289 billion dollars in aid to Colombia in 2000, a package that came to be known as Plan Colombia, with funding approved every year since. A major component of Plan Colombia is the aerial fumigation of coca (cocaine) and poppy (heroin) crops. Illegal crops are sprayed with a mixture of water, herbicide (glyphosate), and surfactants (polyoxyethylene alkylamine, cosmoflux 411f, and an unknown surfactant). Spray aircraft, escort helicopters, pilots, fuel, herbicide, and technical and scientific advice are provided by the U. S. Department of State.

This aerial fumigation is extremely unpopular among the Colombian people and some branches of the Colombian government. Governors of four Colombian provinces have spoken out against the herbicide sprayings for causing "economic destruction, environmental degradation and illness, including birth defects."

It is unclear whether the aerial fumigation is successful in decreasing the amount of drug crops grown in Colombia. Some reports indicate that after their fields are fumigated, drug farmers simply move their fields elsewhere in Colombia or to neighboring Peru and Bolivia. Known as the "balloon effect," this phenomenon results in the destruction of virgin rainforest to create new coca fields and irreversibly damages delicate ecosystems. Another source claims that land devoted to coca production has decreased by 38% in Colombia and by 22% in South America. A State Department official, while claiming that overall production of illicit crops in Colombia has decreased, conceded that production in some areas of Bolivia and Peru increased.

The glyphosate spraying has triggered many complaints of negative health effects including headaches, dizziness, fever, skin rashes, red eyes, and vomiting. In 2003, the Department of State logged thousands of health complaints related to the spraying, but dismissed all as caused by other factors.

The spraying also damages ecosystems. U.N. experts described an area in which a coca field was aerially eradicated as a "desolate scene" with "indiscriminate destruction of the jungle, legal crops, medicinal plants, and fish-ponds. There is clear evidence that wildlife has fled, rivers are contaminated and production in the region has fallen."

Furthermore, the herbicide spraying has profound economic and social effects. Many farmers have no other way to support themselves and "tens of thousands have fled the [coca growing] region, a vast exodus of poor, uneducated people looking for money to feed themselves in an economy in which unemployment hovers at 15%." These farmers converge in Colombia's cities or flee to neighboring countries, alarming those countries' governments. While some funding for alternative crop programs exists, alternative crop programs are not comprehensive and are only meant to last a few years. Without the infrastructure to assure long-term success, it is unlikely that these farmers will have any choice but to resume growing drug crops.

Several commentators have vehemently criticized Plan Colombia for its failure to provide viable economic alternatives to farmers. Noam Chomsky writes that "the 'drug war' is crafted to target poor peasants abroad and poor people at home; by the use of force, not constructive measures to alleviate the problems that allegedly motivate it, at a fraction of the cost." Another commentator argues, "emphasis on aerial eradication undermines the economic stability of the country, exacerbates international displacement, and creates resentment of the citizens toward the state, undermining citizen confidence." Finally, "the rural population of Colombia ... is unlikely to be weaned off of drug traffickers or guerrillas without fundamental political reform and economic development. It will take the equivalent of a Marshall Plan to turn the tide."

Concerned about the potential environmental and social effects of aerial fumigation, Congress attached an environmental reporting requirement to the Foreign Operations Appropriations Act of 2002. This provision placed conditions on the funds to be used for herbicides and aerial fumigation of coca plants in Colombia. The Department of State was required to certify that "(1) aerial coca fumigation is being carried out in accordance with regulatory controls required by the Environmental Protection Agency as labeled for use in the United States, and after consultation with the Colombian Government to ensure that the fumigation is in accordance with Colombian laws; (2) the chemicals used in the aerial fumigation of coca, in the manner in which they are being applied, do not pose unreasonable risks or adverse effects to humans or the environment; and (3) procedures are available to evaluate claims of local citizens that their health was harmed or their licit agricultural crops were damaged by such aerial coca fumigation, and to provide fair compensation for meritorious claims; and such funds may not be made available for such purposes after six months from the date of enactment of this Act unless alternative development programs have been developed, in consultation with communities and local authorities in the departments in which such aerial coca fumigation is planned ..." The certification requirement was renewed in 2003, 2004, and 2005.

In its 2002 Certification report, the State Department claimed that the glyphosate spraying in Colombia was being conducted in accordance with Congressional requirements. The report mentions that EPA expressed concern about the herbicide's potential for acute eye toxicity, and recommended use of a lower toxicity glyphosate formulation until further testing could be done. The Department promised to switch to a lower toxicity formula as soon as one became available.

In the 2003 report, the Department again claimed to have met Congress's requirements and noted that it had switched to lower toxicity glyphosate formula. In this report, the EPA expressed concern that the spray would drift and that nearby, non-targeted vegetation would be killed by the herbicide spraying. The Department reported that it was developing mechanisms and pilot training programs to minimize spray drift.

In the 2004 report, the Department noted that it had expanded monitoring of human and environmental issues related to Plan Colombia. According to this report, effects from spray drift are "temporary in nature and small in extent" and "to date, no relation of reported human health problems to spraying has been substantiated by the rigorous evaluations of toxicologists hired by the Embassy's Narcotics Affairs Section (NAS)." The 2005 report made similar claims.

These certification reports have been heavily criticized as misleading and incomplete. For example, the Institute for Science and Interdisciplinary Studies notes that the State Department report assumes that glyphosate is being used in accordance with the manufacturer's instructions, which is not the case in Colombia. The State Department also focuses its report on the effects of the herbicide itself, and does not take into account potential toxic effects of the added surfactant. The Inter-American Association for Environmental Defense raised similar concerns, adding that the State Department did not study health effects suffered by those directly sprayed with the herbicide mixture. The Senate Appropriations Committee also expressed dissatisfaction with the report, delaying the release of funding until after State Department staff appeared before the Senate to answer questions.

However, even if it were established that the Department of State did not fulfill the environmental conditions attached to Plan Colombia funding, reports to Congress are arguably not subject to judicial review.

While Colombia's crop eradication program is perhaps the most well known, the U.S. has supported fumigation efforts in other nations as well. *See, e.g.,* Luz Estella Nagle, *Global Terrorism in Our Own Backyard: Colombia's Legal War Against Illegal Armed Groups*, 15 Transnat'l L. & Contemp. Probs. 5, 60–62 (2005) (describing crop eradication efforts in other South American countries and reporting that in 2001, 10,000 Ecuadorians filed a complaint against Virginia-based DynCorp. based on its involvement in that country's aerial spraying program); Alyssa Greenspan, Note: *Are We Fighting the Right War?*, 16 Cardozo J. Int'l & Comp. L. 493, 518–23 (2008) (describing U.S.-led opium eradication efforts in Afghanistan).

5. The U.S. Drug Certification Process

As discussed above, a number of international leaders—particularly within Latin America—have begun to call for an end to the global drug war. This development is consistent with Seth Harp's argument in *Globalization of the U.S. Black Market: Prohibition, the War on Drugs, and the Case of Mexico* that the costs and benefits of drug prohibition are unevenly distributed, with consumer countries like the United States receiving the benefits of any decrease in use and producer countries bearing the costs of violence and corruption. But if drug prohibition visits its costs primarily on producer countries, why haven't any legalized the manufacture of drugs within their borders? The answer may lie, at least partially, in United States policies designed to encourage producer countries to adopt and actively enforce drug prohibition laws. *See generally* Allegra M. McLeod, *Exporting U.S. Criminal Justice*, 29 YALE L. & POL'Y REV. 83 (2010) (examining methods used by the U.S. to advance its transnational criminal enforcement priorities abroad). In particular, the U.S. has developed a certification process that ties trade status and aid packages to participation in the drug war.

Fighting Bad Guys with International Trade Law
Raj Bhala
31 University of California Davis Law Review 1 (1997)

Congress and the President have used international trade law not only to deal with the threat to Americans from terrorists, but also to combat the scourge of drugs in American society. As former Secretary of State James Baker suggested, both are national security threats: "there is no foreign policy issue short of war or peace which has a more direct bearing on the well-being of the American people" than the international trade of illicit drugs. Secretary Baker's statement is not hyperbole. The United Nations estimates that the international trade in illicit drugs is worth $400 billion—approximately 8% of world trade— more than the trading in iron, steel, or motor vehicles. There are very few commodities that the United States is more heavily dependent upon foreign countries than drugs. Approximately 95% of the illegal narcotics consumed in the United States is imported.

Among the particularly severe drug threats to the United States are cocaine and heroin.

Both drugs originate almost entirely from overseas: Bolivia, Colombia, and Peru account for essentially all of the world's coca cultivation, and the "Golden Triangle" countries of Myanmar (Burma), Laos, and Thailand account for 75% of the world's opium production. Most of the balance of the world's opium production occurs in the "Golden Crescent" countries of Iran, Afghanistan, and Pakistan. During the early 1990s, the share of the illicit drug industry in the gross domestic product was 6% in Peru, more than 7% in Colombia, and more than 9% in Bolivia. The most important Burmese and Afghan exports are also drugs.

In an effort to combat the scourge of drugs, Congress amended the Trade Act of 1974 with title IX of the Drug Enforcement, Education, and Control Act in 1986, also known as the 1986 Narcotics Act. The 1986 Narcotics Act is a "carrot and stick" approach to dealing with the problem of illegal drug smuggling into the United States and the threat of foreign[-]sourced drug production. The 1986 Narcotics Act empowers the President to take unilateral trade actions against a country producing or transporting drugs if that country does not cooperate fully with the U.S. government in keeping drugs out of the United States. These "stick" actions are to be taken as of March 1 of each year. The "carrot" is the possibility of obtaining presidential certification that would exempt a country from trade sanctions.

The carrot and stick approach of the 1986 Narcotics Act reflects an important development in U.S. strategy in the war on drugs. Until Congress passed this Act, the United States concentrated much of its effort on interdiction—intercepting drug shipments during transit from the source countries of the drugs to the U.S. border. Interdiction is a game of cat and mouse that raises the cost of doing business for drug producers and traffickers each time a seizure occurs. However, interdiction cannot stem the wave of drug smuggling. As the State Department declared in 1995, "We are not satisfied with simply raising the cost of doing business for the traffickers." The 1986 Narcotics Act reflects what might be called a "source country" strategy. The major source countries of drugs are identified; the weak link in the chain from drug production overseas to drug sales in the United States is attacked, namely the drug crops lying dormant in the field. This strategy is attractive because the bulk of world production of cocaine and heroin is concentrated in a relatively small number of countries.

The 1986 Narcotics Act identifies two target classes of possible unilateral trade sanctions: "major drug producing countries," and "major drug-transit countries." A major drug producing country is defined by the annual output of opium, cocaine base, or marijuana produced in that country. Specifically, it is a country that illegally produces at least five metric tons of opium or opium derivative, 500 metric tons of coca, or 500 metric tons of marijuana during one fiscal year. A major drug-transit country is a conduit for narcotics or a money laundering center. It is a country "that is a significant direct source of illicit narcotic or psychotropic drugs or other controlled substances significantly affecting" the United States. In addition, the country's government must either know or be in complicity with drug transporting and money-laundering of significant sums of drug-related profits. To establish a suspect country as a major drug producing country, it is unnecessary to demonstrate that a country's government is involved in producing or trafficking drugs.

The 1986 Narcotics Act establishes the stick — five sanctions the President must impose on a major drug producing or drug[-]transit country. Although the sanctions are mandatory in most cases, the President has some discretion whether to impose any or all of the sanctions. First, the President may revoke any preferential treatment afforded to the country's products under the Generalized System of Preferences ("GSP"), Caribbean Basin Initiative ("CBI"), or other preferential scheme. Second, the President may impose an additional duty of up to 50% ad valorem on any or all of the country's products, and he may impose a duty of up to 50% on duty-free products. Third, the President may suspend air carrier transportation between the United States and the country, and may terminate any air service agreement with the country. Fourth, the President may withdraw U.S. personnel and resources that are participating in a service arrangement for customs pre-clearance. Finally, a country whose government is involved in illegal drug trade or that fails to cooperate with U.S. narcotics enforcement activities cannot receive a quota allocation for sugar imports into the United States. In the abstract, these sanctions may not appear particularly severe. In some cases, however, the first and second sanctions may inflict harm on another country and thereby cause it to alter its behavior with respect to drug production or transit.

The 1986 Narcotics Act contains an important exception to these sanctions. The United States will not impose sanctions on a major drug producing or drug-transit country if the President determines and certifies to Congress that, during the previous year, the country "has cooperated fully" with the United States, or "has taken adequate steps on its own," to change its behavior. The four certification criteria are the carrot in the 1986 Narcotics Act because they attempt to compel a major drug producing or drug-transit country to alter its behavior and thereby avoid the stick of trade sanctions. Because there is no definition of "cooperation fully" or "adequate steps," the President has considerable discretion in using the carrot.

First, a major drug producing or drug-transit country must reach a bilateral or multilateral narcotics agreement with the United States and cooperate fully with the U.S. government in satisfying the agreement's goals. The statute contemplates an agreement with specific objectives: to reduce drug production, consumption, and trafficking within the country, and address illicit crop eradication and crop substitution. Under the agreement's terms, a nation must also increase drug interdiction and enforcement, drug education and treatment programs, cooperate with U.S. drug enforcement officials, and participate in extradition, mutual legal assistance, sharing of evidence, and other treaties aimed at drug enforcement. The country must also identify and eliminate illicit drug laboratories, as well as the trafficking of essential precursor chemicals used to produce illegal drugs. If a country has already been designated as a major drug producing or drug-transit country during the previous year, the President similarly cannot certify a country as cooperating fully with the United States unless that country enacts a bilateral or multilateral narcotics agreement. This requirement induces countries to enter into such an agreement.

Second, a country must cooperate fully with the United States to prevent illegal drug sales and transports to U.S. government personnel and their dependents. Unfortunately, the statute does not specify how a country is to prevent drugs from being sold to U.S. government personnel, particularly where a U.S. government official is determined to buy drugs. Certainly, a country cannot be expected to police the behavior of U.S. officials within a U.S. embassy, which is U.S. property, and where U.S. officials may enjoy diplomatic immunity.

Third, before the President certifies a major drug producing or drug-transit country, that country must also cooperate fully with the United States to prevent and punish the laundering of drug-related profits in that country. This requirement may prove especially difficult for smaller countries with limited law enforcement resources and little experience in prosecuting sophisticated white-collar crimes. Money laundering cases typically involve extensive and painstaking investigation. For example, it may be necessary to trace wire transfers of funds among banks around the world, which may require obtaining exemptions from applicable bank secrecy laws. These tasks are likely to require the assistance of bank regulators in relevant countries. Further, money laundering is a criminal offense requiring proof that the funds in question were generated by drug sales and that they were laundered.

The final requirement for certification takes aim at official corruption that often is connected with drug production and trade. A major drug producing or transit country must cooperate fully with the United States to prevent and punish bribery and other public corruption that facilitates the production, processing, and shipment of illegal drugs, or that discourages the investigation and prosecution of these acts. This requirement may prove difficult in a country whose government is riddled with corruption. "Clean" government officials may lack the political clout to punish bribery and other corrupt acts by "dirty" officials. Indeed, they may fear for their own lives. Even in a less extreme situation, rooting out corruption may be difficult.

The statute imposes one further requirement to obtain presidential certification, pertaining to a major drug producing or drug-transit country that produces licit opium. The opium producing country must take steps to prevent significant diversion of its licit cultivation and production into the illicit market, maintain production and stockpiles at levels no higher than those consistent with licit market demand, and prevent illicit cultivation and production. This requirement acknowledges the legitimate reasons for producing opium and induces countries to act against the illicit market.

Consider the 1997 certification of Mexico granted by President Clinton under the Foreign Assistance Act of 1961 ("1961 Assistance Act"), as amended. The President certified Mexico as a full partner in the U.S. war on drugs despite the arrest of Mexico's top antinarcotics law enforcement official on charges of collaboration with drug traffickers. The House of Representatives voted 251 to 175 against the President's certification, and the Senate voted ninety-four to five in favor of a non-binding resolution criticizing the certification. This congressional action was not surprising in the wake of the arrest. While the arrest signified that Mexico was making some progress, many members of Congress questioned the integrity of Mexico's entire law enforcement apparatus. Moreover, by 1996, more than half of all cocaine entering the United States came through Mexico. Mexico had become a major money laundering center even though it had introduced legislation to criminalize money laundering and fight organized crime.

However, the President's certification was foreseeable. The Clinton administration had invested considerable time and money in forging closer ties with Mexico and helping it develop economically through two controversial events: Mexico's inclusion in the North American Free Trade Agreement ("NAFTA") and the multi-billion dollar rescue package arranged for Mexico after its peso crisis. Politically, President Clinton was not in a position to reverse course and impose trade sanctions on Mexico. At the same time, the Republican Congress assuredly did not fail to point out Mexico's shortcomings in the war on drugs. The end result reflected this political stand-off.

The 1961 Assistance Act and 1986 Narcotics Act work in tandem, in a manner analogous to a cross-default clause in an international loan agreement. For example, suppose a country fails to obtain certification and does not qualify for the "vital national interests waiver," discussed below, under the 1961 Assistance Act. Because the certification and waiver criteria are similar to the criteria in the 1986 Narcotics Act, the country should not be certified under the 1986 Narcotics Act. The result would be a loss of foreign assistance and the imposition of trade sanctions under the 1961 Assistance Act.

The 1986 Narcotics Act provides guidance to the President in administering the above four certification criteria to determine whether the government of a major drug producing or transit country is cooperating fully with the United States, or making adequate efforts on its own in the war on drugs. The 1986 Narcotics Act lists eleven issues the President must consider when evaluating a government for potential certification. First, has the government of that country acted to effect "the maximum reductions in illicit drug production" that the U.S. government has determined to be achievable? Second, has the foreign government adopted judicial and law enforcement measures to eliminate illicit drug production and trafficking, as evidenced by seizures of drugs and illicit laboratories and prosecutions of violators? Third, has the foreign government adopted judicial and law enforcement measures to eliminate money laundering, as evidenced by the enactment of anti-money laundering laws and cooperation with U.S. anti-money laundering efforts? Fourth, has the foreign government adopted judicial and law enforcement measures to eliminate bribery and other forms of public corruption that facilitate drug production and trafficking and discourage investigation and prosecution? Fifth, has the foreign government, as a matter of policy, encouraged or facilitated the production or distribution of illegal drugs? Sixth, does any senior official of the foreign government engage in, encourage, or facilitate the production or distribution of illegal drugs? Seventh, has the foreign government aggressively investigated cases in which a U.S. drug enforcement official has been the victim of acts or threats of violence, inflicted by or in complicity with a law enforcement officer, and has the government "energetically sought to bring the perpetrators ... to justice?" Eighth, has the foreign government failed to provide reasonable cooperation to U.S. drug enforcement officials, including the refusal to allow these officials to pursue aerial smugglers a reasonable distance into the airspace of the foreign country? Ninth, has the foreign government revised its conspiracy and asset seizure laws to combat drug traffickers more effectively? Tenth, has the foreign government expeditiously processed U.S. extradition requests relating to drug traffickers? Finally, has the foreign government protected or granted safe haven to known drug traffickers?

While the President must consider these eleven questions in applying the certification criteria, the precise statutory language used to frame several of these questions leaves considerable room for the President to maneuver. For example, the second, third, and fourth questions contain the phrase "to the maximum extent possible." Thus, using the fourth question as an example, the President must decide whether a foreign government has taken measures against money laundering to the maximum extent possible. Similar flexible wording is contained in other questions. For instance, the sixth question uses the term "senior official" but does not define this term; the seventh question asks the President to determine whether a foreign government has investigated cases aggressively and brought perpetrators to justice energetically; the eighth question inquires about reasonable cooperation and a reasonable invasion of airspace; and the ninth question addresses expeditious processing of extradition requests. In sum, while the statute provides the President with a checklist of issues to consider in applying the certification criteria, this subjective checklist invites the President to exercise discretion.

Even if a country is a major drug producing or transit country and even if it fails to meet the four certification criteria, the country may still avoid the stick of sanctions under the 1986 Narcotics Act. This possibility depends upon whether, from the U.S. perspective, sanctions would be counterproductive. The President may determine and certify to Congress that the "vital national interests" of the United States require that it not apply sanctions.

Countries are likely to obtain a vital national interests waiver in five scenarios. For example, in 1987 and 1988, President Reagan found that Laos had failed to cooperate fully with the United States on narcotics control and to take adequate steps on its own. Nonetheless, he gave Laos a vital national interests certification in both years to promote continuing investigations of Americans missing in action and prisoners of the Vietnam War. Plainly, the United States has a unique issue to address with Laos that qualifies as a vital national interest. Second, suppose the non-certified country is a principal U.S. supplier of a precious commodity, and there is no other readily available substitute source. Examples include oil from Saudi Arabia, or certain minerals like uranium from countries such as Russia. The non-certified country's supplier status may effectively immunize it from sanctions. Third, suppose the non-certified country could inflict significant economic damage to U.S. businesses through a denial of market access or government procurement contracts. China would be an obvious example of a country that may be too big to penalize. A fourth category of non-certified country is one that might be too dangerous to penalize. Such a country may be able to inflict significant damage to American military and civilian personnel working abroad. Egypt and Turkey might be examples. Finally, consider a country in which the United States has too much invested to sanction. Surely Mexico, a partner in NAFTA, is a case in point.

Our trading partners may consider the 1986 Narcotics Act to be an imperialistic statute.

[T]he 1986 Narcotics Act focuses and visits blame entirely on drug-supplying countries. It pays no attention to the tremendous demand for drugs by Americans. Consider the statement of former Singapore Prime Minister Lee Kuan Yew: "Let me give you an example that encapsulates the whole difference between America and Singapore. America has a vicious drug problem. How does it solve it? It goes around the world helping other anti-narcotic agencies to try and stop the suppliers. It pays for helicopters, defoliating agents and so on. And when provoked, it captures the President of Panama and brings him to trial in Florida. Singapore does not have that option. We can't go to Burma and capture the warlords there. What we can do is pass a law which says that any customs officer or policeman who sees anybody in Singapore behaving suspiciously, leading him to suspect the person is under the influence of drugs, can require the man to have his urine tested. If the sample is found to contain drugs, the man immediately goes for treatment.... In America if you did that it would be an invasion of the individual's rights and you would be sued."

[Moreover,] even the State Department admits that some governments of drug-supplying countries lack the ability, assuming they have the will, to reduce or eliminate drug production in their territory. Consider the context in which the governments of Laos, Afghanistan, and Burma, all major heroin-producing countries, must lead an anti-heroin campaign. Laos has "a difficult geography, an impecunious central government that has delegated fiscal responsibility to regional entities and thus lost some measure of control, and a dependency on international institutions for external financing." In Afghanistan, years of warfare diverted government attention from the problem of poppy cultivation; without a vigorous central government, Afghanistan fell under the thumb of regional commanders who are akin to feudal warlords. Moreover, Afghanistan is plagued by a "devastated economy and a large refugee population." In Burma, the ruling State Law and Order Restoration Commission is hardly a sympathetic government. Insurgent armies in Burma control the poppy fields in areas largely out of the central government's reach. The Rangoon government allows poppy cultivation in return for peaceful coexistence with these armies.

Imagine the reaction in the United States if our trading partners enacted a converse piece of legislation. This hypothetical bill would mandate the identification and publication of major drug-consuming countries; the United States surely would be blacklisted. Such legislation would require the United States to cooperate fully with its trading partners to reduce drug demand or take steps on its own according to criteria set by our trading partners. These criteria would include creating drug rehabilitation programs, prosecution initiatives, and the commitment of specific budgetary allocations to support these efforts. Failure to satisfy these criteria could lead to denial of access to our trading partners' markets in key sectors like agriculture, services, and aviation. This hypothetical legislation, if enacted by a trading partner, would undoubtedly provoke outrage in the United States; however, the 1986 Narcotics Act is precisely this sort of legislation visited upon our partners.

————————

In 2011, Bolivian President Evo Morales called for the development of a certification process for drug consuming countries like the United States. "The origins of drug trafficking are in the demand, not the supply," said Morales. "So I'd like for some international organism to certify or decertify the United States for their responsibility on the issue of drug trafficking." CNN Wire Staff, *Morales Wants Drug Certification for U.S.*, CNN.com, Sept. 21, 2011. Morales's comments followed increased tensions between the two countries surrounding U.S. drug policy, including the 2008 expulsion of U.S. DEA agents and the U.S. ambassador from Bolivia. *See, e.g., Bolivia's Morales Insists No Return for US Drug Agency*, BBC News, Nov. 8, 2011.

D. Controlled Substances Laws in Comparative Perspective

As discussed above, almost every country in the world is party to one or more of the three major drug prohibition conventions. Nevertheless, within the boundaries of global prohibition, there is a diversity of approaches to domestic drug control, including a handful of policies that verge on a legal, regulated domestic market for some substances.

The relationship between domestic drug policies and drug usage is difficult to measure. Principles of supply and demand would seem to dictate that prohibition laws should result in lower usage of prohibited substances than a loosely regulated legal market. But the range of variables in domestic drug laws and the influence of cultural attitudes toward drug use make comparisons difficult. In 2008, the World Health Organization (WHO) conducted the first major cross-national evaluation of illegal drug use rates in all regions of the world. The study considered 17 countries and the findings did not indicate a significant correlation between the restrictiveness of a nation's drug laws and its drug use rates. The WHO researchers found that "countries with more stringent policies toward illegal drug use did not have lower levels of such use than countries with more liberal policies." Indeed, the report noted that the "United States stands out with higher levels of [drug] use ... despite punitive illegal drug policies[.]" Louisa Degenhardt et al., *Toward a Global View of Alcohol, Tobacco, Cannabis and Cocaine Use: Findings from the WHO, World Mental Health Surveys*, 5 PLOS MEDICINE 1053 (2008).

This section considers a sampling of different drug control policies. Though the apples-to-oranges quality of comparing drug laws may make it impossible to draw definitive conclusions about effectiveness, the material below provides a helpful perspective on the diverse set of policy options and philosophies that guide domestic drug control strategies.

1. The Dutch Marijuana Coffee Shops

What Can We Learn from the Dutch Cannabis Coffeeshop System?
Robert J. MacCoun
106 Addiction 1899 (2011)

In 1976 the Netherlands adopted a formal written policy of non-enforcement for violations involving possession or sale of up to 30 g of cannabis. The 'gateway theory' has long been seen as an argument for being tough on cannabis, but interestingly, the Dutch saw that concept as a rationale for allowing retail outlets to sell small quantities. Rather than seeing an inexorable psychopharmacological link between marijuana and hard drugs, the Dutch hypothesized that the gateway mechanism reflected social and economic networks, so that separating the markets would keep cannabis users out of contact with hard-drug users and sellers.

This essay examines what the available data can tell us about how these retail coffeeshop sales may have influenced cannabis use and its consequences. Three types of indicators are examined: the prevalence and intensity of cannabis use; market indicators, including prices, purity, seizures and enforcement; and treatment data as a partial indicator of harms to users. Other types of consequences (for public safety, public order, economic productivity, family life, health and personal enjoyment) are not examined because they are so difficult to quantify and because they pose such severe causal identification problems.

This essay does not seek to judge the Netherlands or critique its internal policy decisions—which as we will see are undergoing significant change. Rather, the goal is to see what other jurisdictions might learn about potential policy options and outcomes by drawing upon the Dutch experience and their energetic efforts to document their policies and outcomes. There are daunting analytical challenges in making cross-national comparisons of drug policies and outcomes, but if we want to identify more effective policies we need to make comparisons across jurisdictions, and it is surely better to make provisional judgments than provincial ones.

Although the numbers are currently dropping, the most recent systematic count identified around 700 retail cannabis outlets in the Netherlands—about one per 29,000 citizens (one per 3,000 in Amsterdam). The industry employs 3,000–4,000 workers, and the owners have their own union (the Bond van Cannabis Detaillisten). The shops sell somewhere between 50 and 150 metric tonnes of cannabis at a value of perhaps €300–600 million a year. They do not pay VAT—the European Court of Justice will not let them—but they pay various income and corporate taxes. It is estimated that a quarter of the 4–5 million tourists who visit Amsterdam visit a coffeeshop, and that 10% of them cite that as a reason why they came.

The Dutch experience is challenging to characterize, because it is a moving target. The Dutch policy has continued to evolve in response to internal and external political pressures as well as the nation's inherently pragmatic 'learning by doing' orientation to drug problems. In 1995, the 30-g limit was reduced to 5 g, and a 500-g limit was set for coffeeshop stocks. Since the late 1970s, a set of guidelines has emerged for regulating the technically illicit retail sales in open commercial establishments. As formalized by the Public Prosecution Service, coffeeshop owners are not to be prosecuted for selling cannabis provided that they comply with five rules (the so-called 'AHOJ-G' rules): (1) they may not sell more than 5 grams per person per day; (2) they may not sell ecstasy or other hard drugs; (3) they may not advertise drugs; (4) they must ensure that there is no nuisance in their vicinity; (5) they may not sell drugs to persons aged under 18 or even allow them on the premises.

The sale of cannabis will continue to be an offense. If the rules set out above are not observed, the premises are closed down and the owners or management may be prosecuted. Under the official drug guidelines, coffeeshops may stock up to 500 g of cannabis without facing prosecution. Municipalities may impose additional rules on coffeeshops in order to avoid nuisance.

Enforcement of these rules did not have real teeth until 1997, when officials began closing coffeeshops for non-compliance. Between 1997 and 2007, the number of retail cannabis outlets dropped 40%, from 1179 to 702.

In the past few years, the Dutch have had lively debates about the coffeeshop model. In 2008 the Netherlands banned tobacco smoking in the coffeeshops (and all other commercial establishments) and they have been closing shops located near schools. To eliminate the so-called 'backdoor' problem of legal inconsistency, some officials argue that municipalities or coffeeshop owners should be allowed to cultivate cannabis legally. In 2010, the European Court of Justice ruled that the town of Maastricht may ban foreigners from buying cannabis there.

However, the most significant development was the Dutch cabinet's announcement on 27 May 2011 that the coffeeshops would be run as private clubs for Dutch citizens. Memberships per club will probably be initially capped at 1500, and foreign visitors [even those from the European Union (EU)] will be excluded. As discussed in more detail below, this change will significantly impact the sizable 'drug tourist' market, and is likely to result in a significant reduction in the number of active coffeeshops. The proposed policy change is startling, because Dutch officials have long resisted international pressure, standing by the coffeeshop model as an expression of Dutch *gedoogcultuur* ('culture of permissiveness') and as a pragmatic 'least worst' solution.

So why this change, and why now? The Cabinet cited nuisance, sales to tourists and increases in problematic use by youth, but the complexities of recent coalition politics are probably a factor as well; in particular the rising influence of Geert Wilders' far-right party. The 2009 Lisbon treaty may also have played a role: Articles 83 and 86 allow for the establishment of a European Public Prosecutor's office that could pursue 'cross-border' crimes such as drug trafficking. What is striking is that the proposed policy shift would not actually eliminate the 'backdoor problem' that many see as an unworkable contradiction. Rather, the Dutch will have essentially internalized the contradiction, accepting it for their own citizens but no longer allowing it to influence foreigners.

When Reuter and I examined Dutch cannabis trends for the 1980s and 1990s, the data were very sparse and of uncertain comparability. In 2010 there are a great deal more relevant data, and are generally of better quality, due largely to the tremendous efforts of two international consortia, the European Monitoring Centre for Drugs and Drug Addiction (EMCDDA) and the semi-annual European School Survey Project on Alcohol and Other Drugs (ESPAD).

Table 1 (columns 2, 3 and 4) shows ESPAD and US (Monitoring the Future; MTF [20]) data for 15–16-year-old students. Three features of the prevalence data are noteworthy. First, the US rates exceed the Dutch rates, but they are roughly equivalent within sampling and measurement error. Secondly, both the United States and the Netherlands rank highly relative to most other nations. Thirdly, in recent years many European countries have rates of student marijuana use that either match or exceed the Dutch rate — including Italy, Belgium, Ireland, the United Kingdom, France and Switzerland.

Are Dutch youth more likely to try cannabis than they might be without the coffeeshop system? One way of addressing this question is to compare how Dutch youth rank relative to other European nations with respect to the use of other substances. Table 1 suggests that Dutch students do indeed rank higher for life-time prevalence of cannabis than for getting drunk or the use of other illicit drugs.

[A]s one might expect, Dutch youth report higher than average availability of cannabis. Nevertheless, they fall well short of the levels reported in the United States and some other countries, and the Dutch data fit right on the trend line.

By facilitating relatively easy access to cannabis, it is conceivable that the Dutch system might alter the intensity and duration of a cannabis using 'career'. Table 1 shows some evidence for this in student data. Dutch youth are somewhat more likely to have used frequently, and they are somewhat more likely to start using early (before age 13) compared to their European neighbors, and in this respect they bear a closer resemblance to students in the United States.

One might expect that Dutch citizens would be more likely to escalate from casual experimentation to regular use, but student data … show that the current use rate among Dutch students is quite close to what we would predict knowing only their life-time prevalence rates. When we include data for adults…, we find that the Dutch 'continuation rate' is actually lower than one would predict based on similar rates in other countries.

Regarding regular Dutch users, do they use more cannabis than they might in other countries with less availability? A comparison of regular users in Amsterdam and San

Table 1 Drug use and perceived availability among students aged 15–16 years, averaged for the years 2003 and 2007.

	Cannabis			Other				
	Life-time prevalence	Last year preva-lence	Past month preva-lence	Mean use 40+ times	Mean first use by age 13	Fairly/ very easy to obtain	Been drunk in past 12 months	Ever used other illicit drugs
Austria	19.0	15.0	8.0	3.0	4.0	33.5	62.5	9.5
Belgium	28.0	23.0	14.5	5.5	6.0	44.5	38.0	8.5
Bulgaria	21.5	16.5	7.5	3.0	3.5	38.5	50.5	6.5
Croatia	20.0	14.5	7.0	3.0	3.0	45.5	45.5	5.0
Cyprus	4.5	3.5	2.5	1.0	1.5	12.5	21.5	4.0
Czech Republic	44.5	35.5	18.5	8.0	7.5	62.0	58.0	10.0
Denmark	24.0	19.0	9.0	3.0	5.5	55.5	77.5	6.0
Estonia	24.5	16.5	6.0	2.5	4.5	28.5	55.0	9.5
Finland	9.5	7.0	2.5	0.5	1.5	15.5	54.5	3.0
France	34.5	27.5	18.5	7.5	8.0	44.5	32.5	9.0
Germany	23.5	18.0	9.5	3.5	7.5	39.5	55.5	9.5
Greece	6.0	5.0	2.5	1.0	1.0	21.0	31.5	4.0
Hungary	14.5	10.5	5.5	1.0	2.0	26.5	44.0	6.0
Ireland	29.5	23.0	13.0	5.5	7.5	51.5	59.5	9.5
Italy	25.0	20.5	14.0	5.5	4.0	40.0	32.0	8.5
Latvia	17.0	10.0	4.0	1.0	3.5	25.5	51.0	8.0
Lithuania	15.5	11.5	5.5	1.0	2.0	24.0	54.5	7.0
Malta	11.5	10.0	4.5	1.0	2.5	23.5	38.0	6.5
Netherlands	**28.0**	**24.0**	**14.0**	**6.5**	**7.0**	**45.5**	**41.0**	**6.5**
Norway	7.5	5.0	2.5	1.0	2.0	27.0	47.0	3.0
Poland	17.0	13.0	7.0	2.0	2.0	36.0	39.5	7.0
Portugal	14.0	11.5	7.0	2.5	3.5	29.0	27.0	6.5
Romania	3.5	2.0	0.5	0.0	0.0	11.0	31.0	2.5
Slovak Republic	29.5	22.0	10.5	3.5	6.0	50.5	53.5	7.5
Slovenia	25.0	20.5	11.5	4.5	6.0	51.0	49.5	6.5
Sweden	7.0	5.0	1.5	0.5	1.5	25.5	46.0	3.5
United Kingdom	33.5	26.5	15.5	7.0	11.0	54.5	62.5	9.0
United States	33.5	26.4	15.6	9.0	8.0	71.5	34.5	19.0
Mean	20.4	15.8	8.5	3.3	4.4	36.9	46.2	7.2
SD	10.4	8.5	5.3	2.6	2.7	15.3	12.8	3.2
Median	20.8	15.8	7.3	3.0	3.8	37.3	46.5	6.8

Source: Author's calculated averages using data from European School Survey Project on Alcohol and Other Drugs (ESPAD) (2003, 2007) and Monitoring the Future (MTF) (2003, 2007). MTF (2003 and 2007); Table 1 (life-time) 2 (last year), 3 (past month), 6 (risk), 13 (availability); ESPAD (2003, Table 28c; 2007, Tables 31A and 41A), MTP (2009, Tables 1–3, 6 and 12). SD: standard deviation.

Francisco found quite similar rates of self-reported use. The most common response in both Amsterdam (41%) and San Francisco (52%) was 'less than 2 grams' in the past 3 months, well short of the maximum allowed coffeeshop purchase (5 g). Almost all (89% in Amsterdam and 91% in San Francisco) reported using less than 15 g over 3 months.

Past-month prevalence, 2001

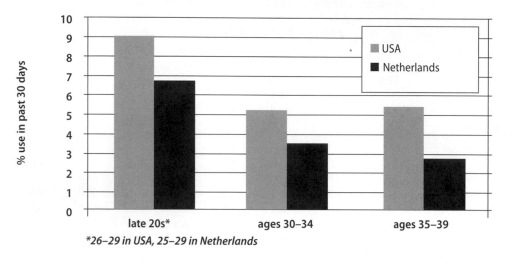

26–29 in USA, 25–29 in Netherlands

Last-year prevalence, 2005

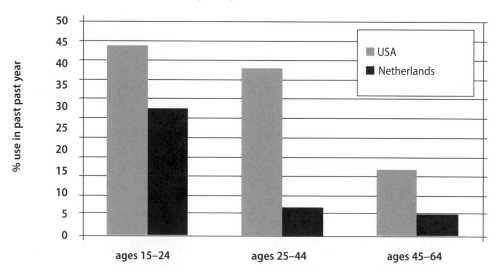

Figure 3 Past-month prevalence (2001) and last-year prevalence (2005) by age group. Sources: US data from National Survey on Drug Use and Health (NSDUH) 2001 and 2005 (Tale 20B); 2001 Dutch data from Abraham, Kaal & Cohen [2002; Centrum voor Drugsonderzoek (CEDRO); Table 4.5]; 2005 Dutch data from Rodenburg *et al.* [Addiction Research Institute Rotterdam (IVO), 207 [23], Table; 4.3]

One might also expect that the ready availability would serve to extend the length of a using career. Figure 3 examines this issue using Dutch national surveys in 2001 (top panel) and 2005 (bottom panel). Both comparisons tell the same basic story: Dutch users appear to 'mature out' of cannabis use at a faster rate than their American counterparts.

As noted earlier, a key part of the rationale for the Dutch coffeeshop system was the hypothesis that 'separating the markets' would weaken the statistical 'gateway' association between cannabis and hard drug use.... The estimates all suggest that cocaine and amphetamine use are below what one would predict for the Netherlands. Although hardly conclusive, these data are consistent with the notion that the coffeeshop system might 'weaken the gateway'.

Reuter and I have suggested that the Dutch cannabis system emerged in two phases, with distinct effects—an initial 'depenalization' phase with no detectable effects on cannabis use, and a second phase (approximately 1984 and 1996) in which the percentage of 18–20-year-olds who had ever used cannabis rose from 15% to 44%, with past-month prevalence rising from 8.5% to 18.5%. During this latter period, prevalence trends were either flat or declining in the United States, Oslo, Catalunya, Stockholm, Denmark, Germany, Canada and Australia. We characterized this period as the Dutch 'commercialization era', arguing that it was plausibly attributable to the rapid expansion of retail cannabis outlets, at least in Amsterdam. The differences between Amsterdam and smaller Dutch cities were more pronounced than one sees in urban-non-urban comparisons for the United States, perhaps due to Amsterdam's disproportionately large share of the coffeeshops in the Netherlands.

This commercialization thesis has been debated in the literature. The available data fall far short of what contemporary methodological standards require for strong causal inference, but there is simply no other source of evidence on the effects of tolerated retail sales of cannabis in modern times, and we have argued that a commercialization effect is both theoretically plausible and arguably consistent with evidence from experiences with the commercialization of tobacco, alcohol and gambling.

Between 1997 and 2005, past-year use among Dutch 15–24-year-olds declined from 14.3 to 11.4% during a period when other European countries (Germany, Spain, Italy and Sweden) were seeing increases. Although it is difficult to establish causation, this pattern is also consistent with the commercialization thesis, because the legal age for coffeeshop purchases was raised from 16 to 18 years in 1996, and the number of cannabis coffeeshops dropped nearly 40%, from 1179 in 1997 to 729 in 2005.

One might expect a decline in the number of coffeeshops to be a response to declining prevalence, rather than a cause, but this is unlikely to be the primary story. First, it is doubtful that 'drug tourism' was declining during this period. Secondly, the majority of coffeeshop closings were due to complaints or violations of the AHOJ-G rules rather than economic considerations.

Fewer shops meant less visibility and salience and greater search time and hassle for customers.

Statistically, perhaps the most distinctive feature of Dutch cannabis use is that their users seem to have a higher likelihood of being admitted to treatment for cannabis use than is true for most countries in Europe. It is difficult to know how to interpret this high treatment rate. It could reflect a greater need for cannabis treatment in the Netherlands, but that is difficult to reconcile with their relatively modest cannabis continuation rates (relative to Europe) and quantities consumed (at least relative to San Francisco).

One possibility is that the Dutch are more generous and proactive in providing treatment. Reuter estimates that the Dutch government spends about €9200 per 'problematic drug user' on treatment; the comparable estimate for Sweden—a country with an active coerced treatment tradition—is approximately €7600.

[I]t appears that on a per-capita basis, the United States has about four marijuana treatment admissions for every Dutch admission; on a per past-month user basis the ratio is 1.8 : 1. About half the US admissions are criminal justice referrals versus about 10% of the Dutch admissions. If we exclude these referrals, we end up with six admissions per 1000 past-month users in each country, so it appears that users are more likely to find their way into treatment in the United States than in the Netherlands, but that the difference is probably attributable to the much greater use of criminal justice referrals in the United States.

It is very likely that full-scale legalization would significantly reduce cannabis prices. The Dutch do not have a true legalization regime; it is best characterized as *de facto* legalization, and even then only at the retail level.

The 'typical' retail price reported by government officials circa 2007 (UNODC [41]), was about $7 per gram of cannabis herb in the Netherlands, slightly higher than in Spain ($4), lower than the United States ($10) and considerably lower than in Norway ($27). It is not clear how officials in each country generate these estimates, or whether they do so in a similar way. The comparisons are muddied further by the stark difference in policy between the Netherlands and the other nations.

Two recent studies provide more rigorous estimates of Dutch prices on a purity-adjusted basis. Pijlman and colleagues estimates that for 2004, the average Euros-per-gram price was 6 for Nederwiet, 4.9 for imported marijuana, 12.5 for Nederhasj (hashish produced in the Netherlands) and 6.6 for imported hashish. This is in the $6 to $15 range per gram for 2004. Hazekamp found prices in the €5–9 per gram range—about $6–11 per gram. (All but two of his 13 samples were less than the advertised 10 g.) Across the two studies, the 9-D-tetrahydrocannabinol (THC) content ranged from 7% (imported marijuana, at $5.88 per gram) to 39% (Nederhasj, priced at $39 per gram). Prices ranged from around $3.50 to $8.50 per 100 mg THC.

Synthesizing price data from the System to Retrieve Information from Drug Evidence (STRIDE), the National Survey on Drug Use and Health (NSDUH) and *High Times* magazine, Gettman suggests that the typical price per gram in the United States circa 2005 was around $7.87. Using a more elaborate structural estimation model, Caulkins & Lumibao estimate that a more accurate figure for 2005 would be around $4.81, and possibly as low as $3. (A third estimate falls in between, at $5.78.) US samples of seized marijuana in 2005 averaged 8.14% THC. This implies a price per 100 mg of THC of around $6.41 (using Gettman's price estimate) to $3.92 (using the Caulkins & Lumibao price estimate).

Under the Gettman estimate, 2005 prices were comparable for Dutch Nederwiet and US marijuana herb on a per-gram basis, but the Dutch product was cheaper on a purity-adjusted basis. Using the Caulkins & Lumbibao estimate, the Dutch and US prices were roughly comparable on a purity-adjusted basis, but the US price would actually be lower on a per-gram basis. Differences in sampling and statistical analysis make these comparisons very approximate; US consumers also buy less often in larger packages, receiving a quantity discount.

Why are the Dutch prices so high in a quasi-legalization regime—does this indicate that legalization has no effect on prices? The Dutch price data include retailer mark-ups to cover the costs the owners incur in operating retail outlets in commercial neighborhoods. However, it is also likely that prices in the Netherlands are elevated by their unusual hybrid regime which approximates legalization at the user level, but European style prohibition at the level of the growers and traffickers—with coffeeshop owners in a gray area somewhere between. If high-level Dutch traffickers face an enforcement risk, they presumably pass this along in higher prices down the supply chain.

It is extremely difficult to find good comparative data on the stringency of enforcement against cannabis growers and traffickers anywhere in Europe. In 2004, roughly 40% of Opium Act cases were for 'soft' drugs (primarily cannabis); they accounted for about 2% of the total detention years imposed that year. Figure 6 shows that by a less direct measure — convictions for any drug offenses (averaged for 4 years to reduce noise) — the Dutch are more lenient than many but by no means all their neighbors. Unfortunately, these figures are not broken out by drug or specific criminal charge.

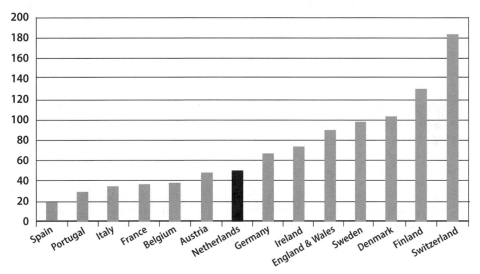

Figure 6 People convicted of drug offenses per 1000 citizens, averaged for 2000–2003 in varous European nations. Source: author's calculations using data from European Sourcebook of Criminal Justice Statistics, Table 3.2.1.12.

During the years 2005–07, the Dutch seized about 37 kg of herbal cannabis per 100 000 citizens, about the same as the United Kingdom (38 kg/100,000) and well above the seizure rates for Denmark, Finland, France, Germany, Italy, Portugal, Spain and Sweden (0.7–6.8 kg/100,000). This could reflect aggressive Dutch enforcement, the sheer amount of herbal cannabis available to seize, or both. At best, we can take these data — together with routine reports of particular police actions in the Dutch media — as an existence of proof that the Dutch are clearly enforcing prohibition at the higher end of the supply chain. This presumably raises prices for consumers.

The impact of the Dutch system on other countries has been a constant source of contention, especially in the EU. More than a million tourists a year may have been visiting the coffeeshops, and an even larger amount of cannabis is exported from the Netherlands by professional traffickers.

Data on drug tourism and smuggling are too sparse to permit a direct statistical test of Dutch influence. A weaker test is geographic: across 12 nations (Belgium, Denmark, Finland, France, Germany, Italy, Norway, Portugal, Spain, Sweden, Switzerland and the United Kingdom) there is an inverse association ($r = -0.50$) between students' perceptions of availability (see Table 1) and the distance from the center of their country to the center of the Netherlands; but this simply reflects shared features of culture and geography: it turns out that perceived availability within a nation is better predicted by its proximity to Portugal, Belgium, France, Switzerland or the United Kingdom (rs ranging from -0.74 to -0.59) than by proximity to the Netherlands.

While it seems likely that the coffeeshop system has facilitated the development of a cannabis export industry, the nature and extent of that linkage is not entirely clear. The coffeeshop supply system certainly facilitates production and reduces suppliers' risks, but less so than one might expect in a true legal market, and the Netherlands might be a significant cannabis exporter even without a coffeeshop system. The Dutch are a leading horticultural exporter; they are near the geographic midpoint of western Europe; they have perhaps the busiest railway system in the EU and the busiest port (Rotterdam) in Europe, and the Netherlands is a prominent European exporter of other drugs that are fully prohibited by Dutch law and policy. It may be easier to infer the impact the coffeeshop model has had on other countries a few years after tourist sales have ended.

Whether the Dutch should go forward with some variant of this coffeeshop model in the future is uncertain, and Dutch citizens may feel it is none of our business anyway. However, the Dutch experience is potentially informative for people in other countries who are debating whether to legalize cannabis sales. The best available evidence paints a nuanced picture. Dutch citizens use cannabis at more modest rates than some of their neighbors, and they do not appear to be particularly likely to escalate their use relative to their counterparts in Europe and the United States. Moreover, there are indications that rather than increasing 'the gateway' to hard drug use, separating the soft and hard drug markets possibly reduced the gateway.

However, the Dutch experience also raises some cautionary notes. There are several lines of circumstantial evidence that the Dutch retail system increased consumption, especially in its early years when coffeeshops were spreading, open to 16-year-olds and advertised more visibly than they do today. If so, this increase occurred in a hybrid system in which high-level enforcement probably served to keep prices from dropping the way they might in a full-scale legalization scheme. Many people look to the Netherlands as a model for what might happen if cannabis were legalized, but what the Dutch have done is quite different, and far more nuanced, than the kind of full-scale legalization that is usually debated in other countries. The Dutch system is ambiguous by design, and it is ambiguous in ways that give officials leverage over prices and sales in ways that might be far harder to achieve in a full-scale legalization regime.

2. Drug Treatment Courts and Portugal's Decriminalization Law

The Decriminalization Option: Should States Consider Moving from a Criminal to a Civil Drug Court Model?
Alex Kreit
2010 University of Chicago Legal Forum 299

Today, we have over two thousand drug courts in the United States, a number that ... is likely to increase in the coming years along with the expanding budget.

Drug courts vary widely in the details of their operations, but in essence they allow some drug offenders to obtain treatment under the close supervision of a drug court in place of a traditional sentence. Drug courts are designed to be nonadversarial, with the prosecutor, defense attorney, and judge working together for the goal of promoting public safety. Drug court judges typically monitor and evaluate defendants through regular status hearings, frequent drug and alcohol testing, and other methods. If a drug court participant fails to comply with program requirements—by, for example, testing positive for drugs—the judge may impose sanctions. These sanctions are generally imposed on a graduated basis and can range from the imposition of work detail or community service to brief jail sentences to termination from the program. Judges can likewise reward participants who are on track with intermediate benefits, such as complimentary public transportation passes.

In 1997, the National Association of Drug Court Professionals, in partnership with the U.S. Department of Justice, formalized this basic structure by publishing a report with "ten key components" for drug courts and requiring state and local drug courts to abide by them in order to be eligible for federal funding. Beyond these ten components, however, there is a wide diversity in the operation of drug courts. In terms of procedural posture drug courts can be grouped into three basic models: (1) pre-plea/pre-adjudication, (2) post-plea/pre-adjudication, and (3) post-adjudication. In the first category, prosecution is deferred while the defendant goes through the drug court process. A defendant will typically be required to waive certain procedural rights (such as the right to a speedy trial), but will retain her right to challenge the charge against her should she fail to complete the program and be returned to a traditional court. In the "post-plea/pre-adjudication" scenario, a guilty plea is part of the price of admission into the drug court, but the plea is held in abeyance during the defendant's participation in the program. If the defendant succeeds in the drug court, the charge will be dismissed, but if she fails, the plea is entered and a sentence is imposed. Finally, in the post-adjudication model, a defendant pleads guilty and is convicted. The sentence is then suspended pending the successful completion of the drug court program. Some post-adjudication programs provide a method for a successful defendant to have her record expunged. In others, however, a successful defendant will escape imposition of the suspended sentence but will still have a conviction on her record.

Eligibility requirements also vary significantly from court to court, though typically a defendant who wishes to gain entry into a drug court program must be charged with drug possession or another nonviolent offense and must demonstrate that she has a substance abuse problem.

For all their differences, perhaps the most important quality that unites American drug courts is that they are uniformly a part of the criminal system. Drug possession remains criminalized and those caught with drugs are arrested and processed by the police as usual. Drug court programs only enter the picture at this stage, offering a way out for individuals who are facing a prison sentence or who would simply prefer not to have a criminal record. In every instance—whether pre-plea or post-adjudication—the threat of a criminal sanction hangs over the treatment process, and judges are responsible for meting out graduated sanctions. As a result, within the drug court system, "the court, rather than treatment center, becomes the focal point of the treatment process." Similarly, though drug courts operate on the premise that drug addiction is a disease that should be treated and not punished, criminal sanctions ultimately await those who fail the program and those who either choose not to participate or are excluded from participating.

[U.S. d]rug courts appear to have been born primarily out of necessity. As drug war arrests and prosecutions reached a crescendo in the late 1980s, many urban court and prison systems were having a hard time keeping pace. Drug courts were conceived as a method for helping to control rapidly increasing court caseloads and prison populations. But as the courts spread during the early 1990s, drug court advocates began to look beyond the immediate benefits in managing caseloads and jail populations and focused their attention on drugs courts as a potentially more effective and therapeutic alternative to the status quo.

Today, most drug court advocates view them as both a less expensive method for processing low-level drug offenders through the criminal justice system and a more humane and effective approach to addressing the problem of substance abuse than conventional options. Whatever faults that drug courts may have, there does appear to be a fairly broad consensus for the proposition that drug courts produce better results than incarceration and at a reduced cost. Various studies have found that drug courts reduce criminal justice and victimization costs as compared to incarceration or even simple probation, and others have found long-term savings have been achieved in counties where drug court programs have been instituted. An analysis in California, for example, found that the drug courts studied cost only $3,000 on average per client while generating an average savings of $11,000 per client in reductions in recidivism and costs to victims. A systemic review of drug court research by the Government Accountability Office (GAO) in 2005 found that the studies showed net benefits ranging from $1,000 to $15,000 per drug court participant. As the 2009 National Drug Control Strategy put it when summarizing the research into the efficacy of drug courts, "Over a decade of drug court research shows that drug courts work better than jail or prison."

[In sum], there is a great deal of evidence that when it comes to dealing with low-level drug offenders, drug courts are less expensive and far more effective than incarceration. And yet, drug courts that operate within the criminal system are still a very cumbersome way to address the underlying concerns in this area: drug demand, drug abuse, and drug addiction.

The criminal prohibition of the possession and distribution of small quantities of controlled substances turns all drug users into criminals, whether or not they are addicted, violent, or otherwise law abiding. A substantial percentage of drug users, however, do not have a drug abuse problem and will never develop one. Indeed, the available evidence shows that most people who use an illegal drug will stop using entirely within five years. Many more will continue to use drugs regularly or sporadically without any negative impact on their lives. And, even among users who do go on to abuse drugs (including alcohol), many will simply outgrow the problem without treatment. Of course, someone who is arrested for drug possession or sale is more likely than the average user to suffer from an abuse or addiction problem. A person who has an addiction or abuse problem may be more likely to engage in risky behavior that would lead them to encounter the police and be arrested for drug possession. And a drug abuser is more likely to be in possession of a controlled substance at any given time than a casual user simply because someone who abuses or is addicted to drugs will use and carry them more frequently. Nevertheless, in any system that criminalizes the possession, cultivation, and distribution of small quantities of controlled substances, a substantial percentage of those who are arrested and prosecuted will inevitably be nonaddicts and nonabusers.

For these reasons, drug courts that operate within the criminal justice system run into the problem of overinclusiveness and run the risk of funneling nonaddicts into treatment that they don't need. Not surprisingly, then, drug courts often require would-be participants to have either tested positive for drugs or to demonstrate that they suffer from an abuse problem in order to gain entry. These requirements are undermined, however, by the relative ease with which an individual can fake an abuse or addiction problem and by incentives that tend to result in the admission of nonaddicts into drug court programs.

Nonaddicted defendants will often have a very strong motivation to embellish the extent of their use in order to prove that they have an abuse problem and become eligible to participate in a drug court. This is because, for an individual without addiction or abuse problems, a drug court will often be a far more preferable alternative to a drug conviction. Even if the punishment a person is facing is relatively minimal, an otherwise law-abiding recreational drug user will generally have an especially strong interest in avoiding a drug conviction. A drug conviction carries with it a wide array of collateral legal consequences (in addition to the social stigma associated with a criminal conviction), including the loss of a range of federal benefits and professional licenses. A non-addict, who may be a student or have a regular job, is likely to be more concerned with these types of consequences than someone who is suffering from an abuse or addiction problem and living on the margins of society. At the same time, participating in a drug court program is a low-risk endeavor for a nonaddict because he will not have much difficulty passing drug tests and adhering to other program requirements. As one commentator put it: "Defendants understand that they have to play the treatment game to pass through the criminal hoops." And, because addiction and abuse are imprecise disorders the diagnosis of which will typically depend on an individual's self-reported behavior, it would be difficult to stop a determined defendant from entering a drug court program under false pretenses even in a system that was firmly dedicated to weeding out nonaddicts.

At the same time, despite the letter of their eligibility requirements, drug courts generally have a very strong interest in admitting nonaddicted clients. This is because drug courts rely on funding that is contingent, implicitly or explicitly, upon demonstrating results and treating a sufficient number of defendants. Indeed, a substantial amount of anecdotal evidence indicates that many drug courts actively seek out "low-risk" nonaddicted clients and do their best to "skim" high-risk clients away from their programs in order to boost their success rate. Many drug court gatekeepers may also have less self-interested reasons for admitting nonaddicts. [A National Association of Criminal Defense Lawyers] report recounted the testimony of a drug court judge who "favors opening the door 'as wide as we can' because 'treatment court is the best game in town.'"

Few studies have attempted to quantify the prevalence of drug court participants who do not have addiction or abuse problems within drug court programs. Drug court studies that have attempted to assess rates of drug dependency among participants, however, indicate that a substantial number of drug court clients do not have a substance use disorder. One team of researchers that has measured drug dependency in drug court found that "nearly one half of misdemeanor drug court clients, one third of felony drug court clients, and two thirds of pretrial clients in a drug treatment and monitoring program produced 'sub-threshold' drug composite scores on the Addiction Severity Index."

An examination of past-month use rates of individuals entering treatment from the Substance Abuse and Mental Health's Treatment Episode Data Set suggests that the findings in the handful of individual studies to address the issue are not anomalous. The data set includes the frequency of a treatment client's drug use prior to entering treatment for his or her primary drug substance of abuse, as well as the person or entity responsible for referring the client to the program. Looking at the frequency of use by referral type from the most recent available year (2007) reveals that an unusually large number of individuals referred to treatment by the criminal justice system had used their primary substance of supposed abuse either not at all or only rarely within the month before entering treatment. Specifically, 38 percent of individuals who entered treatment because of a referral from a state or federal court had not used drugs at all within the past month. Another 17 percent had only used their primary substance of abuse one to three times in the one month prior to entering treatment. That means 55 percent of all individuals who were referred to treatment by a court program had used their primary drug of abuse less than three times in the month before they entered into treatment. By comparison, only 21 percent of individuals who referred themselves to treatment had used their primary drug of abuse less than three times in the past month.

These statistics are, of course, inherently limited in their ability to tell us the total number of drug court participants who do not have a genuine abuse or addiction problem. It is certainly possible, for example, for a person to suffer from a substance abuse or addiction problem without having used (or having used only infrequently) within the month prior to their admission into treatment. Similarly, some criminal justice treatment clients might be motivated to conceal their use or to scale back their use before entering treatment in order to demonstrate their compliance to the court. While these statistics cannot tell us the scope of the overinclusiveness problem with specificity, however, the abnormally large number of criminal justice treatment clients who had used three times or fewer prior to entering treatment seems to provide strong corroboration for the general proposition that a not-insubstantial number of drug court participants do not have a substance abuse or addiction problem. Rather, these individuals are gaming the system and entering treatment not because they have any need for it but because it is a preferable alternative to the punishment they would otherwise receive.

It is self-evident, of course, that sending an individual who does not have a drug abuse or addiction problem to receive drug treatment is not an efficient use of scarce and costly drug treatment resources. Processing nonaddicts through the machinery of drug courts— including regular drug testing, drug court appearances, and other requirements—is also unlikely to provide significant benefits in return for the investment. Indeed, participation in drug court programs may be counterproductive for nonaddicted defendants since meeting program requirements are likely to interfere with their work and family responsibilities. Because drug courts generally attempt to tailor their treatment regimens to the participant, it is worth noting that low-risk offenders without abuse problems may cost drug courts less than the average drug court participant. And drug courts are still less expensive than incarceration. This fact, however, is precisely why there is unlikely to be a solution to the overinclusiveness problem within criminal drug courts. As long as treatment or typical criminal justice solutions like incarceration are the only options, drug courts will be seen as the most cost-effective option for low-risk defendants, even those who do not have substance abuse problems.

Even if criminal drug courts may have their shortcomings, it does not necessarily mean that they are not our best option. Drug use—along with abuse and addiction—has existed in almost every society in recorded history. There is no silver bullet that will solve the problem of drug abuse and addiction, and any system that we design is going to involve trade-offs.

The inefficiencies discussed above, however, seem to be preventable problems that flow primarily from a single source: the criminalization of drug use and abuse. Because drug courts are located within the criminal system, they put individuals who are caught in possession of drugs to a choice between a drug court treatment program and the (more costly and less effective) traditional criminal penalty. In some cases, this choice will lead defendants who do not have a drug abuse problem and are unlikely to develop one to obtain treatment they do not need to avoid the punishment they would otherwise face. In others, defendants who might benefit from a detailed course of treatment or a brief medical consultation about their substance use are counseled by their attorneys not to enter drug court programs because the punishment they face does not justify the risks or burdens of drug court. As a result, drug courts can, in some instances, waste scarce treatment resources on those without drug problems while allowing others who truly need treatment to pass through the system without so much as speaking with a treatment or addiction specialist.

That criminal drug courts retain these inefficiencies is not surprising. Criminal laws against possession of small quantities of drugs for personal use are not really concerned with possession itself or even with drug use generally. They exist in order to address the problems of drug abuse and drug addiction—problems that are medical in nature and that only affect a small percentage of those in possession of drugs. As a result, criminal laws against possession of small drug quantities are a very imprecise method for addressing the chief problem with which they are concerned.

[Recent experience in Portugal suggests that a civil drug court system may offer advantages over criminal drug courts.]

Under Portugal's law, passed nearly a decade ago, simple possession of small amounts of drugs is no longer a crime. And yet, the possession and use of drugs remains subject to close scrutiny by the Portuguese government.

A brief overview of Portugal's system is instructive. Beginning in July of 2001, Portugal implemented a "decriminalization model" for drug users. The law removes criminal penalties for the purchase, possession, and cultivation of all drugs for personal-use quantities, which the law defines as an amount sufficient for ten days' usage for one person. The sale of drugs in any quantity, meanwhile, remains illegal in Portugal.

What distinguishes Portugal's approach from the traditional decriminalization model is what happens to users who are caught with drugs in personal-use amounts. Rather than receiving no penalty or being given a fine, individuals who are found in possession of personal-use quantities of drugs are referred into what we might think of as a civil drug court system. Because drug possession has been decriminalized, when a police officer in Portugal encounters a person under the quantity limit, she is not permitted to make an arrest. Instead, she issues a citation for the person in possession of drugs to appear before what the law calls a "dissuasion panel." Typically, a person will appear before the commission within seventy-two hours of receiving the citation.

Dissuasion panels are organized to be as nonadversarial in nature as possible. They are made up of three members—typically two people from the medical or social services fields and one attorney. The panels meet with the individuals who appear before them in order to try to assess their treatment needs and to assist them in addressing any abuse or addiction problems. The "offender" is not represented by counsel when he appears before the commission, though he does have the right to request a therapist of his choice to take part in the proceedings or to have a medical examination conducted to aid in the panel's review.

One of the primary objectives of the dissuasion panel structure is to try to foster a supportive atmosphere that is focused exclusively on the health of the offender. Every effort is made to guard against creating an impression that the panels are there to assess guilt or that drug usage is morally blameworthy conduct. So, for example, the commission members sit at a table with the offender, as opposed to behind an elevated bench as in a courtroom.

Consistent with this approach, the dissuasion panel has a good deal of flexibility in terms of how it will handle cases where an individual appears to have an abuse or addiction problem. If, however, the panel determines that an offender is a nonaddicted consumer of drugs with no prior offenses, the law requires it to suspend proceedings and impose no sanction. This is the result in approximately 80 percent of all proceedings. Of course, in these cases the panel still has the opportunity to talk with and advise the individual about drug addiction and abuse issues as part of the meeting.

For offenders who do not fall into the dismissal category, the panels can take a range of action, including issuing a warning to the offender, requiring the offender to check in with the panel at specified times, ordering the offender to enter into a treatment program, and even banning the offender from visiting certain places or associating with certain people. The panels can also impose a fine, but the law provides that fines are to be imposed as a last resort. The more common course with regard to a fine is that a panel may order treatment or some other sanction along with a fine, but suspend the fine contingent upon meeting the required treatment. Because drug possession has been decriminalized, the panels cannot, under any circumstances, impose prison sentences or even send someone to treatment through civil commitment—instead fines are the only mechanism for enforcing compliance with orders to seek treatment.

Portugal's decriminalization law was, perhaps unsurprisingly, strongly criticized by United States and United Nations drug enforcement officials and in the international press. Critics worried that the country would become a destination for "drug tourism." Nearly ten years later, however, these fears have not been realized and Portugal's program appears to have been quite successful at reducing the harms associated with drug use in a cost-effective manner. A 2009 CATO Institute Report on Portugal's decriminalization policy by Glenn Greenwald concluded that "usage has declined in many key categories and drug-related social ills have been far more contained in a decriminalized regime." There has, for example, been a substantial decline in HIV infections among drug users, with instances of new cases dropping from 1,400 to 400. Likewise, drug overdose deaths dropped from 400 to 290. Meanwhile, the reforms have helped to alleviate some of the burdens on Portugal's criminal justice system and contributed to progress in addressing prison overcrowding. The savings in criminal justice spending has allowed Portugal to increase its treatment capacity and helped lead to a 147 percent increase in the number of people in substitution treatment from 1999 to 2003.

Joao Castel-Branco Goulao, the director of Portugal's principal drug policy agency— the Instituto da Droga e da Toxicodependencia—is careful to emphasize that he does not believe decriminalization by itself has been the driving force behind the successes of Portugal's model. Rather, in his view, decriminalization has provided Portugal with a framework for the noncriminal dissuasion commission system to operate and to treat drug supply and demand as distinct problems. By detaching drug use from the criminal justice system and treating the issue through a civil system, Portugal was able to create an atmosphere in which addiction is viewed purely as a medical and public health problem.

While the available studies indicate that Portugal's decriminalization law has been successful on its own terms, there has been little discussion of what the benefits and drawbacks of such a system might be in comparison to other approaches. [There is good reason to believe that a] civil drug court system similar to Portugal's, in which possession of personal-use quantities of drugs has been decriminalized and those found in possession are given medical consultations before civil panels, is likely to be more cost effective than [the] criminal drug court model.

A civil drug court like Portugal's model would remedy the overinclusiveness problem of spending treatment resources on those who do not need them. When drug courts are incorporated within the criminal justice system, drug court treatment programs exist only as an alternative to the traditional penalty the offender would otherwise face. As a result, drug defendants who do not have an abuse or addiction problem often have a strong incentive to enter into treatment through drug courts whether or not they truly need it. Moving drug courts from the criminal to civil system would squarely address this problem by allowing the court or treatment panel to base the outcome in each case entirely on the individual's treatment needs. Those without abuse or addiction problems—who constitute a substantial majority of offenders—could be sent on their way with nothing more than a warning and a consultation, accompanied by information about the benefits of cessation and how to recognize the early signs of addiction in their own behavior. Nonaddicted defendants, in turn, would no longer have an incentive to exaggerate their drug use. Because there are few, if any, conceivable benefits from treating or punishing individuals in this category of offenders, this would yield substantial cost savings over criminal drug courts while incurring minimal additional costs.

While the flexibility of a decriminalized drug court system may provide some substantial benefits over the rigidity of our current criminal drug court model, critics may counter that any benefits ... would be outweighed by losses from removing the deterrent value of the criminal justice system. Deterrence-based objections to a civil drug court system might proceed on two fronts. First, some might argue that removing criminal penalties for possession of small amounts of drugs would lead to an increase in new and casual drug users who may presently be dissuaded by the possibility of criminal punishment. Second, some might argue that treatment courts will not be as effective if judges are unable to deter bad behavior through the use of short jail stints to punish those who slip up or the threat of a prison sentence for those who fail the programs entirely.

The fear that decriminalization may lead to an increase in use, particularly by new users, while understandable in theory, is belied by the experience in Portugal. In the decade since Portugal enacted its decriminalization policy, drug use rates in the country have largely remained stable or declined. Use rates among the key demographics of thirteen to fifteen-year-olds and sixteen to eighteen-year-olds fell by approximately 4 and 6 percent respectively in the years following decriminalization in Portugal.

The argument that removing drug courts' access to criminal sanctions will diminish their ability to incentivize treatment is a more serious and realistic concern. For example, in his insightful book *When Brute Force Fails*, Mark Kleiman points to the successes of an innovative probation program in Hawaii as evidence that a regime with increased drug testing and criminal sanctions may be more effective that current models that focus on treatment at the outset. In the program, named Hawaii's Opportunity Probation with Enforcement (HOPE), a state judge tired of probation violations put problem probationers on a strict program in which any violation—from a failed drug test to a missed appointment—would result in an immediate but short jail sentence. The results were impressive, with a decrease of over 90 percent in the violation rates of program participants and rearrest rates less than half than the comparison group. Kleiman argues that the lesson to be learned from Project HOPE is that successful diversion programs should include "frequent drug tests and quick and consistent sanctions for failure to comply."

Although the HOPE program persuasively demonstrates that sanctions can be a successful tool for problem probationers, evidence on the effectiveness of sanctions in drug court programs remains inconsistent. While some studies have shown sanctions to be effective, others have found that they have little, if any, effect. A study in Clark County, Nevada, for example, even indicated that imposing sanctions was associated with higher rearrest rates and lower graduation rates.

The inconsistent evidence may be due, in part, to differences in the make-up of offenders in the studies. Specifically, sanctions for failed drug tests might be expected to be more effective in deterring use in programs that include large percentages of individuals without drug abuse or addiction problems. This is because those without addiction or abuse problems are better able to abstain from drug use and more likely to respond more rationally to threats of punishment than are addicts. In assessing the implications of the HOPE program and the usefulness of sanctions, then, it is important to consider that HOPE's participants were not primarily drug offenders, but rather felony probationers who had been convicted of a wide range of offenses—from sexual assault and burglary to drug dealing—and were facing five- to ten-year prison terms. Likewise, the program's aim was to reduce probation violations, not address substance abuse or addiction problems. Accordingly, while HOPE provides strong evidence that incorporating swift and certain sanctions for probation violations is an effective method for deterring such violations and recidivism among serious felony offenders, it does not necessarily mean that the availability of sanctions provides better outcomes among drug court populations. This is not to say that sanctions may not be an effective method for persuading some drug addicts to stay on track in drug court programs, only that we should be careful not to overstate their importance.

Even if we grant that the deterrent effect of sanctions is likely to help some drug court participants stay on track, civil drug courts may offer other benefits that would counter the loss of a deterrent effect and leave treatment success rates unchanged. In particular, a civil drug court system modeled after Portugal's might be able to achieve better outcomes for some participants than a coercion-based system. There is a wealth of evidence that indicates internal motivation to be a strong predictor of treatment success and reveals that voluntary treatment is more successful than compulsory treatment. There is good reason to believe that a decriminalized civil drug court system, in which addicts meet with a treatment panel to determine the outcome in their cases, would be better positioned to convince participants that they need treatment than a criminal system in which their participation is based entirely on external coercion. Rather than facing a judge who is mandating sobriety as evidenced by clean drug tests, an offender would meet with treatment professionals who would have the opportunity to discuss his use and convince him that he is in need of treatment. If civil drug courts are successful at inspiring internal motivation among participants, the benefits from that effect may balance any possible negative consequences from the loss of criminal sanctions as a deterrent tool. And, while a civil system would remove the availability of jail sanctions, sanctions in the form of fines or other civil remedies would remain an option in the event of noncompliance. Finally, we must keep in mind that jail sanctions are not cost free. Indeed, they are quite expensive, both in terms of the direct costs of incarceration and the collateral costs of disrupting the treatment client's social bonds and ability to maintain employment.

Even if those who argue that eliminating criminal sanctions would decrease the overall rate of success among treatment participants are correct, the benefits of addressing the over- and under-inclusiveness problems inherent in a criminal drug court system might still make a civil drug court system more efficient overall. Solving those problems would result in substantial cost savings by ensuring treatment resources are not wasted on those who do not need treatment. It would also dramatically expand the net of drug users who have the opportunity to consult with treatment professionals [because all users found with drugs would be sent to a dissuasion panel, rather than the current system in which many users found in possession of drugs are given a fine or probation without any treatment opportunity]. By sending all users directly to a treatment panel, we could expect to see dramatic long-term savings through "brief interventions" that reach casual users before they have become addicted, as well as treatment of addicts who may not have a sufficient incentive to enter a drug court in a criminal system. Thus, even if the success rate for treatment in a civil drug court system were lower than in a criminal drug court system, the significantly larger pool of individuals receiving treatment consultations in a civil system, in combination with the savings achieved by removing nonaddicts from costly treatment programs, make a compelling case for the proposition that civil drug courts are likely be more cost effective than criminal drug courts.

Harm Reduction and the American Difference: Drug Treatment and Problem-Solving Courts in Comparative Perspective
James L. Nolan, Jr.
13 Journal of Health Care Law and Policy 31 (2010)

In my recent book, *Legal Accents, Legal Borrowing*, I examine the development of problem-solving courts in the United States and observe the process by which these courts have been exported to five other common law countries: England, Scotland, Ireland, Canada, and Australia. A comparison of the development of problem-solving courts in these six cases reveals an important difference between the U.S. and the other countries as it concerns the salience of defining treatment philosophies. In the five non-U.S. regions, one finds a treatment philosophy—typically characterized as "harm reduction" or "harm minimization"—that is clearly distinct from the sort of sensibilities and treatment practices common in the U.S. The harm reduction approach popular in these other countries manifests itself in a number of ways, including in the defining practices of new problem-solving court programs.

By most accounts, the problem-solving court movement began in 1989 in Dade County, Florida, with the initiation of America's first drug court. Since then, the burgeoning drug court movement has expanded in two important directions. First, a number of other specialty courts—largely based on the drug court model—have been developed throughout the United States, the most prominent of which are community courts, domestic violence courts, and mental health courts. Currently, there are more than three thousand problem-solving courts in the U.S. Second, over the past decade, a variety of problem-solving courts have been exported internationally. England, Scotland, Ireland, Canada, and Australia are among the countries where this process of legal transplantation is most advanced.

Although problem-solving courts vary considerably from place to place, it generally has been observed, particularly in the U.S., that these courts share five common features: (1) close and ongoing judicial monitoring, (2) a multidisciplinary or team-oriented approach, (3) a therapeutic or treatment orientation, (4) the altering of traditional roles in the adjudication process, and (5) an emphasis on solving the problems of individual offenders. In the process of transplanting these courts, importers have attempted to adapt or indigenize the American model to suit the conditions of their local legal-cultural context. One important difference revealed in this process of adaptation is the extent to which the countries outside of the U.S. embrace a harm reduction philosophy.

This approach is evident in a variety of problem-solving court venues. One of the more interesting can be found in Melbourne, Australia's prostitution court. Euphemistically referred to as the "Tuesday afternoon list," this court-based program is overseen by Magistrate Jelena Popovic, whose judicial orientation is clearly guided by a harm minimization perspective. Popovic explains that there are three types of sex workers in Melbourne: the higher-class "call girls," the prostitutes who work in brothels, and those who work the streets. Many of those working the streets have serious drug addiction problems and are the ones who most often find themselves on Popovic's Tuesday afternoon list. One of the aims of the court is to move offenders from the streets to the brothels. From a harm reduction perspective, according to Popovic, such a move represents a positive step for offenders because the brothels pose fewer dangers as it concerns matters of health and safety. However, this does not represent an endorsement of brothels, only an acceptance that reduced exposure to the hazards of life on the streets is a preferable situation and thus a worthy if modest goal.

The same sort of thinking informs contrasting perspectives on the appropriateness of needle-exchange programs. With respect to drug control, harm minimization is often invoked to support needle-exchange programs, a drug control strategy practiced in both Canada and Australia, among other places. Catherine Rynne, the first treatment coordinator of the Sydney drug court, speaks proudly of Australia's "needle- and syringe-exchange programs," which, according to Rynne, "have left us with one of the lowest rates of HIV infection among injecting drug users in the world." Similarly, the Canadian cities of Toronto and Vancouver both have needle-exchange programs. Vancouver even has a "safe injection site" or "harm reduction hotel" called Insite, which provides addicts with a safe, sanitized, and supervised space to inject their drugs of choice.

Dr. Gabor Mate, a counselor at the Vancouver site, offers an explanation of the harm reduction philosophy that is central to the program. Dr. Mate illustrates the philosophy by first discussing medical practices used to treat the harmful consequences of cigarette smoking: "If a smoker comes to me with an infection, I will give him an inhaler to suppress the inflammation in his lung and I will give him an antibiotic to fight the infection. I didn't treat their disease of addiction. Nothing I have done there will stop them from smoking. They will continue to smoke, but I have reduced the harm of their habit to them. That is a legitimate medical goal."

The difference between the U.S. and other countries with respect to a harm reduction philosophy is also apparent in the differing styles of drug court programs found internationally. The goal of most U.S. drug courts is "total abstinence," or what some have referred to as "demand reduction." That is, clients (as they are commonly called in drug court) usually must be both drug-and alcohol-free for a specified period of time in order to graduate from a U.S. drug court program. In contrast, other countries often view reduced use as a success, and clients can sometimes graduate without being entirely drug-free. A central treatment practice in many programs outside of the U.S. is the prescription of a maintenance drug, such as methadone or naltrexone. A few American drug courts use methadone maintenance, but this is actually rare in the U.S. Twenty percent of American drug courts, in fact, specifically prohibit the use of any pharmacological interventions.

Importers of American-styled problem-solving courts are aware of the differences between the United States and their countries as it concerns the acceptability of methadone maintenance practices. Justice Paul Bentley, Canada's first drug court judge, observes that, "unlike most [U.S.] drug courts, the Toronto [Drug Treatment Court] incorporates methadone maintenance as part of its treatment arsenal for heroin addicts. The abstinence model of most [U.S.] courts does not permit methadone to be used." Catherine Rynne observes the same in Australia and associates this difference with the existence of public health systems in both Australia and Canada. As she puts it, "harm-minimization really is a public health approach." Because both countries are "welfare states" and have "universal healthcare," Rynne believes the courts are able to offer a range of services without requiring participants to pay for treatment, as sometimes happens in U.S. programs. Again, the primary treatment offered in these programs is prescribed methadone.

One finds a similar attitude toward the use of methadone in both Ireland and Scotland. That is, judges identify harm-reduction as a defining treatment philosophy and see this philosophy as very different from the sort of thinking that informs U.S. drug court programs. Judge Gerard Haughton, who helped start Ireland's first drug court, understands that "most American models are based on total abstinence from drugs and alcohol." He explains, however, that in Ireland, "the principal determining factor as to the success or otherwise of the drug court was whether or not there was significant reduction in crime" and that the treatment service working with the court uses a "methadone maintenance program" to meet this objective. Haughton concedes that "while total abstinence might be an ideal goal, it was unlikely to be realistic in many cases." An important government report issued in Ireland prior to the start of the Dublin drug court expresses a similar sentiment. The report acknowledges that "whereas total abstinence is the optimal object of a drugs treatment programme[,] the alternative system of methadone maintenance should not be excluded" from Irish drug courts.

In fact, in both Ireland and Scotland, methadone maintenance has been a central part of their respective drug court programs. In Ireland, participants can graduate from the program while still on a maintenance prescription for methadone. While participants may be encouraged to "come off the methadone," as a Dublin probation officer explains, it is not required in order to "graduate from the drug court program." The importance of methadone treatment in the Glasgow program is illustrated by the story of a delegation of Russian officials who visited the Glasgow drug court. The visit evidently made it very clear to the Russians that the Scottish drug court model was not transferable to a Russian context, due in part to the court's use of methadone in treating offenders. Moira Price, program director of the Glasgow drug court, recalls the visit of the Russian delegation: "We use methadone to a great extent here in our treatment, and methadone is an illicit drug in Russia. So ... where we'd use methadone as an alternative therapy, they just could not use that at all.... They just could not get their heads around the concept of substitute prescribing as a way to deal with addicts. They seemed to think the way to deal with addicts was work therapy in prison."

As in Scotland, Ireland, Canada, and Australia, methadone maintenance is often a main staple of the treatment program associated with England's drug court and drug court-like programs. Such an orientation is attributable in no small measure to Britain's particular history of drug control, in which doctors have played a more central role, and where providing maintenance drugs for the "stable addict" has been a more common practice. Doctors can still prescribe heroin in the U.K., though in recent years methadone has become the preferred maintenance drug. The important point here is that from a British perspective, prescribing for maintenance purposes, given Britain's particular history of drug control, is not unusual. Given this history, it is not surprising that methadone maintenance is a central feature of treatment practices in U.K. drug courts.

It should be noted that while the British are comfortable with a harm reduction philosophy in which a medical doctor oversees treatment—the central component of which is the prescription of a maintenance drug—they are much less comfortable with the sort of therapeutic, self-help treatment that is often part of American drug court programs. In interviews with British judges and other problem-solving court officials, I discovered high levels of discomfort with the confessional, expressive style of the group therapy format. As a drug court judge in London explains, "Brits won't talk to each other in the free and easy, relaxed, and very open way that Americans will talk to each other." This is particularly the case among British men for whom this kind of discourse "doesn't come naturally," but rather is viewed as "a sign of weakness." According to this judge, the only way British men can speak in such an open manner is "when they get very drunk," a method unlikely to find much support in a criminal justice program aimed at reducing substance misuse.

An official with Scotland's first drug court observes much the same: "It's just hard to picture many Scots standing up in a group and saying all the things that you're meant to accept.... And that can only be cultural; it's just that we're reticent." Like the London judge, the Scottish official observes that the only way Scots would behave in such a manner would be if they were intoxicated: "We don't like speaking up, particularly in front of groups.... I'd have to be drunk to stand up in a group and say I'm an alcoholic.... If I was sober, nothing on earth would induce me to stand up among a crowd of strangers and talk about myself."

Practices in these other countries, then, are characterized less by the therapeutic self-help format of American programs, and more by a clinical, medical model—an important feature of which is methadone maintenance. Such practices are in keeping with the overall treatment philosophy of harm reduction that is in place in these other countries. Just as the British have been reluctant to embrace self-help treatment modalities that have become popular in the U.S., Americans too have been hesitant to embrace harm reduction as a guiding treatment philosophy. Instead, at least as it concerns drug courts, the U.S. prefers a total abstinence or demand reduction approach, an orientation that practitioners in the other countries find unrealistic.

In full agreement with the Scottish official cited above, I believe that these differences are attributable, in part, to distinctive cultural predilections, and are reflective of differing "legal accents" found in the six countries. In other words, a preference for a harm reduction model is indicative of the more moderate orientation of the other countries—one that stands in contrast to the bold and enthusiastic disposition of American practitioners. Australian criminologist, Arie Freiberg, observes: "Where the United States treads boldly, rapidly, and sometimes foolishly, Australia tiptoes carefully, slowly, and most times reluctantly." Arguably, the slow, modest, and cautious qualities of the Australians are also evident in the four other non-U.S. common law countries considered here.

This contrast with the U.S. is even reflected in the nomenclature used to describe these courts, at least in the early years of this international legal movement. That is, some outside of the U.S. were reluctant to embrace the concept of problem-solving, preferring instead the more modest expression problem-oriented. In 2001, Arie Freiberg noted that, at the time, there was "no generally accepted terminology" regarding these new court innovations. Freiberg preferred problem-oriented, which "is slightly less hubristic" than problem-solving. Australian criminologist John Braithwaite has also used the term problem-oriented, as has Susan Eley in her analysis of the Toronto K Court; she notes that problem-solving is the terminology used "in the American literature." In spite of this initial reluctance, problem-solving has become the preferred term internationally. Nevertheless, the resistance, if only initial and short-lived, is still telling.

It reflects a perspective held by many outside of the U.S. that these courts will not solve all of society's problems; they are not a panacea, as a number of American practitioners often seem to suggest. Those in the non-U.S. regions harbor fewer illusions that the perennial problems addressed in these courts will ever be fully solved. Arie Freiberg acknowledges that problem-oriented in contrast to problem-solving represents a view that "is slightly more pessimistic than [that of] American promoters of this concept." Freiberg sets himself apart from the Americans in another sense when he writes that though he "can be identified as a supporter of the problem-[solving] ... experiment," he is "not messianic about it," a not very subtle allusion to attitudes found in the U.S. Jocelyn Green, a member of the Ministry of Justice in the U.K., thinks Frieberg's preference for using the term problem-oriented to characterize these courts "is a good point" and notes that in England and Wales, "they're quite realistic about what they believe these courts can achieve." Compared to the U.S., Green believes the U.K. is more realistic.

One manner in which this "more realistic" perspective is revealed is in perceptions of what constitutes success. One of the early applications of the drug court model in the U.K. was Drug Treatment and Testing Orders (DTTOs). Inspired by the U.S. drug court model and launched in 1998, DTTOs were first tested out as a pilot scheme in Gloucestershire, Liverpool, and Croydon (South London). Upon completion of the pilot, the Home Office declared DTTOs a success and rolled them out nationally, as indicated in the following press release issued in the fall of 2000: "The national roll-out follows three successful pilot schemes in Croydon, Liverpool and Gloucestershire which ran from 1 October 1998 to 31 March 2000.... The average number of crimes committed per month by offenders on DTTOs fell dramatically from 107 to 10, while their average weekly spend on illegal drugs showed a significant reduction from £ 400 to £ 30."

Notice that offenders in these programs were still using drugs and were still participating in criminal activity, albeit at reduced rates. From a British perspective, however, this is still interpreted as a success. As Paul Hayes, Chief Probation Officer of the Southeast London Probation Service, explains: "the indications are that everything we hoped for in terms of reduced offending and reduced drug use is true. Across the three pilots, instead of people averaging thirty acquisitive crimes a week they are averaging three. So, in those terms it is clearly a success, [even though] everyone is testing positive for continued drug use." As noted above, such a position has historical precedence. As Hayes explains, "the whole harm reduction philosophy has dominated U.K. drug policy for a long time."

This medically informed perspective can sometimes be very difficult for Americans to understand. Philip Bean, a British criminologist who for years studied the U.S. drug court movement on behalf of the U.K. Home Office, made note of this difficulty when speaking to a group of British and American criminal justice professionals: "I think it's sometimes very difficult for North Americans to realize that it's still possible in Britain for heroin to be prescribed as maintenance and is often prescribed. I'm not talking about methadone; I'm talking about heroin. There isn't the culture in Britain as there is occasionally in certain parts of America to talk in terms of complete abstinence of all drug substances, including alcohol. I think that really does make a difference because the debate in Britain isn't about abstinence, it's about harm reduction."

3. Heroin Maintenance Programs

Can Heroin Maintenance Help Baltimore?
Peter Reuter
The Abell Foundation 2009

Baltimore City in particular has been adversely affected by the problem of heroin addiction. Whether measured by the number of heroin-related deaths per capita, heroin treatment admissions, or HIV related to heroin injecting, Baltimore City has for decades been the leading or close to the leading city in the United States. Even the massive expansion of Baltimore City's treatment programs that has occurred since 1995 has failed to rid the city of the problem.

Given that tougher enforcement and greater treatment provisions have not managed to make a large dent in the harm that heroin causes Baltimore City, there is a continuing desire to consider more radical solutions. In November 2007, the Baltimore City Council once again considered a bill proposing the legalization of drugs, hardly a realistic option given the federal government's views on, and role in, drug policy.

There is, however, a less radical, though still bold, innovation that has received attention from time to time in Baltimore City: heroin maintenance. Under this option, heroin users who have tried and failed in other kinds of treatment, including methadone maintenance, are provided heroin in the context of a medically supervised facility. The assumption is that if an addict has cheap access to heroin in safe conditions, many of the harms of the drug will disappear; the risk of overdose will become minimal, and the addict will no longer have to commit numerous property crimes, or sell to other users, in order to finance an extremely expensive habit.

There are many arguments against this assumption, involving both principle and pragmatic considerations. For example, in the heroin maintenance program, the government appears simply to be providing addicts with what they want rather than curing them of a dependence that prevents them from leading productive and socially engaged lives. Others assert that these programs lead to an increase in heroin initiation because they make the consequences less harmful. Nonetheless, a small but growing number of Western nations are experimenting with heroin maintenance. In two European countries, the Netherlands and Switzerland, heroin maintenance is now a routine treatment option, available to most heroin addicts, though taken up by few. Germany, the United Kingdom, and Spain are seriously considering the option. Canada has experimented with heroin maintenance in two cities, Vancouver and Montreal. The treatment evaluations, which are of varying quality, generally show positive results; none show negative results.

There are now 23 facilities in Switzerland providing heroin-assisted treatment (HAT); two are located in prisons. The total number of clients in treatment has stabilized at about 1200, constituting less than 5 percent of the estimated heroin-addict population. The total number of places available for treatment has been capped, but there is no indication of substantial waiting lines.

A decision to allow addicts to choose their own dose was critical. It removed any incentive to supplement the clinic provision with black-market purchases. A patient could receive heroin three times daily, 365 days of the year; very few now receive it more than twice daily. The average daily dose stabilized at 500 to 600 milligrams of pure heroin, a massive amount by the standards of U.S. street addicts.

The programs, by design, offer a very sterile, indeed clinical, environment. Operators make every effort to reduce this experience to medicine rather than recreation. Patients must turn up on time, take the drug promptly, and leave the premises. There is to be no congregating and socializing. For example, in one facility there are few chairs in the waiting room; the aim is to move patients in and out as soon as they have recovered from their dose. They are expected, here and elsewhere, to leave within 20 minutes of taking their heroin.

The patient population is aging and, mostly, very troubled. They have long-standing problems in all aspects of their personal lives and little prospect of being able to improve their conditions.

Perhaps the most significant evaluation of the Swiss experience appeared in a 2001 issue of *The Lancet*, a leading British medical research journal. The study followed 2,000 addicts admitted to HAT over a six-year period. One thousand were discharged for some reason but the retention rate was high; even at the six-year mark nearly 30 percent remained in the program.

Of particular note was the analysis of reasons for discharge; more than 60 percent of those who left HAT did so in order to take up another treatment option. Most of those seeking other treatment went into a methadone maintenance program (60 percent) but almost 40 percent went into an abstinence program.

What these data suggest is that heroin maintenance is not a terminal state, as most critics have (plausibly) alleged, but that it is mostly a transitional state. The Swiss experience suggests that the transition might take a few years and that some will stay in heroin assisted therapy. Nonetheless, it does potentially change assessments of the desirability of the program if perhaps one-third of those who enter have transitioned to other treatment within a few years.

[There have been a total of three major studies of HAT programs to date.] All evaluations so far have been positive. Retention in treatment has been high and drop-out has often been into other treatment modalities. Reductions in crime and improvements in health and social functioning are somewhat, but not greatly, better than the results to be expected for a good methadone program. However, the clients in HAT have a record of repeated failure in methadone maintenance treatment (MMT) so that crude comparison may be misleading. It is difficult to find any evidence that HAT has caused additional harms either to users or to the broader population. There is no indication that heroin has leaked from the facilities, dispensing the drug into the black market. Though it is difficult to develop a research design that would assess changes in initiation, no one has claimed that the availability of HAT has led to an increase in the number of persons experimenting with heroin.

One concern is that heroin assisted treatment is substantially more expensive than MMT. That has been the experience in both Switzerland and the Netherlands. The heroin patients costs were much higher not because of the cost of the heroin itself but primarily because of all the associated program costs. However, studies in both countries found that the additional benefits outweighed the additional costs. For example, adding the social costs to the costs of provision of services, a patient in treatment for a given period of time in the heroin arm of the Dutch trials cost 37,000 Euros compared to 50,000 Euros for the methadone arm of the trial. Reductions in crime were a large part of the gains, as was true in the Swiss studies. This comparison points to a chronic problem of substance abuse treatment funding; the expenditures are borne by the health-care sector, while the benefits are primarily reaped by the criminal justice sector and the community.

Heroin assisted therapy is clearly a supplement to methadone maintenance rather than a substitute for it. In no site where the HAT has been available has it attracted a substantial share of the heroin users who seek treatment; 10 percent is a high estimate of the potential share of treatment slots that might be occupied by HAT clients. Given the political and programmatic challenges that confront HAT in Baltimore, the question for the community is: Is the undertaking worth the effort for such a small share of clients?

At best there is a case only for an experiment. There are too many potential differences between Baltimore City and the other sites in which HAT has been tried to allow confident predictions of the outcomes. Visits to facilities in other countries hardly provide an inspiring model. The client population in Baltimore City is highly troubled so even if HAT leads to better outcomes for the group as a whole, many of the clients will remain unemployed, marginalized, and in poor health conditions. There will be some poster children but not many.

The potential for gain, however, is substantial. Even in the aging heroin-addict population, there are many who are heavily involved in crime and return frequently to the criminal justice system. Their continued involvement in street markets imposes a large burden on the community in the form of civil disorder that helps keep investment and jobs out. If heroin maintenance could remove 10 percent of Baltimore's most troubled heroin addicts from the streets, the result could be substantial reductions in crime and various other problems that greatly trouble the city. That is enough to make a debate on the matter worthwhile.

4. Sweden's Vision of a Drug-Free Society

Drug prohibition critics are likely to favor the Dutch marijuana coffee shops, Portugal's drug decriminalization law or Switzerland's heroin maintenance sites as models for drug regulation. Drug war proponents, by contrast, often cite Sweden as an example of achieving low drug use rates through strict zero-tolerance drug policies. *See, e.g.,* JOSEPH A. CALIFANO, JR., HIGH SOCIETY: HOW SUBSTANCE ABUSE RAVAGES AMERICA AND WHAT TO DO ABOUT IT 131 (2007) (arguing that "Sweden offers an example of a successful restrictive drug policy").

What Can We Learn from Sweden's Drug Policy Experience?
Christopher Hallam
The Beckley Foundation Drug Policy Programme, Briefing Paper 20 (2010)

Sweden is well-known for its commitment to a vision of "the drug-free society". In recent years, Sweden's drug policies have been the focus of considerable attention and debate, which may be seen in the context of both the ten year United Nations General Assembly Special Session on the World Drug Problem (UNGASS) review of international drug control and a much broader discourse of drug policy reform that has achieved growing political salience in many parts of the world. The Swedish example has been deployed by those arguing for a zero tolerance approach to drug policies and abstinence-driven treatments for dependent use (for example, the UK Conservative party), together with those (such as Antonio Maria Costa at the United Nations Office on Drugs & Crime) seeking to defend the current UN treaty-based system from widespread calls for change. In a 2006 report entitled *Sweden's Successful Drug Policy,* the United Nations Office on Drugs and Crime (UNODC) reviewed the country's policy model and tracked the development of its progressively more restrictive approach following a brief experiment with relatively liberal policies in the 1960s. In its conclusions, the report argued strongly that Sweden's unambiguously repressive stance had resulted in low levels of the prevalence of drug use, that these policies were therefore successful and should be adopted by other nation states. As a consequence of this and other interventions, Sweden has begun to function as a symbol of the efficacy of restrictive drug laws and policies, a utopia against which the allegedly dystopian potentials of more tolerant societies can be measured. At the same time, for drug policy reformers and advocates of harm reduction, the country encapsulates the failures that may be expected to flow from policies driven by an over-arching ideological commitment to abstinence. This briefing paper will analyse Swedish drug control policy in its legal, clinical, political, social and cultural dimensions and consider the claims and policy-objectives it has been used to support. In the course of this analysis, it will explore the implications of Sweden's model, if any, for other countries. Such an undertaking is, of necessity, a complex one, involving a wide-ranging discussion of the factors implicated and an argument possessed of many strands.

Sweden is a country which, in general, has relatively low levels of illicit drug use. Historically, the country's experience of substance use issues has changed considerably over time; while alcohol has been problematized and viewed as an issue for social intervention since the 19th century, it was amphetamines that first drew governmental attention to the use of other psychoactive substances. These stimulants were widely used in the 1930s and 40s, when they were legally available on prescription. Popular use of all drugs increased in the 1960s, and it was at this point that the influence of the medical profession, which had until then tended to dominate the drugs field, was largely replaced by popular social movements and the professional association of social workers. After receding across the intervening decades, prevalence increased steeply during the 1990s, in common with many European societies. Lifetime drug use rose from 7% to 12% amongst 15–75 year old Swedes in the decade to 2000, while problematic use expanded by more than a third, drug-related deaths doubled and treatment demand grew by more than half. Drug prices decreased sharply despite increased seizures. Prevalence trends have reduced since 2000, though they remain above their pre-1990s levels; problem drug use has stayed fairly constant at around 26,000 people, although this figure is subject to some dispute. Sweden's major form of problematic use centres on the injection of amphetamines, which made up 34.7% of the 6,480 clients entering treatment in 2007, and on heroin, with opiate users constituting 25.7% of that population. As in most European countries, cannabis (originating in Morocco and entering Sweden via Spain or Portugal) is the most widely used and frequently seized of illicit drugs.

In February 2008, the Swedish Ministry of Health and Social Affairs produced a fact sheet on its *Action Plan on Narcotic Drugs 2006–2010.* The primary objective of the country's strategy is there summarized as follows: "The drugs policy is based on people's right to a dignified life in a society that stands up for the individual's needs for security and safety. Illegal drugs must never be allowed to threaten the health, quality of life and security of the individual or public welfare and democratic development. The overall objective of the Swedish drugs policy is: *a drug-free society.*" (Original italics). The 2006–2010 Action Plan breaks down into three programmatic areas: prevention, or "recruitment to drug abuse must decrease", treatment or "drug abusers must be induced to give up their abuse" and supply reduction.

By the term *strategy,* we refer here to the fundamental philosophical underpinning of a country's drug control policy. Whereas the Netherlands, for example, has a pragmatic, health-oriented strategic focus that seeks to manage the consequences of drug consumption, Sweden seeks to realize the goal of a society without drug use. While rhetorical support for a drug-free social landscape is a familiar political tactic in many societies around the world, Sweden is unusual in making such explicit linkage of this objective to policy formulation.

This strategic vision has a number of specific practical consequences for Sweden's policy responses. At the level of legislation and enforcement, it results in an emphasis on the end-user which, again, is unusual in contemporary European policy; whereas enforcement resources in other EU states are directed mainly at networks of supply and distribution, in Sweden the consumer is deemed equally or more worthy of intensive police attention, being viewed as the fundamental unit of the illegal drug market. Likewise, in its treatment interventions, Sweden is untypical in its determination to enforce abstinence upon the recalcitrant drug user, rather than manage the consequences of use and ameliorate their severity. This emphasis, it should be noted, is not viewed in punitive terms by its advocates, but rather as providing protection, assistance and support; it bears a strong resemblance to the American discourse of 'tough love'. As Goldberg has observed, a key assumption underlying the Swedish conception of drugs is that the user is 'out of control', with individual self-will having been replaced by the drug's own 'chemical control', or, in a version theoretically elaborated by the psychiatrist Nils Bejerot (discussed below), controlled by instinctive drives that subvert rationality. Thus, the dependent user needs the society to take control back from the drug, by coercive means if necessary.

The most important element of [Swedish] drug control legislation is the 1968 *Narcotics Drugs Punishment Act* (NDPA), which has been amended several times over subsequent years and which defines those acts and substances to be prohibited. These include the standard categories such as possession, production and distribution of narcotic drugs, in addition to drug use *per se,* which is explicitly criminalized and can result in a prison sentence. Drug use itself was made a criminal offence in 1988, "in order to signal a powerful repudiation by the community of all dealings with drugs." Within the terms of the Act, narcotic drugs are viewed as medicines or other substances which are hazardous to health, possess addictive properties, and/or produce a state of euphoria in the consumer. The law provides three degrees of severity of offences: *minor, ordinary* and *serious,* the designation as one or another determined principally by the substance involved and its quantity. Minor offences are punished by fines or up to six months imprisonment, ordinary offences up to three years imprisonment, and serious offences by between two and ten years imprisonment. Alternatives to incarceration do exist in Sweden, and drug offenders can receive suspended sentences or probation; however, cases classed as serious must be dealt with by either a prison sentence or treatment. In 1993, the government announced that the minor offence category would apply only in the very mildest of cases. In the same year, the police were given legal authority to enforce drug testing on those they suspected of having consumed drugs. Drug testing plays an important role in the Swedish model and will be discussed further below. Trafficking activities are dealt with under the auspices of the *Law on Penalties for Smuggling* (2000), which includes penalties identical to those contained in the NDPA. Supply offences almost invariably result in incarceration. A further group of laws may also be applied to drug offences, such as those regulating the compulsory institutionalization of adults and compulsory drug treatment of the young. As discussed below, the Swedish drug control regime has become increasingly restrictive during the course of the last few decades. On the ground, in the quotidian existence of drug users, the Swedish approach is characterised by the continuous application of a generalized repression. As stated by the Police representative to a government task force in 1990: "We disturb them (the drug users) in their activities, and threaten them with compulsory treatment and make their life difficult. It *shall* be difficult to be a drug misuser. The more difficult we make their living, the more clear the other alternative, i.e. a drug-free life, will appear." (Original emphasis).

According to the Social Welfare Act of 1980, "The Social Welfare Committee shall actively ensure that the individual addict receives the help and care that he or she needs to escape from addiction." The treatment system is closely tied to the notion of a drug free society and to the enforcement of abstinence; abstinence-based interventions form the greater part of Sweden's treatment provision.

As pointed out by the UNODC in its very positive account of the country's approach, Sweden was the first European country to make Methadone Maintenance Therapy (MMT) available, at Uppsala in 1966, using the model developed by Dole and Nyswander. Despite this historical provenance, MMT has not been widely utilized in Sweden in the intervening years. According to the country's 2002 Reitox Report, methadone maintenance is provided in only four locations (Uppsala, Stockholm, Lund and Malmo), and patient numbers have been limited by parliament to a maximum of 800 persons. Entry protocols are restrictive, with entrants required to have been known to the authorities for at least two (formerly four) years, to have tried other treatment methods unsuccessfully, and so forth; they are tested regularly to enforce compliance. If they are found to have used illicit opiates, they are removed from the programme. The 2006 Reitox Report states that new regulations on substitution treatment came into force in 2005, and have apparently expanded the use of methadone, as well as providing detailed regulations around the prescribing of buprenorphine, the only other medication employed in Swedish substitution therapies. According to the 2006 Reitox Report, 62 treatment units (including 20 private) had "expressed an interest" in offering substitution treatment by October 2006. The Report states that 2,700 patients were in medically assisted treatment in the year to June 30th 2006, of whom 1,500 used buprenorphine. It is unclear how many of the methadone patients were in short-term detoxification, using medication in a "reduction" context, as opposed to MMT.

Compulsory or coerced treatment is permitted in Sweden, though its use is less prevalent than is often supposed. As of November 2005, 6% of drug users in institutional treatment were there on a coerced basis. Both adults (of 20 years and above) and juveniles can be committed to coerced institutional treatment, the former by reference to the *Care of Alcohol and Drug Abusers Special Provisions Act,* the latter by the *Care of Young Persons Special Provisions Act.* Though coercive treatment is in general used comparatively rarely, it is employed rather more often in the case of alcohol dependence. The compulsory treatment of adolescents is more frequent, as is the employment of threatened coercion as a device to "encourage" participation in voluntary treatment.

Therapeutic communities have traditionally been the most popular treatment modality in Sweden; these communities are usually located in rural districts, and many are privately run. In the 1980s, a two year stay in such a facility was commonplace for an injecting drug user in recovery, but, partly as a result of the more stringent economic climate prevailing in subsequent years, the duration of stay has decreased to something in the region of 6 months. Moreover, outpatient treatment has become increasingly popular over recent years. Most outpatient treatment is based around the '12 Step' model.

The role of social workers is very important in the Swedish treatment system, as these professionals provide the links within the 'care chain'. Composed of outreach, detoxification, institutional facilities, aftercare and rehabilitation, the care chain is an important concept that ties together the various elements of the drug control regime. Thus, working in close cooperation with the police, social workers play a key role in the initial identification of drug users on the streets; if the police locate a drug user, they bring him or her to the attention of a social worker who will decide upon the proper course of action.

Harm reduction is not a phrase that is used in Swedish drug control discourse; its founding assumption, that some people cannot or will not stop using drugs and therefore require services that minimise the associated damage, is, indeed, alien to the Swedish approach. With the advent of HIV in the 1980s, the provision of needle and syringe exchange services — perhaps the paradigmatic harm reduction intervention — was debated at length. The government subsequently announced that needle exchange would be made nationally available in 1988. The proposal was greeted by a storm of protest from pressure groups and professional associations, and was quashed by the Swedish parliament the following year. New legislation passed in 2006 does permit needle exchange services to be set up by local authorities, but there are, to date, only two such services, one in Malmo and the other in Lund, both having been set up on an experimental basis in the 1980s and operating successfully since that time. These services cater for roughly 1,200 individuals, or some 5% of the nation's total injecting population. Injecting equipment is not obtainable in pharmacies except on prescription.

Since 1993, the police have had the power to enforce drug testing on those they suspected of using drugs. This, along with legislation permitting the imprisonment of even minor drug cases, was a fundamental part of the increasingly restrictive measures that accompanied Sweden's steep rise in drug prevalence and severe economic downturn during the 1990s. It should be noted that blood and urine tests could only be deployed where offences were of sufficient seriousness to warrant a prison sentence, and that these two laws should therefore be seen as mutually enabling. The objective of testing was defined as follows: "to provide opportunities to intervene at an early stage so as to vigorously prevent young persons from becoming fixed in drug misuse and improve the treatment of those misusers who were serving a sentence." In defence of the policy of testing, then Health Minister Bengt Westerberg claimed that it was necessary to target the user, who was "the motor of the whole drug carousel."

Normative interventions are an important and ongoing aspect of the Swedish regime. The government ran a 2006 media campaign, based largely on the use of the internet but also involving youth media such as MTV, entitled *Drugs Are Poo*. This was aimed at reinforcing in young people the continued disapproval of drug use; according to the 2007 Reitox Report, the campaign was successful. Surveys reported that 9 out of 10 young urban Swedes support the government in such interventions, and 56% had heard someone repeat the slogan *Drugs are Poo*. Nonetheless it seems likely that those drawn to such interventions are likely to be those who do already support the orthodox stance.

We have provided an overview of the main elements in Sweden's drug control regime. However, in order to comprehend its objectives and the terms in which it is framed, one must take into account certain aspects of Swedish history and culture; without doing so, it is impossible to understand how and why the current system developed. We will briefly explore the most important of these factors here. At the outset, it is important to avoid a possible misunderstanding. In the course of this discussion, we will identify various tendencies within Swedish culture that we believe help to explain the country's attitudes and responses to illicit drug use; these should be read as general trends and characteristics present within the social milieu, and not as referring to some essential, fixed or innate Swedish or Nordic 'personality-type'. They are generalizations that nonetheless do reflect the realities of Sweden's social and cultural life, and are the result of specific and discernible social and historical circumstances.

By 2008, Sweden's population had risen to just over 9 million. Its transition from a feudal society, with wealth and power controlled by a tiny aristocratic elite, to a modern social democracy was, in comparative terms, a very rapid one. While 2008 figures put the urban population at 85%, most people still have relations and cultural roots in the countryside, lending Swedish culture a distinctive blend of the traditional and the modern. The social democratic party was the driving force behind the building of the *folk-hemmet* or 'people's homeland' in the 1930s; the *folk-hemmet* offered its citizens prosperity and security; the latter category, *trygghet* in Swedish, has proven to be of critical importance in the nation's political life, and has deeply infused the national culture. The state has endowed Swedish citizens with one of the world's highest standards of living, combining a dynamic market economy with extensive welfare provision and an exemplary human rights record. The state or system has thus been experienced in Sweden as an over-whelmingly beneficent force, and a belief in the effectiveness of state-sponsored solutions to political, economic and social problems, or 'social engineering', has been widely diffused throughout Swedish society. A powerful ethic of conformity has co-existed with this implicit faith in the Good State, generating a suspicion of social difference and its identification with social *deviance.* Boekhout von Solinge points out that Sweden's geographical location on the western limit of Europe, far from the cosmopolitan melting-pots of Paris, Berlin and London has perhaps contributed a certain provinciality and insularity to the country's outlook. In short, despite its social democratic tradition, it appears that Sweden is, in the social and cultural register, a conservative country.

The Social Democratic party elected in the 1930s instituted a political culture based on consensus; both private sector employers and trade unions were committed to this consensus, leading to the success of the corporatist and collectivist 'Swedish Model', and resulting in extended periods of full employment, generalized prosperity and a capacious safety net of social welfare measures. Another essential element in the establishment of this harmonious order has been the influence of popular social movements, groups and associations, often organized around a specific cause or set of values. These trends anticipated the single-issue pressure groups that have been influential in other contemporary democracies. Though membership in Sweden's popular social movements has declined — partly because they have been so successful, and their objectives largely integrated into the state and its mechanisms — many of the older generations of Swedes can still recall their personal participation in constructing the Good State. Swedish society is, perhaps understandably, proud of its social and political achievements.

This very active political pluralism has had a large impact on the development of Swedish drug policy, which has widespread popular support. The country remains to this day a strongly protestant society, with some 87% of the population belonging to the Lutheran church. The denomination has a strong temperance tradition, and has been politically influential since the 19th century, when its campaigning resulted in the passing of laws forbidding the home distillation of alcohol. Temperance has historically coexisted with a Nordic drinking tradition in which alcohol is consumed with the objective of getting very drunk, very quickly. The discourse of temperance, in a form strongly committed to the achievement of abstinence, was central to two social movements highly active in the drug policy field from the late 60s onward: *The National Association for a Drug Free Society* (RNS) and *Parents Against Drugs* (FMN). As Lindberg and Haynes observe: "RNS was started by a doctor, Nils Bejerot, who believed that the solution to the narcotic problem was to restrict supply and to compel addicts to enter treatment. Bejerot saw the cause of drug addiction as a social illness, like a transmitted infection, and that older drug addicts taught younger people how to use drugs. Prohibition was believed to be the only answer and this was to be achieved by strict law enforcement and the compulsory treatment of drug misusers. RNS was supported by many social workers, some doctors, teachers and members of the general public. RNS also was supported by the FMN which had the same philosophy and solution to the problem." It should be noted, in addition, that the police play a powerful political role in Sweden, and have tirelessly advocated the restrictive model. Bejerot was consulting psychiatrist to the Stockholm police in the late 1950s and 60s, his ideas finding immediate favour in the service, which was strongly against the Stockholm experiment with legal prescribing.

Between 1965 and 1967, Sweden experimented with the medical prescription of drugs to dependent users. This phase is regarded by some as the root of the country's drug problem, and advocates of its zero-tolerance model argue that the repressive policies introduced subsequently were responsible for reducing the prevalence of drug use. However, the prescribing experiment was not scientifically planned or structured; no control group was established against which to measure its effects, and it is consequently difficult to draw conclusions from it. The project was much smaller than is sometimes supposed, with a total of 120 patients being prescribed over the two year period. Claims that injecting drug use increased during the project's lifetime and were lower before and after it are based on the work of Nils Bejerot. Bejerot's work in this regard—which, despite being subjected to intensive scientific critique, attracts widespread belief both in Sweden and internationally—is based on police statistics on the prevalence of injection marks amongst arrestees. Such data lack sufficient scientific validity and reliability to ground any but the most tentative of conclusions, since they may reflect police practice rather than the reality of drug use (increased searching, the over-zealous use of interpretive categories and so on). Even if injection *was* more widespread, this cannot be safely attributed to the effect of the prescribing experiment: the 1960s saw a generalized expansion of drug use in all forms, and the police data used by Bejerot do not offer any way of isolating the effect of the prescribing project from the general social and cultural context in which the behaviours were situated.

Altogether, Nils Bejerot has nonetheless had an enormous impact on Sweden's drugs strategy. He became active in the field following the experiment with prescribing, and was at the centre of the dissemination of the zero tolerance model. Despite Bejerot's own medical qualifications, however, the most powerful professional input into the groups pressing for more restrictive policies came not from doctors but from social workers. Already having a higher professional status than their counterparts in Britain, Swedish social workers became, according to Lindberg and Hayes, the leading elite grouping in Swedish drug policy formation at this time. Closely involved with both RNS and FMN, they were able to exert influence on policy makers by successfully deploying their expert status and specialized knowledge, in a way somewhat analogous to the medical profession in the UK, though with very different results. Unlike UK medics, Swedish social workers were able to tap into an anti-expert strand in the culture, contrasting their own 'hands-on' engagement with the problem on the streets with the allegedly remote pronouncements of doctors and academics. The call for widespread needle exchange services in Sweden to counter the HIV epidemic in the 1980s was effectively defeated by this alliance.

The cultural conservatism referred to above is compounded by Sweden's high degree of ethnic and social homogeneity. Until the last couple of decades, the majority of such immigration as there has been has involved people from other Scandinavian nations, especially Finland, with which Sweden shares a border. In a work exploring the links between social anxieties, immigration and drug policy, Gould describes a Swedish government report entitled "We *will Never Surrender*"; the cover displays some significant iconography, with the title emblazoned over a photograph of Sweden's rocky coastline, standing eternally vigilant against the depredations of the ocean and that which might try to come across it. The report develops the theme of drugs as alien material, coming from outside Sweden, whose borders must be defended against the intrusion of disorder from without. Gould recognizes that, "there is a rational connection between migrant labour and drugs (it would be surprising if migrants did not take their native drug habits with them on their travels, as they do other aspects of their cultures) ...", but points out that "the concern ... has been with the irrational, exaggerated, mutually reinforcing fear of both." While Sweden has been a tolerant, liberal society in respect of its immigrant labouring populations in the past, recent immigration patterns have generated a more ambivalent response, particularly in the case of asylum seekers and refugees. Extreme Right-wing parties have had some local successes, while instances of crime by foreigners have generated public outrage amongst "normal" Swedes.

In a case which fits a well-established historical pattern, it seems that drugs in Sweden have assumed a symbolic role in which they have become linked with foreigners and with fears of 'the outside' in general. The fact that Sweden has very little historical experience with intoxicating substances from other parts of the world (comparable with Britain or France and their Asian and North African colonies, for instance,) has helped to establish the essentially 'foreign' quality of drugs originating from these regions. As Pratt notes, "'Getting tough on crime' then becomes a way of providing gestures of reassurance against a common enemy—uniting the public, restoring security, reaffirming homogeneity and solidarity." This is particularly the case with drugs. The more that homogeneity has come under threat, he states, "the more the dangers of drugs become … acute. There is a symbolic link between the two sets of concerns. In all societies, purity (represented here by Scandinavian homogeneity) and danger (drugs) are important symbols. Purity conveys a sense of order and homogeneity; danger conveys disorder and disintegration … The more that which is pure comes under threat, the more it becomes necessary to take dramatic action against that which endangers it." Pratt makes reference here to the anthropologist Mary Douglas's celebrated work *Purity and Danger* and the way these categories work to establish sacred and profane spaces and materials in human societies. The reason that Swedish culture constructs drugs as an extreme danger, despite the fact that their prevalence is relatively low in the country, is related to a specific set of historical and cultural factors that add to the sense of risk, threat and uncertainty. These may be said to be linked in one way or another to the phenomenon of globalization.

While we provided a brief overview of Sweden's drug market above, we will now look in a little more detail at the claims made about the successes and failures of its drug policy. The low prevalence of drug use in the Swedish population is one of the major areas to which advocates of the model point. In terms of prevalence of drug use amongst the general population, it does indeed appear that Sweden is 'successful', being below European and North American averages in most of the key indicators. The general rise in drug use in the 1990s was mentioned previously, as was the fact that trends have fallen once again since the year 2000. In 2007, lifetime prevalence of cannabis use amongst young adults (15–34) was 18.1%, against an EU range of 2.9% to 48%. For comparative purposes, we might note that countries with similar prevalence figures include Hungary (19.1%) and Portugal (17.0%). Amongst all adults (15–64), the Swedish figure was 12.8% against an EU range of 1.5% to 38.6%; similar figures are found for Latvia (12.1%), Luxembourg (12.9%) and Portugal (11.7%). For last year cannabis use amongst young adults, Sweden's figure was 4.8% (EU range 0.9% to 20.9%), and for all adults it was 2.1% (EU range 0.4% to 14.6%). Interesting comparisons arise with Portugal, for which these figures were respectively 6.7% and 3.6%. For school students, Sweden's figures are even lower, lifetime prevalence of cannabis use for 15–16 year olds standing at 7% (EU range 4% to 45%), and last year prevalence at 2% (EU range 1% to 5%). To reiterate, it seems from these data that the prevalence of cannabis use is lower than the EU average, sometimes much lower. The same general trend may be observed for other illicit drugs. Low prevalence data is the primary measure used by the UNODC in concluding that Sweden's is a 'successful drug policy.' However, it should be noted that a number of other countries, including Portugal, which employs a very different set of drug control measures, have broadly similar prevalence levels (and lower levels in some categories), and could, in principle, have been selected as exemplary policy templates by the UNODC.

Some further reservations must be made. Firstly, in terms of the content of these data, one must very careful about drawing any firm conclusion that they accurately reflect the reality of drug consumption. Prevalence data are based on surveys of the general population, conducted by face to face interview or postal questionnaire. In a country where the authorities adopt such a restrictive posture in relation to drug use, and where community disapproval is so powerful, it would be somewhat surprising if citizens *did* provide entirely candid replies: so it is very likely that the figures underestimate consumption. Moreover, anecdotal narratives speak of rising levels of drug use among young Swedes as they become progressively more integrated into global youth cultures. Researchers have identified club-based dance cultures in which drug use is part of the process of forging identities defined against the tightly enforced norms of Sweden's mainstream society. Schools-based research, in its latest 2008 study, discovered that cannabis use had increased from 5% to 7% amongst female students and from 7% to 9% for males over the past year. Notwithstanding this, it is likely that prevalence rates of recreational drug use remain relatively low. This leads us onto a second point: a comparatively low overall prevalence rate of drug use tells us little about the patterns of use that *do* exist, and the problems that may be associated. It is necessary to ask, what levels of problematic drug use are there, what kinds of harms cluster around it, and how effective is the policy response to these harms?

[O]fficial figures estimate there to be approximately 26,000 problem drug users in Sweden, though again the actual numbers may be higher. The problem drug use prevalence rate is put at 0.45% by UNODC, slightly below the EU average of 0.51%. Nonetheless, UNODC acknowledges that problematic drug use *as a proportion of overall drug use* is very high in Sweden. 1 in every 5 to 6 Swedish users is included in this category, compared with 1 in every 12 or 13 in the UK. Amphetamines and opiates are widely injected by this population, and the drug and policy-related harms are significant. While HIV infection rates in Sweden are relatively low, injection-related HIV increased by 52 new cases in 2007 compared to an average of 21 new cases annually over the previous five years. It may be significant that these were very strongly centred in the Stockholm area (49 of the 52 new cases in 2007). Though Stockholm is by far the largest population centre in Sweden, it does not have needle-exchange facilities. The two cities that do, Malmo and Lund, saw no new HIV cases between 2001 and 2006. Furthermore, injecting drug users (IDUs) represent 57% of all hepatitis C infections in Sweden, and the Swedish Institute for Infectious Disease Control estimates that 95% of IDUs will test positive for hepatitis C infection within two years of initiating injecting.

In the late 1990s, the then Director General of the Swedish National Institute for Public Health spoke out against the tightly restricted use of methadone, stating that: "Mortality among heroin addicts is twice as high in Stockholm as in other European cities. The only treatment method that is reasonably effective, methadone, is held in check by Swedish drug policy." The remark was made in the context of steeply climbing drug-related mortality seen during the 90s, and the longstanding and still evident tendency for discussion of drug-related deaths to be seen in terms of the 'international legalization movement', the perceived threat of which drives Swedish debate to be extremely cautious about sending out the 'wrong message'. The adoption of measures to minimize harms to drug users is seen as condoning and even encouraging drug use. According to the National Cause of Death Registry, drug-related deaths rose to a peak of 403 in 2001, and have declined gradually since then to 310 in 2006.

The lack of harm reduction measures in the face of this serious situation led Paul Hunt, the UN Special Rapporteur on the Right to Health, to criticize Sweden following his mission to the country in 2006. He noted that, while Sweden's international commitment to human rights is exemplary and its government has signed up to many international treaties recognizing the right to health, "this human right is less firmly entrenched in Sweden's domestic laws and policies." Expressing his "surprise" that the very successful needle exchange in Malmo, which he visited, was one of only two in the country, Professor Hunt concluded that, "The Special Rapporteur emphasizes that the Government has a responsibility to ensure the implementation, throughout Sweden and as a matter of priority, of a comprehensive harm-reduction policy, including counselling, advice on sexual and reproductive health, and clean needles and syringes."

During the preparation of this Briefing paper, a further significant intervention has been made in support of harm reduction measures in Sweden, this time from within the country itself. The Director General of the National Board of Health and Welfare, together with the Directors of the Infectious Diseases Institute and the Institute of Public Health have called for local authorities to make use of the provisions under the 2006 Act enabling them to set up needle exchange services for drug users. These three prominent clinicians point out that this is a health measure supported by the United Nations, the World Health Organization, the International Red Cross and the World Bank, and that neighbouring Finland, which shares a restrictive approach, has successfully introduced low threshold needle exchanges that are "free, non-judgmental and ... anonymous". Amongst EU countries, only Sweden and Greece continue to deny this health service to their citizens, the authors go on to say, urging their country's authorities to act according to the principles of the Dublin Declaration, which Sweden signed in 2004. The Dublin Declaration commits signatories to ensure that syringe exchange services are available to at least 60% of [injection drug users]. As already noted, the two services presently operative in southern Sweden reach some 5% of this vulnerable population.

UNODC has argued that while causal relations are notoriously difficult to establish, "in the case of Sweden, the clear association between a restrictive drug policy and low levels of drug use is striking." ... While overall prevalence remains low, the extent to which this is due to Sweden's drug policy, or to wider social, historical and geographical factors, cannot be easily surmised from the available information. Judgements regarding the efficacy or otherwise of Swedish policies therefore inevitably involve wider sets of value and belief, firm or otherwise.

Addendum

On November 6, 2012, voters in Washington and Colorado approved ballot measures legalizing marijuana. Though eighteen states now have medical marijuana laws and others have enacted some form of marijuana decriminalization, Washington and Colorado are the first to have legalized the manufacture and sale of marijuana for recreational use.

In both states, the production and sale provisions will not take effect until 2013. This is because both laws charge state agencies with adopting regulations for the licensing and oversight of marijuana manufacturers, distributors and retailers. By contrast, protections for individual users in possession of marijuana took effect as soon as the results were certified.

The new laws raise a host of legal and policy questions. As a practical matter, the most pressing issue may be how the federal government will respond. At the time this book went to press, the Department of Justice had not yet announced whether, or to what extent, it will seek to interfere with the laws. Legally, the laws are on a similar footing as state medical marijuana laws, which also conflict with federal law. The federal response to state medical marijuana laws is covered in Chapter 7. Do you think it is likely that the federal government will take the same approach to the marijuana legalization laws in Colorado and Washington? If so, how successful do you think the federal government will be at blocking the new laws?

The Colorado and Washington ballot measures could also influence laws outside the United States. As discussed in Chapter 9, a growing number of prominent international leaders have begun to question aspects of the war on drugs, including marijuana prohibition, in recent years. The United States has opposed these calls for reform. Indeed, the U.S. maintains a certification process (also covered in Chapter 9) that ties trade status and aid packages to participation in the drug war. Shortly after the votes in Colorado and Washington, outgoing President of Mexico Felipe Calderón suggested that marijuana legalization by U.S. states is "a paradigm change on the part of those entities in respect to the current international system[.]" E. Eduardo Castillo and Michael Weissenstein, *Colorado, Washington Marijuana Legalization: Latin American Leaders Ask for a Review of Drug Policies*, Associated Press, Nov. 12, 2012. Will the measures in Colorado and Washington impact the standing of the U.S. to oppose drug policy reform proposals in other countries?

Of course, there is also the question of what impact the laws will have within Colorado and Washington. How will the measures affect marijuana use and availability, the criminal justice system, and the problems that come with black market drug distribution? Interestingly, Washington's ballot initiative includes a provision requiring the state to conduct cost-benefit evaluations of the law in 2015, 2017, 2022, and 2032. Until then, the material on the marijuana legalization debate in Chapter 2 is a useful starting point for considering the policy implications of these laws.

The text of Colorado's Amendment 64 and Washington's Initiative 502 appear below. These excerpts, which include most of the provisions from each law, may take some time to review. As with any statute, it is critical to consider how the different provisions fit with one another. Reading both laws in detail is also a useful exercise for thinking about how to translate policy preferences into law. What do you think are the key differences between the two laws? Do you think these legal differences will translate into significant differences in how each law is carried out on the ground?

Colorado Amendment 64

Be it Enacted by the People of the State of Colorado

Article XVIII of the constitution of the state of Colorado is amended BY THE ADDITION OF A NEW SECTION to read:

Section 16. Personal use and regulation of marijuana

(1) **Purpose and findings.**

(a) In the interest of the efficient use of law enforcement resources, enhancing revenue for public purposes, and individual freedom, the people of the state of Colorado find and declare that the use of marijuana should be legal for persons twenty-one years of age or older and taxed in a manner similar to alcohol.

(d) The people of the state of Colorado further find and declare that it is necessary to ensure consistency and fairness in the application of this section throughout the state and that, therefore, the matters addressed by this section are, except as specified herein, matters of statewide concern.

(2) **Definitions.** As used in this section, unless the context otherwise requires,

(a) "Colorado Medical Marijuana Code" means article 43.3 of title 12, Colorado revised statutes.

(b) "Consumer" means a person twenty-one years of age or older who purchases marijuana or marijuana products for personal use by persons twenty-one years of age or older, but not for resale to others.

(c) "Department" means the Department of Revenue or its successor agency.

(d) "Industrial Hemp" means the plant of the genus cannabis and any part of such plant, whether growing or not, with a delta-9 tetrahydrocannabinol concentration that does not exceed three-tenths percent on a dry weight basis.

(e) "Locality" means a county, municipality, or city and county.

(f) "Marijuana" or "Marihuana" means all parts of the plant of the genus cannabis whether growing or not, the seeds thereof, the resin extracted from any part of the plant, and every compound, manufacture, salt, derivative, mixture, or preparation of the plant, its seeds, or its resin, including marihuana concentrate. "Marijuana" or "marihuana" does not include industrial hemp, nor does it include fiber produced from the stalks, oil, or cake made from the seeds of the plant, sterilized seed of the plant which is incapable of germination, or the weight of any other ingredient combined with marijuana to prepare topical or oral administrations, food, drink, or other product.

(g) "Marijuana accessories" means any equipment, products, or materials of any kind which are used, intended for use, or designed for use in planting, propagating, cultivating, growing, harvesting, composting, manufacturing, compounding, converting, producing, processing, preparing, testing, analyzing, packaging, repackaging, storing, vaporizing, or containing marijuana, or for ingesting, inhaling, or otherwise introducing marijuana into the human body.

(h) "Marijuana cultivation facility" means an entity licensed to cultivate, prepare, and package marijuana and sell marijuana to retail marijuana stores, to marijuana product manufacturing facilities, and to other marijuana cultivation facilities, but not to consumers.

(i) "Marijuana establishment" means a marijuana cultivation facility, a marijuana testing facility, a marijuana product manufacturing facility, or a retail marijuana store.

(j) "Marijuana product manufacturing facility" means an entity licensed to purchase marijuana; manufacture, prepare, and package marijuana products; and sell marijuana and marijuana products to other marijuana product manufacturing facilities and to retail marijuana stores, but not to consumers.

(k) "Marijuana products" means concentrated marijuana products and marijuana products that are comprised of marijuana and other ingredients and are intended for use or consumption, such as, but not limited to, edible products, ointments, and tinctures.

(l) "Marijuana testing facility" means an entity licensed to analyze and certify the safety and potency of marijuana.

(m) "Medical marijuana center" means an entity licensed by a state agency to sell marijuana and marijuana products pursuant to section 14 of this article and the Colorado Medical Marijuana Code.

(n) "Retail marijuana store" means an entity licensed to purchase marijuana from marijuana cultivation facilities and marijuana and marijuana products from marijuana product manufacturing facilities and to sell marijuana and marijuana products to consumers.

(o) "Unreasonably impracticable" means that the measures necessary to comply with the regulations require such a high investment of risk, money, time, or any other resource or asset that the operation of a marijuana establishment is not worthy of being carried out in practice by a reasonably prudent businessperson.

(3) **Personal use of marijuana.** Notwithstanding any other provision of law, the following acts are not unlawful and shall not be an offense under Colorado law or the law of any locality within Colorado or be a basis for seizure or forfeiture of assets under Colorado law for persons twenty-one years of age or older:

(a) Possessing, using, displaying, purchasing, or transporting marijuana accessories or one ounce or less of marijuana.

(b) Possessing, growing, processing, or transporting no more than six marijuana plants, with three or fewer being mature, flowering plants, and possession of the marijuana produced by the plants on the premises where the plants were grown, provided that the growing takes place in an enclosed, locked space, is not conducted openly or publicly, and is not made available for sale.

(c) Transfer of one ounce or less of marijuana without remuneration to a person who is twenty-one years of age or older.

(d) Consumption of marijuana, provided that nothing in this section shall permit consumption that is conducted openly and publicly or in a manner that endangers others.

(e) Assisting another person who is twenty-one years of age or older in any of the acts described in paragraphs (a) through (d) of this subsection.

(4) **Lawful operation of marijuana-related facilities.** Notwithstanding any other provision of law, the following acts are not unlawful and shall not be an offense under Colorado law or be a basis for seizure or forfeiture of assets under Colorado law for persons twenty-one years of age or older:

(a) Manufacture, possession, or purchase of marijuana accessories or the sale of marijuana accessories to a person who is twenty-one years of age or older.

(b) Possessing, displaying, or transporting marijuana or marijuana products; purchase of marijuana from a marijuana cultivation facility; purchase of marijuana or marijuana products from a marijuana product manufacturing facility; or sale of marijuana or marijuana products to consumers, if the person conducting the activities described in this paragraph has obtained a current, valid license to operate a retail marijuana store or is acting in his or her capacity as an owner, employee or agent of a licensed retail marijuana store.

(c) Cultivating, harvesting, processing, packaging, transporting, displaying, or possessing marijuana; delivery or transfer of marijuana to a marijuana testing facility; selling marijuana to a marijuana cultivation facility, a marijuana product manufacturing facility, or a retail marijuana store; or the purchase of marijuana from a marijuana cultivation facility, if the person conducting the activities described in this paragraph has obtained a current, valid license to operate a marijuana cultivation facility or is acting in his or her capacity as an owner, employee, or agent of a licensed marijuana cultivation facility.

(d) Packaging, processing, transporting, manufacturing, displaying, or possessing marijuana or marijuana products; delivery or transfer of marijuana or marijuana products to a marijuana testing facility; selling marijuana or marijuana products to a retail marijuana store or a marijuana product manufacturing facility; the purchase of marijuana from a marijuana cultivation facility; or the purchase of marijuana or marijuana products from a marijuana product manufacturing facility, if the person conducting the activities described in this paragraph has obtained a current, valid license to operate a marijuana product manufacturing facility or is acting in his or her capacity as an owner, employee, or agent of a licensed marijuana product manufacturing facility.

(e) Possessing, cultivating, processing, repackaging, storing, transporting, displaying, transferring or delivering marijuana or marijuana products if the person has obtained a current, valid license to operate a marijuana testing facility or is acting in his or her capacity as an owner, employee, or agent of a licensed marijuana testing facility.

(f) Leasing or otherwise allowing the use of property owned, occupied or controlled by any person, corporation or other entity for any of the activities conducted lawfully in accordance with paragraphs (a) through (e) of this subsection.

(5) **Regulation of marijuana.**

(a) Not later than July 1, 2013, the department shall adopt regulations necessary for implementation of this section. Such regulations shall not prohibit the operation of marijuana establishments, either expressly or through regulations that make their operation unreasonably impracticable. Such regulations shall include:

(i) Procedures for the issuance, renewal, suspension, and revocation of a license to operate a marijuana establishment, with such procedures subject to all requirements of article 4 of title 24 of the Colorado Administrative Procedure Act or any successor provision;

(ii) A schedule of application, licensing and renewal fees, provided, application fees shall not exceed five thousand dollars, with this upper limit adjusted annually for inflation, unless the department determines a greater fee is necessary to carry out its responsibilities under this section, and provided further, an entity that is licensed under the Colorado Medical Marijuana Code to cultivate or sell marijuana or to manufacture marijuana products at the time this section takes effect and that chooses to apply for a separate marijuana establishment license shall not be required to pay an application fee greater than five hundred dollars to apply for a license to operate a marijuana establishment in accordance with the provisions of this section;

(iii) Qualifications for licensure that are directly and demonstrably related to the operation of a marijuana establishment;

(iv) Security requirements for marijuana establishments;

(v) Requirements to prevent the sale or diversion of marijuana and marijuana products to persons under the age of twenty-one;

(vi) Labeling requirements for marijuana and marijuana products sold or distributed by a marijuana establishment;

(vii) Health and safety regulations and standards for the manufacture of marijuana products and the cultivation of marijuana;

(viii) Restrictions on the advertising and display of marijuana and marijuana products; and

(ix) Civil penalties for the failure to comply with regulations made pursuant to this section.

(b) In order to ensure the most secure, reliable, and accountable system for the production and distribution of marijuana and marijuana products in accordance with this subsection, in any competitive application process the department shall have as a primary consideration whether an applicant:

(i) Has prior experience producing or distributing marijuana or marijuana products pursuant to section 14 of this article and the Colorado Medical Marijuana Code in the locality in which the applicant seeks to operate a marijuana establishment; and

(ii) Has, during the experience described in subparagraph (i), complied consistently with section 14 of this article, the provisions of the Colorado Medical Marijuana Code and conforming regulations.

(c) In order to ensure that individual privacy is protected, notwithstanding paragraph (a), the department shall not require a consumer to provide a retail marijuana store with personal information other than government-issued identification to determine the consumer's age, and a retail marijuana store shall not be required to acquire and record personal information about consumers other than information typically acquired in a financial transaction conducted at a retail liquor store.

(d) The General Assembly shall enact an excise tax to be levied upon marijuana sold or otherwise transferred by a marijuana cultivation facility to a marijuana product manufacturing facility or to a retail marijuana store at a rate not to exceed fifteen percent prior to January 1, 2017 and at a rate to be determined by the General Assembly thereafter, and shall direct the department to establish procedures for the collection of all taxes levied. Provided, the first forty million dollars in revenue raised annually from any such excise tax shall be credited to the Public School Capital Construction Assistance Fund created by article 43.7 of title 22, C.R.S., or any successor fund dedicated to a similar purpose. Provided further, no such excise tax shall be levied upon marijuana intended for sale at Medical Marijuana Centers pursuant to section 14 of this article and the Colorado Medical Marijuana Code.

(e) Not later than October 1, 2013, each locality shall enact an ordinance or regulation specifying the entity within the locality that is responsible for processing applications submitted for a license to operate a marijuana establishment within the boundaries of the locality and for the issuance of such licenses should the issuance by the locality become necessary because of a failure by the department to adopt regulations pursuant to paragraph (a) or because of a failure by the department to process and issue licenses as required by paragraph (g).

(f) A locality may enact ordinances or regulations, not in conflict with this section or with regulations or legislation enacted pursuant to this section, governing the time, place, manner and number of marijuana establishment operations; establishing procedures for the issuance, suspension, and revocation of a license issued by the locality in accordance with paragraph (h) or (i), such procedures to be subject to all requirements of article 4 of title 24 of the Colorado Administrative Procedure Act or any successor provision; establishing a schedule of annual operating, licensing, and application fees for marijuana establishments, provided, the application fee shall only be due if an application is submitted to a locality in accordance with paragraph (i) and a licensing fee shall only be due if a license is issued by a locality in accordance with paragraph (h) or (i); and establishing civil penalties for violation of an ordinance or regulation governing the time, place, and manner of a marijuana establishment that may operate in such locality. A locality may prohibit the operation of marijuana cultivation facilities, marijuana product manufacturing facilities, marijuana testing facilities, or retail marijuana stores through the enactment of an ordinance or through an initiated or referred measure; provided, any initiated or referred measure to prohibit the operation of marijuana cultivation facilities, marijuana product manufacturing facilities, marijuana testing facilities, or retail marijuana stores must appear on a general election ballot during an even numbered year.

(g) Each application for an annual license to operate a marijuana establishment shall be submitted to the department. The department shall:

(i) Begin accepting and processing applications on October 1, 2013;

(ii) Immediately forward a copy of each application and half of the license application fee to the locality in which the applicant desires to operate the marijuana establishment;

(iii) Issue an annual license to the applicant between forty-five and ninety days after receipt of an application unless the department finds the applicant is not in compliance with regulations enacted pursuant to paragraph (a) or the department is notified by the relevant locality that the applicant is not in compliance with ordinances and regulations made pursuant to paragraph (f) and in effect at the time of application, provided, where a locality has enacted a numerical limit on the number of marijuana establishments and a greater number of applicants seek licenses, the department shall solicit and consider input from the locality as to the locality's preference or preferences for licensure; and

(iv) Upon denial of an application, notify the applicant in writing of the specific reason for its denial.

(h) If the department does not issue a license to an applicant within ninety days of receipt of the application filed in accordance with paragraph (g) and does not notify the applicant of the specific reason for its denial, in writing and within such time period, or if the department has adopted regulations pursuant to paragraph (a) and has accepted applications pursuant to paragraph (g) but has not issued any licenses by January 1, 2014, the applicant may resubmit its application directly to the locality, pursuant to paragraph (e), and the locality may issue an annual license to the applicant. A locality issuing a license to an applicant shall do so within ninety days of receipt of the resubmitted application unless the locality finds and notifies the applicant that the applicant is not in compliance with ordinances and regulations made pursuant to paragraph (f) in effect at the time the application is resubmitted and the locality shall notify the department if an annual license has been issued to the applicant. If an application is submitted to a locality under this paragraph, the department shall forward to the locality the application fee paid by the applicant to the department upon request by the locality. A license issued by a locality in accordance with this paragraph shall have the same force and effect as a license issued by the department in accordance with paragraph (g) and the holder of such license shall not be subject to regulation or enforcement by the department during the term of that license. A subsequent or renewed license may be issued under this paragraph on an annual basis only upon resubmission to the locality of a new application submitted to the department pursuant to paragraph (g). Nothing in this paragraph shall limit such relief as may be available to an aggrieved party under section 24-4-104, C.R.S., of the Colorado Administrative Procedure Act or any successor provision.

(i) If the department does not adopt regulations required by paragraph (a), an applicant may submit an application directly to a locality after October 1, 2013 and the locality may issue an annual license to the applicant. A locality issuing a license to an applicant shall do so within ninety days of receipt of the application unless it finds and notifies the applicant that the applicant is not in compliance with ordinances and regulations made pursuant to paragraph (f) in effect at the time of application and shall notify the department if an annual license has been issued to the applicant. A license issued by a locality in accordance with this paragraph shall have the same force and effect as a license issued by the department in accordance with paragraph (g) and the holder of such license shall not be subject to regulation or enforcement by the department during the term of that license. A subsequent or renewed license may be issued under this paragraph on an annual basis if the department has not adopted regulations required by paragraph (a) at least ninety days prior to the date upon which such subsequent or renewed license would be effective or if the department has adopted regulations pursuant to paragraph (a) but has not, at least ninety days after the adoption of such regulations, issued licenses pursuant to paragraph (g).

(j) Not later than July 1, 2014, the General Assembly shall enact legislation governing the cultivation, processing and sale of industrial hemp.

(6) **Employers, driving, minors and control of property.**

(a) Nothing in this section is intended to require an employer to permit or accommodate the use, consumption, possession, transfer, display, transportation, sale or growing of marijuana in the workplace or to affect the ability of employers to have policies restricting the use of marijuana by employees.

(b) Nothing in this section is intended to allow driving under the influence of marijuana or driving while impaired by marijuana or to supersede statutory laws related to driving under the influence of marijuana or driving while impaired by marijuana, nor shall this section prevent the state from enacting and imposing penalties for driving under the influence of or while impaired by marijuana.

(c) Nothing in this section is intended to permit the transfer of marijuana, with or without remuneration, to a person under the age of twenty-one or to allow a person under the age of twenty-one to purchase, possess, use, transport, grow, or consume marijuana.

(d) Nothing in this section shall prohibit a person, employer, school, hospital, detention facility, corporation or any other entity who occupies, owns or controls a property from prohibiting or otherwise regulating the possession, consumption, use, display, transfer, distribution, sale, transportation, or growing of marijuana on or in that property.

(7) **Medical marijuana provisions unaffected.** Nothing in this section shall be construed:

(a) To limit any privileges or rights of a medical marijuana patient, primary caregiver, or licensed entity as provided in section 14 of this article and the Colorado Medical Marijuana code;

(b) To permit a medical marijuana center to distribute marijuana to a person who is not a medical marijuana patient;

(c) To permit a medical marijuana center to purchase marijuana or marijuana products in a manner or from a source not authorized under the Colorado Medical Marijuana Code;

(d) To permit any medical marijuana center licensed pursuant to section 14 of this article and the Colorado Medical Marijuana Code to operate on the same premises as a retail marijuana store.; or

(e) To discharge the department, the Colorado Board of Health, or the Colorado Department of Public Health and Environment from their statutory and constitutional duties to regulate medical marijuana pursuant to section 14 of this article and the Colorado Medical Marijuana Code.

(8) **Self-executing, severability, conflicting provisions.** All provisions of this section are self-executing except as specified herein, are severable, and, except where otherwise indicated in the text, shall supersede conflicting state statutory, local charter, ordinance, or resolution, and other state and local provisions.

(9) **Effective date.** Unless otherwise provided by this section, all provisions of this section shall become effective upon official declaration of the vote hereon by proclamation of the governor, pursuant to section 1(4) of article v.

Washington Initiative 502

BE IT ENACTED BY THE PEOPLE OF THE STATE OF WASHINGTON:

PART 1—INTENT

NEW SECTION. **Sec. 1.** The people intend to stop treating adult marijuana use as a crime and try a new approach that:

(1) Allows law enforcement resources to be focused on violent and property crimes;

(2) Generates new state and local tax revenue for education, health care, research, and substance abuse prevention; and

(3) Takes marijuana out of the hands of illegal drug organizations and brings it under a tightly regulated, state-licensed system similar to that for controlling hard alcohol.

This measure authorizes the state liquor control board to regulate and tax marijuana for persons twenty-one years of age and older, and add a new threshold for driving under the influence of marijuana.

PART II—DEFINITIONS

Sec. 2. RCW 69.50.101 and 2010 c 177 s 1 are each amended to read as follows:

(g) "Department" means the department of health.

(p) "Lot" means a definite quantity of marijuana, useable marijuana, or marijuana-infused product identified by a lot number, every portion or package of which is uniform within recognized tolerances for the factors that appear in the labeling.

(q) "Lot number" shall identify the licensee by business or trade name and Washington state unified business identifier number, and the date of harvest or processing for each lot of marijuana, useable marijuana, or marijuana-infused product.

(s) "Marijuana" or "marihuana" means all parts of the plant Cannabis, whether growing or not, with a THC concentration greater than 0.3 percent on a dry weight basis; the seeds thereof; the resin extracted from any part of the plant; and every compound, manufacture, salt, derivative, mixture, or preparation of the plant, its seeds or resin.The term does not include the mature stalks of the plant, fiber produced from the stalks, oil or cake made from the seeds of the plant, any other compound, manufacture, salt, derivative, mixture, or preparation of the mature stalks (except the resin extracted therefrom), fiber, oil, or cake, or the sterilized seed of the plant which is incapable of germination.

(t) "Marijuana processor" means a person licensed by the state liquor control board to process marijuana into useable marijuana and marijuana-infused products, package and label useable marijuana and marijuana-infused products for sale in retail outlets, and sell useable marijuana and marijuana-infused products at wholesale to marijuana retailers.

(u) "Marijuana producer" means a person licensed by the state liquor control board to produce and sell marijuana at wholesale to marijuana processors and other marijuana producers.

(v) "Marijuana-infused products" means products that contain marijuana or marijuana extracts and are intended for human use. The term "marijuana-infused products" does not include useable marijuana.

(w) "Marijuana retailer" means a person licensed by the state liquor control board to sell useable marijuana and marijuana-infused products in a retail outlet.

(ff) "Retail outlet" means a location licensed by the state liquor control board for the retail sale of useable marijuana and marijuana-infused products.

(ii) "THC concentration" means percent of delta-9 tetrahydrocannabinol content per dry weight of any part of the plant Cannabis, or per volume or weight of marijuana product.

(kk) "Useable marijuana" means dried marijuana flowers.The term "useable marijuana" does not include marijuana-infused products.

NEW SECTION.

Sec. 3. A new section is added to chapter 46.04 RCW to read as follows:

"THC concentration" means nanograms of delta-9 tetrahydrocannabinol per milliliter of a person's whole blood. THC concentration does not include measurement of the metabolite THC- COOH, also known as carboxy-THC.

PART III—LICENSING AND REGULATION OF MARIJUANA PRODUCERS, PROCESSORS, AND RETAILERS

NEW SECTION.

Sec. 4. (1) There shall be a marijuana producer's license to produce marijuana for sale at wholesale to marijuana processors and other marijuana producers, regulated by the state liquor control board and subject to annual renewal. The production, possession, delivery, distribution, and sale of marijuana in accordance with the provisions of this act and the rules adopted to implement and enforce it, by a validly licensed marijuana producer, shall not be a criminal or civil offense under Washington state law. Every marijuana producer's license shall be issued in the name of the applicant, shall specify the location at which the marijuana producer intends to operate, which must be within the state of Washington, and the holder thereof shall not allow any other person to use the license. The application fee for a marijuana producer's license shall be two hundred fifty dollars. The annual fee for issuance and renewal of a marijuana producer's license shall be one thousand dollars. A separate license shall be required for each location at which a marijuana producer intends to produce marijuana.

(2) There shall be a marijuana processor's license to process, package, and label useable marijuana and marijuana-infused products for sale at wholesale to marijuana retailers, regulated by the state liquor control board and subject to annual renewal. The processing, packaging, possession, delivery, distribution, and sale of marijuana, useable marijuana, and marijuana-infused products in accordance with the provisions of this act and the rules adopted to implement and enforce it, by a validly licensed marijuana processor, shall not be a criminal or civil offense under Washington state law. Every marijuana processor's license shall be issued in the name of the applicant, shall specify the location at which the licensee intends to operate, which must be within the state of Washington, and the holder thereof shall not allow any other person to use the license. The application fee for a marijuana processor's license shall be two hundred fifty dollars. The annual fee for issuance and renewal of a marijuana processor's license shall be one thousand dollars. A separate license shall be required for each location at which a marijuana processor intends to process marijuana.

(3) There shall be a marijuana retailer's license to sell useable marijuana and marijuana-infused products at retail in retail outlets, regulated by the state liquor control board and subject to annual renewal. The possession, delivery, distribution, and sale of useable marijuana and marijuana-infused products in accordance with the provisions of this act and the rules adopted to implement and enforce it, by a validly licensed marijuana retailer, shall not be a criminal or civil offense under Washington state law. Every marijuana retailer's license shall be issued in the name of the applicant, shall specify the location of the retail outlet the licensee intends to operate, which must be within the state of Washington, and the holder thereof shall not allow any other person to use the license. The application fee for a marijuana retailer's license shall be two hundred fifty dollars. The annual fee for issuance and renewal of a marijuana retailer's license shall be one thousand dollars. A separate license shall be required for each location at which a marijuana retailer intends to sell useable marijuana and marijuana- infused products.

NEW SECTION.

Sec. 5. Neither a licensed marijuana producer nor a licensed marijuana processor shall have a direct or indirect financial interest in a licensed marijuana retailer.

NEW SECTION.

Sec. 6. (1) For the purpose of considering any application for a license to produce, process, or sell marijuana, or for the renewal of a license to produce, process, or sell marijuana, the state liquor control board may cause an inspection of the premises to be made, and may inquire into all matters in connection with the construction and operation of the premises. For the purpose of reviewing any application for a license and for considering the denial, suspension, revocation, or renewal or denial thereof, of any license, the state liquor control board may consider any prior criminal conduct of the applicant including an administrative violation history record with the state liquor control board and a criminal history record information check. The state liquor control board may submit the criminal history record information check to the Washington state patrol and to the identification division of the federal bureau of investigation in order that these agencies may search their records for prior arrests and convictions of the individual or individuals who filled out the forms. The state liquor control board shall require fingerprinting of any applicant whose criminal history record information check is submitted to the federal bureau of investigation. The provisions of RCW 9.95.240 and of chapter 9.96A RCW shall not apply to these cases. Subject to the provisions of this section, the state liquor control board may, in its discretion, grant or deny the renewal or license applied for. Denial may be based on, without limitation, the existence of chronic illegal activity documented in objections submitted pursuant to subsections (7)(c) and (9) of this section. Authority to approve an uncontested or unopposed license may be granted by the state liquor control board to any staff member the board designates in writing. Conditions for granting this authority shall be adopted by rule. No license of any kind may be issued to:

(a) A person under the age of twenty-one years;

(b) A person doing business as a sole proprietor who has not lawfully resided in the state for at least three months prior to applying to receive a license;

(c) A partnership, employee cooperative, association, nonprofit corporation, or corporation unless formed under the laws of this state, and unless all of the members thereof are qualified to obtain a license as provided in this section; or

(d) A person whose place of business is conducted by a manager or agent, unless the manager or agent possesses the same qualifications required of the licensee.

(2)

(a) The state liquor control board may, in its discretion, subject to the provisions of section 7 of this act, suspend or cancel any license; and all protections of the licensee from criminal or civil sanctions under state law for producing, processing, or selling marijuana, useable marijuana, or marijuana-infused products thereunder shall be suspended or terminated, as the case may be.

(3) Upon receipt of notice of the suspension or cancellation of a license, the licensee shall forthwith deliver up the license to the state liquor control board. Where the license has been suspended only, the state liquor control board shall return the license to the licensee at the expiration or termination of the period of suspension. The state liquor control board shall notify all other licensees in the county where the subject licensee has its premises of the suspension or cancellation of the license; and no other licensee or employee of another licensee may allow or cause any marijuana, useable marijuana, or marijuana-infused products to be delivered to or for any person at the premises of the subject licensee.

(4) Every license issued under this act shall be subject to all conditions and restrictions imposed by this act or by rules adopted by the state liquor control board to implement and enforce this act. All conditions and restrictions imposed by the state liquor control board in the issuance of an individual license shall be listed on the face of the individual license along with the trade name, address, and expiration date.

(5) Every licensee shall post and keep posted its license, or licenses, in a conspicuous place on the premises.

(6) No licensee shall employ any person under the age of twenty-one years.

(7)

(a) Before the state liquor control board issues a new or renewed license to an applicant it shall give notice of the application to the chief executive officer of the incorporated city or town, if the application is for a license within an incorporated city or town, or to the county legislative authority, if the application is for a license outside the boundaries of incorporated cities or towns.

(b The incorporated city or town through the official or employee selected by it, or the county legislative authority or the official or employee selected by it, shall have the right to file with the state liquor control board within twenty days after the date of transmittal of the notice for applications, or at least thirty days prior to the expiration date for renewals, written objections against the applicant or against the premises for which the new or renewed license is asked. The state liquor control board may extend the time period for submitting written objections.

(c) The written objections shall include a statement of all facts upon which the objections are based, and in case written objections are filed, the city or town or county legislative authority may request, and the state liquor control board may in its discretion hold, a hearing subject to the applicable provisions of Title 34 RCW. If the state liquor control board makes an initial decision to deny a license or renewal based on the written objections of an incorporated city or town or county legislative authority, the applicant may request a hearing subject to the applicable provisions of Title 34 RCW. If a hearing is held at the request of the applicant, state liquor control board representatives shall present and defend the state liquor control board's initial decision to deny a license or renewal.

(d) Upon the granting of a license under this title the state liquor control board shall send written notification to the chief executive officer of the incorporated city or town in which the license is granted, or to the county legislative authority if the license is granted outside the boundaries of incorporated cities or towns.

(8) The state liquor control board shall not issue a license for any premises within one thousand feet of the perimeter of the grounds of any elementary or secondary school, playground, recreation center or facility, child care center, public park, public transit center, or library, or any game arcade admission to which is not restricted to persons aged twenty-one years or older.

(9) In determining whether to grant or deny a license or renewal of any license, the state liquor control board shall give substantial weight to objections from an incorporated city or town or county legislative authority based upon chronic illegal activity associated with the applicant's operations of the premises proposed to be licensed or the applicant's operation of any other licensed premises, or the conduct of the applicant's patrons inside or outside the licensed premises. "Chronic illegal activity" means (a) a pervasive pattern of activity that threatens the public health, safety, and welfare of the city, town, or county including, but not limited to, open container violations, assaults, disturbances, disorderly conduct, or other criminal law violations, or as documented in crime statistics, police reports, emergency medical response data, calls for service, field data, or similar records of a law enforcement agency for the city, town, county, or any other municipal corporation or any state agency; or (b) an unreasonably high number of citations for violations of RCW 46.61.502 associated with the applicant's or licensee's operation of any licensed premises as indicated by the reported statements given to law enforcement upon arrest.

NEW SECTION.

Sec. 7. The action, order, or decision of the state liquor control board as to any denial of an application for the reissuance of a license to produce, process, or sell marijuana, or as to any revocation, suspension, or modification of any license to produce, process, or sell marijuana, shall be an adjudicative proceeding and subject to the applicable provisions of chapter 34.05 RCW.

NEW SECTION.

Sec. 8. (1) If the state liquor control board approves, a license to produce, process, or sell marijuana may be transferred, without charge, to the surviving spouse or domestic partner of a deceased licensee if the license was issued in the names of one or both of the parties. For the purpose of considering the qualifications of the surviving party to receive a marijuana producer's, marijuana processor's, or marijuana retailer's license, the state liquor control board may require a criminal history record information check. The state liquor control board may submit the criminal history record information check to the Washington state patrol and to the identification division of the federal bureau of investigation in order that these agencies may search their records for prior arrests and convictions of the individual or individuals who filled out the forms. The state liquor control board shall require fingerprinting of any applicant whose criminal history record information check is submitted to the federal bureau of investigation.

(2) The proposed sale of more than ten percent of the outstanding or issued stock of a corporation licensed under this act, or any proposed change in the officers of such a corporation, must be reported to the state liquor control board, and state liquor control board approval must be obtained before the changes are made. A fee of seventy-five dollars will be charged for the processing of the change of stock ownership or corporate officers.

NEW SECTION.

Sec. 9. For the purpose of carrying into effect the provisions of this act according to their true intent or of supplying any deficiency therein, the state liquor control board may adopt rules not inconsistent with the spirit of this act as are deemed necessary or advisable. Without limiting the generality of the preceding sentence, the state liquor control board is empowered to adopt rules regarding the following:

(1) The equipment and management of retail outlets and premises where marijuana is produced or processed, and inspection of the retail outlets and premises;

(2) The books and records to be created and maintained by licensees, the reports to be made thereon to the state liquor control board, and inspection of the books and records;

(3) Methods of producing, processing, and packaging marijuana, useable marijuana, and marijuana-infused products; conditions of sanitation; and standards of ingredients, quality, and identity of marijuana, useable marijuana, and marijuana-infused products produced, processed, packaged, or sold by licensees;

(4) Security requirements for retail outlets and premises where marijuana is produced or processed, and safety protocols for licensees and their employees;

(5) Screening, hiring, training, and supervising employees of licensees;

(6) Retail outlet locations and hours of operation;

(7) Labeling requirements and restrictions on advertisement of marijuana, useable marijuana, and marijuana-infused products;

(9) Application, reinstatement, and renewal fees for licenses issued under this act, and fees for anything done or permitted to be done under the rules adopted to implement and enforce this act;

(11) Times and periods when, and the manner, methods, and means by which, licensees shall transport and deliver marijuana, useable marijuana, and marijuana-infused products within the state;

(12) Identification, seizure, confiscation, destruction, or donation to law enforcement for training purposes of all marijuana, useable marijuana, and marijuana-infused products produced, processed, sold, or offered for sale within this state which do not conform in all respects to the standards prescribed by this act or the rules adopted to implement and enforce it: PROVIDED, That nothing in this act shall be construed as authorizing

the state liquor control board to seize, confiscate, destroy, or donate to law enforcement marijuana, useable marijuana, or marijuana-infused products produced, processed, sold, offered for sale, or possessed in compliance with the Washington state medical use of cannabis act, chapter 69.51A RCW.

NEW SECTION.

Sec. 10. The state liquor control board, subject to the provisions of this act, must adopt rules by December 1, 2013, that establish the procedures and criteria necessary to implement the following:

(1) Licensing of marijuana producers, marijuana processors, and marijuana retailers, including prescribing forms and establishing application, reinstatement, and renewal fees;

(2) Determining, in consultation with the office of financial management, the maximum number of retail outlets that may be licensed in each county, taking into consideration:

> (a) Population distribution;

> (b) Security and safety issues; and

> (c) The provision of adequate access to licensed sources of useable marijuana and marijuana-infused products to discourage purchases from the illegal market;

(3) Determining the maximum quantity of marijuana a marijuana producer may have on the premises of a licensed location at any time without violating Washington state law;

(4) Determining the maximum quantities of marijuana, useable marijuana, and marijuana-infused products a marijuana processor may have on the premises of a licensed location at any time without violating Washington state law;

(5) Determining the maximum quantities of useable marijuana and marijuana-infused products a marijuana retailer may have on the premises of a retail outlet at any time without violating Washington state law;

(6) In making the determinations required by subsections (3) through (5) of this section, the state liquor control board shall take into consideration:

> (a) Security and safety issues;

> (b) The provision of adequate access to licensed sources of marijuana, useable marijuana, and marijuana-infused products to discourage purchases from the illegal market; and

> (c) Economies of scale, and their impact on licensees' ability to both comply with regulatory requirements and undercut illegal market prices;

(7) Determining the nature, form, and capacity of all containers to be used by licensees to contain marijuana, useable marijuana, and marijuana-infused products, and their labeling requirements, to include but not be limited to:

> (a) The business or trade name and Washington state unified business identifier number of the licensees that grew, processed, and sold the marijuana, useable marijuana, or marijuana- infused product;

> (b) Lot numbers of the marijuana, useable marijuana, or marijuana-infused product;

> (c) THC concentration of the marijuana, useable marijuana, or marijuana-infused product;

> (d) Medically and scientifically accurate information about the health and safety risks posed by marijuana use; and

> (e) Language required by RCW 69.04.480;

(8) In consultation with the department of agriculture, establishing classes of marijuana, useable marijuana, and marijuana-infused products according to grade, condition, cannabinoid profile, THC concentration, or other qualitative measurements deemed appropriate by the state liquor control board;

(9) Establishing reasonable time, place, and manner restrictions and requirements regarding advertising of marijuana, useable marijuana, and marijuana-infused products that are not inconsistent with the provisions of this act, taking into consideration:

(a) Federal laws relating to marijuana that are applicable within Washington state;

(b) Minimizing exposure of people under twenty-one years of age to the advertising; and

(c)The inclusion of medically and scientifically accurate information about the health and safety risks posed by marijuana use in the advertising;

(10) Specifying and regulating the time and periods when, and the manner, methods, and means by which, licensees shall transport and deliver marijuana, useable marijuana, and marijuana-infused products within the state;

(11) In consultation with the department and the department of agriculture, establishing accreditation requirements for testing laboratories used by licensees to demonstrate compliance with standards adopted by the state liquor control board, and prescribing methods of producing, processing, and packaging marijuana, useable marijuana, and marijuana-infused products; conditions of sanitation; and standards of ingredients, quality, and identity of marijuana, useable marijuana, and marijuana-infused products produced, processed, packaged, or sold by licensees;

(12) Specifying procedures for identifying, seizing, confiscating, destroying, and donating to law enforcement for training purposes all marijuana, useable marijuana, and marijuana-infused products produced, processed, packaged, labeled, or offered for sale in this state that do not conform in all respects to the standards prescribed by this act or the rules of the state liquor control board.

NEW SECTION.

Sec. 11. (1) On a schedule determined by the state liquor control board, every licensed marijuana producer and processor must submit representative samples of marijuana, useable marijuana, or marijuana-infused products produced or processed by the licensee to an independent, third-party testing laboratory meeting the accreditation requirements established by the state liquor control board, for inspection and testing to certify compliance with standards adopted by the state liquor control board. Any sample remaining after testing shall be destroyed by the laboratory or returned to the licensee.

(2) Licensees must submit the results of this inspection and testing to the state liquor control board on a form developed by the state liquor control board.

(3) If a representative sample inspected and tested under this section does not meet the applicable standards adopted by the state liquor control board, the entire lot from which the sample was taken must be destroyed.

NEW SECTION.

Sec. 12. Except as provided by chapter 42.52 RCW, no member of the state liquor control board and no employee of the state liquor control board shall have any interest, directly or indirectly, in the producing, processing, or sale of marijuana, useable marijuana, or marijuana-infused products, or derive any profit or remuneration from the sale of marijuana, useable marijuana, or marijuana-infused products other than the salary or wages payable to him or her in respect of his or her office or position, and shall receive no gratuity from any person in connection with the business.

NEW SECTION.

Sec. 13. There may be licensed, in no greater number in each of the counties of the state than as the state liquor control board shall deem advisable, retail outlets established for the purpose of making useable marijuana and marijuana-infused products available for sale to adults aged twenty-one and over. Retail sale of useable marijuana and marijuana-infused products in accordance with the provisions of this act and the rules adopted to implement and enforce it, by a validly licensed marijuana retailer or retail outlet employee, shall not be a criminal or civil offense under Washington state law.

NEW SECTION.

Sec. 14. (1) Retail outlets shall sell no products or services other than useable marijuana, marijuana-infused products, or paraphernalia intended for the storage or use of useable marijuana or marijuana-infused products.

(2) Licensed marijuana retailers shall not employ persons under twenty-one years of age or allow persons under twenty-one years of age to enter or remain on the premises of a retail outlet.

(3) Licensed marijuana retailers shall not display any signage in a window, on a door, or on the outside of the premises of a retail outlet that is visible to the general public from a public right-of-way, other than a single sign no larger than one thousand six hundred square inches identifying the retail outlet by the licensee's business or trade name.

(4) Licensed marijuana retailers shall not display useable marijuana or marijuana-infused products in a manner that is visible to the general public from a public right-of-way.

(5) No licensed marijuana retailer or employee of a retail outlet shall open or consume, or allow to be opened or consumed, any useable marijuana or marijuana-infused product on the outlet premises.

(6)The state liquor control board shall fine a licensee one thousand dollars for each violation of any subsection of this section. Fines collected under this section must be deposited into the dedicated marijuana fund created under section 26 of this act.

NEW SECTION.

Sec. 15. The following acts, when performed by a validly licensed marijuana retailer or employee of a validly licensed retail outlet in compliance with rules adopted by the state liquor control board to implement and enforce this act, shall not constitute criminal or civil offenses under Washington state law:

(1) Purchase and receipt of useable marijuana or marijuana-infused products that have been properly packaged and labeled from a marijuana processor validly licensed under this act;

(2) Possession of quantities of useable marijuana or marijuana-infused products that do not exceed the maximum amounts established by the state liquor control board under section 10(5) of this act; and

(3) Delivery, distribution, and sale, on the premises of the retail outlet, of any combination of the following amounts of useable marijuana or marijuana-infused product to any person twenty-one years of age or older:

(a) One ounce of useable marijuana;

(b) Sixteen ounces of marijuana-infused product in solid form; or

(c) Seventy-two ounces of marijuana-infused product in liquid form.

NEW SECTION.

Sec. 16. The following acts, when performed by a validly licensed marijuana processor or employee of a validly licensed marijuana processor in compliance with rules adopted by the state liquor control board to implement and enforce this act, shall not constitute criminal or civil offenses under Washington state law:

(1) Purchase and receipt of marijuana that has been properly packaged and labeled from a marijuana producer validly licensed under this act;

(2) Possession, processing, packaging, and labeling of quantities of marijuana, useable marijuana, and marijuana-infused products that do not exceed the maximum amounts established by the state liquor control board under section 10(4) of this act; and

(3) Delivery, distribution, and sale of useable marijuana or marijuana-infused products to a marijuana retailer validly licensed under this act.

NEW SECTION.

Sec. 17. The following acts, when performed by a validly licensed marijuana producer or employee of a validly licensed marijuana producer in compliance with rules adopted by the state liquor control board to implement and enforce this act, shall not constitute criminal or civil offenses under Washington state law:

(1) Production or possession of quantities of marijuana that do not exceed the maximum amounts established by the state liquor control board under section 10(3) of this act; and

(2) Delivery, distribution, and sale of marijuana to a marijuana processor or another marijuana producer validly licensed under this act.

NEW SECTION.

Sec. 18. (1) No licensed marijuana producer, processor, or retailer shall place or maintain, or cause to be placed or maintained, an advertisement of marijuana, useable marijuana, or a marijuana-infused product in any form or through any medium whatsoever:

    (a) Within one thousand feet of the perimeter of a school grounds, playground, recreation center or facility, child care center, public park, or library, or any game arcade admission to which is not restricted to persons aged twenty-one years or older;

    (b) On or in a public transit vehicle or public transit shelter; or

    (c) On or in a publicly owned or operated property.

(2) Merchandising within a retail outlet is not advertising for the purposes of this section.

(3) This section does not apply to a noncommercial message.

(4)The state liquor control board shall fine a licensee one thousand dollars for each violation of subsection (1) of this section. Fines collected under this subsection must be deposited into the dedicated marijuana fund created under section 26 of this act.

Sec. 19. RCW 69.50.401 and 2005 c 218 s 1 are each amended to read as follows:

(3) The production, manufacture, processing, packaging, delivery, distribution, sale, or possession of marijuana in compliance with the terms set forth in section 15, 16, or 17 of this act shall not constitute a violation of this section, this chapter, or any other provision of Washington state law.

Sec. 20. RCW 69.50.4013 and 2003 c 53 s 334 are each amended to read as follows:

(3) The possession, by a person twenty-one years of age or older, of useable marijuana or marijuana-infused products in amounts that do not exceed those set forth in section

15(3) of this act is not a violation of this section, this chapter, or any other provision of Washington state law.

Sec. 21. It is unlawful to open a package containing marijuana, useable marijuana, or a marijuana-infused product, or consume marijuana, useable marijuana, or a marijuana-infused product, in view of the general public. A person who violates this section is guilty of a class 3 civil infraction under chapter 7.80 RCW.

NEW SECTION.

Sec. 22. RCW 69.50.412 and 2002 c 213 s 1 are each amended to read as follows:

[The amendments in this section of the Initiative removed marijuana-related paraphernalia from Washington's drug paraphernalia laws.]

PART IV — DEDICATED MARIJUANA FUND

NEW SECTION.

Sec. 26. (1) There shall be a fund, known as the dedicated marijuana fund, which shall consist of all marijuana excise taxes, license fees, penalties, forfeitures, and all other moneys, income, or revenue received by the state liquor control board from marijuana- related activities. The state treasurer shall be custodian of the fund.

(2) All moneys received by the state liquor control board or any employee thereof from marijuana-related activities shall be deposited each day in a depository approved by the state treasurer and transferred to the state treasurer to be credited to the dedicated marijuana fund.

(3) Disbursements from the dedicated marijuana fund shall be on authorization of the state liquor control board or a duly authorized representative thereof.

NEW SECTION.

Sec. 27. (1) There is levied and collected a marijuana excise tax equal to twenty-five percent of the selling price on each wholesale sale in this state of marijuana by a licensed marijuana producer to a licensed marijuana processor or another licensed marijuana producer. This tax is the obligation of the licensed marijuana producer.

(2) There is levied and collected a marijuana excise tax equal to twenty-five percent of the selling price on each wholesale sale in this state of useable marijuana or marijuana-infused product by a licensed marijuana processor to a licensed marijuana retailer. This tax is the obligation of the licensed marijuana processor.

(3) There is levied and collected a marijuana excise tax equal to twenty-five percent of the selling price on each retail sale in this state of useable marijuana and marijuana-infused products. This tax is the obligation of the licensed marijuana retailer, is separate and in addition to general state and local sales and use taxes that apply to retail sales of tangible personal property, and is part of the total retail price to which general state and local sales and use taxes apply.

(4) All revenues collected from the marijuana excise taxes imposed under subsections (1) through (3) of this section shall be deposited each day in a depository approved by the state treasurer and transferred to the state treasurer to be credited to the dedicated marijuana fund.

(5) The state liquor control board shall regularly review the tax levels established under this section and make recommendations to the legislature as appropriate regarding adjustments that would further the goal of discouraging use while undercutting illegal market prices.

[The initiative also included provisions addressing, in detail, how monies from the "dedicated marijuana fund" are to be disbursed among government agencies and programs.]

NEW SECTION.

Sec. 30. (1) The Washington state institute for public policy shall conduct cost-benefit evaluations of the implementation of this act. A preliminary report, and recommendations to appropriate committees of the legislature, shall be made by September 1, 2015, and the first final report with recommendations by September 1, 2017. Subsequent reports shall be due September 1, 2022, and September 1, 2032.

(2) The evaluation of the implementation of this act shall include, but not necessarily be limited to, consideration of the following factors:

(a) Public health, to include but not be limited to:

(i) Health costs associated with marijuana use;

(ii) Health costs associated with criminal prohibition of marijuana, including lack of product safety or quality control regulations and the relegation of marijuana to the same illegal market as potentially more dangerous substances; and

(iii) The impact of increased investment in the research, evaluation, education, prevention and intervention programs, practices, and campaigns identified in section 16 of this act on rates of marijuana-related maladaptive substance use and diagnosis of marijuana-related substance-use disorder, substance abuse, or substance dependence, as these terms are defined in the Diagnostic and Statistical Manual of Mental Disorders;

(b) Public safety, to include but not be limited to:

(i) Public safety issues relating to marijuana use; and

(ii) Public safety issues relating to criminal prohibition of marijuana;

(c) Youth and adult rates of the following:

(i) Marijuana use;

(ii) Maladaptive use of marijuana; and

(iii) Diagnosis of marijuana-related substance-use disorder, substance abuse, or substance dependence, including primary, secondary, and tertiary choices of substance;

(d) Economic impacts in the private and public sectors, including but not limited to:

(i) Jobs creation;

(ii) Workplace safety;

(iii) Revenues; and

(iv) Taxes generated for state and local budgets;

(e) Criminal justice impacts, to include but not be limited to:

(i) Use of public resources like law enforcement officers and equipment, prosecuting attorneys and public defenders, judges and court staff, the Washington state patrol crime lab and identification and criminal history section, jails and prisons, and misdemeanant and felon supervision officers to enforce state criminal laws regarding marijuana; and

(ii) Short and long-term consequences of involvement in the criminal justice system for persons accused of crimes relating to marijuana, their families, and their communities; and

(f) State and local agency administrative costs and revenues.

PART V—DRIVING UNDER THE INFLUENCE OF MARIJUANA

Sec. 31. RCW 46.20.308 and 2008 c 282 s 2 are each amended to read as follows:

[The amendments in this part of the Initiative established a per se cut off for drivers of 5 nanograms of active THC metabolite per milliliter of whole blood. Legally, this policy is similar to a blood alcohol level cut-off, although the scientific evidence regarding the relationship between different THC levels and impairment is less certain than for alcohol.]

Index

Countries and Regions

People and Organizations

Commissions

Constitutional Provisions

Legislation

International Meetings and Agreements

Legal and Policy Issues